Short Story Criticism

Guide to Thomson Gale Literary Criticism Series

For criticism on	Consult these Thomson Gale series
Authors now living or who died after December 31, 1999	*CONTEMPORARY LITERARY CRITICISM (CLC)*
Authors who died between 1900 and 1999	*TWENTIETH-CENTURY LITERARY CRITICISM (TCLC)*
Authors who died between 1800 and 1899	*NINETEENTH-CENTURY LITERATURE CRITICISM (NCLC)*
Authors who died between 1400 and 1799	*LITERATURE CRITICISM FROM 1400 TO 1800 (LC)* *SHAKESPEAREAN CRITICISM (SC)*
Authors who died before 1400	*CLASSICAL AND MEDIEVAL LITERATURE CRITICISM (CMLC)*
Authors of books for children and young adults	*CHILDREN'S LITERATURE REVIEW (CLR)*
Dramatists	*DRAMA CRITICISM (DC)*
Poets	*POETRY CRITICISM (PC)*
Short story writers	*SHORT STORY CRITICISM (SSC)*
Literary topics and movements	*HARLEM RENAISSANCE: A GALE CRITICAL COMPANION (HR)* *THE BEAT GENERATION: A GALE CRITICAL COMPANION (BG)* *FEMINISM IN LITERATURE: A GALE CRITICAL COMPANION (FL)* *GOTHIC LITERATURE: A GALE CRITICAL COMPANION (GL)*
Asian American writers of the last two hundred years	*ASIAN AMERICAN LITERATURE (AAL)*
Black writers of the past two hundred years	*BLACK LITERATURE CRITICISM (BLC)* *BLACK LITERATURE CRITICISM SUPPLEMENT (BLCS)*
Hispanic writers of the late nineteenth and twentieth centuries	*HISPANIC LITERATURE CRITICISM (HLC)* *HISPANIC LITERATURE CRITICISM SUPPLEMENT (HLCS)*
Native North American writers and orators of the eighteenth, nineteenth, and twentieth centuries	*NATIVE NORTH AMERICAN LITERATURE (NNAL)*
Major authors from the Renaissance to the present	*WORLD LITERATURE CRITICISM, 1500 TO THE PRESENT (WLC)* *WORLD LITERATURE CRITICISM SUPPLEMENT (WLCS)*

ISSN 0895-9439

Volume 102

Short Story Criticism

Criticism of the
Works of Short Fiction Writers

Jelena Krstović
Project Editor

THOMSON
™
GALE

Detroit • New York • San Francisco • New Haven, Conn. • Waterville, Maine • London

THOMSON
GALE

Short Story Criticism, Vol. 102

Project Editor
Jelena Krstović

Editorial
Kathy D. Darrow, Jeffrey W. Hunter, Michelle Lee, Thomas J. Schoenberg, Noah Schusterbauer, Lawrence J. Trudeau, Russel Whitaker

Data Capture
Frances Monroe, Gwen Tucker

Indexing Services
Factiva®, a Dow Jones and Reuters Company

Rights and Acquisitions
Margaret Abendroth, Margaret Chamberlain-Gaston, Edna Hedblad

Imaging and Multimedia
Dean Dauphinais, Leitha Etheridge-Sims, Lezlie Light, Mike Logusz, Dan Newell, Christine O'Bryan, Kelly A. Quin, Denay Wilding, Robyn Young

Composition and Electronic Capture
Tracey L. Matthews

Manufacturing
Rhonda Dover

Associate Product Manager
Marc Cormier

LIBRARY OF CONGRESS CATALOG CARD NUMBER 88-641014

ISBN-13: 978-0-7876-8899-8
ISBN-10: 0-7876-8899-1
ISSN 0895-9439

Printed in the United States of America
10 9 8 7 6 5 4 3 2 1

Contents

Preface

Short Story Criticism (*SSC*) presents significant criticism of the world's greatest short-story writers and provides supplementary biographical and bibliographical materials to guide the interested reader to a greater understanding of the authors of short fiction. This series was developed in response to suggestions from librarians serving high school, college, and public library patrons, who had noted a considerable number of requests for critical material on short-story writers. Although major short-story writers are covered in such Thomson Gale series as *Contemporary Literary Criticism* (*CLC*), *Twentieth-Century Literary Criticism* (*TCLC*), *Nineteenth-Century Literature Criticism* (*NCLC*), and *Literature Criticism from 1400 to 1800* (*LC*), librarians perceived the need for a series devoted solely to writers of the short-story genre.

Scope of the Series

SSC is designed to serve as an introduction to major short-story writers of all eras and nationalities. Since these authors have inspired a great deal of relevant critical material, *SSC* is necessarily selective, and the editors have chosen the most important published criticism to aid readers and students in their research.

Approximately three to six authors, works, or topics are included in each volume, and each entry presents a historical survey of the critical response to the work. The length of an entry is intended to reflect the amount of critical attention the author has received from critics writing in English and from foreign critics in translation. Every attempt has been made to identify and include the most significant essays on each author's work. In order to provide these important critical pieces, the editors sometimes reprint essays that have appeared elsewhere in Thomson Gale's Literary Criticism Series. Such duplication, however, never exceeds twenty percent of an *SSC* volume.

Organization of the Book

An *SSC* entry consists of the following elements:

- The **Author Heading** cites the name under which the author most commonly wrote, followed by birth and death dates. Also located here are any name variations under which an author wrote, including transliterated forms for authors whose native languages use nonroman alphabets. If the author wrote consistently under a pseudonym, the pseudonym will be listed in the author heading and the author's actual name given in parentheses on the first line of the biographical and critical introduction. Uncertain birth or death dates are indicated by question marks. Single-work entries are preceded by the title of the work and its date of publication.

- The **Introduction** contains background information that introduces the reader to the author and the critical debates surrounding his or her work.

- The list of **Principal Works** is ordered chronologically by date of first publication and lists the most important works by the author. The first section comprises short-story collections, novellas, and novella collections. The second section gives information on other major works by the author. For foreign authors, the editors have provided original foreign-language publication information and have selected what are considered the best and most complete English-language editions of their works.

- Reprinted **Criticism** is arranged chronologically in each entry to provide a useful perspective on changes in critical evaluation over time. All short-story, novella, and collection titles by the author featured in the entry are printed in boldface type. The critic's name and the date of composition or publication of the critical work are given at the beginning of each piece of criticism. Unsigned criticism is preceded by the title of the source in which it appeared. Footnotes are reprinted at the end of each essay or excerpt. In the case of excerpted criticism, only those footnotes that pertain to the excerpted texts are included.

- Critical essays are prefaced by brief **Annotations** explicating each piece.

- A complete **Bibliographical Citation** of the original essay or book precedes each piece of criticism. Source citations in the Literary Criticism Series follow University of Chicago Press style, as outlined in *The Chicago Manual of Style,* 15th ed. (Chicago: The University of Chicago Press, 2006).

- An annotated bibliography of **Further Reading** appears at the end of each entry and suggests resources for additional study. In some cases, significant essays for which the editors could not obtain reprint rights are included here. Boxed material following the further reading list provides references to other biographical and critical sources on the author in series published by Thomson Gale.

Indexes

A **Cumulative Author Index** lists all of the authors that appear in a wide variety of reference sources published by Thomson Gale, including *SSC*. A complete list of these sources is found facing the first page of the Author Index. The index also includes birth and death dates and cross references between pseudonyms and actual names.

A **Cumulative Nationality Index** lists all authors featured in *SSC* by nationality, followed by the number of the *SSC* volume in which their entry appears.

An alphabetical **Title Index** lists all short-story, novella, and collection titles contained in the *SSC* series. Titles of short-story collections, separately published novellas, and novella collections are printed in italics, while titles of individual short stories are printed in roman type with quotation marks. Each title is followed by the author's last name and corresponding volume and page numbers where commentary on the work is located. English-language translations of original foreign-language titles are cross-referenced to the foreign titles so that all references to discussion of a work are combined in one listing.

In response to numerous suggestions from librarians, Thomson Gale also produces an annual paperbound edition of the SSC cumulative title index. This annual cumulation, which alphabetically lists all titles reviewed in the series, is available to all customers. Additional copies of this index are available upon request. Librarians and patrons will welcome this separate index; it saves shelf space, is easy to use, and is recyclable upon receipt of the next edition.

Citing *Short Story Criticism*

When citing criticism reprinted in the Literary Criticism Series, students should provide complete bibliographic information so that the cited essay can be located in the original print or electronic source. Students who quote directly from reprinted criticism may use any accepted bibliographic format, such as University of Chicago Press style or Modern Language Association (MLA) style. Both the MLA and the University of Chicago formats are acceptable and recognized as being the current standards for citations. It is important, however, to choose one format for all citations; do not mix the two formats within a list of citations.

The examples below follow recommendations for preparing a bibliography set forth in *The Chicago Manual of Style,* 15th ed. (Chicago: The University of Chicago Press, 2006); the first example pertains to material drawn from periodicals, the second to material reprinted from books:

Morrison, Jago. "Narration and Unease in Ian McEwan's Later Fiction." *Critique* 42, no. 3 (spring 2001): 253-68. Reprinted in *Short Story Criticism.* Vol. 57, edited by Jelena Krstovic, 212-20. Detroit: Gale, 2003.

Brossard, Nicole. "Poetic Politics." In *The Politics of Poetic Form: Poetry and Public Policy,* edited by Charles Bernstein, 73-82. New York: Roof Books, 1990. Reprinted in *Short Story Criticism.* Vol. 57, edited by Jelena Krstovic, 3-8. Detroit: Gale, 2003.

The examples below follow recommendations for preparing a works cited list set forth in the *MLA Handbook for Writers of Research Papers,* 6th ed. (New York: The Modern Language Association of America, 2003); the first example pertains to material drawn from periodicals, the second to material reprinted from books:

Morrison, Jago. "Narration and Unease in Ian McEwan's Later Fiction." *Critique* 42.3 (spring 2001): 253-68. Reprinted in *Short Story Criticism.* Ed. Jelena Krstovic. Vol. 57. Detroit: Gale, 2003. 212-20.

Brossard, Nicole. "Poetic Politics." *The Politics of Poetic Form: Poetry and Public Policy.* Ed. Charles Bernstein. New York: Roof Books, 1990. 73-82. Reprinted in *Short Story Criticism.* Ed. Jelena Krstovic. Vol. 57. Detroit: Gale, 2003. 3-8.

Suggestions are Welcome

Readers who wish to suggest new features, topics, or authors to appear in future volumes, or who have other suggestions or comments are cordially invited to call, write, or fax the Associate Product Manager:

Associate Product Manager, Literary Criticism Series
Thomson Gale
27500 Drake Road
Farmington Hills, MI 48331-3535
1-800-347-4253 (GALE)
Fax: 248-699-8054

Acknowledgments

The editors wish to thank the copyright holders of the excerpted criticism included in this volume and the permissions managers of many book and magazine publishing companies for assisting us in securing reproduction rights. Following is a list of the copyright holders who have granted us permission to reproduce material in this volume of *SSC*. Every effort has been made to trace copyright, but if omissions have been made, please let us know.

COPYRIGHTED MATERIAL IN *SSC*, VOLUME 102, WAS REPRODUCED FROM THE FOLLOWING PERIODICALS:

Américas, v. 45, 1993. © 1993 Américas. Reproduced by permission of *Américas,* a bimonthly magazine published by the General Secretariat of the Organization of American States in English and Spanish.—*Arizona Quarterly,* v. 52, autumn, 1996 for "Philip Roth's Jewish Family Marx and the Defense of Faith" by Emily Miller Budick. Copyright © 1996 by the Regents of the University of Arizona. Reproduced by permission of the publisher and the author.—*Comparative Literature,* v. 29, summer, 1977. Copyright © 1977 by University of Oregon. Reproduced by permission of *Comparative Literature.*—*Contemporary Literature,* v. 32, winter, 1991. Copyright 1991. Reprinted by permission of the University of Wisconsin Press.—*Crítica Hispánica,* v. 6, 1984. Reproduced by permission.—*English Studies,* 1987. Copyright © 1987 Swets & Zeitlinger. Reproduced by permission.—*Hispanic Journal,* v. 4, fall, 1982; v. 4, spring, 1983. Copyright © 1982, 1983 IUP Indiana University of Pennsylvania. Both reproduced by permission.—*Journal of the Short Story in English,* spring, 1999. Copyright © 1999 by Presses de l'Universitè d'Angers. Reproduced by permission.—*Kentucky Romance Quarterly,* v. 30, 1983. Copyright © 1983 by Helen Dwight Reid Educational Foundation. Reproduced with permission of the Helen Dwight Reid Educational Foundation, published by Heldref Publications, 1319 18th Street, NW, Washington, DC 20036-1802.—*Latin American Literary Review,* v. 9, spring-summer, 1981. Copyright © 1981 *Latin American Literary Review.* Reproduced by permission of the publisher.—*Literature/Film Quarterly,* v. 19, October, 1991. Copyright © 1991 Salisbury State College. Reproduced by permission.—*MELUS,* v. 11, summer, 1984; v. 15, winter, 1988. Copyright *MELUS: The Society for the Study of Multi-Ethnic Literature of the United States,* 1984, 1988. Both reproduced by permission.—*The New Criterion,* v. 13, October, 1994 for "Fantastic Argentine" by Alexander Coleman. Reproduced by permission of the Literary Estate of the author.—*Nineteenth-Century Contexts,* v. 18, 1994 for "The Monstrous Other: The Chimera of Speculation in Balzac's 'The Girl with the Golden Eyes'" by Marie Josephine Diamond. © 1994 OPA (Overseas Publishers Association). Reproduced by permission of Taylor & Francis, Ltd. (http://www.informaworld.com), and the author.—*Nineteenth-Century French Studies,* v. 16, spring, 1988. Copyright © 1988 by *Nineteenth-Century French Studies.* Reproduced by permission.—*Notes on Modern American Literature,* v. 9, winter, 1985 for "Plotting Against Chekhov: Joyce Carol Oates and 'The Lady with the Dog'" by Matthew C. Brennan. Copyright, 1985, Edward Guereschi and Lee J. Richmond. Reproduced by permission of the author.—*Prooftexts: A Journal of Jewish Literary History,* v. 21, winter, 2001. Copyright © Indiana University Press. Reproduced by permission.—*Queen's Quarterly,* v. 111, fall, 2004 for "Surprised by Love: Chekhov and 'The Lady with the Dog'" by Robert Fulford. Reproduced by permission of the author.—*Romance Studies,* autumn, 1993. Copyright © Romance Studies 1993. Reproduced by permission of Maney Publishing.—*Shofar,* v. 19, fall, 2000. Reproduced by permission.—*South Atlantic Bulletin,* v. 42, November, 1977. Copyright © 1977 by the South Atlantic Modern Language Association. Reproduced by permission.—*South Central Review,* v. 19, spring, 2003. Copyright © 2003 The Johns Hopkins University Press. Reproduced by permission.—*Studies in Jewish American Literature,* v. 7, 1988; v. 8, fall, 1989. © 1988, 1989 by The Kent State University Press. Both reproduced by permission.—*Studies in Short Fiction,* v. 27, spring, 1990; v. 30, summer, 1993. Copyright © 1990, 1993 by *Studies in Short Fiction.* Both reproduced by permission.—*Symposium,* v. 51, 1997. Copyright © 1997 by Helen Dwight Reid Educational Foundation. Reproduced with permission of the Helen Dwight Reid Educational Foundation, published by Heldref Publications, 1319 18th Street, NW, Washington, DC 20036-1802.—*Twentieth Century Literature,* v. 51, spring, 2005. Copyright 2005, Hofstra University Press. Reproduced by permission.—*Yale French Studies,* 1981. Copyright © Yale French Studies 1981. Reproduced by permission.

COPYRIGHTED MATERIAL IN *SSC*, VOLUME 102, WAS REPRODUCED FROM THE FOLLOWING BOOKS:

Balderston, Daniel. From "Murder by Suggestion: *El sueño de los heroes* and *The Master of Ballantrae*," in *Robert Louis Stevenson, Writer of Boundaries.* Edited by Richard Ambrosini and Richard Dury. The University of Wisconsin Press,

Thomson Gale Literature Product Advisory Board

The members of the Thomson Gale Literature Product Advisory Board—reference librarians from public and academic library systems—represent a cross-section of our customer base and offer a variety of informed perspectives on both the presentation and content of our literature products. Advisory board members assess and define such quality issues as the relevance, currency, and usefulness of the author coverage, critical content, and literary topics included in our series; evaluate the layout, presentation, and general quality of our printed volumes; provide feedback on the criteria used for selecting authors and topics covered in our series; provide suggestions for potential enhancements to our series; identify any gaps in our coverage of authors or literary topics, recommending authors or topics for inclusion; analyze the appropriateness of our content and presentation for various user audiences, such as high school students, undergraduates, graduate students, librarians, and educators; and offer feedback on any proposed changes/enhancements to our series. We wish to thank the following advisors for their advice throughout the year.

The Girl with the Golden Eyes (La Fille aux yeux d'or)

Honoré de Balzac

French novella.

The following entry presents criticism of Balzac's *La Fille aux yeux d'or* (1835; *The Girl with the Golden Eyes*). For further discussion of Balzac's short fiction, see *SSC,* Volumes 5 and 59.

INTRODUCTION

Balzac's dark tale of a young man's pursuit of sexual pleasure was shocking in its day, dealing as it does with themes of seduction, jealousy, unorthodox love, and sexual identity. The novella concerns the infatuation of the young dandy Henri de Marsay with an exotic, golden-eyed Creole, Paquita Valdès. After seducing her, Henri discovers that Paquita is being kept by another, and vows to kill her. All the characters are deeply flawed, but their story is compelling and carries readers along on a breathless ride to its outrageous conclusion. While the novella examines Henri's relentless quest for an idealized sexual object, it serves also to comment on post-Napoleonic French society, with its insatiable desire to consume and its fixation on possession. In its description of the world of the young protagonist, the tale censures the decadence of nineteenth-century Parisian society, driven by love of money and pleasure. Balzac's story, which he included in the *Histoire des treize* (*History of the Thirteen*) trilogy in the multivolume *Comédie humaine* (1842-50), also inspired numerous other writers, notably Henry James, as well as a 1961 film adaptation of the work. While *The Girl with the Golden Eyes* has not generated a great deal of critical commentary in English, several scholars have undertaken detailed readings of the story. Many commentators have noted that the story contains sexist and racist elements, but show, too, how with his work Balzac overturns assumptions about sexuality and gender. Themes in the novella that critics have paid particular attention to include gold, blood, decadence, pleasure, slavery, the interrelatedness of masculinity and femininity, monstrosity, exoticism, sexual and racial hybrids, and sexual domination.

PLOT AND MAJOR CHARACTERS

Part I opens with a lengthy description of Paris and its inhabitants. For almost the entire section—one fifth of the novella—Balzac's narrator ruminates on Parisian society, showing how at all levels people are enslaved by the lusts of "gold and pleasure." Parisians are "gaunt, yellow, tawny," in a state of decay and in relentless pursuit of money and gratification. The city is likened to hell, and its social structure compared to the concentric circles of Dante's *Inferno*. Paris is a place of extremes, brimming with moral corruption but also, paradoxically, "the crown of the world," that "leads human civilization." After twenty pages of this harsh and often bitter portrait, the story proper opens with a description of the young protagonist, Henri de Marsay. Henri, the illegitimate son of Lord Dudley and the famous Marquise du Vordac, the narrator explains, is not only a bastard, but has no ties at all, having been abandoned by his parents and raised first by an elderly aunt and then a clergyman.

In the first paragraphs of Part II the narrator describes Henri and his background more fully. After his aunt (the only mother he had known) died, Henri inherited a fortune, and now, at twenty-two has no obligations in the world and is "free as an unmated bird." Henri, who looks barely seventeen, is also described as "pretty" and "possessing the skin of a young girl." While not effeminate, he has certain feminine qualities. He is also courageous, agile, artistic, and intelligent. But his most terrible vice is that he believes in no one and nothing. The narrator also explains that Henri has a half-sister he does not know about, Lord Dudley's daughter by a Spanish woman, Euphémie. She is married to Don Hijos, Marquis de San-Real, and lives in Paris.

The action of the novella begins as Henri is walking one fine Sunday in April 1815 along the avenue of the Tuileries. He meets his friend Paul de Manerville, and tells him that on Thursday he had seen a beautiful young woman who is his "ideal," who possesses a sort of "animal magnetism" and golden yellow eyes like a tiger's. Paul knows the woman, too, and presently she appears, looks at Henri, and Paul and Henri follow her and her chaperone. The woman waves her handkerchief from her carriage, and Henri pursues her in his own coach to a fine house in the Rue Saint Lazare. The next day, Henri sends his valet, Laurent, to the house and learns from the postman that it belongs to Don Hijos, Marquis de San-Real. The Marquise, the wife of Don Hijos, is away in London. According to the postman, the young woman Henri has seen is Paquita Valdès, mistress of Don Hijos. No one is allowed into the hotel where she stays, he informs them. On learning this, Henri's excitement builds, and the idea of the difficulty of obtaining her increases the value of Paquita in his eyes.

In Part III, Henri devises a plan to meet and seduce Paquita. He sees her again as he walks on the Terrasse des Feuillants and follows her along the terrace. As he is walking, he sees the aged Marquis de San-Real. Paquita exchanges glances with Henri, but she is chastised by her chaperone. Paquita does not reappear for days afterwards. Henri then writes a letter to her and asks her to send him a letter over her wall. The following day, two mysterious people come to see Henri: a mulatto, or man of mixed African ancestry, and an old, bearded, and dilapidated man, his translator. The mulatto returns the letter Henri wrote to Paquita, and the translator tells him to be at the boulevard Montmartre at 10:30 the next day and wait for a carriage. Henri does as he is told, and the next day goes to Paquita's chambers. Before he sees her, he encounters her decrepit and emotionless mother, an Asian hag who is as old and ugly as Paquita is young and beautiful. She is a former slave who was once beautiful and who has now sold her daughter into her present situation. Paquita tells Henri they have twelve days together. Henri flies into a jealous rage, and says he will kill her before anyone else has her. They reconcile, and agree to meet again and begin their affair.

At the beginning of Part IV, Henri and Paquita have been involved for two days. Henri is only allowed to go to see her under secret and mysterious conditions, led by the mulatto, whose name is Christemio. Henri tries to resist this insult to his honor, but capitulates and agrees to continue to see her only on her terms. Paquita's boudoir is perfumed and exotic, and contains a divan fifty feet in circumference made of white cashmere. The room is punctuated by red cushions, covers, and curtains. The room, Henri learns, is soundproof—Paquita's lover made it so in order that no one learn of this private place. Paquita and Henri begin their lovemaking. At one point Paquita dresses Henri in a woman's robe and bonnet, and they laugh together. Henri finds that while Paquita is a virgin, she is not innocent.

When he meets Paul one day, Henri denies that he has been thinking about Paquita, and does not let on that he has been seeing her. He begins to think about Paquita's virginity and skill in lovemaking, and he realizes he has been fooled. That night, when he goes to her, she begs him to go away with her. Her chaperone has begun to suspect, and she must escape from the lover who enslaves her in case her secret becomes known. She explains to Henri that she has been locked up since she was twelve years old, and wants him to free her.

As the fifth and final part of the novella opens, Henri and Paquita talk about going away together. Henri suggests they go to the exotic Indies, the Orient where the "birds sing of love." But they cannot go to Asia, he says, if they have no gold. She says there is some in the house where she is enslaved. Henri says he cannot take it because it is not his. But Paquita says he has already taken what is not his—he has taken her—so surely it makes no difference. As they make love later, Paquita suddenly calls out "Margarita," and Henri is incensed, crying, "Now I know all that I still tried to disbelieve." He tries to kill Paquita with a knife but he is stopped by Christemio, who vows to kill him if he hurts her. Henri leaves.

A week later, Henri returns to the hotel where Paquita stays and finds that the Marquise has returned from London. When he arrives at Paquita's chamber, he finds his lover in a pool of blood, speaking her last words. The Marquise, it turns out, has killed Paquita. She was the young woman's lover, and she has exacted her revenge before Henri could do so. Henri confronts the marquise, and they both recognize that they are half-siblings, that Lord Dudley was their father. The Marquise is Henri's sister, Margarita Euphémie Porrabéril. Paquita's mother enters, and the Marquise throws her a bag of gold to clean the room and dispose of her daughter's dead body. The old hag for the first time shows emotion—joy at the prospect of the gold. The Marquise tells Henri she will now go to Spain to enter a convent, and they part. A week later, Henri encounters Paul, who asks him what has become of the "girl with the golden eyes," and he tells her that she has died of consumption.

MAJOR THEMES

From its opening lines depicting the insatiability of Paris to its ending, when Henri idly remarks that his lover has died of consumption, *The Girl with the Golden Eyes* is about the relentless, unthinking, and ultimately unfulfilling pursuit of gold and pleasure. At the heart of the novella is Henri's obsessive desire, not for Paquita herself but for an ideal, and more importantly, for an ideal that is difficult to attain. Henri is the epitome of the Parisian aristocrat: gifted, wealthy, and refined, but with no substance, concerning himself with trivialities such as fashion and gossip. He is infatuated by Paquita's beauty and exotic nature. His desire for her increases once he finds that she is a prize he must fight for—that the pursuit of her will not be easy. Having nothing else to occupy his time—he does not have to pursue the other type of gold because he is independently wealthy—Henri makes it his mission to go after this girl with the golden eyes, his ideal of ultimate sensual pleasure. The color gold is used to symbolize the ideal that is pursued, as in the color of money and Paquita's eyes, but it is often shown, too, in a decayed and dirtied form—yellow. Yellow is the color of decaying Parisian society, of Paquita's mother's eyes, of bile. It is seen in the novella that the pursuit of pleasure is never-ending, leading to ever more desire. Desire in the novella is shown as monstrous when Henri's desire for Paquita becomes obsession, when the marquise's jealousy becomes murderous, and when Paquita's mother's desire for gold becomes more important to her than the life of her own daughter.

Another important theme in the novella is that of blood. When Henri is introduced, the first thing the narrator explains about him is his illegitimacy. Henri's bloodlines play an important part in his makeup. Having been abandoned by his real parents, he has no attachments, is free, yet enjoys the benefits of being the offspring of a rich father. Henri is an aristocrat, and thus his blood is important. The racial makeup of Paquita is also significant. At first it is assumed that she is Henri's sister, because she appears to be the wife of the Marquis de San-Real. Her racial makeup and exoticism are part of her attraction for Henri and much is made of her Asian and Creole ancestry. The novella also includes other characters of various races—Paquita's mother, her mulatto servant, and the Spanish-English Euphémie. The shock at the end of the story is not merely that Paquita has been enslaved by a lesbian lover, but that her lover is Henri's half-sister. The siblings recognize that they share the same blood, and that Paquita was attracted to it.

Related to this question of blood is that of identity. The identity of Paquita is not known by Henri immediately, which titillates him and heightens his sense of the chase. She is the exotic "Other," at first nameless and until the end a mystery. The identity of her lover remains a mystery as well, although it is assumed that he is a man, the Marquis. Henri's identity is also a complex one, as he is of mixed ancestry, as is the identity of his Spanish-English sister. The novella also explores the nature of sexual identity. Paquita's faith-

ful servant Christemio, the mulatto, is a eunuch, but his love for his mistress surpasses any other love in the novel. The sexual identity of Henri is also examined closely in the story. On the one hand, Henri seems to be a traditional rake, pursuing heterosexual relationships and taking many women as lovers. But he is described as having feminine traits and allows Paquita to dress him in women's clothes before they make love. Traditional masculine and feminine roles are overturned, too, in the figure of the Marquise, who is discovered at the end to be Paquita's lover, and whose obsession with her object of desire surpasses even that of her brother.

CRITICAL RECEPTION

When *The Girl with the Golden Eyes* was first published in 1835, Balzac was already a successful writer, having produced several novels and collections of short stories. While many nineteenth-century readers found the novella shocking, it was widely read. It also gained the attention of other writers; James's 1885 novel *The Bostonians* was based on the story. Since then, the novella has become one of Balzac's most celebrated works and is recognized as one of the first stories to openly treat the subject of lesbianism. Many modern critics who have written about the novella have had mixed feelings about the piece. Some have noted that while, stylistically, it has moments of great beauty, it also suffers from long passages that are ranting and unfocused. The plot, too, is criticized for being melodramatic and overblown, and the final section, in which Henri discovers that his rival is his half-sister, is seen as bordering on camp. Several critics, including Shoshana Felman, have emphasized as well that *The Girl with the Golden Eyes* is filled with patriarchal discourse, that it is misogynistic, that it exoticizes the "Other," that it is filled with racism, and that it depicts brutal violence against women. Despite these criticisms, scholars have found much in the novella to praise. They have noted that the treatment of gender and sexuality in the novella was ahead of its day, and have admired its insightful treatment of masculine/feminine roles and sexual psychology. The novella's sensational elements notwithstanding, it is seen as offering a penetrating portrait of the dark side of sexual love and of the pursuit of sensual pleasure. The novella has also been praised for its commentary on French mores of the nineteenth century and its portrait of Paris in the opening pages is frequently cited by historians as offering an accurate portrait of the social, economic, and cultural climate of post-Napoleonic France.

PRINCIPAL WORKS

Short Fiction

Scènes de la vie privée (short stories) 1829-30; enlarged, with a novella 1832

Romans et contes philosphiques. 3 vols. (novels and short stories) 1831; revised as *Contes philosphiques* 1832

Les Cent Contes drolatiques: Premier dixain [*Contes drolatiques; Droll Stories Collected from the Abbays of Touraine*] 1832

Les Nouveaux contes philosophiques (novel and short stories) 1832

Etudes de mours au XIXe siècle. 12 vols. (novels, novellas, and short stories) 1834-37

Le Livre mystique (novels and short stories) 1835

OEuvres complètes de H. de Balzac: La Comédie humaine. 17 vols. (short stories, novels, and novellas) 1842-50

Les Célibataires (short stories, novellas) 1844

Honorine (novella) 1844

OEuvres complètes de H. de Balzac. Edition définitive. 26 vols. (short stories, novellas, novels, drama, letters, and essays) 1869-1906

La Comédie humaine. 40 vols. (short stories, novels, and novellas) 1895-98

OEuvres complètes de H. de Balzac. 40 vols. (short stories, novellas, novels, drama, letters, and essays) 1912-40

Other Major Works

Le Dernier Chouan; ou, La Bretagne en 1800 [*The Chouans*] (novel) 1829; also published as *Les Chouans; ou, La Bretagne en 1799* 1834

Physiologie du mariage; ou, Meditations de philosophie eclectique sur le bonheur et le malheur conjugal [*The Physiology of Marriage*] (novel) 1830

Le Peau de chagrin [*The Wild Ass's Skin*] (novel) 1831

Notice Bibliographique sur Louis Lambert [*Louis Lambert*] (novel) 1832

Le Medecin de campagne [*The Country Doctor*] (novel) 1833

La Recherché de l'absolu [*The Quest of the Absolute*] (novel) 1834

La Père Goriot: Histoire parisienne [*Father Goriot*] (novel) 1835

Séraphita (novel) 1835

Le Lys dans la vallée [*The Lily of the Valley*] (novel) 1836

Eugénie Grandet [*Eugénie Grandet; or, The Miner's Daughter*] (novel) 1837

La Vielle fille (novel) 1837

Histoire de la grandeur et de la decadence de César Birotteau, parfumeur [*History of the Grandeur and Downfall of César Birotteau*] (novel) 1838

Beatrix; ou, Les amours forcés (novel) 1839

Ursule Mirouët (novel) 1842

Les Trios amoureux [*Modest Mignon; ou, Les trios amoureux*] (novel) 1844

Histoires des parens [*sic*] *pauvres: La cousine Bette et Les deux musiciens* [*Poor Relations*] (novel) 1847

Lettres à l'étrangère. 4 vols. (letters) 1847

Théâtre (plays) 1853

Correspondence de H. de Balzac, 1819-1850 (letters) 1876

Honoré de Balzac: Letters for Madame Hanska, 1833-1846 (letters) 1900

The Dramatic Works of Honoré de Balzac 1901

The Love Letters of Honoré de Balzac: 1833-1842 (letters) 1901

CRITICISM

Adeline R. Tintner (essay date summer 1977)

SOURCE: Tintner, Adeline R. "James and Balzac: *The Bostonians* and *La Fille aux yeux d'or.*" *Comparative Literature* 29, no. 3 (summer 1977): 241-54.

[*In the following essay, Titner argues that* The Girl with the Golden Eyes *provided Henry James with the inspiration, plot structure, and themes for his 1880 novel* The Bostonians.]

During a short period in the 1880s Henry James appears to have been influenced by the contemporaneous French decadent novel. This "curious" strain surfaced most visibly in *The Bostonians* which is usually approached solely in terms of its political theme. James was able to assimilate the decadent material only under the acceptable auspices of his master, Balzac. A close analysis of *The Bostonians* reveals how James appropriated one of the progenitors of the decadent movement, **La Fille aux yeux d'or,** which enabled him both to combine his interest in "the antagonism of the sexes" with exoticism and to "correct" the excesses of the decadent movement proper by his characteristic technique of criticizing a work of literature by "redoing" it. "To criticize," James wrote in his Preface to *What Maisie Knew,* "is to appreciate, to appropriate, to take intellectual possession, to establish in fine a relation with the criticized thing and make it one's own." By making one of the classical examples of decadent fiction his own, he transformed its structure into a vehicle for his view of society.

"The essential, latent antagonism of the sexes—the armed opposed array of men and women, founded on irreconcilable interests. Hitherto we have judged these interests reconcilable, and even practically identical. But all that is changing because women are changing, and their necessary hostility to men—or that of men to them, I don't care how you put it—is rising by an inexorable logic to the surface. It is deeper—ah, far deeper, than our need of each other, deep as we have always held that to be; and some day it will break out on a scale that will make us all turn pale . . . We shall be united by hate."[1]

In the 1880s Henry James was preoccupied by the relationship between the sexes and wrote a good deal about how far a woman could determine her own happiness and to what extent she was dominated by a male society. *The Portrait of a Lady* (1881) demonstrated how a young woman, thinking herself mistress of her fate with "the world all before her," ends as a slave to her Pateresque theory of life and to her husband. In this novel James offered a full range of possibilities for freedom, from the case of Mrs. Touchett who lives the way she wants to at the price of her husband's discomfort yet protected by her social privileges, to the case of Henrietta Stackpole, the "new woman" (based partly on Margaret Fuller), independent, career minded, and lucky enough to find a husband willing to engage in an egalitarian marriage. In his next novel, *The Bostonians* (1884-86), James carried his inquiry further. From his *Notebooks* we know that he wished "to write a very *American* tale, a tale very characteristic of our social conditions." He believed that "the situation of women, the decline of the sentiment of sex, the agitation on their behalf" was "the most salient and peculiar point in our social life."[2] He gave as the germ for his story Daudet's *Évangéliste,* and the reader of both novels can see a certain resemblance between Olive Chancellor and the religious fanatic, Madame Autheman, who also willfully takes a young girl away from her mother in order to use her for her own cause. However, in Daudet's novel the drama is the girl's mother's, not the lover's. Following his clues which, indeed, he does not conceal in his fiction, we can track down James's true models. However, no source has been offered for the central issue in *The Bostonians:* the struggle between a man and a woman to master and emotionally dominate a young girl, a struggle in which the woman loses out to the man and in which the girl herself is destroyed by her passive, slave-like role.

There is another well-known work in nineteenth-century European fiction which corresponds strikingly to this basic drama, one which James knew well and admired, Balzac's *La Fille aux yeux d'or* (*F*). James quotes from it at length twice in his 1875 essay on Balzac. It was probably one of the most widely read of Balzac's stories in America, especially by boys who, like James, could read French, and was published with two other related romantic adventure stories as *L'Histoire des Treize.* The story opens with a long section in which the author analyzes Parisian society, showing how the obsession with "or et plaisir" differs in every social class, and by means of this introduction prepares the reader for the abnormal emotional occurrences in the story (a narrative device which may be a model for James's seemingly awkward introduction to the first part of *The Bostonians*). Henri De Marsay, a dandy and a member of a secret society ("Les Treize," or "Les Dévorants"), dedicated to pursuing eastern sensual pleasures and accomplishing by a conspiracy of fellow sybarites what one man could not do by himself, vies with his as yet unknown half-sister, the Marquise de San-Réal, for the possession of the soul and body of a gifted illiterate girl, Paquita Valdès, who has been secluded in the Marquise's house and kept in virtual slavery. Her jealous jailer has kept her from knowing anything about the world of men. When she discovers that the girl has been having relations with a man, she ferociously kills her and retires to a convent to devote herself to God. The basic agon of *The Bostonians* is the struggle between Olive Chancellor and her cousin, Basil Ransom, for the possession of the body and soul of Verena Tarrant, a gifted girl who has been secluded by Olive and also kept in virtual slavery. Although linked with Olive in the cause for women's rights, she is kept from the world of men by Olive. When Basil finally wins Verena from her, Olive retires not to a convent but to a nineteenth-century Boston episcopalian version of one, a continued life of zeal in the cause of women.

Before we consider certain echoes of Balzac's tale which corroborate the similarity suggested by the basic structure it may be well to note that James felt a lifetime indebtedness to Balzac which he often mentioned in the five essays on his master. He admitted that Balzac was so completely in his bloodstream that it would be hard for him to say where Balzac ended and he himself began. He wrote that Balzac's books "exist for us, with the lapse of time, as the substance itself of knowledge . . . They have become part of our personal history."[3] In 1884 when he began to write *The Bostonians* he had long been immersed in the *Comédie* [*La Comédie humaine*] and had produced the long essays of 1875 and 1876 (the latter on Balzac's letters). He had just taken a trip into the Balzac country around Tours where he had ferreted out the sites of his favorite stories as if they had been real places where real events had taken place, since for him they *were* real events. An entire day was spent locating Mlle Gamard's boarding house where a poor, good abbé had been victimized by a wicked one. It existed only in *Le Curé de Tours,* a story which James was to rework in *The Spoils of Poynton,* his story of furniture and people.[4]

James's return to America for his mother's funeral had placed before his eyes the woman question in America. His sister's neurasthenia, her morbid attachment to her nurse and companion, Miss Loring, and her passionate feelings had become his personal concern when he installed her and her nurse near Bournemouth while he was writing *The Bostonians*. By following Balzac's strategem of providing a bird's-eye view of Parisian society as a background for the extensions of vice possible among the aristocracy,[5] James transformed his focus from one of pleasure in sex, as in Balzac, to Olive's and her fellow agitators' struggle for the cause of freedom for women. The answer Balzac gives to the woman question is that woman can do pretty much whatever she wants if she acts within the limits that society allows her, and nineteenth-century society allowed the aristocratic woman to do a great deal. Her power can be wielded in a masterly fashion in politics by creating a training ground in worldliness for rising young men who are still powerless. Even in these conditions, as countless stories in the **Comédie** reveal, woman is considered a species inferior to man. Her emotions are her downfall and only a rare hardheaded Madame d'Espard or a Diane de Maufrigneuse can manage to skirt the dangers to which their own passion exposes them. However, it is inexcusable for woman to transgress society's limits, to go beyond the boundaries in her desire to master circumstances and people, in her challenging of man's concept of his own masculinity. For what lies behind the fantastic romantic realism of the Balzac story is the hidden threat to De Marsay's masculinity. This representative of male power at its youthful high, described as a potentate, an underground king who satisfies his need for "the infinite" in Paquita's exotic lovemaking, finds his real challenge in Margarita-Euphémia Porrabéril, the Marquise de San-Réal, who preempts his role. Margarita comes back to murder Paquita after she finds out that she has been betrayed by a man, a member of the sex which, like Olive, she has taught Paquita to distrust and hate. The young girl, like Verena after her, has reacted to this starvation diet by developing a consuming desire to get to know men. She then learns to enjoy men, and finally to prefer them to women. Both Balzac and James are nineteenth-century men in that the "natural" as they conceive it must triumph over the "unnatural." Their presumptuous women, Margarita and Olive, must fail: the Marquise because of her ferocity and resemblance to an animal, and Olive because of her emotional morbidity and ideological fanaticism. What is more important is that both women in their urge to become masters of their loved ones find themselves enslaved by their feelings. They are trapped by their need to go to desperate lengths in their fight against the "natural" attraction between their girls and men. In addition to imprisoning the girls they must bribe the mothers of their protégées. Mrs. Tarrant, Verena's mother, is satirically presented as the daughter of an abolitionist who spent his life trying to free the southern slaves, yet she has permitted the daughter's enslavement to her father's mesmerism with typical slave-to-her-husband psychology. Like Paquita, Verena has her own magic; like Paquita's, too, that magic can only be used by others—first by her father, then Olive and, finally, Basil. The mothers in both stories are the most abject slaves, not bothered by the revolution of rising expectations caused by their daughters' taste for men. Not only are they slaves but slaves corrupted by western society, not even enfranchised in their imaginations as are their daughters. They sell their daughters and are addicted to other vices of the Western world. Paquita's mother wants gold because of her passion for gambling, a vice she has adopted from European society without ever learning either to read, write, or speak anything but her own primitive language. Mrs. Tarrant, too, has her vice, ironically the last one we would expect the daughter of a social reformer to adopt—snobbery and social conformity. The innocent daughters of such parents are tainted from childhood and conditioned to subservience. They do not wish for freedom but for a new captor, one who conforms more to their "natural" drives. In this sense the woman who has assumed the role of master or substitute male has made her biggest mistake, for in barricading her young girl from her "natural" partner, she has encouraged the girl to make the fatal move toward the man simply out of curiosity. Olive tells Verena, "Don't listen to men. They don't care for us. They care only for their pleasure. It is war upon us to the knife." But Verena finds that her walks with Basil have given her, on the contrary, her greatest pleasure. Paquita's reaction to her imprisonment after meeting De Marsay is "cette vie cachée n'est que ténèbres en comparaison de la lumière."[6] She wants him to "prends-moi comme un jouet" as Verena is "the toy" to Basil. Balzac invokes Richardson's Clarissa as the only kind of woman whose character and predicament would excite the blasé De Marsay. Verena is also a Clarissa and her tears when she elopes with Basil prefigure her married life. The last line of *The Bostonians* hints that James must have known that Balzac had at first intended to call his story "The Girl with the Red Eyes"!

Although Balzac has presented the Marquise de San-Réal as a monster, at the end of the story after she has exhausted her rage and murderous vengeance he does show sympathy for her grief and remorse. James, following Balzac, also shows sympathy for Olive in her suffering after the loss of Verena. But both authors clearly are critical of women who assume the basically masculine desire for total possession of the loved one for they condemn them to failure. Olive fails, like the Marquise, because her spell cannot possibly compete with the attraction Verena feels for Basil. (It is interesting that the language of the occult to explain animal magnetism distinguishes both stories; James repeats Balzac's figures of speech showing the resemblance of Basil to a tiger with his yellow eyes and "leonine" hair!) But the conquering element in the male is his ability to keep cool. Both De Marsay and Basil know how to wait. Their basic cynicism (Balzac gives his hero an education by a disenchanted priest, James calls Basil a "cynic")[7] and desire to protect their masculinity (Basil "wants to save his sex from feminization") make them triumph. The victimized girls can at first accept the men who have been presented as deadly enemies only by a feeble attempt to feminize them. At first Paquita can only make love with De Marsay after she dresses him as a woman, but the second time she wants him as he is. At the time of the Burrage lecture Verena tells Basil, "I wanted to convert you. Now I want you to remain as you are." They both slip very easily into the new cadres of love, for they have no wills of their own; they have only *instincts*. The woman who has been enslaved since her early years will remain a slave, and because of the very nature of her emotional blindness the willful woman who fights against the inferior role of woman will be enslaved by her uncontrolled desire for freedom. This is the point of view that both Balzac and James take, although James will revise it in his later fiction. The heroes go on, deflected from their way of life for a moment but not radically changed in their thinking. Whether Basil will ever become President of the United States or even the southern senator he appears to have been based on, Lamar[8] (as De Marsay becomes premier of France outside the time of the story), is doubtful, but he surely will persist in his male-dominated, southern slave-based philosophy. James, whose attitude toward women is more generous and hopeful than Balzac's, allows for such saintly and dedicated types as Miss Birdseye and Dr. Mary Prance who, thoroughly desexed herself, has become simply a functionary with no illusions about either men or women.

James has taken his basic triangle and organized it around the pitting of woman's power against man's power, as Balzac had done ("tu oublies le pouvoir féminin," says Paquita to De Marsay) (*F,* p. 394). However, he has eliminated the cruelty of the marquise which Balzac had explained by her kinship with "les animaux faibles," for "elle avait calculé sa vengeance avec cette perfection de perfidie" (*F,* p. 403), typical of weaker animals. Olive's philosophy—here we may see James "correcting" Balzac's point of view—is one not of vengeance but of renunciation

(she often quotes from *Faust:* "Entsagen sollst du, sollst entsagen!"). James further corrects Balzac's view of women. Instead of emphasizing the duplicity and lack of decency that the French author usually attributes to women, the American author analyzes in depth the failings of the women in his novel—the absurdity of their beliefs and their uncontrolled passion. The ironic detached tone with which James concludes *The Bostonians,* however, links him to the author of the **Comédie,** for it echoes the oblique almost contemptuous ending of *La Fille aux yeux d'or.*

James's unsentimental acceptance of the coming battle between the sexes, cited in the epigraph to this paper, was written at the end of the decade in which James was concerned with the effort of women to transcend their limits in late nineteenth-century society. The options open to an independent-minded woman ended in a stalemate chiefly because her will to influence mimicked but could not take the place of the dominant male patterns of emotional and sexual conquest. Olive "consumed and was consumed"; Paquita died "de la poitrine" (of consumption).

James's appropriation of **La Fille aux yeux d'or** for his own use in *The Bostonians* is more than just another example of his reworking of any piece of fiction which interested him, and Balzac, as we have seen, interested him during his whole literary life. It is also part of a short-lived period of experimentation in which James flirted with the decadent novel. Discussion of James's relationship to the decadent movement is difficult because of the ambiguities that surround the definition of this genre. Certain aspects of Balzac's work, especially **La Fille aux yeux d'or** and **"Une Passion dans le désert"** served as germinating influences for the decadent writers of the 1880s. James himself, in a review of the 1870s, considered that both *Salammbô* and *La Tentation de Saint Antoine* by Flaubert "abounding in the grotesque and the repulsive, the abnormal and the barely conceivable" belonged to this stream. "Behind M. Flaubert," he wrote, "stands a whole society of aesthetic *raffinés,* demanding stronger and stronger spices in its intellectual diet."[9] That other classic of the decadent school, *Mademoiselle de Maupin,* had occupied James's thinking considerably and in a review of Gautier's posthumous works written in the 1870s, he refers to it as "that tremendous monument of juvenile salubrity . . . in which the attempt to seem vicious is like a pair of burnt-cork moustaches smirched over lips still redolent of a mother's milk."[10] James owned all the works of Huysmans, the outstanding decadent of the 1880s, and he owned a first edition of *A Rebours,* perhaps the "bible" of the decadents, which appeared the year James began to write *The Bostonians.*[11] Although James's public view of these writers, especially ten years before he came to write *The Bostonians,* was critical, the important point is the use to which he put them in his novel about a morbid passionate relationship between two women.

James intended *The Bostonians* to be "curious." Writing to Gosse in 1915, he regretted his lack of opportunity to revise it for the New York Edition. If he had, "it would have come out a much truer and more curious thing (it was meant to be curious from the first)."[12] Even Miss Birdseye, he wrote to William in 1885, was meant not only to "be sympathetic, pathetic, picturesque," but also to be presented in a "grotesque way." It is not a matter of accident that the word "curious" (as adjective or in its substantive form) appears at least thirty-three times. "Peculiar" and "peculiarities" appear at least seventeen times, "perverse" at least a dozen. "Queer," "monstrous," "exotic," "oddity," "oriental" are scattered liberally so that the reader is constantly reminded that he is reading a story about "abnormal" events or behavior. The novel, like Dr. Prance, has "an air of taking everything abnormal for granted" (p. 701). This is a device shared by other stories James wrote during these years. As Olive Chancellor represents the witch, so Christina Light of *The Princess Casamassima* represents the *belle dame sans merci* of the romantic tradition,[13] symbols reappearing in the decadent novels of the 1880s which Mario Praz tells us dominated the literary world of the time.[14] "Pandora" (1884) uses "curious," "queer," "peculiar," "singular" a number of times in its short span. Pandora has become a "peculiar" Daisy Miller, driven by perverse male drives to secure an ambassadorship for her fiancé who accepts a passive female role in relation to his aggressive fiancée. All the events are seen through the eyes of a German and references to Goethe and Byron unite this story, as well as *The Bostonians,* to romantic models ("Pandora" repeats the very title of a dramatic fragment by Goethe). "Georgina's Reasons" presents a willful woman who, curiously, for reasons hard to understand, commits bigamy and condemns her husband to a solitary life.

"Curious" seems also to connote strange or unusual sexual behavior. In a letter of this period to Miss Reubell,[15] when James must surely have known of the reputation of the notorious homosexual whom he had just met, he calls Robert de Montesquiou "curious." James remarked to John Buchan when they both handled some private and scandalous Byron papers: "singular . . . most curious, nauseating perhaps."[16]

The novels, stories, and letters of 1884-1886 also indicate an overt interest in the "perverse" and the "curious." In 1875 when he took Swinburne to task for a "perversity of taste in alluding jauntily and *en passant* to Gautier's *Mademoiselle de Maupin*" as "the most

perfect and exquisite book of modern times," James criticized not Swinburne's immorality but the fact that "he does not at all understand immorality." He added that Swinburne's tale about Hugo's "great criminals and monstrosities" is "worthless as anything but amusing fantasy. As psychology it is, to our sense, extremely puerile."[17]

In 1888 he appreciates the *Journal* of the Goncourt brothers which, although inexcusably indiscreet, in his judgment, shows at least "a curious mind moved by sympathy with the curiosity of a coming age."[18] They are "névrosés," and in their uncomfortable style "they offer a lot," for "if you *are* curious . . . where will you get to the same degree as in these patient pages the particular sensation of having your curiosity stimulated and fed?"[19] In fact, this interest in the "curious," and the stimulation of curiosity in the writer and reader, combine and define a new phase in the following work of James: *The Bostonians, The Princess Casamassima* (1886) (where "curious" occurs at least seventeen times, "perverse" or "perversely" even more) and "The Author of 'Beltraffio,'" (1884) in which we find the entire panoply of decadent terms—"monstrous," "grotesque," "curious," "queer," "peculiar"—along with the mention of Balzac and Browning who both dealt with the strange personalities of men and wrote about the tension of abnormal human relations. One of the most "perverse" things in "The Author of 'Beltraffio'" (1884) is the flirtatious behavior of the small boy, Dolcino, son of the author, Mark Ambient, toward the narrator. We know now what James may not have known at the time: that Symonds, the model for Mark Ambient, was homosexual. What James could feel was a wife's fear that the child would be corrupted by the father's writings and tastes and James's depiction of the child's behavior shows that he viewed him as already corrupted.

Having met Edmond de Goncourt with Zola and Daudet just before writing *The Bostonians* and having been exposed to the popular decadent novels of the time, James, in a diluted manner, incorporated the atmosphere of French decadent literature into his works written from 1884 to 1886 in what I have attempted to identify as his "curious" strain—a strain that appeared quite briefly, had no public success, and was soon abandoned. When it came to using actual models from French literature, he seemed, out of genuine literary taste and a dread of what he called the "unclean" in the fiction of both naturalists like Zola and the decadent writers to prefer the earlier "frénétique" romanticism of a few stories by Balzac to the contemporary lush and extreme versions of sensual decadence. However, with Praz's exhaustive catalog at hand we can see characteristics that stamp him here as one of the decadents, although a timid, transmogrified, and exclusively psychological one. In *The Bostonians* he repairs Swinburne's ignorance of decadent psychology and in Olive Chancellor he creates a study of a lesbian personality. The analysis of Olive's morbid fixation on Verena rationalized by her fanatical devotion to the women's rights movement is James's original contribution. Although critics have pointed out that Priscilla's submission to Zenobia in *The Blithedale Romance* is a model for Verena's relation to Olive, and although the Cape Cod episode and the character of Dr. Mary Prance betray the effect of Howells' *Dr. Breen's Profession,* these resemblances are only superficial. Hawthorne's Zenobia, far from wishing to control Priscilla, exerts her power involuntarily and in losing her man to Priscilla is part of a conventional heterosexual triangle. In fact, James found the "least felicitous" part of Hawthorne's novel that part "which deals with Priscilla and her mysterious relation to Zenobia."[20] The only character in *Dr. Breen's Profession* that critics agree has a connection with James's novel is the heroine-worshipping Miss Gleason who admires Dr. Breen, but with no morbidity involved. Olive Chancellor belongs emotionally and psychologically to a class of women different from those appearing in the spate of decadent novels that Praz tells "were the keynote in literature from 1880 on." Olive, however, confined to the tag ends of Puritan society, is ignorant of her drives although she expresses these impulses in a "curious" and "peculiar" pattern.

The music of Wagner, the poetry of Byron, Africa, Faust, Mephistopheles, and "the witches on the Brocken" all appear in *The Bostonians.* In their discreet but unmistakable presence, they attest to this novel's belonging to decadence, focusing on the psychology of "abnormality" *per se* rather than on its sexuality or sensuousness. The green eyes which Praz sees as the signature of the perverted female appear in Olive Chancellor—the "curious tint of her eyes—the glitter of green ice" (even Verena has "curious, radiant, liquid eyes"). As Olive with the "green eyes" is a "fatal woman," so Basil Ransom whose eyes have "yellow lights" is a "fatal man."

More central to *The Bostonians* than the mention of the books and music dear to the decadents or the reiteration of perverseness, peculiarities, curious elements, monstrous characteristics (the latter usually used in a form of hyperbole by Mrs. Luna in describing Olive) is the struggle between a man and a woman for the possession and domination of a young girl. Not in *Faust,* nor in Byron nor Péladan, not in Gautier[21] nor Swinburne can any example of such a struggle be found. In *La Comédie humaine* of Balzac, a constant quarry of themes and technical help for James, the structure of *La Fille aux yeux d'or* alone is unmistakably that of *The Bostonians.* James lifted it out of its

"frénétique" frame in Balzac's pleasure-conspiracy of *L'Histoire des Treize* and concentrated on the one element partially hinted at which really interested him and which Balzac totally ignored, the psychology of the lesbian Marquise de San-Réal. Balzac, always at James's elbow, was a far better model than the effusive, wordy, and fantastic rantings of the decadents which James took as a joke, at least in the case of Gautier.

Balzac tells a tale so perverse and exotic that only Eugène Delacroix, the symbol of exotic romanticism in painting, deserves and gets the dedication. In a story one-sixth the length of *The Bostonians,* Balzac plants images and tropes that James will incorporate into his novel. Balzac uses words referring to the "curious" or "monstrous" twenty-two times, "bizarre," "singulier," "drôle," "monstrueux" sharing the burden. Balzac unlike James uses the word "curieux" to signify the quality that produces interest in something, rather than to specify the peculiar or unusual. The French language offers "bizarre," "singulier," "drôle," "monstrueux" as synonyms for the second meaning. However, James uses "curious" in *both* its senses so the reader feels it is appearing constantly. In Balzac the variety of alternatives refreshes his prose, but one feels that James emphasizes the word to keep the reader constantly aware that "the work was meant to be curious from the first." Balzac also insists on the "unnatural" aspects of the situation which he emphasizes by key words. As Ransom "had grown curious" (p. 439) about the women's rights movement, so Henri de Marsay was interested in "des aventures qui stimulassent sa curiosité" (*F,* p. 359) and as things become more peculiar in this new escapade, the more de Marsay claims "je suis devenu curieux" (*F,* p. 353).

In addition to this noticeable echoing of Balzac's language, the comparison of his hero to lions and tigers is adopted by James for Basil. "Henri avait un courage de lion" (*F,* p. 343); he and the other twelve in his conspiracy of pleasure-seekers are "tigres"; he looks like a tiger (*F,* pp. 349, 351) and roars like a tiger when angry; Paquita's eyes are "deux yeux jaunes comme ceux des tigres"; Henri had "le pouvoir aristocratique du despote oriental" and "une conscience léonine" (*F,* p. 378). *La Fille aux yeux d'or* is centered around other images of exotic character. Paquita's boudoir is an oriental dream and her pleasures are the perversions of the Orient. Balzac presents all this as an example of the hidden corrupt life of pleasure that "une réligion de plaisir et d'égoisme" can unearth in Paris. Henri de Marsay is one of "treize rois inconnus, mais réellement rois," and because of his power can experience an episode filled with "la bizarrerie des contrastes" (*F,* p. 9), Balzac writes in his preface to *L'Histoire des Treize.* When Basil Ransom is introduced at the beginning of *The Bostonians,* he, too, is presented as "strange," "exotic"; he too is a "roi," a king in actual name (the root of Basil is the Greek word for "king") whose discourse had "something almost African in its rich . . . tone" (p. 425), with his black hair "rolled back in a leonine manner" (p. 425), and he too was a personage at once "so exotic" and "peculiar."

The literary ideals of the decadent writer already appear together in the Balzac story. In addition to the Anne Radcliffe novels and *Clarissa Harlowe* with its villain-hero, Lovelace, Balzac mentions the three great romantic classics: "Paquita répondait à cette passion . . . mystérieuse si dramatiquement exprimée dans Faust, si poétiquement traduite dans Manfred, et qui poussait Don Juan à feuiller le cœur des femmes" (*F,* p. 397). James, too, invokes Faust at least three times with special attention to "the witches on the Brocken" (p. 426). He alludes to Byron by mentioning Manfred, and he names an important character, Adeline Luna, after one of the chief heroines in *Don Juan.* Although James refers to the creations of the exotic romanticists who appear after Balzac, such as the Esmeralda of Hugo and the music of Wagner, Balzac had created the mode. Not only had he invoked Delacroix in the dedication to *La Fille aux yeux d'or*—but he probably had in mind a Delacroix painting, *L'Indienne et le tigre,* which shows a wild beast devouring a young Indian girl (vide "Les Dévorants"). This is the kind of image behind the savage murder of Paquita by Margarita, the female counterpart of De Marsay, the tiger. Although Verena does not have the yellow tiger eyes of Paquita, the yellow eyes found their way into the other story of this period of "exotic" references, "Pandora" (1884). They underline the fact that James was holding the Balzac story in his hand at that time. Verena's costume is also like Paquita's, amber beads (p. 463) and a gypsy dress, and as Paquita is described as an "houris de l'Asie . . . à l'Europe de l'éducation, tropique par sa naissance" (*F,* p. 388), so Verena is the granddaughter of an abolitionist and the daughter of a mesmeric healer, exotic offshoots of American life. As Paquita is "la femme du feu," so Verena has "hair of fire." James sees the entire cast of characters as, if not "corrupt" in the sense that Balzac's are, at least "perverse." Though Basil is not so corrupt as Henri, who enjoys an incestuous kiss with his half-sister over the dead body of the girl he has so recently loved passionately, in the eyes of Mrs. Luna he is the essence of "duplicity and perversity" (p. 721).

Lesbianism was a characteristic theme of the French decadent novel. Péladan's *Le Vice suprême* (1884) set the mode, and others followed in profusion. However, the manner in which James handled the subject of Olive's obsession with Verena is typical of the way in

which he translated the concerns of the decadents. In this respect, Olive Chancellor is typical, as James wrote in his *Notebooks,* of New England society, and one feels that he was not only happy in his choice of a locale and movement that could reasonably shelter this morbid and jealous fixation of one woman on another, but that he was also an astute psychologist in noting that such abnormal emotions could be reenforced by an ideology catering to its peculiarities. In fact, the entire predicament enchants him because of its psychology alone, and that is why it is inaccurate to call the attachment simply lesbian. Yet when Basil Ransom meditates on Olive's sex—"what sex was it, great heaven? he used profanely to ask himself" (p. 661)— James is obviously aware of the sexual aspects of Olive's "passionate admiration" for Verena.[22]

Thus it is not strange that James should refer to **La Fille aux yeux d'or** to launch his tale of the "curious." And having done so he would characteristically look at the other "decadent" tale Balzac devoted to "peculiar" attachments, **Sarrasine,** a story within a story, told by La Palférine to help break up Madame de Rochefide's affair with Calyste de Guénic. Sarrasine is a sculptor who mistakenly falls in love with a castrato, the favorite of a powerful cardinal. What James appears to have taken from this story for *The Bostonians* is the scene where Zambinella, the castrato, sees Sarrasine in the audience as he is singing:

> Son regard flamboyant eut une sorte d'influence magnétique sur Zambinella, car le *musico* finit par détourner subitement la vue vers Sarrasine, et alors sa voix céleste s'altéra. Il trembla! Un murmure involontaire échappe a l'assemblée, qu'il tenait comme attachée à ses lèvres, acheva de le troubler; il s'assit, et discontinua son air . . . Cependant Zambinella, s'étant remis, recommença le morceau qu'il avait interrompu si capricieusement; mais il l'exécuta mal, et refusa, malgré toutes les instances qui lui furent faites, de chanter autre chose.[23]

The scene in *The Bostonians* where Verena's beautiful voice falters corresponds to this situation. Verena says to Basil, "As soon as we got here I went out to those steps that go up to the stage and I looked out . . . and saw you in a minute. Then I felt too nervous to speak! I could never, never, if you were there! . . . Olive guessed as soon as I came back." So, too, the cardinal finds out the reason for Zambinella's failure to sing, and sends his men to destroy the castrato. It is interesting that this detail should come from the only other Balzac story centering around human sexual inversion. (Vautrin's attraction to Eugène de Rastignac and Lucien de Rubempré does not determine the plots of the larger novels in which it manifests itself.)

The decadent strain of the contemporary French novel surfaced for only a short period in James's work of the 1880s, but its features were assimilable by him only with the sanctions of the author of *La Comédie humaine*. It is in this fashion that *La Fille aux yeux d'or* entered into the very language and structure of *The Bostonians*.

Notes

1. Henry James, "An Animated Conversation," in *Essays in London and Elsewhere,* by Henry James (New York, 1893), p. 271.

2. The *Notebooks of Henry James,* ed. F. O. Matthiessen and Kenneth B. Murdock, (New York and Oxford, 1947), p. 47.

3. Henry James, *Notes on Novelists* (New York, 1914), pp. 109-10.

4. Adeline R. Tintner, "'The Old Things': Balzac's *Le Curé de Tours* and James's *The Spoils of Poynton*," *NCF,* 26 (March 1972), pp. 436-56.

5. The icons from Balzac's "La Fille aux yeux d'or" spill over even to *The Princess Casamassima.* The English Lord Frederick and his French mistress, the demimondaine Florentine, Hyacinth's parents, repeat the structure of the English Lord Dudley and his French mistress, Florine (often confused with the dancer, Florentine, both courtesans in *La Comédie humaine*), although it is still another French girl who is the mother of De Marsay. The latter's tutor, the Abbé Moronis, is echoed in Mr. Vetch, Hyacinth's equally cynical protector and educator.

6. Honoré de Balzac, "La Fille aux yeux d'or," *La Comédie humaine,* ed. Marcel Bouteron et Henri Lognon: Étude de Moeurs: Scènes de la Vie Parisienne (Paris, 1933), I, 396. All references to "La Fille aux yeux d'or" are indicated by *F.*

7. Henry James, *The Bostonians,* in *The American Novels and Stories of Henry James* (New York, 1947), p. 659. References to *The Bostonians* are indicated only by page number.

8. George Monteiro, *Henry James and John Hay* (Providence: Brown University Press, 1965), p. 97.

9. *Literary Reviews and Essays by Henry James,* ed. Albert Mordell (New York, 1957), p. 150.

10. Ibid., p. 97.

11. Leon Edel, personal communication.

12. *The Letters of Henry James,* ed. Percy Lubbock (New York, 1920), II, 498.

13. Adeline R. Tintner, "James and Keats and *The Princess Casamassima*," *NCF,* 28 (Sept. 1973), 179-93.

14. Mario Praz, *The Romantic Agony* (London and Oxford, 1933), passim.

15. Leon Edel, *Henry James: The Middle Years, 1882-1895* (Philadelphia, 1962), p. 150.

16. John Buchan, *Pilgrim's Way* (Cambridge, 1940), p. 149.

17. Henry James, *Views and Reviews,* ed. LeRoy Phillips (Boston, 1908), p. 59.

18. Henry James, *Essays in London and Elsewhere,* p. 189.

19. Ibid., p. 201.

20. Henry James, Jr., *Hawthorne* (New York: Harper, 1879), p. 132.

21. In *Mademoiselle de Maupin* Gautier presents a young woman who is attracted to and sexually functions with both a man and a woman and cannot make up her mind which to choose. There is a reminder of this ambivalence, even a precedent for it, in Verena's wavering in her final choice between Basil and Olive. However, in Gautier's novel there is no interest in the psychology of such a choice and no passionate struggle between the man and woman lovers to possess the young girl, no actual lesbian passion, since the heroine performs as a hermaphrodite and perverse sexual pleasure is the sole concern of the author. There is no hint of personal passion nor of the fight to possess a human soul.

22. *The Notebooks of Henry James,* p. 46.

23. Honoré de Balzac, *La Comédie humaine,* Études de Moeurs: Scènes de la Vie Parisienne, "Sarrasine," (Paris, 1913), IV, 427-28.

Marthe Robert (essay date 1980)

SOURCE: Robert, Marthe. "Marthe Robert on the Oedipal Family Romance." In *Balzac,* edited by Michael Tilby, pp. 201-20. Harlow, England: Longman Group Publishers, 1995.

[*In the following excerpt, originally published in 1980, Robert contends that Henri de Marsay, the protagonist of* The Girl with the Golden Eyes, *enjoys certain freedoms, rights, and power because of his bastard status.*]

Henri de Marsay may be seen as the first of this generation of indolent and ambitious Bastards, compelled by circumstances rather than by nature to go to the dogs or to achieve the highest honours and the most responsible situations (de Marsay becomes Prime Minister under the July Monarchy, Rastignac is Under

Secretary of State in his cabinet, then Minister of Justice). The hero of *La Fille aux yeux d'or* has precisely the family background and history his lightning ascent requires—this novelettish Bastard could not have written his autobiography otherwise had he been paid to do so, for everything happens to him according to the *convention* to which such literature conforms (Balzac's contemporaries were not entirely unjustified in classifying him with Eugène Sue: the novelettish aspect of a number of his stories could easily lead them to overlook the difference in quality and even influenced the judgement of such a distinguished and authentic novelist as Dostoevsky).

> Lovely as the day, everywhere at ease, a thoroughbred with a schoolgirl's complexion, gentle and modest of appearance, slim, aristocratic and possessing beautiful hands, Henri is (let us conceal it no longer) a love-child, the natural son of Lord Dudley and the well-known Marquise de Vordac . . .

In other words he is a genuine bastard whose characteristic inconsistency is given ample scope until he achieves a fortune and a government post which, at the time, was equivalent to Royalty. Henri's mother had been married off by her lover to an old nobleman called Monsieur de Marsay, 'a faded butterfly', who adopts the child 'in exchange for the usufruct of a one-hundred-thousand francs income automatically devolving to his presumed son . . .' 'The old nobleman died without having known his wife. Madame de Marsay then married the Marquis de Vordac; but before becoming a Marquise she had not shown much interest for the child she had borne to Lord Dudley . . .' Here indeed we have a typical Oedipal Family Romance situation, what Dostoevsky called an 'accidental family' where everything conspires to enable the hero to create his own life unfettered and be able to transgress and transcend human laws. As a foundling who knows neither his mother's nor his father's identity, 'the only father poor Henri de Marsay was to know was, of the two, the one who had no obligation to be such. Monsieur de Marsay's paternity was naturally most unsatisfactory.' Moreover, first entrusted to the care of one of his adopted father's aged sisters, then to a learned, alcoholic priest, an atheist who was particularly interested in the one-hundred-thousand francs income into the bargain, this youthful Adonis grew up without ever feeling any 'dutiful' affection. And such a total lack of ties is precisely what makes his future supremacy possible. Unlike Don Juan, with whom he shares a complete lack of faith 'in men, women, God and the Devil', he will make everyone submit to his charm without himself having to pay for it in any way (it should be noted however that he dies young and, like Balzac, shortly after having taken the marriage vows).

If Balzac's highly-praised realism is not always as thorough as one tends to believe—indeed for certain psychological reasons we shall discuss later it is often totally inadequate—in this case, notwithstanding or perhaps because of the novelettish course of events, it must be admitted that he fully deserves his reputation, at least insofar as subjective personal realism is concerned. For this story, which combines extravagance with conventionality and where the most incredible clichés of Romantic folklore are heavily underscored, is absolutely true to life—not actually true, of course, but in its portrayal of an 'accidental family' such as that where Balzac himself experienced the ordinary, ever-changing tragedy of an unhappy childhood. With his distinguished father, generously distributing bastards throughout the neighbourhood, his notoriously unfaithful mother whose lover, a neighbouring worthy, was the official family friend, a beloved younger sister on whom he doted to compensate perhaps for the mother's neglect of her legitimate offspring, and a young brother (called Henri like the Comte de Marsay) whose illegitimacy was an open secret and who was the sole object of his mother's affections, the child Honoré would find in his immediate surroundings confirmation of the Family Romance's most daring inventions. First of all he would be entitled to believe that an illegitimate child is gifted with peculiar qualities that invite affection (both he and his sister Laure were very fond of Henri whom they never ceased to protect while trying to repair the havoc he made of his life). Furthermore, since he had countless brothers in the neighbourhood who did not bear his father's name and one under his roof who bore it without being his father's son, he had more reason than most young Bastards to question the legitimacy of his own birth and to solve the problem without more ado to the advantage of his Oedipal dreams (since Henri bears my father's name without being his son, who can prove that I, Honoré, bear the name of my real father?). Thus on the one hand an illegitimate child enjoys almost magical powers that make his irregular situation particularly enviable, but on the other anybody may be illegitimate given the uncertainty which generally—and especially in this family—surrounds the notion of paternity and descent. With the help of a child's imagination, always ready at the best of times to add flattering touches to irreversible fate, Honoré appropriates the supposedly incalculable prerogatives of his younger brother, without renouncing the unchallenged rights of his own legitimacy. But the basis for the whole operation is the uneasy reality of a particularly suspect 'accidental family' which, seen through the eyes of a precocious, sensitive child, contributes to his fiction an element of realism and a partiality for the concrete and for verisimilitude which he maintains even in his most striking overstatements. (R. Judrin observes that 'a sane mind has never raved more wildly',[1] and conversely: never has a madman been so rational—suffice it to remember the German story-tellers.) The youthful maker of romances who acts on the authority of a questionable civil status—always questionable but especially so in the Balzac family—to reinvent his biography *rationally,* will become the all-powerful novelist capable not only of creating countless existences but of competing with the one institution entitled to name individuals and legalise descents. Far from being a belated addition to art and intellect his famous competition with the registry office may be said to be an old habit, a familiar practice whose resources Balzac had exploited during the formative years of his intellectual pre-history, long before he was capable of formulating the idea.

Thus Henri de Marsay and similar young upstarts in *La Comédie humaine* illustrate the incredible luck of having claims to illegitimacy—a blessing for which the child Honoré could only envy his younger brother Henri who automatically enjoyed its prerogatives: incomparable charm together with more power and freedom. Henri and Honoré de Balzac, both raised to the peerage by the spurious particle the elder decided one fine day to affix to his name,[2] merge into the single figure of the irresistible charmer, gifted with a man's strength and the grace and beauty of a girl, who effortlessly captivates whomsoever he meets because, free from the emotional constraints of family ties, he *belongs* to no living creature. Having become in his own imagination the illegitimate child his brother really was, Honoré invents another Henri, a true Bastard this time, a favourite of both nature and society precisely insofar as, being born outside official relationships, he outrageously breaks off the sequence of generations.

> He had grown up in mysterious circumstances which invested him with immense, inexplicable power. This youth held a sceptre more mighty than that of a modern king who is nearly always restrained on every side by laws and regulations. De Marsay possessed the autocratic power of an Oriental despot. But whereas in the East such power is squandered on besotted men, here it was supported by a Western mind, a French intellect, indeed by one of the liveliest and sharpest instruments of knowledge . . . His imperceptible sway over society had invested him with a real but invisible majesty, unemphatic and self-contained. He saw himself, not as Louis XIV saw himself, but as the proudest Khalif or Pharaoh who believes he is of divine origin and appears veiled before his subjects because, like the gods, he cannot be contemplated face to face without causing instantaneous death . . .

Invisible majesty, immense, inexplicable power, the awareness of being greater than Oriental despots—who indeed could not boast of having held sway over all Paris—all these prerogatives were de Marsay's as a result of illegitimacy and a neglected childhood which entitle him even to the most terrible of divine privileges, murder (he kills, unhesitatingly, anybody he considers has insulted him).

Among the extraordinary advantages derived from his hero's divine, outlawed status there is one Balzac refers to less frankly, even if in *La Fille aux yeux d'or* it is precisely what sparks off a sequence of strange events. It consists in the peculiarity of 'accidental families' such as Henri's to favour and even condone incest, because in them kinship is more obscure and hypothetical than elsewhere. Lord Dudley—similar in this respect to Bernard François Balssa, if we are to take Balzac's word for it—never bothered to 'notify his off-spring of all the siblings with whom he had favoured them', so that Henri is unaware of the existence of the sister he happens to meet when he is about twenty (incidentally in the most risky circumstances, since this unexpected sister is furthermore his rival for the affections of the golden-eyed girl whom she jealously sequestrates to prevent her from knowing the love of a man). Thus Henri might just as easily have fallen in love with Lord Dudley's daughter, in which case not he but his father would have been to blame for their incest, were it only because of his amazing frivolity ('Who is this handsome youth? My son? Oh what a nuisance!'). Conversely Honoré, were he truly the bastard he hopes and believes he is, might indulge his secret attraction to Laure, the beloved sister he incessantly pursues in the guise of all the Laures with whom he seeks to perfect his sentimental education and to find happiness (Laure de Berny, Laure Sallambier, Laurence de Montzaigle, Laure d'Abrantès, so many 'sisters' whose names foredoom them to revive a forbidden childhood inclination and, in the context of Oedipal transference, so many mothers won over from an abhorred father).[3] However Henri de Marsay does not commit the incest circumstances seemed to favour. He is precluded from doing so because the author had already concentrated on him all his hopes for a successful social ascent, and cannot therefore submit him to the supreme retribution automatically reserved for Oedipal transgression (Oedipus must be a king and full of honours when Fate strikes him down). Incest is thus averted and only occurs as it were by proxy, in the person of this strange golden-eyed girl who seems to be indiscriminately susceptible to the charms of all Lord Dudley's children, bestowing her favours simultaneously on the brother and the sister and thus creating an incestuous situation more compatible, doubtless, with the hero's lofty ambitions, if not with the requirements of ordinary ethics. The golden-eyed girl pays for this indirect incest she has innocently perpetrated, with her life—she is stabbed in the end, not by

Henri, though he had considered killing her and been deterred at the last minute, but by Euphémie, who can easily be sacrificed since she has no role to play in Balzac's ambitious pilgrimage.[4]

Notes

1. Cf. *Encyclopaedia Universalis,* under *Balzac.*

2. His earlier works, published under his own name were signed Honoré Balzac. When criticised for suddenly adding the particle to his name, Balzac defended himself by asserting that his father, member of an aristocratic provincial family, had decided to resume his legitimate title. (Cf. Preface to *Le Lys dans la vallée.*) However this is not very convincing. In the end he admitted that he called himself de Balzac just as Monsieur Arouet had called himself de Voltaire ('He knew he would dominate his century, and such premonitions justify every audacity').

3. R. Judrin (*Encyclopaedia Universalis*) observes 'Is it not remarkable that most of Balzac's relationships with women were grouped under a single first name?' Indeed, very remarkable but also very understandable in an accidental family where circumstances favoured incestuous relationships and encouraged its members to collaborate in a single Family Romance (furthermore we know that Laure de Surville collaborated with her brother in some of his books and 'provided' him with plots). The author takes his suggestion no further but his conclusion corresponds to our theory: 'It seems obvious that in *La Comédie humaine* Balzac was inspired by this natural coincidence, *rather as Napoleon, less permanently, set Bonapartes over Europe.*' (My italics.)

4. *La Fille aux yeux d'or* is usually highly praised by Balzac enthusiasts, though the story itself is more melodramatic than tragic and the pomposity, overstatement and inconsistent similes (Henri rules over 1828 Paris like an Oriental despot!) border on the absurd. This is because Balzac, *a great novelist but not a greater writer,* has the knack of somehow dreaming right, like all those who have delved deep enough into their unconscious to be scorched by the flame of truth they find there.

Shoshana Felman (essay date 1981)

SOURCE: Felman, Shoshana. "Rereading Femininity." *Yale French Studies,* no. 62 (1981): 19-44.

[*In the following essay, Felman argues that* The Girl with the Golden Eyes *explores issues of sexual identity as well as the fundamental nature and interrelatedness of masculinity and femininity.*]

Rereading, an operation contrary to the commercial and ideological habits of our society, which would have us "throw away" the story once it has been consumed . . . so that we can then move on to another story, buy another book . . . , rereading is here suggested at the outset, for it alone saves the text from repetition (those who fail to reread are obliged to read the same story everywhere).

(Roland Barthes)

"The Riddle of Femininity"

"Today's lecture," wrote Freud in 1932, "may serve to give you an example of a detailed piece of analytic work, and I can say two things to recommend it. It brings forward nothing but observed facts . . . , and it deals with a subject which has a claim on your interest second almost to no other":

Throughout history people have knocked their heads against the riddle of the nature of femininity. . . . Nor will *you* have escaped worrying over this problem— those of you who are men; to those of you who are women this will not apply—you are yourselves the problem.[1]

Intended for "an audience gathered from all the Faculties of the University,"[2] the lecture, entitled "Feminity," was in fact never delivered. Having undergone an operation for mouth cancer, its author was no longer in a condition to deliver public lectures. And thus he wrote, prefacing his own unspoken lecture:

A surgical operation had made speaking in public impossible for me. If, therefore, I once more *take my place in the lecture room* during the remarks that follow, it is only by an artifice of the imagination; it may help me not to forget to *bear the reader in mind* as I enter more deeply into my subject.[3]

I would here like to take my place as reader—as a reader of "Feminity" and as a reader of femininity—by reflecting, first, on its relation to Freud's place: to Freud's place in the lecture room, at once real and imaginary, of the University of Vienna; the place which he addresses and from which he asks the question of femininity. In quoting Freud's introductory remarks as an introduction to this paper—itself originally delivered as a public talk—I have displaced, however, the locus of the question to another lecture room and to another structure of address. Thus, when I said along with Freud, "Today's lecture . . . has a claim on your interest second almost to no other," and "I can say two things to recommend it," "today" was not 1932 but 1979; the "you" addressed was not the Viennese University public but a contemporary American audience gathered for a feminist colloquium at the University of Wisconsin-Milwaukee; and my usage of the first person "I" introduced into the quotation a discrepancy of genders, since Freud's "I" implied the male gender, whereas I addressed the public as a woman. Consequently, when I then went on to quote, throughout history men have knocked their heads against the riddle of femininity. . . . Nor will *you* have escaped worrying over this question—those of you who are men; to those of you who are women, this will not apply—

the audience—as I had expected—did not fail to laugh.

What are the implications of this laughter? It was brought about by an awareness—at once spontaneous and historical—of the spatial, temporal and sexual displacement that my enunciation operated in Freud's statement. But this historical awareness—the discrepancy named "history" which my reading introduced into Freud's text as a difference from itself—only made apparent the inherent textual discrepancy between Freud's *statement,* opening up the question *of* the Woman, and his *utterance,* closing it *for* women, excluding women from the question: "to those of you who are women, this will not apply; you are yourselves the problem."

"Those of you who are men," on the other hand, will not "have escaped worrying over this problem." A question, Freud thus implies, is always a question of desire; it springs out of a desire which is also the desire for a question. Women, however, are considered merely as the *objects* of desire, and as the *objects* of the question. To the extent that women "*are* the question," they cannot *enunciate* the question; they cannot be the speaking *subjects* of the knowledge or the science which the question seeks.

In assuming here my place as a speaking subject, I have then *interfered,* through female utterance and reading, in Freud's male writing. I have *enacted* sexual difference in the very act of reading Freud's interrogation of it; enacted it as precisely difference, with the purpose not of rejecting Freud's interrogation, but of displacing it, of carrying it beyond its *stated* question, by disrupting the transparency and misleadingly self-evident universality of its male enunciation.

Freud, indeed, in spite of his otherwise radical approach, still articulates "the riddle of femininity" in typical nineteenth-century terms. His question: "what is femininity?" in reality asks: "what is femininity—*for men*?" My simple (female) reiteration of Freud's question—with the rhetorical effect of the public's laughter—has somewhat redefined the "riddle" and implied a slightly different question: what does the question—"what is femininity—*for men*?"—mean *for women*?

It is this question which I propose to address in the present study, through a reading of an ingenious text by Balzac which, in its turn, dramatizes the "riddle of femininity" as the double question of the reading of sexual difference and of the intervention of sexual difference in the very act of reading.

"GOLD AND PLEASURE": SOCIAL CLASSES AND SEX ROLES

The text in question, Balzac's short novel entitled ***The Girl with the Golden Eyes***[4], is in fact literally a provocative erotic *riddle,* specifically addressing the question of sexual difference: dramatizing, in a triangular complication, the interferences of an affair between a man and a woman with an existing affair between two women, depicting both the interplay and the conflict between homosexual and heterosexual loves, the text at once explores and puts in question the very structure of opposition between the sexes, as well as the respective definitions of masculinity and femininity.

The erotical narrative, however, is preceded by a long discursive preamble in which the narrator depicts a panoramic analytical picture of Paris and its social classes. The classes are *separated,* economically distinguished, according to their material wealth, according to the amount of gold that they possess or do not possess; but they are also *united* by their common desire for "gold" and for "pleasure": the self-destructive drive for ever-increasing amounts of money and enjoyment canalizes the social energies on all class levels. Paris is thus viewed by Balzac as a battlefield of interests and of passions in which "everything stimulates the upward march of money" (p. 318), each "sphere" throwing its "spawn into a superior one," each class endeavoring to rise to a higher social rank, in order "to obey that universal master, gold or pleasure" (p. 316, TM). "Who . . . is dominant in this country . . . ? Gold and pleasure. Take these two words as a light," says Balzac (pp. 310-311, TM).

What is then the connection, the question arises, between Balzac's "light" and Balzac's darkness, between this discursive sociological treatise on Parisian society and the rather obscure erotical narrative that follows? How does the *class struggle* depicted in the prologue relate to the *sex struggle* around which the story revolves?

It would seem, at first sight, that what is common to the two struggles is the very structure of *division* from which they spring, as well as the principle of *hierarchy* which, in both cases, organizes the division as an authoritative *order.* The prologue's hierarchical division of social classes would thus correspond to the story's hierarchical division of sexual roles according to which, in Balzac's society as well as in ours, the female occupies the inferior position whereas the male, in much the same way as the class possessing the gold, occupies the superior, ruling position.

It is no coincidence that the feminine heroine, Paquita, is a slave, whose origin is "a country where women are not human beings, but chattels. One does what one likes with them, sells them, buys them, kills them. In fact one uses them to indulge one's whims, just as here you make use of your furniture" (p. 390). The alibi of a *foreign* country's cultural manners should not, however, mislead us, since it is in Paris that Paquita is thus disposed of, being sexually used and unscrupulously murdered. It is equally in Paris that Henri de Marsay pronounces his contemptuous verdict on women:

> And what then is woman? a little thing, a bunch of twaddle. With two words spoken in the air, can't she be made to work for four hours? She is sure that the fop will take care of her, because he does not think of great things. . . . Indeed, a fop cannot help being a fop if he has a reason for being one. It's the women who give us this rank. The fop is the colonel of love, he is a lady killer, he has his regiment of women to command. . . . So therefore foppishness . . . is the sign of an unquestionable power conquered over the female population.
>
> (pp. 348-349, TM)

It is in these terms, by this verdict on women, that Henri de Marsay defines his own foppishness as well as his own male role in the story, the typical male role of the Parisian civilization. According to these well-defined masculine/feminine social roles, the relationship between man and woman is one of sexual hierarchization, in which the man is the master whereas the woman is reduced to the state of a mere slave, at once man's pleasure-object and his narcissistic assurance of his own importance, value and power.

GOLD AND FEMININITY

This culturally determined male attitude can also, more subtly, be analyzed, not through Henri's *contempt* for "the female population" of Paris but through his *admiration* for an exceptional woman—the girl with the golden eyes—whose desirable image strikes him as his feminine ideal, the very incarnation of the woman of his dreams:

> Last Thursday . . . I was strolling about . . . , I found myself face to face with a woman. . . . This was no case of stupefaction, nor was she a common streetwalker. Judging from the expression on her face, she seemed to be saying: "What! you are here, my ideal, the being I have thought of, dreamed of night and morning! . . . Take me, I am yours . . ." And so on. . . . So I looked at her closely. My dear fellow, from a physical standpoint, this incognita is *the most adorably feminine woman I have ever met. . . . And what most struck me straightaway,* what I still find fascinating, is *her two eyes,* yellow as a tiger's; yellow as *gleaming gold; living gold, brooding gold, amorous gold, gold that wants to come into your pocket. . . .* Ever since I have taken interest in women, my un-

known *she* is the only one whose virginal bosom, whose ardent and voluptuous curves have realized for me the unique woman of my dreams. . . . *She is the very essence of woman,* an abyss of pleasures whose depths may never be sounded: *the ideal woman.*

> (pp. 337-339, TM; italics mine)

Clearly Henri is here attracted to the girl's golden eyes because they are for him the sign of feminine desire and sexuality, the very incarnation of femininity *per se.* However, what are the connotations of the metaphor of gold which, through her eyes, comes to symbolize the girl and, thus, to embody ideal femininity? By virtue of its very brilliance, the "gleaming gold" ("*jaune d'or qui brille*") is essentially a *reflective* substance, which reflects a source of light external to itself; the light reflected comes indeed from the object contemplated by the woman—Henri himself: the golden eyes of femininity are fundamentally a *mirror* in which the male—Henri—can contemplate his own idealized self-image so as to admire himself:

> Judging from the expression on her face, she seemed to be saying: "What! you are here, my ideal, the being I have thought of, I have dreamed of night and morning!"
>
> (p. 338)

The golden brilliance of the girl with the golden eyes is fascinating, says Henri, because it is an "amorous gold, gold that wants to come into your pocket." Paradoxically, gold as the metaphor of the utmost value is an image, at the same time, of *possession* and *appropriation,* through which the ideal woman is again reduced to a mere *object,* whose sole function is to be possessed and owned by man. But the metaphor evoked by Henri of the gold that wants to come into his pocket is even more ambiguous than that, since, carrying a clear erotic connotation suggestive of the sexual act, it grants the golden eyes of femininity a fantasmatic masculine—phallic—role. Ironically enough, femininity itself thus turns out to be a metaphor of the phallus. To the extent that the girl with the golden eyes is here viewed by Henri as the tool for his purely narcissistic satisfaction, Henri's desire for the ideal woman can be said to be a sort of masturbation fantasy: his own phallus is indeed the prize he seeks. In much the same way as, in the prologue, gold was said to be the ruling principle, a principle of domination and of hierarchy, so the golden phallus in the story, beckoning from behind the mask of woman's beauty, is to be wishfully recuperated and restored to its proper place: man's pocket.

The girl with the golden eyes is thus the very name of woman and of femininity *as a fantasy of man.* The name, indeed, was given to the girl by a group of men—Henri's friends. Defined by man, the conventional polarity of masculine and feminine names woman as a *metaphor of man.* Sexuality, in other words, functions here as the sign of a rhetorical convention, of which woman is the *signifier* and man the *signified.* Man alone has thus the privilege of proper meaning, of *literal* identity: femininity, as signifier, cannot signify *itself;* it is but a metaphor, a figurative substitute; it can but refer to man, to the phallus, as its proper meaning, as its signified. The rhetorical hierarchization of the very opposition between the sexes is then such that woman's *difference* is suppressed, being totally subsumed by the reference of the feminine to masculine identity.

A QUESTION OF ADDRESS

When Henri decides to possess, i.e., to place in his pocket, the gold of the girl with the golden eyes, he has first to find out who she is. Having followed the girl to the house where she lives, he charges his valet to spy on the mailman and shrewdly extort from him the name of the target of his desire. In order to ward off the mailman's suspicion, the valet is furnished with a false package which he supposedly has to deliver to the golden-eyed girl. Having learnt from the mailman that the house belongs to Don Hijos, Marquis de San Réal, the valet mistakenly concludes that the woman desired by his master must be the Marquis's wife. "My package," he thus tells the mailman, "is for the Marquise." (p. 342). But he soon realizes his mistake when the mailman, responding to a bribe offer, informs him of the presence of still another woman in the Marquis's house. The mailman then shows him the address on a letter he has to deliver: the real name of the golden-eyed girl is Paquita Valdès. On the basis of this information, the valet, and Henri in his turn, will make a second mistake, assuming that Paquita must then be the mistress of the Marquis. The drama of desire being a triangular one, the Marquis, Henri mistakenly thinks, must therefore be his rival and his enemy.

> The report made by his valet Laurent had enormously enhanced the value of the girl with the golden eyes. Battle had to be given to some secret antagonist, as dangerous, it seemed, as he was cunning. To gain the victory all the forces at Henri's command would not be superfluous. He was about to act the eternally old, eternally new comedy with three characters: an old man, Don Hijos, a girl, Paquita, and a suitor, de Marsay.
>
> (p. 347)

If Henri's story seems, at its outset, to follow indeed the conventional triangular pattern of erotic competition, of rivalry in desire, the seemingly banal triangle is an uncanny one to the extent that Henri has no real knowledge, in fact, of his partners in the triangle. Engaged as he is in the very act of desiring and of struggling, of opposing, Henri does not really know who it

is that he truly desires, who it is that he truly opposes, who are the two other poles of the triangle which implicates him and structures his own sexual involvement. The episode with the mailman, more crucial than it appears to be, outlines thus the basic unconscious inquiry which governs Henri's adventure: the question is indeed one of *addresses.* Through his valet, Henri asks the mailman: what is the real address of the message of my desire? Whom do I really desire? For whom, in fact, is my package? And what, on the other hand, is the true address (the true addressee) of my hostility, of my aggressivity? Who is my real enemy? These two basic questions, pertaining to the address of desire and to the identity of the enemy, immediately translate themselves into two *interpretative mistakes:* "my package is for the marquise," says Laurent; the enemy is the marquis, thinks Henri. Whereas the first mistaken assumption is quickly dispelled and corrected, the second mistake is there to stay, in Henri's interpretation as well as in that of the reader, until the dénouement of the story, in which Henri, along with the reader, discovers that Henri's rival is not the *marquis* but the *marquise.* The mistake, in other words, consists in the substitution of the *masculine* for the *feminine.* It is therefore governed by the logic of the rhetorical hierarchy of the polarity masculine/feminine, according to which the signified (i.e., meaning) is as such necessarily *masculine,* can only be *read in the masculine.* But the story on the contrary shows this rhetorical presupposition to be indeed an ironic error. Henri, as well as the reader, has to learn, as the text puts it, to "read this page, so brilliant in its effect, and guess its hidden meaning" (p. 376, TM). If Henri's drama springs from a *misreading of femininity,* consisting in a blind substitution of the masculine for the feminine, what Henri has to learn is precisely how to read femininity; how to *stop reading* through the exclusive blind reference to a masculine signified, to phallocentric meaning.

THE SEX OF READING

The substitution, by Henri, of the masculine for the feminine in his attempt to read the proper name of his enemy, is by no means the only error in the story. Ironically enough, Paquita commits a strikingly similar, although diametrically opposed, mistake. In much the same way as Henri—a typical ideological product of the ruling male civilization—is unable to read in the feminine, Paquita, by reason of the coercive and restrictive education to which she has been subjected, is unable to read in the masculine. Having been confined as a slave since the age of twelve, in sexual bondage to the marquise, Paquita—in the most literal manner—does not know what a man is, before her encounter with Henri. That is why her understanding of the opposition masculine/feminine takes the feminine as its point of reference. When she sees Henri for the first time, she is struck by his resemblance to the *woman* she knows and loves—the marquise—who, we will later learn, is really Henri's sister. "It's the same voice," said Paquita in a melancholy tone, "and the same ardent passion." (p. 361) Paquita then falls in love with Henri because of his very resemblance to the woman she knows. In their first sexual scene, Paquita makes Henri dress as a woman, so that he might better resemble the original model, the feminine referent: a wish which Henri unsuspectingly obeys as a pure fantasy. Paquita's very innocence thus becomes an ironic reversal of the conventional functioning of the polarity masculine/feminine: like the feminine for Henri, the masculine for Paquita signifies not itself but its symmetrical, specular opposite. The feminine is at first for Paquita the *proper meaning* of the masculine. Whereas Henri's ideal woman is a metaphor of the phallus, Paquita's ideal man is a metaphor of a woman.[5]

Since Paquita makes Henri wear a woman's dress, Henri, unwittingly, thus becomes a transvestite. Balzac's text could be viewed, indeed, as a rhetorical dramatization and a philosophical reflection on the constitutive relationship between transvestism and sexuality, i.e., on the constitutive relationship between sex roles and clothing. If it is clothes, the text seems to suggest, if it is clothes alone, i.e., a cultural sign, an institution, which determine our reading of the sexes, which determine masculine and feminine and insure sexual opposition as an orderly, hierarchical polarity; if indeed clothes make the *man*—or the woman—, are not sex roles as such, inherently, but travesties? Are not sex roles but travesties of the ambiguous comlexity of real sexuality, of real sexual difference? Paquita's ideal man is but a travesty of feminine identity, in much the same way as Henri's ideal woman is a travesty of masculine identity; Henri's masculine sex role, for Paquita, in the same way as Paquita's feminine sex-role for Henri, are thus but transvestisms of the other sex's deceptively unequivocal identity; that is, they are travesties of a travesty.

If transvestism then refers sexuality to clothes, to the cultural institution of the sign, travesty is possible because signs function not just grammatically, according to a norm, but rhetorically, through substitutions. Transvestism is indeed an arbitrary sign whose signifier is displaced onto a signified not "its own," an exiled signifier which no longer has, in fact, a "proper" signified, a "proper" meaning, a claim to literality. Transvestism, in Balzac's story, links sexuality to rhetoric, and rhetoric to sexuality: *"Tu travestis les mots"* ("You disguise—you travesty—your words," p. 377), says Henri to his friend Paul de Manerville, unwittingly suggesting that transvestism as well as trav-

esty are conditioned by the functioning of language; that sexes can be substituted, that masculine and feminine can be exchanged, or travestied, because words can be.

ACTIVE DISCRETION

Henri, indeed, exposes a whole theory of rhetoric relating sexuality to language through two principles of "discretion":

> When you find yourself in need of discretion, learn this: there are *two kinds, one active, one negative. Negative discretion* belongs to the dolts who have recourse to *silence, denial,* frowning faces, the discretion which takes effect behind closed doors—sheer impotence! *Active discretion proceeds by blunt assertion.*
>
> (p. 375, italics mine)

Active discretion, in other words, consists not in denying what one wants to hide, nor in simply keeping silent about it, but in positively saying something else, in making a concrete erotic *affirmation* altogether different, so as to displace the focus of attention, to divert suspicion from the fact to be concealed. Active discretion, says Henri,

> The best kind of discretion . . . , consists of compromising a woman we're not keen on, or one we don't love or don't possess, in order to preserve the honor of the one we love sufficiently to respect her. The former is what I call the *screen-woman.*
>
> (p. 375, TM)

The rhetoric of sexuality is thus a rhetoric of screens: of what Henri calls "negative discretion"—euphemisms and understatements—or of what he calls positive, "active discretion," the ostentatious use—in a kind of erotic overstatement—of a *screen-woman.*

The question here arises: if a woman can as such be but a screen, what can she screen? Is there, in Balzac's text, a screen-woman? Who is she? Where are the screens? And what is being screened? Can the polarity of masculine and feminine itself be modified, affected by the screen procedure, by the subversive power of linguistic travesty, by the potentiality of transvestism built into language?

A screen can have a triple function: it can serve to divide or separate, to conceal or hide, to protect or shield. In a sense, it could be said that the marquise, Henri's sister, is the screen-woman, since she literally tries to screen Paquita—to hide Paquita from the world and to hide the world from Paquita. In so acting, she constitutes a screen between Paquita and Henri. Henri's attempt, of course, is to break through, to traverse that screen. But the marquise inadvertently reemerges as a screen—as a barrier—between the lovers when Paquita, by mistake, cries out her name at the very height of her ecstatic sexual intercourse with Henri.

> At the very moment when de Marsay was forgetting everything and was minded to take possession of this creature for ever, in the very midst of ecstasy a dagger-stroke was dealt him which pierced his heart through and through: the first mortification it had ever received. Paquita, who had found strength enough to lift him above her as if to gaze upon him, had exclaimed: "Oh! Mariquita!"
>
> "Mariquita!", the young man roared out. "Now I know all that I didn't want to believe."
>
> (pp. 383-384)
>
> Paquita's exclamation was the more hateful to him because he had been hurled down from the sweetest triumph which had ever exalted his masculine vanity.
>
> (p. 385)

Paquita's exclamation is a double insult to Henri, and a symbolic emasculation, first, because the name she calls out in her ecstasy is not his own, and second, because not only is he a mere substitute, but he is obviously being substituted for a *woman*. It is thus the very name Mariquita which becomes a screen between the lovers: a screen because it separates them; a screen because it is a woman's name which names a man; a screen in that it is a substitute, a *proper* name which names *improperly:* the very name, indeed, of impropriety.

The screen is thus a *signifier,* and the signifier's implications could extend beyond its simple referent, the woman it refers to. Mariquita, indeed, is not just a woman's name; it also means, in Spanish, an effeminate man; its implicit connotation of homosexuality, although obviously linked to the marquise's name as well as to her sexual mores, cannot but reflect back upon Henri, whom it re-names. Furthermore, the name "Mariquita" can be read as a composite, either of "*mar*quise" and "Pa*quita*" or of *Mar*say (Hen*ri*) and Pa*quita;* as a signifier, the word "Mariquita" thus names both Paquita's ambiguity, as part of two different couples, and the linkage of de Marsay and Paquita in Mariquita; i.e., the triangular linkage which ties together de Marsay, Paquita, and Mariquita. Paradoxically, the screen between the lovers, the name Mariquita, while it separates them, also metonymically links them to each other. The screen is a triangle. And the triangle is a screen in that it cancels out, precisely, the propriety of its three proper names, setting them in motion, as interchangeable, in a substitutive signifying chain which subverts, along with their propriety, their opposition to one another, subverting, by the same token, the clear-cut polarity, the symmetrical, dual opposition, of male and female, masculine and feminine.

Effects of Impropriety

No longer pointing to opposed "*proper* places," to literal referential poles, but to successive *roles* in a triangular, dynamic spatial figure, to respectively opposed but interchangeable positions in a structure which subverts propriety and literality, the polarity of masculine and feminine itself becomes dynamic and reversible. However, the substitutions of woman for man and of man for woman, the interchangeability and the reversibility of masculine and feminine manifests a discord which subverts the limits and compromises the coherence of each of the two principles.

The male-centered cultural division of sex roles, the hierarchical model of male domination which conventionally structures the relationship of man and woman, and through which Henri indeed expects to dominate Paquita, is thereby equally subverted or unsettled, since the master-slave relation of male to female presupposes the transparent, unified identity of each, and particularly, the coherent, unequivocal *self-identity* of the ruling male. This male self-identity, however, and the mastery to which it makes a claim, turns out to be a sexual as well as a political fantasy, subverted by the dynamics of bisexuality and by the rhetorical reversibility of masculine and feminine. If Paquita is indeed a slave, she nonetheless undermines Henri's delusion that he is her master when it turns out that she has still another master. But the marquise is not Paquita's real master either, since her hierarchical claim as Paquita's owner is equally frustrated by Paquita's love affair with Henri. If both Henri and the marquise treat Paquita as an object (be it a precious object—gold—to be owned and guarded in one's pocket), Paquita usurps the status of a subject from the moment that she takes *two lovers*—has two masters. The golden eyes of ideal femininity thus turn out to be deceptive: having two lovers, subject to a double visual fascination and infatuation, the mirroring, brilliant golden vision no longer reflects the idealized *unified* self-image of the lover, but his *division,* his fragmentation. The golden eyes do not keep their fantasmatic promise: the gold is not to be possessed; all it does is *disown* the marquise, and *dispossess* Henri of the illusion of his self-identical master-masculinity. The signifier "femininity" no longer fits in the code of male representation, or in any representative unequivocal code; it is no longer representative of the signified masculinity, nor is it any longer representative of *any* single signified. It is precisely constituted in *ambiguity,* it signifies itself in the uncanny space *between two signs, between* the institutions of masculinity and femininity. It is thus not only the conventional authority of sovereign masculinity that Paquita's femininity threatens, but the authority of any representative code as such, the smooth functioning of the very institution of representation.

THE SECRET ENEMY

It is this threat which Henri plots to eliminate through Paquita's murder: the physical suppression of Paquita's life, repressing femininity as difference, as otherness, would eliminate ambiguity as such, stabilize the suddenly drifting cultural signs, insure the principle of hierarchy and of representation, reestablish the univocality of the political institution of sexuality, i.e., of culture.

It is, however, once again the marquise who precedes Henri and kills Paquita. Henri arrives at the murder scene only to find the dagger—an obvious phallic symbol—already thrust into Paquita's chest; the masculine sign of power has once again been usurped by a woman. "Ah!" de Marsay cried. . . . "This woman will even have robbed my of my revenge!" (p. 387) In the very moment of his attempt to deny, through an act of violence, woman's power, Henri finds himself in the dénouement, once again, face to face with its castrating image. But most uncannily, this terrifying image has suddenly become his own.

> Faced with the spectacle that offered itself to his eyes, Henri had more than one cause for astonishment. The marquise was a woman. . . . The girl with the golden eyes lay dying. . . . The marquise was still holding her blood-stained dagger. . . . The marquise was about to fling herself on the divan, . . . stricken with despair. . . . This movement enabled her to notice Henri de Marsay.
>
> "Who are you?" she said, rushing upon him with raised dagger.
>
> Henri seized her by the arm, and thus they were able to look at each other face to face. A shocking surprise chilled the blood in the veins of both of them and they stood trembling like a pair of startled horses. In truth, the two Menaechmi could not have been more alike. In one breath they asked the same question: "Is not Lord Dudley your father?"
>
> Each of them gave an affirmative nod.
>
> "She remained true to the blood line," said Henri, pointing to Paquita.
>
> "She was as free of guilt as it is possible to be," replied Margarita-Euphemia-Porraberil, throwing herself on Paquita's body with a cry of despair.
>
> (pp. 388-390, TM)

This recognition scene finally provides the answer to the question which has obsessed Henri throughout the story: who is the secret enemy? What is the identity of the rival, of the third term in the triangular drama of desire? But the answer, at last revealed and clarified, is by no means a simple one, since Henri's enemy is his duplicate in every sense: in this uncanny mirror-game of doubles over the corpse of their mutual vic-

tim, Henri beholds in his enemy the exact reflection of his own desire and of his own murderous jealousy; the enemy has his own voice, his own face; the enemy, in other words, *is himself*. The recognition scene thus meets and illustrates, in a striking, unexpected manner, Freud's psychoanalytic definition of the "uncanny" (*Das Unheimliche*) as the anxiety provoked through the encounter with something which, paradoxically, is experienced as at once foreign and familiar, distant and close, totally estranged, unknown, and at the same time strangely recognizable and known. What, indeed, could be more distant from oneself, more foreign and estranged, than one's very enemy? What, on the other hand, is closer to oneself than oneself? But Balzac's text, in much the same way as Freud's text, postulates the meeting of extremes. The enemy—the embodiment of foreignness and distance—here uncannily turns out to be the very image of familiarity and closeness.

> "We will meet again," said Henri. . . .
>
> "No, brother," she said. "We shall never meet again. I shall return to Spain and enter the convent of Los Dolores."
>
> "You are too young and beautiful for that," said Henri, taking her in his arms and kissing her.
>
> (p. 391)

What could be suspected in the recognition scene, and becomes apparent in these lines, is the connotation of incestuous desire between the brother and the sister. Narcissistic incest is indeed the implied logical consequence of the narcissistic structure of their mutual desire for Paquita; it is the secret figure which, throughout the novel, this particular triangle geometrically builds up to: since Paquita's golden eyes are but a mediating mirror in which the brother and the sister, each in his turn, behold their own idealized self-image, fall in love with their own reflection, it is but natural that they would equally desire *their own image* in each other, each being an exact *reflection* of the other.

THE PURLOINED PACKAGE

What the dénouement reveals, then, is that, paradoxically enough, it has been Paquita—the apparent female center of the story—who has in fact all along been the *screen-woman*, screening an incestuous (unconscious) narcissistic fantasy. The golden eyes themselves were thus the screen: the screen has been a mirror, blinding in its refractions, dazzling in its bright intensity, screening through its very golden brilliance and its play of ray deflections and reflections. It is therefore through Paquita's murder—through the physical annihilation of the screen—that the face to face encounter between the brother and the sister is made possible.

In this manner, the dénouement provides a second un-expected answer to the second question outlined by the story: what is the true *address* of Henri's desire? Looking back again at the initial scene in which Henri's valet interrogates the mailman in the hope of finding out the true address of Henri's false package, the name of the desired woman, the true address, in other words, of Henri's message of desire, we can now fully understand the dramatic irony and symbolic impact of the valet's mistake, in saying: "my package is for the marquise." For as it turns out, Henri's package is, indeed, unwittingly, *for the marquise.* Let it be recalled, in this conjunction, that the mailman shows the valet Paquita's name and address on the envelope of a letter sent from London, sent—as we will later gather—by the marquise. Symbolically, it is therefore from the start the marquise who *gives* Henri the *address* of his desire; and indeed, materially and literally, Paquita's address and the address of the marquise are the same. Furthermore: the phonetic resonance of the name Paquita resembles the phonetic resonance of the French word *paquet,* "package." In much the same way as the true address of Henri's message of desire is mediated by the false package, Paquita herself, as the screenwoman, turns out to be but a false package whose function ultimately is to be eliminated, having brought together brother and sister, the addressor and his real addressee. Paquita, in other words, can be said to be, ironically, Henri's uncanny *purloined package.*

THE FATHER'S NAME

The narrative's completion of the suggestive figure of incestuous desire brings back to the text the forgotten father-figure of Lord Dudley. This rhetorical return of the father, both doubled and materialized by the actual return of the marquise from England, the father's country, illustrates again Freud's definition of the uncanny as a return of the repressed, as the recurrence of "something familiar and old-established in the mind that has been estranged only by the process of repression."[6] Lord Dudley has indeed *rhetorically* been repressed at the beginning of the story, where he is mentioned, as it were, for the last time, as *that of which the text will speak no more:*

> But *let us finish with Lord Dudley* [Lord Dudley, *pour n'en plus parler,* vint . . .]: he came and took refuge in Paris in 1816 in order to escape from English justice, which gives its protection to nothing exotic except merchandise [qui, de l'Orient, ne protège que la marchandise]. The itinerant lord saw Henri one day and asked who the beautiful young man was. On hearing his name, he said: "Ah! He's my son. What a pity!"
>
> (p. 331)

This euphemistic passages seems to point to Lord Dudley's homosexuality: Dudley must have fled to Paris to escape prosecution for his homosexual mores, eu-phemistically referred to as an Oriental import outlawed by the English courts. Lord Dudley's cynical understatement, "He's my son; what a pity!" seems to imply that, having come across Henri in Paris, the father has unwittingly lusted after his own handsome son. The rhetorical return in the dénouement of the rhetorically repressed Lord Dudley thus connotes the return both of incest and of homosexuality.

But Lord Dudley, let us not forget, is equally involved with women: it is indeed his unwanted, multiplied and disseminated fatherhood which accounts for the story:

> To make this story comprehensible, we must at this point add that Lord Dudley naturally found many women ready enough to strike a few copies of so delightful a portrait. His second masterpiece of this kind was a girl called Euphémie. . . . Lord Dudley gave his children no information about the relationships he was creating for them here, there, and everywhere.
>
> (p. 331)

If, therefore, in the recognition scene between the brother and the sister, the father's name suddenly emerges in the very place of the erased name of the girl with the golden eyes, it is not just because both names evoke bisexuality, but because they both occupy a symmetrical place in two symmetrical triangles: in much the same way as Paquita, having two love affairs, occupies the mid-position between her first love and her second, between Euphémie and Henri, Lord Dudley, in the primal scene-triangle, occupies the mid-position between his first love-affair, Henri's mother, and his other love affair, Euphémie's mother, and consequently also between Henri and Euphémie. Furthermore, being a foreigner in Paris, as is the father, Paquita can only speak to Henri and communicate with him in English: his father-tongue.

Occupying thus the same position in the symbolic structure, Paquita's gold ultimately comes to symbolize the father. The signifier *gold* is itself inscribed in the father's name: the French pronunciation of the word *Lord* (lor') would phonetically resemble, be in fact a homonym, of the word *l'or* (gold). The desired golden eyes turn out to be, indeed, the family jewels. And just as in Paquita's case, the golden eyes themselves ultimately constitute a screen, so in the father's case it is gold which *screens* the *Father's Name,* which conceals the fatherhood, since it is gold which buys the "artificial" father, the parental substitute, de Marsay, who, for the money he is paid by Dudley, accepts to act as father, to recognize Henri as his son and give Henri his name.

The return of the lost *Name of the Father* in the dénouement therefore strips Henri of his (adoptive) proper name, de Marsay, leaving him, indeed, with *no name* that he can claim to be *his own;* that he can claim to be his *proper* name. The cultural procedure of name-giving as insuring representative authority is no longer valid in the story: the (male) authority of name givers, customarily father and husband, is here disrupted: the father is no longer truly and legitimately *represented* by the son, in much the same way as the masculine is no longer truly and legitimately represented by the feminine. The Name of the Father, which traditionally is supposed to symbolize and to guarantee both propriety (proper name) and property (gold), here turns out to symbolize both *impropriety,* loss of proper name, and *dispossession,* loss of gold: it emerges in the very place of the symbolic loss of the golden eyes.

GOLD AND MEANING, OR THE PATERNITY OF THE PROLOGUE

Gold itself, the very fetish of desire, the very principle which the prologue establishes as that which makes society go round, no longer incarnates the economic principle of *property* and of possession, but rather the economic principle of *substitution* and replacement, the very principle of endless circulation of screening substitutes and their blind fetishization.

It is because the fetish is a screen, the very screen of substitution, the screen of screening, that Henri, so as to join the girl with the golden eyes, had to agree to be blindfolded, and that he has symbolically to lose the golden eyes so as to face the gold inscribed—as signifier, not as signified—in the father's name.

The opposition between "gold" as signified and "gold" as signifier, the displacement and disruption of the one by the other, was indeed prefigured at the outset by the *narrative's first word:* the word which serves as a *transition* between the prologue and the story. It is noteworthy and quite striking that, right after the prologue has established the word *or* ("gold") as an all-encompassing explanatory guiding "light," as *the* authoritative sign of meaning, the narrative is, in its turn, introduced by the word "or." This "or," however, is just a homonym, and not a synonym, of the prologue's "gold": since it is used as a *coordinate conjunction,* it is a signifier not of the (luminous) precious substance but of the *logical relation* between the prologue and the story, a logical relation which is by no means clear and whose meaning (although ironically articulated by the signifier *or*) can no longer be "taken as a light":

> *Or,* par une de ces belles matinées du printemps . . . , un beau jeune homme . . . se promenait dans la grande allée des Tuileries . . .
>
> [*Now,* (thus? however?), on one of those beautiful spring mornings . . . , a handsome young man . . . was sauntering along the main avenue of the Tuileries gardens
>
> (p. 327, TM)]

Constituting the ambiguous *transition* between the introductory authoritative discourse and the narrative, joining the prologue's gold and the story of the girl with the golden eyes, does the signifier, the conjunction *OR,* mean "thus" (logically introducing an argument in support of a thesis) or does it mean "however" (logically introducing an objection)? Through this conjunction, does the story serve to *illustrate* the prologue, as a slave would serve its master[7] (OR = "thus"), or is the story, on the contrary, a rhetorical *subversion* of the authority (of the paternity or consciousness) of the prologue (OR = "however")?

NARRATIVE INSUBORDINATION

It could be said that, through the chiasmus, the reversal operated by the story's dénouement within the very import and significance of the sign "gold," the narrative indeed ends up subverting, to some extent at least, the "guiding light" of the prologue, the authoritative truth which was supposed to be its "proper" meaning and which it had to "demonstrate" as a self-evident principle of identity and value which, while distinguishing between the social classes, organizes Paris as a social universe of *order* and of ascending *hierarchy.* But in the narrative, on all three levels of the story—the level of the economical class struggle, of the political sex struggle, and of the rhetorical sense struggle—the signifier "gold" turns out to be no longer a principle of identity, of order, and of hierarchy, but rather, on the contrary, a principle of universal economical *equivalence* which subverts the "proper" in every sense and thus upsets the hierarchical coherence and legitimacy of classification and of class, whether political (social classes, poor as opposed to rich), rhetorical (substitutive metaphorical as opposed to literal; figurative meaning as opposed to "proper" meaning), or sexual (female as opposed to male). The prologue can no longer be *represented* by the narrative, in much the same way as, in the story's dénouement, the father can no longer be represented by the son, or the signified "gold" by its signifier, or the signified "male" by the signifier "female."

DIFFERENCE

The principle of identity is subverted along with the principle of opposition when Henri discovers, in the recognition scene, that the Same is uncannily Other and that the Other is uncannily the Same: what he had expected to be Other—his rival's face—is Same; what he had expected to be Same—his rival's sex—is Other. Difference, Henri thinks, is determined by sexual identity. As it turns out, identity itself is determined by sexual difference. What the uncanny mirror-game of the recognition scene suddenly reveals to Henri is womanhood, not as manhood's specular reflection, but as the disorienting incarnation of real sexual difference.

> Faced with the spectacle which offered itself to his eyes, Henri had more than one cause for astonishment. The marquise was a woman.
>
> (p. 388, TM)

What is the significance of this final revelation of the woman to Henri, as the ultimate signifier of the story?

The incestuous desire for the feminine sisterly double can be read as a fantasy of a return to the womb, to femininity as mother, a fantasy which Freud precisely mentions in his discussion of "The Uncanny": "It often happens," writes Freud, "that male patients declare that they feel that there is something uncanny about the female . . .":

> This *unheimlich* place, however, is the entrance to the former *heim* [home] of all human beings, to the place where everyone dwelt once upon a time and in the beginning. There is a humorous saying, "Love is a homesickness," and whenever a man dreams of a place or a country and says to himself, still in the dream, "this place is familiar to me, I have been there before," we may interpret the place as being his mother's . . . body. In this case, too, the *unheimlich* is what was once *heimlisch,* homelike, familiar; the prefix "un" is the token of repression.
>
> (p. 153)

Since Henri's sister is a marquise, she can equally evoke Henri's mother, who was also a marquise. Henri's entire drama within the close interiority of the boudoir of the San-Real Mansion betrays a womb nostalgia, a nostalgia for the woman as a familial and familiar essence, a nostalgia for femininity as snug and canny, *heimlich,* i.e., according to Freud's definition, "belonging to the *house* or to the *family,*" "tame, companionable to man" (p. 126).

Paquita, however, let us not forget, must be sacrificed, eliminated, killed, so that this incestuous return to the womb can occur. The nostalgia for heimlich femininity, for the woman as the tame, domesticated essence of domesticity and homeliness turns out to be a deluded, murderous narcissistic fantasy which in reality represses femininity as difference, kills the real woman.

Furthermore, the narcissistic *heimlich* union with familial and familiar femininity itself turns out to be *un*-heimlich and *un*canny. For in the mirror, Henri has to recognize, incarnated by his double—by his sister—his own feminine reflection: he sees *himself*—as a woman. Henri uncannily thus finds himself face to face with his own castration, symbolized at once by this reflection of his woman's face, and by his loss of the golden eyes, through which he could complacently behold his own idealized male self-image, his univocal masculine literality. Dethroned from the privilege of unequivocal self-present literality, the masculine can no longer signify itself with a sign of plenitude. If femininity becomes indeed a signifier of castration, it is by no means here the embodiment of *literal castration,* the literalization of the figure of castration (as it sometimes is in Freud), but rather, (as I understand the most radical moments of Freud's insight—as well as of Balzac's text), castration as a differential process of substitution, subverting, on the contrary, literality as such.

Masculinity, Henri discovers, is not a substance, of which femininity would be the *opposite,* i.e., at once the *lack* and the negative *reflection.* Since Henri himself has a woman's face, the feminine, Henri discovers, is not *outside* the masculine, its reassuring canny *opposite,* it is *inside* the masculine, its uncanny *difference from itself.*

THE UNCANNY AND THE WOMAN

"What interests us most in this long extract," writes Freud in his study on "The Uncanny," after having examined the lexicological and philological implications of the term, of the word "unheimlich" as opposed to "heimlich,"

> What interests us most . . . is to find that among its different shades of meaning the word *heimlich* exhibits one which is identical with its opposite, *unheimlich.* What is *heimlich* thus comes to be *unheimlich.* . . . In general we are reminded that the word *heimlich* is not unambiguous, but belongs to two sets of ideas . . . : on the one hand, it means that which is familiar and congenial, and on the other, that which is concealed and kept out of sight. The word *unheimlich* is only used . . . as the contrary of the first signification and not of the second.
>
> (p. 18)

> . . . Thus *heimlich* is a word the meaning of which develops towards an ambivalence, until it finally coincides with its opposite, *unheimlich.*
>
> (p. 131)

One might say, following Freud's analysis, that what is perhaps most uncanny about the uncanny is that it is not the opposite of what is canny, but rather, that which uncannily *subverts the opposition* between "canny" and "uncanny," between "heimlich" and "unheimlich." In the same way, femininity as real otherness, in Balzac's text, is uncanny in that it is not the opposite of masculinity, but *that which subverts the very opposition of masculinity and femininity.*

Masculinity is not a substance, nor is femininity its empty complement, a *heimlich* womb. Femininity is neither a metonymy, a snug container of masculinity, nor is it a metaphor—its specular reflection. Femininity *inhabits* masculinity, inhabits is as otherness, as its own *disruption*. Femininity, in other words, is a pure difference, a signifier, and so is masculinity; as signifiers, masculinity and femininity are both defined by the way they differentially relate to other differences. In *The Girl with the Golden Eyes,* femininity, indeed, is rigorously *the substitutive relationship between different screens.*

The dynamic play of sexuality as *difference* in the recognition scene between the brother and the sister takes place, indeed, not only *between* man and woman, between Henri and Euphémie, but between the masculinity and femininity of each. If the girl with the golden eyes was thus a *screen* between Henri and Euphémie, her symbolic screening function was not just to screen the other woman, but to be a screen between Henri and his own femininity, to travesty, disguise, or hide from Henri's eyes his own split otherness, his own division as a subject, his own castration, reassuringly projected outside of himself onto his external female partner. Paquita, in other words, was a screen to the extent that she embodied the bar of censorship which separates consciousness from the unconscious. The golden eyes therefore function precisely as the prefix *un* in "unheimlich," a prefix which Freud defines as the very "token of repression," screening the unconscious differential energy. Paquita as the bar of censorship insures the deceptively unequivocal ideological functioning of the fantasmatically reified and fetishized *institutions* of masculinity and femininity.

THE COVER-UP

With Paquita's death, the golden veil is torn, the bar of censorship is for a moment lifted, Henri and Euphémie can see into their own difference from themselves, into their own constitutive division and castration; but this uncanny moment of intolerable insight and of terrifying knowledge will itself be soon repressed with the cover-up of Paquita's murder and the new linguistic screen, the final euphemism which commits the murder—and the whole adventure—to forgetfulness:

> A week later Paul de Manerville met de Marsay in the Tuileries Gardens. . . .
>
> "Well now, you rascal, what has become of our lovely GIRL WITH THE GOLDEN EYES?"
>
> "She's dead."
>
> "Of what?"
>
> "A chest ailment [*De la poitrine*]."
>
> (p. 391)

"La poitrine," or the ailing "chest"—a euphemism for consumption—is of course a lie, a social cover-up, which at the same time euphemistically and cynically describes the truth of Paquita's death through the dagger thrust into her chest; it can also euphemistically mean that Paquita has indeed died of the heart, as a metaphor for her love; she has died of her emotional and passionate involvement with Henri. The chest, however, can also euphemistically, through a dramatic textual irony, point to a sign of female difference, a signifier of femininity. In this sense, the text could here be answering that the girl with the golden eyes has died *because she is a woman;* she was sacrificed, repressed, because she incarnated femininity as otherness, as real sexual difference.

Paquita's death is thus a rhetorical transition from "active discretion" to a passive, "negative discretion," from an erotical affirmation, from the overstatement of a screen-woman, to an erotical negation, to euphemistic understatements. It is no coincidence that Henri's sister, the woman who is revealed to Henri through Paquita's murder, through the erasure of the screen-woman, is called Euphémie, Euphemia, Euphemism.[8] Femininity is in this text at once the relationship and the difference between "positive" and "negative" discretion, between a screen-woman and a euphemism. Ultimately, femininity itself becomes a euphemism, a euphemism at once for difference and for its repression, at once for sexuality and for its blindness to itself; a euphemism for the sexuality of speaking bodies and their delusions and their dreams, determined by a signifier fraught with their castration and their death. With the novel's final euphemism, however, with Paquita's death of "a chest ailment"—*de la poitrine*—femininity becomes indeed a *euphemism of euphemism,* a figure of the silencing of the very silencing of woman, of the repression of the very functioning of repression. The text, nonetheless, through its very silencing of death by language, opens up an ironic space which articulates the force of the question of femininity as the substitutive relationship between blind language and insightful, pregnant silence—between a language threatened and traversed by silence, and the silence out of which language speaks.

Notes

1. Sigmund Freud, "Femininity," in *New Introductory Lectures on Psychoanalysis,* tr. James Strachey (New York: Norton, 1965), p. 112.

2. Freud, Preface to *New Introductory Lectures on Psychoanalysis,* op. cit., p. 5.

3. Ibid., p. 5; emphasis mine.

4. Honoré de Balzac, "La Fille aux yeux d'or," in *Histoire des Treize*. Page references following quotations in English are to: "The Girl with the

Golden Eyes," in *History of the Thirteen,* tr. Herbert J. Hunt (Penguin, 1974). When the English translation has been modified by me, the page reference will be followed by the abbreviation "TM" (translation modified).

5. Unlike Henri, however, Paquita, in time, renounces her model of sexual hierarchization, her rhetorical subordination of the masculine to the feminine pole. In their second sexual encounter,

> "Put my velvet gown on me," said Henri coaxingly.
>
> "No, no" she impetuously replied. "*Remain where you are,* one of these angels I had been taught to detest and whom I looked upon only as monsters."

> (p. 380; italics mine)

6. Freud, "The Uncanny," tr. Alix Strachey, in *Sigmund Freud on Creativity and the Unconscious* (New York: Harper Torchbooks, 1958), p. 148.

7. As the prologue indeed paternalistically affirms: "*quod erat demonstrandum,* if one may be permitted to apply a Euclidean formula to the science of manners" (p. 327). What the "demonstration" consists of, however, is by no means clear.

8. Cf. the remarkable article by Leyla Perrone-Moisès, "Le Récit euphémique," in *Poétique,* no. 17, 1974.

Janet L. Beizer (essay date 1986)

SOURCE: Beizer, Janet L. "Thrice-Told Tale: *Une Passion dans le desert.*" In *Family Plots: Balzac's Narrative Generations,* pp. 48-100. New Haven, Conn.: Yale University Press, 1986.

[*In the following excerpt, Beizer considers various metaphors found in* The Girl with the Golden Eyes, *concentrating on imagery comparing women to wild animals.*]

La Fille aux yeux d'or presents the most systematized assimilation of a woman to a creature of the wild.[1] Even the Parisian apartment where the intrigue unfolds recalls the desert seclusion of *Une Passion,* for the exotic Oriental decor is an oasis-like enclosure as far from the Parisian mainstream as if one were "au milieu du Grand Désert"[2] (in the middle of the Great Desert). This shift of contexts will be of particular interest later when we find references to France and vestiges of civilized life intruding into the wilds of the Egyptian desert.

Most striking is the physical resemblance between Paquita (la fille aux yeux d'or) and Mignonne. Mignonne's feminization is matched by Paquita's "felin-

ization," and Mignonne's gleaming golden eyes reappear in Paquita, who has "deux yeux jaunes comme ceux des tigres"[3] ("two yellow eyes like a tiger's").

Although intriguing, the physical analogy becomes really useful only when replaced in the larger narrative context, where it becomes evident that the beast-woman and the woman-beast play similar roles within their respective texts, for the very reason that the nature of each of these roles is inherently dualistic. Neither woman nor panther can be conceptualized independently, though each text accords dominant (literal) status to one of the two and subordinates (metaphorizes) the other. Such a relationship of complementarity means that the wild fille aux yeux d'or can tell us something about the woman disguised in panther's clothing.

When considering Paquita Valdès, we cannot avoid observing "la femme" as well as "la fille," for Paquita is symbolically—and almost literally—welded to her mother, an old slave originally purchased "for her rare beauty" but now described as "la terrible harpie" (p. 1081). Despite Paquita's beauty, she is an ironic replica of her monstrous mother. The mother, too, has yellow eyes, eyes in which appear "l'éclat froid de ceux d'un tigre en cage qui sait son impuissance et se trouve obligé de dévorer ses envies de destruction" (p. 1081; the cold glare of a caged tiger who knows he is powerless and is obliged to swallow his hunger for destruction). Her quarters are referred to as her "tanière" (p. 1108; lair). She is "une hyène à laquelle un jaloux a mis une robe" (p. 1065; a hyena upon whom some jealous man has put a dress)—which description carries a very distinct echo of the panther Mignonne.

Never was the question of origins—and of endings—more inescapable. A rendezvous between Paquita and her lover, de Marsay, takes place before her mother's vigilant eyes, and leads to the following reflection, on his part:

> Cette femme décrépite était là comme un dénouement possible, et figurait l'horrible queue de poisson par laquelle les symboliques génies de la Grèce ont terminé les Chimères et les Sirènes, si séduisantes, si décevantes par le corsage, *comme le sont toutes les passions au début.*

> [p. 1080; emphasis added]

> [This wasted woman was there like a potential denouement, and called to mind the horrible fish-tail with which the allegorical geniuses of Greece completed their Chimeras and Sirens, whose bodices are so seductive, so deceptive, *just like the beginning of all passions.*]

This rather complicated three-tiered metaphor first tentatively compares Paquita (and the passion she represents) to her mummified mother: "un dénouement possible." The potential outcome of love is figured by this decayed female creature who stands for aging and death. But the metaphor is gripping, because it is doubled by an implicit metonymy; we know that the mother was once beautiful, like the daughter, and she thus represents the continuation of the daughter's life and image. The temporal metaphor is next spatialized, and the original subject and vehicle are conflated to form the subject of the following comparison. Now passion and hag together are likened to "l'horrible queue de poisson" (literally a fish-tail, but figuratively an arbitrary or insignificant ending) attached by the Greeks to "les Chimères et les Sirènes." At this point, an extension of the vehicle (the upper region of the mythical beings whose nether parts figured earlier) quite dexterously turns back to the original subject. Despite their horrible termination, chimeras and sirens are "si séduisantes, si décevantes par le corsage, comme le sont toutes les passions au début." As Paquita and her mother are metonymically related, they together form a Chimera, a Siren, the image of passion's course; as they are metaphorically related, either one of the two figures all the other elements of the chain.

Several points should be extricated from this tangled string of metaphors. We should take special note of the metaphorical and metonymical equivalence of Paquita and her mother; this rapport, coupled with an almost constant spatial proximity, leads to the postulation of a profound primary identity which is only secondarily split or divided into two personae. This means that we, like de Marsay, have to deal with a composite figure which juxtaposes the enticement of beauty and sensuality with the threat of violence and the menace of death.

The queue de poisson metaphor can be singled out and juxtaposed to the similar category of reptilian women so common in Balzac. We find another version of this in the person of Paquita, who seizes her lover's body, "s'entortillant autour de lui comme un serpent" (p. 1083; twisting around him like a serpent). But the queue de poisson metaphor is of particular interest because it presents an internal contradiction. In its literal acceptation, a fish-tail appended to a woman makes a mermaid and creates an alluring visual presence. In a figurative sense, a woman (or a passion) ending "en queue de poisson" amounts to nought, signifies little, evanesces, *entails a lack*. Once again we find presence—very insistent presence—used to express absence.

We can locate another (and ultimately similar) ambiguity in the person of Paquita. The denouement clears up a mystery that has pervaded the text up to this point: that of Paquita's knowing innocence. Paquita is bisexual; she belonged to the marquise and was a woman's erotic slave before meeting de Marsay and being enthralled by a man. This symbolic hermaphroditism defies Henri's sense of his own masculinity and brings about a symbolic castration. In a moment of ecstatic transport, Paquita, the incarnation of female perfection for Henri, cries out to him, *using a woman's name* instead of his own (Mariquita, the marquise's nickname). Thereupon "il reçut au milieu de sa joie un coup de poignard qui traversa de part en part son coeur mortifié pour la première fois" (p. 1102). Using metaphors of emasculation, the text records the dual movement whereby Paquita inadvertently reveals her own ambiguous sexual identity (her Sapphic past) and unwittingly calls into question de Marsay's sexuality:[4]

> L'exclamation de Paquita fut d'autant plus horrible pour lui qu'il avait été détrôné du plus doux triomphe qui eût jamais agrandi sa vanité d'homme. L'espérance, l'amour et tous les sentiments s'étaient exaltés chez lui, tout avait flambé dans son coeur et dans son intelligence; puis ces flambeaux, allumés pour éclairer sa vie, avaient été soufflés par un vent froid.
>
> [p. 1104]
>
> [Paquita's exclamation was all the more horrible for him because he had been dethroned from the sweetest triumph that had ever inflated his male vanity. Hope, love—all emotions—had been excited in him, his heart and his wit had been ablaze; then these torches, kindled to light up his life, had been blown out by a cold wind.]

Such an itinerary of sexual illusion and loss is traveled many a time by Balzac's characters. Representations of men whose masculinity is compromised by involvement with women whose femininity is both less than and more than it should be (because supplemented by apparently masculine attributes or characteristics) are legion.

Notes

1. See Léon-François Hoffmann's more detailed argument for a permuted relationship betwen Mignonne and "la fille aux yeux d'or" in "Mignonne et Paquita," *L'Année Balzacienne*, 1964, pp. 181-86.

2. Quoted by Hoffmann, "Mignonne et Paquita," p. 185.

3. Balzac, *La Fille aux yeux d'or*, in *La Comédie humaine* V, p. 1089. Subsequent references appear in the text.

4. Paquita of course problematizes all sex roles in this novel, for the Marquise is as virile as Henri is effeminate.

Doris Y. Kadish (essay date spring/summer 1988)

SOURCE: Kadish, Doris Y. "Hybrids in Balzac's *La Fille aux yeux d'or.*" *Nineteenth-Century French Studies* 16, nos. 3 and 4 (spring/summer 1988): 270-78.

[*In the following essay, Kadish argues that the hybrid nature of Henri de Marsay and Margarita-Euphémia Porrabéril's nationality and sexuality are important and overlooked features of* The Girl with the Golden Eyes.]

I wish to read Balzac's *La Fille aux yeux d'or* along the symbolic lines that Fredric Jameson has proposed in *The Political Unconscious* in order to understand the relative importance of a number of its curious semantic features. One feature, which has received little attention, is the mixed nationality—half French and half foreign—of the protagonist Henri de Marsay and his female counterpart and half-sister (by marriage the marquise of San-Réal), Margarita-Euphémia Porrabéril. Another feature, which has perhaps received too much isolated attention, is the mixed sexuality—half male and half female—of de Marsay, the marquise, and their shared lover Paquita Valdès. The two women's deviant sexuality has often been assumed, wrongly to my mind, to be the chief subject of the short novel. I use the general concept of hybrid for the mixed nationality and the mixed sexuality of the characters in *La Fille aux yeux d'or,* along with other related elements; and it is their interrelation that I shall study in this paper.

Balzac's use of the structure of the hybrid is characterized by the presence of heterogeneous parts, an uneasy cohabitation in one living organism of different and incongruous elements. Those elements mix but do not combine in the hybrid; as a result, elimination or transcendence of difference is only partially achieved. De Marsay, for example, is manifestly both French and English, an individual in whom a seamless, harmonious blend of the nationalities of his two parents has not occurred. To borrow an analogy from chemistry, one could compare de Marsay to a mixture, as of oil and water, as opposed to a compound, as of sodium and chlorine in salt. Whereas the parts in the compound lose their individual identity and a new identity results, the parts in the mixture retain their original identity to a large extent and can be separated out easily.

The hybrid structure underlies the various parts of *La Fille aux yeux d'or*: its lengthy prologue, the presentation of de Marsay immediately following the prologue, and finally the remaining part in which the story is recounted. (It similarly underlies the clandestine group of the Treize, to which de Marsay belongs.) Re-gardless of which part is at issue, however, the structure of the hybrid remains the same, thus producing narrative coherence. Moreover, the function of the hybrid also remains the same. That function is to make the political statement that in Restoration society, class differences have been obscured and undermined, but not wholly obliterated. Thus there has arisen a new impure, adulterated, upper class—a hybrid class, personified by hybrid figures like de Marsay and the Treize—which stands in the place of a legitimate aristocracy that has allowed itself to be relegated to a position of marginality in French society. In short, rather than deviant sexuality being the only subject, it, together with mixed nationality—the hybrid—is but a symbol for the further subject of deviant politics. In contrast with a number of important critics who accord sexuality the major role in the interpretation of *La Fille aux yeux d'or,* I shall follow Jameson in attempting to "transcend individualistic categories and modes of interpretation," such as sexuality, by viewing the text "in terms of the collective or associative." (Jameson, 68)

The inordinately long description of the sociology of Paris in the prologue of *La Fille aux yeux d'or*—roughly one-fifth of the work—focuses on form as well as content. Form helps to explain the prologue's close and crucial ties with the rest of the text. Consider the relationship highlighted in the prologue between "or et plaisir," the two forces that motivate Parisians at all social levels, according to Balzac. While these two forces initially are presented disjunctively ("or *ou* plaisir"), they subsequently come to be presented conjunctively ("or *et* plaisir"). (Debreuille, 152-153) Whereas initially the reader was led to understand that Parisians are motivated by either gold or pleasure, he subsequently understands them to be motivated by both, but without any clear understanding of what that dual motivation entails. The development of the theme of "or *et* plaisir" in the prologue is thus the development of the hybrid: the mixture of two terms that remain separate rather than achieving some meaningful harmony and synthesis. But because the nature of their interrelationship is not clearly spelled out, confusion and incoherence result. As Serge Gaubert observes about Balzac's treatment of Paris generally in the prologue, "Tout et rien, vie et mort, jeunesse et caducité, pouvoir et impuissance ne se distinguent plus." (Gaubert, 172) The emphasis on the relationship between gold and pleasure in the prologue of *La Fille aux yeux d'or* highlights the key structural and symbolic pattern of the entire work.

Another instance of the prologue's focus on form, and of the same mixture of elements as with "or et plaisir," occurs in the presentation of social classes. In most of the prologue, with the exception of a few passages in which difference is sharply delineated, classes are conceived as interrelated spheres or domains rising inevitably out of one another. With the passage of time and the dogged pursuit of gold and pleasure that marks all social classes, upward mobility occurs. The various classes are thus different, but are also the same in their pursuit of the same goals and their natural historical and sociological ties to one another. That such a conception of society contrasts sharply with the Marxist view, in which classes are dialectically opposed, is not only important for historical reasons (Debreuille, 155; Gheude, 48; Mozet, 101) but for literary reasons as well. Classes are related to one another in the prologue as de Marsay is to his half-sister and as "or" is to "plaisir." Difference exists, but not in a distinct and clearcut manner. The distinction between upper and lower classes that is absolute for the Marxist is unclear and problematic for Balzac. In short, such apparent disjunctions as gold versus pleasure or upper versus lower classes cease to be clearcut disjunctions in Balzac's prologue. Similarly, other disjunctions—noble versus bourgeois, legitimate versus illegitimate—are shown later in the text to be inoperative in the degraded modern world.

The presentation of de Marsay in the part immediately following the prologue again furnishes evidence of the structure of the hybrid and its political significance. One of the very first details presented concerns the different nationalities of de Marsay's parents, Lord Dudley and "la célèbre marquise de Vordac." (1054) The text then goes on to explain about Henri de Marsay that "Cet Adonis . . . naquit en France, où lord Dudley vint marier la jeune personne, déjà mère d'Henri, à un vieux gentilhomme appelé monsieur de Marsay." (1054) Although the different nationalities of de Marsay's parents may seem to be a gratuitous detail at first glance, that detail marks de Marsay with the structural pattern of the hybrid. Indeed, Balzac explicitly identifies his protagonist later as the instantiation of that pattern:

> L'union si bizarre du mystérieux et du réel, de l'ombre et de la lumière, de l'horrible et du beau, du plaisir et du danger, du paradis et de l'enfer, qui s'était déjà rencontrée dans cette aventure, se continuait dans l'être capricieux et sublime dont se jouait de Marsay.
>
> (1091)

After identifying de Marsay with the hybrid structure through his parents' different nationalities, the text relates that structure to his physical appearance:

> De son père, lord Dudley, il avait pris les yeux bleus les plus amoureusement décevants; de sa mère, les cheveux noirs les plus touffus; de tous deux, un sang pur, une peau de jeune fille, un air doux et modeste, une taille fine et aristocratique, de fort belles mains.
>
> (1057)

De Marsay's hybrid nature is apparent in this passage by the fact that he combines his father's blue eyes with his mother's dark hair and the fact that, as a male, he displays such feminine characteristics as "une peau de jeune fille, un air doux et modeste, une taille fine." Thus not only is de Marsay half English and half French, he is also half man and half woman. Elsewhere in the initial description, he is presented as half human and half animal through the use of animal imagery and even a direct allusion to the hybrid figure of the centaur: "Henri avait un courage de lion, une adresse de singe. Il . . . montait à cheval de manière à réaliser la fable du centaure . . . était leste comme Chérubin et tranquille comme un mouton." (1057)

De Marsay's close association with the structure of the hybrid also assumes political significance. For one thing, the emphasis on nationality suggests that he embodies larger social or political forces. The reader learns later that de Marsay "devint un des hommes politiques les plus profonds du temps actuel." (1096) Other comments that appear later also cast his personal qualities in a political light:

> Il avait grandi par un concours de circonstances secrètes qui l'investissaient d'un immense pouvoir inconnu. Ce jeune homme avait en main un sceptre plus puissant que ne l'est celui des rois modernes presque tous bridés par les lois dans leurs moindres volontés. De Marsay exerçait le pouvoir autocratique du despote oriental. Mais ce pouvoir . . . était décuplé par l'intelligence européenne, par l'esprit français.
>
> (1084-1085)

De Marsay's hybrid nature also assumes political significance because a number of factors in his private life closely parallel comparable factors in the public life of his times: his English and French parents separate at the very time that war separates their respective countries (1054-1055, 1056); the Church, in the person of the abbé de Maronis, acts as a mother to him (1056) at the very moment when the Church resumed its traditional nurturing social function; de Marsay's "real," biological father Lord Dudley seeks a substitute to replace him, de Marsay's stepfather ("un vieux gentilhomme appelé monsieur de Marsay," 1054), around the time that the "real" king Louis XVI was replaced by substitutes. Moreover, the main events of the story take place "vers le milieu du mois d'avril, en 1815" (1058), that is, during the Hundred Days. Just as de Marsay's father chose to be replaced by a substitute, so too according to Balzac and other monarchists did Louis XVIII and his followers "choose" to hand over control of the country to Napoleon by allowing the substitution to occur.

On the basis of such political overtones in the presentation of de Marsay's hybrid character, I propose viewing him as a figure in the kind of political allegory that Jameson identifies with Balzac and defines as "symbolic narratives of class representatives or 'types.'" (Jameson, 80) The specific political figure depicted in *La Fille aux yeux d'or* belongs to a mixed race, which arose when the monarchy abdicated its legitimate control of the country. For there can be no real aristocrats without a strong and active monarch, according to Balzac. Indeed, there can be no clearcut differences at all. The very process of creating difference and meaning in society depends on the presence of such paternal figures as the father and the king, as Gaubert aptly observes:

> la rupture de la barre paradigmatique qui garantit le jeu des différences et celui des significations manifeste la perversion de l'ordre, celui du Père. . . . *La Fille aux yeux d'or* est une . . . analyse dominée par la figure d'un roi indécis qui a laissé fuir le pouvoir.
>
> (173)

The structure of the hybrid assumes the same thematic importance in the main part of *La Fille aux yeux d'or* as in the prologue and the presentation of de Marsay. That importance can be discovered in the role of two groups of foreign characters referred to or actively developed in the novel: male political figures, and female sexual figures. Whether male or female, however, the characters emerge as similarly heavy with political significance.

The role of male foreign characters in Balzac's work is to be heterogeneous and non-harmonious with the indigenous French characters. Thus France herself and French society become hybridized. Because the elements are non-harmonious, Balzac suggests that there is no enrichment of the country, even when the foreign elements embody positive qualities. Thus despite the presence in France of foreign aristocrats such as Lord Dudley and the marquis de San-Réal, the French aristocracy is in no way strengthened since there is no meaningful integration of the foreign elements into French society. Nor is the country strengthened by Christemo's manifestation of passionate loyalty or Paul de Manerville's adoption of English habits (1062). The implication is that France is pervasively marked by foreign culture; as de Marsay says at one point, "Nous prenons tant de choses des Anglais en ce moment que nous pourrions devenir hypocrites et prudes comme eux." (1071) But instead of achieving some meaningful integration, the culture of England and other countries, as presented in *La Fille aux yeux d'or,* stands merely as a heterogeneous element alongside corresponding French elements.

By failing to achieve a meaningful integration, foreign elements in Balzac's work not only contribute to the hybrid nature of French society but implicitly threaten national unity and political control. According to Jean-Pierre Richard, Balzac's political mythology is "marquée par le désir (le plus souvent nostalgique) d'une autorité centrale, fixe, prédominante, durable—et donc de préférence héréditaire—qui soit capable d'imposer sa loi à toutes les variations individuelles ou périphériques du pays"; and Richard then goes on to suggest that central authority is threatened by any forces located "dans les marges—géographiques, idéologiques, sociales—d'un groupe toujours prêt à se défaire." (14) When strength and nobility are found in the geographical margins of society, unity and control are undermined.

A threat is also posed by the uneven composition of the elements within the structure of the hybrid. Whereas positive qualities such as strength, passion, imagination, and vigor find clearcut embodiment in foreign and exotic elements, their embodiment in French elements is often partial and problematic. De Marsay himself is a prime example. On the one hand, as seen earlier, he is described as invested with "un immense pouvoir inconnu." Allusions to the Treize at the beginning and end of the work also enhance de Marsay's positive, powerful side, not only because he is shown to have powerful friends but because he is said to share their physical and moral strengths. (The Treize are described in the preface of the *Histoire des Treize* as "tous doués d'une assez grande énergie pour être fidèles à la même pensée, assez probes entre eux pour ne point se trahir . . . criminels sans doute, mais certainement remarquables par quelques-unes des qualités qui font les grands hommes, et ne se recrutant que parmi les hommes d'élite," 787). But on the other hand, de Marsay also displays negative qualities such as shallowness, materialism, and egotism, as can be seen in his more than two-hour long toilette and his profound indifference to all forms of enduring love. Like Balzac's treatment of the castrato and bourgeois money in *Sarrasine* (see Barthes's *S/Z,* 47), de Marsay is sapped to a significant extent from within and made to embody an internal void.

The female foreign characters in *La Fille aux yeux d'or,* notably de Marsay's half-sister Margarita and her lover Paquita Valdès, again provide evidence of the structure of the hybrid that gives coherence to the heterogeneous narrative elements of Balzac's novel. The text casts Margarita in the role of a hybrid not only because her parents, like de Marsay's, had different nationalities but more importantly because she is involved in homosexual practices: the implication is that although she is a woman, and indeed a strikingly feminine and beautiful one, she acts like a man by loving a woman and playing a dominant, masculine role in their relationship. With Paquita, the hybrid structure is ontological in nature, involving a heterogeneous mixture within her of the forces of both being and non-being. On the one hand, her passion for life and love can be associated with the vigor and fullness of being that foreigners tend to embody in Balzac's work. But on the other hand, her preeminently feminine role as a sexual object condemns her to a status of nothingness. As Margarita observes at the very end of the novel, "Elle est d'un pays où les femmes ne sont pas des êtres, mais des choses dont on fait ce qu'on veut." (1108) It is indeed as *nothing,* as non-being, that she assumes her role as a sex object for both de Marsay and Margarita.

A number of particular features of the female hybrids in *La Fille aux yeux d'or* are reminiscent of the relationship between *or* and *plaisir* in the prologue. Those features hold out a false promise of a meaningful combination of elements, which turns out to be merely the haphazard mixture of parts characteristic of the hybrid structure. Consider Margarita's partially English origin, which she shares with de Marsay. Their common English parent, like their similar appearance, initially suggests the union between brother and sister that Balzac depicts in *Séraphita.* But instead, as Geneviève Delattre observes, *La Fille aux yeux d'or* recounts "l'histoire de l'androgyne brisé, non réalisable sur la terre." (186) In a similar vein, Paquita has recourse to the English language as her sole means of communicating with de Marsay, despite her clearly exotic origin. Yet as with the brother and sister's failed union, so too with the lovers', no truly unifying principle exists.

Names also hold out a false promise of unity. As a number of critics have observed (see, e.g., Gaubert, Laugaa, Felman), the names of the triad of lovers suggest linkages of various sorts. Most striking perhaps is the syllable "mar" common to de Marsay, Margarita, and the marquise: their names, like their common English origin, suggest unity. And there is more. "Mariquita" is a nickname in the novel; and as Shoshana Felman observes,

> Mariquita, indeed, is not just a woman's name; it also means, in Spanish, an effeminate man. . . . Furthermore, the name 'Mariquita' can be read as a composite, either of '*mar*-quise' and 'Pa*quita*' or of *Mar*say (Hen*ri*) and Pa*quita;* as a signifier, the word 'Mariquita' thus names both Paquita's ambiguity, as part of two different couples, and the linkage of de Marsay and Paquita in Mariquita.
>
> (30-31)

Another critic observes that "le toponyme Paris est la condensation des prénoms Pa(quita)-(Hen)ri." (Laugaa, 64) But although the names of the three main characters suggest combinations of all sorts, those combinations ultimately produce no profound or lasting unity.

On the contrary, as the tragic denouement reveals, their coming together has been disharmonious and discordant.

Concerning the political significance of the female hybrids in *La Fille aux yeux d'or,* both Margarita and Paquita play roles similar to de Marsay's as social types or symbolic political figures. As women, they are inextricably linked with the city of Paris' vices and destructive powers. (Czyba, 144) Consider the following description of Paris: "Là règne l'impuissance; là plus d'idées, elles ont passé comme l'énergie dans les simagrées du boudoir, dans les singeries féminines." (1051) The degraded female side of Paris highlighted in this description can be contrasted with that city's elevated male side in another description: "Paris est la tête du globe, un cerveau qui crève de génie et conduit la civilisation humaine, un grand homme, un artiste incessamment créateur." (1051) Like de Marsay, then, the female characters in *La Fille aux yeux d'or* represent an impure, degraded and degrading force in modern society. In the name of that illegitimate, non-aristocratic force, a woman like Paquita can proclaim, "Si je suis esclave, je suis reine aussi." (1090) Paquita Valdès emerges thus as the ultimate symbol of Restoration society. In the prostituted world inhabited by male hybrids like de Marsay, only a female hybrid and enslaved sex object like Paquita could appropriately serve as queen.

To conclude, this analysis has discovered a series of hybrids in *La Fille aux yeux d'or,* beginning with such neutral, general phenomena as "or et plaisir" or the relationship between upper and lower classes, then progressing to more individually and politically specific cases like de Marsay, and culminating in the sexually deviant female characters who occupy center stage at the end. But those characters should not be viewed in isolation from the other manifestations of the hybrid structure. They are neither more important as individuals than those other manifestations nor less important as political symbols. They are merely more egregiously hybrid to Balzac, as they are undoubtedly to society in general. For, as Julia Kristeva notes, forces that threaten the breakdown of firm and clearcut sexual, linguistic, or political barriers are typically conceived as both degrading and female. (See, for example, Kristeva, 58-61.) Not surprisingly then, women are effectively eliminated from society, through death or exile, at the close of *La Fille aux yeux d'or.* If, as a politically conservative pragmatist, Balzac realized that the day of the hybrid had arrived in modern French society, with its breakdown of what he considered meaningful political difference, he could at least strive to minimize the losses by keeping the unbridled impurity and threatening presence of female hybrids at bay.

Texts Cited

Balzac, Honoré de. *La Comédie humaine,* V. Paris: Gallimard, Pléiade, 1977.

Barthes, Roland. *S/Z.* Paris: Seuil, 1970.

Czyba, Lucette. "Misogynie et gynophobie dans *La Fille aux yeux d'or.*" *La Femme au XIXᵉ siècle.* Lyon: Presse Universitaire de Lyon, 1979, 139-149.

Debreuille, Jean-Yves. "Horizontalité et verticalité dans *La Fille aux yeux d'or.*" *La Femme au XIXᵉ siècle.* Lyon: Presse Universitaire de Lyon, 1979, 151-165.

Delattre, Geneviève. "De Séraphita à *La Fille aux yeux d'or.*" *L'Année balzacienne* (1970), 183-226.

Felman, Shoshana. "Rereading Femininity," *Yale French Studies,* 62 (1981), 19-44.

Gaubert, Serge. "*La Fille aux yeux d'or:* Un Texte-charade." *La Femme au XIXᵉ siècle.* Lyon: Presse Universitaire de Lyon, 1979, 167-177.

Geheude, Michel. "La Vision colorée dans *La Fille aux yeux d'or* de Balzac." *Synthèses,* 289-290 (1970), 44-49.

Jameson, Fredric. *The Political Unconscious.* Ithaca: Cornell University Press, 1981.

Kristeva, Julia. *Powers of Horror: An Essay on Abjection.* New York: Columbia University Press, 1982.

Laugaa, Maurice. "L'Effet *Fille aux yeux d'or.*" *Littérature,* 20 (1975), 62-80.

Mozet, Nicole. "Les Prolétaires dans *La Fille aux yeux d'or.*" *L'Année balzacienne* (1974), 91-119.

Peronne-Moïsés, Leyla. "Le Récit euphémique." *Poétique,* 17 (1974), 27-38.

Richard, Jean-Pierre. "Balzac, de la force à la forme." *Poétique,* 1 (1970), 10-38.

George Moskos (essay date winter 1991)

SOURCE: Moskos, George. "Odd Coupling: Duras Reflects (on) Balzac." *Contemporary Literature* 32, no. 4 (winter 1991): 520-33.

[*In the following essay, Moskos compares and contrasts the plot structure and themes of sexual tension in* The Girl with the Golden Eyes *with those of Marguerite Duras's* La Maladie de la mort.]

A comparison of Honoré de Balzac's **La Fille aux yeux d'or** (1834-35) and Marguerite Duras's *La Maladie de la mort* (1986) reveals strikingly and surprisingly similar plot lines. In **La Fille,** a Parisian dandy,

Henri de Marsay, becomes obsessed with a mysterious Creole, Paquita Valdès, after catching sight of her in a public park. The story is centered exclusively on a series of four visits to her closed bedchamber during which Henri attempts to conquer and possess her. The repeated visits are punctuated by his growing desire to murder Paquita. The story ends with her brutal stabbing at the hand of Henri's sister. In *La Maladie,* a man invites a woman, a stranger, to spend several nights in his room in order that he might learn to love. Duras's plot is also centered on a series of repeated encounters during which the man slowly comes to the realization that the only proper end to this series would be the death of the woman.

The movement of these two narratives from erotic arousal through a series of repetitions leading finally to death retraces the trajectory of what Peter Brooks in *Reading for the Plot* has described as Freud's "masterplot." Brooks's "literary" rereading of Freud's theories of the repetition compulsion and the death instinct elaborated in *Beyond the Pleasure Principle* leads him to propose this "masterplot" as a "model for narrative." For Brooks, the beginning is "the arousal of an intention in reading, stimulation into a tension" and as such always displays a "specifically erotic nature" (103). It marks the divergence from the unnarratable (the quiescent or inanimate) to the narratable. The narrative itself, "the Aristotelian 'middle,'" maintains the tension of the beginning as "an ever more complicated postponement or *détour,*" manifested in patterns of repetition (103). These repetitions have the conservative function of leading the text forward to its end, which is in fact the quiescence of the time before the beginning. The repetitious detours of the middle seek to insure that the narrative reaches "the right death, the correct end" (103). Brooks analyzes the conservative working of repetition in terms of metaphor and metonymy: "Repetition . . . may . . . work as a . . . binding of textual energies that allows them to be mastered. . . . To speak of 'binding' in a literary text is . . . to speak of any of the formalizations, blatant or subtle, that force us to recognize sameness within difference" (101). Brooks associates sameness with metaphor and difference with metonymy. The privileging of metaphor is apparent throughout his essay; indeed, the fundamental desire of plot is summed up as "metonymy in the search to become metaphor" (106).[1] Meaning itself is predicated on the subjugation of metonymy, for it "depends on the . . . structuring force of the ending: the interminable would be meaningless." Freud's masterplot, and Brooks's literary use of it, could perhaps more properly be called a plot for mastery.

It may surprise us that Duras's novel follows the same "masterplot" as Balzac's, given that Brooks bases his analysis for the most part on nineteenth-century (male) fiction and that Duras is known to us as a late twentieth-century (female) innovator of form. Should we then conclude that there is something "universal" in this masterplot, something anchored in the human psyche that transcends both history and, I would hasten to add, gender? I will argue otherwise. Shoshana Felman prefaces her project of "rereading femininity" in Balzac's **La Fille** with Roland Barthes's exhortation to reread texts: "rereading is here suggested at the outset, for it alone saves the text from repetition (those who fail to reread are obliged to read the same story everywhere)" (19). I propose to reread Duras's *La Maladie* as a rewriting of Balzac's **La Fille,** taken as a representative of traditional narrative, that literally turns Barthes's advice on its head. Rather than saving her text from repetition, Duras carefully repeats, "mimes," the essential structures and strategies of the masterplot *in order* to undo the same story—or more precisely the story of the masculine Same—that is the very condition of its narratability. My analysis will center on four thematic structures, common to both texts, which serve as the motors for the masterplot: masculine desire as the original catalyst for the movement of the text, the ambiguous role played by repetition, the privilege of the masculine gaze, and finally the question of the proper end of the story, which in both cases seems to be the "erasure" of the feminine, whether by death or disappearance. The question of the proper end will be linked to the gender-dependent functioning of metaphor and metonymy in the texts.

In **La Fille aux yeux d'or,** from the moment he lays eyes on Paquita, Henri knows that he must possess this "femme idéale" ("ideal woman" [282]).[2] The arousal of his desire is directly linked to what Freud has called the "epistemophilic impulse": "plus qu'amoureux," Henri says, "je suis devenu curieux" ("more than in love, I have become curious" [283]). Paquita becomes a "mystère" ("mystery" [308]), a "charade vivante" ("living riddle" [320]) which must be deciphered. More important at this point is the role *localization* plays in his desire; in order to solve this feminine puzzle, Henri must first *find* Paquita. His manservant is able to pinpoint Paquita by following her carriage through the streets of Paris; but this does not guarantee access to her since she lives behind an impenetrable "porte mystérieuse" ("mysterious door" [287]). Since "l'attrait de la passion" ("attraction of passion" [290]) hardly touches Henri, this obstacle to the immediate satisfaction of his desire is precisely the condition necessary for its continued existence. Furthermore, it will determine the repetitious series of visits to Paquita which constitutes the essential movement of the plot. Interestingly enough, the fatal end of the story is announced at the very beginning of their

first meeting in the person of the "vieille momie" ("old mummy" [305]), Paquita's mother, whom Henri sees even before Paquita appears: "Cette femme décrépite était là comme un dénouement possible" ("This decrepit old woman was there like a possible denouement" [305]). However, this preordained and fatal end is constantly deferred as Henri moves back and forth between the outside world and Paquita's hermetically sealed bedchamber. There will be no end to this repetition, and to the story, until Henri has mastered Paquita.

Before each of their rendezvous, Henri must be in the same place at the same time and say the same words to the same man who takes him to Paquita and then drives him back to his point of departure. At first, however, Henri literally does not know where he is being taken. As Balzac makes clear in a passage punctuated with geographical imagery, Henri's desire threatens literally to lose him(self): "il fut entraîné par-delà les limites,,, jeté par-delà cette ligne où l'âme est maîtresse d'elle-même, il se perdit dans ces limbes délicieuses . . . que le vulgaire nomme . . . *les espaces imaginaires*" ("he was carried beyond the limits . . . thrown beyond that borderline where the soul is master of itself, he lost himself in that limbo full of delights . . . that the vulgar call . . . imaginary spaces" [338]). Henri's emotions are running too high for him to notice where he is being taken during the first trip. During the second he is blindfolded, although Balzac remarks that he could have deduced the itinerary if he had been able to concentrate. It is only during the last trip that, even though blindfolded, Henri applies his intelligence and divines the route. He will leave this last rendezvous with his blindfold off. And when he returns to kill Paquita, he will have the keys to her house and a map in hand. There are two important points to be noted here. First, the effect of Henri's repetitious movement is a progressive recognition of his own whereabouts that parallels an increasingly strong desire to kill Paquita. Second, the localizing function of desire has shifted from Paquita to Henri. The operative question is no longer "Where is Paquita?" but rather "Where is Henri?" By a curious inverted movement, then, having set out to find and know (*connaître*) Paquita, Henri instead comes to recognize (*reconnaître*) his own place. This (self-)recognition will lead directly to Paquita's death.

The rebounding of desire's trajectory from its object back to its subject can be better understood in relation to the working of the "gaze" in **La Fille.** From the beginning, it is clear that Henri's desire is a narcissistic fantasy, a need to see himself reflected in Paquita's golden eyes, which he describes as "un jaune d'or qui brille . . . de l'or qui pense . . . qui aime et veut absolument venir dans votre gousset!" ("a gold-colored yellow that shines . . . gold that thinks . . . that loves and wants absolutely to come into your pocket!" [281]). As Shoshana Felman so rightly concludes, this metaphor of the gold that wants to come into his pocket "shows that femininity itself turns out to be a metaphor of the phallus . . . Henri's desire [is] a sort of masturbation fantasy: his own phallus is indeed the prize he seeks" ("Rereading" 25). When Henri exclaims, "Je veux être seul, là où je suis" ("I want to be alone, here where I am" [319]), we understand that in placing himself, he is himself re-placing the supposed feminine object of his desire. Paquita's fate is sealed at the moment she fails to provide Henri's self-reflection. Gazing into his eyes, she misnames him Mariquita, Spanish for an effeminate man, thus unwittingly revealing what Luce Irigaray would call Henri's "hommo-sexual" desire to eliminate feminine Difference (168).[3] The dramatic visual confrontation of Henri and his sister Euphémie, who has herself just killed Paquita, is the text's climactic fantasy solution to Henri's desire. He finds himself face to face with—himself: "deux Ménechmes ne se seraient pas mieux ressemblé" ("two Menaechmi could not have looked more alike" [347]). The Menaechmi were of course twin *brothers*.[4] In the person of Euphémie, the feminine becomes nothing more than a euphemism, a metaphor, for the masculine. Feminine Difference is effectively denied, reduced to a mirror image of the masculine Same.

If, as Lacan maintains, the phallus only operates when veiled, then Duras's *Maladie* throws a wrench into the masculine works from its very first sentence: "Vous devriez ne pas la connaître, l'avoir trouvée partout à la fois . . . au hasard de ton sexe dressé dans la nuit qui appelle où se mettre, où se débarasser des pleurs" ("You wouldn't have known her, you'd have seen her everywhere at once . . . when your sex grew erect in the night, seeking somewhere to put itself, somewhere to shed its load of tears" [7, 1]).[5] Like a beacon in the night seeking desire's direction, the erect phallus is unveiled as the stimulation and origin of the masterplot. The insistence of directional prepositions, especially *où*, figures in the overall pattern of repetition in the text: "vous avez moins peur de ne pas savoir où poser votre corps ni vers quel vide aimer" ("you may be less afraid of not knowing where to put your body or at what emptiness to aim your love" [11, 5]). As in *La Fille*, the man in *La Maladie* risks losing himself in desire: "Vous dites que vous êtes perdu. Vous dites que vous ne savez pas à quoi, dans quoi vous êtes perdu" ("You say you're lost. But that you don't know what you're lost to. Or in" [50, 47]).

It is through the man's gaze that his desire is directed, ostensibly, on the woman: "Ensuite vous allumez des lampes pour la voir. Pour la voir elle." "Vous voudriez tout voir d'une femme, cela autant que puisse se faire" ("Then you switch some lights on, to see her. Her." "You want to see all of a woman, as much as possible" [28-29, 39; 24, 36]). As in *La Fille*, *tout voir* (see everything) also means *tout savoir* (know everything): "Vous croyez savoir vous ne savez quoi, vous n'arrivez pas au bout de ce savoir-là, vous croyez être . . . à l'image d'un destin privilégié. Vous croyez être le roi de cet événement en cours" ("You think you know you know not what, you can't go through with that knowledge, you think you . . . are the image . . . of a special fate. You think you're the master of the event now taking place" [43, 40]). Knowledge would bring privilege and dominance over the woman. Here we can juxtapose Balzac's description of Henri as a "despote oriental" ("oriental despot" [312]) with Duras's masculine "roi" ("king" [Bray translates as "master"]). Duras cuts straight to the ultimately narcissistic direction of masculine desire by eliminating the diversion of locating the woman—from the first paragraph she has already been found "partout à la fois" ("everywhere at once" [7, 1]). When the woman asks the man why he wishes to spend these nights with her, he responds: "pour dormir sur le sexe étale . . . pleurer là, à cet endroit-là du monde" ("so as to sleep with your sex at rest . . . to weep there, in that particular place" [9, 3]). Her response makes it clear that this *là* (there), pointing to the object of his desire, has nothing to do with her: "Elle sourit, elle demande: Vous voudriez aussi de moi?" ("She smiles and says: Do you want me, too?" [9, 3]). Her smile and the tone of her response are the first examples of the irony which will become the text's principal weapon in undoing the pretense of masculine desire. In fact, she is invisible to him: "Vous lui dites: Vous devez être très belle. Elle dit: Je suis là, regardez, je suis devant vous. Vous dites: Je ne vois rien" ("You say: You must be very beautiful. She says: I'm here right in front of you. Look for yourself. You say: I can't see anything" [21-22, 16-17]). The *connaissance* (knowledge) the man seeks through the woman is again but a screen for the self-recognition that would assimilate and eliminate feminine Difference: "Vous regardez . . . les seins sont bruns. . . . Vous les mangez, vous les buvez. . . . Une autre fois vous lui dites de prononcer un mot . . . celui qui dit votre nom, vous lui dites . . . ce nom" ("You look . . . her breasts are brown. . . . You eat them, drink them. . . . Another time you tell her to say a word . . . the one that's your name, you tell her what it is" [25-26, 21]). As in *La Fille*, desire rebounds from its supposed object back to the masculine subject: "De ce corps vous voudriez partir, revenir vers le corps des autres, le vôtre, revenir vers vous-même" ("You'd like to start from that body and get back to the bodies of others, to your own, to get back to yourself" [16-17, 11-12;

"partir" could also be read as "to leave"]). Masculine desire is ultimately narcissistic and homosexual: "Vous n'aimez rien . . . même cette différence que vous croyez vivre. . . . Vous ne connaissez que la grâce du corps . . . de vos semblables" ("You don't love anything . . . you don't even love the difference you think you embody. . . . All you know is the grace of the bodies . . . of those like yourself" [37, 33-34]).

Repetition constitutes both the general movement of the plot, a series of daily rendezvous, and the specific acts during these meetings: "Vous prenez le corps, vous regardez . . . vous le retournez, vous le retournez encore, vous le regardez, vous le regardez encore." "Vous lui demandez de répéter encore les mots. Elle le fait, elle répète les mots" ("You take hold of the body and look. . . . You turn it round, keep turning it round." "You ask her to say the words again. She does. Repeats them" [22, 23; 17, 18-19]). Each time the man can no longer tolerate the sight of the woman, he moves outside on the balcony to look at the sea, only to return later to the room. The adverb *encore* (again) persists throughout the text, emblematic of this repetition and, at the same time, of the excess of this feminine body—*en-corps* (in the body), as Lacan writes it in *Seminar XX* (11)—that escapes the man's desire to control it. The woman's body seems to grow before his very eyes until it encumbers "le monde tout entier" ("the whole world" [28, 24]). The threat posed by this feminine body becomes even clearer in the description which immediately follows the woman's refusal to speak the man's name, to recognize him:

> Mais toujours l'esprit affleure à la surface du corps, il le parcourt tout entier, et de telle sorte que chacune des parties de ce corps témoigne à elle seule de sa totalité, la main comme les yeux, le bombement du ventre comme le visage, les seins comme le sexe, les jambes comme les bras, la respiration, le coeur, les tempes, les tempes comme le temps.
>
> (26-27)
>
> (But all the time the spirit shows through the surface of the body, all over, so that each part bears witness in itself to the whole—the hand and the eyes, the curve of the belly and the face, the breasts and the sex, the legs and the arms, the breath, the heart, the temples, the temples and time.
>
> [22])

There exists perhaps no more elegant illustration of the working of metonymy, the relation of contiguity in which the part is taken for the whole. The final reference to time links the metonymy of the woman's body to the linear and seemingly interminable movement of the plot itself.

The correspondence between the woman's body and the metonymy of the narrative becomes explicit in the pivotal passage, located precisely at the midpoint of the text, in which the man decides that the she should die ("devrait mourir" [30, 26]). Time, like the woman's body, is excessive: "Ce sont des heures aussi vastes que des espaces de ciel. C'est trop, le temps ne trouve plus par où passer" ("These hours are as vast as stretches of sky. It's too much, time can't find a way through" [30, 25]). It quickly becomes apparent that what is at stake here is not so much the passage of time but more its *end:* "Vous vous dites que si maintenant . . . elle mourait, ce serait plus facile, vous voulez dire sans doute: pour vous, mais vous ne terminez pas votre phrase" ("You tell yourself that if now . . . she died, it would be easier. For you, you probably mean, but you don't finish the sentence" [30, 26]). Two pages later he will finish his sentence: "Vous terminez votre phrase. Vous vous dites que si . . . elle mourait ce serait pour vous plus facile de la faire disparaître de la face du monde" ("You finish your sentence. You tell yourself that if . . . she died, it would be easier for you to make her disappear off the face of the earth" [32, 28]). The end of the sentence and the death/disappearance of the woman are interdependent events. The passage between the beginning and the end of this sentence repeats the plot of *La Maladie:* the man gazes on the woman; unable to tolerate this view, he leaves the room and turns his gaze on the sea instead. There seems to be no end in sight for either the sentence or the text. Indeed, it is the constant movement of the sea that is most threatening to him: "Elle bouge. Elle n'arrête pas de bouger" ("moving, always moving" [31, 27]). It is at this point that a dynamic of *metaphorization* begins to take shape within what had been a relation of contiguity between the sea and the woman: "l'eau noire" ("black water" [31, 27]) replaces "sa forme plus sombre" ("[her] darker shape" [30, 26]). Like Paquita's eyes, the phallic "longues lames blanches" ("long white rollers" [31, 27]) are substituted for the "flaque blanche des draps blancs" ("white expanse of white sheets" [30, 26; *lame* can be translated either as "wave" or "blade, sword," while *flaque* could be translated more precisely as "pool" or "puddle," thus underscoring the correspondence between the woman and the sea]). The culmination of this process of substitution directly precedes and enables the completion of the sentence and, by extension, the story: "L'idée vous vient que la mer noire bouge *à la place d'autre chose,* de vous et de cette forme sombre dans le lit. Vous terminez votre phrase" ("It occurs to you that the black sea is moving *in the stead of something else,* of you and of the dark shape on the bed. You finish your sentence" [32, 28; emphasis added]). Unwilling to accept the "admirable impossibilité de la rejoindre à travers la différence" ("the marvelous impossibility of reaching her through . . . difference" [56, 54]), the man's desire is to immobilize and control this excessive, interminable metonymy of feminine Difference by reducing it to a metaphor of the masculine Same. This metaphorical reduction—"la mer noire, le corps qui dort" ("the black sea . . . the sleeping body" [42, 39])—gives him the illusion of "penetrating" her for the first time: "Et puis vous le faites . . . vous revenez vers le corps. Vous le recouvrez complètement du vôtre, vous le ramenez vers vous . . . vous revenez vers le logement nocturne, vous vous y enlisez" ("And then you do it . . . you go back towards the body. You cover it completely with your own, you draw it towards you . . . you return to the nightly dwelling, you are engulfed" [42, 39-40]). It is clear that their coupling is no more than an attempt to make her disappear into him; the slippage from "vous vous y enlisez" ("you sink down into") to the homonymic alternative "vous vous y (en) lisez" ("you read yourself there") suggests the same mirror-image game of reading (himself) we found in **La Fille**. If the relation between the sexes is impossible, it is "à cause de ce mensonge de dire que la mer est noire" ("because you lied and said the sea is black" [46, 44]), because of this metaphorical reduction that effectively eliminates the "other," the "second," sex.

Analogously to the relation of terms in a metaphor, the man's control depends on the woman's simultaneous presence (as mirror) and absence (as subject). Duras, however, provides no fantasy solution for him: "Un jour elle n'est plus là. Vous vous réveillez et elle n'est plus là. Elle est partie dans la nuit" ("One day she isn't there anymore. You wake and she isn't there. She has gone during the night" [53, 51]). Her self-imposed disappearance robs his story of its proper end, rendering it unnarratable: "D'abord vous la racontez comme s'il était possible de le faire, et puis vous abandonnez. Ensuite vous la racontez en riant comme s'il était impossible qu'elle ait eu lieu ou comme s'il était possible que vous l'ayez inventée" ("At first you tell it as if it were possible to do so, then you give up. Then you tell it laughing, as if it were impossible for it to have happened or possible for you to have invented it" [55, 53]). Finally, all that will be left of the story will be four words, "ces mots qui disent ce dont vous êtes atteint: Maladie de la mort" ("the ones [words] that tell you what's wrong with you: the malady of death" [56, 55; we should note that Duras capitalizes *Maladie,* suggesting a correspondence between this sickness and her own text]). Interestingly enough, Balzac wrote a *postface* to **La Fille** that can also be considered a meditation on the proper end as the fundamental enabling factor of narrative. In this story (of his story), Balzac tells how Henri came to him asking that his adventure be published. Balzac, like the man in *La Maladie,* at first judges the enterprise to be an "impossible" one, in great part because of its "unpoetic" ending: Paquita is

in fact *not* dead. Indeed, her repression turns out to have been a linguistic play, a literary staging of the murder: "Si quelques personnes s'intéressent à [elle], elles pourront la revoir après le rideau tombé sur la pièce, comme une de ces actrices qui, pour recevoir leurs couronnes éphémères, se relèvent bien portantes après avoir été publiquement poignardées" ("If anyone is interested in [her], they can see her again after the curtain has fallen on the play, like one of those actresses who, in order to receive their ephemeral wreaths, get back on their feet after having been publicly stabbed" [373]).[6] In order to narrate Henri's story, to give it coherence and meaning, Balzac must bring an end to this interminable repetition represented by Paquita's daily resurrection—she must die once and for all. In *La Maladie* Duras refuses this closure; the man can get no further in his own narrative than the four words which are the title of the book we hold in our hands.

Duras will reclaim as her own this same old story, this old story of the (masculine) Same. I would argue that *La Maladie* and all Duras's later texts are in fact a play on the mirroring function so essential to masculine identity. They at least appear to reflect, repeat, mime the essential *mise en scène* necessary for the elimination of feminine Difference—what we might call the scene of the crime. Duras's strategy is summed up well in Irigaray's concept of *mimésis* as a subversive feminine activity: "Jouer de la mimésis, c'est donc, pour une femme, tenter de retrouver le lieu de son exploitation par le discours, sans s'y laisser simplement réduire. C'est se resoumettre . . . à des 'idées,' notamment d'elle, élaborées dans/par une logique masculine, mais pour faire 'apparaître,' par un effet de répétition ludique, ce qui devait rester occulte: le recouvrement d'une possible opération du féminin" ("To play at mimesis, is therefore, for a woman, the attempt to find [again] the place of her exploitation by discourse, without letting herself simply be reduced to it. It is to resubject herself . . . to certain 'ideas,' in particular about herself, developed in/by a masculine logic, but in order to render 'visible,' by an effect of ludic repetition, what is supposed to remain hidden: the covering up of a possible operation of the feminine" [74]). Duras's texts have over the years diminished in length, moving toward what Xavière Gauthier has called a "dépouillement de tout ce qui . . . n'est qu'accessoire" ("stripping away of everything that is only of incidental interest" [Duras and Gauthier 60]. Balzac's story, as we might expect, is embroidered with a long introduction to Parisian society and, between visits, a running commentary on Henri's place in it. These "embellishments" have served as a screen, effectively focusing critical attention on what Rose Fortassier in her preface to **La Fille** calls Henri's "voyage initiatique" ("initiatory voyage" [40]), from which he will return "plus fort" ("stronger" [40]) and ready to take his place in society. Our gaze is diverted from Paquita, who becomes a metaphor for inversion, incest, and death. In *La Maladie* this basic plot has been completely denuded of any social reference and of all "embellishments" which might distract our attention from its fatal progression. *La Maladie* is a bare-bones distillation of Balzac's text—all that is left is the unadorned masterplot.

Duras underlines her intentionally repetitive strategy by choosing the only words of the story that the man remembers as the title for her text.[7] Like the woman, "Elle sourit, elle dit qu'elle a entendu et lu aussi beaucoup de fois cette histoire, partout, dans beaucoup de livres" ("She smiles, says she's heard and read it [this story] too, often, everywhere, in a number of books" [51-52, 49]). Repetition in *La Fille* serves to defer the preordained "dénouement" until Henri's mastery has been fine-tuned. Brooks explains this postponement as necessary if the narrative is to find its proper end. Repetition would serve to bind the text, to send it back on itself, to delay the "pleasurable discharge" of the end that confers meaning. Hence the meandering arabesque of plot that wrests "meaning" from "life"—metonymy becomes metaphor, even as Difference becomes Sameness. Duras, on the other hand, will mime this repetition *au pied de la lettre*. Her plot will not meander and permit us to find a self-reflexive Sameness. There will be no end imposed on this repetition that would permit us to make "sense" of this malady of death; rather, it is revealed as non-sense that has always already omitted Difference. In so doing, Duras undoes the plot for mastery.

Peter Brooks's analysis of plot as *détour* repeats the man's speculative mirroring of the woman in *La Maladie*. The fascination this scenario holds for critics resides, I believe, in its promise of mastery over the text. Tempting though this mastery may be, it makes the reader into a mirror image of the man gazing at the woman in search of his own reflection. Literature itself becomes a mirror for our own critical desire to control. From that position we are doomed to see the same thing and to tell the same story, as though no other were possible. We turn away, with the man at the end of *La Maladie,* from the implications of this mirroring—the elimination of sexual difference in the service of a masculine model of sameness. Only by focusing on these implications and by moving as best we can away from the mirror will we begin to see what has always been hidden. But that is a different story entirely.[8]

Duras re-creates the scene of the crime in such a way as to mirror the male fantasy of control and power. The woman, "comme les femmes de ses ancêtres" ("like the women of her ancestors" [10, 4]), exhibits every "feminine" stereotype: she is passive—"Elle vous laisse faire" ("She offers no resistance" [14, 9]); acquiescent—"C'est comme vous voudrez" ("Whatever you say" [14, 8]); and silent—"Elle ne crie plus" ("She doesn't [cry out anymore]" [14, 9]). Indeed, she spends most of her time sleeping. This scene should be a comforting and familiar one for the man, yet it is not. The insistence on stereotypes serves rather to underscore the irreconcilable difference between the man and the woman in such a way that, for instance, her weakness becomes simultaneously her strength: "Vous regardez cette forme, vous en découvrez . . . la puissance infernale . . . la force invincible de la faiblesse sans égale" ("You look at this shape . . . you realize its infernal power . . . the unconquerable strength of its incomparable weakness" [31, 26-27]). This voluntary miming of her "feminine condition" opens up an ironic space in the text through which the woman slips out of the man's grasp: "Vous découvrez qu'elle est bâtie de telle sorte qu'à tout moment . . . sur son seul désir, son corps pourrait . . . disparaître à vos yeux, et que c'est dans cette menace qu'elle dort, qu'elle s'expose à être vue par vous" ("You realize she's so made that it's as if at any moment, at her own whim, her body could . . . disappear from sight, and that it's in this threat that she sleeps, exposes herself to your view" [33, 29]). Or as Irigaray has written: "Si elle peut si bien jouer ce rôle, si elle n'en meurt pas tout à fait, c'est qu'elle . . . subsiste encore, autrement et ailleurs que là où elle mime si bien ce qu'on lui demande" ("If she plays this [feminine] role so well, if she does not die completely as a result, it is because she . . . still lives on, otherwise and elsewhere than there where she mimics so well what is asked of her" [148]). It is from this other place, from her Difference, that the woman in *La Maladie* "se moque . . . en dormant" ("smiles ironically . . . in her sleep" [51, 49]). The room that he thought was his own, recognizable and safe, turns out to be an illusory image of that space reconstructed to undo the man's power by revealing it as no more than the repetition of a very old and worn fiction. Duras shows us, as Shoshana Felman has written, "that authority is a *language effect,* the product or creation of its own *rhetorical* power: that authority is the *power of fiction;* that authority, therefore, is likewise a fiction" ("To Open" 8). A fiction so powerful that no (Other) story has yet to take its place. Duras's narrative is in some real sense condemned to repeat it. It is nonetheless through this very gesture of repetition that Duras opens up a "faille . . . dans la logique de l'univers" ("lapse in the logic of the universe" [52, 50]) through which her women exit, elsewhere and other-wise.

Notes

1. "Mere" seems to be Brooks's adjective of choice to describe metonymy: "We read the incidents of narration as 'promises and annunciations' of final coherence, that metaphor that may be reached through the chain of metonymies. . . . The sense of adventure . . . has something of the rigor . . . provided in poetry by meter and rhyme, the pattern of anticipation and completion which *over-codes mere succession*" (93-94; emphasis added). Or similarly: "repetition . . . recall . . . all these journeys back in the text . . . that allow us to bind one textual moment to another in terms of similarity or substitution rather than *mere contiguity*" (101; emphasis added).

2. Except those for *La Maladie de la mort,* translations throughout the article are my own. Page references after my English translations refer to the French editions.

3. The doubling of the *m*—elsewhere Irigaray writes "hom(m)o-sexuality"—is a play on "homme" (man) and "homo-," underlining the exclusionary, male organization of society. See also Eve Kosofsky Sedgwick's analysis of "male homosociality" in *Between Men: English Literature and Male Homosocial Desire.*

4. The reference is to the twin brothers in Plautus's comedy *The Twin Menaechmi.*

5. The first page reference is to the French edition; the second is to Barbara Bray's English translation.

6. Here we cannot but think of Madeleine, the actress in Duras's *Savannah Bay,* who despite all the various plays in which she has acted claims to have always played out the same story of the disappearance of the *jeune fille de la Pierre Blanche:* "Pendant des mois il m'est arrivé de mourir chaque soir au théâtre" ("For months I have died every night at the theater" [69]). Duras's play itself will be nothing more, nor less, than a repeated evocation of this same story in an unsuccessful attempt to "understand" it: "Désir violent d'appréhender l'inconnaissable du passé. . . . Echec" ("Violent desire to understand the unknowable of the past. . . . Failure" [55]).

7. In her fascinating essay "The Forgetfulness of Memory: Jacques Lacan, Marguerite Duras, and the Text," Mary Lydon deftly entwines reading, repetition, and memory in yet another fashion: "Memory, then, would be the repetition, the re-enactment of loss . . . and I wonder if I am alone in recognizing in this description my experience after reading one of Lacan's or Duras's own texts" (363).

8. In "Coming Unstrung: Women, Men, Narrative, and Principles of Pleasure," Susan Winnett begins to theorize this other story. She notes that it is "only in the context of the androcentric paradigm that Brooks's Freudian reading of . . . male nineteenth-century novelists can be considered the model for all narrative—or even for all 'traditional narrative'" (511). Winnett suggests readings that take into account "the difference of women's pleasure" (505). She does not propose her alternative perspective "as a scheme competing for authority with the Masterplot" (508), clearly realizing that such a move would fall into the Same (totalizing) trap. Its value, she argues, lies rather in its "relativizing function" (508). Jay Clayton, in his piece "Narrative and Theories of Desire," recognizes that Brooks's "model of desire, and hence, of narrative, is based almost entirely on a male sexual paradigm" (40). However, the formulation of Clayton's desire for a "radically historicizing mode of criticism" reproduces many of the elements of the "male sexual paradigm" with and against which Winnett and Duras write. When he concludes that "a historical account of desire in narrative *would look for* the system of relations that prevailed at a given historical moment rather than for the *substantive identity* between two universals (53; emphasis added), Clayton manages to invoke the identificatory mirror even as he gestures at its removal. The critic's *gaze* ("would look for"), which is meant to fix its object and to "make sense" of metonymy, is the predominant metaphor in his closing paragraph: "I would like to conclude by asking if such a radically historicizing mode of criticism would eliminate both narrative and desire as *stable objects* of analysis. Would *viewing them* as variable social constructions condemn us to the *mere enumeration* of unique historical instances? I think not. . . . This system of relations . . . would evolve slowly enough [rather, I would imagine, like a Brooksian plot] to provide a *stable field of study* (53; emphasis added). Brooks's use of "mere" as an antidote to the slippery dangers of metonymy (and in praise of metaphor) seems to be contagious (see my note 1). The "relativizing function" of which Winnet writes is of no interest to Clayton, who chides even Brooks for his willingness to "acknowledge the fictiveness of all totalizing interpretations." "This is a halfhearted way to defend narrative understanding," he writes, "since understanding is still trapped within an entirely fictive realm" (37).

Works Cited

Balzac, Honoré de. *La Fille aux yeux d'or.* Paris: Gallimard, 1976.

Brooks, Peter. *Reading for the Plot: Design and Intention in Narrative.* New York: Knopf, 1984.

Clayton, Jay. "Narrative and Theories of Desire." *Critical Inquiry* 16 (1989): 33-53.

Duras, Marguerite. *La Maladie de la mort.* Paris: Editions de Minuit, 1986.

———. *The Malady of Death.* Trans. Barbara Bray. New York: Grove, 1986.

———. *Savannah Bay.* Paris: Editions de Minuit, 1982.

Duras, Marguerite, and Xavière Gauthier. *Les Parleuses.* Paris: Editions de Minuit, 1984.

Felman, Shoshana. "Rereading Femininity." *Yale French Studies* 62 (1981): 19-44.

———. "To Open the Question." *Yale French Studies* 55/56 (1977): 5-10.

Fortassier, Rose. Préface. *La Fille aux yeux d'or.* By Honoré de Balzac. Paris: Gallimard, 1976. 7-40.

Freud, Sigmund. "The Infantile Genital Organization of the Libido." *Sexuality and the Psychology of Love.* New York: Macmillan, 1963.

Irigaray, Luce. *Ce sexe qui n'en est pas un.* Paris: Editions de Minuit, 1978.

Lacan, Jacques. *Encore: Le Séminaire XX, 1972-73.* Paris: Seuil, 1975.

Lydon, Mary. "The Forgetfulness of Memory: Jacques Lacan, Marguerite Duras, and the Text." *Contemporary Literature* 29 (1988): 351-68.

Sedgwick, Eve Kosofsky. *Between Men: English Literature and Male Homosocial Desire.* New York: Columbia UP, 1985.

Winnett, Susan. "Coming Unstrung: Women, Men, Narrative, and Principles of Pleasure." *PMLA* 105 (1990): 505-18.

Owen N. Heathcote (essay date autumn 1993)

SOURCE: Heathcote, Owen N. "The Engendering of Violence and the Violation of Gender in Honoré de Balzac's *La Fille aux yeux d'or.*" *Romance Studies,* no. 22 (autumn 1993): 99-112.

[*In the following essay, Heathcote concentrates on Balzac's depiction of violence against women in* The Girl with the Golden Eyes, *which, the critic contends, should not be viewed simply as a representation of the author's misogyny.*]

('La volupté mène à la férocité')

(De Marsay in *La Fille aux yeux d'or*[1])

The following analysis of *La Fille aux yeux d'or* offers a contribution to an extended examination of the representation of gender-related violence in literature, film, the media, and the written press. Various areas of the media have already been examined for their representation of violence, particularly towards women.[2] It is, however, not just the so-called popular representations of sexuality and violence which need reappraisal, but also the established literary canon and avant-garde literature. Here, a number of recent works illustrate critics' determination to analyse and expose the interdependence of art and gender-related violence and abuse.[3]

Honoré de Balzac's *La Fille aux yeux d'or* is a useful and interesting text to continue such analyses. It is, after *Ferragus* and *La Duchesse de Langeais,* the third and final episode of the *Histoire des Treize,* or of the undercover Parisian brotherhood of thirteen 'flibustier[s] en gants jaunes et en carrosse' (791), who act in unison to further each other's interests or take vengeance on their enemies. After an extended overview of Parisian society and its obsession with 'or et plaisir', this final episode describes another, more fleeting, obsession,—that of the dandy and future politician, Henri de Marsay with the Creole from Havana, Paquita Valdès, known as 'la fille aux yeux d'or.'[4] Despite the various bodyguards surrounding Paquita, she and de Marsay conspire to arrange two passionate meetings in her red-and-white draped boudoir, in the course of which Henri realizes that 'il avait posé pour une autre personne' (1096). He resolves to revenge himself by enlisting the help of the Thirteen to execute Paquita, but is forestalled by that 'other person', the marquise de San-Réal, who is taking her vengeance in her own way, by slaughtering Paquita with a dagger: ' *La Fille aux yeux d'or* expirait noyée dans le sang' (1106). A shock of recognition then strikes Paquita's two lovers: they are like two Menaechmi, like male and female identical twins with the same father, Lord Dudley. The 'fille aux yeux d'or', who lived and loved in red-and-white, remains, while dying in her own blood, 'fidèle au sang' (1108). She dies, as de Marsay later quips to his friend Paul de Manerville, 'de la poitrine' (1109).

It can be seen that Balzac's text raises a number of issues in relation to gender-related violence. The first concerns the fact that the novel ends with the murder of a woman. As Armine Kotin Mortimer notes in her book, *Plotting to Kill:* 'A woman's death is certainly one of the most common of clotural conventions, one that we accept uncritically.'[5] It is, therefore, necessary to establish whether the reader of *La Fille aux yeux d'or* is, as Mortimer writes of other works, 'coopted into participating in an anti-woman plot',[6] or whether other features of the novel inhibit such an uncritical, un-gender-aware, response. At this point, two further, related questions arise: in what way is it important that the killer is both a woman and a lesbian? and what is the role of de Marsay as potential killer, as murder witness, and as a man of androgynous beauty who dresses in women's clothes before making love with Paquita? In other words, do the real or apparent transgressions of gender in *La Fille aux yeux d'or* contribute to, or detract from, the violence of the dénouement? A third set of questions concerns the role of the group, whether of Paris or of the Treize: is the murder of Paquita in any way coloured by the opening descriptions of Paris and by the underground activities of the violent brotherhood? Finally, a fourth set of questions concerns the role of representation itself: do for instance the colourful descriptions of Paquita's boudoir so prepare the reader for her death, that her murder is 'naturalized' and 'normalized' in such a setting? Do they create and corroborate what Joel Black has called 'the aesthetics of murder'?[7] These are some of the questions I shall examine.

I

The sexual politics of *La Fille aux yeux d'or* has given rise to a variety of reactions from earlier critics. Rose Fortassier, who has written introductions to both Pléiade and Folio editions, traces what she sees as the profound misogyny of the whole of the *Histoire des Treize,* including *La Fille aux yeux d'or,* both to Balzac's own 'déceptions amoureuses' and to Otway's *Venice Preserv'd.*[8] Michel Lichtlé, who, more than any other critic, has highlighted the violence in *La Fille aux yeux d'or,* comments: 'Aussi dans ce roman si fortement teinté de misogynie, est-ce finalement l'homme qui fait figure de bourreau.'[9] Maurice Regard, for his part, doubtless bearing in mind de Marsay's indirect allusion to Sade in the pages of *La Fille aux yeux d'or* (1097), finds Paquita's boudoir 'une petite maison sadienne.'[10] Pierre Barbéris, however, has a different interpretation of the 'scène sanglante' of Paquita's death: 'Un point en tout cas semble clair: dans cette page, *les femmes sont belles,* et c'est de Marsay qui est déclassé, pâli. Il ne s'agit en rien d'une page misogyne.'[11]

If Barbéris seems to be in a minority here, it may be because both the *Treize* as a whole, and *La Fille aux yeux d'or* in particular, can be read as an indictment of women. One of the criticisms levelled at women is their hypocrisy. Or, as Balzac writes in *Ferragus:* Toute femme ment' (834).[12] However technically innocent or however well-intentioned, the women protago-

nists of the *Histoire des Treize,* delude, disappoint, and deceive. In *Ferragus,* Clémence Desmarets conceals from her husband the identity and 'profession' of her father. In *La Duchesse de Langeais,* Antoinette de Langeais deceives Montriveau as to the nature of her feelings for him—or, perhaps, as to the lack of such feelings; her whole life is a personal and social lie (see p. 962). In *La Fille aux yeux d'or,* Paquita conceals, however confusedly, desperately, and understandably, the existence and nature of her other relationship. It is this unwillingness or inability to *speak* that damns her in the eyes of the male. Paquita's love cannot or will not speak its name and that spells death: 'Ce que les gens qui se trouvent dans la situation sociale où était de Marsay [. . .] savent le mieux reconnaître, est l'innocence d'une fille. Mais, chose étrange! si la *Fille aux yeux d'or* était vierge, elle n'était pas certes innocente' (1901). In the *Treize* Balzac seems to have taken three non-virginal innocents, or non-innocent virgins—the faithful wife, the coquettish aristocrat, the lesbian lover—the better to warn men against what he calls, in the opening passages to *La Fille aux yeux d'or,* 'les simagrées du boudoir' and 'les singeries féminines' (1051). It would seem, therefore, that there are fewer differences than might be hoped between the provocative *boutades* of the *Physiologie du mariage* and the 'straight' novels of the *Comédie humaine.*[13] As Ross Chambers has written of *Autre étude de femme:* 'Women are either respectable or scandalous and guilty, but in either case they are hypocritical and deceptive—damned, it seems, if they do and damned if they don't.'[14] Hence the leitmotiv of the hybrid which Doris Kadish has noted in *La Fille aux yeux d'or.*[15] Hence, too, Balzac's woman is, as Nicole Ward Jouve has shown in relation to *Une fille d'Eve,* a mass of 'impossible contradictions', needing both to know and not to know, to be both in circulation and out of reach. Inevitably and congenitally duplicitous and double, Balzac's woman is, like Paquita and Mariquita, inevitably and congenitally *split,* or *two.*[16]

The duality and the duplicity of woman in the *Histoire des Treize* relates to another motif in *La Fille aux yeux d'or*: that of the mythological monster or *chimère.* Paquita is born of a mother who, having sold her daughter at an early age, is both a physical grotesque and a moral monster: she would, Balzac notes, be a success in China, 'où le beau idéal des artistes est la monstruosité' (1079). This fusion of Oriental and artistic themes both anticipates the description of Paquita's boudoir and recalls Paquita's identification with 'la délirante peinture appelée *la femme caressant sa chimère*' (1065).[17] Paquita is, therefore, not only double but multiple: as a product of a monster, she can both *be* a monster and *possess* a monster: Henri de Marsay. (See p. 1065.)[18] She thus assumes strange shapes in his dreams—'des images monstrueuses, des bizarreries insaisissables' (1085). This identification of Paquita with the chimera is not, however, mere exotic fancy, mere tantalizing enigma. It also condemns her to death. For, as Chantal Massol-Bedoin has pointed out, the enigma of the chimera, unlike that of the sphinx, offers little prospect of knowledge: 'Avant que le romantisme lui redonne vigueur et positivité, le terme est investi d'une valeur essentiellement péjorative, il n'est qu'un synonyme d' "illusion."'[19] If Paquita is a kind of illusion, then murdering her seems either immaterial or a final path to the knowledge she would otherwise withhold. For, as Joel Black has shown, killing can be cognition; it can represent 'in a narcissistic culture awash in inauthenticity', the last, desperate, 'means of clarifying the real.'[20] And even if her existence is seen as 'real', it is the reality of the monster which invites the blades of the avenging angels which are Henri de Marsay and his half-sister, the marquise de San-Réal.

Doing violence to Paquita can, therefore, be seen as an obvious and natural response to her 'nature': *dédoublement* invites further splitting; fission invites further incision. It is appropriate, therefore, that death in *La Fille aux yeux d'or* is associated primarily with sharp blades. From the opening lines on Paris, characterized by 'une moisson d'hommes que la mort fauche plus souvent qu'ailleurs' (1039), to the closing description of Paquita's body, 'déchiqueté à coups de poignard par son bourreau' (1107), there are repeated references to death by stabbing—whether by Paquita herself (1090), by her mulatto, Christemio (1086), or by de Marsay (1103). This motif reinforces, through its literary, pictoral, and Oriental associations, the previously mentioned 'aesthetics of death': death becomes a spectacle in the theatre of Paquita's boudoir, with both Henri and Mariquita vying for the leading role of executioner. This motif also recalls the preceding episode of the *Treize, La Duchesse de Langeais,* with its earlier title of *Ne touchez pas la hache:* although duchess and Montriveau are, in their different ways, equally dangerous, it is Montriveau who has the 'real' axe. As Antoinette writes to him, his is the axe of the executioner, whereas hers is that of God (1028). Small wonder, then, that Ronquerolles advises Montriveau: 'N'aie pas plus de charité que n'en a le bourreau. Frappe. Quand tu auras frappé, frappe encore. [. . .] Les duchesses sont dures, mon cher Armand, et ces natures de femme ne s'amollissent que sous les coups' (982). Such sentiments are echoed in *La Fille aux yeux d'or,* where Balzac writes: 'Les femmes aiment prodigieusement ces gens qui se nomment pachas eux-mêmes, qui semblent accompagnés de lions, de bourreaux, et marchent dans un appareil de terreur' (1085).

Thus, on repeated occasions, Paquita urges de Marsay to use her, to treat her like a toy 'jusqu'à ce que tu me brises' (1100), and even to kill her: 'Enivre-moi, puis tue-moi' (1090; see 1103). If the marquise's cruelty turns the boudoir into 'une petite maison sadienne', then Paquita's appeals to de Marsay to kill her exemplify what Pierre Danger has called 'le caractère fondamentalement masochiste du désir sexuel' in Balzac.[21] If the misogynist takes pleasure in the humiliation, torture, and slaughter of a woman, then there seems to be indeed such material in *La Fille aux yeux d'or,* where Balzac writes: 'Et qu'est-ce que la femme? Une petite chose, un ensemble de niaiseries' (1072). For Paquita, like her mother, no doubt comes from a country where 'les femmes ne sont pas des êtres, mais des choses dont on fait ce qu'on veut, que l'on vend, que l'on achète, que l'on tue' (1108).

II

Although the above remarks seem to offer convincing evidence of misogynistic sadism and masochism in *La Fille aux yeux d'or,* it is tempting to respond as Paquita herself does to de Marsay: 'tu oublies le pouvoir féminin' (1099). For it must be remembered that the afore-mentioned comments about Paquita's mother are spoken not by a man but by Margarita-Euphémia Porrabéril, marquise de San-Réal. It is, moreover, she, not de Marsay, who controls Paquita. Although great play is made of the power of de Marsay, 'despote oriental' (1085), he is quick to realize that not he, but another, rules the boudoir (1089). He also realizes that he is controlled even more directly by Paquita herself: 'de Marsay s'aperçut qu'il avait été joué par la *Fille aux yeux d'or*' (1096). This lack of authority extends, moreover, to all his dealings with Paquita. As Nicole Mozet has pointed out: 'Jamais il n'a l'initiative des rencontres.'[22] Jean-Yves Debreuille has also signalled 'cette étrange passivité de Henri',[23] which allows him, however reluctantly, to be abducted blindfold, to Paquita's apartments and to yield to her sexual advances: 'Elle le pressa de tous les côtés à la fois [. . .] lui présenta ses lèvres, et prit un baiser' (1083). It is, moreover, she who begins to undress him (1089) before redressing him in 'une robe de velours rouge', 'un bonnet de femme', and a shawl (1091). Thus, if Paquita seems to be the passive, Oriental slave, she has sufficient initiative and skill to bend Henri de Marsay to her wishes: '"Mets-moi donc à ton goût," dit Henri' (1091).[24]

The ease with which Paquita induces Henri to cross-dress in their first amorous encounter has received relatively little attention from critics. After all, in the early stages of the narrative, Henri was seen to have 'une peau de jeune fille' (1057) and 'cette suave figure qui n'eût pas déparé le corps de la plus belle d'entre elles [les femmes]' (1058). Women admire him in the same way as men admire women (1054). It has, therefore, been easy to see de Marsay as one of many vaguely androgynous dandies in the *Comédie humaine* such as Lucien de Rubempré and, on occasion, Eugène de Rastignac. The presence of Paul de Manerville during the hours Henri spends on his *toilette,* and Henri's closeness to Paul, along with Paul's own 'délicatesse de femme',[25] both in *La Fille aux yeux d'or* and in *Le Contrat de mariage,* have suggested to at least one critic that 'en plus du thème lesbien, l'on retrouve dans *La Fille aux yeux d'or* une préoccupation de l'homosexualité masculine.'[26] Although such a reading helps confirm Camille Paglia's verdict that 'Balzac's manipulations of gender are the most complex in literature',[27] it also has two less useful results. For such a reading not only conflates transvestism, androgyny, and homosexuality, but also makes men once again the focus of attention at precisely the moment when a man is shown to be losing ground to women. For if Paquita feels the urge to make Henri cross-dress, and if Henri so willingly complies, it is surely because both of the lovers thereby reproduce the lovemaking between Paquita and the marquise, with, as Pierre Danger has pointed out, de Marsay as little more than a dildo.[28] Like his frined Paul de Manerville in *Le Contrat de mariage,* de Marsay has been controlled and effectively demolished by an alliance of women, and, again like Paul, by two Creoles. No 'flibustier en gants jaunes' can match such an amalgam of female power.

It is at this point that it is important to examine that other under-discussed aspect of *La Fille aux yeux d'or*—the lesbianism of Paquita and the marquise. For although de Marsay is, at the end of the novel, disparaging about 'la manière dont se traitent leurs querelles de ménage' (1106), and although Paquita seems to renege on her earlier passion once she experiences 'real' heterosexual feelings ('Quoique bien remplie, cette vie cachée n'est que ténèbres en comparaison de la lumière [1100]), de Marsay's reaction with Paquita herself is different. The mixture of innocence and experience he finds in Paquita acts as a stimulus to his lovemaking—'il fut entraîné par-delà les limites dans lesquelles il avait jusqu'alors enfermé la passion'— and her 'other' love represents a challenge and an incentive: 'il ne voulut pas être dépassé par cette fille qu'un amour en quelque sorte artificiel avait formé par avance aux besoins de son âme' (1101). De Marsay is fascinated by Paquita not *despite* her lesbianism but *through* and *because of* her lesbianism. In the same way, perhaps, is he drawn towards his half-sister, the marquise, at the end of the story.[29] In both cases, however, de Marsay is rebuffed—by Paquita's exclamation of 'Oh! Mariquita!' (1102) at the height of her pas-

sion, and by the marquise who is inconsolable in her loss. In both cases the male is finally excluded in an assertion of lesbian sexual fulfilment and lesbian loyalty and love. The bitter dramatic irony of Paquita's final words to her would-be murderer, de Marsay: 'Trop tard, mon bien-aimé!' (1106), confirms that lesbians have little or nothing to learn from heterosexual men.

It must, however, also be admitted, that, if *La Fille aux yeux d'or* is to be believed, then the reverse is also true, and heterosexual men have little to learn from lesbians if their 'querelles de ménage' simply replicate or anticipate male violence. Whether de Marsay cross-dresses, goes bisexual, or, as happens elsewhere in the *Comédie humaine,* marries an English heiress called Dinah Stevens, makes little difference if he is so ready to murder at the slightest slight to his male dignity. Whether the marquise de San-Réal is empowered as a woman, sister, lesbian, or nun, makes equally little difference, if she imprisons, harasses, and then slaughters her hitherto devoted partner. Neither the empowerment of women nor the emasculation of de Marsay's masculinity puts a stop to incarceration, cruelty, and killing.[30] Indeed the empowerment of the marquise, and the disempowerment of de Marsay, simply seem to make their roles more complementary: like Valmont and Mme de Merteuil they could indeed twin into an unholy alliance. It would appear that if any transgression of gender-roles or of sexual positioning in *La Fille aux yeux d'or* does little either to elucidate or eliminate violence, then solutions must be sought elsewhere. The next sections will, therefore, turn to the remaining two themes: the role of the group—the Treize and Paris—and of representation.

III

When Balzac added the *dédicace* to Eugène Delacroix to the Furne edition of *La Fille aux yeux d'or* in 1843, he can hardly have had any idea of the influence this would have on later analyses of the novel. From Albert Béguin's *Balzac visionnaire* of 1946,[31] to Henry Majewski's 'Painting as Intertext in Balzac's *La Fille aux yeux d'or*' in 1991,[32] comparisons between the two artists have fuelled critical debate on the novel, often with the assumption that, as Olivier Bonard wrote in 1969: 'Balzac était habité par la figure et l'oeuvre de Delacroix lorsqu'il travaillait à *la Fille aux yeux d'or.*'[33] Critical attention has thus concentrated on parallels in chromatics—the use by both artists of the colours red, white, and gold—on parallels in relation to exoticism, the Orient and animals, and, less frequently, on violence. Paintings of Delacroix cited range from his *Desdémone,*[34] to *Femmes d'Alger dans leur appartement* (1834),[35] and *La Mort de Sardanapale* (1827).[36]

The search for parallels between painter and writer has, however, tended to obscure the importance in Balzac of painting as a model for representing or mediating a particular image. It obscures the importance of studying the dynamics of painting and writing *within* the Balzacian narrative, of examining what Jean-Loup Bourget has called, in his critique of Bonard's book, the pictural as having 'une fonction dans la trame du récit.'[37] It is, in other words, possible to see the chromatics linking the verbal and visual arts in the description of Paquita's boudoir as simply a particularly salient example of a thematics of representation in *La Fille aux yeux d'or.* Such a thematics of representation would link the personalities and actions of the characters to more generalized notions of artistic performance, mediatization, and image-creation.

From the very moment we are introduced to Henri de Marsay, we are conscious of him as an artist and as a performer, as, indeed, a performing artist or an artist in performance—both in the sense of *in* a performance, and as an expert *at* performance. We see him as one of the many handsome young Parisian dandies promenading one Spring morning in the Tuileries in 1815 (1058). He is, therefore, highly visible, conscious of image, out to see and be seen. As Jean-Yves Debreuille writes of this scene: 'il s'agit [. . .] d'une promenade, d'un 'parcours' où l'activité essentielle est de l'ordre du voir', recalling, with its 'esthétisme pastoral', the traditional 'spring opening' of the courtly lyric.[38] Both he and fellow-dandies are, moreover, first struck by Paquita's *eyes,* those celebrated 'deux yeux jaunes comme ceux des tigres' (1064). It is interesting that de Marsay, although known for his independence and force of character, immediately uses the name given to Paquita by his fellow Parisians: la *Fille aux yeux d'or.*[39] He immediately absorbs language which is, like gold, already common currency, which is, like himself, already in circulation, and which is, being based on her two eyes, already a double visual representation. From the outset, then, the dandies commute Paquita's reality into an image, in the same way as alchemists seek to commute baser metals into gold. Both Paquita and gold are essentially *signs,* and signs of a willed and possibly violent transformation of an earlier, rejected commodity into 'precious bane.' Even at this early stage, Paquita is, then, in a sense, mere language and image. She is circulating as art. Her body is, as Teresa de Lauretis might say, 'continually and inevitably caught up in representation.'[40]

At the same time, of course, so is de Marsay, although in different ways and for different reasons. Henri has the unusual background of having no visible mother and four possible fathers: Lord Dudley, Monsieur de Marsay, the marquis de Vordac, and, finally, the abbé de Maronis. None of his four fathers shows any inter-

est in him, except the one with least biological or legal connection to him, the abbé, who strives to replace 'virilement la mère' (1056). With such a background, it is perhaps inevitable that Henri should see his role as more important than biology, blood-ties, or other forms of socially legitimated relationships. He, too, has undergone a transformation, a transformation painstakingly engineered by the abbé de Maronis. De Marsay, too, has been commuted from a human base metal into a golden youth, blooming in the Paris spring. He, too, is now a work of art—the Parisian dandy, spending two-and-a-half hours on his *toilette* which the *Traité de la vie élégante* tells us is 'l'expression de la société' and 'une science, un art, une habitude, un sentiment.'[41] If sexuality is the physical body, and if gender is the meaning imposed on that body, or, perhaps more radically, the stylization of that body,[42] then de Marsay does indeed engender himself in representation—as the dandy. At the same time, he also denies such engendering by disassociating himself from the band of male dandies to Paul de Manerville (1071-73). The only way he can salvage an identity from such engenderings and de-engenderings, from such violations and self-violations, is to engage in an action which enables him to assume that violence and to exploit it to his own advantage: he allies himself to a violent group, the *Treize,* and engages in an action which combines the characteristics of violence and performance: 'Il s'agissait de livrer bataille à quelque ennemi secret [. . .] Il allait jouer cette éternelle comédie qui sera toujours neuve, et dont les personnages sont un vieillard, une jeune fille et un amoureux [. . .] "Il va falloir jouer serré," se dit Henri' (1070-71). In this way, de Marsay demonstrates that if, as Teresa de Lauretis has argued, 'the representation of violence is inseparable from the notion of gender', then 'violence is en-gendered in representation.'[43]

It is not possible in the course of this paper to look at all the examples of links between violence, gender, and representation in *La Fille aux yeux d'or.* These culminate, however, in the descriptions of Paquita's boudoir, whose configuration evokes either a theatre or a church,[44] with the divan centre-stage as eventual sacrificial altar and with the marquise as high priestess. The Oriental furnishings and weaponry figure as décor in a setting which, as has been noted, bears similarities to a Delacroix canvas, whether the *Femmes d'Alger* or *Sardanapale.* Rather than similarities of mood or even technique, what is important about the reference to Delacroix is the way violence in *La Fille aux yeux d'or* is fashioned through the artistry of its execution into a spectacle to be admired both by the executioner and the audience. It is the transformation of killing into an art which *La Fille aux yeux d'or* both exploits and exposes. As Joel Black remarks:

'"Out-lawed" in real life as a moral transgression, murder could only be legitimated, and made socially acceptable, in art. Insofar as it defied reason itself, murder could only become minimally comprehensible *as* art.'[45]

The ultimate performance is, therefore, at the end of the narrative, and is the murder itself:

> *La Fille aux yeux d'or* expirait noyée dans le sang. [. . .] Cet appartement blanc, où le sang paraissait si bien, trahissait un long combat. Les mains de Paquita étaient empreintes sur les coussins. Partout elle s'était accrochée à la vie, partout elle s'était défendue, et partout elle avait été frappée.
>
> (1106)

What is striking about this scene is that it is, precisely, a scene, a tableau, which is both static and without human agency. The murder as *action* is already in the past, transposed into colour and décor. For Jean-Luc Bourget, tableaux in Balzac represent 'un moment d'équilibre', '[une] illusion statique': 'Peinture de l'illusion, illusion de la peinture: son illusion (d')optique, c'est qu'elle croit pouvoir immobiliser le drame.'[46] This congealing of the action has the effect of congealing Paquita's blood almost before it has been shed. She is always already dead, and the aesthetics of death does away with actual murder.

Once murder has become a spectacle, the presence of the marquise can be registered:

> La marquise avait les cheveux arrachés, elle était couverte de morsures, dont plusieurs saignaient, et sa robe déchirée la laissait voir à demi nue, les seins égratignés. Elle était sublime ainsi. Se tête avide et furieuse respirait l'odeur du sang.
>
> (1107)

Here the violence of the marquise is also arrested, immobilized, and frozen in her pose of avenging priestess. Once again, the eye of de Marsay as artist turns death into aesthetics. At the same time, his gaze is distracted from the transgression of murder by, on the one hand, his fascination with the semi-nudity of the marquise, and, secondly, by the other, more unspeakable, transgression of lesbian love. The representation of death pales into insignificance beside the *unrepresentable* transgression that is lesbianism. The final twist to Balzac's aesthetics of murder is that even what art does *not* say still supersedes a killing. Even artistic silence is more eloquent than death. Mariquita's withdrawal into a convent and de Marsay's final quip that Paquita died of a chest complaint—'De la poitrine'—do, moreover, ensure that Paquita's death is so sealed in art that it can never escape and be retold. It, and she, are condemned to become another *chef d'oeuvre inconnu.*

IV

It can be seen that there are two seemingly incompatible ways of viewing *La Fille aux yeux d'or*: as a narrative shot through with misogyny and homophobia; as an exposure of the attractions and the dangers of welding together gender, violence, and representation. In order to bring these two views into a more harmonious perspective, it may be useful to return to the beginning of the novel, to the descriptions of Paris, and, once again, to the character and times of Henri de Marsay.

De Marsay's spring walk in 'la grande allée des Tuileries' (1058) takes place in 1815. In the course of the walk, Paul de Manerville tells Henri that he had seen *La fille aux yeux d'or* in the Tuileries 'quand les Bourbons y étaient' (1064). It follows that the events of the novel, of short duration, are situated in a 'période charnière' which is neither Napoleonic nor Restoration, but can be seen as looking back to one and anticipating the other. As Pierre Barbéris has indicated: 'L'histoire va [. . .] se développer dans une sorte d'entre-deux politique.'[47] However, the *Fille aux yeux d'or* episode is, for de Marsay, only a beginning. Although it occurs after his betrayal by Charlotte, recounted in *Autre étude de femme,* it still belongs to a period of his youth when there remain illusions to be shed. The failure of his affair with Paquita helps to confirm him in a resolve to marry for ambition not love, and to devote his energies to politics, in which he develops a brilliantly successful career, culminating in his being made Prime Minister of France in 1831. He dies, however, shortly afterwards in either 1833 or 1834.

If this chronology is placed alongside that of the composition of *La Fille aux yeux d'or* (1834-1835), an interesting fact emerges: de Marsay is almost certainly 'dead' in the *Comédie humaine* before *La Fille aux yeux d'or* is published. Although the novel traces de Marsay's golden youth, it is, for Balzac, seen from the perspective of knowledge of his maturity, apotheosis as Prime Minister, and death. Although, then, the narrative seems to trace a birth and a beginning, it is also tempting to see that beginning as 'une recherche du temps perdu', like Félix de Vandenesse's 'imposants souvenirs ensevelis au fond de [s]on âme, comme ces productions marines qui s'aperçoivent par les temps calmes, et que les flots de la tempête jettent par fragments sur la grève.'[48] No wonder, then, that Paquita's body can be so easily passed over, and her death seem so distant. It *is* distant. Twenty years distant.

So, too, are the exploits of the Treize, As Rose Fortassier points out, they are disbanded at the death of Napoleon, in 1821. For they did, like Montriveau in

La Duchesse de Langeais, take from Napoleon 'le culte de l'énergie et de l'action.'[49] By the time of writing of *La Fille aux yeux d'or,* such Byronic gestures belong essentially to the past. The Donjuanism which P.-G. Castex has associated with de Marsay,[50] has changed, has become 'embourgeoisé en carriérisme.'[51] This may well explain why de Marsay, *already* in 1815, disavows the life of the dandy while using it to his own advantage. He is already moving towards the conformisms of 1830, like the rest of the Treize, who are also now going *straight,* 'paisiblement rentrés sous le joug des lois civiles' (787). No wonder that he so easily dismisses the *roman noir* of his affair with Paquita, and the extraordinary marquise de San-Réal: he has, in his later political career outlined in *Le Contrat de mariage,* more in common with his influential father, Lord Dudley, than with his wayward Creole half-sister, Mariquita. He has more need of the actual money of his future wife, Dinah Stevens, than of Paquita's golden eyes. The welding of sexuality, art, and the subversive, Satanic violence of the *Treize* is no longer appropriate to de Marsay, *grand politique.* Equally inappropriate is the violence of the sharp, straight, cutting instrument which has been shown to characterize the Treize. For as de Marsay explains in *Une fille d'Eve*: 'les ambitieux doivent aller en ligne courbe, le chemin le plus court en politique.'[52]

Although such observations cannot retrospectively justify either murder, misogyny, or homophobia, they do, at least, expose as misguided and outmoded the ethos in which such actions and attitudes were found. They demonstrate that all that has followed an aesthetic of death is the death of that aesthetic. For this aesthetic seems to have announced less the destruction of others than the destruction of itself. Hence the manifest *failure* of the Treize to achieve any of their objectives—vengeance on or for Clémence, the duchess, and Paquita. As Balzac himself writes: 'les Treize ont vu leur pouvoir [. . .] brisé, leur vengeance trompée' (1038). If some of their members succeed in the future, it will be in the new incarnation of a political oligarchy 'où demeure une pensée fixe de gouvernement et qui dirige les affaires publiques dans une voie droite au lieu de laisser tirailler le pays en mille sens différents.'[53] The aesthetics of death is giving way to an aesthetics of politics. This may not be an ideal solution, for the aestheticization of politics has been shown to characterize fascism,[54] but at least it marks a very radical shift in purpose from the artistic assassination of women.

This shift is accompanied by another change, signalled in the introduction to *La Fille aux yeux d'or,* 'Physionomies parisiennes.'[55] Some critics have found this introduction too unwieldy, too disparate, and too self-contained, to sit easily with the later narrative, espe-

cially when de Marsay is presented as a rarity in relation to the system described (1054). However, if the introduction is seen to offer a description of the period of its composition (1833-1834), then its relation to the rest of the novel can be viewed very differently. If, as Chantal Massol-Bedoin has argued, 'le prologue offre un tableau de la société parisienne au début de la monarchie de juillet',[56] then the de Marsay-Paquita episode of 1815 can be seen as a *flashback,* again like Félix de Vandenesse's recollections of the same period in *Le Lys dans la vallée.* For *La Fille aux yeux d'or,* like *Le Lys* [*Le Lys dans la vallée*], was originally conceived as a first-person narrative, related by Ronquerolles,[57] and thus as a memoir historicized from both individual and social perspectives.

Seen in this light, the prologue offers a very different view of society from the later episode, if only because it does offer a *view of society,* not of a few exceptional individuals. Even as a dandy, de Marsay wants to be different, whereas, as Balzac points out in the *Traité de la vie élégante* (1831), 'dans notre société les différences ont disparu.'[58] Thus, in the introduction to *La Fille aux yeux d'or,* Balzac is concerned with 'l'aspect général de la population parisienne', with 'une moisson d'hommes que la mort fauche plus souvent qu'ailleurs' (1039). Death is, therefore, generalized and depersonalized, the result of social position,[59] overwork, squalor, and disease such as cholera, rather than an act of vengeance, jealousy or love. The undermining and the destruction of whole swathes of the Parisian population, swept along on a tide of 'or et plaisir', thus offers a very different view of death and violence from the later narrative. Death and destruction are not planned as an art, but endured as an evil. Hence even the artists themselves are being destroyed: 'La concurrence, les rivalités, les calomnies assassinent ces talents. Les uns, désespérés, roulent dans les abîmes du vice, les autres meurent jeunes et ignorés' (1049). There is no place for Henri and Paquita in such a world, except as exceptions, illusions, fictions. An aesthetics of death in such a context is indeed a perversion, a perversion which *La Fille aux yeux d'or* as a whole can be seen to depict and expose. The future of the 1830s may not be any less bleak. But at least murder and death are no longer beautiful. The exotic dandy, the mythic *chimère,* and the sublime murderess are all laid to rest. Thus, long before the prophets of postmodernism, of *la société du spectacle,* of simulation and seduction, Balzac offers his own exposure of the ideology of an aesthetic, his own deconstruction of an aesthetics of death.[60]

Notes

1. Honoré de Balzac, *La Fille aux yeux d'or,* p. 1097. All page references to *La Fille aux yeux d'or,* as to *Ferragus, La Duchesse de Langeais,* and pref-

aces, refer to *La Comédie humaine,* edited by P.-G. Castex (Paris: Gallimard, Bibliothèque de la Pléiade), V (1977). Subsequent references to this volume will be given parenthetically in the text. An earlier version of this paper was presented at the Eighteenth Colloquium of Nineteenth-Century French Studies, Binghamton, 1992.

2. See, for example: Carol J. Clover, *Men, Women and Chain Saws. Gender in the Modern Horror Film* (London: British Film Institute, 1992); Deborah Cameron and Elizabeth Frazer, *The Lust to Kill* (Oxford: Polity Press, 1987); Keith Soothill and Sylvia Walby, *Sex Crime in the News* (London: Routledge, 1991); Jalna Hanmer and Sheila Saunders, *Reading Between the Lines* (Basingstoke: Macmillan, 1992, forthcoming).

3. Recent examples are: *Rape and Representation,* edited by Lynn A. Higgins and Brenda R. Silver (New York: Columbia University Press, 1991); Elisabeth Bronfen, *Over Her Dead Body. Death, Femininity and the Aesthetic* (Manchester: Manchester University Press, 1992); Joel Black, *The Aesthetics of Murder* (Baltimore: Johns Hopkins University Press, 1991). See also Susan Rubin Suleiman, *Subversive Intent. Gender, Politics, and the Avant-Garde* (Cambridge, MA: Harvard University Press, 1990).

4. For studies of the graphics of *La Fille aux yeux d'or,* title and character, see Maurice Laugaa, 'L'Effet *Fille aux yeux d'or*', *Littérature,* 20 (1976), 62-80 and his 'Système des marques graphiques et du nom propre', in Université de Paris VII: *Recherches en sciences des textes. Hommage à Pierre Albouy* (Grenoble: Grenoble University Press, 1977), pp. 190-218.

5. Armine Kotin Mortimer, *Plotting to Kill* (New York: Peter Lang, 1991), p.xi.

6. Mortimer, p.xiii.

7. See the title of Black's volume, above, note 3.

8. Pléiade, pp. 741-42. See also Honoré de Balzac, *La Duchesse de Langeais, La Fille aux yeux d'or,* Préface de Rose Fortassier (Paris: Gallimard, Folio, 1976), p. 8.

9. Honoré de Balzac, *Histoire des Treize: Ferragus, La Fille aux yeux d'or,* edited by Michael Lichtlé (Paris: Flammarion, 1988), p. 47.

10. Maurice Regard, 'Balzac et Sade', *L'Année balzacienne,* 1971, 3-10, p. 7.

11. Honoré de Balzac, *Histoire des Treize,* edited by Pierre Barbéris (Paris: Livre de Poche, 1983), p. 534. Barbéris's italics.

12. Quoted by Lichtlé, p. 43.

13. The *Physiologie* can, however, itself be seen as a parody: see Marie Maclean, 'Narrative and the Gender Trap', *AUMLA 74* (1990), 69-84.

14. Ross Chambers, 'Misogyny and Cultural Denial (Balzac's *Autre étude de femme)*', *L'Esprit Créateur,* 31.3 (1991), 5-14, p. 10.

15. See Doris Y. Kadish, 'Hybrids in Balzac's *La Fille aux yeux d'or*', *Nineteenth-century French Studies,* 16 (1988), 270-78 and her chapter 'Mixing Genders in *Marat assassiné* and *La Fille aux yeux d'or*' in her *Politicizing Gender. Narrative Strategies in the Aftermath of the French Revolution* (New Brunswick: Rutgers, 1991), pp. 37-63.

16. See Nicole Ward Jouve, 'Balzac's *A Daughter of Eve* and the Apple of Knowledge', in *Sexuality and Subordination,* edited by Susan Mendus and Jane Rendall (London: Routledge, 1989), pp. 25-59, pp. 37 and 56).

17. For a possible source for this reference, see Henri de Latouche, *Fragoletta. Naples et Paris en 1789* (Paris: Pour la Société des Médecins Bibliophiles, 1929), pp. 42-43. It must be remembered, however, that this 'femme caressant une Chimère' is a picture, not a woman. It is also important not to confuse the themes of the hermaphrodite *(Fragoletta),* the transvestite *(Mademoiselle de Maupin)* and lesbianism.

18. In *Balzacian Montage. Configuring 'La Comédie humaine',* (Toronto: Toronto University Press, 1991), pp. 63-73, Allan H. Pasco emphasizes the themes of the monster and the monstrous in *La Fille aux yeux d'or.*

19. Chantal Massol-Bedoin, 'La Charade et la chimère. Du récit énigmatique dans *La Fille aux yeux d'or*', *Poétique,* 89 (1992), 31-45, p. 42. The roles of ambiguity, secrecy and silence in *La Fille aux yeux d'or* have also been analysed by Leyla Perrone-Moisés, 'Le récit euphémique', *Poétique,* 17 (1974), 27-38, and by Nils Soelberg, 'La narration de *La Fille aux yeux d'or*: une omniscience encombrante', *Revue Romane,* 25.2 (1990), 454-65. The undecidable contours of the chimera also recall Frenhofer's plea to abolish the line in art as in nature.

20. See Black, pp. 123, 158.

21. Pierre Danger, *L'Eros balzacien. Structures du désir dans 'la Comédie humaine'* (Paris: Corti, 1989), p. 35. In a long chapter on masochism in Balzac (pp. 119-69) Danger argues that for Balzac 'le sadisme était l'autre face du masochisme' (p. 143). Gilles Deleuze would, however, distinguish between these scenarios.

22. Nicole Mozet, *Balzac au pluriel* (Paris: PUF, 1990), p. 126.

23. Jean-Yves Debreuille, 'Horizontalité et verticalité: inscriptions idéologiques dans *La Fille aux yeux d'or*', in *La Femme au XIXe siècle. Littérature et idéologie* (Lyon: Presses Universitaires de Lyon, 1979), pp. 151-65, p. 158.

24. For the Orientalism of *La Fille aux yeux d'or,* see Pierre Citron, 'Le Rêve asiatique de Balzac', *L'Année balzacienne,* 1968, 303-36, and Pierre Saint-Amand, 'Balzac oriental: *La Fille aux yeux d'or*', *Romanic Review,* 79 (1988), 329-40. For the theme of fire, see Juliette FrØlich, 'Une phrase/un récit: Le jeu du feu dans *La Fille aux yeux d'or* de Balzac', *Revue romane,* (1979, 1), 59-73.

25. See *Le Contrat de mariage,* Pléiade, III, p. 634.

26. Victor-Laurent Tremblay, 'Démasquer *La Fille aux yeux d'or*', *Nineteenth-Century French Studies,* 19 (1990), 72-82, p. 77. It is true that Lord Dudley seems disappointed that the handsome Henri is his son (p. 1058).

27. Camille Paglia, *Sexual Personae* (London: Penguin, 1991), pp. 404-05.

28. Danger, p. 44.

29. In 'Rereading Femininity', *Yale French Studies,* 62 (1981), 19-44, p. 40, Shoshana Felman argues that in this recognition scene 'Henri has to recognize, incarnated by his double—by his sister—his own feminine reflection: he sees *himself*—as a woman.'

30. For the novel as an exposure of masculinity in crisis, see Lucette Czyba, 'Misogynie et gynophobie dans *La Fille aux yeux d'or*', in *La Femme au XIXe siècle,* pp. 139-49.

31. Republished in his *Balzac lu et relu* (Paris: Seuil, 1965). For the analysis of *La Fille aux yeux d'or,* see pp. 81-87.

32. Henry F. Majewski, 'Painting as Intertext in Balzac's *La Fille aux yeux d'or*', *Symposium,* 45 (1991), 370-84.

33. Olivier Bonard, *La Peinture dans la création balzacienne* (Geneva: Droz, 1969), p. 157.

34. Fortassier, Pléiade, V, p. 784. It is not clear which of Delacroix's Desdemona pictures is alluded to here. Despite the reference to *Othello* in *La Fille aux yeux d'or* (p. 1075), there seems little connection with a picture such as *La Malédiction de Desdemona* (1852).

35. Although Majewski deals with this picture at some length (pp. 372-76), he also notes the considerable differences between the two works (p. 375).

36. One link here is the male as passive witness to murder (Majewski, p. 380).

37. Jean-Loup Bourget, 'Balzac et le pictural', *Romanic Review,* 64 (1973), 286-95, p. 295.

38. Debreuille, p. 156.

39. Communication is often only achieved through an intermediary in *La Fille aux yeux d'or,* whether the postman, Moinot (p. 1069), an interpreter (p. 1077), or another language such as the English used by Paquita and de Marsay (p. 1081). This effort and this mediation—what Félix de Vandenesse calls 'le travail que nécessitent les idées pour être exprimées' (Pléiade, IX, p. 970)—turn even the most anodine exchanges into an *art.*

40. Teresa de Lauretis, 'Feminist Studies/Critical Studies: Issues, Terms, and Contexts', in *Feminist Studies/Critical Studies,* edited by Teresa de Lauretis (Basingstoke: Macmillan, 1986), pp. 1-19, p. 12.

41. Pléiade, XII, pp. 250, 253.

42. See Morag Shiach, '"Gender" and Inequality', Paper read at Inequality/Theory Conference, University of Nottingham, July 1992, pp. 6, 14. Reference is being made, respectively, to Elaine Showalter and Judith Butler.

43. Teresa de Lauretis, 'The Violence of Rhetoric', in *The Violence of Representation,* edited by Nancy Armstrong and Leonard Tennenhouse (London: Routledge, 1989), pp. 239-58, p. 240.

44. For a detailed analysis of the form of Paquita's boudoir, and the church analogy, see John R. O'Connor, *Balzac's Soluble Fish* (Madrid: José Porrúa Turanzas, 1977), pp. 198-205.

45. Black, p. 102.

46. Bourget, pp. 291, 294, 295.

47. Barbéris, p. 531. See also Michele Hannoosh, 'La Femme, la ville, le réalisme: Fondements épistémologiques dans le Paris de Balzac', *Romanic Review,* 82 (1991), 127-45, p. 135, and André Vanoncini, 'Les "Trompettes de 1789" et "l'Abattement de 1814." Moments du tableau parisien dans *La Fille aux yeux d'or*', *L'Année balzacienne,* 11 (1990), 221-32.

48. Pléiade, IX, p. 970.

49. Fortassier, Folio, p. 7. See Lichtlé, p. 36.

50. Honoré de Balzac, *Histoire des Treize,* edited by P.-G. Castex (Paris: Garnier, 1956), pp. 364-65.

51. Barbéris, p. 15.

52. Pléiade, II, p. 306.

53. De Marsay writing to Paul de Manerville in *Le Contrat de mariage,* Pléiade, III, p. 647. It is worth noting that for Lichtlé (p. 13), the Treize are essentially individuals rather than a true collective.

54. See David Carroll, 'Literary Fascism or the Aestheticizing of Politics: The Case of Robert Brasillach', *New Literary History,* 23 (1992), 691-726. On aesthetics and the left, see for example James Rolleston, 'The Uses of the Frankfurt School: New Stories on the Left', *Diacritics,* 21.4 (1991), 87-100. For Terry Eagleton, the aesthetic can function as an emancipatory or as a hegemonic force *(see The Ideology of the Aesthetic* (Oxford: Blackwell, 1990), p. 28).

55. The chapter divisions are retained in some editions (Folio, Flammarion) but not in others (Livre de Poche, Pléiade).

56. Massol-Bedoin, p. 32.

57. See Pléiade, V, p. 1526.

58. Pléiade, XII, p. 224.

59. As Debreuille (p. 155) notes, Balzac evokes society in metaphorical terms—the 'spheres'—as, historically, he could not speak in terms of the class struggle. Debreuille's further suggestion that this metaphorical construction is then reinvested in the second part of the novel casts an interesting new light on the role of aesthetics and representation in *La Fille aux yeux d'or.*

60. This deconstruction seems to be corroborated by Balzac himself who, in a note to the 1835 edition of *La Fille aux yeux d'or* (see Lichtlé, p. 302), claims that Paquita is like the actress who rises from the dead after a theatrical performance and is, therefore, still alive, relatively well, and living in Paris. In the same note, however, he states that the *dénouement* is 'un fait périodique à Paris, dont les chirurgiens des hôpitaux connaissent seuls la triste gravité.'

Marie Josephine Diamond (essay date 1994)

SOURCE: Diamond, Marie Josephine. "The Monstrous Other: The Chimera of Speculation in Balzac's *The Girl with the Golden Eyes." Nineteenth-Century Contexts* 18 (1994): 249-62.

[*In the following essay, Diamond examines the psychological context of* The Girl with the Golden Eyes *as well as Balzac's depiction of early-nineteenth-century French society.*]

Balzac's **The Girl with the Golden Eyes** (1834-1835) is rhetorically, structurally, and thematically a monstrous, excessive text. The extended descriptive analysis of post-Napoleonic Restoration Paris that opens the narrative operates on a number of contending interpretive registers. In a tone of unrelenting hyperbole, the narrator describes the functioning of the metropolis in terms of a spectacle, a Dantesque allegory of suffering and damnation, a personification based on a study of physiognomies, a classification of economic and class structures, and a synecdochic evocation of the modern industrial city as a giant engine in a ship of trade and colonization. Paris is a giant desiring machine. Driven by the allegorized monster, Speculation, its different social classes consume themselves in the pursuit of gold and/or pleasure. At the pinnacle of the social hierarchy is the aristocracy, which, representing the possession of wealth and access to pleasure, embodies an ultimate standard of value and mediates the desires of the striving working class, the petty bourgeoisie, the high bourgeoisie, and ambitious writers and artists. This descriptive social analysis functions as a prologue and appears generically at odds with the narrative body of the text.

The story of **The Girl with the Golden Eyes** tells of a brutal sexual liaison between Henri de Marsay, the epitome of the rich and admired aristocrat devoted to the pursuit of pleasure, and the Creole Paquita Valdès, an ideal object of desire. Sold into a domestic, sexual slavery by her once enslaved, Asian mother, she is the exotic possession of the jealous and passionate marquise de San Réal, who confines her to a closely guarded "oriental" space of luxury and indulgence. When de Marsay overcomes all obstacles to possess Paquita, he is horrified to find that her owner and his rival is a woman. In a passion for revenge he plans to kill his mistress only to find that the marquise has preceded him and has hacked their mutual victim to death. In a final recognition scene, he discovers that the murderous marquise, still holding aloft her bloody knife, is his half-sister. Shadowing the narration of this aberrational sexual triangle is the silent figure of Paquita's grotesque and abject mother, who is finally called upon to clean up the room in which her daughter has been killed.

One of the problems that immediately confronts the reader of this novel is the aesthetic disjunction between the generalized, social analysis of modern Paris and the particularized, psychological context of the ensuing story. However, the transition between these two very different generic modes is so blurred as to be almost imperceptible. The narrator closes the scathing, descriptive introduction of Paris with a general statement that, like real devotion and noble friendships, extraordinary faces—all the more remarkable for being rare—can still be found in the aristocracy. He then goes on to evoke such a face as a fusion of youthful English beauty and southern French strength, intelligence and purity. This preamble is followed by the conjunction "or" ("now") that introduces de Marsay— the son of an English lord and a French marquise.

This indirect and abrupt transition seems to present de Marsay as a contradiction to the generality of Parisian egotism and moral ugliness. However, as is immediately clear in the brief biographical summary of his life, his external appearance, unlike all other physiognomies in the social taxonomy of Paris, does not reflect an inner equivalent. His beauty is deceptive. The conjunctive "or" is thus ironic, disrupting the equation between physical appearance and moral value, and its homonymic double meaning "gold" figuratively relates de Marsay to the general analysis of the speculative order of Parisian society.

Nevertheless, in one of the most interesting and innovative analyses of *The Girl with the Golden Eyes,* Shoshana Felman interprets Balzac's rewriting of the classic, male dominated love triangle and the complex gender displacements among de Marsay, Paquita, and the marquise as disruptive of the hierarchies of gender, money, and class described in the "prologue." She brilliantly articulates how de Marsay almost loses control of his own master plot of sexual conquest as he becomes enmeshed in the subversive triangle that locates him in the place of the feminine—he even cross-dresses to satisfy Paquita's desire. From this perspective, the gold that is the sign of identity, order, and hierarchy, and which de Marsay first pursues in Paquita's golden eyes as the reflection and confirmation of his masculinity and superiority, turns out to be an unstable currency. What de Marsay discovers in his bizarre adventure, to quote Felman, is "a principle of universal economical *equivalence* which subverts the 'proper' in every sense and thus upsets the hierarchical coherence and legitimacy of classification and class, whether political (social classes, poor as opposed to rich), rhetorical (substitutive metaphorical as opposed to literal; figurative meaning as opposed to 'proper' meaning), or sexual (female as opposed to male)" (39). The discovery of the "feminine" as a subversive sign within rather than resolutely other to masculinity thus culminates in de Marsay's recognition that the marquise is his half-sister, his feminine "double." Felman raises the possibility that this crucial encounter may mask a desired reunion with the lost mother, the threat of an incestuous longing to return to the womb and a negation of otherness. However, she dismisses this potential reading and asserts that the recognition of his half-sister allows de Marsay an authentic but fleeting moment of the discovery of the other in the self, of femininity as the very principle of difference, which he negates when he returns to his "normal" life as though nothing has happened, completely suppressing the reality of Paquita's murder with the euphemism that she died *de la poitrine* (literally, "of the chest"—a synonym for consumption). Felman also relates de Marsay's discovery of the femi-

nine as difference with the impropriety of his father, Lord Dudley, whom she reads as subversive of the Law of the Father, of the patriarchal principle of social order: Lord Dudley does not pass on his patronym to his children; he is bisexual/homosexual (his "oriental" inclination, according to the text), and a general figure for transgression.

In Felman's reading, the repressed of the hierarchical, patriarchal social order is the "monstrous" instability of sexual identity, the feminine as a principle of "difference." Mary Jacobus in her *Reading Woman* generalizes this insight when, speaking of *Orlando,* she describes the monster in literary texts as sexual vacillation: "The monster in the text is not woman, or the woman writer; rather, it is this repressed vacillation of gender or the instability of identity—the ambiguity of subjectivity itself which returns to wreak havoc on consciousness, on hierarchy, and on unitary schemes designed to repress the otherness of femininity" (5). Indeed, the figure of an actual monster, a chimera, mediates the representation of de Marsay's liaison with Paquita. Describing the girl with the golden eyes shortly after he has met her, de Marsay evokes a painting, "The Girl Caressing Her Chimera," in which he identifies the girl as Paquita and himself as the chimera. Recalling that this painting refers to Henri Latouche's novel *Fragoletta* (1829) in which the chimera is related to the hermaphrodite and the bisexual as the representative emblem of love, Jacobus concludes that the monster in *The Girl with the Golden Eyes* represents the uncanny of repressed femininity as bisexuality (14-17).[1] I shall return to this figure of the chimera, which recurs at crucial articulations of the story and assumes a metacritical function in the text.

By "bisexuality" Jacobus clearly means the principle of a deconstructive difference defined as feminine. However, bisexuality may indicate male appropriation, colonization, or neutralization of the feminine. In her "The Laugh of the Medusa," Hélène Cixous warns against reading bisexuality as necessarily transgressive of the hierarchical patriarchal order since, in its classic conception, "it fantasizes a total being and does away with difference experienced as an operation incurring loss, conjuring away the fear of castration" (254). Sure of his dominant position, de Marsay allows himself to be dressed up as a woman to intensify his desire and satisfy Paquita's curiosity, becoming, thereby, a "merger-type bisexual," to use Cixous' formulation, a travesty of the unifying phallic mother. Rather than locating her lover in the place of the feminine as difference, Paquita's insistence on dressing him as a woman is to confirm what has been missing in her lesbian relationship with the marquise: the presence of the phallus. And her experience and expertise in sensuality, combined with her technical virginity, constitutes an ideal male fantasy of desire, of having it all. She represents an exciting paradox for de Marsay, an embodiment of a romantic ideal of the fusion of opposites: "of the mysterious and the real, shadow and light, the horrible and the beautiful, pleasure and danger, heaven and hell" (322).[2] Projected as an oriental poem, her sublimity for de Marsay derives from her affirmation of her pleasure in phallic sexuality: "She was an oriental poem filled with the sun of the sprightly stanzas of Saadi and Hafiz. However, neither the rhythms of Saadi or of Pindar could have expressed the extasy full of confusion and amazement that siezed this young girl when she discovered the error in which she had been held with an iron grip" (322).

De Marsay is finally enraged, not at a suspicion of his own possible bisexuality but because he erroneously believes that he has been betrayed, outplayed, and disempowered in the competitive game of sexual conquest. The chilling and uncanny recognition that his rival is his half-sister dissolves both his rage and his passion for Paquita. Indeed, he is erotically drawn to the marquise's youth and beauty as his own mirror image. Felman's deconstructive reading of the recognition scene as de Marsay's discovery of the feminine in himself that subverts hierarchies and dualisms comes up against, as she herself acknowledges, the potential opposite reading in which he encounters an incestuous desire for unity rather than difference. In effect, what he does encounter with his sister is the unity of the identity of "blood," the sign both of genetic sameness and of aristocratic hegemony. Seeing his own face in that of his half-sister, he realizes that their identity locates them in the same position in relation to Paquita, who was "faithful to the blood." Thus he is reconciled with the marquise in the affirmation of aristocratic power and a narcissism unscathed by the otherness of the bloodied and mutilated body of their victim. His apparent feminization—his titillation with transvestism, his travesty of bisexuality, and his narcissistic fascination with his half-sister—does not seriously threaten his phallic mastery. Indeed, his appropriation of the feminine does not subvert but is inscribed within the social ideal he represents. In the context of his erotic escapade, it supports relationships of power constructed upon and denigrating the consumed body of a "different" feminine: the monstrous body of the exploited and racial other.

The notion of the "feminine" as subversive difference has to be distinguished from its use as a pejorative epithet to criticize the aristocracy for a loss of virile power. The description of the aristocracy as femininized is typical of criticisms of the *ancien régime*. It coincided with an indictment of women's influence in public spaces—such as salons and political clubs—and with the rigid separation of a masculine, public,

from a feminine, private sphere that was advocated by Rousseau, implemented in the last phase of the Revolution, and codified by Napoleon. Thus among many others, the aristocratic Chateaubriand blamed women for the distractions of salon society, for the trivialization of men, and the contamination of public, political life: "Women, among modern people, independently of the passion they inspire, influence all other feelings. They have in their being a certain abandon which affects us; they make our male character less decisive and our passions, softened by contact with theirs, unstable and tender" (63). "Feminized," in this case is a misogynistic epithet for inconstancy, emotional weakness, and the degradation of male, political and public power. Balzac continues and complicates the conventionally negative meaning of the feminine in his description of the aristocracy, whose pursuit of women for physical pleasure leads to ennui, sterility, and nothingness: "[A]ristocrats have appetites rather than passions, fancies inspired by novels and cold affairs" (262). In their world "impotence reigns," and ideas and energy have been absorbed into the "affections of the boudoir and feminine pretence" (262). Encoded as weakness, vanity, and a threat to virility, the "feminine" negatively undermines the masculine aristocrat. Thus, the difference between the feminized, homosexual, bisexual, impotent, or sterile aristocrat is one of degree rather than kind.

In this context, bisexuality and male homosexuality are more obvious signs of the political "effeminization" of the aristocracy. The illegitimate son of a bisexual father whom he never knew and a mother whose success as an elegant woman of the world "had distorted all maternal feeling" (268), de Marsay acquired his French patronym through his mother's marriage (arranged for a suitable price by his fugitive father) to the dying and impoverished scion of an exhausted aristocratic line. His education by a corrupt Jesuit father in the intrigues of Parisian society and financial speculations was as successful, the narrator ironically notes, as might be expected from such a tutor. Thus Balzac contextualizes de Marsay, the standard of value that regulates the frenzied activity of Parisian society, within a broken aristocratic and "devirilized" genealogy: the bisexual biological father, the impotent and wasted legal father, the corrupt Jesuit father all signify the impotence of an unproductive but rich aristocracy of speculators and consumers.[3]

De Marsay, however, seems to combine a conventionally encoded masculine energy and virility with feminine beauty and talents. He looks like a woman, has "the skin of a young girl, a gentle and modest appearance, a slender and aristocratic shape and very beautiful hands" (271), and he is accomplished at playing the piano and singing. He is also strong, brave, a skilled horseman and fighter, and member of a secret society, the Treize, that adheres to a "virile" chivalric and Napoleonic code.[4] It is a commonplace in the writings of Balzac that Restoration aristocracy is a pale imitation of its feudal ideal. And despite de Marsay's energy and virility, his real field of conquest is the bedroom not the battle-field. He borrows his strategy from his "enemy," spending hours at his toilette, he explains, not only because women love men who take care of their appearance but because such a preoccupation signifies a man who "does not belong to himself" (293), one who will not neglect a woman—"a little thing, an ensemble of trivialities" (293)—for glory, ambition, politics, and art. His incorporation and cultivation of the feminine is that of the dandy who seduces women while despising them and who "feminizes" and aestheticizes himself in the name of emotional control and detachment.[5] He believes in nothing, "neither men, women, god nor the devil" (263). He boasts that his studied fatuity and inanity make him the commander of a regiment of women, any one of whom, in exchange for two flattering words, will work to further his interests. Although success over women guarantees him social ascendancy in the salons, his deliberate "feminization"—attention to his toilette and display of lack of seriousness—means constant attention to his image, a narcissistic preoccupation that reflects the priority of appearances and emotional vacuity: "Embraces mask a profound indifference, and politeness a perpetual contempt. One never loves another" (262).

Although de Marsay represents the ultimate, ideal image for the rest of society, he is as implicated as other social classes in the order of calculations and profit. All relations are a matter for speculation. Thus he speculates on his "best friend," Paul de Manerville: "De Marsay had taken him into his friendship as someone who could be of use to him in his social transactions, as a daring speculator uses a trusted employee" (278). Women are the mediators of his social transactions, both as means to pleasure and the confirmation of power. As objects of sexual consumption, they are constantly replaced, renewed, and reinvented to awaken desires that become jaded with every new satisfaction.

The narcissism of de Marsay that epitomizes the feminized aristocracy psychologically manifests the order of the imaginary (in the Lacanian sense) that defines Parisian society in general. Indeed, the opening sentence of the novel evokes Paris as spectacle in which the population is presented through its alienated and frightening appearance: "One of the most frightening spectacles is doubtless the general appearance of the Parisian population . . ." (246). Guy Debord's analysis of modern consumer society as spectacle is prefigured by Balzac in his depiction of mercantile, industrial, and speculative Paris.[6] The spectacle, in Debord's

analysis, constitutes a deceptive image of unity, masking the alienation of labor, the divisiveness of competition, the fragmentation of community, and it absorbs, as in Balzac's description of Paris, all differences into the same world of phantasmatic appearances. In this unreal world, metaphors mix, images collide in an explosion of figurality in which the only stable reference is the priority of the spectacular itself. The faces of the people of Paris, which we are invited to wonder at, turn out to be masks hiding nothing. What is so remarkable in this representation of the post-Revolutionary structure of industrial and mercantile capitalism is that not only mechanized workers and bureaucrats but the exceptional individuals who rise above their class (the exemplars of bourgeois initiative and "individualism") are depicted as automatons, phantasms without any access to the real. This transitional economic and political stage in the development of bourgeois society is mediated by persistent feudal structures, and it is possible to equate the "appearance effect" (to rephrase Barthes's "effect of the real") of Balzac's description of Restoration society with the instability of shifting social codes. Doris Kadish interprets the many images of hybridity in the novel, physically embodied in the monstrous image of the chimera, in terms of a generalized collapse of legitimate aristocratic order within a social structure made up of heterogeneous and discordant elements that combine but do not coalesce. She reads Paquita, "in the prostituted world inhabited by male hybrids like de Marsay" (279), as the ultimate symbol of an impure and degraded Restoration society. And, in his interpretation of *The Old Maid* (written in 1836 but situated, like *The Girl with the Golden Eyes,* during the early Restoration), Fredric Jameson similarly describes a clash of competing political codes at a time of transition and points to what he defines as Balzac's dream of a synthesis between feudal, aristocratic values and bourgeois industry (151-285). Such hybridity and heterogeneity certainly characterize Balzac's evocation of the Restoration, but the "appearance effect" of his depiction of society as spectacle is not just a temporary effect of the decline of the aristocracy and the concomitant social crisis but is intrinsically related to the mercantile, commodifying, and speculating new order. Indeed, Balzac wrote *The Girl with the Golden Eyes* after the July revolution of 1830 and the establishment of the bourgeois monarchy; the consolidation of the bourgeoisie and its "derealizing" structures is retroactively reflected in his description of Restoration society.

Caught in the mirror of the personal and social imaginary, de Marsay, despite his possession of gold and access to pleasure cannot escape the cycle of restless self-consumption and consumption. Every "other" is psychologically and socially an object of speculation. And, just as all social classes exhaust themselves in endless and pointless striving, he must endlessly subordinate the other to the image of his golden perfection. In this narcissistic structure, women represent only the possibility of specular or speculative gain, but every satisfaction of desire brings him closer to an encounter with impotence. Thus his tastes become increasingly rarefied and exotic. It is in the context of a desire for the exotic dialectically produced by the banality of materialism and its illusory satisfactions that de Marsay turns to Paquita.

The Orient and the "orientalized" feminine is intrinsic to Balzac's evocation of the modern commercial city. Thus, the petty-bourgeois traders "extend their hands to the Orient" for shawls "disdained by the Turks and the Russians" (253) and reach out as far as India for objects that will catch the eye of their customers and bring in a profit. At the opera, the same exhausted men lose themselves in exotic oriental fantasies and vicarious passions. The Orient represents an escape from the relentless toil of metropolitan existence. Thus the narrator praises the serenity of oriental philosophers "who despise movement and hold it in horror whereas in Paris the lower, middle and upper classes run, jump and turn somersaults, whipped by a pitiless goddess, necessity: the necessity of money, fame and amusement" (264). The upper classes seek an "oriental" opiate in food, sex, and gambling, and the courtesans who live in seclusion "*à l'orientale*" and never venture into the dirty and busy streets create the illusion of some transcendent oasis. Orientalism, of course, was much in vogue since the beginning of Romanticism.[7] Balzac dedicates his story to Delacroix, whose Moroccan paintings he admired, particularly "L'Odalisque couchée" and "Les Femmes d'Alger,"[8] which give vivid form to the Western fantasy of the seraglio, of women eternally available for an infinity of pleasures. It is this image of the sensuous—and potentially violent—Orient that dominates Balzac's story. Paquita is not only an erotic object for de Marsay and his sister, she is an exotic "orientalized" other. Although she is a Spanish speaking Creole, she is the daughter of a slave from Asian Georgia, sequestered in luxury for sexual pleasure and guarded by a faithful, mulatto eunuch.

De Marsay also imagines himself as an oriental pasha whose will is the only law. His dream of absolutism reflects his nostalgia for a feudal, aristocratic power of which his own secret society is an anachronistic imitation. It masks his dependence on the speculations and manipulations of an economic structure in which he is thoroughly implicated.

Narcissism, consumerism, and speculation contextualize de Marsay's pursuit of the unavailable, "oriental" Paquita, whose golden eyes emblematize her value: "First of all, what struck me the most are her eyes, as yellow as a tiger's; a golden shining yellow, a gold that thinks and absolutely desires to come into your pocket" (281). As Felman points out, Paquita's eyes are mirrors in which de Marsay seeks the reflection of his power and masculinity. The phallic function he attributes to them reflects a desire for the reinforcement of his potency. However, they also reflect back to him the mediations of the economic order, the desirability of the exotic other as an ideal luxury object and sexual commodity.

Paquita herself indulges in dreams of a flight to the Orient and proposes to de Marsay that they leave the boudoir/seraglio in which she is held prisoner for Asia, "the only country where love can spread its wings" (339). He indulges her sentimental fantasy and evokes an idealized colonial vision of "slaves, sunshine, white palaces, perfume and birds singing of love" (339), but raises material objections—the difficulty of acquiring a large sum of money at short notice—to the possibility of its realization. To her suggestion that they abscond with the marquise's abundant supply of gold, he protests that they cannot take what does not belong to them. Paquita exposes this transparent bad faith by reminding him that he has in fact stolen her: "Haven't you taken me? When we have taken the gold it will belong to us" (339). What he dismisses as her ingenuousness is, in effect, an exposure of his moral hypocrisy, the discrepancy between his respect for the wealth and power of his class and his casual appropriation of her as colonized other.

De Marsay is first attracted to Paquita because she seems to belong to an adventure novel, and he is excited by the prospect of playing the role of courageous and ingenious hero who must confront the threat of violence and overcome dangerous obstacles to satisfy his desire. His transition into Paquita's world is a transition into a Gothic melodrama. As if in a dream, he is blindfolded and transported by her African eunuch, first to a shabby garret in an unfamiliar part of Paris, and then to the enclosed, soundproofed room in the mansion belonging to the marquise's old and absent husband. The phantasmatic world of Paquita not only evokes oriental sensuousness and adventure but the sinister other side of Europe's fantasy of the Orient—violence and ugliness. She is surrounded by figures, connoted by the general epithet "Chinese," whom de Marsay despises for their otherness. Thus he pejoratively refers to Christemio, her mulatto protector, as "that Chinese," but it is Paquita's mother who emblematizes his vision of oriental monstrosity: she is mysterious, inscrutable, silent, and wears a turban that "would be very successful in China where the aesthetic ideal of beauty is the monstrous" (303).

If Paquita is a projection of de Marsay's desire, the ultimate luxury object for the jaded European palate, the old "oriental" woman, enslaved, impoverished and ugly, appears to function as the absolute antithesis of the young, beautiful, wealthy male aristocrat. However, although she plays a small part in the story, she frames, as it were, de Marsay's adventure with Paquita. Her appearances are structurally crucial: she is present at their first rendezvous and in the final scene following her daughter's murder.

On the threshold of his first encounter with Paquita's mother, de Marsay experiences a chilling sense of the uncanny, which he compares to the sensation of reading one of Ann Radcliffe's Gothic novels. The old woman conjures up images of the most threatening and castrating monsters—Medusa, harpy, witch, and Egyptian mummy. De Marsay experiences her presence as evil and uncanny, and she seems to embody hideous desire. Her faded yellow eyes grotesquely parody Paquita's golden ones, indicating what Paquita will become once consumed and expended. The narrator compares her to the monstrous tail of a chimera or siren of which Paquita is the seductive face: "That woman was there like a possible ending [*dénouement*], and emblematized the horrible fish tail with which the Greek geniuses of symbolism concluded the Chimeras and Sirens, so seductive and deceptive by their first appearance [*corsage*], as are all passions in the beginning" (305). An emblem for Paquita and her mother, the chimera is also the emblem for the narrative that describes de Marsay's adventure. Thus, through such semantic and figurative parallels, Balzac creates an affiliation among Paquita, the old woman, and the young dandy.

When de Marsay first sees Paquita he imagines her as the original of the hallucinatory (*délirante*) painting, "The Woman Caressing her Chimera." She epitomizes the terrifying pleasure embodied in woman, "the most infernal inspiration of the genius of antiquity" (282), and he identifies himself with the chimera, which he calls the monster of the fresco. As a concrete emblem of the monstrous in the context of aesthetic representation, a painting of a fresco, the chimera assumes a metacritical, self-reflective function that becomes even more apparent when it is used to describe Paquita and her mother in juxtaposition as a text. The chimera not only stands as a figure for narrativity itself—the old woman representing the "end" of the story—but poses a riddle not unlike that asked of Oedipus: how can Henri, Paquita, and her mother be one and the same?

In his reponse to the painting, de Marsay inverts the real power relationship between himself and the girl with the golden eyes, in which he is the master and she the slave, by projecting her as the ultimate enchantress. The painting opens up the unconscious. Although de Marsay desires to be the caressed "monster

of the fresco," the double image of the chimera embodies a threatening fantasy. An expression of the beautiful and the ugly, the seductive and the monstrous, it reveals the murderous ambivalence of de Marsay's image of woman. From this perspective, his sense of the uncanny which prefaces his encounter with Paquita's mother, can be understood in classical Freudian terms as a fear of the unfamiliar in the familiar, the threat of castration associated with fusion with the maternal body (Freud 122-61). By the logic of the Law of the Father, feminine Eros fatally invokes Thanatos. In his *The Melodramatic Imagination,* Peter Brooks defines melodrama in Balzac as the struggle between good and evil in a desacralized world in which inner psychic conflict replaces conflict between transcendent forces. Thus he writes of encounters with the uncanny, "We are led back to the sources of the 'uncanny' in the processes of desire and repression analyzed by Freud. The desacralization and sentimentalization of ethics leads us—as Diderot discovered in reading Richardson—into 'the recesses of the cavern,' there to discover 'the hideous Moor' hidden in our motives and desires" (19). Balzac's Moor, the old oriental woman, may uncannily represent the return of the repressed on a psychological register, but she also represents the oppressed. As the narrator pervasively indicates, Paquita and her mother are as much inscribed in a colonial as in a libidinal economy. What de Marsay represses in wishing to be Paquita's chimera is not only the otherness of death embodied in the erotic figure of woman, but the image of oppression and the fear of the other's rage. However, his monsters remain only fantasies. The double meaning of chimera as the monstrous and the imaginary connects the articulation of Paquita, her mother, and de Marsay within the overall speculative and psychic economy that contextualizes their story: in the social order mobilized by the monster Speculation there are only imaginary encounters.

De Marsay is haunted by Paquita's mother and horrified by her faded yellow eyes that, as it were, devalue those of her daughter. If he fantasizes Paquita's golden eyes as money in his pocket, a return on his investment in terms of an increase in the value of his masculinity, her mother's yellow eyes expose the meaninglessness of the transaction. The gold standard that would guarantee his value turns into the faded eyes of an exhausted woman, the alien and enslaved body that is the ultimate object of exploitation. This demystification takes place through an analogous semantic association of de Marsay, Paquita, and her mother in which the mother specifically designates impotence. Thus Henri is compared to a lion in his imperiousness and social power, Paquita to a graceful tiger and cat, and her mother to a tiger trapped in a cage forced to devour its own rage: "Her eyes had the cold glint of those of a caged tiger which knows its impotence and finds itself constrained to devour its desire for destruction" (306). Just as her faded yellow eyes demystify de Marsay's golden image of himself, as well as revealing the real woman behind his oriental fantasy, her impotent rage reflects not only the rage of the oppressed other but the impotence stalking his own desire. Thus he is haunted by the image of the old woman as a monster that he must cast out at any cost, "for she had remained in his imagination like something infernal, crouching, cadaverous, vicious, savagely ferocious which the fantasy of painters and poets had not yet fathomed" (311). What he sees in her eyes is the rage and resentment that is also potential in Paquita's masochistic sexual abandon and social powerlessness, and the impotence that haunts his pursuit of mastery and pleasure. In the double image of the oriental woman—luxurious commodity and enraged slave—he encounters the other of oppression and projects it as chimerical monster. While he may joyously accept his own femininity in the beautiful face of his aristocratic sister, he blocks out the feminine or feminized other on which his commodifying desire feeds. Thus he understands not a word of Christemio's language, not a word of that of Paquita's mother, who herself remains nameless. Nor can he read her face, which "possessed to the highest degree the gravity of savage peoples, the impassivity of a statue on which observation founders" (309). Unlike Wilde's Dorian Gray, who consciously makes a pact with the devil to embody his moral corruption in some alienated image, de Marsay does not recognize that the monstrous face of the old slave is related to himself.

As emblematized by the tail of the chimerical monster to which de Marsay compares her, the grotesqueness of Paquita's mother prefigures the grotesque ending of the story. She appears after the marquise has hacked Paquita to death. Again, she is represented as absolute monstrosity, as she shows no emotion at the bloody scene and accepts payment to clean up the traces of the murder. She is the savage exotic other, outside of humanity, indifferent even to her own "blood."

The importance of the trope of blood in this narrative is reflected in Balzac's original title, "La Force du Sang" ("The Power of Blood"), which remains as the title of the final chapter. It is as rich in its implications as the title *The Girl with the Golden Eyes*. The last scene of the novel counterposes the spilled blood of the murdered slave, to be erased by her "unnatural" mother, and the affirmation of the superiority of aristocratic blood. Blood for de Marsay and his sister has primarily a figurative significance.[9] Paquita's blood need not have been spilled because she was faithful "to the blood." As we have seen, in this extraordinary

interweaving of the patterns of economic and erotic speculation, de Marsay does not bridle at playing with feminine identity as long as it furthers his mastery. And he plays with Paquita as long as he can subordinate her otherness. He finally screens her out in the name of the hegemony of the same, the superiority of his "blood." Her role in their sexual play as racial and colonized other is erased. Gender difference is here superseded by a class identity that negates the trace of the exploited other. Similarly, Lord Dudley may not be a proper figure for the representation of the Law of the Father, but his sexual ambiguity, like that of his children, does not radically undermine the power of his class and wealth. Exiled from England, he neverthless pursues pleasure in the far corners of the earth. His own orientalism, the quest for sexual pleasure as exotic commodity, may be outlawed; but it both extends and caricatures his country's quest for foreign goods and markets.

The obliteration of the figure of Paquita's mother is explicit in her silence. She never speaks, even when she sees her daughter's mutilated body. The marquise speaks for her: "You are going to tell me that you did not sell her to me so that I would kill her. . . . I know why you have crept out of your lair. I'll pay you for her twice over" (348). However, the old woman's smile remains enigmatic as the marquise flings gold coins at her feet. Neither Paquita nor her mother have any redress for this murder. When de Marsay raises the question of possible blackmail, the marquise explains that the old woman will be indifferent because she comes from a country where women are not beings but things "that are sold, bought, killed, used, finally, as a caprice, as here you might use a piece of furniture" (348). Given Balzac's detailed description of such reification not only in the description of Parisian society but in the story of Paquita, the marquise, de Marsay's double, is transparently projecting her own economic and psychic reality onto this alien other represented as monster.[10] Moreover, the old woman will keep quiet, according to the marquise, because a fateful passion for gambling has succeeded in erasing all maternal feeling. (It is an ironic statement, given the general emotional anomie described in the novel; de Marsay's own aristocratic mother is portrayed as the model of the nonmaternal.) And when de Marsay asks who will help her to remove "the traces of this fantasy" (349), the marquise, in a gesture that expresses her sadism as much as the monstrosity of the Georgian slave, points to Paquita's mother. The old woman's love of gambling is the final ironic pastiche of the order of speculation represented by de Marsay. A simulacrum of the risks of high finance, it plays at life and death in an imaginary mode. It is only a game.

De Marsay enters his adventure with Paquita as though he is entering a world of fantasy, and his project to kill her, accompanied by his valiant comrades, concludes this novelesque charade. In effect, the chivalric ideal of the Treize is travestied by the sordid dénouement. Not only does the secret brotherhood fail to kill Paquita, but it is foiled by the rage of a woman who has also killed Christemio, the embodiment of physical force and devotion who was always a match for de Marsay. What is most impotant for de Marsay is that the traces of the adventure, "this fantasy," be covered up.

The monster Speculation that the prologue defines as the driving force behind the pursuit of gold and pleasure etymologically contains the speculum, the mirror. The story of de Marsay and his half-sister relates the order of economic speculation to psychic narcissism and the negation of otherness. The other might be projected as absolute ideal or absolute monstrosity—hence the double image of the racially exotic—but finally remains, in the more common meaning of the word, only a chimera. As monstrously constructed as Balzac's novel appears, his descriptions of modern Paris and de Marsay's oriental adventure are, in effect, two sides of the same counterfeit coin.

Notes

1. Pierre Saint-Amand proposes a different and incompatible interpretation of the chimera; that is, Henri's identification with the chimera in Paquita's lap signifies his desire to be the phallus, but that he discovers that the marquise, whose phallic power terrorizes Paquita, is the real chimera of the text.

2. All English translations of Balzac are my own.

3. De Marsay belongs to a genealogy of dandy/aristocrats that culminates in the fin de siècle decadence of Huysmans' Des Esseintes, the end of the line. Situated at the beginning of the explosion of bourgeois, industrial and speculative power, he is ready to harness his energy and vitality to a new political order. Des Esseintes, of course, is sickly and withdrawn, but he also is enamored of images of power and virility. His aestheticism is futuristic and anti-natural. Thus, he eulogizes the locomotive, the embodiment of technological and economic mastery. And whereas de Marsay's sexual ambiguity remains potential and inseparable from his sexual power over women, Des Esseintes becomes impotent with women, turns towards men, and fantasizes destruction of and by woman/nature as the ultimately monstrous other.

4. The Treize is a secret society of restless aristocrats founded during the Empire and dissolved in 1821. It embodies both a code of male chivalry and an ideal of energy and action. *The Girl with the Golden Eyes* is part of the *Histoire des Treize*, Balzac's first group of novels about Parisian life. For further information, see Fortassier.

5. De Marsay has many of the attributes—wealth, leisure, the cult of self, a haughty disdain of triviality—of Baudelaire's classic definition of the dandy in "Le Peintre de la vie moderne." Moreover, Baudelaire situates the dandy in the transitional space between the declining power of the aristocracy and the rise of the bourgeoisie: "Le dandysme apparait surtout aux époques transitoires où la démocratie n'est pas encore toute-puissante, où l'aristocratie n'est que partiellement chancelante et avilie" (485).

6. Obviously, this application of Debord's understanding of spectacle to Balzac is perfunctory and schematic, but it suggests an area for further investigation.

7. See Kabbani (especially chs. 2 and 3).

8. The "Odalisque couchée" was exhibited in 1832 at the Galerie Colbert and "Femmes d'Alger" in the Salon of 1834.

9. This priority given to blood as an essential sign of aristocratic identity and superiority is on a continuum with the marquise's use of her own blood in the letters she sends to the illiterate Paquita. The literal marks of her blood replace conventional written symbols and signify a narcissistic denial of otherness.

10. Kabbani writes that an important aspect of the West's perception of Oriental villainy is the trade in female bodies: "The villainy of Oriental men is aggravated by the fact that they are portrayed as traders in female bodies. They are the cruel captors who hold women in their avaricious grasp, who use them as chattels, as trading-goods, with little reverence for them as human beings" (78). In Balzac's story, it is the marquise and de Marsay who have made a trade of Paquita. The marquise's blindness to her own use of Paquita—mirrored by that of de Marsay—is glaring to the reader.

Works Cited

Balzac, Honoré de. *La Duchesse de Langeais/La Fille aux yeux d'or* [*The Girl with the Golden Eyes*]. Ed. Rose Fortassier. Paris: Gallimard, 1976.

Baudelaire, Charles. *Curiosités esthetiques/L'Art romantique*. Paris: Gallimard, 1962.

Brooks, Peter. *The Melodramatic Imagination*. New York: Columbia UP, 1985.

Chateaubriand, Francois René Vicomte de. *Atala/René.* Paris: Flammarion, 1964.

Cixous, Hélène. "The Laugh of the Medusa." *New French Feminisms.* Ed. Elaine Marks and Isabelle de Courtivron. New York: Schocken Books, 1981. 245-264.

Debord, Guy. *La Société du spectacle.* Paris: Editions Gerard Lebovici, 1987.

Felman, Shoshana. "Rereading Feminity." *Yale French Studies* 62 (1981): 19-44.

Fortassier, Rose, ed. *La Duchesse de Langeais/La Fille aux yeux d'or.* By Honoré de Balzac. Paris: Gallimard, 1976.

Freud, Sigmund. "The Uncanny." *On Creativity and the Unconscious.* New York: Harper, 1958. 122-161.

Jacobus, Mary. *Reading Woman.* New York: Columbia UP, 1986.

Jameson, Fredric. "Realism and Desire: Balzac and the Problem of the Subject." *The Political Unconscious.* Ithaca: Cornell UP, 1981. 151-285.

Kabbani, Rana. *Europe's Myths of Orient.* Bloomington: Indiana UP, 1986.

Kadish, Doris. "Hybrids in Balzac's *La Fille aux yeux d'or.*" *Nineteenth-Century French Studies* 16 (1988): 270-278.

Saint-Amand, Pierre. "Balzac's Oriental: *La Fille aux yeux d'or.*" *Romanic Review* 79 (1988): 329-340.

T. Denean Sharpley-Whiting (essay date 1997)

SOURCE: Sharpley-Whiting, T. Denean. "'The Other Woman': Reading a Body of Difference in Balzac's *La Fille aux yeux d'or.*" *Symposium* 51, no. 1 (1997): 249-62.

[*In the following essay, Sharpley-Whiting focuses on the character of Paquita Valdès and the significance in* The Girl with the Golden Eyes *of her race, sex, class, exoticism, and position as slave and as "Other."*]

> Et qu'est-ce que la femme? Une petite chose, un ensemble de niaiseries?
>
> **Balzac, *La Fille aux yeux d'or***

In his undelivered lecture entitled "Femininity," Sigmund Freud ventured to decipher what no man before him had ever successfully discerned—the nature of femininity:

> To-day's lecture, too[,] should have no place in an introduction. . . . It brings forward nothing but observed facts, almost without any speculative additions. . . .

> Throughout history people have knocked their heads against the riddle of femininity. . . . Nor will you have escaped worrying over this problem—those of you who are men . . . to those of you who are women this will not apply—you are yourselves the problem.
>
> (102)

Freud's inquiry reflects the tendency of Western patriarchal discourse to render unintelligible and incomprehensible peoples and cultures that do not conform to the normative gaze. The lecture "Femininity" is an attempt to capture "woman" through observation and in writing in order to make her more accessible to those people who have knocked their heads against her riddled nature: men. And while the psychoanalyst maintains that his work offers no speculative additions, "Femininity" is pure speculation, a mirroring project/projection that uses the masculine as its point of departure to discern the nature of the feminine.

And because Freud never discovered the nature of the feminine, some 42 years later, a re-reading of "Femininity" was undertaken by one of its objects of inquiry, Luce Irigaray. In her re-reading of "Femininity" in *Speculum de l'autre femme*, Irigaray determines that "woman" as she exists in phallocentric thought is a lesser man with a clitoris as an equivalent of the penis. In "Femininity" woman is defined by male subjects, by male parameters. In this logic of sameness, the masculine is mediated through the feminine; femininity is repressed, erased. The nature of femininity that Freud found so puzzling and analyzed in "unfriendly" terms is the result of woman's position as "un petit homme désavantagé, un petit homme plus narcissique du fait de la médiocrité de ses organes génitaux" (Irigaray 26).

In both the writings of Freud and Irigaray a particular erasure and universality occurs. If Freud privileges white male hegemony, Irigaray privileges a white female hegemony. Indeed, one could argue a privileging of a particular class as well. Certainly, the opportunity to observe the nature of the "Other woman" did not present itself to Freud in Austria—nor perhaps was the subject of particular importance. In her albeit insightful critique, Irigaray sets up the very logic of sameness against which she argues. Her repressed woman becomes the universal body that defines all female experiences. White femaleness and white maleness dominate both economies of representation. The Freudian question, What does femininity mean for men? and the Irigarayian re-reading, What does femininity for men mean for women? ask in reality: What does white femininity mean for white men? and What does white femininity for white men mean for white women?

What are the implications of this politics of domination for nonwhite women? Are they even lesser men, lesser beings—slaves even—than white women by virtue of their racial and sexual differences? What does Other femininity for white men mean for Other women? It is precisely this polemic that I wish to take up in a reading of the erotic Balzacian narrative **La Fille aux yeux d'or,** whose female protagonist, Paquita Valdès, functions as a racial and sexual Other and a slave.

Considerable attention has been given to the themes of orientalism and the questions of sexual and class differences in Balzac's short tale at the expense of a rigorous analysis of the racial difference that manifests itself in the body of the female protagonist. Generally, the category of race has been understandably analyzed along the lines of Balzac's *rêveries orientales* or neatly subsumed into a reading of class and sex differences (that is, master and slave, man and woman), without taking into consideration the veritable socioeconomic and political differences between a slave woman and a woman. I would argue that Paquita's sex and race are intimately linked to her position as a slave. The differences between white femininity and Other femininity, between woman and racialized slave woman, between Euphémie and Paquita, become apparent at the novel's tragic end. Yet, in a novella rampant with what Doris Kadish calls "hybrids," the dilemma with reading race may stem from the ambiguity emanating from the text itself (Kadish 270).

The situating of Paquita is somewhat frustrated by a fluid Balzacian cartography that traverses countries (France, Spain, Cuba, England, and Georgia) and cultures. Her mysterious origins begin with her denatured mother—a slave woman bought in "Géorgie" for her rare beauty. Georgia's Eurasian locale points to the text's all-too-well noted oriental bent. Racial difference inserts itself immediately with Balzac's description of the mother as possessing "au haut degré cette gravité des peuplades sauvages" (375). In Balzac's tediously class-delineated Paris (those who have gold [*l'or*] and those who do not), it is only fitting that distinctions be drawn between "civilized" and "savage" races, between Europeans and Eurasians, between Western and Eastern cultures. Cultural differences are perceived as concrete racial differences. Paquita is a slave because of her mother's racial and cultural differences. Yet, her racial otherness equally manifests itself outside of orientalism. Alternately referred to as "l'Espanole" (372), "l'inconnue" (351), and "une jeune créole des Antilles" (343), Paquita presents a tropical disruption to oriental readings. She is, in a word, Other, a body of utter difference: "l'Asie par sa mère, Europe par son éducation, Tropiques par sa naissance" (388).

A Creole, from the Spanish *criollo* or *criar,* which means to breed or nurture, is a person of European descent born especially in the West Indies or Spanish America. *Creole* was equally used to differentiate New World blacks—that is, blacks born in the New World—from Africans newly imported to the colonies (*Grand Larousse de la langue française*). Creolization thus describes European and African naturalization in the New World; creolity is a purely geographic marker. Yet, the nineteenth-century discourse on creolity in the *Larousse du XIXème siècle* is clearly racialized:

> C'est dans les grands yeux spirituels des femmes créoles qu'on trouve le contraste si rare d'une douce langueur et d'une vivacité piquante. Elles sont surtout remarquables par la beauté de leur chevelure, qui est d'un noir incomparable, par la petitesse de leurs pieds cambrés. . . . Leurs membres sont presque toujours doués d'une souplesse qui les rend éminemment propres à tous les exercices du corps. . . . La seule différence qui existe entre eux [les noirs] et les créole blancs à peu près est dans la couleur de la peau et dans la forme de la chevelure.

By drawing on physical and emotional specificities and, therefore, distinctions from the French born in France and similarities between Caribbean-born blacks, creolization is racialized. Creoles appear to be a separate and distinct race formed on the basis of their colonial experiences. The "white" creole is, in fact, biracial. The biracial characteristics exhibit themselves particularly in the French stereotypes of the creole woman; suppleness of the body, small, arched feet, incomparably dark and beautiful hair distinguish the Creole woman from the French woman. With the black woman, the Creole shares culture, nationality, and geographic space. Even her gaze represents a rare contrast—biraciality: blackness is equivalent to languor and whiteness to vivacity. In *Curiosités esthétiques,* Baudelaire also evokes the biracial gaze in his description of the Creole poet Leconte de Lisle (Miller 69-138). The exoticism, timelessness, and sensuality—the blackness—associated with the colonies envelops the Creole woman and filters osmotically into her blood. Blackness is contracted through proximity. The whiteness of flesh and the texture of her hair are the only distinctions from her black female counterpart.

The "remarquables" attributes of the Larousse's *femme créole* are strikingly consonant with those of **La Fille aux yeux d'or.** Balzac pays particular tribute to Paquita's "pied bien attaché, mince, recourbé" (353) and "beaux cheveux noirs" (375). Paquita's creolity marks her racial alterity, her biraciality. In his description of Paquita, Henri de Marsay evokes this "two-ness":

> cette fille semblable à une chatte qui veut frôler vos jambes, une fille blanche à cendrés, délicate en apparence . . . mais dans les mouvements de laquelle se devine la volupté qui dort . . . c'est une femme idéale.

> (351-2, 383)

A dichotomy is drawn between Paquita's appearance and her sexual nature. She is delicate in appearance, yet bestial and sexual. Balzac's contrasting of her slumbering voluptuous nature and beautifully placid, white exterior coincides with the romantic discourse on the *mulâtresse* as described by Léon-François Hoffman:

> Admirable pour les uns, criminelle pour les autres, la Mulâtresse deviendra une des grandes figures de l'éros romantique . . . Réputation de beauté, réputation de légèreté egalement. La sensualité lascive des Nègres coule dans leurs veines, mais raffinée par l'apport blanc. . . . La Mulâtresse est la maîtresse idéale proposée à l'imagination érotique du Français moyen.
>
> (248)

Both are white, yet inescapably black, and thus unable to shake the lascivious and sexually ardent stereotypes that govern characterizations of black female sexuality.[1]

The French conceptualizations of the *femme créole* and the *mulâtresse* are virtually interchangeable.[2] It is from the sexually racialized stereotypes of the *négresse* that the sexual nature of both the mulatta and the Creole woman are conceived. The *négresse* is not ideal; she does not represent beauty but sexuality. The canon of feminine beauty is constructed around whiteness, whereas voluptuous sexuality is mysterious and dark: black. In a Pygmalion-like fashion, two erotic, exotic, and idyllic forms of femininity are created from the combination of the négresse and white femaleness.

Physically white yet epitomizing racial difference, Paquita, like the *mulâtresse* of the nineteenth century, is indeed de Marsay's ideal mistress in the story:

> Jeudi dernier . . . je me trouve nez à nez avec une femme . . . Ah! mon cher physiquement parlant l'inconnue est la personne la plus adorablement femme que j'aie rencontrée. Elle appartient à cette variété féminine . . . la femme de feu. Et d'abord, ce qui m'a le plus frappé, ce dont je suis encore épris, ce sont deux yeux jaunes comme ceux des tigres; un jaune d'or qui brille, de l'or vivant, de l'or qui pense, de l'or qui aime et veut absolument venir dans votre gousset! . . . Depuis que j'étudie les femmes, mon inconnue est la seule dont le sein vierge, les formes ardentes et voluptueuse m'aient réalisé la seule femme que j'aie rêvée, moi! tandis que c'est une femme idéale, un abîme de plaisirs où l'on roule sans en trouver la fin . . . c'est une femme idéale qui ne se voit . . . presque jamais en France. . . . J'aurais décidément cette fille pour maîtresse.
>
> (351-52, 364)

Paquita is the essence of sensuality and beauty. She evokes purity, on the one hand, with her "virginal bosom," and voluptuousness, on the other, signified by her "ardent curves." She is white and black in the flesh; she is ideal.

Henri desires to possess the girl with the golden eyes, to become the slave woman's master and to master her sexually. Desire is fundamentally the narcissistic drive to impose oneself on another and to be recognized by the Other (Gates 85). Henri clearly imposes/ projects himself onto Paquita: "Moralement parlant, sa figure semblait dire: '"Quoi te voilà, mon idéal, l'être de mes pensées, de mes rêves . . . Prends moi, je suis à toi . . ."'" (351). Paquita not only "recognizes" Henri but begs that he take possession of her. She is reduced to mere object: the object of Henri's sexual desires, but equally an object to be possessed—a slave woman. And as a slave, Henri's "jouet" (396), she has no will, desire, or subjectivity other than to be a "plaisir" (398) for Henri. Void of subjectivity, Paquita is invested with masculine desire. Her desires are those of the master, the white male, Henri.

And Henri, a fop par excellence, must "dormir et vivre devant un miroir"[3] (Baudelaire 1:687). Paquita is that mirror. She is *plaisir* and *or,* a never-ending harvest of rich, sensual self-indulgence and reflexivity. She is "un chef d'oeuvre de la nature" (368), created to sexually satiate and envelop him and to constantly reflect and recognize his idealized self-image.

Henri's quest for this mirroring abyss of perfection is realized with the help of the Othello-like *mulâtre* Christemio, Paquita's "père nourricier" (376). The mulatto surrogate father further colors Paquita's creole origins. Balzac's portrait of Christemio is rather generous in its use of racialized language:

> Jamais figure africaine n'exprima mieux la grandeur dans la vengeance, la rapidité du soupçon, la promptitude dans l'éxecution d'une pensée, la force du Maure et son irréflexion d'enfant. Ses yeux noirs avaient la fixité des yeux d'un oiseau de proie . . . comme ceux d'un vautour. . . . Son front, petit et bas, avait quelque chose de menaçante.
>
> (366)

In uncanny Gobineauesque language (see Gobineau), Balzac credits the character with "irreflection," a void of intellect. From Christemio's physiognomy—front petit et bas—Balzac reads his emotional and mental capacity. Propelled by violent, hasty emotions and vengeance rather than calculated rational thoughts— like Shakespeare's Othello the Moor—Christemio is a brute of a man, a black beast, in his use of strength to compensate for his "irréflexion d'enfant."

His presence in the text is not only symbolic of Paquita's alterity, but cliché. Reading *La Fille aux yeux d'or* along orientalist imaginations, Christemio functions as a eunuch. However, reading against the grain of orientalism, pushing this creolized reading further, Christemio would appear to serve as a reminder of the primitive sensuality of the colonies. He represents the contagious blackness that has filtered into the Creole woman's blood—the slumbering passion in Paquita's movements. He is an exotic backdrop, thrice used to take Henri to his out-of-this world, dreamlike sexual experience.[4] The possibility of Henri's sexual gratification is mediated through Christemio, his "guide" (369) to the "femme idéale," to the abyss of sexual pleasure. And as Henri navigates his way to Paquita through Christemio, he experiences the sensation of being in an Anne Radcliffe novel "où le héros traverse les salles froides, sombres, inhabitée, de quelque lieu triste et désert" (369). Blackness represents the primal, as it is only through a black (Christemio) that sexual gratification can be realized.

True to form, during the two love scenes, Paquita invites Henri into her "coquille de Vénus" (369) and takes him "sur ses ailes pour le transporter dans le septième ciel de l'amour" (394). However, during the last celestial sexual encounter, Paquita exclaims in ecstasy, "Mariquita!" (401).[5] The fop is brought abominably low; "sa vanité d'homme" (401) is usurped by not another man but a woman. At this moment of emasculation—effeminization—Henri vows to kill Paquita.

Rather than re-explore the overwrought, but nonetheless accurate, readings of the triangularity encoded in the names *Mariquita, Paquita,* and *Henri de Marsay;* lesbianism and the ambiguous sexuality present in the name *Euphémie Porrabéril;* Paquita's use as a mask for the incestuous relationship of the half-brother and sister, Henri and Euphémie; and Henri's clearly effeminate beauty and resemblance to his sister, which led to Paquita's misnaming, I will move directly to the tragic denouement where the meaning of Other femininity is disclosed.

Paquita is viciously murdered by the jealously enraged marquise for her sexual indiscretion. She lies drowning in her own blood; with the dagger dripping, the marquise looks up to see Henri. This scene of recognition is followed by a mutual affirmation of common paternity—Lord Dudley. Henri then points to the expiring slave woman and declares, "Elle était fidèle au sang." This critical sentence has been translated and interpreted as "She was faithful to the bloodlines"— that is, she was attracted to the brother and sister, the same blood.[6] Yet, this same sentence has also been translated as "She was true to the instincts of her race" (Ives and Walton 423).[7] The latter translation best captures Paquita's status as a slave woman. In essence, Paquita is void of subjectivity; she is commodified into a prototypical specimen of her race, a stereotyped being "true to the instincts of her race" (Gates 86).

Reduced to a generic, racially stereotyped object, Paquita can be exchanged for an "other" slave woman. This commodification is further revealed by Euphémie when Dona Concha sees her daughter's ravaged body:

> Tu vas me dire que tu ne l'avais pas vendue pour que je la tuasse. . . . Je sais pourquoi tu sors de ta tanière. Je te la paiera deux fois.
>
> (406)

Paquita is a readily disposable and exchangeable object, whose death is redeemable for gold. She is a lesser being, a lesser woman, because of her racial and sexual otherness. The otherness translates into her subjugation, enslaved objectification and unscrupulous murder. She is, as Doris Kadish relates, "a non-being" (276).

Exchangeability and disposability seem to accurately define the meaning of Other femininity for Balzac.[8] Yet, the veritable unveiling of the meaning of "Other femininity" begins with de Marsay's contemptuous response to the riddle of femininity: "Et qu'est-ce que la femme? Une petite chose, un ensemble de niaiseries" (360). Woman is a little thing, a bundle of absurdities, silliness; woman simply makes no sense; she is nonsense. If woman is but a little thing, what of the Other woman? This non-rhetorical question brings us to Balzac's pronouncement on woman: "Woman and paper are two white things that suffer everything" (Balzac, *Pensées,* 45). As Peter Brooks has remarked, that statement implies that woman, like paper, is written/inscribed on by men (84). The male writer's pen penetrates the page and woman, thus marking both. Woman suffers penetration/inscription. But more important, woman is white. Therefore the Other woman does not exist for Balzac. She is less than a little thing: therefore invisible, nothing, a no-thing. And when she attempts to rear her quintessentially different head, to articulate desire outside of the dominant economy of representation, and thus subjectivity, she is physically suppressed, bludgeoned out of existence. In sum, the combination of racial and sexual otherness in this erotic novella is deadly.

Notes

1. For more on French stereotypes of black femininity in literature and culture, see my forthcoming *Sexualized Savages, Primal Fears, and Primitive Narratives in French.*

2. Flaubert writes in *Le Dictionnaire des idées reçues* under the rubric *négresse:* "elles sont plus voluptueuses que les blanches" (61). In his *Historie naturelle du genre humain,* Jean-Joseph Virey describes the négresse as "très ardente en amour": "elles portent la volupté jusqu'à des lascivetés ig-

norées dans nos climat" (150.) The mulâtresse, having black blood, will share some of the négresse's characteristics.

3. From Baudelaire's *Oeuvres complètes* in which he writes that the fop or "le dandy doit aspirer à être sublime sans interruption, il doit vivre et dormir devant un miroir."

4. Sander Gilman notes that the black servant in visual arts represents the sexualization of the society in which he or she is found. This observation could equally be said of literary representations of blacks.

5. According to Shoshana Felman *mariquita* means homosexual man in Spanish.

6. See Felman for this translation and also Edward Ahearn's interpretation.

7. Though this translation may be a bit faulty, it nonetheless invokes the Balzacian unconscious concerning racial/sexual difference at work throughout the novella.

8. One could plausibly argue that because of the sadness expressed by the marquise at the novella's end and Henri's description of Paquita as an ideal woman that Paquita represents more than an exchangeable and disposable object. However, this argument is flawed when one considers that despite the marquise's sadness, when asked about the police, she says that no one would avenge Paquita's murder except Christemio, whom she has also murdered—hence, Paquita's disposability. Paquita's exchangeability is glaringly apparent through the exchange of gold for her murder. De Marsay's idyllic characterizations of the slave woman are at best perverse. Henri is attracted to Paquita's differentness, which he describes in sexually racialized language. She is a sexual *object,* an abyss of pleasure. Paquita represents a prototype, "that feminine variety" that one "rarely sees in France" but in other countries. She is unique because she has been imported to a place—France—where "other" women are rarely encountered. And just as easily as de Marsay dreams of her, he wants to murder her and then he quickly forgets her after she is murdered.

Works Cited

Ahearn, Edward. *Marx and Modern Fiction*. New Haven: Yale UP, 1989.

Balzac, Henri de. *La Duchesse de Langeais suivi de La Fille aux yeux d'or*. Paris: Le Livre de Poche, 1958.

———. *Pensées, Sujets, Fragments*. Ed. J. Crépet. Paris: Blaizot, 1910.

———. *Cousin Bette, Pierre Crassou, The Girl with the Golden Eyes*. Trans. George Ives and William Walton. Philadelphia: George Barrie & Son, 1896.

Baudelaire, Charles. *Oeuvres Complètes*. Paris: Gallimard, 1975.

Brooks, Peter. *Body Work: Objects of Desire in Modern Narrative*. Cambridge: Harvard UP, 1993.

Felman, Shoshana. "Re-reading Femininity." *Yale French Studies* 62 (1980): 19-44.

Flaubert, Gustave. *Le Dictionnaire des idées reçues*. Paris: Aubier, 1951.

Freud, Sigmund. *New Introductory Lectures on Psychoanalysis*. Trans. James Strachey. New York: Norton, 1965.

Gates, Henri Louis, ed. *Race, Writing, and Difference*. Chicago: U of Chicago P, 1986.

Gilman, Sander. *Difference and Pathology: Stereotypes of Sexuality. Race and Madness*. Ithaca: Cornell U P, 1985.

Gobineau, Arthur Comte de. *Essai sur l'inégalité des races humaines*. Paris: Pierre Belfond, 1967.

Hoffman, Léon-François. *Le nègre romantique: personnage littèraire et obsession collective*. Paris: Payot, 1973.

Irigaray, Luce. *Speculum de l'autre femme*. Ithaca: Cornell UP, 1985.

Kadish, Doris. "Hybrids in Balzac's La Fille aux yeux d'or." *Nineteenth-Century-French-Studies* 16 (1988): 270-78.

Miller, Christopher. *Blank Darkness: Africanist Discourse in French*. Chicago: U of Chicago P, 1985.

Sharpley-Whiting, T. Denean. *Sexualized Savages. Primal Fears, and Primitive Narratives in French* (forthcoming).

Virey, Jean-Joseph. *Histoire naturelle du genre humain*. 1st ed. Paris: Crochard, 1801.

Owen Heathcote (essay date spring 2003)

SOURCE: Heathcote, Owen. "Hermeneutic Circles and Cycles of Violence: *La Fille aux yeux d'or, Histoire d'O, Les guérillères*." *South Central Review* 19, no. 4 (spring 2003): 44-62.

[*In the following essay, Heathcote compares themes of gender-based violence in* The Girl with the Golden Eyes, *Pauline Rèage/Dominique Aury's* Histoire d'O, *and Monique Wittig's* Les guérillères.]

I

Violence is always gendered but it is sexed in different ways. Although the title of Oliver Stone's notorious 1994 film *Natural Born Killers* suggests that both male and female members of its killer couple Mickey and Mallory are indeed "natural born killers," the violence of Mickey and Mallory is never symmetrical. Whereas the violence of Mickey is so natural that it is hardly necessary for him to proclaim or explain it, the violence of Mallory has to be motivated by her history of sexual abuse. As in Ridley Scott's *Thelma and Louise* (1991), where again the protagonists' violence is prompted by sexual attack, the violence of women has to be explained in order to make it intelligible.[1] Since female violence, even for the increasingly popular "tough girls," or gun-toting *femmes fatales*,[2] is always already "naturally" counter-cultural, it is difficult for the violence of women to be countercultural in other, less explicitly, or differently gendered ways. As Margarita Stocker has shown in her study of *Judith Sexual Warrior,* the violence of the biblical figure of Judith is frequently seen as either unnaturally deviant or co-opted to support male power—or both. As Stocker writes: "The most striking element in the Book of Judith is that it is so conscious and deliberate in its acknowledgement of the phallic concept of power. If power is patriarchal, then the only possessor of supreme masculinity is God."[3] The only way of providing feminist alternatives to the seemingly natural violences of patriarchy is to make Judith's violence so explicit and so self-conscious that it has to be taken as more, or as other, than (just) recuperable women's violence. The only way of avoiding the co-option of female violence is, according to Stocker, by disavowing as well as repeating the association between women and violence, by showing that Judith and her avatars are "sited at points of ideological difficulty" that expose, exploit and undercut traditional notions of femininity and violence: "[Judith] is an image of the autonomy that is constantly being wrested from us all, and an icon of the ways to recover it."[4]

Given Stocker's emphasis on Judith as a potential counter-cultural myth, it is interesting that the works of Monique Wittig have also been cited for their similarly radical, contestatory character. As Christiane P. Makward and Madeleine Cottenet-Hage write in their *Dictionnaire littéraire des femmes de langue française* (*Literary Dictionary of Women's Writing in French*): "Monique Wittig has always insisted on the need to compensate for the alienating myths of mainstream culture by creating these counter-mythologies."[5] Characteristic of these counter-mythologies is Wittig's espousal of "the darkest side of the imagination," which would include, in *L'opoponax* (*The Opoponax*), "a gleeful game massacring all the representatives of the phallic order, with a corpse in every chapter," and, in *Le corps lesbien* (*The Lesbian Body*), recourse to "fragmentation, staged through the use of double pages with large print which details the female anatomy."[6] Although the violence done to human bodies, whether male or female, is linked to Wittig's parallel dislocation of French grammar (her habitual use of the solecistic "quelqu'une" in *Les guérillères*[7] and the notoriously split "j/e" in *Le corps lesbien*) and to her iconoclastic dismantling of sex and gender categories that, for Makward and Cottenet-Hage, combine to work towards "a new poetics,"[8] this combination of physical, formal and conceptual violence can remain a site of *unwelcome* "ideological difficulty" for Wittig's readers. This may be because some, while not endorsing the traditional "unnaturalness" of female violence, are, after Hannah Arendt, more interested in power than in violence, if only because "the Woman with A Gun is deployed by reactionary ideology to instigate revalorized manhood in antagonism to it."[9] Or it may be because, according to Jean Duffy, "[t]he pragmatic feminist who can see no further than equal opportunities and a discursive space within a social structure that has been engendered by men will find little or no constructive guidance in Wittig."[10] Or, finally, it may be because Wittig's seeming demolition of sex and gender categories "by opposing woman and lesbian" simply reiterates "the binary structure in a different way."[11] If, then, the physical, formal and conceptual violence in Wittig appears problematic, it is not just because of some ill-considered squeamishness, but because this violence arguably no longer *works*. Unlike at least some instances of the violence of Judith, it seems it can no longer be harnessed to what Stocker calls "a complete overhaul of [our] mental furniture."[12]

Given the above, it is clearly an opportune moment to reconsider the relationship between violence and sexual politics in Wittig's work. Since an attempt has already been made to revisit the violence of her *Le corps lesbien* and *Virgile, non,*[13] this essay will concentrate on *Les guérillères* which raises interesting questions in relation to violence, gender and representation. Firstly, it is important to ask whether the violence of the *guérillères* as a group is the same as the violence of *Les guérillères* as text: is the explicit circularity attached to the group of *guérillères* the same as the circularity of the text? A first section of this paper will, therefore, examine the circularity or non-circularity of spaces and bodies in *Les guérillères* and the relation of that circularity to violence. In order to explore this, it will be helpful to compare *Les guérillères* with two other texts which foreground circles, sexuality and violence: Honoré de Balzac's *La Fille aux yeux d'or* (*The Girl with the Golden Eyes*) and Pauline Réage/Dominique Aury's *Histoire d'O*

(*Story of O*). Secondly, if there is a (violent) disjunction between the (violent) form and the (violent) content of *Les guérillères,* what is the role and the meaning of the violent content—the violence of the *guérillères* as a group—and the violence of the form—the violence of *Les guérillères* as text, and what is the function of the violent disjunction between the two? Is it that *Les guérillères* as text does violence to the *guérillères* as content in order to show both the violences of patriarchy towards women and that the very gendering of women as women does violence to identity? If this is the case, then the violence of *Les guérillères* may seem more programmatic than "real"—an important intervention in sexual politics but not about "real" violence, such as torture as in Ariel Dorfman's *Death and the Maiden* or in women growing up after the Holocaust as in Ronit Lentin's *Songs on the Death of Children.*[14] A second section of this paper will, therefore, examine the relations between sex, gender and violence in *Les guérillères.* Finally, a third section will examine the role of language in *Les guérillères* in order to see whether the violence of its language endorses the violence described, or offers leverage for a critique both of its own violence and of gendered violence in general. Does the violence of *Les guérillères* enclose its "characters" within its own circles of violence, and its readers in an unreflecting hermeneutic cycle of violence, whether violent form or violent content? Or does the violence of *Les guérillères* encourage a critical distance both from itself and its violences that break with the circles of the group of *guérillères* and with the cycles instititued by *Les guérillères* as text? Throughout this essay it is, therefore, important to ask if the violence in *Les guérillères* is a means or an end and, if a means, what precisely is the end it is seeking to achieve.

II

Circles and cycles are key features of Balzac's **La Fille aux yeux d'or** and of Réage/Aury's *Histoire d'O.* If O is the name of the protagonist—and the only name revealed to the reader—it is a sign of both her openness to invasion through her three orifices ("her loins . . . her mouth . . . her womb") and of her imprisonment "in a closed circle, a sealed universe." Thus, of Sir Stephen, "she knew he could see her, however she could not see him, and once again she felt happy with this constant exposure, with the constant imprisonment in his gaze where she was trapped."[15] If Paquita Valdès in **La Fille aux yeux d'or** is similarly available to Henri de Marsay in a horse-shoe-shaped boudoir, the area where Henri stands "formed a gently gracious circular line,"[16] and this boudoir is for Paquita a prison in a Paris characterized in terms of the circles of Hell, by "[a] girdle of the most immodest of Venuses" (**Fille** [*La Fille aux yeux*

d'or], 1041), and by the spiralling "ascending movement" of "gold and pleasure" (**Fille,** 1046, 1049). It can be seen that the circle in both texts associates the female body, enclosure and, more specifically, through the Orientalized Paquita and the gynaeceum of Roissy, the reputedly exotic sensualities of the harem. Both sets of circles are, moreover, shot through with violence: of O it is said "she loved the idea of torture" (*Histoire,* 197) and Paquita exclaims to Henri: "Intoxicate me, then kill me" (**Fille,** 1090). In addition, in both texts violence is particularly associated with women: the cruellest flagellator for O is Anne-Marie (*Histoire,* 197) and Paquita is slaughtered by her female lover, Mariquita: "The *Girl with the Golden Eyes* was expiring, steeped in blood" (**Fille,** 1106).

Despite these similarities, there is a sense in which the circles of **La Fille aux yeux d'or** and of *Histoire d'O* are very different. One of the features of *Histoire d'O,* at least in Just Jaekin's 1975 film version, is that the narrative is also circular: not only does the film end as it begins, with the introduction of a new woman into the house at Roissy, but, at the end, O leaves Jacqueline with the same words as René used to her at the beginning: "I will be there" (*Histoire,* 22). The end of the novel thus continues and indeed intensifies the association of cloistered femininity and violence. Even if physically absent, O's ghostly presence during Jacqueline's sequestration seals Jacqueline and her sisters in the rituals of Roissy. At the end of **La Fille aux yeux d'or,** however, Henri leaves the dead Paquita and her avenging lover, never to return to the fateful boudoir. Paquita and her passion are dismissed with a quip and then forgotten. It would seem then, that the heightened "femininity" of the end of *Histoire d'O* contrasts with the reasserted "masculinity" at the end of **La Fille aux yeux d'or**: whereas the circles of *Histoire d'O* represent unending cycles of violence towards women, the circles of Balzac's Parisian Hell can be a launch-pad for the dandy's tangential thrust into a new and different future. This contrast between the heightened interiority at the end of *Histoire d'O* and the regained exteriority at the end of **La Fille aux yeux d'or** is, however, deceptive, for both works leave intact the association of circles, femininity, violence *and art.* Although seemingly different, the freeze-framing of Paquita's death in a tableau of blood and silks is as unchanging and as unchangeable as the rituals of women's punishment at Roissy. Whether sealed in the ironic detachment of Henri or in the complicitous presence-absence of O, both works are the vehicles for an aesthetic of violence towards women. Whether the departing character is *inside* the aesthetic of violence as is O at the end of her narrative, or *outside* the aesthetic of violence like Henri at the end of his, the result is the same. Whether inside or outside, whether "male" or "female," circles and cycles encase (other) women in aestheticized violence.

Given that Paquita Valdès's boudoir has the shape of a horseshoe, it is interesting that in *Les guérillères* Wittig writes: "They say that the horseshoe which is a representation of the vulva has long been considered a lucky charm."[17] What remains at the level of implication in Balzac is thus made repeatedly explicit in relation to the *guérillères* whose sung Os recall "the zero or the circle, the vulvic ring" (*Guérillères*, 14) and whose circular dance reminds its practitioners that "the circle is your symbol" (*Guérillères*, 53). Since the *guérillères* also inhabit circular alveoli "which resemble an egg, a sarcophagus, an O" (*Guérillères*, 86), there is a manifest homology between the vulva and the songs, the dances and the habitats of the *guérillères*. In the same way, moreover, as Réage's O wears her Roissy finger—and later vulvic—rings, the *guérillères* display oval rings: "According to the feminaries rings are contemporaneous with such expressions as jewels treasures gems to designate the vulva" (*Guérillères*, 49). Since, moreover, the text includes several blank pages inscribed only with the outline of a large, black ring, it would seem that Wittig's text is indeed simply a more explicit, celebratory take on traditional associations between circles and femininity, even, or perhaps especially, when these are also imbued with violence.

It is, however, important to note that although Wittig seems to be making the analogies between, for example, vulva and circle, *more* explicit than in *La Fille aux yeux d'or* and even more incantatorily repetitive than in *Histoire d'O*, the attribution of these analogies is shown to be a citation, whether underscored by "*elles disent*" ("the women say"), by "*d'après les féminaires*" ("according to the feminaries"), or by express references to symbolic representation, culminating in the actual black circles that could hardly be more graphic—but *only graphic*. For whereas the homology between Paquita's body and her semi-circular boudoir is all the more incontrovertible for being suggested rather than stated, any homology between the actual bodies of the *guérillères* and the circles is nowhere mooted and, if the reader makes the connection, it can only be by consciously repeating other textual representations such as the feminaries—or *Les guérillères* itself. Thus at the same time as Wittig seems to be defining the *guérillères* in terms of their internal and external vulvic circles, she is in fact (also?) doing the opposite: attributing the supposedly "essential" characteristics of woman to legend, hearsay and song. Unlike Balzac and Réage/Aury who turn femininity into

art, Wittig is exposing, and celebrating, the artistic constructedness of femininity.

The essentially symbolic role of the circle in *Les guérillères* is further exemplified by its ability to signify not only forms of shelter and enclosure such as the above-mentioned alveoli, but also more military forms of protection such as "rounded shields" (*Guérillères*, 138) and of attack such as the ospah (*Guérillères*, 104) and ray-propelling spheres (*Guérillères*, 107-08). By turning the mirror, which, in *Histoire d'O*, reflected O's self-oppression and imprisonment in the male gaze, into a weapon (*Guérillères*, 120), Wittig shows that, as she writes at the beginning of *Les guérillères*, "all action is overthrow" (*Guérillères*, 5) ("*tout geste est renversement*"), and that any so-called essential femininity is itself reversible and thus unstable. To the internal circles of vulvas and alveoli can be added the dynamic, externally oriented circles that release the tangents of rays and, with its particularly Amazonian connotations, the arrow. *Les guérillères* thus combines the enclosures of *Histoire d'O* with the external projection of *La Fille aux yeux d'or*. In addition to the closed and static circles and cycles of *Histoire d'O*, the circles of *Les guérillères* are also associated with the activity of dance and song,[18] of the series, of the "geste" ("action")—with the onward movement of de Marsay in the *Comédie humaine*: "The women say that, to complete a cycle, a series of brilliant deeds or extraordinary and baleful events is required" (*Guérillères*, 90). Here again, however, the circle is essentially symbolic, combining opposites such as positive and negative, internal and external, movement and stasis and, through a reference to "a circle drawn in black" on corpses (*Guérillères*, 124), inscriptions of death as well as creativity. What emerges here is not just connotations of contrast and multiplicity, but, more importantly, the multiplicity of connotation. The very variety of the connotations of the circle demonstrates that what matters is connotation and symbol: the circle itself is (literally) almost immaterial except as a paradigm for multiple myth. Thus, at the same time as Wittig draws on age-old emblems of femininity, she shows these emblems to be poetically powerful but perhaps no more than powerful poetics: "They do not say that vulvas with their elliptical shape are to be compared to suns, planets, innumerable galaxies. . . . They do not in their discourses create conventional figures derived from these symbols" (*LG*, 61). Given that "*tout geste est renversement*," the negations and the violences associated with the circle also turn Wittig's *Histoire d'O* into what Erika Ostrovsky has termed "an anti-*Histoire d'O*,"[19] or, perhaps more accurately, into a kind of *Histoire d'anti O*, whose implications for the representation of sex, sexuality, gender and violence in *Les guérillères* can now be examined.

III

In its ability to shock through its association of sexuality and violence, Wittig's work is by no means unique in French literature. Not only is the French literary tradition punctuated by a considerable number of "*poètes maudits*" from the marquis de Sade to Octave Mirbeau, the surrealists and Georges Bataille, but a privileged vehicle of that sexual violence or violent sexuality has been homosexuality and homosex, not only in the works of Sade himself but, much more recently, in writers such as Jean Genet, Pierre Guyotat, Hervé Guibert and Cyril Collard. The breaking of sexual taboos is, moreover, increasingly associated with women's writing, from Rachilde and Violette Leduc to, more recently, *Histoire d'O* itself, and to other iconoclastic texts authored by women, such as Alina Reyes's *Le boucher* (*The Butcher*), Marie Darieussecq's *Truismes* (*Pig Tales*), Christine Angot's *L'inceste* (*Incest*) and Catherine Millet's *La vie sexuelle de Catherine M.* (*The Sexual Life of Catherine M.*).[20] These writings have given rise to repeated "*succès de scandale,*" matched only in the film world by Virginie Despentes's *Baise-moi* (*Fuck me*) and *Romance* by Catherine Breillat who writes: "With 'Romance' I have gone over to the other side of Judeo-Christian-Islam guilt. Crossing taboos is my preferred cinematic space."[21] Although many of these latter works can be seen, like *Histoire d'O,* to reinforce male power and male violence towards women, they are nevertheless contributing to what Alex Hughes and Kate Ince see as "a canon of French women's erotic writing."[22] As Lucienne Frappier-Mazur has written of women's erotica: "Their contribution is double: they develop a new erotic model, and they are introducing this model into mainstream literature."[23]

As the examples of *Histoire d'O, Le boucher, Truismes, L'inceste* and *Romance* all show, one of the common features of this "new erotic model" is the centrality of a single female figure and her gradual initiation into, or disclosure of, new, conventionally taboo, forms of sexual practices. Whether that sexual practice is sadism, masochism, incest, bestiality or simply lust, it is—and this is one of its claims to originality—relayed through the perspective and the experience of its central narrator, whether in a kind of free indirect speech as in *O,* or, more usually, through the first-person narrative. These writers are, challengingly, seeking "*les mots pour le dire*" ("the words to express it") or "*parole de femme*" (woman's word").[24] As with "*écriture féminine,*" if with a very different style and approach, they are seeking to give a voice to a woman's experience as it is inscribed in and on that woman's body. Whether writing in milk, according to Hélène Cixous, or in blood, like Jeanne Hyvrard,[25] they are giving that female body a new language.

It can be seen that, however different in their aims and sexual politics, the above positions can all seem to depend not only on a single female figure, but on a single female figure who seeks to re-valorize herself as female and to reclaim desires and practices that have been prohibited to her as woman. Thus Jeanne Hyvrard, for example, deplores but also seeks to rehabilitate her position in "femitude": "It is my castrated sex which cries out the love of life."[26] In *Les guérillères,* however, Wittig uses a variety of strategies to avoid speaking from a position of "femitude." First of all, she seemingly follows writers like Hyvrard and Leclerc in identifying the *guérillères* in terms of their female bodies—notably by vulvas and breasts (*Guérillères,* 72)—but at other points denies the importance of vulvas ("They say that they must now stop exalting the vulva." [*Guérillères,* 72]) and uses breasts neither positively nor "essentially," but strategically: the *guérillères'* exposure of their breasts is interpreted, incorrectly, by their enemy as "a gesture of submission" (*Guérillères,* 100).[27] Breasts are thus both asserted and denied—because they are asserted in order to be *misread.* The use of female body parts is thus neither metonymical—for vulvas and breasts, read "femaleness" or female wholeness—nor is it an example of the Surrealist "*corps morcelé*" and thus, through its dismembering of the female body, complicitous with the murdering of women.[28] In an adroit and strategic use of multiple violences, Wittig manages to avoid *both* essentializing *and* deconstructing women. To say, then, that Wittig replaces one set of binaries (male/female) with another (women/lesbian) does a signal disservice to the subtleties and the strengths of the sexual politics of *Les guérillères.*

It is at this point that mention should be made of the use of "elles" (they) whose utterances and whose actions notoriously frame the text of *Les guérillères.* Here the effect is twofold. Firstly, the use of a plural "elles," contrasting with the singular experiences recounted in other texts such as *Truismes* and *L'inceste,* blocks any extrapolation from the "elles" to the female body or female condition because the female is, in a sense, never particular but always already generalized. The plural "elles" of the *guérillères,* like the plural *écolières* (schoolgirls) in *L'opoponax,* blocks the metonymical totalization or hypostasization of female identity, as does the simultaneous valorization and devalorization of female body parts. Thus, as Wittig has famously remarked: "In *Les guérillères,* I try to universalize the point of view of *elles.* The goal of this approach is not to feminize the world but to make the categories of sex obsolete in language."[29] At the same time, however, as with the references to vulvas and breasts, the use of "elles" inevitably and productively also effeminizes. As with the references to vulvas and breasts, the "elles" are, inevitably, not only de-gendered but also residually and subliminally feminine. The success of "elles" is that it usurps the conventionally generalized "ils" but retains some of its conventional freight of femininity. In this way, Wittig creates a new language but retains some of the advantages of the old, in that the palimpsestic femininity of the "elles" (and the *guérillères*) leaves space for a potentially universalized lesbianism.

At the same time, her treatment of the men in the work goes in the opposite if ultimately complementary direction. Unlike the "elles," the men are specifically sexed as "*jeunes hommes*" ("young men") who are acknowledged as differently male with a promise of sexual dalliance with a *guérillère*: "Taking him in their arms, the women bear him to the side of the young weeping woman, applauding when they recognize each other and embrace. . . . They inform the young man that he is the first to have joined them in their struggle. They all embrace him" (*Guérillères*, 141). At the same time, however, as promising heterosexual congress, the young men are also devirilized by their softness and their lack of muscularity (*Guérillères*, 106, 138) and de-gendered or re-gendered through their association with flowers, new language, emotivity and circularity (*Guérillères*, 122, 137, 138, 140-01). Thus, whereas the "elles" are de-gendered but residually effeminized, the "jeunes hommes" are retained as men but actively de-masculinized. In this way the goal of the *guérillères* is completed: the young male is coopted into a feminized and yet unfeminized narrative of conquest and complicity while the female does not exist as such but still has a monopoly of both voice and action. Even the promise of heterosexual congress is, moreover, enlisted into a potentially lesbian paradigm: the "straight" men are devirilized and colonized by universalized non-feminized femaleness, or, again, a universalized lesbianism.[31] The advantage of enlisting these devirilized males into the company of *amantes* (*female lovers*) is not only to show that heterosex is absorbed into lesbian sex but to ensure that the circle—and the narrative—are also *in process*. Deconstruction is a dynamic. The text has telos.

It follows that, in terms strangely reminiscent of **La Fille aux yeux d'or** where lesbianism (or at least a lesbian relationship) is the hidden but finally acknowledged ground of a supposedly heterosexual attraction between Paquita and Henri, lesbianism in *Les guérillères* is the unspoken but logical result of combining a universalized "elles" with the initially violent but finally peaceful deconstruction of sex and gender categories. It is, in *Les guérillères,* not a case of using

lesbianism (or gayness or queerness) to rework sex and gender categories, but of showing that reworking sex and gender categories clears the ground for a universalized lesbianism. This strategy, and, perhaps, this "reality," gives *Les guérillères* its uncompromising and gleeful violence but also its empowering and liberating serenity. Given, however, that this reworking of sex and gender categories may itself be one of the (mere) myths alluded to in *Les guérillères,* and may thus itself be subject to what Namascar Shaktini has called "Wittig's deconstructive conception of circulation,"[32] it is now necessary to turn to the narrative *énonciation* as a whole. To what extent is the move through sexual complementarity and gender convergence vitiated by the violence of Wittig's own language? To what extent is the utopian promise of universal lesbianism infected by the violence needed for its own creation?

IV

If *Les guérillères* has been seen as a novel of violence, then this violence is primarily associated with its language. Unlike previously mentioned texts such as *Truismes,* where the violence is associated with the transfiguring monstrosity of the protagonist, and unlike *Histoire d'O* which Jean Paulhan categorizes by "*the word* decency,"[33] the violence of *Les guérillères* is first and foremost explicitly linguistic: "They are heard on all sides crying hate hate" (*Guérillères,* 116); "They say, War, rally! They say War, forward!" (*Guérillères,* 120); "They say that they are more barbarous than the most barbarous" (*Guérillères,* 130). It can be seen from these three examples that the violent language of *Les guérillères* has three main features: firstly, repetition ("hatred" and "war," to which can be added the insistence of "they say" itself); secondly, cooption: the violent language *of* the text is (re)articulated by violent voices *within* the text: "crier," "elles disent"; thirdly, exaggeration: through being repeated in the text by voices from the text, the violence acquires a hyperbolic crescendo of energy: "The cries they utter are so terrifying that many of their adversaries drop their weapons . . . they utter shouts of victory" (*Guérillères,* 102,103). If Wittig writes of the *guérillères* that "their violence is unleashed they are in a paroxysm of rage" (*Guérillères,* 118), then that violence is doubly linguistic—the war-cries of the *guérillères* as characters combine with the war-cry that is *Les guérillères* as a text, with both these violences being encapsulated by that very neologism that is the word *guérillères* itself: taboos are first broken in language. For this linguistic violence is, in fact, a linguistic *counter*-violence, mounted against the power of hegemonic language—the language that, for example, essentializes the binaries of male and female in grammatical genders and that perpetuates the distinctions between heterosexuality and a (marked) homosexuality in those very terms. Thus if, according to Jennifer Birkett, "[t]he apparatus and the structures of repressive power relationships are [in Wittig] turned into a rhetoric," then, as Birkett also points out, "the political force of the text is precisely in the violence of its rhetorical ploys."[34] The violence of hegemonic language can only be countered by the violence of linguistic dislocation and by the iconoclastic linguistic creativity of "this new species that seeks a new language" (Guérillères, 131).

One of the problems associated with destroying and replacing hegemonic language is that the critique of the old language is inevitably at least partially expressed via that same outmoded and repressive discourse. Since, if the text is to be intelligible, it cannot consist exclusively of neologisms or solecisms, other ploys have to be adopted that suggest both the violence of oppressive power relationships and the counterviolence of revolt. One ploy is to re-deploy the violence associated with insistent repetition in favour of the community of guérillères themselves by listing individual female names which replace patronymic or family name and re-place individual female identity in the community of "amantes." Another ploy is to constantly repeat the "elles disent" alongside multiple narratives within the main narrative, both to give individual guérillères a voice, and yet to suggest the situatedness and therefore the possible unreliability of the narrative perspective. Hence, at the same time as creating a myth of feminaries and of the guérillères themselves, such myths are, as Frances Bartkowski has noted, eventually suspect and short-lived: "They say, we must disregard all the stories" (Guérillères, 134); "The women say that it may be that the feminaries have fulfilled their function" (Guérillères, 49).[35] A third, related ploy is to exploit but also to condemn the recourse to symbols, comparisons and lists: "the comparisons present no problems" (Guérillères, 48); "In speaking of their genitals the women do not employ hyperbolic metaphors, they do not proceed sequentially or by gradation" (Guérillères, 66). But since comparisons are a problem when it comes to evoking the vulva (Guérillères, 48) and since the text does use both hyperbole and accumulation, the violence of oppressive language is used in order to be denied and is itself enlisted in the process of reaffirmation and renewal. Thus, if, as Diane Crowder argues, "[w]hat is missing prior to Les guérillères is the female presence in language and culture, symbolized in the text by the circle O," and if, according to Jean Duffy, "[t]he recurrent O points to the gaps in which a female discourse may take root,"[36] then a certain linguistic violence is necessary. And even a certain playfulness with violence. When one of the guérillères, Anne Damien,

plays at "Sister Anne do you see anything coming" (Guérillères, 12), she plays not only with the quotation from Bluebeard, but with the violence of the traditional narratives which play on the violence of men and the fears of women. Anne Damien's play is necessarily violent because she is playing misogyny at its own game. Laughing, perhaps with Medusa, she is powerful enough to play with Bluebeard—and win. At the same time Wittig herself both exploits and defuses that violence by incorporating it within her own language, her own play and her own new "conceptual furniture."

It can be seen from the above that one of the main features of Les guérillères is its ability to co-opt, incorporate and displace previous, phallocentric discourses within its own, self-conscious énonciation which is also a dénonciation of its others and itself. What Shaktini refers to as overwriting[37] does, therefore, relate not only to the theme of ingestion in Wittig—common for example in Le corps lesbien—but to the persistent intertextuality of/in Wittig, whereby, as in the case of Blue Beard, quotations or references to other texts are productively absorbed and re-signified in the discourse of the guérillères or of the "amantes"—the community of "companion lovers."[38] By combining the overwriting of intertextuality with the insistent repetitiveness of the plural "elles disent," Les guérillères establishes and reiterates a highly self-conscious performativity. Unlike the more individualized discourses of Annie Leclerc's Parole de femme, or Marie Cardinal's Les mots pour le dire, this "parole" is always already plural, always already multiple, always already able to replace and displace what are henceforward its differently marked others—including the other in itself and, potentially, itself as other. The originality of Les guérillères is to combine the enclosed, autotelic énonciation of Histoire d'O with the distanced, external point of view of the Marsay in La Fille aux yeux d'or. Combining the narrative points of view of Histoire d'O and La Fille aux yeux d'or Les guérillères is both closed and open-ended; it is dynamically, critically and therefore non-voyeuristically self-reflexive.

It has to be said, however, that this process of performativity via ingestion and regurgitation of discourses is, as the above quotation from Le corps lesbien and the reference to Bluebeard show, still persistently and provocatively violent. And, as Judith Butler has argued, it is precisely the quality of citationality, of iterability, that characterizes the violence of hate speech. For Butler hate speech is, like the language of Les guérillères, always already said. As we (re-)read in Les guérillères: "They are heard on all sides crying hate hate" (Guérillères, 116). At the same time, what may be seen as the "hate speech" of Les guérillères is not just repetition, since it is not, in Butler's words, simply *"a citation of itself"* but a highly self-consciously de-contextualized and re-signified quotation or reference,[39] and its very self-consciousness as *language* ensures that it creates a gap between itself as speech and any violent action. This ensures the possibility of moving beyond mere iterability, beyond the mere sedimentation of speech *acts* that identify with the hypostasized body and with the identifiable subject in discourse. Hence the importance of plurality and community in *Les guérillères,* and hence the importance of "Wittig's deconstructive conception of circulation." For it is the combination of plurality and performativity that ensures that violent language is not (mere) hate speech against identifiable individuals or groups—whether *guérillères, jeunes hommes* or any other category. For the importance of the self-conscious naming and re-naming in Wittig is that it ensures that naming is, as Butler writes, "kept separate from what is nameable, if only to guarantee that no name finally claims to exhaust the meaning of what we are and what we do."[40] Paradoxically but crucially, therefore, it is the very insistence of Wittig's violent language within the framework of its explicit and plural performativity that ensures that it enjoys the full power of its sexual politics without the opprobrium of targeted hate speech—and, incidentally, without the frenzy of the sexually visible as in *Romance* or *Baise-moi.*[41] It follows that *Les guérillères* is a more radical, more truly counter-cultural representation of re-gendered or de-gendered empowerment than many of the reworked myths of Judith. Unlike *Histoire d'O* and **La Fille aux yeux d'or** which, in their different ways, confirm the identification of violence, gender and aesthetics, the self-consciously plural and layered *énonciation/dénonciation* of *Les guérillères* disrupts any such identifications. Its constant foregrounding of the performative constructedness of violence and language combines with its dismantling of gender to show that the link between violence, language and gender is neither natural nor inevitable as in *Natural Born Killers,* but, like the discourses incorporated in *Les guérillères* itself, eminently *deconstructible* once no longer constantly re-enacted in discourse. Unlike in *Histoire d'O* and **La Fille aux yeux d'or,** the association between violence, language and gender is, in *Les guérillères,* an explicit, strategic, anti-mythical myth. But this association remains at the level of explicit, strategic, anti-mythical myth. The hermeneutic circle, like the textual circle, and like the circles and cycles of violence, is always open. Despite, or rather because of, its resounding title, violence in *Les guérillères* is never aestheticized, hypostasized or commodified as feminary, propaganda, pornography or art.

Notes

1. For an extended exploration of this position, see Karen Boyle, "Violence and Gender in Contemporary Cinema" Ph.D. diss., University of Bradford, 1998.

2. On the "tough girl," see Sherrie A. Inness, *Tough Girls: Women Warriors and Wonder Women in Popular Culture* (Philadelphia: University of Pennsylvania Press, 1999), 21 and on the gun-toting *femme fatale,* Margarita Stocker, *Judith Sexual Warrior: Women and Power in Western Culture* (New Haven: University of Yale Press, 1998), 173-97. As an indication of the increasing interest in violent women, see Helen Birch, ed., *Moving Targets: Women, Murder and Representation* (London: Virago, 1993), Lynda Hart, *Fatal Women: Lesbian Sexuality and the Mark of Aggression* (London: Routledge, 1994), Patricia Pearson, *When She Was Bad: How Women Get Away With Murder* (London: Virago, 1998) and Bev Zalcock, *Renegade Sisters: Girl Gangs on Film* (London: Creation Books, 1998).

3. Stocker, 7.

4. Stocker, 252.

5. Christiane P. Makward and Madeleine Cottenet-Hage, *Dictionnaire littéraire des femmes de langue française: De Marie de France à Marie NDiaye* (Paris: Karthala, 1996), 626. Unless otherwise noted, all translations in this essay are my own.

6. Makward, 626, 627.

7. A neologism invented by Wittig, combining *guérrières* (female warriors) and *guérilla.* See below note 17.

8. Makward, 625.

9. Stocker, 232.

10. Jean H. Duffy, "Monique Wittig," in *Beyond the Nouveau Roman: Essays in the Contemporary French Novel,* ed. Michael Tilby (New York: Berg, 1990), 226.

11. Margrit Shildrick, "Queering the Master Discourse: Lesbians and Philosophy," in *Straight Studies Modified: Lesbian Interventions in the Academy,* ed. Gabriele Griffin and Sonya Andermahr (London: Cassell, 1997), 192.

12. Stocker, 213.

13. See Jeannette Gaudet, *Writing Otherwise: Atlan, Duras, Giraudon, Redonnet and Wittig* (Amsterdam: Rodopi, 1999), 162-203; Owen

Heathcote, "Violent exclusion or the exclusion of violence? From Balzac's *Les proscrits* to Wittig's *Virgile, non*" (forthcoming); Diane Griffin Crowder, "Amazons and Mothers? Monique Wittig, Hélène Cixous and Theories of Women's Writing," *Contemporary Literature* 24.2 (1983): 117-44; and Claire Whatling, "Wittig's Monsters: Stretching the Lesbian Reader," *Textual Practice,* 11.2 (1997): 237-48. *Virgile, non* has been translated as *Across the Acheron* by David Le Vay in collaboration with Margaret Crosland (London: The Women's Press, 1987).

14. Ariel Dorfman, *Death and the Maiden,* trans. Ariel Dorfman (London: Nick Hern Books, 1994); Ronit Lentin, *Songs on the Death of Children* (Dublin: Poolbeg Press, 1996).

15. Pauline Réage, *Histoire d'O* (Paris: Jean-Jacques Pauvert, 1975), 106. Further references to this work will be indicated in the essay with the abbreviation *Histoire* and an accompanying page number. The persistent link between the 'O' and the feminine received interesting confirmation by the launch of *O. The Oprah Magazine,* May-June 2000.

16. Honoré de Balzac, *La comédie humaine,* ed. Pierre-Georges Castex, vol. 5 (Paris: Gallimard, 1977), 1087. Further references to this work will be indicated in the essay with the abbreviation *Fille* and an accompanying page number.

17. Monique Wittig, *Les guérillères,* trans. David Le Vay (Boston: Beacon Press, 1985), 44. Further references to this work will be indicated in the essay with the abbreviation *Guérillères* and an accompanying page number. The original French edition (Paris: Minuit, 1969) will be cited where necessary, for example for the repeated "elles disent" for which neither "they say" nor "the women say" is a true equivalent. It is interesting that Le Vay did not in his title try to translate Wittig's French neologistic *guérillères* which will also be retained in this essay.

18. According to Lyn Webster Wilde, groups identifiable as "actual" Amazons indulged in "orgiastic dancing" which was "both erotic and aggressive" (*On the Trail of the Women Warriors* [London: Constable, 1999], 145, 146). See also Batya Weinbaum, *Islands of Women and Amazons: Representations and Realities* (Austin: University of Texas Press, 1999). The circular weapons of the *guérillères* also recall the chakram of *Xena: Warrior Princess,* the cult television series, analyzed by Inness, *Tough Girls,* 160-76.

19. Erika Ostrovsky, *A Constant Journey: The Fiction of Monique Wittig* (Carbondale: University of Southern Illinois Press, 1991), 42.

20. Alina Reyes, *Le boucher* (Paris: Seuil, 1988); Marie Darrieussecq, *Truismes* (Paris: P.O.L., 1996); Christine Angot (Paris: Stock, 1999); Catherine Millet, *La vie sexuelle de Catherine M.* (Paris: Seuil, 2001).

21. *Le Nouveau Cinéma* (January 2000), 31.

22. Alex Hughes and Kate Ince, introduction to *French Erotic Fiction: Women's Desiring Writing, 1880-1990* (Oxford: Berg, 1996), 19.

23. Lucienne Frappier-Mazur, "Marginal Canons; Rewriting the Erotic," *Yale French Studies* 75 (1998): 128.

24. See Marie Cardinal, *Les mots pour le dire* (Paris: Grasset, 1975) and Annie Leclerc, *Parole de femme* (Paris: Grasset, 1974).

25. For an analysis of the violence in Hyvrard and Cixous, see Owen Heathcote, "Reinventing Gendered Violence? The Autobiographical Writings of Jeanne Hyvrard, Hélène Cixous and Marguerite Duras," *Modern and Contemporary France,* 8.2 (2000): 203-14.

26. Jeanne Hyvrard, *Les prunes de Cythère (The Plums of Cythera)* (Paris: Minuit, 1975), 62, 145.

27. See Crowder, "Amazons and Mothers?," 120.

28. The invasion/mutilation of the lover's body in Wittig's *Le corps lesbien* (Paris: Minuit, 1973) has been a frequent source of controversy. One of its functions is doubtless to detach amputation from its traditional association with phallocentric castration. See also above note 12 and below note 35.

29. Monique Wittig, "The Mark of Gender," in *The Straight Mind and Other Essays* (New York: Harvester Wheatsheaf, 1992), 85. It has to be said that other feminists are phasing the category woman back in. See for example Alison Butler, "Feminist Theory And Women's Films At The Turn Of The Century," *Screen,* 41.1 (2000): 73-9 and Toril Moi, *What is a Woman? And Other Essays* (Oxford: University of Oxford Press, 1999).

30. According to Lyn Webster Wilde the Amazons were above or beyond the sex/gender distinction: "There is no room for trivial gender-sniping here; . . . it is quite impossible to say to which sex the power belongs. In fact, it belongs to neither, only to the divine source of both" (*On The Trail Of The Women Warriors,* 81-82). Wilde also scotches the myth of the single-breasted Amazon (82) and that they were men-haters (50).

31. The notion of universalized lesbianism makes for an interesting comparison with Leo Bersani's deployment of "homo-ness" as "an antiidentitarian

identity" in *Homos* (Cambridge: University of Harvard Press, 1995), 101. By "universalizing" lesbianism—a strategy she describes in "The Point of View: Universal or Particular?," *Feminist Issues* 3.2 (1983): 63-69 and "The Trojan Horse," *Feminist Issues,* 4.2 (1984): 45-49—Wittig avoids defining it in terms such as "woman-identified-woman," "feminist-separatist" or "queer anarchist" like Susan Gubar, *Critical Condition: Feminism At The Turn Of The Century* (New York: University of Columbia Press, 2000), 46.

32. Namascar Shaktini, "Figuring Circulation: Claude Lévi-Strauss and Monique Wittig," *Contemporary French Fiction by Women: Feminist Perspectives,* ed. Margaret Atack and Phil Powrie (Manchester: University of Manchester Press, 1990), 148.

33. Jean Paulhan, "Le bonheur dans l'esclavage," foreword to Pauline Réage, *Histoire d'O,* iv.

34. Jennifer Birkett, "*Sophie Ménade:* The Writing Of Monique Wittig," *French Erotic Fiction,* 113, 112.

35. Frances Bartkowski, *Feminist Utopias* (Lincoln: University of Nebraska Press, 1989), 38. See also Ostrovsky, 56 and Laurence M. Porter, "Writing Feminism: Myth, Epic and Utopia In Monique Wittig's *Les Guérillères*," *L'Esprit Créateur,* 29.3 (1989): 99.

36. Crowder, 128; Duffy, 221. According to Crowder, "one of the primary tasks of 'lesbian writing' is to strip the female body of its heavy burden of metaphor and imagery imposed by male culture" (119). Crowder claims, however, that the feminaries contain "accurate descriptions of the vulva" (120). *Les guérillères* also resists the allegorization of woman as charted by Marina Warner in her *Monuments And Maidens: The Allegory Of The Female Form* (London: Picador, 1985).

37. See Namascar Shaktini, "Displacing the Phallic Subject: Wittig's Lesbian Writing," *Signs* 8.1 (1982): 32. The notion of overwriting is stronger than that of "reverse discourse" (see Jonathan Dollimore, "The Dominant And The Deviant: A Violent Dialectic," *Critical Quarterly,* 28.1 & 2 [1986]: 179-92) and perhaps even than "tout geste est reneversement." In "Quelques remarques sur *Les guérillères*," *L'Esprit Créateur,* 34.4 (1994): 121, Wittig emphasizes the *mise en abyme* effect of "the book in the book" in the work.

38. See Crowder, 123 and, on the importance of intertext in *Les guérillères,* Birkett, 105-15. For an earlier analysis of its violence, see Owen Heathcote, "Masochism, Sadism And Women's Writing; The Examples Of Marguerite Duras And Monique Wittig," *Nottingham French Studies,* 32.2 (1993): 71-84.

39. Judith Butler, *Excitable Speech: A Politics Of The Performative* (New York: Routledge, 1997), 80.

40. Butler, 125.

41. See Linda Williams, *Hard Core: Power, Pleasure, And The "Frenzy Of The Visible"* (London: Pandora, 1990).

Michael Lucey (essay date 2003)

SOURCE: Lucey, Michael. "Balzac and Same-Sex Relations in the 1830s." In *The Misfit of the Family: Balzac and the Social Forms of Sexuality,* pp. 82-123. Durham, N.C.: Duke University Press, 2003.

[*In the following excerpt, Lucey concentrates on actual events in early-nineteenth-century Paris that influenced the narrative and themes of* The Girl with the Golden Eyes.]

THE POSTFACE TO *LA FILLE AUX YEUX D'OR*

La Fille aux yeux d'or ends with the bloody spectacle, witnessed by Henri de Marsay, of the death of the beautiful Paquita at the hands of her aristocratic lover Euphémie, the marquise de San-Réal. There was a postface to the first edition of *La Fille aux yeux d'or* (1835) which unfortunately is missing from many modern editions. In it the author claims that the events of the preceding tale are mostly true and were told to him by the protagonist of the story. He adds that one of the most difficult things to believe about the story would doubtless be the incredible "half-feminine" beauty of the male hero (Henri de Marsay) at age seventeen, although traces of it were still apparent in the man of twenty-six who told the story to the author. The passage then continues:

> If there should be anyone interested in the *Girl with Golden Eyes,* they can see her again after the curtain has come down on the play, like an actress who, to receive her ephemeral crown of glory, rises up in perfect health after having been publicly stabbed. Nothing ends poetically in nature. Today, the *Girl with Golden Eyes* is thirty years old, and her beauty has faded. The marquise de San-Réal, who has rubbed elbows with certain readers of this tale this very winter at the Opera or at the Bouffes, is now of an age that women do not admit to, but which can be surmised from the frightful hairdos that certain foreigners allow themselves to display in the front rows of certain theater boxes, much to the dismay of the younger folk seated behind them. This marquise was raised in the tropics, where Girls with Golden Eyes are accepted by custom to such an extent that they are practically an institution.

> [Si quelques personnes s'intéressent à la *Fille aux yeux d'or,* elles pourront la revoir après le rideau tombé sur la pièce, comme une de ces actrices qui, pour recevoir

leurs couronnes éphémères, se relèvent bien portantes après avoir été publiquement poignardées. Rien ne se dénoue poétiquement dans la nature. Aujourd'hui, la *Fille aux yeux d'or* a trente ans et s'est bien fanée. La marquise de San-Réal, coudoyée pendant cet hiver aux Bouffes ou à l'Opéra par quelques-unes des honorables personnes qui viennent de lire cet épisode, a précisément l'âge que les femmes ne disent plus, mais que révèlent ces effroyables coiffures dont quelques étrangères se permettent d'embarrasser le devant des loges, au grand déplaisir des jeunes personnes qui se tiennent sur l'*arrière*. Cette marquise est une personne élevée aux îles, où les mœurs légitiment si bien les Filles aux yeux d'or, qu'elles y sont presque une institution.]

(5:1111-12)[1]

The passage is ambiguous and enigmatic while still being forthright about the presence of a lesbian subculture in Paris in the 1830s. Rose Fortassier has suggested Balzac is making a slightly veiled reference to Marie Dorval, the lead actress in Alexandre Dumas's play *Antony,* in which she appeared regularly in Paris from 1831 to 1834, and throughout the rest of France even longer.[2] At the end of the play, in order to protect her reputation, she is stabbed by her lover as her husband breaks down the door. The lover then declares to the husband, "I killed her because she resisted me."

Rumors were circulating regarding an affair between Dorval and George Sand. Alfred de Vigny, with whom Dorval was involved, wrote in the margins of one 1833 letter from Sand to Dorval, "I have forbidden Maria to reply to this Sappho who is pestering her."[3] It is also often suggested that the relationship between Lélia and Pulchérie in Sand's novel *Lélia* draws on Sand's relationship with Dorval. Rather like the correspondence between Balzac and Sue or Balzac and Latouche, the correspondence between Sand and Dorval provokes a wide range of critical speculation. Lillian Faderman refers indecisively to "a very sensual but not unambiguously sexual relationship between them." The editor of a 1950 edition of *La Fille aux yeux d'or,* on the other hand, declares that "some of Sand's texts leave no doubt as to the intimacy of their relation, nor as to the vice that they shared."[4] Arsène Houssaye, a contemporary of Sand, gives a long description in his *Les Confessions* of the passionate and intimate relation of a dark-haired woman novelist and a blond actress, without ever giving names: "It was more than a libertine affair of the heart; it was an oriental, an Indian, a Japanese passion. The two bacchantes would finally take their leave of each other at daybreak, still drunk on the paleness of the dreams they had lived out. And the woman of eloquence would be more eloquent on that day, just as the woman of the theater would have more caresses in her voice, more fire in her eyes, a wilder passion."[5] Houssaye also refers to the rumors circulating about the same-

sex liaisons of the Princess of Belgiojoso. He notes that she was extremely fond of George Sand. "Why did they enjoy seeing each other so much? Doubtless in order to emancipate women and the people" (3). Houssaye also remarks that around this time Balzac was finishing *La Fille aux yeux d'or*—making clear that Balzac's contemporaries associated the story with a culture of same-sex relations between women that they knew to exist around them (3). In a letter to Sand, written on January 27, 1833, Gustave Planche, an aspiring suitor, warns her of Dorval's reputation:

> One of my friends who is close enough to J—te to be able to judge her truthfulness impartially has assured me that Madame A. D. [Allan Dorval] had for her a passion of the same nature as the passion Sappho had for the young Lesbians—it's terrible that I tell you such an ugly thing, isn't it? Perhaps it's disrespectful. But I don't think so. Between now and February 15, if by chance you find yourself alone with Madame A. D., you could easily find out if I have been misled. In any case, please burn this letter, and cover these preceding revelations in deep silence and forgetfulness. I don't care much about public opinion, yet I would still not like to be known as a stool pigeon.[6]

Doubtless, many letters such as Planche's were in fact burned. Yet enough testimonials remain to indicate not only the reigning curiosity about the Sand/Dorval connection, but a general awareness of and interest in same-sex relations between women.

It is thus not surprising that Balzac's postface should refer relatively openly to a subculture of women sexually interested in other women in Paris. (The sentences from the postface cited above are ostentatiously constructed with the feminine substantive *personnes* and its corresponding pronoun *elles* in order to suggest that women in particular among his readers may be interested in knowing the current whereabouts of Paquita and Euphémie.) The postface further suggests that it suffices to be sufficiently well-informed in order to be able to see members of this subculture all around.

At the same time, the postface deflates the spectacular violence marking the end of the story just told. It reveals both female participants in the story's bloody final scene to be still alive, and also unkindly notes how much less attractive they have become with the passage of time. The ridicule attached to the older marquise de San-Réal is particularly noteworthy. Why would the postface be so carefully constructed as to force us to recognize the artifice of the spectacular ending of the tale that has just been told?

The concluding pages of *La Fille aux yeux d'or* are themselves tonally rather unstable or even incoherent. One finds in them an excessive use of melodrama (bordering on camp), as an unknowing brother rides through Paris to the mansion in which he plans to kill a woman who is already in the process of being murdered by the sister that the brother does not even know he has. There is a somewhat ironic reference to the stylized representations of murder in the gothic novel that would shortly be taken up with gusto in France with the appearance of the *roman feuilleton* (serial novel): one of Henri's accomplices is pleased to note that the marquise has forgotten to soundproof the chimney, thus allowing the noise of her crime to be perceptible from the street, a mistake the men would not have made. The tabloid sensationalism in effect as brother and sister head for the shocking revelation that they have been sexually involved with the same woman suddenly gives way to a startlingly detailed painterly description (the tale is dedicated to Eugène Delacroix) of a room in bloody disarray due to the successful attempt of one woman to kill another after having sex with her. The very tonal instability of the passage (camp and the portrayal of intense violence) might indicate a certain indecisiveness on Balzac's part as to what sense to make of same-sex relations involving two women. It is nearly reduced to nothing but the material for a spectacular display.[7]

In my next chapter, I return to the question of Balzac's interest in and ways of thinking about same-sex couples. The novels I consider there, *Le Cousin Pons* and *La Cousine Bette,* date from 1846 and 1847, more than a decade later. In the interval, Balzac will have filled out his understanding of same-sex relations with a great deal more sociological content. That content, fascinating in its own right, will not ultimately prove sufficient to restrain the novelistic impulse to bring samesex couples to a melodramatic end. Again in *La Cousine Bette,* Balzac will reserve a particularly sensational and mostly gratuitous violence for the end of the female couple, thereby furthering the kind of masculinist dissymmetry already apparent in his treatment of couples of women and couples of men a decade earlier. In *La Cousine Bette,* Balzac will, in speaking of Bette's feelings for Valérie, refer to "the most violent sentiment we know of, the friendship of one woman for another [le sentiment le plus violent que l'on connaisse, l'amitié d'une femme pour une femme]" (7:433, 424). As we will see more fully in the next chapter, that statement itself has several aspects. It is, on the one hand, a recognition of the ways in which women are at a disadvantage in the economic system that governs marriage and family formation for most people in France at the time: to escape from or to revolt against that system requires an immense effort for a woman. On the other hand, Balzac's pronouncement is also a kind of pop-psychological justification for the melodramatic treatment of same-sex eroticism between women.

Anne-Marie Meininger, who edited *La Cousine Bette* for the Pléiade edition of *La Comédie humaine,* annotates that sentence on the violent sentiment found in female friendships by recalling the violence of the conclusion of *La Fille aux yeux d'or.* She then reminds us that Balzac, in a letter to Madame Hanska, named the poet Marceline Desbordes-Valmore as one of his models for Bette:

> The passionate friendship of Marceline for Pauline Duchambge, who had been mixed up in the twists and turns of Marie Dorval's affair with Vigny, might have given Balzac some reason to wonder about the possible existence of a network of singular feminine friendships in Paris.
>
> [L'amitié passionnée de Marceline pour Pauline Duchambge, laquelle avait été mêlée aux péripéties de la liaison de Marie Dorval et de Vigny, a pu donner à Balzac quelques raisons de s'interroger sur l'existence d'un réseau de singulières amitiés féminines à Paris.][8]

The unnecessarily tentative quality of the claim regarding what Balzac *may* have known is unfortunate. The ideological constructs that produce that hesitant mode of expression are both tenacious and intellectually frustrating. Of course Balzac, moving in the circles he moved in and friends with the people he was friends with, and author of *La Fille aux yeux d'or* and its postface, as well as of *La Cousine Bette,* did more than wonder about the possible existence of same-sex relations between women. He knew of them, thought about the social forms through which they were enacted, theorized them (sometimes in sexist ways), and historicized them, just as he did with same-sex relations between men. I now turn to examine more closely how he does this within *La Fille aux yeux d'or.*

LA FILLE AUX YEUX D'OR

In 1900 the New York publishing house of P. F. Collier brought out a work titled *Honoré de Balzac in Twenty-Five Volumes: The First Complete Translation into English,* which was a reprint of the edition prepared by George Saintsbury and first published in England in 1895. When, however, in the "complete" Collier edition one reaches page seven of volume twelve, one finds a note from the editor that states: "In its original form the *Histoire des Treize* consists—or rather, it was originally built up—of three stories: **'Ferragus'** or **'The Rue Soly,'** **'La Duchesse de Langeais'** or **'Ne touchez-pas a la hache,'** and *La Fille aux yeux d'or.* The last, in some respects one of Balzac's most brilliant effects, does not appear here, as it contains things that are inconvenient."[9] So much for the completeness of the edition. Indeed, *La Fille aux yeux d'or* itself seems to foreshadow this reticence on the part of what the French call the Anglo-

Saxon world. The protagonist of the story, Henri de Marsay, is the illegitimate son of a certain Lord Dudley, of wide-ranging sexual proclivities. The story tells us that in 1816 Lord Dudley "came to seek refuge in Paris in order to escape legal proceedings in England, where, of all things Oriental, only merchandise is protected" (5:1058, 331).[10] Just in case that reference is not clear, the narrator continues by recording Lord Dudley's reaction on catching sight of his son, whom he has apparently never before seen, and on whose extraordinary beauty (at twenty-two going on twenty-three, he barely looks seventeen and is as handsome as a spring morning) the narrator had just been expatiating: "On hearing his name, he said, 'Oh! He's my son! How unfortunate!'" (5:1058, 331).[11]

The prudery that gives rise to the legal situation from which Lord Dudley flees—the prudery testified to by the first "complete" English translation—is also inscribed in the novel in interesting ways. When Henri de Marsay receives a morning visit from his friend Paul de Manerville, who asks him to lunch, Henri in turn asks if Paul will be shocked if he gets ready to go out in front of Paul. (His toilet is going to take two and a half hours.) Paul says he will not be shocked, and Henri expresses ironic relief: "We are taking on so many English things at the moment that we are in danger of becoming as hypocritical and prudish as they are [Nous prenons tant de choses des Anglais en ce moment que nous pourrions devenir hypocrites et prudes comme eux]" (5:1071, 347). Yet, Paul *is* shocked by watching Henri and his servant in the elaborate process of getting Henri dressed. As we have seen, this same duo of Paul de Manerville and Henri de Marsay had also been used by Balzac in *Le Contrat de mariage,* published the same year. They made the same contrast there as here: Henri's well-maintained aristocratic dandyism contrasts with Paul's slow slide into bourgeois subjectivity. The contrast between these two ways of being—indeed, two ways of perceiving—structures the story in more profound ways as well.

La Fille aux yeux d'or opens with a prologue that apparently has little to do with the plot that follows. The prologue is one example of the endless pop-sociological descriptions of Paris popular at the time. It had been published separately elsewhere by Balzac before being roped into service for this story.[12] One of its functions is to construct the image of a reader objectively different from all of the Parisian types described in the preface and, in particular, from those images described in several passages at the prologue's end, as the presentation of Henri de Marsay and his family approaches:

> Is not seeking after pleasure a sure way of finding boredom? Society people have warped natures from an early

age. Having nothing to do but to invent ways of enjoying themselves, they have been quick to misuse their senses, as the working man misuses alcohol. Pleasure is like certain medicaments: in order to keep on obtaining the same effects one has to double the doses, and death or besottedness is contained in the last one.

> (5:1050, 323)

> One finds, in the feminine world, happy little colonies which live after the Oriental mode and are able to preserve their beauty; but these women are rarely seen out in the streets on foot. They lie hidden, like rare plants which only unfold their petals at certain times of day and really are exotic exceptions.

> (5:1053, 326)

> In Paris, in high aristocratic circles, may sometimes be seen, here and there, a few ravishing young faces, the fruits of educations and mores that are quite exceptional.

> (5:1053, 326)

As the narrator strives to tie the almost hackneyed, stereotypical "analysis" of Paris with which the tale opens to the plot of the story he has to tell, he does so by referencing what we might think of as a tabloid-level set of prejudices about the perverse sexual mores of the aristocracy. It is as if he invites us to become prudish (English or American?) in order to relish the shock to our bourgeois sensibilities that may be coming, to be ready to feel outraged at the queer spectacle that is to follow.

On the other hand, or perhaps at the same time, the narrator assumes that the reader is savvy enough to figure out the ending of the story long before it happens, and so to take a different form of (French?) pleasure in watching the sophisticated Henri de Marsay be a dupe where the reader is not. Shortly after introducing the stunning de Marsay and his profligate father, the narrator comments:

> To make this story comprehensible, we must at this point add that Lord Dudley not unnaturally found many women ready enough to strike a few copies of so delightful a portrait. His second masterpiece of this kind was a girl called Euphémie, the daughter of a Spanish lady, brought up in Havana, conveyed back to Madrid with a young creole girl from the Antilles, both of them burdened with the ruinous tastes customary in the colonies. But she was luckily married to an old and phenomenally rich Spanish hidalgo, Don Hijos, Marquis of San-Real. . . . As much out of unconcern as through respect for youthful innocence, Lord Dudley gave his children no information about the relationships he was creating for them here, there and everywhere. Such situations are one of the inconveniences in civilization, though the latter has so many advantages that we must shut our eyes to its defects in view of the benefits it brings.

> (5:1057-58, 331)

The hint the narrator gives is hardly subtle: Henri has a half-sister, Euphémie. They don't know of each other's existence, and their ignorance will be important in the story. The sentences that follow the passage cited show Lord Dudley entranced by the gorgeous vision of his son, and disappointed, on learning of their rather close family relation, to feel obliged to remove him from consideration as a sexual object. Watch out! The incest train is coming.

A few pages later, Henri forms an attraction to a beautiful and mysterious girl with golden eyes who is walking in the Tuilerie gardens. He recounts his meeting with her to Paul de Manerville, as follows: "I found myself face to face with a woman . . . who, if she refrained from throwing her arms round my neck, did so . . . through one of those paralysing shocks which robs your arms and legs of movement" (5:1063, 337). Paul de Manerville, on hearing the girl described, tells Henri that everyone calls her "the girl with golden eyes," and that she has been seen in the garden previously with another young woman, more beautiful than she, whom Paul begins to describe before exclaiming, "Why now, upon my word, she takes after you!" (5:1064, 338).

On making inquiries as to where the girl lives, Henri finds that she lives in a palace belonging to Don Hijos, marquis de San-Réal (5:1067, 343). When Henri finally, fifteen or twenty pages later, makes it into the girl's presence, she comments to herself, "He has the same voice!" (5:1083, 361). Even before publishing the story, Balzac had, as a post-face to **La Duchesse de Langeais,** announced that the story that was on its way would deal with "a terrible passion, one which our literature has never dared face up to [une passion terrible, devant laquelle a reculé notre littérature]" (5:1038). That sentence was published in 1834, which makes it in fact a bit inexact. George Sand's *Lélia* was published in 1833, and it included a character named Pulchérie whose same-sex interests were clear, and whose relation with her sister Lélia was affectively very charged.[13] (Balzac had been friends with Sand in the early 1830s, but in 1833-34 had little to do with her after she broke up with Jules Sandeau, with whom Balzac sided; indeed, Sandeau would move in with Balzac for about a year in late 1834. Balzac says nasty things about *Lélia* and Sand in a letter to Madame Hanska in October 1834, wondering why a woman with children would have been interested in characters who are *inféconds*.)[14]

Lélia successfully provoked outrage among critics. Leyla Ezdinli points to the reaction of a certain Alphonse du Valconseil, who expresses particular outrage at the enthusiasm with which Pulchérie "lost her innocence among the infamies of Sodom complicated by incest [perdit son innocence dans les infamies de Sodome compliquée d'incestes]."[15] Ezdinli also cites an article that appeared in *Le Figaro* on August 24, 1833, titled "Il ou Elle: Énigme" ("He or She: Enigma") that, without explicitly mentioning Sand, made clear what a stir she was making in literary circles: "They say that *she* writes books and that *he* smokes, that *she* left her husband and that *he* (this woman) drinks rum and punch; they maintain that she shaves. She requires her male lovers to call her/him sir and her female lovers, in the midst of the sweetest hugging and kissing, to call her/him miss [On dit qu'*elle* écrit des livres et qu'*il* fume, qu'*elle* a quitté son mari et qu'*il* (cette femme) boit du rhum et du punch; on assure qu'elle se rase. Elle exige que ses amants l'appellent monsieur, et que ses amantes, dans les plus doux embrassements, l'appellent mademoiselle]."

Any informed literary reader in Paris in the mid-1830s would thus have found nothing particularly enigmatic about **La Fille aux yeux d'or,** unless they willfully cast themselves in the role of the bourgeois prude feigning ignorance as to the existence of same-sex relations between women or between men. The story seems to be structured to allow readers to be perfectly "in the know" while they simultaneously try out what it would feel like to be surprised and shocked by the denouement. This particular situation—knowing while pretending not to know in order to see what kind of sensation might arise from that pretense—perhaps encapsulates a certain specific historical confrontation, the clash of several cultures, each with different epistemologies.

If there were not necessarily anything enigmatic about the story in the 1830s, it is not clear why there should be anything particularly enigmatic about the story for anyone who reads it carefully today. It is therefore somewhat surprising to find it so often read precisely as an enigmatic text. Shoshana Felman, for instance, writes:

> I remember that the textual ambiguity I was attempting to decipher was entirely baffling and astonishing to me: it took me time and labor even to understand it literally, to figure out that what the text was so elliptically narrating was the story of a triangular affair, of a woman loving both a woman and a man, and that the story's ambiguities derived, primarily, from the confusion, the misreadings, the mistakes made by (experienced by) a man (a suitor) in his difficulty—and indeed his impossibility—of grasping the situation from his male perspective: a predominant, stereotypical perspective that puts men (himself included) at the center of women's lives and that cannot conceive of femininity except as subordinate to man (himself, or else a rival who must surely in turn be male) as its only center. The protagonist, Henri, thus fails to guess that his rival

is in fact a woman, and tragic consequences ensue. Henri is deluded, and his reading of the sexes and of sexual difference is ironically demystified and subverted by the text. But are we not all, in fact, the cultural progeny—and cultural hostages—of this perspective? This is why it was a text so hard to read in the beginning: its interpretation had to go against the grain of universal sexual error.[16]

La Fille aux yeux d'or is filled with patriarchal discourse, misogyny, exoticizing discourse, racism, and brutal violence against women, and readings such as Felman's that critique this aspect of the story are much to the point.[17] Yet her claims about the "universal sexual error" that the story enacts in order to subvert seem hard to credit.

First, we might note that while Henri is more of a dupe than any reader of the story need be, he is not as thick-headed as Felman claims. He does figure out, slowly, that Paquita, the girl with the golden eyes, is having an affair with a woman for whom he is only a substitute, and this even before, in the midst of passionate lovemaking with him, she "lifts him vigorously into the air" and cries out "Oh! Mariquita!" (5:1102, 384). The first time he had slept with her, he had noted that she was "virgin," but "by no means innocent" (5:1091, 370).[18] The narrator admits that Henri is sometimes so attached to life in the present that it takes him a while to put two and two together, but notes that after having reflected on his first night of lovemaking he does add things up:

> At that moment then, de Marsay perceived that he had been deceived by the girl with the golden eyes, for now he could see the past night in perspective, beginning as it had done with a trickle of pleasures which in the end has swollen into a torrent of voluptuousness. By now he was able to read that page, so brilliant in its effects, and divine its hidden meaning. Paquita's purely physical innocence, the amazing quality of her joy, the few words, at first obscure but now clear, which had escaped her in the midst of that joy, everything showed him that he had posed for another person. Since no form of social corruption was a closed book to him, since he professed perfect indifference with regard to all kinds of moral deviation and believed them to be justified by the mere fact that they were capable of being satisfied, he took no umbrage at vice, being as familiar with it as one is with a friend; but he smarted at the thought of having provided it with sustenance.

> [En ce moment donc, de Marsay s'aperçut qu'il avait été joué par la *Fille aux yeux d'or*, en voyant dans son ensemble cette nuit dont les plaisirs n'avaient que graduellement ruisselé pour finir par s'épancher à torrents. Il put alors lire dans cette page si brillante d'effet, en deviner le sens caché. L'innocence purement physique de Paquita, l'étonnement de sa joie, quelques mots d'abord obscurs et maintenant clairs, échappés au milieu de la joie, tout lui prouva qu'il avait posé pour une autre personne. Comme aucune des corruptions so-

ciales ne lui était inconnue, qu'il professait au sujet de tous les caprices une parfaite indifférence, et les croyait justifiés par cela même qu'ils se pouvaient satisfaire, il ne s'effaroucha pas du vice, il le connaissait comme on connaît un ami, mais il fut blessé de lui avoir servi de pâture.]

(5:1096, 377)

The text is a little roundabout, but not that hard to decipher. Henri understands that Paquita has been given to the "vice" of same-sex love-making, and that his sexual penetration of her was the first time she had ever been penetrated. *Une autre personne* (another person) is thus precisely *une autre* (some woman). He is not bothered by the vice. He is bothered by the fact that he has been used as a stand-in for a woman. (Paquita actually dressed him up as a woman before taking him to bed, which didn't seem to bother him while it was going on.) He returns to her palace a few nights later, in fact, in order to see if he cannot somehow make love to her so passionately that she can no longer mistake him for anything but a man. He imagines himself to be doing precisely this at the moment she cries out "Mariquita," cruelly dashing his hopes, arousing his masculinist ire once and for all, and causing him to begin laying plans to return once more to kill her. When he arrives to kill her, and hears the noises of someone else already doing so, he assumes that the person is the marquise herself.

Henri is thus *not* a dupe regarding same-sex relations between women. He seems perfectly familiar with them—as would have been any number of readers in the 1830s. What he does not know is that the woman who is his rival is also his half-sister. But the attentive reader is aware of this before the plot is even underway, and thus should be waiting with little surprise for the final scene, in which Henri returns to kill Paquita, only to discover that his rival has beat him to it. Discovering that Paquita is no longer a virgin ("For the blood you have given over to him, you owe me every drop of yours! [Pour le sang que tu lui as donné, tu me dois tout le tien!]" [5:1107, 389]), Euphémie has stabbed her to death. The reader may not be surprised by the revelation, but certainly she or he may have eagerly been awaiting the tabloid conflagration that these decadent, perverted aristocrats were heading for.

Felman universalizes the final meeting between Henri and Euphémie into a lesson about the loss of the paternal function in post-Revolutionary French society. She does this based on the identical sentence uttered by the two half-siblings as they apprehend the full significance of the other's presence: "Is not Lord Dudley your father? [Lord Dudley doit être votre père?]" (5:1108, 390). Felman writes:

> The return of the lost *name of the father* in the dénouement therefore strips Henri of his (adoptive) proper name, de Marsay, leaving him, indeed, with *no name*

that he can claim to be *his own,* that he can claim to be his *proper* name. The cultural procedure of name giving as insuring representative authority is no longer valid in the story: the (male) authority of name givers, customarily father and husband, is here disrupted: the father is no longer truly and legitimately *represented* by the son, in much the same way as the masculine is no longer truly and legitimately represented by the feminine.[19]

This is well and good, although one might want to substitute "always already not" for both of the occurrences of "no longer" in the citation, for the artifice of the social construction of paternity is, for Balzac, a historical constant, not a modern novelty. Yet I think there is something that may be a bit flat-footedly obvious about the meeting between murderous half-brother and half-sister that risks being forgotten via this sophisticated attention to the father's name. Both Henri and Euphémie immediately think of "blood" when they see each other. "She remained true to the blood [Elle était fidèle au sang]," Henri states. Euphémie replies, "She was as free of guilt as it is possible to be [Elle était aussi peu coupable qu'il est possible]" (5:1108, 390). Paquita's faithfulness to the bloodline compensates for her falling away from same-sex fidelity to the sister and for her implicit attack on the masculinity of the brother. That is, faithfulness to the bloodline here trumps anything we might think of as possessiveness regarding sexual identity.

Balzac may well have both a historical and an epistemological point to make. Regarding the historical point, it seems similar to the one Proust's narrator makes in *La Prisonnière* when the bourgeois Verdurins try to shame Charlus in front of his aristocratic friends for his sexual relations with the plebeian Morel. As Proust's narrator puts it, etiquette trumps scruples. There is a possible place for and a possible way of recognizing and assimilating same-sex practices within the aristocratic ethos, especially when the family (with its "identité pleinement consciente") is threatened from the outside. The bourgeois system for understanding sexuality (the one that Felman seems unwittingly to universalize) is not the only one at people's disposal. It is only slowly coming into being.

The epistemological point in *La Fille aux yeux d'or* has something to do with the rapidity with which brother and sister assimilate into something unremarkable the various sexual histories that meet in their confrontation. There is no surprise or self-consciousness or shame expressed about anything that anyone else might construe as a "vice," nor is there any narrative punishment meted out to either of them—they even get away with murder. In this regard, the tabloid sensibilities of one segment of the reading public might be less than satisfied. We might say of Henri and Eu-

phémie (as of the story itself) that they are not fully heterosexualized. And this is the paradox of the story, as well as the paradox of the way it is read by someone like Felman: it is possible for some to be surprised at what is not surprising in the story; it is possible for some to be ignorant of what is not ignored in the story; different ways of knowing and not knowing the world and its sexual relations seem able to coexist without noticing each other. Here history and epistemology perhaps meet, for it will be the work of the rest of the nineteenth century to produce the surprise that Balzac's story does not fully offer—a surprise we have perhaps most clearly seen in the reaction of Heppenstall to the Balzac novel he translates, but a surprise that Felman claims to experience as well. Yet the *lack* of surprise of someone like Henri, who "ne s'effaroucha pas du vice, il le connaissait comme on connaît un ami [took no umbrage at vice, being as familiar with it as one is with a friend]" (5:1096, 377), if it was present in 1815 when the action of the story is set and was available to the story's readers in the 1830s, would surely be worth recovering for today.[20]

Notes

1. The translation from the postface is my own.

2. Fortassier, introduction to *La Fille aux yeux d'or,* 5:771-72.

3. George Sand, *Correspondance inédite George Sand—Marie Dorval,* ed. Simone Andre-Maurois (Paris: Gallimard, 1953), 27. Editors of *La Fille aux yeux d'or* also often point to source material in *Souvenirs et mémoires* by the countess Merlin, whose salon Balzac frequented and whose maiden name was Maria de las Mercedes. She was born in Havana, and she mentions in the memoirs (which were published starting in 1836, but which Balzac may have read in manuscript or heard read in a salon) an aunt she had named Paquita, as well as another relative in Madrid named Mariquita (see 5:775 of *La Comédie humaine;* see also Castex's comments in his edition of Balzac's *Histoire des treize,* 362-64). Merlin's memoirs have recently been republished as: *Souvenirs et mémoires de madame la comtesse Merlin: Souvenirs d'une créole,* ed. Hector Biancotti and Carmen Vásquez (Paris: Mercure de France, 1990): Paquita is found on p. 48; the devout, patriotic, and unmarried Mariquita on pp. 246-53. The countess Merlin was also good friends with Custine. Later in the 1840s, she would compose a book that was both a travelogue and a sociological analysis of the colonial situation in Havana, *La Havane;* sections of which were dedicated to Custine, George Sand, and others. Carmen Vásquez suggests that Merlin was helped in the composition of *La Havane* by the intellectual with whom she was involved at

the time, Philarète Chasles (see *Souvenirs et mémoires,* 12-13). Later in life, Chasles would publish a particularly perfidious set of memoirs that found ways to discuss the sexual deviance of several of his acquaintances. Those memoirs contain a particularly virulent description of Custine:

> Chez la comtesse Merlin, je vis entrer un jour, annoncé comme marquis par le laquais, sans que je saisisse parfaitement son nom, un homme . . . qui s'assit après avoir serré la main de la comtesse. . . . La comtesse avait retiré promptement, mais non vivement sa main, sans presser celle du marquis. La nuance était légère; car dans les mouvements des personnes bien élévées de ces régions il n'y a jamais une brusquerie anguleuse ou une véhémence trop accentuée. . . . Une heure se passa comme une minute; et il prit congé sans bruit, comme les gens du dix-huitième siècle. La comtesse regardait sa petite main et la secouait légèrement. 'Ce pauvre marquis, me dit-elle, il est charmant. Mais je ne peux pas le toucher, sa main me répugne.—Pourquoi?—Elle ne serre pas, elle colle. . . . C'est Custine!—Ah! lui dis-je.' Cette exclamation la fit sourire. Je n'ai connu que depuis lors la véritable vie de cet être extraordinaire et malheureux, problème et type, phénomène et paradoxe, que le vice le plus odieux à mon tempérament chevauchait, domptait, opprimait et ravalait; qui, au vu et au su de toute la société française, y pataugeait, y vivait comme Fiévée avec son ami Théodore Leclerc, qui subissait, tête basse, le mépris public; et qui d'autre côté était, sans se racheter, loyal, généreux, honnête, charitable, éloquent, sprituel, presque philosophe,—distingué, presque poëte. Ces mélanges d'éléments compliqués et contradictoires, fondus dans un même type unique sont fréquents aujourd'hui. Mais jamais je n'ai rien vu de tel que Custine. Mon irrépressible curiosité me poussa donc à connaître ce caractère unique. Mon herbier de cryptogames, ma collection de phénomènes sociaux, mon répertoire de nosologie monstrueuse, n'auraient pas été complets, si ce catholique fervent, ce sensuel mystique, ce talent subtil, poétique, élévé,—perdu dans un vice,—cette conscience austère pliant sous le fardeau de sa honte; cette maladie et cette misère du paria social, tout en pleurs, devant une société qui valait peut-être moins que lui,—avait manqué à mon grand musée d'originaux. Je l'étudiai donc très-attentivement; je le plaignis beaucoup; et je rêvai souvent avec tristesse sur les effets que les vieilles civilisations produisent, sur ce gentilhomme déchu, et sur certains organismes exténués et avachis qui se développent comme les lichens chez les peuples qui finissent.

> [One day at the Countess Merlin's a man whose name I did not catch entered and was announced as a Marquis . . . who sat after taking the countess's hand. The countess had promptly (but not overly quickly) withdrawn her hand without holding onto his. It was a slight nuance, for in the movements of people in these elevated spheres nothing is jarring or overly accentuated. . . . An hour flew by, and he took his leave unostentatiously, like someone from the eighteenth-century. The countess looked at her hand and gave it a little shake. 'The pour Marquis,' she said, 'is a charming fellow. But I cannot bear to touch him; his hand revolts me.' 'But why?' 'It does not take hold of yours; it sticks to you. . . . He's Custine!' 'Ah ha!' I replied. At that she smiled. It was only after this time that I learned the true details of this extraordinary and unhappy fellow's life. He was a type, a problem case, a phenomenon and a paradox, hounded, overtaken, oppressed and swallowed whole by what is for me the most odious vice. In full view of all of French society, he wallowed in this vice, as did Fiévée and his friend Leclerc [*sic*]. He lowered his head and endured the public's scorn. In his own way, he was, without in any way redeeming himself, loyal, generous, honest, charitable, eloquent, witty, philosophical, even,—distinguished, practically a poet. These odd complicated and contradictory mixtures are common nowadays. But I had never seen a case like Custine. I was led on by my irrepressible curiosity to get to know this unique fellow. My herbarium of cryptogams, my collection of social phenomena, my repertory of monstrous nosologies would have been incomplete had this fervent Catholic, this sensual mystic, this subtle, elevated, poetic talent, lost in vice, this austere conscience weighed down by shame, this sick and miserable social pariah, tearfully facing a society that was perhaps less worthy than he, not been included in my museum of originals. I therefore studied him extremely closely. I felt sorry for him. I often sadly thought of the effects produced by aged civilizations, about this fallen gentleman, about the extenuated and shapeless organisms that develop like lichens among peoples that are coming to an end.]

(Chasles, *Mémoires* [Paris: Charpentier, 1876], 1:308-11)

4. Faderman, *Surpassing the Love of Men,* 456 n.6. Albert Prioult, ed., writing in *La Comédie humaine* (Paris: Hazan, 1950), 11:620. Others who share Prioult's position are Antoine Adam, in *Le Secret de l'aventure vénitienne: La Vérité sur Sand et Musset* (Paris: Perrin, 1938); and René Jasinski, in *Les Années romantiques de Théophile Gautier* (Paris: Vuibert, 1929), esp. 289-326.

5. Arsène Houssaye, *Les Confessions: Souvenirs d'un demi-siècle, 1830-1880* (Paris: Dentu, 1888), 2:13-14.

6. Maurice Regard, *Gustave Planche, 1808-1857: Correspondance, Bibliographie, Iconographie* (Paris: Nouvelles éditions latines, 1955), 71.

7. On the function of melodrama in *La Fille aux yeux d'or*, see the helpful pages in Prendergast's *Balzac*, 63-68. Prendergast concludes his analysis by commenting: "The extension, by way of the analogical play of the text, of the sexual and familial intrigue into the social, and specifically urban, domain of modern life, with its tentative gesture at the comprehension of a whole social structure, marks the first stage in a literary intinerary that will result in deeper and more complex realizations" (68).

8. Balzac's letter to Madame Hanska is from June 28, 1846, *Lettres à Madame Hanska*, 2:232. (Two days earlier he had had dinner with Custine at Madame Merlin's.) Meininger's comments are from *La Comédie humaine* 7:1366-67. (see also 7:24-26). Pauline Duchambge was a composer who set to music poems by, among many others, Desbordes-Valmore and Custine. In an article written shortly after her death, Pierre Hédouin comments ambiguously: "Dans sa première jeunesse, la calomnie, ce fléau des grandes et des petites villes, qui fait la proie de tout ce qu'il y a de distingué, n'a point épargné Mme du Chambge. . . . Tendre rêveuse, un peu romanesque, elle a pu se laisser entraîner par excès de sentiment et de pitié, mais son cœur est resté pur de toute action pouvant torturer sa conscience [In her early youth, she was not spared calumny, that scourge of both small and large towns that attaches itself to anyone of any distinction. . . . Perhaps, being a tender-hearted dreamer, and taken with novels, she let herself be drawn to certain excesses of feeling and of pity, but her heart remained unsullied by any action that might have tortured her conscience]" (Hédouin, *Mme Pauline du Chambge* [Paris: Mourgues, 1858], 5). Hédouin also recounts that Duchambge kept many souvenirs from old friends in her apartment, including a model of the spiral staircase from the set of the first production of Vigny's *Chatterton*, a play that starred Marie Dorval, and which included a famous bit of acting in which Dorval's character, Kitty Bell, in a moment of profound emotion, slid down the staircase.

9. Balzac, *Honoré de Balzac in Twenty-Five Volumes: The First Complete Translation into English* (New York: Collier, 1900), 12:7. Harper and Row apparently also published an American version of Saintsbury's edition of Balzac around the same time. That version did include a translation of *La Fille aux yeux d'or*, and excised the sentence about its inconvenience from the preface.

On the English reception of Balzac, see the helpful work of Sharon Marcus, "Comparative Sapphism," in *The Literary Channel: The International Invention of the Novel*, ed. Margaret Cohen and Carolyn Dever (Princeton: Princeton University Press, 2002), 251-85.

10. The English translation cited here is *The Girl with the Golden Eyes*, in *History of the Thirteen*, trans. Herbert J. Hunt (Harmondsworth: Penguin, 1974). I will often have silently modified the translation.

11. The idea of English prudery was a commonplace in nineteenth-century France, and French writers such as Balzac or Gautier poked fun in particular at the prudery regarding male same-sex relations. It was, in fact, more than prudery. Balzac and Gautier both make plain that men risked their lives in England by having sex with other men. In *La Maison Nucingen*, Balzac writes of a "well-known English lord" who had to fire the handsome young groom to whom he was deeply attached because a journalist wrote an article that suggested there might be something "improper" (not to say inconvenient) in their relationship. From "improper" to the gallows, the narrator of the story notes, is only a short step (6:344-45). Gautier, in his pornographic *Lettre à la Présidente*, about a trip to Italy in 1850, writes of coming across a bottle of oil in the restroom of an inn where a handsome young male servant worked. He deduces that "this oil served to lubricate the behind of this pretty boy, highly sought after by the Englishmen who go to Italy to satisfy their pederastic tastes, which are punished by a rope on their friendly island—a touching attentiveness on the part of their government, which thereby guarantees a few fucks to some Englishwomen who wouldn't get them otherwise [cette huile servait à lubrifier le derrière de ce joli garçon, fort recherché des Anglais qui vont en Italie satisfaire leur goût de pédérastie, punie de la corde dans leur aimable île; attention touchante du gouvernement, qui procure ainsi quelques vieux coups aux Anglaises, qui ne seraient jamais baisées sans cela]" (Gautier, *Lettre à la Présidente: Voyage en Italie, 1850* [n.p.: Les Perspective, n.d.], 13). As we have seen, Stendhal was aware of this situation, and the migrations it caused. See Birnberg, "Stendhal, l'Évêque de Clogher et l'Irlande," esp. 150-51. See also Crompton, *Byron and Greek Love*.

12. Rose Fortassier, the editor of the story for the Pléiade edition, tells us that "Balzac also recycled in *La Fille aux yeux d'or* the text of a 'physiologie' that he offered at the same time to Mme Béchet for her *Nouveau Tableau de Paris au XIXe siècle*" (5:781). Chantal Messol-Dedoin informs us that part of the material had even been published in

1830 in *La Caricature* (Messol-Dedoin, "La Charade et la chimère: Du récit énigmatique dans 'La Fille aux yeux d'or,'" *Poétique* 89 [February 1992]: 32). There are endless examples of this genre at the time, such as *Les Français peints par eux-mêmes* (1840-1842) or *Paris; ou, Le Livre des cent-et-un* (1831-1832). See Judith Wechsler, *A Human Comedy: Physiognomy and Caricature in Nineteenth-Century Paris* (Chicago: University of Chicago Press, 1982).

13. One could profitably compare the kiss between brother and sister at the end of *La Fille aux yeux d'or* with the kiss between two sisters at the end of part 2 of *Lélia*.

14. Balzac, *Lettres à Madame Hanska*, 1:196.

15. Valconseil, *Revue analytique et critique des romans contemporains* (Paris: Gaume frères, 1845), 90; cited by Ezdinli, "Rumor and Reputation." Ezdinli suggests persuasively that this 1845 volume collects articles published much earlier in the press.

16. Shoshana Felman, *What Does a Woman Want?* 18. See also Messol-Dedoin, who in "La Charade et la chimère" states that "the point of departure for the story is a mysterious situation that requires clarification" (35).

17. See also Owen N. Heathcote, "The Engendering of Violence and the Violation of Gender in Honoré de Balzac's *La Fille aux yeux d'or,*" *Romance Studies* 22 (autumn 1993): 99-112.

18. It seems unlikely that Balzac actually imagined sex between women to be non-penetrative, if only given the evidence that he was a reader of Sade (to whom de Marsay makes an oblique reference within *La Fille aux yeux d'or*). Yet it serves his purpose to portray the sex between Paquita and Euphémie as non-penetrative, because to do so provides a mechanism for dropping hints about the sexual relation between the two women (as in the sentence about Paquita being a virgin, but not an innocent one). Moreover, it also allows him to link Euphémie's possessiveness about Paquita's virginity to an aristocratic ethos concerned with blood lines; allows Euphémie to ascertain physically from Paquita's body that she has been "unfaithful"; and allows for an ending to the story that is all the more lurid.

19. Felman, *What Does a Woman Want?* 60.

20. A similar kind of reading of the story *Sarrasine*, written a few years before *La Fille aux yeux d'or*, can be offered. *Sarrasine* was, of course, transformed into one of Balzac's most well-known texts by Roland Barthes, who reprinted it and subjected it to a bravura line-by-line analysis in *S/Z: An Essay* (trans. Richard Miller [New York: Hill and Wang, 1974]). Like *La Fille aux yeux d'or,* *Sarrasine* shows an analytic as well as a melodramatic interest in sexual forms that are passing into obscurity, and in the effects of the uneven distribution of knowledge that remains about those increasingly little-known forms. As is the case with *La Fille aux yeux d'or,* it is possible melodramatically to overread the story's emphasis on *enigma* ("the mystery of the Lantys [l'histoire énigmatique de la maison Lanty] presented a continuing source of curiosity, rather like that contained in the novels of Ann Radcliffe" [6:1046; *S/Z*, 224]), and so miss the story's interest in the ways the enigma experienced by certain characters (Sarrasine and Béatrix Rochefide, to whom his story is narrated) is not a generalized or a generalizable one but is produced by the social and historical forces bearing on their specific persons. *Sarrasine,* like *La Fille aux yeux d'or,* can be read as a story investigating the social distribution of ideologies and epistemologies of sexuality, of historical knowledge about sexuality's evolving forms. It performs a demonstration of the way that distribution shifts over time and thereby affects our abilities to perceive and act in the world.

Sarrasine is, of course, filled with clues to the "shocking revelation" at the story's end, just as is *La Fille aux yeux d'or*. At the party at which the story opens, Marianina sings the cavatina from Rossini's *Tancrède,* one of Rossini's most famous contralto trouser roles—the kind of role that would, in an only slightly earlier period, have been sung by a castrato. Within certain circles in Balzac's moment (within even narrower circles in our moment) this reference would have been clear. Gautier's poem "Contralto," in *Émaux and Camées,* which explicitly links the question of that kind of voice to sexual indeterminacy, makes clear that this frame of reference was active and available to Balzac's readers. When Prince Chigi finally forces Sarrasine to notice what Zambinella is, the prince understands Sarrasine to be astonishingly ignorant: "Where do you come from? Has there ever been a woman on the Roman stage? And don't you know about the creatures who sing female roles in the Papal States?" (6:1072; *S/Z*, 250). As Roland Barthes puts it, "ignorant of the code of Papal customs, Sarrasine dies from a gap in knowledge" (*S/Z*, 185). Yet Barthes's analysis moves toward the psychoanalytic rather than the historical or sociological: "To make *being-castrated,* an anecdotal condition, coincide with *castration,* a symbolic structure, is the task successfully carried out by the performer (Balzac), since the former does not entail the latter" (*S/Z,*

163-64). This allows a universalizing conclusion that might recall Felman's: "*Sarrasine* represents the very confusion of representation, the unbridled (pandemic) circulation of signs, of sexes, of fortunes" (*S/Z*, 216). Yet such universalizing is only possible by implicitly insisting that the single critical point of view on the story somehow coincide with a particular point of view within the story: that of Sarrasine, or that of a reader not sufficiently informed (i.e., not having had a particular formation), or that of a reader drawn to melodramatic scenes of what we have learned to think of as castration anxiety, a form of social policing that usually functions in the service of very precise historical interests. Those historical interests are invested in certain aspects of Balzac's oeuvre, without, however, having a monopoly over it.

Deborah Houk Schocket (essay date 2005)

SOURCE: Houk Schocket, Deborah. "Seduction's Power Games: Domination and the Social Order." In *Modes of Seduction: Sexual Power in Balzac and Sand*, pp. 104-34. Madison, N.J.: Farleigh Dickinson University Press, 2005.

[*In the following excerpt, Schocket analyzes Balzac's unconventional characterization of erotic domination and submission in* The Girl with the Golden Eyes.]

POLARITY UNGROUNDED IN *LA FILLE AUX YEUX D'OR*

In *La Fille aux yeux d'or* (*FYO*) Balzac creates a setting for erotic relations that play with masculine and feminine positions. A seemingly straightforward opposition gets contaminated, and subversive ambiguity takes over as the reigning principle. Here domination and submission do not take the path of gender complementarity traditionally imagined for these polar opposites in patriarchal ideology. Instead, the partners Henri de Marsay and Paquita Valdes oscillate between dominant and submissive positions. This phenomenon is even prefigured by the text's opening section on the different spheres of Parisian society, where the narrator carefully differentiates between hierarchical circles only to admit later that these categories are plagued by a seepage from one to the other, as some people rise on the social ladder while others fall. Moreover, the two coveted objects of desire in this society, gold and pleasure, are also assigned a changing relationship in rhetorical terms; first it is "l'or et le plaisir" (*FYO*, 1040) [gold and pleasure], then "le plaisir et l'or" (*FYO*, 1045) [pleasure and gold]. The theoretical principles of the prologue establish a link between it and the seduction narrative that follows, for throughout this text Balzac proceeds by evoking contrasting terms whose opposition proves unstable.

Early in the story, many elements suggest that the reader is presented with a traditional tale of the Don Juan-esque seducer who envisions seduction as a game of conquest and Paquita as "yet another" victim to add to his list (*FYO*, 1064). Success has left de Marsay bored, and, in a situation that recalls Sand's Raymon de Ramière, the obstacles surrounding de Marsay's project to seduce Paquita seem to excite him more than the woman herself. After first meeting her in the Tuileries gardens, he does not immediately follow Paquita's carriage to determine her identity; rather, he lets the enigma surrounding his new erotic interest subsist. When his servant, Laurent, informs him of the tremendous obstacles blocking the path to Paquita, de Marsay is overjoyed by the challenge this project presents him. He thus proceeds in his pursuit of Paquita as if he were cast in "l'éternelle vieille comédie" (*FYO*, 1071) [the eternal old play] of triangular rivalry with another man. And, through the use of military rhetoric, the narrator links this text to mythical representations of masculine seduction.

However, de Marsay's own behavior suggests that he is not quite the dominating seducer the text sometimes represents him to be. Further, the narrator's physical description of him evokes the image of an effeminate man by its notation of such details as "une peau de jeune fille, un air doux et modeste, une taille fine et aristocratique, de fort belles mains" (*FYO*, 1057) [a young girl's skin, a sweet and modest air, a thin and aristocratic waist, very beautiful hands]. In describing his first encounter with Paquita to his friend Paul de Manerville, de Marsay positions himself as her object of desire, a status most often gendered feminine. For instance, he envisions Paquita as the image that inspired the artist who created *La femme caressant sa chimère* and calls her "cette fille dont je suis la chimère" (*FYO*, 1065) [this girl whose chimera I am], further objectifying himself. However, Paquita does not continuously occupy the dominant position in de Marsay's fantasies, for in this same conversation he describes how Paquita's expression seemed to tell him submissively, "Prends-moi, je suis à toi" (*FYO*, 1064). [Take me, I belong to you.] Thus, for this seducer, domination and submission are not mutually exclusive principles.

The series of three meetings de Marsay has with Paquita involves a vacillation between conventional masculine and feminine sexual roles; de Marsay and Paquita alternately adopt the positions of domination and surrender. In effect, their relationship is marked by the kind of mutual tension Daniel Sibony evokes as a feature of seduction when he writes, "[I]n seduction, one cannot say who is the seducer and who is the seduced, who began and who is at the beginning. . . ."[1] The first time de Marsay goes to see Paquita, he does so motivated by a desire to obtain an *emprise* over her. The narrator paints the portrait of a powerfully dominating man: "De Marsay exerçait le pouvoir auto-cratique du despote oriental. [. . .] Henri pouvait ce qu'il voulait dans l'intérêt de ses plaisirs et de ses vanités" (***FYO,*** 1084-85). [De Marsay exercised the autocratic power of the oriental despote. . . . Henri could do whatever he wanted in the interest of his pleasure and his vanity.] However, in their second meeting, the dynamics of control and submission have subtly shifted, a difference signaled at the very mo-ment de Marsay submits to being blindfolded and pas-sively led to Paquita. Rather than a true reversal, though, their roles are marked by a mutual give-and-take. At one moment, de Marsay appears to have re-gained the master's position, with Paquita as his sub-missive slave: "Comme un aigle qui fond sur sa proie, il la prit à plein corps, l'assit sur ses genoux, et sentit avec une indicible ivresse la voluptueuse pression de cette fille dont les beautés si grassement développées l'enveloppèrent doucement" (***FYO,*** 1089). [Like an eagle that pounces on its prey, he took her in his arms, seated her on his knees, and felt with an inexpressible intoxication the voluptuous pressure of this girl whose generously developed beauty sweetly enveloped him.] But no sooner has he seemingly established his posi-tion of dominance than he senses that he is not the reigning master in his lover's boudoir. Paquita reas-serts herself by asking him repeatedly, "Veux-tu me plaire?" (***FYO,*** 1089, 1091). [Do you want to please me?] Her fancy of dressing de Marsay as a woman adds a gender-bending twist to the tale of erotic domi-nation. In the course of this exchange, de Marsay comes to the realization that Paquita represents a co-existence of contradictory terms: "l'union si bizarre du mystérieux et du réel, de l'ombre et de la lumière, de l'horrible et du beau, du plaisir et du danger, du para-dis et de l'enfer" (***FYO,*** 1091) [the strange union of mysterious and real, of shadow and light, of the hor-rible and beauty, of pleasure and danger, of paradise and hell]. If the text emphasizes Paquita's hybrid na-ture as someone who is virginal without, somehow, being innocent, one cannot forget that de Marsay's masculinity has certainly not been homogeneous itself. Thus, Balzac does not portray a seduction that simply subverts masculine domination, but instead offers a more complicated picture.

Balzac's representation of the third meeting between de Marsay and Paquita reveals a divergence from the traditional eroticism of seduction that serves to bolster the seducer's subjectivity. The intensity of this en-counter causes de Marsay to lose the control of his senses he had previously fought so hard to maintain. At this point, eroticism seems to have exerted itself above and beyond the will of the people involved, tak-

ing them past a game of rational control to a point where neither one dominates. However, de Marsay re-ceives a startling blow when Paquita, looking at him, cries out "Oh! Mariquita!" (***FYO,*** 1102). Due to this symbolically violent attack on de Marsay's sense of masculinity, one would expect his identity as a confi-dent seducer to be completely destroyed. Indeed, the narrator does not hide the crushing significance of this event: "L'exclamation de Paquita fut d'autant plus horrible pour lui qu'il avait été détrôné du plus doux triomphe qui eût jamais agrandi sa vanité d'homme" (***FYO,*** 1104). [Paquita's exclamation was all the more horrible for him in that he had been dethroned from the sweetest triumph that had ever increased his male vanity.] Because vanity is such a large part of the se-ducer's sense of self, as we also saw in the case of Sand's Raymon, de Marsay is struck at the very core of his subjectivity. In this narrative, then, the effects of uncontrolled eroticism are compounded by Paquita's revelation, robbing the seducer of the sweetness of his triumph.

In contrast, the controlled eroticism of seductions that take the form of erotic domination effectively protects against the chaos of a violent eroticism that, according to Georges Bataille, confronts the subject with a break-down of the limits of the individual self. For Bataille, "Sexual activity is a moment of isolation crisis. This activity is known to us from the outside, but we know that it weakens the sense of self, that it puts it in ques-tion."[2] Seducers who aim to dominate their victims are preoccupied by issues of their own subjectivity and use seduction to reinforce their sense of self. They do not seek to experience the weakening of the bound-aries of the self that Bataille describes. By taking a controlling approach to erotic relations they are essen-tially trying to gain recognition of their agency while simultaneously skirting the self-threatening potential of sexual activity. Taking Bataille's work on eroticism as a point of departure, Benjamin describes the protec-tive aspect control assumes in the context of sadomas-ochistic relations:

> Excitement runs in the *risk* of death, not in death itself. And it is erotic complementarity that offers a way to si-multaneously break through and preserve the bound-aries: in the opposition between violator and violated, one person maintains his boundary and the other allows her boundary to be broken. One remains rational and in control, while the other loses her self. Put another way, complementarity protects the self.[3]

These same words could be applied to domination in seduction, underscoring the fact that the sexual experi-ence is not the main goal of seduction; instead, a se-ducer seeks power, control, and domination. The oth-er's submission serves to affirm the seducer's sense of self and feelings of desirability. Motivated by anxiety, the dominating seducer tries to affirm the opposite by performing an identity that displays confident self-assurance. In effect, seduction as domination serves to tame eroticism and disguise the subject's fundamental fragility.

While Balzac created this outbreak of chaotic forces in his text, by the conclusion he has eliminated the subversive elements from his narrative. He evokes a feminine sexuality whose power is threatening to men, but then reduces this force that menaces masculine domination. Following the marquise's murder of Paquita, the text isolates this violent and sexually deviant woman by having her withdraw to a convent. The restoration of masculine power is further signaled by de Marsay's resumption of a normal life: his return to the Tuileries gardens where he can see and be seen by other fashionable people in Paris, and potentially can find a future object for seduction. The social order gets restored, and traditional power structures reassert themselves; the man's life will continue as usual, whereas the women involved end up murdered or in self-exile. But this return to "normalcy" could only take place by dint of the text's previous revelation of the potential for disorder. De Marsay is not entirely a Don Juan-esque figure, nor is Paquita's identity that of the submissive female promoted by patriarchy; instead, both lie somewhere in between. In her analysis of the text from the perspective of psychoanalysis, Shoshanna Felman reads Balzac's narrative as a dramatization of sexual difference, and she writes, "[F]emininity is uncanny in that it is not the opposite of masculinity but *that which subverts the very opposition of masculinity and femininity.*"[4] In this light, femininity appears as a disruptive force, one that subverts the smooth functioning of the masculine social order. At least in its initial stages, then, Paquita's version of femininity allows this seduction to proceed in such a way that the domination and power asymmetry are not locked into traditionally gendered positions, but instead allow for playful reversibility.

Even the fact that the status quo of masculine domination gets restored in the end does not erase the significance of Balzac's representation of alternative possibilities for the configuration of relations between the sexes. *La Fille aux yeux d'or* reveals that masculine domination is not an essential ingredient in sexual relations, thereby exposing the constructed nature of the patriarchal social order. Although Balzac portrays these alternatives as threatening, he also reveals their fascinating appeal. This tendency to expose multiple perspectives, even to evoke possibilities he does not personally espouse, is true for the writer's works on a larger scale as well. Commenting on Balzac's relatively undogmatic approach to representing society, Pierre Barbéris has observed: "*La Comédie humaine,*

in effect, is not a peremptory and monocolored work; it does not flow in one direction. If Balzac had been royalist or republican, . . . he would not have written *La Comédie humaine.* He then would only have seen one side of things, and his work would be psychologically and sociologically dead."[5] Indeed, Balzac's works display great diversity in the sexual, political, and social ideas they represent. Balzac seems to delight in exploring the ambiguities of human nature and social interaction. By letting his desire to reproduce society as he observed it drive his narratives rather than being ruled by a fixed moral or social agenda, Balzac expanded the horizons of nineteenth-century narrative.

Notes

1. Daniel Sibony, *Le féminin et la séduction* (Paris: Le Livre de Poche, 1987), 9.

2. Georges Bataille, *L'érotisme* (Paris: Editions de Minuit, 1967), 110.

3. Jessica Benjamin, *The Bonds of Love: Psychoanalysis, Feminism, and the Problem of Domination* (New York: Pantheon, 1988), 64.

4. Shoshanna Felman, "Textuality and the Riddle of Bisexuality (Balzac, 'The Girl with the Golden Eyes')," in *What Does a Woman Want?* (Baltimore: Johns Hopkins University Press, 1993), 65; italics in the original.

5. Pierre Barbéris, *Mythes balzaciens* (Paris: Librairie Armand Colin, 1972), 245.

FURTHER READING

Criticism

Belenky, Masha. "Gender Reversals: Reading Balzac with Rachilde." In *Visions/Revisions: Essays on Nineteenth-Century French Culture,* edited by Tim Unwin and Jennifer Yee, pp. 275-86. Oxford: Peter Lang, 2003.

Compares Balzac's treatment of women and jealousy in *The Girl with the Golden Eyes* with portrayals of these themes by other nineteenth-century authors.

Houk, Deborah. "Self Construction and Sexual Identity in Nineteenth-Century French Dandyism." *French Forum* 22, no. 1 (January 1997): 59-73.

Investigates dandyism in *The Girl with the Golden Eyes* and in texts by Charles Baudelaire, Charles-Marie-Georges Huysmans, and Rachilde.

Majewski, Henry F. "Painting as Intertext in Balzac's *La Fille aux yeux d'or.*" *Symposium: A Quarterly Journal in Modern Literatures* 45, no. 1 (spring 1991): 370-84.

Examines the role of painting and analyzes the influence of Eugène Delacroix in *The Girl with the Golden Eyes.*

Mortimer, Armine Kotin. "Problems of Closure in Balzac's Stories." *French Forum* 10, no. 1 (January 1985): 20-39.

Discusses the endings of several short works by Balzac, including *The Girl with the Golden Eyes.*

Additional coverage of Balzac's life and career is contained in the following sources published by Thomson Gale: *Authors and Artists for Young Adults*, Vol. 68; *Beacham's Guide to Literature for Young Adults*, Vol. 14; *Contemporary Authors*, Vol. 124; *Contemporary Authors—Brief Entry*, Vol. 104; *Dictionary of Literary Biography*, Vol. 277; *DISCovering Authors*; *DISCovering Authors 3.0*; *DISCovering Authors: British*; *DISCovering Authors: Canadian Edition*; *DISCovering Authors Modules*, Eds. DRAM, MST; *Drama Criticism*, Vol. 9; *Drama for Students*, Vol. 1, 5, 10, and 12; *Encyclopedia of World Literature in the 20th Century*, Ed. 3; *European Writers*, Vol. 7; *Exploring Short Stories*; *Literature and Its Times*, Vol. 3; *Literature and Its Times Supplement*, Ed. 1:1; *Literature Resource Center*; *Reference Guide to Short Fiction*, Ed. 2; *Reference Guide to World Literature*, Eds. 2 and 3; *Short Stories for Students*, Vol. 5, 13, and 14; *Short Story Criticism*, Vol. 2, 28, 41, 51, and 85; *Something about the Author*, Vol. 90; *Twayne's World Authors*; *Twentieth-Century Literary Criticism*, Vol. 3, 10, 31, 55, 96, and 163; and *World Literature Criticism.*

Adolfo Bioy Casares
1914-1999

(Also wrote under the pseudonyms Martín Sacastru, Javier Miranda, B. Suárez Lynch, B. Lynch Davis, H. Bustos Domecq, and Honorio Bustos Domecq.) Argentinean short story writer, novelist, essayist, and screenwriter.

For further discussion of Bioy Casares's short fiction, see *SSC,* Volume 17.

INTRODUCTION

Bioy Casares's highly imaginative stories blend science fiction, fantasy, and mystery to comment on social and political conditions in his native Argentina. His best-known work, the novella *La invención de Morel* (1940; *The Invention of Morel*), was praised by Julio Cortázar, Gabriel García Márquez, and Octavio Paz, and is recognized as a masterpiece of fantastic fiction. The futuristic tale about a man who falls in love with a virtual woman contains elements of realism and fantasy, and opened up an important new phase in the development of Latin American fiction. Bioy Casares's work was also admired by his friend, mentor, and collaborator, Jorge Luis Borges, but it is still relatively unknown outside Latin America. Most critical discussion of Bioy Casares's short fiction in English has focused on *The Invention of Morel* and the novella *Plan de evasión* (1975; *Plan for Escape*). Critics have discussed the author's innovative and complex plots; his treatment of simultaneity (the occurrence of past, present, and future at the same time), time travel, invisibility, metamorphosis, and other supernatural happenings; and his explorations of love, identity, human nature, and the absurdity of the human condition.

BIOGRAPHICAL INFORMATION

Bioy Casares was born in Buenos Aires to wealthy parents. His father frequently read gaucho epics to him when he was a boy. At an early age Bioy Casares began to compose stories and poetry that revealed a fascination with the supernatural. His first published work, *Prólogo* (1929; *Prologue*), edited by his father and published at his father's expense, appeared when he was only fifteen. One of the most significant events

of Bioy Casares's life was meeting Borges at the home of Victoria Ocampo, a fiction writer and publisher of the literary magazine *Sur.* Bioy Casares was only seventeen, Borges thirty-two, but the two began a friendship and mentorship. Bioy Casares also began a relationship with Ocampo's sister, Silvina, who was eleven years his senior; the two would eventually marry in 1940. Borges's encouragement led Bioy Casares to transfer from the study of law to philosophy and literature, and ultimately, to choose a writing career. Rejecting the then-prevalent historical approach to literary criticism, Bioy Casares and Borges in 1936 began a magazine of avant-garde criticism called *Destiempo* (*Out of Time*). Although the magazine did not remain in circulation for long, it initiated their collaboration on a variety of projects such as short stories; anthologies of Argentinean fantastic fiction, detective stories, and their favorite gaucho poetry; and *Cuentos breves y extraordinarios* (1955; *Extraordinary Tales*), a miscellany of quotes and epigrams by popular writers from classical to modern times. In 1990 Bioy Casares's outstanding literary career was recognized with the prestigious Cervantes Prize, the highest distinction for writers in Spanish. He died in 1999 in Buenos Aires.

MAJOR WORKS OF SHORT FICTION

In Bioy Casares's short fiction, the characters experience what one critic has described as an "adventure . . . whether plausible or fantastic, in order to reveal their cosmic puniness." In *Guirnalda con amores* (1959; *A Garland of Love*), Bioy Casares deals with issues of identity and the comic ironies that surround romantic love. Several of the stories use politics as a subplot to the major drama, as in a collection written with Borges entitled *Seis problemas para don Isidro Parodi* (1942; *Six Problems for Don Isidro Parodi*). The protagonist in *Six Problems* solves crime mysteries through deductive reasoning from a prison cell, having been framed for a murder committed by a public official. In *Plan for Escape,* set on a small island off the coast of French Guiana, the protagonist, Enrique Nevers, attempts to observe the activities of the French governor who is stationed on nearby Devil's Island. The novella centers on Nevers's changing perceptions and the disparity between what he knows and what is actually taking place. The governor, in fact, is overseeing a surgical experiment that produces permanent synaesthesia in prisoners on the island.

Bioy Casares's interest in film and the medium's capacity for mimicking dreams and fantasy figures prominently in his most famous work, the novella *The Invention of Morel.* Inspired by the author's obsession with the silent movie actress Louise Brooks, it tells of a man who falls in love with a woman projected by a machine that transforms people into holographic images of themselves. The novella uses Bioy Casares's trademark techniques of concise dialogue, brief sentences, and an omniscient narrator who comments on events about which the protagonist is unaware. In the short story "El otro laberinto," collected in *La trama celeste* (1948; *The Celestial Plot*), the metaphysical phenomena of temporal simultaneity and time travel serve as ways to solve the mystery of a death that took place centuries earlier. *Crónicas de Bustos Domecq* (1967; *Chronicles of Bustos Domecq*) features vignettes and fictional essays satirizing modern aesthetic theories and figures from Argentinean literary and artistic circles.

CRITICAL RECEPTION

Bioy Casares began publishing his writing when he was a teenager, but it was not until the appearance of *The Invention of Morel* that he attracted wide notice. Borges declared the novella a masterpiece of plotting, compared it to works by Henry James and H. G. Wells, and said he found it to be "perfect." Cortázar, Márquez, Paz, Juan Carlos Onetti, Alejo Carpentier, and other literary luminaries have praised it highly, declaring that it ushered in a new phase of Latin American fiction, one that blended realism with elements of the supernatural. The story was also an important inspiration for the avant-garde film *Last Year in Marienbad* (1961) by Alain Resnais and Alain Robbe-Grillet. Initially, critics regarded Bioy Casares's social criticism and satires of Argentinean political society as too obscure, but more recent studies of the fiction praise his inventive plots, sardonic humor, and concise language.

Despite his renown in Argentina, Bioy Casares has still not received much attention in English-speaking countries. His collaborative works with Borges have tended to emphasize Borges's authorship and commentators therefore focus on Borges's contribution. English-language criticism of his short fiction has focused on the use of the fantastic and the treatment of time and time travel. Critics have noted the influence

of Wells, and one scholar has argued that the "island novellas," *The Invention of Morel* and *Plan for Escape,* are carefully constructed parodies of H. G. Wells's *The Island of Dr. Moreau.* Bioy Casares has a small but ardent following among lovers of science fiction, and a new edition of *The Invention of Morel* appeared in 2003.

PRINCIPAL WORKS

Short Fiction

Prólogo (short stories and essays) 1929

Diecisiete disparos contra lo porvenir [*Seventeen Shots against the Future*] [as Martin Sacastru] 1933

Caos [*Chaos*] 1934

La nueva tormenta; o, La vida multiple de Juan Ruteno (novella) 1935

Luis Greve, muerto [*Luis Greve, Deceased*] 1937

La invención de Morel [*The Invention of Morel*] (novella) 1940

Seis problemas para don Isidro Parodi [*Six Problems for Don Isidro Parodi*] [with Jorge Luis Borges] 1942

Los mejores cuentos policiales [*The Greatest Detective Stories*] [editor, with Jorge Luis Borges] 1943

Dos fantasias memorables [*Two Memorable Fantasies*] [with Jorge Luis Borges, published under the joint pseudonym H. Bustos Domecq] 1946

La trama celeste [*The Celestial Plot*] 1948

Las visperas de Fausto 1949

Cuentos breves y extraordinarios [*Extraordinary Tales*] [with Jorge Luis Borges] (quotations, epigrams, and stories) 1955

Historia prodigiosa [*Prodigious History*] 1956

Guirnalda con amores: cuentos [*A Garland of Love: Stories*] 1959

El lado de la sombra [*The Shady Side*] 1962

Crónicas de Bustos Domecq [*Chronicles of Bustos Domecq*] [with Jorge Luis Borges] 1967

El gran serafin [*The Great Seraph*] 1967

Historias de amor (short stories) 1972

Plan de evasión [*A Plan for Escape*] (novella) 1975

Historias fantásticas 1976

Nuevos cuentos de Bustos Domecq [with Jorge Luis Borges] 1977

El héroe de la mujeres [*The Hero and the Woman*] 1978

Historias desaforadas [*Colossal Stories*] 1986

Una muñeca Rusa [*A Russian Doll and Other Stories*] 1991

Selected Stories 1994

Other Major Works

Antologia de la literatura fantástica [*The Book of Fantasy; Anthology of Fantastic Literature*] [editor, with Silvina Ocampo and Jorge Luis Borges] (anthology) 1940

El perjurio de la nieve [*The Perjury of Snow*] (novel) 1944

Los que aman, odian [*Those Who Love, Hate*] [with Silvina Ocampo] (screenplay) 1946

El sueño de los héroes [*The Dream of Heroes*] (novel) 1954

Diario de la guerra del cerdo [*Diary of the War of the Pig*] (novel) 1969

Dormir al sol [*Asleep in the Sun*] (novel) 1975

La aventura de un fotografo en La Plata [*The Adventures of a Photographer in La Plata*] (novel) 1985

Diccionario del Argentino Exquisito [*Dictionary of the Exquisited Argentine*] 1990

CRITICISM

Suzanne Jill Levine (essay date spring-summer 1981)

SOURCE: Levine, Suzanne Jill. "Science Versus the Library in *The Island of Dr. Moreau, La Invención de Morel (The Invention of Morel),* and *Plan de Evasión (A Plan for Escape)."* *Latin American Literary Review* 9, no. 18 (spring-summer 1981): 17-26.

[*In the following essay, Levine analyzes the plots, themes, and characters of Bioy Casares's novellas* The Invention of Morel *and* Plan for Escape *and maintains that they should be viewed as parodies of H. G. Wells's* The Island of Dr. Moreau.]

This paper is part of a lengthy chapter of my dissertation which deals with Bioy Casares' novellas, *La invención de Morel* [*The Invention of Morel*] *(1940) and* **Plan de evasión** [***A Plan for Escape***] *(1945), as parodic reductions or mirrors of H. G. Wells' "scientific romance" The Island of Dr. Moreau.[1] This chapter discusses Bioy and his companion-in-letters, Borges, as readers of Wells and of a whole tradition of utopic literature which encompasses works of Jules Verne, Edgar Allan Poe, Mary Shelley, Johnathan Swift, Daniel Defoe, Voltaire, Shakespeare, and last but not least, Sir Thomas More. Besides analyzing the echoes of Wells and company in the theme, plot, and "characters" of Bioy's novels, I also attempted, in this chapter, to trace*

the spiralling repetitions and variations of certain narrative devices such as *"the first-person account of extraordinary events."*

It is not difficult to discover, in *La invención de Morel* (*M*) and in *Plan de evasión* (*P*), that the scientific content of the experiments carried out in these novels are used as metaphors of a textual experiment. Morel's machine, "scientifically" explained by Morel himself (*M,* 102-115), while prophetic of a scientific possibility, is, as Alfred MacAdam has observed, a metaphor of the work of art.[2] In *Plan,* a similar deception is involved. Castel, governor of the penal colony on an apocryphal Devil's Island and mad scientist in his spare time, takes synesthesia, a psychological and esthetic phenomenon, to unheard-of surgical consequences, making use of scientific theories of William James and Sir Francis Galton. Again, the synesthetic experience of the men in the prison cells works as a metaphor of the experience of the reader of the text, *Plan*: he sees signifiers—words—and interprets them; his interpretation is an illusion. There is no possible way of reaching for an absolute reality beyond the text, because the text, the signifiers, are the only reality within his reach.

Again, Dr. Moreau's experiment, the acceleration of Darwin's laws of evolution through surgery and behavioral conditioning, is, in this case, a metaphor of not a literary reality but a moral truism: man is biologically an animal disguised in a thin layer of training and of biological difference. As Dr. Moreau pontificates:

> Very much, indeed, of what we call moral education is such an artificial modification and perversion of instinct; pugnacity is trained into courageous self-sacrifice, and suppressed sexuality into religious emotion. And the great difference between man and monkey is the larynx . . .
>
> (*Island of Dr. Moreau* [*IDM*], 114)

This "message" is expressed most strongly by the book's apocalyptic close: when Prendick, the hero of the story, finally returns to civilization, he cannot stand the nearness of man in whose gestures he sees the sickening echoes of the beast men, among whom he had been forced to live during his last months on the island. Prendick isolates himself in the country (far from the "animal"-ridden city). Here we can see echoes of Part IV of Gulliver's Travels in which Gulliver prefers life among the horses to life with people. Prendick's last words are:

> I have withdrawn myself from the confusion of cities and multitudes, and spend my days surrounded by wise books, bright windows, in this life of ours lit by the

shining souls of men . . . whatever is more than animal within us must find its solace and its hope. I hope, or I could not live. And so, in hope and solitude, my story ends.

Edward Prendick (*IDM,* 218-219)

It isn't only the metaphoric intention of the scientific experiments in Wells, and more evidently so in Bioy, that make their works more fiction than science. There are also the intrusions of books, and even of the library, which "interfere" with the scientific content. In Bioy's texts, we know that this bookish interference is self-consciously signalled. In Wells, the presence of the book, though not a self-conscious signal, is an inevitable reality—as indeed it is in all literature. For example, when Dr. Moreau "explains" his experiment to the horrified Prendick, he places his "surgical" methods in a "historical" perspective:

A similar operation is the transfusion of blood, with which subject indeed I began. These are all familiar cases. Less so, and probably far more extensive, were the operations of those medieval practitioners who made dwarfs and beggar cripples and show-monsters; some vestiges of whose art still remain in the preliminary manipulation of the young mountebank or contortionist. Victor Hugo gives an account of them in *L'Homme qui rit* . . . But perhaps my meaning grows plain now. You begin to see that it is a possible thing to transplant tissue from one part of an animal to another, or from one animal to another, to alter its chemical reactions and methods of growth, to modify the articulations of its limbs, and indeed to change it in its most intimate structure?

And yet this extraordinary branch of knowledge has never been sought as an end, and systematically by modern investigators, until I took it up! Some such things have been hit upon in the last resort of surgery; most of the kindred evidence that will recur to your mind has been demonstrated, as it were, by accident—by tyrants, by criminals, by the breeders of horses and dogs, by all kinds of untrained clumsy-handed men working for their own immediate ends. I was the first man to take up this question armed with knowledge of the laws of growth.

Yet one would imagine it must have been practised in secret before. Such creatures as the Siamese Twins . . . And in the vaults of the Inquisition. No doubt their chief aim was artistic torture, but some, at least, of the inquisitors must have had a touch of scientific curiosity . . .

(*IDM,* 112-113)

In the midst of a discourse of vivisection, in which scientific words like "grafting," "physiology," and "chemical" are used, Moreau cites as a historical source, Victor Hugo's *L'Homme qui rit* [*The Man Who Laughs*]. And, he also refers to vivisectors as "artistic" torturers who practice an "*extraordinary* branch of knowledge." Both in his sources and his explanations, Moreau's scientific discourse is invaded by the language of art and of literature.

The mention of Hugo is another of the many cross-references which would appear to establish the relationship between Bioy's text *Plan,* and *Dr. Moreau.* In *Plan,* not only is the mention of Hugo synonymous with a mockery of traditional literature, but also a possible salute to the Hugo who appears in Wells, as the fictional source at the basis of Moreau's scientific experiment.

Moreau's "scientific" explanation is Wells' derision of science's pretense to be whole and coherent. It is a mumbo jumbo of scientific ideas mixed in with sadistic obsessions about "artistic torture," and Faustian urges of taking God's creation into his own hands, a collage of Darwin and Victor Hugo. Indeed, Moreau's explanation is not far from the Beast-Men's chant of the Law, a mumbo jumbo of religion and fear which they sing to try to keep themselves from reverting to beastly habits. Moreau criticizes the chant because it is only evidence of their imprisonment in their animality:

There's something they call the Law. Sing hymns about "all thine." . . . But I can see through it all, see into their very souls, and see there nothing but the souls of beasts, beasts that perish—anger, and the lusts to live and gratify themselves . . . It only mocks me . . .

(*IDM,* 125)

If Moreau is mocked by the "Law," a poor simulacrum of civilized thought, he is mocked by his own discourse. It was, after all, Dr. Moreau who implanted certain "fixed ideas" in the heads of the Beast-Men[3]—ideas about what they could and could not do—on which they base their chant. (*IDM,* 128) Indeed, the statement, "It only mocks me," is a possible indication of self-commentary intended by the text. Moreau's science is revealed as myth, and superseded by the fiction of the text. Levi-Strauss' concept of the scientist as myth is already recognized, perhaps not so unconsciously, by the scientist-writer, H. G. Wells. This concept has been described by Jacques Derrida:

The engineer, whom Levi-Strauss opposes to the *bricoleur [tinkerer],* should be the one to construct the totality of his language, syntax, and lexicon. In this sense the engineer is a myth. A subject who would supposedly be the absolute origin of his own discourse and would supposedly construct it "out of nothing," "out of whole cloth," would be the creator of the *verbe* itself. The notion of the engineer who had supposedly broken with all forms of *bricolage [tinkering]* is therefore a theological idea; and since Levi-Strauss tells us that *bricolage* is mythopoetic, the odds are that the engineer is a myth produced by the *bricoleur.*[4]

Moreau, like Wells, the writer-*bricoleur* who brings together Darwin and Hugo to create a text of science and fiction—a Frankenstein stitched-together text—is the scientist-*bricoleur* who brings to life the metaphor of this patchwork activity, the piecing together of parts of animals to create a Frankenstein breed of men. The myth of the scientist, so secure in the fantasies of Jules Verne, is exploded in *Dr. Moreau.*

Bioy Casares, in his "reworkings" of the *Island of Dr. Moreau,* brings to the foreground this exposure of science as myth. Wells at least considered that he was using Darwin's theories as a real pretext to develop a philosophical "message." Bioy, on the other hand, is aware that his starting point is the text that is made from other texts, from *Moreau,* from a whole tradition of utopian-island works. If Moreau's explanations are mumbo jumbo, then Morel's and Castel's explanations are even more apocryphal and fragmentary.

But perhaps one of the most effective images in Wells and in Bioy which reveals the text's progressive awareness (from Wells to Bioy) of its own textuality, is the intrusion of the library upon the scientific adventure. At the beginning of Prendick's adventure on the island of Dr. Moreau, the doctor attempts to distract Prendick from discovering the true nature of the experiment. One of his diversionary tactics is to point Prendick's attention to something else:

> He called my attention to a convenient deckchair before the window, and to an array of old books, chiefly, I found, surgical works and editions of the Latin and Greek classics—languages I cannot read with any comfort—on a shelf near the hammock.
>
> (*IDM,* 45-46)

The first protagonist of **Morel [*The Invention of Morel*]** makes a similar discovery when he first enters the building called the "museum" on the island:

> In one room there is a large but incomplete collection of books, consisting of novels, poetry, drama. The only exception was a small volume (Bélidor, *Travaux: De Moulin Perse,* Paris, 1737), which I found on a green-marble shelf . . . I wanted to read it because I was intrigued by the name *Bélidor,* and I wondered whether the *Mulin Perse* would help me understand the mill I saw in the lowlands of this island.
>
> (*M,* 13-14)

And in **Plan,** Nevers makes a similar discovery during his early explorations of Castel's domain:

> In Castel's library there were books on medicine, on psychology, and some nineteenth-century novels; there were few classics. Nevers was not itnerested in medicine. The only benefit he got out of *Tropical Diseases Made Easy* was a pleasant but ephemeral prestige among the servants in his house . . .
>
> (*P,* 15)

The similarities and differences between the model, Wells' text, and its two parodies, are telling. Dr. Moreau's library, "an array of old books," is really just a selection of useful scientific books, dealing specifically with surgery, which would be guides for his experiments in vivisection, and for more "philosophical" reading, he has some Greek and Latin classics. Their presence too is in keeping with Moreau's "classicism." That is, in his explanation to Prendick, he claims that his ultimate goal is a truly Platonic quest for an ideal, within the principles of Stoicism—the indifference to Pleasure and Pain which justifies his cruel surgery. (*IDM,* 116-124) Moreau carries his surgery to a classically poetic extreme by creating a Satyr-Man, or, as Prendick comments: "The Satyr was a gleam of classical memory on the part of Moreau . . . " (*IDM,* 137) Prendick, a biologist, not a literary man, admits with gentlemanly irony that he is not up to Greek and Latin, though he attempts to read Horace. (*IDM,* 55)

On the other hand, **Morel,** not pretending to have its basis in a scientific reality like Wells' romance, but rather which is inscribed within a science *fiction, Moreau,* contains "bibliotecas inagotables"—that immediately suggest to the Borgesian reader the infinite library of Babel. This library is a parodic reversal of Moreau's not only because of its size, but also its content which is almost all fiction and no science, except for a book titled *Le Moulin Perse* [*The Persian Mill*]. As the **Morel** narrator later explains, it is a book about tides which must have helped Morel figure out how to run his machine by tidal energy—the "molino" [*mill*] on the island exists for that purpose. (*M,* 84-85) The book, whose apparent author is someone named Bernardo Forest de Belidor, is an "invention" of Bioy's—indeed, it would seem an attempt to confuse the reader with the double association to the *Moulin rouge* [*Red Hill*], and Montesquieu's *Les lettres persannes* [*Persian letters*].[5]

In the **Morel** library, the protagonist seems to echo Prendick's complaint about the presence, the intrusion of literary works. He is not a scientist like Prendick, but as he is writing an *Elogio de Malthus [Tribute to Malthus],* his interests would seem to be more scientific than literary. For him, Morel's library is "deficiente" because it doesn't contain scientific works, and indeed, he grabs the only "scientific" work there. Later, as spectator and then actor in Morel's movie, he complains that the lack of scientific information may lead him, in his ignorance, to threaten the immortality of the machine. (*M,* 70) But Morel's library, like Moreau's, is an index of the book's intention: Morel's science is mere pretext; it is its fiction, and not its science, that "immortalizes" it.

Castel's library, which is in many ways more similar to Moreau's than Morel's, contains an element of more complete reversal of the Moreau library. Like the latter, it contains an array of scientific books which would relate to Castel's experiment. Unlike Moreau's, but like Morel's more literary library, it contains novels. Nevers, a more "literary" type than Prendick and than the **Morel** diarist, seems to be in an intermediate position between Prendick and Nevers. Though not a scientist, he seems more interested in science than literature. He specifies that they are nineteenth century novels. He also seems to express disappointment at the lack of classical literary texts, in opposition to both Prendick, who is almost uncomfortable in their presence, and the **Morel** diarist who also disapproves of the abundance of literary books.

Indeed, whereas the **Morel** diarist reads *Le Moulin Perse* throughout his adventure—it is true, more to be able to deal with his immediate situation than for pure scientific interest-Nevers, who brought with him and read briefly the medical book only because of a morbid fear of catching a tropical disease,[6] spends his reading time with the classic text of Plutarch on symbols, *The Treatise of Isis and Osiris.*

Nevers consistently avoids scientific "useful" matters; his own personal library that he brings with him consists mainly of the books of Jules Verne. (*P*, 2) His lack of knowledge of scientific matters is emphasized by the fact that in order to discuss prison matters at the Frinziné party (*P*, 5), he resorts desperately to the Larousse.[7] Nevers' cousin Xavier tries to encourage Nevers to do some solid research writing during his stay on the islands, aware of Nevers' poetizing Bohemian tendencies. (*P*, 16) And Castel criticizes Nevers' wasting his time on Plutarch, and in general denigrates the study of the classics when one should be more involved with the "progress" of modern culture. This is clearly Castel's message when he starts a conversation with Nevers by asking the young man:

> "What are you reading?"
>
> "Plutarch." It was useless to pretend.
>
> "Why are you wasting time? Culture must not be confused with the study of elementary men," pronounced the puppet voice.
>
> "Students of philosophy still pour over Plato's dialogues, and the most demanding readers laugh again and again at Molière's jokes about doctors. The future is black."
>
> "Black, camouflaged," said Nevers shrewdly.
>
> There was a silence. Cut out of weakness, Nevers continued,
>
> "This book interests me. It deals with symbols."
>
> "With symbols? Perhaps. But don't you think that in eighteen hundred years the subject might have been enriched?"
>
> (*P*, 32)

The total belief in scientific progress, already disturbed by the pessimism of Wells in *Moreau*, is certainly undermined here by Nevers' burlesque attitude toward the demogogic words and puppet-like image of Castel, the scientist.

While all three novels are inscribed within the *topos* of the library, it becomes obvious that not only are **Morel** and **Plan** more self-consciously so, but that **Plan** is the more "bookish" of the two. This has already been pointed out in terms of the fact that **Plan** has many more allusions than **Morel**, and also is inscribed within the text of **Morel**, which makes **Plan's** textual texture more dense. This difference between **Plan** and **Morel** is also verified by the comparative treatment of the library. While the **Morel** diarist, like Prendick, rejects the literary texts in the library, Nevers does the opposite by fleeing, *escaping*, from the scientific, and into the literary.

Another indication of the fact that these three novels are enclosed within the library is that their characters, apart from being readers, are writers. Indeed, so is More's Utopia traveler, and Defoe's islander, which again emphasizes the textuality of the whole utopian tradition.

In *Moreau*, Prendick, after all, has left his nephew a "narrative." (*IDM*, vii) Prendick talks about the writing of his "chronicle":

> There is much that sticks in my memory that I could write, things that I would cheerfully give my right hand to forget. But they do not help the telling of the story.
>
> (*IDM*, 199)

Here Prendick is revealing that he is not merely noting down facts, but he is, in a sense, editing the story, according to how he, the writer, thinks it should best be told.

The *topos* of the writer becomes, logically, more dominant in Bioy's self-commentative texts. At the beginning of both **Morel** and **Plan** we discover that the chief characters are writing works of a factual nature, in the case of **Morel**, a *Defensa ante sobrevivientes* [*Apology for Survivors*] and an *Elogio de Malthus* [*Tribute to Malthus*] (*M*, 10), and in the case of **Plan**, an *Addenda a la Monografía sobre los juilcios de Oléron* [*Addenda to the Monograph on the Judgements of Oléron*]." (*P*, 2) *Though Malthus' prophecy of overpopulation and Les jugements d'Oléron*—an anonymous maritime code—are historical referents, these "documentary" projects of both protagonists are as fictional as the adventure they narrate. They are fictional because—as they are never written—they exist only in the text, and because their appearance in the text is a result of their relation to its fictional theme. That is, in *Morel,* Matlthus is mentioned in counterpoint with Morel's invention which is, after all, an antidote to overpopulation since it insures immortality without the need of procreation. The mention of the maritime code relates to *Plan* in that the legality of Nevers' actions as a naval officer and Castel's as governor are among the many elements in question within the complex plot of *Plan.*

However, even in the use of these documentary referents as commentaries on the text, *Plan,* again, is the more self-commentative: the fact that Nevers is writing addenda to a monograph on a document is a kind of joke on the act of writing which is about writing about writing. This burlesque commentary is further compounded when Castel reveals that one of his reasons for wanting Nevers as a collaborator is that he thinks Nevers is the "autor de *Los juicios de Oléron* [author of *The Judgements of Oléron*]." (*P,* 97) This clownish mistake on Castel's part is not a simple joke; if, indeed, Bioy's books are about writing which is about writing, they are about writing as a continuous process that transcends the individual "author." In *Les judgements d'Oléron,* it is the text that matters, not the author, who could be one or many, i.e., a collaboration, like the many works written by "Bustos Domecq." The pseudo-concepts of the *original* and of authorship are surely being mocked here.

What is perhaps most significant about the historical projects of the *Morel* diarist, and of Nevers, is that, as Prendick leaves history behind when he ventures upon Moreau's island, they leave behind these documents, and sacrifice themselves, as writers, to fiction. Or as the *Morel* diarist writes:

> Although I have been making entries in this diary at regular intervals, I have not had a chance to work on the books that I hope to write as a kind of justification for my shadowy life on this earth. And yet these lines will serve as a precaution, for they will stay the same even if my ideas change.

> (*M,* 18)

Though not a dabbler in metaphors and poetry like Nevers, the *Morel* diarist, like Nevers, communicates to the reader "I am a writer." (*M,* 54) He will be immortalized by fiction, not History. Nevers, too, ceases to mention his Addenda and becomes more involved in writing his account. The diarist and Nevers bring to the written page the "inventions" of Morel and Castel whose names unite the science fiction of Wells and the expressionist fiction of Kafka.

Notes

1. Abbreviations:

    M = The Invention of Morel, tr. Ruth L. Simms (Austin: University of Texas Press, 1964).

    P = A Plan for Escape, tr. Suzanne Jill Levine (New York: E. P. Dutton, 1975).

    IDM = The Island of Doctor Moreau (New York: Duffiled and Green, 1933).

2. Alfred MacAdam, "Satire and Self-Portrait," *Modern Latin American Narratives: The Dreams of Reason* (Chicago: University of Chicago Press, 1977), pp. 32-33.

3. Again, another parallel between *Moreau* and *Plan* comes into view. Castel fixes in the minds of his altered men the idea that paradise is a solitary, desert island so that they will enjoy the illusion they will experience. As in Moreau, the fixed idea is parodic of Castel's scientific experiment, a fixed idea in Castel's mind, as well as parodic of the text itself, a "fixed idea" of the writer and the reader.

4. Jacques Derrida, "Structure, Sign, and Play in the Discourse of the Human Sciences," *The Structuralist Controversy* (Baltimore: The Johns Hopkins University Press, 1972), p. 256.

5. The name Bernardo Forest de Belidor suggests a mixture of nationalities (Spanish-French-English) as the names in Bioy often do. Again, this mixture is more Latin American than purely Spanish names, since Latin America, like the U.S., is a melting pot. At the same time the names in *Morel,* like those in *Plan,* suggest a bookish reality. Just to mention a minor character that appears in *Morel,* Jane Gray, for example, could suggest to the reader Mark Twain's *The Prince and the Pauper* where Jane Grey—a real life personage of the Elizabethan court—appears. Bioy's Jane Gray differs by one letter—again, like the modification "l" to "au" in Morel; indeed, his spelling of Gray is the American spelling. (Samuel L. Clemens, *The Prince and the Pauper, The Writings of Mark Twain* (New York & London: Harper & Brothers, 1909), vol. 15.

6. One of his "hypotheses" about the mystery "behind" Castel's activities is that there is an epidemic in the colony and Castel is trying to hide the fact.

7. Resorting to the Larousse (or the Encyclopedia Britannica) is what Bioy does in real life; thus this comic episode at the house of the Frinziné's has certain autobiographical echoes. Indeed, Nevers' bumbling speech on prisons at the Frinziné house is perhaps a repercussion of a bungled public performance that Bioy attempted in his youth. During his student days he was asked by a professor to give a speech in Paris, from memory and in French, for his class. He insisted that he was not good at public speaking, but the professor per-

sisted. Bioy's father quickly copied the speech out of the Encyclopedia Larousse, and Bioy failed miserably to remember his lines. (See "Cronología" in S. J. Levine's *Variations on Topoi: Locus Amoenus,* Pastoral and Romance in Two Works by Adolfo Bioy Casares," Ph.D. diss., 1977, p. 263)

The apparently frivolous joke about Nevers' getting his information from the Larousse involves a constant theme in Borges as well: the use of apocryphal or second-hand erudition, i.e., another form in which the veracity of the text is undermined. The Frinzinés—who represent a colonial cultural mileu that could be a mirror of Argentinian society—are another sign of apocryphal or false knowledge, since while pretending to know about poetry, they admire such a third-rate poet as Ghil. Although Nevers mocks them, his knowledge and sensibility is just as apocryphal: his main source is the Larousse, his favorite poet: also René Ghil.

Maribel Tamargo (essay date fall 1982)

SOURCE: Tamargo, Maribel. "*Plan de evasión*: The Loss of Referentiality." *Hispanic Journal* 4, no. 1 (fall 1982): 105-11.

[*In the following essay, Tamargo argues that in the novella* Plan for Escape *Bioy Casares intentionally undermines the reader's ability to understand the deeper meaning behind the text's mysteries, symbols, and literary allusions.*]

Developing in a tradition in which the very activity of writing is posed as a problem, the contemporary novel offers interesting possibilities regarding the relationship between the text and the reality it describes. The discourse in these texts is not constructed on the appropriation of a referent outside itself; instead it presents itself as the production of its possibilities, limits and forms of articulation. This is what Stephen Heath, in his book on the "nouveau roman," defines as "a shift of emphasis in the novel from a monologistic 'realism' to . . . the practice of writing."[1] Heath later explains the "practice of writing" in this way:

> Its foundation is a profound experience of language and form and the demonstration of that experience in the writing of the novel which, transgressed, is no longer repetition and self-effacement but work and self-presentation as text. Its "realism" is not the mirroring of some reality but an attention to the forms of the intelligibility in which the real is produced, a dramatization of possibilities of language, forms of articulation, limitations of its own horizon.[2]

Bioy Casares' discourse inscribes itself in this tradition, a tradition in which the novel recognizes its autonomy from "reality" and thus, develops parallel to

it, without pretending to capture or repeat it. The novel is no longer the repetition on a mirror but rather the repetition through a mirror. It is useful here to cite a passage from Lewis Carroll's *Through the Looking Glass* which describes Alice as she goes through the mirror:

> Then she began looking about, and noticed that what could be seen from the old room was quite common and uninteresting, but that all the rest was as different as possible. For instance, the pictures on the wall next to the fire seemed to be all alive and the very clock on the chimney piece (you know you can only see the back of it in the Looking Glass) had got the face of a little old man, and grinned at her.[3]

The text's "autonomy" from reality does not imply that it is not the reconstruction of something. For example, *Plan de evasión*,[4] the novel I will deal with in this essay, is the reconstruction (since the events have already taken place and are being recounted) of Enrique Nevers' adventures on Devil's Island. But this reconstruction cannot be compared to the one which a mirror presents, that is to say a reconstruction that hides its mechanisms. *Plan de evasión*'s discourse reconstructs Nevers' story in such a way that the rules of functioning are made manifest. It is for this reason that it is very difficult to imagine a naive reading of this text, since the novel's self-reflexive gesture points to what Roland Barthes has called a "structuralist activity":

> The goal of all structuralist activity, whether reflexive or poetic, is to reconstruct an "object" in such a way as to manifest thereby the rules of functioning (the "functions") of this object.[5]

Let me now take a closer look at the text of *Plan de evasión.* The novel is narrated by Antoine, the uncle of Enrique Nevers. Antoine receives his nephew's letters and pretends to give the reader an objective look at what has taken place. He often quotes directly from the letters and then proceeds to comment in his own words. The sections of Enrique's letters which we are allowed to read directly present him as a paranoic man who is searching for the truth of a mystery he believes exists on the island. His fears never seem to have justification. As a matter of fact, they are never justified by the explanation he gives. Thus, the reader himself becomes suspicious.

On the other hand, Antoine also explains that, through his discourse, he wants to arrive at true events. One of the ways he tries to be objective in his narration is by acting as a chronicler, that is, by including documentation, for example, the text of Castel's experiments. Dr. Castel, the governor of Devil's Island, is developing a series of experiments through which he tries to better the situation of his prisoners. Through a complicated operation he modifies the sensory system of the prisoners so that they perceive their cells as islands where they gain their freedom. Antoine's intention of objectivity is nevertheless betrayed. He states that he wants to help Nevers, but soon after he makes comments that are obviously damaging to his nephew. The following remark is an example: "Debería saber que es el signo de una idiosincrasia que lo distingue, tal vez en la historia de la psicología morbosa" (p. 26).

The dialogue between these two narrators, Enrique Nevers' letters and Antoine's apparent chronicle, integrates the novel. This chronicle has, besides Castel's text, another document: the letter which Xavier Brissac (Enrique's cousin who comes to Devil's Island once Enrique disappears) writes to Antoine. After making several comments that complicate the plot, Xavier Brissac includes a very suggestive paragraph that implicates Antoine in still another complot, underlining once again his unreliability. Brissac writes that he does not hate Nevers, as Antoine insinuates, and that he doesn't want to accuse Antoine:

> No esperes que perdone al autor de esta infamia. Sé que no eres tú. Sé que repetiste lo que te han dicho. Sé, también, que descubriré a quien lo dijo: no eran muchos los que me oyeron hablar.
>
> (pp. 65-66)

The possibilities of **Plan de evasión** lie in the tension produced by this plurality of "tramas" in which none is privileged. The two narrators are in search of the true story, the real story, but they both betray themselves, introducing a doubt about their reliability. They both seem to be hiding something, but that something never appears and the text folds back upon itself, calling attention to its own production, its own *readability*. It has been pointed out that in this text everything is made relative by the presence of the lie. This lie is not present as the opposite of truth, which would be its affirmation, but rather it presents itself as an empty lie, a lie which does not point to a truth but rather to the process of lying.

We have now seen how this text deconstructs the reconstruction that seems to be its intention. This is accomplished through the superposition and interweaving of different versions which are all rendered relative precisely because of the presence of the other versions. In this way it performs what I have called a "structuralist activity."

The mechanism I have studied with respect to the plurality of "tramas" repeats itself in the use of quotations or of names that refer to historical figures or literary characters. To quote or to use a proper name that points to something outside of the text, that is, to give

a symbolic value to a name, is to give depth to the discourse. These references seem to be there in order to give clues to the reader as to how he should interpret the text; that is, they seem to be pointing toward a truth, the true story, or at least the correct version of the story. But they don't point anywhere except at themselves and their own mechanisms.

There are numerous references to this type in the text and any reading of the novel must take them into account. The island where Enrique's adventures take place is none other than Devil's Island in the year 1913. In it he finds a prisoner who goes by the name of Dreyfus. The association is almost too plain. But the relationship with the historical Dreyfus is no more than a confusion, actually a misnaming. The only reason this man is called Dreyfus (we are told this by Antoine who has received the information from Nevers) is because he often talks about Dreyfus even though he does not know anything about the historical figure. This misnaming is made very obvious later on in the novel when Enrique meets another prisoner of the island, a man called Bernheim. Bernheim will tell Enrique: "Yo soy una llaga en la conciencia de Francia" (p. 26) and Enrique replies to Dreyfus: "Entonces a él, y no a usted, habría que llamarlo Dreyfus" (p. 50). Bernheim himself is another reference that misleads the reader. He reminds the reader of the French doctor of the same name who wrote a book entitled *Nature and Uses of Hypnotism*. The association with hypnotic powers makes Bernheim a very suspicious character since he always seems to be planning something, and follows Nevers around in what the latter interprets as an intention of telling him something that he does not want to hear. Antoine writes: "En la noche del 22 no podía dormir. Insomne, atribuyo importancia a la revelación que no quiso oírle a Bernheim" (p. 41). In spite of all this Bernheim will not be privileged, that is to say he will function within the text, he will carry the associations attributed to him but they will never be confirmed.

Literary references are also frequent: Rimbaud, Verlaine and Rene Ghill and from the Symbolist movement; a significant quote from William Blake translated into Spanish: "¿Cómo sabes que el pájaro que cruza el aire no es un inmenso mundo de voluptuosidades, vedado a tus cinco sentidos?" (p. 153); Nevers reads Plutarch's *Tratado de Isis y Osiris* because: "Este libro me interesa. Trata de símbolos" (p. 51); the detective plot is mentioned with regard to the *Misterio del cuarto amarillo;* and finally there is a comparison between Castel and "un anciano debilísimo, con planes para volar la Opera Cómica" (16). As we can see, all these references reinforce the positions of our narrators (and also of the reader) as "decifradores de enigmas," as searchers for a hidden truth.

But this mystery, this truth, escapes the text, denies itself, that is, denies its possibility to exist within the text. Nevers will be permitted to say "cualquier cosa es símbolo de cualquier cosa" and Castel will explain in agreement with Blake's quote:

> Nuestro mundo es una síntesis que dan los sentidos, el microscopio da otra. Si cambiaran los sentidos cambiaría la imagen. Podemos describir el mundo como un conjunto de símbolos capaces de expresar cualquier cosa.
>
> (p. 154)

Rather than symbols, these allusions should be called ciphers, underlining their emptiness. The referent is not important as an end but as a process. What is important is its formulation, its articulation, its functioning. This is not to deny that these references allude to something. They are effective within the text's mechanism precisely because they are obvious references to something specific. It is when these ciphers present themselves, negate themselves and make themselves unreliable, that the reader perceives the game of which he is a part. He perceives the rules of functioning and ceases to be concerned about the content, about the referent of these empty signs. We could now say that Bioy's discourse is a discourse of surface, it takes place on the surface, it lacks depth. It is not the mask of something else that is under it, but rather it is the mask itself.

Thus, the reading of *Plan de evasión* provokes a frustration which is necessarily the effect of a text that eludes being the representation of anything other than itself. Through a play with certain (empty) allusions, which appear to have the intention of revealing truth, yet at the same time undermine such an intention; and by the constant presence of the possible lie, we see that what actually is uncovered is a mechanism in movement. This same effect is produced with respect to the camouflages that Nevers discovers on the island: "la nefasta verdad se reveló: la isla del Diablo estaba camouflada" (p. 20). In reaction to this discovery Nevers writes to his uncle:

> ¿Qué significa esto? . . . ¿Que es un perseguido el gobernador? ¿Un loco? ¿O significa la guerra? . . . Todavía no he visto a Castel, no pude interpelarlo sobre estos camouflages, no pude oír sus mentiras.
>
> (p. 20)

The camouflage is repeated in the cells of the prisoners with whom Castel is doing his experiments. Antoine writes about Nevers' first encounter with the cells: "Confusamente vio en las paredes manchas coloradas, azules, amarillas. Era el famoso 'camouflage' interior (p. 113). *Plan de evasión* is a series of camouflages. First, with respect to its symbols, since even possibilities that are eliminated suggest others and, therefore, go on indefinitely, second, with respect to the different versions which are all called into question, and finally with respect to the camouflaged island itself. Nevers, therefore, is faced with a camouflage of a camouflage, while the reader is faced with an open text. Open because it ends with the word "Etcétera" suggesting the existence of certain information that has not been included. Open, also, because it articulates the reader himself in the complot, implicating him and thus not allowing him to solve the mystery, not allowing him to close the text. The question might now be formulated as to whose plan to escape this is: Nevers', Castel's, the novel's? Nevers himself, when speaking to two prisoners of the island, asks the same question: "¿Castel los preparaba para una evasión?" (p. 90) It is not until the end of the novel, however, that the reader finds out that the escape is accomplished precisely by placing the prisoners in the cells that Castel has constructed:

> Una de las celdas es interior. Si tuviera que encerrarme en una de ellas—escribe Nevers—elegiría esa. Por lo menos estaría libre del caliente horror de los espejos. Alude, con su habitual dramatismo, a los grandes y baratos espejos que hay en las otras celdas. Cubren, del lado de adentro, todas las paredes que dan al patio.
>
> (pp. 117-118)

In his manuscript Castel explains, in more detail, his experiments with human senses:

> Si hubiera un cambio en los movimientos de los átomos este lirio sería, quizá, el golpe de agua que derrumba la represa, o una manada de jirafas, o la gloria del atardecer. Un cambio en el ajuste de mis sentidos haría, quizá, de los cuatro muros de esta celda la sombra del manzano del primer huerto.
>
> (p. 153)

The camouflaged cells, then, are actually liberty for the prisoners locked within. They are cells covered by mirrors on their interior walls—unfoldings. They are closed space but at the same time opened space because of the possibility of escape. They are a metaphor of the paradox of representation that makes the text possible:

> Nuestro mundo es una síntesis que dan los sentidos, el microscopio da otra. Si cambiaran los sentidos cambiaría la imagen. Podemos describir el mundo como un conjunto de símbolos capaces de expresar cualquier cosa; con sólo alterar la graduación de nuestros sentidos, leeremos otra palabra en ese alfabeto natural.
>
> (p. 154)

Plan de evasión is a constant changing of the senses, which in this way, avoids the privileged version of the univocal referent.

It is apparent that in the same way that the camouflage of the cells hides nothing, the camouflage of the island does not reveal anything beneath its surface. This repeats Jean-Louis Baudry's comments about the mask as a surface that invites us to believe in a level that hides nothing but itself.[6] Through the reading of the play between the "tramas," and through the mechanism of quoting, *Plan de evasión* functions as a mask and produces itself on the surface of the text.

What then is the plan to escape? As we can now see, a hint of the answer to this question appears to be revealed in the state of the island's prisons. Just as the camouflaged cells meant freedom for those prisoners enclosed within them, so too, the text gains freedom from the prison of referentiality when it limits itself to the surface, despite the invitation to examine beneath the camouflage of multiple levels. It is in this way that the text gains freedom, for there is no longer any necessity for it to mean anything more than its own production.

Notes

1. Stephen Heath, *The Nouveau Roman* (Philadelphia: Temple University Press, 1972), p. 22.

2. Heath, p. 22.

3. Lewis Carroll, *Through the Looking Glass* in *The Annotated Alice,* ed. Martin Gardner (New York: Bramhall House, 1960), pp. 185-86.

4. Adolfo Bioy Casares, *Plan de evasión,* 2nd ed. (Buenos Aires: Editorial Galerna, 1969). The page numbers following each quotation from this text refer to this edition.

5. Roland Barthes, *Critical Essays;* trans. Richard Howard (Evanston, Illinois: Northwestern University Press, 1972), p. 214.

6. Jean-Louis Baudry, "Ecriture, fiction, ideologie" in *Thèorie de'ensemble* (Paris: Editions du Seuil, 1968).

Suzanne Jill Levine (essay date spring 1983)

SOURCE: Levine, Suzanne Jill. "Parody Island: Two Novels by Bioy Casares." *Hispanic Journal* 4, no. 2 (spring 1983): 43-49.[1]

[*In the following essay, Levine argues that the novellas* The Invention of Morel *and* Plan for Escape *are masterfully constructed parodies that function as commentary on the nature of a wide assortment of literary genres.*]

Parody in the new Latin American novel has become a central theme in Hispanic criticism, and one of the first writers to theorize on this subject was Cuban novelist Severo Sarduy. In an essay-parody[2] on Manuel Puig's *Boquitas pintadas* in which (in the spirit of *Don Quijote,* Part II) Puig's provincial Argentine women gossip about the sophisticated Parisian transvestites of Sarduy's *Cobra,* Sarduy defines a concept of parody which goes beyond that of "burlesque imitation." His point of departure is the cathartic theory of carnivalesque laughter in Mikhail Bakhtin's study of *Rabelais and His World*[3] in which the symbolic spectacle of carnival, a syncretic and universal folkloric tradition, parodies the values and hierarchies of everyday life, in the double sense that carnival both destroys and renews, mocks and pays homage to man's existence. Bakhtin studies the carnivalesque function of literature in Rabelais, but also refers to the Greek satires as well as *Don Quijote* as models of carnivalesque parody which share in common the same literary mechanisms, i.e. the fusion of genres, the grafting of different types and levels of discourse, and the abolition of narrative autonomy.

Sarduy notes, in the same essay, that Jorge Luis Borges and Bioy Casares, in their Bustos Domecq take-off on the detective genre, *Seis problemas para don Isidro Parodi* (1942), use parody in the carnivalesque sense suggested by Bakhtin: they mock the local color and excessive intricacy of archteypical detective novels, but also glorify and renew the tired genre with their own inventions.

In a discussion on the baroque and neo-baroque, Sarduy[4] goes beyond Bakhtin to point out that parody, in the sense that it is self-conscious revelation of one's sources, is a baroque device that appears in much of contemporary Latin American literature: the baroque text (and he doesn't limit his commentary on the baroque to literature but extends it to the plastic arts, architecture, etc.) is that which allows the reader to discover, to decipher an ever-present sub-text, of which the visible text is always a reflection, a commentary, a re-working or a "memory."[5]

Bioy Casares' two island novels, *La invención de Morel* (1940) (this novel inspired Robbe-Grillet's script of Alain Resnais' movie *Last Year at Marienbad*) and *Plan de evasión* (1945), a more caricaturesque, overtly self-reflexive version of a utopic island adventure, are pioneering works in this rebirth of the baroque in Latin American fiction not only because they reflect each other in this wider sense of parody as commentary on the nature of literature as a process of destruction and re-creation, but also because they synthesize a whole tradition of utopic works beginning, at least, with Plato's *Republic* and Greek bucolic poetry and culminating perhaps in Victorian science fiction.

It is not new that, in the self-revelatory literature being produced by Borges, Bioy Casares and other twentieth-century American writers, their writing is self-reflexive, since Theocritus' idylls, More's *Utopia,* and H. G. Wells' *The Island of Doctor Moreau* were also. (As Borges shows in "Tlön, Uqbar, Orbis Tertius" (*Ficciones,* 1941) all writing is inevitably self-reflexive, contained in a reality that differs from, though somehow mirrors, flesh and blood reality. In the filigree of Theocritus' poems, the reader can glimpse epic poetry, mythological legends; in *Utopia,* Plato's *Republic,* in Wells' "scientific romance," Jules Verne's *Mysterious Island,* or *Robinson Crusoe,* or *Gulliver's Travels.*) What is new, or neo-baroque, is that contemporary writers not only use models but that they expose them, they write explicitly about this reality of artifice. And ***Plan de evasión (A Plan for Escape)*** is certainly an apotheosis of the text as produced by many texts not only because it reflects, in its strategies and allusions, the texts previously mentioned and many others (Poe's *Narrative of Arthur Gordon Pym,* Kafka's *Penal Colony,* Julien Green's *Voyageur Sur la Terre,* James' *Turn of the Screw,* not to mention underlying occidental and oriental myths and legends), but because it exists as a mirror-text of *La invención de Morel,* a fantastic adventure centered around a love obsession, very much in the spirit of the Surrealist *amour fou.* Borgesian fantastic fiction, a Frankenstein-ian fusion of science fiction, detective story and philosophical essay, to which Bioy Casares has added the archetypal love story, is quintessentially carnivalesque in that it cannibalizes all literatures, high and low, Western and Eastern.

The Sub-Version of a Sub-Text

I will limit myself here to revealing in some detail what Borges has signalled, in his preface to ***Morel,*** as the obvious text which **Morel** [*La invención de Morel*] , remembers (as well as ***Plan*** [*A Plan for Evasion*], I shall add) which is the already-mentioned *The Island of Doctor Moreau* (1896) by H. G. Wells. (To follow all the allusions threading through **Morel** and **Plan** is an infinite voyage, undertaken in part, already, in my Ph.D. dissertation.)

The Island of Doctor Moreau recounts the adventure of Edward Prendick, shipwrecked in the Pacific and picked up by a schooner which happens to be shipping animals to an island (uncharted, of course). On this ship Prendick meets Montgomery, a renegade medical student who, because of some unspecified disgrace (remember this is a Victorian setting), has fled England and is now the assistant of an eccentric scientist, Moreau, who is running a "biological station" of sorts. When they reach Moreau's island, Prendick is left stranded by the unfriendly captain who dislikes Moreau and his strange shipments. The rest of the short book deals with Prendick's gradual discovery of

the atrocious nature of Moreau's experiments, the terrifying outcome of these experiments, and Prendick's miraculous salvation from the island. Moreau, as we know, attempts to transform beasts into men and women, by means of surgery that is cruelly performed without anesthesia. Moreau is a kind of Faustian Darwin, and one of the moral (or metaphysical) lessons that Wells' reader is supposed to extract is that man is inevitably and tragically a beast yearning to transcend his mortal prison of flesh and blood (be it through science or religion) but doomed.

Obviously, the parallels between *Moreau* and **Morel** go beyond a graphic modification of "au" to "1," even beyond the theme of a scientific invention that is produced on an "unchartered" (i.e. nonexistent except in the text) island in the Pacific. Like Montgomery, the protagonist-narrator of **Morel** is a renegade from society who is forced, for unspecified reasons (the convenient device of vagueness in "scientific" fantasies, a device already present in More's *Utopia*), to take refuge on a vaguely-identified Pacific island. Like Prendick, he is isolated because he is stranded on an island which the world either ignores or distrusts. The narrator of **Morel** also discovers gradually an atrocious "reality" which involves an unheard-of process of transformation: mad scientist-artist Morel kills human beings (who happen to be his friends) and himself in order to transform them into three-dimensional movie images (How prophetic fiction writers can be: the holograph had not yet been invented!). Morel's purpose: to live in eternity with Faustine, the woman he loves but who is indifferent to him. The nameless narrator also falls in love with the distant Faustine and, once he discovers the fantastic machine, decides to sacrifice life and transform himself into an eternal image as well. **Morel,** a novel overtly about the romantic sacrifice of life for love, and art, through the metaphor of fantastic transfigurations, is also a metamorphosis of *Moreau,* a novel about metamorphoses. The scientific content in both is really a "pre-text."

At this superficial level of plot it is not difficult to recognize **Plan** as a further stage in this series of changes. While mad Dr. Castel's name (a salute to Kafka's *Castle* perhaps) does not echo Moreau's as Morel's does, Castel's experiment is, in many ways, more reminiscent of Moreau's. Like the latter's, Castel's involves surgery: Castel, the governor of a penal colony on an apocryphal Devil's Island, is performing a kind of post-symbolist synesthetic surgery on the prisoners, changing their powers of perception so that when they look upon their cell walls they will perceive a paradise island. Nevers, the innocent bystander, (forced by his family because of some unspecified disgrace, again!) to accept a military assignment on Devil's Island) is yet another avatar of the unwilling outsider who gradually discovers (and becomes involved) in the "awful truth" of a science fiction experiment. When Nevers first encounters Castel he sees him surrounded by a flock of animals and finds out later that Castel did his first operations on animals. At this point, Bioy Casares does more than allude to Moreau; he openly exhibits his "source"; that is, the narrator, Nevers' Uncle Antoine, basing his story on Nevers' letters, writes: "Tal vez Castel fuese una especie de doctor Moreau. Le costaba creer, sin embargo, que la realidad se pareciera a una novela fantástica."[6] No apparent ambiguity here: the Moreau alluded to in *Morel* is spelled out clearly in the more parodic text *Plan*.

However, just as the above quotation is ironic—it is a novel, *Plan,* and not "reality" which resembles a "fantastic novel" (*Moreau*)—so are the references to *Moreau* in *Morel* and *Plan* tricks that the writer is playing on the reader. The mention of Doctor Moreau in *Plan* sugests one plot to the reader when the "plot" is actually another (just as, indeed, Bioy Casares' novels are not transparent transmitters of messages but metaphoric elaborations on the solitary, self-reflexive nature of perception and of writing). *Morel* and *Plan* continue to tease the reader even after the "truth" is discovered because we never really know if it is true (too many unreliable narrators as intermediaries); indeed, particularly in the case of *Plan,* an open-ended labyrinth, the final fate of the protagonist is never known.

Specific signs of parody of Wells' text abound in *Plan*. When Nevers finally meets Castel's mysterious assistant and "collaborator," a young man named De Brinon (actual name of a French Nazi collaborator), a kind of comic synthesis of Montgomery and M'ling, Nevers describes De Brinon's voice as follows:

> Dice Nevers que tuvo la impresión de que la distancia que lo separaba de De Brinon había desaparecido y que la voz—atrozmente—sonaba a su lado. Dice que llama voz al sonido que oyó porque, aparentemente, De Brinon es un hombre; pero que oyó el berrido de una oveja. Añade que parecía una voz de ventrílocuo imitando a una oveja y que De Brinon casi no abría la boca al hablar.
>
> (*Plan,* p. 126)

Again, in this slapstick version of terror, the echo of *Dr. Moreau* rings clear: the fact that De Brinon sounds like an aminal though he is a man, suggests Dr. Moreau's conversion of beasts into men whose original nature is not eradicated but is insidiously visible, between the lines, so to speak. But at the same time the echo turns out to be a false clue not only because of the discovery of the "true" nature of Castel's experiments, but because of Bioy's ironic, comic way of revealing Nevers' "impression" which contrasts with

Wells' authentically suspenseful narration of Prendick's impression when he first sees M'ling abroad the schooner: "I . . . had a disconnected impression of a dark face with extraordinary eyes close to mine, but that I thought was a nightmare, until I met it again."[7] And when he meets it again: "In some indefinable way the black face thus flashed upon me shocked me profoundly. It was a singularly deformed one. The facial part projected, forming something dimly suggestive of a muzzle" (*Moreau,* p. 13). Wells' tone is one of insidious horror, and what is suggested here—M'ling's beastly nature—is later confirmed.

On the other hand, Nevers' nightmarish encounter with De Brinon is described with comical, ambiguous distance, especially Nevers' first view of De Brinon which immediately precedes the unexpected bellow:

> Allí estaba De Brinon. Nevers no tuvo un momento de duda. Era la primera vez que veía a ese joven atlético, de cara despierta y franca, de mirada inteligente, que se reclinaba, abstraído, sobre un enfermo. Ese joven tenía que ser De Brinon.
>
> (*Plan,* pp. 125-26)

After this comforting view of De Brinon as an intelligent-looking youth, comes the shocking contrast of the demented voice, comic not only because of the abrupt juxtaposition but because of Nevers' incoherent description of a sheep's voice as a bellow (instead of baaing).

Whereas in Wells there is a rational sequence of events leading from first suspicions to final discoveries, in Bioy Casares, the logic is that of the White Knight in *Through the Looking-Glass,* or of *The Cabinet of Dr. Caligari,* i.e. dream logic. Unlike M'ling, whose beastliness becomes gradually apparent, the handsome De Brinon is abruptly reduced to a strange animalistic, disembodied voice: the extraordinary suddenly invades everyday reality. But while this extraordinary factor could appear to be explained by *Moreau,* i.e. the text between the lines, it isn't: Nevers thinks there is something beastly about De Brinon but also remarks that he could be "mentally retarded" (*Plan,* p. 127). The absolute truth about De Brinon as about everything else can never be ascertained. Infinite uncertainty is what the reader of contemporary fantastic fiction is left with.

The shipwreck incident is a cliché of the island adventure without which the three plots would be imcomplete but again, though the adventure of the *Morel* protagonist is closer to Prendick's in that both are stranded on an island while Nevers is officially dispatched to one, there are greater anecdotal similarities between *Moreau* and *Plan.* The shipwreck tale of one of the prisoners on Devil's Island, called the Priest, is, in many of its details, a reduction, a condensed version and thus a parodic commentary of Edward Prendick's adventure (*Plan,* pp. 57-58). Like Prendick, the Priest, when his "ship wrecked," was in the only boat that was not picked up until many days later, after many privations; just as Prendick's dinghy loses sight of the others, so does the Priest's. In Prendick's case, the water soon runs out and the men start going mad: indeed, madness drives two of them to kill each other, as madness probably drives the Priest to kill off his companions. Prendick himself feels threatened by madness and laughs insanely when his companions fall into the water, a laugh, he says, that "caught me like a thing from without" (*Moreau,* p. 6). The Priest (an ironic name, of course) remains crazed after his ordeal, and sees only hallucinations and monsters, all of which leads to disastrous consequences when he is operated on by Dr. Castel.

The slight suggestion in *Moreau* that Prendick's story may not be credible because the whole thing may have been a hallucination (he mentions seeing M'ling's face as if in a nightmare) becomes a labyrinth of doubts in *Morel* and *Plan,* where not only minor characters like the Priest are crazy but where there are many doubts as to the sanity or credibility of the protagonists, all unreliable narrators. Here again, if one explanation of Prendick's experience on the island is that it was all a hallucination, then the Priest's island drama, a parody of Prendick's, is infinitely more "unreal."

The echoes of *Moreau* in *Morel,* and even more pronounced in *Morel*'s mirror-text, *Plan,* are false leads which are true leads. While *Morel* and *Plan* deal with different "experiments" (having more to do with art than with science), the fact that both of Bioy Casares' novels suggest that their "source" could be another book rather than an empirical reality, points to an ultimate "truth," to a textual reality. And *Morel* and *Plan* are parodies not so much in the sense that they are renewing the science fiction genre, as perhaps Bustos Domecq has done for the detective genre, but in the sense that they are commenting on the "nature" of all literature: Texts represent not a presence but an absence; the referent is always, already out of reach.[8]

Elsewhere I have examined a useful strategy in utopic island adventures, the already-mentioned first-person narrative, and how what in *Robinson Crusoe* guaranteed an illusion of authenticity in the early eighteenth century, in *Morel*[9] and *Plan* emphasizes the very literariness, the very artificiality of the account of an extraordinary adventure. But here it will have to suffice to say that the concept of parody, in the wider sense of commentary, of creation as re-creation, not only illuminates the mode of Bioy Casares' two novels but of many of the more original works of Latin American literature today.

Notes

1. This article is an excerpt from *Guía de Bioy Casares* (Madrid: Editorial Fundamentos, 1982). Translation is mine.

2. Severo Sarduy, "Notas a las Notas . . . A propósito de Manuel Puig," *Revista Iberoamericana,* Nos. 76-77 (Pittsburgh, July-Dec. 1971), 555-67.

3. Mikhail Bakhtin, *Rabelais and His World* (1929; Cambridge: M.I.T. Press, 1968).

4. Severo Sarduy, "El barroco y el neobarroco," en *América Latina en su literatura,* César Fernández Moreno (México: Siglo XXI Editores, 1972).

5. Eugenio Donato, "Topographies of Memory," *SubStance,* No. 21 (U. of Wisconsin, 1978), pp. 37-48. This essay appeared after the completion of my dissertation on intertextuality in the works of Bioy Casares; it would be interesting to pursue Donato's formulation which approaches intertextuality by examining the presumed relationship that a text bears to its "memory" (used metaphorically here), or as he writes," . . . a text necessarily stages a metaphorical memory in the form of a 'pre-text' which, though generated by the text, always seems to precede it, and from 'another' place appears to control the strategic presentation of the text."

6. A. Bioy Casares, *Plan de evasión* (2nd ed: Buenos Aires: Editorial Galerna, 1968), p. 70. Referred to in the text as *Plan.*

7. H. G. Wells, *The Island of Doctor Moreau* (New York: Duffield & Green, 1933), p. 7. Referred to in text as *Moreau.*

8. See Jacques Derrida, "Structure, Sign and Play in the Discourse of the Human Sciences," *The Structuralist Controversy* (Baltimore: The Johns Hopkins Press, 1972), pp. 249-65.

9. A. Bioy Casares, *La invención de Morel* (Buenos Aires: Editorial Losada, 1940), preface by Jorge Luis Borges.

Thomas C. Meehan (essay date 1983)

SOURCE: Meehan, Thomas C. "Temporal Simultaneity and the Theme of Time Travel in a Fantastic Story by Adolfo Bioy Casares." *Kentucky Romance Quarterly* 30, no. 2 (1983): 167-85.

[*In the following essay, Meehan analyzes the themes of time and travel in the short story "El otro laberinto," which, the critic asserts, is a literary mystery as well as a masterpiece of fantastic fiction.*]

Western prose fiction of the twentieth century reveals something approaching an obsession with time. From the themes themselves and the radical innovations in narrative structure and technique, such as stream of consciousness and fragmented temporal sequence, to the rekindled interest in timeless universal myths, much of contemporary literary expression bespeaks a sometimes anguished metaphysical contemplation of the fourth dimension. Through their fictitious worlds writers have consistently suggested symbolic ways for man to refute the existence of time, to overcome its irreversible flow, to escape the restricting confines of the present and enter into the refuge of eternity.

Fantastic fiction in particular is characterized by the frequent appearance of themes which bear witness to this temporal preoccupation. Representative of such themes are the Nietzschean eternal return, circular time, dilation, contraction and stopping of time, reversible time, parallel and simultaneous temporal zones and, perhaps one of the most interesting, the theme of time travel. Illustrious Anglo-American examples of the latter theme which come to mind immediately are H. G. Wells' *The Time Machine,* Max Beerbohm's short story "Enoch Soames," Virginia Woolf's *Orlando,* Mark Twain's *A Connecticut Yankee in King Arthur's Court,* and Henry James' unfinished *The Sense of the Past.* In Argentina, a nation of the Hispanic world with a long and rich tradition of fantastic fiction,[1] the theme has received treatment in works by Jorge Luis Borges, Julio Cortázar, Enrique Anderson Imbert, and Adolfo Bioy Casares, among others. Indeed, in a 1949 lecture Borges singled out time travel and simultaneous, parallel actions as two of the principal themes of fantastic fiction.[2]

The limited scope of the present study precludes an extensive theoretical discussion of the fantastic as a literary genre or subgenre. However, certain of Louis Vax's general concepts regarding this type of literature will be helpful.[3] In fantastic fiction, "se borra la frontera entre lo real y lo imaginado" (p. 17), yet the world depicted is still familiar and secure to us; it is our own world (p. 6). That is to say, the fantastic "se deleita en presentarnos a hombres como nosotros, situados súbitamente [or sometimes gradually, p. 13] en presencia de lo inexplicable, pero dentro de nuestro mundo real" (p. 6). The fantastic further demands "la irrupción de un elemento sobrenatural en un mundo sujeto a la razón" (p. 10). Thus, the fantastic usually represents some kind of threat, physical or metaphysical, to our traditionally accepted notions of reality. Our smug complacency is shaken and overturned. Our faith in a world governed by reason, systematic order, and natural laws is challenged (pp. 17-18).[4] Hero and reader are left in a state of hesitation, ambiguity, and uncertainty vis-à-vis the events described.[5]

In the course of a fantastic narrative, then, a familiar, comfortable set of circumstances is often transformed into a nightmarish, sometimes philosophically anguishing, reality. Finally, most critics are in agreement that good fantastic fiction may be, but is usually not, merely escapist, in the pejorative sense of that word. Although fantastic fiction includes mysterious, uncanny happenings, if it is also serious literature it is paradoxically and simultaneously calling our attention back to the real, to "the most central aspects of our existence."[6]

Among the group of Argentine writers mentioned above, Adolfo Bioy Casares is probably best known as the author of *La invención de Morel* (1940) and as long-time friend and collaborator of his more famous compatriot, Jorge Luis Borges. However, over a period of forty-three years Bioy Casares has also created an impressive personal corpus of original prose fiction which includes eleven books of short stories and seven novels and novelettes. The bulk of Bioy's writings, largely overlooked by critics,[7] may, like that of Borges, be broadly classified as fantastic literature.

The purpose of this essay is to examine the narrative structure and the fantastic themes of temporal simultaneity and time travel in **"El otro laberinto,"** one of six stories which make up an important early collection of Bioy Casares' fantastic fiction titled **La trama celeste** (1948). **"El otro laberinto"** is an adventure story, but it is also a sort of literary mystery which challenges the reader to solve its enigma and perceive the intellectual underpinnings of its intricate organization before the narrator clarifies matters towards the end.

In a manner reminiscent of the cosmopolitan settings, events, and characters of Borges' writings, the action of the tale unfolds in Hungary in early 1904 against a background of Austrian political and social oppression of Magyar nationalist sentiment. Anthal Horvath, a prolific but unsuccessful novelist, reluctantly returns from an extended stay in Paris to his native Budapest only to be drawn irresistibly into a network of former university friends and conspirators plotting the murder of a despised Austrian police chief. István Banyay, Horvath's wealthy, lifelong friend and member of the Hungarian patriots, is a historian obsessed by an incident which had occurred exactly three centuries earlier. In 1604, a dead man was found in a sealed room of the Tunnel Inn of Budapest. The same ancient building now forms part of the Banyay family estate, and István occupies bachelor quarters in rooms contiguous to that in which the corpse had been found so long ago. Found on the dead body was a mysterious manuscript, apparently the biography of the deceased. This document had disappeared and subsequently became the object of a three-hundred year scholarly search. István Banyay, with more than a passing interest in seventeenth-century Hungarian history, finds the manuscript, but then he himself vanishes unexplainably. Anthal Horvath's investigation of his friend's disappearance leads to the astounding discovery that István, in possession of the manuscript, and in an attempt to escape the Austrian secret police, had entered the ancient room. In doing so, he magically stepped back (or "over") into the seventeenth century, whereupon he dropped dead of heart failure. Horvath subsequently offers his explanation of the facts in the case. He reveals his motive for and the events which led up to his forgery of the manuscript, which had brought about his friend's tragic death. Horvath's profound remorse over the senseless trick he had played on his friend seems to him ample justification for his contemplated suicide. The action comes full circle just preceding Horvath's entry into the fatal room where a glass of water and arsenic await him.

The foregoing schematic summary of **"El otro laberinto"** conveys only the barest idea of the story. It does not, however, communicate any notion of the rigorous plot structure or the richness of the fantastic themes and their metaphysical connotations which pose stimulating literary and intellectual challenges to the reader. My remaining comments will attempt to illuminate these facets of the tale. I will first examine the structure and then the themes.

STRUCTURE

"El otro laberinto" is organized into two large narrative configurations. Part I, subdivided into ten short, numbered chapters, is narrated completely in the third person by an omniscient author. It is, however, told largely from the point of view of Anthal Horvath, who will later unmask himself as the great dissimulator and forget of the fateful manuscript. Part II combines Horvath's first person confession or "Comunicación a los amigos," conveniently printed in italics, with interspersed third person omniscient author entries that comment and elaborate upon Horvath's confession. Although the time span of the action remains somewhat vague, it comprises a period of several months to, at most, a year. The narrative present is 1904, and the climax occurs at the end of the story, at dawn of 17 March. Toward the end of the first part Bioy Casares introduces the mysterious disappearance of a main character, thus creating an enigma. The second part presents, again toward the end, the revelation of a fantastic explanation for that vanishing act. As Horvath announces, *"Intentaré la simple relación histórica de los hechos. . . ."*[8]

Although the form of the story follows the guidelines of the classic *relato fantástico*, Bioy has also drawn upon certain resources of detective fiction in shaping his fictional material. The quotation just above, for example, reveals that certain events have happened prior to the main action and that information has been cunningly and intentionally withheld from the reader in the manner of a mystery novel. The trajectory of the action, like that of the detective story (or gothic romance) moves from the "descripción de una situación ambigua o sobrenatural (mundo 'desconocido')" to an "explicación *racional* o verosímil del fenómeno (mundo 'conocido')."[9] (The difference here, of course, is that the "explanation" of the enigma, unlike that of the detective story, is not rational or verisimilar, but fantastic.) In addition, facts and incidents appear, as in a mystery, in an apparently haphazard manner, but these elements are then repeated and clarified. If the reader picks up the artist's ingenious system of cross-references, every detail eventually produces its resonance, and all is justified and explained. The puzzle is worked out.

Other features of mystery fiction[10] are the use of the sealed room motif (here the magic room called the *museo*), the surprise ending, Horvath's investigation of four versions of István's disappearance,[11] and the planting of several clues for the alert reader in the course of the story's first part. For example, in the first chapter of Part I Horvath casually remarks that the day after his arrival in Budapest he had visited Professor Liptay in the library. Not finding Liptay, Horvath left him "un pequeño recuerdo que le envió una muchacha francesa . . . (p. 111)." Only in Part II will the reader discover that the "little souvenir" was the manuscript of the seventeenth-century dead man's biography forged by Horvath and Madeleine in Paris (p. 139). Professor Liptay contends that only a man who expects little out of life, a man without hope, would make the best assassin of the police chief (p. 115). This constitutes a foreshadowing clue to what will happen to both István Banyay and Anthal Horvath. The former gives up all hope upon losing his beloved Erzsebet to Horvath, and the latter can expect little from a life of remorse after causing the death of his best friend.[12]

In its most prominent structural contours, however, **"El otro laberinto"** is more aptly a model of the fantastic genre. In distinguishing between detective fiction and the *relato fantástico,* Vax points out that the former introduces the supernatural, usually at the outset, only to suppress it in the dénouement so that reason and logic may have the last word: "En el cuento fantástico, el planteamiento es inverso; lo sobrenatural, ausente al principio, domina el proceso que lleva al desenlace; es necesario que se insinúe poco a poco, que adormezca a la razón en lugar de escandalizarla."[13] Bioy Casares himself has drawn a structural blueprint for the fantastic tale in similar terms. The author's ideas might be simply paraphrased as follows: into the midst of a realistic, credible atmosphere there intrudes a single incredible occurrence which surprises, bewilders, and strikes fear and doubt. For the surprise to be most effective it should be carefully prepared, foreshadowed, and thus slightly attenuated.[14]

It now becomes more apparent that the basic components and narrative functions of the story's two main structural units coincide precisely with the above theories of both Bioy Casares and Vax with regard to the fantastic. The narrative strategy of Part I, and a characteristic of the author's style in general, is the deliberate creation of a believable atmosphere "full of localizing connotations,"[15] or what one critic has called "una densidad vital concreta."[16]

The impression of such a dense, specific reality is achieved by four technical means, the general lines of which may be only adumbrated here. First, there is the creation of a vivid impression of space made up of a country (Hungary), its capital (Budapest), the previous existence of a character in the capital of another nation (Paris, France), and other towns and places (Nyiregyhaza, Nagy-Banya, Tuszer). This general fictional space is further filled by more specific references to the names of streets, parks, lakes, plazas and fountains, a family estate, old buildings, cafés and coffeehouses, a tailorshop, and a university library. In addition, it is teeming not only with well-sketched secondary personages (Palma Szentgyörgyi, Erzsebet Loczy, Professor Liptay, Ferencz Remenyi), but also other anonymous people (vendors, students, conspirators, police), as well as trolleys, horse-drawn coaches, trains, etc. Secondly, there is the creation of convincing human personalities and attention to character development (of the two protagonists, Horvath and Banyay, especially) which go well beyond those found in the normally shorter Hispanic *cuento* and the usual fantastic tale (of a Borges, e.g., with whom the author is frequently compared).

Third is the presentation of a strong impression of human psychology: memories, faults and virtues (loyalty and disloyalty, courage and cowardliness), the interplay and conflict of emotions (anger, fear, loneliness, timidity, tenderness, indifference, arrogance, guilt, and remorse). Principal factors here, and in most of Bioy's works, are the elements of friendship and love, which achieve the result of humanizing a content and style which tend toward being almost coldly cerebral at times, perhaps owing to the metaphysical, abstract themes treated. Horvath and Banyay are depicted as lifelong friends, and the former's remorse upon discovering the awful truth about István's death seems genuine. Illustrative of the amorous element is the fact

that five man-woman relationships develop in **"El otro laberinto"**: Horvath-Madeleine; Horvath-Palma; Horvath-Erzsebet; István-Palma; István-Erzsebet. Indeed, love even emerges as a "magic" force in the strange, forged manuscript. Horvath writes: *"Y aquí debo señalar algo mágico en ese manuscrito fraguado, una anticipación que, en cierto modo, lo redime de su condición de impostura: hay una descripción del amor que inspira Erzsebet que es una pálida pero fiel descripción del amor, de la adoración, que ahora siento por ella"* (p. 137; Bioy's italics). A fourth and final technique used to build a believable atmosphere is the careful elaboration of a realistic socio-political background. This is made up here of elements such as the Magyar struggle against Austria for local national autonomy, economic class distinctions, academic politics, student unrest and violence, police brutality, etc.

The purpose of this elaborately constructed reality, this dense atmosphere, is to create a medium receptive to the entrance of the fantastic element, a "real" world which will bear the weight of its impact, contain and absorb it naturally. The reader's disbelief has now been willingly and sufficiently suspended. His reason has been adequately lulled so as to accept the intrusion of the fantastic without undue shock.[17] Absent throughout Part I[18] and most of Part II, the fantastic emerges only toward the end of the second section and dominates the *desenlace,* as Vax had indicated (see above, p. 170). When the story's single fantastic incident makes its appearance, it is stated in an almost matter-of-fact manner, almost as an afterthought, as if to downplay its importance: "Por su parte, István sólo entró en el pasado. . . . Pero István no cayó muerto en el 'museo'; cayó en el cuarto de la posada del Túnel, en el siglo XVII" (p. 141). The reader is thus left wondering whether it might not have happened after all; he is in that state of uncertainty so essential to the fantastic genre, according to Todorov (see above, p. 168 and note 5). One even wonders whether Anthal Horvath is about to follow István into the past.

THEMES

The main fantastic themes of **"El otro laberinto"** are the simultaneous existence of past and present time zones and the ability of a man to travel from one of those temporal dimensions to another. At one point in his confession, Horvath provides the key in words that might well be applied to the story as a whole: *"La clave de este proceso es una cuestión de tiempo; si el tiempo es sucesivo, si el pasado se extingue, es inútil que yo busque una excusa. . . ."* (pp. 133-34; Bioy's italics). István's trip to the simultaneous past proves, as Horvath ultimately asserts, that *"el tiempo sucesivo es una mera ilusión de los hombres y que vivimos en una eternidad donde todo es simultáneo. . . ."* (p. 141; Bioy's italics).

However, as Bioy Casares stipulated (see above, p. 169), the reader discovers that the fantastic surprise ending can become all the more effective and aesthetically rewarding when it is carefully prepared for. The writer's masterful interweaving of the themes into the artistic texture of his narrative bears ample witness to his remarkable craftsmanship as a storyteller. In numerous subtle ways, the narrator is constantly pointing toward his fantastic dénouement with clues, symbols, motifs, and foreshadowing. For example, the opening lines of a fantastic tale are often very significant, and the present story is no exception. Horvath's first thoughts of István are an initial hint at the temporal theme: "Es como si detuviera el tiempo, o como si yo no hubiera estado en París; antes de irme, [István] hablaba de esto; ahora sigue hablando. Insiste en este episodio del pasado; olvida el presente (p. 101)."

Another important device used to prepare the terrain for the emergence of the fantastic is a technique frequently employed by Bioy Casares: he indirectly provides a key to his themes through literary references worked into the plot functionally. Although **"El otro laberinto"** is replete with literary, philosophical, and historical allusions, I will consider only those that directly bear upon the theme and form of the story. Each of the two large structural divisions is prefaced by an epigraph. That of Part I quotes a line from Ovid's *Tristia:* "dissimulare velis, te liquet esse meum" (p. 101). ["You wish to dissimulate, but clearly you are mine."][19] These words evidently allude to some form of deception, and the reader soon discovers that the author is about to lead him a merry chase. The source is not III, iii, 18 of *Tristia,* as Bioy's quote stipulates, but I, i, 62, which is the proem to the Latin poet's book. Writing from exile, Ovid apostrophizes his collection of poems in this line and sends it on its way to Rome as an emissary to plead for his pardon. Ovid goes on to say that, although his work still lacks a title, its style should enable readers to recognize him as its author. Bioy Casares is hinting at a secret author and possibly spurious document. The epigraph of Part I thus becomes a clue to the fact that the manuscrupt found by István is a hoax, a document forged by Anthal Horvath as a joke on his friend. This epigraph also covertly suggests the form of the story, which is based upon a system of shifting perspectives. We observe an illusory reality in Part I, and only in Part II are we permitted to see the true face of that reality.

István later discovers that a different hand had interpolated another verse from Ovid in the manuscript: *"nulla venit sine te nox mihi, nulla dies,"* (p. 118) ["no night comes to me without you, no day either"]. The *Tristia* verse number indicated (I, v, 7) is again incorrect. (Bioy's "game" with the reader continues.) Horvath will later confess to having added the beauti-

ful, amorous verse as a "last countersign and as a greeting (p. 140)." He asserts that the "contraseña" was concealed in the intentionally wrong verse number (I, v, 7), which was addressed to István in the hope that his friend would discover the hoax of the apocryphal manuscript. The *Tristia* verse which does bear that number thus takes on a significance also. It appears in a letter of Ovid *to a friend* (like Horvath to Banyay), and reads: *"scis bene, cui dicam, positis pro nomine signis"* ["you know well to whom I am speaking by means of these symbols substituted for your name."]. The love "greeting" was directed either to Madeleine or Erzsebet (in his bewilderment, Horvath is no longer sure for which woman he intended the verse, p. 140). The correct number of the Ovidian verse *"nulla venit sine te . . ."* is III, iii, 18. This line is from one of the many poetic letters the Roman poet composed to his wife. Two things are noteworthy here. First, Ovid's letter begins with words which, in the context of **"El otro laberinto,"** become another cryptic allusion to a "shadow writer": *"Haec mea si casu miraris epistula quare / alteris digitis scripta sit . . ."* ["If haply you wonder why this letter of mine is written by another's fingers . . ."] (*Tristia,* III, iii, 1-2). Secondly, the reader now discovers that the verse number given for *"nulla venit sine te . . ."* (III, iii, 18) corresponds, in labyrinthine manner, to the reference which Bioy Casares had originally affixed to the epigraph of Part I, *"dissimulare velis, te liquet esse meum!"* All these dissimulations and deceptions point indirectly at the big deception perpetrated on mankind, namely, that the traditional concept of linear time in a past-present-future continuum is a fraud. István Banyay's entry into the seventeenth century proves that all time is simultaneous. Eternity is now.

Two further allusions to writers of antiquity mirror the temporal theme. In a frieze around the ceiling of the university library, Horvath reads "una cita del libro undécimo de las *Confesiones,* de San Agustín (p. 120)." He also observes a bust of Boethius[20] and reads the inscription: *"HI OCULI VIDERVNT AETERNITATEM"* (p. 120). ["These eyes saw eternity."] This Latin phrase obviously interrelates with the closing words of Horvath's confession, which are an overt statement of the theme of simultaneous times. On the basis of István's escape to the past, Anthal deduces that "successive time is a mere illusion" and that "we live in an *eternity* where everything is simultaneous" (p. 141; my translation). Book Eleven of St. Augustine's *Confessions* contains (Chaps. XI-XXXI) his meditations on the problem of time. He demonstrates that "time and creation are cotemporal" and reaches conclusions that point to a completely subjective theory of time.[21]

The epigraph to Part II of the story quotes a verse from a poem by Thomas Chatterton, "The Storie of William Canynge," which relates a dream vision of the past. The quotation appears in the original English, but it is deliberately incomplete: "*Straight was I carried . . .*" (p. 128). Upon reading Chatterton, the reader will discover that the complete verse immediately casts a bright spotlight upon the theme of time travel: "Strayte was I carryd back to times of yore. . . ."[22] However, the implications of this literary reference are multiple since they further reinforce the motif of forgery and dissimulation alluded to in the epigraph to Part I of the story. It is significant that Bioy Casares should draw his epigraph from the writings of Thomas Chatterton, for the latter, like his contemporary, James Macpherson (1736-96), author of the controversial Ossian poems, was one of the notorious forgers of English literary history.[23]

There are intriguing thematic parallels between the plot of **"El otro laberinto"** and certain circumstances pertaining to Chatterton's "The Storie of William Canynge." In the latter work, the poet (supposedly Rowley), while resting beside a river, recollects the bellicose recent past of the now peaceful, scenic locale. The allegorical figure of Truth appears, puts the poet to sleep, and transports him back in time (like István's temporal journey) so that he may reconstruct the earlier life of his new friend, William Canynge, heroic lord mayor of nearby Bristol. Although Chatterton published the poem as if it were merely his own transcription of an authentic fifteenth-century manuscript by Rowley, literary historians are now certain that it is a hoax. Taking a leaf from Chatterton's book, Anthal Horvath, a struggling young writer like Chatterton, forges a three-hundred-year-old document to play a trick on his friend, István Banyay. While living in Paris, Horvath had been inspired by a performance of Alfred de Vigny's play *Chatterton,* and aided by Madeleine, his French mistress, he had created the fake biography later ("earlier!") found on the corpse in the seventeenth century. "*Después leí todo lo que pude hallar sobre el poeta que inventaba manuscritos y poetas*" (p. 135; Bioy's italics). Bioy Casares hinted at such a development in Part I when he referred to Anthal's projected biography of Chatterton (p. 108). Furthermore, again like the English poet, Horvath errs frequently in his attempt to duplicate the style of writing of an earlier period. Anthal's apocryphal manuscript is written mainly in modern Hungarian, but with occasional missing z's or diereses, many lexical archaisms, old orthographic forms, and even anachronisms (pp. 137-38). Since Madeleine, who was copying Horvath's rough draft to prevent István from identifying the handwriting, knew no Hungarian, misspellings abound in the document.

But the story of Chatterton informs **"El otro laberinto"** in even more subtle ways. If the reader consults Alfred de Vigny's play, he will discover that all the tragedy of the English poet's short existence, including poverty, literary forgery, futile struggle for recognition and, ultimately, suicide, is entirely mirrored in the life of Anthal Horvath. Throughout the story Horvath's brooding and his somewhat melodramatic, even phony, romantic posturing suggest that he views himself as a modern-day Chatterton, another unrecognized, misunderstood genius. The despondent tone of Horvath's "Comunicación a los amigos" is imbued with the melancholy spirit of Chatterton's final hours, as they are presented in de Vigny's drama. During the redaction of that confession, Anthal is so obsessed with the memory of the tragic, young English bard, with whom he obviously identifies, that he even inserts a line from another Chatterton poem, "Bristowe Tragedie," which expresses Horvath's own feelings at the moment of death: "Hay que morir, dijo el valiente Carlos. / Eso no temo." (p. 134).[24] Finally, by taking arsenic in water, Horvath imitates precisely the manner of Chatterton's suicide.[25] Bioy Casares thus introduces another fantastic motif, the reversal of a traditional aesthetic principle, i.e., "life imitates art."

There is evidence pointing to the functional presence in the story of two other traditional fantastic motifs which further buttress the theme of time travel. The first is that of the double or *doppelgänger.*[26] Upon the disappearance of István Banyay, Anthal Horvath immediately begins to assume his friend's identity and, in all probability, his destiny. Horvath is received "like a son" (p. 123) by István's parents, practically adopted into the wealthy family and invited to occupy their son's quarters next to the *museo* (p. 124). As István's father reasons, "Horvath es la persona más cercana de István; faltando István, en cierto modo lo representa (p. 126)."

Anthal now proceeds to pursue István's activities. He continues the latter's work on the *Enciclopedia Húngara* (p. 125), attends meetings of the Magyar patriots in István's place, takes up with Palma first and then transfers his love to Erzsebet, just as Banyay had. He even declares he will write the biography of the seventeenth-century dead man who had so obsessed István (p. 126). The similarities and repetitions of the twin protagonists accelerate at dawn of 17 March. Horvath is seated at the same table in front of the window where Banyay was last seen by both Janós, the family coachman, and the Dollseller (pp. 124-25; 133). Like István, Horvath also has now become a man without hope, as Professor Liptay had foreseen (p. 115): upon reading in the newspaper of the students' assault on the office of the university rector, Anthal knows that police security will be increased, and that he will have no chance to kill Liptay who has been branded as a traitor to the patriots (p. 130). Horvath's own capture is imminent, and his heart pounds rapidly, "pesado y enorme" (p. 133), which recalls reiterated references to István's weak heart (pp. 110, 133). When Janós leaves the room, Horvath writes furiously because he now realizes that things are repeating and that he is about to follow István Banyay into the old room where death awaits (p. 134). Toward the end, the image of a beckoning, open door to the *museo* further strengthens the suggestion that Anthal, like István, will find the temporal warp and escape into the past (p. 133). When Anthal sees the same secret police agent dressed in gray whom István had seen approaching his apartment, he announces: "Ahora yo pasaré por la misma puerta . . . (p. 141)." As he steps through that door, Horvath says he does not possess his friend's supernatural powers: "Yo tengo solamente un vaso de agua, un poco de arsénico y el ejemplo de Chatterton" (p. 142).

The fantastic motif of the double is closely related to the theme of time travel. Although Bioy Casares lets the reader draw his own conclusions, by story's end the narrator has carefully prepared the suggestion that Anthal Horvath, as István Banyay's *doppelgänger*, will repeat some form of the latter's temporal journey. Given the extent to which Horvath assumes the identity (and destiny?) of the vanished Banyay, there is every reason to believe that the former, upon entering the magic *museo,* will likewise be whisked away to another simultaneous past, perhaps to the time of his much admired Chatterton.

The *ámbito cerrado* is a second traditional motif from fantastic literature which becomes a central image in **"El otro laberinto."** The *ámbito cerrado* may be a secret space, an enchanted garden, for example, where magic things happen, or some hermetically sealed room or recess. It is usually set off from the rest of reality, and it is always conductive to the fantastic. Such locations have been defined as "lugares aptos para construir otra realidad, ámbitos físicos y metafísicos aislados por el mar separador de lo real y lo posible."[27] Such a place is István Banyay's *museo*, which is the same room in which the dead man was found three centuries earlier. The building containing it is significantly isolated, being located far from the manor house, "en los fondos del jardín" (p. 103). The stuffy, hermetic atmosphere of the whole area is further emphasized by the stagnant air found even in the adjoining rooms which serve as István's quarters (p. 105).[28]

The *museo* is appropriately named since a museum is a place where the past lives on in the present, so to speak, thus reflecting the theme of simultaneous time dimensions. In Banyay's museum the past has "con-gregated" and has, quite literally, been "accumulated." The room once served as a kind of warehouse for a great uncle of István, who heaped up in the semi-darkness the countless objects bought to pamper his collector's whims (p. 103). Here the past exists *in* the present, and here István Banyay, through an act of supernatural mental projection, finds a warp in the barrier dividing the simultaneous temporal dimensions and steps from present into past.

Careful scrutiny of the narrator's lengthy enumeration of objects and artefacts in the *museo* (p. 103) reveals that most are symbolically linked to various motifs and thematic threads of the story. Each antique is invested with thematic resonance, or as Kovacci expresses it, "Cada objeto es al mismo tiempo unidad y manifestación de pluridades como simbólicos laberintos."[29] For example, the clocks designed like little villages with houses and figurines and the astronomical instruments can, of course, be related to the general theme of time. The same can be said of the legend of the immortal Wandering Jew which decorates a Russian doll bearing the date 1785. Its presence in the collection proves, as the narrator cryptically states, that the origin of the legend is previous to the nineteenth century. A contrasting parallel to the Wandering Jew, who lives in successive incarnations *forward* in time, is the reference to Philip the Englishman, whose successive avatars apparently take place *backwards* in time. He was first "clockmaker to Hume" (eighteenth century) and then, moving back in time as István does, mimic ("mono") of Pope Sylvester II (tenth century) who is often credited, incidentally, with the invention of the mechanical clock (circa 996).

The elaborate chess set and billiard table are images related to the idea of "games" or "jokes," a motif repeated throughout the story. The big "joke," of course, was Anthal Horvath's innocent joke played on his friend. The forged manuscript was a game which got out of control, however, and turned into a grim joke for all of them in the end: "Pero él [Horvath] no podía sospechar la terrible aventura que los esperaba" (p. 101). The torture instruments, including a Turkish version of the *demoiselle,* may foreshadow the strongly intimated fact that Ferencz Remenyi, a member of the patriots, is tortured by the Austrian authorities before they play a cat and mouse game with him instead of killing him outright (again the game and joke motif). He is given forty-eight hours to escape across the border, an illusory escape in space which parallels the "real" escape in time effected by István Banyay (p. 132).

The optical instruments in the *museo* suggest the play of visual perspectives inherent in the structure of the narrative points of view employed in the story. Until the reader is placed in Anthal Horvath's first-person perspective in Part II, his vision of reality is only partial. Our eyes, like those of István and Professor Liptay, have been closed or blinded to the deception practiced in the manuscript forgery. In Part I we are not permitted to see this hidden side of reality, although there are hints and clues scattered throughout.

The copies of the wooden dove and the bronze fly built by Regiomontanus are spurious ("ejemplares apócrifos," p. 103), and as such relate directly to the motif of forgery and deception. Regiomontanus ("belonging to the royal mountain," i.e., to Königsberg, where he was born) was a German mathematician and astronomer (1436-76) whose real name was Johannes Müller. (Again the motif of concealment, dissimulation: note that Horvath also uses a pseudonym. He claims to be working on a "rigurosa novela de peripecias, que se publicará con mi seudónimo . . ." [p. 108].) Regiomontanus, one of those mysterious historical figures which fascinate Bioy Casares and Borges, was called to the court of Hungary (scene of the action of Bioy's tale) in 1468 to make a collection of Greek manuscripts. (A manuscript is a central image in the story.) He also assisted in reforming the calendar while at Rome in 1475 (theme of time).

Central in the development of the dual themes relating to time is the role of István Banyay who is soon revealed as a man who feels out of place in the twentieth century and more at home in the seventeenth: "Estoy acostumbrado a esa época; las demás se me figuran irreales. . . . Si no me vigilo creo que el siglo XVII es la época natural de la vida humana; más aún de mi propia vida. . . ." (p. 107). He is convinced that the century which so fascinates him actually exists in the room he calls the "museum": "Cuando trabajo en mis biografías para la Enciclopedia, imagino que el siglo XVII está en ese cuarto" (p. 109). Anthal Horvath attributes personality defects to his friend: István must attend to matters successively, one thing at a time; he is also unable to establish relationships and comparisons (p. 104). Yet these same characteristics may be seen in a positive light. The first hints at István's great powers of concentration and his supernatural gift of mental projection which ultimately enable him to recreate "los objetos y los siglos" (p. 142), and thereby to seek refuge in the past. The second allows him to overlook certain inconsistencies in Anthal's forged manuscript, to intuit his own life in the false seventeenth-century biography, and to live out the life depicted therein: "Me pierdo en la vida que relata" (p. 113). It also enables him to overcome (or overlook) a "small matter" like the cause-and-effect relationship of reality by transporting that manuscript of the present into an apparently bygone time wherein it was lost and then eagerly sought by scholars for three centu-

ries. The past is thus envisioned as vulnerable to the present, since the present can alter and affect the past.

István's supernatural powers of mental projection are suggested early in the story (p. 104). They are later described in greater detail (p. 116), but Banyay refers to a major difficulty he encounters in performing the feat: "Proyectar la forma, el color, la solidez, la temperatura . . . nunca me costó mucho. El peso da más trabajo." (p. 116) Supposedly, then, István managed to overcome this obstacle because he succeeded in lifting his bulky body and projecting it back three centuries. But the attentive reader has watched the author subtly preparing even this small detail of the fantastic surprise ending. The description of the corpse found in the Tunnel Inn in the seventeenth century stated: "Era corpulento, pero no obeso" (p. 101). However, the early descriptions of István emphasize his enormous size (p. 105), his huge round head (p. 107), and his "ponderoso busto" (p. 113). The reader is thus tempted to hesitate, to doubt the intervention of the fantastic, i.e., to question whether the cadaver found in the inn was István Banyay. However, Horvath soon notices that his friend seems "algo más flaco" (p. 115). Professor Liptay later reports that Banyay is in an alarming condition: he is sick, has lost more weight, and Horvath finds him "casi flaco" (p. 120). István no longer has "excess baggage," and is now ready for his fantastic "flight through time!"[30]

Anthal Horvath, as co-protagonist with István Banyay, plays a role no less important in the development of the temporal themes. Horvath also is convinced that the past is in the *museo,* but for him it is no consolation, but rather produces an unpleasant feeling: "Según Anthal Horvath, la visión de ese cuarto producía una desilusionada tristeza, como si allí estuviera todo el pasado, como si desde allí acecharan todas las esperanzas, todas las frustraciones y todas las modestas locuras de los hombres" (pp. 103-4). Anthal has come home to Hungary seeking refuge in his time of troubles, economic and professional, but to him this return to his "provincial" homeland is humiliating and repugnant. He recalls verses by a Hungarian poet, Janos Aranyi, which should serve as a warning to him that he will find no external refuge. The reference to the Garden of Paradise is clearly a symbol of a place outside of time, in eternity: "*No busques el Jardín del Paraíso / el abismo arde ya en tu corazón / o florece la paz, que a tu alma educa*" (p. 105). Longing for Paris, for Madeleine and for wider cultural horizons than those afforded by Hungary, he angrily revises the last line: "*O florece París, que a tu alma educa*" (p. 105). The sight of the familiar street scene outside his window and the recollection of a Hungarian folk song give him the impression that time has stood still here during his absence, that Budapest and the past represent, in the words of the song, his "montaña nativa, donde todo, hasta el pasado, nos ampara" (p. 110). Other lyrics of the same song proffer a second, unheeded warning and a premonition: Horvath looks at the street "por donde viene . . . el infortunio y la muerte" (p. 110). It is along this very street that he will later observe the approach of the thin man dressed in gray, an investigator for the Austrian secret police, the same person that István had seen before vanishing (p. 141).

Nevertheless, Horvath feels safe in his well-known reality. Time has stood still here; all is as it was before. Despite the claims of the patriots that the city has changed (p. 111), the evidence to the contrary seems to be everywhere before Anthal's eyes as he strolls through well-remembered streets. The enumeration of familiar things, which makes up the entirety of the brief second chapter of Part I, is intended to reinforce the thematic impression that the past lives on in the present. Anthal again flirts with the tailor's wife by whistling a German love song ("Wenn die Liebe in deinen blauen Augen"), and he feels now the same sentiments he had felt when younger "frente a esa misma puerta en muchas tardes de años anteriores" (p. 112). This impression that nothing has changed, that the past exists simultaneously in the present is intensified at the outset of Chapter III as Horvath drinks beer with his good friends at the familiar Turf café and listens to the music of traditional old czardas: "Horvath sintió con desagrado que los años de París se desvanecían de su vida como si nunca hubieran existido, y que el repetido y pobre laberinto de sus costumbres en Budapest volvía a encerrarlo" (p. 112). Indeed, Anthal Horvath is entering a labyrinth, the "other labyrinth" of past time which will lead him to his death. In a sense, Horvath, like István, is returning to the past, his own past, as he gradually accepts and settles into the familiar ways of his previous life: "Reconoció que ninguna música le conmovía como las czardas, que le gustaba estar con sus amigos y que, en última instancia, él había nacido en Budapest (p. 114).

No sooner, however, does Anthal accept his past reality than it begins to change (p. 115). Since he has reentered the temporal flow, he naturally becomes more aware of the changes wrought by time. There are two reasons for this ambiguous, fluctuating reality. First, the tense political situation is turning the city into a prison for the Hungarian patriots. Second, and more importantly, Horvath knows something that the reader does not: he realizes that his little joke, the forged manuscript, is backfiring on him. István continues to believe in the authenticity of the document. Not yet a committed member of the patriots, a forger, doubly disloyal to his best friend, even unsure as yet of his love for Erzsebet (p. 122), Horvath formulates a thought which is one of those frequently appearing sentences in fantastic literature which call the reader's attention to the real, "the most central aspects of our existence" (see above, p. 168). Perhaps the most profound comment on life made by **"El otro laberinto"** is summed up in these words: "Debemos cuidarnos de que nuestras propias mentiras no nos engañen" (p. 122). Anthal later confesses: *"Estuve engañado sobre el alcance de mi obra"* (p. 139; Bioy's italics).

After the discovery of Horvath's spurious manuscript and István's subsequent disappearance, the events involving Anthal begin to move so quickly that he loses all control of the situation. Helpless now to change political matters and seemingly paralyzed before the snowballing effects of his "joke," Anthal's safe, familiar world of reality gradually turns completely nightmarish, thus following the classic pattern of the fantastic story. Horvath emphasizes this at the beginning of his confession to his friends: *"Todo ha cambiado. . . . [Los amigos] participaron, día a día, en ese proceso de transformación; nunca sabrán cómo se apresuró el tiempo en Hungría, cuánto cambio trajo. Yo mismo, al regresar de París, no advertí inmediatamente que ya era otro mundo este mundo familiar. Ni siquiera lo advertí cuando István desapareció. De un modo gradual, sin revelaciones patéticas ni sobresaltos, penetré en esta pesadilla"* (p. 128; Bioy's italics).

Two facts bring Horvath to a full realization of just exactly how nightmarish his secure world has become. With regard to the situation in Budapest, Anthal refers to his last meeting with Ferencz Remenyi as a "símbolo sobre la verdadera naturaleza de las cosas" (p. 128). The reader soon discovers the brutal truth that the real world of spies, police, dungeons and torture have reduced the once brave, happy, idealistic Ferencz to a sobbing, cringing, terrified animal (p. 132). Their encounter took place in a grove of trees, and was enveloped, as Anthal states, in a "sombra de irrealidad" (p. 128). The real has thus become unreal and monstrous.

Second, what had seemed fantastic, unreal, has been realized. Aware of Banyay's supernatural powers, of the latter's obsession with the seventeenth century, and of descriptions of the manuscript found on the dead man, Horvath finally understands that what had begun as an innocent joke has ended in tragedy. His friend has entered the "other labyrinth," the endless labyrinth of time. He concludes, awestricken: 1) that the cadaver found in the Tunnel inn of Budapest in 1604 was that of the young historian, István Banyay (p. 141); 2) that the manuscript was István's photocopy of his (Horvath's) own counterfeit handiwork (p. 140). Realizing that István was doubtlessly fleeing from the Austrian secret police, Anthal reconstructs what probably happened on the day of Banyay's disappearance: "*Istvàn comprendió que era la policía secreta; pensó, con desesperada intensidad, en el cuarto que estaba más allá de la puerta de la izquierda, en el 'museo.' Siempre había imaginado que allí estaba el siglo XVII; ahora, su imaginación de aquel siglo se concentraba obsesivamente en una pieza de la posada del Túnel, de la posada que había entonces en el sitio donde sus abuelos edificaron el pabellón. Guardó el documento en el bolsillo de su capa, abrió la puerta y pasó . . . Tuvo tiempo de cerrar el pasador. Estaba muy agitado. Su corazón, que siempre había sido débil, falló. Pero Istvàn no cayó muerto en el 'museo'; cayó en el cuarto de la posado del Túnel, en el siglo XVII*" (p. 141; Bioy's italics).

When Istvàn informed Horvath that *in 1637* a French writer of travel books, Jean Baptiste Tavernier (1605-89), found an error in the manuscript concerning the source of a quote from Ovid's *Tristia,* Horvath had turned inexplicably pale and was unable to speak (pp. 118-19). We learn much later that Anthal had intentionally planted that error in his forged manuscript *of 1904* in order to assure that Istvàn would discover the hoax (p. 140). Tavernier's discovery of Horvath's error, supposedly mentioned somewhere in the Frenchman's multivolumed *Six voyages . . .* (p. 118), makes Anthal aware that his reality has turned completely unreal and nightmarish, that forces beyond his comprehension are at work.

Horvath's fear and astonishment are brought on by his numbing realization of the fantastic reversal of the cause-and-effect relationship of things. In linear time, cause precedes effect; here the opposite prevails. Anthal's deliberate error in the manuscript of 1904 takes place "*before*" the 1637 discovery of that error by Tavernier. For such to happen, however, it was necessary for a twentieth-century man to travel to the seventeenth century with the forged manuscript containing the mistake. Istvàn's temporal journey to the past alters the subsequent three hundred years and influences the present actions of both protagonists. Since Anthal's fraudulent manuscript in a sense triggered that voyage in time, the reader must conclude that future (i.e., 1904 seen from 1604) has determined past (1604). Effect precedes cause, thereby negating the traditional concept of time. Here, past, present and future become one. As the bewildered Anthal Horvath concludes: ". . . comprendí que yo había entrado en un mundo mágico" (p. 141).

In the foregoing analysis of **"El otro laberinto,"** we have seen how the artist, Adolfo Bioy Casares, has skillfully woven the dual themes of temporal simultaneity and time travel into the entire creative fabric of his story. Plot, characters, setting, atmosphere, motifs, foreshadowing devices such as literary allusion, etc., and all other details are tightly bound into a well unified narrative structure. **"El otro laberinto"** is a masterful and aesthetically pleasing example of the contemporary tale of fantastic fiction.

Notes

1. Useful studies and anthologies of Argentine fantastic fiction include the following: Ana María Barrenechea y Emma Susana Speratti Piñero, *La literatura fantástica en Argentina* (México, 1957); *Cuentos fantásticos argentinos,* Selección e Introducción de Nicolás Cócaro (Buenos Aires, 1960), pp. 11-39; *Cuentos fantásticos argentinos: Segunda Serie,* Selección e Introducción de Nicolás Cócaro y Antonio E. Serrano Redonnet (Buenos Aires, 1976), pp. 9-26; Julio Cortázar, "The Present State of Fiction in Latin America," *Books Abroad,* 50, No. 3 (Summer 1976), 522-32; Enrique Luis Revol, "La tradición fantástica en la literatura argentina," *Revista de Estudios Hispánicos,* 2 (1968), 205-28; Donald A. Yates, "*Sobre los orígenes de la literatura fantástica argentina*" in *La Literatura Iberoamericana del Siglo XIX. Memoria del XV Congreso Internacional de Literatura Iberoamericana* (Tucson, 1974), pp. 213-20. Two recent anthologies of fantastic stories contain further valuable introductory material on the subject. See: *Antología de literatura fantástica argentina, 1. Narradores del siglo XIX.* Selección, Estudio Preliminar y Notas de Haydée Flesca y María Hortensia Lacau (Beunos Aires, 1970) and *Antología de literatura fantástica argentina. 2. Narradores del siglo XX,* Selección, Estudio Preliminar y Notas de Alberto Manguel (Buenos Aires, 1973).

2. Cited in Emir Rodríguez Monegal, "Borges: Una Teoría de la Literatura Fantástica," *Revista Iberoamericana,* 42, No. 95 (abril-junio 1976), 185-87. Borges' earlier lecture was repeated years later, on April 7, 1967, at the "Inauguración del ciclo cultural 1967 de la Escuela Camillo y Adriano Olivetti" and was published as a fourteen-page monograph by that institution. See Jorges Luis Borges, *La literatura fantástica* (Buenos Aires: Ediciones Culturales Olivetti, 1967). Other fantastic themes discussed by Borges in this informative lecture include metamorphosis, invisibility, supernatural beings, the double or *Doppelgänger,* and the penetration and alteration of reality by oneiric elements.

3. See Louis Vax, *Arte y literatura fantásticas,* trans. Juan Merino (Buenos Aires: EUDEBA, 1965). All further citations are from this edition, and will appear in the text.

4. Cf. the following remarks by another authority on the fantastic: "The fantastic . . . manifests a scan-

dal, a rent, an extraordinary, almost unbearable ir-ruption in the world of reality. . . . But the fan-tastic is not a milieu [like fairyland]: it is an aggression. . . . The fantastic supposes the solid-ity of the real world, the better to ravage it. . . . The essential step in the fantastic is the Appari-tion: what cannot happen but *does* happen, at a given moment and point in the heart of a perfectly ordered universe, from which one believed mys-tery to have been forever banished. Everything seems as it was yesterday, quiet, ordinary, without anything unusual—when the Inadmissible slowly slips upon us or suddenly bursts upon the scene." Roger Caillois, "The Fantastic," trans. Will McLendon, *Forum* (Houston, Texas), 2, No. 2 (May 1958), 51.

5. Tzvetan Todorov centers his definition of the fan-tastic in the duration of this uncertainty of charac-ter and reader. See *The Fantastic: A Structural Approach to a Literary Genre,* trans. Richard Howard (Ithaca, N.Y.: Cornell University Press, 1975), p. 25.

6. Edmund Fuller, "A Note on the Fantastic" in *Books with Men behind Them* (N.Y., 1960), pp. 135-36. Cf. Yates, *Literatura Iberoamericana del Siglo XIX . . . ,* p. 220: "La literatura fantástica mod-erna no es escapista: es una literatura de retorno. Con ella, uno se libra de los confines y de las limitaciones de la realidad cotidiana para después volver la vista, desde *otra* perspectiva, sobre las preocupaciones humanas de todos los tiempos."

7. Noteworthy exceptions are Ofelia Kovacci's thirty-two page introduction to her anthology of works by Bioy Casares, *Adolfo Bioy Casares* (Buenos Aires: Ediciones Culturales Argentinas, 1963) and D. P. Gallagher, "The Novels and Short Stories of Adolfo Bioy Casares," *Bulletin of His-panic Studies,* 52 (1975), 247-66. See also my study, "Estructura y tema de *El sueño de los héroes* por Adolfo Bioy Casares," *Kentucky Romance Quarterly,* 20 (1973), 31-58.

8. Adolfo Bioy Casares, *La trama celeste* (Buenos Aires: Sur, 1967), p. 135; Bioy's italics. All sub-sequent quotations from "El otro laberinto" refer to this edition and will be indicated by page num-ber in the text. "El otro laberinto," the other tales from *La trama celeste,* and Bioy's major novel, *La invención de Morel,* have been translated into English. See Adolfo Bioy Casares, *The Invention of Morel and Other Stories (from La Trama Celeste),* trans. Ruth L. C. Simms (Austin: Uni-versity of Texas Press, 1964).

9. Jorge B. Rivera, "Lo arquetípico en la narrativa argentina del 40" in Jorge Lafforgue, ed., *Nueva Novela Latinoamericana 2* (Buenos Aires: Paidós, 1972), p. 180.

10. István had even suggested to Horvath that the story of the dead man found in the Tunnel Inn in the seventeenth century would be good material for an exciting detective novel (p. 104), an idea which Horvath pompously scoffs at because, as Anthal says, "István no conoce las reglas del género." (Bioy is, of course, hinting at his own narrative method at the same time that he makes fun of Horvath. István was right. The story is, in part, a good mystery.) The reader learns later that Horvath is engaged in writing, among other things, three works of detective fiction for the publisher, Hellebronth (p. 108). They would, no doubt, fol-low the general (foolish!) "reglas del género" which Horvath had previously mentioned: "que la acción ocurra en ese incomparable París del Seg-undo Imperio o, al menos, en las brumas de Lon-dres; que la Sûreté no se omita (p. 104)." Bioy's story, "El otro laberinto," proves that a good mys-tery can be made of other, more subtle stuff.

11. Horvath's own account (p. 122-23), István's par-ents' version (p. 123), the coachman Janós' testi-mony (p. 123), and finally the true version, the "revelación" of the dollseller (p. 125).

12. Although neither protagonist murders the police chief, both of them ultimately die themselves.

13. Vax, *Arte y literatura fanásticas,* p. 13.

14. See the "Prólogo" by Adolfo Bioy Casares to Jorge Luis Borges, Silvina Ocampo, Adolfo Bioy Casares, eds., *Antología de la literatura fantás-tica,* 2a ed. (Buenos Aires: Editorial Sudameri-cana, 1965), pp. 8-9.

15. Kovacci, *Adolfo Bioy Casares,* p. 35.

16. Jaime Rest, "Las invenciones de Bioy Casares," *Los Libros,* No. 2 (agosto 1969), 8. This charac-teristic feature of Bioy's fiction partially explains the unusual length of his *cuentos.*

17. "Los planos de la realidad y la fantasía se relacio-nan en las obras de Bioy Casares sin violen-cia. . . . Se entre en este último terreno con toda naturalidad, como a un orbe feliz en ciertos ca-sos." (Kovacci, p. 28.)

18. With one exception, the dual references to István Banyay's supernatural powers of mental projec-tion (pp. 105, 116).

19. The verse has also been translated as follows: "Though you should wish to play the deceiver, it is clear that you are mine." Ovid, *Tristia * Ex Ponto,* ed. and trans. Arthur Leslie Wheeler (London: William Heinemann Ltd., 1965), p. 7. All further quotes and translations included throughout this section are from this edition of Ovid's *Tristia.*

20. The invention of the first wheel clock is often attributed to Boethius (A.D. 470-525).

21. Augustine, *Confessions and Enchiridion,* trans. and ed. Albert C. Outler, VII, The Library of Christian Classics (Philadelphia: The Westminster Press, 1955), p. 244. One can only speculate on what passage from St. Augustine's lengthy eleventh book Bioy Casares has in mind (or perhaps examine the frieze on the ceiling of the library at the university in Budapest, if such should exist). Any of the following quotations from the edition of the *Confessions* cited above would be appropriately related to the theme of simultaneous time or eternity: "In the Eternal . . . nothing passes away, but the whole is simultaneously present" (p. 252); "All thy years stand together as one, since they are abiding" (p. 254); "Thy years are but a day, and thy day is not recurrent, but always today" (p. 254); "For if there are times past and future, I wish to know where they are. But if I have not yet succeeded in this, I still know that wherever they are, they are not there as future or past, but as present" (p. 257); "It is in you, O mind of mine, that I measure the periods of time" (p. 266).

22. *The Works of the English Poets,* ed. Alexander Chalmers, XV (London: C. Whittingham, 1910), p. 399. In modern English, the line would read "Straight was I carried back to times of yore."

23. The English poet, Thomas Chatterton (1752-70), was the posthumous son of a poor Bristol schoolmaster. At the age of twelve, after immersing himself in the medieval history of his native city of Bristol and teaching himself Gothic lettering, he began to compose his famous "Rowley Poems" in a pseudo-Middle English. Thomas Rowley was a creation of Chatterton, an imaginary, Anglo-Saxon priest-poet of Bristol whose supposed patron was the historical lord mayor of the city, William Canynge. According to Chatterton, Canynge had been the original owner of Rowley's fifteenth-century manuscripts which Chatterton had chanced upon in a chest left in the Church of St. Mary Redcliffe at Bristol. Chatterton's use of an elaborately archaic lexicon and pseudoarchaic spelling did not suffice, however, to conceal the interior evidence of a rhyme and meter based on eighteenth-century pronunciation. Nevertheless, his medieval literary hoaxes were apparently so authentic in appearance that in 1769 he even succeeded in duping, at least temporarily, so discerning a reader as Horace Walpole. Unmasked and crushed by Walpole's subsequent rebuff, Chatterton tried, with little success, to sell his poetry to various London magazines. Half starved, but too proud to beg or borrow, he poisoned himself by taking arsenic at the early age of seventeen. Although Chatterton died in dis-

grace, he was later widely recognized both for his adept imitations of medieval poetic style and for his original artistic genius. For such talents, the gifted, rebellious, and pathetic Chatterton soon became a hero to many European romantic writers who saw in him a symbol of the inspired artist whom an ignorant, crass society failed to understand. Keats and Coleridge wrote poems about him and Alfred de Vigny immortalized the youthful bard in his play, *Chatterton* (1835).

24. A direct translation of the line, "'Wee all must die,' quod brave syrr Charles; / 'Of thatte I'm not affearde.'" *The Works of the English Poets,* p. 393.

25. *The Works of the English Poets,* p. 375.

26. Rivera also seems to consider Anthal Horvath and István Banyay as doubles, for the refers to them as *pares* or *gemelos míticos. Nueva Novela . . . ,* p. 184.

27. Kovacci, *Adolfo Bioy Casares,* p. 21.

28. Kovacci points out that in Bioy Casares' fiction, "Un ámbito donde van a ocurrir sucesos prodigiosos se presenta con ciertos rasgos extraordinarios" (p. 35). Another reader of "El otro laberinto" suggests that the errie, magic atmosphere of the room is produced by the unlikely objects accumulated there which contribute to the occurrence of the temporal warp essential to István's escape into the past: "La tenacidad evocativa y *desrealizadora* de las cosas se verifica en forma pugnaz en 'El otro laberinto,' donde los objetos antiguos acumulados por el tío abuelo de Banyay . . . tienen una capacidad contaminante tal que coadyuvan a la realización del alabeo temporal que transporta al siglo XVII a uno de los personajes . . . ellos existen para tomar parte en el 'warp' temporal. Su *realidad* es eminentemente *desrealizadora.*" (Rivera, pp. 197-98.)

29. Kovacci, p. 35.

30. The motif of weight is present in Horvath's case also, and is further evidence supporting the interpretation of the double, developed above (p. 174). Ferencz Remenyi earlier noticed how thin Horvath was (p. 113), and on the last day of his life, Anthal weighs himself (p. 129).

Anthony J. Cascardi (essay date 1984)

SOURCE: Cascardi, Anthony J. "Reading the Fantastic in Darío ('La Pesadilla de Honorio') and Bioy-Casares ('En Memoria de Paulina')." *Crítica Hispánica* 6, no. 2 (1984): 117-30.

[*In the following essay, Cascardi traces similarities in the employment of fantastic literary devices in Rubén Darío's "La pesadilla de Honorio" and Bioy Casares's short story "En memoria de Paulina."*]

To propose, as the title of this essay does, that certain works of literature are "fantastic" is not to invoke an *a priori* category, a fixed model or established class. Even less is it to consecrate a revolt against verisimilitude. To denote the fantastic in literature is, rather, to engage in the interminable process of defining that which constitutes it, of differentiating it from all else. To name the fantastic is to confront as well the more disconcerting question: what literature is not in some way fantastic? And although such queries are imposing in the very scope they imply, the notion of the fantastic persists as a useful, even fertile concept in literary criticism. It is in part because the fantastic is a term of ever evolving and renewable significance— one that induces us to seek in the text, each and every text, its measure of difference from the world outside it—that modern practitioners of this species of literature have so held the interest of structuralist critics, themselves concerned with the verbal object as an autonomous whole.[1] Yet the fantastic also brings an immediate awareness of the referential nature of language, of the inescapable fact that while each text establishes its own coherence, it must also make reference to that which is outside its verbal confines. Thus, an interest in the fantastic extends beyond the limits of structuralism, and is germane to the criticism that has followed in its wake, much of it concerned with the problematic borders of verbal and extra-verbal worlds.

To think of the fantastic both in terms of the text itself and all that is outside the text is not merely useful for a reading of Darío's "La pesadilla de Honorio" and Bioy-Casares' **"En memoria de Paulina"**: it is an approach demanded by the texts themselves. These two fantastic stories revolve around the differences between the text and the vast world outside it—the world of empirical reality, that of the reader himself, and of those others readers and texts that serve as the defining points of reference for the work at hand. While recognizing the referential nature of the verbal work of art, we must at the same time seek to discover the traits which it defines for itself and with which it marks off the borders of its own world. Simply to quantify the "ángulo de desviación entre el tema de un cuento y la realidad de todos los días" is a false science, as Anderson-Imbert avers.[2] Rather, we must recognize the constantly emerging outlines which the text shapes and which are ambivalently set in both the imaginary and empirical worlds.

The narrative "contract" in Darío's "La pesadilla de Honorio"—those facets which enable the reader to recognize an intelligible, however unfamiliar, world—is not founded on the presence of referents whose sole function is to confirm a mimetic intent.[3] From the start, however, the narrator suggests plainly enough the coordinates of a cohesive world: "¿Dónde? ¿Dónde?

A lo lejos . . . ;" "¿Cuándo? Es en una hora inmemorial . . . ;" "¿Cómo y por qué apareció en la memoria de Honorio esta frase . . . ?"[4] Whereas conventional stylistic analysis would detect in these interrogatives an indirect suggestion of mood, it is particularly important that we ask, as Roland Barthes might, "who speaks here?"[5] For, insofar as the "¿Dónde?" "¿Cuándo?" "¿Cómo y por qué . . . ?" intimate the referential quality of the text and solicit from the reader the anticipation of a world he knows, the narrative voice is here a reflection of the reader's expectations.

The opening paragraphs of Darío's story call into play the full range of dualities latent in the interrogatives. The narrative voice that poses these questions also supplies the reader with answers; and because the answers are imprecise, evasive, or indicative of that which is unfamiliar to the reader, this voice is not *simply* an echo of the reader's world but an autonomous narrative voice as well—doubly valent. The initial narrative response to "¿Dónde?" consists of a deft slight-of-hand, a description not of an immediate locale but of a distant vision: "A lo lejos, la perspectiva abrumadora y monumental de extrañas arquitecturas, órdenes visionarios, estilos de un orientalismo portentoso y desmesurado" (p. 39). And yet, even in a description such as this the narrator continues to acknowledge the reader's world, implicitly marking the difference between the two in the adjectives *extrañas, visionarios,* and *desmesurado.* While the principal human subject of the story is present in the opening paragraph only by allusion ("a *sus* pies . . . "), the more immediate physical location becomes a point of the narrator's direct concern. Again, his voice marks off that which is familiar and known—because it is living—from that which is, by suggestion, dead and therefore radically strange: "A sus pies un suelo *lívido;* no lejos, una *vegetación* . . . " (*ibid.*).

Similarly, the referential elements which are induced by the interrogative time-coordinate delineate the temporal moment of the action as at once familiar and different: it is both "una hora inmemorial," and a "grano escapado quizás del reloj del tiempo" (*ibid.*). Moreover, the narrative voice relieves the reader of the burden of recognition, while implicitly acknowledging his world, through the otherwise superfluous *quizás.* And, perhaps more important, the subsequent description of the light ("*no es* la del sol; *es como* la enfermiza y fosforecente claridad de espectrales astros") at once limits the province of the narrative world and reverses the essential narrative task of naming specifically the components of that world. As Jean Ricardou commented *à propos* of a perplexing passage in Poe,[6] a fundamental law of narration is that which allows the author to limit his world by a process of inclusion: "si une narration présente un ou deux attributs d'une chose, la nécessité d'en présenter un troisième en règle générale diminue car le texte, du fait de sa linéarité, verserait dans une inesthétique insistence."[7] Darío's description does not evade the narrative task of inclusion; by a subtle inversion of the process of naming and specifying, it fulfills the more important function of delimiting the components of a world: it names that which is *not* and, furthermore, defers the essence of the light (while nonetheless differentiating it) through a simile.

Darío's final interrogative ("¿Cómo y por qué apareció en la memoria de Honorio esta frase de un soñador: *la tiranía del rostro humano*?" p. 40), however, ushers in a change in the narrative voice. Rigorously considered, the question produces a reply that is no less equivocal than the previous descriptions I have discussed. In addition to the continued intimations of uncertainty that in effect allow the reader to lend his own world to the text, the direct response to these final questions is a curious *non sequitur;* while pretending to answer the questions of motivation and means, it is but a description of Honorio's experience—an experience which, it should be added, the narrator denotes as inexplicable: "El la escuchó dentro de su cerebro, y cual si fuese la víctima propiciatoria ofrecida a una cruel deidad, comprendió que se acercaba el instante del martirio, del horrible martirio que le sería aplicado. . . . ¡Oh sufrimiento inexplicable del condenado solitario! Sus miembros se petrificaron . . . " (*ibid.*). By virtue of the fact that the linear configuration of prose approximates the line of human reason, a passage such as this is made to pass as a more or less logical answer to the questions that have been posed. And yet, does not the linear quality of prose mark the passage both as familiar to the reader and as something quite strange, as following a linearity which it establishes for itself? From this point in the narration on, the narrative voice ceases to play on the dualities of reference which mark the precarious contours of the textual world; rather, Darío makes increasing use of the very flow of language to delimit a verbal world apart from that which the reader knows and at the same time to secure the reader's faith in that world as valid, while neither logical nor familiar. "L'homme poursuit noir sur blanc," Mallarmé said, and for the major portion of "La pesadilla de Honorio" the reader is given over to the very force of the written word, in its plenitude as both bridge and barricade between imaginary and empirical worlds.

Yet, we should add that from the start Darío engages the reader's awareness of the limited self-control which he will ultimately come to experience as a function of the language of the text. In the opening description, for example, the trees (with "sus ramas su-

plicantes, en la vaga expresión de un mudo lamento") face a "cielo implacable." It is significant for the narrator's final and deepest pact with the reader that, at the outset, Honorio is seen almost exclusively as a passive figure, unable to constitute himself sufficiently enough to exert a force over himself or over that which surrounds him: "Honorio siente la posesión de una fría pavura . . . " (p. 39); "Honorio sufre el influjo de un momento fatal" (*ibid.*); "Honorio deja escapar de sus labios, oprimido y aterrorizado, un lamentable gemido" (p. 40). The tormenting "tiranía del rostro humano"—De Quincey's phrase—is, in effect, a ceaseless recognition of both the sameness and difference of Honorio with respect to the innumerable members of the human race, a horrific recognition and loss of self. Yet Honorio, who is more a creature of the text than a subject of the story, also acts as a bridge for the reader's entry into the text, for it is *vis à vis* this singular character that the reader can judge the measure of his own difference from the narrative world.[8]

Ostensibly, the marked change in style that begins in this central paragraph is a verbal transfiguration of Honorio's nightmare. The prose becomes animated, and flows with a spontaneous energy; gone are the hesitant dualities of certainty and doubt—question and camouflaged reply—that prevailed in the opening paragraphs. It is for this reason that once again we ask "who speaks here?" For not only does the narrative voice exhibit its difference with respect to that of the interrogatives, the "subject" of the narration—the faces and masks to which it refers—is not bound by the constraints of the rational world which the reader knows. Each phrase, each word revises (and contradicts) the previous one: "Pierrot indiferente, Pierrot amoroso, Pierrot abobado, Pierrot terrible, Pierrot, desmayándose de hilaridad; doloroso, pícaro, inocente, vanidoso, cruel, dulce, criminal" (*ibid.*). The referential function of language is blocked and the reader is no longer able to recognize a familiar logical world; yet precisely where Darío's language asserts its own difference, the text is freed as its own writing.

Who indeed speaks here? On one level, it could be said that this voice is that of Honorio and that Darío has lapsed into *le style indirect libre.* And yet such a reply does nothing more than evade the deep question; for, we must also then ask, in what capacity does Honorio speak? Certainly not as a reflection of the reader. And to propose that Honorio speaks here as a function of the "other world" of his own nightmare is only to reaffirm the unfamiliarity of this voice, its radical difference from the world of the reader. In this passage and, indeed, in much of the second portion of the story, we can only ascribe the narrative voice to itself and to a text which follows its own verbal laws. Honorio exists solely as a function of the strange coherence of the dream, which is to say as part of the purely verbal world governed by the linear force of prose, by a purely verbal logic. The recognizable change in style which occurs in the story moves us from a world of reference, intelligible on the basis of the reader's world, to a verbal world intelligible on the basis of its own writing. As Ricardou stated, "Loin de se servir de l'écriture pour présenter une vision du monde, la fiction utilise le concept de monde avec ses rouages afin d'obtenir un univers obéissant aux lois de l'écriture" (*op. cit.,* p. 25). Or, adapting the vocabulary of Roland Barthes, we could say that "La pesadilla de Honorio" moves from readerly (*lisible*) to writerly (*scriptible*).

Despite the fact that Darío is commonly recognized as a renovator of the Spanish literary language, both his prose and his poetry are marked by a fundamental conservatism, a conservatism which stems from his will to achieve a carefully crafted form that would incarnate his ideals of beauty—however elusive such a form might be, e.g. "Yo persigo una forma. . . ." As Raimundo Lida put it, "Darío no se abandona al culto romántico de la improvisación. Si sus sueños son de poeta . . . lo son, además, de escritor consciente y enamorado de su oficio. . . . El ideal de forma pulcra y vigilada asoma en Darío inequivocadamente."[9] Darío, who lived to know the more audacious innovations of the Avant-Garde, resisted its linguistic experiments; his most innovative period ends with *Prosas profanas* (1896), as Octavio Paz has said: "después de *Prosas profanas* los caminos se cierran: hay que replegar las velas o saltar hacia lo desconocido. Rubén Darío escogió lo primero y pobló las tierras descubiertas."[10] Yet, "La pesadilla de Honorio" (1894) remains an uncontestable example of innovation on Darío's part. In the prose that characterizes the second portion of the story we can detect a language that anticipates the automatic writing of the true pioneers and colonizers of the world of dreams, the surrealists.

Not only does Darío sustain for several paragraphs the kind of verbal energy that we have seen in the description of Pierrot. The narrative voice takes on a dynamic, self-propagating character and follows no laws other than those which it generates for itself. The "suave color de oro oriental" (p. 41), a phrase which already contains internal echoes, comes to describe the masks of the gods as well ("todas de oro," p. 42). The laughing mask becomes a "*gárgola* surtidora de *chistes*" (p. 41), and, by association, Honorio sees before him "un *diluvio* de máscaras niponas" (*ibid.*). Finally comes Darío's *tour de force,* the vertiginous sequences of adjectives whose order breaks the borders of all pre-conceived rational categories:

> Todos los ojos: almendrados, redondos, triangulares, casi amorfos; todas las narices: chatas, roxelanas, bor-bónicas, erectas, cónicas, fálicas, innobles, cavernosas, conventuales, marciales, insignes; todas las bocas: arqueadas, en media luna, en ojiva, hechas con sacabocado, de labios carnosos, místicas, sensuales, golosas, abyectas, caninas, batracias, hípicas, asnales, porcunas, delicadas, desbordadas, desbridadas, retorcidas. . . .

> (p. 42)

The series are generated by a more or less free association of ideas ("erectas, cónicas, fálicas, innobles") as well as by purely phonic associations ("delicadas, desbordadas, desbridadas").[11] This is not the pageantry of masks Darío knew from Gérard de Nerval, and which he later used in the "Cuento de Pascuas" (1911), but rather a purely linguistic encounter with the terror of human nature, a recognition of infinite human difference, and also a shocking encounter with the self.

The reader has no choice here, if he is to continue to read, but to submit himself to the text, much as Honorio is submitted to the dream. The reader is called upon to reaffirm his participation in the narrative pact, but now on the terms of the text itself. That aspect of language which is referential has given way to a purely verbal world. Honorio, we have said, exists not so much as a function of his dream as a function of the discourse of the text; in a similar way, the reader's world ceases to exist and he too becomes a function of the writing of the text. This transformation allows Darío to suggest a more subtle blurring of the borders between verbal and referential worlds: "Y Honorio no pudo más: sintió un súbito desmayo, y quedó en una dulce penumbra de ensueño, en tanto que llegaban a sus oídos los acordes de una alegre comparsa de Carnestolendas . . . " (p. 42). The "comparsa de Carnestolendas" recalls immediately the "enjambre carnavalesco" of masks of the previous paragraph and, as well, "todas las farsas" of "las encarnaciones simbólicas" suggested by the figure of Pierrot (p. 40). Yet, the music of the Lenten carnival is perceived not during Honorio's nightmare, but afterwards; it is a final suggestion that the world outside the text has been subsumed into the verbal world. The narrative voice—no longer either questioning or melding with Honorio's dream—marks itself as clearly distinct and apart from Honorio and the reader. Honorio has become a creation of the narrative voice, not an autonomous character, in the same way that the extra-verbal world is now a function of the text.

Honorio begins to come out of his dream into an autonomous physical world, but never completes the passage. Rather, he remains "en una dulce penumbra de ensueño." We might take Darío's phrase as a metaphor for the text itself, existing apart from both the imaginary and the physical worlds, or rather, between the two. The verbal world, both referential and autonomous, is engaged in the constant forging of its own difference, of marking itself off from all that it is not, of acknowledging the reader and his world and at the same time affirming its own autonomy. Darío's fantastic story, an adventure into the emerging profiles of black on white, is an invitation to partake in the fundamental linguistic process of differentiating. Like Poe's adventurers exploring parts unknown, the reader seeks in the unfamiliar and unrecognizable the outlines of his own image. By confronting that which is different, he comes to recognize the measure of his own difference, and hence of his identity. The singular characteristic of the waters encountered by Poe's adventurers—which has elicited comment from Ricardou and others[12]—remains ineffable, yet just the same compulsively intriguing, because so different. Those waters, much like the text itself, can yield a world which helps the reader form an image of his own uniqueness, the singular and precise cipher of his identity.

As modeled in Darío's story, the fantastic is not so much a special brand of literature as an example of textuality as such. Contemporary fantastic fiction, like the *nouveau roman* in this sense, has been well received because it accepts the reader's willingness to enter into the narrative pact: the world of his reference is recognized, even if it is to be fragmented, contradicted, torn asunder. Yet unlike Darío's fantastic tale, more recent fantastic literature plays less on those purely textual and linguistic functions of differentiation and more on temporal and narrative technique.

Considered in this light, Bioy-Casares' **"En memoria de Paulina"** is a text in which the reader's image is not obfuscated but resolved, his identity placed in equilibrium with his "otherness." The story is not the mere reflection of the world of the reader's reference, yet neither is it an intractable verbal expanse. Unlike Darío's "La pesadilla de Honorio," which consumes the reader's world of reference, **"En memoria de Paulina"** transforms the world of reference, leaving the reader with a clear vision of his own image, at once the same and new. Here, both text and reader are remitted to their most singular characteristics as functions of each other.

The story broaches one of the most formidable of all narrative challenges—that of recovering the past—at the start. Indeed, the first phrase is the victorious salvation of the narrator's past, accomplished by simply stating it as fact, by fixing it with all the firmness that the word "siempre" and the preterit tense can bestow: "Siempre quise a Paulina."[13] The reader, pre-disposed to alliance with the narrator, is able to enter the text by virtue of the narrator's own memories: "En uno de mis primeros recuerdos, Paulina y yo estamos ocultos en una oscura glorieta de laureles . . . " (*ibid.*). The

narrator not only recalls his past, but seeks to give it order as well; his narrative act thereby differentiates the past from the world of human experience—which is, by contrast, a world of continuous present and constant projection into the future. How different the reader's past, which is ceaselessly extinguishing; how different indeed the unordered future of which the narrator comes to tell and which confounds his expectations: "La vida fue una dulce costumbre que nos llevó a esperar, como algo natural y cierto, nuestro futuro matrimonio . . . Muchas veces nosotros imaginábamos un ordenado porvenir . . . " (*ibid.*). As the narration proceeds, not only does the future reveal itself to be radically unexpected (or, rather, unexpectable), but the narrator's own memories become increasingly fragmentary. They remain, nonetheless, the primordial means by which the past is made a knowable, if not familiar, landscape: "Me dije que se trataba de una superposición de recuerdos anacrónicos (el más antiguo, del caballito; el más reciente, de Paulina). La cuestión quedaba dilucidada, yo estaba tranquilo y debía dormirme" (p. 21). Memory becomes a refuge from the growing distance between the narrator and Paulina: "No cavilaría más sobre la conducta de Paulina. . . . Ya que no podía hacer un vacío en la mente y dejar de pensar, me refugiaría en el recuerdo de esa tarde" (p. 20).

The narrator-protagonist undergoes a differentiation which in essence parallels the reader's experience of the text. ("Hablar—he says—hubiera sido, en cierto modo diferenciarnos," *ibid.*). While the opening passages tell of a past that is sufficient evidence of itself, the events narrated thereafter become increasingly strange. We are called upon to share in the unexplainable as the narrator himself negotiates the ever-growing unfamiliarity of Paulina. The opening paragraphs bring us first the world of familiar reference: "Paulina me dijo: Me gusta el azul, me gustan las uvas, me gusta el hielo, me gustan las rosas, me gustan los caballos blancos. Yo comprendí que mi felicidad había empezado, porque en esas preferencias podía identificarme con Paulina. Nos parecíamos tan milagrosamente que en un libro sobre la final reunión de las almas en el alma del mundo, mi amiga escribió en el margen: *Las nuestras ya se reunieron.* 'Nuestras,' en aquel tiempo, significaba la de ella y la mía" (p. 11). Gradually, however, the presence of Julio Montero imparts a strange and unfamiliar cast to the narrator's world: "Cuando salimos del ascensor, Montero descubrió el jardín que hay en el patio. A veces, en la tenue luz de la tarde, viéndolo a través del portón de vidrio que lo separa del hall, ese diminuto jardín sugiere la misteriosa imagen de un bosque en el fondo de un lago" (pp. 12-13); "Ignoraba dónde vivía Paulina. El portero me prestó la guía de teléfonos y la Guía Verde.

Ninguna registraba la dirección de Montero. Busqué el nombre de Paulina; tampoco figuraba. Comprobé, asimismo, que en la antigua casa de Montero vivía otra persona" (p. 22).

One of the few physical objects mentioned in the story, the china statue of a horse (a gift to Paulina, "hermoso como la primera pasión de una vida," p. 13), becomes a forgotten object in the presence of Montero, whose otherness begins to divide the narrator and Paulina. And yet the china statue acquires a permanence—much like the text, written *in memoriam*—and takes on the qualities of a commemorative object that is capable of saving the past. It is a familiar point of reference in new and different surroundings: "Yo no estaba seguro de que *[el espejo]* reflejaba la habitación. Tal vez la reflejaba, pero de un modo vago y sumario. En cambio el caballito se encabritaba nítidamente en el estante de la biblioteca" (pp. 21-22). What is more, the statue is set within a library that reveals the narrator's self as transformed and made new by his estrangement from Paulina and their once familiar surroundings: "La biblioteca abarcaba todo el fondo y en la oscuridad lateral rondaba un nuevo personaje, que no reconocí en el primer momento. Luego, con escaso interés, noté que era yo" (p. 22). In effect, the narrator is undergoing here the transformation, the process of self-discovery, that allows the very act of his narration. As a fully constituted narrator, however, he can also see himself before the literary metamorphosis: "No me atrevía a encarnar el papel de enamorado . . . " (p. 11). The narrator also conceives of Montero in literary terms, as defined by his activity in a literary context: "La víspera, Montero me había visitado por primera vez. Esgrimía, en la ocasión, un copioso manuscrito y el despótico derecho que la obra inédita confiere sobre el tiempo del prójimo" (p. 12). In the substratum of Bioy's prose, there lies the conviction that literature is among the most characteristic and individualizing of all human activities. As is illuminated from a different angle in "Un león en el bosque de Palermo," precisely those activities which impel man to confront the strange, the Other, are the projects which differentiate him from the indistinct beasts.

While the subject of **"En memoria de Paulina"** (not unlike that of Montero's unpublished book) is that of radical estrangement, the narrative act is an assertion of the past as a permanent world. The text is on this level an object greatly dissimilar to the world of the reader's experience, which is made only of the evanescent present. Yet to consider **"En memoria de Paulina"** as a text which is experienced by the reader—more as force than static form[14]—and not simply the narration as object or fact, is also to recognize that in the text the reader can find an image of the familiar world he so instinctively seeks. The forces

which enter into the narrative process of the formation of self and past are antithetical to the narration as a verbal *object,* and yet they make possible the very existence of that verbal object: the paradox is resolved for the reader, for through the operation of these forces the world of his experience is included in the text itself. A closer inspection of certain passages will help illustrate this point.

While the initial paragraphs of the story are fixed firmly in the narrator's memory, the past soon becomes less stable for him. The narrator comes to doubt and question; he frankly admits to uncertainties: "No recuerdo qué me contestó. Creo que me invitó a su casamiento" (p. 16); "No había una persona más incompatible con Paulina (y conmigo) que Montero. ¿O me equivocaba?" (*ibid.*). Moreover, he exerts a will to forget, and thereby to distance himself from Paulina: "Quería olvidar a Paulina. En mis dos años de Inglaterra evité cuanto pudiera recordármela. . . . Eludí obstinadamente su recuerdo" (p. 18). This self-imposed distancing is crucial, for it allows him to recognize Paulina in all her otherness. And yet, Bioy, as narrator must proceed further before the verbal object can be formed. Not only does the narrator accept the fiction of Paulina's visit ("Nunca nos habíamos querido tanto. Nunca estuvimos tan cerca. . . . Nuestro pobre amor no arrancó de la tumba a Paulina. No hubo fantasma de Paulina," p. 24); more important, he admits that his own desires are not his at all ("Yo abracé un monstruoso fantasma de los celos de mi rival," *ibid.*), that Paulina is not a projection of his but rather of Montero's ("la imagen proyectaba por Montero se condujo de un modo que no es de Paulina. Además, hablaba como él," p. 25), and that he is not himself at all: "No me reconocí en el espejo, porque Montero no me imaginó claramente" (*ibid.*). Already on the thematic level, this awareness of otherness, which incorporates an awareness of the otherness of self (in Rimbaud's phrase, "je est un autre") is analogous to the reader's encounter with the text, with a world that is at once his and not his. Yet, precisely because the reader must actualize that otherness through the text, and follow the tracks of a forgetting narrator, the experience of reading acquires the temporal traits of human existence and the spiritual aspects of self-definition.

The closing paragraph of the story begins to complete the narrator's self-effacement, and offers the fruits of his sacrificial self-destruction. Here, in addition to the acceptance of his own otherness as a result of his estrangement from Paulina (" . . . al tomarla de la mano—en el supuesto momento de la reunión de nuestras almas—obedecí a un ruego de Paulina que ella nunca me dirigió y que mi rival oyó muchas veces," *ibid.*), the narrator assumes a conviction with regard to his own non-existence. In this, he is paradoxically once again reassured; once again he is sure of the past. And yet this voice speaks with a maturity that differentiates it from the more ingenuous narrator of the opening paragraphs: "Urdir esa fantasía es el tormento de Montero. El mío es más real. Es la convicción de que Paulina no volvió porque estuviera desengañada de su amor. Es la convicción de que nunca fui su amor. Es la convicción de que Montero no ignoraba aspectos de su vida que sólo he conocido indirectamente" (*ibid.*).

The process of narration is a coming to terms with self and past that culminates in the victorious erection of the verbal object as a whole. For the narrator in **"En memoria de Paulina,"** this process is catalyzed not by memory but by its antithesis, by the sacrificial act of forgetting.[15] The reader too is asked to engage in self-denial as he approaches the text and enters into the narrative pact. Bioy-Casares' **"En memoria de Paulina"** demands self-denial from the reader as the price of this covenant, for the reader must follow the narrator in his process of shaping the past. Yet, at the same time, this is a text which welcomes the reader, for the narrator also offers him an analogue of human experience. The text is both object and process; it is both an autonomous verbal world and a part of the world of the reader's experience. Through his encounter with the text, the reader is left transformed into a more singular, more mature self. As a function of the reader's wager, of his reading, the text will in turn impart a new and deeper reading of his world. As Borges wrote,

> A veces en las tardes una cara
> Nos mira desde el fondo de un espejo;
> El arte debe ser como ese espejo
> Que nos revela nuestra propia cara.
> . . . . .
> También es como el río interminable
> Que pasa y queda y es cristal de un mismo
> Heráclito inconstante, que es el mismo
> Y es otro, como el río interminable.[16]

The verses from this "Arte poética" could serve as well for a reading of the fantastic.

Notes

1. The most important structuralist study of the fantastic is that of Tzvetan Todorov, *Introduction à la littérature fantastique* (Paris: Editions de Seuil, 1970). His approach not only admits, but actually codifies a definition of the fantastic in literature. A detailed discussion of this book would be out of place here, for its methods and goals are quite different from mine: I am more concerned with reading the fantastic than with describing, classifying, and codifying it. Also of interest, and of a broad methodological base, is the study of Eric S.

Rabkin, *The Fantastic in Literature* (Princeton: Princeton University Press, 1976).

2. *Los cuentos fantásticos de Rubén Darío* (Cambridge, Mass.: Harvard University, 1967), p. 24. (Victor S. Thomas Inaugural Lecture).

3. See Jonathan Culler, *Structuralist Poetics* (Ithaca: Cornell University Press, 1975), pp. 192-193.

4. I cite from the edition of José Olivio Jiménez, *Rubén Darío: Cuentos fantásticos* (Madrid: Alianza Editorial, 1976); here, pp. 39-40. The story was first published in *La Tribuna* (Buenos Aires, 1894).

5. See his *S/Z* (Paris: Editions de Seuil, 1970), p. 157.

6. The passage in question is from "The Narrative of Arthur Gordon Pym." Although it is too long to cite in its entirety here, I have excerpted particularly important fragments: "On account of the singular character of the water, we refused to taste it, supposing it to be polluted; . . . I am at a loss to give a distinct idea of the nature of this liquid, and cannot do so without many words. Although it flowed with rapidity in all declivities where common water would do so, yet never, except when falling in a cascade, had it the customary appearance of *limpidity*. It was, nevertheless, in point of fact, as perfectly limpid as any limestone water in existence, the difference being only in appearance. . . . It was *not* colorless, nor was it of any one uniform color—presenting to the eye, as it flowed, like the hues of a changeable silk. . . . We perceived that the whole mass of liquid was made up of a number of distinct veins, each of a different hue; that these veins did not commingle. . . . The phenomenon of this water formed the first feeble link in that vast chain of apparent miracles with which I was destined to be at length encircled." (*The Works of Edgar Allen Poe*, vol. V [1895; rpt. Freeport, New York: Books For Libraries Press, 1971], pp. 237-238.) Perhaps equally significant are portions of the preceding passage: " . . . the conviction forced itself upon us that we were in a country different essentially from any hitherto visited by civilized men. We saw nothing with which we had been formerly conversant" (p. 236).

7. *Problèmes du nouveau roman* (Paris: Editions de Seuil, 1967), p. 200.

8. Cf. Jacques Derrida, "La différance," *Marges de la philosophie* (Paris: Les Editions de Minuit, 1972), pp. 1-29.

9. "Los cuentos de Rubén Darío," *Letras hispánicas* (México: Fondo de Cultura Económica, 1968), p. 227.

10. "El caracol y la sirena," *Cuadrivio,* 3ᵃ ed. (México: Joaquín Mortiz, 1972), p. 36.

11. Darío commented on similarly self-generating passages in his two essays, both called "Tentativas de expresión," dated Paris, October and November, 1911, and published in November of that year in *La Nación;* they were later collected in the posthumous *El mundo de los sueños* (Madrid: Librería de la Viuda de Pueyo, 1917). See the recent edition of Angel Rama, *Rubén Darío: El mundo de los sueños* (Puerto Rico: Editorial Universitaria, 1973), pp. 118-125.

12. Ricardou discusses the commentaries of Borges ("El arte narrativo y la magia," in *Discusión*), Gaston Bachelard (in *L'Eau et les rêves*), and Marie Bonaparte (in *Edgar Poe, sa vie, son oeuvre; étude analytique,* vol. II).

13. Adolfo Bioy-Casares, *Cuentos fantásticos* (Buenos Aires: Emecé Editores, 1972); here, p. 11.

14. See Jacques Derrida, "Force et signification," *L'Ecriture et la différence* (Paris: Editions de Seuil, 1967), pp. 9-49, *à propos* of Jean Rousset, *Forme et signification* (Paris: José Corti, 1964).

15. There is much that remains to be said about the process of recollection and forgetting, not only in the fantastic, but in all narrative. Samuel Beckett's brief comment about Proust nonetheless says a great deal: "Proust had a bad memory. . . . The man with a good memory does not remember anything because he does not forget anything." From *Proust* (Edinburgh: The University Press, 1931), p. 17.

16. Jorge Luis Borges, "Arte poética," *Obra poética,* 9ᵃ ed. (Buenos Aires: Emecé Editores, 1972), p. 226.

Caleb Bach (essay date 1993)

SOURCE: Bach, Caleb. "The Inventions of Adolfo Bioy Casares." *Américas* 45, no. 6 (1993): 14-19.

[*In the following essay, Bach discusses Bioy Casares's literary association and friendship with fellow Argentinean Jorge Luis Borges.*]

To visit the workroom of Adolfo Bioy Casares, in his apartment high above the La Recoleta district of Buenos Aires, is to step back into a golden moment in the history of Latin American letters. In the book-lined study, with photographs of literati on nearly every shelf, one is transported to those halcyon years of the early 1940s when a remarkable trio conspired with youthful verve to invent an entirely new tradition of fantastic literature. In 1940 Bioy himself came forth with perhaps his most original work, *La invención de Morel* while a year later, Jorge Luis Borges hatched his metaphysical masterpiece, *El jardín de senderos que se bifurcan*. Simultaneously Bioy's wife, Silvina Ocampo, already recognized as an author of dark, disturbing tales of life's "small horrors" collaborated with Borges in an *Antología de la literatura fantástica* for which Bioy, at age 26, composed the prologue. Therein he observed that "old like fear itself, fantastic fiction comes *before* (modern) letters. It populates *all* literature: *The Zendavesta, The Bible,* Homer's sagas, *The Thousand and One Nights.*" That terrifying "sense of the marvelous" often common to both ancient fable and contemporary science fiction also was the realm of Bioy and his colleagues. They explored it continually during their long careers.

Within this circle of fantasists there was a strong spirit of collaboration. Ocampo (who had studied in Italy with the surrealist painter, Giorgio De Chirico) doubled as illustrator for Bioy's early effort, *La nueva tormenta* (1935). A few years later he also persuaded Borges' artist sister, Norah, to furnish line drawings to accompany the first edition of *La invención de Morel.* By far, the most celebrated collaborative "partners in crime" were Borges and Bioy who created as their mouthpiece the fictitious "H. Bustos Domecq"—a combination of the pseudonym "H. Bustos" Borges had used as author of his first story, *Hombre de la esquina rosada* and "Domecq," the family name of Bioy's paternal grandmother. In his later *Crónicas,* Bustos Domecq as essayist would "invert, deflate, and dismantle most of the aesthetic fads of our time" (*Atlantic Monthly*), but in his earlier guise as parodist he made an inspired assault upon the detective story genre. *Seis problemas para don Isidro Parodi* (1942) satirized clichés and gleefully twisted traditional whodunnit plots. Four years later, in *Un modelo para la muerte,* the rascal in these two great writers surfaced again through the words of an equally fictitious "B. Suárez Lynch."

What was it like to collaborate with a "certifiable genius" like Borges who was fifteen years older than Bioy and whose reputation tended to cast a shadow upon those around him? Bioy, with affection and not the slightest tinge of envy, believes it grew out of genuine respect that went in both directions. "First of all, we were two people who had complete confidence and trust in one another. In a total sense we were friends. We didn't hold back things from one another." As to the specific dynamics: "One of us would tell the other an idea he had for a story. Borges came here every night for dinner and we'd go to the dining room and during perhaps three evenings we'd discuss the story, always in an unhurried way. Eventually the moment arrived and I'd sit down over there (at a type-writer on a table in the corner) and whomever had the first phrase would propose it and so it went with the second and the third. Normally when one writes a story this way, you would think a moment arrives when you don't know how to proceed, when you get stuck in the mud. But it never happened because we never had the bad luck of getting stuck at the same time. For us writing this way was quite easy. Unfortunately, we ended up writing in a way we didn't want to. Our goal was to present the story economically, in a simple manner but we didn't always do this. Instead, there emerged a "third writer" whom we had not invited who was a *burlesco,* who made one joke after another. Something emerged full of jokes that was entirely outside our intention. What we did receive was a lesson in humility. We wanted one thing and ended up with another. At any rate, I think we had a good time."

Although Borges would emerge a cult figure in Argentina (a fact not wasted on publishers who still print Borges' name several time larger than that of Bioy on the covers of their collaborative efforts) the unassuming Bioy has never resented the unequal treatment nor his friend's celebrity. "Life has filled me with many happinesses and the friendship with Borges was one of them. I have had many. Life with Silvina was another. I've been very lucky. It wasn't hard to love Borges. He was an extraordinary fellow. He'd come to the house and say to me, 'I have news from the Baroness Puffendorf de Ambois. There was always something happening with this personality invented by H. Bustos Domecq.'"

To some degree, the literary careers of "Georgie" (Borges' nickname at home where English often was spoken) and "Adolfito" (to differentiate from his father who was also named Adolfo) were launched by their fathers. Both men exposed their sons at an early age to great books in many languages and, frustrated as writers themselves, they encouraged the younger generation to pursue a kind of professionalism that had eluded them. The self-effacing Bioy is disinclined to confirm that it takes two generations to "make a master" but he does acknowledge he enjoyed an advantage. "I know my father gave me all the help he could, I mean he facilitated things. When I had done my first book, I didn't know he had gone to a local editor named Torrendell where he arranged things beforehand. Then back home he said to me, 'Why don't you go to Torrendell. He's an excellent editor.' I went and the editor accepted my book. I admitted to Torrendell I had written poorly in the past but that I thought this effort was worthy of publication. And he said, 'Enough of that. I am willing to publish the book (**Prólogo,** published by Editorial Tor in 1929).' It didn't occur to me at the time that my father already had talked with

the editor and agreed to pay for the edition. I never discussed this with my father because only many years later did I put it all together and realize what had happened. By then he had died."

As in the case of Mario Vargas Llosa or Manuel Puig, did the movies play an important role in Bioy's formation as a writer? "Probably they did," concedes Bioy, "but at first I didn't get to see many because my mother said if I went to the movies all the time, I'd become fat and soft!" Still trim and fit as he nears the end of his seventh decade, Bioy admits to a life-long love affair with tennis and excellence as a youth in boxing and rugby (he was captain of his team). "I did sports every afternoon, then read and studied and so I didn't have much time for the movies. It took time to not hear my mother and start going. If I had had a brother, I would have done my best to help him become a movie director." Bioy believes that the multiple viewpoints characteristic of some of his stories may have been influenced by seeing in a cinematic way: "To tell a story through a series of visible scenes, that's what I try to do. Stevenson said all stories need a scene at the beginning, another in the middle, and one at the end—at least three, better if there are more. I agree. Right now I have this image, for example. There's a little lighted plaza. Two men approach, one with a club. He walks in a labored manner. When they pass, he hits the other with the club. This is a scene I have in my mind." Chuckling to himself, Bioy says, "It would be a good way to start a story."

In the early 1930s, the young writer first studied law at the Universidad de Buenos Aires and then transferred to the Facultad de Filosofía y Letras where he stayed for a year. But Borges and Silvina Ocampo reinforced his own inclination to abandon college entirely and write full-time, as did his father, and soon Bioy and Ocampo were living at the family *estancia,* Rincón Viejo, several hours drive from Buenos Aires. "I was young, just twenty. A couple days before I arrived, there was a crime. There was a man who had forgotten his native French but didn't speak Spanish well so he could hardly communicate at all. He dressed in other peoples' clothes, used clothes; he looked like a bundle of burlap sacks. He collected lots of money from a property he rented out and for that money he was killed. The police suspected the neighbors who lived nearby. One kind but dirty fellow had been tortured by the police to extract a confession. A second also was tortured by sticking his head in a trough full of water and rotten meat. Then they hung him by his feet all night from a roof beam. To the third one they did nothing because someone had said he'd had intercourse with the animal. The third fellow left the area. I saw the dead horse with a bullet hole in the chest. When I arrived at the *estancia* after the murder had occurred, I was asked to solve the mystery. I was "tested" for the first time and I failed immediately." Bioy never succeeded in building a story around this event, just one of many adventures during his five years as ranch administrator for his father, but he has included it in his reminiscences. Entitled *Memorias,* his autobiography is nearing completion and will be ready for publication next year by Editorial Tusquets in Spain.

Of the seven novels Bioy has produced over the year, for many *La invención de Morel* remains one of his most engaging works. It is a complex tale that requires readers to pay close attention to critical details in order to decypher the author's ingenious plot (it involves an invention that anticipates holography, virtual reality, and several other recent high-tech innovations). Does Bioy make his readers work hard? "I hope so," he responds. "I write for people who like to read. But do you think many readers exist these days?"

Borges greatly admired *Morel La invención de Morel.* Indeed, it moved him to write a prologue for the story which is famous in its own right. He used the opportunity to reject the psychological and realistic novel in favor of the adventure story. He called for novels of "reasoned imagination" with a narrative—a "verbal artifice" intolerant of superfluous elements. Borges closed his commentary by saying, "I have discussed with the author the details of his plot. I have reread it. To classify it as perfect is neither an imprecision nor a hyperbole." Bioy treasures that appraisal but is quick to point out that Borges admired the structure, not the style. "It had too many short phrases. In writing the complicated book, I didn't aim to succeed but rather not to commit mistakes. So, by short phrases it was safer because my previous books had been ruined by mistakes I made. But the short phrases produced a style like *pan rallado* (chopped up bread)." Whatever the case, over the years film adaptions of *Morel* have been attempted but in Bioy's opinion, only with limited success. "I always say to the director, 'Don't do that story! It's a trap!' Well, they do it and it *is* a trap. That's how it functions."

La invención de Morel as well as the novel that followed, *Plan de evasión* (1945), both depend on mysterious events that occur on a remote island for which reason sometimes they are called Bioy's *novelas isletas.* Each employs a kind of abstraction in a visual sense and they offer the reader ample opportunity to participate. "I think there are very few works that function that way," Bioy points out. Another test is how the work translates: "When I like what I've written in another language, it's because it's good. I might add that it is very difficult to write a book and continue admiring it." As to the motif of an island and

how this theme started, "I imagined a fugitive who by boat reaches the island and, well, the process took over and the story revealed itself." As to whether the motif fits as a metaphor for Bioy himself—his life in isolation, hard work in his study, a private man removed from the tumult—he accepts the idea. "It is a gift given me by destiny. It is a motif that fits."

Travel is another element around which Bioy has built many an account, especially his short stories. Author Barbara Mujica, in her review of *El lado de la sombra* (*Américas,* Volume 44, Number 3), quotes Bioy's position: "Traveling frees the spirit. It exposes the individual to new experiences and predisposes him to accept the mysterious and inexplicable. If you want to die, the fastest means is routine, sweet routine. On the other hand, if you want life and memories, travel." The author got his first taste of international travel at age eight when he accompanied his father to France. At age 14 he visited Egypt and the following year he accompanied his parents to New York. Currently, as part of *Memorias,* he is incorporating notations from personal diaries of his wanderings through Europe, also Turkey and Brazil. Are these real trips or voyages of the mind? "Oh, no, they're real trips," he smiles, "You can trust me!" Bioy admits still to having itchy feet: "I've not seen every place I'd like to because once I get somewhere, I want to stay. I don't like short visits. Buenos Aires is my home base but I have bases elsewhere. I wrote a novel in Pau in the Pyrenees of Southern France (from where the family of Bioy's father originates) and I did another in Spain." Sometimes, Bioy's objective is to track down places associated with authors of interest to him. In 1988, Bioy was invited to Sulmona, Italy because of his interest in Ovid. "I had been writing a tale about Ovid which I didn't finish. I went with an Argentine friend and at first the town seemed to have nothing of particular interest. But inside I found remains of the aqueduct that crosses the center of town and then through a door there was a little plaza and there was Ovid (his statue) and I greeted him!"

In 1990, Bioy received the Premio Miguel de Cervantes de Literatura, often thought of as the Nobel Prize of Spanish letters. His acceptance speech was full of the wry humor and self-deprecating modesty for which he is famous. He admitted his first attempt at writing was to impress a girl friend while the second was to imitate Conan Doyle and Gaston Leroux. "My ambitions then were not literary. I wanted to run one hundred meters in nine seconds and be a tennis or boxing champion. But after reading the opening episode of Cervantes' masterpiece, when Quijote abandons that implacable life to leave in search of adventures, if I do not recall incorrectly, after concluding the first chapter I knew I wanted to be a writer." Given

Bioy's solitary nature, has the Premio Cervantes been a kind of punishment? "It was a great pleasure, a great surprise for me. But as a result, social life entered my life and this cost me a great deal. A journalist asked me if I would keep on writing and at first I was almost offended. But as time went by, I feared he might be right, that it might be difficult to continue." After receiving the prize in November 1990 at Alcalá de Henares, Cervantes' birthplace, Bioy went to Paris. "In order to prove that I could still do it," he recalls, "I wrote a story to reassure myself that I was the same fellow. It was like a tranquilizer!"

As Mujica points out in her analysis of Bioy's short story, *La obra,* its author believes that "an individual's only defense against misfortune is his work." Bioy lives by that credo working long hours at his desk on different writing projects, all the while assiduously defending his right not to be interrupted. What is he working on now? "I thought it was a full-sized novel. I was very proud of it. Now it's going to be just a short story called *El fondo del campo,* part of a collection. In one of the other stories, someone discovers that when he opens the faucet, the water talks to him and starts directing his life. It's very entertaining." Is that a new idea or does Bioy have ideas on the shelf? Well, no, it's not a new idea. Yes, I do have ideas on the shelf for two or three novels. Before, they were a resource, now they cause worry that I won't get to them. It doesn't matter. Someone else will write them up from my notebooks, from the notations and outlines."

Bioy's inventive story lines have attracted several filmmakers. Aside from *La invención de Morel,* his *Diario de la guerra del cerdo* (which deals with savage, youthful resentment directed towards old people) made its way to the screen in a film directed by Argentina's Leopoldo Torre Nilsson. Currently, another local filmmaker, Maria Luisa Bemberg (a niece of Silvina Ocampo) has responded to the author's suggestion that she do a film version of his short story, *Cavando un foso.* The Gothic tale involves a young couple's attempt to rescue their failing business by murdering a rich older lady. However their mounting guilt and double dealing creates an ever deeper pit of guilt that eventually destroys them. The project is only at an exploratory stage, but both Bioy and Bemberg believe it holds considerable promise.

Today Bioy occupies a spotlight solely his. He has earned it for the remarkable quality of his ideas and his inspired writing, not because he happened to be an associate of Borges. Currently serving as a juror on the panel that will select the next winner of the Premio Cervantes, Bioy is rereading a large body of literature so that he can vote in a responsible manner.

(Near at hand, he had a notebook full of carefully indexed comments regarding the works of other writers.) In late October, after traveling to Madrid to participate in the final selection process, he will be in London "to talk with the public, not a press conference. I'm a writer. I abhor press conferences." He will be feted in Paris and then continue on to the University of Grenoble where he will speak on Stendhal and the University of Clermont-Ferrand where he will lecture on Pascal. On both occasions he will be awarded honorary degrees, as will be the case at the University of Bayonne. Appreciative of all this attention, Bioy nonetheless knows the rigors of the trip will also take its toll. With a broad grin, he says, "Thereafter the remains of Adolfo Bioy Casares will return to Argentina to be interred."

In a recent interview with Daniel Riera and Miguel Russo (*La Maga,* 30 June 1993) Bioy was asked what was most important in a story and he responded, "One writes to touch the reader with great truths. When I asked him whether he really meant that, he said, "Well, sometimes. I hope so. Yes." Given Bioy's reputation for multiple truths, even a measure of deception or intentional obscurity designed to oblige readers to think some things out for themselves, I proposed a revision: "Bioy Casares writes to touch his readers with great lies." Laughing, he responded, "That's all right, that's all right. Maybe it is true!"

Alexander Coleman (essay date October 1994)

SOURCE: Coleman, Alexander. "Fantastic Argentine." *The New Criterion* 13, no. 2 (October 1994): 65-70.

[*In the following essay, Coleman discusses Bioy Casares's role in Latin American literature, his literary collaborations with Jorge Luis Borges, and the structure and themes of a collection of his stories written between the 1950s and the 1980s.*]

Generalizations about contemporary writing from Spanish America are neither advisable nor recommended for general use. There is nothing coherent to be said about the literary production of twenty distinct countries, where the situation of the writer, the place accorded literature in that society, and the author's particular response to the societal and political mix are a special case in each instance, applicable not even to a neighboring country. This is so in spite of the fact that Spanish American authors all seem to write in the same language and have a common history of conquest, colonization, and apparent liberation from the political and cultural models that were Spain's legacy from the age of discovery. Though such things are not known or acknowledged in the U.S.A., it is good to keep in mind that an Argentine arriving in Mexico is a Martian to most Mexicans, as is a Cuban arriving in Chile—utterly different worlds on all fronts. All the more reason for insisting on specificity when talking about a particular author today.

For instance, within the Peruvian context, where literature is rarely granted any distance from society, and where fiction is more likely to be valued for its documentary value than for its imaginative qualities, it was logical that Mario Vargas Llosa would feel compelled to offer his candidacy for the presidency of Peru. Vargas Llosa is a devourer of reality, a manic Flaubertian, scrutinizing and exposing the fossilized structures of Peru's authoritarian feudalism. But unlike Flaubert (although similar to other Peruvian writers before him), he possesses a messianic compulsion to cure the nation of its ills by his own magisterial hand—a vocation for martyrdom. Writers turning into politicians and failing miserably are an old story in parts of Spanish America, and literature is not the better for these dalliances. In any case, it was a Peruvian phenomenon, not readily replicable elsewhere. For instance, a "committed" writer such as the Colombian Gabriel García Márquez, who apparently has ideas similar to those of Vargas Llosa, has always insisted that the only social responsibility of the writer is to write well, and that's that. He has consistently refused (and there have been many) offers of ambassadorships, consulates, and possible candidacies for the presidency of Colombia. He's been wise to do so.

If generalizations are perforce shaky, it is nonetheless true that the North American reader does have an *impression* of and about contemporary fiction from Spanish America, more likely than not drawn from a recent and cursory reading of a few works of, say, García Márquez or Isabel Allende. Such an impression, nebulous and vague as it is, is widespread, and it always seems to point to a kind of performance practice which distinguishes Spanish American fiction from its North American counterpart, and this in turn relates to the uses and misuses of the fantastic. It would seem that most American readers are under the impression that the only mode practiced in Spanish America is something called "magic realism," or, to use another term, coined by the Cuban novelist Alejo Carpentier, "the marvelous real." The two terms mean quite different things, but no matter; for the North American reader, the terms have come to be equivalent. García Márquez's *One Hundred Years of Solitude* is the touchstone for this visionary literature. Examples abound therein. Along with the many gory and exorbitant events in that novel, Father Nicanor Reyna levitates twelve centimeters above the ground upon sipping a cup of chocolate, while Remedios the Beautiful is swept up

into the heavens accompanied by a gaggle of airborne bedsheets. Many readers have taken these magical episodes as examples of a piquant fancy, suggestive of the author's addiction to medieval chronicles and chivalric novels. This is very much to the point, since García Márquez has always expressed his contempt for slice-of-life literature and for European realism in general, and has tended to veer toward adventure stories, fairy tales, and children's literature as nurturing elements for his own writing—the world of the romance. Most occasional readers of Spanish American fiction have taken this style as the coin of the realm, as if fantasy, hyperbole, and dream were always present.

Historically, just the reverse is the case. Since the first recognizable novel in all of the colonies was not published until 1816 in Mexico, the founding novels of the nineteenth century in each of the newly independent nations were born under the successive novelistic aesthetics of what then reigned in France and Spain—romanticism, realism, and, markedly, naturalism. In these novels, Nature itself—or rather the unequal contention between man and nature—was the protagonist. Zola was a hidden master behind these novels, which came in many guises and have had many labels in the histories of the Spanish American novel—the "novel of the earth," "the protest novel," "the *indianista* novel," "the novel of the Mexican Revolution"—and they carried on a hardy existence in across the continent until well into the 1940s. García Márquez, whose grand novel was published as recently as 1967, was one of the first of today's writers to lament the persistence of parochial realism in Spanish America. Things could have been quite different in terms of literary evolution had Spanish American writers reached back to pre-nineteenth-century, even medieval, models:

> The authors of chivalric novels succeeded in inventing a world in which the imagination was possible. The only important thing for them was the validity of the account, and if they deemed it necessary for the knight to have his head cut off four times, it would be cut off four times. This amazing capacity for inventing fables penetrated the reader of that period in such a way that it became the emblem of the conquest of America. The sad part is that Latin American literature should have forgotten so soon about its marvelous origins.

If García Márquez and his contemporaries (Alejo Carpentier, Julio Cortázar, Carlos Fuentes, and Mario Vargas Llosa, to name a few) represent the new canon that has spead *urbi et orbi* throughout college curricula as "representative" of the Spanish American novel, the old canon survives only as subject for revisionist readings and an exemplar of historical interest.

One of the main agents in displacing the old with the new was the Argentine novelist and essayist Adolfo Bioy Casares. Born in 1914 in Buenos Aires, he found himself in such fortunate financial circumstances that he was able to dedicate himself to a writing career, with the passionate encouragement of his littérateur father. His older friend and compatriot Jorge Luis Borges (b. 1899) had similar luck—a well-off family and a father who, frustrated by his own lack of literary talent, poured his unrealized ambitions into his son. The two met for the first time in 1932, and although they were always to be quite different as writers, a unique friendship developed over the years which resulted not only in their reviewing and commenting upon each other's literary production, but also in their jointly creating a "third party," an author dubbed *"Biorges"* by one of Borges's biographers.

The two collaborated in five works of fiction, most of them parodies of detective stories modeled on their avid readings in Chesterton and Conan Doyle. They also produced (with Silvina Ocampo) an anthology which was to make its mark on the future of much of Spanish American writing, the *Anthology of Fantastic Literature* (1940), where Lewis Carroll abuts Cocteau, Alexandra David-Neel, and Kafka, and Lord Dunsany finds himself in the company of Chuang-Tzu, Saki, and Swedenborg. The editors included one of Borges's finest early short stories, "Tlön, Uqbar, Orbis Tertius" (where Bioy Casares appears as a literary character on the first page of the story—the purported reader of the false, pirated encyclopedia which in due course gives birth to the invading planet Tlön). Bioy Casares also put his name on the truculent prologue to the anthology, which is as much a manifesto as anything else. He there notes that in "Tlön, Uqbar, Orbis Tertius" Borges "created a new literary genre, part essay, part fiction. This new genre of Borges is an exercise in a rigorously applied intelligence and felicitous imagining, a story without padding, without the 'human element,' neither emotional nor heart-rending, all aimed at intellectual readers, students of philosophy, some specialists in literature."

In a similar vein, Borges and Bioy Casares, during a long conversation one afternoon in 1939, compiled a list "of what was to be avoided in literature." The anathemata included "works in which the real protagonist was the pampa, the virgin jungle, the sea, a deluge, or monetary profit," or "works which have situations with which the reader identifies," or "works which pretend to be menus, albums, itineraries, musical concerts"; also, works "which ask for illustration, which suggest films." It should be added that Borges and his friend had the good sense to pull their own legs and include, in their list of prohibitions, works which "include in their plot development vain plays with time and space as found in Faulkner, Borges, and

Bioy." During this same conversation, Borges described to Bioy Casares the outline of one of his finest literary spoofs, "Pierre Menard, Author of the Quixote."

Throughout the groves of academe, more than a few doctoral dissertations are surely in preparation concerning the multiple significance of this friendship, which ended only with the death of Borges in 1986. In his "Autobiographical Essay," Borges recognized the complexity of their relationship and made a telling remark about the debt he felt he owed to the younger writer:

> It has always been taken for granted in these cases that the elder man is the master and the younger his disciple. This may have been true at the outset but several years later, when we began to work together, Bioy was really and secretly the master. . . . Opposing my taste for the emotional, the sententious and the baroque, Bioy made me feel that quietness and restraint are more desirable. If I may be allowed a sweeping statement, Bioy led me gradually to classicism.

As Borges's biographer Emir Rodríguez Monegal noted in his lengthy discussion of the relationship, Bioy Casares published his most famous work, ***The Invention of Morel,*** with a prologue by Borges, just a few weeks before the publication of the "fantastic" anthology in November 1940. Like Bioy's manifesto for the anthology, Borges's prologue to his friend's work rails against the psychological novel in general and its most particular manifestation—the Russian novel, with Dostoevsky probably the principal target. Borges finds such novels to be loose, baggy monsters, as did Henry James, but in terms unique to his own perception of the nature of literature: "The Russians and their disciples have demonstrated, tediously, that nobody is impossible. A person may kill himself because he is so happy, for example, or commit murder as an act of benevolence. And one man can inform on another out of fervor or humility. In the end, such complete freedom is tantamount to chaos." Turning to Bioy Casares's rigorously plotted novel, he places it on a level of achievement equal to any other work of the time or of the previous few decades:

> I believe I am free from every superstition of modernity, or any illusion that yesterday differs intimately from today or will differ from tomorrow; but I maintain that during no other era have there been novels with such admirable plots as *The Turn of the Screw, Der Prozess, Le voyageur sur la terre* (of Julien Green), and the one you are about to read, which was written by Adolfo Bioy Casares.

A selection from the fiction of Bioy Casares has just been published by New Directions.[1] The deft translator of these stories, Suzanne Jill Levine, points out in her introduction that while H. G. Wells's novel *The Island of Dr. Moreau* (1896) provided the point of departure for Bioy Casares, *The Invention of Morel* should not be taken as mere science fiction. Alfred Mac Adam described *Morel* [*The Invention of Morel*] as "a text about a man who becomes first an artist and then a work of art." The plot is simple: a fugitive, shipwrecked on an island, spies on an alluring group of elegant vacationers who fill their days with drink, fine talk, a good selection of records of the Twenties, and innumerable games of tennis. He soon becomes enamored of the *belle dâme* of the group, Faustine. As he observes all of them over a period of weeks without his presence being noted, he realizes that they repeat every conversation, every move and gesture, cyclically over a fixed stretch of time. They have died, or have been killed, after having been filmed in three dimensions by the sinister group leader, Morel. Finally concluding that what he sees is a kind of continuous holographic film loop whose projected images have bulk and move about the island as if alive, the fugitive determines to master Morel's invention (powered by the fluctuation of the tides) so that he will be able to intercalate himself into this revolving time machine of images. He wants to stand (or lie) next to the already pre-programmed Faustine, who will of course never know of his presence. Intimacy will be denied him, but the anguishing approximation of it is better than nothing. The young lover forever on the brink of possession, encased in a work of art, has some consolations—Keats's "Ode on a Grecian Urn" being the classic formulation.

Bioy Casares's brief novel represents the proto-artist who is at once writing in a diary (inscribing on the urn, if you will) and making himself into a component part of (and a collaborator on) an art object, a permanence of images. *The Invention of Morel* is one of the first instances of a movement away from representation in literature in Spanish America. By the way, the work attracted the attention of Alain Robbe-Grillet, who reviewed it in *Critique* in 1953; in can be seen as a subtext to his screenplay for the film *Last Year at Marienbad* (1961). Robbe-Grillet admitted to as much in an interview. He tells how, after the première of the film, a friend (Claude Ollier) called to congratulate him on his achievement, but began with a memorable exclamation: "Mais, c'est L'Invention de Morel!" At any rate, Bioy Casares has hardly been idle since then. Aside from the collaborations with Borges, he has published some fifteen books—novels, novellas, and short stories—along with a number of critical articles in Argentine journals; he has also continued on as a sometime anthologist. One of his more mordant works of recent years is his *Dictionary of the Exquisite Argentine* (second edition, 1990), a compilation of barbarisms and pompous anglicisms that have crept into daily use in Buenos Aires. The growing corruption of meaning in daily language usage has always been a major concern.

By now it is probably impossible to extricate the name of Bioy Casares from its association with Borges and his work. They are, however, quite distinct writers, though they both share a penchant for the metaphysical and the sense of life-out-of-mind-and-body. But Borges always had a leaning toward the epic sense of life, what with his celebration of Walt Whitman, his addiction to the major films of the "Western" genre, his espousal of *Ulysses,* his avoidance of the intimate tone, his real aversion to the confessional aspects of literary expression. On the contrary, Bioy Casares "tends toward the lyrical," in the words of Ms. Levine, with a special attention to Baudelaire, Rimbaud, and especially Verlaine, authors who find little favor indeed in Borges's eccentric pantheon. Furthermore, Bioy Casares's stories flow in realms that Borges would never acknowledge as proper for his own writing.

All of the pieces in the present collection are taken from four books dating from the mid-1950s through the late 1980s; they revolve around the subject of love, which manifests itself in a hallucinatory and obsessive way within each story. Most of the pieces are variations on the theme of *l'amour fou,* described in an offhand and oblique way that makes each character something of a phantom, a mental event rather than an evolving person on the page.

The most intriguing thread running through these stories is the repetition of a kind of child's adventure tale, only eroticized: each story rehearses a search for the beloved across space and time which more often than not ends in grinding frustration and a hallucinatory dénouement. Bioy Casares's art draws upon the world of the child as a diagram for the deceptions and disillusions of adulthood. Still, the child remaining within always has the option of returning home to the cozy world of uncomplicated parental affection. In a brief chronology of his life written in 1975, Bioy Casares recalls that in early childhood, at around age five, "my mother [told] me stories about animals who stray from the nest, are exposed to danger, and in the end, after many adventures, return to the security of the nest. The theme of the safe, or apparently safe, haven, out of the dangers that lurk outside still (in 1975) appeals to me." The way this plays out is elusive; the stories tell of events in a monochromatic stream of time without much tonal variation or carefully prefigured surprises within the ongoing flow of things. The machismo of the errant male, a favorite target, is subverted, put at a loss, while women's sensibilities and questing are no luckier but are seen in an immensely more generous light. Like the protagonist of *The Invention of Morel,* Bioy Casares's people are losers, they are always out of joint. Often physically together, "adjoining" each other as it were, they are at an unbreachable psychic distance.

For instance, in **"Women Are All the Same,"** a young wife, over the objections of her much younger suitor, allows her elderly husband to intern her in an insane asylum; she thereby "achieves security," suggests Ms. Levine, "by making fidelity into a form of suicide." In **"Men Are All the Same,"** a young widow leaves her lover in favor of a much younger man; she later discovers that her new husband is interested in her only because of the splendid automobile she lets him drive. In **"Pearls before Swine,"** a woman's passion for a young gentleman goes wholly unrequited; only years later does the man come to see that he has thrown away his one chance at love in his lifetime. In **"Dorotea,"** a father's search for his estranged wife in the south of France ends in his finding his daughter, but not his wife. She has died, and the daughter is now unreachable and distant. What might have been ends in frustration and isolation. Bioy Casares's fluent manipulation of time and space is evident in **"About the Shape of the World"** and **"The Hero of Women,"** but these are not "escapist" pieces; the political realities of Argentina intrude throughout. **"The Myth of Orpheus and Eurydice"** is based on the torching of Buenos Aires's elegant Jockey Club by enraged *Peronistas.* Inside the political anecdote, the story tells of a dramatic and failed search for love as the hordes plunder this bastion of the old aristocracy. As in Borges, dream is the bedrock of Bioy Casares's reality. Ms. Levine quotes Borges to good effect on this matter: "Nobody knows whether the world is a natural process or whether it is a kind of dream which we may or may not share with others."

Robbe-Grillet said of *The Invention of Morel* that it was "un livre étonnant," which might be variously translated as an "astonishing" or "amazing book." It is most certainly that—a revelation—and should be read anew by every generation. The stories in this collection, however, are not at that level of intensity; they artfully echo Bioy Casares's major achievement of 1940, exploring the obsessions implicit in the earlier masterpiece. Still, that should be more than enough to explain why Bioy Casares is now Argentina's most distinguished living man of letters and is considered a founding father of the new novel in all of Spanish America. When Carlos Fuentes noted that "without Borges, there would be no new Spanish American novel," he misspoke—he should have said "*Biorges.*"

Note

1. *Selected Stories,* by Adolfo Bioy Casares. Translated from the Spanish, and with an introduction, by Suzanne Jill Levine. New Directions, 176 pages, $21.95.

Margaret L. Snook (essay date 1998)

SOURCE: Snook, Margaret L. "Introduction," "Seeing and Knowing: The Reenactment of the Oedipal Drama," and "Discourse and Desire: The Struggle between Self and Other." In *In Search of Self: Gender and Identity in Bioy Casares's Fantastic Fiction,* pp. 1-4; 43-81; 87-116. New York: Peter Lang, 1998.

[*In the following excerpt, Snook concentrates on a number of Bioy Casares's stories that explore triangular relationships and display variations on Oedipal inclinations.*]

Most critics view Bioy Casares as one of the first in South America to develop the self-conscious novel and the modern fantastic story, both of which enjoyed sustained popularity and were cultivated by Borges and Cortázar, among others. Studies tend to analyze the devices that call attention to the artifice of the text and the theme of the artist, or they explore fantastic themes such as the negation of time and space. Tamargo, for example, demonstrates how Bioy's texts, like those of the vanguard movement, expose the artificiality of the fictional invention and the problematic nature of language. According to her, Bioy's prose presents an example of "esa variante de la narrativa contemporánea que se realiza en obras que cuestionan su propia naturaleza, problematizan el lenguaje y desarrollan una tarea autocrítica" (11). Unlike such experimental writers as Cortázar, who plays with narrative strategies and disorders reading sequences, Bioy does not attack traditional narrative forms. His prose remains conventional in style and, consequently, lacks an appearance of "modernity."

The self-reflecting nature of Bioy's works has also been studied by MacAdam, Borinsky and Levine, among others. MacAdam observes that Bioy does not usually express his ideas about literature through dialogues or monologues, as Cortázar does, but presents them in metaphoric fashion (43). MacAdam interprets *La invención de Morel* as a metaphor for art and the artist and *Plan de evasión,* as a "totally metaphoric text whose subject is metaphor" (42). In her analysis of *Plan de evasión,* Borinsky shows how the image of camouflage is central to the text's concern with language and the masking of meaning (117-119). Not only is the island camouflaged, but the characters and their actions all allude to the use of masking devices and deception. Nothing is what it initially appears to be nor can the reader arrive at any real referent hidden or concealed beneath the cloaking device. Levine analyzes the self-consciousness of Bioy's works in their relationship to traditional forms. In particular, she studies the author's parody of anti-utopian science fiction popularized by writers such as H. G. Wells (*Guía de Bioy Casares* 73-115). She also traces the connection between the Argentine writer's novels and the bucolic tradition, which deals with the same themes of death and resurrection and similarly exposes the text's artifice or literary mechanisms (132). The pastoral poem situates its protagonists in an idyllic setting, separate and remote from the rest of the world. The island locations of Bioy's earlier novels initially evoke this setting, but all illusions of a tropical paradise soon are transformed into nightmares of isolation and fear.

Other critics, such as Meehan, have discussed fantastic themes and narrative strategies that characterize the author's fiction. In his study of the short story **"El otro laberinto,"** Meehan analyzes the theme of time, one of Bioy's central preoccupations, focusing on two aspects common to fantastic fiction: simultaneity and time travel (5-14). Meehan also alludes to Bioy's use of the resources of detective fiction in shaping his subject, a characteristic, one might add, found in other works of the author.

Scheines, in her article "Claves para leer a Adolfo Bioy Casares," studies three key recurring elements in the author's texts. The first is the voyage that allows the character access to another dimension where new rules and roles govern life (14). Secondly, Scheines observes that the incursions into the unknown usually occur in restricted, isolated places that separate the protagonist from surrounding reality: "Pese a su aparente variedad, estos lugares comparten la condición de circunscriptos, es decir separados del entorno por un límite definido . . . Este límite que marca la diferencia esencial con la realidad circundante, a menudo se lo acentúa por medio de elementos aisladores: agua, bosques, desiertos, paisajes inhóspitos, murallas, llaves y candados" (17). Finally, Scheines states that masks are recurrent motifs that reflect the author's concept of life or life as play (rehearsal, theater). These motifs are important clues to the author's concepts of personal identity and the construction of the subject.

Cardounel explores different terrain in his study of the role of women in Bioy's works. Cardounel considers the physical and moral aspects of Bioy's women and the real and unreal elements that characterize their portrayal. He concludes that the male's unsuccessful spiritual pursuit for union with the female, apparent in the earlier works, is subsequently abandoned. Both males and females become more materialistic, and the women take on a more aggressive role in their relationships with men. Cardounel also observes that "en la obra de Bioy Casares la persistencia y variedad de formas del triángulo amoroso es significativa" (118). Commonly, two men and a woman form the triangle. The psychological significance of this triangularization of desire is examined in the second chapter of this study.

Another new perspective on Bioy's work appears in Filer's study of *Dormir al sol*. She states that this novel and other works by the author have a substratum of collective or institutional violence and indicate the presence of social commentary (115). According to Filer, the work presents a synthesis of the author's philosophical, psychological and social interests, which remain to be more fully explored. My analysis of Bioy's works explores the psychological interests referred to by Filer, focusing on the issue of identity and how Bioy's protagonists struggle to maintain a sense of self.

In her article, Scheines asserts that identity is a recurrent theme in Bioy's stories: "La identidad constituye una de las obsesiones de Adolfo Bioy Casares. Saber quiénes somos, si somos lo que jugamos, si detrás del rostro habitual escondemos otros insospechados, son inquietudes que el escritor logra conjurar por vía fantástica" (19). Although a number of critics have discussed the theme of selfhood, including some previously cited, the issues of identity and gender warrant more in-depth study. The chapters that follow contribute to that study.

Although Bioy's stories are masculine in orientation, the female is inextricably linked to the events that shape the male's history and sense of self. Bioy Casares refers to the theme of love as a constant in his texts (Paley Francescato 17). The author's texts, and therefore our discussion, inevitably turn to the woman in relation to the man. In order to analyze male/female relationships and the structuring of their gender and identity roles, two critical approaches are combined: psychoanalytical theory and feminist criticism. A reading of Bioy's works within the parameters of both critical perspectives reveals three recurrent forms of experience that shape the protagonists' sense of self: separation and loss, self-sacrifice and denial, opposition to and struggle with the other. These experiences expose the protagonists' awareness of difference and boundaries and correspond to three characteristic forms of interaction. At times, the male protagonist seeks to deny separation, attempting to engulf the other within his own boundaries. On occasion, the male protagonist competes with a rival for the affection of the female, refusing to suppress or deny his desire. Often, interaction with the female reveals a struggle for power and control over the other. All three forms of experience and interaction may overlap in any given text, as the protagonist moves from one psychological register to another. To provide an in-depth study of each pattern of relationship, my analysis focuses on each one separately, illustrating how the pattern is developed in representative works.

The illustrative works chosen for this study were selected from both the author's earlier and later production. The reader will be able to apply many of my observations to other texts not specifically addressed. My reading of well-known and less-studied works casts new insight into the previously obscure functions of many small details often omitted in discussions of Bioy's works.

. . . . .

In her study of literature and cinema, Teresa de Laurentis argues that male-centered narrative is governed by Oedipal logic (140). In developing her argument, de Laurentis recalls Roland Barthes's observation that "it is at the same moment (around the age of three) that the little human 'invents' at once sentence, narrative, and the Oedipus" (104). Narrative is conceived within a society ruled by the incest prohibition and retells in multiple forms the story of frustrated and displaced desire. According to de Laurentis, there are certain recurring components in the literary manifestations of the Oedipal drama. The hero or male subject attempts to overcome obstacles and cross boundaries, represented by the Sphinx in the original myth, in order to penetrate another space. By doing so, the hero "is constructed as human being and as male" (119).

In his theoretical discussions of infantile psychology and the Oedipal complex, Freud states that the male subject begins his sexual history by desiring his first object, the mother, as did the mythical hero (Lacan, *Feminine Sexuality* 9). The father becomes his rival. The father's claim to possession is based, in part, on his relation to time, for he exists in the mother's world prior to the son. The father functions as the prohibitive figure who intervenes on behalf of society to deprive the son of the desired object. According to Freud, the threat of castration causes the young male child to relinquish the forbidden object of desire and identify with the father; in time he will become, not his father, but a father. The sight of the female genitals, symbolic of lack, confirms the male's fear of castration.

Lacan later expanded upon Freud's theory, stating that the Oedipal drama presents yet another form of alienation from self that constitutes the process of identifi-

cation. For Lacan, the Oedipal stage marks the subject's entrance into the Symbolic Order, characterized by the introjection of the discourse of the other. The subject renounces and displaces his desire for the mother "through the introjection of the Father's Name (embodying the Law of incest prohibition), which becomes constitutive of the child's unconscious" (Felman 1029). The unconscious is thus "the discourse of the other" (Felman, 1025). The subject is no longer conscious of the original object of desire since knowledge of this origin has been barred by the process of denial and substitution. Through the Oedipal conflict, the subject becomes aware of positionality for the successful outcome "leads the subject from the dual relationship with mother to the triad of other, ego and object" (Lemaire 80). This awareness of positionality is reflected in linguistic terms as the subject now recognizes the third person, he/she, *él/ella*. These pronouns not only introduce positionality, they contain a gender differentiation absent in the pronouns I/you and *yo/tú*.

The Oedipal complex provides the core narrative of Freudian psychoanalytical theory, the basic explanation of how the male subject arrives at gender identification. Freud sought confirmation of his theory not only in his patients' cases but in myths and literature. Stories, like dreams, are the products of the unconscious, and Freud believed interpretation uncovered many veiled references to castration anxiety. In his well-known essay on Medusa, for example, Freud equates decapitation with castration. The decapitated head of Medusa, which represents the female genitals, creates terror in the male beholder by confirming his inner fears. It is important to remember that Freud links the terror of castration to the sight; once the male is lured to look upon the female, a potential horror is revealed to him.

Freud's discussion of the Oedipal myth links Oedipus's self-inflicted blindness to the act of castration: "In blinding himself, Oedipus, that mythical lawbreaker, was simply carrying out a mitigated form of the punishment of castration—the only punishment that according to the *lex talionis* was fitted for him" (*On Creativity and the Unconscious* 137). Later, in his analysis of the uncanny in the works of Hoffmann, Freud equates the fear of blindness with the dread of castration: "A study of dreams, fantasies and myths has taught us that a morbid anxiety connected with the eyes is often enough a substitute for the dread of castration" (137). The intense emotion attached to the incapacitating loss of any organ is created precisely by the original threat of loss, mutilation, and impotence. Freud thus sees throughout literature a validation of his theories in unconscious narrative reenactment of the Oedipal drama.

Recent feminist criticism has expanded upon or reinterpreted the Freudian model. A number of feminist writers identify castration with the feeling of impotence that arises from the frustration of desire, an experience which is universal. Flieger, for example, observes that what Freud identifies as the threat of castration manifests itself "as universal human experience of the obstruction of desire or the limitations of personal power, which often only masquerades in patriarchal garb as a "phallic catastrophe."[1] Gallop, who analyzes Lacan's interpretation of Freud, states that castration is not only sexual but linguistic. All humans are left impotent by a symbolic system, which commands them. According to Gallop, "we are inevitably bereft of any masterful understanding of language, and can only signify ourselves in a symbolic system that we do not command, that, rather, commands us" (20). Everyone, regardless of sexual organs, is castrated, and the realization of this fact offers a new perspective on feelings of inadequacy.

In observing the male's relationship to the female in a number of Bioy's works, the reader is struck by certain recurring features that suggest modern reenactments of the Freudian model of the Oedipal drama. This Oedipal model offers the most fertile terrain in exploring many of the conflicts in Bioy's works. Bioy's male figures seem to relive childhood fantasies in which they usurp the father's role. This type of infantile fixation is revealed in their choice of love object. The female is someone over whom another male figure has a prior right of possession, either husband, friend or deity. The female in this triangle arouses intense jealousy, occasioned by her possible infidelity or betrayal, or a strong longing to help her. This female soon becomes an overriding obsession for the protagonist, who views her as unique and irreplaceable.[2] According to Freud, such overestimation of the female object fits into the infantile set of ideas regarding the mother, for "no one possesses more than one mother, and the relationship to her rests on an experience which is assured beyond all doubt and can never be repeated again" (*On Creativity and the Unconscious*, 167). Sexual union with the female is consciously or unconsciously viewed as threatening in Bioy Casares's works, and the desire for the mother figure is followed by blindness or incapacitating illness, symptomatic of castration anxiety. In each instance, the male protagonists fail to successfully negotiate the Oedipal stage; they refuse to renounce their desire for the "mother" and are "punished." At the conclusion of the story, they are left diminished or powerless.[3]

The Oedipal allusion also emerges in Bioy's treatment of the father figure. It is worth noting that the figure of the biological father is infrequent in Bioy's fantastic tales. When mentioned at all, this figure is conspicuous by his absence in the important events that structure the son's identity. Powerless, he serves as a complement to vigorous or rebellious wives and daughters. The symbolic role of the father, the authoritarian prohibitor who functions to introduce the protagonist to positionality and relationality by affirming his own position to the female, is conferred upon another in the text. There is, however, an interesting exception to this general pattern in one of Bioy's more recent tales, **"Margarita o el poder de la farmacopea,"** from the collection *Una muñeca rusa* (1991). This story is told from the perspective of the strong, triumphant father who destroys the weak son who would usurp his place of authority. The father uses as his instrument of destruction an apparently innocent female child.

The triangularization of relationships involving two males and a female is apparent in a number of Bioy's fantastic tales. The male intruders who impinge on the original dyad on occasion are the imaginative products of jealousy and obsession. They may also be absurd, unworthy rivals, which makes the female's betrayal seem all the more unjust (Monmany 122). A study of three illustrative works reveals how the characteristic pattern of triangularization is usually developed in the author's works. The first tale, **"Los ídolos,"** from *Trama Celeste* (1945), surrounds the protagonists in a dream-like aura of ancient rites and rituals. The second work, **"La sierva ajena,"** from *Historias fantásticas* (1972), is an ironic tale of dwarfs and midgets that contrasts the literal and figurative meanings of greatness and smallness.[4] The third story, **"Máscaras venecianas,"** from *Historias desaforadas* (1986), presents a tale of doubles and clones amidst the masked havoc of carnival in Venice. Finally, a fourth narrative, **"Margarita o el poder de la farmacopea,"** presents a bizarre tale of cannibalism that transpires in what initially appears to be an everyday domestic setting. The story shifts the usual focus of the Oedipal drama from mother/son to father/son and confers the power over narrative voice to the father rather than the son.

"El ídolo"

The narrator of **"El ídolo"** is an antique dealer and a professional decorator. His vocation expresses a desire to reclaim objects from a lost past, while his constant rearrangement of these objects reveals his need to create order. His tendency to convey life to these objects reveals an infantile perception of his world, like the child who animates his toys: "Baste apuntar que los objetos que pasan por mis manos adquieren una vida, un poder y acaso un encanto del todo propios" (42) ["I should merely like to point out that the objects I touch acquire a life, vigor, and perhaps a charm of their own" (121)].

The narrator's preliminary remarks call attention to the act of writing, the serious purpose behind the engendering of the text. The process of writing will enable him to elude the threat of sleep and fearful dreams while the text may provide an important message for the readers. The narrator concludes these introductory remarks with a reference that ostensibly draws the reader's attention to the beginning of the tale. As author of the text, he is conscious of the importance of narrative structure, of having a beginning for his story. Yet the same introductory reference apparently dismisses the importance of beginnings: "Un comienzo parece tan bueno como otro: propongamos este:" (41) ["One beginning seems as good as another; I propose this one:" (121)]. The use of contradiction or denial becomes characteristic of his discourse and suggests inner conflict. In this particular instance, it reveals conflict surrounding the question of origins. The narrator's remarks imply a link between the role of writer/creator and that of paternal figure as source of origins. The narrator perceives origins, on the narrative level, as intentional beginnings that represent a deliberate rupture with the temporal world.

The authorial *we* with whom the introduction concludes marks his stance as writer as opposed to his function as protagonist in the body of the text. The split between the I as writer and the I as subject of the writing is thus clearly marked. This divided nature of the subject is subsequently developed in the text as the conscious I of daytime reality as opposed to an unconscious I of dreams.

The narrator begins the body of his text by discussing the origins of his relationship with his friend and client, Garmendia. The narrator has sold Garmendia objects that cannot be authenticated and feels intense guilt. Once again, the reader is met with a preoccupation with origins and beginnings, not on the level of the narrative act but on the level of interpersonal relationships and objects. His comments contain a veiled allusion to paternity in the sense of issuance or engendering of objects. The narrator is concerned with knowing and proving who created the objects: the age-old question of proving paternity, now metaphorically displaced to the realm of things. Moreover, the narrator claims a paternal function for himself when he asserts that the objects that pass through his hands acquire a life and personality all their own. These issues of origins and authenticity, in turn, are linked initially to feelings of guilt and subsequently to fear.

The narrator travels to Europe to acquire new objects that can meet the criteria of historical authenticity. He journeys to the castle of Gulniac, where he purchases an old Celtic idol, a wooden statue of a god with a dog-shaped face. The narrator compares the wooden figure to what he believes to be the Egyptian equivalent, Anubis. The mythical figure of Anubis is highly suggestive, since Anubis assisted Isis in uniting the dismembered body of her husband Osiris, but according to some versions of the tale, the reconstituted body lacked the phallus. The allusion to Anubis thus brings up implicitly the theme of castration.

The body of the Celtic idol is covered with nails, which, according to legend, represent the souls won by this nameless god. Legend also relates that every man in the Gulniac family, sole owners of the statue, has died blind. The theme of blindness is also linked to the idol through an anonymous fifteenth century poem that compares the nails on the statue to the lifeless eyes of its worshipers.

The wooden idol, associated with ancient rites, cruel priestesses, and blindness points to universal myths of incest and castration. According to Jung, snakes and dogs were traditionally depicted as guardians of treasure, defenders of the entrances to the caves or caverns, forces that intervene to impede penetration (2:372). The association between the mythical role of the dog as guardian and the idol's function is reinforced when the narrator describes the idol's head as that of "un tosco perro de guardia" (46) ["a course watchdog" (125)]. Jung also tells us that the infantile son in love with his mother often views the father as a monster who guards the treasure (I, 261). He cites as an example the monster that guards the garden of Ishtar in the Gilgamesh myth. After the monster is destroyed, Ishtar makes sexual advances toward Gilgamesh (I: 261). In Bioy's tale of veiled desire, the Celtic idol may be interpreted in psychoanalytical terms as the guardian of the female, the authority figure that threatens castration, the father/monster.

The female who will soon disrupt the narrator's world, Geneviève Estermaría, brings to mind the figure of Ishtar. The first part of her surname, Ester, is derived from Ishtar, goddess of the moon. Ishtar is traditionally depicted as wearing a ring on her left hand; Geneviève Estermaría will also wear a ring given her by a suitor. The second part of Geneviève's surname, María, refers to yet another maternal figure. The binary nature of her surname also reflects the narrator's subsequent dualistic perceptions of her as pagan priestess and innocent, nurturing mother/madonna.

Upon his return to Buenos Aires, the narrator sells the wooden idol to Garmendia. Geneviève then appears unannounced, a plain peasant girl who had accompanied the narrator on his tour of the Gulniac Castle. She arrives in springtime, a season that reveals itself "en cierta hondura de la tibieza, en cierta vehemencia del verde, en cierta reducción del catarro—" (48) ["by a certain warmth in the air, a special vehemence of the verdure, an easing of respiratory congestion—" (126)]. The narrator thus associates the season with gratifying and calming sensations, such as warmth and protection from illness. At the same time, however, he describes the greenery of the season in terms ("cierta vehemencia") that are associated with intense emotion or passion. His description thus expresses the polarities of emotion that the season arouses in him. Geneviève is linked to this season by her attire, which the narrator describes as "un traje extremadamente verde," (48) ["a dress that was extremely green," (126)]. Moreover, the arrival of Geneviève and the beginning of a cyclic pattern of events occurs in the spring, a season linked to the beginning of a cyclic pattern in nature. The season of birth/rebirth affirms the existence of a temporal, biological world and its reproductive cycle. It is precisely the existence of this pre-ordained cyclic order that the narrator attempts to deny earlier in his narrative act through the concept of intentional beginnings.

The color green, which suggests a springtime that is both comforting and disquieting, and which is clearly associated with Geneviève, reiterates her dual nature. During the day, Geneviève is the simple, nurturing peasant, while at night, in the dreams of the narrator and his friend, she becomes an alluring priestess who blinds her victims. According to the critic Cirlot, the color green is a bivalent symbol; it is the color of life and death. Cirlot adds that for this reason the Egyptians used the color green to depict Osiris, god of vegetation and of the dead (138). Ishtar is also linked to a dual existence, spending part of the year in the sky giving life and the other part in the underworld taking life (Magnarelli 21).

The narrator becomes preoccupied with Geneviève's immediate future and cannot abandon her in a foreign city. He feels a need to help or protect her and temporarily concedes an unfurnished room on the upper level of his establishment. The narrator then suggests that Geneviève prepare some food and she responds to his request with a concoction that she names "omelette à la mère." Once again, the narrator feels sensations of gratification and contentment, and he begins to think that Geneviève is special. Compared to her, the women of Buenos Aires seem opaque and unsubstantial. The narrator's tendency to view Geneviève as unique among women corresponds to the infant's perception of the mother. In psychoanalytic terms, there is a transference of feelings for the mother to the love object.

This domestic scene is typical in Bioy Casares's tales. The male derives pleasure from eating food prepared or served by the female or shared in her company.

Such an act brings a sense of relaxation and well-being. Women, and in particular the mother, have always been associated with food and nurturing, not only because they planted the crops and prepared the meals, but because there own bodies were a source of sustenance. Thus, the image of the nurturing female originates in early experiences of hunger and satisfaction. Moreover, psychoanalytical theory tells us that pleasant and unpleasant physical sensations (satisfaction and hunger) trigger memory traces in the adult and in the process revitalize the affect originally attached to them. Thus, the sensation of well-being the male experiences triggers a subconscious association between food, satisfaction, and mother. On the unconscious level, Geneviève is once again linked to symbols of maternity and pleasurable feelings that surround the maternal figure.

At the same time, however, the narrator is mortified by the thought that a continual diet of rich food would lead to "el fantasma de los kilos," and the uncomfortable necessity of "la gimnasia y el footing" (51). Thus he decides to remove Geneviève from his home. The narrator's declaration offers a typical instance in which gratification is opposed to self-denial, in which pleasure is linked to possible negative consequences. Thus the narrator's struggle between gratification and renunciation of pleasure is played out on various levels of experience.

The maternal light in which Geneviève is initially cast becomes more focused when the narrator asks her to care for Garmendia during his illness.[5] When the narrator visits his friend some days later, Garmendia declares that Geneviève "lo cuidó maternalmente" (p. 53) ["had taken care of him like a mother" (130)]. In gratitude, Garmendia presents the narrator with his latest publication on *matés, yerberas* and *azucareras* from the period of *Mama Inés.* All the while, Geneviève is serving them tea and food. Thus the function of maternal nurturer linked to Geneviève continues to appear in the text together with another reference to a maternal figure and food, *Mama Inés.*

On this same occasion one of the two men, which one is never clarified, comments on how maddening it would be to fall in love with a woman like Geneviève (53). The declaration at first seems mystifying. They never articulate why they view such a love as hopeless and frustrating. Why is the plain, nurturing woman so inaccessible? The answer is not verbalized because their association of Geneviève with mother is hidden from their consciousness. They fail to recognize the Oedipal structure of their desire according to which satisfaction must be "forever differed and forever ruled by the threat of death . . ."[6] The narrator's inability to identify the origin of such a love in the Real/Mother corresponds to his difficulty in ascertaining the true "beginning" of his narrative.[7] The narrator both relives and retells the narrative of Oedipus unconsciously, unaware of the regressive symbolic displacements that have drawn him back to the very origins of desire. Although lucid, he is not insightful, and he cannot tell what he cannot "see."

Garmendia subsequently describes the first of his dreams about Geneviève, in which he implores her love and is told his desire can be fulfilled only if he consents to one condition too dreadful to recall. Garmendia's dreams become progressive, each continuing where the previous ended. In them, he gives Geneviève a ruby ring that had belonged to his mother, a ring the narrator later glimpses on her finger. The subsequent removal of both Geneviève and the idol from Garmendia's home does not stop his dreams or restore his peace of mind. He jealously accuses the narrator of stealing Geneviève, although she returned to the narrator's shop at his own request.

The narrator duplicates Garmendia's history. He begins to dream of Geneviève as seductive priestess, poised by the altar and the idol. In his early dreams, the narrator acts as voyeur, witnessing the events of Garmendia's dreams, filled with horror and dread. He cannot see the consummation of the sexual act, but the mechanics of his dream allow him knowledge of what transpires beyond his view. As Geneviève grasps a hammer and nails, the narrator covers his eyes. The following day, the narrator discovers two new nails in the idol and learns that Garmendia has lost his sight; in reality, Garmendia has gone mad, believing himself blind.

In psychoanalytical terms, Garmendia has imposed a dreadful punishment for the releasing of his repressed, forbidden desires. Like Oedipus, his blindness is self-inflicted, caused by his own remorse and repugnance. Earlier in the story, he covered his eyes with his hands when relating his dreams in an attempt to cover or remove from sight his terrifying erotic visions. At the same time, the gesture is also meant to protect his eyes from some external threat, real or imagined. In the end, Garmendia's loss of reason or hysterical blindness results in a figurative death, the surrender of control over his life; he has entered a world of blackness, the underworld over which the other side of Ishtar rules.

In the conclusion of the story, the narrator fears for his sight and sanity. His dreams draw him progressively closer to the chamber where the rites of initiation occur. During his dreams, he initially feels relief and gratitude as he moves through endless corridors. These feelings change to fear and disgust: "Mi pavor y mi asco fueron tan vehementes que me despertaron" (62) ["My fear and my disgust were so vehement that they caused me to awaken" (137)]. Like Garmendia, he also experiences feelings of jealousy and betrayal when he discovers Geneviève talking with a stranger who wishes to contract her services. His desire for her exclusive possession is implied in his statement to the man: "Geneviève no saldrá de esta casa. No me importa de amigos ni de compromisos, ni permitiré que nadie la trate a mis espaldas" (61) ["Geneviève is not leaving this house. I don't care about friends or previous arrangements, and I shall not permit anyone to speak to her behind my back" (137)].

The narrator, like Garmendia, feels a prisoner in his own house. Like many of Bioy's other characters, he is seized by a desire to flee, but he recognizes the futility of such an attempt. He would be like a bird that flew away carrying his cage with him (67). The trap or cage that he cannot escape, that goes where he goes, is the body. The body is inexorably linked to the self. The body is a manifestation of materiality, biological reproduction, temporal order, all of which the narrator attempts to reject. The body is corruptible, subject to the laws of nature and death and, it is from this decaying part of self that the narrator would flee.

The narrator also experiences feelings of fear and disgust, the same emotions evoked in describing his dreams. The cause of these emotions is located in the narrator's objects and what they represent: "Me encontré en la butaca (no recuerdo cuándo me había sentado). Miré con asco sus monstruosos brazos de cuero . . . Sentí horror por todos los objetos, por todas las manifestaciones de la materia que me acechaba y me rodeaba como un cazador infalible" (67) ["I found myself sitting in my easy-chair, but I did not recall having sat down. I regarded its monstrous leather arms with disgust . . . I felt horrified by all the objects, all the manifestations of the matter that was ambushing me and pursuing me like an infallible hunter" (141)].

This attitude marks a sharp reversal in the narrator's affective relationship with his objects. One cannot interpret this change from love to dread unless one takes into account the source of the narrator's original love and pride. As noted previously, the narrator is the one who confers life into these objects. In psychoanalytical terms, he now feels threatened by the separate life he has engendered, knowing that in the course of events this life will survive and replace him, just as the father is replaced, hence symbolically "murdered," by the son. The objects thus represent not only the death encoded in all perishable matter but the fantasized threat of patricide, of displacement or substitution by the other encoded in the Oedipal drama.

The Oedipus complex, as Felman reminds us, involves two fantasied murders, that of the father by the son and that of the son by the father through castration (1029). The narrator has unconsciously placed himself in both roles of father and son. Thus, he is menaced by the idol/father in desiring Geneviève/mother and threatened by the objects/sons to which he has given life. According to Lacan, "the intermediary of death can be recognized in every relation through which man is born into the life of his history" (*Écrits: A Selection* 104). The narrator intensely fears losing his sanity, surrendering his reason to the chaotic impulses of instinct that would result in psychic death. Like other of Bioy's characters, the narrator fears loss of control, of power, resulting in impotence.

The narrator decides to occupy himself with the writing of his tale in order to ward off the allure of sleep and avoid the threatening visions. The writing process deters or opposes death. Instead of objects, the narrator now consciously arranges words, dealing with a different representational act and a different code of signifiers. Psychoanalytically, writing may be seen as a final attempt to affirm culture over nature, the symbolic over the lure of the mother's body. Both the child and the artist/writer, as MacCannell reminds us, must create metaphoric substitutes for the desire the Real incites in them because the Law "has already barred them from directly fulfilling that desire" (914). The use of symbols that constitute language removes both child and writer from the Real while providing them the means to create substitutes. According to MacCannell, narratives, as the burying of primal wishes originating in the Real "become in effect the triumph of civilization over the primal, the violent, the instinctual" (911). Although not a writer by profession, the narrator thus chooses to defer sleep by means of narration so that he may vanquish the instinctual.

While the narrator writes, Geneviève paces below in the basement like a caged animal. Earlier descriptions of Geneviève's feline eyes and her unusual gait also suggest the presence of the animal lurking below the surface of the woman. In this manner, Geneviève is linked to the natural world of instincts and the unconscious, and she too is momentarily trapped or repressed while the writer remains awake. Geneviève's physical location in the lower regions of the house dramatizes the metaphorical value assigned her. She represents the baser instincts; that is, forbidden sexual desires that lie beneath conscious reality.

At the end of the story, the narrator concludes that the events he recounted were largely a fabrication of his imagination. He denies a threat exists so that he may no longer deny himself gratification or fulfillment of his unconscious desires. He will abandon himself to

sleep, "con el consuelo de quien retorna, tras un penoso intento de separación, a la mujer querida . . ." (68) ["with the relief of a man who returns to his beloved after a painful attempt at separation . . ." (143)]. The struggle is over, surrender is near, the attempt at separation from the *mujer querida* has failed. His final words tell the reader that Geneviève has come with singular solicitude to inform him that he should rest, that he must sleep. The story ends here with the suggested fulfillment of desire and its consequences. The narrator abandons his writing or his attempt at substitution and surrenders to his desire for the Real/Mother. However, desire is fulfilled in the dream but is not revealed or recognized by the conscious subject. The "I" of Bioy's tale, the narrator, fails to recognize the origin of his desire. Moreover, just as the narrator fails to identify the origin of his desire or ascertain the true beginning of his narrative, he fails to perceive or "see" the end.

The story's abrupt conclusion is also explicable within the structure of the Oedipal. With the implied castration of the narrator or his loss of control and power, continuation is impossible. Continuation is also meaningless, since the story of Oedipus Rex, the possession of the mother and the punishment of blindness, has been recounted. He can only retell the same story rather than add to it.

In this fascinating tale of erotic love, Bioy reveals the struggle between conscious and unconscious desires through the combination of waking reality and dream. This binary opposition is reflected and enhanced by other dyadic contrasts, particularly in the settings. The ancient, mysterious, European castle with its oneiric ambiance contrasts with the stylish shop of Buenos Aires, while the shop's crowded exhibition rooms oppose the bare, stark quarters of the upper level. Objects are also ambivalent. The statue of Horus in the narrator's shop offers one such example. The narrator describes Horus as the god of libraries and thus consciously associates him with culture and the symbolic. Horus, however, is usually identified as the son of Osiris. Jung says that Horus is sometimes confused in legend with Osiris becoming the husband/son of Isis. The suppression of one identifying element and the privileging of the other testifies to the narrator's attempt to privilege the conscious and the symbolic and repress any references to Oedipal drama.

As in other tales by Bioy Casares that deal with the mind/body split, the protagonist of **"El ídolo"** exemplifies the Cartesian duality of the subject that privileges one element over the other: mind over body, culture or the symbolic over nature, conscious over unconscious. In each instance, the female is associated with the body, nature, and the unconscious. As body or nature, woman is an enigma, since she is not a product of the male mind. In **"El ídolo,"** the narrator refers to Geneviève as an enigma when he first encounters her in Buenos Aires, and his subsequent failure to understand her leads to the ambivalent portrayal of her. The female, as equivalent to nature, is threatening and mystifying. To be rendered safe and comprehensible, she must be recreated by man, a feat the narrator symbolically attempts by verbally recreating her in the narrative. However, Geneviève is also associated with the objects that obsess the narrator. Like his material possessions, Geneviève also undergoes a transformation in value. In a sense, he conveys a meaning or life to Geneviève as he does to his art objects; his words create her roles as the Good and Bad Mother. She is an object endowed with some subjectivity.

The ambiguity that surrounds Geneviève may also reflect the male's attitude toward the female and her ambiguous role in society. According to Gallop, woman's traditional role in culture is neither that of subject or object, "but disturbingly both" (15). In developing this argument, Gallop quotes Levi Strauss's assertion that woman is both a sign and an exchanger of signs. Consequently, woman evokes another primitive epistemology "in which all objects were considered endowed with subjective status" (15). In Freudian terms, the ambiguous status of the female may also be attributed to remnants in the adult of the infant's perception of the mother prior to its ability to distinguish between subject and object. Within the Freudian perspective, the narrator's association of Geneviève with mother leads to his ambiguous portrayal of her as both good and evil, nurturing and destructive; that is, as the complementary opposite to his desires. In the end she is still an enigma for the reader.

Triadic components of the text reiterate and enhance the many triangular relationships of the story (Garmendia/idol/Geneviève; Garmendia/Geneviève/the narrator; the narrator/ Geneviève/the stranger; the narrator/Geneviève/the idol). Among these components the most notable is the opposition between three cultures that imply three different epochs: modern European, ancient Egyptian and medieval Celtic. The reader may speculate that the triangularization of temporal and spatial components (that also includes the triadic division of the narrator's shop into basement, exhibition floors and barren attic) reflects the narrator's triangular perspective. The narrator's description of the house in which his dreams occur also divides the setting into three parts: a series of rooms, a dark, narrow corridor and a dim chamber. This description, in turn, echoes the portrayal of the Gulniac Castle and in particular the chamber where the dog/god is enthroned. Psychoanalysts have recognized the strong identification between house, body and mind. Teillard claims that in dreams the house represents different levels of the psyche (Cirlot, 120). While the upper levels stand for the superego, the basement is identified with the unconscious and instincts. Viewed within this perspective, the narrator's house and the activities assigned to each level of the house represent aspects of his psyche and his struggle between the call of civilization and the lure of nature.

The flexibility of the first person narration allows the narrator to incorporate myths and legends of other time periods, just as his profession allows him to collect and combine multiple objects that represent different epochs. In this respect, his shop and his text are alike. Both the explicit and veiled references to past dramas allude to the timeless repetition of the Oedipal drama itself. This endless duplication from ancient to medieval times is carried over into present time in the narration when one character duplicates the dreams of the other and shares the same object of desire. Garmendia's drama becomes the narrator's. Even the stranger in the shop and the reader may subsequently be players in a similar drama.

"La sierva ajena"

The ambiguity that surrounds the female in **"El ídolo"** resurfaces in a later tale, **"La sierva ajena."** Although the title apparently refers to a female protagonist, once again the narrative structure centers on the male and his inner drama. The tale, like others, concludes with a tragic outcome for the male and seems to take no interest in what subsequently occurs to the female.

The tale exhibits Bioy's talent for ironic humor, constructed on a play of opposites in physical forms and linguistic meanings. The dramatic contrasts between small and great, light and dark, together with the epic dimensions accorded to descriptions of the mundane, confer a baroque tone to the narrative. The spiral of binary opposition is evidenced on the structural level in the presentation of two different narratives: the longer, fantastic tale of Keller contained within the open frame of the shorter, realistic tale of the anonymous narrator.[8]

"La sierva ajena," like other tales of Bioy Casares, is a story within a story. The main protagonists do not relate the bizarre events of which they are victims, as their capacity to do so has been eliminated before the time of narration. This task is delegated to secondary characters whose undesirable traits distance them from their intended audience. In this tale, as in others by the author, the narrative logic reflects the power status of the characters; their silence, or linguistic castration, mirrors their physical or social reduction and their loss of social identity.

The anonymous narrator, tongue in cheek, begins his verbal play of linguistic contrasts by characterizing himself as "un sujeto oscuro y apocado," ["an obscure and common fellow"] who is nonetheless privileged to witness a brilliant moment of epic proportions: the social collapse of a great society matron. The use of terms that contradict, negate, or diminish a previous effect contribute to this humorous tone, establishing a bubble only to burst it. Thus, the narrator describes this episode and the grande dame of *porteño* society, Tata Laserna, in this manner: "no (es) menos inovidable porque hoy muy pocos la recuerdan. No describiré a Tata como una señora obesa, pero tampoco afirmaré que era alta" (123) ["She isn't less unforgettable because today few remember her. I will not describe Tata as an obese woman but I wouldn't state either that she was tall"]. Tata Laserna, depicted as short, obese, wearing heavy makeup, and followed like a hen by the latest young man, is brought to ruin by the discovery of the death of her former lover. The dashing Don Juan and world explorer was captured by pygmies, and his shrunken head is revealed in the midst of a social gathering.

The initial tale does more than simply introduce the subsequent story of another Don Juan and explorer who is shrunk to the size of a rat and yet lives to dominate the female. It presents and valorizes a phallocentric definition of desire according to which the female attempts to appropriate the power or privilege of the male through servitude. According to the narrator, the female is like the moon or other satellite; she has no light of her own but can only reflect the male's. Thus, Tata Laserna is diminished, reduced socially when her lover is reduced physically, for she gained her position through her association with him: "La luna, tenue y perentoria, brilla por la luz de un sol que no vemos; de igual modo, la considerable Tatá conquistó su lugar de privilegio, se afirmó en él, porque la fama la ha vinculado a un hombre extraordinario . . ." (125) ["The moon, tenuous and fixed, shines because of the light of a sun we do not see; in the same way, the worthy Tata conquered her position of privilege, and maintained herself in it, because fame linked her to an extraordinary man . . ."]. The cry the hostess utters on seeing the shrunken head is not an expression of sorrow over the horrible fate of her lover but, as the narrator declares, the last gasp of a woman witnessing her social collapse.

In this introductory and framing narrative, the author plays on the literal and figurative meanings of greatness and smallness and their relationship to power. To reiterate this message, he also remarks on another woman from a prominent family, who scandalized society by marrying a wealthy industrialist. It was not money that attracted her, however. According to the narrator, the industrialist is the modern version of the prince and the factory towers represent castles. The female can only appropriate these envied and desire symbols of authority and phallic power through her association with, and servitude to, the male. The relationship between male and female is thus defined by possession and lack, and difference accordingly is viewed as opposition (sun/moon, master/servant) rather than otherness. However, the affirmation and measure of the male's greatness is dependent upon the degree of the female's desire; the master is dependent on the servant, a relationship developed in the longer tale, narrated by one of Tata Laserna's guests.

The second narrative is told to the narrator by Keller after they and other guests have left the site of Tatá Laserna's social demise. Keller's narration details the strange events that have befallen his friend Urbina, as recounted to him and recorded in Urbina's diary. According to Keller, Urbina fell into the trap of a manipulative, seductive, and unstable woman, who conceals a secret in her isolated mansion: a former world explorer and Don Juan, shrunk by pygmies to the size of a rat.[9] Urbina suggests the image of a rodent when he recalls his first encounter with Flora, the object of his desire. He hears some faint squealing from behind a massive curtain and assumes the sound emanates from the household rodent. It creates such a strong impression that he later includes it in a poem commemorating their first encounter.

This initial representation and subsequent identification of the explorer, Rudolph, with the figure of the *rata* is suggestive. Cirlot says that the rat has been symbolically assimilated with the figure of the devil and the phallus: "se le superpone significado fálico, pero en su aspecto peligroso y repugnante" (382). Rudolph becomes the rival of the timid and naive Urbina and blinds Urbina on the eve of his departure with Flora. In the end, Flora abandons the rich but impotent Urbina and remains Rudolph's servant. The conclusion thus provides a tacit recognition of the fact that the phallic power envied and desired by Flora resides in Rudolph. Rudolph's authority, based in part upon his prior possession of the female, is symbolized in the trident that he carries like a regal scepter and with which he blinds Urbina.

The reader recognizes in Keller's narration certain recurrent motives that figure in Bioy's tales. First, the female figure is again split between the asexual mother and the fallen seductress, Eve. The Edenic scenario is suggested on the occasion of Urbina's first visit to Flora. Her mansion is surrounded by an overgrown garden: "Todo era extremadamente verde, no solo el follaje, sino los troncos de los árboles, cubiertos de musgo" (128) ["Everything was extremely green, not only the foliage but the tree trunks, covered with moss"]. The evocation of extreme green leads the reader to recall a similar phrase in **"El ídolo."** Flora is linked to this green garden by her name. The garden scene evokes some vague memory that is veiled from Urbina like the shrouded mansion: "Envuelta en un halo de bruma y en la desorbitada vegetación, la casa aparecía en la vaguedad de un recuerdo" (128) ["Enveloped in an aura of mist and in exorbitant vegetation, the house appeared in the vagueness of a memory"].

The image of Flora as fallen seductress, however, also remains veiled from Urbina, who does not "open his eyes" until it is too late, until Rudolph pierces them with his scepter. Until the end, Urbina "sees" Flora as candid, honest, and maternal; moreover, the primordial nature of his desire remains hidden even after he gains new insight. His initial descriptions of Flora reveal an idealized, artistic image of a woman with large dimensions, who from the beginning places him in the position of dwarf/child. On one occasion, Urbina declares: "Yo era, ante ella, como un niño . . ." (132) ["I was, before her, like a child . . ."]. Although a poet, Urbina resorts to sculpture to convey the looming presence of Flora, comparing her first to *Palas Atenea* and then to the allegorical image of the Republic and finally to "la reina emblemática de una escultura" (130) ["the emblematic queen of a sculpture"]. At her side, Urbina always feels morally and physically puerile. Although Flora diminishes his manhood, converting him into child/little man, Urbina's desire is to be with this maternal figure: "'*Ser*,' mumuró, 'únicamente *ser* junto a ella: esto basta.' Flora le sonreía con dulzura maternal" (143; emphasis added) ["'To be,' he murmured, 'just to be next to her: this was enough.' Flora smiled at him with maternal sweetness"]. The use of the verb *ser* as opposed to the verb *estar* indicates how essential Flora is to his existence. In psychoanalytical terms, the narrator seeks libidinal, pre-Oedipal pleasure in his pursuit of Flora, a form of pleasure that Rousseau once described as "the pleasure of sheer contiguity, of 'being with . . .'" (MacCannell, 77).

Flora becomes a model against which all other woman are measured, the outstanding figure for which other women merely form a complementary chorus or bas relief. Urbina views Flora's home, to which she initially denies him access, as a forbidden castle, and he subsequently views Rudolph as a rival with a prior claim. The title of the story, **"La sierva ajena,"** draws attention to this issue of prior claim. It is derived from a verse by Saint Paul with which the story concludes, but the original gender of the Spanish translation is altered to fit the narrative context: "Tú quién eres que juzgas al siervo ajeno? Para su señor está en pie o cae" (161) ["Who are you to judge another man's ser-

vant? To his own lord he stands or falls"]. The title, **"The Other's Servant"** thus clearly evokes Flora's role of servitude and emphasizes her possession by another.[10]

The rival figure in this bizarre triangle, Rudolph, is the only one whose complete biography is revealed; Flora relates this information to Urbina. She supplements by displaying Rudolph's numerous trophies that attest to his early athletic prowess and the photographs adorning his room that reveal his erotic conquests. Thus, although reduced or shrunken, Rudolph appears a more complete character. Meehan suggests that this abundance of details lends the fantastic figure verisimilitude. At the same time, this technique confers upon Rudolph a wholeness that contrasts with the other characters' lack; his "narrative" completeness seems to reflect his privileged position and authority over the female Flora (the female as defined ideologically in the text as a sign of lack). Cruel, tyrannical, and childish, Rudolph wields a power over Flora that is not based on threatening physical stature or economic position. The symbolic or phallic origin of this power is veiled, implied rather than revealed, just as Rudolph is initially veiled behind the massive curtains in Flora's home.

In his study of *La de Bringas*, Smith refers to the veiled nature of the phallic order: "Lacan says that the phallus must remain veiled in order to perform its function as empty marker of difference. Thus it cannot be embodied by a single character, still less by the all too visible figure of Bringas, the 'little mouse' . . ." (83). Like Rosalía of *La de Bringas*, Flora's submissiveness corresponds not to a particular man but to the phallic order that speaks through him.

Rudolph, as "whole" character, also contrasts with the child/Urbina who seeks completeness in Flora, as his words clearly indicate: "Yo era, ante ella, como un niño; como niño que, por no estar formado, puede ser impuro o procaz. Para distinguir el bien del mal debía mirarla" (132) ["I was, before her, like a child; like a child who, because he isn't formed, can be impure or precocious. To distinguish good from bad I had to look at her"]. At the same time, however, Rudolph is dependent on Flora for the satisfaction of his needs, and this dependency is demonstrated in his childish outbursts. Once again, one encounters the discourse of the master/servant in male/female relationships.

Flora uses the term *señor* when referring to Rudolph. The Spanish word Señor is used in prayer to refer to the Lord, but *señor* also refers to the lord and master of the manor and evokes a feudal, patriarchal system. Flora calls Rudolph "un señor odioso," he is the authority that exists above her, who possesses the power she envies and desires. Flora claims that Rudolph's uncontrollable temper will lead to some act that will justify her abandoning him. The servant threatens the master with revolt. Events prove the inverse of this prediction. Following Rudolph's foul deed, Flora abandons Urbina, not Rudolph. This outcome is foreshadowed in Urbina's observation of the contradiction between Flora's harsh words and her obedience to Rudolph's demands.

The lack of absolute authority over one's life (or one's desire) is reflected in the narrative strategy of the text by the absence of one, centered, authoritative narrative voice. The text actually has four narrators: the anonymous narrator of the framing tale, Keller, Flora, and Urbina, whose comments and poems are indicated by quotation marks and italics. Keller's comments are contained within, and thus subjugated to the anonymous narrator's tale and are determined by what Urbina told him. He is not a direct witness to the events he portrays. Flora does not tell her own story but rather explains Rudolph's origins based on what he has told her, and her comments are contained within Keller's story. The fact that man's life story, his sexual history, is predetermined by another, prior narrative, the Oedipal narrative, is reflected in this narrative strategy, in the predetermined nature of the stories. All the narrators tell someone else's story that has been previously recounted to them. They do not spontaneously create but rather re-create the history of another's desire. Only the anonymous narrator has observed the events he recounts, but his interpretation is shaped by tales of princes and castles and social, ideological values he has learned from others. Moreover, all these narrators are characterized by undesirable traits that alienate them from their intended audience and thus deprive them of an authoritative voice. The snobbism and pedantry of the anonymous narrator distance the reader from him. This narrator ridicules Keller. Early in his narration, Keller categorizes Flora as unstable, secretive, and manipulative. Furthermore, none of the principal victims have direct access to the reader. These circumstances reflect their loss of power at the time narration commences.

The association of power and authority with voice is implicit in two apparently minor episodes. Keller tells us that Urbina's father moaned and perhaps cried when he discovered that his son's rival was the size of a finger, hardly the reaction one would expect from an authoritative figure. Shortly before he is blinded, Urbina has a dream about his father. His father shouts a warning "en un tono autoritario, que Urbina no le conocía . . ." (160) ["in an authoritarian tone, which Urbina didn't recognize in him . . ."]. Only in Urbina's dream is the father given the authoritative tone that one would

normally associate with his position. The only biological father in the text is thus shown to be a powerless figure. The father's lack of "un tono autoritario" is reiterated in the lack of authoritative voice in the narrative. The text has no one central creative voice, the voice of the father/author

The meaning and value the male speakers attribute to male/female difference in their narratives also reflect the ideological concepts that men learn during the Oedipal transition, according to the theories of Chodorow. Chodorow states that at this time the male learns to define maleness as human and female as not-me (110). His self-definition is the result of a conflictive process based on denial of the feminine aspects learned from the mother and integrated within the core self during the pre-Oedipal stage. The ideological constructs acquired during the Oedipal stage are reflected in the anonymous narrator's definition of difference as possession and lack (sun/moon), for example. The positive/negative values assigned to difference are also reflected in Keller's assertion that men, as compared to women, are naive and immature in matters of sentiment while women are cunning: "El hombre es un desheredado que debe aprenderlo todo . . . En la mujer obran casi intactos los defectos y las virtudes del instinto; cada una hereda la experiencia acumulada desde el origen del mundo" (131) ["Man is a disinherited person who must learn everything . . . In women, the defects and virtues of instinct function almost intact; each one inherits the experience accumulated since the beginning of the world"]. In Keller's statements, acquired knowledge is opposed to instinct, mind to nature, with the former of each category being privileged in patriarchal society. Urbina's view of the female world, as recounted by Keller, also attributes negative or inferior values to the feminine: "Se dijo que el mundo de las mujeres—opresivo, indefinido, psicológico, malsano, prolijo—no convenía a la salud de esa noble planta, la mente del varón . . ." (143) ["He told himself that the world of women—oppressive, indefinite, psychological, unhealthy, tedious—was not suited to the health of that noble foundation, the male mind . . ."].[11] Throughout their narratives, the male speakers repeatedly describe attributes as masculine or feminine. These references attest to the importance they attribute to signs of gender and the crucial role of difference in shaping their definition of self.

Just as the male subject learns the meaning and value of feminine and masculine during the Oedipal transition, so too it learns what to desire through the internalization of the incest taboo. The fact that desire is not wholly spontaneous but orchestrated from without is suggested on the dramatic level by Flora's prearranged "chance" meetings with Urbina and on the thematic level by Urbina's references to the theatrics that people perform for the benefit of others. Urbina's remarks exhibit an awareness of the roles people play as actors and spectator in a drama that does not originate in themselves. Keller's description of the scene that precedes Urbina's introduction to Rudolph abounds in terms that evoke the theatrical:

> La escena continuó, por una inolvidable fracción de minuto, como si no hubiera testigos. Los actores estaban absolutamente entregados a la situación . . . Contra el espejo, como en un escenario, con el vestido blanco, con el chal amarillo, que movía como alas fantásticas, Flora, sola, de pie, con los brazos en alto, exclamaba: -(Por favor, basta de melodrama!
>
> (146)

> [The scene continued, for an unforgettable fraction of a minute, as if there were no witnesses. The actors were completely absorbed in the situation. . . . Facing the mirror, like on the stage, with a white dress, with a yellow shawl, that she moved like fantastic wings, Flora, alone, standing, with arms held high, was exclaiming:—Please, enough melodrama!]

Urbina characterizes the violet curtains that surround the monumental mirror in Flora's home as theatrical. The curtains conceal Rudolph while the exposed portion of the mirror reflects Flora playing the role of irate servant. The curtains both conceal and reveal. The theatrical curtains frame a scene, like the framing narrative, revealing its artificiality or fictionality, while concealing the mechanisms or reality of the off-stage author/other from spectator or reader. For a brief moment, Urbina empowers himself by casting Flora as the object of observation and the (male) gaze. His position allows him to see the character and the performer, inside and outside the framed scene. At the same time, the scene evokes an earlier one, when Urbina deliberately arrives late for a date at the London Grill. He observes Flora while she is unaware of his presence. Urbina also images Flora as an *object d'art* when he likens her to a work of sculpture.

When Urbina is finally introduced to Rudolph, however, he does not look upon him but rather gazes at his image in a mirror. Urbina claims that modesty and shame cause his reluctance to face Rudolph directly. Urbina chooses to look at something in order not to see something else that is barred by the demon of shame. Later, Urbina reflects a similar attitude when he laughs at Flora's "blind" love for Rudolph while failing to recognize his own "blindness"; that is, the nature of his desire and what he seeks in the person of Flora.

Thus, as in **"El ídolo,"** Bioy presents in this story of triangular desire the conflictive process that constitutes the male subject. The search for self remains problem-

atic, since it is based on denial and seeks origins that are necessarily occluded from the sight or insight of the subject. The subject is blinded not only by Rudolph's trident but by the protective fictions and metaphors created by the Oedipal, which spare him the painful knowledge of the real object of his desire.

"MÁSCARAS VENECIANAS"

In **"Máscaras venecianas,"** from the collection ***Historias desaforadas*** (1986), Bioy again presents a story of triangular desire, although some narrative features depart from the earlier paradigm.[12] The narrator is a journalist aimlessly wandering between one love and another until he meets Daniela, the ideal woman. The narrator's acquaintance with Daniela coincides precisely with the onset of mysterious attacks of fever, which are diagnosed as an incurable illness. These attacks incapacitate the narrator and prevent what promise to be romantic interludes with Daniela. One such attack occurs on the day they are to leave for a weekend in Montevideo, during which Daniela is participating in a scientific conference. When Daniela returns from the conference, the narrator tells her about his illness and claims that he has no right to burden her with it. He secretly hopes she will reject his apparent renunciation, but Daniela hears the words and does not apprehend their hidden appeal. She leaves the narrator for Europe, where she pursues her scientific studies. This initial episode draws attention to one of the central issues of the text: the ambiguity of the spoken word and its ineffectiveness in reaching the heart of the other. Words, like the masks that figure prominently in the second part of the narrative, conceal meaning; while they provide the symbols to describe reality, they also bar the subject from the direct apprehension of reality.

It becomes clear that while the narrator accepts the deferment of libidinal pleasure, he has not renounced it. He entertains fantasies of overcoming his illness and being reunited with Daniela even after she marries his friend and confidant. This may be read, in psychoanalytical terms, as a desire to overcome the castration threat and recover the original object of desire. The narrator's journey to Europe for health reasons conceals his secret desire to encounter Daniela and snatch her from his rival, Hector Massey. The narrator meets Massey and Daniela in Venice during the time of carnival, when *women* are flurrying about in costumes and masks.

At this point, the narrator, like Bioy's other narrators, is confronted with a mystery or riddle the woman is concealing. One recalls, for example, the mystery surrounding Geneviève's identity and Flora's mansion, and one notes the obvious parallel with the Oedipal tale. The narrator of this tale phrases the riddle in the form of a question concerning Daniela's identity. He is confronted with two identical women, one who greets him indifferently in the opera house and one who moments later secretly arranges a meeting with him. The gaze of the second Daniela, the "brillo de sus ojos," convinces the narrator he has discovered the real Daniela. The importance the narrator attributes to the gaze associates Daniela's with the primordial objects and reenforces her identification with the mother figure. However, pursuing her through the streets of Venice culminates in another incapacitating attack of fever, which may be viewed psychoanalytically as symptomatic of castration anxiety.

Massey provides the true solution to the riddle, not the narrator. The narrator's failure to do so reflects his disempowerment and foreshadows the denial of access to the beloved. Massey tells the narrator that Daniela has developed a cloning process and created in her own image the woman with whom Massey lives. Andrée Mansau compares Daniela's clone to Fasutine's image in *La invención de Morel*: the clone like the hologram deceives the anxious male's senses and is created by science (457). Both allude to a representation or a drama observed by the deluded male spectator (462). Daniela rejects any reunion with the narrator but offers to create a clone for him as she did for Massey. While the narrator rejects the offer and insists on obtaining the *original* woman, Massey is content in transferring his desire to the replacement, as his words clearly indicate:

> —Parece increíble, pero realmente es una mujer hecha a mi medida. Idéntica a la madre pero, ¿cómo decirte?, tanto más adecuada a un hombre como yo. Te voy a confesar algo que te parecerá un sacrilegio: por nada la cambiaría por la original. Es idéntica, pero a su lado vivo con otra paz, con genuina serenidad.
>
> (53)
>
> [—It seems incredible, but really she is a woman made to suit me. Identical to the mother but, how can I explain it to you, so much more satisfactory for a man like me. I am going to confess something to you that may seem a sacrilege: I wouldn't exchange her for the original for anything. She is identical, but at her side I live with a different peace, with genuine serenity].

Initially, the reader may conclude that Massey represents the successful Oedipal transition, sacrificing the original object of desire and displacing that desire onto the substitute, leading to the reward or happy ending that civilization has promised in return. The narrator, on the other hand, insists upon a desire that cannot be satisfied; he desires the woman Massey has called "la madre" and not any representation of her. However, this unexpected and perplexing turn of events also leads to a re-evaluation of the tale's appar-

ent Oedipal triangle. Massey, it appears, is not a rival for the affections of Daniela. What intervenes in the satisfaction of libidinal desire is not Massey as other but Society as Other. In wanting Daniela, the narrator unconsciously desires "mother," a desire which cannot be satisfied. Society, which codifies interhuman relations, prohibits mother/son gratification. The narrator's desire then can still be read in terms of transgressive; that is, opposed to civilization's goals in socializing the human being and defining his object of desire. But one might also read a transgressive desire in Massey's relationship, which he suggests may be interpreted as "*un sacrilegio,*" for he has opted for the "daughter" and the pleasure that familial eros provides.

A desire to transgress the Oedipal code may also be implied in the story's fantastic hypothesis, the cloning of a complete person. Like other tales of Bioy's in which doubles are created through mirror images, mental projections or mind/body splits, the self is duplicated or multiplied without recourse to sex. It is precisely during the Oedipal transition that the subject learns to center pleasure on a particular erogenous zone as opposed to the multiple erogenous zones experienced during the pre-Oedipal stage. By shaping the subject's gender identification and restructuring its "first passions" and sources of pleasure, the Oedipal attempts to foster heterosexuality and procreation, viewed as essential for the perpetuation of civilization. The creation of the clone subverts the Oedipal by reproducing outside heterosexual activity. One should note that Daniela's male mentors are clearly credited with providing the means or scientific knowledge through which she accomplishes her experiment. One may read this as yet another attempt to grant the male some form of creative role, the ultimate word or control over the birthing process. In either case, Daniela's clone, whether engendered by male or female invention, contradicts the traditional Oedipal scenario; it cancels the need for heterosexual love.

The concept of duplication, as opposed to original production, is reiterated in the text in various forms. For example, the narrator sees an opera in which there is an amorous triangle, a situation with which he identifies. The triangle on stage mirrors his own. When he pursues Daniela through the streets of Venice, he encounters many women disguised in the same costume, that of the dominó, as though Daniela is reflected in many mirrors, making the apprehension of the original impossible.

The mask, often referred to in the text, both conceals and reveals, and this ambiguity establishes an equivalency between it and another code of signifiers, words. According to Lacan, the function of the word is to mask meaning. The word as signifier is devoted to ambiguity; it cannot be restricted to a single meaning:

The word is instituted in the structure of a semantic world, that of language. The word never has only one use. Every word always has a beyond, sustains several functions, envelops several meanings. Behind what discourse says, there is what it means (wants to say), and behind what it wants to say there is another meaning, and this process will never be exhausted.

(I, xix, 267)

The word as mask and the accouterment of the mask place a bar between the subject and the object; they conceal or stand for the real while implying that the real lies behind or beyond them. With this in mind, Bioy's tale of a frantic search during carnival may be read as a search for self and other within a system of signifiers (masks and words) that reveal significance while veiling meaning.

The reader is informed that only women go to the opera in costume. The difference between male/female is thus underscored by the duality of unmasked/masked. The mask as sign of the female suggests her ambiguity to the male and also links her to the function of the word. As a male writer, the narrator attempts to abolish the ambiguity of both through his control of discourse. In his study of Spanish literature, Smith observes that such scenes of masked characters and operatic performance also suggest "the artifice of woman under patriarchy, her existence as masquerade"(198). The relationship between the sexes is viewed as one of *teatro*.

Throughout the story, the narrator gives great importance to the spoken word as well as to the word that is silenced or omitted from recorded speech. For example, on two occasions the narrator omits from his account the special name that Daniela has given him and that they alone share:

Daniela se echó en mis brazos, mumuró un sobrenombre (ahora lo callo porque todo sobrenombre ajeno parece ridículo) . . .

(31)

[Daniela threw herself in my arms, she murmured a nickname (now I don't mention it because other people's nicknames seem ridiculous). . . .]

Dijo también otra palabra: un sobrenombre, que sólo ella conocía.

(46)

[She said also another word: a nickname, that only she knew].

The word or name, as something given or exchanged just between them and not uttered publicly, creates a secret both pleasurable and embarrassing, something appropriately veiled from others. It attempts to establish a code within the broader code of language, as-

signing a unique meaning to a signifier. As such, this form of exchange attempts to create an intimate bond from which others are excluded. The verbal form of exchange suggests or stands for the sexual.

But what can be inferred about the proper name brought to the level of speech? Again, the occasions of its omission reveal the significance of its inclusion. The narrator, for example, dreads hearing Daniela's name uttered by Massey: "Sentí impulsos de preguntar por Daniela, pero también aprensión y disgusto de que Massey la nombrara" (42) ["I felt an impulse to ask about Daniela, but also apprehension and disgust that Massey might mention her name"]. In fact, in the recorded dialog of the narrator's story, Daniela's name does not cross Massey's lips. On the one hand, the narrator tells us what Massey said and on the other he allows Massey to speak for himself in the form of dialog. In the dialogs he records, Massey does not speak Daniela's name. The narrator controls the exchange with Massey, preventing Massey's utterance of Daniela's name. Daniela's name does occur in reported speech, but only the narrator employs it; he speaks for Massey thus appropriating his words.[13] To name something is to symbolically apprehend or appropriate it, and for this reason, the narrator does not want to hear Massey name Daniela. For the same reason, the narrator places great significance on the fact that Massey initially refers to Daniela as "mi mujer" instead of using the proper noun. The narrator is not forced to recognize Daniela as the object possessed; her identity is left unstated.

Two other circumstances surrounding Daniela's name are equally revealing. The narrator never uses her surname. When he murmurs her name in the presence of the double, he experiences sadness. The ways the narrator omits and includes Daniela's name suggest various interpretations. On the one hand, the word brought to the level of direct speech introduces it into the public code of language or discourse. This form of exchange, in psychoanalytical terms, implies the presence and intervention of a third party, the other or society, who shapes and validates the significance of the signifier and the code. Once the word is voiced and heard, the presence of a third party is thus implied. Such an exchange supersedes the dual relationship (beloved/lover, mother/son) the narrator wishes to establish. As previously stated, naming an object is a means of mentally or symbolically grasping it, of appropriating it. For this reason the narrator denies or limits Massey's opportunity to exercise this function over Daniela. The omission of Daniela's surname, either maiden or married, similarly evinces a tendency to deny her prior possession or belonging to another and, perhaps, her social-public existence.

The sadness and confusion the narrator experiences upon uttering Daniela's name in the opera house leads to yet another consideration of the nature of language. This incident triggers doubt and an intuition that the woman is not the original. The narrator intuitively recognizes the gap between the name and the object, the loss or absence of the real referent who has been substituted for the symbolic that stands in its place. Daniela, the real referent, is initially replaced by her double and subsequently by the word, the name, which frequently appears in the narrator's discourse. In the end, the narrator has only the empty word or symbol, for the real referent is lost to him forever.

The opposition between the word and the thing, between the real referent and its representation, is echoed in the narrator's reference to the contrast between literal and figurative meaning. As he chases Daniela through the streets of Venice, a figurative expression ["no debo perder la cabeza" (48)] takes on a literal meaning for him as he experiences a loss of equilibrium. In a sense, the narrator's thought process reverses the process of the Symbolic Order, which proceeds from the real to the metaphoric or figurative. This reversal, in turn, may be symptomatic of an underlying attempt and unconscious desire to devalue or negate the symbolic in favor of the real. The Symbolic Order, according to Lacan, is based on denial and displacement, but the narrator does not renounce or displace his desire; he does not wish to relinquish the Real/Mother.

The story concludes abruptly when Massey tells the bedridden narrator that Daniela has boarded a plane with no intention of ever renewing her relationship with the narrator, a relationship that the narrator had characterized as "ideal." The narrator fantasized the relationship, and this circumstance conveys significance and irony to his statement that imagination is the real obstacle to happiness. The inability to renounce the fantasy of pre-Oedipal, familial love leads to the narrator's often mentioned sadness. The narrator is nostalgic for a former state of being that only existed in his imagination. In the end, the female/mother, rather than the male, creates the separation by abandoning the male, as in **"La sierva ajena."**

This episode is concluded in the narrator's life and so is his romantic quest, although not his desire. In fact, the conclusion implies that the narrator will remain trapped within the past, unable to renounce his desire. The futility of any future pursuit, the unattainability of satisfaction, is captured in Massey's sad but firm response to the narrator's demand for the original Daniela: "Entonces, no conseguirás nada" (53) ["Then, you won't obtain anything"].

The reader notes a parallel between the nature of the narrator's desire, which is insatiable, and his illness, which is incurable. Neither are brought to conclusion in the story and can only end with death. The conclusion of the story thus closes an episode but lacks a sense of finality, reflecting the unending nature of both desire and illness. This parallel may also lead one to read the narrator's desire for origins as illness. The narrator, like Bioy's earlier protagonists, is rendered impotent because of his desire, the true nature of which remains masked, veiled from sight or insight. Like Bioy's other narrators, he ends alone, the absence of social ties or bonding being the price that is paid for transgressing the Oedipal logic. This state of incapacitation is reflected, as in other of Bioy's tales, by narrative voice, since Massey, not the narrator, utters the concluding remarks.

The narrator, like the protagonists in **"El ídolo"** and **"La sierva ajena,"** does not recognize the nature of his desire; all three male protagonists have been "blinded" by the fictions of the Symbolic Order and therefore cannot name what they do not perceive. In Lacanian terms, they have been castrated or disempowered by language itself, by the ambiguity and hollowness of the word that separated them from the Real. As writers, Bioy's protagonists attempt to master language and master through language only to be defeated in the end, relinquishing all control over speech or composition.

"Margarita o el poder de la farmacopea"

While the tale **"Margarita o el poder de la farmacopea"** may at first appear quite different from the works previously studied, the reader observes a similar underlying preoccupation with the temporal and relational boundaries that define human existence. However, in this story, it is the narrator/father who puts into motion the bizarre event that results in the death of the son. The death of the son by cannibalism evinces a generational conflict that has at its core a negation of genealogy or succession, a sort of recasting of the myth of Cronos devouring his young. The self affirms its autonomous being by denying any future replacement. Like Morel with his holographic images and the narrator of **"El ídolo"** with his objects and his text, the father/author/inventor of this tale attempts to place himself at the center of creative origin. Origin is not conceived in a genealogical perspective but rather as an intentional beginning, representing a deliberate rupture with the temporal, biological world and its reproductive cycle.

The tale comes from a volume of short stories titled, *Una muñeca rusa* (1991). While a number of interpretations may be offered for the suggestive spatial image evoked in the title, one is particularly pertinent to this discussion. The figure of the Russian doll may stand for the divisibility of the self, or rather, the inability to locate the self in one, continuous, inalterable form.

In **"Margarita o el poder de la farmacopea,"** the narrator's two-year-old granddaughter, Margarita, is transformed into a monster that devours her family. The horror of this situation is mitigated by the black humor or irony of the text: Margarita's insatiable hunger and subsequent cannibalism are caused by the tonic her grandfather invented to remedy her lack of appetite. However, this very short story is not solely concerned with body issues expressed through Margarita's transformation. The work begins and ends with references to family and specifically to reproaches from the narrator's son; thus it calls attention to relational or kinship boundaries as well.

This first person narrator of this tale is not only a type of inventor or creator, in this instance, one credited with curative balms and ointments, but a biological father as well. His role as father figure is reiterated in his multiple functions: creator of tonics, origin of biological life, and author of the narrative.

The narrator demonstrates similarities with Bioy's other protagonists who desire to place themselves at the center of creation, in the role of the autonomous God the Father. Like the biblical omnipotent Father, his power is manifested in the body alterations he can bring about in others, producing both life and death, pleasure and pain. Margarita is a sign and manifestation of this power, "el poder de la farmacopea." Although Margarita is at the center of the one significant event in this story, the work really focuses on the narrator, his drive to affirm his ego boundaries and his autonomy, as the outcome of the story, the son's death, suggests. Margarita unwittingly provides him the means to accomplish this outcome. Through her, his son and grandsons are eliminated; thus the threat to his autonomy, the menace of genealogical succession and replacement, is removed. There is no heir to carry on the family name; endless duplication of self in progeny is negated. The narrator does not literally devour his offspring like Cronos, but he does bring about this end. The son's final words implicitly place the blame for his death on his father by exonerating the daughter: "—Margarita no tiene la culpa" (161) ["It's not Margarita's fault" (116)]. Both the son and the reader recognize the origin of the son's death in the narrator's creative endeavors. The outcome thus enacts one of two Oedipal fantasies described by Felman: the death of the son by the father.

The nature of the narrative conflict can be uncovered in the narrator's choice of words, in his mode of rep-

resentation, as well as in the implications of the story's outcome. The narrator chooses to begin his tale with a recollection of his son's reproach: "—A vos todo te sale bien" (159) ["Everything always goes so smoothly for you" (114)]. The reproach is located in the tone of voice rather than in the words themselves; that is, the significance of the son's words depends upon the narrator's interpretation. From the narrator's perspective, the son is viewed as an antagonist who envies the father's triumphs, his power. The narrator tells us little else about his son, except that he lives at home with his wife and four children, a fact that suggests limited financial success and independence. There is no physical description, no characterization through action or dialog. The son is absent or suppressed in most of the text, limited to two brief reproachful statements at beginning and end. The reader cannot envision a body or persona that corresponds to his voice of reproach. Thus, as author or father of the text, the narrator linguistically and figuratively eliminates the body of the son from the narrative while Margarita literally dismembers and discards it from the fictional world.

The son's initial reproach leads the narrator to ponder the nature of triumph and to consider his own successes. His eyes glance inward; he is preoccupied with himself. It is worth noting the very insistence on the word *triunfo* to describe the narrator's accomplishments, a term which aggrandizes his contributions and belies his attempts at modesty. The word *triunfos,* meaning successes or triumphs, evinces his desire to be victorious over others, to view himself as supreme. Other descriptive terms used to represent his *triunfos* link his supremacy with authority and origins, qualities also associated with a patriarchal figure. For example, he observes that: "Mis triunfos, si los hubo, son quizá auténticos . . ." (160) ["My successes, if there were any, have been authentic perhaps . . ." (115)]. His triumphs are authoritative, of undisputable origin, original. They preceded any repetitions or imitations in the pharmaceutical world. His formulas, extensions of himself, are the origin of balms and ointments that alleviate the sick, that produce change in others (160). His assertion that his formulas appeared on *every* shelf in his *vast* country exposes his pride and vanity, his tendency to aggrandize his creative role. The narrator further reveals his desire for triumph when he subsequently describes the certainty of *triunfo* he experienced when he foresaw the invention of his new tonic, *Hierro Plus.*

The narrator continues his discussion of the pharmaceutical world in his belittlement of vitamins, the successors that replaced tonics. Of course, the heirs apparent were failures and the world now seeks in vain the original tonics (160). The superficial discussion of tonics and vitamins provides the narrator with the means to articulate an underlying preoccupation with generational conflict, the opposition between the original authority and the potential usurper of privilege. Moreover, his tone suggests that antagonism and resentment also characterize the position of the threatened authority. The world of pharmaceutical transactions thus enters into a symbolic relation with the narrator's world of kinships; it parallels or represents his familial situation, in which an heir apparent, already deemed unsuccessful, waits in the wings to replace the original.

Margarita, the only named character in the text, is the sign and instrument of the narrator's power. As an infant female, she is the least threatening person in the story. As a two-year-old, she is incapable of formulating a narrative; her limitations are thus linguistic as well as physical. The child becomes actor following her transformation. The narrator precipitates and witnesses the event; he narrates the event but it is the child who performs it. As such, Margarita may be viewed as a projection or extension of the narrator's self, one which enables an action to be performed that results in his ultimate triumph. The privileging or apparent individualization of Margarita by assigning her a proper name could then be read as actual individualization or privileging of the narrator's manifested power, of his performing self. The narrator's interpretation of his son's last words paint the outcome as his triumph, for he sees in his son's remark the usual reproach that accompanied his successes: "Las dijo en ese tono de reproche que habitualmente empleaba conmigo" (161) ["He said this in the same reproachful tone that he always used with me" (116)]. The narrator reads the same meaning into the final words as he did with the earlier complaint: "A vos todo te sale bien" (159).

Margarita's role as actor/character who preserves and manifests the power of the original/author by cannibalizing the family/successors presents further complexities. Margarita is also distanced from a truly physical body, although the narrator employs linguistic means or metatropes to accomplish this act of disembodiment. The title of the story begins this process of distancing the character from the physical body by linking her to pharmacopeia. Rather than suggesting the story is about one or the other, the title actually reflects the identicalness of both, the fact that two terms refer to the same entity. Margarita stands for or is the power of pharmacopeia. She is to be read like a pharmacopeia, a book published by an authority containing standard medical formulas and methods. Michie describes this mode of representation, in which the female character is likened to text or painting, as metatrope, a typical device in nineteenth century literature.[14]

In his first description of Margarita, the narrator utilizes other modes of representation that recall the disembodied characterization of Victorian heroines. He resorts to descriptive clichés of nineteenth century females in depicting Margarita as golden blonde, with blue eyes and pale complexion. He employs another typical metatrope in comparing her to a print or image; she is like a product of the visual arts. He concludes his initial characterization by comparing her to angels, symbols of disembodied being. This use of cliché or conventional descriptive terms in nineteenth century female portraiture expresses the male's perspective on the female body and its lack of uniqueness (See Michie, 88-97). The narrator underscores the fact that Margarita is a repetition of something that is itself a repetition by clearly labeling as nineteenth century the imagery he borrows to describe her (160-161). The representation of Margarita thus underscores the fact that her uniqueness, signified by her proper name, does not reside in personal attributes but in the power of performance injected or projected into her by the creator/narrator.

As representative of text and fictional actor, Margarita serves to introduce other symbolic, generational relationships of conflict: the conflict between literary precursors and their followers, the opposition between original works and their imitations, the struggle between author and character for supremacy and autonomy. Through Margarita, the narrator seems to affirm the fantasy of the original, autonomous author by disposing of the successors; his character or text cannibalizes or ingests them. The original contains all that follows rather than the successors engulfing their predecessor. Although the narrator/author projects part of himself into the character of Margarita, he remains supreme and autonomous. Even after her transformation, the narrator describes Margarita as only a toy, "una muñeca rubia" (161) ["blonde doll" (116)], something that must be animated from without. The objective tone of his voice and the absence of guilt or remorse suggest an inventor/creator who feels removed and above the rest.

It is apparent that in this ironic tale of metamorphosis Bioy explores the role of ego and rivalry in professional and familial relationships. Under closer scrutiny, the tale discloses a fear of the voracious energies and desires of offspring and the horror of being consumed by them. The father/artistic self imagines itself imperiled in others and the text dramatizes a fantastic revenge on the potential usurpers of privileged position. In the end, the original inventor/father remains, his autonomy affirmed by the destruction of his male progeny.

However, like the characters in Bioy's other stories of rivalry in which the protagonists attempt to subvert the logical progression of the Oedipal, the protagonist does not recognize or name his desire. In fact, in a discussion with his daughter-in-law, the narrator had declared at the beginning of the story that triumph (success or phallic power) is not vulgar or repulsive but rather the desire for triumph. To be powerful is not bad but to seek or desire the power of the other is repugnant. The narrator then adopts a false modesty, allowing the remarks or actions of others to attest to his success and power. This tactic is transparent and the reader not only sees through his ploy but beyond it. The reader recognizes what the protagonist cannot: that his sense of identity is constructed on an errant vision or misrecognition of the self. The protagonist sees himself as successful although his latest invention is a scientific failure. He sees himself as possessing rather than seeking autonomous power. In a sense, he has a psychological blind spot. He has no insight into the difference between his life history and his story. He does not recognize himself in his quest to be The Father.

The Oedipal, as MacCannell asserts, offers a promise as well as a threat in its attempts to shape the identity of the social being: "Oedipus is a patterned set of reversals, in which the threat of privation is turned into the promise of completeness, unity, and fullness. As 'castrated' you give something up . . . in exchange for a certain freedom from the organic, the necessaritarian. It is the freedom from nature that only culture could provide" (69). In the tales we have considered, Bioy's protagonists reject the promise of the Oedipal and challenge its logical progression. This challenge is manifested in the relationships of the characters and in the narrative strategies they employ. Through their actions, it becomes apparent that the protagonists do not accept the displacement of the real/original by the symbolic/substitute. In some instances, their texts overtly attack the process of socialization by putting it on display as comic drama or melodrama. For example, the narrator of **"La sierva ajena"** labels some attitudes or actions as histrionic and describes Flora performing before the large curtained mirror as if she were on stage. The narrative strategies of the texts also evince a desire to subvert the closed structure of the Oedipal in favor of the open-ended conclusion.

Although the protagonists attempt to break the triangular enclosure and subvert traditional patterns of socialization, their efforts result in failure. They are "punished": left incomplete, incapacitated or "blind." Meaningful relationships or bonds of love are destroyed or rendered impossible. Attempts to cross boundaries established by society lead not to fulfillment but self-destruction: loss of sight or insight, loss of control or esteem.

The texts explore the relationship between conscious and unconscious desire in the structuring of subjectivity and gender relationships. This relationship is suggested by many references to sight and blindness and to the protagonists' visual perspectives as voyeur or exhibitionist, performer or spectator. It is also developed in references and allusions to display and concealment. The texts' many references or allusions to sight and insight or their lack generates an awareness of blindness to or ignorance of the hidden truths that shape individual identity and gender roles. In **"El ídolo,"** the protagonist cannot see what transpires between Garmendia and Geneviève as it is hidden from view, but the mechanics of the dream allow him to know what has happened. However, both the narrator and Garmendia fail to "see" the site or origin of their desire which is barred from conscious knowledge. In **"La sierva ajena,"** Rudolf is initially concealed behind theatrical curtains, but even after Urbina sees Rudolf he fails to recognize the power and danger Rudolf represents. Urbina also makes several references to the pretexts employed by him and Flora to avoid or seek each other, thus calling attention to the gap between apparent and hidden motives. In **"Máscaras venecianas,"** the narrator attempts to recognize the real woman concealed behind the mask while failing to recognize his desire for the Real. In **"Margarita o la farmacopea,"** the narrator emphasizes his role of spectator by referring to the demise of his family as "un espectáculo que no olvidaré así nomás" (161) ["a spectacle that I won't forget so easily" (116)]. He fails to really "see," however, the small, fleeting nature of his triumphs which is referred to in the epigraph of the story: "Tus triunfos, pobres triunfos pasajeros (Mano a mano, tango)" (159) ["Your success, poor brief success from Holding Hands (a tango)" (114). Balderston, in his review of Levine's translation, notes that a better meaning for the phrase *mano a mano* would be "We're even" since that phrase is more relevant to the story (15). It captures the adversarial nature of the interpersonal relationships. In the end, all four texts generate in the reader an awareness of "blindness" or ignorance of hidden motives that structure one's sense of identity and shape gender relationships.

. . . . .

In the previous chapters, we have seen how Bioy's male protagonists struggle against rivals or other obstacles, including powers beyond their comprehension or control, to be united with the female object of desire. Analysis of individual works demonstrated the pre-Oedipal or Oedipal nature of desire in the protagonists' quests for their lost-self and the other. A number of these texts reveal another pattern of interaction, where the protagonist strives to assert authority over the other and inscribe the actions of the other within a male-conceived hierarchy. In Bioy's narratives, such personal struggles for power often occur between the male and female characters. According to Bioy, male/female relationships provide the most interesting source of dramatic conflict.

The dualistic vision that underlies many fantastic hypotheses and other aspects of the author's texts is evident in his depiction of the female, whose role is usually defined by her relationship to men. Consequently, she is often cast in one of two stereotypical molds: the good, passive woman or the devious schemer. Bioy has said that, at times, he feels women are more intelligent than men or psychologically superior, and men, as a result, are reduced to the role of the fool or child at their sides (Snook 109). In such a situation, the woman is not protective or nurturing, but domineering and manipulative. On occasion, as in **"La sierva ajena,"** the dominance of the female is suggested by her large physical dimensions. The relationship between male and female in many of Bioy's tales is thus conceived in terms of a power struggle. Intelligence or psychological superiority is a covert form of power that the female exercises, symbolically castrating the male and annihilating his individuality. This deceptive woman often resembles the Jungian concept of the "Devouring Mother," who betrays the child or entraps him in her womb.[15] She destroys the male, bringing about a figurative death, for his subsequent incapacitation or withdrawal from life results in a demise of authority and identity. The role of the schemer may thus be interpreted as a projection of the male's conflicting fear of and desire for a return to the center or to origins. It is worth reiterating at this point that the biological mother seldom appears in Bioy's works. The traits usually attributed to her are subsumed in other female characters.

Although struggles for power most often occur on the interpersonal level, on occasion the author presents issues of authority and control in broader, social terms. For example, in "La pasajera de primera clase" ["The first-class passenger"], an older female protagonist portrays the encroachment by the popular masses into the social space of a fading upper class. The story may be interpreted as a metaphor for the class conflict that occurred during the Peronist years, but it uses the same language and techniques that suggest more personal "boundary disputes."

Before analyzing in detail the conflictive relationships dramatized in **"La pasajera de primera clase"** and two other representative works, let us consider more closely the definition of power and how power often manifests itself. Webster's New Twentieth-Century Dictionary defines power as "the ability to do" or "the ability to control others." Magnarelli demonstrates that

this definition suggests "that power is not absolute but relative, dependent on the other and the other's position" (*See(k)ing Power/Framing Power 14*). In narrative, power is revealed through the dynamic activity or interaction of characters, through the ability to perform and to control others' performance. According to Magnarelli, "those in power manipulate space and movement through space, their own and others', as they control the location of objects or bodies (animate or inanimate, theirs or others'). In this respect, power is related to possession; those in power position valued (and thus valuable) objects (of desire), animate or inanimate, in proximity to themselves, as they designate themselves their sole possessors (dictators of their spatial movement) in a circular maneuver that simultaneously determines which objects can be defined as desirable" (14).

As Magnarelli demonstrates, positions of power are often expressed through spatial metaphors, such as "control over" or "to serve under." Hierarchy is revealed through the privileging of one spatial term over its binary opposite, such as in the contrast inner/outer. The opposition of native/foreigner might also be viewed in this category as it suggests political and cultural boundaries that are inclusive or exclusive.

Magnarelli discusses two other ways in which power manifests itself in the literary text. Power may manifest itself as control over discourse or control over vision. In the first instance, those in power control who will speak and "the validity of what will be spoken" (15). Such grammatical indicators as demonstrative pronouns reveal physical or social proximity as opposed to distance and difference while pronouns reveal positions as subjects or objects in the events that unfold. In the second instance, those in power determine what will be viewed and how it will be viewed. By focusing on certain details and relegating others to a blurry background, the author/narrator may enhance or reduce those elements that affirm or threaten his/her power. The use of a framing tale calls attention to the boundaries in the text and reflects an ideology of inclusion or exclusion.

These characteristics of power relationships are evident in a number of Bioy Casares's stories. Analysis of three illustrative stories, **"Moscas y arañas,"** from *Guirnalda con amores* (1959), **"Los afanes,"** from *Historias fantásticas* (1972), and **"La pasajera de primera clase,"** also from *Historias fantásticas,* will illustrate how Bioy develops the power struggle.[16]

"MOSCAS Y ARAÑAS"

The text's title, **"Moscas y arañas"** [**"Flies and Spiders"**], refers to the concept of predator and prey, victim and victimizer, and informs the reader immediately of the underlying nature of the story's conflict. It derives from a phrase uttered by the male protagonist, Raúl Gigena, when he instructs his wife, Andrea, about the Darwinian nature of life: "Este mundo se divide en moscas y arañas. Tratemos de ser arañas que se comen a las moscas" (156-157) ["This world is divided into spiders and flies. We'd better be the spiders, so that we can eat up the flies" (91)]. Raúl's allusion to the natural order shows how men base many of their myths and patterns of behavior on biological observations. According to Simone de Beauvoir, the myths that shape male/female relationships are also traceable to the male tendency to identify woman with Nature.[17] Man entertains an ambivalent relationship with Nature; he exploits her, but she crushes him; she is the womb that creates his being and the tomb to which he must return. She thus inspires conflicting feelings of admiration and fear. Moreover, the male myth of devouring femininity has crystallized around the image of certain predatory females, such as the spider and praying mantis, who consume their mates (de Beauvoir 15). The model conceptualizes life as a battle between the sexes, a struggle between the powerful and the weak.

At the same time, man's tendency to identify the female with nature may be viewed as a consequence of the male process of differentiation. As psychoanalytical theory informs us, it is only through the recognition of separation and difference from the other that the self achieves a sense of its own identity. The perception of same and other thus underlies our experience of the world and self as well as the manner in which we portray them through language. According to Chodorow, the male learns to interpret separation and difference as "me" and "not me." He recognizes in nature and the female that which is "not me." Magnarelli also refers to male transformation of difference in her discussion of the strange bond between woman and animals:

> . . . as I have discussed at length in *The Lost Rib,* our comprehension of the world and our language itself are ultimately based on our ability to differentiate between X and not X, between the same and the other. We have two words for two objects because they are somehow not identical. Now for man, the other or not man has always had two forms: the animal and the female. Thus, the very fact that both animals and women can be defined as not man or as man's opposite assuredly produces some of the overlapping of connotation between the two terms.
>
> (*Reflections/Refractions: Reading Luisa Valenzuela*, [69])

As a consequence of the emphasis placed on difference, the male also valorizes boundaries which mark separation and difference. Moreover, the male not only

groups the three categories of male, female, nature into two, man and not man, through the Oedipal he also learns to evaluate and give meaning to the members of the dyad. Thus evolves the privileging of one element over the other, the establishing of hierarchies: male over the female, the master over the slave.

Raúl transposes the power struggle to the socioeconomic plane and thus quickly establishes a successful business as a wine broker upon his arrival in Buenos Aires. Subsequently, Raúl turns their large home into a boarding house to efficiently utilize the unoccupied space and to gain additional revenue. His business acumen and competency are contrasted against the sentimentality and domesticity of Andrea, who would have preferred the romantic coach house to the ugly *caserón* her husband bought. Even though the boarding house eventually provides more than adequate financial income, Raúl refuses to relinquish the brokage business which requires long hours away from home and which leaves him exhausted upon his return from work. This refusal can be interpreted as an expression of Raúl's need to assert his masculinity through his own economic power in as much as the boarding house is successful mainly through the industrious efforts of his wife Andrea. In their interpersonal relationship, it is clear that Raúl conceives of a dominant role for the husband, the role of the "araña" once again, through the exercise of the power to make decisions. The passive role attributed to Andrea is evidenced, in turn, in her acquiescence to these decisions.

Shortly after the arrival of the Hertz couple to the boarding house, Raúl begins to experience disturbing dreams in which Andrea betrays him with the men in the boarding house and with total strangers. During the daytime, his doubts about his wife's fidelity persist and drive a wedge between them. Raúl cannot decide if his wife is the devoted and loyal woman he daily experiences or the wicked seductress revealed in his nightly fantasies. It is only after Andrea's suicide that Raúl discovers the source of these disruptive dreams and realizes that the reunion that he now desires with Andrea is impossible. Shortly after learning of Andrea's death, Raúl discovers that he has been a pawn in a psychological power struggle waged by one of their boarders, the elderly and crippled Helene Jacoba Krig. Helene had telepathically transmitted thoughts to Raúl to separate him from Andrea and claim him for herself.

The association of Helene with the role of the spider or predator is first suggested by her physical attributes. Her depiction as a relatively motionless entity, whose activities are confined to restricted spatial parameters, recall the inactivity of the patient spider within the borders of its web. The salient features of her physiognomy also invoke the image of the devouring spider: "La señorita tenía . . . la boca grande, los labios rojos, que descubrían dientes irregulares y mucha saliva" (157) ["The lady had . . . a large mouth, and quivering red lips which exposed crooked teeth and a lot of saliva" (92)]. The words she utters on revealing her diabolical scheme to Raúl at the conclusion of the story also reiterate the roles of victimizer and victim into which they have been cast: "Hace mucho que tendí mis redes, que usted cayó. ¿Supone que revoltea por acá, por acullá? Dasvaríos. Le juro que está en la red, por así decirlo, práticamente. No proteste, no se altere" (166-67) ["You see, I spun my web and caught you in it a long time ago, so to speak. Did you think you were flying here and there and yonder? Nonsense. Rest assured that you are and have been mine, for all practical purposes, completely at my service. Don't protest, don't get upset" (99)]. Raúl, consequently, is reduced to the role of the subservient, obedient child by the Jungian "Devouring Mother" who will feed on his youth and mobility. Helene's final words to Raúl, which repeat those used earlier to refer to her dog, whom she also controls through telepathy, underscore Raúl's humiliating and dehumanizing subjugation: "Al principio nadie me quiere. Poco a poco lo conquistaré. ¿Descubrirá algo, no es verdad, Raúl, en su Helene Jacoba?" (167) ["Nobody loves me at first. Slowly but surely, however, I will conquer you. You'll find something to love, isn't that so, Raúl, in your Helene Jacoba?" (99)].

In the interaction between Helene and Raúl, two traditional binary operations which signify relationships of power or authority, master and pet, predator and prey, are metaphorically enacted and reduced to one: man and woman. Moreover, if one considers Raúl's ultimate circumstances as a surprise reversal from his customary role and as a dramatic shift within the binary opposition, one must also conclude that the position of victim or conquered he now occupies is ordinarily assigned to the other member of the dyad, the female. The role reversal, furthermore, suggests the unnatural and malevolent nature of the subversion of male authority, for Helene has resorted to covert, mysterious means to gain control. She has employed and abused means which are not at the disposition of the average mortal male to rid herself of the wife and claim the husband/son. As such, she may be viewed as a relative of the witch who gains no societal approval for her victory, whose exercise of power is not sanctioned or condoned.

If the reader considers in broader terms, however, the nature of the power struggle alluded to in the title of the text, some additional light can be shed on the concept of the victim. In a sense, both Helene and Andrea are also victims, trapped in the web of binary opposi- tion transmitted by language and culture, that allows for only winner or loser, saint or seductress, conqueror or conquered, predator or prey. Such a system contains no terms to mediate these extremes or provide gradations between them.[18] Andrea is thus viewed by Raúl as alternately pure or deceitful; Helene is totally evil. Both are created to provide Raúl his complementary opposite, that is the suitable mate or the formidable enemy. In the case of Helene, the female may also represent a projection or extrication of the evil half or flaws within Raúl.[19] Helene's remarks allude to this relationship between them when she states that she, in fact, is a more compatible match for Raúl than Andrea since she shares his interest in power and his materialism (167). The female is thus circumscribed by a binary linguistic and cultural code which defines her role in terms of her opposite, the male. Her ultimate domination by the masculine control of the word is reflected in the manner in which her story is inscribed within and dependent upon the male's story. Thus, **"Moscas y arañas"** concludes with the figurative death of Raúl, his loss of authority, when he is finally caught within the web.

Raúl's figurative movement toward the center of the web is mirrored in the text by allusions to other movements of characters from the periphery or outside to the center. In the beginning of the story, Raúl and Andrea move from the province to Buenos Aires, the center of commerce. This is the only decision which Andrea makes, for she sees the need to be free of the influence of outsiders, presumably her in-laws. In terms of Andrea's aspirations, the movement would be termed centrifugal, directed away from the center. In terms of Raúl's materialistic ambitions, this movement is directed toward the center. Furthermore, and although somewhat paradoxical, Raúl's initial reluctance to detach himself from home is another indication of an attachment to center and provides an early indication of a child-like dependency. Once they have established their house in Buenos Aires, Raúl decides to take in boarders. The penetration of the outside world into the inner world of the boarding house is further emphasized in the case of Helene by her foreign status. The penetration of Raúl's mind by Helene offers the culminating instance of this play on the binary opposition of inside/outside. Moreover, this centripetal movement of the text is seen as negative in as much as it leads to the ultimate downfall of Raúl.

The movement from outside to inside, implicit in the activities of the characters, is reflected in a similar shift in the positions of the narrative voices that relate the events of the tale. The first part of the story is recounted by a public, heterodiegetic narrator, that is a person who apparently is not a character or participant in the fictional world. His comments are addressed to a public narratee, who also exists outside the fictional world and with whom the real reader or historical audience may identify. The narrator appears to possess privileged information about the characters' thoughts, feelings and their lives since he describes scenes and events he did not witness. Moreover, he provides no indication of any secondary sources for his knowledge.

As the story progresses, the narrator departs from the convention of omniscience that characterizes the authorial stance of the preceding section. He implies that his knowledge of events is based on memory and therefore subject to limitations and error: "Si no me equivoco, la aparición del matrimonio Hertz coincidió con los primeros sueños de Raúl" (158) ["If I'm not mistaken, the arrival of the Hertz couple coincided with the first of Raúl's dreams" (92)].

The unexpected departure from the conventions of unrestricted knowledge marks a new role and a status for the narrator of the story. Up until this point, no clear separation or distinction has been made between the heterodiegetic author and the narrating voice. Since the story begins in the third person mode and the narrating voice possesses an unlimited view of his characters, an identification between implied author and narrator might be assumed by the reader. According to Susan Snaider Lanser:

> Ordinarily, the unmarked case of narration for public narrator is that the narrating voice is equated with the textual author (the extra-fictional voice or "implied author") unless a different case is marked—signaled—by the text. In other words, in the absence of direct markings which separate the public narrator from the extra-fictional voice, so long as it is possible to give meaning to the text within the equation author-narrator, readers will conventionally make this equation.
>
> (257)

In **"Moscas y arañas,"** a definite textual signal of case differentiation is sent to the reader by the abrupt shift from the third person to first person mode, expressed by the pronoun *yo,* and not the conventional collective *nosotros* previously used to imply author and reader. Furthermore, by suggesting at this point in the text that the narrator has in some way learned of the story's events, his relationship to the narrative act and the fictional world is suddenly cast in a new light. The distance between the extra-fictional voice and the narrating voice is clearly established. Narration now appears to come from someone who, although not a participant in the events, is nonetheless related to the world of the characters. Thus, the discourse marks a movement of internalization into the fictional world.

Subsequent passages denote a further progression away from external mediation. The use of tagged direct dis-

course in the form of monologues and dialogues is extensive, thus allowing the characters to speak with minimal authorial intervention. The process of internalization of narrative voice reaches its culmination in the conclusion of the story, presented in the form of a dramatic monologue delivered by Helene Jacoba Krig. Minimal tag expressions, such as "she said," disappear from the text. Explanation of events is now given solely by a character or persona belonging to the fictional world who acts as a private narrator, that is, someone who has no direct access to the extra-fictional world. Her remarks are directed to Raúl, another fictional character, who serves as a private narratee in the communicative act. The process of internalization and reduction of authorial mediation is completed as narration now comes from the other side of the fictional act, from within the fictional world itself.

The character's power relationships with others are reflected in these shifts in narrative voice and in their ability to exercise control over discourse situations. During the first part of the story, the narrative is controlled by an anonymous third person narrator whose voice, as we have seen, is often identified by the reader with that of the implied author, which in this case is masculine. The absence of significant dialogue in this section between Andrea and Raúl not only reflects their status of authority or independence in relationship to the narrator, but to each other as well. It is clear that Raúl is reluctant to include Andrea in his activities and that Andrea is reticent to question or complain. The limitation of dialogue between Andrea and others may also denote her inability to participate effectively in discourse addressed outwardly and enunciated in the outside world. Her silence underscores her resignation, apparent in the narrator descriptions: "Andrea se dejó persuadir por las razones de su marido" (150) ["Andrea was swayed by the same reasoning as her husband's" (90)] and "Andrea se resignó" (155) ["Andrea accepted the situation reluctantly" (90)].

The occasional use of narrated monologues also alludes to the subordinated or dependent roles of the characters. Such statements, like those of indirect style, are narrated in the third person mode but usually transpose the future tense of direct discourse to the conditional, and the past to the pluperfect. Also notable is the use of grammatical forms (i.e. possessive adjectives and pronouns) which are characteristic of direct discourse and reflect the spatial, temporal and ideological perspective of the protagonists. Andrea's thoughts on the prospect of boarders in her home are conveyed through such a technique: "Ya no estarían solos, pero compartir la casa con los desconocidos que depara la suerte no es como compartirla con gente de la familia, que se cree con derecho a dirigir nuestras vidas y opinar sobre todo" (155) ["They wouldn't be alone, of course, but sharing the house with any stranger that fortune provided at least wasn't like sharing it with one's own family, who always thought they had the right to run one's life and pass judgements on all matters" (90)]. The reader notes the use of the possessive *nuestras* in the Spanish version. The narrated monologue fuses the authorial voice with that of the character, suggesting that it could issue from either source.[20] Thus Andrea does not speak independently of the narrator nor is she seen as directly communicating with Raúl. The narrated monologue attributed to Raúl in the first part of the story, on the other hand, reveals a naivete or child-like dependency on others. His ability to be manipulated by others is underscored by his use of words that are suggested or imposed by another. Specifically, his discourse discloses an influence of the advertisement media in adopting its phraseology while extolling the virtues of the ugly *caserón* he decides to buy instead of the carriage house preferred by Andrea (154-155). In both the case of Raúl and Andrea, the presence of the narrated monologue reflects the characters' limited authority or power status by underscoring the control or manipulation by the other of discourse situations.

The second part of the story is marked by the presence of two separate dialogues in which Raúl and Andrea verbalize their doubts about the other's fidelity. Each chooses an unreliable confidant as their interlocutor. The narrator thus exercises less control or less mediation, but the role that Andrea and Raúl play in these conversations still denotes their gradual loss of control over their existence or submission to superior authority. Each is placed in the position of asking questions of the corresponding male or female interlocutor, who is thus situated in the power position for they seemingly possess the knowledge or the answers that Raúl and Andrea do not.

According to Martínez Gómez, a relationship of inequality and dependency between characters is frequent in Bioy's more recent narratives and this relationship is effectively portrayed through dialogue. Martínez Gómez also states that the inequality that Bioy depicts is not based on social inequality but rather on the different degrees of knowledge or power that the interlocutors possess.[21] This basis for determining privileged position is exemplified in the verbal exchanges between Raúl, Andrea and their confidants in **"Moscas y arañas."**

However, the dismissal of social roles in determining the authority with which one ultimately speaks in Bioy's narratives leads to only a partial picture of the dynamics of discourse. It also poses some questions the reader must answer to arrive at a more complete understanding of the text. If the female character in Bioy's recent fiction follows the traditional path of subordination to the male, as Martínez Gómez contends, does not her social role determine the authority with which she speaks vis à vis the male character (72)? If her role is defined by tradition, is it acceptable for her to possess greater knowledge or power than the male? These issues of social role, knowledge and power and their relationship to the control of discourse are very central to the interpretation of the text and its conclusion.

The conclusion of the story is narrated in the form of a dramatic monologue delivered by Helene Krig in which she reveals that she is the true predator. The use of monologue in this instance allows Helene the opportunity to reveal her malevolent intentions without recourse to the narrator. She also assumes the task of disclosing the thoughts or reactions of other characters, a privilege originally exercised by the narrator. The monologue effectively portrays her control of Raúl by keeping her interlocutor, now her passive victim, silent and unheard. Her control of the situation is reiterated in her control of the narrative for in the conclusion her voice is the only one that is heard.

Although the voice with which the story concludes is feminine, the discourse still appears masculine. The lines Helene recites, and indeed her role, seem predetermined by male-created stereotypes and myths of devouring femininity. She serves as a projection of the male's wishes and fears. Helene and her web may thus be interpreted as a metaphor of the dangers and undesirability present in a return to the center or origins. Moreover, although Helene traps Raúl within her web of conspiracy and domination, she also is trapped within and dependent upon Raúl's story because the narrative itself is centered on the male. In this respect, Helene occupies a position on the periphery. Ultimately, the reader may conclude that both Raúl and Helene are victims of a power struggle generated by a culturally and linguistically determined binary system of operations that can conceive of relationships only in terms of "insider" and "outsider," "winners" and "losers." In such a system, both male and female may suffer the loss of individual identity and become a complementary object constructed by and for the other.

"LOS AFANES"

The short story **"Los afanes"** begins with a description of a group of friends that includes the narrator and the story's primary and secondary characters: "El primero de mis amigos fue Eladio Heller. Lo siguieron Federico Alberdi, para quien el mundo era claro y sin brillo, los hermanos Hesparrén, el Cabrío Rauch, que descubría los defectos de cada cual; mucho después llegó Milena" (237). ["The first of my friends was

Eladio Heller. There followed him Federico Alberti, for whom the world was clear and without lustre, the brothers Hesparrén, Cabrío Rauch, who uncovered the defects in everyone; much later Milena arrived"]. As Maldavsky observes, the relationship between the members of this group is characterized by competition and the search for difference in three main areas: "Los puntos básicos en que se derime la competencia (y la búsqueda de la diferencia) consisten en el vigor físico (incluido el muscular tanto como el sexual), el poder económico y la capacidad intelectual" (8). The rivalry between the male friends for the affections of Milena is resolved early on in the story with her marriage to Eladio Heller. Subsequently, the narrator's story focuses on the struggles between Eladio and Milena.

Unlike **"Moscas y arañas,"** it will be the male, Eladio Heller, who exercises the covert mental power to control and manipulate his wife, Milena. However, none of the malevolent intentions attributed to Helena Krig are assigned to this story's protagonist. Since the male protagonist is a member of the group that normally exercises power, his attempts to control do not lead to any characterization of schemer. Moreover, benevolent motives are attached to his intervention: the establishment of peace and harmony. Since he realizes his goal through scientific means, his accomplishment affirms rather than contradicts the hierarchy of values in patriarchal society.

The division of male/female is reflected from the beginning in the bivalent title of the story. The title draws upon two meanings of the word *afanes,* both of which allude to some manner of separating or distinguishing the sexes. As a translation for the word labors, it suggests the traditional way in which men have been differentiated from women by their daily tasks. This meaning of the term is suggested in the implicit comparison of Heller's scientific endeavors with his wife's domestic obligations. As a signifier for desire, the term *afanes* also alludes to the passions or motives that underlie the actions of the male and female protagonists, upon which the primary attention of the text is focused. Milena is characterized by her desire to appropriate her husband's wealth and authority while her husband desires to control his wife and the private world that surrounds them.

Eladio Heller is a shadowy figure who never appears in scenes and never directly addresses either characters or reader. Even before his death, Heller is depicted by the anonymous narrator and his wife as "un fantasma," a term which draws attention to his lack of physical presence and voice within the text. In his description of Heller, the narrator focuses on two principal traits, Heller's wealth and his exceptional scientific brilliance. Heller's economic power and intellectual capacity set him apart from the other members of the group. While the former is considered an attractive quality, Heller's intellect and scientific experiments distance him from his wife and friends.

Heller's duality is reflected in the story's fantastic hypothesis, which dramatizes the mind/body split through an experiment that succeeds in separating the thinking self from the body.[22] Heller invents a nickel frame into which he can transmit and preserve human consciousness, a process that also brings about biological death. Driven to despair by the constant fights with his wife, Heller transmits his own mind into the frame, confident that he can achieve immortality. He thus recreates himself as pure thought and then attempts to manipulate his argumentative and aggressive wife through telepathy. Heller's transformation or rebirth thus enables him to control Milena's actions and discourse; it empowers him to exercise the authority he was unable to exercise as mortal man.

Heller's attempts to control his wife fail, however, when she learns of the existence of the frame from her brother-in-law and destroys it. Enraged, "como una fiera hambrienta" ["like a starving wild animal"], Milena seeks to discover and destroy that which she considers a monstrous and hideous act against nature. She engages in her last struggle with Heller and apparently wins: "'Peleamos a brazo partido' me dijo, con la respiración entrecortada, 'a ver quien podía más: Eladio para alejarme, y yo para encontrarlo. Yo pude más. Fue nuestra última pelea'" (258) ["'We fought bitterly,' she told me, with labored breath, 'to see who could win: Eladio (trying) to make me go away, and I (fighting) to find him. I won. It was our last fight'"].

Milena not only apparently dominates her husband but the narrator as well. This domination is revealed, according to the narrator, by the position he occupies in space in relation to Milena when he visits the latter at her home: "Que yo eligiera, para sentarme, en ese cuarto abarrotado de muebles, una silla tan baja y tan frágil, no fue un infortunio fortuito, sino un hecho fatal, símbolico de mi relación con Milena" (245) ["That I should choose to sit on such a low and fragile chair, in that room stuffed with furniture, was not a fortuitous mishap but a fated event, symbolic of my relation with Milena"].

On first reading, the story seems to suggest the subversion of patriarchal society, a triumph of woman/body over the hegemony of male power and the symbolic order. This interpretation is supported further by the conclusion of the story. In the hope of preserving Heller's discovery, the narrator has kept an earlier experimental model of the nickel frame, in which Heller had transmitted the mind of his dog.[23] The frame, however, is beyond anyone's comprehension and becomes "una curiosa peculiaridad" in the narrator's home. Heller's last chance to gain authority posthumously through recognition is shattered, like the frame previously shattered beneath his wife's feet.

Upon re-reading, however, the story suggests an affirmation of patriarchal myths and values, particularly those surrounding the female figure. Milena's actions in the story are circumscribed by patriarchal stereotypes that emphasize a complementary function or negative role. Milena's most notable trait is negating what has been said or done by others through her verbal contradictions and her impetuous destruction of the frame, which negates Heller's accomplishment. The tendency to define Milena by her opposition to others is also underscored in the narrator's recollections of her behavior: "acometía contra las preferencias, las costumbres, la familia, los amigos, el mundo de cada cual" (239) ["She attacked preferences, costumes, family, friends, everyone's world"]. Although the narrator informs the reader that he feels intimidated at her side, like a fool or child who can neither speak nor think clearly, he later states that Heller "vivió con Milena y con nosotros como entre chicos una persona grande" (248) ["lived with Milena and with us like an adult among children"]. Milena, in comparison to the husband, assumes the role of child, a role in which the wife is frequently cast in patriarchal society. But Milena is also viewed by Heller's friends as the manipulative, castrating female, desirous of appropriating male power and authority. It is suggested that she chose Heller from among all her intimidated suitors precisely because he was the richest, wealth being equated with power.

Thus, Milena is reduced to the role of the complementary opposite for her intellectually brilliant husband. Unlike the disembodied Heller, Milena is associated with the corporeal world. She is the only character whose physical appearance is detailed, providing her with a concreteness the other characters lack. Moreover, Milena is endowed with physical traits that reflect the psychological traits attributed to her. Milena's domineering character, for example, is reflected in her imposing stature. Her will to master or lead is suggested in the many sores on her hands obtained through the frequent contact with her horse's harness. Thus, who or what Milena stands for is revealed through the body.

The association of Milena with the corporeal world is also emphasized by her role as biological mother, a role which is rare in Bioy's texts. The female birth role and procreation, represented by Milena, are im-plicitly contrasted and pitted against male scientific creation, represented by Heller. Through his attempts to re-create himself or provide for his rebirth into immortality, Heller attempts to negate or overcome the female birth role and the subjugation to the life-death cycle that is the result of man being born of woman. The location of the generative power within the male may also be symbolized by the site Heller chooses to hide his frame. He places it within a hollow bust of Gall, the father of Phrenology; thus the site of rebirth is located within the male.

As complementary opposite, Milena also functions as female object for the male subject. The opposition between subject and object is revealed in the descriptions of Milena's and Heller's disputes. Heller roams about like "un fantasma" during their arguments and refuses to recognize Milena as subject by his refusal to voice a response. He tries to silence her with his own silence. Moreover, this treatment of Milena as object is reiterated in Heller's attempts to control her from the nickel frame. In a sense, Heller acts as voyeur, perceiving Milena without being transformed from subject to object of perception.

Milena is also limited to the private world of the house, unlike her husband who is capable of becoming a nationally known and recognized figure. Her labors or "afanes," are limited to the domestic sphere. In fact, Milena seldom appears outside the home. When Milena remarries, it is with her brother-in-law, Diego; she remains within the family. Her relationship with Diego mirrors her relationship with Heller; once again she is the aggressive and irrational foe for the reasonable male. Moreover, her second husband, an avid photographer, takes many pictures of Milena, rendering her as the object of the gaze and confining her within the "frame" of the camera lens. Limited by patriarchal myths and roles, the parameters of Milena's actions are thus very restricted.

Heller, as opposite to Milena, is also limited by his complementary role. Heller represents one extreme polarity, the mind, in contrast to Milena, who represents the body. His pure reason confronts Milena's irrationality. The sphere of his movements is also spatially restricted to his room, where he studies, and the garage, where he conducts his experiments. Once confined within the nickel frame, the parameters of Heller's activity become even more restricted.

The enclosure or entrapment of the subject within the binary process created by patriarchy is not only reflected in the framing devices mentioned in the plot and the physically restrictive confines of its setting, but in the narrative strategy of the text as well. In

"Los afanes," the public narration provided by the anonymous narrator frames or encloses the private narration provided by Milena and Diego.[24] The anonymous narrator is the only speaker who addresses his remarks specifically to a public narratee, that is, to someone who is not a participant in the story's events. Both Milena and Diego address their remarks to the anonymous narrator, who functions as their intended private narratee. Their account of events are contained within and dependent upon the anonymous narrator's framing tale. In the case of Milena, her narrative stance as private narrator reflects her dramatic stance, which is limited to the private world.

The characters' positions of power and authority are reflected in their ability to exercise control over discourse situations. Narration is primarily controlled by the anonymous narrator who is a third party or observer of events. The masculine voice of this third party is privileged over the voices of Milena and Diego by the very act of mediating their discourse. By describing or rather inscribing Milena and Diego within a given order, this narrator/other structures the desires, "los afanes," of the subjects that it subjugates to its own fictional narrative.

The authority and control of this narrative voice, is in turn, limited. The anonymous narrator plays a role within the fictional world, and as a fictional character with limited knowledge and objectivity, he is clearly distinguished from the implied author of the text. This separation between extra-fictional voice and narrating voice draws attention to the role of external mediation in the narrator's discourse as well. At the same time, this process of mediation creates distance between the narrator and the real reader. Since the narrator is not a heterodiegetic narrator, that is one who exists outside the fictional world, he does not coexist on the same plane or level as the real reader. This distance allows the reader to perceive that which the narrator cannot: the ironies of the text and the true nature or mediated structure of the struggles the narrator portrays.

The female protagonist, Milena, has limited opportunities to participate in discourse situations, and when she does speak through dialog with the narrator, the reader wonders if she does so in her own voice. The words which Milena utters seem predetermined by the masculine generated stereotype of the domineering female and serve only to confirm her definition of self through opposition to the male. This opposition is presented dramatically in the argumentative tone and posture with which she addresses the male narrator and in the message of her words. Milena does not speak about herself but about her husband and his first invention. Milena's limited intervention in the text in the form of dialogue serves to characterize her husband and reen-force the opposition between the two of them. Thus, although the speaker is female, the discourse seems governed or controlled by patriarchal ideology. Moreover, the masculine control of Milena's discourse is suggested dramatically in the conciliatory remark she addresses to her in-laws, which is attributed directly to Heller's telepathic intervention. This scene highlights the male's desire to control all utterances directed outwardly.

The fact that the narrator views encounters with Milena as struggles for dominance is evinced in the choice of words with which he describes their lengthy conversation concerning Heller. The narrator resorts to military terminology to depict his discursive strategy.[25] Failing to calmly reason with Milena and score an initial victory, he uses another tactic: "Miré a mi alrededor. Intenté lo que en terminología militar se llama una diversión" (245) ["I looked around me. I tried what in military terminology is called a diversion"]. After discussing household furniture, the narrator again returns to the topic of Heller: "Juzgué que la diversión debía concluir. Volví a la carga" (246) ["I judged that the diversion should end. I charged again"]. Apparently Milena convinces the narrator that Heller is indeed a monster, that is, she seems to win in the battle to persuade. However, it is clear that the narrator was always predisposed in her favor and her victory cannot necessarily be attributed to the force of her argument or the authority of her voice, which is undermined from the beginning by her negative traits and the motives attributed to her.

Although Diego is granted more lines of direct discourse than Milena, Diego's intervention in the text is completely limited to dialog with the narrator; that is, Diego is totally dependent on the narrator in order to engage in discourse. As in the case with Milena, Diego acts as a private, secondary narrator who recounts the story of others, principally the discovery of Heller's telepathic presence and Milena's subsequent destruction of the frame. Diego's limited control over discourse situations is also reflected in the narrator's manipulation of their last conversation, in the manner in which the narrator skillfully interrogates his interlocutor. The narrator obliges a reluctant Diego to recount his story so that, once again, dramatic stance, the position of authority between the characters, is reflected in narrative strategy, in the ultimate subjugation of one narrative to the other.

Although there are some recorded remarks attributed to Eladio Heller, he never participates in direct discourse. While Heller's lack of narrative voice suggests his lack of authority, it is not a sign of submission or resignation. In fact, his resistance to Milena, his principal adversary, is confirmed in the narrator's brief observation: "Heller nunca se entregó plenamente" (240) ["Heller never completely surrendered"]. Moreover, through his telepathic endeavors, Heller does strive to be heard and to exercise control over discourse situations. Ultimately, however, Heller's inability to maintain control over discourse is reflected from the beginning of the story by the absence of his voice. Heller, in effect, has been silenced by the intervention of others.

In conclusion, the antagonisms that arise between the characters in Bioy's tale of failed relationships originate in a system of binary opposition that is perpetuated by traditional society. Such a system or narrative not only emphasizes the division between male and female, mind and body, but also attributes value to difference by establishing hierarchies between the opposites. Thus, as in **"Moscas y arañas,"** each member of the male/female dyad struggles to affirm his or her privileged position over the other. In such a system, both male and female suffer the loss of individual identity and become a complementary object constructed for the other. Moreover, the story's narrative strategy mirrors the cultural ideology of the text. The entrapment of the characters within the binary system of opposition is reflected in the narrative's framing structure and in the characters' inability to participate in discourse addressed outwardly and enunciated in the outside world. The tale's complex chain of transmission thus draws attention to the role of mediation in the structuring of discourse. In the end, none of the characters speak with an authoritative voice or control their (hi)stories of desire; their utterances, and indeed their roles, are controlled or mediated from without, from beyond the "frame" in which they are enclosed.

"La pasajera de primera clase"

The focus on difference and boundaries that is manifested in the spatial relations, discourse, and narrative strategies of the previous tales is also evident in the short story **"La pasajera de primera clase"** [**"The First-Class Passenger"**]. However, in this story, the power struggle unfolds between social groups rather than individuals. The title suggests markers of difference, economic and social status, that separate the characters of the story. Wealth and social class, reflected in the choice of travel accommodations, shape the physical and social space in which two antagonistic groups move; they are indicators of difference but not, as we shall see, clear indicators of power.

The story begins with the words of an anonymous narrator who, in the absence of markers to the contrary, may be identified as masculine. The narrator provides the brief framing structure into which the tale of *la pasajera* will be inserted. The anonymity of this narra-

tor and the female protagonist who recounts the body of the story enables them to function as representatives of social groups.

The frame establishes distance (difference and boundaries) between the narrator, the passenger, and the reader. This separation is enforced by the gender difference between the public narrator who addresses the reader and the private narrator who addresses the consul. Gender also establishes distance between the real author and the private narrator, attributing to her the portrayal of events that may represent metaphorically the Peronist period and the cultural/political conflict between the working classes and the country's affluent, intellectual elite. As an elderly upper-class voice, the passenger provides a diametrical opposite to the young Eva Perón, speaker for, and patron of, the *descamisados* during the Perón years. According to this interpretation, the author distances himself from the real events by concealing them beneath metaphor and himself beneath a feminine mask.

The ideology of inclusion and exclusion, expressed by the use of a framing device, is reiterated in the remarks that constitute it: the description of setting and protagonists establishes distance or proximity, the polarities of here/there, insider /outsider. The narrator's initial words, describing the scene introduce these polarities: "En aquella ciudad tropical . . ." (337) ["In that tropical city . . ."]. The demonstrative adjective *aquella,* which relies on the spatial concept of here/there, indicates the physical and cultural distance the narrator wishes to establish between himself and the location of the narrated events.

The narrator then states: "Cuando algún barco fondeaba en el puerto, nuestro cónsul festejaba el acontecimiento con un banquete en el salón morisco del hotel Palmas" (337) ["When some ship anchored in the port, our consul celebrated the event with a banquet in the Moorish hall of the Hotel Palmas"]. The words *nuestro cónsul*/our consul reenforce the narrator's position as outsider in this country while revealing that he is addressing his comments to those who share a similar cultural background. He is not addressing a general public but rather a select audience, part of an inner circle from which others are excluded. The narrator does not identify with this tropical city, which apparently has not undergone the transformations wrought by technology and post-colonialism. There, the arrival of a ship is cause to celebrate, while the absence of modern refrigeration makes the food served at its banquets suspect.

The narrator's remarks also call attention to the difference between geographic and cultural boundaries and their relationship to sense of self. Modern transportation makes it easier for many to travel and to cross geographical borders, but location in a particular country does not necessarily shape the parameters of the self. For example, one can still be an Argentinean although located in Central America. Cultural boundaries, on the other hand, are seen as more resistant to change and penetration than geographic demarcations and contribute more to the structuring of identity. In regards to this underdeveloped country, the narrator is the outsider/foreigner, and it is important to him to establish this difference and maintain his cultural boundaries. Moreover, while one culture may borrow an object from another, that object remains identified with the other, like the Moorish hall of the hotel. The architectural style is used but not assimilated or identified with the native.

The politics of inclusion/exclusion are further reiterated in the description of the banquets held in honor of a ship's arrival. The consul would invite the ship's captain and a group of his selection. Thus, the person of most authority and those of his inner circle are included while the other passengers are excluded. It is in this manner that the passenger arrives to this tropical city, at which point the framing tale ends and the passenger's begins. One may conclude that the framing narrative, technically and thematically, lays the groundwork for the tale of insider versus outsider, self versus other, that the passenger recounts.

The narrator casts a shadow of speculation on the veracity of the passenger's tale by suggesting the role of mediation in its telling. He states that his country's consul heard this tale directly from the passenger, but he does not indicate how he came into possession of her story (335). One notices also the narrator's vacillation in qualifying her narration as explanation or story, implying it may be truth or paranoid fiction. Moreover, he suggests that the passenger's expansiveness may be due to a fine white wine that the consul often served to important visitors.

The passenger begins her tale by describing an advantage her class has lost to the popular classes. She claims that the crew's preference for the popular classes leads them to send the most exquisite dishes to the second-class dining room (337). The privilege she enjoys on shore at the consul's *banquete* is denied on board ship. As her story progresses, it becomes clear that the losses or disadvantages suffered by her social class become increasingly serious.

Unlike the popular classes, young and numerous, her group is aging and small. The fading, moribund status of her group is represented by the decrepit characters she describes at a dance: "En primera, los bailes, cuando los hay, parecen de cadáveres resucitados, que se han echado encima la mejor ropa y todo el alhajero, para celebrar debidamente la noche. Lo más lógico sería que a las doce en punto cada cual se volviera a su tumba, ya medio pulverizado" (338) ["In first class, dances, when there are any, look like the dead have risen, put on their best clothes and the whole jewel box, to duly celebrate the evening. The most logical thing would be that at twelve sharp, each one would return to his tomb, already half converted into dust"]. The upper classes have lost not only their numbers but their vigor.

On occasion, the second-class travelers present themselves in the first-class area where no one presents any barrier to their entrance (338). They are well received although recognized immediately as being other: "Estas visitas de la gente de segunda son bien recibidas por nosotros, los de primera, que moderamos nuestros agasajos y efusividad para que los ocasionales huéspedes no descubran que los identificamos, en el acto, como de la otra clase . . ." (338) ["These visits by the people of second-class are well-received by us, those in first-class, who moderate our hospitality and effusiveness so that the occasional guests do not discover that we identify them, in the act, as the other class . . ."]. On the other hand, the first-class passengers are not accorded the same mobility for their incursions into the space of the second-class passengers are regarded as slumming (338).

The passenger's group receives far less favorably the raids conducted by the second-class passengers under the cloak of darkness. During these incursions, they capture and throw overboard any first class-passenger who has lingered outside the safety of a locked cabin. The first-class passengers, out of decorum and fear of spies, never discuss those who have disappeared nor do they take any action. The increasing progression of loss described by the *pasajera*, that began with the loss of certain advantages, culminates in loss of life. However, despite the losses and perils, she concludes her story by stating that she cannot reconcile herself to becoming a second-class passenger.

The ship on which these bizarre events occur represents mobility and changes in spatial/social relationships. It provides the means to cross frontiers or geographic borders. Geographic location is fluid; people are not confined or defined by a country's boundaries. Furthermore, the privilege of leisurely travel, once reserved for the wealthy, is now enjoyed by the masses, who can enter the realm of the other. On board ship, the second-class travelers outnumber the first, penetrate their physical/social space with impunity, and bring about their disappearance and demise. The ship's voyage and the events that occur during it represent changes and challenges to boundaries on a sociopolitical plane. They represent the repositioning of the popular masses and the dislocation of the elite, driven by economic factors and the rising numbers of the *segunda clase*. They also allude to the possible violent consequences of some sociopolitical schema that advocate the abolishment of boundaries to achieve personal and social utopia. As Kirby states, "Equalizing the members of binary pairs, leveling hierarchies and destroying the boundary may be necessary to promote equality and the transformative knowledge of the other, but violence may be its necessary price" (117). In Bioy's tale, the breaching of the walls of social space results in the death of one of the "participatory" members in the binary opposition.

The passenger's stance toward these events indicates a need to establish difference (boundaries) in order to maintain a sense of identity. The text suggests that a collapsing of any boundaries represents, for her, an abolishment of difference and the inability to separate herself from the other. In telling her story to the consul, she rejects being a silent, complacent agent in the elimination of boundaries. In her refusal to *become* a second-class passenger, she rejects transformation into the other: ". . . no me avengo a convertirme en pasajera de segunda" (339) [". . . I do not resign myself to becoming a second-class passenger"]. The loss she will not accept is the loss of sense of self, which is irrevocably linked to social/class difference and demarcations.

It is important to note that the passenger chooses an option and a space outside the binary structure of relationships, the space of resistance. Her words, *no me avengo* state this position of resistance. She chooses neither aggression nor passivity. She opts for a third position that suggests a space that neither attacks nor recedes. This renegotiated space would maintain difference as necessary and nonthreatening, accepting others as other, neither pressuring others to conform nor accepting pressure to become the other. While some boundaries, e.g. geographic boundaries, may be temporal and changeable, individual borders must remain firm. Firmness is precisely one of the terms used initially to characterize the passenger: "—una acaudalada señora, entrada en años, de *carácter firme* . . ." (337, emphasis mine) ["—a wealthy woman, advanced in years, of firm character"].

It is also significant that the character who gives voice to this stance is an elderly woman. The gender difference between her and both narrator and author draws attention to the issue of otherness and boundaries. Furthermore, this type of character is usually considered nonthreatening; the stereotype portrays such women as physically weak and non desiring. The passenger also

describes herself as devoid of expectations, of any personal or political agenda (338). Thus there is a harmonious combination of the messenger and the message, both presenting firm, nonthreatening stances. A traditionally marginalized voice, the woman speaks for a once-privileged and now decentered group, *la primera clase*.

However, the passenger's use of some hostile terminology must be reconciled with a position of nonaggression. Otherwise, the reader might conclude that her voice is used to express male ideology, and that she lends support to the autonomous subject of patriarchy created by recognition of inside/outside.

The passenger uses two different registers to depict the crossing of first-class passenger space. At first, she refers to the second-class passengers as guests and their appearances as visits, terms denoting friendly and temporary crossing of borders to know the other. These instances are, according to her, well received. The second type of interaction, however, involves the kidnapping and killing of first-class passengers; the hostile intentions of the second-class passengers toward the other then leads her to describe the penetration of her physical and social space as *incursiones,* or *indiadas*. The second-class travelers, previously described as young and beautiful, are now referred to as *invasores* and *adversario*. Although the passenger may opt for a space of resistance and nonaggression, this does not mean that she will be exempt from the operations of the prevailing binary system. The limitations of her stance and space may be reflected in her limited narrative stance. She is restricted to addressing a private narratee, and her story is framed by a man's, which determines with what validity and authority she speaks.

The passenger's observations on social interactions and the forces that influence them reveal her perceptions of power. Most notably, she asserts that power structures or hierarchies are not based on any natural law: "En cuanto a la referida preferencia por las clases populares, no se llame a engaño, no tiene nada de natural . . ."(337) ["As for the previously mentioned preference for the popular classes, don't be deceived, there is nothing natural about it"]. As Kirby notes, "We like to suppose that the organization of the external world, best symbolized by the layout of the land, is natural and necessary and that our representation of the external world merely reflects a 'natural' order. But what if, instead, human patterns and mediation come first?" (109). The passenger refers specifically to one mediating force: writers and journalists, who control the medium of language. She states that it is they who have instilled a preference for the popular classes: ". . . la inculcaron escritores y periodistas, individuos a los que todo el mundo escucha con incredulidad y desconfianza, pero que a fuerza de tesón a la larga convencen" (337) [". . . it was instilled by writers and journalists, individuals to whom everyone listens with incredulity and distrust but who in the end convince by dint of their persistence"]. By implication, her remarks cast doubt on the trustworthiness and objectivity of the narrator/author who communicates with the public reader and mediates the telling of her tale. In comparison, the first-class passengers are silent in response to the violent acts committed against them. They opt for a silent complacency or complicity. They do not use language to negotiate or renegotiate their position: "Todas las mañanas los pasajeros de primera nos miramos con ojos que están a las claras comentando: 'Así que a usted no le ha tocado.' Por decoro nadie menciona a los desaparecidos . . ." (339) "Every morning we first-class passengers look at each other with eyes that are clearly commenting: 'So your turn hasn't come up yet.' Because of decorum, nobody mentions those who have disappeared . . ."]. Only the female narrator breaks this silence, on land, not on board, by relating the events to the consul.

The first-class passenger's remarks reveal the transactional, intersubjective and transitory nature of power. As transaction, power depends on the ability to do and act, to negotiate and to renegotiate one's position. In the story, the first-class passengers do not act or negotiate their position; they have no control over their physical or social space or language. Only the female narrator attempts to negotiate a different, third position of resistance. As intersubjective, power depends on where and in what relationship one is located. On the ship, the female narrator and the first-class travelers occupy a position of inferiority vis à vis their fellow travelers, while on land, among the invited guests of the consul, they occupy a superior position. The victim in one location may be the privileged in another. The challenge to the older, wealthy travelers occurs on board ship; it is confined in space and time. The power position of the second-class travelers, like their position in physical space, is transitory, limited to an interlude between two destinations. They as a class will prevail only while the trip lasts: "—una clase que mientras dura el viaje constituye su más auténtico orgullo—" (338)["—a class that, while the trip lasts, constitutes its most authentic pride—"]. The choice of the indicative over the subjunctive suggests the limitations to power as opposed to indefinite duration.

This tale, like the two preceding, shows power fluctuating with position. In all three, the roles of victim and victimizer shift. In **"Moscas y arañas,"** Raúl is both predator and prey; in **"Los afanes,"** Milena dominates and is dominated; the *pasajera* of the last tale experiences privilege and its loss. All three demonstrate that within a binary structure, attempts by one member of the dyad to cancel the boundaries of the other leads to violence or death. In **"Moscas y arañas,"** Raúl suffers the demise of his personal identity when he is controlled by Helene's telepathic powers. In **"Los afanes,"** Eladio Heller is destroyed when his wife crushes the frame containing his consciousness. In **"La pasajera de primera clase,"** the first-class passengers disappear as they are hurled into "la negra inmensidad del mar" ["the black immensity of the sea"]. **"La pasajera de primera clase,"** the only story in *Historias fantásticas* not previously published in any volume of author's works, suggests a position outside the dichotomy of interpersonal struggles, the position of resistance. It creates a space from which the other may be viewed as other and subject. However, the story indicates that such a position does not necessarily exclude one from the consequences of a prevailing binary system in which one member of the hierarchy seeks to dominate the other.

Notes

1. For a feminist interpretation of Freud's Oedipal complex, see Jerry Aline Flieger, "Entertaining the Ménage à Trois," *Feminism and Psychoanalysis,* Ed. Fieldstone and Roof (Ithaca: Cornell UP, 1989) 185-208.

2. Freud discusses these characteristics of male object choice in his essay, "A Special Type of Object Choice," in *On Creativity and the Unconscious,* 621-63. He concludes that these conditions, which surround the choice of object, are derived from "a fixation of the infantile feelings of tenderness for the mother and represent one of the forms in which this fixation expresses itself' (166).

3. In his study of Bioy's works, David Maldavsky states that the author's narratives constitute a manifestation of "el lenguaje fálico-uetral." He presents a pattern for Bioy's fiction which has several points in common with the one outlined in this chapter. He summarizes this pattern as follows: ". . . podemos sintetizar diciendo que el estado inicial se presenta como rutina, el surgimiento de la tensión como emergencia de un deseo ambicioso, mientras que la tentativa de consumación aparece como penetración de un objeto prohibido y enigmático. La consecuencia de ello es el develamiento del engima contenido en el objeto: posee la señal, la firma de un origen extraño y hostil, y de allí se accede al estado final: quedar marcado por un equivalente de dicha firma que expresa la procedencia simbólica, y que abre a un mundo siempre diferente" (6).

4. "La sierva ajena" first appeared in *Historia prodigiosa,* published in Mexico in 1956. This volume

of stories was later published in Buenos Aires, 1961. "La sierva ajena" next appeared in *Historias fantásticas* 1972. Translations are mine.

5. In a number of Bioy's stories the figure of the nurse or nanny appears. Although the female may appear as a professional nurse or nanny, as in *Dormir al sol,* more often the woman is assigned the role of nurse as in "El 'ídolo.'" Sprengnether associates this role with the male tendency to divide the female into asexual mother and erotic object. In this regard, Sprengnether mentions Jim Swan's article, "Mater and Nanny: Freud's Two Mothers and the Discovery of the Oedipus Complex." According to Sprengnether, Swan describes "the evolution of Freud's concept of the Oedipus complex as the outcome of his split image of mother into *mater,* his idealized and 'pure' biological mother, and 'nannie,' the nurse whom he regards as the agent of his first sexual arousal and humiliation." By disassociating the two, Freud "not only preserves an image of asexual motherhood, he also avoids an acknowledgement of his dependency in relation to a mother who has the power both to elicit his desire and to shame him" (305). In *Dormir al sol,* the narrator is sexually confronted by the nurse who wishes to aid his escape from the sanatorium, which results in the narrator's embarrassment and childish response. In "El ídolo," Garmendia's erotic dreams commence after Geneviève begins to "nurse" him. Thus, Geneviève plays two roles in Garmendia's house, that of nurturing mother and that of nurse who arouses erotic feelings.

6. MacCannell states that the Oedipus, by placing a bar between the child and the fulfillment of desire, forces the child to create metaphoric substitutes and frees him/her from the painful knowledge of the object of his/her desire. She further states that "through Oedipus, through the fictional, we can look for our (guilty) origins, secure in the fact that we will never have to find them. Like God they will always, thanks to Oedipus, remain hidden by the protective veil of these fictions, these metaphors. The narrative quest for origins and for ends will and must always be frustrated by Oedipus . . ." (915).

7. For a discussion of the term "the Real," see MacCannell, "Oedipus Wrecks: Lacan, Stendhal and the Narrative Form of the Real." In this article, MacCannell states that Lacan, "has a third element in his system, an element that exists beyond (or behind?) the opposition of the Imaginary and the Symbolic. It is an element that, for good or for ill, has resisted specification, discussion and exposition: the Real" (914). In a footnote, MacCannell goes on to say that the Real "may well turn out to

be that signified which has slid under the domination of the (phallic) signifier: the *only* signified, the mother" (914). MacCannell also states that clues to the Real can be found in Lacan's formulation of the Real as that "which resists symbolization absolutely." She asserts that Stendhal's writings are the very epitome of the Real for Stendhal rejects the sacrifice of the desire for the mother; he rejects the law of the *lack of satisfaction of desire* and never gives up hope for satisfaction. A similar observation may be made in regards to Bioy's texts and characters.

8. There are also notable contrasts between this tale and an earlier version, "Como perdí los ojos," which is included in the collection, *Luis Greve, muerto* (1937). In his study of both works, Thomas Meehan concludes that the later tale is more realistic than the original and that the figure of the little man changes from mythical being to one created by man. For further discussion, see "The Motifs of the Homunculus and the Shrinking Man in Two Versions of a Short Story by Adolfo Bioy Casares."

9. The appearance of the shrunken man in this tale demonstrates the author's continued preoccupation with issues of body boundaries. Unlike the tales described in the previous chapter, there is no mind/body split or fragmentation of the body; however, there are dramatic changes in the body from without. This interest in body boundaries is also evident in a more recent tale, "Historia desaforada," from the collection *Historias desaforadas* (1986), in which a doctor transforms a patient into a monstrous giant.

10. In a note to his study of this tale, Meehan refers to the title and the biblical passage from which it is derived. He concludes that "the protagonist's blindness and suffering *may* be interpreted as punishment for attempting to seduce away the 'servant' (woman, wife) of another man, but the moral implications in such a reading would seem a bit unlike Bioy Casares" (87). Meehan's observation is correct, for the author is more interested in displaying the psychological implications of this Oedipal triangle. At the same time, the reader recognizes in this paradigm of blindness and seduction of another man's servant some basic elements of "El ídolo," in which Geneviève literally works as a servant in the narrator's shop and is coveted by another man.

11. The reader notes Bioy's typical irony in this episode, which serves to unmask the arbitrariness of the qualities attributed to male and female. Urbina, having disdained the tedious world of female discourse, becomes engaged in a "fascinating" discussion of barbershops, noting he shares an af-

finity of tastes with Antonescu in type of blades, shaving soap and water temperature. This scene of male bonding suggests that male conversation may often be banal rather than intellectually stimulating. At the same time, this incident reveals the male's preoccupation with attributes of manliness and his attempts to define the self by emphasizing difference from the female. The male need to establish boundaries between male and not-male and distance himself from the feminine are symbolized in Urbina's physical withdrawal and separation from Flora as he moves from one room to the other.

12. Translations of the text are mine

13. The two writing styles being compared here are also referred to as indirect and direct discourse. For a discussion of direct and indirect discourse and its relation to issues of authority, see Susan Snaider Lanser, "The Poetics of Point of View: Status, Contact, Stance," *The Narrative Act: Point of View in Prose Fiction,* 149-225.

14. For a detailed discussion of metatrope and its use in the depiction of nineteenth century heroines, see: Helene Michie, *The Flesh Made Word: Female Figures and Women's Bodies,* 102-123.

15. For a discussion of the Jungian concept of the "Bad Mother," see: C. J Jung, *Symbols of Transformation,* 2:306-394.

16. The story "Los afanes" originally appeared in *El lado de la sombra,* (Buenos Aires: Emecé, 1962). However, quotes are from the 1972 version contained in *Historias fantásticas.* Translations of "Los afanes" and "La pasajera de primera clase" are mine.

17. For further discussion of this theme, see Simone de Beauvoir, 133-36.

18. Sharon Magnarelli discusses this binary aspect of language in her study of the Latin American novel. She concludes that "at the center of the literary depiction of the female we encounter the question of power which is generated by the linguistic trap of envisioning and thus idealizing the world in terms of polar opposites . . . The Hispanic emphasis on machismo merely intensifies this polarity" (191).

19. In her study of the Latin American novel, Sharon Magnarelli states that the female character often represents an extrication of the good or evil within the male (186). In this respect, Bioy's treatment of the female is similar to that of his contemporaries.

20. For a discussion of narrated monologue, see Dorrit Cohn, 110.

21. Martínez Gómez analyses Bioy's use of narrative voice and dialogue in three recent collections of short stories and states that the author seldom presents friendly conversations in which the interlocutors are on equal terms: "En cambio, existe otro tipo de relación más frecuente entre los personajes de Bioy, determinada por la distancia, la desigualdad, no la desigualdad social sin la proveniente de un distinto acopio de conocimiento o de fuerza que produce un trato jerarquizado en virtud del saber o el poder que cada cual ostenta. Entonces es cuando el diálogo se torna más efectivo y transmite la verdadera dimensión del personaje, hecho dueño de la palabra del texto. Según el tipo de interlocutores que intervengan, el diálogo adquirirá variadas y sutiles tonalidades significativas siempre en torno a los dos centros axiales que determinan la relación de dependencia de los hablantes: sabiduría y poder" (71).

22. It is interesting to note that the basic outline for this fantastic hypothesis is given by a character, Julio Montero, in Bioy's earlier tale, "En memoria de Paulina."

23. The figure of the dog appears in a number of Bioy's tales and suggests a variety of interpretations. In this story, the dog, as the most domesticated of animals, mirrors the "civilized" nature of his master. The dog's name, Marconi, provides further testimony to Heller's devotion to science and the world of symbols. The tempestuous Milena abhors the dog and often threatens to do away with it.

24. For a discussion of the terms public and private narrator, see Susan Snaider Lanser, 142-47.

25. Martínez Gómez also finds that Bioy's choice of words reveals a power relationship between male and female: "No sería erróneo pensar que, también entre sexos, se establece una relación de poder a juzgar por el tipo de léxico empleado por los personajes masculinos para designar el acercamiento a la mujer" (73).

Works Cited

Bal, Mieke. "Sexuality, Sin and Sorrow: The Emergence of Female Character (A Reading of Genesis 1-3)," *The Female Body in Western Culture* Ed. Susan R. Suleiman. Cambridge: Harvard UP, 1986.

Balderston, Daniel. "Fantastic Voyages," *The New York Times Book Review* (November 29, 1992): 15.

Beauvoir, Simone de. *The Second Sex.* Trans. H. M. Parshley. New York: Batam Books, 1961.

Benjamin. Jessica. "The Bonds of Love: Rational Violence and Erotic Domination." *The Future of Difference.* Ed. Hester Eisenstein and Alice Jardine. Boston: G. K. Hall & Co., 1980, 41-70.

Bioy Casares, Adolfo. *Asleep in the Sun.* Trans. Suzanne Jill Levine. New York: Persea Books, 1978.

———. *Dormir al sol.* Buenos Aires: Emecé Editores, 1973.

———. *Guirnalda con amores.* Buenos Aires: Emecé Editores, 1959.

———. *Historias desaforadas.* Buenos Aires: Emecé Editores, 1972.

———. *Historias fantásticas.* Buenos Aires: Emecé Editores, 1972.

———. *La invención de Morel.* Buenos Aires: Emecé Editores, 1953.

———. *The Invention of Morel and Other Stories (from La Trama Celeste).* Trans. Ruth L. C. Simms. Austin: U of Texas P, 1964.

———. *Una muñeca rusa.* Barcelona: Tusquets Editores, S. A. 1991.

———. *A Russian Doll and Other Stories.* Trans. Suzanne Jill Levine. New York: New Directions, 1992.

———. *Selected Stories.* Trans. Suzanne Jill Levine. New York: New Directions, 1994.

———. *La trama celeste.* Buenos Aires: Sur, 1967.

Borinsky, Alicia. "Plan de evasión de Adolfo Bioy Casares: la representación de la representación. *Otros mundos, otros fuegos: Fantasía y Realismo en Iberoamérica.* Ed. Donald A. Yates. Michigan State University, Latin American Studies Center, 1975, 117-119.

Camurati, Mireya. *Bioy Casares y el alegre trabajo de la inteligencia.* Buenos Aires: Ediciones Corregidor, 1990.

Cardounel, Humberto I. "La mujer como elemento real objetivo e imaginario en la narrativa de Adolfo Bioy Casares." Diss. U of Maryland, 1977.

Cascardi, Anthony. "Reading the Fantastic in Darío ('La pesadilla de Honorio') and Bioy Casares ('En memoria de Paulina')." *Crítica hispánica.* 6 (1984): 117-130.

Chodorow, Nancy. "Gender, Relation and Difference in Psychoanalytic Perspective." *The Future of Difference.* Ed. Hester Eisenstein and Alice Jardine. Boston: G. K. Hall & Co., 1980, 3-19.

———. *Feminism and Psychoanalytic Theory.* New Haven: Yale UP, 1989.

Cirlot, Juan-Eduardo. *Diccionario de símbolos.* Barcelona: Editorial Labor, S. A., 1985.

Cohn, Dorritt. "Narrated Monologue: Definition of a Fictional Style." *Comparative Literature.* XVIII (1966): 97-112.

De Laurentis, Teresa. *Alice Doesn't: Feminism, Semiotics, Cinema.* Bloomington: Indiana UP, 1984.

Dowling, Lee H. "Derridean 'Traces' in La invención de Morel by Adolfo Bioy Casares," *Discurso: Revista de Estudios Iberoamericanos.* 9 (1992): 55-66.

Felman, Shoshana. "Beyond Oedipus: The Specimen Story of Psychoanalysis," *Lacan and Narration: The Psychoanalytical Difference in Narrative Theory.* Baltimore: John Hopkins UP, 1985, 1021-1053.

———, ed. *Literature and Psychoanalysis:* The Question of Reading: Otherwise. Baltimore: Baltimore: John Hopkins UP, 1989.

Filer, Malva. "Dormir al sol de Adolfo Bioy Casares: fechoría de un discípulo del Dr. Moreau." *Alba de América: Revista literaria* 6 (1988): 109-15.

Flieger, Jerry Arline. "Entertaining the Mènage à Trois." *Feminism and Psychoanalysis.* Ed. Feldstein and Roof. Ithaca: Cornell UP, 1989, 185-208.

Freud, Sigmund. *Civilization and Its Discontents.* Trans. Joan Riviere. London: The Hogarth Press, LTD., 1953.

———. *On Creativity and the Unconscious.* New York: Harper, 1958.

Gallop, Jane. *Reading Lacan.* Ithaca: Cornell UP, 1985.

González Lanuza, Eduardo. "Adolfo Bioy Casares: La invención de Morel (Editorial Losada)." No. 75 *Sur* (1940): 159-161.

Jung, C. J. *Symbols of Transformation.* Trans. R. F. C. Hull New York: Harper, 1956.

Kirby, Kathleen M. *Indifferent Boundaries: Spatial Concepts of Human Subjectivity.* New York: The Guilford Press, 1996.

Lacan, Jacques. *Speech and Language In Psychoanalysis.* Trans. and Commentaries by Anthony Wilden. Baltimore: John Hopkins UP, 1984.

———. *Écrits: A Selection.* Trans. Alan Sheridan. New York: Norton, 1977.

———. *Feminine Sexuality and the école freudienne.* Ed. Juliet Mitchell and Jacqueline Rose. New York: Norton, 1985.

Lemaire, Anika. *Jacques Lacan.* Trans. David Macey. London: Routledge, 1977.

Levine, Suzanne Jill. *Guía de Adolfo Bioy Casares.* Madrid: Editorial Fundamentos, 1982.

———. "Parody Island: Two Novels by Bioy Casares," *Hispanic Journal* IV, 2 (1983): 43-49.

MacAdam, Alfred J. *Modern Latin American Narratives: Dreams of Reason.* Chicago: U of Chicago P, 1977.

MacCannell, Juliet Flower. "Oedipus Wrecks: Lacan, Stendhal and the Narrative Form of the Real." *Lacan and Narration: The Psychoanalytical Difference in Narrative Theory.* Baltimore: John Hopkins UP, 1985, 910-940.

———. *Figuring Lacan: Criticism and the Cultural Unconscious.* Lincoln: U of Nebraska P, 1986.

Magnarelli, Sharon. *The Lost Rib: Female Characters in the Spanish American Novel.* Lewisburg: Bucknell UP, 1985.

———. *Reflections/Refractions: Reading Luisa Valenzuela.* New York: Peter Lang Publishing, Inc., 1988.

———. "See(k)ing Power/Framing Power in Selected Works of José Donoso." *Structure of Power: Essays on Twentieth Century Spanish-American Fiction.* Ed. Peavler and Standish. Albany: State Univ. of New York P, 1996, 13-37.

Maldavsky, David. "La narrativa de Bioy Casares y sus parentescos. Un estudio sobre el lenguaje erótico," *Hispamérica* Vol. 24 No. 71 (1995): 3-21.

Mansau, Andrée. "Máscaras venecianas y amores con la muerte en la obra de Adolfo Bioy Casares," *Studies in Honor of Gilberto Paolini.* Ed. Mercedes Vidal Tibbitts. Newark, Delaware: Juan de la Cuesta, 1996.

Martínez Gómez, Juana. "Conversadores viajeros y nostálgicos en los últimos cuentos de Adolfo Bioy Casares." *Adolfo Bioy Casares.* Barcelona: Antropos, 1991, 65-79.

Meehan, Thomas C. "The Motifs of the Homunculus and the Shrinking Man in Two Versions of a Short Story by Adolfo Bioy Casares." *Hispanofila* 28 (1985): 70-87.

———. "Temporal Themes in a Fantastic Story by Adolfo Bioy Casares," *Perpectives on Contemporary Literature.* 4 (1978): 5-14.

Michie, Helene. *The Flesh Made Word: Female Figures and Women's Bodies.* New York: Oxford UP, 1987.

Monmany, Mercedes. "Las mujeres imposibles en Bioy Casares." *Cuadernos hispanoamericanos.* 513 (1993): 117-22.

Navascués, Javier de. "Perspectivas y espacios del engaño en un cuento de Bioy Casares," *Revista de filología hispánica* 10, 2 (1994): 83-96.

Paley Francescato, Martha. "Adolfo Bioy Casares." *Hispamérica* 9 (1975): 75-81.

Scheines, Graciela. "Claves para leer a Adolfo Bioy Casares." *Cuadernos hispanoamericanos* 487 (1991): 13-22.

Silverman, Kaja. *The Subject of Semiotics.* New York: Oxford UP, 1983.

Smith, Paul Julian. *The Body Hispanic: Gender and Sexuality in Spanish and Spanish American Literature.* Oxford: Oxford UP, 1992.

Snaider Lanser, Susan. *The Narrative Act: Point of View in Prose Fiction.* Princeton: Princeton UP, 1981.

Snook, Margaret L. "Entrevista con Adolfo Bioy Casares." *Prismal/Cabral* 7/8 (1982): 104-117.

Sprengnether, Madelon. "(M)other Eve: Some Revisions of the Fall in Fiction by Contemporary Women Writers." *Feminism and Psychoanalysis.* Ed. Feldstein and Roof. Ithaca: Cornell UP, 1989, 298-322.

———. *The Spectral Mother: Freud, Feminism and Psychoanalysis.* Ithaca: Cornell UP, 1990.

Tamargo, María Isabel. *La narrativa de Bioy Casares.* Madrid: Editorial Playor, 1983.

Winnett, Susan "Coming Unstrung: Women, Men, Narrative, and Principles of Pleasure." 105 No. 3 *PMLA* (1990): 505-518.

Daniel Balderston (essay date 2006)

SOURCE: Balderston, Daniel. "Murder by Suggestion: *El sueño de los héroes* and The Master of Ballantrae." In *Robert Louis Stevenon, Writer of Boundaries,* edited by Richard Ambrosini and Richard Dury, pp. 348-58. Madison: The University of Wisconsin Press, 2006.

[*In the following excerpt, Balderston examines the literary relationship between Bioy Casares's* The Dream of Heroes *and sections from Robert Louis Stevenson's* The Master of Ballantrae *that Bioy Casares and Borges excerpted as a short story.*]

It was a slightly odd experience for me to be at the Stevenson Conference in Gargnano. I finished a dissertation on Borges and Stevenson in 1981 and published it in Spanish in Argentina in 1985, and apart from an occasional reference to Stevenson's work (and its importance to Borges) I haven't really worked on the Scottish writer since. I was quite surprised to learn that some kind people—some of whom are here—had consulted the microfilm version of my dissertation, just as I was surprised to find my interviews with Borges and Bioy Casares (from 1978) in French translation[1] in the volume of L'Herne that Michel Le Bris devoted to Stevenson in 1995 and to find a somewhat misleading reference to my "thèse, hélas inédite" [alas unpublished thesis] in Le Bris's *Pour saluer Stevenson* (2000)—my book had, as I've mentioned, been published by a major Argentine publisher in 1985, but obviously its Spanish language version didn't find its way to many Stevenson scholars. Today I'm going to talk not about Borges but about his friend and close collaborator Adolfo Bioy Casares (1914-1999), whose work in the crucial period of their collaborations (roughly 1940 to 1955) provides important evidence of Borges's ideas about narrative theory and favorite reading. Bioy has long been known to have been enthusiastic about Stevenson—he mentions him in several essays and interviews—but his own fiction has not been examined much for evidence of the relation. So here goes.

In 1943, Borges and Bioy Casares included an excerpt from Stevenson's *The Master of Ballantrae* in their first anthology of crime fiction (***Los mejores cuentos policiales***). They titled it "La puerta y el pino" ("The Door and the Pine Tree"), a title they invented themselves, because in the original the tale comes in the middle of a chapter titled "Mr Mackellar's Journey with the Master" (the eighth chapter in some editions, the ninth in others). In their headnote they call Stevenson "el preclaro escritor escocés" [the eminent Scottish writer], and comment: "Escribía con felicidad, pensaba con precisión e imaginaba con lucidez" [He wrote joyfully, thought precisely, and imagined lucidly].[2] The list of Stevenson's fiction in the headnote consists of the stories of the *New Arabian Nights* and *Island Nights' Entertainments,* as well as *Dr. Jekyll and Mr. Hyde* and only four of the novels: *Treasure Island,* the unfinished *Weir of Hermiston,* and two of the books written in collaboration with Lloyd Osbourne, *The Wrecker* and *The Ebb-Tide.* Two secondary works are listed: Chesterton's book *Robert Louis Stevenson,* and Sir Walter Raleigh's *R. L. Stevenson,* one of the first works of criticism to appear after Stevenson's death.

The excerpt from *The Master of Ballantrae* is clearly a detective story, though a highly unusual one, especially when it is considered in relation to the detective story of the time, dominated by the figures of Auguste Dupin and Sherlock Holmes: that is, by the figure of the detective, an individual marked by his mannerisms and opinions, whose way of conducting an inquiry into a case takes precedence over the original crime of violence. Borges, in an article on the detective fiction of Chesterton, says that one of the rules of detective fiction is "primacía del cómo sobre el quién" [predominance of the how over the who] (Borges 1935: 93), but the Holmes stories tend to stress the *who* and *how* of the detective more than the identity of the criminal and the mechanics of the crime. The Stevenson story, by way of contrast, dispenses with the detective altogether, and even with any discussion of the prehistory (or motivation) of the crime or of its later consequences: that is, with the investigation that normally takes precedence in the classic detective story. The story plunges us directly into the working out of a

crime, a murder that is a pure act of imagination or, as De Quincey says, "one of the fine arts."

In the Stevenson novel, the narrator (an unimaginative old servant, Mackellar) is forced to cross the Atlantic in company of the Master of Ballantrae, the evil older brother of his master, Henry Durie, whom he insists on seeing as purely good in contrast to the monstrosity of the brother. In the middle of a storm, the Master "must tell me a tale, and show me at the same time how clever he was and how wicked. . . . [T]his tale, told in a high key in the midst of so great a tumult, and by a narrator who was one moment looking down at me from the skies and the next peering up from under the soles of my feet—this particular tale, I say, took hold upon me in a degree quite singular" (Stevenson 1889: 209). Borges and Bioy (who we must assume are the translators for lack of evidence to the contrary) provide a fairly faithful translation of the tale, omitting only occasional references to Mackellar and the Master, and sharpening the effect of the tale as a whole by isolating it from its context.

The Master's story consists of four distinct moments or scenes and includes only two characters: a count (a friend of the Master) and a German baron, whom the count hates for some undisclosed reason. The first scene shows the count riding outside of Rome one day and discovering an ancient tomb by a pine tree. He enters a door in the tomb, takes the right fork of a passage, and barely escapes falling down a deep well. Reflecting on the event, he asks himself: "a strong impulsion brought me to this place: what for? what have I gained? why should I be sent to gaze into this well?" (210). In the second scene he makes up a dream about himself and the baron, in order to tempt the baron to enter the tomb; besides describing the place, he says that when the baron entered the door and turned to the right, "there was made to you a communication, I do not think I even gathered what it was, but the fear of it plucked me clean out of my slumber, and I awoke shaking and sobbing" (212). The third scene shows them riding together, passing the tomb, and the count feigning an attack of fright—which he will not explain, but which is sufficient motive for the baron to look around and recognize the place from the description of it in the supposed dream. On their return to Rome, the count "took to his bed and gave out he had a touch of country fever" (213). The fourth scene is the briefest of all: "The next day the baron's horse was found tied to the pine, but himself was never heard of from that hour." And the Master, "breaking sharply off," adds: "And now, was that a murder?" (213).

The tale, brief and understated as it is, is structurally quite complex. The first and last episodes involve only one of the two characters, first with the near death of the count, and later with the death of the baron. In each case the approach to the well provokes a question and a story: the count's questions about why he has been brought there (which he answers by making up a plot, and by slightly changing his experiences in making of them a "dream," which satisfies his own and the baron's wishful thinking in different ways), and the Master's question whether the death of the baron was a murder (which provokes Mackellar to try to kill the Master by pushing him overboard, but which even in the fragment published in Borges and Bioy's anthology demands an answer from the reader, a sequel, or supplement). The second and third episodes mirror each other in a similar fashion. Both consist of excursions on horseback by the two characters together, first in a fiction (the count's "dream"), and later in fact. In both the count pretends (the dream, the attack), and the pretense allegedly portends ill for him (he wakes in a fright from his "dream," he takes to bed after the excursion). And in both episodes something mysterious is communicated without being stated: in the "dream," according to the count, "there was made to you a communication," but he doesn't know what it was; during the excursion, the count refuses to say what has upset him, and his silence serves to "make a communication."

The story's success depends on its being told in an understated way, that is to say, on the narrator's keeping silent about a number of essential issues (the motive for the tale, the communication from the well, the exact manner of the baron's death, the question of whether or not this was a murder). Thus, the reader has to fill in the gaps, to supplement what is given by work of the imagination, to answer the questions posed by the text. The reader is made to perform the same mental operations that the count performed when he concocted the plan; the tale is a question directed at the reader, and challenging his or her morality by stating baldly: if murder can be accomplished by the mere power of suggestion, then what is the reading of imaginative literature but the enactment in the mind of every kind of crime? And the question is a telling one within the frame tale of *The Master of Ballantrae*: the narrator, staid old Mackellar, after listening to the Master's tale, answers it in his own way by trying to shove him overboard. Such, indeed, is the power of suggestion.

The tale functions within the whole of *The Master of Ballantrae* as an only too literal *mise-en-abyme*: a story within a story that, by mirroring the whole of which it is a part, but only in essence, in outline, serves to reveal the shape of the whole more clearly.[3] The hatred that the Master feels for his brother Harry, and which is repaid in kind, is as unmotivated as the count's hatred for the baron and as lethal. In the tale

the Master dramatizes the immense power of suggestion (which allows him, in the novel as a whole, to control his brother so completely that the latter ends an abject parody of himself), as well as the moral ambiguity of that suggestion. He forces Mackellar to confront the question, at the very moment when the narrative is passing from home and Scotland to the American wilderness, of who is responsible when violence is done—the author or the actors. Even after the excursion into the wilderness that has left both brothers dead, Mackellar is left with the question of who is to blame for the tragedy, if blame is to be assigned; and by abnegating his role when he presents a simplified view of the story to the reader, in which the Master is villain and Henry is martyr, he passes the question along to us.

Speaking of the famous "problem of the closed room" in the history of crime fiction, Borges says: "En alguna página de algunos de sus catorce volúmenes piensa De Quincey que haber descubierto un problema no es menos admirable (y es más fecundo) que haber descubierto una solución" [In some page of one of his fourteen volumes De Quincey affirms that to have discovered a problem is no less admirable (and is more fruitful) than to have discovered a solution] (Borges 1938: 24). He credits Poe (in "The Murders in the Rue Morgue") with having discovered the problem of the closed room; I don't know whether to credit Stevenson with the *discovery* of the problem of murder-by-suggestion in the tale we have been discussing, but can affirm with confidence that it was a problem that was fruitfully and passionately explored in the crime fiction of Borges and Bioy Casares (and in that of their joint creation Honorio Bustos Domecq). To cite a few examples: Borges's "La muerte y la brújula" (1943) explores the manipulation and eventual murder of the detective by the criminal, who bases his plot initially on some chance events (just as the count begins with his chance experience of discovering the tomb), which he later elaborates into a complicated system;[4] Bustos Domecq's **"Las previsiones de Sangiácomo"** (1942)[5] tells of the enormously intricate plot by which a father forces his supposed son (who is actually the product of an adulterous relation on the part of his wife) to commit suicide;[6] Borges's "Abenjacán el Bojarí, muerto en su laberinto" (1951) recounts the trap set by Zaid, servant of Abenjacán, for his master, using the telling symbols of the labyrinth and the spider web. However, the closest parallel to "La puerta y el pino" is Bioy Casares's novel *El sueño de los héroes* (1954), the whole of which can be viewed as an attempt to answer the questions posed by Stevenson's brief text, or to pose those questions in a different, more insistent, way.

El sueño de los héroes is the story of a young Argentine man, Emilio Gauna, who becomes obsessed with a mysterious event in his past, until the obsession leads to his death. Shortly before carnival in 1927, Gauna wins a lot of money at the races, which he decides to spend in a three-day drinking spree with a number of friends, led by an older father figure, Sebastián Valerga, who is at once sinister and brave. Toward the end of the three days, Gauna's hold on the situation becomes increasingly loose, and when he is found in the Bosque de Palermo, he has vague, contradictory memories of what has happened to him, including one very intense memory of something that did not happen—a fight at knife-point between him and Valerga. Three years pass, during which Gauna gets married and draws away from the group and from Valerga; then, during carnival in 1930, Gauna again wins a sum of money and decides to try to repeat the earlier experiences, hoping to penetrate the mystery of the third day of the 1927 carnival. Valerga and his friends play along with his obsession, and on the third day of the 1930 carnival, after an approximate repetition of the earlier spree, Gauna faces Valerga in the Palermo woods, each with knife in hand, and is killed by him. The narrator explains that the first time Gauna was protected by the intercession of a sorcerer, Taboada, whose daughter will become Gauna's wife; the second time Taboada is dead, and the events take the course they were fated to take the first time when Taboada interrupted them.

The parallels with the Stevenson story are numerous and striking. Bioy also uses the motif of the asymmetrical repetition of a series of events, which the first time almost leads to death (that of the count, and that of Gauna), and which the second time does lead to death (of the baron, of Gauna). The driving force of the middle portion of the novel, as of the tale, is the principal character's fascination or obsession with his near death, which leads to investigations and plans that include other people. In both fictions one person controls another by the power of suggestion, leading him to his death in a very subtle way, so that it appears that it is always the latter who is seeking his own death. Control is exerted over the victim by the suggestion that something was communicated to him, or was about to be communicated, at the moment of the near death: I have already cited the count's remark, and although Valerga doesn't say anything so explicit, his conduct leaves Gauna "muy resuelto a ver lo que había entrevisto esa noche, a recuperar lo que había perdido" [very decided to see what he had glimpsed that night, to recover what he had lost] (41). And in both stories, this hidden communication spurs the victim on, working on his curiosity (that is to say, on an incomplete faculty of the imagination, since it

cannot recapture the whole communication except by leading to the death of the "curioso impertinente"), until the moment of his death, on the outskirts of a great city.[7]

Furthermore, in both the motif of the dream is of utmost importance. The count invents a dream to tantalize the baron, by giving him a vicarious sense of *déjà vu* when they "chance" to pass the tomb in the course of their excursion. Gauna, toward the end of the second carnival, dreams "the dream of the heroes" that gives the book its title: in his dream the heroes play a card game to decide who will have the right to walk down a red carpet and take his place on a throne as the greatest of the heroes (212). At the end of the book, Gauna recalls the red carpet and understands that it is spread for him (239): as a brave man, but also as a dead one, since the red is that of his own blood. Both dreams serve to inspire the victims to hurry on to their encounter with death, which will reveal the significance of the dreams and of the heroes (though it must be added that we are privy not at all to the baron's point of view at the decisive moment, so we cannot say with confidence whether he meets death with Gauna's resolution and conviction of his own courage—and one suspects that he has no time to reflect on these questions before sliding into the slimy hole).

Furthermore, *El sueño de los héroes* makes an enigmatic question of the death of the hero, much as the Master's tale ends with the question: "And now, was that a murder?" Is the death of Gauna the death of a hero or that of a suicide? Or is it murder? Bioy and his narrator leave these questions open at the end. In his review of the book, Borges touches on the enigmatic nature of the ending:

> Al final se revela que este mentor es un hombre siniestro; la revelación nos choca y hasta nos duele, porque nos hemos identificado con Gauna, pero confirma las fugaces sospechas que inquietaron nuestra lectura. Gauna y Valerga se traban en un duelo a cuchillo y el maestro mata al discípulo. Ocurre entonces la segunda revelación, harto más asombrosa que la primera; descubrimos que Valerga es abominable, pero que también es valiente. El efecto alcanzado es abrumador. Bioy, instintivamente, ha salvado el mito. ¿Qué pasaría si en la última página del Quijote, don Quijote muriera bajo el acero de un verdadero paladín, en el mágico reino de Bretaña o en las remotas playas de Ariosto?
>
> (Borges 1955: 89)

[At the end it is revealed that this mentor is a sinister man; the revelation shocks and even pains us, because we have identified with Gauna, but it confirms the passing suspicions that disturbed our reading. Gauna and Valerga have a knife fight and the master kills the disciple. Then the second revelation occurs, which is much more surprising than the first one: we discover that Valerga is odious but is also brave. The effect that is achieved is striking. Bioy, instinctively, has saved the myth. What would happen if on the last page of Don Quixote the hero were to die beneath the sword of a true paladin in the magic kingdom of Briton or on the remote beaches of Ariosto?]

The reference to Don Quixote and heroic legend is far from casual. Gauna, like Don Quixote, has sought the death of a hero, and through his obsession has been granted some measure of fulfillment. But Bioy is kinder to his hero than is Cervantes:[8] he doesn't demand that his hero wake up and die sane according to the norms of the everyday world, granting him instead access to the heroic world of myth.

If we consider the Master's little tale as part (a *mise-en-abyme*) of the whole of *The Master of Ballantrae*, we notice some further parallels with *El sueño de los héroes.* Both novels are concerned with a relation between two people marked by animosity and attraction: the antagonists need each other to be themselves, to fulfill their destinies. This rivalry leads first to the near murder of one by the other (Henry's duel with the Master, whom he leaves for dead, and Valerga and Gauna's shadowy duel in the first carnival, which allegedly only happens in Gauna's imagination), and then to death (of both brothers in the Stevenson novel, of Gauna in *El sueño*). The stronger of the two rivals—and the older in both cases—is evil ("siniestro," as Borges says in his review), and yet strangely brave and attractive, a heroic figure after all. And the victim in both cases is the focus of the narrators' sympathy, yet that sympathy is highly ambivalent—Mackellar insists on taking Henry's part throughout, but portrays his weaknesses only too clearly, while the enigmatic narrator of *El sueño de los héroes* seems to take Gauna's part and yet makes fun of him throughout the novel (as do Gauna's "friends" in the group).

An important difference between *El sueño de los héroes* and both the Stevenson pieces we have been considering—the whole of *The Master of Ballantrae*, and the interpolated story of the count and the baron—is that Valerga's evil influence on Gauna is offset in Bioy's novel by the protection afforded him by the sorcerer Taboada, while both the baron and Henry are helpless before their adversaries, although Henry has the benefit of Mackellar's common sense and good advice. The existence of Taboada as well as Valerga—a good as well as a bad influence—gives Gauna freedom to resist the call of death, a freedom not granted the baron or Henry Durie. His destiny is equivocal (more so, perhaps, than he is ready to admit), as the sorcerer points out to him: "En ese viaje no todo es bueno ni todo es malo. Por usted y por los demás, no vuelva a emprenderlo. Es una hermosa me-

moria y la memoria es la vida. No la destruya" [On that journey not everything is good and not everything is evil. For your own sake and that of others don't try to take it. It is a beautiful memory and memory is life. Don't destroy it] (47-48). So when he chooses to repeat the earlier adventure, it is a choice, an act of will on his part, a decision to obliterate a memory *qua* memory by realizing or enacting it.

The juxtaposition of "La puerta y el pino" and *El sueño de los héroes* is useful because it helps us interpret a number of factors that would otherwise be difficult to discuss. In the Stevenson tale we are given a skeletal form of the intricate plot of the Bioy novel: a chance event that almost leads to death, the elaboration of that event by means of imagination and memory, and a repetition of it leading to death. By contrasting the dynamics at work in the earlier tale, which is acted out by only two characters, with that of the group of characters in *El sueño,* we can see more clearly the specific kinds of complexity introduced by the figures of Taboada, Clara, and Larsen, and the ambivalent nature of Gauna. More importantly, the intertext of "La puerta y el pino" serves to explain the presence of elements of the detective story in *El sueño de los héroes,* as well as the deviations from the norms of the genre: Gauna's investigations lead to his own death (as in "La muerte y la brújula"); the initial act of violence turns out to be a mere rehearsal of the final one; and the process of revelation or explanation that usually pertains to the detective is—with the death of Gauna—fulfilled by the narrator instead, though the latter's explanations may not be completely convincing.

Moreover, the noting of the similarities between Bioy's novel and "La puerta y el pino" points up the need to study Bioy's (as well as Borges's) interest in Stevenson, an interest that should not surprise us, in view of the close association of Borges and Bioy and of Borges's fondness for Stevenson's fiction, but which has not been explored up to now.[9] It also serves to explain the inclusion of the Stevenson story in an anthology with the provocative title *Los mejores cuentos policiales,* since Stevenson's treatment here of some elements of the detective story—stressing the plotting or imagination of a crime more than the investigation of it,[10] omitting the superfluous character of the detective, and achieving a high degree of ambiguity—anticipates the experiments with the genre some half-century after Stevenson's death in Samoa by the Argentine writers Borges, Bioy Casares, Bianco, and H. Bustos Domecq.

Notes

1. The interviews were also published in the original English in Balderston 1999.

2. This glowing comment is very different in tone from the other headnotes in the volume, which tend to be mere lists of biographical and bibliographical data.

3. The classic example of this device, discussed in Borges 1949, is the play within the play in *Hamlet*.

4. The story further resembles "La puerta y el pino" in its open ending: Lönnrot's posing of a geometrical problem at the end invites the reader to go on with the story in much the same way as the Master's posing of the final question.

5. This story, co-authored by Borges and Bioy under the pseudonym of Honorio Bustos Domecq, appeared in *Seis problemas para don Isidro Parodi* (1942), and is included in Borges et al. 1979.

6. "Sangiácomo" is similar to "La puerta y el pino" (unlike the other stories mentioned here) in that no murder is committed directly: the baron's death, like Sangiácomo's, could be interpreted as suicide.

7. The Italian name of the park where Gauna meets his death, Palermo, perhaps is meant to recall the Italy of Stevenson's story, though of course it is also a real park in Buenos Aires, and the neighborhood is central to Borges's early poetry.

8. Cf. the comments in Borges 1956 on Cervantes's final cruelty to his hero, a note that is almost contemporary to his review of Bioy's novel.

9. The only critic I know of who touches on Stevenson's anticipations of some of Bioy's fiction is Julio Matas (1978: 123).

10. Cf. Borges's review of Bianco's *Las ratas:* "su tema es la prehistoria de un crimen, las delicadas circunstancias graduales que paran en la muerte de un hombre" (Borges 1944: 76). Dorothy L. Sayers included the same extract, titled "Was It Murder?" in *Tales of Detection: A New Anthology* (1936), which Borges reviewed in *El Hogar* (19 Feb. 1937).

References

Balderston, Daniel. 1985. *El precursor velado: R. L. Stevenson en la obra de Borges.* Buenos Aires: Editorial Sudamericana.

———. 1999. Interviews with Borges: Buenos Aires, August-September 1978. *Variaciones Borges* 8: 187-215.

Bioy Casares, Adolfo. 1954. *El sueño de los heroes.* 1969. Buenos Aires: Emecé.

Borges, Jorge Luis. 1935 Los laberintos policiales y Chesterton. *Sur* 10: 92-94. In del Carril et al. 1999: 126-29.

———. 1938. [Column.] *El Hogar* (March 4, 1938): 24.

———. 1944. [Review of José Bianco's *Las ratas.*] *Sur* 111. In del Carril et al. 1999: 271-74.

———. 1949. Magias parciales del Quijote. *La Nación* (November 6, 1949): 1. In *Otrás inquisiciones.* 1952. Buenos Aires: Sur. 55-58.

———. 1955. [Review of Adolfo Bioy Casares's *El sueño de los heroes.*] *Sur* 235. In del Carril et al. 1999: 284-86.

———. 1956. Análisis del último capítulo del "Quijote," *Revista de la Universidad de Buenos Aires* 1: 28-36.

———. 1974. *Obras completas.* Buenos Aires: Emecé.

———, et al. 1979. *Obras completas en colaboración.* Buenos Aires: Emecé.

———, and Adolfo Bioy Casares, eds. 1943. *Los mejores cuentos policiales.* Buenos Aires: Emecé.

del Carril, Sara Luisa, and Mercedes Rubio de Socchi, eds. 1999. *Borges en Sur 1931-1980.* Buenos Aires: Emecé.

Le Bris, Michel. 2000. *Pour saluer Stevenson.* Paris: Flammarion.

———, ed. 1995. *Robert Louis Stevenson.* Paris: l'Herne (Les Cahiers de l'Herne, 66).

Matas, Julio. 1978. Bioy Casares o la aventura de narrar. *Nueva Revista de Filología Hispánica* 27:112-23.

Sayers, Dorothy, ed. 1936. *Tales of Detection: A New Anthology.* London: Dent.

Stevenson, Robert Louis. 1889. *The Master of Ballantrae.* Thistle Edition, second issue. Vol. 9.

FURTHER READING

Criticism

Borinsky, Alicia. "Adolfo Bioy Casares—1975." *MLN* 91, no. 2 (March 1976): 356-59.
　　　Brief overview of Bioy Casares's writings.

Dowling, Lee H. "Derridean 'Traces' in *La Invencion de Morel* by Bioy Casares." *Revista de Estudios Iberoamericanos* 9, no. 2 (1992): 55-66.
　　　Argues that many previously unexamined aspects of Bioy Casares's *The Invention of Morel* can be seen as anticipating the subsequent deconstructionist ideas of Jacques Derrida.

Meehan, Thomas C. "Temporal Themes in a Fantastic Story by Adolfo Bioy Casares." *Perspectives on Contemporary Literature* 4, no. 2 (November 1978): 5-14.

> Early version of an essay that analyzes themes of temporal simultaneity and time travel in the story "El otro laberinto."

Swanstrom, Lisa. "Records, Projections, and the Dixie Flatline: Character Loops in *La Invención de Morel* and William Gibson's *Neuromancer.*" In *Selected Proceedings of the Fifth Annual Graduate Student Conference on Lusophone and Hispanic Literature and Culture,* edited by María Luis Collins, Gustavo Collins, and Alicia Ruedo Acedo, pp. 161-76. Santa Barbara: Department of Spanish and Portuguese, University of California, Santa Barbara, 2004.

> Compares Bioy Casares's *The Invention of Morel* with the 1984 American science fiction/cyberpunk novel *Neuromancer.*.

Additional coverage of Bioy Casares's life and career is contained in the following sources published by Thomson Gale: *Contemporary Authors,* **Vol. 29-32R;** *Contemporary Authors New Revision Series,* **Vols. 19, 43, and 66;** *Contemporary Authors—Obituary,* **Vol. 177;** *Contemporary Literary Criticism,* **Vols. 4, 8, 13, and 88;** *Contemporary World Writers,* **Ed. 2;** *Dictionary of Literary Biography,* **Vol. 113;** *DISCovering Authors Modules,* **Ed. MULT;** *Encyclopedia of World Literature in the 20th Century,* **Ed. 3;** *Hispanic Literature Criticism,* **Ed. 1;** *Hispanic Writers,* **Eds. 1 and 2;** *Latin American Writers; Literature Resource Center; Major 20th-Century Writers,* **Eds. 1 and 2;** *Major 21st-Century Writers (eBook),* **Ed. 2005; and** *Short Story Criticism,* **Vol. 17.**

Kay Boyle
1902-1992

American short story writer, novelist, poet, essayist, translator, editor, and children's author.

For further discussion of Boyle's short stories, see *SSC,* Volume 5.

INTRODUCTION

The author of almost forty volumes of fiction, poetry, essays, and translations, Boyle was an important figure during her heyday in the 1920s and 1930s. Her short fiction, much of which concerns the search for love, won popular and critical acclaim. As an American expatriate, Boyle moved in influential circles of writers in Paris and wrote about the changing social and political climate of post-World-War-I Europe. Using terse understatement, interior monologue, stream-of-consciousness narrative, and flights of surrealist prose, her fiction reflects the atmosphere of alienation and disillusionment that permeated Europe during those troubled years. Deeply informed by her experiences, Boyle's works are characterized by intense psychological portraits of individuals looking for love and meaning in a disordered world. Despite being faulted by early critics for focusing on style rather than substance, Boyle received two O. Henry Awards and several of her stories and novellas—notably "The White Horses of Vienna" (1936), and *The Crazy Hunter* and *The Bridegroom's Body* (both included in *The Crazy Hunter: Three Short Novels,* 1940)—are hailed as among the finest short prose works of the twentieth century. Although she continued writing and publishing until the end of her life, critical interest in Boyle's work waned considerably after the 1970s. Issues in her work that have interested scholars include the author's revolutionary ideas, her virtuosic style, and her carefully drawn portraits of isolated people and situations. In her later life, Boyle was active in the social justice movement in the United States.

BIOGRAPHICAL INFORMATION

Boyle was born on February 19, 1902 in St. Paul, Minnesota to affluent parents. Her mother tutored her at home and Boyle traveled extensively in the United States and Europe throughout her youth. Boyle began writing as a teenager under the encouragement and guidance of her mother, and by 1922 she had secured a position at the magazine *Broom.* In 1922 Boyle married Robert Brault, a French engineer, and moved to France. She would remain in Europe until World War II necessitated her return to the United States in 1941. Through the 1920s and 1930s, Boyle lived and worked within the expatriate community in Europe, assisting Ernest Welsh with *This Quarter,* an avant-garde journal that featured the writings of such revisionists as James Joyce, Gertrude Stein, and Ernest Hemingway. By the 1930s, Boyle's fiction was becoming increasingly well known and respected. She won her first O. Henry Award for "The White Horses of Vienna" in 1934 and her second in 1941 for "Defeat." In 1943, Boyle married her third husband, Joseph Franckenstein, an Austrian baron. She returned to occupied Germany in the late 1940s as a foreign correspondent for the *New Yorker,* remaining there until the anticommunist hearings of Senator Joseph McCarthy precipitated her final return to the United States. Throughout the postwar period, Boyle continued to write about her experiences and to protest social injustices such as McCarthyism, the treatment of minorities, and the American involvement in the Vietnam War. She served a short prison sentence for her participation in antiwar demonstrations. From 1963 until 1980, Boyle taught creative writing at San Francisco State University. She died in Mill Valley, California in 1992.

MAJOR WORKS

Boyle's first book of short stories appeared in 1929, but it was not commercially successful. The following year she published *"Wedding Day," and Other Stories,* containing the stories from the earlier volume as well as pieces that had appeared in literary magazines. That volume received good critical reviews and Boyle was praised for her command of language, adept metaphors, and passionate concern for her subjects. As in much of her work, an enduring theme in these early stories is the vagaries of love. Another predominant theme in Boyle's early short fiction is the moral and emotional impact on individuals of Europe's changing social and political climate after the first world war.

By the 1930s, Boyle's work was being published frequently in American magazines. "Kroy Wen," from *"The First Lover and Other Stories"* (1933), was the first of many Boyle stories to appear in the *New Yorker,* initiating a relationship that lasted several decades. In 1936 Boyle published *365 Days,* an anthology of short stories she co-edited with her second husband, Laurence Vail, and Nina Conarian, and to which she contributed nearly one hundred of her own stories. Also in 1934, Boyle was awarded her first Guggenheim Fellowship and won her first O. Henry Memorial Award for the short story "The White Horses of Vienna." This story is exemplary of much of Boyle's writing, as it articulates an urgent need for art to engage with political and social issues. In this story, set in Austria in the early 1930s, the Viennese Dr. Heine travels into the mountains to assist an older doctor whose knee has been sprained during covert socialist maneuvers, and who can no longer attend to his patients. While the young Dr. Heine argues that art, science, and everyday life are fundamentally more important than politics, the older doctor seems to believe that as long as human dignity is threatened, art is meaningful only in the service of freedom. This same basic theme is played out, with numerous variations and immense subtlety, in the majority of Boyle's short stories, including such acclaimed pieces as "Defeat" (1941), which won Boyle her second O. Henry Memorial Award, and "Winter Night" (1946).

Two of Boyle's most acclaimed works are her novellas *The Crazy Hunter* and *The Bridegroom's Body,* both of which appeared in the collection *The Crazy Hunter: Three Short Novels* (1940). In these works, Boyle used a blinded horse and a pair of nesting swans respectively to objectify her characters' fear of and need for love. After World War II, Boyle served as a foreign correspondent for the *New Yorker* in Europe until 1953. Her experiences from these years are treated in many pieces from the collections *Thirty Stories* (1946) and *The Smoking Mountain* (1951). Boyle published three more novellas in the volume *Three Short Novels* in 1958 and a new collection of stories *Nothing ever Breaks Except the Heart* in 1966. Her later short fiction collections in the 1980s reprinted her early works, to much critical acclaim.

CRITICAL RECEPTION

Throughout her career, Boyle was admired for the range, depth, and technical brilliance of her prose. Although she also produced what was labeled slick, commercial fiction, her more literary works were also recognized for their conveyance of the evolution of individual sensibility amid historical experience. Her short fiction was admired by her contemporaries as eminently readable, elegant, and moving in its treatment of love and war. Although she continued writing

novels and poems into the 1990s, critics and audiences paid little attention to her works after the early 1970s. Despite her distinguished and prolific career, Boyle's work is little known or read today. Critics who continue to study her short fiction acknowledge her central role in the American expatriate period of the 1920s and 1930s, note her unceasing personal dedication to social and political activism, discuss her revolutionary style and ideas, and demonstrate how her imaginative vision is grounded in the concrete world, and how public events shape private experience in her work. Modern scholars of Boyle's work have lamented that such an original short story writer has achieved so little recognition and have called for more discussion of her writings.

PRINCIPAL WORKS

Short Fiction

Short Stories 1929
"Wedding Day," and Other Stories 1930
"The First Lover," and Other Stories 1933
365 Days [editor and contributor, with Laurence Vail and Nina Conarain] (fiction anthology) 1936
"The White Horses of Vienna," and Other Stories 1936
The Crazy Hunter: Three Short Novels 1940
Thirty Stories 1946
The Smoking Mountain: Stories of Postwar Germany 1951
Three Short Novels 1958; reprinted 1990
Nothing ever Breaks Except the Heart (short stories) 1966
Fifty Stories 1980
"Life Being the Best," and Other Stories 1988

Other Major Works

My Next Bride (novel) 1934
Death of a Man (novel) 1936
A Glad Day (poetry) 1938
Monday Night (novel) 1938
The Youngest Camel (juvenile) 1939
Primer for Combat (novel) 1942
An American Citizen Naturalized in Leadville, Colorado (poetry) 1944
Avalanche (novel) 1944
A Frenchman Must Die (novel) 1946
1939 (novel) 1948
His Human Majesty (novel) 1949
The Seagull on the Step (novel) 1955
Generation without Farewell (novel) 1960
Collected Poems (poetry) 1962

Being Geniuses Together, 1920-1930 [with Robert McAlmon] (nonfiction) 1968

The Long Walk at San Francisco State, and Other Essays (essays) 1970

Testament for My Students, and Other Poems (poetry) 1970

The Underground Woman (novel) 1975

This Is Not a Letter, and Other Poems (poetry) 1985

Words That Must Somehow Be Said: The Selected Essays of Kay Boyle (essays) 1985

CRITICISM

Peter Monro Jack (essay date 1940)

SOURCE: Monro Jack, Peter. "Three Unusual Stories by Kay Boyle." In *Critical Essays on Kay Boyle*, edited by Marilyn Elkins, pp. 48-9. New York: New Directions, 1997.

[*In the following essay, originally published in 1940, Monro Jack gives mixed praise to the three novellas in Boyle's* The Crazy Hunter, *concluding that the best piece of the collection, "The Bridegroom's Body," places Boyle among the premier American short fiction writers.*]

Miss Boyle is an expert in the psychiatry of fiction and there is no story of hers that does not send a delicate thrill of apprehension and recognition of the neurotic even in the most normal reader. The lines from Mr. Eliot's tortured Love Song of J. Alfred Prufrock should accompany her stories:

> It is impossible to say just what
> I mean!
> But as if a magic lantern threw
> the nerves in, patterns on a
> screen:

That is what Miss Boyle does, to throw the jangled nerves in delicate patterns on a screen that is only indirectly and often obscurely reflective. It is a technique developed (in the short story) through Chekhov and Katherine Mansfield and it is evident in the work of Katherine Anne Porter (to whom this book [*The Crazy Hunter: Three Short Novels*] is dedicated) and Djuna Barnes, whose early story, "A Night Among the Horses," has perhaps some relation to Miss Boyle's extended story of the crazy hunter. Possibly it is a peculiarly feminine art, a nervous exacerbation combined with a small but most acute perception of character and style.

The Crazy Hunter takes the space of half the book, a long short story stopping short of the development of a novel. It is followed by *The Bridegroom's Body,* a story of average length—not, as the publishers say, a short novel—and one of Miss Boyle's best; and by an unsuccessful hugger-mugger called **"The Big Fiddle."** The first two are of English county life, as distinguished from her earlier French or Austrian sophistication; but of English county life as only a visitor would see it in all of its clarity and ambiguity, as Henry James saw it, for instance, in "The Turn of the Screw." Miss Boyle's excellence is her extraordinary and unfailing knowledge. If it is horses that turn the story, then Miss Boyle knows all about horses; if it should be swans, then Miss Boyle knows them from cob to pen, better than their owners.

The first long story is about a horse, an unhappy marriage, and a young sensitive girl, almost a compendium of Miss Boyle's work. The husband is a pleasant impecunious Canadian painter who has married a moneyed English-woman and fallen under her domination. Her hobby is pedigreed horses, about which he knows nothing; but in an effort to assert himself he buys with her money, and he gives to their daughter a stag-faced hunter that turns out to be stone-blind. His wife insists that it should be "put down," killed, immediately. The daughter, who has fallen in love with her blind horse, wins a delay while she hopes to prove that he can still be a useful animal.

But while the daughter has gone down to London (and here is the beginning of the love story that Miss Boyle has not developed into a novel) her mother determines to kill the horse, and her father, fortified with whisky and an unusual sense of responsibility, overcomes his fear and keeps vigil over the horse for his daughter. Miss Boyle's men get drunk too easily and rather implausibly and there is a general sense of unreality in the last scene. What remains in the memory is Miss Boyle's uncanny feeling for the animal life of a horse and the tender and disciplined, though overstrained, solicitude of the girl. The strain lies in Miss Boyle's writing, with its burden of emotional words and its Irish rhythms that have a sort of intellectual blarney to them.

But for the second story, *The Bridegroom's Body,* there can be nothing but praise. All of Miss Boyle's undeniable artistry in the short story, all of her intuitions into the curious motives of human behavior and her startling and peculiar guesses at animal behavior, even her studied mannerisms and tricks of style seem to come to the proper terms of her narrative. With the savage sexual life of the swans as a counterpoint, Miss Boyle delicately, meticulously and admirably suggests the impotent desire of the owner of the swannery,

Lord Glourie; the restless, unsatisfied energy of his wife; the tenacious habits of the old swanherd; the new blood of the young farmer; and, to focus all this, the clear and honest innocence of a young Irish nurse who comes up from a London agency. Of course there is a certain ambiguity and symbolism, without which Miss Boyle would not be herself, but here it seems natural and as if it wrote, so to speak, its own ticket.

The last story is a made-up story and reminds us too violently of Miss Boyle's worst fault of artificiality, and her habit of making a neurotic excitation take the place of a sober and more difficult realism. Sentences like "the fragile, the peaked, the almost-ailing, almost-tainted quality of her flesh lured him speechlessly and terribly toward love" and "the childish neck turned, the small breakable white jawbone visible, beneath the skin" are made up for the psychology of a crime story; they never ring true, the intention is too obvious, and Miss Boyle is caught in her own network of alarming words.

But at her best in this book Miss Boyle demonstrates that she is one of the best short-story writers in America, and probably the most careful, percipient and unusual.

Richard C. Carpenter (essay date 1953)

SOURCE: Carpenter, Richard C. "Kay Boyle." In *Critical Essays on Kay Boyle,* edited by Marilyn Elkins, pp. 89-95. New York: New Directions, 1997.

[*In the following essay, originally published in 1953, Carpenter provides background for Boyle's literary career and laments the fact that such an original short story writer achieved such minor fame and received so little formal recognition.*]

In her autobiography, *The Passionate Years,* Caresse Crosby says of Kay Boyle: "Kay is built like a blade—to see her clearly you must look at her from one side and then from the other; both are exciting." This is an assessment which can be equally well applied to her writing, as can Mrs. Crosby's description: "neat as a needle . . . like a breeze or a bird's wing"—it is exciting, and it must be looked at from more than one angle to appreciate it thoroughly. After twenty-five years of writing short stories and novels, Miss Boyle manages to bring to her work the same vividness, the freshness of style, the subtle insights, and the craftsmanship that marked her first writing. Several of the tales in her most recent book, *The Smoking Mountain,* are as taut and clean as those which appeared in *"First Lover" and Other Stories*

twenty years ago and as intense in their emotional currents as her first novel, *Plagued by the Nightingale,* which was published in 1931. The stories that appear from time to time in the *New Yorker* show no diminution of ability, and the chances are that reading one will bring an absorbing experience.

Yet Kay Boyle is singularly little known; even college English professors are as a rule only vaguely aware of her existence and may recall with some difficulty having read a story in one of the several anthologies in which her tales have appeared. Her some dozen novels and over a hundred short stories, while frequently praised and often reprinted, have not given her a wide reputation. Few people have encountered such fascinating tales as *Monday Night* or *The Bridegroom's Body,* both of them eminently worth reading. However, the fact remains that Miss Boyle has done much excellent work and should be better known.

Encouraged by her mother, she started to write early and had by the age of seventeen written "hundreds of poems, short stories, and a novel." Married at eighteen and settled abroad, presumably for a visit, but actually as a permanent expatriate as it turned out, she wrote stories throughout the twenties and had her first collection published at the Black Sun Press in Paris by Caresse and Harry Crosby in 1929. This was republished in the United States as *"Wedding Day" and Other Stories.* In 1931 she started a full-fledged career of writing and, following her first novel, *Plagued by the Nightingale,* brought out four novels and two collections of short stories in the next five years. *Year before Last, Gentlemen, I Address You Privately,* and *My Next Bride,* all of them concerned with the pathos of love lost through weakness or circumstance, proved that she was a very subtle analyst of personality and established (together with *"First Lover" and Other Stories* and *The White Horse of Vienna*) her reputation as a stylist—an exquisite manipulator of the nuances of phrase and a craftsman with image and metaphor. By 1938 it appeared that she had laid claim to this title, for the blurbs on her books announced it, and the critics in general followed suit. While they praised her stylistic ability, they did, however, regret that her situations were not more realistic and that her people lived too much in the pale light of another world. At the same time they noted her uncanny immediacy and impact, for these tales are without doubt weirdly fascinating.

That she was an expatriate, using European backgrounds and characters largely, and that she soon came to be engrossed with political and social themes also were noticed—to her irritation, for she feels that she is writing about people, not places or politics. Still, such novels as *Death of a Man,* with its sympathetic analysis of the ideas and feelings of an Austrian Nazi; *Avalanche* and *A Frenchman Must Die,* "elegant potboilers"; and the short stories of this period show a preoccupation with the effect of political turmoil and war on quite ordinary people. Probably her weakest book, *His Human Majesty* (1949), is the result of her attempt to write on such a problem, the lives and loves of ski-troops, a task eminently unsuited to her kind of fiction.

A selection from her stories of the last twenty years or so, *Thirty Stories* (1946) affords ample evidence, nevertheless, that she is more than either a stylist or a writer mesmerized by the confusions and alarums of our weary world. It becomes clear, on reading through these stories, that her twice winning the O. Henry Memorial Prize for the best short story of the year, her constant appearance in such magazines as the *New Yorker* and *Harper's Bazaar,* and the recent inclusion of her novella *The Crazy Hunter* in Ludwig and Perry's *Nine Short Novels* (in the company of James, Kafka, and Mann) have been no mere flukes and are due to more solid virtues than are comprised in style or political consciousness, good though those may be.

Of course, it is undeniable that she is an able manipulator of language. She enjoys the play of words; she has a keen eye for the striking image; and she can fascinate with the bold trenchancy of her metaphors: "Here then was April holding them up, stabbing their hearts with hawthorn, scalping them with a flexible blade of wind," or "The waves came in and out there, as indolent as ladies, gathered up their skirts in their hands, and with a murmur, came tiptoeing in across the velvet sand." Especially is it true that she can create amazingly sharp, vivid pictures: "Prince and Star were black as seals and here they stood in the white unmelting world, the two black horses steaming against the hard, bright, crusted snow. The white boughs of the trees were forked full in the woods around, and the twigs of the underbrush were tubed in glass the length of the frozen falls."

Still, this mastery of style accounts for only one side of the blade that is Kay Boyle—the side that glitters and dazzles and, perhaps, blinds some readers to the more significant things she has to offer. Style is obviously integral to her work and makes it peculiarly her own; it undoubtedly helps heighten the intensity and immediacy which most readers recognize as the hallmark of Miss Boyle's writing. Dagger-sharp images and crackling metaphors do assist in raising the temperature of a story. Other qualities, however, seem to me to be more basic. First of all, a thorough acquaintance with the bulk of her work leads to an increasing appreciation of her mastery of her own kind of fictional technique. She has a most delicate touch in un-

folding the lives of her characters, an exquisite sense of reticence and balance, all the while that the tale is trembling on the edge of pathos or sentimentality. Much of this effect she manages by carefully limiting the area of perception (something she may have learned from Chekhov or perhaps from Faulkner, whom she admires most highly), so that the reader becomes *aware* in the form of a gradual revelation, as do the principal characters. This contributes greatly to developing the "specification of reality," the sense of immediacy which James desired of fiction. When used, as Miss Boyle frequently does use it, with judicious foreshadowing, it creates a considerable current of tension without having much "happen" in the sense of the usual well-plotted story. We do not leisurely savor her stories but breathlessly turn pages, sure that these apparently innocuous events are somehow tremendously vital.

Beyond technique, Miss Boyle's basic themes are also productive of suspense and intensity. Her fiction world is not a happy one: she deals with disease, war, perversion, cowardice, frustration. Her people are complex souls undergoing a variety of torments, prevented either by their own weaknesses or by the devils of circumstance from living the rich and full lives which should be theirs. To make things worse, her people are not degraded but *potentially* fine and *potentially* happy. They are sensitive, courageous, artistic, profoundly emotional. We like them, usually, and would like to see them happy, but they are the beautiful and the damned. Miss Boyle achieves her characteristic force by showing us a vision of humanity in need of pity and understanding, a central idea that does not make for light reading but one which accounts for the realism and effectiveness we inescapably feel as we read through her work. While probably not the end result of a reasoned philosophy, it is a telling and significant attitude toward life that makes of her writing much more than a pretty toy or a tract. Miss Boyle is not simply *interested* in people; she is vitally *concerned* with people and profoundly moved to write about their struggles with themselves and with their dreams. She does not write just to tell a tale, to make money, to create a thing of beauty, even though these may sometimes be her motives; but, as she has said, she also writes "out of anger, out of compassion and grief . . . out of despair." This is truly the other side of the blade.

From her earliest work we can see Miss Boyle working out this idea. *Plagued by the Nightingale* and *Year before Last* explore the relations between people whose happiness is shadowed by disease; *Gentlemen, I Address You Privately* is an analysis of perverted love. *Plagued by the Nightingale* is the story of an American girl who has married into a French family cursed with a hereditary disease which cripples the legs of the men. The conflict grows out of the insistence of the family, particularly Papa, that the young couple have a child, even though everyone knows the risk. A silent but bitter struggle, beneath the surface of an idyllic family life, is waged, with the family using the lever of promised money to weaken the son's resistance. The family loses, eventually, but the girl loses as well, for she leaves her husband, and her love, at the end. The novel is almost a parable, with Bridget and Nicholas—youth, beauty, and love—defeated by age and corruption, symbolized by the nature of the disease, a "rotting of the bone" as it is called. The corruption comes closer to home in her second novel, *Year before Last,* since Martin, the hero, is handsome, brave, sensitive, deeply in love, as well as tuberculous. He is, perhaps, a bit too much of these things and a trifle impossible, but he and his inamorata, Hannah, reiterate for us that the beautiful *are* often the damned. As we watch them flee across the south of France, with the hemorrhages becoming more frequent and deadly, we find our feeling of pity and our sense of irony steadily increasing until the inevitable death at the conclusion.

An interesting aspect of these novels is that they ought to be merely depressing instead of enthralling. However, through the poetic use of language and the method of implication and reticence, Miss Boyle lifts the story. Besides, because the reader creates the emotional tone for himself, as he gradually becomes aware of the situation, the essential tragedy is not sharply emphasized. The tale unfolds slowly, flower-like, so that we are almost able—almost, but not quite, like the characters themselves—to close our eyes on the worm i' the bud. The enervation of some of her later work is undoubtedly due to a partial abandonment of this method of implication for that of stream of consciousness and interior monologue where we are brought directly and explicitly into contact with the people's thoughts and emotions, usually in italics. In her weaker writing Miss Boyle tells us too much; in her better we float on a placid, shimmering current, all the time aware of the cold, black, rushing depths beneath.

Naturally, this method can be overdone, as it is in her third novel, *Gentlemen, I Address You Privately,* where we see everything through a glass most darkly, so much so that it is difficult to realize what the theme is. An analysis of the chiaroscuro, however, shows that all the characters are twisted in some way: the cast is composed of two homosexuals, two Lesbians, a prostitute, a fanatic, a sadist, and one fine woman starved for love. In general, love is perverted in this novel; the characters are lost souls, whirled through the darkness of their desires.

The tale comes to a flat and tasteless end, despite some tension in the last chapters, and its people are too much for us to swallow—possible perhaps, but hardly probable. Still, with all its frigidity and confusion, it somehow sticks in the mind, like a reflection in a distorting mirror, concentrating for us the pathos and irony of Miss Boyle's theme. It is, as well, the furthest advance she has made in the use of implication and memorable for that reason.

Throughout Miss Boyle's writings prior to the war we can see the same techniques, the same quivering emotion held in tight leash, the concern with the interrelations of personality, the same bitter brew. Though the short stories naturally play many variations, they show the same fundamental theme, not difficult to recognize once it has been analyzed.

In some stories the problem is pride, as in **"Keep Your Pity,"** where the Wycherlys, impoverished Englishmen in the south of France, preserve appearances even beyond death. In others, such as **"The White Horses of Vienna,"** it is the pathos of prejudice and misunderstanding. The young Jewish student-doctor, who has been called in to assist the injured Austrian Nazi, ought to be able to be a friend—he and the Austrian are really much alike, the Austrian with his worship of power and the Jew with his nostalgic idealism, his memory of the royal white horses of Vienna, "the relics of pride, the still unbroken vestiges of beauty bending their knees to the empty loge of royalty where there was no royalty any more." But of course they cannot be friends.

Other stories are tales of initiation, in which an innocent or unknowing character learns evil—as in **"Black Boy,"** where a young white girl learns that she cannot have an innocent friendship with a black boy, at least not as far as her grandfather is concerned; or in ***The Bridegroom's Body*** (a novella), where Lady Glourie realizes that the young nurse who has come from the city has not been, as Lady Glourie suspected, in love with Lord Glourie or the farmer Panrandel but really with Lady Glourie herself. In **"Natives Don't Cry"** we see the beautifully low-keyed treatment of the real pathos in the old maid's life as the governess tries to pretend she is getting letters from her young man, when the mail was not delivered that day.

"Wedding Day," one of Miss Boyle's best, a light and delicate study of personal relations between brother and sister on her wedding day, does not force theme on our attention, but there is still the sense of loss, of youth left somewhere behind, forever. **"Count Lothar's Heart"** concerns itself with what has happened to a young man who has had a homosexual experience during the war and cannot get it out of his mind, his perversion symbolized by the swans of the Traunsee, emblems of passion. **"One of Ours"** studies through image and symbol the hidden feelings of a most proper Englishwoman who thinks a savage at an exposition is lusting after her—a projection of her desires, for he is really interested in the doll she is holding. The theme of distortion is carried out by her fascination with the savage's maleness as well as her fear of him.

It might be wondered whether or not Miss Boyle offers anything but utter blank and bitter pessimism with this constant iteration of the theme of a world out of joint. Indeed, it could be maintained that there is nothing else. A novel like *My Next Bride* (1934) leaves about as bad a taste in our mouths as anything we could find, with an American girl who deserves no evil falling into utter degradation through her love for another woman's husband. Perversely she becomes promiscuous rather than having her affair with Antony, making her pregnancy by some unknown especially fruitless. Probably the most unpleasant sequences Kay Boyle has ever written are to be found in the account of Victoria's attempts at abortion.

Yet the novel, *Monday Night* (1936), which has a protagonist who is repulsively dirty and possesses a nauseatingly mutilated ear, manages to distil something more positive from the flowers of evil. The contrast between the clean and the filthy, the innocent and the obscene, is implicit perhaps, but it is still there to provide a kind of counterpoint to the basic theme. In fact, this counterpoint may be seen running through many of her writings, indicating a corollary to the pessimism. A passage in **"Count Lothar's Heart"** symbolizes what this may be; speaking of the swans, she writes:

> Some of them had thrust the long stalks of their throats down into the deeper places before the falls and were seeking for refuse along the bottom. Nothing remained but the soft, flickering short peaks of their clean rumps and their leathery black elbows with the down blowing soft at the ebony bone. In such ecstasies of beauty were they seeking in the filth of lemon rinds and shells and garbage that had drifted down from the town, prodding the leaves and branches apart with their dark, lustful mouths.

Miss Boyle seems to be saying that the polarity between the beautiful and the ugly, the good and the bad, is central in our lives. Wilt, in **Monday Night,** disreputable and dirty, is yet a dreamer of beautiful dreams which he conveys to us in long monologues written in an incantatory style strongly reminiscent of Faulkner, who, Miss Boyle says, strongly influenced the book. Wilt ought to be a great writer, yet he is a seedy drunk. Miss Boyle is not telling us that he is going to triumph over himself; rather she is showing us that he cannot possibly do so: the fact that he and his friend never reach the goal they seek is the only logic that the underlying theme will permit the plot. Yet Wilt is somehow noble. He is giving himself to an ideal; the tale is almost an allegory, a *Pilgrim's Progress* of this modern world, where modern man fails of heaven as a goal but finds his soul in the quest itself. Here, as in other places, we can see Miss Boyle implying that devotion, integrity, and courage are the means by which we transcend our fate.

This implication is particularly evident in the tales since the war; dealing with social and political themes, they throw the contrast between what is and what ought to be into clearer light. In the backwash of a war-world, the need for undramatic devotion and integrity is particularly great. A number of tales since 1938 benefit from this larger context. There is less tendency toward attenuating the situation; the characters are often more believable, their suffering justified, their bravery less self-conscious, their defeat more real. It must be admitted that they transcend their fate but seldom. Many tales are vitiated by Miss Boyle's indiscriminate tenderness toward those who are the victims of war. Her best work in this type of writing is rather that which grows out of indignation, the failure of devotion and integrity. **"Defeat,"** which won the O. Henry Memorial Prize in 1941, shows this indignation combined effectively with tenderness, the indignation coming from the failure of the French girls to resist the German blandishments of food and dance music, the tenderness for the men who realize their country is defeated only when its women are defeated.

Her most recent book, **The Smoking Mountain,** rings the changes on Miss Boyle's preoccupation with the war: there are some good stories in it and some that strain after sentiment. She is trying to show us the atmosphere of an occupied land in which all the old hatreds still smolder under the ashes of defeat. Probably the most interesting part of the book is the long, nonfiction Introduction, the account of Germans against German in the trial of a former Gestapo brute, a new kind of venture for her and one that may lead to more significant writing. A new venture is needed; to this reader it does not seem that Miss Boyle has lost any of her ability to perceive and convey human feelings and relations, there is no slackening of her mastery of prose style, and she has certainly not turned into a shallow optimist. Yet it would be a pleasant change to see a tale not tied to particular "conditions and conflicts," as she calls them, as universal as, let us say, the novelle *The Crazy Hunter* and *The Bridegroom's Body,* tales rich in background and symbol, powerfully motivated from within the characters themselves, subtly reproducing the conflicts of personality. To my mind, these two short novels are the cream of her writing, together with such stories as **"The White Horses of Vienna," "Wedding Day,"** and **"Natives Don't Cry."** It is fortunate that Professors Ludwig and Perry have reprinted *The Crazy Hunter,* and it would be well if someone would do the same for *The Bridegroom's Body,* that eerie yet unforgettable re-creation of the swannery on the rain-drenched coast of England, with the magnificently vital yet tragically lonely Lady Glourie and the bitter irony of Miss Cafferty's love for her. Then more readers might be able to see that Miss Boyle not only can dazzle us with style but also can move us to a deeper understanding.

Maxwell Geismar (essay date 1966)

SOURCE: Geismar, Maxwell. "Aristocrat of the Short Story." In *Critical Essays on Kay Boyle,* edited by Marilyn Elkins, pp. 67-9. New York: New Directions, 1997.

[*In the following essay, originally published in 1966, Geismar argues that the short stories and novellas in* Nothing ever Breaks Except the Heart *showcase Boyle's finest, most mature literary achievements and place the author among the finest American short story authors.*]

Kay Boyle has been one of the most elusive characters in contemporary American fiction. I say this with some feeling, because I have tried to categorize her work in every decade since the early 1930's, and each decade, it seems, I have been wrong.

She is the author of 13 novels, some of them very good, but she is not quite a major novelist. Her major medium has always been the short story and the novelette. (And it is typical of this aristocrat, whose earlier work lay in the tradition of Edith Wharton and Henry James, not to use the fashionable word, novella.) But even here, she was in the early thirties, a writer of superior sensibility—or so I thought—using a foreign scene more successfully than her native one, and belonging, in essence, both to the expatriate line of James and Wharton and to that later "lost generation" of the 1920's.

What this new collection of Miss Boyle's short stories and novelettes [*Nothing ever Breaks Except the Heart*] does prove is that while all of the speculation above is somewhat true, none of it is really true, or profoundly true. She has all these elements in this new collection of her mature work. But, as in the case of every first-rank writer, she rises above the disparate elements in her work or in her temperament, to become something else. What *Nothing ever Breaks Except*

the Heart proves, in short, is that Kay Boyle has at last become a major short-story writer, or a major writer in contemporary American fiction, after three decades of elusiveness, sometimes of anonymity, almost of literary "classlessness," while she has pursued and has finally discovered her true metier. It is a joy to discover such an event: not a new talent, which is rare enough, but an established and mature talent which has developed and perfected itself—and particularly in an epoch when so many false talents are proclaimed every year.

Unlike her earlier collection of *Thirty Stories* which was arranged chronologically—and that earlier volume is fascinating now to read over and to compare with the present one—*Nothing ever Breaks Except the Heart* is arranged topically: **"Peace," "War Years"** and **"Military Occupation."** And perhaps one should add, in the selfish concern of pure art, that nothing better could have happened for Kay Boyle than World War II and the periods of military occupation, by the German and then the Allied forces. For even in the present volume, the first section, **"Peace,"** is less effective than the remainder of the book—and still Kay Boyle is less effective about the American than she is about the European scene. When it comes to a story like **"Anschluss,"** dealing with a world-weary Parisian fashion-writer and a marvelously gay brother and sister in a dying Austria, she is superb.

Here, as in so many of her earlier stories and novels, her satiric strain works unrelentingly upon the German character and physique. Here, more convincingly than in earlier books, her romantic lovers are destroyed by the dissolution of a society; and here, just as in her work of the early forties, she dramatizes the pageantry of a dissolute and amoral social scene over and above the sensibilities of her characters.

In Miss Boyle's writing, there has always been a traditional sense of character—romantic, pagan at heart and best exemplified in her heroines rather than her heroes—but the European *Walpurgisnacht* of the late thirties gave her a dramatic social background that she could hardly afford to ignore. Thus, too, in her first novel, *Plagued by the Nightingale,* first published in 1931 and just recently reissued, the central theme was of an ingrown and diseased French bourgeois family, of an American heroine's struggle against this family. (Miss Boyle herself was born in St. Paul in 1903, married a Frenchman, and went to live in France in the early twenties; but her "expatriatism," as she recently wrote to me, was enforced by circumstances rather than by choice.)

The style, too, of her first novel is more precious, studied and "literary" than her present, apparently more prosaic, and truly more beautiful style. As late as

1938, she could still turn out such a mediocre novel as *Monday Night,* a picaresque mystery, still about that "family romance" which any true novelist must have in his bones, but which, in itself, is never enough. Perhaps it was only with **Primer for Combat,** in 1942—which is curiously close to the place and theme of the "Anschluss" story—that the *larger* European scene of social and moral disintegration and corruption appeared so firmly and so incisively and so brilliantly. And it was in **Generation without Farewell** (1960) that she added the American Occupation Forces to her Nazi conquerors, in order to prove that human debasement—the evil soul, the vicious soul, the lost soul—can be a matter of social circumstance rather than of national origins.

Indeed, in **Nothing ever Breaks Except the Heart,** it is a toss-up as to who the true villains are, Germans or Americans or just plain Occupiers—while the heroes, to Miss Boyle, are those who have been conquered and occupied, those who have resisted, those who have put to the acid test their property, their career and their lives. To her earlier vision of sensibility, she has added what every first-rate writer must have, a standard of human morality—and the fact that human morality is usually, if not always, related to a specific social or historical context.

It is this familiar concept, missing in so much current and "new" American fiction, that is embodied in the magnificent stories of her maturity. (For conversely, it is of no use to an artist to have a perfect sense of morality without an adequate art form to project it.) The title story of the present collection is another beauty: a Hemingway tale, so to speak (about a pilot who is finished), but produced by an intensely feminine talent, and with an anti-Hemingway moral. (By this I mean anti-late-Hemingway, when all that remained in him was the killer pitted against a hostile, menacing universe.) What is so remarkable in these late tales of Kay Boyle, by contrast, is the increased sense of sympathy in them for all the losers, all the defeated persons and peoples of contemporary history.

Here again, an earlier sense of nostalgia in her work has become an intense sense of compassion. I don't pretend to know the secrets of this fine craftsman, but I do realize how many of these stories leave you on the brink of tears. And a world in tears; since Kay Boyle has become the American writer to express the texture of European life after Chamberlain and Daladier and Munich.

There is still a final phase of writing in **Nothing ever Breaks Except the Heart,** still another epoch of our modern history: the period of the Occupation, the black market and the reappearance of the same old people, asking for privilege and power and "deals" all over again, after the heroism, the gallantry, the selflessness of the liberation battle. No wonder that the last one of these stories describes an American State Department official returning to a McCarthyite America—ironic sequel to the war for European freedom. And no wonder that the last of these beautiful tales describes an American mother, who agrees with "a terrified race"—the French peasants of the atomic age. "'I am American,' she said to that unseen presence of people in the silent room, 'and the wrong voices have spoken out for me, and spoken loudly, and I too, I too, am terribly afraid.'"

Sandra Whipple Spanier (essay date 1988)

SOURCE: Whipple Spanier, Sandra. "Introduction." In *Kay Boyle: "Life Being the Best" and Other Stories,* pp. vii-xviii. New York: New Directions, 1988.

[*In the following essay, Spanier provides biographical information on Boyle's six-decades-long literary career, concentrating mainly on her early stories of protest and disappointment written while living in France in the 1920s and 30s.*]

When Kay Boyle's first book, a collection of short stories, was published in Paris in 1929, William Carlos Williams wrote: "Her short stories assault our sleep. They are of a high degree of excellence; for that reason they will not succeed in America, they are lost, damned. Simply, the person who has a comprehensive, if perhaps disturbing view of what takes place in the human understanding at moments of intense living, and puts it down in its proper shapes and color, is anathema to United Statesers and can have no standing with them. We are asleep."

He was only too accurate in his prediction of the commercial success of Kay Boyle's writing ("Surely excellence kills sales.") But she has never faltered in the bold articulation of her vision. In the course of her six-decade career, Kay Boyle has written over thirty-five books, including fourteen novels, eleven collections of short fiction, five volumes of poetry, two essay collections, and a memoir of Paris in the twenties. She has also translated three *avant-garde* French novels, ghostwritten two books, and edited several more volumes. Her first publication was a poem in Harriet Monroe's *Poetry,* when Boyle was in her teens, later followed by a number of others in that magazine. Hundreds of her stories, poems, and articles have since appeared in periodicals ranging from the "little magazines" published in Paris to the *Ladies' Home Journal* to *The Nation.* She has twice been awarded Guggenheim fellowships, won the O. Henry Award for best short story of the year in 1935 and again in 1941, holds a number of honorary degrees, and occupies the Henry James chair of the American Academy of Arts and Letters (one of only six women members of that select body of fifty writers, artists, and musicians). In 1981 she was awarded a Senior Fellowship for Literature from the National Endowment for the Arts for her "extraordinary contribution to contemporary American literature over a lifetime of creative work." And in 1987 she received an endowment from the Fund for Poetry "in support and appreciation of her contribution to contemporary poetry."

In 1978, the *San Francisco Chronicle* asked several contemporary writers for sketches of how they saw themselves. Kay Boyle's self-portrait was a line drawing of an angel in flight, complete with wings and halo, bearing a small round smoking bomb in each hand. Her caption reads, "Since receiving several volumes of censored data through the Freedom of Information Act, I see myself as a dangerous 'radical' (they themselves put it in quotes) cleverly disguised as a perfect lady. So I herewith blow my cover." (Her 2000-page FBI file contains a report that she had had an affair with Ezra Pound before World War I. "I would have been no more than ten," Boyle says. She did not meet Pound until 1927, in Paris, and she disliked him then.)

If outspoken political activism makes one a "radical," then probably the label fits. Since roughly the beginning of World War II, nearly everything Kay Boyle has written has been overtly political. Her 1944 novel *Avalanche* was the first book about the French Resistance (and, incidentally, her only bestseller). From 1946 to 1953, she was a foreign correspondent for *The New Yorker,* assigned to write articles and fiction on conditions in France, Spain, and Occupied Germany, until she and her diplomat husband, Joseph von Franckenstein—an Austrian baron who fled Nazism, became a U.S. citizen, and later was decorated for his heroic work with the OSS behind enemy lines—endured a McCarthy-style loyalty-security hearing. Despite their being cleared, Franckenstein was fired as "surplus," *The New Yorker* withdrew Kay Boyle's accreditation, and for the rest of the decade she found herself blacklisted. From the time she began teaching at San Francisco State University in 1963 and settled permanently in the United States, Kay Boyle has continued to voice her social and political concerns—protesting the war in Vietnam (and going to jail with Joan Baez and others for blocking the entrance to the Oakland Induction Center), participating in the student strike of 1968 (and getting herself publicly—but only temporarily—fired by university president S. I.

Hayakawa), marching with California farm workers, founding a San Francisco chapter of Amnesty International, and continually speaking out on behalf of human rights around the globe.

Such are the signs of "radicalism" that a J. Edgar Hoover would recognize. What William Carlos Williams saw in her work and what these thirteen early stories represent is perhaps a less obvious but no less revolutionary approach to life and art. For Kay Boyle was in Paris in the twenties among the pioneers of modernism who called their aesthetic revolt "the Revolution of the Word."

Kay Boyle went to France in 1922 with her first husband, a French exchange student whom she met while he was studying engineering at the University of Cincinnati. Because by law at that time an American woman who married a foreigner automatically assumed her husband's citizenship, she was not technically an expatriate. But she was very much a part of the group of writers and artists that has since come to be known as the Lost Generation—a term she hates. Her friends included James Joyce, William Carlos Williams, Samuel Beckett, Hart Crane, Black Sun Press publishers Harry and Caresse Crosby, *This Quarter* editor Ernest Walsh (she left her husband to live with him in the South of France, and he was the father of her first child), and Robert McAlmon, that largely forgotten but enormously important figure of the Left Bank. At the time of his divorce from the poet Bryher (who wanted to be free to continue her relationship with H.D.), a generous settlement from his wealthy British father-in-law enabled McAlmon to found the Contact Press and to publish the first work of Ernest Hemingway and other young unknown writers, as well as that of Gertrude Stein.

But Kay Boyle's revolutionary training in the arts had begun long before she ever got to Paris, and her contacts with the *avant-garde* were not limited to writers. Alfred Stieglitz was a friend of her mother's, and from the age of eight or nine, Kay Boyle considered him a mentor. A show of children's art at his "291" Gallery included paintings by Kay Boyle and her sister. When her mother took her, aged eleven, to see the Armory Show in New York in 1913, Kay Boyle could hardly have imagined that in 1927 Francis Picabia would become the godfather of her first child, that with Constantin Brancusi she would design a carving for the marble crypt of that child's father, Ernest Walsh (who died five months before his daughter was born), that she would be photographed in Paris by Man Ray, or that Marcel Duchamp would be a close friend and the godfather of her sixth and last child, her son Ian, born in 1943. (She describes Duchamp as a "wonderful man, absolutely dauntless," and she dedicated *Ava-*

lanche to "Monsieur et Madame Rrose Sélavy"—Duchamp and his longtime companion, Mary Reynolds. Reynolds was active in the French Resistance and provided many details for the novel; in turn Kay Boyle shared the profits from the book with the couple.)

Kay Boyle's early poems and stories appeared in the *avant-garde* magazines of the twenties alongside the work of Ezra Pound, James Joyce, Gertrude Stein, William Carlos Williams, Carl Sandburg, Djuna Barnes, and Ernest Hemingway. Her contemporaries considered her one of the most promising writers of their generation. Archibald MacLeish declared in 1929, "She has the power and the glory. I believe in her absolutely when she writes—even when I want not to." In 1931 Katherine Anne Porter wrote: "Gertrude Stein and James Joyce were and are the glories of their time and some very portentous talents have emerged from their shadows. Miss Boyle, one of the newest, I believe to be among the strongest." William Carlos Williams considered her Emily Dickinson's successor.

Of Paris in the 1920s, Kay Boyle has said, "all this glorification of that wonderful Camelot period is absurd." She firmly maintains that all those Americans were gathered in Paris mainly because of the favorable exchange rate. The writers did not sit around in cafes and talk about art. Most worked in isolation—many, including Kay Boyle and her second husband, painter and surrealist writer Laurence Vail, lived outside Paris or in the South of France and visited the city only occasionally—and none among them ever discussed their work. When she was with James Joyce, he talked mainly about white wines and his wife Nora talked about clothes. Had anyone mentioned his writing, she claims, he would have got up and left the table.

But if Kay Boyle debunks the legend of the Lost Generation, she does not deny that a revolution was taking place in Paris: "The recovery of the self was what we were seeking in the twenties, although we never gave it such a grand sounding name. Our daily revolt was against literary pretentiousness, against weary, dreary rhetoric, against out-worn literary conventions. We called our protest 'the revolution of the word' and there is no doubt that it was high time such a revolution take place. There was *then,* before the twenties, no lively, wholly American, grandly experimental, furiously disrespectful school of writing, so we had to invent that school."

In 1929 Kay Boyle and Laurence Vail were among sixteen writers and artists who signed a twelve-point manifesto, written by Eugene Jolas and published in his magazine *transition,* calling for the "Revolution of the Word." It declared, among other things, "The writer expresses. He does not communicate," and "The plain reader be damned." Yet in the course of the thirties, living in Austria, England, and France with Vail and their children, she witnessed first hand the historical events brewing toward cataclysm. By the time the family fled war-torn Europe in 1941, she had come to the belief that the artist must not retreat into a heady solipsism, but must recognize a responsibility to communicate his or her fervent convictions to as many readers as possible—"plain" ones included. In most of her later work she takes as her material events of contemporary history and writes in a far more accessible style than earlier.

The stories in this volume—originally published in the collections *Wedding Day* (1930), *The First Lover* (1933), and *The White Horses of Vienna* (1936)—show an artist in transition. Some are products of her experience in Paris in the twenties and exhibit the idiosyncratic subject matter and complex, experimental style of the Revolution of the Word. In **"I Can't Get Drunk,"** whose protagonist she later identified as Robert McAlmon, Boyle experiments with what the *transition* manifesto called the "language of hallucination," presenting a dialogue between a man and woman in a Paris bar through the woman's stream of consciousness. The disillusioned young woman of **"Art Colony,"** trapped by poverty in a squalid commune of toga-clad *artistes,* is closely modeled on Kay Boyle herself, who after Ernest Walsh's death, lived with her infant daughter at the Neuilly colony of Raymond Duncan (Isadora's brother), whose followers wore togas and sandals and subsisted on yogurt and goat cheese. Like the woman in the story, Kay Boyle worked at the colony's gift shops—one on the Boulevard St. Germain and the other on the Rue de Faubourg St. Honoré—selling hand-woven tunics, hand-dyed scarves, and leather sandals to American tourists. She became disillusioned when Duncan (who delighted in introducing her as "the honey who drew the bees" to his shops) used the proceeds from his lectures on the virtues of the simple life to buy a luxurious American automobile. With the help of Robert McAlmon, she "kidnapped" her young daughter from the group and escaped the prison of the commune in late 1928.

But while Kay Boyle never loses sight of the personal struggle, other stories reflect a growing concern for matters of what she once called "the functioning world." In these stories the fate of the individual is inextricably bound up in larger political and social struggles. Kay Boyle delicately mocks the maiden fervor of three vacationing German sisters awaiting **"The First Lover,"** but their eager expectancy takes on poignance when the attraction of the fine, fit Englishman is set so firmly in the context of their defeated nation's poverty and suffering: "They were in a new country of greed and plenty and they would forget, by turning their faces away, they would forget everything that made their hearts like winter apples."

Kay Boyle strove to write "with an alertness sharp as a blade and as relentless." (She wrote that Harry Crosby, who died in 1929 in a tragic suicide pact with a mistress he called the "Fire Princess," stood "singularly alone" in his "grave acknowledgement of that responsibility.") Typically in a Kay Boyle story, very little "happens." Her stories most often end not in resolution but in revelation—in a supercharged moment of truth that James Joyce would have called an "epiphany." Beneath the deceptively placid surface rushes a treacherous current that imperils our complacency. It is interesting how consistently reviewers and critics over the years have used metaphors of quiet disaster to describe Kay Boyle's work. An early reviewer wrote of her stories in the 1930s: "Here is poison—in the small doses in which arsenic is prescribed for anemia." In the 1980s, Margaret Atwood noted that while Kay Boyle's writing is sometimes spoken of as approaching the surreal, "there is nothing of the ant-covered clock about it": "One thinks rather of Breughel, a landscape clearly and vividly rendered, everything in its ordinary order, while Icarus falls to his death, scarcely noticed, off to the side."

Kay Boyle early gained a reputation as a brilliant stylist. Her skill is evident in her ability to fix an instant with photographic clarity or to animate a landscape as a reflection of the inner state of the perceiver. She captures with equal precision the voices of a drunken artist on a barstool, a jaded Italian surgeon about to perform his fourth mastoid of the day "and this one done in sterling," and a deceived but cleverly undaunted English lady who exacts her revenge on an insincere suitor in a series of impeccably correct epistles. Boyle is a master of the fresh, surprising metaphor, and she is capable of revealing character through complex internal monologues that rival those of Joyce and Faulkner in their psychological authenticity.

William Carlos Williams noted in Kay Boyle's work a distinctly female perspective. "Few women have written like this before," he said, "work equal in vigor to anything done by a man but with a twist that brings a new light into the whole Sahara of romanticism, a twist that carries the mind completely over until the male is not the seeing agent but the focus of the eye." Her work incorporates a wide swath of human experience simply relegated to invisibility in most fiction written by men. Her keen eye takes in the details of daily life that form the inevitable backdrop of existence for most women—"the vegetables, stiff as dead men on the table, waiting for water and fire to bring them life again," the slices of cold potato "browning sweetly in the butter." Her work reflects the experience of a woman who has raised eight children, six of her own and two from Laurence Vail's previous marriage to Peggy Guggenheim. She displays a keen ear for the voices of children, an aching concern for their vulnerability, and an astute and unsentimental observation of their ways. ("The stone hearts of little girls belonged, like those of perverts, in a privy world of their own," she writes in **"Convalescence."**)

Despite the surface diversity of her work, set anywhere from a Paris art colony to an English estate to the Australian outback, written in the "language of hallucination" or the language of the *Saturday Evening Post,* Kay Boyle's is a unified vision. F. Scott Fitzgerald claimed that in a lifetime a writer writes only two or three stories, over and over. Kay Boyle did not know Fitzgerald in Paris (she encountered him only once, in New York in 1922, when she and her sister went to see the young celebrity at a book signing at Columbia University, where he was surrounded by adoring autograph-seekers) but she probably would agree with the observation. At the heart of Kay Boyle's central story is a belief in the absolute essentiality of love—both on a private and a public scale—and a sense of tragic loss when human connections fail, leaving individuals who are desperately in need of contact bouncing off one another like atoms. The plight of the young man of **"I Can't Get Drunk"** is the plight of all lonely and isolated humanity: "To see him with his lean mouth closed like a wallet, his eye like iron and as cold as, would it ever have come into your head that the mouth of his heart was open, was gaping wide like a frog's in dry weather, requesting that into it be drained not glasses with frost on their faces but something else again." He is gasping for love like oxygen, not even knowing what he needs.

The plumber tells the astronomer's wife as he leads her away from her egotistical husband, "There's nothing at all that can't be done over for the caring." But with the exception of a few stories like **"Astronomer's Wife"** and **"His Idea of a Mother"** that end in a glimmer of hope for rescue, Kay Boyle's work explores the tragedy of love not lost but never gained. Kay Boyle is an idealist in her view of human possibilities but a pessimist about their chances for fulfillment.

Boyle's stories are a catalog of the ways in which love can fail. In some, connection is blocked by quirks of the individual psyche, by misunderstanding, by pride—and in the case of **"The Meeting of the Stones"** and **"To the Pure,"** the problem is complicated by a conflict in sexual orientation. But in other stories in this volume and in much of Kay Boyle's later work, the barriers to contact are institutionalized and large scale; the forces keeping human beings apart are social, political, historical. In **"Life Being the Best,"** the humanistic teachings of the gentle schoolmaster begin to transform the imagination of a motherless Italian boy whose family has taken refuge from Mussolini's black shirts in the South of France. "The words he used were never on anyone else's tongue in the country: such things as 'the might of thought,' and 'the power of the soul,' he spoke of, and undid Jesus from the cross and made a wounded weeping man of him." But Kay Boyle ultimately forces us to the tragic conclusion that in our time the simplest values of brotherly and sisterly love and respect for human life are no match for the crushing forces of militarism, poverty, and oppression.

Kay Boyle's world most often is a grim place. But it is not a meaningless Waste Land. In her youth, she and her companions burned T. S. Eliot and Ezra Pound in effigy on the Rue de Montparnasse. Then, as now, she had little patience for the high art of alienation and despair. She believes that there are still responsibilities to be taken, choices to be made. Her stories are mined with bitter ironies, but she is never ironic about her basic belief in the power of human compassion and understanding to transform the world. In Paris in the twenties and thirties, she has said, stories "were written in protest, and also in faith, and they were not unlike fervent prayers offered up for the salvation of man, for the defense of his high spirit, for the celebration of his integrity." The irony that pervades so much of her work is not the mark of cynicism but the scar of a betrayal of faith, of a deep disappointment in humanity's failure to live up to its infinite capacity.

Suzanne Clark (essay date 1991)

SOURCE: Clark, Suzanne. "Revolution, the Woman, and the Word: Kay Boyle." In *Critical Essays on Kay Boyle*, edited by Marilyn Elkins, pp. 157-82. New York: New Directions, 1997.

[*In the following essay, originally published in 1991, Clark analyzes the experimental and revolutionary nature of Boyle's writing and its relation to the emergence of literary modernism and feminism.*]

Women's experimental writing had an especially problematic relationship to modernist experiments with poetic language because the women were part of the culture of modernism, representing attachments to everyday life that were not literary. Even though it may now seem that modernist men and women were

inventing a kind of *écriture féminine,* challenging paternal conventions by a maternal authority, the men and women of modernism repressed the specific innovations of women writers because they denied these feminine connections. Kay Boyle's early work put the old categories into motion and marked out a new literary space of intense descriptive prose. Yet her impact on literary history has not seemed so powerful as her writing would warrant. In 1928, Boyle signed the manifesto for *transition* calling for "The Revolution of the Poetic Word."[1] Other signers included Hart Crane, Harry and Caresse Crosby, and Eugene Jolas. The "Proclamation" asserted, among other things, that "the literary creator has the right to disintegrate the primal matter of words" and that "we are not concerned with the propagation of sociological ideas except to emancipate the creative elements from the present ideology."

It must be admitted that Boyle's rewriting of the new word was a different matter from the poetics of someone such as Hart Crane, a difference she in fact had signaled herself in a critique of his obsession with the primacy of words, in **"Mr. Crane and His Grandmother."**[2] Although she shows herself to be in the tradition of Baudelaire and Rimbaud as well, Boyle prefers the American renewals of William Carlos Williams and Marianne Moore. Her innovations in prose style qualify her as a revolutionary of lyric language.[3] In her early works, such as **"Episode in the Life of an Ancestor," "Wedding Day,"** or **"On the Run,"** she swerves her narratives into a language of illumination and intensity that disorders story sequence and the familiar forms of remembering.[4] She experiments in a way that recalls the hallucinatory surrealism of Rimbaud's prose and fulfills the aspiration of the poetic revolution for "the projection of a metamorphosis of reality." But what does this powerful disintegration of conventional writing have to do with writing as a woman?

The strong old forms of the sentimental novel were part of what this modernist poetics—and she too—rejected. And yet, for the modernists, the cultural image of women and writing was deeply involved with that past. A shattering of language seemed to be at odds with writing like a woman, and challenging the image of woman seemed itself feminist and sentimental. Like other modernist women who felt they had to separate themselves from that conventional past, Boyle herself has taken pains to dissociate her work from the older tradition of women's writing and from the politics of feminism. Nevertheless, her reworking of the relationship between time and place, narration and description, also makes the connection between the time of poetic revolution and the place of the woman. I am going to suggest that Boyle shows us how the transition was made, from a representation of woman as the author of conventional romance to the function of woman as a disruptive, disturbing—and so revolutionary—difference in the rhetoric of fiction.

Julia Kristeva, herself a woman who has complicated relationships with revolution and women's writing, may help us to see how time operates in Boyle's work. In her essay "Women's Time," Kristeva redefined Nietzsche's idea of monumental or mythic time, a kind of temporality that is left out of rational discursive history.[5] Kristeva defines "women's time" as "repetition" and "eternity," in contrast with the linear movements of history. Women's time is characterized by

> the eternal recurrence of a biological rhythm which conforms to that of nature and imposes a temporality whose sterotyping may shock, but whose regularity and unison with what is experienced as extrasubjective time, cosmic time, occasion vertiginous visions and unnameable jouissance.
>
> (191)

If the order of production defines the time of history, it is the order of reproduction which seems to define this other kind of time, time which is so bound to the monumental, and the regional, that it is almost a kind of space. The cyclic and monumental forms of time associated with female subjectivity are far from the linear times of progress and project. But we must proceed very carefully, with Kristeva as with Boyle, for it would be wrong to suggest that either of them advocates a splitting away of a woman's order from human history.

In her *Revolution in Poetic Language,* when Kristeva associates certain innovations in avant-garde poetics inaugurated by writers in the tradition after Mallarmé with a breaking open of the possibilities of language, she is ambiguous about how women writers might participate in that fracturing.[6] If language itself oppresses, the language itself must be broken in order that marginal subjects, such as women, may be able to speak. And the woman, as marginal subject, is in a position of privilege to do this. But Kristeva's theoretical practice, like Boyle's prose, has been at odds with the discourse of feminism. Let us be careful not to see her antifeminism or Boyle's as simply oldfashioned modernism (let the paradoxical vocabulary resonate for us), for it is attached to some of the most unsettling and promising aspects of modernist experiments with subjectivity.

Boyle, in her practice, resists the binary coding of opposites which would make clear gendered structures for her stories, working instead at multiple and complex borders. Her early work practices this resistance

to extremism in the midst of the 1920s modernist extremism about gender. She defies the ideological either/or which would either deny the existence of gender difference in the name of equality or, in a move which Catharine Stimpson calls the "modern counterreformation in support of patriarchal law," claim gender difference, as D. H. Lawrence does, for example, to be the final truth.[7]

If Boyle refuses to write polemically, in behalf of an alternative woman's reality, she also refuses to omit gendered, female elements from her writing. Working within a culture of gendered extremism, she softly moves to put the contradictions into motion. The word *soft* has a certain significance; in an age which favored the tough over the tender, Boyle uses it so frequently it is almost a stylistic marker. A certain radical fluidity characterizes the forward movement of her narration. Hers is not a strikingly avant-garde text, not even at its most experimental, in the sense that such a text by its mode of presentation challenges the reader's ability to read, or breaks flagrantly with the bourgeois norms of realistic prose. But she makes visible the movement of what is left unspoken by the controlling enigmas of realism. So the luminous otherness of her work might well pass unremarked, since it is "soft," since it is neither an embrace nor a refusal of modernism's radical gendered Other.

Boyle's work resists certain categories, traps of ideology, and this includes the categorical oppositions of male and female. It would be too easy to imagine that time could be divided and separated into the two orders: the male order of linear plots, the female order of cycle and reproduction. But, as Julia Kristeva has argued, women's time cannot escape history, and the question for women today is, "What can be our place in the symbolic contract?"[8] Given that our language sacrifices the specific moment as it sacrifices the individual's bodied, material relations to others, Boyle like Kristeva is interested in an aesthetic practice which would make the excluded felt and known. The attention to structures based on linear time and productivity has left us separated from reproduction, from the maternal, from the moral and ethical representations once provided by religion—that is, from cyclical and monumental forms of time. Radical feminists of the seventies, recognizing this, began to talk about a separate female utopia, as if women's time and space could be wholly separated and alternative to the linear forms which organize modern culture. Language does not bridge the gap between individuals because they are identical or identically subjected, inscribed within it, but makes the connection across difference, metaphorically.

II

Kay Boyle's work might be thought of as revolutionary, then, not only because of the shattering of syntax which connects her experimental writing to the avant-garde. She makes the metaphorical connection between individuals, across difference. Her writing subverts the male plot, linear time, by a recursive, anaphoric temporality. And perceptions flow with the voice of the speaker across the boundaries of subject-object, rewriting the romantic identifications with exterior images which Ruskin criticized as the "pathetic fallacy." Boyle uses the fluidity of poetic forms to wash out the one-track temporality of male discourse and to undermine the singularity of gender ideology by a multiple sympathy. She unsettles the stabilities of identity. Women's time enters into history, making it less singular, undoing its regularities.

Three of her early stories will serve as examples of how Boyle's writing might participate in such a project. What kind of narrative time is operating in the story called **"Episode in the Life of an Ancestor"**? What kind of story is an "episode"? Is it singular or plural? A kind of turning point, or a repeated event?

In the story, a young woman defies her father's conventional desires for her to act like a submissive woman. The masterful way she treats their horses is like the mastery she exercises over her father and a would-be suitor, the schoolmaster. But the conflict between the father and daughter is framed by the long view of history. This is the story of an ancestor, very close to that of Boyle's own grandmother as a young woman.[9] The whole shimmers ambiguously between the backward long vision of memory and the immediacy of a present moment: "But at a time when the Indian fires made a wall that blossomed and withered at night on three sides of the sky, this grandmother was known as one of the best horsewomen in Kansas" (17-18).

The point of view also shifts to produce discontinuities in the linear structure of the plot. It is her father's egoistic will to dominate which provides the conflict in the story: "Her father was proud of the feminine ways there were in her. . . . It was no pride to him to hear [her voice] turned hard and thin in her mouth to quiet a horse's ears when some fright had set them to fluttering on the beak of its head" (17). The daughter/grandmother, however, is not drawn into the conflict. Her perceptions involve the repeated, habitual, physical world, and her mode is exclamatory, even joyful: "What a feast of splatters when she would come out from a long time in the kitchen and walk in upon the beasts who were stamping and sick with impatience for her in the barn" (19). From the daughter's point of view, sympathy is a strong recognition of difference, and her "way with horses" is mastery without egotism. Her point of view flows into the animal sensations of the horse:

> This was tame idle sport, suited to ladies, this romping in the milkweed cotton across the miles of pie-crust. Suddenly he felt this anger in the grandmother's knees that caught and swung him about in the wind. Without any regard for him at all, so that he was in a quiver of admiration and love for her, she jerked him up and back, rearing his wild head high, his front hoofs left clawing at the space that yapped under them.

(23)

The wildness of the horse seems to represent some kind of primeval vigor and sexuality that might remind us of D. H. Lawrence. It is, however, an energy both shared and directed by the woman. Against this energy, the father's will appears as unreal imaginings: he longs for "the streams of gentleness and love that cooled the blood of true women" (18). He doesn't know what is going on inside her or outside her. As he sees it, she goes off into the unknown for her ride into a night "black as a pocket." The ironic folds in the fabric of their relationship turn about the schoolmaster, a "quiet enough thought" by comparison to the woman and the horses until the father imagines him in the sexualized landscape of her midnight ride. Then his rage produces a paranoid close-up of the schoolmaster's face in his mind's eye—the detail of hairs and pores—in a failure of sympathy which wildly reverses itself again at the end with his unspoken cry: "What have you done with the schoolmaster?" (14). The father's fantasies are chairbound and disconnected from life. In the end, he cannot even put them into words.

The grandmother has hot blood, a heat that spreads and permeates the vocabulary of the story in a membranous action. The woman is woven into the fabric of the moment as she is into the words of the text, part of the whole cloth of experience. This displacement of human energy onto the surrounding objects of perception makes the descriptions seem luminous, surreal—not imaginary but strongly imagined. The grandmother's intensity spreads into the landscape with its contrasts of soft and hard, white and red, domestic flax and wild fire: "soft white flowering goldenrod," "Indian fires burning hard and bright as peonies" (20). The deep valleys and gulfs and the blossoming prairies form a topology of pocketing and hollows. The father registers how the daughter is a very figure of thereness: "When she came into the room she was there in front of him in the same way that the roses on the floor were woven straight across the rug" (23). He, on the other hand, is the very figure of absence, speechless, longing nostalgically for someone "of his own time to talk to" (23). On the recommendation, apparently, of the schoolmaster, the woman has been reading the passage from *Paradise Lost* about the creation of Eve. Milton's lines expose Boyle's poetic figure, the mutuality of flesh and landscape, and the spousal emotion. But this revelation of poetic influence offends the father, perhaps as much as the sexuality implied in the passage.

Like Milton, her father takes an accusatory stance toward the woman's sexuality. However, the daughter's refusal to be feminine his way, "the cooking and the sewing ways that would be a comfort to him" (20), undoes his ego-centered plot, an undoing which opens possibilities for the woman to be heroic in more multiple ways. Instead of a single hero dominating a single plot in time, Boyle produces the double figure of the daughter grandmother and a narrative which circles back from a lifetime to an episode. Instead of a hero who would make the woman over in his own image she produces a heroine who moves through mastery—of the horses, the schoolmaster, even her father—to a sympathy which is not identification with a male voice. The story is contained by long-distance temporality, as if written on a tapestry, a legendary mode which mimics the male heroic modes only to name them "episode." Female desire reshapes the forms of narrative as well as the forms of description: the woman is a hero who changes the forms of the heroic.

But in **"Wedding Day,"** Boyle does not shrink from showing us female power of a less attractive kind, allied with the bourgeois projects of family and possessions, and the literary mode of "realistic" representation. In this story, it is the mother who works to dominate, through organizing the details of the daughter's wedding day which will initiate her all-too-energetic children, the too-loving brother and sister, into the empty exchanges of proper social relations. The wedding will initiate—and separate—them. It is the mother who makes the violent cut that institutes order—as if she were founding the very system of culture by preventing the incest of brother and sister—but the gesture is also absurd and grotesque. So it finds its image in the "roast of beef" that "made them kin again" as "she sliced the thin scarlet ribbons of it into the platter" (26).

Not that the mother has, exactly, forced this marriage; she says it was not her idea, and her son defends his sister's choice—whose choice it was is confused. The issue is more primitive; the mother's negativity is on the side of the cut, the ceremonial structure, against any outbursts of trouble or love. She opposes her son

with a prayer for "dignity," but they find her, returning from a last excursion together, on her knees tying "white satin bows under the chins of the potted plants" (28).

She must maintain the objects of family life as intact mirrors—so it is that she counts the wedding "a real success, . . . a *real* success" when "no glass had yet been broken." Of course, it is the bride at the wedding who is "broken," but that happens beyond the precincts of the "real" which the mother so carefully maintains. Thus, from the point of view of the mother, the story has a happy ending; if she were the author of it, the incestuous energy of the brother and sister's love would be repressed.

Just as the brother and sister threaten the social order and its objects with their desire, the descriptive intensity of Boyle's style violates the decorum of the ceremony with a contradiction and violence that threatens to flood out the containing devices of concrete objects. What are these images doing at a wedding? The red carpet was to "spurt like a hemorrhage." "No one paid any attention" to the wedding cake, "with its beard lying white as hoar frost on its bosom." What is this negativity? There is the "thunderous NO" of the mother, who refuses to give the copper pans to her daughter as the spirit of a family inheritance might suggest. The mother must keep the pans orderly and unused, the "pride of the kitchen," "six bulls—eyes reflecting her thin face." She wishes, indeed, for the orderly household objects to serve as mirrors for the son and daughter as well, representations of the selves she would have them take on.

The young people challenge the civilizing project. These two are Nietzschean creatures, with "yellow manes," "shaggy as lions," "like another race." Like a refrain, the brother keeps repeating, "It isn't too late." But what else might they do except enter into the schemes laid out for them? Something, this story suggests, as it exceeds and overwhelms the bourgeois "real" of the mother: "in their young days they should have been saddled and strapped with necessity so that they could not have escaped. . . . With their yellow heads back they were stamping a new trail, but in such ignorance, for they had no idea of it" (27).

The necessity of youth, of freedom, of a new race encounters the violence of April, like Eliot's April the "cruelest month," bringing the death, here, of childhood. "Here then was April holding them up, stabbing their hearts with hawthorne, scalping them with a flexible blade of wind" (26). "Over them was the sky set like a tomb, the strange unearthly sky that might at any moment crack into spring" (28). The brother and sister take a ride in a boat together. If the boat ride were solitary, it would be an easy allegory; the wedding would represent the shackling of the poetic spirit. However, they are two; what is between them we are less likely to see as a visitation of the romantic imagination than as incestuous desire. Neither they nor we know if they should act on what they feel. "And who was there to tell them, for the trees they had come to in the woods gave them no sign" (27).

The signs of the story produce not a judgment about how the plot should have gone but a negativity that opens up the forms of the wedding and the story to something else, something which like the sister and brother does not wholly fit in the bourgeois "real," something full of energy, destructive and exuberant. At the end the daughter's "feet were fleeing in a hundred ways throughout the rooms, . . . like white butterflies escaping by a miracle the destructive feet of whatever partner held her in his arms" (29). The wedding, far from locking her exclusively to one person, has propelled her into an anonymity of social exchange. The brother's antagonism scatters the calling cards around the rooms. An exotic, almost romantic, energy inhabits the mother's performance as she dances, undermining her decorum, and destroying the very syntax of the sentence: "Over the Oriental prayer rugs, through the Persia forests of hemp, away and away" (30).

In **"Wedding Day,"** Boyle reveals the hidden violence of the social contract and releases the energy of exposure to work on the forms of prose. At the same time, she does not wholly cast the mother as executioner, the daughter as victim. Rather, she exposes the sacrificial violence of the wedding itself, and the relentless secularity of its bourgeois forms. Boyle resists a "women's writing" which would trap her in an oppositional category identified with the bourgeoisie; she neither endorses nor combats but rather eludes capture in the mother's forms.

Boyle's elusiveness produces an unsettling. She is always in favor of something which illuminates the landscape with significance—call it love, something which bends the narrative plot away from its resolutions, which turns the eye inescapably to the detail, apparently decorative, but now repeating anaphorically the interestedness of the subject who writes. These are stories not about isolated selves but about the mutual imbrications of relationships among people, and so they do not disguise the complexity of perspectives which our feelings for each other are likely to generate.

Even a story as purely focused as **"On the Run"** shows the contrary motions of resolution coming up against one another and that language of significance

breaking closures, keeping the time itself open. The situation is close to autobiography: two lovers, like Boyle herself with Ernest Walsh, are wandering across the south of Europe, unable to find a place for the sick man to rest—thrown out of hotels because he is dying. In **"On the Run,"** memory is left permeable—fragile, undecided, unpunctuated, determined only by the universal timelessness of death that thus seems everywhere. David Daiches says that Boyle's stories are like parables, with "a special kind of permanence" about them.[10] In our culture, this sense of permanence may be identified with women's time, appearing as a contrary narrative that works across the linear, historical plot. This is especially visible in **"On the Run,"** where the history is known, and the story exists nevertheless not in a past but in a recurring present, like a parable.

The young couple must deal with a woman who orders them to leave rather than helping them. It is not just a person but social convention itself which opposes them. The proprietress of the hotel is, in fact, in mourning. She seems to know all about death:

> Bereaved in the full sallow of her cheeks bereaved and the tombstones rising politely polished with discreet sorrow bereaved and remembered with bubbles of jet frosted on her bosoms and mourned under waves of hemmed watered crepe. I have mourned people for years and years this is the way it is done.
>
> (105)

She seems also to possess a kind of knowledge about religious conventions of sacrifice: there was her "rosary hanging like false teeth," and "the Christ bled with artistry" on her crucifix. But her knowledge has all been projected onto the objects, reduced and transformed to fetishes. So what she says is: "Your husband cannot die here . . . we are not prepared for death" (106). Here is the terrible irony, that the sick man must keep on going. Like the mother in **"Wedding Day,"** the proprietress does not seem to know what women are supposed to hold in custody: the value of relationship, the cycles of time, of the generations, of biological time. And like the mother, she has translated all of it into the social symbolic.

Thus women's time must return through the narrative of the story. Boyle's writing stops the forward pressing of historical time, like the train stopped at "Saint-Andre-les-Alpes," and sidetracks it into sensuous, loaded detail: "As the train stopped a soft pink tide of pigs rose out of the stationyard and ran in under the wheels of the wagon. The crest of little alps was burning across the roofs of the town, with the dry crumbling linger of the church lifted and the sky gaping white and hot upon decay" (103). She strips the sick man's words of their history to let them fly out as if prophetic, repeated, stripping them even of punctuation: "Get her out of here he said I am going to cough Christ is this where the death will get me take the cigaret and when I cough walk around the room and sing or something so they won't hear me" (104). There is no period after his words.

The conflict with the proprietress does not appear as a single plot with a conclusion but as the anaphoric structure of enduring betrayal. The message of betrayal is repeated three times, each introduced by the phrase "The bonne came back to say." It is a sacramental structure. At the end, too, the man's words seem to escape the symbolic conventions of the story and sound in the mind like stream of consciousness, recurring. This is anamnesis, a resurrection of the past and not just memory: "Keep on keep on keep on he said maybe I'm going to bleed" (107). Such a resurrection takes place in the process of a narrative dialectic between the linear time of history that is past and the personal time of remembrance, anamnesis. Anamnesis is the form of recollection which Plato associated with eros—and with access to eternal truth. It is the word for the "remembrance" of Christian communion. And it is the unforgetting of the past which Freud advocated, the healing memory of pain which psychoanalysis could effect. This time which Boyle produces is associated, as well, with what Julia Kristeva calls "women's time."

This resurrection—and not just recollection—of a moment of pain and love inserts difference into the history. The position of difference which we may associate with women's time here is different from the polarized opposition which some of Boyle's characters, like the mother and the proprietress, seem to inhabit. This alternate version of narrative, with its descriptive intensity overwhelming the forward movement of plot, opens language up to the surreal, the hallucinatory. Narrative time gives way to descriptive space.

The energy is not in the story, or the forward movement of plot, but rather in the metaphorical connections among people and places—in relationship. Even though these connections shift and develop through time, so that it looks as though there is an elaboration of plot, the motive force of the story is not erotic in the masculine mode. That is, the displacement of desire does not take the form of an adventure. The energy here is moral, even if the situations are unconventional.

Let us look a little more closely at this descriptive language which so many of Boyle's readers have noted—which Margaret Atwood cites as one of her most strik-

ing attributes.[11] Sandra Whipple Spanier associates it on the one hand with a Joycean project and on the other with the romantic perspective in Boyle: she "depicts the external world as a reflection or projection of the perceiver's consciousness."[12] Like Joyce, Boyle writes a "lyric" novel, which decenters the lyric subjectivity, the image of an ego. Boyle opens language to the pressure of the unspeakable; her words are saturated with the residues of what cannot be said but can be mutually felt. In doing this, she changes the way we might think about the so-called pathetic fallacy.

Boyle rewrites the romantic reflexivity, shattering the mirror relationship of self and nature under the pressure of a point of view that flows everywhere and comes from no single or stationary ego, or subjectivity. In this, she eludes the very categories of romantic, unified selfhood, of the "true and false appearances" with which Ruskin had thought through his influential critique of the "pathetic fallacy."[13] Ruskin, let us recall, had argued that it is "only the second order of poets" who delight in the kind of description produced by violent feeling, a "falseness in all our impressions of external things" which "fancies a life" in foam or leaf instead of maintaining distinctions. Ruskin's "great poet" masters feeling:

> But it is still a grander condition when the intellect also rises, till it is strong enough to assert its rule against, or together with, the utmost efforts of the passions; and the whole man stands in an iron glow, white hot, perhaps, but still strong, and in no wise evaporating; even if he melts, losing none of his weight.[14]

The whole man arises in the imaginary as if forged in the steel mills, the image of reason. This nineteenth-century vision of the strong ego, the rational individual, has retained its heavy influence in twentieth-century criticism, visible in the work of critics such as John Crowe Ransom and Yvor Winters, and visible in the great fear of a "sentimental" softening which permeates criticism.

Boyle's practice, like Joyce's, breaks open this paranoid logic of the subject. In the place of individual heroic figures, she has the multiple connections of relationships; against the center of a linear plot she brings a counternarrative to bear. Words do not simply mirror subjects; the luminosity of her language tracks the energy of a freed desire to make connections. Hers is the logic of a poetic revolution which makes room for the woman, as for others. In this it is not simply experimental, and indeed, the chief characteristics I have observed here are to be found, in slightly different forms, in her later, apparently more conventional work.

Boyle works to rewrite the extreme imagination of reason which erases woman from the place of the subject or installs her as the singular Other of male discourse. Hers is instead a lyric refiguring of the story which produces more multiple possibilities. It might simply be called the logic of sympathy.

Freud introduces the sentimental into the heart of rational discourse, and that is the formula of modernism, but he also strengthens the rhetoric of countersentimentality, which forbade not only happy endings but also love stories. Boyle's fiction allows this anamnesis of the sentimental to overwhelm the tragic plot, so that her insistent interruption of forgetting produces a certain politics of solidarity not with family ideology but with women's lives.

The struggle of narratives appears in fiction by men and by women. Ernest Hemingway's *A Farewell to Arms* is like much fiction written in the painful aftermath of World War I, seized by the desire for some kind of return to human relationships. As Sandra Spanier has convincingly argued, critics have lost sight of the context of Hemingway's work. Catherine has the qualities Hemingway most admired, attributes usually associated with his male heroes.[15] Her death because of childbirth in the novel should not, then, be attributed to a cynicism about love on the part of Hemingway. The novel is an example not of countersentimentality but of the increasing impossibility felt by writers of producing an anamnesis of love and of maternal themes which would not be contained by a more tragic plot: it is an example of Hemingway's sentimentality. And it is an example of the deep longing to escape the tragic plot which would permeate modernism from Proust's *madeleine* to Eliot's rose garden, and emerge as the dominant chord of postmodernism, whether as carnival or as nostalgia.

This struggle with love and desire appears in literature at the time when the efficiency of the machinery for regulating and organizing human labor had been ratcheted up several notches, first by the military in the war, and then by the Taylorization of industry and the invention of the assembly line. As the forces of work become more and more demanding, it becomes increasingly important that work contradicts the domestic plot which it pretends to support—work drives the family underground. That is, the separation from the maternal leads to not a *paternal* role but a rejection of the whole enterprise—the father absents himself, and the family, not just the woman, is repressed. The military attitude was surely no more antifemale than the industrial, though the military has been more forthright about its stance: "If we wanted you to have a wife, we'd have issued you one" was a Marine Corps commonplace as late as the war in Vietnam.

The important place of irony in modernist literature is related to this repression of the domestic. The wife that used to make it all possible is now a hindrance;

technology takes over the wifely work, as Barbara Ehrenreich and Deirdre English have detailed in *For Her Own Good.*[16] Sandra Gilbert has argued that women's culture and men's culture separated dramatically before the 1920s because of the First World War, when women found themselves newly powerful and men found themselves disillusioned.[17] Paul Fussell's *The Great War and Modern Memory* greatly influenced Gilbert's notion of the war's impact.[18] He argues that the horror-filled and nightmarish experience of the infantryman grounds a sense of reality which patriotic optimism denied. Irony is the only possible point of view. Gilbert goes on to conclude that women's experience was excluded from a literature with such assumptions. But our ability to read even Hemingway is severely affected as well.

The dialectic of love and tragedy, the personal and the public which generated male modernism hardened into a critical party line which excluded not only women but attitudes that seemed feminine, or sentimental. Fussell, says Ian Hamilton in a 1989 review of his book on World War II, is so driven by his own terrible years as an infantryman in World War II that he rejects all but the ironic stance and "his hostility to America's 'unironic' temper, to its earnestness and sentimentality, is of such depth and ferocity that it leads him to over-value almost any piece of writing that is not actively soporific or mendacious."[19] This suggests that, while Fussell has helped us to interpret modernism, it is because he represents the modernist attitude, and the obsession with the repetition of military horror which reproduces it. The ironic stance is thus more than irony; in the form of this horror it has seized the imaginary and come to seem the only credible stance for the whole of this century's literature.

Yet neither Freud's sense of tragedy nor the postwar bitterness of disillusionment provides an alternative to the overdetermination of a single narrative plot and the domination of an image of separation and loss extended as linear time. And even though the story seems to entail growing up to face reality, it involves denial of the human bonds which situate the maternal real. It is a plot writers have struggled to rewrite, and the struggle between irony and American sentimentality does not belong to women writers alone. The dominance of a thematized irony has meant exploring alternatives to the alienated individual who spins off into war and into the free-market economy, free as well from any complicated or novel-length human connections. The pain of these explorations surfaces as the recollection of feeling in style. In that respect, Kay Boyle is both innovative and paradigmatic in her writing. Her attention to the issues of women places her closer to the borders of the problem. Far from giving us the sentimental as an escapism, she makes us recognize how a love story might be closest to the real problem.

III

The "revolution of the word" appears to precipitate a crisis of the family by rejecting domestic claims along with domestic, genteel fiction. Thus the themes of free love appear and reappear, and challenges to the old codes of a social Puritanism make up an important part of what seems revolutionary, from Emma Goldman through Henry Miller. D. H. Lawrence and James Joyce both celebrate sexuality at the same time that they open up family structures to intensities of disequilibrium, so that the carnivalesque of style which undermines conventional prose also undermines conventions of sexuality and family relations. The family order of mothers, fathers, daughters, sons seems not the origin of emotional freedom but the very structure which oppresses. Freud's narrative sequence dominates narrative form, directing plot toward separation. At the same time, the family romance provides the fictional matrix, so that the more the discourse is about escaping the maternal, the more it is contained by the maternality thus conjured, which operates as an unconscious eternal return of the same. The conflicts generated by this internalizing of narrative mark modernist fiction and modernist life with extreme violence.

Writing inside this extremity, Kay Boyle nonetheless seems to discover a style which opens up the crises of the family. That is, she puts the sentimental narrative back into play, not as a mode of mastering the plot and rescuing it for family values but as a discourse which softens and disputes the forms of revolution. Nothing, at the end, could be more like having it all than the multiplicity of loves for which she manages to find a place. Yet this protean inventiveness is not quite comic; it has, in fact, its own irony. She does not deny violence and pain, and she resists the narrative closures which might provide a contemplative or satirical distance.

The first pair of novels she published operate like a counterpoint opening up the impossibilities of love in a culture dominated by bourgeois manipulations. The descriptive voice—speaking the American speech as Williams heard it, as an empirical, democratic voice which believes in perception—establishes a strangeness relative to its setting in European bourgeois culture. This descriptive empiricism separates patriarchy from the ordinary American observer. In *Plagued by the Nightingale* and *Year before Last,* Boyle writes the kind of closely observed love story that a French sensibility might recognize, but this does not mean that

the style is European, not at all. The negativity and questioning evoked by the revolution of the word are directed against the European patriarchal orthodoxy instead of the middle-class gentility of American culture, where, Boyle claims, it is merely derivative and translated.[20] Thus Boyle's modernist critique of the domestic and the genteel is very different from that of Eliot or Pound, who are critical of American culture but, like James as well, identify with European conservative attitudes.

Furthermore, the narrator representing the ordinary American free individual is a woman. Such a point of view is already well connected to themes of feminism, independence, and even free love in American literary traditions, and after Daisy Miller and Edna St. Vincent Millay, readers may have almost expected Boyle to present such a female narrator. But Boyle separates her critique of the bourgeois family from the conventions of free love, with its rebellions against the connectedness of individuals and its unholy alliance with Mill's rationalistic feminism. This sensuous narrative voice lodges its critique in the body, the figure, the symptom—not accepting the family romance in any of its formulas. The narrator rebels against the bourgeois family's manipulative economy, for example, by deciding to do exactly what the family apparently desires: have a baby. There is no retreat from the sexuality of the maternal.

In *Plagued by the Nightingale* Boyle critiques a classic French bourgeois family. Two newlyweds arrive for a summer with the family and find themselves trapped, Nicolas the victim of the family's disease, and both without escape from its "safe" imprisonment. Family imperatives are diseased, crippling in themselves, and parallel the crippling illness imposed by the family genes on the young husband. The new American wife, Bridget, who tries to learn both French and the family language, finds herself at odds even with her husband, who fights and is ever more entangled.

European patriarchy constructs domesticity as a feminine world, "a world of women who lived without avarice or despise . . . a woman's world built strongly about the men's fortune and the men's fortitude" (69), and Maman's forceful management extends to the village, where she organizes the people to fight a fire. It is the men who have the disease, who act like children—Jean, with his fortune, is forever dissolving in tears—but it is the men, too, who police the bourgeois standards: there is "Papa's intense feeling about immoral literature" and Oncle Robert, who presses past Maman's defenses to discover the glass ring left on her cabinet, and leaves a judgmental remark with the others about Bridget's earrings. Nicolas feels the disease is the family's, that they never should have had him knowing the crippling heritage, that they are responsible for him now. His rage is murderous— "imagine the joy of slowly killing Maman . . . ripping Papa up the middle!" (50)—but the family's desire is always for more children, for babies, and the family desire is inexorable.

The story is told from the point of view of Bridget, who does not speak French and who comes from an American family which let its members go off as individuals. Thus the book is written as if outside language and culture, in objects and gestures and places, without judgments. The bourgeois feminine world is "strange." Bridget enters it first to last as a body, as the object of the family gaze and the design for more babies. When she goes for a swim, her legs are bare, but the others cover themselves in bathing dresses, and Bridget sees Annick, the daughter who would be a nun, look at her with "half-revulsion for her exposed legs and arms" (13). She is a female body, the object of reproductive desire but also of revulsion.

The family plots revolve around the family's own reproduction. Charlotte has married the first cousin, Jean, brought his fortune next door, and produced five children. The three girls—Annick, Marthe, Julie—are in long-term pursuit of the young doctor, Luc, who visits each year and seems ready to be ensnared by the family. And Nicolas has brought home the American bride, who must now produce a child. The men's control of the fortune is all directed toward managing the family's reproductive will. Papa promises fifty thousand francs to the couple if they have a child, while Jean and Oncle Robert refuse to lend them any money to make an escape. If it is a feminine world, the women's only power rests in maintaining themselves in this time of reproduction, apart from history and change. When Charlotte's body becomes repulsive in her last pregnancy, as she grows more horribly sick, her breath foul, her tongue white and swollen, her revolting body confined to her dark bedroom, the family's ruthlessness becomes more apparent: they delay the necessary surgery too long and she dies. The woman is the sacrificial body, and woman's work is having children.

What Bridget's American point of view brings to this family plot is not a male alternative—not escape, not adventure. Instead she finds some mutual attraction and encourages Luc's resistance until he decides not to marry into the family: "What was the nightingale's small liberty to the deep wide exemption she had given Luc, she thought" (334). She agrees with Nicolas, that she brought him back to "the heart of his family and now it is up to me to get him out" (211). She listens without denial to his proposals that she have a child

with another man, to avoid the disease. At last she resolves to have a child. Whether Nicolas will be the father is left decidedly open. Thus the reproductive realm of "women's time" comes to operate not as the defining center of the bourgeois family but as a maternal irony that recognizes the family's deadly exploitation of Charlotte's body—and Bridget's enduring ability to escape family regulation altogether by the freedom to make love with someone else. This maternal, female irony is not the utopian vision of total escape associated with advocates of free love—it is the irony always available to the oppressed, to colonized, domesticated peoples (including America) as to women.

As the novels work out the implications of sensuous style on an external scale, on the level of culture as well as experience, one of the chief consequences is that style works to elaborate a borderline individuality, not isolated but rather metaphorically related to others, to place, and to context, woven into the tapestry. The experimentalism in linguistic point of view that crosses boundaries and denies isolation works not only in Boyle's early stories, where condensation and stream of consciousness make the form private, intense, and lyrical. Comparing the short story **"On the Run"** with her second novel, *Year before Last*—written after the death of Ernest Walsh—may suggest how the shift from internal to external focus operates.

The scene represented in **"On the Run"** appears again in *Year before Last,* greatly changed. Instead of concentrating all the times when hotels rejected the dying man into a single, symbolic moment, the scene is one added chapter in a painful series. The novel externalizes the private experience, extending it across many spaces: the northern town, the southern chateau, the restaurants, train stations, hotels, Saint-André, St. Jean-les-Pins. The question is not whether Hannah and Martin will love each other—there is no courtship, only consequences. Nor is it whether or not he will die: he is living on a pension, on externally funded time. He has, in a sense, already been killed in the war:

> There's nothing to me, said Martin. I'm not here at all. My boots were found on a tree-top, sticking up to scare the crows from their direction. My clothes, he said, and he touched his cloak, are now hung on a peg and stuffed with straw to make them human. Touch me, Lady Vanta, said Martin softly leaning forward. Touch me. That was the night I died.
>
> (182)

What changes as the story develops is, instead, the relationship with the other woman, the relationship between Hannah and Eve (was she always already other?). It is not allegorically simple; the two women are like sisters, rivals, and like mother-daughter. Eve is a difficult, strong—and "virginal"—woman who owns the magazine which Martin is at work editing. "But there was Eve as well, between them there on their first morning together: the woman who could go to prison for a thing. . . . She was a brave woman, thought Hannah" (5).

The question between the women is whether the erotic young love of Hannah and Martin has any moral force. Hannah has left her husband, Dilly, to be with Martin, and Martin's alliance with Hannah has caused Eve to leave him, withdrawing not only her financial support but also her magazine.

> Now if I were a brave and a simple woman, thought Hannah . . . I would see sin and virtue and be able to distinguish between them. I only believe in sin when I see the fury on Eve's face, and I must be the sinner. When I see the look she has now with him I know there can be no virtue in having come between these two.
>
> (67)

The two women are reconciled at the end, at the scene of Martin's death: "Hannah, Hannah, my darling, Eve cried out like a woman gone mad. Hannah, will you save him! Can you save him, Hannah, Hannah, my lamb?" (219). The women seem to occupy two points of a Freudian family triangle. This is not to argue, however, that Eve represents the maternal and Hannah the erotic in a straightforward psychological allegory: Hannah cares for Martin as she did for her husband in a motherly way, starching the collars of his shirts, administering his medicines. Eve, on the other hand, is cruel and jealous and flirtatious.

Nonetheless, the elements of plot are a familiar triangle: they are the endlessly recombining elements of the family drama, and like the soap opera, they have no necessary conclusion but death. That is, the forms that structure this work are continuous with the forms that structure the texts of mass culture—the best sellers and romances for women as well as the soaps.

That does not mean that we should be critical of such forms. Like the experimental structure of the short stories, the relational plot lets Boyle overthrow the hero-centered formula of fiction. Tania Modleski's argument in *Loving with a Vengeance* for the interest of women's mass culture texts will perhaps help us to carry on this discussion in a way that continues to take these forms seriously.[21] That women's plots are easy to recognize should not make them any more trivial than masculine plots with more action and less moral agonizing. Modleski suggests that the pleasure women take in the soap opera might be something feminists would want to build on rather than reject, because the apparent limitlessness of the text has the

effect of "decentering" the classic (masculine) heroic self or ego: "soap operas may not be an entirely negative influence on the viewer; they may also have the force of a *negation,* a negation of the typical (and masculine) modes of pleasure in our society" (105).

I am arguing as well that another kind of plot needs to be put into dialectical relationship with the linear plot of action and adventure. In *Year before Last,* Boyle writes a love story, refusing to make it carry some other significance about the tragedy of desire. Words, almost a good in themselves like the colors aroused by paint or the light of perception, take up the energy of a desire for connection. Another kind of temporality is installed. Boyle's style performs the drama, making precise the metaphorical nature of subjectivity. Thus objects—like words—become acts: they dramatize not only the self but the way the self connects to others, to the world. Take, for example, Eve's dresses:

> She had taken a room on the other side of the hall. And there were her frocks shaking out on their hangers. Five pairs of elegant shoes were out of her bags already and set along the wall, waiting, with their toes turned in. Waiting for tangoes, waiting for rhumbas, waiting till Martin could go stepping out again. I've been taking dancing lessons to fill in the time.
>
> The time, said Eve and the word gaped wide before them.
>
> (209)

It is as if the motive force for action were not lodged in a singular "I" but rather was dispersed into all the environment. The point is to resist "the time" of inexorable death. The law of cause and effect seems beside the point, and morality is not a matter of rules and consequences. But the acts of individuals are not wholly irrational either; they take place as a function of context, as a matter of what can be described rather than analyzed. *Year before Last* coheres around the intensity of lost love, and the tragedy that not heroism but the loss of a connectedness brings. The metaphor of relationship proves to be the figure of a moral law.

Boyle's early fiction seems experimental but not political, and as her later fiction becomes less experimental, it also seems more involved in the context of history, more firmly embedded in historical time. Superficially, her career seems to follow an evolution of writing away from the personal and toward more public forms. But this is misleading. Contrary to this appearance, her early work already establishes the basic moral principle, the metaphor of intersubjectivity. Furthermore, I believe that her later work becomes more difficult and less accessible in a way that is significant for feminism. As the novels become "clearer," and more clearly lodged in a sense of political history that defies dominant positions, they also become more rhetorically challenging to familiar (family) ideologies of human relationship and more clearly *different* from familiar male narratives.

Boyle's soft revolution defies convention by describing the intensity of relationships that should not be "interesting," like the relationships of women to one another, or that should not be seen sympathetically, like the love of an American woman for a Nazi doctor in *Death of a Man,* or the pain of a prisoner of war returning to Germany in *Generation without Farewell.* She does not give us predictable American attitudes or relationships. Jaeger, the protagonist of *Generation without Farewell,* is a man who identifies with women. But more than that, couldn't we say that the narrator, winking at us over the heads of these characters, is a woman? Nancy Miller's *The Heroine's Text* explored how male narrators looked at the reader through the texts of their heroines, so that the story is still governed by a male exchange.[22] It would be interesting if we could show that Boyle institutes a female narrator who does the same. But if so, how do we explain this femininity in a narrator looking into a phallogocentric culture? Isn't this move out of the hands of the author?

Boyle works this by identifying her female narrators with other oppressed subjects and subjects of colonization. Jaeger, displaced, is a returned German prisoner of war, working in ersatz-wool clothes and secondhand shoes, identifying with the Jews and with the resistance. And is the female narrator, looking past him at her readers, not in a similar position? The character who at once represents his German culture and yet resists it resembles the American Kay Boyle, and the resistance of women. Thus there is an exploration of the complexities of complicity, of loss of power, of subversion. But this figure—Jaeger—is a difficult hero. Who is to identify with him? What reader will be able to read such a point of view? When Boyle lodges subversion in this kind of resistance, a negativity which depends upon the response of readers, and does not direct it, she makes her text vulnerable to the other readings of history which surround her. And indeed, she has suffered.

Boyle is a modernist writer, but not in the mainstream of American modernism. Description in her work is different from both journalistic reporting of historical events and a certain line of modernist metafiction. In her work description is infused by an ideology of democratic appeal—call it sentimentality—which *represents* the problem of the feminine, thematizes it. Yet her description also problematizes the woman in language at the level of the signifier, forcing language back upon itself into internal reflection and disrupting

its paternal functioning. Alice Jardine's comparison of American and French writers can perhaps help to clarify Boyle's position. In *Gynesis,* Jardine argues that modernity operates differently for the two traditions.

> The American interpretive response to twentieth-century crises in legitimation has not been one of exploding paternal identity, concepts, and narrative to get at their feminine core, through a rearrangement of *techne* and *physis,* a radical rearrangement of gender. . . . The writing subject and his sentence both remain integral unto themselves—and very male—by shoring up textual barriers against the "Nature" that threatens them (Burrough's "virus") or by deriding and dismembering that body, which, if explored, would disturb their satire as technique (Barthelme's Mother and Julie). . . . [The American version of *gynesis*] seems to exist here only at the level of *representation.*
>
> (236)[23]

But, as Jardine points out, the insertion of female voices into this dichotomy reveals new possibilities for feminists to take advantage of the interrogations modernity has inaugurated. Boyle's work identifies the narrator with other suppressed voices—challenging male modernity at the level of representation—and at the same time puts the gendered subject under question at the level of the signifier, a practice which differentiates her work from American modern and postmodern texts. What Jardine means by "modernity" begins with the period which includes American modernism but is really most of all what we call postmodern. Boyle needs to be seen within this cosmopolitan modernity, as a writer who has written after modernism from the beginning, and a writer who has directed European sensibilities and American speech to a practice American interpreters cannot quite recognize, inserting the question of the woman into *style.* Nonetheless, the confusion or even the disregard of Boyle's readers may signal for us how difficult such work must be, and how the revolution of modernism has not finished.

In a speech titled "Writers in Metaphysical Revolt," Boyle tries to specify the nature of the literary revolution of which she was a part. It is democratic. It involves putting the voice of the people into writing. She sees herself, like William Carlos Williams, like William Faulkner, as part of a particularly American project: "There was . . . before the twenties, no lively, wholly American, grandly experimental, and furiously disrespectful school of writing, so we had to invent that school" (3). American culture, however, is not necessarily receptive to the disrespectful, especially when the woman furiously subverts the panaceas of family respectability. What Boyle submits to the experimental cauldron of her prose is the most threatening of cultural forms, the very plot of the family romance.

Forty years after those novels of the late twenties and early thirties, Boyle wrote a closely autobiographical novel from inside the events of the late sixties in San Francisco: the protests against the Vietnam War, the jailing of protesters, the concurrent struggle for civil rights engaging black Americans, and the darkness of the Hell's Angels and the cult of Charlie Manson. *The Underground Woman* thematizes a politics grounded in personal attachments and confronts the pain of a family order which comes apart on the level of representation. Boyle might well remind us here of Emma Goldman's voice telling of the same descent into the other world of prisons, outrage fueled by the same maternal sympathy. The political is personal. "Believe that our separate lives are of no importance? . . . Is anybody ever prepared for that? Isn't that the thing they always forgot to make convincing in church or school or whenever we asked for advice?" (55). And the fiction is rhetorical, filled with argument for a moral stance. By its overt advocacy it is kin to Harriet Beecher Stowe and the old traditions of women's prose. Its appeals are sentimental. It is hard to read, and for different reasons than *The Waste Land* was hard.

In *The Underground Woman,* Boyle tells the horror story of a mother whose daughter is taken away by a cult, juxtaposed with the more public story of the woman's protests against Vietnam. Athena, the Kay Boyle character in the book, is a professor of mythology—an interpreter of ideologies, not a writer. The members of the cult invade Athena's house, propelled by the fury of "Pete the Redeemer" who had declared, "I hate the world, and I'll hate it until it's completely destroyed" (119). There are different orders of destruction in the book: the cancer that killed Athena's husband, the cult that takes her daughter, the government that goes on with the war. But Athena is not propelled by hate. The mother's solidarity with another protesting mother, Calliope (Joan Baez's mother was the model), is absolutely dependent on their moral commitments. When they go for a climb up Angel Island on a free day, they find disengagement from the antiwar effort very difficult, almost immoral.

> "This is the one day in our lives we can have away from everyone!"
>
> "We can start by rejoicing that we're free" and at once the shadow of guilt fell on their hearts.
>
> (257)

The guilty freedom seems escapist. Deer follow them, and Boyle turns to one of the most conventional of sentimental emblems to express the commitments that mobilize their fellow feeling. In spite of the two women's shared experiences in jail, in the free pleasures of

the hike there is a veil between them. "Yet if one of these deer, just one, should be felled by an illicit hunter, Athena pictured how she and Calliope would turn as one person, inseparable in its passionate defense" (259).

Is this use of sentimental rhetoric something we should criticize in Boyle? A sort of need for irony may be generated in us by these emotional appeals, even though they ground the argument through history for all humanitarian appeals. As readers, we are well trained in modernism. It is extremely difficult to talk about a feminine rhetorical *tradition* as "sentimental" which connects the political fiction of Boyle to the political autobiography of Emma Goldman without seeming to denigrate both writers. The tradition comes into view always already discounted. And yet Boyle's appeal is to a convention so familiar that postwar Americans would think of it as the "Bambi" appeal—this is public rhetoric, not a less accessible literary imagery. Boyle extends the pain and love of experiences between mother and daughter, man and wife, woman and woman, across the limits of family into the politics of protest against the war. This fiction is rhetorical. We have great difficulty reading this kind of work. Boyle herself thought it had problems. We have been brainwashed by antifeminist constraints to think of it in literary terms that narrow and reduce literature itself.

And what appears strongly in *The Underground Woman* is the solidarity of women in the very scene of oppression. In the jail they learn to question the isolation of individuals: "they were learning that night that they were not, and had never been, a hundred women lying on their cots in the dark, isolated, and thus lost, in their own identities, women now who were neither black nor white nor Chicano, but all with interchangeable skins. The attack upon one girl in the darkness of her cell was an attack on their flesh . . ." (113). At the same time, no social form can be adequate to the revolution, and the potential for evil influence is great. In spite of Pete the Redeemer's promises, "the commune was not for an instant a revolutionary place," and "the redemption he offers is fame and fortune, these words of promise given his followers like a Bank of America card or a Master-Charge plate" (116). Freedom finds its act in resistance to the story, "there isn't any *story*" (184).

The plot of the book moves from one form of imprisonment—the jailing of protesters—to another—the malign influence of the commune—and returns to another jailing. There is no progress. Martha, an alcoholic prisoner who hoped to reform, returns at the same time as the protesters, with her eye black, her face a "wreck." The conclusion is a return, not only to the "barren walls" of jail but to the recognitions of personal loves and personal losses: "Sybil and Paula would write, but Melanie and Rory were gone forever, somewhere far, far away. *Oh, reality, hold me close, hold me close* the underground woman asked in silence of the barren walls" (264).

The "reality" which Boyle as underground woman here faces is configured as the bare walls of jail. This "reality" is metaphorically connected to the reality of oppressive state societies addressed by a literature of subversion since Dostoyevsky's *Notes from the Underground.* The prison metaphor is also a fact of life, a part of contemporary history which Boyle recalls in her essay on her imprisonment, "Report from Lockup." She sees a connection between the unfortunate women she finds in prison and twentieth-century history, from the prison memoirs of Emma Goldman's old friend Alexander Berkman, to the Birdman of Alcatraz, the Chinese once imprisoned on Angel Island, and the Native Americans who took Alcatraz back for a time. Imprisonment is a feminist tradition: she cites Alice Paul (whom her mother had brought home to lunch) and Doris Stevens's report of the force-feeding of Paul in a psychiatric ward.[24] The prison metaphor is a modern matrix, calling up a kind of new mythology. The new commonplaces of twentieth-century literature are these scenes of violence and despair, in prisons, in confrontations with the police. In *The Underground Woman,* Boyle invokes these images and at the same time she juxtaposes them to the other set of commonplaces, the interior scenes of family relations, the domestic, the sentimental. She finds the violence at home. *Home.* The horror stories of European culture are relocated inside American institutions and inside the experience of the ordinary American individual—that is, of course, inside the woman.

IV

The solidarity of women in Kay Boyle comes out of family feeling but also defies the family romance. Boyle makes us see the alternatives within canonical modernism—she is, or ought to be, part of the modernist canon. She practices the revolution of the word in a way that should be visible from a postmodern point of view. She writes, that is, in full recognition of both the possibilities of style and a need to recuperate love as the final metaphor, the best subversion. She allows the antiplot to emerge into rhetoric only in later works, particularly in *The Underground Woman* and then explicitly in essays. But she maintains the political commitments that the modernist revolution seemed to imply in the beginning. Her childhood experience with feminism joins with a perspective about the place of the intellectual that most American modernists shared with Europeans in the time of the expatriates:

It is *always* the intellectuals, however we may shrink from the chilling sound of that word, and, above all, it is *always* the writers who must bear the full weight of moral responsibility. Frenchmen will tell you that the decision to speak out is the vocation and life-long peril by which the intellectual must live. . . . American intellectuals . . . prepared and oriented our revolution: the only revolution in history . . . which did not destroy the intellectuals who had prepared it, but which carried them to power.

(190)

This resistance to the fatalities of irony is not an anti-modernism. It is inherent in modernism as part of the struggle—the sentimental *within* modernism: what, in fact, makes the literature so powerful. Boyle's relationship to modernism is that of a second generation which has really absorbed the implications of the first. Like young women growing up right now, seventy years later, Boyle heard *Tender Buttons* from her feminist mother. The family in Boyle is divided into a patriarchal order of violence and oppression—or failure—and a maternal order of subversive pleasure and morality. In her essay **"The Family,"** Boyle describes her extraordinary mother, who was responsible for her most important education and introduced her not only to the words of Stein but to a virtual honor roll of the revolution:

George Moore, Dreiser, Shaw, Isadora Duncan, Caruso, Roman Rolland, George Santayana, Oswald Garrison Villard, Mary Garden, James Joyce, John Cooper Powys, Alice Paul, Alfred Stieglitz, Norman Angell, Susan B. Anthony, Mozart, Upton Sinclair, Margaret Anderson, Jane Heap, Bach, Eugene Debs, Jules Massenet, Cezanne, Monet, Picasso. . . .

(6)

Her mother was in fact friends with some: Alice Paul, Alfred Stieglitz, Mary Garden, John Cooper Powys. Boyle attributes her mother's involvements to simple human motives such as "her wish to help a beautiful and talented young woman," Marie Lawall, on whose behalf her mother contacted Mary Garden. But the mother's knowledge is mysterious.

I do not know how . . . she realized it was important to take me to the Armory Show in New York in 1913 to see Marcel Duchamps' "Nude Descending a Staircase" and Brancusi's "Mlle. Pogany" and his "Bird in Space." . . . Isolated as Mother was from the literary scene, I also cannot explain her understanding of the urgent need to send word of support to Margaret Anderson, who was threatened with arrest for publishing in the *Little Review* chapters of Joyce's banned *Ulysses.*

(8)

But it was probably the very isolation of women that propelled her, "an unending loneliness."

The first experience Boyle had of the solidarity of women was with the alliance of her mother and herself against the men in the family, an alliance connected specifically with the modernist revolution:

> It was difficult to speak at the dinner table at night of the acts of moral courage achieved by total strangers, inasmuch as the men of the family spoke of more familiar things. It was because of instances such as these that Mother and I became part of a conspiracy of silence and discretion, one that involved a great many people, some of whom lived in other countries, a conspiracy to bring to life another reality in which one could put one's faith and it would never be betrayed.
>
> (8)

The "moral courage" to present "another reality" is joined to social action: "There was another complicity in her life, and that was her covert alliance with the underprivileged, the lost, the poor" (8). In Boyle's mother, as in Boyle's fiction, the revolution of the word is joined to a moral revolution, a conspiracy on behalf of "another reality."

Boyle's modernism implies a political practice. In her 1947 essay **"Farewell to New York,"** she remains critical of writers who failed to support the Spanish struggle against Franco in 1939: "if I feel guilt . . . it is because there are writers and poets to whom the invitation to speak was given, a long time ago, and they gave their answers" (76). She cites Pound, Evelyn Waugh, and T. S. Eliot. In 1953, she wrote **"Farewell to Europe,"** juxtaposing the voices of Europeans who counseled staying away from an America transfixed by McCarthyism, and her decision to return: "This is one of the times in history when one must go back and speak out with those of the other America clearly and loudly enough so that even Europe will hear" (98). This reflects her conviction that it is an American voice, an American speech, which is revolutionary. Nothing about the disillusionment of the twenties challenged that assumption so violently as the McCarthyism of the fifties must have done. Boyle and her husband, Joseph Franckenstein, were victims, the subjects of a loyalty hearing. The *New Yorker* dropped Boyle as a writer. Her writing was blacklisted—for a decade she could not publish anywhere. If she spoke for the "other America," that voice was indeed not to be allowed.

If we read Boyle as a daughter of feminism and modernism, we will begin to understand the particularly contemporary complexity of her project. At the same time that she rejects patriarchy, she asserts continuity with women; at the same time that she destroys narrative continuities, she softly moves to enlarge the province of sensuous perception so that the perception itself is imbued with emotion and the experience of commitment. These are texts like a body of pleasure but also an embodiment of moral perspective, texts like Emma Goldman.

Boyle is one modernist who does not revolt against the maternal tradition, whose maternal tradition *is* modernism and the promise of moral progress. She is in the lineage of strong women such as Emma Goldman and Gertrude Stein. She reminds us that there is such a lineage. She is decidedly not in the lineage of submissive women who subsume their own moral certitudes to the "realities" of jails and Mastercards or to the masters of the house. Boyle's work upsets the hierarchical order and reminds us again and again of women's time as a space of freedom and love.

In *The Underground Woman,* Boyle violates the sense of direction implied by Freudian narratives. She deplores the isolation of individuals, she sees the loss of her daughter as tragic, and she claims that bonds of compassion are the foundation of political action. The book is not about justice, or violations of law or even of principle. It advocates a return to the maternal enclosure of human relationship—even though this solidarity has to be located within the barren walls of prison. This is not, in other words, the substitution of a woman's story leading to togetherness instead of the male story leading to separation; it is a recollection of another order which ruptures the story and stops the movement of separation, which drives language itself to turn aside. That opening up of language to the pressure of emotion is both modernist and womanly.

Whether or not a writing which practices this kind of revolution may be powerful enough to work larger changes in literary culture remains, however, an open question. This writer offers us an artistic practice which can say things that could not be said otherwise. As her readers, it is up to us now to find ways to speak about Kay Boyle's words and the revolution of the woman.

Notes

1. For an account, see Sandra Whipple Spanier, *Kay Boyle: Artist and Activist* (Carbondale and Edwardsville: Southern Illinois UP, 1986) 25-26.

2. Kay Boyle, *Words That Must Somehow Be Said,* ed. Elizabeth S. Bell (San Francisco: North Point Press, 1985) 31-34.

3. For a convincing discussion of Boyle's experimental writing, her collection of stories in *Wedding Day and Other Stories,* and her contribution to the "revolution of the word," see Spanier, *Kay Boyle* 30-56.

4. These stories appear in *Wedding Day and Other Stories* (New York: Jonathan Cape and Harrison Smith, 1930). "Episode" and "Wedding Day" also appear in *Fifty Stories* (New York: Doubleday, 1980), and "On the Run" was reprinted in the spe-

cial issue on Kay Boyle of *Twentieth Century Literature* (Fall 1988). References are to the most recent editions.

5. This essay, published originally in French as "Le temps des femmes" in *33/44: Cahiers de recherche des sciences des textes et documents,* no. 5 (Winter 1979), first appeared in English, translated by Alice Jardine and Harry Blake, in *Signs: Journal of Women in Culture and Society* 7 (1981), and has been reprinted a number of times. My references are to the text in *The Kristeva Reader,* ed. Toril Moi (New York: Columbia UP, 1986) 187-213.

6. Julia Kristeva, *Revolution in Poetic Language,* trans. Margaret Waller (New York: Columbia UP, 1984).

7. Catharine R. Stimpson, "Stein and the Transposition of Gender," *The Poetics of Gender,* ed. Nancy Miller (New York: Columbia UP, 1986) 2.

8. "Women's Time" 199.

9. She writes in "The Family," in *Words That Must Somehow Be Said,* that her own grandmother was a strong woman who worked in the Land Grant Division of the federal government and lived a life of independence: "I knew she ran, and danced, and sang before the horses in the beginning of the day because she wasn't afraid of the Indians or of anything else in life" (23). Boyle does not know "where Grandma Evans had found the courage to leave Kansas and a grandfather I was never to see and to move with her two young daughters to Washington D.C." (23).

10. In the Introduction to Boyle, *Fifty Stories* 14.

11. See Atwood's introduction to Boyle's *Three Short Novels* (New York: Penguin, 1982) ix.

12. *Kay Boyle* 36.

13. See John Ruskin, "Of the Pathetic Fallacy," *Critical Theory since Plato,* ed. Hazard Adams (New York: Harcourt Brace Jovanovich, 1971).

14. "Pathetic Fallacy" 619.

15. Spanier's argument about Catherine as a heroic figure is set out in "Catherine Barkley and the Hemingway Code: Ritual and Survival in *A Farewell to Arms,*" *Modern Critical Interpretations: "A Farewell to Arms,"* ed. Harold Bloom (New Haven and New York: Chelsea House, 1987) 131-48. Spanier goes on in another article to situate the novel in the context of the aftermath of the Great War, and to argue that critical interpretations have often missed the significance of love and the personal to Hemingway in that novel because they have lost sight of the context: "Hemingway's Unknown Soldier: Catherine Barkley, the Critics, and the Great War," *New Essays on "A Farewell to Arms,"* ed. Scott Donaldson (Cambridge: Cambridge UP, forthcoming 1990).

16. Barbara Ehrenreich and Deirdre English, *For Her Own Good: 150 Years of the Experts' Advice to Women* (Garden City: Anchor Books, 1979).

17. Sandra Gilbert, "Soldier's Heart: Literary Men, Literary Women, and the Great War," *Signs* 8.3 (Spring 1983): 422-50.

18. Paul Fussell, *The Great War and Modern Memory* (London and New York: Oxford UP, 1975).

19. *London Review of Books* (September 28, 1989): 6.

20. See the speech "Writers in Metaphysical Revolt," *Proceedings of the Conference of College Teachers of English of Texas* 36 (September 1971): 6-12.

21. Tania Modleski, *Loving with a Vengeance: Mass-Produced Fantasies for Women* (New York: Methuen, 1982).

22. Nancy Miller, *The Heroine's Text: Readings in the French and English Novel, 1722-1782* (New York: Columbia UP, 1980).

23. Alice Jardine, *Gynesis: Configurations of Woman and Modernity* (Ithaca: Cornell UP, 1985).

24. An elaboration of the subject of imprisonment appears in "A Day on Alcatraz with the Indians," "The Crime of Attica," and "Report from Lockup," *Words That Must Somehow Be Said* 104-51.

Elizabeth S. Bell (essay date 1992)

SOURCE: Bell, Elizabeth S. "Part I." In *Kay Boyle: A Study of the Short Fiction,* pp. 3-85. New York: Twayne Publishers, 1992.

[*In the following excerpt, Bell assesses Boyle's major short stories and novellas, contending that the author was a revolutionary literary stylist.*]

INTRODUCTION

As a young writer, Kay Boyle experimented with the English language in ways that are evident in both the form and content of her short fiction. Ignoring many of the conventions deemed sacrosanct by the literary establishment, she wrote stories that detailed little more than the nuances of a relationship or the thought process that would lead to action taking place after the story's conclusion or offstage, beyond the reader's sphere of knowledge. The terms that had traditionally defined narrative—rising action, climax, denoue-ment—held no meaning in Boyle's early fiction, for she was shaping language with the same technical vir-tuosity other artists were using on clay, bronze, and metal.

In many ways, Kay Boyle's sensibility was informed by the avant-garde concepts with which Europe was brimming in the early decades of the century. When she was 11 her mother took her to New York City to see the 1913 Armory Show, at which Marcel Duch-amp's *Nude Descending the Staircase* caused an up-roar by flouting the established ideas of what consti-tuted art. Her mother also read to her the works of Gertrude Stein and counted the photographer Alfred Stieglitz as a personal friend. After moving from her native Minnesota to New York in 1922, Boyle became associated with *Broom* magazine and was put in close contact with some of the founders of American mod-ernism: Marianne Moore, William Carlos Williams, Lola Ridge. Her association a few years later with Ernest Walsh of *This Quarter;* Maria and Eugene Jo-las of *transition,* Robert McAlmon of Contact Press, and Harry and Caresse Crosby of Black Sun Press led her into the heart of the European/American artistic revolution of the decade. Boyle was alive to the eclec-tic and electric currents sweeping the artistic commu-nity. Her contributions and promise as a young writer received the praise of writers and critics alike.

Boyle drew heavily and unself-consciously from her personal experience in writing her fiction. She probed her responses to situations as private as abortion and as public as divorce; she recorded in courageous detail her liaison with the dying Ernest Walsh. She wrote of damaged relationships, the sense of rootlessness, hu-man perfidy, and the hope of human love. The 1920s were heady times both for a generation trying to find itself and for Boyle herself. Intensely traumatic, these years shaped her perception and response to the hu-man condition and thus established the direction of her literary work.

By the 1930s, Boyle had earned a reputation as a pre-mier stylist and was establishing a relatively reward-ing private life. Her relationship with the unpredict-able Bohemian Laurence Vail provided her the opportunity to enter another facet of the avant-garde world. She met Samuel Beckett and Marcel Duchamp, personal friends for life; Duchamp, in fact, was godfa-ther to one of her children. As she traveled through Europe with Vail and six children—one of hers, three of theirs, and two of his—Boyle wrote and published an astonishing array of novels, stories, poems, and es-says. She was published in the most prestigious and popular magazines and by respected and established publishing houses. She received two Guggenheim fel-lowships and such coveted awards as the O. Henry Memorial Award and the Edward J. O'Brien Award.

During these years Boyle witnessed firsthand the forces at work throughout the Continent creating rifts between nations, classes, races, and generations that led to the outbreak of war in 1939. To the intensely personal subject matter of her earlier works, Boyle be-gan adding the more outwardly focused issues of in-ternational affairs. Still not overtly political in the early 1930s, Boyle's works translated these larger is-sues into the realm of individual lives and human con-sequences. She continued to write from her personal experience but learned to draw on the influences of the outside world. Thus, from the mid-1930s, Boyle began her tireless exploration of the human face be-hind national and international political movements. She had found the subject matter that would engage all genres of her writing for the rest of her life.

Her marriage to Vail ended, in fact, at least partially because of this matter, for he believed the artist had no quarrel and no concern with politics. Boyle found this position untenable, and as the 1930s drew to a close, so did her marriage to Vail. With Joseph Franck-enstein, whom she married in 1943, Boyle launched a life of political and human rights involvement that ex-tended from war-torn Europe to the draft boards of California, from foreign correspondent work for the *New Yorker* to organizational work for Amnesty Inter-national.

During the 20 years of their marriage, Boyle and Franckenstein lived a very public life, finding them-selves often in the forefront of public action. Such was the case in the 1950s as they spent nearly a de-cade fighting the hysteria of the McCarthy era witch hunts and the resulting blacklist that robbed Joseph of his career and kept Boyle from attaining the publish-ing exposure she deserved. These years changed the direction of Boyle's professional life, for realizing that their personal difficulties were but symptoms of a far larger national danger, she focused her work more di-rectly on the social and human rights ills of contempo-rary society. Although she had always touched on these issues in her writing, her approach now became more visible, partially because she more overtly politicized her fiction and partially because she developed her tal-ents as an outspoken essayist. In the 1960s, 1970s, and 1980s, much of Boyle's most eloquent writing takes form as essays and extended pieces of nonfiction writing, on such subjects as Vietnam and worldwide civil rights violations. She has spoken on virtually all of the major issues of the twentieth century.

Boyle has seen the world change. She has recorded her insights and perceptions with the consummate de-votion and skill of the writer. Her craft developed both technically and thematically as her life experiences took her on strange journeys. Her growing body of admirers have watched as she perfected new techniques or adopted new themes or explored again the deep recesses of the human spirit. Yet, in the midst of these changes, we also find the familiar, for Boyle returns to some of the same themes throughout her writing career.

These familiars, however, bear witness to Boyle's changing approach to life. As she lived her life, learning and maturing, stretching the parameters of her experience, her outlook of necessity transformed her message as writer. Thus, although she touches again and again on certain ideas, she does so with a freshness born of her connection to the volatile spirit of the twentieth century. She does not shrink from exploration of the major issues of our world, as the following examples illustrate.

Boyle was among the few white writers who dealt directly with racism in the early half of the century. Several of her stories revolve around the issue, but as the century aged, Boyle's patience with injustice waned. Thus, the later stories—**"Home"** (1951), **"The Lost"** (1952), and **"One Sunny Morning"** (1965)—project a much different outlook from the early ones, **"Black Boy"** (1932) and **"White as Snow"** (1933), for example. While Boyle portrays the injustice of racism in personal terms in the early stories, they ultimately express a form of impotence that was all too realistic in the 1930s when they were written. In **"Black Boy"** the title character, the only black person in the story, finds his dreams unobtainable and his acts of human kindness misinterpreted by the unofficial arbiter of society's mores. The grandfather strikes him in the face for carrying the injured granddaughter home. The title character ends the story speechless, with no recourse, no way to redress the situation. Likewise, in **"White as Snow"** Boyle shows an even more damning side of racism. Carrie, the black nursemaid for the vacationing English family, wants desperately to appear white; she uses heavy layers of light powder on her face and hopes the sun will straighten her hair. She chafes under the restrictions of Jim Crow. As understandable as this denial of her heritage might have been in the 1930s, it marks the depth of damage racism can cause in its victims. Damage to the spirit cannot be measured solely against the victim, however. For in this story, a young white aristocrat, Adamic, well known in the area, finds himself attracted to Carrie, but he is unwilling to break society's racial taboos. He courts Carrie, but only as long as no one else notices. When they do, he abandons her. Adamic's prevarication and cowardice reveal his own weakness, his own fear of societal censure. He, too, has been damaged by the role he has adopted. His racism per-

haps is worse than that of the grandfather in **"Black Boy,"** for Adamic bears the stamp of his craving for approval, even if his personal wishes differ. At worst, he willingly jettisons any conception of personal integrity in his relationship with Carrie and with himself, all for the shallow rewards of societal acceptance. Boyle portrays the injustices and the personal costs, but in the 1930s she could not realistically offer any solutions.

By the 1950s, however, Boyle was projecting a more active response to racism. Her black characters no longer want to appear white; they want only the dignity and respect due human beings. In addition, they respond through the channels open to them to the racist attitudes they encounter. **"The Lost"** points out the inhumane and far-reaching implications of racism and race's irrelevance in issues universally human. Both this story and **"Home"** demonstrate that the particulars of racial discrimination can be extremely local, for black soldiers in Europe pose no threat in the minds of Europeans. They live with a dignity and respect denied them "at home." In **"The Lost"** and **"Home"** the men have recourse—they can take action, they can work toward their goals—unlike the boy or Carrie in Boyle's earlier stories. In the 20 ensuing years, at least action had become possible, if not yet particularly effective. In **"One Sunny Morning,"** Boyle posits a corrective for racism—the individual acts of well-meaning people. These personal acts—acts such as those the earlier Adamic was unwilling to undertake—can dispel the power of racism.

These thematic changes reflect the ever-so-slow progress of the human spirit and Boyle's awareness of it. All of these stories appeared before the massive restructuring of American society in the late 1960s. If Boyle's stories seem timid today, it is only because of the great strides made during the decade following the latest of these stories. At the time, Boyle's voice was one of the most strident and poetic to be raised in both fiction and nonfiction against the racial injustices of American society. Her essays of the period continue in more direct fashion the battle she launches in her short stories.

As Boyle matured as a writer and gained experience as a mother, she developed a profound concern for children, asking often in her fiction the unstated questions: "What will happen to them; who will care for the children; what kind of world will we leave for them?" Sometimes Boyle allows her narratives to be told through the personae of children, for their voices can say things adults hesitate to face about such issues as racism, neglect, dishonesty, and lack of courage. Always maintaining the child's innocence and naïveté in these stories, Boyle magnifies the emotional impact of these topics through the simple ploy of having the child describe events he or she does not understand. The child does not know the labels to apply to what he or she has witnessed, but merely feels the emotions locked inside. The reader, however, views the events with a much more critical eye; he or she knows the labels and makes judgments in broader terms than those the children can understand.

In later stories, peopled much more frequently with children, Boyle portrays both children who are betrayed by the adult world (**"Ballet of Central Park," "The Lost,"** and **"Winter Night"**) and those who speak with wisdom far beyond their years (**"Should Be Considered Extremely Dangerous"**). Often, she spotlights the parent-child relationship in her stories, frequently—especially in *The Smoking Mountain* (1951) and *Nothing ever Breaks Except the Heart* (1966)—father and son bonds. She always strives to protect the children, or—as she says in **"The Ballet of Central Park"**—to save them. In them she sees both the literal future and the metaphorical health of society. She voices a warning that we need to be concerned about the fate we hand our children before it is too late. Boyle calls for a society that cares for its children, all of them, regardless of age or gender or race.

. . . . .

DEPARTURES AND ENDINGS: *WEDDING DAY AND OTHER STORIES*

"Wedding Day" and Other Stories was published in 1930 at the end of a period of great instability for Kay Boyle. In the preceding five years, as she wrote and reworked her stories, publishing several of them, she divorced her husband, lost her lover to tuberculosis, bore a child out of wedlock, joined and escaped a communal artists' colony, and kidnapped her own child from that colony. Boyle openly portrayed these events in her novels *Plagued by the Nightingale* (1931), *Year before Last* (1932), and *My Next Bride* (1934), in addition to several of her short stories, some of which served as studies for the novels.[1]

By 1930, Boyle had met Laurence Vail, who was to be her husband for the next decade, and had begun collecting her stories and working on her novels. From the chaos and personal anguish of her recent past, she was entering what was to be one of her most productive decades. During the 1930s, she produced her three most praised collections of stories, four novels, and a book of poetry in addition to the uncollected pieces of writing she regularly published.

Seven of the stories in *"Wedding Day" and Other Stories* had been published the previous year at the request of Caresse Crosby as *Short Stories* in an ex-

tremely limited edition by the Crosbys' Black Sun Press. The six new stories Boyle added for the more commercial *"Wedding Day" and Other Stories,* published in 1930 in New York by Jonathan Cape and Harrison Smith, include the title story, as well as **"Episode in the Life of an Ancestor,"** which as homage to her Grandmother Evans was one of Boyle's favorites. The English edition, published in London by Pharos Editions, appeared in 1932. The stories in *"Wedding Day" and Other Stories* are, therefore, both remnants of her personal past and portents of her future stylistic innovations, for Boyle explored in them the various kinds of closures and stopping places she had experienced in her life. To do so, she used her style and form in experimental ways, some of which she subsequently abandoned and some of which became part of her canon.

Critical response to the collection was generally very favorable, praising Boyle's style and inventiveness while at the same time prodding her to explore more substantive issues. Very little agreement exists, however, on which of the stories are the best. Helen Moran, writing for the *London Mercury,* comments favorably on the "sharp clarity and crisp beauty" of **"Life of an Ancestor"** and the "controlled strength and disarming simplicity" of **"Letter of a Lady."**[2] In the *Nation,* Gerald Sykes, even as he calls for Boyle to root her fiction in something substantive, finds **"Life of an Ancestor"** and **"Summer"** to "mark the highest stage of her development,"[3] while E. B. C. Jones of the *Adelphi* spotlights **"On the Run"** as a "poignant trifle" and **"Letters of a Lady"** as "delightful."[4] Katherine Ann Porter, however, praises the entire collection even as she indicates the stories are uneven. Basing her opinion on the stories and on Boyle's previously published novel, *Plagued by the Nightingale,* Porter recognizes that Boyle "is part of the most important literary movement of her time."[5] In fact, Porter sees in Boyle the virtual embodiment of that movement, for Porter credits her with spirit, courage, vitality: "her own attitude and idiom, a violently dedicated search for the meanings and methods of art" (Porter, 279). Earlier in *transition,* William Carlos Williams also offers Boyle his own version of high praise in a somewhat rambling and quarrelsome critique of her writing. He finds in Boyle the best in American writing, trailing—as he explains it—hints of forest and wilderness, but he decries what he believes to be the American habit of ignoring those who produce its highest accomplishments. He fears this fate for Boyle.[6] Thus this first major volume of Boyle's short stories captured the attention of reviewers who found much promise in its pages, and it was recognized by writers who were Boyle's contemporaries as an exciting collection of fiction.

SAYING GOOD-BYE

As a collection, *"Wedding Day" and Other Stories* explores the many faces of leave-taking. Three of the stories deal with the separation of parent and child, two with the dissolution of other relationships within a family, six with the severing of love or romantic relationships, one with the loss of one's dreams, and the other with social ostracism. Boyle approaches her themes, however, from different perspectives, making each piece of fiction an unpredictable tour de force.

The title story of the collection demonstrates Boyle's use of the unexpected. She bases the story on the wedding of Laurence Vail's sister Clothilde, but she transforms a family occurrence into something quite different. In **"Wedding Day"** she completely reverses the usual marriage theme; instead of the joy and union of two lovers, her story chronicles the sadness and separation of a brother and sister on the sister's wedding day. This wedding clearly marks the dissolution of a valued relationship, the nature of which is at best ambiguous, for Boyle hints at an incestuous attraction between the siblings. In a scene containing a beautifully sensuous description of the two walking in the April wind, their "yellow manes" of hair "turning them shaggy as lions,"[7] Boyle declares that they could have started a new race, so magnificent were they. Moving as a refrain throughout the story the brother reiterates his pained plea to the sister to abandon her marriage plans: "It's not too late." While she does not respond, she conveys as well as he the mood of sadness that pervades the story. Even after the ceremony, the two, who recognize the wedding as "the end, the end they thought," share "hearts sobbing like ring-doves" (33). Yet, despite the paralleled sadness they feel, the possibility of canceling the sister's wedding never even appears as a real option.

The mother, too, shares mixed feelings about the wedding. While she prays the ceremony will "pass off with dignity," she admits her daughter's choice of husband-to-be appalls her. She refuses to pass along the family's prized copper saucepans as a wedding present, but nevertheless clearly wants the wedding to proceed without incident. She fears her son's behavior at the ceremony. When he does nothing more than dance with a silver tray over his head and scatter the calling cards placed on it, the mother realizes with relief that the celebration will be peaceful enough: "What a real success, what a *real* success" (35). The disturbing undercurrents that sustain the story do not erupt.

Ironically, Boyle has divorced the concept of wedding from that of marriage, for the story remains fixated on the ceremony itself. The husband-to-be is totally un-

important to the story, so much so that he never appears. He remains faceless and nameless. Nor is there any suggestion of future plans or of the kind of life the wedding couple will share tomorrow, all the tomorrows of their lives. With so much ambivalence about this wedding from everyone involved, the reader is forced to ask why it must take place at all. Boyle declines to answer and, thus, creates the tension of the story. Its very uncertainty and the deliberate refusal to provide explanatory details increase the impact of the story by recreating a fragmentary glimpse into the events of one day in the life of a family about which the reader will never know more. It becomes, thus, a "slice of reality" for the reader to ponder.

Among the earliest previously published stories in this collection, **"Theme"** (1927) touches tangentially on one of the subthemes in **"Wedding Day,"** for it deals with the departure of an adult son from his mother's home. Unlike stories of this type told from the adult child's point of view, with rebellion and breaking of bonds as primary themes, Boyle chooses the mother's perspective and explores through her personality the contradictory emotions that arise. The themes that emerge subtly differ from those one might expect; Boyle deals in this story with abandonment more than rebellion, with stifling isolation more than the breaking of bonds. She creates a picture of a complex relationship that has different realities for each of the parties in it, for it is a relationship completely devoid of communication.

During the day the mother pretends conversation with her son, who is away. She fears the mirror, for she sees herself not as the ideal mother, but as someone ugly. Through this ploy, Boyle emphasizes the mother's discomfort with reality. When the son comes home at night, the mother remains silent, unable to communicate with him as she had in her fantasies. In response to the son's declaration that he is moving to Chicago, the mother wants to tell him she will survive. Instead, she tells him she is an old woman and asks him how she will be able to survive if left alone. She follows him to Chicago, beseeching him to return with her, but he turns on her in bitterness: "'You never wanted a son,' he said to her. He saw her face ugly with crying." Her response is poignant in its insufficiency but clearly communicates to the reader the mother's realization of the extent of her estrangement from the son: "'Yes, yes,' she said. 'Yes, I wanted a son.'" (44).

Boyle uses the repetition of thematic motifs to underscore the underlying tone of the story. She plays, for example, with the pun involved in the mother's repeated desire to be a "slavic [Slavic] mother," a concept romanticized by the mother as meaning no existence beyond slavish motherhood. Boyle contrasts the mother's desire with her behavior, which belies her ability to live such a life. This kind of irony becomes the pivot on which the story turns. On a more sophisticated level, the works of George Moore and Chekhov act as a motif throughout the story, with Boyle telling the reader the mother can no longer read Moore "because of what had happened in her heart" (37). The mother can no longer read of families in disrepair and disruption; Moore and Chekhov write of situations too close to her own emotions. The delicacy of Boyle's touch in creating this motif signals the promise more fully developed in her later, more mature, style. Instead of belaboring her point, she relies on the reader's sense of language and knowledge of Moore and Chekhov to fully reveal the complexities of her theme.

Boyle enlarges her exploration of the growing apart of parents and adult children in what is one of her favorite stories from this collection and her first story to win inclusion in Edward J. O'Brien's "Roll of Honor" for best short stories of 1931. **"Episode in the Life of an Ancestor,"** based loosely on the relationship of Boyle's grandmother to her father in nineteenth-century Kansas, focuses on the communication gap that exists between the young female protagonist (called "the grandmother") and her widowed father. Although the character of the young woman is the focus of the story, Boyle shifts attention from the young woman's consciousness to that of the father, for through his mind the reader constructs an image of the vital and strong young woman the father cannot understand. From him the reader learns the issues of conflict between them. He wants a traditional feminine life for her, fears for her the premature loss of her virginity, imagines scenarios in which her actions cause her harm, and reacts with the anger of a father unable to deal with his adult child's choices.

In this story, Boyle experiments with narrative form, for in contrast to traditional plot lines, her story ends at the point at which the conflict becomes manifest, the point at which the father and daughter confront each other. The story, then, consists of assembling pieces of a puzzle that—long after the story on the page is over—must be fitted together. The action of the story, if action is defined as the working out of conflict, takes place "offstage" long after the reader has been dismissed.

Boyle also experiments with narrative voice, adding yet another consciousness to the story to contrast the father's perspective. Boyle takes the reader into the consciousness of the horse that carries the grandmother across the Kansas prairie on long nocturnal rides. Through the instinctive reactions of the horse to the young woman, the reader gains a more positive recognition of the spirit of the young woman than the father can possibly relay. Thus, Boyle uses the unexpected perspective of the horse to balance the judgment of the father about the young woman. This story, which Boyle envisioned as an homage to her grandmother's strength and courage, is the only one from this collection selected for publication in Boyle's *Thirty Stories* (1946).

"Polar Bears and Others," perhaps the most successful story in the collection, previously appeared in *transition* (1927) and later in a collection of stories, *23 transition Stories* edited by Eugene Jolas and Robert Sage (New York, W. V. McKee, 1929). The story begins with the description of polar bears in a zoo. The tone is laborious, emphasizing the contrast between the bears' life in the wild and their new redefined and limited life in the confines of the zoo: "The polar bears came slowly, slowly. . . . They came with their prejudiced bodies and their jaws gaping out for fish in empty water" (67). Even though they may want the old life, they must live in the new. Boyle then compares the bears to "people who live in small countries and who go out of them with their small grudges strapped to their backs" (67). At this point, the reader realizes the depiction of the bears serves as a frame device, as the analogy that leads into the real story. On another level, the people from small countries become yet another analogy for the situation that provides the main energy and focus of the narrative: the growing apart of the narrator and her lover, the necessary trading of the old way of life for a new one that is much less comfortable.

Through the consciousness of the narrator, Boyle explores the process by which the narrator realizes she and her lover are in different stages of their relationship: he is becoming restless and wants to move on to other relationships; she still clings to him emotionally and fails to prepare for his loss. As she watches him—"gentle, a lover of flowers and vegetables and also of young women"—in the garden working with the plants, she contrasts her old confidence that other women didn't matter because "they stood on the edge of him and saw no deeper than the reflection of their own faces" (69) with her new realization that he is thinking of someone else as he works with the soil and roots. She becomes, she tells us, afraid of this unnamed, faceless, perhaps imaginary woman who occupies his mind in the private solitude he has established. After the fear comes another emotion, for she finds herself bitter at his perfidy: "Yes, yes, the heart knoweth that for a little while I was something carried in his wrists and I fell drop by drop from him until his blood was clean of me" (70). But after the bitterness, the narrator comes to the realization that her love for him is not permanent either and that when she no longer loves him, she will "be off without a thought for him" (72).

The lover, perhaps from guilt, postpones his trip to visit his new love in Havre. The narrator, looking from the window as he works in the garden, calls to him to go, for she knows her time will come also. Boyle suggests a touch of surprise in the narrator's appraisal of her own behavior. The narrator begins to understand through her own actions that one does not know how one becomes a changed person until it happens.

Thus, during the course of the story, the characters' positions change dramatically. At the beginning of her story, the narrator is the one who wants to hold on to her lover; by the end of the story, she urges him to leave. He, on the other hand, begins the story already having left her emotionally; he ends the story hesitating to leave physically. Boyle charts the course of their changing emotional outlook through circumstantial means: never in the lover's consciousness, the reader must make from his actions assumptions about his perspective and his motives, always seen at a distance and through the perceptions of the narrator. Conversely, the reader sees very little action on the part of the narrator, but must surmise the course of actions the narrator will take from what she reveals of her thoughts and feelings.

REVOLUTION OF WORDS

Six of the thirteen stories in this collection previously appeared in *transition* between 1927 and 1929. During these years, Boyle was familiar with the workings of *transition* and with the ideas about contemporary language and literature promulgated by its editor, Eugene Jolas. He felt strongly that the traditional language of literature could no longer contain the reality of life in the early twentieth century. As a result, in the combined sixteenth and seventeenth issues of *transition,* published in 1929, Jolas and 15 other writers including Kay Boyle signed "The Revolution of the Word Proclamation," which called for an end to what they described as banality, monotony, stasis, and naturalism. The proclamation gave the writer the right to "disintegrate the primal matter of words imposed on him by text-books and dictionaries," to fashion his own words and to "disregard existing grammatical and syntactical laws." Its final two provisos stipulated that ". . . the writer expresses. He does not communicate," and ". . . the plain reader be damned." Under Jolas's guidance, *transition* established itself as a haven for unconventional writers, especially surrealists and the Jolas-led vertigralists, an offshoot of the surrealists. Their writing deviated in almost every conceivable way from conventional prose or poetry.

While Kay Boyle signed the proclamation and agreed with its general intent to revitalize literary language,

her writing did not typically adhere to the principles outlined, especially the last two, which struck at the heart of her storytelling talents. Boyle freely experimented with narrative form and with some of the conventions of punctuation, particularly of dialogue, but she seldom distorted language to the extent that communication with the reader became secondary. Two stories in *"Wedding Day" and Other Stories* prove exceptions to this rule and serve to demonstrate both the influence of Jolas and the point at which Boyle diverged from the experimental writing of her immediate circle of colleagues.

"Spring Morning," originally published in *Short Stories* in 1929, highly surreal and fragmented, appears to deal with death as a form of leave-taking. It contains two predominant, but unsustained, strands of images: that of art (canvas, Cézanne, photographed faces) and that of death (rotting corpses, holding the nose "from the smell of Pruter rotting and still above sod a lively feeding ground" [101]). Yet the lack of connection between or among images diffuses their individual effect. Thus the sketch contains no images that startle, none that communicate beyond creating a sense of pain and chaos. Its clearest reference comes at the end, with the narrative voice in a near soliloquy addressing the reader: "This I would never escape or find words to whisper / *I have waited so badly I have waited but so badly I have waited so badly I have waited so badly for you what are you going to do.*" The sketch conveys a mixture of emotions, a confusion of sights, sounds, odors. The turmoil it invokes is mirrored in the pattern of the prose. In short, the sketch works most effectively as a mood piece, but cannot—perhaps does not intend to—sustain either mood or involvement.

Its companion piece, **"Vacation-Time,"** published originally in *transition* in 1928, combines the rudiments of plot as a frame for the stream of consciousness that makes up the interior of the story. The train has left and the narrator has tears making mascara run down her face, for she has sent her young child away for the season. She goes for comfort to a bar where she meets a man she knows. They binge on drink and cocaine, falling into a kind of pseudoreality. Merged sentences and fragments, jumbled images, interweave with a refrain from her companion: "cocaine ringing like hell in my head." Repeated several times throughout the story, this refrain keeps her companion from hearing or, indeed, having to hear the narrator's anguish, her fear her child will not feel loved. She goes home to beat her fists against her mirror, only to hold onto it because it contains a human face. She lies with her "arms around the mirror soothing the sad old face that was crying in the glass" (96). Again, the story creates the mood of anguish and despair, of the narrator's inability to deal with loss, but her equal inability to prevent it either. Thus, the title of the story provides an ironic counterpoint to the mood it creates.

A third story, more narrative than the other two, joins the periphery of this group, for it contains some passages of stream of consciousness used very effectively. Published previously in *transition* (1929) and developing themes Boyle would later explore in *Year before Last* (1932), **"On the Run"** chronicles the plight of a young couple made outcasts by society's fear of the man's tuberculosis. As the story begins, the two find lodging in a hotel in Saint-André-les-Alpes. The man, with forced bravado, tries to hide his condition by ordering hearty, heavy food, but the look of death shadowed him, for the servants all seem to know this and to withdraw from him. The protagonist, meanwhile, must face the proprietor, herself a widow, who tells her they must leave: "'Your husband cannot die here,' she said, 'we are not prepared for death'" (106). Against the fear and decisiveness of the proprietor, the protagonist reacts with anger, turning against the town and their harshness to a human being in mortal need; she tries to protect her lover by telling him not to worry, for they can easily find better accommodations than this hotel. His reaction, on the other hand, implies the long-term price of his illness: "This time I am afraid to go on" (107). As he begins coughing, he urges the protagonist to sing, to cover up the noise of his attack: "Keep on keep on keep on he said maybe I'm going to bleed" (107). These words end the story, and fittingly enough, they have no end punctuation, for the situation facing the young couple is chronic. They will continue their odyssey, looking for a resting place, a place to call home until at last they are met by the death that shadows them.

Here, and in similar passages, Boyle's use of the stream-of-consciousness technique serves well to convey the panic and desperation the man feels as his illness becomes too public. In this story, Boyle contrasts emotional responses that transform fear: first the townspeople's fear of death turns to rejection and lack of compassion; then the protagonist's fear for her lover becomes anger at the ostracism they must face; finally, his fear of both death and rejection becomes bravado that dissolves into panic. Based obviously on her experiences with Ernest Walsh, this story differs from others in the collection in its approach to leave-taking. The undercurrent of violence—expressed as anger and as the uncontrollable coughing of the young man—envelops the conclusion, yet presents also the occasion for courage under pressure, displayed by the young woman's willingness to sing in the face of her lover's approaching death and their mutual homelessness.

Significantly, Boyle did not develop stream of consciousness or surrealism as major elements of her writ-

ing beyond the late 1920s. As she grew as a writer, she worked instead on other elements of language, shown clearly even in the early stories contained in this collection. She consistently tried to create fresh images and metaphors, producing a contemporary version of the seventeenth-century metaphysical conceit. In addition, she pared narrative to its bare bones, reducing plot to an afterthought or an irrelevancy. She told stories from unexpected angles and through unexpected voices. She recreated the passions and pains of her own life in fictional forms, establishing as her hallmark the autobiographical connection.

A STUDY OF CHARACTER: *"THE FIRST LOVER"*
AND OTHER STORIES

Boyle dedicated her second collection of short stories, *"The First Lover" and Other Stories* (1933), to Eugene Jolas, "who wrote 'Follow the voice that booms in the deepest / dream, deeper go, always deeper.'" This dedication pays tribute to the artistic and personal debt Boyle felt she owed Jolas and which she gladly tried to repay. Yet, even as she penned the tribute, she had grown in her own directions and matured as writer.

The collection arose from a period of travel and a measure of domestic stability Boyle had not experienced for almost a decade. Its stories were written largely between an earlier period of intense personal struggle and a yet-to-come period of intense international disruption. Even so, the volume addresses potentially explosive issues, such as emotional abuse, gender identity, racial prejudice, and poverty. It received mixed reviews when first published. Many reviewers noted the collection was uneven, with stories of startling power next to stories that lacked depth and virtuosity. Yet even the negative reviewers, such as Desmond Hawkins writing for *Criterion* (1938), saw the ineffective stories as aberrations, as artifacts not of the quality one usually associated with Kay Boyle's short fiction.[8] Even the less successful stories, few in number, present stylistic eloquences of startling beauty, although as some reviewers pointed out, their techniques and devices are sometimes excessive and artificial. The reviewers seem in agreement, however, that at her best, Boyle's stories verge on "pure poetry."[9] As a group, however, critics largely ignored the issues she raised in her stories. By the early 1930s, Kay Boyle was virtually always described as a stylist; in fact, the words "her Boyle style" were self-explanatory to those who knew her writing.

In *"The First Lover" and Other Stories* her style is paramount, for Boyle creates a series of character studies remarkable for their economy of detail and for their sharp, clear focus. In this collection, Boyle strips her characters to their essential elements, usually choosing even to forgo naming them in order that their actions or, most frequently, their thoughts serve alone to define them. Settings are minimal, as is plot, for Boyle again focuses on the interior of her characters. She experiments with narrative form, her trademark, but does not let her innovations interfere with her role of storyteller throughout the collection.

Among the more extreme—and successful—examples of these techniques in the volume is the story **"Three Little Men,"** in reality a triptych of character sketches. Divided into three sections, the story provides an unspecified narrator's description of "him." The reader has no indication of the narrators' gender or even whether the narrators of the separate sections are different people or the same. Indeed, the interior monologues of the narrators are given no context. Each section, however, explores a different kind of relationship between the narrator and the man spotlighted in the section. A quotation from *Through the Looking-Glass* establishes a perspective the reader holds for the story's duration: "I'm very brave generally, he went on in a low voice: only to-day I happen to have a headache." The quotation suggests the theme that ties the three sections of the story together—courage and its absence, especially in social interaction—and each section reveals a different element of the comparison.

The first section is told by the narrator about his or her father, a man seemingly desperate for love. The narrator finds pitiful some of the lengths to which he goes, but on discovering the torn fragments of a love note to "Mary" written at the narrator's desk by the father, the narrator's pity turns to anger at the "pale flowers" of his passion.[10] The narrator concludes that the father, somewhat like a hooded falcon, abdicates his feelings by refusing to engage with the world around him.

The second section, addressed to "A.C.," presents the narrator and a writer who engage in literary discussions. The writer reads to the narrator from a story he has written of love and of a girl with "Chinese blue eyes" (66), but the narrator finds no passion in it. At the writer's revelation that the story is personal and based on a real event, he and the narrator change the topic. Yet the narrator finds they do not communicate, for as much as the narrator would like to offer passion to the writer, the narrator finds no corresponding capacity to receive it in the writer.

The third and final section, for "G.M.," concerns the narrator and a priest who hates religion because he feels it destroys all that sustains life. He does not read, for he finds ideas stale. Instead he reveres art, but not aesthetics. His advice to the narrator is to avoid strong feeling, whether it be anger or love or determination. The narrator, on the other hand, sees art as the form that contains "the torrent of man's belief" (69) and, in recognizing the priest's avoidance of the possibility of passion, considers him barren and sterile.

Although they represent different roles—father, writer, priest (father of another kind)—all three men fear passion in any form and have arranged their lives to protect themselves from it. As the various narrators decide, these men lack the courage to really live. Unlike many of Boyle's stories, this one contains a resolution of sorts, but only a highly fragmented one. At the end of each section, the narrator draws conclusions and makes value judgments about the choices taken by the man in the segment. Thus, Boyle presents a resolution of internal realizations, but not of external action or circumstance. She presents the reader with negative definitions: This is what lack of courage is like.

HISTORICAL SETTING

Boyle continues the theme of courage in its many facets throughout the collection with stories containing varying degrees of detail about character or setting. While she rarely names her protagonists, she frequently provides more information about them than she did in **"Three Little Men."** The title piece of the collection, **"The First Lover,"** reprinted in both the *O. Henry Award Stories of 1932* and Edward J. O'Brien's "Roll of Honor" for *The Best Short Stories of 1932,* provides more background information, especially in historical setting, while it continues Boyle's exploration of the meaning of courage in personal relationships.

Set in an opulent hotel, which serves as counterbalance to an austere and vanquished post-World War I Germany, the story explores the relationships of three sisters, the daughters of Professor Albatross, who have been sent to the hotel on holiday and who are attracted to the same young Englishman. His world has not been as circumscribed as theirs; he takes his relative affluence for granted, but in a way the sisters envy this. As they fantasize about their possible relationships with him, the oldest of the sisters creates a new scenario for her life. She will intrigue the Englishman with tales of their prosperity and of their father, the imaginary Baron. As fate would have it, the Englishman nullifies their dreams by asking if they are the daughters of Professor Albatross with whom he once studied. The sisters, now faced with reality, prefer the world of their imagination, a more congenial world. Realizing the Englishman can never inhabit that world, the sisters can only watch as he walks out of their lives, unaware of their infatuation with him, leaving them with nothing.

Unlike her choice in **"Three Little Men,"** which succeeds because of its lack of context, in this story Boyle relies on the socioeconomic and political milieu she has invoked to add depth. At contrast are the sisters' poverty-stricken bleak world in the devastated Europe of the late 1920s and early 1930s and the world of their imaginations and longings.

In terms of traditional narrative, the plot of this story is virtually nonexistent, for very little external action occurs. This story internalizes action, looking at potential personal conflicts and changes through the psyches of the main characters, through their moods and the subtleties of their emotional reactions. Although successful on this level, the story makes a yet deeper impact, one that rests in the reader's knowledge of the real-world events alluded to as undercurrents in the narrative. In **"The First Lover,"** Boyle has wedded her narrative to its place in history.

Boyle also relies on historical setting in **"Black Boy,"** originally published in the *New Yorker* (14 May 1932) and reprinted in *Editor's Choice* edited by Alfred Dashiell (New York: G. P. Putnam's Sons, 1934) among other publications. The story begins at an undefined time ("At that time . . .") and with an undefined subject matter. Its setting is the beach, modeled on Atlantic Beach where Boyle spent some time during her childhood. Three characters interweave throughout the story: the narrator, who is a young girl of 10 or 12, her "little grandfather, Puss," and the young black man who earns his living pushing tourists in chairs along the boardwalk. He sleeps on the beach and dreams of being a king, a dream he confides to the narrator.

Grandfather does not approve of the child's talking with the young man and warns her that the young man will steal her money. He tells the narrator to stay away from him. She ignores the grandfather, and, as she takes her horse for a ride along the beach, she stops and lets the young man ride the horse. She hears his dreams of being a jockey and sees his skill with the horse. The narrator, too, is comfortable on horseback, but the animal is scared and throws her, knocking her unconscious. The young man comforts her and carries her home where he is met by the irate grandfather. "Puss was alive then, and when he met the black boy carrying me up to the house, he struck him square across the mouth" (145).

This story, too, is about courage, the courage of the child defying her grandfather and the courage of the young man defying the conventions of society. Boyle depends on her readers to understand societal undercurrents she does not explain. For example, the narra-

tor's age is significant, for she is just approaching puberty. The grandfather's warning that the young black man could "steal her money" serves metaphorically to articulate a darker fear on his part. The narrator's relationship with the young man skirts the edge of sexuality, certainly implying the potential for it. The grandfather's almost palpable fear of this smothers his ability to see or appreciate kindness on the part of the young man. Instead he lashes out at the implied "insult" to his sensibilities. In 1930s America, the stereotypical image of the black male's sexuality, as well as the societal stigmatizing of blacks in general, was well known to Boyle's readers. Thus, the undercurrents serve to produce a story that deals not just with individual conflicts and insensitivity, but also with the entire society's psychology.

One of the less successful stories in the collection (nevertheless another of Boyle's "Roll of Honor" stories for Edward J. O'Brien's 1933 anthology) deserves notice for Boyle's exploration of national character. **"The Man Who Died Young,"** based partially on Boyle's grandmother's experiences as a government worker, blends the narrative of the protagonist Eva's life with the metaphor of the growth of the nation. The story fails, in part, because the narrative is less compelling than the metaphor that moves it. As a child Eva met General George Washington and, growing up later in Kansas, retains her enthusiasm and admiration for now President Washington and other leaders of the new nation. In conflict is her desire to be part of the shaping of the United States and the expectation her family holds that she will marry and live a more traditional life for a nineteenth-century woman. In a scene submerged in melodrama, she marries Jem at gunpoint, but leaves him immediately for the new national capital where she plans to find work. He vows to give her some time to complete her dream, but also promises to come for her if she does not return to him eventually. The story progresses with Eva's involvement in her work, as mapmaker and filer of land grants and deeds, and her obliviousness to the passing of time. Poor Jem dies alone in Kansas of a broken heart, yet Eva barely notices his death or the passing of years because of her work in Washington. The story ends with the now much older Eva imagining the long-dead Jem has come to Washington to retrieve her. As narrative, the story is a rather elaborate retelling of the lost love theme.

As metaphor, however, the story takes on new dimensions. The birth and early development of the nation is chronicled in Eva's life, paralleling in time the events of the narrative. Eva's job as mapmaker allows her both literally and figuratively to see the shape of the new nation as it grows into ever larger portions of the continent, and her correspondence with the people who file land claims with her office allows her to hear the voices of the nation as it expands westward and to respond to them, adding her own observations and opinions to the formal legal notices. Thus, symbolically she accomplishes what she has always wanted: to help shape the character of the new nation. On this metaphorical level the story produces genuinely compelling images, reminiscent of the conceits of the metaphysical poets of the seventeenth century. One is reminded of John Donne's use of the map as metaphor in his sermons and poems.

Yet ultimately the story fails because it lacks unity. The melodrama of Eva's personal story with its patently unhappy ending conflicts with the message of the metaphorical story. While Boyle's fiction typically adopts successfully a neutral narrative tone, in this particular story such neutrality serves merely to confuse its meaning.

TIMELESSNESS

In contrast to **"The First Lover," "Black Boy,"** and **"The Man Who Died Young,"** which rely on a given historical milieu, other stories in the collection occur in a timelessness that frees them from societal or cultural parameters, thus allowing the study of character to remain central. In **"His Idea of a Mother,"** Boyle captures the attractiveness of illusion and fantasy as a young boy's escape from harsh reality, but through her manipulation of narrative patterns she also presents a more complex and ambiguous story than is indicated at first glance. The setting for this story is rural and bleak, pitting a small lonely boy against a world that starves him. Not unexpectedly the boy finds a kind of solace in fantasy, in the romance of imagination. Boyle describes the landscape through the child's eyes as a magic place where willows dry their hair and trees form castles at the top of hills. Populated with wildlife and with cows that both intrigue and frighten the child, this landscape forms the backdrop against which stands the more ordinary, but essentially more frightening, environment of the boy's home.

The unnamed protagonist, orphaned so young that he does not remember his mother at all and has only the scantiest of memories of his father, lives with his Aunt Petoo, a harsh woman concerned primarily with her garden and with rules. While not portrayed as an unloving woman, she is completely unsuited to nurturing a small child. The work of the garden, transplanting and weeding, pruning and shaping, seems more natural to her than the gentleness and guidance the child craves. The only other adult close by is Reynolds, the hired man, who personifies cruelty. He has raised the killing of kittens and rabbits to an art form, and when the reader is first introduced to him, he has "an ur-

chin" in tow, caught stealing cherries from Aunt Petoo's tree. Reynolds, too, lives a rule-bound life and responds by thrashing the child with a whip. Aunt Petoo demands only that he do it behind the stables so the child's cries will not disturb her.

At this point Boyle changes the story from a Dickensian depiction of the orphan's hardships into an exploration of courage under adversity. The protagonist, himself vulnerable, intercedes for the urchin, begging his aunt to stop Reynolds's punishment of the child. She refuses, telling him his childish behavior should embarrass him and that his Uncle Dan, a soldier coming that very day for a visit, will not tolerate his actions.

The boy runs away from home to the hillside and the cows that have drawn his imagination. In the dark of evening, all seems natural to him. He sees the gentleness of the cows, reaches out and strokes one of them. She in turn lies down beside him and, as he snuggles closer to her, licks him as if he were her calf. She becomes a mother figure for him, comforting and secure next to him, providing him with the only form of nurture he has ever known. After she leaves him, he returns home to find his uncle waiting. The boy assumes he will receive a thrashing himself for running away from home. The story ends ambiguously, but hopefully, for Uncle Dan, surprised by the boy's assumption, takes him away from the house in order that they can talk undisturbed.

The story posits no resolution, Boyle offers no hints about the nature of the talk the boy and his uncle will share. Nor does she suggest any future action or change in his situation. She merely holds out the faintest possibility of a positive human relationship. By ending the story as she does, Boyle dramatically alters narrative and plot conventions. No matter what results from the boy's encounter with his uncle, dramatic conflicts and changes are virtually unavoidable, either between the uncle and Aunt Petoo or between the boy and Aunt Petoo. The story concludes with action taking place "offscreen," beyond the scope of the narrative as told. This deemphasizing of plot as action opens the story to more subtle explorations.

As a character study, the story focuses on the boy who must sort out questions of courage and "manliness" in an atmosphere devoid of love, kindness, and gentleness. Ironically, in pleading for mercy for the other child and in admitting to his uncle that he had run away from Aunt Petoo, the boy displays the only element of courage within the story. Fittingly, Boyle pares the conventions of storytelling to their thinnest, not naming the main character, not giving an ultimate resolution, but allowing the boy to confront his fears in their most elemental forms.

"Rest Cure," another story from this collection chosen by Edgar J. O'Brien for inclusion in *Best Short Stories of 1931,* also fits this pattern; it, too, explores the definitions of courage, this time in the face of approaching death, while having the protagonist remain anonymous and leaving out a resolution. The protagonist—a writer resembling in circumstance D. H. Lawrence—his wife, and his publisher spend a late afternoon on a terrace overlooking the Mediterranean. The movement of the story resides in the protagonist's grappling with the knowledge of his rapidly approaching death and with his resentment of the health and liveliness of his companions. His emotional isolation from them grows as the story develops, but his separateness from others gives him an opportunity to delve deeper into his own consciousness. He feels a mystical connection to the live langouste his wife brings for lunch, for this creature, too, faces an imminent sentence of death with no chance for reprieve. The langouste reminds the protagonist of his father because its shoulders are sprinkled with a black luminousness just as his father's shoulders were always black with the dust of the coal mines that bound his life. In the late afternoon sunshine, the writer remembers those dark, dank coal mines, even smells them, and they, too, remind him of death awaiting. As the story ends, the protagonist recognizes a connection to his long-dead father and calls out to him to save him from his own death.

This story successfully blends symbol and event, for every detail, from the time of day to the shape of the protagonist's hand—a "skeleton of [a] hand" (190)—serves to prefigure death. The details of the story associate the writer with darkness and with confinement, for just as the langouste has his claws shackled and gropes "about as if in darkness" (202) and the father lived beneath the earth consigned economically to the mines, so the protagonist finds himself imprisoned in his dying body, picturing his death as a descent into the pits of a coal mine. Contrasting symbols full of the imagery of light, such as his desire for "buckets" of the "clear living liquid" golden champagne and his love of the sun he wishes would not set, at least not yet, achingly suggest the protagonist's love of life and his regret that he will soon be leaving it. Boyle's choices and patterns of images draw on the traditional symbolic dichotomy of light and dark, but embody them in unexpected forms, again very much on the order of a conceit of the seventeenth-century metaphysical poets. As in other of her most successful stories, this one—a stylistic masterpiece—shows few of the strings and pulleys of technique. Instead, its elements work together to create a smooth and flawless whole.

PERSONAL EXPERIENCES

Frequently, Boyle draws on her own family circumstances and childhood experiences for the stories in this collection, focusing on elements of character inspired by her ancestors rather than on events. She uses this technique in **"Black Boy"** with a portrait of her grandfather and in **"The Man Who Died Young"** with a portrait of her maternal grandmother, but she also extends her autobiographical fiction to later periods in her life, basing her protagonists on herself as an adult. **"I Can't Get Drunk"** and **"Art Colony,"** for example, both deal with Boyle's Paris years.

"I Can't Get Drunk," based loosely on a brief period during Boyle's relationship with Robert McAlmon in Paris, follows the narrator and Denka, a man drowning in his own despair. Because of his emotional pain, Denka detaches from the world around him, preferring to spend all his time in bars "looking for something that might catch his curiosity" (208). The narrator, obviously a friend of Denka's, has lost patience with him, even though the narrator clearly recognizes the depth of his pain. Denka, however, obstinately denies anything is wrong except that he can't get drunk, a posture he holds throughout the story. As the story progresses, the reader begins to realize that Denka has loved the narrator and that his trouble emerged as the result of the end of their romantic involvement. They speak of past plans, things that now will never come to pass.

Denka begins telling the narrator a story of "a little boy who had no mother and no father" (213). As he continues, frequently observing that he needs to get drunk, the reader realizes the story is about himself. The more he tells, the more pain he feels and the more imperative his need to get drunk. Boyle's use of the story-within-a-story adds a dimension to her exploration of Denka's personality. He cannot speak of his own life except in third-person terms. Thus, he fantasizes his own memories. But he must pay a price for doing so, as he acknowledges through his actions and his search for the oblivion induced by alcohol. He seeks in every way he can to separate himself from his life, preferring the cloudy fantasy world of drunkenness to the real world in which he must face his past and current problems. The story ends with Denka assuring the narrator they must try even harder tonight to drink themselves into oblivion. Denka obviously runs from his pain, but ironically carries the source of it with him.

The narrator plays a dual role as both Denka's guardian and his tormentor. While the reader sees Denka clearly, the narrator remains more of a mystery, for

Boyle gives little indication of the narrator's feelings or of the shape of the relationship between them. Yet, the narrator plays a central role in the story. Boyle ignores traditional demarcations of dialogue in this story, creating the impression of conversation once removed. The reader, then, becomes aware not so much of two characters joined in conversation, but rather of the narrator's retelling of the substance of a conversation that occurred earlier. The effect is to place the narrator in closer communication with the reader than with Denka. The story, then, becomes a virtual soliloquy given by the narrator.

"Art Colony," which served as an early attempt to shape the material that would later become Boyle's novel, *My Next Bride,* draws on her experiences as a member of Raymond Duncan's communal colony of artists and artisans during the late 1920s. While a few particulars differ from the later novel—the protagonist's name, for example—the substance and tone of the story accurately reflect those of the novel. Nevertheless, **"Art Colony"** stands as a successful story by itself in this collection, as indicated by its inclusion in Edward J. O'Brien's *Best Short Stories of 1933* and other anthologies.

The short story begins with Boyle's swift and sure setting of scene: "Paris has a grief of its own some nights in December . . ." that "dries its tears with your hands" (237). The setting mirrors the protagonist's admission of disillusionment at the filth and the hollowness of the colony. She returns to the central house late one winter evening to find a belligerent Russian woman, who plans to join the colony in order to have food to eat. She has been sitting for hours in the cold, bleak house next to a sleeping child from the commune too lightly clothed to be warm in these conditions. She berates Shiloh, the protagonist, for the horrible conditions of the colony and then begins to tell of her life as servant to the Baroness. She has been sent away because the Baroness believed she gossiped about the Baroness's affair with Sorrel, leader of the colony. Since that time, her life has been one of poverty and hunger. Her attitude toward Shiloh softens as Shiloh prepares food for them and, in a confiding mood, she asks why Shiloh stays in the colony and whether the child's mother ever visits. Shiloh's answer—"She hasn't any money . . . and its father is dead" (249)—responds to both the spoken and the unspoken questions and ends the story with a note of deep pessimism.

While the story establishes a somber mood full of despair, Boyle also explores the interrelationship of two women, very different in background, who nevertheless share desperation in a situation that repulses them,

but from which they have few avenues of escape. A communion of sorts, born of their poverty, their concern for the child, and fittingly enough their sharing of food, binds the women together, however briefly. This story, too, contains a subtle, understated commentary on social issues, for Boyle has placed her characters in a situation clearly and severely circumscribed by their lack of money. What they would like to do—leave the squalor and phoniness of the colony—is impossible because of their economic condition. Again, as with so many stories in the collection, Boyle provides no final resolution, no indication of future action.

Throughout the collection, Boyle explores character types, specifically as they relate to the concept of courage in human relationships. The definitions that result are as varied as the individual characters she creates. She places her characters in a variety of circumstances and situations that draw forth their best or their worst, their facing of reality or their withdrawal from it. Throughout it all, however, Boyle continues to tell her stories with startling candor and, on occasions, a lyricism akin to poetry. Drawing on her own experiences and her own dark vision, Boyle produces a microcosm of human possibility.

CHRONICLING THE CHANGING AGE: *"THE WHITE HORSES OF VIENNA" AND OTHER STORIES*

With what was to become the title story of this volume, first published in *Harper's* in 1935, Boyle achieved her first major critical recognition, winning the O. Henry Memorial Prize for 1935. Altogether 10 of the 18 stories included in this collection won critical recognition of some kind, and 3 of the 10 appeared twice in the O'Brien "Rolls of Honor," once for the original publication and once for the English reprint. She was at this time writing and publishing with enormous energy. In the three years since her last collection of short stories, **"The First Lover" and Other Stories,** she had published three novels, numerous short stories and poems, and several essays and reviews. While the O. Henry Award and critical acclaim validated her prodigious literary efforts, the recognition she began receiving was a mixed blessing.

Reviewers of **"The White Horses of Vienna" and Other Stories** (1936), perhaps because of the temper of the Depression years, cast a jaundiced eye at the collection. They saw the collection as romantic or trivial in content. Most reviewers commented on Boyle's stylistic prowess, but some qualified their commentary with the notice that the absence of what they recognized as significant content marred the book. Edith Walton, writing for the *New York Times Book Review,* decided that only the title story of the collection had any connection to the dramatic issues of the day.[11] *Punch* echoed the sentiment,[12] while Mark Van

Doren in the *Nation* concluded that the stories in the collection were inconsequential.[13] Boyle's stylistic and narrative subtlety misled these reviewers. At the core of the volume Boyle deals pervasively with political and moral issues as she found them in the early 1930s.

Fortunately, these disparaging and mistaken opinions were not the only ones voiced at the time. Reviews such as Peter Quennell's in the *New Statesman and Nation*[14] and "The New Novels" in the *Times Literary Supplement* evidence a more perceptive reading of the fiction.[15] Both of these reviews respond to the human drama being played out in Boyle's stories behind the floodlights focused on the political events of the day. The perspective of an additional 50 or so years finds in these latter reviews a more judicious perception of Boyle's accomplishment, for her fiction intimately and movingly reflects the daily reality of Europe during the early 1930s.

While most reviewers complimented the topical nature of **"The White Horses of Vienna,"** some did not understand the events in Europe that provided the backdrop for the story. For example, Sylvia Pass of the *Christian Century* finds the story obscure, but she mistakenly sets the story in Switzerland instead of Austria and—because she does not realize that the story grows from the particular situation brewing in Austria—naturally grumbles that the central piece of satire, the doctor's marionette show, fails to communicate.[16] Howard Baker, writing for *Southern Review,* dismisses this central episode as well, failing to realize that it provides the underlying explanation for the story itself.[17] Pass's and Baker's confusion points out a central feature of Boyle's relationship to her reader: she expects her reader to know the shape of world events; she refuses to mar her stories with explanations of events the reader jolly well should already know.

Briefly stated, Austria—and indeed most of Europe—suffered from massive unemployment and crushing inflation during the 1930s. Part of the problem, of course, was the worldwide Depression that began in the United States in 1929 and spread with some rapidity to Europe. Yet another element of the problem grew from the stringent treaties that ended World War I, designed to stifle economic growth for Germany and its allies. As Boyle points out in several of her stories, an entire generation of young people had grown up in poverty, with no opportunity to find productive employment in a moribund economy. By the 1930s, people found that ways of life that had sustained them for generations no longer worked. Most of the vanquished European countries developed strong nationalistic movements as a result of what they considered the humiliating conditions of the World War I treaties. These nationalistic movements flourished because they

reestablished a sense of pride and worthiness that World War I had shaken, and they promised hope for rebuilding the prosperity of the land.

Austria in the 1930s was ruled by a so-called Christian dictatorship headed by Engelbert Dollfuss, made up of right-wing political and military supporters. Rabidly antisocialist, the government also fought to counter the growing German presence on its border, yet economic conditions throughout Austria became more and more desperate. A growing number of Austrians saw Dollfuss as incapable of providing the leadership they needed. In July 1934 Dollfuss was assassinated, and a new dictatorship headed by Kurt von Schuschnigg took charge. However, the new government shared many of the same weaknesses that marked the old one, and many Austrians began to look more favorably at what appeared to be a stronger, more promising government in Germany. Indeed, the Austrian Nazi party began demanding the union of Austria and Germany. This situation prevailed as Boyle wrote and published the stories she collected in *"The White Horses of Vienna" and Other Stories,* just after Dollfuss's assassination and during the four year's respite before Germany marched into Austria and made the Austrian nationalistic movement a moot issue.

"The White Horses of Vienna," set in Austria immediately before Dollfuss's assassination, develops the interplay between political movements and personal lives amid the confusion of a rapidly changing international situation. Its three parts are chronologically and narratively related, but intentionally offer different kinds of information about the people and situations of the central story. Part I provides the personal context of the story, the reason the fastidious doctor and his wife must deal with the young Jewish doctor whom the wife, at least, detests. Boyle mentions that in World War I, the older doctor was a prisoner of war in Siberia. He has studied throughout Europe, but has returned to the Tyrol as a kind of haven, a land that provides him with the distance from people and the vistas of mountains he craves. An injury to his knee occurring on one of his frequent nighttime trips into the mountains, where mysterious swastika fires burn, necessitates his calling for a student doctor to come help him in his practice until the knee heals. Boyle highlights the physical contrast between the two doctors, describing the older one as immaculate in white clothing and somewhat neurotically concerned with cleanliness, while young Dr. Heine is dark and alien, appearing on the doctor's property with mud on his shoes and sweat pouring from him.

The doctor's wife provides a barometer for the anti-Semitism of the community, first through her own distress at the doctor's obvious Jewish looks: she begins recoiling from him at first sight. She mentions that the community will feel the same way. The doctor agrees, but does not overtly join in his wife's distress. This section of the story ends with a scene between Dr. Heine and the older doctor's wife, as she offers to mend his coat for him, then realizes she has offered to help a Jew. With this episode, Boyle contrasts the nature of relationships forged between people responding to each other as individuals with those broken or truncated relationships that sometimes exist between groups of people.

Part 2 of the story deals with a more metaphorical kind of information. Boyle has both doctors present an analogue for reality as they see it. Dr. Heine tells of the royal Lippizaner horses of Vienna, still performing as if for a royalty that no longer exists. An incredibly wealthy Indian maharajah, seeing the horses, decides he must have the best for himself. The state, in chronic need of money, sells the horse to him, but on the day of the scheduled departure for India, the horse develops a mysterious cut on its hoof. The groom who has loved the horse from its birth cannot bear to see it leave Austria and has taken measures to delay the process. After the first cut heals, he makes another, this time causing blood poisoning. The horse must be destroyed; the groom commits suicide. Both have died senselessly for a way of life no longer possible.

The doctor's wife, accepting the stereotypical image of Jewish people, assumes Dr. Heine tells the story from his appreciation of the sharp deal the state made or of the marahajah's incredible wealth. She gloats on the moral she attaches to the story: money can't buy everything. But Dr. Heine recognizes the irony of the Lippizaner's training to please a royalty that will never exist again. He and the doctor's wife continue their mismatched conversation, with the young doctor asserting his belief in art and science, while the doctor's wife interjects her own disdain for art and her concerns for the people starving and unable to find productive work. The two speak on different planes, for although Dr. Heine is virtually apolitical, the doctor's wife is unable to view life on any terms except the political.

Austrian authorities come to ask the old doctor about the swastika fires and reveal he has been arrested previously for his pro-Nazi activities. In the face of his refusal to cooperate, they leave, indicating they always feel better when the doctor is safely behind bars. This exchange troubles Dr. Heine, but he fails to connect the doctor's political activities with anything that could possibly affect his own life.

The old doctor then presents his analogue with a marionette show, peopled by puppets he has made. He provides a thinly disguised satire of the ineffective Doll-fuss, portrayed as a clown called "Chancellor" and a magnificent Hitler, embodied as an elegant grasshopper referred to as "The Leader." The clown bears artificial flowers in a setting of Austrian wildflowers, contributing to his ludicrous and lifeless character. The grasshopper, however, belongs in the setting and appears to uphold the natural order of things. While Boyle refers neither to Dollfuss nor Hitler by name, their characters are unmistakable. Dr. Heine, distinctly uncomfortable during the presentation, realizes that even the playfulness of the doctor is political.

This section of the story illustrates metaphorically the underlying philosophical conflict between the two doctors. Boyle objectively presents the perspectives of both: through the old doctor she suggests the desperation of a people crushed by economic instability and political humiliation, grasping at any promise, especially a political movement promising salvation. Through Dr. Heine she shows the deadly nature of the solution being promised and a naive reliance on the intellect as a saving power. She portrays his gentleness and his sensitivity, his love of art and learning, but also his virtual indifference to the political storm gathering around him. Both men, taken individually, have valid human concerns. Their choices, however, are mutually exclusive.

The third part of the story occurs on an evening in July, the evening after Dollfuss's assassination. The Austrian authorities come to arrest the old doctor. Dr. Heine asks what he can do to help the doctor, who responds with ironic humor that Dr. Heine can throw peaches and chocolates to him through the prison's window bars. Last time, he says, his wife was such a poor shot he could not catch all the oranges she threw to him. For that biting edge of irony, Boyle plays on the reader's knowledge of contemporary reality in Europe, for in the economic disaster of Europe, peaches, chocolates, and oranges are unobtainable luxuries. As the authorities carry away the doctor, Dr. Heine thinks in anguish of those Lippizaner horses and their bond to a way of life gone forever.

Both doctors use their analogues to shape their own choices, believing them to be true and accurate. The old doctor's worldview leads him to action that counters his personal experience, for as prisoner of war he has seen political movements fail; the young doctor's leads him to no action at all, but merely a philosophical musing on the conditions of the world. In 1935, at the time Boyle wrote this story, the full horror of Hitler's Reich was still incomprehensible. She accurately portrays the human concerns and frustrations rapidly coming to boil in central Europe and delves into the mind-sets that allowed nazism to come to power. **"The White Horses of Vienna,"** perhaps more cogently and certainly more humanly than news reports of the day, outlines the forces at work in Europe in the decade preceding World War II.

THE CIVILIAN LIFE

While most critics willingly granted that this story dealt with contemporary issues, they overlooked the topical nature of some of the other stories in the collection, dismissing many of them as overtly or unhealthily romantic. However, this volume marks the beginning of what we see in Boyle's later collections: a profound understanding of the "civilian" life in a volatile political world and of the human issues that need attention in an insensitive society. She writes of the world in growing turmoil, as the everyday citizen would see it. She draws heavily on her own experience in her fiction, but as this collection begins to indicate, that experience includes her observations of societal conditions around her, cast through the lives of individuals dealing in daily necessity with rapidly deteriorating personal circumstances. She sees the problems facing the old, the poverty-stricken, the young, the lost, the people displaced literally or metaphorically by events they cannot control. Particularly in a Europe still trying to rebuild economies and governments shattered by World War I, the 1930s held sweeping social changes. Thus, Boyle's stories increasingly deal with class distinctions, racial issues, lives forever changed. Again, Boyle demands of her reader a knowledge of world events, especially in Europe, to grasp the resonances of these stories.

"Count Lothar's Heart" masquerades as a romantic look at a bygone day, but in reality it explains part of the desperation of Europe in the 1930s. To fight in World War I, which he sees as his patriotic duty, young and handsome Count Lothar leaves his ancestral estate and the woman, Elsa, his parents have chosen to be his wife. His mother heartily disapproves of his action, for she believes the noble have no role in war. In bitterness she sends him off, refusing even to say goodbye.

Six years pass; the war ends, the old Countess dies, and Elsa hears nothing of Lothar. She knows he either is dead or will return only when he has nowhere else to go. She knows only that he has been in a prison camp in Siberia and has wandered as far as China. Meanwhile, the war has dramatically circumscribed life for Elsa and the old Count. Boyle mentions little of what they have faced, leaving the details to be imagined from Lothar's reaction when he returns.

When Lothar eventually comes home from his experiences, he is shocked at the changes war has brought to his estate: once covered in lush forest, it now lies waste with vistas of broken stumps bearing evidence of the poverty that has fallen on the old Count. Lothar notices, too, how old and ugly Elsa has become as a result of the poverty, hard manual labor, and worry. He learns that his life, also, must change even more than it already has because he must find some kind of work to support himself, his father, and Elsa. Indeed, all the stability of the past has vanished, and the three of them must forge another kind of security in order to survive, as the old Count and Elsa already understand.

Lothar finds solace in watching the swans each afternoon, and one day their flight triggers his memories of the horrors he has seen: in the prison camps he has seen women given to men, men given to men, haunted faces given to haunted faces with no joy, no spark of life. As Elsa joins him, he begins to tell her what he has experienced, and she realizes that such revelations bind them together. But he cannot communicate it all; some of what he has experienced cannot be transmitted by words alone. He turns silent and never again discusses the subject with her. The story ends with an authorial projection of the surface of their life together—in Salzburg each winter where he works in a bank and at the estate to which they return each summer.

In this story, Boyle contrasts pre-World War I life in Europe among the nobility with postwar life. She suggests, through one family's story, the sweeping changes Europe's old aristocratic classes had to face. She chronicles the closing of one way of life and the search for another to replace it. In addition, she creates in Lothar a modern version of the brooding Byronic hero, full of noble intentions but beset by a crushing fate. But he is a twentieth-century vision, and as befits the worldview of the age, sinks ultimately into the ordinary life, lived without nobility or heroism, marked only by endurance.

"Keep Your Pity" continues the same theme, but explores the plight of the aging aristocracy left without a young Lothar and Elsa to forge a new way of life for them. This story projects the dismal life of those who previously led a privileged life but now find themselves too old to adapt to the new social and economic conditions under which they must live. It operates on a complex theme of clashing cultures, between the naive and relatively unscathed American culture personified by an ordinary businessman, Mr. Jefferson, and the older, more experienced, more devastated culture of Europe. Boyle adds to this mixture the cultural clash the aged Europeans Mr. and Mrs. Wycherly encounter between their former life of elegance and prestige and their current life of inescapable poverty. On a third level, Boyle also touches on the clash between American wealth, based on Mr. Jefferson's hard work, his business prowess, and his shrewd dealing in selling his business just before the Depression hit, and the older couple's poverty, resulting from a pre-World War I life-style that required nothing of them and left them with no place in the Europe that remained after the war. They have only their pride, their haughtiness, and their will for survival with which to face the world.

Mr. Jefferson sees Mr. and Mrs. Wycherly as frail and fragile; they see him as a court jester to their own royalty. But he possesses one thing they do not have: money. Boyle hints at the depth of their poverty with subtle references to a past elegance and present privation: Mrs. Wycherly wears velvets, but they are faded and worn; the two of them have lived in an apartment for 12 years, pointedly—if one is inclined to the arithmetic—exactly the number of years since the end of World War I, suggesting a sharp decline in their fortunes. Oblivious to the implications of their actions, they have systematically ignored the accumulation of bills and warning notices that have littered their world. They evaluate stray cats in language suggesting a decidedly carnivorous intent.

Faced with eviction from their apartment and with the forced auction of all their belongings, Mr. and Mrs. Wycherly resort to elaborate means of preserving what is left to them, and they show the cunning that has allowed them to survive so far. Boyle interjects dark humor into their situation by having the two concoct outlandish responses to the inevitable threat of eviction. In a futile attempt to deny their desperate situation, Mr. Wycherly builds a foolish and elaborate trap for anyone who would dare knock at their door; with a false cheerfulness and bravura, Mrs. Wycherly tells Mr. Jefferson of her husband's inventions, sadly lost without a wealthy backer. Mr. Jefferson, thinking he understands the situation, in pity provides a monthly income for them, ostensibly to pay for a share in Mr. Wycherly's inventions. They take his money without even an expression of appreciation.

Several years pass, with Mr. Jefferson's money arriving regularly to support the Wycherlys. Ultimately the authorities find Mr. Wycherly dead and decaying at his desk, with Mrs. Wycherly's assurances to them that, appearances notwithstanding, he is just intensely involved in inventing something important. Back in Ohio, Mr. Jefferson reads the news reports of the case and still does not believe the Wycherlys capable of such a thing. He has never understood them, the conditions that establish their behavior, or the social stratum that produced them.

While not defending any of the characters in this story, Boyle deliberately tells it from the European view. She hints in this story—as in others of the time—of the post-World War I European resentment of America's relative prosperity. It sets Mr. Jefferson apart from other characters, even the Wycherlys, who regard him with predatory sharpness. Picking up on Henry James's classic observations of the relationship of American and European worldviews, again through the Wycherlys, Boyle also hints at the European disdain for the brash and uncultured American character. Thus, Mr. Jefferson never becomes a sympathetic character in this story; he serves merely as a foil for the Wycherlys. Unimaginative, hard-working, and lucky, he provides the perfect victim for the crafty, desperate, unlucky Wycherlys. The Wycherlys, however, also fail to become sympathetic characters, for despite the humor Boyle attaches to them, she consistently reminds the reader they have a hard edge. They refuse to give up the imperial attitudes of their former life, just as they deny the need to find realistic solutions to their current problems. They survive by whatever means available. Ultimately, not even Mr. Jefferson's money can provide them with a comfortable life. The world in which they could fit vanished, leaving them as anachronisms in a harsh reality.

"Dear Mr. Walrus" also deals with people ill prepared to face the Depression. In the suddenly circumscribed lives of Fanny and Lydia Walrus, maiden sisters to Stuyvesant Walrus, an aspiring but no longer young writer, Boyle captures some of the human tragedy of the 1930s, times so demanding no one could afford to be foolish or naive. The sisters' hopes are pinned on Stuyvesant because years ago he received a promising letter from a publisher. They believe that letter to be a guarantee that once he finishes writing his masterpiece, it will bring fame and fortune. At 57, Stuyvesant, the youngest of them, becomes the head of the household, and when their parents die announces dramatic changes in their lifestyles, such as closing off large portions of the house and dismissing some of the servants. The sisters make their sacrifices willingly, pretending they do not realize the changes are dictated by financial considerations.

As the months pass, the sisters cut more from their own food allowance in order that Stuyvesant might have the energy and peace of mind to continue his work. When an old family friend suggests Stuyvesant contact the publisher to show some progress on his masterpiece, Stuyvesant refuses. He wants to finish the entire work, all 10 volumes of it, before he speaks to the publisher. Finally the work is completed—ironically on the very day the publisher dies. Stuyvesant attends the funeral, carrying the original letter from the publisher in his pocket. The full text of the letter, revealed here for the first time, shows it to be a gracious rejection note. The next day, the old family friend discovers the sisters and Stuyvesant have committed suicide, and in the fireplace he finds a huge mound of burned paper.

Much as Mr. and Mrs. Wycherly, the Walruses find themselves adrift in a world to which they are not suited. At their ages and with their lack of practical preparation, they are unlikely to find any employment. They also suffer from the same kind of class consciousness as the Wycherlys: Stuyvesant refuses to allow the sisters to follow through with their one attempt at obtaining genteel work because he finds the prospect of his sisters working demeaning. In effect, he chooses the prospect of starvation rather than that of breaking an ancient social tenet.

While these two stories lack the immediate political connections of **"The White Horses of Vienna,"** they deal intimately with an issue that contributed to the political conditions of the time. People living in a shattered economy that offers them no hope may turn in desperation to systems that make promises. Dr. Heine's parable of the Austrian Lippizaner horses provides an appropriate metaphor for the people in these stories as well.

RACISM

Boyle also dealt with social problems that were to become major issues after the 1930s in her stories in this collection. Told through the narrative voice of a child observing the actions of adults, **"White as Snow"** explores a particularly devastating form of racism. Carrie, the young black nursemaid with a family on vacation, hates her blackness. She wants straight hair and light skin and so wears a heavy pale face powder and refers to her color as "suntan." She believes the sea air and sun will straighten her hair and bleach her skin. She fantasizes about a life containing more romance and excitement. Adamic, a popular regular at the vacation hotel, finds Carrie attractive, but, aware of the social barriers separating their races, makes no public commitment to her. Instead, he invites her to the movies, but refuses to walk there with her. He walks ahead, pretending he does not know her, but clearly expects her to follow. Even when he buys candy for her, he refuses to give it to her if anyone is watching. When they arrive at the movie, Adamic learns they cannot even sit together because she will be confined to the Jim Crow gallery. Rather than defy social convention, Adamic makes a lame excuse for leaving without seeing the movie—pointedly enough *The Birth of a Nation*—and Carrie goes back to her life as nursemaid.

Boyle explores two manifestations of racism in this story. Adamic—like the doctor's wife in **"The White Horses of Vienna"**—will not allow his personal appreciation of Carrie to temper his judgement of her based on her race. His lack of moral integrity leads him to reject his own preference for some kind of relationship with Carrie in deference to the racist practices of society. He refuses to challenge the existing order. On the other hand, Carrie suffers from her own form of racism, perhaps ultimately more damaging than Adamic's. Carrie's racism is directed toward herself. A product of a society that defines beauty and worth in skin tones, pointedly tied to holiness by the allusion in the very title of the story, Carrie devalues herself and her heritage by trying to become something she cannot be. She, too, refuses to challenge the existing order.

By choosing to tell the story through the perspective of the child narrator, Boyle addresses the emotional content of the issue in remarkably neutral tones. The child accepts as normal Adamic's treatment of Carrie and reports it with an absence of moralizing. The stark contrast between the child's view and that of the reader creates much of the underlying tension in the story. The ploy also demands of the reader some form of judgment, for unlike the child, the reader cannot view the events of the story neutrally.

Boyle reverses this narrative technique in a story that appears to have no relationship to contemporary issues of the 1930s, but in fact, draws heavily on societal context for its impact. **"Security,"** told by an adult viewing in retrospect events of her childhood, attempts to define what security is to a child. Two little girls, one of which is the adult narrator, start a newspaper written and illustrated mostly by themselves. They are cherished by a doting grandfather who, because he loves doing things for others, gives each a Union Iron and Steel Preferred bond. He also offers to back the newspaper for them, providing them with 100 copies and a color cover for each issue. In addition, he promises not to control the content of the paper. However, he submits articles on political topics to two issues, and the children's mother angrily accuses him of using the children's paper to air his own prowar views. She advises the narrator to reject his patronage and, therefore, be free to print whatever she wishes. After witnessing a heated argument between her mother and grandfather, the narrator informs him she cannot accept his aid and, in order to return to him the money he has already invested in the endeavor, hands to her grandfather her Union Iron and Steel Preferred bond. Sadly, she recognizes her returning the bond and his accepting it as marking a breach between them. Several days later, however, on her birthday, the grandfather gives her as a present one Union Iron and Steel Preferred bond "for security."

On one level the story provides a sentimental vision of childhood security: the grandfather's love of the child survives a disagreement between them. The title of the story plays the financial connections of bonds against the emotional "bond" between the grandfather and the child. But on another level, Boyle's use of the adult narrator adds an ironic cast to the story. The adult voice, speaking in the 1930s, knows just how fragile the security provided by any bond, even a Union Iron and Steel Preferred, can be in the mid-Depression. Here again, Boyle reminds her audience of how much the world has changed in the process of only part of a lifetime and how old standards and old securities have dramatically lost their value.

PLAYFUL AND SOMBER

Other stories in this collection show Boyle in other moods. She creates two playful anecdotes. **"Rondo at Carraroe,"** which re-creates in rapid fashion the conflicting versions of a crime, has each witness contradicting the other witnesses on all particulars except one. By the end of the tale, no one knows what happened, except that there was a pattern at Carraroe. On this they all agree. The sketch ends with the case dismissed. The second of these short, fast-paced pieces, entitled **"First Offense,"** offers a dated romp through a conversation between Bishop Delicatatem, who has just been arrested, and the concerned Elder Ornament, who has come to offer aid. The sketch plays on the stereotype of the womanizing, gambling, drinking, fighting preacher who lives off his congregation. It turns on the irony of Bishop Delicatatem's claim that he has been arrested for his first offense, even as he reels off a string of previous ones.

These two anecdotes, examples of "shaggy dog" stories because each episode within them repeats the narrative pattern and, indeed, some of the language patterns already established by the first episode of the group, illustrate a particularly American adaptation of a standard popular formula: they mimic the rhythms and spirit of the vaudeville stage. They aim for humor by the most direct and rapid route possible and, thus, both dwell on stereotypes and surface action, unfortunately so in the case of **"First Offense."** They reveal a departure for Boyle, without a doubt, but one that adds variety to the collection's mood.

On a more somber note, two of the collection's latter stories showcase the darker side of human nature. **"Your Body Is a Jewel Box"** weaves a study of mental illness into a discussion of the changing mores of the new generation. Action centers on two sisters, Olive and Mildred, who must each in her own way deal with the effects of mental illness. Mildred cannot cope with the existing world, so she retreats into one she has created even though she remains uncomfortable and frightened. As she sits on the roof in the rain, her mother worries about what the neighbors will think,

but also about Mildred herself. Olive, an attractive young woman with a sense of style, long ago lost patience with the whole situation and looks with relief on the quiet young constable who comes to capture Mildred and on the consequential decision to send Mildred to an asylum.

Part 2 of the story takes place that afternoon as Olive, the young constable now in plain clothes, and two male friends load Mildred into the car for the journey. She begs them not to do to her what she knows they are planning, but they assure her that they are only going for an afternoon ride. Her pleas, delivered with dignity, punctuate the journey. As they continue, the young constable finds himself aroused by the animal strength he feels in Mildred, but he also finds himself repulsed by her personally. At last they arrive at their destination, Mildred's fate, a building with bars on the windows.

Part 3 portrays the return journey of Olive and the three young men, as they try to reassure themselves that Mildred will be all right. Perhaps in an effort to drown the doubts that arise or to block out the image of the window bars, they stop frequently for drinks at roadside bars. At first the young constable refuses to join them, but as Olive becomes more and more inebriated and the other two young men more sexually aggressive, the constable, too, joins in. Olive arouses him, as she has the others, and as he grabs her to kiss her, the driver who wants his chance with her turns to watch. The car pitches off the road into a lake and all four drown, caught as it were in the act.

With this story, Boyle tricks the reader, for the element that at first appears to present the most conflict, Mildred's mental illness, in reality serves merely a peripheral role in the events that follow. Rather, Boyle directs her attention to the reactions of other characters to Mildred's condition and to the solution her family adopts for the problem. Her condition serves as catalyst for both the constable's erotic tension and Olive's growing displeasure with the strictures she feels on her behavior. Together the strains these two characters feel force a response aimed, not at the problems they face, but, through Mildred's situation, at a surrogate.

Pointedly, Boyle places the explosive action of the story in what many social commentators of the 1930s saw as the focal point of the sexual revolution: the back seat of an automobile, especially one stocked with free flowing alcohol and eager young people. Without Mildred's story, the events would point to a traditional—and atypical for Boyle—warning about the dangers of moral promiscuity; with the addition of

Mildred's story, however, **"Your Body Is a Jewel Box"** becomes a multidirectional exploration of subconscious fears and the consequences of not dealing with them.

Boyle closes her collection of stories with **"Winter In Italy,"** which again deals with more than one topic. Three characters—Dr. Contento, the child Lorenzo, and the child's mother, an opera singer—engage in a conflict of differing agendas. The child has been ill for several days with severe pain behind his ear. His mother has waited until after her performance in *Tosca* to take him for medical treatment. The doctor, attracted to the mother, genteelly propositions her while he examines the boy. The mother toys with the idea of abandoning her vacation plans with the son in order to remain close to the doctor. Meanwhile, the doctor orders an operation for the son, who before he is anesthetized overhears Dr. Contento discussing with a colleague that only four such operations a day keep him in a life-style he enjoys.

Boyle indulges in a touch of dark humor with the ironic name Dr. Contento. Anything but contented, he exudes both a personal and a professional greed. To him the boy's mother represents a trophy, while the boy becomes a source of revenue. But the humor evaporates as Boyle concentrates on Lorenzo, for both his mother and Dr. Contento exploit him. He becomes merely a prop, an excuse, for the casual seduction they plan.

These two stories explore the unpleasant sides of human nature, those without a place for courage or honor. The individuals in them, by design, fail to gain our sympathies, except for young Lorenzo, who finds himself a pawn in someone else's game. They round out the parade of character studies Boyle presents in this collection. She portrays all-too-human people, some of whom respond to the particular social and political situations in which they must live, and others who must find and fight their own individual demons. Rather than ignoring the world situation, as some of her reviewers claimed, Boyle explores how individuals respond when world events inevitably affect their lives.

RECOLLECTIONS: *THIRTY STORIES*

Thirty Stories (1946) is a significant departure from Boyle's earlier short story collections. Each of her three previous volumes contains either stories that appeared only in magazine or journal publications or those written specifically for that collection. As the circumstances under which Boyle lived changed, so did the tone and direction of the stories she wrote, published, and collected in these early volumes. In contrast, 14 of the stories in **Thirty Stories** come from

these three earlier compilations and, instead of being labeled by the title of the original collection, are divided in this new volume into sections identified by time period and the country in which they were written. Three previously uncollected stories from the 1930s appear in this volume: **"Ben"** (*New Yorker,* 24 December 1938), **"How Bridie's Girl Was Won"** (*Harper's Magazine,* March 1936), and **"The Herring Piece"** (*New Yorker,* 10 April 1937). The remaining 13 stories, originally published in the early 1940s, are also collected for the first time. These stories, defined in the table of contents as the "French Group: 1939-1942" and the "American Group: 1942-1946," deal with events associated with World War II. Thus, as a collection **Thirty Stories** is a Janus of sorts, with a face looking consciously backward to well-known and highly respected fiction and one looking forward with fresh and timely new writings. This arrangement produces more than merely a group of short stories; it accomplishes a dual task.

First, **Thirty Stories** represents a capsule view of Boyle's writing career and, consequently, her life and concerns. The re-collected stories range from portrayals of her family background and family members from whom she drew strength to glimpses of her life as a young writer in various parts of Europe, sometimes telling of her life with Ernest Walsh, the eccentrics and bohemians she knew, the lands she saw with Lawrence Vail, her shared concerns with Joseph Franckenstein, her life alone, and her life as a young mother traveling from Austria to England and back again. The stories plunge deeply into her emotional life and borrow details from the substance of her everyday existence to document the making of Kay Boyle, the journey of her life, with the forces that shaped her particular consciousness. Thus, **Thirty Stories** becomes a retrospective of sorts for Boyle's career as writer.

Just as important, however, the volume documents some of the major periods of the twentieth century: the deceptively calm and secure years before the First World War, the unsettled and unstructured years of the 1920s in Europe, the strained and volatile years of the 1930s leading to the Second World War, and the war years themselves. The stories embody the journey Boyle saw our world embark on as the century took its shape.

Critical reception of the book was overwhelmingly favorable. Struthers Burt, writing for the *Saturday Review,* praises the collection, especially the European stories for their clarity and focus.[18] He finds the selection of stories effective in showing the range of Boyle's writing. Edith R. Mirrielees, in the *New York Times Book Review,* mentions the commentary Boyle makes on the fractured world of the twentieth century. She recognizes Boyle's special place and voice in a time needing to be chronicled.[19] Indeed, with few dissenting voices, in the opinions of most reviewers of *Thirty Stories,* Boyle demonstrated her mastery of form, content, and vision, and as the earlier pieces of the collection proved, she had been mastering them in individual works from virtually the beginning of her career.

The last two sections of *Thirty Stories* warrant attention, for they contain the previously uncollected stories that chronicle the progress of World War II as reflected in the periphery of the political and military spotlight. Boyle does not show her readers the literal battlegrounds or take them on reviews of troop movements, political conferences, treaty signings, or the like. Instead, she describes the lives and decisions of the misplaced—the foreigners on suddenly occupied soil, the prisoners of war, the resistance fighters whose lives depend on their being able to distinguish friend from foe, the everyday ordinary people riding out the air raids in dismal cellars, the new recruits, and the children who have seen or heard too much of war. The stories in the French section of the book and those of the American section have different personalities, different tempers, different realities.

FRANCE IN THE 1940S

The "French Group," the more extensive section of the two, contains a gamut of moods, beginning with Boyle's gently stinging indictment of misplaced civilian priorities in the ironically entitled **"Major Engagement In Paris,"** originally published in *American Mercury* in 1940. Set during the war, but before France's fall to nazism or America's entry into the war, the story details the relationship between two women who have been friends for years. One of them, Mrs. Hodges, an American who has lived in Paris for 30 years, suddenly becomes much taken with toothpicks and, to the horror of her very proper friend Mrs. Peterson, uses them with glee in her favorite tea shop. Under pressure from Mrs. Hodges to try them out, a flustered Mrs. Peterson accidentally breaks two toothpicks against her teeth. Because of the resulting censure from Mrs. Hodges, Mrs. Peterson develops a mental block against the toothpicks, and when during an air raid, she must again confront both Mrs. Hodges and the dreaded toothpicks, she again fails to use them satisfactorily. Mrs. Hodges reacts in anger and promises never to think of anyone except herself again.

This story has been much misunderstood, as a review from the *San Francisco Chronicle* indicates.[20] That reviewer sees the story as a discussion of senility, perhaps a nice character sketch of two old women no longer aware of the world around them. In fact, this story represents Boyle's mounting displeasure with civilian nonchalance in the face of war. For example, she lets Mrs. Hodges make a cavalier and disparaging comparison of "this war" with World War I in order to show a certain form of apathy too prevalent in 1940, an apathy born of the desire to look at the war as a personal inconvenience—if one had the privilege of distance from it. Boyle contrasts the triviality of "the battle of the toothpicks" with the larger battle surrounding them, as indicated by the tear gas cannisters the characters carry with them and the air raid that precipitates their final confrontation. The extent of the emotions spent in the confrontation between two friends is out of proportion to the issue involved. In the inappropriateness of their responses, Boyle establishes the fundamental conflict of the story.

Boyle returns to this theme in a more biting piece of nonfiction in **"The Battle of the Sequins,"** published in the *Nation* (1944) and referring to the American public's concern for dwindling supplies of consumer goods at a time when the situation in Europe and other parts of the world was deteriorating rapidly.[21] In this essay she again uses the language of battle to describe women fighting over sale items in a department store, as phantom faces from the jungles and battlefields of the real war look on accusingly. While the satirical mood of these two writings may appear at first glance to be light, the satire masks a deeper and darker irony leveled at the egocentrism of the human heart.

Despite its title, **"Major Engagement in Paris"** transcends its national setting, but other stories in the French section of this collection depend for their meanings on a specifically French setting and context. Boyle draws on the unexpectedly rapid invasion and defeat of France by Hitler in 1940 and the resulting establishment of a bitterly received collaborationist government at Vichy as backdrop to her stories. Some of her references to these events are oblique: for example, in several of these stories, she describes her characters' concern for crossing the Channel into England, although she does not specifically explain that they wish to join the Free French movement headed by Charles de Gaulle and fear official reprisals if they are caught in the attempt. In several stories, she alludes to the healthy Resistance in France and to the efforts of people of many nations to support it. And in several stories, she makes a distinction between those who are French men and women by birth and those who are true French men and women by spirit, a distinction born of the contempt with which many French nationals held the Vichy government—and the French citizens who capitulated to Hitler without a fight—for the betrayal of their country. Thus, the stories depend for much of their power on the reader's knowledge of the undercurrents of anger, despair, defeatism, and courage that played across the face of France during the early 1940s.

The showcase story of this section, **"Defeat,"** won the O. Henry Memorial Award for 1941 for its cogent and focused depiction of the disillusionment of one man who serves as a mirror for his nation. The story opens in the summer of 1940 with the return of soldiers who had served in the French army before its armistice with Nazi Germany. Boyle draws a subtle comparison between the disillusionment of these men who are "without victory" and the displacement that American Confederate soldiers must have felt when they returned to a home no longer as they remembered it. The returning Frenchmen explain their defeat through accounts of the superior forces and preparedness of strong young Germans, the outdated and poorly equipped French army, and the corresponding cowardice of the French leaders, many of whom were among the first to retreat. They testify to a shameful episode in French affairs and, in their retelling of the events witnessed, try to purge themselves of the outrage and perhaps guilt they feel.

In contrast, the protagonist of the story, a bus driver by trade, tells his story only once in the quiet atmosphere born of shared glasses of wine with two traveling salesmen, strangers—as if he could not bear to speak to friends of what he has seen. An escaped prisoner of war, he chronicles his travels through the French countryside, finding aid where he can from a courageous schoolmistress and generous farmer, but finding also an unexpected hostility from others who fear German reprisals and who blame the French army for its defeat. As he journeys, the bus driver encourages himself by focusing on the thought that France will never be defeated as long as its women remain strong, for he finds in the defiance he saw in the eyes of the schoolmistress a reminder of the France for which he fought.

His faith in his country, however, appears to be for naught. Throughout the country the German authorities have usurped the preparations being made for Bastille Day celebrations, and they urge the French to come join them in dancing and feasting. Concerning this insult to the spirit of France, the bus driver remains confident the Germans will celebrate alone. To his dismay, later that night, as he looks down on the village square from the window of the hayloft where he hides, he sees the townswomen and men joining the Germans in merriment. He tries to explain away what he has seen by blaming it on the vast display of food the Germans have provided, but at last he must comfort himself by the notion that he saw only one town. Even so, his tears indicate that he does not believe those events to be isolated.

Boyle uses three time settings, which are not chronological in the story: she begins in late June with the soldiers' return, then shifts forward in time—two months after the bus driver's return—to his confession, which takes us back again to July 14 and the events he witnessed. Although the events of the story span very little actual time, they represent a lifetime's journey into betrayal for the protagonist. Boyle suggests the depth of his disillusionment by the simple ploy of contrasting his hesitancy to speak of it with the openness and outspokenness of other returning soldiers. While they broadcast their shock and anger, his choice of confidants and the intimacy of conversation shared over wine point to a deep and abiding despair he cannot exorcise. Through the relatively brief timespan of the story, Boyle contrasts real time with a seemingly much longer emotional time as she explores the gap between one man's—and one nation's—expectations of human behavior and the reality that he—and the world—have to face.

Whether by intent or coincidence, two other stories in the French section provide contrasting definitions of patriotism while they offer an ironic commentary on the pertinent, at that time, question of true French nationalism. **"Effigy of War"** (1940) and **"Their Name Is Macaroni"** (1941), both first published in the *New Yorker*, concentrate on the evolving definitions and self-images of a nation bereft of its traditional identity. Their perspectives differ, but taken either singly or together, these stories raise profound, contemporary questions about the nature of reality and symbol, truth and facade.

In **"Effigy of War,"** none of the principal characters is French, although they all profess loyalty to France. The barman who fought for the Italian army in World War I has not returned to Italy for 15 years and, although he has not taken out citizenship papers, considers himself a Frenchman. When his employer suggests he return to Italy where he belongs, the barman refuses. The Dane who teaches swimming at a local establishment likewise has lived a long time in France, but begins to feel uncomfortable as more and more of the townsmen mobilize for the war; he senses a subtle change in mood within the town. Together the barman and the Dane discuss the changes war is bringing to their daily world and to the way they must conduct business.

Conflict within the story increases as the Greek waiter, naturalized a French citizen eight months ago and scheduled for mobilization within weeks, declares himself "pure French" and assumes the role of protector of the realm. Never having liked the Dane, the Greek waiter begins baiting him, soon drawing the barman into the conflict by proclaiming France was only for the French; no one else should be employed.

The climactic scene of the story shows the Greek waiter and his friends assaulting the Dane and the barman. Boyle describes the violence with graphic physical detail. In one final gesture of his supposed patriotism, the Greek waiter lays out the French flag and as the blood of his victims flows onto it, orders them to repeat allegiance after him. In his uncomprehending, destructive allegiance to the symbols of France, the Greek waiter tramples the meaning and the spirit of them. Boyle contrasts the emotionalism and violence of the Greek waiter with the reason and pacifism of his victims. In the process she exposes the soured, spoiled "patriotism" of the Greek waiter for the horror it is.

"Their Name Is Macaroni" deals with similar distinctions, but from a completely different perspective. Set in Vichy France in a coastal town near Italy, it, too, marks June 1940 as the time when the order of the world changed dramatically and Italy, in its fascist posturing, became a burlesque version of the country it once was. As in **"Effigy of War,"** neither of the story's two main characters is French: the foreman Angostini once was Italian but cannot identify with what Italy has become; Colonel Pinhay is an Englishman in charge of the distribution of food for the town. The southern part of France had been attacked and "conquered" by Mussolini's forces shortly after Hitler secured the northern part, so as the story begins Italian officers have come to the town in victory, only to be met by derogatory graffiti and the disdain of the townspeople. Angostini even tells of taking the officers on a circuitous, needlessly grueling hike to end up only yards from where they began.

Colonel Pinhay, however, puzzles the townspeople. After telling the Italian officers they will get no supplies from him and ordering them off his ship, he resigns his position rather than enforce an order that no food should be given to Italian nationals. The order would mean he could no longer supply the Italian mothers and children of the town with milk and flour. Many in the town do not understand the distinction he makes, for in their eyes an Italian is an Italian. Nevertheless, Colonel Pinhay's actions result in the reconsideration and rescinding of the order. In an anonymous expression of gratitude, the Italian population places a six months' supply of driftwood and charcoal on his doorstep.

In a flashback, Boyle tells of a somewhat similar episode in the Colonel's past. A long time before the French armistice, two Italian bombers flew over the village. Antiaircraft fire missed them, but with a surprising show of misjudgment, the pilots flew into each other, crashing both planes. Colonel Pinhay cheers with the townspeople for this destruction of fascist forces.

At the funeral for the dead pilots—one 19 and the other 21—Angostini looks at his countrymen and spits "Fascist" in the dead faces. Colonel Pinhay, however, looks at the two of them and sees in the face of one something too young for the horrors of Mussolini's Italy. He places in the dead hand a 1920 souvenir flag of the other Italy, before Mussolini. Although he can cheer the destruction of the fascist airplanes and pilots, he respects the deaths of the young men themselves.

Again, Boyle explores the meaning of patriotism, but a kind that extends beyond national boundaries. Angostini, after all, rejects his countrymen, for they represent an ideology abhorent to him. In contrast, Colonel Pinhay looks beyond nationality and ideology to find human bonds and human worth, perhaps in the Italian children of his town or even in the shattered youth of the dead pilots. Here, again, patriotic and national labels conflict with human bonds and human responsibility. Colonel Pinhay, with clearly defined distinctions in his own mind separating ideology from humanity, quarrels not with Italians, but with the Italy of Mussolini.

AMERICA IN THE 1940s

Most of the stories in the French section explore the meanings of honor and betrayal in one context or another. The American section, however, owns another agenda altogether. The United States, while very much involved in the war by this time, nevertheless remained geographically untouched. The fighting belonged to other shores, and this physical separation from the battlefields produced a much different emotional response from American soldiers and civilians. All of the stories in this section describe a form of emotional isolation, produced by individual commitments to a war far away or a dissonance that intrudes in the preparations for that war.

"The Loneliest Man in the U.S. Army" takes place in a reception center for new recruits before they are shipped out to assignments overseas. Some of them will be there for a matter of hours, others for days or weeks. O'Mallory and Dryden serve as the main vehicles for the story, for through their eyes the reader sees the parade of men traveling through the facility, four of whom provide the content of the story. O'Mallory and Dryden originally choose as "loneliest man in the U.S. army" a dark foreigner known only as "Merde" who speaks to no one, except late at night to Dryden in French. To Dryden he confides that his wife is pregnant and on welfare and that the two of them barely escaped from France. Yet, he also conveys in his language in the darkness his longing for the land of olive trees he has been forced to leave. He, however, soon loses his title to the young Chinese recruit who cannot even speak English. Dryden must help him understand the orders, which document his shipping out in less than a day, delivered by a seemingly unfeeling sergeant.

That same sergeant, viewed as an outsider by the lower rank, announces with excitement that his girlfriend will be coming to spend a week with him, and in the confined atmosphere of the reception center, the recruits begin imagining what the two of them will do. Her impending visit becomes a topic of conversation that keeps the men occupied for several days—except, she doesn't come or even send a message to the sergeant who, in despondency, gets drunk and assaults an M.P., thereby losing his rank as sergeant. To O'Mallory's and Dryden's attempt at moral support, he offers only rebuff. The story ends with Dryden finding a handwritten note pinned to the door of the women's restroom at a local canteen. The note from O'Mallory begs for someone to write to him because he is "the loneliest man in the U.S. army."

Boyle parades the individual men through the story to illustrate that in spite of their separate experiences and backgrounds, they share isolation, a loneliness for the context in which they have names and identities. Each of them presents appropriate credentials for the designation of "loneliest man in the U.S. Army," for each of them survives in a separate shell created from past experience. Thus, the reception center becomes a kind of purgatory where no relationships can be permanent and no bonds can flourish; each man must find his own comfort. Human emotion—sympathy, curiosity, humor, despair—has no lasting meaning, for the situations and people that inspire human responses depend on a degree of personal interaction unobtainable in this context. Some of the men reach out to escape the isolation that surrounds them, Dryden through listening, O'Mallory through a search for humor, Merde through his dreams; others, such as the Chinese recruit, do not have the power to reach out. In the end, however, it hardly matters.

"The Canals of Mars" treats the same theme far more complexly and in a far more condensed time period. In this story, the recruited soldier and his wife have four hours before his departure to capture a special moment to remember during their approaching separation. They share memories of an earlier time, when he was sent to a concentration camp, and she was not allowed to even stand on the train platform to see him leave. In the void of her absence, he imagined he was being told farewell by King Arthur, Aldous Huxley, and Heloise and Abelard who had come to the station

just for him. He wanted to take something of their lives with him, although he admitted he should have called up the Abelard of an earlier, less-doomed period.

His wife suggests they go to the Statue of Liberty or to a planetarium to see the stars and the canals of Mars. Either of these would create some lasting special moment for them to take on their separate journeys. She reminds him this leave-taking differs from that earlier one, for then he was alone with his honor. This time he shares the journey with other men going to fight for a mutual cause, and she shares her own journey with the myriad of women of this and other nationalities who wait at home. In her encouragement, he finds the special moment he needs, comparing her to the canals of Mars, for she is as rare and as special as a glimpse of them.

The men are called to their departure, and as they move toward the staircase that will take them to their futures, the families crowding around the wife begin to move also. The two main characters, husband and wife still recognizable to each other, become part of the parallel surges of people heading for the stairway that separates those going from those waiting.

Boyle begins with the personal lives of her protagonists, but shifts gradually into national and universal concerns. In both dimensions, she presents the side of war that has no glory, the side that calls forth just another form of personal sacrifice. Yet, her story is not antiwar; it merely shows the rarely portrayed version of war as seen through the individuals caught up in it, the ordinary, nonglamorous, depersonalized separation of human beings.

In **"Winter Night,"** through the persona of an American child, Felicia, aged seven, Boyle explores the vastly different wartime experiences of children in America and in Europe. Felicia's mother works all day and frequently dines out at night as she waits for the child's father to come home from the war; she hopes then, as she has said to Felicia, life might return to normal. Meanwhile, Felicia returns home daily from nursery school to a succession of maids and a parade of nighttime "parent sitters" who stay with her while her mother does other things. On this night, the sitter begins talking to Felicia of another child, one who just three years ago became her own because her mother went away. As she talks and answers Felicia's questions, describing the camp in which she and the child lived and the conditions under which they survived, Felicia tries to comprehend their lives in terms familiar to her, but irrelevant to the woman's experience. Did the mother go away in a taxi cab? Was she upset when the other child did not brush her teeth or wash up in the evening? She thinks she understands the father's being in another place because she knows her father is away fighting in the war, but other elements of the woman's story puzzle her. As they talk the woman brushes Felicia's hair, telling her of the other child as if it were a story she was narrating. When Felicia's mother returns at midnight, she finds the two of them asleep in each other's arms.

Told starkly, the story seems to be about a loneliness shared by a sitter and a small child. Yet Boyle creates much more depth. She uses light and shadow in the story to suggest the child's sense of isolation. The evening street with streetlights and vehicle lights beneath her window contrasts with the darkness of her apartment; the shadows in which she stands while talking to the young southern girl who serves as day maid indicate the emotional void and lack of connection she feels with this person. Into this setting comes the mysterious and quiet woman of different background and particular experience.

She tells of life in the concentration camps, and the contrast between the witness she bears and the child's lack of comprehension propels the story into a poignant, gentle discussion of experiences no one should have to know. The two fill each other's need: Felicia becomes for one night the child the woman lost; the woman for this one night becomes the surrogate mother for a child who lacks security. Mothers go away (in taxicabs) she knows; do they always come back? Boyle combines the childhood fears of Everychild, embodied in Felicia, with the nightmare life the other child endured, the nightmare specific to a Europe gone mad. Yet, even as the fears share common elements, Boyle also contrasts Felicia's innocence with the woman's experience and in so doing demonstrates the gap separating the American version of war from the European.

As a collection, *Thirty Stories* spans the twentieth century; published in 1946, virtually the century's midpoint, it provides an appropriate stopping place for an examination of our times. Perhaps Boyle had this in mind as she selected the stories. She also established a pattern she would follow in later years; in 1980 and again in 1986, she published new groupings of previously collected stories. *Fifty Stories* (1980) contains the entirety of *Thirty Stories* with the exception of **"Hilaire and the Marechal Petard."** In addition it contains 20 stories selected by Boyle from her other collections. Her choices mark her response to the societal and human issues facing this nation at the beginning of the Reagan years. Drawn from all stages of her life, the stories reflect Boyle's assessment of the first three-quarters and more of the twentieth cen-

tury and demonstrate the growth, maturity, and vision of Boyle the writer.

In *Life Being the Best* (1986), editor Sandra Spanier collects stories of various forms and diverse times, places them outside their political or social context, and provides the reader with the opportunity to reassess them. Spanier chose stories from Boyle's first three collections—*"Wedding Day" and Other Stories, "The First Lover" and Other Stories,* and *Horses of Vienna*—in order to show Boyle as a writer in transition. The works in this collection reflect a collage of moods, explore human nature in many tempers, and picture the world through Boyle's individual perspective. These volumes provide the valuable service of reintroducing Boyle to a generation of new readers who now have the opportunity to experience her development as writer.

OCCUPIED TERRITORY: *THE SMOKING MOUNTAIN*
AS SHIP OF FOOLS

After having written a number of wartime novels many critics dismissed as potboilers, Kay Boyle published in 1951 *The Smoking Mountain: Stories of Postwar Germany,* a collection of narratives that reflected her experiences as a correspondent and an observer of the American military government stationed in postwar Germany. The collection received friendly if mixed reviews and sparked unmistakable puzzlement over the variety of genres included. Beginning with a lengthy factual report of the trial of Nazi war criminal Heinrich Baab, which Boyle covered as correspondent for the *New Yorker,* the book contains 11 narratives, 8 of which are traditional short stories and 3 of which are a more hybrid form that relies heavily on human interest journalism.

Critics were unsure of how to evaluate the collection. For example, while critic Louise Field Cooper, writing for the *Saturday Review,* groused that Boyle's introductory report of the Nazi trial was too derivative of Rebecca West's style and threw the book off center, she granted Boyle wrote her stories with sensitivity and skill.[22] On the other hand, Harry T. Moore, from the *New York Times,* called the introduction "penetrating," but admitted the collection was "an unusual blending of fiction and fact."[23] The book had its supporters, Moore among them, but did not receive the praise or the attention Boyle's earlier collections found. Reviewers dealt with the collection relatively gingerly and seemed somewhat ill at ease with the subject matter, with which Boyle raised difficult questions of complicity and complacency the post-Holocaust world had to face.

Within the collection, she portrays virtually every facet of life in postwar Germany that would be available to the eyes and ears of the non-German associated with the official Occupation government, and she spares her readers none of the tension such a situation contains. She takes us from the courtroom of the war criminal to an American cocktail party, from a clearinghouse for homeless children to the hovels of the devastated, from the nomadic life of the lost to the houses of the arrogant and unrepentant. The Germans in these stories are sometimes presented sympathetically, especially those who with patience and humanity try to exist in a bleak, forbidding world. Those who react arrogantly and with no recognition of their national guilt or those who profited from the war and the Occupation find no sympathy in Boyle's portrayal; they have lost important parts of their humanity and are portrayed as such. The Americans in these stories fare no better; they are not all portrayed as honorable heroes. As was the case with many of the 1920s and 1930s expatriates, these victors-in-occupation keep themselves isolated in American enclaves. They import their familiar life-styles—brand names, supermarkets, music, even Gene Autry ("Home"). Many of them are insensitive to the devastation around them and produce their own version of arrogance that sometimes becomes stark cruelty (e.g., "Summer Evening"); a few are compassionate, but most are merely observant, sometimes providing the backdrop for readers' reactions. In most of the stories there is no real communication between Americans and Germans, not even a "clash of cultures," because the two cultures barely recognize each other. The stories explore in part the chasm that exists in postwar Germany, a gap caused by arrogance on both sides, by contrasts between poverty and wealth, defeat and victory, despair and confidence.

A JOURNALISTIC ACCOUNT

The introductory account of Heinrich Baab's trial, contrary to Cooper's dismissal of it, provides the context from which Boyle wrote the stories and within which they must be evaluated. Here Boyle sets forth the contention that Germany's acceptance of nazism was a moral, not political, consideration, and she uses the occasion of Baab's trial to explore the consequences of that choice in terms of national character. She describes the issues in terms of good and evil, innocence and guilt, and raises the specter of a nationwide acceptance of Nazi brutality and immorality. In discussing the courtroom and the proceedings, Boyle notes that the wealthy and the powerful do not present themselves in the courtroom to witness the murder charges against this relatively minor Nazi; instead the court is full of those who were his victims or family of his victims. Their stories contain details of the horror and inhumanity that marked their treatment at the hands of Baab and the state that legitimized him. The variety of their torture, as well as its crushing similar-

ity, becomes as overwhelming as their number, yet Boyle subtly reminds the reader that Baab was rather mundane, guilty of hundreds of crimes instead of the hundreds of thousands Nuremburg weighed.

Boyle uses the format of this report to instruct her American audience on German customs and mind-set. She discusses the German legal system, including the postwar requirements for jury selection and judge appointment. During the proceedings she uses Baab's background to explain the German vocational education system, which has been the institution solely responsible for creating "rational and cultured beings" of the majority of working class Germans. She inserts flashbacks to her own previous conversations with intelligent, cultured German citizens in which they admit they did not ask questions for fear of what they would be told or passively did nothing for fear of not knowing what to do. She reports other conversations with other Germans in which they indicate no recognition of a national or personal guilt, no responsibility for what happened during the Third Reich. Thus she shows her readers the various faces of Nazi Germany: victim, victimizer, sympathizer, apathetic witness.

From this background, as Boyle explores the particular charges against Baab and recreates the testimonies of specific people, she identifies Baab with the German nation, calling him, in fact, a symbol for it. Of the saner Germany, she can only say that whatever protest they made was not loud enough to be heard. Ironically, she tells us, the Baab trial is being held at precisely the time that, in two other separate trials in different courts, several former Gestapo agents and other Nazis are being acquitted of any culpability in the murders and assaults they committed. Yet, she also observes that as the names of Baab's victims appear in the paper and their testimony becomes known, commonplace citizens in Frankfurt where the trial is being held become convinced of the horror in more personal and profound ways than ever before. Conflicting reactions coexist in the postwar Germany Boyle describes.

The introduction to *The Smoking Mountain* serves, then, as a reminder to the reader of Nazi atrocity, German apathy, and a nation of people coming to terms with both. The narratives that follow it explore individual lives and attitudes that both caused and resulted from the Third Reich. The focus in these narratives centers on the everyday, routine duties of life lived by ordinary people in the aftermath of monumental destruction, in a period of sorting through the remains of a way of life of such dichotomy it defies reason and denies civilization. In Boyle's craftsmanship, the transition from introductory journalistic report to fictionalized story takes place in subtle stages.

THREE SHIPS OF FOOLS

Immediately following the introduction, **"Begin Again,"** presented as a short story, illustrates the hybrid genre Boyle develops in this collection. It adheres only minimally to fictional conventions, yet enough to make an obvious distinction between it and journalism per se. Its setting is the Autobahn, which Boyle uses as microcosm. Its characters are a series of hitchhikers, displaced by the war, in search of new lives in new locations. Its narrative voice belongs to "the American woman" who dominates this collection, but who rarely becomes an active participant in the action. Its plot—which can best be described as minimal—consists of the conversations, almost monologues, of the hitchhikers Boyle's narrator encounters as she travels the Autobahn.

Boyle endows these various hitchhikers with personality, but only in so far as they illustrate particular German interpretations of the postwar world. As they tell the American woman of their lives and destinations, they also reveal prevalent attitudes toward the war and its outcome, from the young medical student who refuses to acknowledge the German military would deliberately destroy the architectural treasures of Italy to the young blond German who unrealistically dreams of joining her GI boyfriend in Missouri and has adopted his bigoted hatred of black people, including the vocabulary of racism that ties Nazi propaganda about Jews to American attitudes toward blacks. A young soldier who lost a leg in the war and whose wife is dying of tuberculosis speaks with fondness of 1943 and 1944, which were "good years for everyone." To herself the American woman notes that those years marked the peaks of activity in the concentration camps and gas chambers. The aristocratic judge for whom the rigid German class structure is absolute and who even now considers "Jewish blood" a taint completes the cast of characters.

In many ways this narrative serves to personify the issues Boyle raises in the introduction. Unlike traditional fiction, however, neither character study nor action provides the purpose for this narrative. Instead its guiding principle is the conjunction of attitudes themselves, representing so much willful self-deceit and avoidance of the moral conundrum of the Third Reich. The narrative is, in fact, a modern enactment of the medieval Ship of Fools motif, which traditionally collected character types representing all facets of life and took them on a journey full of dangers and conflicts from which they learn nothing. In **"Begin Again"** Boyle adheres to the Ship of Fools theme on both a literal and a metaphorical level, but with a modern interpretation. Literally, the journey on which she sends her characters is the fragmented and isolated trip of

each hitchhiker; the ship that carries them on their separate journeys is the American woman's automobile. Metaphorically, the journey includes the distance from the prewar to postwar world within the microcosm of Germany, which contains representatives of American as well as German life.

Boyle continues the exploration of the Ship of Fools motif in the other two journalistic fictions she includes in *The Smoking Mountain,* **"Lovers of Gain"** and **"Summer Evening."**

"Lovers of Gain" exchanges the Autobahn for an equally commonplace setting, the U.S. commissary for the American occupation army. In this microcosm are various German nationals who serve as staff and who daily deal with the occupation forces and their families who depend on the commissary for the life-style they maintain. Again it is through the eyes of an American woman, this time given the name "Mrs. Furley," that the reader becomes acquainted with the workers. Through one of the commissary staff, Mrs. Furley hears of Plato's classification of three kinds of men: lovers of wisdom (who are forgotten), lovers of honor (warriors, she is assured who are now either dead or working as bartenders), and lovers of gain. Providing the title of the story, this allegory also provides its central irony. Boyle subtlely challenges the reader to explore the dimensions of "love of gain" and see it in many forms.

The plot, if it can be called that, follows Mrs. Furley through the shopping aisles of the commissary, bringing her into contact with the German nationals who staff the place as she fills her shopping cart. The commissary is very Americanized: its goods are brand names from the States, its shelves offer variety even if the lines are sometimes long. The German nationals are known to Mrs. Furley by the names of the cigarette brands they prefer, for as is her habit while she shops, Mrs. Furley offers them cigarettes, which they take. She moves among them as one who has access to great luxury (meat, fresh vegetables, cigarettes) denied to them in this their homeland. Thus, she symbolizes to them someone who can help them with their lives because she represents, albeit unofficially, the victorious powers, the holders—as they are reminded everyday—of material wealth beyond their current comprehension.

Over the course of her year there, Mrs. Furley comes to know the workers through what they tell her of their personal pasts and what life was like before the war's end: one was a member of the occupying army in Paris, one a POW in England, one worked in a theater in London, one was a cabaret dancer whose husband is now in jail for trying to kill the man who "denounced" his sister and mother. They imply in their accounts of their private lives a tacit plea that Mrs. Furley make their lives easier.

Although their lives are bleak and much diminished, Mrs. Furley realizes, when she hears the meat counter worker's remark about knowing "a nice [J]ew," that their experiences in war and defeat have taught them nothing about national or personal moral responsibility for what happened in the concentration camps. Again, as passengers on a ship of fools, they have learned nothing and wish to continue their lives as if nothing had occurred.

Yet, Boyle does not leave the reader with a simple moral. Instead she raises difficult questions. Who are the lovers of gain? Are they the German nationals who from their frustration covet the wealth and power so obvious around them? Or are they the occupying forces who import the relative luxury they are unwilling to abandon, even temporarily and in the face of the deprivation surrounding them? As with **"Begin Again,"** Boyle's American woman observes what happens around her and provides the vehicle by which the story is told, but does not provide answers or interpretations.

In these two journalistic fictions, the reader stays outside the consciousness of characters and narrator alike, watching a series of vignettes unfold. The sparse settings, an automobile traveling on the Autobahn and the aisles of an army commissary, parallel the minimal adherence Boyle grants to the conventions of character development and plot in these narratives. "Summer Evening," the third of the journalistic fictions in *The Smoking Mountain,* pushes genre distinctions even further by moving closer to the definition of the traditional short story, but still not quite meeting it.

Departing from the virtual interview format of the other two narratives, Boyle takes the reader in **"Summer Evening"** to an affluent cocktail party for the American occupation forces, wealthy and elegant, with only a brief and understated mention of the physical devastation of the war. This story departs from the stark journalistic technique of the two other narratives, for although its plot is pared to the barest semblance of sustained action, the characters interact with each other and develop small subplots of action. The point of view is that of an impersonal, perhaps even disembodied, observer, moving from one group of people to the next, as one might travel through a real cocktail party, and finding one vignette after another until the whole party is captured as if with a camera.

Boyle tells no one's story completely, but creates a situation which sketches in their essential natures, with fragments of conversation or action serving to

caricature deftly the guests and their principles. The snatches of experiences overheard become emblems of human nature. Again in this context, the narrative perspective itself becomes the major focus.

The major characters of this story are the officers of the American military government and their spouses, along with other civilian Americans, and the lone, aged *Hausmeister,* a German. The host, Major Hatch, exudes officiousness, his wife, shallowness; he is a master of reacting to rank but very insecure with civilians for whom no readily apparent rank exists. The guests all allude to various private grievance or troubles in their lives, but they congregate in this place for temporary companionship of the most superficial kind. The desperate, impoverished, old Hausmeister provides a contrasting desperation. The others' narratives revolve around ironies: the opulence of the party and the food served; the poverty and starvation of the German people; the arrogance of the Americans, and the subservience of the old man. In one vignette Marcia Gruikschank voices displeasure with marriage and begins a flirtation with a young civilian. In another, her husband is repulsed by Marcia's habitual drunkenness. And in yet another the young civilian thinks ambitiously of the benefits of a relationship with Marcia. The most troubling scene, however, portrays the aged Hausmeister begging for a passport to America while the host and other members of the Occupation tease him and laugh at his plight.

A central irony of this story is the Americans' official role as architects of a more humane government in Germany at the same time they are virtually pillaging German society: several conversations discuss the "bargains" the Americans can pick up in art work and antiques because of the people's desperation for food and money. The story paints an ugly picture of the Americans, greedy and insensitive to the point of cruelty. It also presents a picture of a way of German life lost forever.

But again, Boyle does not simplistically portray the human condition. The Hausmeister, while a victim, is not portrayed particularly sympathetically. He is pathetic, willing to beg and grovel to escape the dire conditions of his homeland. He wants his own comfort and survival without regard for the price, but his personal tragedy plays out against the ever-present but deliberately muted backdrop of devastated Europe and the growing awareness of the extent of Germany's acceptance of the Nazis. Again, Boyle raises questions about one's responsibility for others, whether one is a victor or a victim, an individual or a nation.

BIGOTRY

Among the more traditional short stories, **"The Lost,"** set in a "vast" Bavarian manor house that served as a selection camp from 1938-45 but now operates an American children's center, deals with official efforts to reunite "unattended" children, war orphans, with any remaining family or to find new homes and futures for them. The protagonist, 15-year-old Janos, is identified as a "GI mascot"; he has survived the war by following American army units, most particularly the one belonging to Charlie Madden, a sergeant who has been sent back to the United States but who wants to legally adopt the boy. Two younger boys travel with Janos, and despite their youth, have grown a protective rough exterior necessary for their survival. Having existed outside of official channels for so long, the boys find great difficulty in trusting any governmental agency to help them, as their various reactions to the center demonstrate: Anzio immediately melds with the other children, accepting their friendship but not expecting much else, the third boy refuses to enter the center, and prefers to take his chances on his own, and Janos enters and tries to trust its mechanisms for reuniting him with Charlie.

What happens to the three boys represents the fates possible for the lost children, survivors of the war separated from family perhaps at so early an age they no longer remember their real names: Anzio returns home to Italy to a grandfather who has searched all during the war for him; the unnamed other boy decides to strike off on his own, no longer interested in finding a family but relying on his own savvy and instincts to trade for the alcohol and cigarettes that will buy his survival; Janos is found to have no surviving family and, thus, can be recommended for emigration to the United States where Charlie Madden waits to adopt him. Janos's story should have a happy ending, but Boyle adds an additional level of irony to the story: Charlie Madden is "colored," and in postwar, 1940s America, this means Janos cannot live with him.

The American woman who operates the children's center seems to be sensitive and to care about the fates of the children who arrive at the center, but she is also fatalistic in her realization that not all of them can be helped, particularly if they don't want to be. Thus, she encourages Janos to bring the third boy into the center, but she does not demand it, nor does she order a search to find him. She knows the limits to what she can do, for life around her is a constant reminder of that. In fact, she knows she cannot always help even those who want her aid and who trust the system to make things right for them. She treats Janos gently, not trying to explain the senselessness of American segregation even to herself. All she can do to help Janos is suggest alternatives, such as finding a new adoptive family in America. But rather than going to live with strangers and having to reject the man who has been his only human link in the turmoil of Europe

at war, Janos runs away from the center, leaving behind a short thank-you note for the woman and a longer letter to be forwarded to Charlie Madden in which Janos tells Charlie his family has been found and that he will be well and happy with them. For reasons that have nothing to do with him or with Charlie Madden as people, the one family Janos has ever really known cannot be his.

In this story the American woman and the children's center she represents could help only some of the children in its charge. If Boyle presents an accurate ratio in the story, that means only one child of every three seeking assistance could be helped to find a family. Lurking in the background of the story, mentioned only in passing, is the reminder that many more children refused or were unable to work through an official agency such as the center to find or reconstruct their families. Thus, Boyle creates a grim picture of the reality of postwar Germany and of the puny efforts of an impersonal bureaucracy to put things in order.

Boyle takes the reader into the consciousness of the young Janos, having us see with his eyes and think from his perspective in order to fully illuminate the human tragedy in this story. It is a bitter story, but understated. The story calls for strong reactions from the reader, but does so in muted and objective terms. Yet, the questions have been raised: What happens to the children? What kind of lives can they reconstruct and pull from the ruins of civilization? And what about that civilization that supports racial hatred and finds it more acceptable than the fulfilling of individual lives?

Boyle's attack on racism takes a more direct approach in the story **"Home."** A black soldier from Mississippi finds a young German boy in some bushes close to the American shopping center one rainy, cold spring night. The child wears only the thinnest of clothes, certainly not enough to keep him warm or dry, so the soldier takes him inside to buy him warm clothing. The saleswoman, German herself, expresses hostility to the child, who as one of "that kind" of German has no business in the store. Furthermore, she reminds the soldier that, ironically, Germans are not allowed as shoppers inside the Occupation stores. In doing so, the woman seals the bond between the soldier and the child, for the soldier remembers how many places blacks cannot enter in his own country. He knows his uniform buys him respect in Germany, but back home, things remain very different. He makes a variety of purchases for the boy, as if the child were his own. A virtual newcomer to Germany, he speaks to the child through the saleswoman's translation, and through her also, the soldier learns the child and his sister are brought to the center every day by their mother in order to find wealthy Americans to buy food and clothing for them. Yet the black soldier does not feel cheated by the child, for the boy has provided the opportunity for him to offer charity. At home, the soldier has had very little chance to take care of others.

Through the magician's ploy of misdirection, Boyle argues the senselessness of racism in the United States by showing the reader the rigidity and cruelty of the saleswoman's attitude toward the German child, but the presence of the black soldier makes her target unmistakable. The reasoning and the regulations supported by the German saleswoman to exclude the child coincide with the racial barriers prevalent in the United States of the 1950s. A soldier from Mississippi would only too readily see the connection between Occupation policy and Jim Crow law. Thus, Boyle again ties the racism of Germany to that of the United States. The context she presents this time strikes at the heart of America's cherished belief in its moral superiority, especially at the time the countries of the world sought to separate themselves from the events and the attitudes that led Germany to the Holocaust. Boyle's voice of protest against American racism, heard in the early 1950s, raised significant issues with which the United States would soon grapple.

In content and thrust *The Smoking Mountain* marks a dramatic change of direction of Boyle's short fiction. Before this collection, Boyle's work focused on thematic concerns, and what political and social commentary there was dealt mainly with Europe. In *The Smoking Mountain,* primarily about the postwar situation in Germany, Boyle begins to address political and social issues relating to life in the States. The major themes of two stories in this collection and passing references in several others confront the racial tension and injustice that existed in the United States in the late 1940s when the Jim Crow laws and other more informal and widespread forms of discrimination were in full force. Through Boyle's perceptive and passionate consciousness, the conjunction of European postwar trauma and brewing American racial turmoil produced a telling juxtaposition.

In a recent discussion of his own writing, mystery novelist Stuart Kaminsky observed that the most successful fictional attempts dealing with issues focus on people and the effects of those issues on the conduct of daily lives.[24] Boyle, almost 40 years ago, adopted this technique to explore the human injustices she found in the American treatment of racial differences. Never again in either her writing or her life would she be willing to ignore the effects of discriminatory practices on the people involved, both the victim and the perpetrator. **"The Lost"** and **"Home"** play on the irony most Americans did not yet see, of American outrage at the German dehumanizing of Jews and American

complacency at its own national dehumanizing of people of color. Yet, in these stories Boyle does not belabor the moral and ethical travesties of American life; instead she presents the reader with the human tragedies. The reader sees the injustice with new eyes. And therein lies the power of these stories and Boyle's approach as a chronicler of our times.

As a collection, *The Smoking Mountain* is striking for several reasons, not the least of which is the insight with which Boyle established and explored her subject matter, but also its mixture of genres. In this collection Boyle stretches the parameters of the short story and essentially creates a new genre, one claimed more than a decade later by Truman Capote for *In Cold Blood,* but which is amply demonstrated in this work. Capote openly admitted expounding on the story of a group of Kansas murders by re-creating scenes and conversations about them in his imagination, but also by keeping that material consistent with the documented events of the case. In so doing he shifted emphasis from plot to situation and from action to perspective. Boyle did the same with more commonplace experiences, creating a stark re-creation of events totally independent of considerations of plot or traditional narrative.

Ironically, Boyle's exploration in *Thirty Stories* and *Smoking Mountain* of the twin concepts of honor and personal courage soon found a correlative in her own life. In 1952, Joseph Franckenstein was accused of Communist leanings, primarily because of his marriage to Kay Boyle, who was charged with belonging to the Communist Party from 1940-44. She had been named during the McCarthy hearings by three people she had never met and did not know. Franckenstein was cleared of any wrongdoing, but by 1953, with the McCarthy hysteria in full swing in the United States, he was dismissed from his job with the State Department and sent back to the United States. Thus began a long and frustrating campaign to clear his name, as well as that of Boyle.

Magazines and journals that had previously been anxious to print the award-winning author now would not touch Boyle's stories. The blacklisting begun during this time halted the momentum of her career and denied her the American audience she deserved. Yet, both Boyle and Franckenstein refused to name names or to cooperate with the McCarthy tactics in any way. Instead, Boyle issued a statement outlining the principles by which she lived. In it she points to her unalterable opposition to infringement of individual rights and mentions specific evidence of such opposition in many of her stories. She reminds the Senate Subcommittee on Un-American Activities that her work has always stood for a solid belief in the principles of human rights and of things American. However, she says, without her belief in an American spirit that would survive even McCarthy and in her husband's ultimate exoneration, "I must say quite simply that my heart would break." In April 1957, they were cleared, but he was offered no promise of reemployment.

MORAL VISION AND THE UNEXPECTED: *NOTHING EVER BREAKS EXCEPT THE HEART*

Unlike her other collections of short stories, this one is divided into sections recounting Boyle's observations about life in the war and post-war years. The sections are arranged thematically, not geographically or chronologically; the first section, **"Peace,"** deals with the 1950s and early 1960s, while the two remaining sections deal with World War II in **"War Years"** and its immediate aftermath in Germany with **"Military Occupation."** Each section has its own theme and its own personality, as well as its own message, for in this collection Boyle is more didactic than she has been in the past. As we saw in ***"The Smoking Mountain" and Other Stories,*** the war profoundly affected Boyle's perceptions and rather dramatically changed specific elements of her writing. In addition, the years after that collection, spent in the United States, first battling McCarthyism and then racial discrimination and other human injustices, magnified the intensity with which Boyle acted politically and socially, which was reflected in her fiction and the growing body of her nonfiction.

The most obvious change in Boyle's writing concerns her use of plot. In earlier collections of stories, she subordinates action and concentrates almost solely on stylistic innovations and on the development of internal psychological movement. Even in *The Smoking Mountain,* plot remains secondary to other concerns, such as narrative voice and experimentations with genre. In *Nothing ever Breaks Except the Heart* (1966), however, Boyle focuses on plot, on what happened at several levels of the story, as well as on how the story is told. As with her earliest collections of stories, this one still contains remarkable images and narrative techniques, but these stories go beyond virtuosity to establish a moral vision and to reveal the author's consciousness of pressing contemporary issues.

She experiments with narrative voice, especially with the omnipotent storyteller, whose role in several of these stories makes them comparable to fairy tales, but she does so in the context of the events making up her plot. She creates, then, several types of parables and fairy tales, carefully distancing herself as author and/or narrator from the content of the stories in order to provide a clearly articulated moral and ethical stance. This pattern most obviously delineates the stories that make up the **"Peace"** section of the collection.

Ironically titled, this section contains stories of people who for one reason or another lead desperate lives. In most of the stories, a character—usually the protagonist—maintains a stable relationship with society, but sees the problems of societal marginality through the life of another character less able to adapt to the demands or expectations of contemporary life. In all of these stories, the connection between the protagonist and the character who lives on the margins of society is tenuous and fleeting, but it mandates some form of involvement on the part of the protagonist with the problems of the other character. Sometimes the protagonist makes a positive difference (**"One Sunny Morning"**), sometimes not (**"An Evening at Home"**). And sometimes the encounter ends in a disaster (**"Ballet of Central Park"**) through no fault except the nature of contemporary life.

The stories in this opening section of the volume use slices of individual characters' lives to paint a clear picture of contemporary culture in the 1960s. They portray a simmering and smoldering undercurrent running through an American society on the brink of eruption. In all of these stories, tension and the hint of promised violence that may or may not develop support the action of the plot. While Boyle does not posit open warfare in this section, she suggests its promise. Class and race problems, neglect and abuse, generational issues, severely circumscribed lives and spirits suggest the potential for large-scale societal havoc. She personalizes the issues facing the United States in the early 1960s through the lives, actions, and insights of her characters.

One of the most widely recognized and anthologized stories from this section of the book, **"The Ballet of Central Park,"** illustrates both Boyle's use of narrative technique and her involvement with social issues. She creates a frame device for the story by merging the author's voice with that of the narrator, in effect making the author as shaper of events an active participant. Thus, the author speaks directly to readers, establishing a central tension by telling them that this story about children must be told before it is too late. In addition to this sense of urgency, the author establishes a larger context for the story by discussing Dostoyevski's and Freud's theories about the nature of children and why they should not suffer. Finally, as a bridge to the major part of the story, the author admits not having any relationship with the young protagonist, but as observer continues with her story anyway. By distancing the author/narrator from the events of the story, but retaining that omnipotent voice as moral interpreter, Boyle creates a contemporary fairy tale, beginning with a modern adaptation of "Once upon a time . . ." and maneuvering archetypal characters through a landscape almost—but not quite—real.

The protagonist, Hilary, an only child and prodigy talented in poetry and music, a child of privilege from the suburbs, comes into the city twice a week for ballet lessons. During lunch recess one Thursday, she goes to the park where she sees old men playing chess being bombarded by boys throwing water balloons. In the ensuing confusion, Hilary finds herself running off with three of the boys. The three—beautiful Jorge from Puerto Rico, venomous Guiseppe from Italy, and Federico named for a dead Spanish poet—represent a life lived on the streets of the city, far removed in both distance and substance from the security and comfort of Hilary's life. They have seen violence and the deaths of children; they have learned to fend for themselves. Although both Hilary and the boys strive for friendship, their experiences—born of socioeconomic distinctions—forever separate them; Hilary cannot comprehend their lives anymore than they can hers. Even their language as the embodiment of their experience separates them. In the first conversation, Hilary asks them to imagine what kind of animal they would like to be; instead, the conversation turns to stories of death. In response to Hilary's obvious distress, Guiseppe offers no comfort, but merely smiles "his venomous, slow smile."[25] The atmosphere of this scene is charged with the promise of violence, specifically of danger to Hilary, which she senses at some inarticulate level.

Nevertheless, the next Tuesday when she leaves ballet for her lunch recess, the boys are waiting for her, and she blithely follows them to the park. They entertain her by showing her how they panhandle on the subways and perform stunts for money. She is intrigued by their stories of dancing and acrobatics. She romanticizes their struggles to survive and mentally sets them to music. She decides to write a "shoeshine ballet" for a competition at her school, but tells the boys she will need other dancers. Federico, with the soul of a poet and a yearning for Hilary, promises to bring other boys like themselves to dance the parts of her ballet.

On Thursday, almost 20 boys of the street rally to Federico's call. They have come for the promise of food and violence, but Hilary in her innocence does not notice this. The boys dance for practically an hour, then decide they want their reward; the atmosphere is charged with menace, but a menace Hilary cannot understand. She sees only that the time has come for the climax of her ballet, with all the boys laying down their knives and weapons at her feet. Federico, perhaps in homage to her, is the first to do so, and his vulnerability sparks a rampage on the part of the other boys. They attack and kill him, then run away.

As the story's sole representative of the adult world, a police officer responds to Hilary's grief with a callous retort that she should have expected something of the sort when she got mixed up with these boys. As the author/narrator has indicated in the opening frame of this story, the adult world shows a lack of concern for the pain of children; it remains heedless of what happens to them.

"The Ballet of Central Park" explores several themes. Boyle, throughout her career, has dealt with the clash of cultures inherent in the meeting of her typical American protagonist with European civilization. This story, too, explores a clash of cultures, but in two particular contexts. The first, the socioeconomic clash, points out the chasm that exists between the worlds of the privileged, suburbanized, well-educated, secure population and the poverty-stricken, inner-city, uneducated, wary underclass. Hilary is frightened of the boys' world and insensitive to its problems; the boys are oblivious to the graces of her world and predatory toward other representatives of it. Neither Hilary nor the boys understand the differing expectations their lives have created for them, yet each depends for survival on strict adherence to the behavioral standards her or his life is governed by. The mixture explodes, leaving behind victims from both worlds.

On an intrinsic level, Boyle also explores the clash of cultures that exists between the world of the imagination and the world of experience. Hilary creates a world in which she becomes a virtual princess with Federico the young commoner in service to her. In many ways, her ballet celebrates the precepts of courtly love, of the romances of old, in which the warrior class bows before their lady. Indeed, the role she casts for herself projects her accepting the fealty of her subjects, shown in the ritual placing of their knives at her feet. In reality, however, the warriors care nothing of gracious ladies or pledging their loyalty, even to each other. Their world is a concrete one of daily survival and the search for instant reward. Federico, in his attraction to Hilary, forgets his survival skills, and in the moment of trying to join her in the imaginary world she has created, leaves himself vulnerable to the real world he inhabits.

The story, on one level, deals with loss of innocence, for Hilary will never look so freshly or imaginatively at the world again, and Federico will never have the chance. At another level, however, Boyle describes a society that has lost its innocence, a society that has not bridged its chasms nor protected its future, a society that—through the official voice of the police officer—can only say that it was to be expected, that one should not have anticipated anything else. And so the story ends with the boys' senseless physical violence that results in Federico's death and society's equally senseless spiritual violence that destroys something vital in Hilary.

Boyle shows another face of society's senseless spiritual violence in **"One Sunny Morning,"** again using a child as protagonist. This child, a young boy from Philadelphia who has been sent to Delaware to visit his aunt and uncle because his mother has just given birth to a baby, feels lonely and unwanted. As he pedals his bicycle down a country road, on an errand for his uncle who is interested in a Chesapeake Bay retriever owned by the Ticer family, he mulls over the pain and rejection he feels. He wants life as he knew it before; he wants the familiarity of home and family. Instead, he must face an unfamiliar landscape and people. His uncle has told him that the Ticers are "better than most" (51), clearly living in poverty but not in squalor. Yet not until the boy reaches their home does Boyle reveal that the Ticers are black, thus putting the uncle's remark in a more charged context. The boy represents one world, and he is soon to meet Mrs. Ticer and her two children, who inhabit another.

In the Ticer's home, marked by an "ancient" Ford Model A parked precariously in front, the boy begins to learn of the connections between the two worlds. Mrs. Ticer's older children have been sent to New York to live with relatives, just as he has, but they have been sent away in order to obtain a good education. Mrs. Ticer has dreams for them, dreams that cannot be realized in the rural setting of her life. Her sending her children away has nothing to do with convenience; it is a necessity. She also has dreams for her two younger children still at home, Ezra, aged eight, and Alice, aged four. She wants a college education for them, perhaps at the University of Pennsylvania. To the protagonist's comment that he wants to go there also, Mrs. Ticer responds that maybe he'll be able to make Ezra feel at home there. Maybe he'll remember this day of sitting in her house sharing conversation, and he'll return the favor to Ezra.

But there are dramatic differences in the world of the protagonist and the world of the Ticers, and the protagonist must learn them. Ezra tells the protagonist that he, too, hates visiting with relatives, for on a recent trip to Mississippi, his family had to sleep in their car and carry all their food and water with them. Mrs. Ticer tells her son this was only to avoid inconveniencing anyone. The protagonist does not comment on the matter. Boyle, however, expects the reader to know of the Jim Crow laws of the South and plays the naïveté of the children against this knowledge.

At this juncture, a gravel truck barrels down the road, coming to a screeching halt before the Model A. The driver, very angry, begins shouting and threatening Mrs. Ticer, making a slur against her in language the boy cannot process. The protagonist sees the driver as if literally looming over them, expanding as a balloon would, robbing them of the air they breathe. He perceives the driver as a "tower of flesh" and a "floating head" that "pushed aside the landscape" until only the driver and his anger existed (58). In a flash, the protagonist thinks they will all die. Instead, he runs across the yard and jumps into the old Ford, backing it jerkily into the Ticers' driveway and out of the truck's way. With the reason for confrontation removed, the driver diminishes in size, perhaps never having really left the truck, throws it into gear, and drives away. Mrs. Ticer invites the protagonist to stay longer, suggesting her husband might give the boy's uncle the dog he wants. With dignity, she realizes the importance of the boy's actions. The protagonist, too, understands what he has done for her. He has defused a racially motivated scene with an action of such simplicity that its result seems astounding, but not unbelievable.

Ironically, and pointedly, the events of the story happen in Delaware, which Boyle tells the reader "had nothing to do with real South" (50). She wants her reader to know that racial prejudice and the behaviors it spawns are not just a regional problem confined to the South where discrimination and violence were at the time all too common and well publicized. Racial prejudice was, and continues to be, a national reality, and in 1966, as ***Nothing ever Breaks Except the Heart*** was being published, the scope and severity of this national issue was finally being widely examined.

Boyle attacked another controversial issue in this volume of short stories. In **"You Don't Need to Be a Member of the Congregation"** she spoke against the Vietnam War, which in 1966 was not yet the subject of protest and debate that it would become several years later. Her approach to the subject was novel, blurring the distinction between the author as person and the author as participant in the story. In this case, she moved further than she had in **"Ballet of Central Park,"** making the story's author both narrator and a character. The author herself appears in the story and interacts with clearly fictional characters of her own creation.

The author/protagonist/narrator is in search of a way to tell the story she wants to tell, but which exists only in her mind as the image of an old man in a Brooklyn church. She is aware that some catalyst must provide the emotional substance of a story, or there is nothing to tell. The author describes attempts to get some kind of character involved in conversation with the man, by now in the black robes of an Asiatic scholar with papers, scrolls, and a pot of black ink spread before him. The first potential character is a young woman with a white mantilla and an engagement ring. But she doesn't work well in the story, for she informs the author that the only way a conversation between her and the old man would make sense is if she had come to confessional before her approaching marriage. The author is adamant that the church be Unitarian, in which confession is not a common practice, so the young woman leaves to join another story. The second prospective character is a ragged young teenage boy with a green knapsack. Obviously, the author projects, he has stolen something, and she wants him to find words of eternal comfort from the old man. The teenager balks, saying the will be late for biology class, and leaves before the author can persuade him.

Finally, the appropriate character finds the author, although she is afraid of him. He is military, and she recognizes that the old man in the church is Vietnamese, on a hunger strike protesting the destruction of his land and culture. The author is afraid of what the soldier will do; she tries to dissuade him from entering the church, but he insists he knows what he is doing. She wants, then, to go into the church with him, but he insists he must go in alone. He must tell the old man, he assures her, that he refuses to fight in Vietnam. The author then knows the story begins here and that she can finally write it.

Thus, Boyle has written a story about a "prestory," ending it where the "real" story begins. She adapts the traditional concept of the framing device, which may serve to give the pretense of reasonable validity to the narration that follows, to her own purposes. Boyle uses this frame to set a context that reveals the author's intensity and the dilemmas the author must solve before a beginning is possible. In essence, the entire narrative describes the decision-making process an author goes through to create the story that must be written. She includes as well the element of discovery that she believes exists for all writers. In several interviews, Boyle discusses the element of surprise that accompanies writing, with the characters sometimes deciding to travel in directions the author has not consciously intended.

As antiwar statement, **"You Don't Need to Be a Member of the Congregation"** provides a gentle ethical prod to a nation just beginning to build up its military forces in Vietnam.

WAR YEARS

The second section of *Nothing ever Breaks Except the Heart,* "War Years," travels back to a different war and explores it in a variety of contexts through stories Boyle wrote and published predominantly in the 1940s. In Boyle's mind World War II was not the

same kind of endeavor that Vietnam was. It also had the advantage of distance and could be examined within this collection in retrospect instead of in mid-action. Thus, the statements Boyle makes in this section about war are tempered for the reader by the time and the issues.

Boyle does not write the typical war story. She turns instead to another side of war, sometimes in Europe—although never at the front—and sometimes in this country. She again focuses on civilians making their way in life while war goes on somewhere else. She explores a variety of responses and degrees of involvement with the conflict in Europe, sometimes having war touch characters personally with the death of a loved minor character and sometimes leaving war as a theoretical reality the characters see as "over there." She also displays a range of emotional responses in her characters: fear for loved ones, misplaced anger, enthusiasm for the cause, upset over the loss of friendships, patriotism, shame. The juxtaposition Boyle creates of this past war, as portrayed in her stories, and the growing conflict of Vietnam, reported daily in the news for her readers, adds a new dimension and timeliness to her themes.

"Anschluss," widely recognized as one of Boyle's best war stories, features an unlikely protagonist in Merrill, a fashion editor's American assistant who travels twice a year from Paris to Brenau to visit friends. The time is late 1930s, the economic situation in Austria dire, emphasized by the disapproval of Austrians who see Merrill giving sugar to the carriage horses. Boyle also contrasts the frivolity of Merrill's job with the struggle for survival that her friends must face. Fanni and her brother Toni, as most of the young people of their village, have no work; because of the economy, jobs and money are virtually non-existent. Toni engages in political agitation by lighting swastika fires and supporting an Austrian nationalist movement in the hope that it will bring prosperity to his country. Although arrested for treason, he is soon released from prison. Merrill suggests he come with her to Paris where life is better, but Toni refuses to leave his homeland.

The scene shifts to 1938, the spring of the *Anschluss* that brings German troops and nazism to Austria. As Merrill arrives for her usual visit, she wonders if Toni will be ready to leave now that he sees what the Nazis are like. She expects him to be protesting them as he had earlier protested the Catholics and Communists. But the atmosphere has changed dramatically. Both Fanni and Toni have jobs, a new prosperity holds the country, and Toni additionally serves as *Direktor* of the Austrian Youth Local. Swastikas are everywhere.

Boyle captures the more rigid political atmosphere that prevails by describing an exchange between Merrill and Toni. She has appeared at the poolside of her hotel wearing her usual two-piece bathing suit, noticing, however, that other women are more severely covered. For the first time, she feels uncomfortable and out of place here where she has been welcome so many times before. Toni accuses her of looking "like somebody from the theatre" (118), as he bitterly denounces the people who have looked at Austria as Europe's playground. He embraces Germany and the Nazis, for they, he says, have accepted Austria as a serious country. Merrill realizes she no longer has any connection with either Toni or Fanni. She leaves, knowing this political stance marks the end of whatever had existed between them.

In this story, Boyle refrains from heavy moralizing or from obvious statements about the disasters to come. First published in 1939 and reprinted in both *O. Henry Memorial Award Prize Stories of 1939* and Edward J. O'Brien's *Best American Short Stories, 1940,* this story relies on the subtleties that motivate personal relationships to cast a damning indictment at the events shaping up in Europe. At the same time, however, Boyle pointedly acknowledges the economic and nationalistic foundations for nazism's spread in the poverty and desperation of depression-ridden Europe. The story conveys a tone of abiding sadness at the unbridgeable rift developing between peoples of different nations.

"Luck for the Road," although taking its impetus from situations that develop in wartime, seems hardly to be about war at all. Its subject matter relates more specifically to the human condition than the political and to personal loyalties rather than patriotic ones. The action of the story takes place within the consciousness of the protagonist. Indeed, the sole action of the story involves the education of the protagonist, an American, Mrs. Amboy, who learns at her late age a lesson in the relative value of money. A wealthy domineering woman, she idealizes her grandson in whom she sees her own fire and spirit, missing drastically from her son or daughter-in-law. He engages in mischief as a child, some of more serious nature than others, but Mrs. Amboy consistently buys him out of trouble. In her eyes he can do no wrong, until as a young man of 20 he joins the Air Force in order to pilot fighter planes in World War II. Mrs. Amboy views the war as something ordinary people must engage in; clearly it is not meant for people of breeding and privilege such as her grandson. She goes to Washington to buy his way out of service.

In response to the official rebuff given to her efforts, she responds that she has never found anything money could not buy. Even her grandson's insistence that he

wants to fly and that he wants her to stay out of the matter fails to deter her. She travels to the camp where he trains and offers his captain first $50,000 and then $75,000 to ensure that he is not killed as if he were just an ordinary person. The captain responds that he had hoped the war had at least put an end to class distinctions. She then turns to her grandson's crewmates, looking for one desperate for money. She finds a man whose wife is in the hospital after a miscarriage; Ellory needs money for hospital bills and for the mortgage on his house. She offers him $10,000 to keep her grandson out of danger by any means. Ellory tells her he is her grandson's "control officer" and can divert any mission out of danger, even one scheduled for combat. Mrs. Amboy writes the check and goes home, secure in the knowledge that she has bought her grandson's safety.

Shortly thereafter, the grandson is reported missing in action, as is Ellory. Mrs. Amboy learns from her bank that the check she wrote was never cashed and, in her investigation of the matter, discovers that Ellory is a pilot, not a control officer. Realizing she has been tricked, she decides to go to Denver to see Ellory's wife, hoping to learn more about him. There she reads that both men have been rescued floating on a raft. In an imagined conversation between Mrs. Amboy and what she projects as Ellory, he tells of rescuing her grandson from the ocean and of finding a package of cigarettes that the men on the raft can share. Alas, they have no matches. With the use of a magnifying glass one of them carried, they set fire to the check in order to light the cigarettes. Mrs. Amboy's money means much less to him than the camaraderie and bond that exist on that raft.

In reality, Ellory has done what Mrs. Amboy paid him for; he has saved the life of her grandson, but he refuses the money, even though he desperately needs it. He recognizes other values that spur him to action; he recognizes that some values extend beyond money. Mrs. Amboy, aged 75, goes into the hospital to see Ellory's wife with an outlook very much like humility. As the story ends, she, too, has recognized finally that some things in life cannot be bought. However, the newfound knowledge that much of her life has been lived on a false premise does not destroy Mrs. Amboy.

While the ending borders on sentimentality, it also describes the grit of a woman who refuses to become a defeated old fool. Mrs. Amboy may, indeed, have learned a lesson in the size of the human spirit, but she does not retire quietly with her humility. Instead, although somewhat chastened, she embraces her lesson and moves forward, taking decisive action as she has always done, moving forward to new experiences. Her actions, entering the hospital to talk with Ellory's wife, show she has lost none of her spirit, even if she has rechanneled it. Mrs. Amboy refuses to be carried along by the currents of life; she will participate actively in it to the end. Thus, Mrs. Amboy contrasts dramatically with the misplaced aristocrats reeling from World War I's changes as Boyle presents them in earlier story collections.

This section also contains the title story collected in *Best of the Best American Short Stories* (1952) and *Fifty Best American Short Stories, 1915-1965* (1965), both edited by Martha Foley. ***Nothing ever Breaks Except the Heart*** deals with two characters' attempts to deal with the desperation and despair of massive numbers of refugees trying to escape occupied territory. In June Miss Del Monte, an American trying to leave Spain, and Mr. McCloskey, a bureaucrat in the airline office, meet when he tells her she cannot leave Avenida when she wants. Mr. McCloskey and his co-workers face hundreds of requests for air transportation each day and have to tell angry, frightened people that they must wait several months before transportation can be arranged. In Miss Del Monte's case, this means November, even though she tells Mr. McCloskey she has a show opening in September. Their relationship continues over several days as she repeats her case and he repeats his answer. Eventually, they begin seeing each other at night. She takes him to out of the way cafés with which she seems very familiar, where *fado* singers sing of events they've read in the newspaper: a stabbing at the fish market, a murder caused by senseless jealousy. In July he takes her to "the only thing in life [he] cares about," a plane he used to pilot until too much alcohol and too many jitters reduced him to standing in the airline office, unable ever again to fly (128-29). The morning after his confession, he is back in the airline office looking with hopelessness at the supplicants before him.

The rather simple plot of this story disguises the subtlety of Boyle's character depiction. She focuses on two characters whose lives have been shattered, not by the bullets and shrapnel of war, but by the tension and uncertainty civilians must face, civilians who during wartime generally remain unarmed and vulnerable, attendant to the vagaries of the war machine. With gentleness, Boyle shows the underside of the life, populated with somewhat jaded, hopeless people, that defines Miss Del Monte's world. Boyle suggests that these cheap and dark cafés bear relation to the "show" to which Miss Del Monte refers, implying that her life in reality vastly differs from the impression she hopes to make. Likewise, Boyle uses an airplane to indicate the plunge of Mr. McCloskey's world. The poignancy of his feeling for the plane combines with his past as pilot and his present as "gatekeeper" to dramatize his despair. The two are brought together, neither able to

give the other what he or she needs and neither able to change any element of the life they find themselves in. Thus, Boyle's reminder that nothing ever breaks—except the heart—finds embodiment in these two sad souls at the edge of worldwide confrontation.

This second section provides an oblique look at war, for it ignores the usual landscapes and the typical plots that grow up in wartime literature. Boyle's cast of characters in the stories of this section contains ordinary people dealing as best they can with situations over which they have no control. Some of them realize their helplessness; some of them don't. But Boyle takes her reader into a territory with no comforting landmarks, no stories of the heroism and glory of war, or for that matter of the carnage of war. Instead, she takes her reader into the arena of circumstance and coincidence that shapes the face of war most people see.

Military Occupation

The third section of this collection contains stories of military occupation, generally set in Germany of the early postwar years and, with the exception of **"A Christmas Carol for Harold Ross," "French Harvest,"** and **"Fire in the Vineyards,"** all published in 1966, written and published in the late 1940s and 1950s. Unlike *The Smoking Mountain,* which also explores this era, the stories in this collection deal not so much with the tensions between American and German cultures as they do with the clashes that exist within families or within personal relationships. Several of the stories in this section concern relationships between fathers and sons, reflecting perhaps Boyle's own experiences in maintaining family life in the strange world of a military occupation. Many of the stories could occur anywhere, for the location and part-military setting are incidental to the events of the plot. One such story, **"A Disgrace to the Family,"** set in occupied Germany, nevertheless focuses on the emotional journey a father and son must make in order to live at peace with each other. The setting is virtually irrelevant to the events or to the theme of the story.

The father, a career military man, awaits the arrival of his 14-year-old son from boarding school in France. A widower, the father has no other family. Friends assume his joy, and they promise to welcome the young boy. Only gradually does the reader begin to realize that the father does not share his friends' excitement at the arrival of his son, for the father knows what they do not: his son has been expelled from school for theft. During the major part of the story the father's anger develops, revealed through conversations with an accusing tone. The father has been disgraced by his son and finds him an alien creature not worthy of respect or love. His son's rejection of military life in favor of the poetic life of his mother's Irish ancestry cements the father's anger into a wall that separates the two. In fact, the father even begins to wonder if the boy deserves to live.

At the father's insistence, the two go hunting together, and having had several drinks from his flask, the father accidentally shoots the son. Both father and son believe the boy will die. In what he believes to be his final words to his father, the boy confesses that he did not steal the money from his classmates. Rather he allowed himself to be blamed to cover for his best friend. The boy's explanation for his behavior catches the father off guard: the boy knew his friend's father would never forgive him; he also knew his own father would never believe that he could have stolen. The ironic contrast between the boy's faith in his father's love, a faith on which he has risked much, and his father's willingness to believe the worst of his son provides a poignancy that directs the tone of the story. Somewhat dramatically, the father and son are reunited; he, of course, does not die; and the father learns to accept the feminine side of the boy's nature, the poetic qualities he inherited from his mother.

Throughout the story, Boyle uses father and son as foils for each other. She suggests an undercurrent of violence in the father's inability to deal with what he believes to be his son's unworthiness. The father closes a door on the son metaphorically in refusing to discuss the matter with the boy. In literal terms, Boyle represents this through her depiction of the house, large and cavernous for the two of them, to which the father brings his son. The impersonality of the house mirrors the coldness of the father. The undercurrent of potential violence becomes more overt when the father insists his son go hunting; Boyle builds the tension of the story to this point, predicting with almost every word that something will happen. The shooting is inevitable. On the other hand, Boyle presents the gentleness of the boy in all of his actions. He adopts a starving dog they find on the Autobahn and, in naming the dog Famine, suggests the emotional paucity he feels, as well as the dog's physical hunger. He tries to establish a bond with the dog, but events in the dog's past have been too strong; ultimately he cannot be domesticated to life in one place. Yet, while the son cannot talk with his father, he can care for the dog, and his efforts at trying to acclimate the dog to the huge house his father occupies are metaphorical attempts to fill the house with warmth and the bond of shared trust.

The dog becomes the catalyst for reuniting the father and son. On one hand, the father's indifference to the dog and the boy's identification with it form the two extremes of a continuum. The dog accompanies the two on the hunting trip and, because it is undisciplined as a hunter, draws the boy into the range of his father's rifle, providing the father with the opportunity he has fantasized. The shooting forces both father and son to recognize the unfinished business between them and shatters the walls that exist between them. The father's horror at what has happened and the boy's fear that he will be unable to explain to his father meet over the situation created in part by the abandoned Famine, who has since run away again. Despite the father's efforts to find the dog for his son, he cannot. However, having accomplished his task, the dog is no longer necessary to either the characters or the plot of the story. Boyle frequently includes animals in her stories, but they are never mere window dressing. They consistently serve either as analogies to human behavior or, as in this case, catalysts for major changes.

One other story from this collection merits attention because it also deals, at least in part, with the relationship between father and son. In **"The Soldier Ran Away"** the protagonist again is a boy, son of a medical officer in the American occupation army. The events of the story take place while mother and sister are away on a visit, thus creating a closed male world undisturbed by mediating or conflicting influences. Father and son must deal with each other without being able to turn to anyone else for advice.

The father's birthday comes up in two weeks, and the boy wants to build a special pipe rack for him. In order to make it a surprise, the boy takes his tools and wood to the huge and isolated attic to work in the evenings. Old trunks take up some of the space, and several fantastic masks—a parrot, a fox, a devil, and more—hang on the rafters, creating an eerie atmosphere. The first night the boy feels he is being watched and on subsequent nights when he notices that the arrangement of the masks has been changed, convinces himself that perhaps a German refugee meaning no harm and making no threats may have climbed into the attic for warmth, for he has seen the walking shadows of displaced people throughout the streets of Germany. He has trouble fitting the pieces of his pipe rack together and, in frustration because his time is running out, leaves them in disarray on the attic worktable.

When he comes back the next evening, the pipe rack pieces have been arranged in their proper positions, and the boy meets the young AWOL American soldier who has been living in the attic. He tells of his homesickness and admits that leaving his post was a big mistake, one he cannot redress. The boy, however, identifies with the soldier's longing and wants to help him. As they work on the father's pipe rack, the young soldier leaves during a sleet storm to find a special woodworking tool to finish the job. He returns ill with pneumonia, but finishes the rack for the protagonist.

During the next day, as the soldier lies ill in the attic, the young boy debates whether or not he should tell his father. The father as a doctor can help the soldier, but as a military man would be obligated to turn him in to the military authorities as a deserter. Military rules must be obeyed. The protagonist, however, rejects the validity of any kind of rule that does not consider the reasons for contradictory action. Finally, the boy realizes that without help the soldier will die and, as he tells his father of the AWOL soldier, fears his father's actions will cause a breach between them. The boy believes strongly that the young soldier should not be severely punished for giving in to his longing for home. The father senses his son's emotions, perhaps even agreeing with them, and, as he calls the hospital to get an ambulance for the young soldier, tells the authorities the young man was trying to turn himself in and that he, the doctor, will be responsible for him.

The story, then, ends as well as it possibly can, for father and son have reached a compromise born of their mutual respect for each other. The father is bound by military rules he cannot ignore, but bends them as far as he can to accommodate the sensibility of his son. The son fears the result his choice will have for the young soldier, but he must trust the judgment of his father. Their actions and choices strengthen the bond between them. The young soldier's life is saved, literally and probably also metaphorically.

Boyle organizes the story in a circular pattern: The father and son begin with a solid and mutually rewarding relationship, only to have it brought into question by the unfolding events. The story comes full circle, however, with the two characters again united.

Indeed, this story mirrors in some ways the arrangement and movement of the entire collection, for Boyle takes the reader from a peace-time studded with potential violence through a war lived on the periphery to a peace under occupation filled with personal conflict. Different in type from the war stories in **Thirty Stories** or the Occupation stories of **Smoking Mountain,** these narratives carry the reader more deeply into the human heart, as Boyle promised in her title.

Notes

1. In the late 1960s, at the instigation of her friend, editor Ken McCormick of Doubleday, she dealt in a more direct way with this time period in the chapters she wrote and inserted in Robert McAlmon's revised memoirs, *Being Geniuses Together.* In that book, Robert McAlmon wrote of his life in Paris during the 1920s and 1930s. It was published originally by him in 1938. He died in 1956 virtually forgotten by the literary mainstream. Because of her long-standing friendship with McAlmon and her connection with Paris during the time covered by his memoir, Boyle was asked to revise the book, inserting her own material.

2. Helen Moran, review of *Wedding Day and Other Stories, London Mercury* 26 (1932): 567.

3. Gerald Sykes, "Too Good to Be Smart," *Nation,* 24 December 1930, 711-12.

4. E. B. C. Jones, review of *Wedding Day and Other Stories, Adelphi,* n.s. 5 (1932): 73-76.

5. Katherine Anne Porter, "Example to the Young," *New Republic,* 22 April 1931, 279-80; hereafter cited in the text as Porter.

6. William Carlos Williams, "The Somnambulists," *transition* (Fall 1929): 147-49.

7. *Wedding Day and Other Stories* (New York: Cape & Smith, 1930; London: Pharos Editions, 1932), 29; hereafter cited by page number in the text.

8. Desmond Hawkins, "Fiction Chronicle," *Criterion* 17 (1938): 503-4.

9. Review of *The First Lover and Other Stories, Nation,* 19 April 1933, 453.

10. "Three Little Men," in *The First Lover and Other Stories* (New York: Smith & Haas, 1933; London: Faber & Faber, 1937), 61-71; hereafter cited by page number (U.S. edition) in the text.

11. Edith Walton, "Kay Boyle's Stories," *New York Times Book Review,* 9 February 1936, 7.

12. "In and Around the Bull's Eye," *Punch* 192 (1937): 168.

13. Mark Van Doren, review of *The White Horses of Vienna and Other Stories, Nation,* 4 March 1936, 286 and 288.

14. Peter Quennell, review of *The White Horses of Vienna and Other Stories, New Statesman and Nation,* 16 January 1937, 87.

15. "The New Novels: From Many Worlds," *Times Literary Supplement,* 16 January 1937, 43.

16. Sylvia Pass, "What Is It All About?" *Christian Century,* 4 March 1936, 368.

17. Howard Baker, "The Contemporary Short Story," *Southern Review* (1937-38): 588-89.

18. Struthers Burt, "The Mature Craft of Kay Boyle," *Saturday Review,* 30 November 1946, 11.

19. Edith R. Mirrielees, "Stories to Remember," *New York Times Book Review,* 1 December 1946, 9 and 12.

20. J. V., review of *Thirty Stories, San Francisco Chronicle,* 1 December 1946, 32.

21. "Battle of the Sequins," *Nation,* 23 December 1944, 770-71.

22. Louise Field Cooper, "Averted Hearts," *Saturday Review,* 21 April 1951, 17.

23. Harry T. Moore, "In Germany the Ruins Still Smother," *New York Times,* 22 April 1951, 5.

24. Elizabeth Greene, "A Film Professor and Prize-Winning Mystery Writer Whose Books Capture the 'Mythic Power' to Entertain," *Chronicle of Higher Education,* 26 July 1989, A3.

25. *Nothing Ever Breaks Except the Heart* (Garden City, N.Y.: Doubleday, 1966), 39; hereafter; hereafter cited by page number in the text.

FURTHER READING

Bibliography

Chambers, M. Clark. *Kay Boyle: A Bibliography.* New Castle, Del.: Oak Knoll Press, 2002, 360p.
  First comprehensive bibliography of Boyle that describes her individual writings and annotates critical books and articles written about the author and her works; includes a brief biography.

Biography

Mellen, Joan. *Kay Boyle: Author of Herself.* New York: Farrar, Straus & Giroux, 1994, 670p.
  Detailed biography that presents Boyle as a literary figure of consequence who occupies "an indubitable and significant place in the literary history of her century."

Criticism

Cramer, Timothy R. "Kay Boyle: Giving Voice to the Voiceless." *MAWA Review* 11, no. 1 (June 1996): 22-9.
  Discusses Boyle's fiction that deals with the dispossessed.

Additional coverage of Boyle's life and career is contained in the following sources published by Thomson Gale: *Contemporary Authors,* **Vols. 13-16R;** *Contemporary Authors Autobiography Series,* **Vol. 1;** *Contemporary Authors New Revision Series,* **Vols. 29, 61, and 110;** *Contemporary Authors— Obituary,* **Vol. 140;** *Contemporary Literary Criticism,* **Vols. 1, 5, 19, 58, and 121;** *Contemporary Novelists,* **Eds. 1, 2, 3, 4, and 5;** *Contemporary Poets,* **Eds. 1, 2, 3, 4, and 5;** *Dictionary of Literary Biography,* **Vol. 4, 9, 48, and 86;** *Dictionary of Literary Biography Yearbook,* **Ed. 1993;** *Encyclopedia of World Literature in the 20th Century,* **Ed. 3;** *Literature Resource Center; Major 20th-Century Writers,* **Eds. 1 and 2;** *Major 21st-Century Writers,* **Ed. 2005;** *Modern American Literature,* **Ed. 5;** *Reference Guide to American Literature,* **Ed. 4;** *Reference Guide to Short Fiction,* **Ed. 2;** *Short Stories for Students,* **Vols. 10, 13, and 14; and** *Short Story Criticism,* **Vol. 5.**

"The Lady with the Dog" ("Dama s sobachkoi")

Anton Chekhov

(Also translated as "The Lady with the Pet Dog," "The Lady with the Little Dog," and "The Lady with the Lapdog.") Russian short story.

The following entry presents criticism of Chekhov's "Dama s sobachkoi" (1899; "The Lady with the Dog"). For an overview of Chekhov's short fiction, see *SSC*, Volumes 2, 51, and 85; for discussion of Chekhov's short stories "Gooseberries" (1898) and "The Duel" (1891), see *SSC*, Volumes 28 and 41, respectively.

INTRODUCTION

Chekhov's tale of adultery and transformation by love is regarded by many critics as his finest short story, and has been universally praised for its psychological depth and quiet emotional power. The story traces the illicit love affair between an ageing philanderer, Dmitry Gurov, and the younger Anna Sergeevna, after a chance meeting at the Yalta seaside. The action of the story is minimal, but readers are offered a profound glimpse at the interior life of the protagonist and at the unlikely connection between the two main characters that changes their lives. Chekhov does not romanticize the adulterous relationship, nor does he moralize or condemn the actions of the lovers. He presents moments in their experience with such clarity and simplicity that their intimacy becomes real and their struggle deeply affecting. "The Lady with the Dog" has generated a great deal of critical commentary, both in Russian and English. Vladimir Nabokov has noted that it is "one of the greatest stories ever written."

PLOT AND MAJOR CHARACTERS

The story opens with a description of the protagonist, Dmitri Dmitrich Gurov, a banker who is on vacation at the Russian city of Yalta. Gurov is bored, but his interest is sparked by a recent arrival at the seaside town, a young woman named Anna Sergeevna von Diederitz. He sees Anna strolling along the sea-front with her Pomeranian, and later again in the gardens. Since she is not accompanied by a husband, Gurov decides to make her acquaintance. Gurov, it is explained, is not yet forty, but is long married, with three children, and has had many affairs. He married young and now finds his wife intolerable. She is staid, intellectual, and seems older than her years. Gurov thinks very little of women in general—he calls them the "lower race"—but he enjoys their company more than the company of men.

One evening while Gurov is dining in the gardens, Anna Sergeevna sits at the table next to him. He decides that she is married and bored as well, and becomes excited by the prospect of having an affair with this stranger. He calls her dog toward him, as an excuse to start up a conversation, and within a short time they strike an easy friendship. In bed later that night, Gurov continues to think about her and wonders how long ago the woman was still in school, as his own young daughter now is.

A week goes by. It is a warm, windy day, and Gurov and Anna go down to the pier to watch a steamer come in. On impulse, he kisses her and suggests they go to her hotel room. In her room, as he looks at her, Gurov thinks of the other women he has had affairs with, many of them experienced and beautiful, but cold. With Anna, he reflects, there is a sense of life, even if there is diffidence, inexperience, and awkwardness. After Gurov and Anna make love, she becomes distraught. She says she feels guilty not only for deceiving her husband but because she realizes she has been deceiving herself for a long time. She married her husband at twenty and has since realized that he is nothing more than a flunky. She has wanted more—"To live, to live!"—but now she feels her infidelity has shown her to be vulgar and contemptible. She fears too that Gurov will not respect her. Gurov is bored and irritated as he listens to her confession. He feels her remorse is out of place. But he comforts her, and within a short time they are laughing and happy.

They leave the hotel and drive to the town of Oreanda. They sit and look at the sea in silence, and then return to Yalta. For the next few days the two spend all their time together, dining, walking, making love, and enjoying the beauty of their surroundings. Anna continues to express her guilt and fear that Gurov thinks her a common woman. Then Anna receives a letter from her husband asking her to return home. She seems almost relieved at the prospect of leaving, saying it is the "finger of destiny." After he leaves Anna at the railroad station, Gurov reflects on the relationship and thinks of it as yet another episode in his life that has come to an end. He feels a slight tinge of remorse, but thinks too that this young woman he would never see again was not really happy with him, and besides he had not showed her his true self. Gurov decides to go back home to Moscow.

Once home, Gurov tries to return to his familiar routine of work, family life, and entertainment. He assumes that his memories of Anna will fade in a month or so, as the memories of his other lovers have done. He finds, however, that he cannot stop thinking about her. His memories of Anna become more and more vivid, and begin to haunt him. He mentions Anna to an acquaintance, and is horrified that the only response he gets from the man is that the fish they ate at dinner was too strong. Gurov begins to regard his life as nonsensical, empty, and dull. He is sick of his children, his work, and his activities. He decides to travel to Anna's hometown of S—. He finds her house but does not go in, and returns to his hotel. The next day he decides instead to go to the local theater to attend a premiere of "The Geisha," in the hopes of seeing her there. At the theater that night, he sees her in the crowd and realizes she is the most precious and important thing to him in the world. When Gurov confronts Anna during intermission, she is shocked yet thrilled. She too has thought of nothing but him. They kiss passionately but she asks him to leave in case they are seen, and agrees to meet with him in Moscow.

Gurov and Anna meet once every two or three months. As he is walking with his daughter one morning, Gurov reflects that he is living a double life. His everyday life is routine and conventional, but he thinks of it as being full of lies and deceit. He must keep his other life secret, but it contains all that he thinks of as having value, and indeed it represents the kernel of his being. He goes to see Anna, who is waiting at the hotel for him. She is in tears; she believes that their lives have been shattered by their love and the way they must deceive everyone around them. He tries to comfort her, and as he holds her he sees his reflection in the mirror. He has grown old and gray and lost his good looks. But he has fallen in love properly for the first time in his life. The pair talk about how they can change their lives and avoid the travel and secrecy, but they see no solution to their dilemma. The story ends with their ambiguous hope that a solution will soon be found and that a new, beautiful life will begin; but the end is far off and the most difficult part of their life is just beginning.

MAJOR THEMES

The main theme of "The Lady with the Dog" is love: its unexpectedness, its depth, and its power over the human psyche. The protagonists of the story do not seek the type of relationship they eventually find, and when they discover their love it is shocking, painful, and exhilarating. Gurov at first seems to be a shallow philanderer whose view of women shows him to be without emotional or spiritual depth. He sees Anna from a distance and assumes he will have the kind of affair he has had so many times before, one based on physical pleasure and casual intimacy. All his expectations are overturned when he cannot stop thinking of her. Without expecting or wanting it, he discovers an emotional experience that is deep, sincere, and touching. He cannot even pinpoint what it is about Anna that moves him so much, what it is about her that has made her the center of his life. Love, Chekhov suggests, can transform lives, making the most ordinary people seem extraordinary, and endowing life with value.

Another important concern in the story is women. At the beginning of the tale, Gurov is seen as an opportunist who uses women. He thinks of them as the "lower race," but at the same time enjoys their company and is afraid of his intellectual wife. Gurov enjoys women's company because of the intimacy it affords, but only after he has fallen in love with Anna does he realize how deep his need for intimacy is. When Gurov is at his lowest point and seeks someone in whom to confide, his friend dismisses his reference to the fascinating lady he met at Yalta. Gurov is disgusted by the boorishness of males, their savage manners, their unacceptable attitude toward women, and their petty interests such as card-playing and drinking. Women offer true communication, true emotion, and true experience in a way that men do not. When he wants to talk about Anna, his friends do not know what he is saying; ironically, only his wife guesses what he is getting at with his sideways remarks. By the end of the story, Gurov has been transformed by love not only because it has opened up his own emotional life but because it has changed his view of women. Gurov has changed from an oaf who sees women as lower beings to someone who recognizes their ability to understand interior experiences as a source of life's greatest richness. However, the story is told from the point of view of Gurov, and there is far less sense of what Anna thinks and feels about what is going on; most of her emotions and thoughts are filtered though Gurov. Her point of view is never fully presented. Neither are the thoughts of Gurov's wife. Thus, while the story says a great deal about women, it remains very much rooted in a male perspective.

CRITICAL RECEPTION

When "The Lady with the Dog" appeared in 1899, Chekhov had already established his reputation as one of Russia's great short story writers. The tale was immediately popular; Maxim Gorky is said to have remarked that it made him want to "change wives." Gorky also wrote that the work "killed realism" and thus reinvented fiction, because of the way the author required readers to use their imaginations to fill out the story. Early critics noted that the tale opened up the form of the short story through its focus on character and the exploration of one person's moral and emotional growth.

Today, "The Lady with the Dog" is regarded by many critics as one of the greatest short stories in any language and one of the finest psychological studies of love ever written. Recent criticism on the story in English has concentrated on how the work reflects Chekhov's attitudes towards women and love. Other themes of interest to scholars have included the biographical elements in the story, notably parallels with Chekhov's own relationship with Olga Kipper; exactly what type of transformation is undergone by the protagonists; the work's lyricism and structure; the realism, humor, and pathos of the tale; and the story's treatment of memory. Critics have also discussed the influence of the philosophy of Friedrich Nietzsche on the work and the story's vast influence on other artists, from the Russian modernist I. A. Bunin, to the American short-story writer Joyce Carol Oates, to the filmmaker Nikita Mikhalkov. Because of its brevity, simplicity, and lyricism, the work continues to enjoy wide readership. Its appearance in countless anthologies is a testament to its popular appeal and to Chekhov's reputation as a master of the short story.

PRINCIPAL WORKS

Short Fiction

Pestrye rasskazy [*Motley Tales*] 1886
Nevinnye rechi [*Innocent Speeches*] 1887
V sumerkakh [*In the Twilight*] 1887
Rasskazy [*Tales*] 1888
Detvora [*Children*] 1889
Gloomy People 1890
Stones and Tales 1894
Chekhov: Polnoe sobranie sochineniy (short stories and dramas) 1900-04
The Black Monk, and Other Stories 1903

The Tales of Chekhov. 13 vols. 1917-23
Polnoe sobranie sochinenii i pisem A. P. Chekhova. 20 vols. [*Complete Works and Letters of A. P. Chekhov*] 1944-51
The Oxford Chekhov. 9 vols. (short stories, plays, and letters) 1964-75
Polnoe sobranie sochinenii i pisem A. P. Chekhova. 30 vols. [*Complete Works and Letters of A. P. Chekhov*] (short stories, plays, and letters) 1974-83

Other Major Works

Ivanov (play) 1887
Leshy [*The Wood Demon*] (play) 1889
Chayka [*The Seagull*] (play) 1896
Dyadya Vanya [*Uncle Vanya*] (play) 1899
Trei sestry [*The Three Sisters*] (play) 1901
Vishnevy sad [*The Cherry Orchard*] (play) 1904

*During his life Chekhov published most of his short stories individually in periodicals, notably in *Peterburskaia gazeta* and *Novoe vremia.*

CRITICISM

Virginia Llewellyn Smith (essay date 1973)

SOURCE: Llewellyn Smith, Virginia. "The Lady with the Dog." In *Anton Chekhov and "The Lady with the Dog,"* pp. 212-19. London: Oxford University Press, 1973.

[*In the following excerpt, Llewellyn Smith maintains that "The Lady with the Dog" encapsulates Chekhov's attitude toward women and love.*]

It will by now be apparent that Anna Sergeevna, the lady with the dog, can be considered symbolic of the ideal love that Chekhov could envisage but not embrace—that remained, so to speak, behind a pane of glass, as in Heifitz's film. But the significance of the whole story is much greater than that comprised in Anna Sergeevna alone.

No other single work of Chekhov's fiction constitutes a more meaningful comment on Chekhov's attitude to women and to love than does 'The Lady with the Dog.' So many threads of Chekhov's thought and experience appear to have been woven together into this succinct story that it may be regarded as something in the nature of a summary of the entire topic.

Gurov, the hero of the story, may at first appear no more closely identifiable with Chekhov himself than are many other sympathetic male characters in Chekhov's fiction: he has a post in a bank and is a married man with three children. It is because he has this wife and family that his love-affair with Anna Sergeevna leads him into an *impasse*. And the affair itself, involving Gurov's desperate trip to Anna's home town, has no obvious feature in common with anything we know of Chekhov's amorous liaisons.

And yet Chekhov's own attitudes and experience have clearly shaped Gurov's character and fate. The reader is told that Gurov 'was not yet forty': Chekhov was thirty-nine when he wrote **'The Lady with the Dog.'** Gurov 'was married young' (*ego zhenili rano*): there is a faint implication in the phrase that an element of coercion played some part in his taking this step—a step which Chekhov, when he was young, managed to avoid. As in general with early marriages in Chekhov's fiction, Gurov's has not proved a success. His wife seems 'much older than he' and imagines herself to be an intellectual: familiar danger-signals. She is summed-up in three words: 'stiff, pompous, dignified' (*pryamaya, vazhnaya, solidnaya*) which epitomize a type of woman (and man) that Chekhov heartily disliked.

Gurov's wife treats sex as something more complicated than it is, and spoils it for him; and it is also spoilt for him by those mistresses of whom he soon tires: beautiful, cold women with a 'predatory' expression who are determined to snatch what they can from life. 'When Gurov grew cold to them, their beauty aroused hatred in him and the lace on their linen reminded him of scales.' It would seem that exactly some such sentiment inspired Chekhov when he depicted Ariadna, Nyuta, and the other anti-heroines.

Gurov has had, however, liaisons that were, for him, enjoyable—and these we note, were brief: as was Chekhov's liaison with Yavorskaya and indeed, so far as we know, all the sexual relationships that he had before he met Olga Knipper.

'Frequent experience and indeed bitter experience had long since taught [Gurov] that every liaison which to begin with makes such a pleasant change . . . inevitably evolves into a real and extremely complex problem, and the situation eventually becomes a burden.' That his friendships with, for instance, Lika and Avilova should evolve into a situation of this kind seems to have been exactly what Chekhov himself feared: he backed out of these friendships as soon as there appeared to be a danger of close involvement.

Gurov cannot do without the company of women, and yet he describes them as an 'inferior breed': his experience of intimacy with women is limited to casual affairs and an unsatisfactory marriage. Chekhov also enjoyed the company of women and had many female friends and admirers: but he failed, or was unwilling, to involve himself deeply or lastingly with them. That in his work he should suggest that women are an inferior breed can be to some extent explained by the limited knowledge of women his self-contained attitude brought him—and perhaps, to some extent, by a sense of guilt concerning his inability to feel involved.

Gurov's behaviour to Anna Sergeevna at the beginning of their love-affair is characterized by an absence of emotional involvement, just such as appears in Chekhov's attitude towards certain women. There is a scene in **'The Lady with the Dog'** where, after they have been to bed together, Gurov eats a watermelon while Anna Sergeevna weeps over her corruption. It is not difficult to imagine Chekhov doing something similarly prosaic—weeding his garden, perhaps—while Lika poured out her emotional troubles to him.

Gurov's egocentricity is dispelled, however, by the potent influence of love, because Anna Sergeevna turns out to be the ideal type of woman: pitiable, defenceless, childlike, capable of offering Gurov an unquestioning love. Love is seen to operate as a force for good: under its influence Gurov feels revulsion for the philistinism of his normal life and associates. Soviet interpreters have made much of the theme of regeneration,[1] of the idea implicit in the story that 'a profound love experienced by ordinary people has become an enormous moral force.'[2] In fact, although some idea of this sort is certainly implicit in the story, Chekhov is surely attempting above all to evoke what love meant to his protagonists as they themselves saw their situation. Chekhov originally wrote in the conclusion of **'The Lady with the Dog'** that the love of Gurov and Anna Sergeevna had 'made them both better.' He altered this subsequently to 'changed them both for the better'; but still dissatisfied, finally he altered this once more to 'had changed them both', and thus avoided any overt suggestion of pointing a moral.[3]

The point is that we are not seeing the lovers changed in relation to society, but in relation to their own inner lives. Gurov is shaken out of his romantic dreaming by a sudden recognition of the grossness of others in his stratum of society: but he does not give up his job or abandon his social life. Instead, he leads a double existence, and imagines that every man's 'real, most interesting life' goes on in secret. It is this life that Chekhov is interested in, not in Gurov as a representative of his class or his time.

That Gurov and Anna Sergeevna are alone amongst their fellow-men does not point a moral: but it is where the pathos of their initial situation lies. We are not impressed by their moral superiority, but moved by their loneliness. Love is the answer to this loneliness, and there is no need to bring morality into it. Chekhov, where love was concerned, wrote from the heart, not the head.

Chekhov wrote **'The Lady with the Dog'** in Yalta in the autumn of 1899, not long after he and Olga were there together (although they were not, as yet, lovers) and had made the trip back to Moscow together. In the Kokkoz valley, it will be remembered, they apparently agreed to marry: and so by then, we may presume, Chekhov knew what it was to love.

How do Gurov and Anna Sergeevna love one another? Not unnaturally, Chekhov describes the affair from the man's point of view. As one might expect, Gurov's love for Anna Sergeevna has its romantic side. It is associated with the beauty of nature, for it is helped into existence by the view of the sea at Oreanda. When, back in Moscow, Gurov thinks of Anna, he poeticizes her: the whole affair becomes the subject of a day-dream, and ultimately an obsession. So, perhaps, did Chekhov's thoughts dwell on Olga Knipper when she was in Moscow and he recalled their time in Yalta and journey through an area of great natural beauty.

Olga Knipper, however, was no dream. And Anna Sergeevna is not seen solely in terms of 'poetry', even by Gurov. Forced to seek Anna out in her home town, from this point Gurov is back in reality. At the theatre he—and the reader—see her as a 'small woman who was in no way remarkable, with a cheap-looking lorgnette in her hand.' But this does not detract from her appeal for him (and it enhances her appeal for the reader). The romantic heroine has become a creature of flesh and blood, and Gurov still loves her: 'she . . . now filled his whole life, she was his joy and his grief, the sole happiness that he now desired; and to the sound of the bad orchestra, the wretched philistine violins, he mused on how fine she was. He mused and dreamed dreams.'

Gurov dreams—but dreaming is not enough for him. He has tasted happiness: the affair in Yalta was happy, in spite of Anna's sense of guilt. His love there developed from when, after Anna's self-recrimination and his irritation, they suddenly laughed together. This laugh denotes the beginning of communication: the tension relaxes and they behave normally, and find enjoyment in each other's company as well as in 'love.' Love, in fact, has come down to earth. Sex, communication, and simple companionship all play their part in it, in addition to 'poetry.'

And there the problem lies: the love-affair being rooted in reality, Anna and Gurov have to face the world's problems. Gurov, unlike Laevsky and Laptev, has found romantic love: but he also wants the companionship that Laevsky and Laptev had, and because he and Anna Sergeevna are already married, he cannot have it.

The situation, indeed the entire plot of **'The Lady with the Dog,'** is obvious, even banal, and its merit as a work of art lies in the artistry with which Chekhov has preserved in the story a balance between the poetic and the prosaic, and in the careful characterization, dependent upon the use of half-tones. Soviet critics have a valid point when they regard Gurov as a sort of Everyman; **'The Lady with the Dog'** is an essentially simple exposition of a commonplace theme. Unlike in **'The Duel'** and **'Three Years,'** in **'The Lady with the Dog'** Chekhov has made no attempt to investigate the problems of love: the conclusion of **'The Lady with the Dog'** is left really and truly open: there is no suggestion, nor have we any inkling, of what the future may bring: 'And it seemed that in a very little while an answer would be found, and a new and beautiful life would begin. And to both it was evident that the end was far, far away, and that the hardest, most complicated part was only just beginning.'

There can be no doubt but that the policy of expounding questions without presuming to answer them—that policy which Chekhov had declared to be the writer's task[4]—suited his style best. A full appreciation of Chekhov's work requires of the reader a certain degree of involvement, a response intellectual, or, as in the case of his love-stories, emotional, that Chekhov invites rather than commandeers. Ultimately, all depends on how Chekhov is read; but much depends on his striking the delicate balance between sentimentality and flatness.

All must surely agree that the right balance has been achieved in the final scene of **'The Lady with the Dog,'** which is as direct an appeal to the heart as can be found in Chekhov's fiction:

> His hair was already beginning to turn grey. And it struck him as strange that he had aged so in the last few years, and lost his good looks. Her shoulders, on which he had lain his hands, were warm and shook slightly. He felt a pang of compassion for this life that was still warm and beautiful, but which would probably soon begin to fade and wither, like his own life. Why did she love him so? He had always appeared to women as something which he was not, and they had loved in him not him himself, but a creature of their own imagination, which they had sought again and again in their own lives; and then, when they perceived their mistake, they loved him all the same. And not one of them had been happy with him. Time passed, he would strike up an acquaintance, have an affair, and part, but never once had he loved; he had had everything he might wish for, only not love.

And only now, when his hair had gone grey, he had fallen in love properly, genuinely—for the first time in his life.

This passage, read in the light of what we know of the author, gains a new dimension of pathos. The history of Gurov's relationships with women is a transmutation of Chekhov's history, and the essential point of the fiction was reality for him: true love had come too late, and complete happiness—poetry and communication and companionship—was impossible.

Chekhov wrote that Gurov and Anna Sergeevna 'loved one another . . . as husband and wife.' But how are we to explain the incongruity of this bland phrase 'as husband and wife' in the context of Chekhov's entire *œuvre,* in which the love of husband and wife is thwarted and cheapened—virtually never, in fact, seen to exist? Gurov and Anna are, after all, husband and wife, and he does not love his wife, nor she her husband. The irony here, whether conscious or unconscious, finds its origin in Chekhov's apparently unshakeable belief that an ideal love somewhere, somehow could exist.

2

It seems then cruel indeed that he should see fate cheat him of the chance of such love. His happiness was incomplete; and it is difficult not to regard Chekhov's situation as tragic. And yet one question remains. Could Chekhov, so happy as he stood on the threshold of love, ever have crossed that threshold, even in more fortunate circumstances? Could he have lived with love instead of dreaming about it? There is of course no evidence to suggest that his feelings for Olga Knipper would have altered with the passage of time, had she stayed constantly by his side. But evidence there is that, to the last, love as Chekhov conceived it retained its distant, intangible quality.

Konstantin Stanislavsky wrote of Chekhov's last years: 'He dreamed of a new play . . . two friends, both young men, love one and the same woman. Their relationship with one another is complicated by their common love and jealousy. It ends with both of them setting off on a trip to the North Pole. The set for the last act consists of a huge ship wedged in the ice-floes. In the final scene of the play the two friends see a white phantom gliding across the ice. It is clear this is the shade of the soul of the beloved who has died far away in their country.'[5]

Despite the original visual effects this would have entailed—reminiscent of similarly unusual sound-effects in the plays that were realized—the ostensibly prosaic provincial world of those plays seems a far cry from this fantasy, and it is easy to comprehend Stanislavsky's comment that the plot was 'somehow un-Chekhovian.'

And yet it is truly, deeply, Chekhovian. This sketch of a plot shows clearly that, where love was the issue, a dissociation from facts and retreat into a dream world was for Chekhov a continuing process: that the romantic heroine could only be such in apotheosis. In the real world she provokes complications—but her shade is mysterious, beautiful, and fascinating.

And thus before we regard Chekhov's life as tragic, there is an important factor to bear in mind: the possibility that Chekhov, never to experience the reality of a normal marriage, was perhaps by this very misfortune preserved from a disillusionment in his ideal of love which might have proved more bitter than any irony of destiny. Thus the very significance—the supreme significance—which love as an ideal had for Chekhov provides us with an alternative view of his fate. It is not a tragedy: there is no victim. And Chekhov, whose dislike of self-dramatization was one of his most attractive qualities, would surely have preferred this latter view.

Notes

1. B. S. Meilakh in his article 'Dva resheniya odnoi temy' (see bibliography) states that in 'The Lady with the Dog' Chekhov was seeking to present in terms of everyday people (i.e. not the nobility) the problem Tolstoy had posed in *Anna Karenina:* how can there be happiness in the false society that has made it possible for two such dissimilar people as Anna and Karenin to be united? Meilakh writes: Anna Karenina 'perishes as the victim of the cruel mores which constituted the norm of existence for a person of her milieu.' Chekhov, he holds, was showing his lovers to be in virtually the same predicament; but by not resolving the problem in death, Chekhov was suggesting that the more the situation seems impossible, the more one should intensify the search for an exit. In fact, Tolstoy was if anything more concerned with doing away with the evils of the old order than Chekhov: in 'The Lady with the Dog' the lovers blame fate, not society, for their predicament, and the way in which they confront their situation probably only means that Chekhov preferred less dramatic effects and positive statements than Tolstoy, and did not wish to copy the latter too closely. For a discussion of the similarities between *Anna Karenina* and 'The Lady with the Dog', and an interesting analysis of the artistic methods used in 'The Lady with the Dog', see Winner, pp. 216-25.

2. K. M. Vinogradova, 'Stranitsa iz chernovoi rukopisi rasskaza "Dama a sobachkoi"' (see bibliography): Vinogradova maintains that Chekhov's alterations to the first-published text of 'The Lady with the Dog' were made to underline the

theme of Gurov's regeneration. However, the changes she adduces seem rather to have been dictated by artistic considerations, and with the aim of making both lovers appear more ordinary, less wholly good, less wholly bad. Chekhov cuts out, for example, a series of coarse rejoinders that Gurov makes to Anna Sergeevna in the bedroom scene: which would have been better left in, had Chekhov wished to point up the change in Gurov's character to the utmost.

3. Vinogradova, p. 140.

4. See letter to A. S. Suvorin, 27 October 1888, where Chekhov wrote: '. . . you are confusing two things: solving the problem and the correct exposition of the problem. In *Anna Karenina* and [*Evgeny*] *Onegin* not a single problem is solved, but they are wholly satisfying, just because all the problems in them are correctly set out.'

5. Stanislavsky, p. 415.

Abbreviations

The following abbreviations have been used in the notes, references, and bibliography:

(i) *Titles Chvvs A. P. Chekhov v vospominaniyakh sovremennikov,* edited by S. N. Golubov and others, M., 1960

LN Literaturnoe nasledstvo: Chekhov (vol. 68), edited by V. V. Vinogradov and others, M., 1960

Perepiska Perepiska A. P. Chekhova i O. L. Knipper, edited by A. B. Derman, 2 vols., M., 1934 and 1936

Works, Polnoe sobranie sochinenii i pisem A. P. Chekhova, 1944-51 edited by S. D. Balukhaty and others, M., 1944-51

(ii) *Places of publication*

L. London

LG. Leningrad

M. Moscow

N.Y. New York

SPB. St. Petersburg

Works Cited

Works and Letters of A. P. Chekhov

Polnoe sobranie sochinenii i pisem A. P. Chekhova, ed. by S. D. Balukhaty, V. P. Potemkin, N. S. Tikhonov, A. M. Egolin, vols. 1-20, M, 1944-51.

Pis'ma A. P. Chekhova, ed. by M. P. Chekhova, vols. 1-6, M, 1912-16.

Perepiska A. P. Chekhova i O. L. Knipper, ed. by A. B. Derman, vol. 1, M, 1934; vol. 2, M, 1936.

'Perepiska A. P. Chekhova i O. L. Knipper: 1903-1904' (incomplete), ed. by A. B. Derman, *Novy mir,* 1938, no. 10, pp. 271-85; no. 11, pp. 232-59; no. 12, pp. 257-70. *Oktyabr',* M, 1938, no. 7, pp. 171-207. *Teatr,* M, 1960, no. 1, pp. 152-6.

Biography, Memoirs, Criticism, etc.

Meilakh, B. S.: 'Dva resheniya odnoi temy', *Neva,* LG, 1956, no. 9, pp. 184-8.

Stanislavsky, K. S.: *Moya zhizn' v iskusstve,* M, 1954.

———.'Chekhov', *Chvvs,* pp. 371-418.

Vinogradova, K. M.: 'Stranitsa iz chernovoi rukopisi rasskaza "Dama s sobachkoi"', *LN,* pp. 133-40.

Winner, T.: *Chekhov and his Prose,* N.Y., 1966.

Richard N. Porter (essay date November 1977)

SOURCE: Porter, Richard N. "Bunin's 'A Sunstroke' and Chekhov's 'The Lady with the Dog.'" *South Atlantic Bulletin* 42, no. 2 (November 1977): 51-6.

[*In the following essay, Porter compares I. A. Bunin's "A Sunstroke" with "The Lady with the Dog" to highlight the younger Russian writer's indebtedness to Chekhov and to compare how the two authors differed in style and attitude.*]

In reading Bunin one is often reminded of his literary antecedents. In "The Gentleman from San Francisco" there is much of "The Death of Ivan Ilyich" and "Death in Venice." The title and opening passages of Bunin's "Happiness" recall Tolstoy's *Family Happiness.* Bunin's use of *ostranenie* is similar to Tolstoy's; and when one reads "The Dreams of Chang," a story seen through the eyes of a dog, one thinks back to Tolstoy's "Xolstomer," which is told from the point of view of a horse. The description of Nevsky prospekt in "Sinuous Ears" is indebted to Gogol, as is the image of the devil in "The Gentleman from San Francisco." "The Dream of Oblomov's Grandson" goes back, of course, to *Oblomov.* In *Dry Valley,* Bunin acknowledges his debt to Turgenev by using names from *Fathers and Sons.*

One could go on in this vein. In almost every work of Bunin there are echoes from the past. There is, of course, nothing wrong with echoes—Shakespeare is full of them and is not diminished by them. Writing at the end of a long tradition, Bunin chose to avail himself of it. What is interesting about his borrowings is not merely pointing them out, for they are perfectly obvious, but discovering what use he made of them. There was no writer for whom Bunin had greater affection than for Chekhov; and despite Bunin's denial there was no writer from whom he seems to have profited more.[1] Bunin's narrative technique is much like Chekhov's; some of their stories might almost have been written by either one of them. There are, however, important differences between the writers, especially in theme. Chekhov's **"The Lady with the Dog"** and Bunin's "A Sunstroke" have much in common, are frequently mentioned in connection with each other, and lend themselves to comparison. By discerning what features of the stories are alike and unlike one can learn much about the overall similarities and differences of the authors.

The plots of both stories are familiar. **"The Lady with the Dog"** is about Dmitry Dmitrich Gurov, a banker from Moscow, not yet forty, married, and the father of three children, and Anna Sergeevna von Dideritz, who has married two years before and now lives in the provincial city of S. They meet in Yalta, where they are spending their vacations alone. Soon they have an affair. Despite qualms on Anna's part, they are fairly happy, but Gurov is relieved when she goes. At home in Moscow, he is surprised to find that he does not forget her quickly. Instead, he misses her more and more and decides to go to S. to see her. She is surprised but admits that she has thought of him often and arranges to visit him occasionally in Moscow. On her visits, they meet in her hotel room. Although they find some happiness, they realize that the most difficult part of their affair is just beginning.

"A Sunstroke" is about a lieutenant and a young married woman, both of them anonymous, who meet on a Volga river boat. They are immediately drawn to each other and agree to get off at a small town, where they spend the night. When the woman leaves the next morning, the lieutenant does not mind her going; but later in the day he realizes that he misses her desperately. He cannot go after her because she has not told him her name. He tries unsuccessfully in various ways to overcome his sense of loss, and, when he takes the boat that evening, he feels that he has grown ten years older.

Although Bunin's story does not encroach on Chekhov's, there are obvious similarities between them. In both stories, a man of the world meets an attractive young married woman who happens to be vacationing alone. In both stories, he seduces her easily. In both stories, the man enjoys himself but does not expect the affair to last and is relieved when the woman goes. In both stories, the man surprises himself by missing the woman intensely and discovers that he has experienced something new, that he has never before felt so

strongly about a woman. In both stories, the emphasis is on the reaction to the affair rather than on the affair itself.

In an article on Chekhov's place in the development of Russian literature, Dmitrij Tschižewskij suggests that much of Chekhov's work was poorly received by some Russian critics because they were evaluating him as a realist whereas actually he was a literary impressionist. According to Tschižewskij, the principal features of literary impressionism are the vague overall effect of a work, an emphasis on certain details, a tendency not to put into words the thought or idea of the work, the creation of a mood that helps the reader sense the idea of the work, and small details and touches that guide the reader.[2] These are obviously characteristics of Chekhov's work as a whole and by and large of **"The Lady with the Dog."**

Whether or not one wishes to call Chekhov an impressionist, his work does differ from that of many Russian realists in that it favors the nuance and discrete detail over clarity of outline and prefers to suggest themes rather than to state them. The same can be said of Bunin. In his writing generally and in "A Sunstroke" in particular, impressionistic features stand out even more than in Chekhov. Bunin makes little effort to develop a plot as such and has the ability, as Struve says, "to create a story out of nothing."[3] As in "A Sunstroke," he often declines to give his characters names, and one knows little about them. He cultivates a vagueness of outline and concentrates on a few poignant or lyric moments. Although his early prose shows the influence of Gorky and the Znanie circle and deals in part with social issues, his approach to these issues is more universal than it is partisan. In his émigré period, Bunin dropped all topical references, treated various aspects of love, and suggested his themes by nuance and detail. In economy and the emphasis of a few poignant moments, "A Sunstroke" is more typical of Chekhov than is **"The Lady with the Dog."**

It would be misleading to suggest that Bunin owed his prose technique wholly to Chekhov. After all, the approach they both took to the short story was one they shared with a great many European and American writers, one that was until recently called "modern." Nevertheless, Chekhov's contribution to the kind of story that extended roughly from Maupassant to Hemingway was as great as anyone else's, and he was the most attractive and obvious model that Bunin had. "A Sunstroke" is a monument to Chekhov's influence on Bunin, to lessons well learned.

Despite the similarities of "A Sunstroke" and **"The Lady with the Dog,"** they are not entirely alike. The most striking differences are the greater concentration of the Bunin story, its strict focus on the man's reaction, and its termination of the affair after a single night. The stories are also proportioned differently. **"The Lady with the Dog"** is sixteen pages long; the first half is set in the Crimea, the second half in Moscow and S.⁴ "A Sunstroke" is eight pages long;⁵ but within the first two pages the young woman has gone, and she does not reappear. The stories are constructed differently for good reasons. To some extent, Chekhov and Bunin are talking about the same thing; to some extent, they are not.

In the beginning of **"The Lady with the Dog,"** we are told that Gurov disparages women but cannot do without them. He goes about seducing Anna Sergeevna with a poise and skill acquired over years of philandering. When Anna is melodramatic after they have first made love, Gurov grows bored, eats a slice of watermelon, and says nothing for half an hour. Presently, when she dwells on her situation in a maudlin vein, Gurov patronizes her. Yet the scene is the only instance in the story of an extended conversation between the two. One of the striking features of their relationship is that they have so little to talk about. We learn indirectly that they have exchanged a few facts about themselves; they say just enough to keep their affair going; and that is all the talking there is. The problem is not, of course, that Chekhov has shied away from dialogue, but that Anna and Gurov have little in common. The early stages of a friendship are usually uninteresting to outsiders. For that reason, Chekhov generally starts his stories at the crest of the action, as Bunin does in "A Sunstroke." In the case of **"The Lady with the Dog,"** however, Chekhov wishes to cultivate tedium; and he does so in part by passing on the banal remarks of people who have just met.

If Gurov and Anna have so little in common, what holds them together? Chekhov is careful to tell us. Anna is unhappily married to a man who, she says, "is a flunky."⁶ She aspires to something better. Gurov is sophisticated, lives in Moscow, and has the time and means to carry on an affair. From Anna's point of view, he is a reasonably safe lover and is more romantic than her husband. Gurov is motivated largely by thoughts of oncoming age. Age is a motif of the story. At the beginning, we learn that, although Gurov is not yet forty, his tall, intellectual wife seems half again as old as he. At Oreanda, the ocean reminds Gurov of death and eternity, of the indifference of the world to the lives and deaths of people. A moment later, he admires Anna in the light of the dawn, and that is the first time that he seems really to have cared for her. The prospect of oblivion quite literally dawns on Gurov. Thoughts of death make him look at life differently. The realization that he will not always have his women causes him to appreciate Anna and to envy the

immortality of "these fantastic surroundings—the sea, the mountains, the clouds, the broad sky."⁷ When Anna leaves the Crimea to return home, Gurov thinks again of age and realizes that he has been slightly ironic with Anna, that in his attitude there has been the coarse arrogance of a contented male who is almost twice as old as she. Finally, in Anna's hotel room in Moscow, Gurov notices that his hair has begun to turn gray; he has aged in the last few years and has lost his looks.

Only after it is clear that Gurov senses age coming on are we told that he has begun to feel love and compassion. It seems to Gurov that he and Anna are like intimate friends or man and wife. One wonders how much these concepts matter to him in the first place. He and Anna have been intimate friends for some time without achieving real intimacy, and Gurov's marriage is so vapid that the thought of being man and wife cannot appeal to him much. Although in the final scene he is lusty, aware of age, and caught up in the mood of the moment, his relationship with Anna is still unsatisfactory. "The solution" that they hope to find and that they believe will bring a "new and splendid life for them" is illusory. Therefore, "the most complex and difficult part"⁸ is just beginning.

In **"The Lady with the Dog,"** Chekhov brings together two persons who have a great need for each other. Their affair at least enables them to avoid the boredom that each of them has found in married life. In a key passage, Gurov observes that everything that really matters in his life must be kept hidden from the world, and everything that does not matter goes on in the open.⁹ Our habit of keeping important things secret is an aspect of isolation, a theme that runs through all Chekhov's work. In **"The Lady with the Dog,"** the theme has a double application. Gurov and Anna are not really in touch with each other, except in a physical sense, and are essentially isolated. And their affair, which has come to matter to both of them for different reasons, must be kept secret from the world, must be isolated. Chekhov is saying again that no one really knows what goes on within anyone else. Ultimately, we are all set apart from one another, out of touch about things that matter.

Unlike Chekhov in **"The Lady with the Dog,"** Bunin does not bother in "A Sunstroke" to motivate his characters psychologically. When the story begins, his lovers are already attracted to each other; and later they are willing to ascribe their attraction to a kind of sunstroke, an appropriate figure that involves, like their affair, surprise, heat, and prostration. Although we read only a few lines of what the young woman has to say, she appears vivacious enough. Apparently, the two lovers are in fine harmony on their single night together, not restrained as they might have been in a story by Chekhov. Isolation is not the problem in "A Sunstroke." What bothers the lieutenant is that he cannot have the young woman back, not that he could not get across his feelings to her or that he cannot tell others about his emotion. Bunin is concerned with a different theme, that of transience, and it is in theme that his story mainly differs from Chekhov's.

Most commentators on Bunin's later work have noted that in his stories love does not go on for long. As a rule, something soon comes between his lovers. Perhaps one of them dies. The joy of love is brief; the regret that follows is keen. Insofar as both Gurov and the young lieutenant originally underestimate the importance of their affair, the themes of their stories are alike. In Chekhov, however, the theme of value and transience is subordinate to the theme of isolation. In Bunin it is everything.

Transience is what chiefly occupies Bunin, especially in his émigré work. The two most conspicuous results of transience are separation and death, and these subjects engage him almost exclusively after he has passed through his Gorky phase. For that matter, transience and transition are at least subthemes of works such as *The Village* and *Dry Valley*. "A Sunstroke" is devoted entirely to the effect of transience on love. The affair does not begin to take on importance for the lieutenant until he realizes that it is over. At first, he is melancholy at the thought that the woman is even temporarily gone. When he realizes that he will never see her again, that he does not know her name and that she is irretrievably lost, his love and despair are complete. He tries in various ways to get over his emotion. He goes to the marketplace to divert himself; he visits a church; he takes a walk along the Volga; he drinks a great deal; finally, he sleeps until it is time to catch the boat. Nothing helps. In what sense does he feel that he has aged ten years once he is back on the boat? Obviously, he is emotionally drained; but he has also made the sad discovery that value and loss are inextricably connected, that one cares most for what cannot be recovered. The realization brings on despair.

Bunin has been accused of exhausting the subject of love and loss and of repeating himself, especially in the collection *Dark Paths*. Whether or not one agrees is largely a matter of taste and of how one likes Bunin's kind of writing. At any rate, for an author whose theme is transience, love is a convenient subject. Nothing else, besides death, elicits such strong emotions as love; and love is a more versatile subject than death since one can also deal with the aftermath of love.

"The Lady with the Dog" and "A Sunstroke" reveal striking similarities in subject, plot, and construction. Their themes are related; the idea that one desires most what one cannot have is essential to both stories. But in **"The Lady with the Dog"** the main emphasis is on isolation, the isolation of the two lovers from each other and from the world. All the effects of "A Sunstroke" are directed at the theme of transience, at the thought that love depends upon the prospect of loss. This distinction is what ultimately sets apart the mature work of Bunin from that of Chekhov.

Notes

1. I. A. Bunin, "Avtobiografičeskie zametki," *Sobranie sočinenij* (Berlin, 1936), I, 22.

2. Dmitrij Tschiževskij. "Über die Stellung Čexovs innerhalb der russischen Literaturentwicklung," *Anton Čexov: 1860-1960, Some Essays*, ed., T. Eekman (Leiden, 1960), p. 301.

3. G. Struve, "The Art of Ivan Bunin," *The Slavonic and East European Review*, XI (London, 1932-33), 424.

4. A. P. Chekhov, "Dama s sobačkoj," *Polnoe sobranie sočinenij i pisem* (M., 1948), IX, 357-372.

5. I. A. Bunin, "Solnečnyj udar," *Sobranie sočinenij* (M., 1966), V, 238-245.

6. Chekhov, "Dama s sobačkoj," 362.

7. Ibid., p. 363.

8. Ibid., p. 372.

9. Ibid., pp. 370-371.

Beverly Hahn (essay date 1977)

SOURCE: Hahn, Beverly. "The Lady with the Dog." In *Chekhov: A Study of the Major Stories and Plays*, pp. 252-66. Cambridge: Cambridge University Press, 1977.

[In the following excerpt, Hahn views "The Lady with the Dog" as a testimony to Chekhov's belief in the value of love and, by extension, the value of life.]

'The Lady with the Dog' is a tale of adultery which again seems to have the influence of Tolstoy behind it, although this time the Tolstoy of *Anna Karenina*. It is Chekhov's response to the challenge of a subject which *Anna Karenina* had made an occasion for compassion, psychological understanding and tolerance quite unlike anything we find before it in the literature of adultery;[1] and it is, again, a testing extension of sympathies beyond even the point at which Tolstoy's sympathies end. For although Tolstoy presents Anna's predicament with unprecedented compassion, he nevertheless sees her as offending against a social and moral law, and for this there is a price to be paid. He may admire Anna, he may present her death as determined within her as an inevitable consequence of her guilt; but in fact he pursues her, determined that she shall die for what she has done: the moralist in him never quite gives rest to his instinctive sympathies. Chekhov, on the other hand, read *Anna Karenina* time and time again and knew it familiarly as 'dear *Anna*'; and the warmth of his response to Anna herself suggests that she would not have suffered the same eventual fate at his hands. His sense of the preciousness of life itself and of its unpredictability in moral terms would make it unlikely that he should feel impelled to sacrifice her for anything. So it is perhaps not surprising that his own Anna—although she is, within the much-contracted scale of **'The Lady with the Dog,'** less sympathetic, less mature and altogether less splendid than Tolstoy's—is given as much satisfaction and fulfilment as the restricted terms of her situation can possibly offer. Her life as one man's wife—while she loves another—is simply that sad, bitter-sweet combination which Chekhov himself, at this stage, seems to sense and accept as the reality of things.

In all art that reflects upon the sadness of life and is burdened with the sense of its limitations, there is yet perhaps an impulse to serve life and even sometimes to celebrate its persistence and its tragically incomplete satisfactions. It is an impulse that seems to win through especially in the final phase of a great artist's work—for example, in Shakespeare, Rembrandt, Mozart and Beethoven—after earlier phases, first of exuberant discovery of sheer technical power (power exercised over a range of materials and maintaining a certain factual objectivity) and then of deepening psychological understanding and an intense confrontation of the great moral and philosophical issues of existence. That is, in the creative lives of some of our greatest artists (and Chekhov among them) we can observe three distinct phases, the third of which seems to involve a mysterious transcendence of those issues by which it has, in its second phase, been darkened and perplexed. As one would expect, it is a pattern that usually emerges from a long creative life. But there is a small group of artists whose own lives were tragically shortened and who lived in the expectation of an early death, whose apparently instinctive sensitivity to that fact seems to have caused a compression of all three phases into a span of time normally occupied by one. When Chekhov wrote **'The Lady with the Dog'** he had known for some time that he was dying, and the mellowness and tolerance in the story indirectly reflect his awareness of the fact. And we find in Chekhov, as we find in Mozart, a new and quiet confidence emerging strangely but distinctly from among the tragic nuances of the art: a confidence (of which we have had some premonition in **'The Duel'**) that life,

though often sad, can never be worthless and that it may even be self-enhancing—a confidence substantiated by the existence of the creative faculty itself.

The love between Gurov and Anna Sergeyevna, as it eventuates in **'The Lady with the Dog,'** is a love maintained in secrecy and constricted circumstances, and as such it has something of that 'quiet desperation' which Thoreau ascribed to most modern lives. But desperation is not the dominant note of the story, nor is its outcome really tragic, because the hardship of Anna's and Gurov's love cannot be separated from the *fact* of that love and from the fact that it brings each a degree of fulfilment not known before. Anna's and Gurov's position is a willing one, it gives a rationale to their lives, and it retains a strong element of indeterminacy as part of its condition. The story seems deliberately to be presenting us with the ambiguity of their position. Throughout, the tone and detail of the writing are peculiarly balanced between celebration and sympathy—hence the lyricism together with the consciousness of pain. It is a similar sort of ambiguity to that which characterized Chekhov's own life at this time. The pattern of his last years was one both of great promise and of its painful curtailment: his talent was continually expanding, his mind crowded with stories, just as tuberculosis was leaving him less able to write and hastening his end. So it is a triumph, both within the story and outside it, that Chekhov's art should transcend in spirit the ambiguities it portrays in its characters' lives. For if the ambiguity of Anna's and Gurov's position is, in a way, the story's subject, it is important to see that it is not the final quality of the story itself. Over and above it is an unusual formal serenity and a peculiar poise in the narrative voice which encompass even the sad elements in Anna's and Gurov's predicament in a larger—yet cautious—spirit of trust in the residual value of life.

From the beginning, Anna's and Gurov's relationship is treated sympathetically, even though the explanatory sections about each, and about Gurov's background in particular, are not flattering to them. There is nothing specific about their initial attachment and nothing particularly intense: they have come to Yalta separately, aimlessly, in the vague hope of finding some casual amusement in a holiday-resort relationship. But the fact that Anna is a gentlewoman and therefore that Gurov's pursuit of her must observe certain conventions, together with the stylization of life at the resort itself, masks the vulgarity of their motives in an aura of rather attractive gentility. The lady with the little dog appearing on the sea-front—amid the elderly ladies and generals, in a world of hats, bouquets and parasols, and leisurely evening walks down to meet the steamer—is a figure to catch a civilized imagination and impress it with the warmth of desire from out of a picturesquely rarefied atmosphere. In this sense, the Yalta setting itself is probably the first element in the sympathy which Chekhov extends to Anna and Gurov, before there is any suggestion of love between them at all. It has something of the aura of dream, of a fantasy-state where encounters take place and desires are fulfilled without the usual moral complications; and as such it relieves the situation from seeming sordid, though the motives of both characters are indicated bluntly enough:

> He beckoned coaxingly to the Pomeranian, and when the dog came up to him he shook his finger at it. The Pomeranian growled: Gurov shook his finger at it again.
>
> The lady looked at him and at once dropped her eyes.
>
> 'He doesn't bite,' she said, and blushed.
>
> 'May I give him a bone?' he asked; and when she nodded he asked courteously, 'Have you been long in Yalta?'
>
> 'Five days.'
>
> 'And I have already dragged out a fortnight here.'
>
> There was a brief silence.
>
> 'Time goes fast, and yet it is so dull here!' she said, not looking at him.
>
> 'That's only the fashion to say it is dull here. A provincial will live in Belyov or Zhidra and not be dull, and when he comes here it's "Oh, the dullness! Oh, the dust!" One would think he came from Grenada.'
>
> She laughed. Then both continued eating in silence, like strangers, but after dinner they walked side by side; and there sprang up between them the light jesting conversation of people who are free and satisfied, to whom it does not matter where they go or what they talk about. They walked and talked of the strange light on the sea: the water was of a soft warm lilac hue, and there was a golden streak from the moon upon it. They talked of how sultry it was after a hot day. Gurov told her that he came from Moscow, that he had taken his degree in Arts, but had a post in a bank; that he had trained as an opera-singer, but had given it up, that he owned two houses in Moscow . . . And from her he learnt that she had grown up in Petersburg, but had lived in S—since her marriage two years before, that she was staying another month in Yalta, and that her husband, who needed a holiday too, might perhaps come and fetch her. She was not sure whether her husband had a post in a Crown Department or under the Provincial Council—and was amused by her own ignorance. And Gurov learnt, too, that she was called Anna Sergeyevna.

(III.5-7)

The subjects and the strategies of conversation here are those of any seduction which has the compliance of the woman as well as of the man, and Chekhov does not spare his characters the ordinary cheapness of Gurov's coaxing the dog and Anna Sergeyevna's amusement at her ignorance about her husband. There is nothing in the situation that he decides to evade. But the superficial decorum of the conversation, and then the soft lights on the water that seem to release a fuller communion between the two, take away the harshness of the sexual facts, blending them with our sense of the freedom and aimlessness of the place. The lazy days and warm evenings encourage a drifting and delicious but superficial engagement in a world of sensations, which the prose of the Yalta scenes acts out in its unhurried pace. Thus 'They walked and talked of the strange light on the sea: the water was of a soft warm lilac hue, and there was a golden streak from the moon upon it. They talked of how sultry it was after a hot day' has a leisurely peripatetic rhythm which will later contrast with the winter bustle of the scenes in Moscow. There is no pressure about time, and time seems strangely expanded, not only because of the passivity induced by the sea but also because of the almost ritual spectacle of people moving along the Yalta promenades.

I have spoken already of the connection that seems to exist in Chekhov's imagination between warm, sensuous climates and an intensified awareness of human sexuality. Anna Sergeyevna experiences in Yalta a feeling of sensual luxury and liberation similar to that felt by Nadyezhda Fyodorovna in the superbly evoked Black-Sea-port atmosphere of **'The Duel.'** But **'The Lady with the Dog,'** being set at the actual port of Yalta, has additionally potent elements in its setting on which Chekhov can depend. One is the highly stylized sense of fashionable life at the resort, of which Anna's promenading with a 'little dog' is a part, which establishes a genteel atmosphere quite different from the lethargy of life in **'The Duel.'** The other is that elusive quality of reality about a particular place which allows it a whole range of moods which are still characteristically its own. The port in **'The Duel'** is a fictive construct out of any number of places, and it has a certain symbolic quality in that its atmosphere is unchangeable so long as nothing changes in the lives of its people. It is stiflingly hot until the storm suddenly breaks out on the night before the duel. Yalta, on the other hand, can be blustery without reason, simply because it is Yalta:

> A week had passed since they had made acquaintance. It was a holiday. It was sultry indoors, while in the street the wind whirled the dust round and round, and blew people's hats off. It was a thirsty day, and Gurov often went into the pavilion, and pressed Anna Sergeyevna to have syrup and water or an ice. One did not know what to do with oneself.

(III.7)

This intense particularity about the actual place is important: for by keeping Yalta so convincingly itself, unable to be duplicated by any other place because it is so caught up in its own history and its mythology of permissive romance, Chekhov is able to make what happens there seem, by rights, something that does not have to impinge on either Gurov's or Anna's later life. We therefore feel it, as Chekhov I think intends us to do, as a peculiar irony that neither character can actually relegate it simply to memory—that it does remain so durable an influence throughout the rest of their lives.

Of course, not all the landscape images in the story are well managed, and one of the most important—the view from Oreanda with Yalta barely visible in the distance—is probably the most flawed. Along with the particular and quite moving detail describing the scenery, there is too much generalized teleological speculation about our 'unceasing progress towards perfection', which comes with disastrous heaviness in a story that is otherwise so delicate. But the dusty day that precedes Anna's and Gurov's first lovemaking, and then the grand panoramic views they later enjoy high above the mists of Yalta, do have the effect of encompassing their passion, literally, in a special Yalta air. The mode of the story is predominantly naturalistic in the way it represents both the people and the place: Yalta itself is almost lovingly documented. But it is in the nature of the place, as of Anna's youthful inexperience, to have some timeless and emblematic properties. In Anna's case, there is her reaction to her 'fall':

> The attitude of Anna Sergeyevna—'the lady with the dog'—to what had happened was somehow peculiar, very grave, as though it were her fall—so it seemed, and it was strange and inappropriate. Her face drooped and faded, and on both sides of it her long hair hung down mournfully; she mused in a dejected attitude like 'the woman who was a sinner' in an old-fashioned picture.
>
> 'It's wrong,' she said. 'You will be the first to despise me now.'
>
> (III.9-10)

Gurov finds her attitude alternately boring, irritating and ludicrous, and the story implicitly concedes its unexpectedness. But her unconsciously reproduced posture of a classical Magdalen is made to express a genuine shame and humility which give Anna a new depth in our eyes; and it is undeniable that this classical posture and all that it expresses, however apparently incongruous in the story's particular circumstances, is partly why she haunts Gurov's (and in a way the story's own) memory after she has gone.

The case of Yalta is in some ways similar. By the time Anna Sergeyevna leaves for home, Yalta already breathes a 'scent of autumn', and the weather is turn-ing cold. Then, to Gurov, it ceases to seem real at all amid the crisp busy-ness of Moscow to which he returns:

> At home in Moscow everything was in its winter routine; the stoves were heated, and in the morning it was still dark when the children were having breakfast and getting ready for school, and the nurse would light the lamp for a short time. The frosts had begun already. When the first snow has fallen, on the first day of sledge-driving it is pleasant to see the white earth, the white roofs, to draw soft, delicious breath, and the season brings back the days of one's youth. The old limes and birches, white with hoar-frost, have a good-natured expression; they are nearer to one's heart than cypresses and palms, and near them one doesn't want to be thinking of the sea and the mountains.
>
> Gurov was Moscow born; he arrived in Moscow on a fine frosty day, and when he put on his fur coat and warm gloves, and walked along Petrovka, and when on Saturday evening he heard the ringing of the bells, his recent trip and the places he had seen lost all charm for him.
>
> (III.15)

Both the imagery and the pacing of the prose create the new sense of activity, the new sharpness and clarity, which belong to the northern city. The movement, particularly in the last sentences of the passage, is energetic and purposive, to contrast with the aimless superfluity of time in Yalta. But the Yalta landscape, as it turns out, will not allow itself to be forgotten: with its summer ripeness and its ritualized spaciousness of time, it slowly assumes, in retrospect, a dream reality and an archetypal character as a place of freedom and romance. As such, it, too, haunts Gurov more and more as Moscow presses itself upon him as a set of mundane obligations and responsibilities.

'The Lady with the Dog' was, of course, written at a time when Chekhov's major energies were going into his plays, and it is noticeable that during this period his stories contain more straightforward situations and fewer characters than the longer stories of the middle years. It is this which enables the story to concentrate so intensely on Anna and Gurov and their developing love, while making us feel, at the same time, a certain thinness of substance in comparison with the earlier works. Compared with 'The Party,' for example, where the documentation of Olga Mihalovna's domestic environment and her duties at the party is impressively dense, 'The Lady with the Dog'—while highly appealing in visual terms, delicate and deft—does feel only lightly impressionistic. The swift time-transitions and the definition of the stages of Anna's and Gurov's relationship through the way places are imaged remind us of the plays rather than of the novelistic elements of 'The Party' or 'The Duel'; and, in this sort of impressionistic construction, it is much easier for Chekhov to evade or omit aspects of the situation which a fuller and more inclusive account would have faced. I am thinking particularly of the way in which Chekhov represents Anna's husband and Gurov's wife. The shortness of the story and its high dependence on visual imagery allow him to under-create these people and, in doing so, to under-present their claims to consideration and sympathy. Take, for example, the following description of Von Diderits:

> And there really was in his long figure, his side-whiskers, and the small bald patch on his head, something of the flunkey's obsequiousness; his smile was sugary, and in his buttonhole there was some badge of distinction like the number on a waiter.

(III.21)

Here Chekhov is co-operating with Gurov's wish to find Anna's husband unappealing: from the non-Russian name to the endorsing syntax ('And there really was . . .') and the unsympathetic adjectives and similes, everything works against our being able to feel the sort of sympathy which, for example, Tolstoy accorded Karenin. Chekhov is thus directing our sympathies more simply than is arguably required by the difficult and delicate nature of the problem. But the gain associated with that failing is, of course, the sheer intensity of the story's feeling; and the story projects so refined an essence of Anna's and Gurov's feelings, whether of pleasure or of pain, that we are ultimately, perhaps, disinclined to press for greater inclusiveness at the cost of its unusual potency and haunting lyricism.

Like the plays, the story has four parts, and each deftly captures a different phase of Anna's and Gurov's love. The first deals with their meeting and becoming acquainted in Yalta; the second, still in Yalta, tells of their adultery and then their separation; the third gives us Gurov living out the winter in Moscow, finding himself unable to forget Anna and finally seeking her out in a stuffy theatre in a dreary province; and the fourth captures one of their many meetings, years later, in a Moscow hotel. In this highly visual story, each change of scenery reflects significant changes in the emotional atmosphere. In Yalta there is warmth and space, with panoramic vistas for Anna and Gurov to look down on and horizons that seem to sparkle with promise. Even the initial Moscow impressions retain an agreeable sharpness and vivacity. But in Moscow, as the winter sets in and Gurov gradually discovers himself to be a man in love, the imagery of the story begins to project a sense of the difficulties awaiting Anna and Gurov, which will inevitably restrict the promise contained in their love. At S—, the town to which Gurov goes to find Anna again, his hotel room is grey and unattractive; and Anna's house, when he finds it, is sealed off, in effect, by 'a long grey fence adorned with nails.' This is the beginning of a whole sequence of images of hardness, constriction and enclosure whose symbolic purport is clear: we are now to see the difficulty and the sadness of a love begun so carelessly in the summer world of Yalta. But at least there *is* love; and the fullness of that feeling, together with the pitifulness of its context—not contending with one another, but reconciled in a rush of acceptance—are caught as Anna Sergeyevna enters the stalls of the provincial theatre:

> Anna Sergeyevna, too, came in. She sat down in the third row, and when Gurov looked at her his heart contracted, and he understood clearly that for him there was in the whole world no creature so near, so precious, and so important to him; she, this little woman, in no way remarkable, lost in a provincial crowd, with a vulgar lorgnette in her hand, filled his whole life now, was his sorrow and his joy, the one happiness that he now desired for himself, and to the sounds of the inferior orchestra, of the wretched provincial violins, he thought how lovely she was. He thought and dreamed.

(III.21)

Over and above the provincial setting, the difficulty of their position and the sorrow in store for them (things of which the story is most obviously and painfully aware), Chekhov still captures the contraction of Gurov's heart, the sudden new understanding which is to give meaning to the remainder of his life. Anna is to be 'his sorrow *and* his joy': neither is to be thought of as cancelling out the other.

There is, of course, a tragic contrast to their life together in Yalta—alone and free, with time to spend and no real love to spend it on—in the scene which takes place on the crowded theatre staircase. The same movement of retreat which led them up to the mountains high above Yalta now leads them deeper and deeper into the heart of the theatre, where there is a claustrophobic sense of the presence of other people and a pervasive tension and fear. The movement is in each case an upward one towards light and life, but in the theatre it ends on the gloomy and narrow stairway leading to the amphitheatre, which is, in effect, a trap—a dead end. The visual perspectives, instead of opening out to reveal Yalta mistily enshrouded in the lower distance, close in to oppress Anna and Gurov with the narrowness of the staircase and the inescapability of people. As I have said, there is an irony in the fact that this stuffy little theatre should prove the setting of their love, after the enticing but wasted atmosphere of Yalta. But the imagery of this theatre scene is more specifically directed towards reflecting Anna's and Gurov's immediate emotional turmoil, and towards giving, above all, a symbolic embodiment to the restrictions lying in the future of that love. The

figures around Anna and Gurov flit by, as if themselves hurrying away to some secret purpose of time-
ridden urgency. The air on the staircase is stale with
the smell of tobacco; and in place of the picturesque
old ladies and generals of the seaport, there are only
strangely indeterminate figures clad in civil-service
uniforms. Anna's fear of being caught by her husband
or seen by her friends intensifies the urgency about
time which is spatially represented by the closing-in
of people coming up and down the stairs:

> On the landing above them two schoolboys were smok-
> ing and looking down, but that was nothing to Gurov;
> he drew Anna Sergeyevna to him, and began kissing
> her face, her cheeks, and her hands.
>
> 'What are you doing, what are you doing!' she cried in
> horror, pushing him away. 'We are mad. Go away to-
> day; go away at once . . . I beseech you by all that is
> sacred, I implore you . . . There are people coming
> this way!'
>
> Someone was coming up the stairs.
>
> (III.23)

This physical compression of time, in which there is
space only for self-absorbed initial reactions, and in
which any potential happiness is felt only as painful
anguish, is a premonition of the broad terms of Anna's
and Gurov's later meetings in Moscow. But the staircase also symbolically affirms the continuation of
Anna's and Gurov's relationship, whatever the pain
and sense of constriction fated to be theirs. As they
mount the stairs towards their gloomy heights and
Gurov remembers their parting at the train, Chekhov
surely intends us to perceive the difference between
the train's horizontal line of separation and this new
struggle, together, to make of their lives the most that
can be made:

> . . . figures in legal, scholastic and civil service uni-
> forms, all wearing badges, flitted before their eyes.
> They caught glimpses of ladies, of fur coats hanging on
> pegs; the draughts blew on them, bringing a smell of
> stale tobacco. And Gurov, whose heart was beating vio-
> lently, thought:
>
> 'Oh, heavens! Why are these people here and this
> orchestra! . . .'
>
> And at that instant he recalled how when he had seen
> Anna Sergeyevna off at the station he had thought that
> everything was over and they would never meet again.
> But how far they were still from the end!
>
> On the narrow, gloomy staircase over which was writ-
> ten 'To the Amphitheatre', she stopped.
>
> (III.22)

Anna and Gurov declaring their love midway between
landings on this gloomy little staircase epitomizes
their general fate. Their lives are not happy; and in the

last section, the impersonal hotel room and Anna's appearance, pale and tired in her grey dress, reflect the
misery of their struggle to gratify an unsanctioned
love. The signs of age, like Gurov's greying hair, make
us feel the pathos of how little time, in the scheme of
things, is offered to them: all that seems to await them
is continuing secrecy, continuing difficulty and, ultimately, death. But it is a triumph of Chekhov's spirit
and of his art that these things do not overwhelm the
story with pessimism. The intensity of that inner life
of which no one knows but Anna and Gurov, the tenderness and compassion that Gurov displays toward
Anna in her misery, and their love itself, are not sufficient to make the story optimistic, but they do prevent
it from seeming quite tragic. Without that painful secret in his life, Gurov would be merely empty: in his
own almost feminine metaphor, he would be the sheath
without the kernel. Anna is now more heroic, more
able to endure; and Gurov is softer, no longer cynical.
As in 'The Duel,' Chekhov again rejects any view of
people which would hold them to rigidly fixed natures
or even fixed fates. Indeed, the possibility of people's
changing, of their learning to love or to live a better
life, is the small flame of hope that Chekhov, at this
stage in his life, is committed to defend. Thus, even at
the very end of the story, where the image of Anna
and Gurov impresses us as very sad, still we feel a re-
silience, a refusal to give in—not only in the characters but in the author, who in keeping up a spatial
metaphor ('they still had a long, long way to go')
keeps a *future*—however difficult—open for them:

> And it seemed as though in a little while the solution
> would be found, and then a new and splendid life would
> begin; and it was clear to both of them that they still
> had a long, long way to go, and that the most compli-
> cated and difficult part of it was only just beginning.
>
> (III.28)

'The Lady with the Dog' is not one of Chekhov's
most complex stories, nor by any means his greatest.
But, within the limitations of the task it sets itself, it is
a moving and memorable story and one which could
only have come towards the end of his career. It is,
like many of his works, a testimony to his belief in the
worth of human love, which, in this case, is affirmed
even in the most adverse and difficult circumstances;
but few of his stories manifest such mellowness and
so lingering and lyrical an effect of tone. One does not
wish to speak of a 'balance' in the portrayal of the
joys and sorrows of Anna's and Gurov's love: rather,
the story has a strange capacity—felt in the very voice
of the prose—to behold the sad and bitter elements of
life, to accept them for what they are, and yet to perceive even those as having a value in deepening and
giving a more savoured quality to whatever is most
valuable in people's lives. And it is because of this,

and because of the strong sense of the pressures of time on the characters' lives, that one wants to affirm that in 'The Lady with the Dog,' Chekhov's portrayal of the mingled joy and pain of Anna's and Gurov's love is inseparable from what was, at this stage, his sense of life itself.

Note

1. A comparison of *Anna Karenina* with even such acknowledged masterpieces as *Le Rouge et le noir,* with its ironic composure about the subject, or *Madame Bovary* and its rather cynical satire should, I think, make this clear.

Vladimir Kataev (essay date 1979)

SOURCE: Kataev, Vladimir. "'This Is a Great Mystery': 'The Lady with a Little Dog' (1890)." In *If Only We Could Know: An Interpretation of Chekhov,* translated by Harvey Pitcher, pp. 222-34. Chicago: Ivan R. Dee, 2002.

[*In the following essay, originally published in Russian in 1979, Kataev considers exactly how the main characters in "The Lady with the Dog" are changed as a result of their encounter.*]

> They felt that this love of theirs had changed them both.

Numerous critics and readers of **"The Lady with a Little Dog"** rightly see these words from the concluding section as a key point in the whole story. But "changed" in what sense? This is where opinions begin to differ.

The kind of denouement where the characters are shown to undergo a change had been gradually perfected by Chekhov in a number of stories. One of his earliest attempts was in **"Thieves"** (1890), where the hero, Yergunov, gives up his stereotyped existence for a new life based on diametrically opposite principles. Then came **"The Duel"** (1891), in which Layevsky undergoes a similar change. In **"The Wife"** (1892), Chekhov took on an even more difficult task. Here the domestic conflict between Asorin, a man in the Karenin mold, and his young wife unfolds against the grim background of a national disaster: the famine. In Asorin's character there seemed to be no glimmer of light: the hostility and hatred of the people around him, in whose eyes he was "vermin," the universal rejoicing when he left his own house—none of this applied to Layevsky, who was accused by some and defended by others. But even in Asorin's case, after a "strange, crazy, unique" day in his life, a change occurs, as a result of which he feels himself to be "a different person."

But Chekhov makes it clear that these changes are not to be seen as the successful conclusion of the hero's searchings or the discovery of answers, but as the beginning of new questions. In **"Thieves"** the final reflections of Yergunov, whose life has been shaken completely out of its rut, consist of question after question. Layevsky's final reflections about people's searches for real truth seem to be affirmative, but they too contain the question, "Who knows?"—a question that concerns the fate of human searching in general, quite apart from the problems that directly confront the changed Layevsky. Asorin's memoir ends with the phrase, "What the future holds, I do not know."

This kind of denouement, showing how the hero changes after rejecting certain stereotypes and is then faced with new questions, is what Chekhov uses to conclude the story of Gurov and Anna in **"The Lady with a Little Dog."** In contrast to the "resurrection" and "rebirth" endings well known in Russian literature from the works of Tolstoy and Dostoevsky, no solution is found in the conclusion to the problems that have been raised in the story, and no light of truth is revealed.

One should not therefore assume that Chekhov is endorsing Gurov's reflections that "each person" must inevitably lead "a double life." Chekhov shows that for people like Gurov, leading a double life may be the only way out, but he also notes that Gurov "judged others by himself" and always assumed that everyone else's life followed the same course as his own. A person's "real, most interesting life" more often than not runs its course in secret; that is so, and Chekhov points it out with regret, but he does not go on to say: that is how it ought to be.

The relative and individual nature of the character's opinion is further demonstrated by Chekhov's usual method: we simply see that other people view the subject differently. In the last chapter of **"The Lady with a Little Dog"** this is done with special subtlety. In a story where Gurov's point of view prevails (on everything, including their love affair), the author occasionally introduces Anna's "voice," and we see that "this love of theirs" has united two very different people. They take different views of their secret life. For him, "everyone's private existence is maintained in secret," whereas for her, "why could they meet only in secret, hiding from people like thieves? Hadn't their lives been ruined?" But then we come to see that he is adopting her point of view (and this is one of the features of the "new" Gurov). Previously he has used "all kinds of arguments," like the inevitability of a secret life, to reassure himself. But the new Gurov can experience "deep compassion," sincerity, and tenderness, feelings that force him not to object to Anna's logic, as he had done several times before, but to stand up for her point of view. That double life, which the old Gurov might have found interesting and piquant, now seems a life of "intolerable bonds" to him as well as to her. What was no more than an interim conclusion even for Gurov cannot, of course, be regarded as a final conclusion by the author.

No questions are resolved for Gurov and Anna once "this love of theirs had changed them both." On the contrary, only then does the full seriousness of the problems become truly apparent. What stands in the way of their love is not simply "bourgeois morality" or social opinion (in contrast to *Anna Karenina,* society, in so far as it is shown at all in **"The Lady with a Little Dog,"** is completely indifferent to Gurov and Anna's affair). Even if they had managed to overcome the complications of a divorce and to negotiate the problem of the family left behind, etc., questions still remain. "Why does she love him so much?" What is "love" if you can have no conception of it even after participating in dozens of love affairs? Why has love come to them when "his hair had turned grey" and her life is beginning to "fade and wither"? And why does fate compel the two of them, who were destined for each other, "to live in separate cages"? Four more question marks follow in the story's final sentences.

Clearly, no answer is given to these questions which the characters find agonizing and cannot resolve—questions that will always accompany love, for "this is a great mystery"; everything "that has been written and said about love is not a solution but only the posing of questions that remain unresolved," "the causes are unknown," and "we must treat each individual case in isolation, as the doctors say." The solution envisaged, say, by the hero of **"About Love,"** Alyokhin, who was drawn into a similar situation and asked himself similar questions—bitter experience had taught him to take the general view that one ought not to "decorate" love with "these fatal questions" but to cast them aside as "unnecessary and trivial"—is obviously unacceptable to the characters in **"The Lady with a Little Dog."**

Chekhov's changes to the text show how he rejected any form of words that could be taken to mean that the characters' searches were over and their problems solved. He corrected his first version, "Love had made them both better," to "Love had changed them both for the better," before finally deciding on "This love had changed them."

But if the conclusion of **"The Lady with a Little Dog"** evidently has little in common with the "resurrection" or "rebirth" sort of ending, or with the discovery of answers, what exactly is this "change" that has taken place?

The answer is to be found in the way that Chekhov constructs the story. How Gurov's ideas change (for he is the focus of the author's interest) is expressed by means of certain links that are revealed on careful reading. Most prominent among them are two pairs of opposites: "it seemed"/"it turned out that" and "ending"/"beginning."

"It seemed"/"it turned out that" is familiar from a whole series of works, starting with the "stories of discovery," in which Chekhov describes the disappearance of illusions and the rejection of stereotypical thought and behavior.

"Ending"/"beginning" is linked with the particular stereotype that is being rejected in a given story. Both pairs are closely linked from the beginning and run right through the text like musical themes with variations, to merge in the conclusion.

As the reader quickly discovers, the "multiple experience" that Gurov has acquired in his past love affairs stamps its mark straightaway on his affair with the lady with a little dog. This experience has determined his mindset toward all such episodes, of which he is sure there are many more to come ("What strange encounters one has in life!").

The central point in this mindset is that sooner or later all the affairs come to an end (so that new ones can take their place). The first half of the story—the Yalta and Moscow chapters—is designed both to bring out the nature of this stereotype and to show how at first everything develops in full accordance with it. As soon as Gurov's affair with Anna is related to the past, the "seeming" chain of words begins to unfold, and parallel with it a similar chain of "ending" words and phrases.

"It *seemed* to him that he had learned enough from bitter experience . . ."—this is how the story of Gurov's past conquests is introduced (italics added here and subsequently). In line with this experience, each intimacy was pleasant "*to begin with,*" but "*in the end*" it became oppressive. New encounters, however, then followed, past experience was easily forgotten, and "everything *seemed* so simple and amusing." In the first half of the story "seeming" and "ending" are the dominant themes and variations. The course taken by each of Gurov's previous affairs is also a kind of "seeming" game in which both parties accept the conditions. Each intimacy always "*seemed* such a delightfully easy adventure"; Gurov (we learn later) "always *seemed* to women different from what he really was"; and when the affair was coming to an end, the women would become loathsome to him, "and then the lace on their underwear *seemed* to him like the scales on a fish."

Should one of the parties break the rules of this game—by adopting, for example, a serious instead of a playful attitude toward "love" and "passion"—Gurov immediately alludes to this (everything being seen from his point of view) by the use of "seeming" words. These are intended to indicate his unwillingness to take seriously what—as far as he is concerned—are infringements of the rules. For example, we are told that certain women made love to Gurov "insincerely, with superfluous conversations, in an affected, hysterical way, and the expressions on their faces seemed to say that this was not love, not passion, but something more significant." This additional theme accompanies the main one.

Gurov's new affair promises to develop "according to the rules." He and Anna quickly become intimate and with obvious signs of willingness on her part ("when men spoke to her, they had one secret aim in mind that she could not fail to divine . . ."; "'Let's go to your place,' he said quietly. And they set off quickly together"). That the other party in the affair then behaves "strangely and inappropriately" also seems to him like a generally familiar and annoying deviation from the rules: "Anna Sergeyevna, this 'lady with a little dog,' treated what had happened in a curiously personal, very serious sort of way, as if she looked upon it as her downfall. . . . She struck a thoughtful, despondent pose, like some fallen woman in an old-fashioned painting. . . . 'You seem to be trying to justify yourself' . . . had it not been for the tears in her eyes, he might have thought she was joking or playing a part." But taken as a whole the Yalta affair has evidently not broken the stereotype: the theme of "seeming" and "ending" in the background becomes more and more audible in the description of the farewell and of Gurov's first days in Moscow, where Chekhov puts great emphasis on "seeming" and "ending" words:

"We are saying farewell *forever*"; "it was as if everything had conspired to bring that sweet trance, that madness, to a swift *end*"; "So that had been another escapade or adventure in his life, he thought, and now it too was *over*. . . ."; "this young woman whom he would *never* see again, had not after all been happy with him . . . he must have *seemed* different to her from what he really was"; "A month or two would pass, and his memory of Anna Sergeyevna, it *seemed* to him, would cloud over and only occasionally would he dream of her and her touching smile, just as he dreamed of the others."

So the first phase of the story finishes with an idea belonging to Gurov: it seemed to him that everything had come to an end as usual.

But then the new phase begins: in Moscow, memories of "the lady with a little dog" pursue him relentlessly. At first his thoughts are framed in the usual way: "she *seemed* lovelier, younger, and more tender than she had been; and he even *seemed* better in his own eyes than he had been back there in Yalta."

But when for the first time in several months Gurov catches sight of Anna in the crowd at the provincial theater, "his heart missed a beat, and he saw clearly that she was the nearest, dearest, and most important person in the world for him now." Like an echo of the earlier melody, several "seeming" words appear briefly (the husband "*seemed* to spend all his time bowing"; "people *seemed* to be looking at them from every box"). But in contrast to all the earlier "seeming" words, the phrase "and he saw clearly" is heard here for the first time and strikes a distinct and unmistakable note. For Gurov this marks the start of his new life, of his new relationship to life.

Then, at the very center of the composition, the earlier melody returns ("He suddenly recalled that evening at the station, after seeing Anna Sergeyevna off, when he had said to himself that it was *all over* and they would *never* see each other again"), only to be at once reversed: "But how *far* they still were *from the end*!" From now on the two melodies will be heard inseparably together. (The chapter about their meeting in the theater finishes with a paragraph which reverses the old Gurov's stereotyped attitude toward women: "She kept looking back at him, and he could tell from her eyes that she was *truly* unhappy.")

In the last chapter there is a complicated interplay between the story's main themes. The new melody strikes a confident note at first, simply reversing the previous "it seemed, it would end": "It was *obvious* to him that *the end* of this love of theirs *was not near*, was not even in sight." The old Gurov's way of thinking is twice briefly recalled: "And it *seemed* strange to him that he had grown so old and ugly in recent years"; "he always *seemed* to women . . ." But here this is done solely to point up the contrast with his genuine new feeling, for "it was only now, when his hair had turned grey, that he had fallen *well and truly* in love—for the first time in his life." This first real love forces Gurov, who had earlier thought of his feeling of superiority over "the inferior breed" as perfectly natural, to renounce his self-absorption. To underline the two lovers' oneness of thought, Chekhov writes: "*it seemed to them* that they had been destined for each other by fate itself." "Seemed" here seems to mean "self-evident."

So we come to the last sentence of all. Even in the rich musicality of Chekhov's prose, this last sentence of **"The Lady with a Little Dog"** is a rare miracle of harmony. The contrasting melodies running right through the story, enriched in meaning and sound by numerous subtleties, are linked in an inseparable harmony at the end:

> And it *seemed* that in a short time the solution would be found and then a beautiful new life would *begin,* and it was *clear* to both of them that the *end* was still a very long way off, and that the most complicated and difficult part was only just *beginning.*

"It seemed, it would end (easily)"—"it turned out that (the most difficult part) was beginning." This is how Chekhov sums up the change that his hero has undergone. Contrary to his old stereotype, according to which the only prospect ahead of him was a succession of love affairs, Gurov has attained his one and only love and feels that it alone is real. This is the essence of the transformation from the old Gurov to the new; it is the source, too, of "the most complicated and difficult part," but these will be complications arising from "this love of theirs." His one and only love turns out to be not less but more complicated than his previous multiplicity of "escapades or adventures."

Chekhov's last sentence may be misinterpreted. One might suppose that doubt is being cast on the heroes' hopes that "a beautiful new life would begin." This is not so: if a solution is found, "a beautiful new life" will begin without fail. The element of doubt is raised by a different illusory hope: "it seemed that *in a short time* the solution would be found." This, indeed, can only seem to be so; what is clear beyond doubt is "that the end was still a very long way off, and that the most complicated and difficult part was only just beginning."

The transition from "it seemed, it would end" to "it turned out that . . . was beginning" constitutes the essential change in the hero's consciousness. But it does not in itself explain why the stereotype should have been rejected—a stereotype that seemed so firmly fixed in Gurov's consciousness and determined his behavior, and which was only reinforced by each new "escapade or adventure"—including, so it seemed, the affair in Yalta.

Why this particular adventure with the lady with a little dog should have become this inveterate cynic's one genuine love does indeed remain the kind of riddle that forces one to say of love that "this is a great mystery" and "the causes are unknown."

Chekhov does not set out to prove that the mystery of love does not exist. On the contrary, the mystery is what he is writing about. Love is a mystery for Chekhov's characters because there are no general solutions

and each case of love is unique. As Masha says later in *Three Sisters,* "when you read some novel or other, it all seems so stale and obvious, but as soon as you fall in love yourself, you realize that no one knows the first thing about it and you've got to work it out on your own."

Chekhov's characters know and have read about "what love is" in general, and the philosophy of love contains nothing new or interesting for them. The mystery begins with the individualization "of each separate case." Why in that way? Why at that time? Why that particular person? Chekhov's characters in love ask these and dozens of similar "why?" questions. The impossibility of "finding one's bearings" in love is a particular but frequent instance of not being able to find one's bearings in life as a whole.

So it remains a riddle and a mystery why "this quite unremarkable little woman, swallowed up in the provincial crowd, holding a vulgar lorgnette, now filled his whole existence, was his joy and sorrow, and the one happiness that he now craved in life." What we find out about Anna from her speeches of repentance makes us feel sympathetic toward her. But being dissatisfied with one's husband, complaining about the boredom of life, and feeling repentance—all this sort of thing Gurov must have heard many times before in confessions from women. One of the explanations she gives ("*I wanted to live!* To live, to live . . . I was burning with curiosity . . .") sounds so much like Gurov's own usual motivation ("and *he wanted to live,* and everything seemed so simple and amusing") that one would expect his stereotype to be strengthened by all this, not weakened. It is easy to be ironic at Anna's expense, but she is the one who succeeds in becoming Gurov's only true love.

Evidently the reasons for the change depicted in the story are to be sought in Gurov himself. In order to correlate his character's thoughts and actions with the "norm" and "real truth," Chekhov again introduces certain markers—unobtrusively, in passing—that make this correlation possible.

Where do these markers first appear in **"The Lady with a Little Dog"**? Is it at the moment when Anna, after referring to her "lackey of a husband," feels no need to explain herself, since both she and Gurov understand what is meant—and this sounds less like the coded language of lovers than a simple exchange of messages between two people oppressed by their lack of freedom? Or even earlier, in the reference to Gurov's wife as "plain-spoken, sure of herself, imposing, and in her own words, 'a thinking person'"? (Both the "thinking wife" and the "lackey husband" clearly base their lives on certain stereotypes and "general ideas" that are bound to remain unshaken.)

Another marker appears later, in the Oreanda episode: "Gurov reflected on how beautiful everything in the world really was when you stopped to think about it, everything except our own thoughts and actions when we lose sight of the higher aims of existence and our human dignity." This allusion to "the higher aims of existence," like the allusion in **"Gooseberries"** to "our splendid land," would seem to have no connection with the course of the narrative or the demands of the plot. But these allusions are not fortuitous, they are vital. Introduced into a character's train of thought, what they indicate above all is the author's intention to raise a specific individual story to the level of something universal—not known to the characters, but dimly sensed—that would be able to unite everyone. At the start of Chapter 3 the same kind of higher, general note is struck by the reference to "recalling the years of one's youth."

The thoughts that come to Gurov about "the higher aims of existence" are not peculiar to this story. Almost the same feelings that overcome Gurov when he is spellbound by "those magical surroundings of sea and mountains, of clouds and open sky," had been experienced by another Chekhov hero, Dmitry Startsev, on that unique occasion in his life in the moonlit cemetery. Layevsky, Ionych, Gurov—each is moved at a given moment by higher thoughts and reflects on what is eternal. Their thoughts about "the higher aims of existence" come and go, but the "escapade or adventure" continues.

Also outwardly unrelated to the development of the characters' attitudes is the episode in which Gurov tries to strike up a conversation about his affair in the summer, and receives the famous reply:

"You were quite right just now about the sturgeon, it *was* a bit off!"

For some reason these everyday words suddenly roused Gurov's indignation, and struck him as coarse and degrading. What barbaric manners, what ugly people!

Then follows the indignant Gurov's monologue about our "barren, uninspiring life."

This monologue is often seen by critics as an indication of Gurov's rebirth and regeneration under the effects of love, or of the "rebellion" that will give rise to such a regeneration. It is also cited as proof of the social significance of Chekhov's story. Such an interpretation needs to be closely examined, otherwise the whole love story looks like no more than a makeweight addition to the hero's speech of protest.

For a start, Gurov has not yet visited Anna's town and fallen "well and truly" in love. That will happen later; for the moment "he himself had no clear idea" of what was happening to him and what to do; all he wanted was "to see Anna Sergeyevna and speak to her, arrange a meeting if possible." And in the long chain of "how it seemed" expressions, this "struck him as," especially in combination with "suddenly" and "for some reason," looks like a familiar Chekhov example of inconsequential human thoughts, with their unexpected leaps and indiscriminate conclusions. Finally, Gurov's emotional outburst contains nothing that is new or that we have not heard before from other Chekhov characters.

One might suppose that Gurov's companion, who failed to see that love and sturgeon do not go together (especially when the sturgeon is a bit off), was intended by Chekhov to represent a hopelessly crass typical member of society. This is not necessarily so. It is quite clear, after all, from what the companion says, that Gurov himself has just been talking about sturgeon. But right now, at this particular moment, Gurov is someone else, someone who feels in great need of sympathy and of being understood (just like the cabby Iona Potapov in "Yearning"), whereas his companion is too self-absorbed to understand—to be able to understand—him.

Chekhov's characters are submerged in everyday life. There are moments when they expand spiritually and want to break out of the circle of everyday vulgarity, but they do not do this collectively, or at the same time, or even with someone else, but on their own. At each of these moments they are lonely, they are not understood, they obtain no response. This constant Chekhov theme had been expressed very poignantly in **"Ionych"** (written a year before **"The Lady with a Little Dog"**), in the scenes of the two declarations of love that are not understood. In **"The Lady with a Little Dog,"** Chekhov describes with a certain amount of irony how this world of everyday vulgarity is suddenly revealed to Gurov, and the latter explodes with indignation against "these barbaric manners and ugly people . . . these days of unrelieved boredom." What is revealed for a moment to Gurov is shown to be an inescapable constant of human relations.

There is no reason, therefore, to regard this episode as almost more important than the whole of the love story and the change in Gurov's attitude toward the "inferior breed." Such an approach is favored by critics seeking to establish the important social message of **"The Lady with a Little Dog."** But of far deeper and more genuine social significance in Chekhov's world than any words of protest or indignation uttered by one character is the author's unfailing preoccupation with distinguishing the true from the false, the "genuine" from the "nongenuine" in human ideas and actions.

Nevertheless, Gurov's indignant inner monologue *is* important—important in characterizing Gurov. An average man and one of the crowd, he remains so till the end of the story; at all events, nothing is said about a "break" with the society that made him so indignant. But we find out something else about him. Somewhere deep in his soul he carries a feeling of discontent, an awareness that "ordinary" life is a deviation from the "norm" (everything is beautiful "except our own thoughts and actions"), and a consciousness of "the higher aims of existence."

Gurov's monologue repeats almost word for word what Dmitry Startsev, already halfway to becoming Ionych, said about everyday life in the town of S.: "You ask what kind of life we have here? No life at all. We grow old, we get fat, we let ourselves go. Days and nights flash past in a dull blur, without thoughts or impressions. . . . Making money by day and spending the evening at the club, surrounded by gamblers, alcoholics, and vulgarians, whose company I detest. What's good about that?" Both monologues contain the note of "dissatisfaction with oneself and other people" that is felt by so many characters in Chekhov. The outcome of such speeches varies considerably according to the particular individual. It may be, as in the case of Ionych, that everything comes to an end with this surge of indignation, and the "spark in the soul" goes out; or it may lead, as in Gurov's case, to his one and only true love. But these speeches, these thoughts and moods, are like a mark, a sign—a sign of one more ordinary person being drawn unconsciously toward the search for "real truth."

Irina Kirk (essay date 1981)

SOURCE: Kirk, Irina. "Search for Escapes." In *Anton Chekhov*, pp. 105-25. Boston: Twayne Publishers, 1981.

[*In the following excerpt, Kirk analyzes how "The Lady with the Dog," in the words of Maxim Gorky, "killed realism"—because the story appeals to the imagination for its meaning and effect.*]

After reading this story Gorky made the following remark: "Do you know what you are doing? You are killing realism. And you will kill it soon. Kill it for good. This form has outlived its time. It's a fact. After you no one can travel this road. No one can write so simply about such simple things as you do. After any of your insignificant stories everything seems crude, as though it were written not with a pen but with a log of wood. And the main thing, everything seems not simple enough, nor true."[1]

What did Gorky mean by his statement that Chekhov was killing realism? The story seems realistic enough: two people meet at a summer resort and fall in love.

At first it is only a passing diversion to them, but later they discover that they are unable to forget each other and so begin to lead a double life. In summary it sounds like any banal love story.

But the essence of the story does not lie in the plot nor in its realistic quality. This realism is being killed, as Gorky said, because the story appeals to the imagination.

The opening sentence not only gives a full picture of a summer resort with its gossip, boredom, and people looking for adventure, it also unites the hero, Gurov, with the resort crowd. The second sentence shows the lady, separate from the crowd, walking with her white dog. As Gurov's relationship with Anna develops, his sense of identity shifts from an immersion in the superficial world of appearances to an inner, poetic perception of life which he associates with Anna. Through Gurov's love for Anna, her separation from the crowd is transferred onto a symbolic level: it is no longer merely physical, but metaphysical; not only temporary, but permanent. To the crowd Anna will always remain a lady with a lapdog. To Gurov she will become the embodiment of all that is beautiful in life.

"The Lady with a Lapdog" is structured upon two contrasting settings. The first two chapters of the story describe the nature of Gurov's initial attraction to Anna and his brief affair with her in Yalta. When he first sees Anna, Gurov reacts coolly: "If she is here without a husband and without friends," figured Gurov, "it wouldn't be a bad idea to get acquainted with her" (IX, 236). Chekhov uses the calculating, prosaic "figured" to underline the lack of any poetic element in this man. Gurov is bored and in search of a short, enjoyable liaison with a woman. However, Chekhov adds some information about Gurov's background that indicates that he once had romantic longings. He is a philologist by education and at one time was preparing to sing in a private opera. There is also an indication that Anna will touch some other chord in his unloving heart. The closing sentence of this chapter is: "But there is something pitiful in her," he thought, and began to fall asleep (IX, 238).

The second chapter deals with adultery and is built on small details. Anna's eyes sparkle and she loses her lorgnette through which she views the world. Gurov looks around after kissing her to see if anyone had seen his action. There is a lyrical epiphany; when sitting by the ocean with Anna, Gurov feels that "everything, if properly understood, would be entirely beautiful." A single candle barely illumines Anna's unhappy, guilty face after she has become Gurov's mistress.

Anna's remorse following adultery is reminiscent of the Anna-Vronsky scene in *Anna Karenina:*

> It's not right. You're the first person not to respect me . . . God forgive me! I am a wicked woman. I despise myself, and have no desire to justify myself! It isn't my husband I have deceived, but myself! My husband may be a good, honest man but he is also a flunky!

(IX, 239-240)

Chekhov undercuts the scene by having Gurov nonchalantly eat a piece of watermelon during Anna's tearful outburst, and by allowing him to comfort her so that "she was happy again, and they both began to laugh" (IX, 240).

Chapter 3 portrays Gurov's superficial life in Moscow and contrasts it with the lyrical memories he associates with Anna. The rounds of dinners, card games, and conversations no longer distract Gurov from his loneliness. He becomes painfully aware of a lack of communication with other people. This lack is summed up in a conversation between Gurov and an acquaintance to whom he says, "If you only knew what a charming woman I met in Yalta." His friend responds, "You are right. The sturgeon did have a slight smell" (IX, 244). The total poverty of Gurov's emotional life serves as an incentive in his decision to see Anna again.

Gurov's and Anna's reunion is described using a combination of details that parallel earlier observations and draw attention to the changes in their relationship. The description of Anna as "a little, undistinguished woman, lost in a provincial crowd, with a vulgar lorgnette in her hand" (IX, 245) contrasts with her romantic image in chapter 2 after she has just lost her lorgnette because embellishing Anna's appearance is no longer important to Gurov. He loves her as she is. As opposed to Gurov's relaxed cynicism in the first two chapters, he is now nervous and can only murmur, "But do understand, Anna, do understand" (IX, 246). The change in Gurov's feelings is also revealed in that he kisses Anna despite the two schoolboys who are watching, whereas earlier he had made conscious effort to conceal their relationship.

Like chapter 2, in which the seduction takes place, the last chapter is set in a hotel room. Though the social barriers still stand between Anna and Gurov, their feelings for each other and their attitude toward judgment from the outside world have changed. Whereas Anna first wept guiltily because she had committed the sin of adultery, she now cries with the pain of love, "out of sheer agitation, in the sorrowful consciousness that their life was so sad." Gurov is no longer indifferent to Anna's suffering, but shares in it:

> "Formerly in moments of sadness he had soothed himself with whatever logical arguments came into his head, but now he no longer cared for logic; he felt profound compassion, he wanted to be sincere and tender" (IX, 248).

The comfort that Anna and Gurov give each other unites them despite the many obstacles barring their happiness.

> Anna Sergeevna and he loved each other as people do who are very close and intimate, like man and wife, like tender friends; it seemed to them that Fate itself had meant them for one another, and they could not understand why he had a wife and she a husband. . . . They forgave each other what they were ashamed of in their past, they forgave everything in the present, and felt that this love of theirs had altered them both.

(IX, 249)

Although there is no realistic solution to their problem, at least Anna and Gurov know that their pain and sorrow, as well as their love, would always be shared.

Note

1. *Chekhov-Gorki perepiska, stat'i i vyskazyvaniia* (N. Gosizd, 1951), p. 6.

Selected Bibliography

Primary Sources

In Russian:

Chekhov, A. P. *Sorbranie sochinenii v dvenadtsati tomakh.* Moskva: Pravda, 1950.

In English:

Stories 1897-1899. Translated by Ronald Hingley. ("The Oxford Chekhov," vol. IX) London: Oxford University Press, 1975.

Matthew C. Brennan (essay date winter 1985)

SOURCE: Brennan, Matthew C. "Plotting against Chekhov: Joyce Carol Oates and 'The Lady with the Dog.'" *Notes on Modern Literature* 9, no. 3 (winter 1985): item 13.

[*In the following essay, Brennan comments on the influence of Chekhov's "The Lady with the Dog" on Joyce Carol Oates's "The Lady with the Pet Dog," focusing on Oates's overturning of what she viewed as Chekhov's sexist depiction of women.*]

In *Marriages and Infidelities,* Joyce Carol Oates has the main character of "The Dead," the writer Ilena Williams, describe her latest work as "a series of short stories in honor of certain dead writers."[1] Here, in a story honoring James Joyce, Oates autobiographically describes *Marriages and Infidelities*. In another story in this collection, "The Lady With the Pet Dog," Oates honors Anton Chekhov, specifically, his story **"The Lady with the Dog"** (1899). Oates retains the same central characters—two lovers trapped in loveless marriages—and the same kinds of settings—resorts, small and large cities, hotels, concert halls. She even retains the same story line: a man and a woman, both away from their spouses, meet at a resort, make love, and return to their homes expecting never to meet again; however, strong feeling lingers in both lovers and, after the man reappears suddenly at a concert in the woman's home town, they resume the affair, finally realizing that they are truly husband and wife, even if legally married to other people.

Besides these elements, Oates also retains Chekhov's third-person point of view. But unlike Chekhov, who focuses on the male lover, Gurov, Oates makes Anna S., the female lover, the center of consciousness. Because Chekhov privileges Gurov, he represents Anna's feelings only when she speaks to Gurov. In fact, when Anna S. expresses her shame to Gurov, Chekhov says, "The solitary candle on the table scarcely lit up her face"; and rather than reveal her inner thoughts he merely tells us, "it was obvious that her heart was heavy."[2] So, by subordinating Anna S. to Gurov, Chekhov gives readers no way to understand the feminine side of a masculine story. In contrast, Oates presents what Chekhov leaves out—the female's experience—and so relegates the male lover (who in her version is nameless) to the limited status Chekhov relegates Anna S.: Oates privileges the point of view of Anna. Furthermore, because Anna S. says she feels "like a madwoman" (**"The Lady with the Dog"** ["LWD"], 154), Oates fragments Chekhov's traditionally chronological plot, which becomes a subtext against which Oates can foreground Anna's confusion, doubt, and struggle to find an identify.[3] For, as the narrator of "Plot" says, plot is "the record of someone's brain" (*Marriages and Infidelities* [*M & I*], 209), "the record of someone going crazy" (*M & I*, 206).

To record the brain of Gurov, the male lover, Chekhov develops a conventional, sequential plot. He spreads the five-step plot through the four formal divisions of his story. Part 1 consists of the exposition, during which Gurov and Anna S. meet at the resort, Yalta. Part 2 continues the the exposition, as the characters become lovers, and it also introduces the rising action as they separate at the train station, Anna S. returning to her home in the town of S., Gurov to his in Moscow. Then, in part 3, the action continues to rise as Gurov misses Anna and eventually goes to the town of S. Here, at a concert, the two climactically meet again,

and, as part 3 ends, Anna S. agrees to come to Moscow. Finally, in part 4, the action falls as Chekhov describes their affair and dramatizes it in a scene that forms the resolution, through which Gurov realizes, after looking in a mirror, that he is in love for the first time: he and Anna S. really are "as husband and wife" (**"LWD,"** 162), though separated by law.

Oates borrows all these events for her plot, but if Chekhov's is linear, hers is circular. Oates breaks her story into three parts. Part 1 depicts the climax, immediately giving her version the intensity that the high-strung center of consciousness, Anna, is experiencing. We are with her at the concert hall, where her lover appears and she faints, and then with her back home, where her husband clumsily makes love to her while she thinks of her lover. Part 2 opens with a flashback to the rising action—when the lover drives Anna to Albany where they separate, just as Chekhov's lovers separate at the train station; next, part 2 both repeats the climax (at the concert and in the bedroom) and relates, for the first time, the falling action in which the lovers continue their affair. Part 1, then, presents only the climax, and part 2 widens the plot to record not just the center, the climax, but also the rising and falling actions that surround it. Part 3, however, widens the circular plot still further. Expanding outward from the climactic center, first the plot regresses to embrace the exposition (in which the lovers meet and make love at the resort, in this version Nantucket); then it moves inward again, retracing chronologically the rising action, climax, and falling action; and finally, as part 3 concludes, the plot introduces the resolution, rounding out its pattern.

Before the resolution, however, as we witness the falling action (the resumption of the affair) for the second time, Oates stresses the lack of development: Anna says, "'Everything is repeating itself. Everything is stuck'" (*M & I*, 408). By having the plot repeat itself, and so fail to progress toward resolution, Oates conveys Anna's lack of identity: Anna is trapped between two relationships, two "husbands," and hence wavers throughout this version between feeling like "nothing" in her legal husband's house where "there was no boundary to her," "no precise limit" (*M & I*, 395), and feeling defined—as "recognizably Anna"—by her illicit lover, her true "husband," who has sketched her portrait, to which she continually refers as if grasping for a rope (*M & I*, 393, 401-404, 406-408).

Here, then (on p. 408), with the climax repeated three times and the rising and falling actions twice, the plot finally progresses from this impasse to its resolution. And, appropriately, as the plot finally achieves its completion, so too does Anna, discovering as she symbolically looks into the mirror, this man was her husband, truly—they were truly married, here in this room—they had been married haphazardly and accidentally for a long time. In another part of the city she had another husband, a "husband," but she had not betrayed that man, not really. This man, whom she loved above any other person in the world . . . was her truest lover, her destiny.

(M & I, 410)

Significantly, this scene of discovery suggests Lacan's "mirror stage," which embodies the process of constructing a center of the self—an integrated identity or self-image.[4] Not till Anna reaches the "mirror stage," and so discovers the center of her identity, her lover (whom a Jungian might say represents her *animus*)— not till now can the record of her brain, her plot, be resolved. Consequently, Oates allows the plot to progress sequentially to the resolution—to integrity— only as Anna's consciousness discovers its true identity, its integration.

Clearly, then, Oates' version of this story is no mere exercise. Rather, like the narrator of "Plot," Oates was "forced to change things around" in **"The Lady with the Dog"** to create a plot that explains Anna's life (*M & I*, 209). Oates may well be honoring Chekhov in **"The Lady with the Pet Dog,"** but her drastic revision of his treatment of Anna S. nevertheless makes clear that Oates includes Chekhov among those "celebrated twentieth-century writers [who] have presented Woman through the distorting lens of sexist imagination."[5]

Notes

1. "The Dead," *Marriages and Infidelities* (New York: Vanguard, 1972), p. 478. Further references to stories in *Marriages and Infidelities* (hereafter abbreviated *M & I*) will be made parenthetically.

2. "The Lady With the Dog," in *The Norton Introduction to Fiction*, 2nd edn., ed. Jerome Beaty (New York: Norton, 1981), p. 154. Further references to this story (hereafter abbreviated *LWD*) will be made parenthetically.

3. In *Joyce Carol Oates* (Boston: Twayne, 1979), Joanne V. Creighton lists similarities between Chekhov's and Oates' stories, but she ignores changes in plot as well as the importance of the change in viewpoint, concluding that Oates' story is "an exercise," "effective, but in the same way that Chekhov's is" (p. 132). Samuel F. Pickering, Jr., in "The Short Stories of Joyce Carol Oates," *Georgia Review* 28 (Summer 1974): 218-26, and Linda W. Wagner, in "Oates: The Changing Shapes of Her Realities," *Great Lakes Review* 5 (Winter 1979): 15-23, both remark generally on the experimental plots of *Marriages and Infidelities,* but neither cites the plot of "The Lady With the Pet Dog."

4. See Terry Eagleton, *Literary Theory* (Minneapolis: Univ. of Minnesota Press, 1983), p. 164.

5. Oates, "'At Least I Have Made a Woman of Her': Images of Woman in Twentieth-Century Literature," *Georgia Review* 37 (Spring 1983): 7.

Boyd Creasman (essay date spring 1990)

SOURCE: Creasman, Boyd. "Gurov's Flights of Emotion in Chekhov's 'The Lady with the Dog.'" *Studies in Short Fiction* 27, no. 2 (spring 1990): 257-60.

[*In the following essay, Creasman focuses on two incidents in "The Lady with the Dog" that he argues illustrate the protagonist's motivations.*]

In 1921, Conrad Aiken made the following assessment of Anton Chekhov's work: "This, after all, is Chekhov's genius—he was a master of mood" (151). Indeed Aiken's statement is a good starting point for a discussion of the structure of Chekhov's short fiction. Many of Chekhov's short stories—the later ones in particular—are structured around the main character's moments of strong emotion, a feature of the author's short fiction that has never been fully explored, even in discussions of individual stories. For example, much of the criticism of **"The Lady with the Dog,"** one of Chekhov's most revered short stories, has focused on its parallels with his real life love for Olga Knipper, the influence of Tolstoy's *Anna Karenina,* the story's similarities with Chekhov's later plays, and its exemplification of the author's realism and modernity, which have greatly influenced twentieth-century short fiction. In tracing the story's biographical and literary influences and its relation to other literature, though, Chekhov critics have generally ignored an important feature of **"The Lady with the Dog"**—namely, the significance of Gurov's two flights of emotion, the first with Anna at Oreanda, the second outside the Medical Club at Moscow.[1] These two moments of intense feeling are crucial to understanding Gurov's motivations and illustrate the importance of this kind of emotional flight to the structure of Chekhov's short fiction.

In the first of his two flights of emotion, Gurov contemplates the transcendence of love as he sits quietly on a bench with Anna at Oreanda:

> Not a leaf stirred, the grasshoppers chirruped, and the monotonous hollow roar of the sea came up to them, speaking of peace, of the eternal sleep lying in wait for us all. The sea had roared like this before there was any Yalta or Oreanda, it was roaring now, and it would go on roaring, just as indifferently and hollowly, when we had passed away. And it may be that in this conti-

nuity, this utter indifference to life and death, lies the secret of our ultimate salvation, of the stream of life on our planet, and of its never-ceasing movement toward perfection.

Side by side with a young woman, who looked so exquisite in the early light, soothed and enchanted by the sight of all this magical beauty—sea, mountains, clouds and the vast expanse of the sky—Gurov told himself that, when you came to think of it, everything in the world is beautiful really, everything but our own thoughts and actions, when we lose sight of the higher aims of life, and of our dignity as human beings.

(226)

This passage reveals one of the strengths of Chekhov's writing, his superb handling of the theme of transcendence through love. In *Anton Chekhov and the Lady with the Dog,* Virginia Llewellyn Smith discusses the importance of this theme: "In Chekhov's later work, this ideal of love was to become increasingly associated with the concept of something above and beyond the transient, or more precisely, with a quasi-philosophical speculative interest, and a quasi-mystical faith in the future of mankind" (138). Another critic, Beverly Hahn, makes a similar point, finding in some of Chekhov's work a "mysterious transcendence . . . of the great moral and philosophical issues of existence" (253). Finding the eternal in a particular moment, Chekhov's characters can turn away mortality and meaninglessness, if only briefly, by turning to each other. However, it is important to remember that at this point in the story, Gurov clearly has not fallen in love with Anna. At first it is not Anna in particular whom he desires, but rather a pretty woman in general, and the reader is told that Gurov, who refers to women as "the lower race," actually "could not have existed a single day" without them (222). Indeed, Gurov enjoys Anna's company at Yalta but is at first surprised, then bored and annoyed with her sense of having sinned. And when Anna must leave Yalta and return to her husband, Gurov does not seem greatly to regret that the affair has apparently ended: "And he told himself that this had been just one more of the many adventures in his life, and that it, too, was over, leaving nothing but a memory . . ." (227). However, when he returns home, he cannot seem to forget the lady with the dog.

Gurov's second flight of emotion results from his sudden awareness of the grossness and banality of life in Moscow, and the way it pales in comparison to the time he spent with Anna in Yalta. When Gurov starts to tell one of his companions at the Medical Club about her, his friend interrupts him with a comment about dinner, "the sturgeon was just a *leetle* off." At this moment, all of Gurov's pent-up frustrations with his life in Moscow find release in the quintessential Chekhovian flight:

These words, in themselves so commonplace, for some reason infuriated Gurov, seemed to him humiliating, gross. What savage manners, what people! What wasted evenings, what tedious, empty days! Frantic card-playing, gluttony, drunkenness, perpetual talk always about the same thing. The greater part of one's time and energy went on business that was no use to anyone, and on discussing the same thing over and over again, and there was nothing to show for all of it but a stunted, earth-bound existence and a round of trivialities, and there was nowhere to escape to, you might as well be in a madhouse or a convict settlement.

(229)

In some ways, this passage represents the climax of the story, for after Gurov resolves to go to Anna's town, the remainder of the story, in which the characters are forced to keep up appearances by not telling anyone about the affair, has an aura of inevitability about it. In addition to this structural importance, this intense burst of emotion is also very important to an understanding of Gurov's motivations for renewing the affair and thus raises an interesting question: is his decision to find Anna motivated more by love for her or by his desire to escape the tedium of life in Moscow? Certainly the Gurov in the first two sections of the story does not seem like the kind of man who is capable of falling in love with Anna. He becomes bored and uncomfortable, rather than concerned or sensitive, when she gets upset. Does Gurov truly love Anna, or is she simply the natural person for him to turn to in his time of depression?

In his excellent "Chekhov and the Modern Short Story," Charles E. May argues that the question is unanswerable:

It is never clear in the story whether Gurov truly loves Anna Sergeyevna or whether it is only the romantic fantasy that he wishes to maintain. What makes the story so subtle and complex is that Chekhov presents the romance in such a limited and objective way that we realize that there is no way to determine whether it is love or romance, for there is no way to distinguish between them.

(151)

May's otherwise good interpretation is slightly off the mark on this point. While it is true that throughout most of the story it is difficult—because of the objectivity to which May alludes—to determine whether Gurov loves Anna, the reader is directly told just before the conclusion of the story that the two main characters do indeed love each other and that Gurov has "fallen in love properly, thoroughly, for the first time in his life" (234). It is crucial to recognize that the Gurov at the end of the story is not the same as the one at the beginning, and the difference is not merely that he now needs love, but that he has clearly found the woman he loves. Certainly, Gurov does not love less simply because he feels a need for love in his life; in fact, it is precisely this yearning that causes his love for Anna to awaken and grow. And again the key to understanding Gurov's motivations for leaving Moscow and going to Anna is his flights of emotion in which he recognizes the essential truth of the story: his love for Anna is far more noble than his banal, socially acceptable life in Moscow.

Still, at the end of the story, the couple's problem—how to keep their love for each other alive while hiding the relationship from society—remains unresolved. Moreover, neither character seems to have the courage to reveal the truth of their love to anyone else, and therefore, the characters find themselves in a kind of limbo:

> And it seemed to them that they were within an inch of arriving at a decision, and that then a new, beautiful life would begin. And they both realized that the end was still far, far away, and that the hardest, the most complicated part was only just beginning.
>
> (235)

Gurov and Anna find themselves in a desperate situation, but as Beverly Hahn suggests, "desperation is not the dominant note of the story, nor is its outcome really tragic, because the hardship of Anna's and Gurov's love cannot be separated from the *fact* of that love and from the fact that it brings each a degree of fulfilment not known before" (253).

With its elegant language, complex main characters, and realistic detail, **"The Lady with the Dog"** is indeed a masterful story of many moods and, therefore, an illustration of the validity of Conrad Aiken's judgment that Chekhov is a master of mood. Gurov's two intense moments of emotion are important to the structure of the story and demonstrate an important feature of the author's style, for similar Chekhovian flights can be found in many of his other stories, especially his later ones, such as **"About Love," "A Visit to Friends," "The Bishop,"** and **"The Betrothed,"** just to name a few. These flights of emotion are as important in Chekhov's stories as epiphanies are in Joyce's and therefore merit further exploration by those interested in the study of Chekhov's short fiction.

Note

1. A. P. Chudakov, in *Chekhov's Poetics* (Ann Arbor: Ardis, 1983), comes closest to recognizing the structural importance of such scenes in his discussion of how characters' emotional states affect the presentation of physical detail. See chapter 3, "Narrative from 1895-1904," of Chudakov's book.

Works Cited

Aiken, Conrad. *Collected Criticism*. London: Oxford UP, 1968.

Chekhov, Anton. "The Lady with the Dog." Trans. Ivy Litvinov. *Anton Chekhov's Short Stories*. Norton Critical Edition. Ed. Ralph E. Matlaw. New York: Norton, 1979. 221-35.

Chudakov, A. P. *Chekhov's Poetics*. Ann Arbor: Ardis, 1983.

Hahn, Beverly. *Chekhov: A Study of the Major Stories and Plays*. Cambridge: Cambridge UP, 1977.

May, Charles E. "Chekhov and the Modern Short Story." *A Chekhov Companion*. Ed. Toby W. Clyman. Westport, CT: Greenwood, 1985. 147-63.

Smith, Virginia Llewellyn. *Anton Chekhov and the Lady with the Dog*. London: Oxford UP, 1973.

James Palmer (essay date October 1991)

SOURCE: Palmer, James. "Mastering Chekhov: Heifitz's 'The Lady with the Dog.'" *Literature-Film Quarterly* 19, no. 4 (October 1991): 252-57.

[*In the following essay, Palmer discusses Joseph Heifitz's 1960 film adaptation of "The Lady with the Dog," which he says beautifully captures both the humor and pathos of Chekhov's story.*]

Josef Heifitz's film adaptation of Anton Chekhov's **"The Lady with the Dog"** was released in Russia in 1960 in honor of the Chekhov Centenary. In 1987, Russian director Nikita Mikhalkov made **"The Lady with the Dog"** the kernel story for the Russian/Italian co-production entitled *Dark Eyes*. This loose adaptation is more reminiscent of Fellini than Chekhov in its expansive, free-wheeling style and insistent sentimentality.[1] For filmgoers who prefer their Chekhov neat, Heifitz offers a far more literal adaptation in a deceptively simple, unadorned style. Although Mikhalkov's more flamboyant, broadly comic, technicolor film may well be more immediately accessible and appealing to contemporary audiences, Heifitz's restrained, austere style befits Chekhov's prose and produces its own considerable rewards.

Writing a celebratory piece on Heifitz's film in the Swedish journal, *Chaplin*, Ingmar Bergman recalls how he prepared Chekhov's *The Seagull* for a Stockholm theater production by making the cast look at Heifitz's film. According to Bergman, the film "emerges from the work itself, and is enormously faithful towards Chekhov in a way that I have seldom experienced in film."[2] "Faithful" adaptations may call to mind dreary works which follow slavishly their literary sources only to produce plodding, unimaginative films; nevertheless, Heifitz accepts the risks inherent in adhering not only to the plot and structure of Chekhov's story, but also to its slow pace and subtle tonalities. Concluding his tribute to the film, Bergman makes clear the rewards to be found in such attentiveness:

> Consider only the style that dares to be slow, almost motionlessly slow, only afterwards to be able to give the film such an extraordinary craft in the moment when it accelerates. And another thing that I admire so much in *The Lady with the Dog* is that there is not an ounce of sentimentality to be found in the film, . . . Sentiment one finds in rich measure, but sentimentality—never. . . . The film balances at one and the same time the tragedy and comedy that one always finds in Chekhov. This is one film that I shall want to see many times.[3]

Capturing Chekhov's humor and pathos, Heifitz's film invites our attention to the small details and commonplace dialogue of the love affair between two lonely married people, Dmitri Gurov (Alexei Batalov), a Moscow bank official, and Anna Sergeyevna (Iya Savvina), the bored young wife of a provincial bureaucrat. A character study of Gurov and, to a lesser degree, of Anna, the film has little action. Like Chekhov's prose, it achieves its effects through restraint and understatement where the nuance of emotions is often indicated by an apparently insignifcant phrase or fleeting gesture. What is left unspoken between the couple is not absent, just as the film's silent moments—the couple viewing the majestic landscape at Oreanda or Gurov standing in the cold outside of Anna's house in Saratov—are not empty, but infused with the characters' thoughts.

The leisurely pace of the initial scene expand the story's opening sentence—"People were telling one another that a newcomer had been seen on the promenade—a lady with a dog."[4] At the seaside cafe, the men gather to talk of meeting Anna and to tease the one unlucky man whose wife is vacationing with him. The measured tempo of the cafe scenes and the views of people walking along the promenade evoke the lethargy of Yalta shopkeepers and vacationers alike. Through the cafe windows, Gurov and the other men catch a fleeting glimpse of the genteel lady in her white dress as she walks her white Pomeranian. When one of the men encounters the lady on the promenade, he scrutinizes her dog with his binoculars, turns to follow her as she passes by, and then retreats. Such wistful scenes are choreographed like a slow comic dance. This unhurried prologue offers us a glimpse of Gurov and Anna, who differ little from their fellow vacationers, but whose fate will distinguish them.

Both the story and the film are structured in four parts, each section presenting a different stage of the lovers' attachment and charting the transformation of a casual adulterous affair into a desperate and deepening love. In the first section of the story, Chekhov offers an unflattering portrait of Gurov as a somewhat cynical, jaded roué, constantly unfaithful to his wife, yet bored with his many superficial conquests. After describing Gurov's fear of the complications that often accompany a lengthy affair, Chekhov concludes: "But every time [Gurov] encountered an attractive woman he forgot all about his experience, the desire for life surged up in him, and everything seemed simple and amusing." (222) The comic sexual implication of the phrase "the desire for life surged up in him" carries with it the deeper truth of Gurov's real but unacknowledged need to seek an authentic emotional life that he cannot find with his shallow, pseudo-intellectual wife. When Gurov decides on another "brisk transitory liaison," the results prove far from simple or amusing.

The aftermath of their first lovemaking confirms how contrite and morally confused Anna is by her adultery and how trapped Gurov is by his own seductive behavior. Gurov first stands at the window with his back to Anna, then sits down to slice a section of watermelon, carefully picking out the seeds with a small fork. The indifferent Gurov eats the melon and responds to Anna's confession with the cruel comment, "You needn't try to explain. I really don't want to know anything." When Anna describes her Saratov existence, her tedious marriage, her frustrated urge to live and to find something better, she unknowingly depicts Gurov's domestic situation as well. He, in turn, remains unmoved and blind to the revelations her confession holds for him. Even while he embraces Anna and proposes a drive to Orenda. Gurov, vain and self-possessed, calmly brushes his hair. The scene accurately reflects Chekhov's succinct assessment: "Gurov listened to her, bored to death." (225) Their lovemaking seems only to have increased Anna's passive despair and Gurov's cynical coolness.

As in Chekhov's story, the film only gradually makes us aware of the characters' dignity and range of feelings. The film initially depicts Anna as a one-dimensional character, a naive, sentimental victim of an equally stereotyped seducer. On their first stroll together, Anna takes in the romantic view of moonlit water, whereas Gurov hardly acknowledges the view so eager is he to impress Anna with his talk of Moscow and that city's church bells at eventide. In the later scene at Oreanda, however, Gurov seems a different and more sensitive man who now shares Anna's reflective mood. Sitting on a bench overlooking the sea and mountains, they are silhouetted against the skyline. Shots of land, sea, and sky alternate with the two-shots and separate close-ups of each character, the editing clearly indicating Gurov's view of the panorama as well as Anna's. An old peasant wanders by, stops to perform his prayers in the imposing setting, and moves on. Emphasizing both the sacred and the commonplace, this series of shots of the sky, the mountains, and the seated couple conclude with a mundane shot of the carriage horses munching grain from their feedbags. The lyrical music that accompanies these otherwise silent moments, the careful selection and duration of the shots, the nearly motionless characters watching the sea and drifting clouds all contribute to Heifitz's impressionistic rendering of Chekhov's scene. The resonant images center our attention on the characters and their response to the landscape.

Although we sense the nascent ethical changes in Gurov in the Oreanda scene, he reasserts his cool, distant pose as the affair ends. On the way to the train station, Anna describes the dreary view from her house in Saratov: "Our windows face a grey fence. That's all I ever see. Such a long, long fence, with nails in it! I can't bear it . . . It'll pass." Gurov only confirms her fears with his terse reply: "Yes, you're right. It'll pass." But in the farewell scene at the station, Chekhov gives us an introspective Gurov reflecting on Anna and on his own role in their affair:

> And he told himself that this had been just one more of the many adventures in his life, and that it, too, was over, leaving nothing but a memory . . . He was moved and sad, and felt a slight remorse. After all, this young woman whom he would never again see had not been really happy with him. He had been friendly and affectionate with her, but in his whole behavior, in the tones in his voice, in his very caresses, there had been a shade of irony, the insulting indulgence of the fortunate male, who was moreover, almost twice her age. She had insisted in calling him good, remarkable, highminded. Evidently he had appeared to her different from his real self, in a word he had involuntarily deceived her. . . .
>
> There was an autumnal feeling in the air, and the evening was chilly.
>
> "It's time for me to be going north, too," thought Gurov, as he walked away from the platform. "High time!"
>
> (227-228)

Gurov's rationalizing, his self-indulgent feelings, his momentary twinge of conscience, and his brief speculation on his real self are nicely swept away by his eagerness to return to Moscow. We also sense, in Gurov's musing over the end of the affair, that he insists too much on the transitory, fleeting nature of the relationship. Without resorting to a cumbersome voiceover, Heifitz provides an effective, if not analogous, conclusion to the Yalta affair. Gurov, who has not spo-

ken a word during the farewell scene, kisses Anna's hand and watches the train depart. Turning to leave the platform, he finds a glove that Anna has dropped. He holds the glove for several moments, and then as if to confirm the finality of the parting, he drapes the glove over the station fence and silently disappears into the off-screen darkness. His action seems to corroborate our initial impression of him as the inveterate and unsentimental philanderer who neither needs nor wants any memento from a past affair. The image of the lost glove so casually placed on the iron spike fence is especially resonant here as the glove is associated with Anna and with Gurov's past romantic gallantry, while the fence recalls Anna's description of the bleak view from her house in Saratov ("That's all I ever see. Such a long, long fence, with nails in it.").

On his return to Moscow, Gurov finds his memories of Anna becoming more insistent. Idealized recollections of Yalta dominate his thoughts. Chekhov writes:

> When he closed his eyes, she [Anna] seemed to stand before him in the flesh, still lovelier, younger, tenderer than she had really been, and looking back, he saw himself, too, as better than he had been in Yalta. In the evenings she looked out at him from bookshelves, the fireplace, the corner, he could hear her breathing, the sweet rustle of her skirts. In the streets, he followed women with his eyes, to see if there were any like her. . . .
>
> (229)

This passage is the genesis of two sequences in the film. Thinking that he sees Anna's dog on the Moscow street, Gurov follows the animal only to find himself badgered by two men wishing to sell him a Pomeranian.[5] The more important sequence depicts an evening party at Gurov's home where his pretentious wife spends her time giving Gurov orders, playing the salon intellectual, and forcing both her children and her husband to perform for their guests. A single candle lights Gurov's face as he begins to play the piano. When he lapses in reverie, the candle and Gurov's face dissolve to the familiar image of Anna's candle-lit face in the Yalta hotel room. The irony of Gurov remembering that particular image of Anna, given his cold attitude toward her at the time, is matched by the ironic comment of Gurov's wife once he has finished playing. Knowing nothing of the source of his inspiration, she tells him, "You played with feeling today." Gurov's reverie signals the rebirth of his emotional life, intensifying both his disgust with the Moscow social world and his joy and despair in discovering his love for Anna.

Chekhov's brief references to Gurov's participation in the whirl of restaurant and club gatherings in Moscow are greatly expanded in the film. These evenings on the town accurately chart Gurov's growing disenchantment with the crass social world, and they offer Heifitz the opportunity to satirize the dissipated lives of the upper classes in pre-revolutionary Russia. At one restaurant, Gurov meets an old Moscow acquaintance, Alexei Semyonovich, a character who does not appear in Chekhov's story. In Semyonovich, Gurov confronts his worst self, a man equally unhappy and bored with his empty marriage. Cruel and cynical, Semyonovich pays money to hear the guitarist in the restaurant grunt like a pig, throws silverware on the floor for the waiters to retrieve, and finally insults Gurov by offering him five-hundred roubles to sing a solo. The disgusted Gurov leaves the restaurant, but several days later attends Semyonovich's lavish ball where Alexei turns hypocrite by justifying his expensive party because his position in "the firm" demands such extravagance. If such scenes seem typical Socialist propaganda, they also provide strong motivation for Gurov's desperate journey to see Anna.

Repelled by the crude and false world of Moscow, Gurov tells his wife that he must go on business to Petersburg, but plans his trip to Saratov. In providing the brief parting scene between husband and wife, Heifitz, who has until this moment characterized the supercilious, domineering wife much as Chekhov sketched her, adds a moment of comic pathos. When Gurov tells his tearful wife, "Come, I"m not going to America," she embraces him and confesses, "I hate partings." Although his wife's actions may seem conventional enough, giving her the opportunity to play the role of the caring wife, her emotions appear genuine and are emphasized by the close-up of her face resting on Gurov's shoulder. The human dimension of her character momentarily elicits our sympathy and complicates our response to Gurov's actions. No such moment is given to Anna's husband. Sketching this pompous, servile man exactly as Chekhov describes him, Heifitz adds the husband's own philandering, indicated by the man's undue attention to a particular lady at the opera. The actions of this ridiculous character only increase our sympathy for Anna, trapped in such an intolerable marriage.

Arriving at Saratov and failing to meet Anna outside of her house, Gurov goes that evening to the opening of the opera. As he sees Anna and her husband enter the theater, the discordant notes of the musicians tuning up their instruments furnish an apt musical commentary on their dismal marriage. The music works, too, as a counterpoint, an anti-romantic element to Gurov's emotional reaction in finally seeing Anna. Heifitz captures the moment much as Chekhov describes it in the story:

> This little woman, lost in the provincial crowd, in no way remarkable, holding a silly lorgnette in her hand,

now filled his whole life, was his grief, his joy, all that he desired. Lulled by the sounds coming from the wretched orchestra, with its feeble, amateurish violinists, he thought how beautiful she was . . . thought and dreamed. . . .

(231)

Not only do Chekhov and Heifitz show the sympathetic lovers as somewhat foolish, but they also allow the couple's grand passion to be played out amid dingy settings that effectively convey their entrapment. Gurov spends his first hours in Saratov standing in the cold outside Anna's house. Nearly every shot of him in this scene is framed so that the long grey fence, with its inverted nails hammered into the tops of the palings, dominates his isolated figure. The spatial constrictions of the later love scenes make an ironic contrast to the openness and panoramic beauty of Yalta and Oreanda. The crowded, noisy theater provides the ironic setting for the couple's reunion and their frantic confession of love. The soundtrack swells with violin music as they hurry from the theater to climb the seemingly endless flights of stairs in the lobby. Their rush up the stairs might suggest the transcendent power of love, but the lovers' destination is only the dark confines of the theater's upper circles where the distraught Anna promises to come to Gurov in Moscow. There the lovers meet in the small, drab Moscow hotel room.

The lovers' irrecoverable past, desperate present, and uncertain future converge in the time-haunted final scenes in the hotel room. As Anna waits for Gurov, an old man, one of the hotel servants, enters to adjust the noisy clock which he says is running fast "out of sheer nastiness." Gurov's arrival and his silent embrace of Anna are marked by relentless ticking and the low, almost melancholic notes of a street musician's clarinet solo. When Gurov notices Anna's gray dress and urges her to wear it for him even when it is out of fashion ten years hence, the lovers are momentarily distraught by the prospect of their seemingly insoluble situation. Gurov, his aging image reflected in an oval mirror, then expresses his anguish over his wasted past and constricted future: "Why have I met you now, and not before when I was young? Why should we be married to other people? All these years I have been intimate with women, but never loved one. There had been all sorts of things between us, but never love. And only now . . . when my hair's grey. . . ." Although Anna insists that fate brought them together at Yalta, time and circumstances have conspired against them. The clock strikes the hour as Gurov tells her, "We'll think . . . of something." The pathos of this meeting intensifies when Anna, using Chekhov's poetic image of the lovers, tells Gurov, "You and I are like two migrating birds caught and put into separate cages, and pining away with grief!" Moments later, the camera, having moved outside of the hotel room, views the two lovers standing behind the glass of the room's double window. The shot is composed so that the window frames isolate and separate the lovers, visually reinforcing Anna's description of them.

Neither Chekhov's story nor Heifitz's film ends in unrelieved pessimism. Nor does the lovers' commiseration turn maudlin. If their situation seems hopeless, the lovers do not, for they persist in contemplating their uncertain future together. In reviewing the film for *The New Republic,* Stanley Kauffmann claimed that *"The Lady with the Dog . . .* is the best Russian film I have seen since the second part of Eisenstein's *Ivan,"* but he concludes his review with the reservation that "the closing moments are somewhat abrupt, too final. They do not quite catch the mood of Chekhov's last lines: 'To both of them it was clear that the end was still very far off, and their hardest and most difficult period was only just beginning.'"[6] Kauffmann overlooks the film's double ending, where Heifitz provides his own conclusion as well as Chekhov's. Heifitz does include the carefully modulated narrative end to the story by turning Chekhov's final two sentences into dialogue for the central characters:

GUROV:

I sometimes think we're within an inch of arriving at a decision, and that a new beautiful life will begin.

ANNA:

I think so, too. But the hardest part is only beginning.

Whether this exchange strikes us as promising for the characters or simply illusory is certainly debatable, but it does capture the characters' ambivalent attitude toward the future. Gurov's enduring hope and Anna's more guarded optimism accurately reflect the tonal complexities of Chekhov's concluding words. Moreover, this dialogue does not end the film, for Heifitz continues with his own exquisite visual coda when Gurov leaves the hotel. From her high window, Anna watches Gurov cross the snowcovered ground under the street lamp. She raps on the window and nods to him; Gurov stops at the edge of the lamplight, turns to look up at her, and slowly removes his hat. This silent valediction, expressing the affection and mutual respect between the lovers, is followed by the film's final image—a low angle long shot of the towering hotel that blots out the sky. In the center of the image we see the small figure of Anna still standing at her window. The sense of entrapment conveyed by the image (is this the "finality" that Kauffmann objects to?) is qualified by the preceding shots of Gurov's moving, almost chivalric parting from Anna. Even if we grant

that Heifitz's *The Lady with the Dog* is less openended than the story, it is surely no less complex and affecting.

Notes

1. Mikhalkov's *Dark Eyes* stars Marcello Mastroianni, who was nominated for an Academy Award as Best Actor. According to the credits, the film is "based on the short stories of Anton P. Chekhov." Along with "The Lady with the Dog," other sources for the film include "Anna on the Neck" and "My Wife."

2. Ingmar Bergman, "Away with Improvisation—THIS is Creation," *Films and Filming,* September 1961, p. 13.

3. Bergman, p. 13.

4. Anton Chekhov, "The Lady with the Dog," from *Anton Chekhov's Short Stories* ed. Ralph E. Matlaw (New York: W. W. Norton & Company, 1979), p. 221. Subsequent references to the text are from this edition and are included parenthetically in the text.

5. Heifitz makes excellent use of Anna's dog by showing the increasingly isolated pet wandering the hall and waiting outside of Anna's room during the couple's lovemaking. During the walk that leads to this liaison, Gurov kisses Anna for the first time and then glances behind him in alarm to see if anyone has seen him. To convey the couple's urgency and impulsiveness here, Chekhov abruptly ends the scene: "'Let's go to your room,'" [Gurov] murmured. And they walked off together, very quickly." (224) Heifitz omits Gurov's words here but adds a final shot to the scene—a close-up of the dog trotting to keep up with the impatient couple.

6. Stanley Kauffmann, "The Lady with the Dog," in *A World on Film,* (New York: Dell, 1966), pp. 364-366.

Film Credits

The Lady with the Dog, 1960. Black and White. 86 minutes. In Russian with English subtitles.

Director and Screenwriter: Josef Heifitz

Photography: Andrei Moskvin

Dimitri Meshiev

Music: N. Simonyan

Cast: Dimitri Gurov—Alexei Batlov

Anna—Iya Savvina

Distributor: Corinth Films

Charles Stanion (essay date summer 1993)

SOURCE: Stanion, Charles. "Oafish Behavior in 'The Lady with the Pet Dog.'" *Studies in Short Fiction* 30, no. 3 (summer 1993): 402-03.

[*In the following essay, Stanion describes an incident in "The Lady with the Dog" that demonstrates Gurov's transformation from oaf to sensitive lover.*]

Chekhov's **"The Lady with the Pet Dog"** is generally regarded as a story in which a habitual lecher is transformed when he falls in love for the first time. One of the story's most impressive aspects is Dmitry Gurov's gradual metamorphosis: subtle details of action and dialogue illustrate a profound revision of his cynical attitude toward relationships with women. Thomas Winner has noted some of these changes:

> Many other details further support the picture of the change in Gurov. He now respects Anna and he stands before her, while she sits; he addresses her with the polite pronoun *vy*, whereas in their earlier meeting he had addressed her in the familiar form. He no longer looks over her shoulder as he kisses Anna.
>
> (221)

While critics have cited other examples of Gurov's conversion, there is a prominent episode near the middle of the story that has gone unnoticed in this respect. In Moscow again after his affair with Anna, Gurov thinks about her continuously. When leaving a restaurant with an acquaintance, he cannot contain the impulse to mention her:

> "If you knew what a fascinating woman I met in Yalta!"
>
> The civil servant got into his sleigh and was about to be driven off, but suddenly turned round and called out:
>
> "I say!"
>
> "Yes?"
>
> "You were quite right: the sturgeon *was* a bit off."
>
> These words, so ordinary in themselves, for some reason hurt Gurov's feelings: they seemed to him humiliating and indecent. What savage manners!
>
> (Magarshack 274)

The remark disturbs Gurov because it depreciates his veneration of Anna. He is introducing a subject of supreme personal relevance and aesthetic import, and his friend responds by free-associating from women to spoiled fish. The acquaintance not only disregards but deflates the topic of women, much to Gurov's vexation. Yet in an earlier corresponding episode Gurov himself had demonstrated the same inclination:

> there had been . . . women no longer in their first youth . . . and when Gurov had cooled to these, their beauty aroused in him nothing but repulsion, and the lace trimming on their underclothes reminded him of fish-scales.
>
> (Matlaw 224-25)[1]

This allusion relegates women to a category of cold-blooded, unimportant animals—like spoiled sturgeon—exactly as will the later remark by the official in the sledge. However, this attitude is no longer acceptable to Gurov. His indignant reaction to his friend's comment thus represents a 180 degree rotation in his own outlook; women and fish are no longer psychologically linked.

Details such as this—almost subliminal in effect—are important clues in determining the emotional state of Chekhov's characters. With quiet understatement he delineates subtle mannerisms and complex idiosyncrasies, contradictions and evolving convictions, and does so with a simplicity that belies the intricacy of his craft.

Note

1. Yarmolinsky translates this passage: "the lace on their lingerie seemed to him to resemble scales" (417); Magarshack translates: "the lace trimmings on their negligees looked to him then like the scales of a snake" (268); Hingley translates: "the lace on their underclothes had looked like lizard's scales" (130). The original, however, *"chesuya,"* is a general word for "scales," and does not presuppose any specific bestial modifiers; the translators' lizard, fish and snake augmentations are meant to provide a clearer context for the word. Technically, however, fish have scales while lizards and snakes have skin. An insinuation of fish scales, then, while not overt, would seem appropriate.

Works Cited

Chekhov, Anton Pavlovich. "The Lady with the Dog." Trans. Ivy Litvinov. Matlaw 221-35.

———. "The Lady with the Pet Dog." Yarmolinsky 412-33.

———. "A Lady with a Dog." Hingley 127-41.

———. "Lady with Lapdog." Magarshack 264-81.

Hingley, Ronald, ed. and trans. *Stories 1898-1904,* by Anton Pavlovich Chekhov. Vol. 9 of *The Oxford Chekhov.* 9 vols. 1965-75.

Magarshack, David, ed. and trans. *Anton Chekhov: "Lady with Lapdog" and Other Stories.* London: Viking, 1964.

Matlaw, Ralph E., ed. *Anton Chekhov's Short Stories: Texts of the Stories, Backgrounds, Criticism.* New York: Norton, 1979.

Winner, Thomas. *Chekhov and His Prose.* New York: Holt, 1966.

Yarmolinsky, Avrahm, ed. and trans. *The Portable Chekhov.* New York: Penguin, 1988.

Ronald L. Johnson (essay date 1993)

SOURCE: Johnson, Ronald L. "The Master." *Anton Chekhov: A Study of the Short Fiction,* pp. 76-103. New York: Twayne Publishers, 1993.

[*In the following excerpt, Johnson compares Chekhov's depiction of the power of love in "The Lady with the Dog" with his treatment of the theme in his other short stories.*]

"A Lady with a Dog" (Hingley) beautifully illustrates Chekhov's use of a shift in point of view, for in addition to the perceiving consciousness of the protagonist, comment is presented directly to the reader through Chekhov's disembodied narrating persona. Like many of Chekhov's middle-class protagonists, the bank employee Gurov does not have a satisfactory relationship with his wife. He fears her because she is outspoken and intellectual. Any happiness he finds with women occurs in a series of affairs, and while on vacation in Yalta, he engages in what appears to be another such affair. The woman, the "lady with the dog," is named Anne, and on an outing to a church at Oreanda, the couple sit on a bench, entranced by the view. Shifting beyond Gurov's conscious mind, Chekhov adopts a narrating persona who relates that "borne up from below, the sea's monotonous, muffled boom spoke of peace, of the everlasting sleep awaiting us" (IX, 132). This passage has a mystical dimension that recalls the last section of **"Gusev,"** also narrated beyond the conscious mind of the protagonist. The comment becomes more lyrical as it develops in a passage on eternity and the indifference of the universe, which measures not only Gurov but the reader against its endless vastness. It concludes with an optimistic comment on the eternal nature of life—not on the individual, who is mortal, but on life itself which is immortal and constantly progressing, a recurring motif in Chekhov's stories from this period.

The paragraph closes with a return to Gurov's mind as he reflects that "everything on earth is beautiful, really, when you consider it—everything but what we think and do ourselves when we forget the lofty goals of being and our human dignity" (IX, 132). This

thought, mirroring Chekhov's own sensibilities, makes Gurov a more sympathetic character. Although he lives an inauthentic life—in which he speaks disparagingly of women, calling them the "inferior species"—he is capable of this insightful observation when sitting beside Anne. The couple takes a number of excursions which invariably leave an impression of "majesty and beauty," while a subtle transformation begins to occur in each of them. Anne articulates her desire for that transformation when she voices her yearning for a different life—in Chekhov, such a desire is usually the telltale sign of a character's living an inauthentic life. Like Gurov, she does not love her spouse, but her adulterous relationship with Gurov disturbs her because she wants to live a "decent, moral life."

Gurov on the other hand easily dismisses the affair until he returns to his inauthentic life in Moscow. There he resumes his boring life of "futile activities," realizing such meaningless activities "engross most of your time, your best efforts, and you end up with a sort of botched, pedestrian life: a form of imbecility from which there's no way out, no escape" (IX, 135). Gurov's thought recalls the final comments of Nikitin on his domestic life in **"The Russian Master"**: "You might as well be in jail or in a madhouse" (IX, 135). Gurov feels the same desperation Anne felt before her vacation in Yalta, a desperation marked by the feeling she could not control herself. He now flees Moscow to seek out Anne, because their affair has become the most important aspect of his life. This transformation in Gurov's attitude constitutes the dramatic climax of the plot.

After Gurov finds Anne, their situation develops into a prolonged affair, and Gurov begins to live two lives. One is the false life he has been living, full of "stereotyped truths and stereotyped untruth," identical to the life of his friends and acquaintances. He despises this inauthentic life, and feels that "everything vital, interesting and crucial to him, everything which called his sincerity and integrity into play, everything which made up the core of his life" (IX, 139) occurs in his other, secret life with Anne. In contrast to those protagonists from earlier stories such as **"Lights"** and **"The Duel"** who undergo a transformation and throw off their inauthentic lives, Gurov retains his old life in the form of a facade that satisfies the decorum of the age. This compromise makes him a more complex character, a typical modern hero unable to integrate his multiple lives into one.

As the story closes, both Anne and he feel their love has "transformed" them, but the most difficult part of their lives is "only just beginning" (IX, 141). Chekhov's method of ending a story with the suggestion that the lives of his characters will go on developing becomes one of his most effective closures during this period. This conclusion reinforces the theme that through love—one of Chekhov's favorite topics—the characters have been transformed, making them better people.

Chekhov approaches the power of love with a different tone, achieved partially through a shift in point of view, in **"Angel"** (Hingley). Chekhov has a tongue-in-cheek attitude toward the protagonist, Olga, who is "always in love with someone—couldn't help it" (IX, 82). She is a "quiet, good-hearted, sentimental, very healthy young lady with a tender, melting expression" (IX, 82) to whom men are attracted and to whom women respond openly and kindly. At first Chekhov conveys his criticism through light satire as Olga marries a theater manager and adopts his opinions in all matters, especially on the importance of the theater. When the theater manager dies a few years later, she marries a lumberyard manager and in turn adopts his opinions in all matters, including the idea that the theater is a "trifle." Olga is not consciously insincere, merely naive and shallow.

When the lumberyard manager dies after six years—during which the couple prayed for children but had none—Olga falls in love with an army veterinarian who is estranged from his wife, and, in turn, takes up his opinions. But when he is transferred, Olga goes through a crisis because "she no longer had views on anything"—she cannot form her own opinions. She feels she needs a love "to possess her whole being, all her mind and soul: a love to equip her with ideas, with a sense of purpose, a love to warm her ageing blood" (IX, 88). This function of love is the object of Chekhov's satire. Although Chekhov presents some of Olga's experiences from her perspective, he also addresses much of the action directly to the reader. In earlier works, **"Ward Number Six"** and **"Three Years,"** for example, the passages outside the consciousness of the characters are almost always pure exposition, unmediated by the assertive voice of a separate, vital narrating persona.

To this point in the action, **"Angel"** satirizes Olga's sensibility in an amusing series of events without a focused form, reading more like a character sketch than a story. What makes the work a masterpiece is the last episode, in which the tone shifts to one of compassion for the protagonist, much as it does for Jacob in **"Rothschild's Fiddle."** With this shift, the character is redeemed in the reader's eye, becoming worthy of respect and sympathy. After a half-dozen years, the veterinarian returns as a civilian with his wife and son, and Olga emotionally adopts the child, a nine-year-old boy named Sasha. Olga cares for all his needs as her love for him becomes boundless, eclipsing her

earlier loves. Olga's desire to love, which Chekhov has been satirizing, now becomes meaningful by its very compassion: "For this boy—no relative at all—for his dimpled cheeks, for his cap she would give her whole life, give it gladly, with tears of ecstasy. Why? Who knows?" The satire is absent from this statement, which is as straightforward as the closing passage of **"A Lady with a Dog."** The question "Why? Who knows?"—Chekhov directly addressing the reader—deftly deepens the reader's involvement in the action.

"Angel" has generated a number of widely different critical interpretations. One of the more insightful comes from an anonymous reviewer in 1916 who notes Chekhov possessed the "subtlest sympathy," which enables him to "understand and reveal" his characters; this critic maintains that the effect of reading Chekhov's tales is to be "washed free of petty impatience and acerbity of judgement."[1]

Notes

1. *Times Literary Supplement,* 9 November 1916, 537a, quoted in Charles W. Meister, *Chekhov Criticism: 1880 Through 1986* (Jefferson, North Carolina: McFarland, 1988), 143.

Work Cited

Anton Chekhov, *Stories 1897-1899.* Translated by Ronald Hingley. ("The Oxford Chekhov," vol. IX) London: Oxford University Press, 1975.

Vladimir Zviniatskovsky (essay date 1997)

SOURCE: Zviniatskovsky, Vladimir, "Two Ladies with Two Dogs and Two Gentlemen (Joyce Carol Oates and Chekhov)," translated by J. Douglas Clayton. In *Chekhov Then and Now: The Reception of Chekhov in World Culture,* edited by J. Douglas Clayton, pp. 125-36. New York: Peter Lang, 1997.

[*In the following essay, Zviniatskovsky discusses Oates's feminist reinterpretation of "The Lady with the Dog" and her focus on Anna's view of how love has altered her and Gurov.*]

> Love. Either this is the remnant of something which is dying out, which was vastly important at one time, or it is a part of something which will develop in the future into something vastly important; at present though it does not satisfy and gives much less than you expect.
>
> (From a notebook of A. P. Chekhov[1])

> Surely . . . anyone . . . might acknowledge the difficulties that arise when language (or a single term, "androgyny") is evoked to gain an emotional response . . . The synthesis of "masculine" and "feminine" impulses has always been the ideal of all cultures.
>
> (J. C. Oates)

I am putting together a group of short stories called "Marriages and Infidelities," which include stories that are reimaginings of famous stories . . .

　　　　　　　　　　　　　　　(J. C. Oates, an interview)

Marriages and Infidelities by Joyce Carol Oates seems a typical book of the early 1970s. It reflects the situation at the beginning of the crisis after the euphoria of the sixties. In terms of plot this crisis took the form of a "reimagining" of classical stories, and the crisis in behaviour patterns provoked an interest in such types of classical short story as those by Kafka and Chekhov.[2] "The Lady with the Pet Dog" by J. C. Oates differs not only from other "marriages and infidelities" in the book, but from Chekhov's version of the incident as well. This is not just because of the American *couleur locale* of Oates's story, but rather because, unlike Chekhov, the American writer gives us the point of view of the heroine.

Every culture has its own brief description of love as well as its own brief description of culture. By "culture" I mean here elite twentieth-century western culture, which for me includes Chekhov and Russians "educated on Chekhov" on the one hand, as well as Americans "educated on Chekhov" (and also on Kafka, Proust, Faulkner, and others) on the other. I interpret this "education" in the broad sense, not as an assortment of names but as an *education sentimentale*. In this sense both "cultured" Russians and "cultured" Americans have been "educated," in addition to everything else, still more on Bakhtin, even if they have never heard his name, for in a culture of the given type the brief definition of culture and the brief definition of love coincide, moreover they do so in one key word: "dialogue." Dialogue, as a culture of this type understands it, is the opposite of a set of monologues such as we find in every Chekhov play. The theme that unites all of these plays is the characters' longing for love and for culture. These are absent because there is no dialogue, and there is no dialogue because there is no love and not enough culture. It is a closed circle, a Minotaur's labyrinth from which no one knows the way out . . . not even the woman you love, not even if her name is Ariadna, like one of Chekhov's heroines. Ariadna does not have a thread, she has not received an *education sentimentale*.

Unlike drama, a work of prose—nineteenth-century *classical* prose that is—cannot be just a set of self-enclosed monologues. Chekhov's mature prose is not a set of monologues, "voices," or points of view. It expresses one single "voice," one single point of view, although, of course, not the author's but that of one character. It thus becomes of interest to see *whose* point of view is usually selected. **"Ariadna"** and **"About Love"** are key stories about love, for in them

there is not only a storyteller character, but also a narrator-listener. However the function of the latter is to express doubt and incomprehension: if the storyteller (Shamokhin, Aliokhin) understands what he, strictly speaking, does not understand, then the narrator, it seems, is convinced of the fact that the storyteller does not understand even this. The narrator then knows what neither the story-teller nor he himself understands. In the last analysis, the one who is omniscient is the author, who could easily make do without a "story-teller" but not without his point of view, which is expressed by more complex and subtle features of the narration than the overall narrative or the individual voices.

When I was a student, the story **"Lady with Lapdog"** was a mystery to me. I understood that everything was incomprehensible, but it was not so simple to put together a list of the things I did not understand, for it seemed that, taken separately, each individual item was comprehensible. Joyce Carol Oates with her "Lady with a Pet Dog" helped me to discover this "list." "Item one" on her list also remains for me the very first and the most important to this day, as I shall explain.

In her story a certain external event takes place, a certain fact in the biography of the characters, albeit an extremely banal one, precisely defined by the description "adultery" or as the dust-cover of Oates's book has it: "infidelity." Like any fact it must be somehow perceived and evaluated by its participants. Perception and evaluation, not with the intention of moralizing, but in order to depict, is the task of the artist-psychologist whom we imagine Chekhov to be. In essence, his whole story **"Lady with Lapdog,"** as is usual with the later Chekhov, is none other than a detailed picture of the inner world of a character and his evolution: a picture of the perception by Dmitry Dmitrievich Gurov of what has happened between him and Anna Sergeevna von Dideritz, the "lady with the lapdog." If Chekhov wanted to show how the same event in the lives of these two was perceived by the "lapdog," he could have done this easily and brilliantly, as he demonstrated with his splendid, remarkable story **"Kashtanka"** where, in essence, we have no other "narrator" besides the "little dog." But as far as the lady's perspective is concerned, the question is more complicated. "Not often do I have the fortune to meet young ladies who are both young and interesting," says Trigorin in *The Seagull*, "I already *forgot and am unable* to imagine clearly how people feel at age 18 or 19, and *for that reason* in my tales and stories *the young ladies are usually false*." Here the most telling words are "forgot" and "for that reason." Trigorin thinks that, having recalled himself at age eighteen or nineteen, he can easily show "how eighteen year-old girls feel"! And since it is difficult for him or he is too lazy to remember his own feelings, he decides to "get closer" to Nina.

Let us now examine **"Lady with Lapdog"** a little more closely:

> Here there was still the same diffidence and angularity of inexperienced youth—an awkward feeling; and there was also the impression of embarrassment, as if someone had just knocked at the door. Anna Sergeevna, this lady with the lapdog, regarded what had happened in a peculiar sort of way, very seriously, as though she had become a fallen women. So it seemed, and it was odd and disconcerting.[3]

"In a peculiar sort of way"—but *what* sort of way? *To whom* did "it seem" that she regarded what had happened "as if she had become a fallen woman"? *To whom* was it "odd and disconcerting?" Only on the following page do we find out: "*Gurov* could not help feeling bored as he listened to her; he was irritated by her naive tone of voice and her repentance, which was so unexpected and so out of place; but for the tears in her eyes, he might have thought she was joking or play-acting."[4] Only here does the attentive reader receive an indirect indication from the author about what is "odd and disconcerting" on the previous page. This is not the feeling that the author intends the reader to experience, but simply Gurov's feelings. And if the reader manages to experience this feeling after all, then all the worse for the him.

However, further on the attentive reader easily notices that there is an evolution in Gurov's attitude towards "what had happened," which then grows into a new feeling never before experienced by him. At first it is described as "what had happened"; then Gurov calls it, to himself, an "adventure" ("And he told himself that this had been just one more affair in his life, just one more adventure . . ."[5]) then, when the memory becomes obsessive, Gurov, already at home in Moscow, is forced to move it to another shelf, it becomes a "love" ("But at home it was impossible to talk of his love, and outside his home there was no one he could talk to") and hence a "secret" ("was so anxious that his personal secrets should be respected") and, finally, at the highest stage of development, in the finale, it is almost an "eternal love": "It was quite clear *to him* that their *love would not come to an end for a long time, if ever.*"[6] But this is *for him*. What about *for her*? For the answer to this question let us now turn to the story by Joyce Carol Oates.

Unlike extreme feminist treatments, the position of the author of this western, contemporary woman's version of **"Lady with Lapdog"** is by no means cannibalistic or amazon; in general she is not even aggressive.

Moreover, her protagonist, whom we might call the American Gurov, is, for an American, surprisingly Russian. I would even venture to say (and will endeavour to prove) that he is more Russian than Gurov himself. This is all the stranger considering that at the same time that Oates was writing her "Lady with a Pet Dog," the American screen version of *Doctor Zhivago* with Omar Sharif in the title role was popular in America, even among intellectuals (some would say especially among intellectuals). Not long ago I finally saw this film and fell into despair over the level of misunderstanding by westerners of those people whose mother tongue is Russian. An analysis of the film exceeds the framework of my theme. I will say only that that eastern Don Juan who figures into the film could not conceivably write the poem "Meeting" (Svidanie), let alone "The Christmas Star" (Rozhdestvenskaia zvezda), "The Garden of Gethsemane" (Gefsimanskii sad), "In Holy Week" (Na Strastnoi) nor any of the other "Poems of Iury Zhivago" from chapter seventeen of the novel. I might add that the man portrayed by Oates is deeper and more poetic than D. D. Gurov to the same degree that Pasternak's Zhivago is deeper and more poetic than Omar Sharif's . . . but does not the crux of the matter lie perhaps in the fact that we see Oates's hero through the eyes of the heroine? And that the heroines of our novels really do see us with such eyes? (While we see ourselves the way Gurov does).

To be sure, differences are perceivable already at the level of both Russian and English titles, for in the English title the word "lady" suggests the word "gentleman" with all its connotations as inevitably as the Russian word *dama* suggests *kavaler* (womanizer). And indeed, Gurov plays the role of a health-resort "womanizer," a "ladies' man" (as Thomas Winner calls him), so that his attitude towards to a *dama* and especially towards one "with a lapdog" cannot help but be ironic. Oates by contrast even makes the man the owner of the "pet dog," which in no way detracts from his image. But far from being satisfied with this, she devises for him a "detail" that is completely unthinkable for Chekhov—a blind son. This makes his image melodramatic and, for the romantically disposed "lady," truly irresistible: "she thought of that man, the man with the blind child, the man with the dog, and she could not concentrate on her reading."[7]

However, the reader who focusses on reading Oates's story quickly understands what is going on: Oates rejects totally any Chekhovian irony, preferring melodrama instead. The heroine must at all cost become the "lady with the pet dog," not in a primitive health-resort sense, but in a Chekhovian symbolic sense. Here you will probably object that Chekhov does not allow and could not allow the basis for a "pure" symbol (we recall in *The Seagull* two remarks by Nina—first: "This is apparently some sort of symbol, but, I'm sorry, I don't understand" and second: "I am a seagull . . . That's wrong. I'm an actress"). But while for Chekhov's heroine the "seagull" is "wrong," for Oates's heroine "the lady with a pet dog" is absolutely *right*.

In Oates' story there is an episode where *he* draws *her* portrait with *his* dog. A leitmotif emerges from this episode: twice, at the beginning and at the end of the story, the heroine examines the drawing carefully: "Did he see her like that, then?—girlish and withdrawn and patrician?"[8] It is interesting that not only the heroine would like her lover to see her exactly that way, the author would like this too, even if it is contrary to the reality that the author, of course, knows but does not want to know. And if for the slightest moment the author wished to raise an objection to this last point (that she "does not want to know"), I would be ready to defend it with a textual critic's weapons in hand. The textual critic's weapons are, as we know, the early versions and their comparison with later ones. Here is just one example from the magazine version: "'Lady with pet dog,' the man said, *smiling oddly*." In the version in the collection the last two words are missing; the hero has nothing at the back of his mind: his words are a pure symbol like the words of Treplev about the murdered seagull, but unlike Nina, Oates's heroine does not say "I do not understand . . ."

True, the question arises here of the *Chekhovian* peculiarities of Oates's narrative, i.e., the *poetics of the narration.* As Chekhov consistently tries to look at events through Gurov's eyes throughout the story, so Oates tries to maintain exclusively the point of view of her Anna (more consistently in the version in the collection than in the magazine). And she, Anna, does not notice (perhaps she does not want to notice?) the hero's strange smile. If we add to this the fact that the Oates text is intentionally not self sufficient, needing as it does the context of the *Chekhov* story, then it becomes, in the consciousness of the reader who is aware of this context, no longer a "reimagining" but a "deconstruction" (almost exactly in the sense that Jacques Derrida uses this word). In Chekhov's story, as we have seen, the man perceives the woman as "angular" and girlish, in a patently negative sense, while in Oates "girlish" as a trait of the *man's* portrait of the "lady with pet dog" (!) is perceived favourably by the "lady" herself. In both versions the symbolic sobriquet "lady with pet dog" (in quotation marks) is linked precisely to the "angularity of inexperienced youth" and relates contextually to everything that in the heroine's external appearance and inner consciousness is described as "girlish and withdrawn and patrician." True, in Gurov's imagination the picturesque genre-painting

differs somewhat from the American amateur painter's image of the "lady with pet dog." She appears to him in the image of a "sinner in an antique painting" (evidently a repentant Magdalene), but this is because, unlike his American "colleague," the Russian Don Juan looks at his victim not *before* the fall, but *after.* In both cases, however, the look of the man is the look of a refined and cold aesthete, a distant look, what feminist criticism calls "voyeurism."

On the basis of the material under discussion, it would be possible, perhaps, to classify voyeurism into two types: "hard" (e.g., Gurov's in this episode) and "soft," an example of the latter being the poem "Meeting" by Iury Zhivago mentioned above. This poem, by the way, contains an unnoticed yet overt (although it is unclear to what extent it is deliberate) reminiscence of the episode under discussion in Chekhov's story. Contrast Gurov's negative, exasperated attitude towards the humility of the "repentant sinner" Anna, whose "features had lengthened and drooped," with the attitude of the lyrical hero of "Meeting." The poem also contains a "painterly" image, although here instead of a canvas we find the lyrical hero's heart:

> As if with a burin
> Dipped in antimony
> You have been scraped
> across my heart.
> And in it for ever will remain engraved
> *the humility of your trait . . .*

The poem goes on to describe (of course, from a totally lyrical perspective) the evolution of a Gurov-like relationship—in essence the plot of **"Lady with Lapdog,"** for we should not forget that if we are to "insert" Zhivago's poem in the narrative, then the only person to whom he could dedicate it is Lara—and his relationship with her is of the "infidelities" category.

Thus the American who sketches the "lady with pet dog" with such (as it seems to both of them) profound understanding, perspicacity and spiritual warmth has a closer predecessor than Dmitry Gurov—namely Iury Zhivago. Both these heroes of Russian literature, having understood the woman to the degree of which each is capable (and which is different in the two cases), find it necessary to engage her in a dialogue in order to resolve the problems they have in common, in order to find a way out of the impasse: "Let's talk now, let's think of something." Here Chekhov tells the reader that "the most complicated and difficult part was only just beginning"[9] whereas in Pasternak this is where it all ends: "There remained only the discussions,/ But we are no longer in the world." Essentially this is one and the same thing, for it is impossible to "think of something," and what is needed is simply to understand "female logic"—which is also impossible for men with such a mindset and feelings.

In her article "Rereading Femininity" Shoshana Felman makes a remark with which one would like not to agree, but with which it is difficult not to agree, especially since it applies not only to literature, and is valid not only for literary characters, but for authors too: "Women . . . are considered merely as the objects of desire, and as the objects of the question. To the extent that women 'are the question,' they cannot enunciate the question; they cannot be the speaking subjects of the knowledge or the science which the question seeks."[10] To quote the poet (evidently describing men?): "we keep posing the tricky answer, but don't find the necessary question." To be sure, the history of science contains many examples of how science *finds* the question with the same facility with which poetry demolishes formerly immutable idioms ("the tricky question") to create new ones ("the tricky answer"). It is interesting that none other than Chekhov a hundred years ago tried to combine the tasks of science and poetry, declaring that it is the business of the writer to "formulate the question correctly." The vexed "female question" was one of those for which Chekhov tried to find the right formulation—assuming, evidently, that it had not been formulated correctly before him. It was not for nothing that he gave the heroine of **"Lady with Lapdog"**—Chekhov's formulation of the question of mutual understanding between the sexes—the same name as Tolstoy's Anna Karenina (in this sense Oates's Anna is not the *second,* but the *third* in the series). And if we take Chekhov's portrait of a "woman in love" not as a formulation of the question, but as the answer to the question, then of course Virginia Llewellyn Smith is right when she formulates the answer (on Chekhov's behalf) as follows: "For women love is something assumed rather than felt, a kind of acquisition prompted by custom, like an article of clothing."[11]

However, she is not right, for in such a case how would Chekhov differ from Trigorin? They are *almost* no different from each other: both admit honestly that they cannot "imagine clearly how young girls feel,"[12] but Trigorin feels that such an inability to understand is a chance, rectifiable matter (and indeed "rectifiable" in the most primitive manner), while for Chekhov the inability to understand is fatal or at least, at the given point in time, unrectifiable with the means that have been tried thus far. It is this that constitutes the true scientific nature of his thought: that he understands the limits of his competence.

At the risk of far exceeding the limits of my own competence, I will nevertheless say in conclusion that in her version of **"Lady with Lapdog"** Joyce Carol Oates boldly tries to answer the question that Chekhov has posed and look over the edge that she in one of her own critical works described shortly and clearly as "the Edge of Impossibility." I hasten to add that such boldness seems to me justified if only by the fact that the author is a woman herself.

We part for ever from Chekhov's characters at that very point when "they had a long talk" and "tried to think how they could get rid of the necessity of hiding, telling lies, living in different towns, not seeing each other for so long." Gurov, having now become grey-haired and extremely serious, himself resembles a repentant sinner in his gloomy pose, clutching at his head and repeating three times "how?" It is here that we say farewell to him. We will thus never know what Anna was doing at the time that Gurov was clutching his head, although it would seem that in a Chekhov story this is fundamentally unimportant, for the author, we recall, never goes beyond a simple description of his hero's feelings and thoughts, and the hero himself has likewise receded completely into his own seriousness at the end, just as at the beginning of the love affair he had been completely absorbed in his own lightness, irony, and unwillingness to get involved.

When the two Annas—Chekhov's and Oates's—cry, it is totally in the spirit of Anna Karenina, that invention of Tolstoy, who was convinced that he understood women as well as he did men (if not better). The heroines' tears are explicable: they are unhappy, for each of them lives with one man, but loves another. But what Oates said to the world about *her* Anna should evidently shake the male half of humanity as powerfully as it shook the hero of her American story: it turns out that Anna is *happy.* That which Chekhov sought all his life for himself and his characters, that which was in Tatiana's words "so possible, so close," but which always slipped out of his grasp at the end of each work[13]—that occurs in Oates precisely at the point where for Chekhov and Pasternak everything is finished ("But we are no longer in the world").

Before we try to understand how this occurs and thus end our discussion, here is a little "pre-history" to happiness as Oates describes it, based on elements in her story that are not present in Chekhov but which are to be found in Tolstoy, as Thomas Winner notes: "Chekhov's treatment of the adultery theme is . . . different from the expected. There are no dramatic turns of action . . . Parallels to Tolstoy's *Anna Karenina* . . . emphasize this contrast. While both are stories of an Anna who, unhappily married . . . finds a lover, Chekhov's Anna does not think of suicide. Rather, her love affair brings her contentment and some happiness."[14] Oates read Winner, for in her scholarly works there are references to his book; I therefore think that she was influenced not only by Chekhov, but by this Chekhov scholar. Her heroine has constant thoughts of suicide, like Anna Karenina, but she needs them precisely in order to create a foil for the hero-ine's happiness at the end—not just "some happiness," but a large and complete one.

Did Oates's heroine achieve that dialogue of love so sought after by all post-Chekhovian culture?—Un-doubtedly! But with one reservation: it is a *wordless* dialogue. To demonstrate this I must give a long quo-tation. If any commentary is necessary, then it is again a textological one, for in the magazine version of the story the passage reads as follows:

> They would marry, perhaps. Or break off their relation-ship. They would come to rest permanently in each other, pressed permanently together, or they would grow old and forget each other and be free forever . . .
>
> "You look so beautiful. You look so happy," he said, as if jealous at this life inside her, this radiance he could not share. What, was it beginning all over again? Their love beginning again, in spite of them?
>
> "Why do you look so happy? Why?"
>
> "Do I look happy?" she said, startled. "I don't know—I can't help myself."[15]

The book version reads as follows:

> This man was her husband, truly—they were truly mar-ried, her in this room—they had been married haphaz-ardly and accidentally for a long time. [. . .] And she did not hate him, she did not hate herself any longer; she did not wish to die; she was flooded with a strange certainty, a sense of gratitude, of pure selfless energy. It was obvious to her that she had, all along, been behav-ing correctly, out of instinct.

I shall interrupt the quotation here to express a hunch: it would appear that Oates is aware not only of the differences between Anna Karenina and Chekhov's Anna, but also of Tolstoy's opinion of the latter's be-haviour expressed in his diary: "I have read Chek-hov's **'Lady with Lapdog.'** It is pure Nietzsche. People who have not developed in themselves a clear world-view that distinguishes good from evil. For-merly they would be intimidated, would search. Now, thinking that they are beyond good and evil, they re-main beyond it—i.e., they are practically animals."[16] What for Tolstoy is extremely negative—animal in-stinct (although Tolstoy himself had once admired the instinctive life of Natasha Rostova)—is for Oates ex-tremely positive.

The "happy end" of Oates's story is as follows:

> "What triumph, to love like this in any room, any-where, risking even the craziest of accidents!"
>
> "Why are you so happy? What's wrong?" he asked, startled. He stared at her. She felt the abrupt concentra-tion in him, the focusing of his vision on her, almost a

bitterness in his face, as if he feared her. What, was it beginning all over again? Their love beginning again, in spite of them?

> "How can you look so happy?" he asked. "We don't have any right to it. Is it because . . . ?"
>
> "Yes," she said.

Unlike the magazine ending, this is unexpected in a truly Chekhovian way—albeit of a totally different type than the unexpected ending in Chekhov's **"Lady with Lapdog."** There the entire unexpectedness con-sists in the fact that nothing is finished, that it is only "beginning,"—although, as we have seen, this is an il-lusion, and Pasternak's ending "But we are no longer in the world" is more honest. On the one hand, in Oates the purely verbal incomprehension and absence of a dialogue with any abstract concepts in it is brought to an extreme precisely in the finale. The man's remarks are truly exquisite: "Why are you so happy? What's wrong?" and "How can you look so happy? We don't have any right to it"—the last re-mark being a echo not of Chekhov, but of Turgenev's *A Nest of Gentlefolk,*[17] from which Chekhov's idea that "there is no happiness nor should there be" (**"Gooseberries"**) is derived at least as much as from Pushkin (for the latter at least has "peace and freedom"). On the other hand, there exists, it turns out, or at least it is possible to conduct, a dialogue on another, so to speak, non-verbal, instinctual level. Does not the ending of Oates's story simply signify some-thing Chekhov not exactly did not dare say com-pletely, but simply was not sure about, namely whether a woman in such a situation could be truly happy? As for the man (Gurov), he is completely focused on him-self, so that in some measure he is happy. Again Oates would appear to be right: all this clutching of the head was done so as not to appear happy: "How can you *look* so happy?" Woman is able to forgive this too: *comprendre c'est pardonner.*

To be sure, hard-core feminists cannot forgive Oates this ability she has to take a woman's point of view and yet understand and forgive a man. For them this is something pathological, and they have even pinned on her a rare and special label: androgyny. In spite of this, "repeatedly, Oates has called herself a 'feminist' . . . but she acknowledged her sense of the disjunction between masculine and feminine experi-ence: 'Though I don't believe that there is a distinctly 'female' sensibility, I know, of course, that there has been a distinctly female fate.'"[18]

Notes

1. *Sochineniia,* XVII, 77.

2. J. C. Oates's article about Chekhov's impact on Absurdist Drama seems to be an important source for her "reimagining" of Chekhov's story.

3. Anton Chekhov, *Lady with Lapdog and Other Stories* (Penguin: 1984): 268. The translation has been changed slightly to render the Russian more closely (trans.).

4. *Ibid.*, 269.

5. *Ibid.*, 272.

6. *Ibid.*, 280.

7. Joyce Carol Oates, *Marriages and Infidelities* (New York, 1972): 403.

8. *Ibid.*, 403.

9. "Lady with Lapdog," 281.

10. Shoshana Felman, "Rereading Femininity," quoted in Barbara Heldt, *Terrible Perfection: Women and Russian Literature* (Bloomington, 1987): 62.

11. Virginia Llewellyn Smith, *Anton Chekhov and the Lady with the Dog* (London, 1973): 28.

12. In this sense Chekhov's Vera (Faith) and Nadezhda (Hope) from whose point of view respectively the stories "V rodnom uglu" and "The Fiancée" are narrated, are reduced consciously and to an extreme degree to generalized, symbolic names.

13. The only exception is "The Student," in which the "inverted perspective" and the sense of happiness occur precisely at the end. With this story Chekhov proved (first of all to himself) that by nature he was not a "pessimist," but only a "realist" who knows that dialogues like the one in "The Student" occur seldom in life, but are possible. ("How am I a pessimist?" he said to Bunin. "After all my favourite story is 'The Student'" (I. A. Bunin, *O Chekhove: Nezakonchennaia rukopis'* [New York, 1966]: 57.)

14. Thomas Winner, *Chekhov and his Prose* (New York, 1966): 216-17.

15. *Partisan Review*, 30 (Spring 1972): 238.

16. L. N. Tolstoi, *Polnoe sobranie sochinenii*, 54 (M., 1935): 9.

17. In Turgenev's work Lavretskii says to himself the following: "Show me your claim to complete, true happiness! Look around you: who is there who is experiencing bliss or pleasure?" On the influence of this conception of happiness on Chekhov see my article V. Zviniatskovskii, "Zamysel i prototipy (K istolkovaniiu rasskaza Chekhova 'O liubvi'," *Dinamicheskaia poetika* (M., 1990): 147-158.

18. E. T. Bender, *Joyce Carol Oates, Artist in Residence* (Bloomington, 1987): 131.

Elena Siemens (essay date 1997)

SOURCE: Siemens, Elena. "A Tempest in a Tea Cup: Mikhalkov's *Dark Eyes* and Chekhov's 'The Lady with the Dog.'" In *Chekhov Then and Now: The Reception of Chekhov in World Culture,* edited by J. Douglas Clayton, pp. 259-67. New York: Peter Lang, 1997.

[In the following essay, Siemens discusses the important influence of "The Lady with the Dog" on Nikita Mikhalkov's 1987 film Dark Eyes.*]*

Nikita Mikhalkov's 1987 film *Dark Eyes* is based on several stories by Anton Chekhov. To be sure, the connection is rather tentative, for Mikhalkov not only mixes Chekhov with quotations from a variety of other sources, Russian and Western, but also radically transforms Chekhov's narrative. Not surprisingly, the film has not received a very enthusiastic response in Russia. In his recent article on perestroika cinema, Michael Brashinsky described *Dark Eyes* as a "spicy though rather tasteless, cocktail of Western and Eastern sensibilities."[1] Brashinsky's main complaint is this: "What Mr. Mikhalkov presents to us as the essence of the 'Russian spirit' is a total bluff [*kliukva*—'cranberry'].' " In other words, Brashinsky is outraged because the film is too light, too superficial. Brashinsky's harsh criticism may be well justified. However, the question is: is Mikhalkov's film really that different from Chekhov, or has Mikhalkov actually borrowed some of his outrageous strategies from Chekhov himself?

The central theme of Mikhalkov's film comes from Chekhov's well-known story **"The Lady with the Dog"** (1899). This is a love story about a man from Moscow and a woman from a small provincial town. Gurov and Anna Sergeevna meet at the fashionable Black Sea resort of Yalta, fall in love, have a brief affair, and subsequently return to their respective towns and spouses. However, contrary to the canons of literature and life, their summer romance does not end with the advent of winter. Gurov makes a trip to the small town where Anna Sergeevna lives, and thereafter begin her trips—"every two or three months"—to the hotel Slaviansky Bazaar in Moscow. The story ends with a typical Chekhovian conclusion; that is to say with no conclusion: "And they both realized that the end was still far, far away, and that the hardest, the most complicated part was only just beginning."[2]

Mikhalkov's film transforms virtually every aspect of Chekhov's story. Perhaps the boldest of Mikhalkov's transformations concerns the main male character. In the film, the Moscovite Gurov turns into an Italian called Romano. This metamorphosis is rather startling. In Chekhov's story, it is Anna who is described as a somewhat exotic creature, more a Japanese geisha than a typical Russian woman. She is small and slender; her hotel room "smelt of some scent she had bought in the Japanese shop" (224). And, another interesting detail, when Gurov comes to Anna's town, the two of them meet at the local theatre production of the play entitled *The Geisha*. As for Gurov himself, he is certainly a stranger at home and among his acquaintances from the Medical Club. However, there is nothing in the story that suggests his foreignness in the proper sense of the word. There is, to be sure, one remark made by Gurov that may be significant in this respect. During their first conversation at the resort, Anna tells Gurov: "The days pass quickly, and yet one is so bored here." Gurov replies: "It's the thing to say it's boring here. People never complain of boredom in godforsaken holes like Belyev or Zhizdra, but when they get here it's: 'Oh, the dullness! Oh, the dust!' You'd think they'd come *from Granada* to say the least" (223, italics added). This reference to Granada is, of course, too fleeting to serve as a justification for turning Gurov into an Italian, or a Spaniard for that matter. Yet one should remember that Chekhov himself assigned great significance to even the smallest and most irrelevant details. Chekhov's attitude to detail is also registered in the story **"The Lady with the Dog."** Anna and Gurov took the carriage and went to Oreanda. They sat down on a bench by the sea. Both were silent, absorbed by their thoughts: "Someone approached them—a watchman, probably—looked at them and went away. And there was something mysterious and beautiful even in this" (226).

Mikhalkov's film, therefore, may not be that radical after all. Rather, one may argue that Mikhalkov is simply as concerned with details as Chekhov. This argument, however, is also only partially correct, for there does exist one important difference in the way Mikhalkov and Chekhov treat details. In his analysis of **"The Lady with the Dog,"** Vladimir Nabokov writes that Chekhov "seems to keep going out of his way to allude to trifles, every one of which in another type of story would mean a signpost denoting a turn in the action—for instance, the two boys at the theatre would be eavesdroppers, and rumors would spread, or the inkstand would mean a letter changing the course of the story."[3] While treating details as "something mysterious and beautiful," Chekhov at the same time does not elevate their status. In his work trifles remain trifles, nothing more and nothing less. For his part, the director of *Dark Eyes,* while also continually alluding to trifles, seems to pursue an opposite strategy. In his film, Mikhalkov constructs precisely that "other type of story"; that is to say, he elevates Chekhov's trifles, turning every trifle into "a signpost denoting a turn in the action." Mikhalkov's film does in fact include a miniature story about a little boy who is eavesdropping on two adults involved in an emotional exchange. Mikhalkov also develops Chekhov's brief reference to the inkstand and makes Anna write a letter to her lover.

Anna's letter does indeed become a turning point in the film. Having received the letter, Romano sets off on a long journey from Italy to Russia.

In his study *The Imaginary Signifier: Psychoanalysis and the Cinema,* Christian Metz argues that a "referential juxtaposition" (e.g., a character and a coin that he tosses in his hand, as in George Raft gangster films) that appears on the screen does not always develop into a symbolic figure.[4] Metz writes that to turn a "referential juxtaposition" into a symbolic figure, a film must employ a number of operations. Moreover, in some cases, even when a film does employ such operations, "the metonymic process never actually 'solidifies'," and the image still does not become "a real equivalent of the character" but remains "merely a privileged association" (199). Metz's argument applies equally to literature; for in literature an image does not necessarily develop into a symbolic figure either. In what follows, I will show that in Chekhov's story an image is indeed rarely more than "a privileged association." I will also show that, conversely, in Mikhalkov's film an image is rarely only "a privileged association." To solidify an image, Mikhalkov employs a particular operation. Namely, he takes an image, be it an image from **"The Lady with the Dog"** or some other narrative by Chekhov, and turns this image into the protagonist of a short tale which he constructs around it. In this paper I will discuss two such tales and demonstrate that while elevating Chekhov's trifles, Mikhalkov nevertheless produces a truly Chekhovian spectacle, and that, moreover, the strategy that he pursues in film is actually not that different from that pursued by Chekhov in his chosen medium.

Forbidden Fruit, or the Tale of a Watermelon

In the story **"The Lady with the Dog,"** the image of the watermelon appears only once, and the reference itself is very brief. In her hotel room, Anna Sergeevna "assumed a pose of dismal meditation, like a repentant sinner in some classical painting": "'It isn't right,' she said. 'You will never respect me anymore.' On the table was a watermelon. Gurov cut himself a slice from it and began slowly eating it. At least half an hour passed in silence" (225). Anna Sergeevna then resumes the conversation. She tells Gurov that she was married when she was twenty and that she "was devoured by curiosity": "I told my husband I was ill, and came here . . . And I started going about like one possessed, like a madwoman . . . and now I have become an ordinary worthless woman, and everyone has the right to despise me" (225). Gurov remains silent: he "listened to her, bored to death. The naive accents, the remorse, all was so unexpected, so out of place" (225). Anna Sergeevna issues another passionate plea, and then Gurov finally responds: he "soothed her with gentle affectionate words, and gradually she calmed down and regained her cheerfulness. Soon they were laughing together again" (226).

Critics have argued that Chekhov's watermelon is an image of the prosaic that symbolizes "an absence of emotional involvement" on Gurov's part.[5] While this may be true, Chekhov's reference to the watermelon is actually too brief to establish any decisive link between Gurov and the watermelon. Here the watermelon does not become a real equivalent of Gurov, and, while certainly a provocative image, it still remains only an element of decor. Moreover, as regards its symbolic value, it is rather ambivalent as well. Indeed, a watermelon is not necessarily a symbol of the prosaic. After all, a watermelon is not a cucumber or potatoes. To a Russian, and possibly not only to a Russian, a watermelon is an exotic fruit that brings with it thoughts about the South, summer vacations, adventure, romance and passion. Chekhov's watermelon, therefore, may stand not for Gurov's indifference to Anna Sergeevna, but may symbolize his desire. And that is why he is "bored to death" with Anna Sergeevna's confession; for her confession is literally "out of place."

In *Dark Eyes,* the watermelon is featured in two scenes. The first of these resembles that described in Chekhov's story. Like Chekhov, Mikhalkov makes only a brief reference to the watermelon. The scene includes just two close-up shots of the image. There is a close-up of the hands cutting a slice of a watermelon. Another shot shows Romano's face chewing the fruit. To accentuate the image, Mikhalkov employs various lighting techniques. The watermelon is shot in bright harsh light, whereas the rest of the images appear in semi-darkness, lit only by the soft light of an oil-lamp. Mikhalkov also employs a variety of sound effects, contrasting the ticking of the clock by Anna's bed, her sobbing, and her doleful singing, with the sound of Romano's knife cutting a slice of the watermelon. As a result of these manipulations of lighting and sound, Mikhalkov's image of the watermelon is significantly bolder than that of Chekhov. Nevertheless, the link between Romano and the watermelon still remains rather tentative. In this first scene, the image of the watermelon is also only a "privileged association" with rather uncertain symbolic value. Take, for instance, the shot of the hands cutting a slice of the watermelon. What does this image signify: cruelty, passion, hunger?

Mikhalkov, however, adds another scene at Anna's hotel room in which he further develops the link between Romano and the watermelon. In this second scene, images of the watermelon literally invade the screen, and it is no longer clear who is the protagonist of the film: Romano or the watermelon. The scene begins with a shot showing the room from the inside. The door opens, and in the opening appears Romano's hand with a watermelon in it. The watermelon is carved with a laughing face and wearing Romano's hat decorated with straw. A little later, there is another close—up of the watermelon. Having received no response, Romano enters the room. The room is in total disarray: there are scraps of paper on the floor, the bed is unmade, the wallpaper is torn in several places. On the table, there are leftovers from the old watermelon covered with a plate. The flies are buzzing over the plate. Then comes a particularly unusual shot of the watermelon. After the chambermaid gives Romano Anna's letter, Romano sits down on the bed. By the bed there is a little table with Romano's laughing watermelon in its centre. Above the table there hangs a mirror which multiplies the image of the watermelon, showing the reflection of the watermelon's back. The mirror is situated in such a way that it is not certain whether it reflects the back of the watermelon or the back of Romano's own head. Having settled on the bed, Romano smells the envelope and then opens it. But the letter, apart from the first line, is written in Russian. Romano turns the letter in his hands: "Sobachka. But po russki net. No Russian." The final shot of the scene shows a close up of the laughing watermelon.

To sum up, in *Dark Eyes* the link between Romano and the watermelon is fully solidified. Here the watermelon is not simply a "privileged association." Rather, it becomes a symbolic figure, as prominent, or, one may argue, even more prominent than Romano himself.

A TEMPEST IN A TEA CUP

Chekhov's story **"The Lady with the Dog"** includes two references to tea-drinking. The first reference appears in the third chapter of the story: "When he [Gurov] got back to Moscow it was beginning to look like winter; the stoves were heated every day, and it was still dark when the children got up to go to school and *drank their tea,* so that the nurse had to light the lamp for a short time" (228, emphasis added). The second reference is found in the last chapter in which Chekhov describes the meeting of Anna Sergeevna and Gurov at the hotel Slaviansky Bazaar in Moscow: "He [Gurov] rang for tea, and a little later, while he was drinking it, she [Anna Sergeevna] was still standing there, her face to the window" (234). Both of these references are brief, and, as is the case with the watermelon, do not fully develop into symbolic figures. It is also interesting to note that neither of the references directly concerns Anna Sergeevna. In Chekhov's story, it is Gurov who is consistently associated with drinking and eating. As to Anna Sergeevna, Chekhov describes her in relation to things that do not have much to do with food—her hat, fan, lorgnette, and of course her little dog. (Anna's dog, coincidentally, does not appear to eat much either.) Gurov himself does not associate Anna with things gastronomic either: "In the evenings she [Anna Sergeevna] looked out at him from the bookshelves, the fireplace, the corner, he could hear her breathing the sweet rustle of her skirts" (229).

In Mikhalkov's film, Anna is not an ephemeral creature. There is a scene in the film that shows Anna eating and drinking milk in the restaurant at the resort. To be sure, as she is eating, Mikhalkov shows us only the side and the back of her head, and her graceful hand holding a crystal glass. The same scene also includes a frontal shot of a woman who is greedily eating a carrot. The woman looks exactly like Anna. This brief image leaves the viewer puzzled. Is this Anna, or is this her more corporeal and sensual double? Is it how Tina, Romano's flamboyant and perhaps somewhat jealous friend, sees her potential rival? Or is it perhaps Mikhalkov himself teasing Chekhov and his fragile character?

In *Dark Eyes,* tea-drinking or, more precisely, a tea-cup, is associated not with Romano but with Anna. Once again, Mikhalkov makes up a tale in which a common object, this time a tea cup, assumes the status of a protagonist. I refer specifically to the scene which takes place at the Governor's house. The Governor is very happy to greet Romano, the first foreign visitor to the small provincial town of Sysoev. He gives Romano a tour of the house, showing him, among other things, glass cabinets containing costumes of his distinguished ancestors. He then brings Romano to his reception room decorated with the portraits of these same relatives. In the middle of the room, there is a table with a large globe in its centre. Beside the globe there is a beautiful porcelain tea-cup. The cup is shining brightly in the sun, sending reflections all over the room. Romano's face is also caught in this dancing light, and he can no longer hear what the governor says. The Governor turns mute, and from this point on it is the cup that governs the scene.

The Governor eventually notices that Romano is not listening to him. To awaken Romano from his reveries, the Governor claps his hands. He then attempts to continue the conversation. However, as the Governor begins talking, the door to the other room suddenly opens, and a young chambermaid wearing a white apron runs in. As she notices her master, the chambermaid freezes and gives a scream:

GOVERNOR:

> What is it? Get out of here! Who allowed you to come in here when I have a visitor? Out, immediately! How many times have I said that no one is to come here when I am with someone?

MAID

> [whining]: Excuse me, your Excellency. Madame has sent me to fetch her cup.

GOVERNOR:

> What cup? What this about a Cup?

MAID:

> Stepan has put tea into, by mistake . . .

GOVERNOR:

> Take your damn cup and leave! Out! I told you, and I repeat, to you and to Stepan, that you can't come in here.[6]

While the Governor and the maid continue talking, a little white dog sneaks in through the open door. The dog comes towards Romano. The two of them recognize each other. Surprisingly, Romano does not appear to be startled upon seeing Anna's dog. Why is Romano not startled? Because he already knows who the mistress of the house is. The shock of recognition came earlier, at the time when Romano saw the white porcelain cup glittering in the sun.

There are many more similar stories that Mikhalkov narrates in his film. They include, among other things, a delightful story about a hat that gets blown by the wind and lands in a swamp. The film also features miniature tales about a glove, a box of matches, etc. Some of these tales are inspired by the details from **"The Lady with the Dog,"** but the film also refers to other narratives of Chekhov's, as well as alluding to numerous non-Chekhovian sources. The title of the film, *Dark Eyes,* is thus very appropriate. A line from a famous Gypsy love song, it is a good summation of the film's dominant philosophy—the philosophy of a carefree and daring Gypsy. I do not think, however, that Mikhalkov's carefree film is unfaithful to Chekhov. The film, precisely because it is carefree, captures the essence of Chekhov's art, the kind of art in which matters of decorum, however briefly Chekhov may refer to them, occupy a very prominent place.

A screen adaptation of a work of literature is not and can never be a literal translation, but always is an *interpretation.* As we have seen, in his film Mikhalkov gives Chekhov's trifles substance, turning these trifles into the protagonists of short stories. Mikhalkov's intense interest in story-telling makes his film resemble what David Bordwell calls the "classical Hollywood film," that is a film that shows great admiration for "plot."[7] Conversely, Chekhov's story is best compared to Bordwell's category of "art cinema," the kind of cinema that is concerned "less with action, than reaction" (208). Bordwell, in fact, makes this comparison himself: "If the classical film resembles a short story by Poe, the art cinema is closer to Chekhov" (207).

It should be noted, however, that *Dark Eyes* resembles the "classical Hollywood film" only to a degree. For the stories that Mikhalkov narrates are not exactly the type of stories that Hollywood films usually feature. While showing great interest in action, Mikhalkov's film centres this action around mere matters of decor. As we have seen, Mikhalkov continually interrupts his main story-line to stage yet another tempest in a tea-cup. In fact, *Dark Eyes* is so saturated with such side-shows that it is no longer clear which story-line is central, or whether in fact there *is* a main story. But such a structure is actually more akin to Chekhov than it is to the Hollywood cinema. Chekhov's story, when and if it finally begins, also continually deviates from what supposed to be its main direction, so that at times even the characters lose patience, appealing to their interlocutors: "That's a tune from another opera."

Paradoxically, while elevating Chekhov's trifles, Mikhalkov manages to produce a truly Chekhovian spectacle—a spectacle at once absurd, fragmented and profound. To a large extent, Mikhalkov succeeds in his venture precisely because of the boldness of his exaggerations. Films always magnify things, they have to. A filmic shot, as Metz has shown, is an actualized unit. In a film, a watermelon is never just a watermelon, but a concrete watermelon possessing specific characteristics, such as size, colour and shape. Film-makers have often fought the concreteness of their medium by employing, for instance, soft-focus or de-contextualization. Mikhalkov, however, opts for an opposite strategy. Instead of undermining the cinema's concreteness he emphasizes it. In taking full advantage of his medium's capacities, Mikhalkov displays objects the way only cinema can do. He presents his watermelon in every way imaginable: freshly sliced, its flesh crisp and pink; half-eaten and decomposing with flies heard buzzing over it; carved with a laughing face; wearing a hat and without one; placed on a table, and grinning in a doorway; shot close-up, middle-range, and from a distance, as well as multiplied with its back reflected in a mirror. In short, Mikhalkov magnifies and multiplies the concreteness of the already concrete filmic image. But this strategy ultimately is also very similar to that employed by Chekhov in *his* medium. Chekhov was not as gentle as he is often described by critics, at least not when it came to writing. On the contrary, he, too, pushed matters to their ultimate extreme. Only, in his case, he

magnified *ambiguity,* the ambiguity of language, a medium that is already and irrevocably ambiguous.

Notes

1. Michael Brashinsky, "The Anthill in the Year of the Dragon," in: Anna Lawton (ed.) *The Red Screen: Politics, Society, Art in Soviet Cinema* (London, 1992): 326.

2. Anton Chekhov, "The Lady with the Dog," in: *Anton Chekhov's Short Stories: Texts of the Stories, Background, Criticism,* selected and edited by Ralph E. Matlaw (New York, 1979): 221-234.

3. Vladimir Nabokov, *Lectures on Russian Literature,* edited by Fredson Bowers (New York, 1981): 263.

4. Christian Metz, *The Imaginary Signifier: Psychoanalysis and the Cinema,* trans. by Celia Britton et al. (Bloomington, Indiana, 1982):198.

5. Virginia Llewellyn Smith, "The Lady with the Dog," In *Anton Chekhov's Short Stories,* 353.

6. "Les Yeux Noirs, Texte des dialogues," *L'Avant-Scène Cinéma,* No. 365 (November 1987): 93.

7. David Bordwell, *Narration in the Fiction Film* (London, 1985). See especially chapter nine "Classical Narration: The Hollywood Example" (156-205).

Donald Rayfield (essay date 1999)

SOURCE: Rayfield, Donald. "Love." In *Understanding Chekhov: A Critical Study of Chekhov's Prose and Drama,* pp. 198-212. London: Bristol Classical Press, 1999.

[*In the following excerpt, Rayfield comments on the influence of Sydney Jones's operetta* Geisha *as well as of the works of philosopher Friedrich Nietzsche on "The Lady with the Dog."*]

A series of accidents turns a casual affair into a liberation: a candle, a grey fence, dew on the grass, an accidental glance in a mirror alter Gurov's view of Anna Sergeeevna and of himself, weaken his cynicism and change his outlook. (Nevertheless, whenever Anna weeps, Gurov eats or drinks: water-melon at the beginning, tea at the end of the story.) He and Anna follow their impulses and thus free themselves. There is no suggestion of a happy ending: the worthwhile result is that there is no ending in sight, only complications and a mirage of 'a new life' to keep them fully stretched and alive.

Gurov, particularly in the magazine version of 1899, arrives in Yalta as a cold-blooded sensualist, skilfully seducing Anna Sergeevna, with his light talk and predatory patience. We meet him as a type: the womaniser, embittered by each affair, but never able to remember the bitterness. In a way, he is a victim. Chekhov's phrase 'he was married' as 'ego zhenili' (they married him) gives a terse hint at Gurov's vulnerability to outside pressures. Gurov's wife is made repulsive by a few subtle strokes: she calls him Dimitrii, not Dmitrii, calls herself a 'thinking woman', and uses reformed spelling. Once Gurov has picked up Anna, the sexual conquest turns bit by bit into something less easy. Yalta, with its anonymity, makes them 'free people'; the sea predisposes them to sensuality with its 'soft, warm, lilac colour.' Neither Yalta nor Anna fits into Gurov's categories. He divides women into sensualists, intellectuals and predators. Each category repels him as easily as it attracts him: the first by its gratitude, the second by its conceit, and the last by its coldness so that, in Chekhov's unforgettable image, 'the lace of their underwear seemed like fish-scales.' Thus he can plan the beginning of his affair, but not its end.

The second section shows Anna reacting to her fall with a remorse that Gurov cannot believe: only the poetry of the single candle stops him from showing his irritation with her. A seduction, that begins with the conventional suffocating smell of flowers and perfume, ends with an austerity that Gurov cannot yet understand. Up to this point he is remarkable only in his Chekhovian hypersensitivity: his image of fish-scales for the feel of underwear, his smelling flowers on Anna's face after she has sniffed them, indicate his sensuality. Once there is a sense of mystery in the penitent Anna, Gurov shows unsuspected depths. Together they ride up to the mountains at Oreanda (as Chekhov rode with Olga Knipper to Ai-Petri) and stare at the sea. The effect of this nocturnal scene is the same as the cemetery's spell on Doctor Startsev. The sea's roar suggests peace and eternal sleep, and in that suggestion Gurov feels a sense of salvation, an affirmation of beauty, a stimulus to act. All his reactions are conditional: Chekhov says 'it seemed to him', and the absolute beauty of nature leads to an endless chain of qualifications. What man thinks and does seems, to Gurov, to detract from beauty; then he qualifies this by adding 'when we forget about higher aims of being', though at no point in the story do any higher aims of existence become clear. Dawn breaks and shatters the dream, but from this point Chekhov turns an adventure story into a love story. The idleness (*prazdnost'*) of Yalta life transforms Gurov from a mature Don Juan into a naïve lover.

Then the lovers are parted, each in a separate prison. Chekhov's portrayal of Gurov's married life is a remarkable picture of unspoken irritation. In a letter to Meierkhold, advising him how to play the part of Johannes, the unhappily married hero of Gerhart Hauptmann's *Lonely People* (*Einsame Menschen*), Chekhov points out Johannes' *nervnost'* (highly-strung temperament), as something normal: 'Every educated man feels most irritation at home, for the clash of the present and the past is most palpable in the family.' The irritation grows: Gurov needs to talk and no one will listen. His poetic reminiscences evoke from his friends only the remark; 'the sturgeon was a bit off' (the second piscine image in the story). Feeling as if he is in 'a madhouse or a prison, Gurov leaves for S.—the apotheosis of greyness, grey carpet in the hotel room, grey dust on the streets, a grey fence opposite Anna's home. After a long interval, he finds Anna in the local theatre and she agrees to visit him in Moscow.

The story ends where earlier novelists would have begun it; the reader is worried by the talk of 'beginnings' when he can clearly see the white space that marks the end of the story. Gurov now has two lives, a real secret life in the Slav Bazaar—a hotel where many of Chekhov's assignations were kept—and a false public life. There are symbols of trouble everywhere. He tells his little daughter why snow can fall when temperatures are above freezing, why thunder occurs only in summer, hinting at the turbulence in his mental atmosphere. Anna is wearing a grey dress, the colour of S. But the affair will not end. Gurov's scepticism suddenly falters when he catches sight of his grey hair in the mirror, and his love is strengthened as much by self-pity as by pity. Whether his motives are thus selfish (this is the last woman he will be able to seduce), or unselfish (this is Don Juan in love), does not matter to the author who leaves the question open. Love promises a new, beautiful life, as undefinable as the salvation that the sea's roar seems to promise. It does not matter that Gurov and Anna find no answer to the questions they have raised. The complexity and difficulty of the questions, the tangle of deceit and pain, are evidence enough that they are alive, not fossilised. All Chekhov's imagery in the last chapter—'two migratory birds . . . male and female', the snow and the thunder, 'real life under the cover of mystery'—brings out the primitive vitality of love. The imagery of 'two migratory birds . . . forced to live in separate cages', and a number of oriental details in the story, come from a new influence in Chekhov's work, the operetta *The Geisha* by Sidney Jones, which Chekhov mentions as the opera advertised in Anna's grey-fenced town. The idea of a wandering seducer who falls in love with a geisha, entrapped by her provincial governor, and who provides her with brief happiness before he leaves (itself a less tragic pastiche of *Madame Butterfly*) is one element from *The Geisha* which Chekhov is to use in *Three Sisters.*

The other influence is Nietzsche: Chekhov had said a year or two before that it would have been good to spend a night in a train talking to him; his aphorisms had recently been published in *New Times;* and Chekhov had earlier asked a colleague, Dr Korobov, to translate a passage of Nietzsche for *The Seagull.* In *The Cherry Orchard* Nietzsche is cited and lampooned; in **'The Lady with the Little Dog'** Nietzsche is a serious subtext. Gurov's initial philosophy 'Lower race!' echoes Nietzsche's conviction that 'woman is created for the warrior's recreation', that 'if you go to woman, don't forget your whip.' His reflections on a mountaintop, where everything is beautiful except what man does and thinks when he forgets 'the higher purpose of existence' is pure Nietzsche, a paraphrase of *Also sprach Zarathustra,* while the reflections on the necessary exchange of matter through death and birth likewise has a Nietzschean, anti-Christian bias. Gurov's act of commitment, of refusal to conform, his search for his lost love (so unlike the inertia of the narrator of 'The House with the Mezzanine') are proofs of a Nietzschean element in late Chekhov.

Gurov is the last of the few active heroes in Chekhov's work. The final stories and plays show a world in which the men are dying and only the women are prepared to fight on. But the message of **'The Bride'** or *Three Sisters* is the natural consequence of **'The Lady with the Little Dog'**: routine is death, and turbulence—the unknown—is life. The distinction is so important that the happiness or unhappiness which the future may hold for humanity can no longer matter. For Gurov 'this little woman, in no way remarkable . . . now filled his entire life, was his misery and his joy': for Chekhov insoluble anxiety was as good an expression of the life force as was joy. The story's paragraph may start with the usual disclaimer: 'And it seemed . . .', but the authorial and narrative voice are united in the last main clause: 'and it was clear to both of them. . . .'

No work of Chekhov's aroused Tolstoy's ire so strongly: he felt it to be 'animal.' Subconsciously, perhaps, he detected in Chekhov's two dozen pages an explosion of the story-line and conclusion of his own *Anna Karenina,* where adultery destroys both partners and is contrasted with the affirmative course of a marriage in which sexuality has been set aside for patriarchal goals. Tolstoy seems to be vehemently denounced in Gurov's declaration—so at odds too with the Tolstoyan philosophy in 'My Life'—that we must treasure what we tell lies about. It is a vision of human happiness that thirteen years before Chekhov had decried, in a letter to his eldest brother, as 'walking about with a stolen water-melon.' Now he declares it a universal human need:

> He conjectured that everyone, under the veil of secrecy, as under the veil of night, has his real life, the most interesting one. Every individual existence is held together by a secret and, perhaps, this is partly why educated people make such intense efforts to see that personal secrets are respected.

This is Chekhov's most scandalously un-Russian and sophisticated thought. Once *Three Sisters* reinforced the impressions left by **'The Lady with the Little Dog,'** Chekhov was regarded by many critics as a decadent preacher of adultery—ironic for a man who was now finally consenting to marry.

Daria A. Kirjanov (essay date 2000)

SOURCE: Kirjanov, Daria A. "Static and Dynamic Modes of Remembering." In *Chekhov and the Poetics of Memory,* pp. 116-54. New York: Peter Lang, 2000.

[*In the following excerpt, Kirjanov discusses Chekhov's treatment of memory in "The Lady with the Dog."*]

In **"The Lady with a Lapdog"** (1899), the theme of loss is also presented in terms of the memory of place. In this case, the memorable place is the seaside resort of Yalta, a location that becomes intrinsically linked in the protagonist's memory with life's higher ideals, with youth, and with the potential for new beginnings—all of which he feels to be lacking in the vulgarity (*poshlost'*) of the protagonist's present life. In this story, unlike those mentioned above, the protagonist succeeds in his use of memory to overcome spiritual stagnation and to facilitate a regeneration of self in the face of loss. But it succeeds only partially. Memory in this story is presented both in its dynamic aspect and its static aspect. On the one hand, it is the endurance of Anna's image in Gurov's memory of Yalta that leads him to pursue her the following winter and to discover the meaning of "true love" and "real life," signaling the beginning of a "new life."[1] On the other hand, Gurov's behavior toward Anna also reveals a regressive tendency. He is unable to part with his ideal image of Anna, which, in his mind, becomes contiguous with the space of Yalta. Over the course of the development of their relationship he continues to displace Anna's actual presence with his perception of her through the filter of memory. She becomes conflated with an ideal image that represents for Gurov the qualities of youthful vitality and which he is afraid of losing as time moves forward, as he grows older, and as his life settles into the pattern of routine. Gurov's attempts throughout the story to revive the atmosphere of the Yalta episode enclose Anna in an isolated, symbolic space that preserves his memory of Yalta and that sets up a psychological distance between the two lovers. In turn, this distance persists in the background of their growing intimacy. Gurov's love for Anna manifests itself in large part as a desire to preserve the spirit of Yalta and to live in its symbolic space.[2]

As in the other stories investigated in our discussion of the memorability of place, places and physical spaces in **"The Lady with a Lapdog"** are endowed with a strong emotional and psychological tonality. Moreover, the fact that the third-person narration is dominated by Gurov's perspective leads the reader to experience the spaces of Yalta, Oreanda, Moscow, Anna's province, and Anna herself through Gurov's consciousness. Initially, she embodies the quintessential object for Gurov of a male seduction fantasy which the environment of Yalta encourages. Later in the story, she becomes the embodiment in Gurov's memory of all that Yalta and Oreanda represent for him.

The opening of the story sets up a distance in space between Gurov and Anna, relegating her to a marginalized, isolated space that persists at a psychological and temporal level throughout the story. Gurov perceives her as a "new face," (*novoe litso*) a novel diversion that in Gurov gives rise to the tendency to speculate about a casual affair. The reader learns that Gurov is just the type of man to perceive the arrival of this "new face" as encouragement for indulging his fantasies. He is not yet forty with three adolescent children and a wife to whom he has been unfaithful for many years. Gurov, the narrator explains, is a compulsive adulterer each of whose transient affairs begins lightly, with the anticipation of fulfilling the desired fantasy, and then dies in the face of a reality burdened by complications.[3]

When the nameless newcomer appears at Gurov's table later in the day, he begins to fantasize about the romantic pleasures of transient affairs, thereby casting the "new face" into the role of an object of fantasy and placing her in the category of the many women he has seduced and abandoned in the past. Her presence inspires a recollection of stories of easy romantic conquests and of trips to the mountains. Prompted by these memories, he is overcome by a desire to indulge his past behavior and to consummate a "transient" affair with this unknown woman, an affair which, unexpectedly for Gurov, develops into a lasting one.

Their first rendezvous at the seashore is set in the magical landscape of Yalta at dusk. The landscape and seascape is presented as magical and romantic, charac-

terized by the "soft, warm lilac-colored sea" upon which moved a "golden streak of moonlight" ("Voda byla sirenego tsveta, takogo miakogo i teplogo, i po nei ot luny shla zolotaia polosa") (129). The lyrical mood of the evening inspires Gurov to fantasize about Anna when he returns to his room that night. What impresses his memory most are the qualities that make Anna an ideal fulfillment of his fantasy—her naiveté, her youth, her frail neck, and beautiful gray eyes. In short, what is left of her on the filter of his memory is a poetic image associated with the lyrical description of the natural surroundings. Moreover, it is an image that begins to take on aesthetic shape in his memory and to dictate the relationship that develops between them over the course of the story.

In the second chapter, Gurov and Anna watch the new batch of vacationers arrive at the resort. In this scene Anna is again distilled into an image that emerges later in the story as a memory-image. As she looks through her lorgnette at the visitors, the narrator describes her through Gurov's eyes as speaking copiously and disjointedly, then becoming silent and sniffing her bouquet of flowers. Yet, what she says is never articulated to the reader:

> And whenever she turned to Gurov her eyes were shining. She talked a great deal, and her questions were disjointed, as she would all of a sudden forget what she had been asking; then she lost her lorgnette in the crowd . . . Anna Sergeevna was silent and sniffed the flowers, not looking at Gurov.

It is when Anna is silent that she seems most appealing to Gurov, who, as the narrator explains earlier, dislikes such women as his wife who talk too much and express opinions. Thus he rejects everything about Anna except for the qualities which fulfill his image of the ideal woman, the most important qualities of which seem to be youth, beauty, and silence.

Another example of this tendency can be found in the scene describing their meeting in her hotel room that night. The fragrance of exotic perfume in the room prompts Gurov to recall romantic experiences with various women in his past, all of whom he has placed in their respective categories of female types—the carefree and uncommitted, the beautiful and frigid, the overly serious—and all of whom have fallen short of his expectations. The seriousness and sincerity of Anna's attitude toward the night's affair also does not fulfill Gurov's expectations. Anna bursts out with an impassioned monologue about the reasons for her unhappiness, her lack of self-esteem and respect for her husband, her guilt about betraying him, her desire to leave her tedious life. Instead of responding with compassion, he silences her by projecting on to her the image of a "repentant fallen woman in an old painting" ("Tochno greshnitsa na starinnoi kartine"), thus making a melodramatic parody of the scene by distilling her into an image, the same way he has done with the many women who have been preserved in his memory as types. Half an hour passes in silence, during which time Gurov recreates his ideal image of Anna, an image which stays with him until the end of the story:

> There was something touching about Anna Sergeevna; *she had the purity of a well-bred, naive and inexperienced woman.* The single candle burning on the table barely illuminated her face, yet it was clear that her heart was not happy.

It is this image of Anna as a pure, naive, and sad young woman that becomes imprinted on Gurov's memory after leaving Yalta and through the course of the relationship that develops between them. The detail of her face illuminated by the light of a candle further shows the connection with memory. It reappears in various images of illumination later in the text, signaling Gurov's attempt to preserve this image of her in his memory. Everything else about her life he reduces to a vague understanding that her life is not a happy one.

The transformation in the nature of Anna and Gurov's relationship from a casual affair to a deeper commitment is reflected in the story's movement from public, prosaic spaces to more intimate, poetic spaces. The bedroom scene is followed by their stroll along the embankment, now empty of vacationers and pervaded by the sound of the roaring sea. A single light on the barge repeats the image of the candle which illuminated Anna's face in the previous scene, thus functioning as a symbol of haunting beauty and inspiration for Gurov.

This movement in the narrative toward psychologically intimate spaces reaches its climax during their night at Oreanda, high above the city of Yalta, where, the narrator leads the reader to believe, both Anna and Gurov intuit a deeper bond within the sublime harmony between nature, the cosmos, and human existence:

> At Oreanda they sat on a bench not far from the church, looked down at the sea and were silent. Yalta was barely visible through the morning fog; on the mountain tops white clouds sat motionless The leaves on the trees did not stir, cicadas chirped, and the hollow monotone of the sea rising up from below spoke of the peace, the eternal sleep which awaits us. It roared below like this when there was no Yalta or Oreanda yet, and so it roars now and will roar just as indifferently and hollowly when we are no longer here. And in this constancy, in this complete indifference to the life and death of each of us there lay, perhaps, a guarantee of eternal salvation, of the unceasing movement of life on earth, the unceasing movement toward perfection.

The sense of timelessness and the eternal beauty of nature, separate from and indifferent to the course of human time and existence, becomes for Gurov intrinsically linked with Anna, whose very presence next to him on the bench becomes infused in his mind with the expansiveness, timelessness, and silent beauty that characterize the "enchanted" ("ocharovatel'nyi"), "magical" ("skazochnyi") atmosphere of this scene:

> Sitting next to a young woman who in the dawn's light seemed so beautiful, Gurov, comforted and enchanted by the magical surroundings of the sea, the mountains, the clouds, and the broad sky, thought that everything on earth is essentially beautiful when you reflect on it; everything except what we ourselves think and do when we forget about the higher aims of existence and about our human dignity.

As a symbolic extension of this sublime state of balance in nature that makes accessible to Gurov a sort of metaphysical zone beyond articulation, Anna takes on the role of an inspirational muse who connects him with the "higher ideals" of human existence.

The emphasis on the timelessness of this passage is significant in that it stands out in sharp contrast against the background of the rapid passage of time in the rest of the text. There are numerous references in the text to time moving forward. Gurov's life in Moscow is subject to the rigid schedule of clock-time. Days, months, and seasons pass, reminding him that his life and his youth are also passing with the current of time and bringing him closer to a realization of his own mortality. The sense of timelessness here is intensified by the lack of any specific time frame by which the experience is bounded. What appears to the reader to be only a moment in the context of the text appears, by the end of the paragraph, to have taken place over the course of the entire night. The experience passes in complete silence ("they sat on the bench and were silent"/ "sideli na skam'e i molchali"), and it is not until the end of the paragraph, with the intrusion of the guard and Anna's breaking the silence with a suggestion of the time of day ("there was dew on the grass"/ "rosa na trave") that the reader realizes how much time has actually passed. The long period of silence in this passage forms a strong spiritual bond between the two characters. Silence here is connected with the transcendence of chronological time, and we may say that it symbolizes this principle then it may be interpreted as symbolizing this principle each time it is repeated in the story. Since Anna's presence is associated with the element of silence, then it follows that for Gurov she embodies some timeless dimension of existence in which the striving for the "higher ideals" of life overcomes the tendency to lose hope in the face of the tyranny of time.

When Gurov returns to Moscow, he expects that his former way of life will return, Yalta and the summer will be forgotten, and the memory of Anna will be dispelled. His return coincides with the change of seasons from late summer in Yalta to the onset of winter in Moscow. The change in seasonal environments reflects a psychological change in Gurov from a romantic and idle mode to a more active and prosaic one in the face of domestic, professional and social responsibilities. The description of the first snow and the bustle of domestic life contrast sharply with the atmosphere of idleness in the previous two chapters. Initially, Moscow has a nostalgic and revitalizing effect on Gurov. The youthful memories of the first sleigh rides of winter, the snowy birch trees, and the sound of the church bells temporarily efface his memories of Yalta as he happily immerses himself in all aspects of his urban, middle-class lifestyle.

Gurov expects that with his return to the routine of his Moscow life, Anna's memory will "fade into a fog" ("pokroetsia pamiat' tumanom"). Yet, after more than a month, a conflict arises in him as his familiar reality is penetrated by the ubiquitousness of his memory of Anna. Rather than fading into a vague memory, Anna's presence returns in the dead of winter in the form of a vivid memory-image which, like a flame, "flares up more intensely" ("I vospomenaniia razgoralis' vse sil'nee") (138). Significantly, the connection between memory and a flame echoes the images earlier in the text of the candle illuminating Anna's face and the flame on the barge in Yalta. The association here between memory and light is reminiscent of **"Lights"** and prefigures the candle light in the first scene of **"The Bishop,"** which prompts the bishop's memory of his mother (the phrase "I vospomenaniia razgoralis' vse sil'nee" is repeated in the bishop's recollection of his childhood home). Later in the evening, in the silence of his office, the sound of organ music from a restaurant and the sound of the wind in the fireplace wafts into his room, resurrecting in his memory the events of the summer in Yalta:

> *And suddenly everything was resurrected in his memory:* what had happened on the esplanade, and in the early morning with the fog on the mountains, and the steamship from Feodosia, and the kiss. He paced the room for a long time, remembering and smiling, and then his *memories turned into day dreams, and the past mixed together in his imagination with what was to come in the future.* (my emphasis)

So vivid is his memory of Anna that it comes alive, following him everywhere he goes, "like a shadow" ("shla za nim vsiudu, kak ten'"). He hears the sound of her breathing, the rustling of her dress, as she gazes at him from the book shelf, from corners of the room, from the fireplace:

He did not dream of Anna Sergeevna; instead, she followed him everywhere like a shadow and watched over him. Closing his eyes, he saw her as if she were alive, and she appeared lovelier, younger, and gentler than she was. And he himself felt better than he was in Yalta. In the evenings she would watch him from the bookshelf, from the fireplace, from the corner. He would hear her breathing, the soft rustle of her dress.

His memories stand in sharp contrast with the pettiness of his Moscow life, which he once relished and which he can no longer reconcile with his new feelings. In this light his decision to reunite with Anna is motivated by a desire to escape the dull reality of his life, which is made all the more distressing by his realization that he is growing older and is losing his youthful vitality. Gurov's search for Anna is in essence both a desire for escape from his present reality and a desire to reinhabit the space of Yalta through Anna.

Their actual meeting in a theater in Anna's hometown falls far short of the romantic union Gurov had imagined earlier when he stood outside the gray fence surrounding her house and listened to the faint sounds of her piano playing. Anna's entrance is accompanied by the discordant sound of badly tuned violins. Gurov disregards her rather ordinary appearance as he conflates her actual presence with the qualities of his memory of her. The detail of the lorgnette she holds in her hand reminds him of the image of her holding the lorgnette at the port in Yalta. Her presence "now fills his entire life with sadness, joy, and the only happiness which he now desired for himself" ("napolniala teper' vsiu ego zhizn' gorem, radost'iu, edinstvennym schast'em, kakogo on teper' zhelal dlia sebia") (139). Again, Anna serves as a sort of muse through whom Gurov re-experiences the liberating mood of the night at Oreanda high atop the mountain. Even the memory of their ascent up the mountain at Oreanda is evoked in the image of the stairway they climb to the amphitheater. Taking advantage of another opportunity to revive the atmosphere of Yalta, Gurov passionately kisses Anna, turning a deaf ear, once again, to her complaints about her unhappy life which seem to taint his image of Anna.

The final scene in the hotel room is reminiscent of the scene in the hotel room at Yalta. Though they share intimacy at one level, they continue to inhabit their separate zones that are mutually unintelligible to each other. When Anna expresses her sadness about conducting their relationship in secret, Gurov's response is similar to the scene in the Yalta hotel room, except for the fact that this time he drinks tea rather than eats watermelon:

and then, as he was drinking tea, she kept standing with her back to the window . . . she cried from the painful realization that their lives had turned out so sadly; they only see each other in secret and hide from people like thieves! Isn't their life ruined?—"Oh, stop it!" he said . . . He went to her and took her by the shoulder just to be affectionate, to do something funny, and then he saw himself in the mirror.

The visual canvas of the scene again sets Anna apart as a marginalized figure. Both characters are distanced from each other by the fact that the scene portrays the different ways in which they perceive their situation with respect to their individual lives. The narrator presents Anna in a melodramatic pose at the window. Significantly, her back is to Gurov, and what she actually says about her feelings is set off by an ellipsis and followed by the narrator's brief account of her speech. Although the narrator claims that their love has changed them both, the dimension of this change in Anna remains unclear, since she continues to express a profound unhappiness throughout the story, the source of which is not articulated.[4]

The repeated juxtaposition of images of separation and enclosure with those suggesting union indicates that the two lovers continue to live in isolation with regard to society and to themselves. The story ends with an image of unity within separation: two lovers who desire to be together but are grounded, like "two migrating birds, male and female," fleeing the winter toward the warmth of a southern climate, who have been "caught and forced to live in separate cages" ("I tochno eto byli dve pereletnye ptitsy, samets i samka, kotorykh poimali i zastavili zhit' v odel'nykh kletkakh") (143).

The fundamental impasse in their relationship is the reality that they inhabit two different zones. Although these zones intersect at an important point—that is, their mutual love—they nevertheless do not intersect in many other respects, especially in terms of age and past experience. The narrator suggests that a transformation in their relationship lies in the constant renewal of faith that their love will eventually transcend the shackles that burden it and gradually move closer to the ideal that they intuited for a timeless moment at Oreanda. The beginning of a "new and wonderful" life together, an ideal that glows even more brightly for Gurov as he sees his much aged image in the mirror, lies before them, in some distant future. Yet, this ideal is unattainable without a confrontation with the difficulties of the reality that faces them in the present:

> And it seemed that it would not be long before a solution is found, and then a new and beautiful life would begin; and it was clear to both of them that it was still ever so long before the end and that the most complicated and difficult time was just beginning.

The story does point to a transformation in Gurov, but only to the beginning of a transformation. The role of memory in the structure of the story shows that the progress of Gurov's spiritual growth is incremental. As is the case with many of Chekhov's characters, for every step taken in the direction of the new and unfamiliar territory of the future, one takes two steps back into the past. The dynamics of progress in this story, like Chekhov's description of his arduous climb to the summit of Vesuvius in 1891, thus follow the process of regression and progression, with "one step forward and one and a half steps back."[5]

Podgorin, Ognev, Nikolai Stepanovich, and the narrator of "Gospozha NN" all, to varying degrees, are presented as unable to deal with the loss of their past in a productive way. As a result, they experience a spiritual paralysis that leads them to perceive their present lives as stagnant and lacking in personal fulfillment. In "The Lady with a Lapdog," however, Gurov, although he continues to some extent to attempt to preserve his ideal image of Anna in his memory of Yalta, does demonstrate a gradual realization of the pastness of the past and begins the process of a regeneration of self by accepting the idea that what has passed must give way to new beginnings.

For Chekhov all real living is contingent upon overcoming remorse over a lost past and salvaging from it some essential glimmer of truth which will enrich the present and serve as a guide for the future. As we have seen in our earlier discussion of "The House with a Mezzanine," the commemorative aspect of remembering can serve as a dynamic, life-affirming means of dealing with the pain of loss. Commemoration recognizes the temporal "pastness" of the past. Yet, unlike the static nature of nostalgia, which is a self-indulgent form of remembering and a perpetual reiteration of the pain of a lost past, commemoration is primarily oriented to a celebration of the living present, rather than to a mourning of the past. In Russian "commemoration" is translated as "prazdnovanie," the word for celebration and a derivative of "prazdnik" ("holiday") whose literal definition in Russian is "a day of triumph and joy [den' prazdnosti i torzhestva] established in the honor or memory of some person or event."[6] It maintains the importance of preserving essential experiences of the past in order to provide a context for an individual's knowledge of self in the present and a sense of orientation to the future. Commemoration is not about reviving the past, but rather about making constantly present essential knowledge gained from the past in an effort to enhance living in the present.

The need to establish a sense of continuity between the past and the present is, moreover, a way of coming to terms with the finality of endings and preparing the way for the birth of beginnings. It is a way of immortalizing what is mortal. In his discussion of commemoration, Edward Casey defines it is an act of "carrying the past forward through the present so as to perdure in the future," an affirmation of the past in the present by means of a "consolidated re-enactment" which assures a continuation of remembering into the future. Moreover, commemoration is the "creating of memorializations in the media of ritual, text, and psyche; it enables us to honor the past by carrying it intact into new and lasting forms of alliance and participation."[7] By virtue of the fact that it is a contextualizing process, commemoration, unlike personal memory, cannot exist outside the context of place and communication with at least one other individual or group of individuals. The calling for a corememberer who is part of the picture of the past reinforces the desire to reconnect with the experiences of the past, which are preserved in individual memory within the context of place and its community of inhabitants. Commemoration, as Vycheslav Ivanov writes, is a form of "Eternal Memory" (*vechnaia pamiat'*), which he defines as the "continuity of communion in spirit and force between the living and the departed."[8] The impulse to commemorate expresses the need to affirm an individual's sense of continuity with his past and his origins, as well as his sense of belonging to a collective of individuals who share a common past.

Notes

1. Most criticism of the story does not consider the role that Gurov's memory of the past, particularly the summer with Anna in Yalta, plays in the dynamics of his relations with Anna. Most Chekhov scholars maintain that the development of Gurov's relationship with Anna signals a departure from the ways of his past and leads him to a new and regenerated attitude both toward life and toward love. See, for example, V. B. Kataev, *Proza Chekhova: problemy interpretatsii* (Moscow, 1979), 250-68; Thomas J. Winner, *Chekhov and His Prose* (New York: Holt, Reinhart and Winston, 1966), 216-25; Jerome H. Katsel, "Character Change in Cexov's Short Stories," *Slavic and East European Journal* 8 (1974): 377-83.

2. For a discussion of the story that traces both the regressive and progressive dynamics in Gurov's "psychological awakening" and which maintains the centrality of the Yalta episode in this process, see Jan Van Der Eng, "The Semantic Structure of 'Lady with a Dog'," in *On the Theory of Descriptive Poetics: Anton P. Chekhov as Story-teller and Playwright* (Lisse: The Peter de Ridder Press, 1978), 59-94.

3. It is interesting to consider the autobiographical content in Chekhov's depiction of Gurov. In her investigation of the connection between Chekhov's personal relationships with women and his depiction of the women in his stories and dramatic works, Virginia Llewellyn Smith maintains that much of Chekhov's own experience with women and love is expressed in the character of Gurov. For example, Gurov's pompous and domineering wife epitomizes the type of woman whom Chekhov held in contempt. Also, Chekhov, like Gurov, was thirty-nine ("not yet forty"), when he wrote the story shortly after he was in Yalta with Olga Knipper. Before Knipper, his romantic liaisons, like Gurov's, were enjoyable but brief, cut short when they began to signal the danger of a deeper commitment. Gurov's initial behavior toward Anna shows an absence of an emotional involvement which Chekhov himself felt in many of his relationships. The final scene in which Gurov claims to have found true love amidst the realization of his waning youth is, Smith claims, a transmutation of Chekhov's real love for Knipper at a time when he was aware that his own life would soon end. See Virginia Llewellen Smith, *Anton Chekhov and the Lady with the Dog* (Oxford: Oxford University Press, 1973), 212-18.

4. Thomas Winner points to this scene and to the scene in Anna's hotel room in Yalta as revealing Chekhov's response to Tolstoy's treatment of the adultery theme in *Anna Karenina* as a fundamentally moral issue. Chekhov's Anna, like Tolstoy's, continues to suffer, her attitude being presented in a highly melodramatic mode. Unlike Anna Karenina, Anna Sergeevna's hope in the possibility of happiness prevents her from ending her life. Gurov's irritated response to her "theatrics," as he perceives them, reflects, Winner concludes, Chekhov's polemic with Tolstoy and his amoralistic attitude toward his protagonists' affair. See Winner, *Chekhov and His Prose*, 216-25

5. See Chekhov's letter to Maria Chekhova of April 7, 1891, in which he describes his climb up Mount Vesuvius during his visit to Naples in April, 1891. He writes that "you take one step forward and two steps back" (Delaesh' shag vpered i poshaga nazad"),: "The soles of your feet hurt, your chest hurts . . . you walk and walk, and the top is still far away . . . the descent is just as nasty as the ascent. You plow through ash up to your knees. I'm terribly tired. I returned on horseback through the little villages and by the dachas; the fragrance in the air was marvelous and the moon shown. I took in the smell, looked at the moon, and thought of *her*—that is, about Lika Lenskaia" (*PSP*, 4:212-13).

6. S. I. Ozhegov, *Slovar' russkogo iazyka* (Moscow: n. p., 1984), 499.

7. Edward Casey, "Commemoration," *Remembering: A Phenomenological Study* (Bloomington: Indiana

University Press, 1987), 255-57. Casey goes on to define commemoration as an "intensified remembering" in which the categories of place memory and body memory play an integral role.

8. Vyacheslav Ivanov, *Po zvezdam* (Letchworth: Bradda Rarity Reprints, 1971), 393-94. Quoted in Diane Thompson, *The Brothers Karamazov and the Poetics of Memory*, 1.

Bibliography

Chekhov, Anton Pavlovich. *Polnoe sobranie sochinenii i pisem.* Ed. N. F. Bel'chikov et al. 30 vols. Moscow: Nauka, 1974-1983.

Chekhov v vospominaniiakh sovremennikov. Moscow, 1954.

Kataev, V. B. *Proza Chekhova: Problemy interpretatsii.* Moscow: Moskovskii universitet, 1979.

Thompson, Dianne Oenning. *The Brothers Karamazov and the Poetics of Memory.* Cambridge: Cambridge University Press, 1991.

Winner, Thomas. *Chekhov and His Prose.* New York: Holt, Reinhart and Winston, 1966.

Robert Fulford (essay date 2004)

SOURCE: Fulford, Robert. "Surprised by Love: Chekhov and 'The Lady with the Dog.'" *Queen's Quarterly* 111, no. 3 (fall 2004): 331-41.

[*In the following essay, Fulford detects a profound personal investment in love in "The Lady with the Dog" and argues that, for Chekhov, love radically alters the landscape of existence.*]

On the one-hundredth anniversary of Chekhov's death, I happened to pick up the August issue of *Toronto Life* magazine and found myself reading an eloquently Chekhovian story, "Leo fell," by David Bergen. It takes place in the present in two extremely unChekhovian places, Kenora and Winnipeg, but it's melancholy like Chekhov, funny like Chekhov, and tough like Chekhov. And it ends in precisely the way that Chekhov invented and impressed upon the world.

Those who knew Chekhov did not guess that their doctor friend was to be the father of both the modern theatre and the modern short story, but they knew they were dealing with someone exceptional. When Maxim Gorky read Chekhov's **"The Lady with the Dog"** in the December 1899 issue of the journal *Russian Thought,* he wrote to the author: "You are doing a great thing with your stories, arousing in people a feeling of disgust with their sleepy, half-dead existence. . . ."

Gorky's words suggest how variously Chekhov can be read. No one today makes a point of expressing disgust at the people depicted in **"The Lady with the Dog."** On the contrary, we are more likely to notice Chekhov's great-heartedness and the generous treatment of his characters. For Gorky it was natural to consider them symbols of decadent old Russia and to see Chekhov as a potential supporter of the new politics. Gorky's name, which he chose, means "The Bitter." He was on his way to becoming the founder of Soviet socialist realism, driving Russian literature down a blind alley. Chekhov, on the other hand, was striding onto the bright plains of modernity, shaping a literature without limits.

Since then people of every political and intellectual opinion have found reasons to quicken as they read Chekhov or see him performed. Vladimir Nabokov, who of course hated everything about Gorky, loved Chekhov and loved in particular **"The Lady with the Dog."** Long ago, James T. Farrell remarked that the translation of Chekhov early in the twentieth century was a turning point for English-language writers, the signal to revolt against the conventional plot story and draw closer to the true rhythms of life. In the early 1980s a New York editor asked 53 of the leading short story writers of the world, from Updike and Gallant to Kundera and Borges, what writers had most influenced them. The writer most often cited was Chekhov, a result that will surprise no careful reader of the fiction written in the last century.

The story that Gorky admired so much has come into English under various titles—**"The Lady with the Dog," "The Lady with the Pet Dog," "A Lady with a Dog," "Lady with Lapdog,"** and **"The Lady with the Little Dog."** The dog walks into the first sentence, accompanying Anna, a married woman who has come to Yalta by herself from a small provincial city, as she strolls the seaside promenade. Gurov, a banker from Moscow, also alone, seduces her, as he has seduced many women before.

Gurov does not look back on these conquests with affection. In fact, he has discovered that when he loses interest in a woman she becomes hateful to him. As always, Chekhov makes this point with a telling detail, which appears in English in several versions. In different translations Chekhov can be more or less subtle, more or less cruel. The Chekhovian tone persists, but translators inevitably inflect it in different ways.

Consider the way Gurov's sour dislike of the women he has known fixes on their underwear. In 1919 the first great translator of the Russian writers, Constance

Garnett, rendered a certain passage this way: "When Gurov grew cold to them their beauty excited his hatred, and the lace on their linen seemed to him like scales."

The original text contains just one word, *chesuya* (scales), mentioning no creature to which the scales belong. Translators have felt free to elaborate on it in order to convey the revulsion Gurov feels. In 1964 David Magarshack translated the passage as: "the lace trimmings on their negligees looked to him then like the scales of a snake." In the 1970s Ronald Hingley rendered it as: "the lace on their underclothes had looked like lizard's scales." And in 1991 David Helwig put it: "the lace on their underwear became the scales of a reptile." Thus the imagery varies—first scales, then a snake, next a lizard, finally an unnamed reptile. All versions make the point, some with more graphic intensity than others. We who do not read Russian can only guess at the overtones Chekhov wanted us to hear in that single word.

Gurov expects the encounter with Anna to be as brief and casual as his earlier affairs, and the story turns on his surprised recognition that something more significant has happened to him. When he and Anna return from Yalta to their separate home towns and families, he discovers he cannot forget her. She has entered him in some way; she is with him all the time. She's like a safety net (to borrow a simile from the early Alice Munro) that's stretched beneath him; he never knows when he's going to fall into it. He goes to her town, risks a scandal to speak with her, and obtains her agreement to meet him in Moscow. They are in love, yet they can see no way to be permanently together. Eventually they discover that this clandestine love has become their reality, and their lives with their families are now only shadows, meaningless but impossible to escape.

The nineteenth-century feelings running through a Chekhov story like this one could as easily be emotions of the twenty-first century. Beneath his narrative we sense a profound personal investment in love, much like the one most of us still make or long to make. Without quite articulating our purposes, or examining them, we pour into the vessel of love many of the emotions and expectations once connected to religion; at the same time we look to romance and marriage for a concentrated version of the satisfactions once provided by expansive family connections.

Chekhov understood that sexuality, when partially freed from traditional constraints, soon provided its own intricate set of problems. Gurov's customary attitude to lovemaking demonstrates an affliction that of-

ten accompanies liberated sexuality, an aversion to intimacy. In even the most sensitive among us this may well appear as cold-blooded opportunism. It may also lead us into seeing sex as the way to solve the puzzle of a relationship; in this frame of mind you "get it out of your system," purging yourself of a feeling by physically expressing it. In Gurov's case, as in many others, the lovers find instead that unwanted bonds between them have been silently, almost secretly created.

Chekhov characters tend to be trapped: by their marriages, their parents, the rules of their communities, their own lassitude, or the very nature of Russia. They yearn to escape. In Chekhov, yearning is a major theme, like manliness in Hemingway or anger in Philip Roth. Chekhov's people yearn for a different life, one they can just dimly imagine. In the course of a story they often discover that their present existence seems false. They see the truth, announce that they must change, and usually discover that they cannot escape. Bernard Shaw said that Chekhov's genius lay in discovering that for some characters the tragedy is that they do not shoot themselves.

Chekhov bestowed on the writers who came after a magnificent gift: he demonstrated that not every issue raised in a serious work of fiction has to be resolved. Some, in fact, are better left unresolved. He did not believe in what we now (unfortunately, and misleadingly) call "closure." At the end of *Uncle Vanya* we are told explicitly that the dreary provincial frustration we have observed is all that his characters can ever know. Who could have guessed that, a century after the first performance, audiences would demand to see this story enacted again and again? Not Chekhov. He wasn't sure it worked in the first place.

Among its many distinctions, **"The Lady with the Dog"** is, I believe, the only short story to which a book of criticism has been devoted. In 1973 Virginia Llewellyn Smith, in *Anton Chekhov and the Lady with the Dog,* argued that no other work of his better expresses Chekhov's attitude to women and love. In its twenty or so pages, he draws together so many threads of thought and experience that the story becomes a summary of all that he will ever know about the subject.

In 1899, at the age of 39, Chekhov fell in love for the first time. He set his heart on Olga Knipper, an actress eleven years younger. He had been tubercular for some time, and to save his diseased lungs from the Moscow winters he was spending months of each year in what he called "abominable Yalta," the drowsy resort town on the Black Sea. He felt like an exile in the south, but he had no choice. Every autumn, as the first cold winds arrived in Moscow, he would begin coughing blood.

He had a fresh reason for disliking Yalta in 1899. Olga was not there. Earlier in the year they had grown close, and he had slowly come to understand the depth of his feeling for her. Now she was gone, back to her work in the theatre, and he was alone. Boredom afflicted him at the best of times, and now he had to deal with both loneliness and boredom. It was in this state that he wrote, in August 1899, **"The Lady with the Dog."**

Is the story an account of their love? No—and yes. It is not about them because, first, Gurov is a banker rather than a doctor and writer, Anna a housewife rather than an actress. Both have spouses and children back home, so their affair must be secret. Chekhov and Olga Knipper were not married, and though they were discreet they had no need to hide their meetings.

Adultery was not an issue in their lives, and in the story adultery is far from incidental. It takes place, and was written, during a long moment in the history of sensibility that we might call the golden age of adultery, the era that began in 1857 with *Madame Bovary*. A certain kind of "modern adultery" was providing a rich vein of drama and comedy for literature. As an act of love adultery retained the weight of meaning that it would begin to lose in the middle of the twentieth century. The newly emergent bourgeois of Russia placed family at the centre of their concerns. Lifelong marriage vows were embraced with deep seriousness, which made the frisson of sin and fear more intense than it has been for earlier or later generations.

At the same time, changes in social life provided increasing opportunities for breaking those vows. Women were moving toward independence, which might even take the form of holidays on their own. Railroads made it easier for lovers to meet. Anonymous hotels were everywhere. For the prosperous, living a double life was increasingly possible. Like many writers, Chekhov was delighted to exploit the narrative possibilities offered by this new world of erotic mystery and danger.

The experienced Gurov and the innocent Anna see adultery in sharply different ways. After they make love for the first time, Gurov remains aloof. He is satisfied, but she is disturbed. She says, "It's wrong. You will be the first to despise me now." Gurov doesn't bother to reassure her. There's a watermelon on the table. He cuts himself a slice and begins to eat.

And then, Chekhov writes, "There followed at least half an hour of silence." That's an astonishing amount of silence, an eternity in a situation of this kind, and every time I come across it I think for a moment that it's a mistake. It's not. Chekhov is saying that Anna is

paralyzed by shame and cannot articulate her distress. And Gurov has nothing to say to her. Finally Anna begins: "God forgive me. It's awful. . . . I am a bad, low woman; I despise myself and don't attempt to justify myself."

And then, as if this titanic sexual act has somehow cracked open her personality, she confesses to Gurov her feelings about her life:

> It's not my husband but myself I have deceived. And not only just now; I have been deceiving myself for a long time. My husband may be a good, honest man, but he is a flunkey! . . . I was twenty when I was married to him. . . . I wanted something better. . . . I wanted to live! To live, to live! . . . I was fired by curiosity. . . . I told my husband I was ill, and came here . . . and now I have become a vulgar, contemptible woman whom anyone may despise.

And the next paragraph begins: "Gurov felt bored already, listening to her . . ." But she goes on: "I love a pure, honest life, and sin is loathsome to me. I don't know what I am doing. Simple people say: 'The Evil One has beguiled me.' And I may say of myself now that the Evil One has beguiled me."

This scene makes clear why Chekhov has arranged for his lovers to be married. Adultery is not the theme of his story, but adultery charges it with tragedy and guilt. That's why adultery filled so many pages of nineteenth-century literature. It was an event that a woman like Anna could regard as an earthquake in her life.

All of these details distinguish Gurov and Anna from Chekhov and Olga. But the similarities and parallels are equally striking. Gurov, like Chekhov at that time, must be satisfied with occasional moments of love, intermittent and limited, snatched from the demands of their other lives. More important, Gurov's responses to Anna echo Chekhov's to Olga. Chekhov's friends found him loveable and admirable, but a student of his life often encounters references to his detached attitude to women. Like Gurov, Chekhov needed the company of women; by comparison, men bored him. And yet—again like Gurov—he found their emotions hard to deal with and preferred to keep his distance.

In the language of this period we might say he found it hard "to commit." He kept marriage at bay. Ronald Hingley in his biography says Chekhov required his female friends to "be beautiful, elegant, well-dressed, intelligent, witty, and amusing; and above all that they should keep their distance." A more recent biographer, Philip Callow, author of *Chekhov: The Hidden Ground*, writes: "In a feminine part of himself he was drawn to the unpredictability of women, yet their emotional crises threatened his independence and he feared their intrusion into his inner life. The barrier behind which he lived held firm until the arrival of Olga."

There was a secret self he had guarded with care. Now he discovered that Olga had not only penetrated this self, she had become part of it; and this is precisely what happens to Gurov. Chekhov was writing the story in August with Olga on his mind. On September 3 he wrote her the earliest of his love letters that survives: "Dear, remarkable actress, wonderful woman . . . I've become so used to you that now I feel lonely and simply can't reconcile myself to the thought of not seeing you again until the spring."

Chekhov at that moment hadn't reached his fortieth birthday, but he knew that tuberculosis had aged him. He transfers this perception of age to Gurov, who is also just under forty. At the end of the story Gurov, in a hotel room to meet Anna, glances in a mirror and sees himself as old and ugly: "And it was only now, when his hair had turned grey, that he had fallen in love properly, in the way that one should do—for the first time in his life."

"The Lady with the Dog" makes a clear point. What Chekhov says in this sophisticated parable is that love radically alters the landscape of existence. When touched by love, we know the world in a different way. Love changes the inner landscape, too. Under the pressure of love, Gurov looks inside himself and sees someone he has not known before, someone capable of feelings that he barely knew existed.

In the Soviet era Russian commentators used to say that Gurov was regenerated by love, made into a better person. Love had become a moral force. Those critics were not entirely wrong. In fact, Chekhov originally wrote at the end that love "made them [the lovers] both better." But he deleted that idea. He didn't want to dictate a moral. As a thought it lacks the tact we expect from Chekhov; it presumes too much.

The ending he used instead has become a legend. Writing when Chekhov was still something of a novelty in England, Virginia Woolf said that at first he baffles the reader. "A man falls in love with a married woman, and they part and meet, and in the end are left talking about their position and by what means they can be free . . ." And Woolf quoted from the ending, the thought that "the solution would be found and then a new and splendid life would begin." She wrote: "That is the end. But is it the end? . . . it is as if a tune had stopped short without the expected chords to close it." Does that make it inconclusive? No, she decided. With an alert sense of literature we will hear the tune, and in particular the last notes that complete the harmony.

Many others have been fascinated by the ending, but the most surprising treatment of it that I've seen appears in a biography unrelated to Chekhov. In 1968, by some strange means, the closing passage of **"The Lady with the Dog"** migrated from Chekhov's work over to Michael Holroyd's biography of Lytton Strachey, where it appears, undisguised but uncredited.

The closing sentence in the Constance Garnett translation of Chekhov reads: "And it seemed as though in a little while the solution would be found, and then a new and splendid life would begin; and it was clear to both of them that they had still a long, long road before them, and that the most complicated and difficult part of it was only just beginning." Now consider a passage from *Lytton Strachey: The Years of Achievement,* Volume 2, by Holroyd. It's 1917 and Dora Carrington has fallen in love with Strachey; she has learned for the first and last time what it is to love, and Strachey as a homosexual cannot physically return her love. This is how Holroyd ends that chapter: ". . . it seemed as though in a little while a solution must be found, and then a new and wonderful life would begin. And it was clear to her that the end was nowhere yet in sight, and that the most tortuous and difficult part of it was only just beginning."

One of my readers, Doris Cowan, pointed me to the Holroyd passage. I thought of writing to ask him how Chekhov's conclusion ended up in his book. I decided finally that I'd prefer to speculate. My guess is that, like many people, Holroyd read **"The Lady with the Dog"** many times, and read the ending with special care, because of its place in literary history as well as for the pleasure it gives. Eventually the words became a part of him and he innocently placed them inside his own text, where they fit perfectly.

Nabokov was perhaps the most distinguished of all the critics who wrote on that ending: "All the traditional rules . . . have been broken in this wonderful short story . . . no problem, no regular climax, no point at the end. And it is one of the greatest stories ever written." He gave six reasons why it was great, the sixth of which was: "the story does not really end."

In not ending it opens onto other stories; it leaves us with an infinity of possible results; it describes lives in process rather than lives completed. This is the sort of ending that serious short story writers around the world have ever since laboured to achieve. It is the kind of ending now familiar to the readers of Katherine Mansfield and Morley Callaghan, Flannery O'Connor and Tobias Wolf, a score of *New Yorker* writers, and many more authors, all of them in some way Chekhov's descendants.

This hugely influential aspect of his style did not come easily to him. He worried about endings. In 1889 he wrote, "My intuition tells me that it is in the conclusion of a story that I must manage . . . to concentrate the impact that the whole of the story will leave on the reader and to do this, I must remind him, if only to a very small extent, of what has gone before." But he always questioned his work. He was never sure that his endings were right. In 1892 he said in a letter: "Those cursed denouements always escape me. The hero either has to get married or commit suicide—there seems to be no other alternative."

As he knew by then, there was another alternative, the Chekhov ending. He found it, and taught it by example to the writers of a whole century. Beneath it all there was a rule he followed consistently. Maintain the tension to the very last; never stop inserting precise detail, and then—just when the reader wonders how it can possibly end—stop.

FURTHER READING

Criticism

De Maegd-Soëp, Carolina. "Major Works." In *Chekhov and Women: Women in the Life and Work of Chekhov,* pp. 237-327. Columbus, Oh.: Slavica Publishers, Inc., 1987.

Includes a detailed analysis of "The Lady with the Dog," touching on its lyricism, structure, and psychology before surveying the contemporary critical responses to the story.

Gillès, Daniel. "The Last Page of My Life." In *Chekhov: Observer without Illusion,* translated by Charles Lam Markmann, pp. 281-89. New York: Funk & Wagnalls, 1967.

Discusses Chekhov's relationship with Olga Kipper and how it influenced his writing of "The Lady with the Dog."

Greenberg, Yael. "The Presentation of the Unconscious in Chekhov's 'Lady with Lapdog.'" *The Modern Language Review* 86, no. 1 (January 1991): 126-30.

Maintains that in "The Lady with the Dog" Gurov's relationship with Anna is determined by his unconscious attraction to his adolescent daughter.

Meister, Charles W. "Stories: 1898-1904." In *Chekhov Criticism: 1880 through 1986,* pp. 135-61. Jefferson, N.C.: McFarland & Company, Inc., Publishers, 1988.

Surveys critical commentary on "The Lady with the Dog" from its initial appearance through 1985.

Parts, Lyudmila. "Down the Intertextual Lane: Petrushevskaia, Chekhov, Tolstoy." *Russian Review: An American Quarterly Devoted to Russia Past and Present* 64, no. 1 (January 2005): 77-89.

Discusses the influence of Chekhov, and especially of "The Lady with the Dog," on the modern Russian writer Ludmila Petrushevskaia.

Philip Roth
1933-

American short story writer, novelist, essayist, and critic.

For further discussion of Roth's short fiction, see *SSC,* Volume 26.

INTRODUCTION

Although he is best known as a novelist, Roth began his career as a writer of short fiction and his first book, *Goodbye, Columbus* (1959), a collection of five short stories and a novella, is still regarded as a seminal work of postwar American literature. Using wit, irony, and humor to portray Jewish-American life after World War II, the work immediately won the author critical recognition, including the National Book Award for fiction. However, it also earned him condemnation from some within the Jewish community for depicting what they saw as the unflattering side of the contemporary Jewish-American experience. In terms of Roth's subsequent output, the book proved premonitory of his thematic concerns—the search for identity, conflicts between traditional and contemporary moral values, the relationship between fiction and reality—as well as of the controversy that he would generate. In the 1960s and 1970s Roth published a handful of other stories, but he has since produced no other work of short fiction. The early pieces continue to be widely read, anthologized, and discussed, assuring Roth's place as one of the United States's most important short-story writers.

BIOGRAPHICAL INFORMATION

Roth grew up in Newark, New Jersey, the son of Beth Finkel and Herman Roth, a salesman for the Metropolitan Life Insurance Company. He attended Hebrew school and spent one year at Newark College of Rutgers University. From 1951 through 1954, Roth attended Bucknell University, where he majored in English and graduated with honors. He edited and helped found the Bucknell literary magazine, *Et Cetera,* which published his first stories. In the fall of 1954, the *Chicago Review* published "The Day It Snowed." In 1955, the year Roth earned his University of Chicago M.A., his story "The Contest for Aaron Gold" was published

in *Epoch* and anthologized in Martha Foley's *Best American Short Stories. Goodbye, Columbus,* which contains several stories previously published in *The Paris Review, The New Yorker,* and *Commentary,* appeared when Roth was only twenty-six. Three years later he published his first novel, *Letting Go,* to strong reviews. But it was with the 1969 novel, *Portnoy's Complaint,* that Roth achieved real fame. The controversial novel about the sexual life of a young Jewish man was an immediate bestseller. Since then, Roth has continued to write prolifically and has taught writing at the University of Iowa, Princeton, the State University of New York, the University of Pennsylvania, and elsewhere. He is also the most decorated living American writer, having received two National Book Awards, two National Critics Circle Awards, and a Pulitzer Prize for Fiction. In 2007 he published his twenty-seventh novel, *Everyman,* for which he won his third PEN/Faulker Award. Roth was married briefly in the 1960s to Margaret Martinson Williams and in the 1990s to the actress Claire Bloom. He divides his time between New York and Connecticut.

MAJOR WORKS

In addition to the title novella, *Goodbye, Columbus* contains five other short stories: "The Conversion of the Jews," "The Defender of the Faith," "Epstein," "You Can't Tell a Man by the Song He Sings," and "Eli, the Fanatic." Roth's short fiction most often centers on assimilated Jewish-Americans, unlikely heroes trapped within the social constraints of their immediate environment—the family, religion, or American society in general. While Roth's fiction depends heavily on theme, it is replete with dark humor and keen observation, which critics find to be at its best in the novella "Goodbye, Columbus." In that work, Roth examines a summer romance between Neil Klugman, a poor Jewish intellectual, and Brenda Patimkin, a wealthy Jewish suburbanite. Though initially attracted to Brenda's comfortable lifestyle, Neil quickly becomes repulsed by the vacuous materialism of the Patimkin family. So much emphasis is placed on the Patimkins' materialism that some scholars have suggested that the true subject of the novella is American society's predilection to materialism.

The other works in the collection *Goodbye, Columbus* also explore what it means to be Jewish-American in the contemporary world. In "The Contest for Aaron Gold," a summer camp art instructor wrongfully completes a student's project to keep his job. In "The Conversion of the Jews," a Hebrew school student brings to his knees a rabbi who will not allow him to ask questions about his religion. In "Defender of the Faith," a Jewish-American army sergeant has to resist the crass manipulations of a self-serving private who couches his requests for special favors in calls to ethnic solidarity. The title character of "Epstein" suddenly feels, at age fifty-nine, that because he has accepted fully the responsibilities of business, marriage, and parenthood, he has missed out on life. In "Eli, the Fanatic," the assimilated Jews of Woodenton fear that their peaceful coexistence with the Gentiles will be put at risk by the establishment of an Orthodox yeshiva in their community. In the 1973 story "'I Always Wanted You to Admire My Fasting'; or, Looking at Kafka," writer Franz Kafka, a teacher at nine-year-old Roth's Newark school, has a brief affair with Roth's aunt Rhoda, a former puppeteer, before his death. Like Roth's other stories, it dramatizes the conflict between the sensitive man and an insensitive society that limits him and drives him to despair.

CRITICAL RECEPTION

Since he published his first short stories in the 1950s, Roth has been hailed as a master of the genre. His early short fiction appeared in such prestigious magazines as *The Paris Review* and *The New Yorker,* and *Goodbye, Columbus* earned glowing reviews. The title novella was made into a feature film in 1969. Along with achieving great popular and critical success, the stories have inspired much heated debate. Roth's detractors have charged him with antisemitism, of presenting degrading depictions of women, of using obscenity bordering on pornography, of being repetitive, of creating characters that lack humanity, and of using joyless humor. His supporters, on the other hand, regard the stories as richly complex tales and Roth as a deeply moral writer whose dark satires offer insight into the foibles of American life. In his prolific fifty-year literary career, Roth has produced no other collection of short fiction since *Goodbye, Columbus*; in all, he has published fewer short stories than he has novels. But many of his stories have achieved the status of classics. They remain popular with readers and continue to generate a great deal of critical commentary. Among the issues that scholars have discussed in recent years are Roth's portrayal of Black characters, his examination of the quest for identity, his depiction of commodity culture, and his views on cultural assimilation. Critics have noted that what is most remarkable is that Roth's exploration of these themes in his stories still resounds with audiences five decades after they were written.

PRINCIPAL WORKS

Short Fiction

"The Box of Truths" 1952
"The Fence" 1952
"Philosophy, or Something Like That" 1952
"Armando and the Fraud" 1953
"The Day It Snowed" 1954
"The Final Delivery of Mr. Thorn" 1954
"The Contest for Aaron Gold" 1955
"Expect the Vandals" 1958
"Heard Melodies Are Sweeter" 1958
Goodbye, Columbus," and Five Short Stories 1959
"The Love Vessel" 1959
"Good Girl" 1960
"The Mistaken" 1960
"Novotny's Pain" 1962
"Psychoanalytic Special" 1963
"On the Air" 1970
"I Always Wanted You to Admire My Fasting'; or, Looking at Kafka" 1973

Other Major Works

Letting Go (novel) 1962
When She Was Good (novel) 1967
Portnoy's Complaint (novel) 1969
Our Gang (novel) 1971
The Breast (novel) 1972
The Great American Novel (novel) 1973
My Life as a Man (novel) 1974
Reading Myself and Others (essays and criticism) 1975
The Professor of Desire (novel) 1977
The Ghost Writer (novel) 1979
Zuckerman Unbound (novel) 1981
The Anatomy Lesson (novel) 1983
Zuckerman Bound: A Trilogy and Epilogue (novel) 1985
The Counterlife (novel) 1986
The Facts: A Novelist's Autobiography (fictional autobiography) 1988
Patrimony: A True Story (novel) 1991
Operation Shylock: A Confession (fictional autobiography) 1993
Sabbath's Theater (novel) 1995
American Pastoral (novel) 1997
I Married a Communist (novel) 1998
The Human Stain (novel) 2000
The Dying Animal (novel) 2001

The Plot against America (novel) 2004
Everyman (novel) 2006

CRITICISM

Barry Gross (essay date summer 1984)

SOURCE: Gross, Barry. "American Fiction, Jewish Writers, and Black Characters: The Return of 'The Human Negro' in Philip Roth." *MELUS* 11, no. 2 (summer 1984): 5-22.

[*In the following essay, Gross discusses Roth's depiction of Black characters in "Goodbye, Columbus," suggesting that the writer used African Americans in the story to highlight the protagonist's Jewishness.*]

In a number of essays collected in *Shadow and Act*, Ralph Ellison categorizes the typical uses to which modern American white writers have put Black characters: to image "the unorganized, irrational forces in American life"[1]; to image "disorder and chaos"[2]; to image "infantile rebellions [against], fears of, and retreat from reality"[3]; to image "almost everything [the white mind] would repress from conscience and consciousness."[4]

But, Ellison argues, it was not always so. Citing Emerson, Thoreau, Whitman, Melville, and, especially, Twain, Ellison insists on making a positive distinction between American literature of the twentieth century and American literature of the nineteenth in which "the conception of the Negro as a symbol of Man—the reversal of what he represents in most contemporary thought—was organic." For Ellison "the key point" in *The Adventures of Huckleberry Finn* occurs in the scene in which Huck "identifies himself with Jim"[5] and decides to help Jim escape even if it means "going to hell," a "recognition scene" Ellison compares to "that in which Oedipus discovers his true identity."[6] The significance of Twain's use of Jim and Huck's identification with him goes far beyond the novel's "great drama of interracial fraternity." Ellison reads the novel as a great drama of *the* "transitional period in American life": Huck's adolescence is a metaphor for the nation's, "the time of the 'great confusion' during which both individuals and nations flounder between accepting and rejecting the responsibilities of adulthood."[7]

Twentieth-century American literature, on the other hand, does not deal as much or as deeply with national experience, national character, national identity, and, therefore, Ellison does not consider it "accidental that the disappearance of the *human* Negro from our fiction coincides with the disappearance of *deep-probing* doubt [my emphasis]." What doubt there is in twentieth-century American literature Ellison considers "shallow doubt"[8]; the twentieth-century American writer is more interested in "elaborating his personal myth" or "working out a personal" problem than in "recreating and extending the national myth"[9] or working out a cultural problem.

But, as he makes a positive distinction between nineteenth- and twentieth-century American literature, Ellison also makes "a positive distinction between 'whites' and 'Jews'":

> Not to do so could be . . . offensive, embarrassing, unjust. . . . I feel uncomfortable whenever I discover Jewish intellectuals writing as though *they* were guilty of enslaving my grandparents, or as though the *Jews* were responsible for the system of segregation. . . . Speaking personally, both as a writer and as a Negro American, I would like to see the more positive distinctions between whites and Jewish Americans maintained. Not only does it make for a necessary bit of historical and social clarity, at least where Negroes are concerned, but I consider the United States freer politically and richer culturally because there are Jewish Americans to bring it the benefit of their special forms of dissent, their humor, and their gift for ideas which are based upon the uniqueness of their experience.[10]

How valid is the positive distinction in literature? If the distinction is valid then modern Jewish-American writers should portray Black characters more positively than other modern white American writers do. Yet it is certainly true that in *Mr. Sammler's Planet* Saul Bellow is as guilty as any other white writer of using a Black character to personify unorganized and irrational forces in American life. It is also true that in *The Tenants* Bernard Malamud is as guilty as any other white writer of using a Black character to personify disorder and chaos and fears of reality. And it is most certainly true that in "The White Negro" and *An American Dream* Norman Mailer is as guilty as any other white writer of using a Black character to personify infantile rebellions and almost everything the white middle-class mind would like to repress from conscience and consciousness.

But in the name of historical clarity and the uniqueness of experience I do want to insist upon a positive distinction between twentieth-century American literature and twentieth-century Jewish-American literature. The Civil War and post-Civil War period could not be for American Jews the watershed, the dividing line, the great transition and the "great confusion" of adolescent floundering between accepting and rejecting the responsibilities of adulthood, insofar as the Jewish experience in America is uniquely modern. Rather, World War II and the post-World War II period are. Thus, we will not find in the Bellows and Malamuds and Mailers—whose adolescences, like the adolescences of their Jewish-American generation, were spent in a pre-World War II world—that "deep-probing doubt" about Jewish identity and American identity and, most particularly, Jewish-American identity or that attempt, in a Jewish name, to recreate and extend the national myth. We will find, rather, the return of "the human Negro," of "the conception of the Negro as a symbol of Man—the reversal of what he represents in most contemporary thought," in the Jewish-American writers of the next generation, whose most prolific, most proficient, and most representative spokesman is Philip Roth.

In the unfinished basement of the Patimkin house in Short Hills in **"Goodbye, Columbus,"** Neil Klugman finds an old refrigerator, which "had once stood in the kitchen of an apartment in some four-family house" in Newark, had once held "butter, eggs, herring in cream sauce, ginger ale, tuna fish salad," but which now is "heaped with fruit. . . . There were greengage plums, black plums, red plums, apricots, nectarines, peaches, long horns of grapes, black, yellow, red, and cherries, cherries flowing out of boxes and staining everything scarlet. And there were melons—cantaloupes and honeydews—and on the top shelf, half of a huge watermelon."[11] The refrigerator, where it stood and where it stands, what it held and what it holds, is a splendid metaphor for the generational shift from subsistence to affluence and the move the affluence allowed for from the city to the suburb, the shift and move which have forced American Jews to engage in deep-probing doubt about their relationship to the national myth.

The transition can be very accurately dated. Neil's Aunt Gladys, who still lives in Newark, asks him, "Since when do Jews live in Short Hills?" (p. 41), and that is not a rhetorical question: "After Pearl Harbor the refrigerator had made the move up to Short Hills: Patimkin Kitchen and Sinks had gone to war: no new barracks was complete until it had a squad of Patimkin sinks lined up in its latrine" (p. 30). It was after Pearl Harbor that Jews began to migrate from the center of Newark—all the Newarks—to "the edge of [it], then out of it, and up the slope of the Orange Mountains, until they had reached the crest and started down the other side, pouring into Gentile territory" (p. 64).

Neil's Aunt Gladys also adds, "They can't be real Jews, believe me" (p. 41). Like Twain's Huck, Neil Klugman must locate his identity somewhere on the spectrum between the old and new definitions. For Huck the poles define attitudes towards slavery; for Neil the poles define attitudes towards affluence. Neil,

however, is even more conflicted and has harder choices to make than Huck. It is very clear from the very beginning of *The Adventures of Huckleberry Finn* that Twain has no sympathy at all—in fact, has vast distaste bordering on physical revulsion—for the world that Huck must reject; the question is not *will* Huck but *how long will it take Huck to* make the choice Twain means him to make. But Roth allows Neil to be tempted by real and substantial attractions: as so perfectly expressed in **"Eli, the Fanatic,"** suburban America is the answer to what all those Jewish

> parents had asked for in the Bronx, and [what their parents had asked for] in Poland, and theirs [had asked for] in Russia or Austria or wherever else they'd fled to or from. . . . What peace. What incredible peace. Have children ever been so safe in their beds? Never. Parents . . . so full in their stomachs? Water so warm in its boilers? Never. Never in Rome, never in Greece. Never even did the walled cities have it so good! . . . Here, after all, were peace and safety—what civilization had been working toward for centuries. . . . The world was at last a place for families, even Jewish families.[12]

It is not accidental, therefore, that "human" Blacks figure so prominently in **"Goodbye, Columbus."** Roth uses them as Twain uses Jim in *Huckleberry Finn*: as touchstones by which Neil may achieve self-recognition, may resolve confusions, may choose to accept the responsibilities of adulthood, may recreate and extend the national myth. In **"Goodbye, Columbus"** Black characters do not personify unorganized, irrational forces, disorder and chaos, but sanity and sensibility; they do not personify infantile rebellions against, fears of, or retreats from reality, but honest encounters and coping with reality; they do not personify almost everything the white mind would repress from conscience and consciousness, but what conscience and consciousness must deal with.

A lower-middle-class boy from Newark, Neil Klugman comes into contact with Brenda Patimkin only by accident: he is a guest at his affluent cousin's country club, and Brenda asks him to hold her glasses while she swims. Neil, smitten, calls her that night:

> "What's your name?"
>
> "Neil. Klugman. I held your glasses at the board, remember?"
>
> "What do you look like?"
>
> "I'm . . . dark."
>
> "Are you a Negro?"
>
> "No."
>
> (p. 5)

Brenda is being "cute": the only Negroes at Brenda's country club are waiters, locker-room attendants. Neil isn't "Negro" but he is as "dark" as Brenda's country club world will admit in 1957 and his function in it is clearly defined: retainer, if only of eye-glasses.

Neil drives out to Short Hills the next night and they have their first face-to-face conversation. She tells him she goes to Radcliffe and asks where he went to school. "Newark College of Rutgers University," he answers, "too ringingly, too fast, too up-in-the-air" (p. 7). Brenda's motives are irrelevant here; what matters is Neil's self-consciousness, his consciousness of his "place":

> For an instant Brenda reminded me of the pug-nosed little bastards from Montclair who come down to the library during vacations, and while I stamp out their books, they stand around tugging their elephantine scarves until they hang to their ankles, hinting all the while at "Boston" and "New Haven."
>
> (p. 7)

Servant again, waiting on his social betters, and, as a matter of fact, Brenda is, although Jewish, pug-nosed, courtesy of cosmetic surgery. "Is a nose with a deviation a crime against the nation?" Barbra Streisand sings in *Funny Girl*. Well . . . yes.

Brenda invites Neil to dinner the next night. His Aunt Gladys tells him, "Fancy shmancy" (p. 14), and it is: the Patimkins do not, as Jews do in Newark, "eat in the kitchen [but] around the dining room table while the maid, Carlota, a Navaho-faced Negro, . . . serves . . . the meal" (p. 14). Sitting at the table Neil feels for Brenda for the first time "that hideous emotion" he "always felt for her, [which] is the underside of love," and warns the reader that "it will not always *stay* the underside" (p. 19). Feeling a need to express "that hideous emotion," he decides "to run little Julie into the ground" when he shoots baskets with Brenda's younger sister after dinner, but he quickly learns "how the game is played":

> Over the years Mr. Patimkin had taught his daughters that free throws were theirs for the asking; he could afford to. However, with the strange eyes of Short Hills upon me, matrons, servants, and providers, I somehow felt I couldn't. But I had to and I did.
>
> (p. 20)

Already conflicted between what he could do and should do, Neil does what he *has* to do, *has* to if he is to play the game; in order to win whatever glittering prize Brenda represents, he has to lose.

The essential contrast between his life and hers is brought home to him the next morning: remembering his fellow college students "who had worked evenings . . . and had used the commissions they had earned pushing ladies' out-of-season shoes to pay their laboratory fees" (p. 22), watching "wobbly-heeled girls . . . racing down the street toward desks, filing cabinets, . . . and—if the Lord had seen fit to remove a

mite of harshness from their lives—. . . air-conditioners pumping at their windows" (p. 22), Neil wonders if Brenda, in central-non-pumping-air-conditioned Short Hills, "was awake yet" (p. 22). He has to work, she does not; although he does not know it, this fact is a major source of "that hideous emotion." For now, he understands that that fact renders her different from and superior to the "teen-age girls [who] walk twitchingly up the wide flight of marble stairs that led to the main reading room. The stairs were an imitation of a staircase somewhere in Versailles [shades of *The Great Gatsby*!], though in their toreador pants . . . these young daughters of Italian leatherworkers, Polish brewery hands, and Jewish furriers were hardly duchesses. They were not Brenda either" (pp. 22-23).

Into the library comes a Black kid who asks for the art section. Neil's Gentile co-worker is first amused— "Where did *he* ever find out about art?" (p. 25)—then scandalized—"He's been hiding in the art books all morning. You know what those boys *do* in there. . . . Those are *very* expensive books" (p. 25). When Neil notes that "people are supposed to touch them," his colleague replies, "There is touching . . . and there is touching" (p. 25). Also, apparently, there are people and there are people: "You know the way they treat the housing projects we give them. . . . They throw *beer* bottles, those big ones, on the *lawn*. They're taking over the city" (p. 25).

Neil may not know why he feels the need to protect the Black kid from his colleague's bigotry, but we do. Where did a poor boy from Newark ever find out about a rich girl from Short Hills? What will he do to that very expensive girl? Does he know there is touching and there is touching? Will he treat what is "given" him with respect? Or will he try to take it over? Neil identifies with the Black kid to the extent that he volunteers to go up to the art section to see what the boy is doing.

He finds him, "lips . . . parted, . . . eyes wide," looking at Gauguin reproductions: "even [his] ears seemed to have a heightened receptivity [more shades of *Gatsby*!]. He looked ecstatic" (p. 26). The Blacks in the pictures "look cool," he tells Neil, and then asks him if Tahiti is a "place you could go to . . . like a resort" (p. 26). Neil replies, "You could go there, I suppose. It's very far. People live there" (p. 26). Short Hills is, of course, a resort for people who do not live there, but home—air-conditioned, cool—for people who do, far from Newark but not nearly as far as Tahiti. "That's the fuckin life," the boy tells Neil, and Neil, agreeing it certainly is, already sees himself driving "up to Short Hills" that evening, sees Short Hills, "in [his] mind's eye, at dusk, rose-colored, like a Gauguin stream" (p. 27).

As Neil pulls into the Patimkin drive, the Patimkins are heading out the door on an errand, all but little Julie who doesn't want to go. Brenda tells him he has "to sit with" her because "Carlota's off" (p. 27)—maid's night out is Neil's night in, the eye-glass holder is promoted—demoted?—to baby-sitter. Standing in the hall, he feels "like Carlota" (p. 28). He is "bitten with the urge to slide quietly out of the house, into [his] car, and back to Newark, where [he] might . . . sit in the alley [with his aunt and uncle] and break candy with [his] own" (p. 28)—in the alley there might be a welcome breeze—but he doesn't: Julie shouts at him to close the door to keep the air-conditioning in and he "obediently" does, then "stroll[s] in and out of rooms on the first floor," all of which are "totally without . . . smell," even the kitchen—"apparently, with Carlota off, the Patimkins had had dinner at the club" (p. 29).

He wanders down to the finished basement, on the wall of which he examines "a velvet mounting board with ribbons and medals clipped to it: Essex County Horse Show 1949, Union County Horse Show 1950, Garden State Fair 1952, Morristown Horse Show 1953, and so on—all for Brenda, for jumping and running or galloping or whatever else young girls receive ribbons for" (p. 30). Standing before a well-stocked bar, he thinks to pour himself "a drink—just as a wicked wage for being forced into servantry," but he is "uneasy about breaking the label on a bottle of whiskey" (p. 30). In an unfinished room off the finished basement he finds that old refrigerator, "a reminder to [him] of the Patimkin roots in Newark" (p. 30).

As receptive and ecstatic as the Black boy is about Gauguin, Neil touches and takes, grabs a handful of cherries. "They're not washed!" Julie admonishes from behind—"in such a way that it seemed to place the refrigerator itself out-of-bounds, if only for [him]" (p. 31). Chastened, he tells her he "was just looking around" and drops the cherries into his pocket: "Julie was looking at me as though she was trying to look behind me, and then I realized that I was standing with my hands out of sight. I brought them around to the front, and, I swear it, she did peek to see if they were empty. . . . She seemed to have a threat on her face" (p. 31). It is the threat of punishment for the transgressor who does things to very expensive books, the threat of expulsion for the trespasser in the art section of the library. To distract Julie from having caught him cherry-red-handed, Neil offers to play ping-pong with her.

Angry at her for declaring him an interloper, he now does what he didn't do when Short Hills watched him shoot baskets: he runs little Julie into the ground.

> "Can I take that one over? I hurt my finger yesterday and it just hurt when I served."

> "No."

> I continued to win.

> "That wasn't fair, Neil. My shoelace came untied. Can I take it—."

> "No."

> We played, I ferociously.

> "Neil, you leaned over the table. That's illegal—"

> "I didn't lean and it's not illegal."

> I felt the cherries hopping among my nickels and pennies.

> "Neil, you gypped me out of a point. You have nineteen and I have eleven—"

> "Twenty and *ten*," I said. "Serve!"

> She did and I smashed my return past her—it zoomed off the table and skittered into the refrigerator room.

> "You're a cheater!" she screamed at me. "You cheat! . . . And you were stealing fruit!"

> (pp. 31-32)

That night Neil steals the fruit in earnest: he makes love to Brenda for the first time, "takes" what he may not even be supposed to touch, plays the game and wins. The connection is not lost on Neil: "How can I describe loving Brenda? It was so sweet, as though I'd finally scored that twenty-first point" (p. 33).

Nor is the connection between himself and the Black boy lost: "over the next week and a half, there seemed to be only two people in my life: Brenda and the little colored kid who liked Gauguin" (p. 34). Every morning the Black boy is waiting outside the library before it opens, every morning Neil watches him climb "up the long marble stairs that led to Tahiti" (p. 34); one particularly "hot day he was there when [Neil] arrived in the morning and went through the door behind [Neil] when [he] left at night" (p. 34). One morning when the kid does not show up and a man tries to check Gauguin out, Neil tells him "there's a hold" on it, returns it to the stacks, and "when the colored kid showed up later in the day, it was just where he'd left it the afternoon before" (p. 34). Neil will not "go to hell" for protecting the Black boy, as Huck fears he might for protecting Jim, but, given Neil's inability to act decisively about anything, to commit himself by more than half *to* anything is, at least, a stand, as much of one as Neil, product and representative of a timid, hesitant, and silent generation, may be capable of making.

And every evening Neil climbs up the hill that leads to *his* Tahiti, finding Brenda just where he'd left her the evening before. But what if, one night, she *weren't* there? One evening when Brenda takes Neil to swim at the club she asks him if he loves her and Neil, reluctant to commit himself, doesn't answer, but, swimming alone, he has a moment of panic, what the Black boy's panic might be if he found the Gauguin gone: he is suddenly afraid that "she would not be there when [he] returned" and wishes he had "carried her glasses away with [him] so she would have to wait for [him] to lead her back home" (p. 37). When he comes out of the pool and finds her just where he'd left her he tells her, "I love you. . . . I do" (p. 38).

On another night Brenda leads him to "the fruit refrigerator" (p. 38), conferring on him the legitimacy—the *right* to pick and choose, touch and take—he was previously denied. The refrigerator is no longer "out-of-bounds" and thereafter the taking of cherries accompanies his taking of Brenda: every night they take a bowl of cherries from the refrigerator to the TV room and, after everyone is asleep, make love—"when I moved from the darkened room to the bathroom I could always feel cherry pits against my bare soles. At home, undressing for the second time that night, I would find red marks on the undersides of my feet" (p. 40).

Neil's dilemma is crystallized when Brenda invites him to spend his vacation at Short Hills. He sees "awe" in Aunt Gladys' eyes and realizes, "I had come a long way since that day she'd said to me on the phone, 'Fancy-shmancy'" (p. 40).

> "A week?" she said. "They got room for a week?"
>
> "Aunt Gladys, they don't live over the store."
>
> "I lived over a store I wasn't ashamed. . . . Since when do Jewish people live in Short Hills? They couldn't be real Jews believe me."
>
> (pp. 40-41)

Neil assures her that the Patimkins are "real Jews," to which Aunt Gladys replies, "I'll see it I'll believe it" (p. 41). Without admitting it or perhaps even being fully conscious of it, Neil shares her skepticism: he has seen, but does not really believe, that "real Jews" live in the suburbs and get their noses fixed and go to Radcliffe and belong to country clubs and have a Black maid with whom he can more readily identify than he can with any of the Patimkins.

The extent to which Neil is unable to identify with the Jews of Short Hills is measurable by the extent to which he cannot help but identify with the Black boy, cannot help but worry about what will happen to him and about his daily climb up to Tahiti while Neil is on vacation. Just before Neil leaves he goes to talk to the boy in the stacks:

> "I ain't doing anything wrong. I didn't do no writing in *any*thing. You could search me—."

> "I know you didn't. Listen: if you like that book so much why don't you please take it home? Do you have a library card?"
>
> "No, sir. I didn't take *nothing*."
>
> "No, a library card is what we give you so you can take books home. Then you won't have to come down here every day. . . ."
>
> "What you keep telling me take that book home for? At home somebody de—*story* it. . . . Why don't you want me to come round here?"
>
> "I didn't say you shouldn't."
>
> "I *likes* to come here. I likes them stairs."
>
> "I like them too."
>
> (pp. 42-43)

It is the same scene in which Julie catches Neil taking the cherries: the Black boy sees threat and accusation in Neil's face, insists that he has not done anything wrong, has not taken anything. His, like Neil's, is the defensiveness of the interloper. But, as Neil's taking the cherries foreshadows this scene, this scene foreshadows a later one. The boy already knows what Neil is yet to learn: that illusion can be destroyed by reality, that it is the very distance which separates the dreamer from the dream that makes the dream worthwhile, that it is the climb up the marble stairs to Tahiti that *makes* Tahiti Tahiti.

Especially if the dreamer feels unworthy. Before he drives up to Short Hills that night Neil changes his shirt so that when he arrives he will "look as though [he] was deserving of an interlude in the suburbs" (p. 43). It is as if he sees himself as one of those street Blacks who, thanks to the charity of the affluent, gets sent to a camp in the country for one [precious] week in the summer. Keenly conscious that he is as out of place at Short Hills as an urban Black is at Camp Winamakee, he lets his "one shirt with a Brooks Brothers label . . . linger on the bed . . . while the Arrows [he] heap[s] in the drawer" (p. 45).

On some level Brenda also realizes that Neil does not belong and must be made to conform to Short Hills: Brenda plays tennis and wins ribbons at horse shows; her brother Ron was a basketball star at Ohio State; even little Julie shoots baskets and plays ping-pong—the Hellenization of the Jews finally completed in the American suburbs; and Neil, Brenda gratefully discovers one morning at the Short Hills High School track, can run. After she watches him run she tells him approvingly, "You look like me," and Neil understands her to mean that he is "somehow beginning to look the way she want[s] [him] to. Like herself" (p. 50). Every morning he runs and she times him, and Neil is "reminded of one of those scenes in the race-horse movies, where an old trainer like Walter Brennan and a young handsome man clock the beautiful girl's horse in the early Kentucky morning, to see if it really is the fastest two-year-old alive" (pp. 51-52). He is the beautiful southern belle's prize stud, another ribbon for her collection.

The morning that he finally breaks seven minutes he tells him, for the first time, that she loves him. That night Neil has a disturbing dream:

> It had taken place on a ship, an old sailing ship like those you see in pirate movies. With me on the ship was the little colored kid from the library—I was the captain and he my mate, and we were the only crew members. For a while it was a pleasant dream; we were anchored in the harbor of an island in the Pacific and it was very sunny. Upon the beach there were beautiful bare-skinned Negresses, and none of them moved; but suddenly we were moving, our ship, out of the harbor, and the Negresses moved slowly down to the shore and began to throw leis at us and though we did not want to go, the little boy and I, the boat was moving and there was nothing we could do about it, and he shouted at me that it was my fault and I shouted it was his for not having a library card, but we were wasting our breath, for we were further and further from the island, and soon the natives were nothing at all.
>
> (p. 53)

The allusion to *The Adventures of Huckleberry Finn* is unmistakable: Black and white the only crew members, Black and white in the same boat, a pleasant dream. As in *Huckleberry Finn,* however, the pleasantness is only temporary: they must move on even though they don't want to. Because the boy does not have a library card—the ticket of admission, the certification of legitimacy—he will lose his Tahiti. As for Neil, one Brooks Brothers shirt and a seven-minute-mile do not a certification of legitimacy make. The next morning when he says hello to Carlota he feels "a kinship with her" (p. 55), a holdover from the dream, a kinship with the Black boy exiled from Tahiti.

Haunted by the dream of loss, he decides to propose marriage to Brenda but "that proposal would have taken a kind of courage that [he] did not think [he] had"—"I did not feel myself prepared for any answer but 'Hallelujah!' Any other kind of yes wouldn't have satisfied me, and any kind of no, even one masked behind the words, 'Let's wait, sweetheart,' would have been my end" (p. 56). Fearful of rejection but needing to feel that she is his he proposes what he thinks of as "the surrogate" (p. 56)—that she get fitted for a diaphragm. When she balks he accuses her of being selfish. As he sees it their relationship has been based on his obedience to her commands—hold my glasses, baby-sit Julie, run—as if he were her Black retainer, a

male Carlota: "If you asked *me* to buy a diaphragm we'd have to go straight to the Yellow Pages and find a gynecologist open on Saturday afternoon!" (p. 57). Now he wants her to do something just because he has asked her to, a test of his ability to impose his will on her, the servant become master. When she refuses he calls her "a selfish, egotistical bitch" and accuses her of wanting to end their relationship: "In fact, that's the whole thing, isn't it?" (p. 58).

Or is it Neil who wants out and thus makes demands he knows she can't and won't meet? Is it at this point that "that hideous emotion" that is "the underside of love" is no longer the *under*side? The enormous distance between his world and hers is made vividly clear to him when Mrs. Patimkin sends him on an errand to Patimkin Kitchen and Bathroom Sinks which, not accidentally, is located "in the heart of the Negro section of Newark" (p. 64):

> Years ago, at the time of the great immigration, it had been the Jewish section, and still one could see the little fish stores, the kosher delicatessens, the Turkish baths, where my grandparents had shopped and bathed at the beginning of the century. Even the smells had lingered: whitefish, corned beef, sour tomatoes—but now, on top of these, was the grander greasier smell of auto wrecking shops, the sour stink of a brewery, the burning odor from a leather factory; and on the streets, instead of Yiddish, one heard the shouts of Negro children playing at Willie Mays with a broom handle and half a rubber ball. The neighborhood had changed: the old Jews like my grandparents had struggled and died, and their offspring had struggled and prospered, and moved further and further west, towards the edge of Newark, then out of it, and up the slope of the Orange Mountains, until they had reached the crest and started down the other side, pouring into Gentile territory as the Scotch-Irish had poured through the Cumberland Gap. I wondered, for an instant only, if I would see the colored kid from the library on the streets here. I didn't, of course, though I was sure he lived in one of the scabby, peeling buildings out of which dogs, children, and aproned women moved continually. On the top floors, windows were open, and the very old, who could no longer creak down the long stairs to the street, sat where they had been put, in the screenless windows, their elbows resting on fluffless pillows, and their heads tipping forward on their necks, watching the push of the young and the pregnant and the unemployed.
>
> (p. 64)

The sights and smells of the old Jewish section, now the Black section, are more meaningful to him than the sights and smells of the Gentile territory of Short Hills. He is better able to identify with the lingering Jewish smells and the current Black ones than with the smell-lessness of the Patimkin house, with the scabby, peeling buildings than with the suburban split-levels, with the open windows than with the windows shut tight to keep the air-conditioning in, with the

Black children playing at Willie Mays with broom handles than with the basketball hoop on the Patimkin garage, the ping-pong table in the Patimkin rec room, the running track at Short Hills High, the horse shows Brenda wins ribbons at.

At Patimkin Kitchen and Bathroom Sinks he watches Brenda's brother Ron "directing the Negroes" and tries to imagine himself, "the outsider who might one day be an insider" (p. 67), doing that. He hears Mr. Patimkin shout at "the Negro loading gang, . . . 'You guys know how long an hour is? All right, you'll be back in an hour!'" (p. 67) and tries to imagine himself shouting that. Neil bossing Blacks? What is it he is getting into? He has more qualms when, on his way back from Newark, he stops at a deer preserve:

> Young white-skinned mothers, hardly older than I, and in many instances younger, chatted in their convertibles behind me, and looked down from time to time to see what their children were about. I had seen them before, when Brenda and I had gone out for a bite in the afternoon, or had driven up here for lunch: in clothes of three and four they sat in the rustic hamburger joints that dotted the Reservation area and . . . compared suntans, supermarkets, and vacations. They looked immortal sitting there. Their hair would always stay the color they desired, their clothes the right texture and shade; in their homes they would have simple Swedish modern when that was fashionable, and if huge, ugly baroque ever came back, out would go the long, midget-legged marble coffee table and in would come Louis Quatorze. These were the goddesses, and if I were Paris I could not have been able to choose among them, so microscopic were the differences. Their fates had collapsed them into one. Only Brenda shone. Money and comfort would not erase her singleness— they hadn't yet, or had they? What was I loving, I wondered.
>
> (p. 68)

Would he call the goddesses "white-skinned" if he had not just come from the Black section? He is aware that they are as much a product of suburban upper-middle-class money and comfort, as much the goal and natural end result of *their* system, as the southern belle was of *hers*. How different *is* Brenda from these Jewish-American Princesses? And what, after all, is so terrible about being a princess, a goddess?

The Black boy does not have a choice: he *has* to leave Tahiti. But Neil *does* have a choice: he is the outsider who *can* become an insider, but at a certain price, and he is not sure he is willing to pay it (Aunt Gladys' "They can't be real Jews"). The next day while he is waiting for Brenda to be fitted with the diaphragm she has agreed to acquire he asks himself the same questions:

> Can I call the self-conscious words I spoke prayer? At any rate, I called my audience God. God, I said, I am twenty-three years old. I want to make the best of

things. Now the doctor is about to wed Brenda to me, and I am not entirely certain this is all for the best. What is it I love, Lord? Why have I chosen? Who is Brenda? The race is to the swift. Should I have stopped to think?

> I was getting no answers, but I went on. If we meet You at all, God, it's that we're carnal, and acquisitive, and thereby partake of You. I am carnal, and I know You approve, I just know it. But how carnal can I get? I am acquisitive. Where do I turn now in my acquisitiveness? Where do we meet? Which prize is You?

> It was an ingenious meditation, and suddenly I felt ashamed. I got up and walked outside, and the noise of Fifth Avenue met me with an answer:

> Which prize do you think, schmuck? Gold dinnerware, sporting-goods trees, nectarines, garbage disposals, bumpless noses, Patimkin Sink, Bonwit Teller—

> (pp. 71-72)

When he sees her coming out of the doctor's office not carrying anything he is "glad that in the end she had disobeyed [his] desire" (p. 72). Marriage to Brenda—even the one symbolized by the diaphragm— may not be "for the best," that "prize" may not be worth winning. But she tells him she is wearing it, as one *wears* a wedding ring, and for the second time in the novel he tells her he loves her. The first time he told her it was because he thought he had lost her; now he tells her because he thinks he has won her.

The omens are clear: at Brenda's brother's wedding Brenda's uncle tells Neil, "You gotta deal there, boy, . . . don't louse it up, . . . you're next kid, I see it in the cards, . . . you're nobody's sucker, . . . you'll go far, . . . you're a smart boy, you'll play it safe" (pp. 77, 79, 84), and Brenda's father tells him, "Whatever my Buck [cut to the deer preserve!] wants is good enough for me. There's no business too big it can't use another head" (p. 78). But on their last night together before Brenda goes back to Radcliffe and Neil goes back to Newark he watches her sleep and fears he knows "no more of her than [he] could see in a photograph" (p. 84).

When Neil returns to the library his supervisor confronts him with an angry letter from the man Neil denied access to the Gauguin book. Neil bullies his way out of it and wonders if he "had not learned [something] from Mr. Patimkin that morning [he'd] heard him" bullying the Black workers, wonders, "Perhaps I was more of a businessman than I thought. Maybe I could learn to become a Patimkin with ease" (p. 85). But summer *is* over: the Black boy no longer comes to the library and Gauguin is no longer in the stacks. Neil wonders "what it had been like that day the colored kid had discovered the book was gone":

> For some reason I imagined that he had blamed it on me, and then I realized that I was confusing the dream I'd had with reality. Chances were he had discovered

someone else, Van Gogh, Vermeer . . . But no, they were not his kind of artists. What had probably happened was that he'd given up on the library and gone back to playing Willie Mays in the streets. He was better off, I thought. No sense of carrying dreams of Tahiti in your head, if you can't afford the fare.

(pp. 85-86)

The next scene—the ending of the book—is clearly foreshadowed: Neil will discover that Brenda is gone and that it is for the best because he really cannot afford the fare, that the outsider cannot become an insider with ease. Brenda's mother has found the diaphragm where Brenda left it in a dresser drawer and blames Neil's outsiderness, a background which must be "different" and, therefore, wanting: "I cannot imagine what kind of home life he had that he could act that way. Certainly that was a fine way to repay us for the hospitality we were nice enough to show him, a perfect stranger" (p. 92). Mr. Patimkin also makes the same point: "From the beginning I was nice to him and thought he would appreciate the nice vacation we supplied for him. Some people never turn out the way you hope" (p. 91). See what happens when you let someone who does not belong there into the country club? See what happens when you let someone who shouldn't live there into the neighborhood? Neil is no better than the Blacks who litter the housing projects "given" them. Mr. Patimkin assures Brenda that "now that [she] will be away at school and from him . . . [she] will probably do all right" (p. 91)—no "niggers" at Harvard.

Neil and Brenda both blame each other: he accuses her of leaving the diaphragm where it would be found so that their relationship would have to end and she accuses him of always "accusing [her] of things . . . from the very beginning"—"Why don't you have your eyes fixed? Why don't you have this fixed, that fixed? As if it were my fault that I *could* have them fixed" (p. 96). Hers is the more valid claim: the *underside* of love he felt for her *always* vied with the love he felt; he *always* hated her not only for being able to afford to have things fixed but for being the member and product of society that believed such things *should be fixed*. That society has closed ranks against the outsider and Neil ends it by forcing Brenda to assert her membership in that society: he makes her choose between her parents and him, knowing that she will— that she *must*—choose her parents.

He leaves her in the hotel room and walks towards the Harvard Yard which he, graduate of Newark College of Rutgers University, has, of course, "never seen before," and finds himself standing in front of the Lamont Library. Although himself a librarian, he is trespasser here too: the Library, "which, Brenda had once told [him], had Patimkin sinks in its rest rooms" (p. 96), is closed. It is precisely *because* Patimkin sinks are in the Lamont Library—*because* of Patimkin money—that Brenda has had access to and entry into that world from which he is, and will always be, barred. Feeling the anger and rage of the excluded he wants to "pick up a rock and heave it right through" the Library's glass front, "but of course [he doesn't]" (p. 96). Instead, wishing that Brenda "had only been slightly *not* Brenda" but knowing that "then [he] would [not] have loved her," wondering what it was inside him "that had turned winning into losing, and losing— who knows?—into winning" (p. 97), he gets on the train and arrives in "Newark just as the sun is rising on the first day of the Jewish New Year . . . in plenty of time for work" (p. 97).

The last lines of **"Goodbye, Columbus"** are as resonant as the last lines of *The Adventures of Huckleberry Finn*: Huck will "light out for the territory ahead" because he does not want to remain in a "civilization" that, among other things, treats his friend Nigger Jim like an object; Neil rejects the "Gentile territory" of Short Hills and returns to Newark. But the conclusion of **"Goodbye, Columbus"** is much less clear-cut: for Neil there is no "territory ahead" or territory behind to light out to. If he rejects the Gentile territory of Short Hills where no "real Jews" can possibly live, he must also reject the Jewish territory of Newark where no "real Jews" work on the first day of the Jewish New Year. Neil will have to locate his *own* reality, his *own* territory. The "reality" gap between Neil and Short Hills is too vast but so is the generation gap between Neil and Aunt Gladys' Newark. It is not accidental, I think, that the very last word of the novel is "work": the irremediable difference and unbridgeable gulf between Brenda and Neil, between her world and reality and his, has always been—and will always be—made concrete in the fact that she has never had to, and will never have to, work to live and he has and does. It also points, however obliquely, to the future: Neil will find his reality, will accept the responsibilities of adulthood, and will, therefore, recreate and extend the national myth in work, not the library *per se* but in *doing* something rather than in *becoming*—or trying to become—a Patimkin.

"Goodbye, Columbus" is not a retelling—or a recreation or extension—of *The Adventures of Huckleberry Finn*: Roth's characters and subject matter are as unique to his particular time and place as Twain's were to his. But there are some remarkably suggestive parallels, not the least of which are the uses to which both Twain and Roth put their Black characters. If I understand Ellison correctly he is saying that Twain's use of the Negro in *Huckleberry Finn* is acceptable, however stereotypical the portrayal of Nigger Jim is, because of Twain's intentions, and I think the same can be said for Roth's use of Black characters in **"Goodbye, Columbus."** It is not only that Twain intends Jim and Roth intends the Black boy to be symbols of "human value." It is, rather, that both Twain and Roth are, in the best sense of the word, *disinterested* in their Black characters' blackness. Neither Twain nor Roth intends or cares to say anything about Blacks as people or about blackness as a condition. The issue in *Huckleberry Finn* is not Jim's blackness, which is neither negotiable nor in doubt, but Huck's *whiteness,* which is negotiable and in doubt. The issue in **"Goodbye, Columbus"** is not the Black boy's blackness but Neil's Jewishness. How Neil resolves that issue will determine whether he will accept or reject the responsibilities of adulthood and how he will recreate and extend the national myth.

That Roth is *using* Black characters in **"Goodbye, Columbus"**—and for his own ends—is neither to be denied nor apologized for. One must make a positive distinction between writers and people, between literature and life: we cannot allow people to use people but we must allow writers to use people or else every writer would be doomed to be an Aesop and one *Jonathan Livingston Seagull* a generation is quite enough, thank you. But one can—and must—insist upon the distinction between *using* and *abusing*. The question is not *should* white writers use Black characters; the question is *how* are they using them. The answer cannot be to portray the unorganized or the irrational, disorder or chaos, infantile rebellions against or retreats from reality—that would be an *abuse* of any character's humanity. Nor should white writers take it upon themselves to define Black humanity—if that is to be defined at all, it can only be done by Black writers who choose to do it. The only acceptable end for which white writers may use Black characters—the end for which Philip Roth uses them in **"Goodbye, Columbus"** and which, through the process of deep-probing doubt and in the name of recreating and extending the national myth, he achieves—is the end Ellison proscribes: "to recognize the broader aspects of their own [humanity]."[13]

Notes

1. Ralph Ellison, "Twentieth-Century Fiction and the Black Mask of Humanity," *Shadow and Act,* (New York: Random House, 1964), p. 57.

2. Ellison, "Change the Joke and Slip the Yoke," *Shadow and Act,* p. 67.

3. Ellison, "The World and the Jug," *Shadow and Act,* p. 130.

4. Ellison, "Change the Joke and Slip the Yoke," p. 63.

5. Ellison, "Twentieth-Century Fiction and the Black Mask of Humanity," p. 49.

6. Ellison, "Twentieth-Century Fiction and the Black Mask of Humanity," p. 48.

7. Ellison, "Twentieth-Century Fiction and the Black Mask of Humanity," p. 50.

8. Ellison, "Twentieth-Century Fiction and the Black Mask of Humanity," p. 52.

9. Ellison, "Twentieth-Century Fiction and the Black Mask of Humanity," p. 54.

10. Ellison, "The World and the Jug," pp. 132-33.

11. Philip Roth, "Goodbye, Columbus," *Goodbye, Columbus* (New York: Bantam, 1959), pp. 30-31. All subsequent page references to "Goodbye, Columbus" are to this edition.

12. Roth, "Eli, the Fanatic," *Goodbye, Columbus,* p. 202.

13. Ellison, "Twentieth-Century Fiction and the Black Mask of Humanity," p. 58.

Helge Normann Nilsen (essay date 1987)

SOURCE: Normann Nilsen, Helge. "Love and Identity: Neil Klugman's Quest in 'Goodbye, Columbus.'" *English Studies* (1987): 79-88.

[*In the following essay, Nilsen examines Neil Klugman's struggle to find his place in the world as a third-generation American Jew.*]

In [**"Goodbye, Columbus"**] the protagonist, Neil Klugman, is involved in a struggle to develop and preserve an identity of his own amid different environments and conflicting impulses within himself. Throughout the story he makes love to Brenda Patimkin and tries to find a role in society that corresponds to what he regards as his own, unique self. In the process he loses Brenda, but he refuses to compromise and surrender what he regards as his integrity. As a result of this he remains mainly a detached observer in relation to the various settings and role models that make up the social universe of the story. Brenda is the only one that he seeks an intimate relationship with. However, Neil does not choose this outsider role solely for its own sake, as an expression of wilfulness. As a modern, liberal intellectual living in the conservative and repressive American society of the nineteen fifties, he identifies with a set of secular and rationalistic values that are bound to bring him into conflict with the world around him.

Neil's struggle to establish his own identity is highly understandable in view of his circumstances. He represents the third generation of a Jewish immigrant group that has experienced great changes and transitions. His milieu is basically working class or lower middle class and strongly colored by traditional Jewish ethnic attitudes and customs, but he himself is a librarian with a bachelor's degree in philosophy and a modern, assimilationist approach to American society.[1] Neil finds it impossible to accept the narrow-minded concept of life of his relatives, especially his aunt Gladys. He is ready to break away from the lifestyle of the parental generation, and when he meets Brenda, he is attracted both to her beauty and her manners. A resident of the wealthy suburb of Short Hills, she seems to represent a different and better world. Newark and Short Hills constitute two sharply constrasted regions in the symbolic geography of the story, and Neil tries to define his own self mainly in relation to these two extremes, though the library where he works seems to represent a third alternative.

In the Patimkin household Neil is regarded as an outsider and he responds with acerbic inner comments to the various absurdities of this family. They are affluent, but crudely materialistic and snobbish, devoted to appearances, material wealth, social position and athletic prowess. Neil does not hesitate to characterize the whole clan as 'Brobdingnags' who make him feel small and insignificant at their overfilled dinner table. Everything about them and the class that they represent reinforces his conviction that this lifestyle does not correspond to the identity that he seeks for himself.

The library is disappointing to Neil because he cannot identify with the others there and worries that he may end up like one of them, a dusty librarian with a pale skin whose life becomes a bloodless devotion to his duties. Always alert and aware of the imperfections of his surroundings, Neil creates a distance between himself and his colleagues and wants to define himself in terms of his opposition to them, just as he does in relation to his own family and that of Brenda. In the library he achieves such a separation by sympathizing with a black boy who spends hours in the art book section looking at pictures of Gauguin's Tahiti paintings. Another librarian, John McKee, is worried about this little black intruder and what he may be up to in the stacks looking at pictures of nudes. But this racism and sexual anxiety and prudery are repellent to Neil, who has experienced and rejected such attitudes already in his own environment.

Neil appreciates the longings of the black boy for a better world, a freer and more sensuous life, which is so powerfully expressed in Gauguin's colorful scenes and figures. In the story, these pictures are part of a chain of images of an exotic setting which includes Neil's vision of Brenda as a Polynesian maiden and his later dream of a South Sea island. This imagery symbolizes an alternative lifestyle and a happiness which Neil also longs for. Though he is frustrated by the Patimkins, he is not yet ready to given up his dream of a different and more satisfying life which may lie in store for Brenda and himself. Short Hills is the same kind of dream for him that Tahiti is for the black boy, and he envisages the suburb 'at dusk, rose-colored, like a Gauguin stream.'[2]

Neil tries to fulfil his dream by creating a separate realm of love between himself and Brenda which assumes a subversive function in relation to the respectable Puritanism of the Patimkin family. The young couple's erotic activities in the television room are a kind of conspiracy and a parallel to the black boy's hiding in the library to look at pictures. Gauguin himself lived in Tahiti, in voluntary exile from his native French bourgeoisie. Neil's conquest of Brenda and their surreptitious lovemaking are the means by which he not only bolsters his sense of masculinity, but also supports a part of his identity which he feels is threatened by his new situation. His efforts to help the black boy are also an element of this self-protective mechanism.

However, Brenda soon begins to reveal her insecurity and dependence on her parents' approval. They want to know more about Neil and his prospects, and she starts to question him in order to determine his social acceptability or lack of it. She also asks him if he loves her and tells him that she intends to go on sleeping with him whether he does or not. This declaration suggests that she regards her affair with Neil, up to this point, mainly as a sexual fling. She also reveals that she attributes the same motives to himself, something which he finds 'crude' because he has greater hopes for their relationship than that, Thus he is pained by her inability to understand the real nature of his feelings. From the start, it seems that the two of them have different concepts of love. Unable to appreciate Neil's motives for approaching her, Brenda believes that he does not love her yet, telling him that she wants him to do so and that when he does, 'there'll be nothing to worry about' (p. 37). She has a superficial concept of love which has little relation to the actual process which is going on between them. He does love her, and that is the problem, since he wants to aid her in her tentative efforts to liberate herself from her parents' influence.

Brenda is a willing partner for Neil in the physical sense, but in reality she is much less independent than he. She attempts to cover up the whole issue by asserting that everything will be all right once he loves her, but this turns out to be an illusion. However, Neil is not in a position to foresee that this will be the case, and he commits himself to her and declares his love for her. According to one critic, however, the relationship between these two is 'nothing more than a means of escape,' and Neil 'remains without the values of commitment which could take escape beyond itself.' Here, Neil's love for Brenda is seen as pure escapism, whereas he in fact is engaged in a search for something and someone that he can commit himself to in a genuine fashion because they correspond to his real self. This commentator sees no difference between Neil and Brenda and argues that 'neither is willing to face the problems that any involvement entails.'[3] It would rather seem that it is mainly Brenda who shies away from contemplating the deeper challenge that is inherent in Neil's courting of her.

The approaching marriage of Ron Patimkin and his fiancée Harriet is an indication of the kind of life that is expected of a member of the clan, and Neil has a hard time hiding his dislike of the completely unimaginative sort of marriage and life that Ron seems to contemplate quite happily. Neil is aware that Ron is quite nice to him, but the fact remains that the latter's mental horizon does not extend to anything beyond sports and the music of Mantovani or Kostelanetz. As for Brenda, she quarrels with her mother and reveals that she is jealous of Harriet. She complains that Mrs. Patimkin will forget that she exists once Harriet arrives, and Neil suggests that this ought not to be a problem, but rather an advantage. He would like for both himself and Brenda to be as free of parental influence as possible, but Brenda is more hesitant about this. She is very upset about her mother and tells Neil that she would have torn up some of her own hundred dollar bills if she had found them and then put the pieces in her mother's purse. She is crying as she says this, and the whole idea seems to be an expression of her childish need to revenge herself upon her mother for not giving her the love and attention that will now bestowed upon Harriet, the bride to be. Brenda then throws herself at Neil, demanding that he make love to her on the old sofa in the storage room where she had hidden her money. But this, like some of her later actions, is an immature rather than a truly self-assertive rebellion against her parents.

When Brenda asks Neil to take up running with her, he realizes that this is a way in which she tries to make him more acceptable to her by changing his identity so that it becomes less threatening to her and the family. She tells him that he looks like her, and they are wearing similar clothes for the occasion, but Neil feels that 'She meant, I was sure, that I was somehow beginning to look the way she wanted me to. Like herself.' (p. 50). Neil enjoys the running and feels happy afterwards, but this is because both he and Brenda are having a fine time together as young and healthy people in love, not because he has decided to change his attitudes to suit her needs. This, however, is probably what she believes while they are exercising, and hence she gives him the love and attention that contribute to his happiness. In fact, it is only after they have been running for a while on a regular basis that she feels free to tell him that she loves him. Thus their relationship is fraught with misunderstandings and conflicts that come to a head at the end of the story.

The content of Neil's dream about a Pacific island suggests that he is beginning to fear that the affair with Brenda cannot last, that the realities of their situation, the power of the Patimkin environment, may destroy his goal of love and freedom. In the dream, he and the black boy, his fellow conspirator, as it were, are on a boat in the harbor of the island, but soon they drift away from the naked Negro women on the shore and have to watch their island paradise disappear. The natives sing 'Goodbye, Columbus,' the refrain of Ron's college record, as the two of them go, suggesting that they will not possess their dream, their America. The historical parallel is fitting, inasmuch as the real Columbus also became disillusioned in his quest for a better world. Thus Neil is spurred on by his fear that the affair will be over once Brenda returns to Radcliffe, and he begins to contemplate a marriage proposal as a way of securing her for himself. He is, however, afraid to propose since he is not sure of Brenda's reaction and suspects that there are still unresolved issues between them. Instead he decides to ask her to wear a diaphragm both to increase his sexual pleasure and as a symbol of their defiantly intimate relationship out of wedlock.

This diaphragm hardly represents what has been called Neil's dream of a 'classless, creedless hedonism.'[4] It is true that he aims to break down the barriers of class and religious conventions, but hedonism is not a purpose in itself for him, but rather a means by which he affirms his dissenting values and identity. Brenda does not feel mature enough to commit herself to such a deliberate action, but for Neil it is imperative that they are both conscious of what they are doing and that they use the opportunity of their love to define themselves in opposition to the outside pressures that bear upon them. By sustaining their conspiracy, so to speak, they will be changed together and in a direction which Neil finds is right and stimulating. But Brenda rejects the suggestion, making him feel that she also rejects him and what he stands for. The core of the problem is his actual self, which she cannot accommodate herself to.

Neil is offered a new identity, in a manner of speaking, as an employee in Mr. Patimkin's firm, where Ron already works. Mr. Patimkin suggests to Neil that he, too, would be able to learn the business, but the latter recognizes that he is unsuited for such a life. He is not robust enough for the work, but, on the other hand, he is attracted to the neighborhood where the company is located, the black section of Newark that once was peopled by immigrant Jews of his grandparents' generation. This and other parts of Newark are the only locations that Neil feels continuously drawn to throughout the novella. There is an authenticity and vitality in life as it was and as it is lived in these neighborhoods, and the colorful scenes and pungent smells suggest this. The ways of the old Jews as well as those of the blacks of the present are chaotic and poverty-ridden yet more suited to real human needs than the middle-class lifestyle that is replacing them. The old blacks, for example, are not segregated from the community, but are placed in 'screenless windows' where they can watch the throbbing life in the streets. Here, in spite of many problems, there is a freedom and zest for life that Neil appreciates and will not entirely surrender in his own existence either.

Brenda is sufficiently influenced by Neil to finally accede to his request that she obtain a diaphragm. She seems to do this because she wants to act like an adult, but also because she is affected by Ron's marriage and begins to want the same thing for herself. For example, she acquires a new dress which makes her look as attractive as the bride, or even more so. Deep down, it seems, Brenda sees herself in the role that Harriet plays, as a lovely bride with a successful husband, being led to the altar on her father's arm and being protected and cared for by her mother. But for the time being she carries on with Neil Klugman and goes to New York with him to get the diaphragm. For Neil, however, this development is very serious and fraught with consequences. He is both enthusiastic about what he sees as Brenda's affirmation of their rebellious bond and anxious about the responsibilities that lie ahead of him now that their union is about to assume a more permanent aspect.

Neil's uncertainty emerges in his reflections in St. Patrick's Cathedral, where he seeks refuge while Brenda is in the doctor's office: 'Now the doctor is about to wed Brenda to me, and I am not entirely certain that this is all for the best. What is it I love, Lord? Why have I chosen? Who is Brenda?' (p. 71). One crucial question is the first one, concerning the nature of his love. The answer that suggests itself is that Neil loves the possibilities he sees in Brenda, apart from her physical attractiveness, and that he is haunted by a sense that he may be mistaken, that he does not really know her.

Continuing his meditation in the church, Neil adresses God, but his 'prayer' is hardly meant to be serious. In fact, the God he talks to seems to be a pantheistic one

who is present in everything: 'If we meet You at all, God, it's that we're carnal, and acquisitive, and thereby partake of You. I am carnal, and I know You approve. I just know it. But how carnal can I get? I am acquisitive. Where do I turn now in my acquisitiveness? Where do we meet? Which prize is You?' (p. 71).

Neil is hardly a philosophic pantheist, but he makes some good points in this strange inner monologue. If God is identical with a universal process of creation and life, our sexual urges must be manifestations of the divine will. Moreover, if God made us acquisitive, he himself must share that trait in some sense. Neil has no problems with his carnal nature and welcomes it, and he also admits to being acquisitive. He is, however, less certain of the strength of this particular trait in himself and is overwhelmed by the power of the answer that Fifth Avenue gives to his question about the importance of the desire for possessions: 'Which prize do you think, *Schmuck*? Gold dinnerware, sporting-goods trees, nectarines, garbage disposals, bumpless noses, Patimkin Sink, Bonwit Teller' (p. 71).

Neil's concept of God is jocular, but it also embodies his satirical view of religion as an integrated part of the whole bourgeois value system of an acquisitive middle class. To join this class and its gods means joining in the race for wealth and position, and it is here that Neil draws the line as far as he himself is concerned and insists on another self-definition. But he knows that it is difficult to preserve one's identity in the face of society's demands and that it will not be any easier together with Brenda Patimkin. Accordingly, he is momentarily relieved when he sees her coming from the doctor without carrying anything. He thinks that she has broken their agreement, which means that their relationship will be less binding, as he sees it, thus letting him off the hook. However, this relief is only a passing 'levity,' as Neil calls it. He is still committed to Brenda, with or without the diaphragm. But when she tells him that she is actually wearing the device, he is overjoyed and takes it as a sign that she is joining forces with him in their defiance of traditional norms.

But back in the Patimkin house there is no relief for Neil. The wedding of Ron and Harriet offers an array of middle-aged couples that can only serve to confirm Neil's worst expectations of what the Jewish bourgeois lifestyle amounts to. Many of these people are affluent, but they have paid dearly for their success with emotional frustration, physical decay and spiritual emptiness, They are locked into their tradition of hard work, materialism and puritanism coupled with a narrow-minded outlook on everything outside their own circles, and they also suffer from rigid sex roles where the male is the provider and the female the excessively proper housewife. There is no room in their lives for joy, passion or any individualism except mere eccentricity.

Brenda's uncle Leo is the only one who seems to have an inkling of what has happened to him and is aware that only two good things have occurred in his life: finding an apartment in New York and having oral sex with a certain Hannah Schreiber. Otherwise, he has sacrificed all joy and spontaneity as a result of his struggle to survive as a bulb salesman, and his many frustrations have turned into a settled melancholy that is the only emotional content that is left in his life. Neil is touched by the older man's confessions and regards his story as further confirmation that he, Neil, is on the right track in refusing to let his life be controlled by such misery and renunciation. The older generation may have been victims of circumstances, of economic and social necessity, but for modern Jews the situation is different and offers more options.

The end of the novella is ripe with imagery suggesting loss of love as well as of illusions. Leo and his wife leave the wedding, looking like people 'fleeing a captured city' (p. 84), and to Neil, driving on the New Jersey Turnpike, the desolate landscape looks like 'an oversight of God' (p. 84), a phrase that echoes the image of the valley of ashes in *The Great Gatsby*.[5] When Brenda leaves for Boston, 'the wind was blowing the fall in and the branches of the weeping willow were fingering at the Patimkin front lawn' (p. 85). At the library things are also changing, the black boy disappears and Neil is charged with discourtesy by an old gentleman who had wanted to borrow the Gauguin book which Neil had put on reserve, against the regulations, for the boy.

However, by now Neil has also changed his attitude towards his job and his colleagues. He becomes more assertive and sure of himself and invents a story to cover up his manipulations with the book. He is beginning to feel that he belongs in the library as much as the others, but on his own terms and according to his own definition, and he even has Mr. Scapello, the boss, apologizing to him as he is led to his new post and actually receives a promotion. He is aware of the change in himself and half-ironically attributes his new-found strength to the lesson he has learnt in the Patimkin family, where there is a premium on aggressive behavior in the workplace. However, Neil's renewed attachment to the library does not bode well for his relationship with Brenda, who has never shown any appreciation of the job he has chosen for himself and the meaning it may have for him.

The last meeting between Brenda and Neil takes place in a Cambridge hotel where she has reserved a room, pretending that they are married and wearing a fake wedding ring. At this point, Neil, with his strengthened sense of identity as a result of his experiences in the Patimkin family and the library, realizes that he has come to visit her because he wants to ask her to marry him: '. . . it had been long enough. It was time to stop kidding about marriage' (p. 89). Her registering in the hotel also encourages him, since he sees it as a sign that she is getting more liberated and ready to subvert social conventions. However, she tells him that her parents have discovered her diaphragm at home and that she has received two letters from them, an angry one from her mother and a more conciliatory one from her father, who is all too willing to forgive and forget if she will only stop seeing Neil any more. The letters themselves are marvelous examples of the crippling conventionalism in the sexual area on the part of the parents.

Brenda's revelation comes as a shock to Neil, and he feels that her carelessness in leaving the diaphragm indicates her half-conscious wish to prevent their relationship from becoming serious and permanent. She is scared by the prospect, which would force her to take a stand against her parents and risk their enmity. Her decision to take a hotel room with Neil does not suggest any liberation, but rather that she wants him as a casual lover. Again, she indulges in what can be called a pseudo-rebellious act. But Neil is acutely aware of the significance of her forgetting the diaphragm and suspects that this means that they are incompatible. She denies having left it on purpose, and there is no way to prove that this has been the case. However, the fact that she has done it is enough. It clearly reveals her insecurity and insincerity to Neil and makes him desperate, since it suggests that she has never really freed herself from the moral viewpoint of her parents. When he asks her if she thinks that their sleeping together was wrong, she does not answer for herself but refers to her parents' opinion. In other words, she accepts their verdict by refusing to declare herself against it.

Brenda tells Neil that she cannot bring him home for Thanksgiving, once more indicating her compliance with her parents' decisions and attitudes. Without saying so, she seems to agree with them, which is suggested by the 'solid and decisive' (p. 95) look on her face. Her expression reveals the internalized norms that Neil will not stop fighting against, and he tries hard to make Brenda see what she is doing to herself and their relationship. Their dialogue demonstrates the conflict: 'Who can I bring home, Neil? I don't know, who can you? Can I bring you home? "I don't know," I said, "can you?" Stop repeating the question! I sure as hell can't give you the answer.' (p. 95).

Brenda continues to evade responsibility for herself by referring to her family's standards instead of her own opinions, and Neil tries vainly to make her realize that she alone is responsible for what she does with her life, whether she chooses to ally herself with him or not. Neil also suggests that she can stay away from home if she likes, but her only answer is that she has to go home and that 'Families are different' (p. 96). He is forced to conclude that she prefers her family to him and the challenge he represents, and that they have more or less misunderstood each other all along. She complains about his criticism of her, failing to perceive that he was critical because he wanted her to be true to herself instead of to her family. As he sees it, he had offered his opinions because he cared for her.

During this final confrontation the issues between them become clear. Neil declares his willingness to continue the relationship and defy her family, but Brenda chooses the security of the known instead of the uncertainties that she feels that he represents. There is no doubt that Neil is ready to go with Brenda to the Patimkin house for the Thanksgiving feast and defy her parents along with her. To argue that 'To oppose Brenda's parents would have required a decisive commitment which neither is capable or really desirous of making' is to misread the ending of the story.[6] It is only Brenda who shies away from this confrontation. Considering that the story takes place during the fifties, Brenda's choice is understandable, but the fact remains that she puts a stop to a relationship that has a basis in love and that contains the promise of increasing depth and development.

It is likely that Neil would have been accepted by the Patimkins, including Brenda, if he had recanted and followed a path similar to that of Ron, but this is never an option for him. The whole point of the story is to render a protagonist who is determined to retain his own identity and not surrender to outside pressures. It is misleading to interpret Neil mainly as a confused and 'uncoordinated soul' who cannot maintain any sense of selfhood at all and whose life is 'aimless.' Such a view leads to the statement that 'Neil does not know how to be true to himself,' which is the opposite of what the story demonstrates.[7] It is exactly Neil's feeling that he has an inner self that is different and oppositional that makes him act in accordance with his convictions. Both he and Brenda finally realize that there is an unbridgeable gap between them, and he leaves the hotel room, walking into the yard of Harvard University. He stops before the Lamont Library, where he can see himself in a window as if it was a mirror. Frustrated and disappointed as he is, he has an impulse to pick up a rock and throw it through the glass, but instead he gives way to a profound meditation: 'I looked, but the outside of me gave up little information about the inside of me . . . What was it

inside me that had turned pursuit and clutching into love, and then turned it inside out again? What was it that had turned winning into losing, and losing—who knows—into winning? I was sure I had loved Brenda, though standing there, I knew I couldn't any longer' (pp. 96-7).

To become aware of one's real identity, or that of others, is difficult. Ultimately, personal identity is a mystery that can only be partly unveiled, and Neil had felt this also when looking at the sleeping Brenda at the end of the wedding party, wondering if he knew 'no more of her than what I could see in a photograph' (p. 84). But though he admits to a sense of confusion regarding the enigma of his own self, certain answers to his questions do suggest themselves. He has lost Brenda by winning her, since she did not turn out to be what he thought, but by relinquishing, or losing, her, he was won in the only real sense that exists for him, that is, by remaining true to himself.

The final paragraph of the story has a promising ring: 'I did not look very much longer, but took a train that got me into Newark just as the sun was rising on the first day of the Jewish New Year. I was back in plenty of time for work' (p. 97). The image of the rising sun suggests that Neil is doing to make a new start in life, and that Newark, as indicated earlier, is his real home after all. It is not the region associated with the parental generation of Jews, but his own Newark, as it were, a place where he can maintain the self that he has struggled toward during his hectic summer of lovemaking and measuring himself against various temptations and illusions. He returns to the library with a new and greater awareness of its attractions and limitations. It is, after all, an institution where culture, art and dreams are allowed a kind of existence which is impossible in the other environments that he has known, and it is located in a neighborhood that has preserved a certain room for individuality and a measure of freedom. In the library, one must assume that Neil will steer a course of his own, between the pedantry of his colleagues and the anti-social attitudes of the black boy that had spent so much time among the book stacks. If Roth's later novels are anything to go by, it may well be the role of the artist or writer that lies in store for Neil Klugman and which he is preparing for by remaining faithful to his outsider status and to his talent for observing and analysing people and places with such unerring critical accuracy.

Notes

1. Neil Klugman can be seen as a fairly typical example of the third generation, with its 'diminished attachment to Jewish life' and its 'decline' of 'Jewish identification.' Steven M. Cohen, *American Modernity and Jewish Identity* (New York, 1983), p. 60.

2. *Goodbye, Columbus and Five Short Stories* (New York, 1959), p. 6. All citations are from this edition and are given page references in brackets.

3. Norman Leer, 'Escape and Confrontation in the Short Stories of Philip Roth', *Christian Scholar*, 49 (1966), 135-6.

4. Allen Guttman, *The Jewish Writer in America: Assimilation and the Crisis of Identity* (New York, 1971), p. 69.

5. The parallels between 'Goodbye, Columbus' and Fitzgerald's novel are explored in Don Graham, 'The Common Ground of "Goodbye, Columbus" and *The Great Gatsby*', *Forum*, 13 (1976), 68-71.

6. Leer, p. 139.

7. Charles M. Israel, 'The Fractured Hero of Roth's *Goodbye, Columbus*', *Critique: Studies in Modern Fiction*, 16 (1974), 6, 7.

Alan W. France (essay date winter 1988)

SOURCE: France, Alan W. "Roth's 'Goodbye, Columbus' and the Limits of Commodity Culture." *MELUS* 15, no. 4 (winter 1988): 83-89.

[*In the following essay, France discusses Neil Klugman's rejection of the hollowness of the 1950s reification of wealth, status, success, and sexual desire in* "Goodbye, Columbus."]

With growing interest in the historicity of literature and the continuing preoccupation with the 1960s, perhaps it is time to dust off a neglected—if minor—American classic, Philip Roth's novella **"Goodbye, Columbus."** This work occupies the historically anomalous calm at the end of the post-war era but before the student revolt of the following decade. It is thus an excellent introduction to the problems of cultural identity and authenticity at the heart of that revolt, which was a treason not of young Klugmans but of young Patimkins. **"Goodbye, Columbus"** can help today's students see the poverty of a culture idealizing commodity satisfactions, one that continues to bulldoze ethnic and religious traditions to build the shopping malls and entertainment worlds of mass consumption.

Structurally, the plot of **"Goodbye, Columbus"** describes a summer romance between a young, lower-middle-class man and the daughter of a wealthy family recently arrived at upper-middle-class status. Nearly everything in the novella follows directly from this difference in achieved social status.

The setting of the story, first of all, is determined by distinctions of class. Neil Klugman has literally to climb "the hundred and eighty feet that the suburbs rose in altitude above Newark [which] brought one closer to heaven" (18). That is, he must rise out of his home in decaying Newark, New Jersey, to meet with Brenda Patimkin of Short Hills, a suburb already by the later 1950s, having replaced Upper Montclair (home of the snobbish "pug-nosed little bastards" whom Brenda reminded him of [21]) as Essex County's most expensive and thus prestigious bedroom community. The Patimkin family has made the move from Newark to Short Hills permanently, the family business known as Patimkin Sinks having risen on the tide of post-war prosperity.

In the interest of giving his family a better life, Ben Patimkin has bought into the American Dream, erecting a wall of commodity that has cut his family off from their ethnicity and their lower-middle-class roots in Newark. The controlling images of the novella are all directly related, through Neil's perceptions, to the Patimkins' successful struggle to distance themselves from their past, to establish membership in the national, largely gentile, elite.

Refrigerators, those peculiarly American cornucopiae of national abundance, are important emblems of social mobility. Neil's Aunt Gladys is preoccupied with her own refrigerator; her concern to use leftovers efficiently and avoid waste irritates Neil:

> I only hope [he quips caustically] she dies with an empty refrigerator, or otherwise she'll ruin eternity for everyone else, what with her Velveeta turning green, and her navel oranges growing fuzzy jackets down below.
>
> (17)

By contrast, the Patimkins' old Newark refrigerator, transported to Short Hills, has literally borne fruit: "heaped with fruit, shelves swelled with it, every color, every texture" (53). Eating habits also reflect the centrality of consumption in the Patimkins' style of life: Neil is intimidated when he dines for the first time with these "Brobdingnags":

> eating was heavy and methodical and serious . . . sentences [were] lost in the passing of food, the words gurgled into mouthfuls, the syntax chopped and forgotten in heapings, spillings, and gorgings.
>
> (32)

Mr. Patimkin observes that Neil "eats like a bird" (33); and his lack of alimentary gusto suggests his larger inability to join the great banquet of American commodity culture.

Imagery associated with sports also serves to distance the Patimkins from their lower class roots. The family are Yankee fans, first of all. Anyone from the New York metropolitan area old enough to remember the 1950's will perceive at once the social significance of this affinity: the Yankees were the team of success; they had money to buy the best players; and they dominated World Series play in that era. The New York Giants and, even more, the Brooklyn Dodgers ("the Bums") were usually despised by "rich kids." For the Patimkins, Yankee slugger Mickey Mantle is the Messiah, as Brenda jokes: "When the Yankees win, . . . we set an extra place for Mickey Mantle" (29-30).

The Patimkin estate has a basketball court and its trees sprout sporting goods:

> beneath sporting-goods trees . . . like fruit dropped from their limbs, were two irons, a golf ball, a tennis can, a baseball bat, basketball, a first-baseman's glove, and what was apparently a riding crop.
>
> (32)

Brenda is an aggressive tennis player; but significantly, as Neil notes, she will not charge the net when there is any threat to that emblem of upper-class membership, her nose-job. Brother Ron, the hand-pumping Buckeye basketball star, fully subscribes to the American metaphor for economic struggle, athletic competition. But for girls, it is different: Mr. Patimkin uses the basketball court to teach his daughters that "free throws were theirs for the asking" (33). This angers Neil, for whom there are no extra free throws. When he is playing ping pong alone in the cellar with Julie, the youngest Patimkin child, he avenges the privilege that he is forced to accord her in public on the basketball court. In angry petulance at having to play by the rules, Julie accuses Neil of stealing the "fruit," symbolically that fruit of her father's achieved status with which she has learned she can purchase exemption from the rules. She cries, "You Cheat! And you were stealing!" (55). This confrontation brings into relation three patterns of imagery that converge on the social conflict that will ultimately end Neil and Brenda's romance: competition (athletics), mobility (the old refrigerator), and success (fruit).

These three images of the American Dream are brought into focus by the "Goodbye, Columbus" record that Ron Patimkin has brought home with him from Ohio State. Critics have not inquired deeply enough into the significance of the record: it is, after all, the source of the novella's title. Neil refers to the record's narrator as a "Voice, bowel-deep and historic, the kind one associates with documentaries about the rise of Fascism" (114). This Voice of America intones for Ron the verities of the national culture toward which he has been impelled by his father:

> Life calls us, and anxiously if not nervously we walk out into the world and away from the pleasures of these ivied walls. But not from its memories. They will be the concomitant, if not the fundament, of our lives. We shall choose husbands and wives, we shall choose jobs and homes, we shall sire children and grandchildren, but we will not forget you, Ohio State. . . .
>
> (116)

Here we have the great American commodity machine: wives and husbands, work, and homes chosen alike; children "sired" like corn-fed Ohio cattle, living in the bland and faded nostalgia of middle American culture—the America that Ben Patimkin has spent his life buying for his children.

This "Voice of History" mentions "Religious Emphasis Week" and "E. E. Cummings reading to students (verse, silence, applause)," but the real center of interest is competitive athletics. The Voice duly records (in an example of Roth's comic irony) "Ron Patimkin dribbling out. Ron, Number 11, from Short Hills, New Jersey" (115). In fact, Ron's "dribblings" on the job have already been revealed, several pages earlier, during Neil's visit to Patimkin Sinks. Ben expresses a thinly veiled, though patriarchical, contempt for his son's insularity and naivete: "Four years in college he can't unload a truck" (104). Having been acculturated from early childhood into the social elite, the Patimkin children have never learned about the economic struggle by which that elite is supported. In business one must have, Ben tells Neil, "a little of the *gonif* in you," but as he says, of his own children: "They're *goyim*, my kids, that's how much they understand" (105-6). Nevertheless, Mr. Patimkin appears to take considerable pride in having provided the means to isolate his children from the realities of the economic world.

Neil's visit to Patimkin Sinks does in fact reveal a glimpse of the economic underpinnings of class society. The business is located in the Newark ghetto, and Ron's first day on the job is devoted to "directing the Negroes," six of whom are loading trucks with sinks. Driving through the black ghetto, once populated by immigrant Jews, Neil wonder if he might see the black boy who comes to the Newark Public Library to gaze at the volume of Gauguin's dark-skinned South Pacific islanders.

Recently, Barry Gross has observed, of the role of black characters in **"Goodbye, Columbus"** and of Neil's identification with them, that:

> The boy already knows what Neil is yet to learn: that illusion can be destroyed by reality, that it is the very distance which separates the dreamer from the dream that makes the dream worthwhile, that it is the climb up the marble stairs [of the library] to Tahiti that *makes* Tahiti Tahiti.
>
> (Gross 14)

More specifically, the boy's attraction to the idealized, primitive images of Tahitians serves as a central metaphor for Neil's attraction to Brenda and to all that the Patimkins represent for him. The one picture described in the text, "a young brown-skinned maid . . . leaning forward on her knees," elicits from the boy the exclamation, "Man, . . . that's the fuckin life" (47). When Neil tells the boy that Gauguin was white, he smiles and says, "I knew that. He don't *take* pictures like no colored man would. He's a good picture taker" (48).

It is likely that the pictures of naked women a young ghetto boy might be expected to have seen would not be "good"; in other words, they would be, not romanticized images of primitivist art, but raunchy, or clinical, perhaps pornography. Nor is Neil attracted by raw sexuality in his desire for Brenda; he betrays a similar romantic vision of her and her social world. Immediately after his conversation with the black boy, he returns to his seat:

> at the Information Desk thinking about Brenda and reminding myself that that evening I would have to get gas before I started up to Short Hills, which I could see now, in my mind's eye, at dusk, rose-colored, like a Gauguin stream.
>
> (48)

Neil and the young boy each gaze at distorted utopian visions of love. The irony is, as Gross suggests, that Brenda is just as inaccessible to Neil as Gauguin's Tahitian maid is to the ghetto boy. Neither has the power to break out of his subservient position. In Neil's case, the subtle but impermeable barrier of social class makes Brenda more glamorous and desirable but at the same time—as he will discover at the end of the story—ultimately unattainable. The barrier of social reality is like a lens: for the black boy the lens is Gauguin's white-man's eye. For Neil, it is a class system, erected by the dominant (and *goyish*) American commodity culture. His identification with the black boy as a fellow outsider is cemented by the imagery of Neil's dream, the unattainable South Pacific paradise that is seen from the deck of a ship over which neither has any control: it is peopled by "beautiful bare-skinned Negresses" singing "Goodbye, Columbus":

> and though [as Neil relates it] we did not want to go, the little boy and I, the boat was moving and there was nothing we could do about it, and he shouted at me that it was my fault and I shouted that it was his . . . , but we were wasting our breath, for we were further and further from the island, and soon the natives were nothing at all.
>
> (85)

The diaphragm that Neil attempts to impose on Brenda, as the summer draws to a close, is a symbolic attempt to keep the ship of his dreams from drifting out to sea. Both seem to understand its significance as a symbol: by force of will Neil hopes to place his mark of ownership on that limited part of her to which she has given him access. "It would change us," he pleads, but Brenda resists making this commitment to him: "I just don't feel *old* enough for all that equipment. . . . I mean it's so conscious a thing to do" (93).

The exact symbolic nature of the diaphragm becomes clear only later as Neil waits in St. Patrick's Cathedral while Brenda is being fitted for the contraceptive device: "Now the doctor is about to wed Brenda and me" (111), he says during a self-conscious attempt at prayer. The reality of their social differences reasserts itself as soon as Neil leaves the church. His sense of inferiority takes on cosmic proportions, and he identifies God with the emoluments of upper-class commodity culture:

> Gold dinnerware, sporting-goods trees, nectarines, garbage disposals, bumpless noses, Patimkin Sinks, Bonwit Teller—
>
> But damn it, God, that *is* You!
>
> (112)

When Brenda returns to Radcliffe, she leaves behind Neil's one claim on her; and her mother's discovery of the diaphragm leads inexorably to the final break-up of their romance. In separate letters, each parent represents the affair as a violation of a contractual market relationship. Mr. Patimkin assumes that the "mistake" will take care of itself:

> I am willing to forgive and call Buy Gones, Buy Gones, . . . and now that you will be away at school and from him and what you got involved in you will probably do all right I have every faith you will. You have to have faith in your children like in a Business or any serious undertaking. . . .
>
> (139)

Mother Patimkin prefers to call in old debts, complaining:

> you drifted away from your family, even though we sent you to the best schools and gave you the best money could buy. Why you should reward us this way is a question I'll carry with me to my grave.
>
> (141)

Brenda can only choose, ultimately, according to the values that she has grown up with:

> "Neil, you don't understand. They're still my parents. They did send me to the best schools, didn't they? They have given me everything I've wanted, haven't they?"
>
> (145)

Like Daisy Buchanan in *Gatsby,* Brenda must ultimately recognize that self-interest is defined by class interests, which take primacy over romantic inclinations. Love has been reified into commodity. Brenda must affirm her parents' system of value by rejecting Neil's claims on her.

The parting image we have of Neil confirms his status inferiority and the social gulf that separates him from Brenda Patimkin. He has crossed Harvard Yard and is staring at his reflection in a window of the darkened Lamont Library. Examining his image and wishing that he could understand himself, Neil asks: "What was it inside me that turned pursuit and clutching into love, and then turned it inside out again?" (147)

The Lamont Library is, of course, a center of this country's intellectual elite, and the achieved status of Ben Patimkin is represented by the Patimkin sinks in its restrooms: the Patimkins have almost literally become "fixtures" of the American upper-middle-class. Not surprisingly, then, Neil has the impulse to "pick up a rock and heave it through the glass"; instead, he explains, "I simply looked at myself in the mirror the light made of the window. I was only that substance, I thought, those limbs, that face that I saw in front of me" (147). A culturally empty vessel, Neil is nothing more than he sees in the mirror.

With this image we have reached the limits of the post-war reification of wealth, success, status, and sexual desire. For Neil there is no alternative to the hollowness of 1950's commodity culture; he must go back to the Newark Public Library. But the generation that comes after will not bear so quietly its disillusionment with the values of young Patimkins.

Works Cited

Gross, Barry. "American Fiction, Jewish Writers, and Black Characters: The Return of 'The Human Negro' in Philip Roth." *MELUS* 11.2 (1984): 5-22.

Israel, Charles M. "The Fractured Hero of Roth's *Goodbye, Columbus.*" *Critique* 16 (1974): 5-11.

Roth, Philip. *Goodbye, Columbus.* In *Goodbye, Columbus and Five Short Stories.* Cambridge, Mass.: Houghton Mifflin, 1959. 13-148.

Barbara Frey Waxman (essay date 1988)

SOURCE: Waxman, Barbara Frey. "Jewish American Princesses, Their Mothers, and Feminist Psychology: A Rereading of Roth's 'Goodbye, Columbus.'" *Studies in Jewish American Literature* 7 (1988): 90-104.

[In the following essay, Waxman maintains that Roth's depiction of Brenda Patimkin in "Goodbye, Columbus" shows a keen cultural understanding and psychological insight into the phenomenon of the overprotective Jewish mother and her indulged daughter.]

Whether she is enhancing her wardrobe, ensnaring a spouse, decorating her home, planning a bar mitzvah, or ascending the ladder of a corporate law firm, she is identifiable by her daunting self-confidence—even hubris (Tonner 182)—her glamorous appearance, her drive to win, and the arrogant conviction of the perfectionist that nothing but the best will do, both in her own performance and in what is due her. The Jewish American Princess glitters when she walks. She is a fairly new phenomenon in the history of the Jews, emerging a mere seventy or eighty years after the first Jewish immigrants landed in New York. The Jewish American Princess is in stark contrast to her unglamorous pre-America forebears, girls who were raised to be drudges, trained to manage the work of the household and keep the laws of kashruth, and whose status as property was reflected in the dowry by which they enticed prospective husbands (Tonner 17). However, as Leslie Tonner has said, "when Jewish expectation first met the American Dream," the concept of the Jewish American Princess came into existence (19), eventually challenging the traditional position of the firstborn Jewish son as the cynosure of his loving and ambitious parents' eyes. It nevertheless took a generation of adored, hardworking firstborn American sons to acquire the middle-class, upwardly mobile status necessary to elevate the Jewish daughter to this "new American aristocracy of achievement, taste, intelligence and conspicuous consumption" (Sequoia 8). As Anna Sequoia, author of *The Official J.A.P. Handbook,* observed in 1982, "Nothing, absolutely *nothing,* is too good for the child of the self-made man" (47).

References to the Jewish American Princess in popular culture and novels began appearing in the 1950s; Herman Wouk's *Marjorie Morningstar,* whose heroine was an early example of the JAP, was published in 1955. By 1959, with the appearance of Philip Roth's **"Goodbye, Columbus"** and its heroine Brenda Patimkin, whom Sanford Pinsker hails as the "ur-JAP, a Jewish-American Princess, the archetype for Jewish Bitch Goddesses to follow" (266), the JAP was a familiar figure in America, voted by the American public as the female whom they most loved to hate. Of course some JAP researchers claim there were much earlier allusions to the JAP in the Bible—those "daughters of Zion [who] are haughty/And walk with stretched forth necks and wanton eyes" (Isaiah 3 16-26, in Baumgold 31). But more than a hundred years ago, Israel Joseph Benjamin, a Roumanian Jew on tour in America from 1859-62, similarly observed and criticized this Jewish American cultural phenomenon about the daughters of Central European Jewish parents who had already amassed some wealth in America. As reported by Jewish historian Jacob R. Marcus, Benjamin claimed "the education of the Jewish girls here is being neglected . . . for they stop school at fifteen; . . . they start going to balls and dances; they are intent on having a good time. He might also have added [interjects Marcus] they were out looking for husbands. American Jewish girls, he complained, are indulged by their parents"; Marcus then concludes: "From [Benjamin's] description of them, it is obvious that they were the prototypal Jewish American Princesses ('JAP') of the later twentieth century" (60). Newly affluent Central European Jewish immigrants followed the lead of wealthy Gentiles, seeking to fulfill the American Dream "in a country that worshipped success" (Marcus 67); they enabled their daughters to acquire the right wardrobe, secular education and culture to practice all the social amenities, while they offered their sons religious training. The later immigrants, the East European Jews, patterned themselves after their Central European Jewish predecessors (Marcus 182). But what factors besides the Jews' new economic security, which encouraged material indulgence within the American value system, helped to shape this phenomenon of the JAP in American Jewish history?

While Charlotte Baum, Paula Hyman, and Sonya Michel assert that the JAP is formed "by her overwhelming mother and her doting father" (238; cf. Sequoia 12), Baumgold, joined by many others, sees the primary shaping power as the Jewish mother; Baumgold firmly asserts: "A princess is made by only one thing, and that is her mother. Her mother telling her that she is beautiful. Unremittingly, over the years, that she is beautiful; that she is precious, the thing that the man has to earn and deserve" (28). This constant affirmation by the mother helps to establish the JAP's good self-image, her arrogant self-confidence. The Jewish mother's adoration of her daughter is accompanied by her excessive nurturance and guilt-provoking self-sacrifice for her children (Dundes 457, 459), and by a longer period of symbiotic bonding with and supervision of her daughter. This overprotectiveness may stem from the ghetto days of the immigrant Jewish mother, when there were anti-Semitism, poverty, and other unpleasantnesses from which she had to shield her children (Baum 244-45). This hovering mother, when she dwells on prosperous American soil, produces the JAP: "Mothers who overprotect their daughters produce women who expect to be catered to and looked after" (Dundes 461). In return for this overwhelming love, nurturance, indulgence, and protection from the cruel world, the Jewish mother expects from her daughter "eternal loyalty and love" (Dundes 460); the JAP becomes the dutiful, obedient good daughter, or if she does not, she suffers guilt and conflict over her "misconduct." The Jewish mother's love is, thus, not unconditional. Moreover, the Jewish mother's love

may be mixed with some hostility toward her overly demanding children. Beneath this compulsion to feed and indulge her children with the very best is the Jewish mother's own hunger for "the stuff of self and soul, for love and song," and her resentment that this hunger is rarely satisfied, at least in immigrant and first-generation American Jewish mothers (Duncan 28). Hungry mothers may in turn elicit from their children the fear of being devoured (Duncan 28). Such hungers and "helpless rage," Erika Duncan points out, may also be passed down from Jewish mother to Jewish daughter (30), and these feelings combine with her being sheltered and pampered to produce the JAP's acquisitive nature, expectation of being taken care of, and, in stark contrast, her drive to achieve.

Given this combination of positive and negative factors in her upbringing—of parental love, generosity, and affirmation mingled with criticism, resentment, and pressure to achieve in order to gratify parental pride, as well as with longer maternal bonding and an overprotection that encourages childish dependency—it may be surprising that the JAP stereotype is portrayed as so unnervingly self-approving, so well integrated, and so filled with the capacity to achieve and the conviction that she will do so. Why is she not portrayed as more disturbed and paralyzed by her breeding? Of all the popular/folkloric sources I consulted that deal specifically with the JAP stereotype, only Baumgold suggests, somewhat compassionately, that under the JAP's insufferable arrogance, "she is a thin tissue away from hysteria," that she has moments when her self-confidence fails her and guilt assails her because she is unable to be all that her parents expect her to be: "The princess is never as great as she'd been told. . . . And if she was moderately aware, she knew it. . . . She thought she had put something over on her parents" (28). That Baumgold's psychological assessment of the JAP's ego strength *and* insecurity is accurate in its challenging of some stereotypical assumptions about JAPs becomes even clearer when we reexamine Philip Roth's Brenda Patimkin and her mother, using recent concepts and theories garnered from progressive psychoanalyst Alice Miller and feminist psychologists Nancy Chodorow, Carol Gilligan, and Lucy Rose Fischer. This reexamination will enable readers to reassess Roth's JAP in the following ways: to understand some psychological factors behind the negative presentation of the JAP by the narrator Neil Klugman—the "dethroned Jewish Prince" and Brenda's lover—and, hence, to regard Brenda's character from a new angle; to move beyond criticism of the JAP's "selfishness" and "bossiness" in order to acquire more sympathetic insight into Brenda and more understanding of Mrs. Patimkin's conduct in promoting her JAP daughter's egocentrism and expectation of accommodation; to see the symbiotic relationship between Jewish mother and daughter as not really divergent from the mainstream American mother-daughter connection, as not really "neurotic," and even as salutary if the connection is maintained lovingly.

Roth's skill as a thoughtful armchair psychologist emerges in his hero's depiction of Brenda and her mother. Through Neil's narrative, Roth subtly exposes his hero's discomfort with Jewish mothers and daughters and his self-defensive, stereotypically negative thinking about them, thinking that works to "preserve the dualism [in which males are idealistic, females are materialistic] by projecting all materialistic desires onto women, and by locating the roots of ambivalence in them, rather than in men themselves" (Baum 253-54). To Neil, Brenda is, from the beginning, the materialistic JAP who displays all the salient gilded qualities of the type. She is characteristically vain about her attractiveness and its enhancement through rhinoplasty, hallmark of the JAP's penchant for perfection and of her desire to assimilate into American culture by rejecting the image of Jewish woman as *bubbe*. She has been born into wealth and raised to have a taste for luxury and status in her apparel and mode of living. This upbringing also cultivates in her not only a passion for games, but a need to win them and to be admired as a winner. Klugman wryly observes that her "passion for winning a point" in tennis seems outmatched only by a "stronger passion for maintaining her beauty . . ." (7). Readers can observe an even more pronounced penchant in her younger sister Julie, the JAP-in-training for whom her entire family constantly bends the rules of tennis—and probably the rules of the game of life—to "let her win." The drive to win is encouraged from an early age in the Patimkin family, and the expectation of winning is instilled in them in their sheltered environment where the harsh rules of the game of life have been eased.

If Neil complains, however, about his princess's petulant expectation of winning at the cost of his losing, readers have reason to suspect Neil's own Jewish Princely nature, as Sanford Pinsker has observed: ". . . Neil is at least Brenda's match where being 'spoiled' is concerned" (266). Thus Neil is a bit of a sore loser as he endures Brenda's winning streak. Neil's background may not be the gilded one Brenda enjoyed, but he, the adored Jewish son, has been catered to by his parents and resents being ignored in the wake of Brenda's victories. He also seems somewhat envious of Brenda's family's sheltered Short Hills affluence, defensively bristling at Brenda's slighting references to their Newark past, which is still Neil's present. Readers need to bear in mind that all of the qualities depicted in Brenda have passed through the filter of Neil's sensibilities, values, and assumptions

concerning his place in the Jewish social universe. This is not to say that he has misperceived or misrepresented Brenda's penchant for winning and her family's attitude toward it. Yet, however accurate his observations are, he is nevertheless looking at Brenda and her family through a somewhat invidious eye.

In contrast to Neil, psychoanalyst Alice Miller might label Brenda's compulsion to win, her desire to "excel brilliantly in everything . . . she undertakes," as characteristic of grandiosity, a character trait symptomatic of a "narcissistic disturbance," actually a "defense against the real pain over the loss of self" (38). Her core of self may have been lost in her childhood due to certain problems in her relationship with her mother, unfolding a characteristic pattern of interaction between JAPs and their mothers. As Miller would see it, Brenda is unable "to give up symbiosis with the mother and accomplish steps toward individuation and autonomy" because her mother does not show "respect and tolerance for her feelings"; such respect and tolerance are essential "for a healthy narcissism" (7, 10). Thus, despite a thin veneer of self-love or self-confidence, Brenda, perhaps like other JAPs, may not like herself, may not have a healthy self-image, may not have much of a self-image at all, except as reflected in the approving or disapproving eyes of others. Her lack of self-regard and the tacit discontent of her mother may be seen in the Patimkins' desire to obtain plastic surgery for Brenda's nose. That her feelings might have been hurt by her parents' wish to improve on her appearance was probably not considered by the Patimkins. There are additional, more overt, instances of her mother's disapproval of Brenda and discounting of her feelings, too.

For example, Mrs. Patimkin denounces Brenda's aversion to work, which logically accompanies her passion for play. Her mother complains of Brenda's laziness and her attitude that the world owes her a living, that life is all take and no give (46). Of course Brenda has been raised from early childhood to believe the world owes her cashmere sweaters, a straight nose, and points in tennis, so the development of her acquisitiveness is not surprising. As Neil describes it, "life . . . [is] a gathering in . . . for Brenda" (23). While such acquisitiveness is not presented as a positive trait by Neil—nor would it be by many others—readers can see its operation in Brenda more sympathetically by realizing that, for one thing, Neil, still working hard to make it out of Newark into the Promised Land of the affluent New Jersey suburbs, is envious of Brenda's luxurious life, angry that he still lives in Newark (9); and two, that Brenda's passion for acquisition may be a compensation for what she does not receive from her mother: unequivocal, nonjudgmental love. Brenda's mother would love and praise Brenda if she worked harder and demanded fewer cashmere sweaters, instead of loving and approving of her simply because she is Brenda.

Mrs. Patimkin seems to resent Brenda and her taste for luxury, even though she and her husband have cultivated this taste in Brenda, precisely because her daughter has never had to endure the background of poverty that she herself did as a girl in Newark. Mrs. Patimkin values the money her husband has earned because of her own impoverished childhood, but Brenda, having grown up in affluence, seems too cavalier about money, too insensitive to the world's poverty and hardships. Her mother's background of economic insecurity has made her fiscally very conservative and wary of spending indulgently on herself while Brenda's affluent childhood has made her comfortable with spending money on herself, with enjoying money. She dismisses her mother's view of economics, her careful bargain-hunting and wise investing, by declaring that "'money is a waste for her [mother]. She doesn't even know how to enjoy it'" (18). Brenda resentfully perceives her mother's tight view of money, which extends to her outlook on life, as a withholding of affection for and approval of her daughter. It is no wonder, then, that mother and daughter lock horns over "every cashmere sweater" (18), as if each sweater represented not only shelter from the world's hardships, but also the ungenerous doling out of affection. Money becomes a painful substitute for affection, as reflected in Mrs. Patimkin's defense of her fine parenting, "'. . . we sent you to the best schools and gave you the best money could buy'" (92).

Readers can better understand the damaging effects of such expressions of Jewish maternal love by contrasting it to the love of a Jewish mother like Eva in Tillie Olsen's "Tell Me a Riddle." Eva raised her children in a completely self-sacrificing, all-consuming way. She moved "to the rhythms of others" (85), completely driven by fierce primal maternal impulses which Olsen's fire and flood images aptly convey: "The love—the passion of tending—had risen with the need like a torrent; and like a torrent drowned and immolated all else . . . the drowning into needing and being needed" (95-96). Her intense emotional involvement in raising her children contrasts with the more sophisticated and emotionally controlled, calculating involvement of Mrs. Patimkin. This torrent of unreserved, nonjudgmental love successfully carries Eva's children "to their own lives" (96). Unlike Mrs. Patimkin, Eva does not dominate her children, does not dictate how her children should act, probably because she "does not expect to have her needs for achievement or her needs for 'narcissistic gratification' . . . met through the accomplishments of . . . her children" (Bart 139). Her

children can comfortably be themselves and achieve independence, unlike Brenda, who must constantly strive to obtain her mother's approval by trying to be what her mother wants her to be.

Perhaps because she herself was such a private woman, or because she was so busy with the emotional and economic pressures of managing the household, Eva never pried into the lives of her children, never preached to them or declared what kind of people she expected them to be. On her mother's deathbed, then, Clara, the eldest, may reproach her mother for becoming increasingly remote from her over the years: "'*Where did we lose each other? . . . I do not know you, Mother. Mother, I never knew you*'" (111). And Clara's siblings may realize with regret and even alarm, that it is "too late to ask: . . . what did you learn with your living, Mother, and what do we need to know?" (111). Yet, more than Brenda Patimkin, they can function without their mother's protection and instruction. They can really figure out for themselves what they need to know and what values they need to have to lead their lives fully and richly. Eva's son Lennie pays tribute to her ultimate success as a mother, although his tribute seems tinged with regret that her mothering might have prevented her own full self-development, a "martyrdom with no payoff" (Bart 131): "Lennie, suffering not alone for her who was dying, but for that in her which never lived . . . From him, too, unspoken words: *Good-by Mother who taught me to mother myself*" (112). Lennie's farewell suggests that Eva never unduly sheltered her children; of necessity, she made them fend for themselves physically and emotionally, always involving them in running the struggling household, unlike Mrs. Patimkin, who had no struggling household as a backdrop for her children's early years. Eva taught her children how to treat themselves maternally, to think of themselves with kindness and pride, to be self-motivating and self-nurturing, and she enabled them to do so through her unreserved, passionate love for them. Her gifts to her children are surely more nurturing and stabilizing than those Brenda receives: merely "the best that money can buy."

Neil would probably approve of Eva's unstinting, unquantifiable love. He sees Mrs. Patimkin, in contrast, as a servant catering to the spoiled, regal Brenda, but he notes that she is a somewhat resentful catering mother, like "a captive beauty, some wild princess, who had been tamed and made servant to the king's daughter—who was Brenda" (15); this "deposed" Jewish Prince is not fond of his JAP girlfriend's mother (15). His view of Mrs. Patimkin's position with her daughter reflects his own first interaction with Brenda, during which he also caters to her, holding her glasses "as momentary servant" (10) while she takes a swim.

Brenda also divines Mrs. Patimkin's resentment and is unable to feel any of her mother's ministrations as affectionate to herself; she sees her catering, instead, to sister Julie and ignoring her: "'I can't even think of her as my mother. She hates me. Other girls, when they pack in September, at least their mothers help them. Not mine. She'll be busy sharpening pencils for Julie's pencil box while I'm carrying my trunk around upstairs'" (18). Clearly, Brenda does not consider in this observation that Julie is only ten and needs more maternal help than she herself should. She continually complains that her mother never serves her needs, even though these needs should be diminishing as Brenda matures, and that Mrs. Patimkin never gives her anything she wants, acting indifferent to what her daughter's wants are. Brenda claims that Mrs. Patimkin's withholding of "everything" valued by her daughter is due to her rivalry with Brenda, and her jealousy of Brenda's youth, attractiveness, and prowess in tennis. Yet despite her surface confidence, Brenda may not be so sure she could win in this rivalry, never having received essential approval from her mother. Thus, her criticism and resentment of Mrs. Patimkin may be a defense against "her feeling of inadequacy in rivalry with [her mother]"; even more significantly, it may be a defense against her "narcissistic rage" because her mother "is not completely available" to her and because her mother "rejected some parts of . . . [her]self" (Miller 103, 108). Brenda's pain at this maternal neglect and rejection contributes to her wounded self-image and to her overall immaturity.

Brenda's immaturity, or at least Neil's conception of it, is most patent in her childish craving to stay attached to her mother, despite her ongoing anger and sense of emotional deprivation. Her yearning to reattach the umbilical cord, to reestablish the symbiotic relationship, is revealed when her brother Ron's fiancée Harriet visits: "Harriet appeared and Brenda's mother lifted one wing and pulled the girl in towards the warm underpart of her body, where Brenda herself would have liked to nestle" (59). Her desire for reunion with her mother, for her mother's warmth and protection, is well described through this evocative bird imagery Mrs. Patimkin is the mother hen and Brenda is her outcast chick.

This language clearly reveals that Neil finds Brenda's feelings childishly inappropriate for a college girl, that he thinks she should be glad that "'with that goody-good Harriet around she'll just forget I [Brenda] ever exist'" (47). However, his characterization of Brenda's feelings for her mother as atypical and neurotic and his lack of sympathy with Brenda's desire for a close relationship with her mother reflect his limited understanding of women, stemming from his male perspective and male mode of interaction with his mother, especially the typically early detachment from his mother, which contrasts with females' sustained relationships, of extended symbiosis with their mothers. In her groundbreaking book *The Reproduction of Mothering*, Nancy Chodorow elaborates on the function of gender in interactions between mother and child and the different stages at which daughters and sons separate from their mothers to develop their own identity. While the preoedipal attachment of son to mother enables the son to develop his differentness from the mother (since he is male), the daughter's attachment to the mother does not encourage the growth of her separate identity. Mothers also tend to identify more and for a longer period with their daughters. Thus symbiosis between mother and daughter continues through adolescence, with the daughter's ego boundaries not firmly established, as the son's are. Chodorow says: "Because of their mothering by women, girls come to experience themselves as less separate than boys, as having more permeable ego boundaries. Girls come to define themselves more in relation to others" (93). Chodorow's analysis of mother-daughter interaction suggests that Brenda's desire to be taken under her mother's wing is entirely normal. Even in the oedipal stage during adolescence, while the female is turning toward her father and becoming heterosexual, the adolescent girl remains close to her mother, "reseeking . . . her mother as a safe and familiar refuge against her father's frustrating and frightening aspects" (Chodorow 129, 140). What may frighten the daughter in adolescence are the sexual aspects of the father and of her male peers, a fear which is displayed by Brenda in her relationship with Neil when she declares her unreadiness for the sexual equipment of a diaphragm. Again, Neil rather unsympathetically conveys his sense of Brenda's limited passions, failing to understand how her symbiosis with her mother interferes with her sexual expression and sexual identity. She cannot move beyond such symbiosis into sexual maturity and autonomy because her mother has not provided her with the consistent emotional refuge she needs, instead threatening continuously to assault her ego with disapproval. The emotional refuge and identification between mother and daughter can provide "rich, various and vital sources of feminine selfhood" (Kahn 76), which Brenda has been denied at least intermittently. Thus, because her primal trust in her mother had been undermined, Brenda experiences not only the usual identity definition problems which Chodorow observes in most adolescent females, but additional frustration and resentment, impairing her ability to establish her own identity.

Clearly, Neil, as a male, phallocentrically sees separation from the mother as a simple, positive goal; he says only half facetiously to Brenda: "'In high school we had to run a mile every month. So we wouldn't be Momma's boys. I think the bigger your lungs get the more you're supposed to hate your mother'" (50). Desiring dissociation from his mother, he cannot appreciate either the positive elements of daughters' symbiosis with their mothers, or their conflict over attachment versus separation; he cannot fathom that because girls do not reject their mothers unequivocally as males do, they "remain in a bisexual triangle throughout childhood and into puberty . . . [and they] retain an internal emotional triangle," so that they must resolve their oedipal attachments to both mother and father (Chodorow 193). In fact, in her recent study of adult daughters and their mothers, feminist psychologist Lucy Rose Fischer extends this timetable of mother-daughter attachment even further, offering evidence that "adult children continue to seek their parents' approval. . . . Daughters, until at least age forty or so, often sustain some sense of child position in their relationships with their mothers"; moreover, good relationships between mothers and adult daughters exist if the mothers show approval and nurture their daughters (9). If the mothers withhold praise, the adult daughters invariably suffer a lack of self-esteem (Fischer 27). Thus, Neil's denunciation of Brenda as uncommonly immature in looking to her mother for approval and protection in order to shape her own identity is simplistic, unsympathetic, inaccurate, and unfair to Brenda. On the contrary, as feminist psychologist Carol Gilligan says in her important book *In a Different Voice,* "women depict ongoing attachment as the path that leads to maturity," and they define the notion of identity as including "the experience of interconnection" (170, 173). Brenda can thus mature and become more herself through continuing closeness with her mother, if her mother would permit and encourage such intimacy. She is not abnormal in her yearning for interconnection with her mother: for most daughters, "it is the stability of their mothers' attachment to them that allows them to go through the process of separation and develop a sense of independence" (Fischer 24). As careful feminist readers of Roth's story, we need to be aware of these gender issues, how they influence Brenda's behavior and how they color Neil's presentation of Brenda vis-à-vis her mother. Critic Coppelia Kahn has rightly reminded us that "part of our task as feminist critics is to suggest that gray, shadowy region of identification, particularly male identification with the mother [accompanied by 'matrophobia' or fear of becoming like one's mother], and trace its influence on perceptions and depictions of women in patriarchal texts" (79, 88). If we do as Kahn suggests, then Brenda Patimkin becomes more "normal" and a more sympathetic character in her interaction with her mother; Mrs. Patimkin's criticism of Brenda appears more hurtful and damaging; and Neil's own ambivalence toward mothers and their daughters becomes more apparent.

Given this normal attachment between mother and daughter, young women, Gilligan points out, are often in conflict "between personal integrity and loyalty in family relationships"; hence, their desire to avoid hurting their families often results in choices that stymie their self-development (Gilligan 138). This conflict is increasingly apparent in Brenda as her relationship with Neil deepens and she must make some choices between him and her parents, between what Neil demands of her and the kind of behavior her parents expect from her. Early in her relationship with Neil, this conflict in Brenda and the fragility of her own identity are masked by a grandiosity and a superficial self-confidence which encourage her to seek most of the limelight in their interactions (Miller 38); Neil says she rarely asks him any questions about himself and his own feelings (35). In her troubled egocentricity or her "narcissistic disturbance" (Miller 38), Brenda appreciates Neil more as he begins to reflect her; Neil interprets her words about their resembling each other as follows: "She meant, I was sure, that I was somehow beginning to look the way she wanted me to. Like herself" (50). Having a fragile, incompletely formed ego, Brenda needs such a reflection and affirmation of her self through Neil. Her apparently self-confident conviction that Neil will eventually come to love her (37) also reveals her underlying need to be loved and her attempt to convince herself and Neil of her lovableness. Her mother has not convinced Brenda of her endearing qualities, which is why in her conflict over Neil versus her mother, Brenda instinctively moves toward her mother, still seeking Mrs. Patimkin's affirmation of her lovableness.

Brenda is unaware of her own endearing qualities because she is seriously lacking in self-knowledge. Neil describes "the high walls of ego that rose, buttresses and all, between her and her knowledge of herself" (13). Brenda refuses to face up to imperfections in her personality, to feel the pain of being inadequate, perhaps because she fears further loss of her parents' love if she acknowledges her own flaws. Her own impulse toward perfectionism, like her mother's, surely magnifies these flaws (Miller 45). So she doggedly resists self-analysis, will not examine the motives for her own conduct, either in her relationship with Neil or in her interactions with her parents. She, for example, has no idea where her fierce anger at her mother originates and simply attributes to her mother jealousy and vindictiveness in their ongoing battles. She also does not understand her reaction of fear concerning her own sexuality and her desire to retreat to the safety of childhood's maternal protection when Neil raises the subject of her obtaining the diaphragm. When Neil, trying to counter her objections, suggests that "'we're not children,'" she replies, "'I just don't feel old enough for all that equipment'" (58). Furthermore, Brenda does not consider herself "old enough" to have strong feelings for a man. Neil describes her subdued passion for him through several vivid images. He notes, for example, her "cold wetness," which makes him shiver (38). And during the scene where they kiss for the first time, Neil observes in Brenda only a "faint fluttering . . . like . . . tiny wings" (10). The wings of Brenda's passion may be small, or stunted, because she would rather be kept under the warm, safe wing of the mother hen, Mrs. Patimkin, than let the wings of her own passion take off after Neil. She is manifesting the conflict observed by Gilligan in most young women between loyalty to her mother and the need for her approval on the one hand, and, on the other hand, the urge to gratify her own desires and to seek a mature heterosexual relationship that would help her to develop her own identity.

Brenda's decision to obtain a diaphragm and its negative consequences when her mother discovers it bring out the intense nature of Brenda's conflict over Neil and her mother. In addition, Neil's contention that Brenda left the diaphragm home purposely so that Mrs. Patimkin could find it may be accurate: it is Brenda's only way to resolve her conflict between loyalty to her mother and allegiance to herself. Mrs. Patimkin's withholding of unreserved affection and approval from her daughter, a withholding that has prevented Brenda from acquiring a healthy narcissism and autonomy (Miller 7, 10), is evident as she indignantly scolds Brenda for "rewarding" her parents for all they have given her with the "wanton" behavior that she associates with possession of a diaphragm (92). Having been sheltered, pampered, and disapproved of, Brenda is incapable of thinking for herself in this situation. She is still dependent on her parents' value system and still hungry for their approval, especially her mother's. Hence, her guilt at owning a diaphragm is overwhelming. Moreover, the fact of her sexual activity is now known to Mrs. Patimkin, which widens further the distance between them. As Fischer points out, the daughter's usual silence about her sexual activity commonly serves "as a strategy for maintaining continuity in the mother-daughter relationship" and also for maintaining "their parent-child hierarchy" (43-44), this strategy is no longer available to Brenda and her mother. Mrs. Patimkin seems unwilling to accept Brenda's sexual maturity and would like to keep her in the obedient child role, symbolically to regain maternal possession of her daughter's

body (Chodorow 109-110), but the diaphragm's presence will not let her. Her disapproval of Brenda's sexual activity makes Brenda feel negative about her sexuality, unsure about her own identity, and stricken with guilt. She is still willing to accept their construction of her behavior as moral error, willing to merge her identity in theirs. As Gilligan explains, a daughter may suspend "her own interpretation of a morality of responsibility, and suspending her interpretations, she suspends herself" (143).

That Brenda has put her self in abeyance is clear in her final dialogue with Neil, "'How can I face them!/ 'Why can't you face them? Did you do anything wrong?'/'Neil, *they* think it's wrong. They're my parents.'/'But do you think it's wrong—'/'That doesn't *matter*'" (94). Brenda self-effacingly dismisses her own moral beliefs—if she can articulate any—as inconsequential in this family crisis. Only what her parents believe is important to Brenda, and for Mrs. Patimkin, premarital sex is so morally offensive that even mentioning the diaphragm in her letter to her daughter would "degrade [both] of us" (92). As Miller would explain it, Brenda has been unable to discover her true self, including her own value system, because she has been compelled to accommodate herself to "parental needs, . . . to represent [her mother's own] ethical attitudes" (12, 33).

Given these conflicting choices between Neil and her parents, then, Brenda's resolution is to reject Neil and "reward" her parents with an obedience that includes adherence to their moral code, to reward them because they raised her as a JAP. Her own words to Neil tellingly echo her mother's letter to her, and the two passages are worth comparing. Mrs. Patimkin writes, "'I don't know what we ever did that you should reward us this way. We gave you a nice home and all the love and respect a child needs . . . but you drifted away from your family, even though we sent you to the best schools and gave you the best money could buy'" (92). And Brenda replies to Neil's statement that she does not have to choose between bringing him or bringing her roommate home for Thanksgiving, she can choose not to go home: "'They did send me to the best schools, didn't they? They have given me everything I've wanted, haven't they? . . . Then how can I not go home? I *have* to go home'" (95-96). In both passages, the parents' economic "investments" in Brenda take precedence over expressions of affection and concern, and yet Brenda suspends her angry, bitter questioning of her mother's cold interaction and suspends her own search for autonomy, declaring loyalty to her family—like so many of the young women Gilligan observed universally. The shelter of home and the lure of that elusive parental approval draw Brenda more strongly than the chance of a mature relationship with Neil. She simply cannot face a future without her parents' protection and favor. Her parents have molded the classic JAP. They have overindulged and overprotected Brenda. But most important, the affection Mrs. Patimkin has bestowed on her daughter has been provisional, tied to the expectation that she will be the kind of person Mrs. Patimkin wants her to be. Brenda, then, undergoes quite a self-sacrifice; she feels compelled to gratify her "parents' unconscious needs at the cost of . . . [her] own self-realization" (Miller 22).

Thus, Brenda, caught between her parents and Neil and losing her self in the conflict, may become an object of sympathy for the reader, if the reader moves beyond Neil's disparaging characterization of her as an immature, spoiled JAP who is too dependent on her parents materially and emotionally, and instead sees this triangle as a normal, prevalent, and wrenching one for most young women. Neil Klugman has "lost" to the Patimkins in this contest for Brenda, and his description of her and their affair may very well reflect the "sour grapes" attitude of a disappointed Jewish Prince, as well as his ambivalence about his separation from his own Jewish mother, who is "safely" distant from her son in Arizona. In fact, through Neil's rancor toward Brenda and the Patimkins, Roth himself may be attempting, like many male Jewish writers in the 1960s, "to detach [himself] from [the Jewish Mother's] values and expectations" (Bienstock 185). Neil's negative portrait of Brenda as JAP and of Mrs. Patimkin as Jewish Mother may, then, derive at least in part from his "unadulterated male misogynistic hostility" (Dundes 471), which he also displays in a more overt, though facetious, way toward his Aunt Gladys, with whom he has lived in Newark since his mother's departure. Subconsciously, Neil may seek detachment from Brenda and Mrs. Patimkin as he does consciously from the sincerely maternal, clutching mother hen, Aunt Gladys.

Even Neil's parting words to the reader about Brenda, while they express his love for her, are less than completely appreciative of her as a person: "I was sure I had loved Brenda, though . . . I knew I couldn't any longer. . . . If she had only been slightly *not* Brenda, but then would I have loved her?" (97). Neil Klugman in some respects turns out to be unnervingly like Mrs. Patimkin, trying, in order to satisfy his own needs, to turn Brenda into something she is not, or to prevent her from becoming what she can be. And Brenda Patimkin turns out to be less the arrogant and confident "Jewish Bitch Goddess" than the vulnerable young Jewish woman, yearning for autonomy and integrity while struggling to reclaim a place in her uncharitable mother's heart.

Works Cited

Bart, Pauline. "Portnoy's Mother's Complaint: Depression in Middle Aged Women." *Response: The Jewish Woman/An Anthology* 18 (Summer 1973): 131-39.

Baum, Charlotte, Paula Hyman, and Sonya Michel. *The Jewish Woman in America.* New York: The Dial Press, 1976.

Baumgold, Julie. "The Persistence of the Jewish-American Princess." *New York* 4, 12, (22 March 1971): 25-31.

Bienstock, Beverly Gray. "The Changing Image of the American Jewish Mother." *Changing Images of the Family.* Ed. Virginia Tufte and Barbara Myerhoff. New Haven and London: Yale UP, 1979. 173-91.

Chodorow, Nancy. *The Reproduction of Mothering: Psychoanalysis and the Sociology of Gender.* Berkeley: U of California P, 1978.

Duncan, Erika. "The Hungry Jewish Mother." *On Being a Jewish Feminist.* Ed. Susannah Heschel. New York: Schocken Books, 1983. 27-39.

Dundes, Alan. "The J.A.P. and the J.A.M. in American Jokelore." *Journal of American Folklore* 98, 390 (1985): 456-75.

Fischer, Lucy Rose. *Linked Lives: Adult Daughters and Their Mothers.* New York: Harper, 1986.

Gilligan, Carol. *In a Different Voice: Psychological Theory and Women's Development.* Cambridge and London: Harvard UP, 1982.

Kahn, Coppelia. "The Hand That Rocks the Cradle: Recent Gender Theories and Their Implications." *The (M)Other Tongue: Essays in Feminist Psychoanalytic Interpretation.* Eds. Shirley Nelson Garner, Claire Kahane, and Madelon Sprengnether. Ithaca: Cornell UP, 1985. 72-88.

Marcus, Jacob R. *The American Jewish Woman, 1654-1980.* New York and Cincinnati: KTAV, 1981.

Miller, Alice. *Prisoners of Childhood.* New York: Basic, 1981.

Olsen, Tillie. "Tell Me a Riddle." *Jewish-American Stories.* Ed. Irving Howe. New York: Mentor Books, 1977. 82-117.

Pinsker, Sanford. "Philip Roth." *Dictionary of Literary Biography 28: Twentieth-Century American-Jewish Fiction Writers.* Ed. Daniel Walden. Detroit: Bruccoli Clark, Gale, 1984. 264-75.

Roth, Philip. "Goodbye, Columbus." New York and London: Bantam, 1959.

Sequoia, Anna. *The Official J.A.P. Handbook.* New York: NAL, 1982.

Tonner, Leslie. *Nothing But the Best: The Luck of the Jewish Princess.* New York: Coward, McCann and Geoghegan, 1975.

Wouk, Herman. *Marjorie Morningstar.* Garden City, N.Y.: Doubleday, 1955.

Sol Gittelman (essay date fall 1989)

SOURCE: Gittelman, Sol. "The Pecks of Woodenton, Long Island, Thirty Years Later: Another Look at 'Eli, the Fanatic.'" *Studies in American Jewish Literature* 8, no. 2 (fall 1989): 138-42.

[*In the following essay, Gittelman argues that in "Eli, the Fanatic" Roth "made his benchmark" on what it means to be a Jew and that the author's insights into the complexities of the Jewish-American identity still ring true thirty years later.*]

"Eli, the Fanatic" first appeared in the pages of *Commentary* in 1959, the same year that Philip Roth brought forward the collection of short stories under the title of one, **"Goodbye, Columbus."** Much has happened since then to Philip Roth.

What has he *not* been called? Self-hating Jew, marginal Jew, anti-Semite, revealer and concealer—will the real Philip Roth please stand up! Or, if not, let Nathan Zuckerman, after confessional novels and autobiographical conversations with himself, come forward to tell us: what does Philip Roth stand for as a Jew?

Nothing written by Roth over the past thirty years has helped to locate and to identify the "real" Roth. As he grew older, he remained somewhat of the outsider in both the American and Jewish context. Roth sought literary bridges with writers in Eastern Europe, tried to find peace of mind in Zuckerman's carnal hopes, and now, as he approaches the age of sixty, Roth appears—at least according to some of his admirers—to have found in Israel his final anchor as a Jew (Solotaroff 1). My view, however, is that thirty years ago a younger Roth had laid out clearly his value system as a Jew, and although he might have wandered and explored in the intervening decades, what now seems to be a final phase of his "Bildung" is really no more than the closing of a loop which he had started to form in what still may be his finest work of short fiction, **"Eli, the Fanatic."**

In rereading the story, one is astonished to see how the twenty-seven-year-old Roth came right to the heart of Jewish marginality so soon after the Holocaust. Roth's pen bears the anger of a Sholem Asch and the irony of a Sholom Aleichem as it describes the tribulations of a New World *nogid,* the culmination of the postwar American dream in suburbia. Eli Peck is a successful New York lawyer. His partners are Lewis & McDonnell. He lives in Woodenton, Long Island, has a home near Coach House Road in a town where the local supermarket has a colonial design. Since the war Jews have been able to buy in Woodenton by giving up "some of their more extreme practices in order not to threaten or offend" (189). There is no synagogue in town, no *shul* or community activity which brings the Jews together. That would be offensive to the town's fathers who have permitted the Jews to move in, as long as they don't look or act Jewish. And what has this compromise brought Eli? A couple of nervous breakdowns. For the Jews of Woodenton, there is no Torah, and, as far as Roth is concerned, no peace of mind.

But, whatever tentative stability exists for the Jews of Woodenton disappears in the shock of seeing a Hassid walking the streets! With long black caftan, broad-brimmed hat, and tieless white shirt, an apparition from the *shtetl* has appeared in suburbia. The Jews of Woodenton go crazy and run to their lawyer, Eli Peck. It seems that eighteen Jewish children, with a rabbi named Tzuref and a Hassid, have taken over the venerably Protestant Puddington Mansion and have proclaimed "The Yeshivah of Woodenton":

> "Eli, a regular greenhorn," Ted Heller had said. "He didn't say a word, just handed me the note and just stood there, like in the Bronx the old guys who tried to come around selling Hebrew trinkets."
>
> "A Yeshivah!" Artie Berg had said, "Eli, in Woodenton, a Yeshivah! If I wanted to live in Brownsville, Eli, I'd live in Brownsville."
>
> "Eli," Harry Shaw speaking now, "the old Puddington place. Old Man Puddington'll roll over in his grave. Eli, when I left the city, Eli, I didn't plan the city should come to me."
>
> **("Eli, the Fanatic"** 184)

Another note sent to the supermarket turns the Jews of Woodenton to action: "Dear Grocer: Please give this gentleman ten pounds of sugar. Charge it to our account, Yeshivah of Woodenton, NY—which we will now open with you and expect a bill each month. The gentleman will be in to see you once or twice a week. L. Tzuref, Director (5/10/48) P.S. Do you carry kosher meat?" It should be noted that four days later the state of Israel the proclaimed.

But, in Woodenton, the Jews are only interested in ridding themselves of this reminder of their past, and Eli Peck, neurotic, unhappy, and burdened with a guilt he does not understand, is sent to the Yeshivah as emissary, to end the offensive sight of eighteen Jewish orphans and their teachers. The assimilated Jews of Woodenton want no part of Jewish memory in their midst. The fragile paradise has been disrupted, the Holocaust has come to Long Island and the figure of the Hassid walking down Coach House Road has enraged them. But Eli is troubled, and makes a decision: the black outfit offends, not the wearer. If he can get the Jew to dress like everyone else, perhaps Eli's neighbors will accept him. The conversation between Eli and Rabbi Tzuref reveals that Eli cannot forget. Eli tells the rabbi that the Hassidic outfit must go:

> "To take away the one thing a man's got?"
>
> "Not to take away, to replace."
>
> "But, I tell you, he has nothing, *nothing*. You have the word in English? Nicht! Gornisht?"
>
> "Yes, Mr. Tzuref, we have the word."
>
> "A mother and a father?", Tzuref said. "No. A wife? A baby? A little ten-month-old baby? No. A village full of friends? A synagogue where you know the feel of every seat under your pants? Where with your eyes closed you could smell the cloth of the Torah? . . . And a medical experiment they performed on him yet! That leaves nothing, Mr. Peck, absolutely nothing!"
>
> "I misunderstood."
>
> "No news reached Woodenton?"
>
> (191)

With Tzuref's final crushing question Roth cuts to the heart of Jewish indifference during the Holocaust and after. For Eli, the choice has been made. After providing the Hassid with two J. Press suits and appropriate haberdashery, Eli is vindicated: the community accepts the modern dress, and the Jews may stay.

But, for Eli there can be no mere acceptance, no simple accommodation to his Jewishness. When the Hassid returns the favor and gives Eli his old clothes, Peck discovers the roots of his own Jewishness in the box of clothing given to him by a survivor of the Holocaust:

> Inside the box was an eclipse. But black soon sorted from black, and shortly there was the glassy black of lining, the coarse black of trousers, the dead black of fraying threads, and in the center the mountain of black: the hat. For the first time in his lifetime he *smelled* the color of blackness: a little stale, a little sour, a little old, but nothing that could overwhelm you.
>
> (206)

Eli has no other choice. He must accept the clothing and put it on. Eli capitulates to his Jewishness, right down to the fringed undergarment: "He slapped the white fringy surrender flag over his hat and felt it clinging to his chest." (207)

Then, Eli must show the world of Woodenton and explain his epiphany. To his gentile neighbor Harriet Knudson, who paints her rocks pink, Eli says "Shalom," and walks toward the president of the Lion's Club. Eli has to show the world: I am a Jew.

But to his Jewish friends, Eli is sick, is having another nervous breakdown, and needs Dr. Eckman for a little more therapy. Eli's wife Miriam is having a baby, and Eli goes to the hospital to see his new child. His friend Ted asks him, "Should you be walking around like this?", and Eli replies: "Yes" (214). From Miriam he gets little understanding: "Eli, change your clothes. I forgive you."

Finally, convinced that their friend and neighbor Eli Peck has once again gone over the edge, the Jews of Woodenton take matters into their own hands. Two hospital attendants grab his arms and carry him off:

> "Excuse me, Mr. Peck . . ." It was a new rich bass voice. "Excuse me, rabbi, but you're wanted . . . in the temple." His feet seemed to have left the ground some as he glided away from the window, the bassinet, the babies. "Okay easy does it everything's all right—" But he rose, suddenly, as though up out of a dream, and flailing his arms, screamed: "I'm the father!"
>
> (215)

As for the community's understanding of Eli, it is only necessary to see its response. He must be ill, so we will give him a medicine which will calm him and clear his mind of this confusion. But only Eli understood what has happened. His transformation into an East European Hassidic survivor of Hitler's slaughter, a few days before the birth of Israel, has given new strength to the cloth which binds Jew to Jew. At the very moment when it was being dragged away from his child, Roth reaffirms this bond: "In a moment they tore off his jacket—it gave so easily, in one yank. Then a needle slid under his skin. The drug calmed his soul, but did not touch it down where the blackness had reached" (216).

What was Philip Roth onto thirty years ago in **"Eli, the Fanatic"**? Did it take him until now, until *The Counterlife* to establish the relationship of Israel to the modern Jew growing older in America, to Roth's particular generation? In fact, what Roth established in **"Eli"** was not just the relationship of the modern Jew to Israel, but actually the continuity of Jewish life down through the ages. As meaningful as Israel may be, of greater meaning is the world which disappeared in the ovens and gas chambers—but not quite. When Eli Peck, Jewish lawyer and American suburbanite, assimilated and somewhat self-hating, changes clothes with a Hassid in Woodenton, the *shtetl* credentials of American Jewry are validated, and what had been a world of ghosts quite suddenly becomes real once again. Roth may have touched a variety of bases from *When She Was Good, Portnoy's Complaint, The Breast,* to the wanderings of Nathan Zuckerman, but very early in his career, in **"Eli, the Fanatic,"** he made his benchmark on what it meant to be a Jew. It rang true then, and it still does, thirty years later.

For what is Eli Peck if not a *shtetl schlemihl* in a three-piece suit? But the *shtetl* world, marginal as it might have been, was sure of itself in the sense of its Jewishness. Sholom Aleichem's Menachem-Mendl was a *luftmensch* desperately trying to survive by dealing air for air. Gimpel might have been a fool, but he was also blessed by God and knew what it was to be a Jew. So did Peretz's Bontsha. In the *shtetl,* life was hard, but being a Jew was easy.

Not so in Woodenton, Long Island, and Philip Roth was among the very first to see how difficult it was for the Jew to be a Jew, amidst the affluence and the urge to be like everyone else, and above all, to *look* like everyone else. One is reminded of the recurrent Woody Allen daytime hallucination which he used for the first time in *Annie Hall,* when the self-doubting hero thought that in everyone's eyes he looked like a Hassid. For Eli Peck, once he understood the nature of the Jew as survivor, it became a matter of life and death to *look* like a Jew, *and to make certain he was recognized as a Jew,* particularly by his gentile neighbors. On his walk through Woodenton dressed like the Hassid, he made certain that Harriet got the full view: "He lifted his neck so she could see his whole face." (212)

From the very beginning Roth recognized the danger in American affluence for the Jew, and the threat to his identity. From that very first thought, Roth would assure his audience that the future of the Jew in America would be anchored by both the past and the future: the one a memory which would not die; the other a nation just born.

Works Cited

Solotaroff, Ted. "American-Jewish Writers: On Edge Once More." *New York Times Book Review.* 18 Dec. 1988: 1, 31, 33.

Roth, Philip. "Eli, the Fanatic." *Goodbye, Columbus and Five Short Stories.* New York: Bantam, 1963.

Murray Baumgarten and Barbara Baumgarten (essay date 1990)

SOURCE: Baumgarten, Murray and Barbara Baumgarten. "The Suburb of Forgetfulness: 'Goodbye, Columbus' (1959)." In *Understanding Philip Roth,* pp. 21-59. Columbia: University of South Carolina Press, 1990.

[*In the following excerpt, Baumgarten and Baumgarten provide detailed readings of the five short stories in* Goodbye, Columbus, *paying particular attention to their satirical elements.*]

"GOODBYE, COLUMBUS"

The Jewish immigrant past and American present, city and suburb, lower-middle and upper-middle class collide in this comic satire. **"Goodbye, Columbus"** encompasses the conflicts between two generations and two different ways of life. Its narrator, Neil Klugman, is a lower-middle-class Newark boy; Brenda, the girl he loves, is from Short Hills, an elegant suburb; they meet at the country-club swimming pool. Their encounter is the result of a mutual sexual attraction rather than the shared interest of communal life, family connections, or political action. Neil and Brenda define their relationship not in terms of classic Jewish values of family and religious tradition but the chivalric myth of knight and lady.

In its emphasis on seeing, **"Goodbye, Columbus"** has much of the visual impact of a film. Neil as narrator describes what happens as if he were a camera eye and the unfolding experiences in which he participates were a romantic movie of a summer's love affair. He presents himself as detached and disinterested, but what he registers is more complicated than he is willing to admit. "The first time I saw Brenda she asked me to hold her glasses. Then she stepped out to the edge of the diving board and looked foggily into the pool; it could have been drained, myopic Brenda would never have known it." Not only does Brenda as an object of desire for Neil come into focus at the beginning of the tale, so too do Neil's complicated feelings for her, of which he is not fully aware. As the novel begins, Neil quite literally sees what Brenda cannot, and he translates this visual acuity into a presumed moral advantage. While he is indeed a sharp-eyed critic of what Brenda is up to, he does not fully acknowledge what is happening to him. "She dove beautifully, and a moment later she was swimming back to the side of the pool, her head of short-clipped auburn hair held up, straight ahead of her, as though it were a rose on a long stem." Comparing Brenda's head to "a rose on a long stem" makes her into a figure of potential romance. The sentence also suggests that Brenda self-consciously presents herself to the narrator; she is performing for him. Roth's prose makes it clear that Neil is an open-eyed participant in his own seduction.

The response Brenda seeks from Neil takes the rest of the paragraph to emerge. Once more it comes through as a fully realized filmic sequence.

> She glided to the edge and then was beside me. "Thank you," she said, her eyes watery though not from the water. She extended a hand for her glasses but did not put them on until she turned and headed away. I watched her move off. Her hands suddenly appeared behind her. She caught the bottom of her suit between thumb and index finger and flicked what flesh had been showing back where it belonged. My blood jumped.[1]

This exclamation of aroused desire punctuates the vivid opening paragraph, revealing that the young man from Newark who has posed as a wry and somewhat detached, amused, and even cynical observer is no longer merely a spectator. "That night, before dinner, I called her." Neil Klugman, whose name ironically means "smart," in Yiddish, has not been able to resist temptation, and plunges into a summer romance.

In this encounter Roth captures the Jewish moment of suburbanization of American life. Brenda and Neil are not only the quintessential American girl and boy but as well a phenomenon of the 1950s, when the democratic possibilities of upward social mobility were coming true for large segments of the American population which had, up until then, been on the margins of American life. Sharing in the new prosperity, Brenda's family lives in newly elegant Short Hills, while her father commutes to the center of Newark where his plumbing-supply business is located. Neil, however, lives in Newark with his Aunt Gladys and Uncle Max, since his parents have left the humid East Coast climate for Arizona because of their chronic asthma. Working downtown in the Newark Public Library, he does not share in the advantages of an increasingly prosperous American middle-class population that, after World War II, had been moving in ever-increasing numbers from the growing racial, cultural, and ethnic diversity of the American city to the developing suburbs. Neil's meeting with Brenda is his first taste of affluence.

In **"Goodbye, Columbus"** the differences between city and suburb are translated into attitudes toward sexuality. Neil seeks to discover whether there is a necessary connection between Brenda's sexual openness to him and her family's wealth, which he alternately prizes and scorns. Neil is unsure whether he seeks Brenda's social position and money, sexual initiation, or her love. His ambivalence leads him to accept with startling passivity the various tasks she expects him to perform, including holding her glasses while she swims, waiting for her to finish her tennis game, or taking care of her kid sister, Julie. His words, however, consistently have an irritated, angry edge.

Brenda imposes tasks on Neil as if their lives were a chivalric drama of knight and princess, but at the same time she appears to be readily paying him for his services (and leading him on to new challenges) with sexual favors. Neil cannot decide whether Brenda is testing him to find out if he might be a worthwhile partner for her and, despite his lower-middle-class origins and education, is sufficiently malleable to meet her needs, or whether he is simply her summer adventure. Neil's keen city vision and abrasive, aggressive behavior defend him against an acknowledgment of how much he is in love with Brenda and her affluent world.

In this novella Jewish and American history intersect in the two contradictory worlds that come to a focus in the encounter of Brenda and Neil. Neil's city toughness is mirrored in his Aunt Gladys and Uncle Max's matter-of-factness, their tight living quarters, and their understanding that the only way to get ahead is to work very hard. Brenda's summer world is one of endless sport—of swimming, tennis, ping-pong—in which these games become the model for all human activities. Functions are reversed: the Patimkin refrigerator is a horn of plenty, while the trees in the garden literally bear the fruit of sports equipment, as if those expensive toys which are the sign of suburban leisure were a natural part of the Patimkin environment. Brenda's suburban country-club life style is utterly separate from her father's world of dirty, physically taxing work. His prosperous business is still in Newark, the gritty city the Patimkin family left behind in moving to the suburban Garden of Eden of Short Hills.

Though he is fascinated by its abundance and the fullness of possibilities Short Hills offers, Neil also sees its disguises. His skeptical, somewhat distanced perspective reveals the price of entry into the country-club world. Brenda's bobbed nose, surgically altered to make it prettier as well as to make her less obviously Jewish, is but one part of the cost of admission. The growing inability of parents and children to communicate is another. Neil's values, so much closer to the immigrant world committed to work and achievement, make him someone that at one point in the story Mr. Patimkin can respect—by contrast with his feelings for his own son, Ron, who does not share these values. Unlike the lower-middle-class world of Newark with its hard though satisfying physical labor, and the honest, if underpaid, public services of library and state university, the upper-class-world of Short Hills cordons off work and keeps it out of sight; nothing costs too much, and only the right appearance and good looks matter. Suburban men and women are handsome, beautiful, and a homogeneous lot. Like Ron and Brenda they go away to colleges which seal their Americanness. Urban folk, by contrast, come in all sorts of sizes and colors, and have names like Klugman and Patimkin that are the orthographical equivalents of their heterogeneous shapes. They have warts and bumps on their noses, and like Neil they go to school in their ethnically and racially diverse neighborhoods.

The summer heat of Newark relents a little in the evening. Aunt Gladys and Uncle Max sit outside and enjoy the breeze. A vaguely dissatisfied Neil finds their small pleasures frustrating. Aunt Gladys's explanations of why she does things her way irritate him. To expose their distance from each other Roth has his characters speak out of their own terms of reference to characters who no longer share those values and ways. The result is a comedy of misapprehension, as, for example, when Neil suggests to Aunt Gladys that "tonight we all eat together. It's hot, it'll be easier for you." But Aunt Gladys sticks to her own ways. "Sure, I should serve four different meals at once. You eat pot roast, Susan with the cottage cheese, Max has steak. Friday night is his steak night, I wouldn't deny him. And I'm having a little cold chicken. I should jump up and down twenty different times? What am I, a workhorse?" Neil's response—"Why don't we all have steak, or cold chicken"—sounds reasonable, but that is not how Aunt Gladys takes it: "Twenty years I'm running a house. Go call your girl friend" (4-5). Neil is particularly adept at spotting the contradictions in Aunt Gladys's hard-working lower-middle-class life style; nevertheless, this does not make it easier for him to deal with the contradictions in his own life. Though he is scornful of the affluence of the suburbs, Neil wants more than the stifling city can offer him. His ambivalence is resolved temporarily when he interprets Brenda's invitation to visit Short Hills as a promise to stay and taste its pastoral delights.

The plot of the comedy at first mirrors Neil's desire, as boy-meets-girl and then boy-gets-girl, coming to an ironic conclusion with the boy-loses-girl episode that fulfills the romance pattern. Along the way Roth defers the action by interspersing scenes that reveal Neil's divided loyalties. Neil's job in the library is posed against Brenda's country-club afternoons. Her sister, Julie, an obviously spoiled child, is contrasted to a young black schoolboy, with whom Neil identifies, who comes to the library every day to look at the sensual pictures of Gauguin. Neil watches out for him and reserves the books the boy particularly wants even when others ask for them. But he treats Brenda's sister with contempt, taking out on her his frustrations at not having the advantages of the Patimkins.

Even the sexual encounters with Brenda turn out to be unexpectedly frustrating for Neil. He discovers that what their bodies can manage they cannot express more fully. Neil is forced to consider the possibility that except for the fact of their mutual sexual attraction he and Brenda actually have little in common. They do not know how to talk about the meaning of their relationship and build it into a shared world. Their mutual and reciprocal incomprehensibility is most clearly expressed in the childishness of their dialogue, when, for instance, Brenda turns to Neil on what amounts to their first date and asks, "If I let you kiss me would you stop being nasty?" The sexual favors Neil seeks with the intensity of an ambitious working-class boy Brenda bestows with the ease and abandon of the upper-class girl.

> We had to take about two too many steps to keep the approach from being awkward, but we pursued the impulse and kissed. I felt her hand on the back of my neck and so I tugged her towards me, too violently perhaps, and slid my own hands across the side of her body and around to her back. I felt the wet spots on her shoulder blades, and beneath them, I'm sure of it, a faint fluttering, as though something stirred so deep in her breasts, so far back it could make itself felt through her shirt. It was like the fluttering of wings, tiny wings no bigger than her breasts. The smallness of the wings did not bother me—it would not take an eagle to carry me up those lousy hundred and eighty feet that make summer nights so much cooler in Short Hills than they are in Newark.

(14)

Neil's resentment at the advantages of wealth and status, which he does not share with her, drives him toward Brenda at the same time that it blinds him to the causes of their attraction to each other. "Do you love me, Neil?" Brenda asks one night when they are swimming alone at the country club. "I did not answer," Neil says. "I'll sleep with you whether you do nor not, so tell me the truth," Brenda continues her inquiry. "'That was pretty crude.' 'Don't be prissy,' she said. 'No, I mean a crude thing to say about me.' 'I don't understand,' she said, and she didn't" (51). Both are confused as to whether they love or merely lust for each other.

For Brenda and Neil sexual intimacy is easy and difficult at the same time. They discover they can make love in the room where Neil stays over, almost whenever they want to. Unlike the cramped Klugman apartment in Newark where Neil has to lock himself in the closet to phone Brenda and talk to her with some semblance of privacy, the Patimkin house is so large that everyone has a room of her or his own. Privacy is paramount, and everyone is left alone to do what he or she wants to. Nevertheless, Brenda and Neil have a vexed relationship which they carry forward by negotiating the management of their sexual contacts, displacing the possibility of real intimacy into the details of their encounters. Often they sound more like experienced lovers managing an affair than young lovers experiencing the fullness of sexual intimacy for the first time. As Brenda and Neil perform sexually for each other, the social, economic, and psychological differences at the root of their inability to communicate begin to make their presence felt. Masked by their emphasis on sexuality, these difficulties cannot fully be dealt with, and break their relationship apart. "Goodbye, Columbus" repeats the pattern of hopeful encounter and failed relationship of *The Great Gatsby;* like Gatsby, Neil wants desperate romance to blossom into marriage. But despite the link of their common Jewish heritage, the gaps of class and moral consciousness between Neil and Brenda are too great for their relationship to succeed. What Brenda's brother, Ron, manages to do in marrying Harriet, Neil and Brenda cannot achieve.

As he reluctantly takes care of Julie one evening while the family is driving Ron to the airport, Neil wanders through the spacious Patimkin home and discovers the previously unimagined possibilities of suburban life. There are separate bedrooms for all the children; there is a room dedicated to television-watching. Functions that are jumbled together in his aunt and uncle's apartment are honored with their own rooms: for the Patimkins privacy and gracious living go together. The size of the suburban house and its specialization of functions by room make it possible to hide the past, once so integral and jumbled together. Neil discovers that the finished basement—the heart of the suburban ideal—includes a wet bar. In the "bacchanalian paraphernalia" with which it is equipped—"plentiful, orderly, and untouched, as it can be only in the bar of a wealthy man who never entertains drinking people, who himself does not drink, who, in fact, gets a fishy look from his wife when every several months he takes a shot of schnapps before dinner" (41-42)—Neil discovers the ambivalence of this newly rich family. The Patimkins are caught between the demands of their Newark Jewish ethnicity and the desire to show that they have arrived in Short Hills by emulating the ways of its Protestant upper class; their ambivalence echoes the complexity of his own desires. But just as there is no spatial integration of different functions in this suburban house, so there is no spiritual, economic, or communal hierarchy of values. The Patimkins are held together as a family by a system of programmed responses to conspicuous consumption, including food, rather than the values of the close-knit family of the urban Jewish neighborhood.

Brenda's brother, Ron, has no interest in the family business or work ethic. For him the fraternity and collegiate sports are paramount, replacing immediate and local family and neighborhood ties with the abstract and removed loyalties of alma mater. The title of the novella is taken from Ron's fraternity song, "Goodbye, Columbus." The phrase refers to the city of Columbus, Ohio, where Ohio State, the university he has attended, is located, but also ironically evokes the world of the Jewish immigrant by pointing to the discoverer of the New World, Christopher Columbus, and bidding him goodbye. In its focus on sports and college life the "Goodbye, Columbus" song reveals that Ron has substituted the masculine ideals of assimilated American life for traditional Jewish values. The same shallow values color the entire experience of Brenda's family and reveal the superficiality their new wealth has brought. Seeing the process of suburbanization through Neil's eyes, hearing the "Goodbye, Columbus" song through Neil's ears, makes the judgment of their inadequacies possible. The fact that Neil, the city kid, wants Brenda, the suburban girl, further reveals the ways in which the ideal of urban life is no longer functional. In leaving the city for the suburbs, upwardly mobile Jews, like other Americans, are suppressing their urban ethnic past, exchanging it for a luxurious and privileged, if sanitized, present.

In this novella Ron and Harriet, Neil and Brenda, mirror each other ironically. Similarly, the young Negro boy in the library echoes Neil's experiences. Aunt Gladys and Uncle Max are poorer immigrant versions of Mr. and Mrs. Patimkin. As a result of these doublings the reader cannot focus on one character alone, but rather encounters a complex and fuller situation in which a range of roles and character types are deployed. Brenda's country-club world, for example, is paralleled by Ron's fraternity at Ohio State, a school noted more for its football team than its academic standards. Their frat song, "Goodbye, Columbus," expresses the nostalgia for the enclosed happy world of sports achievements. For Ron, leaving Columbus is like Brenda's leaving the Patimkin sheltered, suburban home for the dangerous, anonymous city. Neil's anger and confusion are mirrored in Aunt Gladys's response to his courtship of the country-club girl from Short Hills, and are echoed in Mr. and Mrs. Patimkin's reactions to Brenda's wants and desires.

Like Neil, Brenda is ambivalent about her world. She quarrels with her mother, who treats her in the no-nonsense style of Aunt Gladys. Brenda observes the way her mother and father spoil Julie; she resents her mother's disapproval but is quick to get her father to buy her all the things—especially elegant clothes—she wants. Independent and strong-minded, Brenda is eager to succeed both in sports and academic life; like her father and Neil and unlike her brother, she seizes all her opportunities. Like Neil, Brenda constantly thinks about the meaning of her situation. Unlike Neil, she has put aside the expectations traditional Jewish families have for their children and wants to chart her own way. Her behavior, however, sometimes makes her appear like a girl with a "finishing school" frame of mind.

Despite the fact that Neil is the narrator of this tale, Brenda emerges as a more complex character than he is ready to acknowledge. By contrast with the other women in the stories that make up *Goodbye, Columbus,* she is the most liberated, sexually and socially, the most intelligent, and the one most able to combine her Jewish heritage and American possibility. The surprise with which Neil registers her words reveals how accurately and fully Roth has articulated the power of the new American-Jewish girl. Brenda is not the stereotypical Jewish-American princess of contemporary American folklore (with anti-Semitic overtones, as it has become an entire category of ethnic slurs and jokes);—that is a role her sister Julie will come to fulfill. Rather, Brenda is a figure of the fullness of American female possibility. She is the potentially liberated, new woman of the twentieth century, presented (and this is an indication of the power of Roth's work) through the eyes of a man who comes to challenge but stays to admire.

Despite their suburban home the Patimkins have not been able to change their urban Jewish linguistic usage. All of them are voluble; none of them feels threatened by Neil's verbal aggressiveness. Like Brenda, they can match him line for witty line. They make a theatrical experience of everything, whether it is Brenda's seduction of Neil at the swimming pool or the phone call for Ron from Harriet that brings dinner to an abrupt end and galvanizes everyone into action. Their linguistic virtuosity, like everything else they do, has a rich surplus; like their personal energy, they glory in its excess. For them the pleasure is in the overdoing. Early in the novel when Neil looks in the refrigerator in the Patimkin home he registers the power of abundance and affluence. "I opened the door of the old refrigerator; it was not empty. No longer did it hold butter, eggs, herring in cream sauce, ginger ale, tuna fish salad, an occasional corsage—rather it was heaped with fruit, shelves swelled with it, every color, every texture, and hidden within, every kind of pit." This is not a city icebox, stocked with the few concessions to American supermarkets Aunt Gladys makes, but a transformed fridge that holds the promise of America for the Jews:

> There were greengage plums, black plums, red plums, apricots, nectarines, peaches, long horns of grapes, black, yellow, red, and cherries, cherries flowing out of boxes and staining everything scarlet. And there were melons—cantaloupes and honeydews—and on the top shelf, half of a huge watermelon, a thin sheet of wax paper clinging to its bare red face like a wet lip.
>
> (43)

The sensuality and richness of this description of a Jewish-American household by an American-Jewish writer reveal that the Jews are at home in this new world. Just as Roth can write English as well as the classic English writers, so Jews can live as well as any other Americans. Roth will find the words to represent the experiences of this newly emergent ethnic American community. "Oh Patimkin! Fruit grew in their refrigerator and sporting goods dropped from their trees" (43). This section of the novella, in which Neil discovers the cornucopia in the Patimkin basement, concludes with Brenda and Neil making love for the first time.

In the next section, Neil thinks only of Brenda and, at work, pays attention to the needs of the young black boy, making sure he can look at the sensual pictures of Gauguin's Tahiti. Neil and Brenda briefly discuss his parents and his work: Brenda pointedly asks him whether he expects to make a career of the library. Though these are disturbing developments, they do not at this point puncture the sexual euphoria which envelops Neil and Brenda. Neil announces that he is spending his summer vacation at the Patimkin's home; his stay will extend through Labor Day.

One day Neil journeys to the "heart of the Negro section of Newark," where Patimkin Kitchen and Bathroom Sinks is located. Years ago, Neil muses, at the height of the great Jewish immigration, this had been the Jewish section of town, with its spicy-smelling ethnic stores and Turkish baths. Thinking about the waves of immigrants passing through this city, Neil wonders who will succeed "the Negroes" (90-91). Ron now works for his father, and Neil and Mr. Patimkin have a brief conversation in which Brenda's father comments on Ron's inability, so essential to success in business, to make the most of small advantages. "Here you need a little of the *gonif* in you. You know that that means?" and to Neil's response, "Thief," Mr. Patimkin comments approvingly: "You know more than my own kids. They're *goyim,* my kids, that's how much they understand"; (94). In the intimacy of the talk and the approval which Mr. Patimkin gives Neil for his knowledge of the old ways, the scene suggests he is the true heir to the business—the potential son-in-law who can do what the Americanized son cannot. The encounter of Neil and Brenda thus serves to bridge the values of the immigrant Jewish past and the American future.

As their relationship continues, Neil asserts himself with Brenda; however, he does not ask her to marry him but rather to get a diaphragm. Brenda's response is to claim that Neil is only interested in his own pleasure. Nevertheless, she accedes to his request. As Neil waits for Brenda to emerge from the doctor's office, he goes into a church and muses about his life. He thinks about his eagerness to be a winner and imagines Brenda is the prize. "It was an ingenious meditation, and suddenly I felt ashamed. I got up and walked outside, and the noise of Fifth Avenue met me with an answer: Which prize do you think, *schmuck?* Gold dinnerware, sporting-goods trees, Patimkin Sink, Bonwit Teller"—and Neil reverts to the tough, street-smart kid who won't let anyone, not even himself, get away with anything. "And then I saw Brenda coming out of the Squibb Building. She carried nothing with her, like a woman who's only been window shopping, and for a moment I was glad that in the end she had disobeyed my desire." But Brenda surprises Neil. "'Where is it?' I said. . . . At last she said, 'I'm wearing it'" (100-01). The insouciance with which she manages this transaction expresses her ease and habit of control; by contrast with Neil's identity crisis Brenda, even though she is younger, yet knows who she is.

Later, when Mrs. Patimkin discovers the diaphragm and confronts Brenda with it, the ensuing quarrel of the two lovers leads to the breakup of their relationship. Neil accuses Brenda of purposely leaving it where her mother would find it. Their argument about the diaphragm is again a displacement of the real question of responsibility for continuing (or ending) their relationship. Despite their seeming self-possession, neither Neil nor Brenda can deal with their situation. Reaching for a common future, they are too rooted in their different pasts. Their feelings lead them, but the nature of their emotions is brought into question. As the epigraph to the books suggests, "the heart" here is "only half a prophet." Personal profit is the other half of their relationship. Their hearts are not natural; they are managed.

What the characters of **"Goodbye, Columbus"** do not understand is that their push toward individual mobility and assimilation into the larger American culture will also mean the transformation of their Jewish community. Unlike Bernard Malamud, who relocates the immigrant's Old World village in the American city, Philip Roth recognizes the new opportunities of American Jewish life. By contrast with Saul Bellow, who for the most part views these new opportunities as intellectual problems of thinking and reconceptualization, Roth focuses on them as part of the process of growing up. Education and the family are his central themes as he explores the ways in which people negotiate everyday life, express their deepest feelings and values, and thereby imagine and invent their lives.

The summer comes to a close with the wedding of Ron and Harriet. Brenda's Uncle Leo regales Neil with an account of the heights of his sex life. The ritual moment of the gathering of the clan serves to re-

veal the link between ecstatic sex and Jewish celebration. The rich talk of these exuberant characters becomes an index of their vitality and sexual intensity: Brenda's sharp practical wit, and Uncle Leo's anecdotes echo Aunt Gladys's vivid phrases with their Yiddish inflection. Neil, in whom everyone now confides, draws out their linguistic energy. The affluent Patimkins celebrate the marriage of their firstborn son by overdoing things in good American, rather than strictly Jewish, style. Their excess marks the exuberance with which they have chosen to be Americans. But their Jewish energy shapes their Americanness, expressed in the *chutzpa*—the nerve—with which they address the possibilities of life.

As adventurers the Patimkins are infectious. They seduce the reader into sharing in their daring feats of life and language.

> Near the end of the evening, Brenda, who'd been drinking champagne like her Uncle Leo, did a Rita Hayworth tango with herself, and Julie fell asleep on some ferns she'd whisked off the head table and made into a mattress at the end of the hall. I felt a numbness creep into my hard palate, and by three o'clock people were dancing in their coats, shoeless ladies were wrapping hunks of wedding cake in napkins for their children's lunch, and finally Gloria Feldman made her way over to our end of the table and said, freshly, "Well, our little Radcliffe smarty, what have *you* been doing all summer."
>
> (110)

Brenda's response reveals her ability to defend herself with her native wit and theatrically honed poise. "Growing a penis," she says. Her splendid punch line turns a put-down into a triumphant assertion of self. Like Neil's, her words give her an edge over everyone else. Her talk, like her sexual inventiveness, makes her the queen of this romantic world.

Despite Neil's willingness to follow Ron's example, the romance comes to a painful end in the autumn. Brenda goes back to Radcliffe, and Neil returns to the Newark Public Library and a promotion to head of the Reference Section. After much negotiation Neil agrees to go to Boston over Rosh Hashana, the Jewish New Year. In Boston, however, Neil and Brenda find it difficult to recover their summer intimacy. Instead of sexual encounter they are forced into their long-deferred conversation by the two letters Brenda has received from her parents after they discovered her diaphragm. The resulting quarrel ends up forcing each not only into self-justification but into inadvertent choosing of his and her own family, class, and home.

> "I loved you, Brenda, so I cared."
>
> "I loved *you*. That's why I got that damn thing in the first place."

And then we heard the tense in which we'd spoken and
we settled back into ourselves and silence.

                                                      (134)

Returning to Newark, Neil asks himself the questions
that might help him account for what has happened.
He is left with the bitterness of his ambivalence. He
arrives in Newark "just as the sun was rising on the
first day of the Jewish New Year. I was back in plenty
of time for work" (136). Instead of the old ritual of
family and synagogue, or the newly discovered one of
sexual fulfillment, Neil has only his unsatisfying job
to which to devote himself.

The satire of **"Goodbye, Columbus"** follows the trajectory of the *Bildungsroman*. The events highlight the
lessons Neil must learn about his American and his
Jewish identity. In bringing the values of the past to
bear on the present, Roth's satire implicitly recovers
neglected values. Preserving a people's memory, he
keeps alive the possibility of a vital American Jewish
historical consciousness in the 1950s, a decade devoted to forgetfulness.[2]

"THE CONVERSION OF THE JEWS"

In the five short stories in **Goodbye, Columbus** Roth's
concerns as an American political satirist and as an
ethnographic recorder of Jewish life work together.
Moral pattern, literary strategy, and rhetorical tactic
link American and Jewish themes, revealing them to
be opposite sides of the same coin. Each of these stories builds to a crisis in which the protagonist must
acknowledge his Jewishness by taking a particular
course of action. That recognition has major consequences for the other characters and transforms the
situation. Ironically, in each instance the Jewish course
of action turns out to be identical with, rather than opposed to, the democratic, American choice.

In **"The Conversion of the Jews"** brash young Ozzie
Freedman cannot keep from asking questions in Hebrew school. Unlike his fellow classmates, who content themselves with gestures and grimaces, Ozzie responds to his teacher's sententious statements with
pointed queries. "Anyway, I asked [Rabbi] Binder," if
God "could make all that in six days, and He could
pick the six days he wanted right out of nowhere, why
couldn't He let a woman have a baby without having
intercourse" (141). This and similar questions get
Ozzie into trouble: not only must he defend his intellectual exuberance to his friends, but his mother must
come to school to meet with Rabbi Binder.

Ozzie finds the theological issues fascinating; unlike
his elders, however, he does not privilege Jewish over
American themes. For him they are both part of his

inheritance as an American Jew. Thus he wants to
know how the Jews can be the Chosen People if the
Declaration of Independence claims all men are created equal. And when fifty-eight people are killed in a
plane crash and his grandmother and mother pore over
the lists to detect which of the victims were Jewish,
Ozzie cannot help but raise the problem with Rabbi
Binder. The rabbi's effort to deal with Ozzie's specific
concerns by abstracting them into matters of "cultural
unity and some other things" leads to a confrontation:
Rabbi Binder yells at the boy, and Ozzie "shouted that
he wished all fifty-eight were Jews." Even the chance
to "think it over" in the rabbi's office for an hour does
not convince Ozzie he was wrong in his conviction
that God the Creator is all-powerful. Ozzie suspects
that Rabbi Binder, like the seventy-one-year-old custodian of the synagogue who mumbles his prayers, has
memorized the prayers but forgotten about God.

By contrast, Ozzie's deep religious feelings lead him
to honor the Sabbath: "When his mother lit candles
Ozzie felt there should be no noise; even breathing, if
you could manage it, should be softened." Even though
his mother is tired from work and her daily struggle as
a widow, "when she lit candles she looked like something better; like a woman who knew momentarily
that God could do anything" (143). But when Ozzie
tells her that she will have to see Rabbi Binder again,
this time about the confrontation over the plane crash,
she slaps him. Shocked by the discovery that she does
not share his view of God's power and presence, Ozzie
cries through Sabbath dinner.

The day his mother is to come to Hebrew school,
Ozzie and Rabbi Binder have another fight. Ozzie asks
Rabbi Binder about God's power as creator, and Itzie
gestures obscenely behind the rabbi's back, making
the class burst into laughter. As the rabbi momentarily
turns away, Ozzie yells at him, "You don't know anything about God!" (146), and the angered rabbi turns
and slaps Ozzie, bringing blood from his nose. In the
ensuing confusion Ozzie escapes to the roof of the
synagogue, where he muses on the strange events that
led him there. Down below, the adults misinterpret his
actions; thinking that he will jump, they plead with
him. Struck with his sudden power, Ozzie takes the
opportunity to continue the theological discussion of
God's power.

Ozzie Freedman's innocence makes him take literally
what his teachers interpret allegorically and contextually. A marginal figure, an *isolato,* like so many classic
American literary heroes, he does not participate in
the conventions that limit the adult world. Like Huckleberry Finn, one of his literary ancestors, Ozzie the
outsider thinks for himself. As a result his questions
unintentionally subvert normative values and beliefs

and threaten the social order of his elders. The violence which greets Ozzie's sincere desire for knowledge leads him to the discovery of the political dimensions of the social contract and the extent of his own isolation and marginality.

Like many Jewish communal leaders in the 1950s Rabbi Binder spends the greater part of his energies in separating what is Jewish from what is non-Jewish. As his name suggests, he is eager to bind his flock to their Jewish values; unfortunately that effort blinds him to the values that Americans, whether Jews or Christians, share.[3] Rabbi Binder views his rights as an American as circumscribed by his Jewishness, while Ozzie's actions reveal how vigorously he pursues his rights as an American citizen. There are no limits to what he asks about, and he will not accept the adult response that "it's always been that way." Roth dramatizes both the question and the hostile answer, for he knows that to ask an insecure young rabbi about central Christian dogma with the brash naïveté of the Jewish child is to provoke unthinking, even reactionary responses. The encounter between Rabbi Binder and Ozzie is not only a confrontation between two social unequals—in that case the adult would generally have the upper hand—but between two views of American citizenship. Ozzie's demand makes everyone accept the republican and democratic conditions of American life. Asking questions that are subversive, Ozzie exercises those rights acquired through the process of Jewish Emancipation—the political movement initiated by Napoleon in the aftermath of the French Revolution, which gave the Jews the rights of citizenship in the countries of the West—and that are part and parcel of the conditions making American pluralism possible. The irony of the title—**"The Conversion of the Jews"**—lies in the fact that the Jews are not here converted to Christianity but to the rights of American citizenship guaranteed to all by the American Constitution and the Declaration of Independence.

Much of the force of Roth's ironic tale depends upon parallel sources in American and Jewish culture that emphasize the power of the innocent child. What more American a subject than the outspoken, rebellious young boy; what more Jewish a subject than the smart, questioning student whose understanding far surpasses that of his elders. Ozzie unmasks the implicit arrangements by which adults, Jewish and non-Jewish, rationalize their situations. His innocence brings him to anger; he turns the conventional boundaries that supposedly shore up the individual identities of these adults against them. Unable to tolerate the compromises implied by this particular social arrangement, Ozzie—when he fortuitously gains the upper hand by threatening to hurl himself off the roof—forces his mother, Rabbi Binder, and all those listening to him to

kneel. The title of the story expresses the acknowledgment Ozzie forces Rabbi Binder to make: God "can make a child without intercourse." Then "he made them all say they believed in Jesus Christ." Almost as an afterthought he adds, "Promise me, promise me you'll never hit anybody about God" (157-58). In this way Ozzie takes religion out of the private realm and makes it a public issue. Rabbi Binder is forced to acknowledge the interdependence of the religious beliefs of both Christian and Jew, which depend upon a similar kind of faith. In effect, they are different in degree rather than kind; they exist together in the same universe of discourse. This recognition is one that Rabbi Binder has steadfastly denied in response to Ozzie's clever queries. Rabbi Binder has separated religious from ethnic experience, limiting his moral explorations to what he thinks of as Jewish issues, while refusing to confront larger, more general questions about belief and faith. In "The Conversion of the Jews," Roth, the political satirist and Jewish ethnographer, shows the intertwining of religion, politics, and ethnicity.

"DEFENDER OF THE FAITH"

In the first-person narrative of **"Defender of the Faith"** Sergeant Nathan Marx recounts a confrontation he has had with Sheldon Grossbart, a private in his company and a fellow Jew, late in May, 1945, near the end of World War II. During the course of basic training at Camp Crowder, Missouri, Sheldon has made a point of contacting Marx, the new first sergeant. Playing on their common Jewish heritage, Sheldon begins by asking that he be allowed to celebrate the Sabbath. His requests pile up, and soon Marx discovers that Sheldon is seeking preferential treatment from a fellow Jew. These events are bracketed by a retrospective opening in which Marx muses about his experiences in combat in Europe and a concluding scene which looks toward combat in the Pacific. Together, dramatic confrontation and meditative retrospect and prospect make it possible for Marx to come to a decision about his identity as an American, Jew, and soldier.

Sergeant Marx finds himself caught between Grossbart's requests, which evoke the world of his own Jewish family with its warmth and disinclination to violence or the severity of military law, and the demands of his captain, who admires him "because of the ribbons on your chest, not because you had a hem stitched on your dick before you were old enough to even know you had one" (166). Marx soon finds he must represent the demands of the army and his captain to Grossbart and his two Jewish sidekicks, while at the same time standing up for Jewish traditions and family life to Captain Barrett. Despite his effort to mediate between the two so as to honor both, Marx finds that Grossbart is taking advantage of him, and in his rage interferes with Grossbart's effort to be reassigned to New Jersey rather than the Pacific theater of operations. It is this act which leads to Marx's understanding of the ways in which he is a defender of the faith.

Marx's view of American life does not separate the responsibilities of the Jew from those of the American citizen. Sheldon Grossbart only sees the privileges he is being denied by military service and seeks to recover them by playing on the Jewishness he shares with Sergeant Nathan Marx. For him the ethnic connection is primary and overrules the more abstract, secondary loyalty of soldiers and citizens. In the course of the story Nathan is forced to choose between the Jewishness Grossbart insinuates should entitle him to privileges at the hands of his fellow Jew and a view of Judaism and Americanness as a set of mutual and overlapping obligations.

Nathan has fought against the Nazis in Europe; he has been decorated for bravery under fire. While he is held up to the recruits at the base as an example of someone who has earned his commander's respect, he is also razzed for his name and his Jewishness; it would be easy for him to choose ethnic solidarity over American citizenship. However, unlike Grossbart, Marx does not separate his Jewishness from his Americanness. Like Ozzie Freedman in **"The Conversion of the Jews,"** Marx demands that both be fulfilled: Nathan Marx and Ozzie Freedman both demand that the Jew live up to the highest universal standards of justice and fairness. For Nathan it is not enough for Jews to fight the Nazis; because Jewish and American values overlap, the war must also be brought to a conclusion in the Pacific.

Both the central characters of **"Defender of the Faith"** are Jews. Nevertheless, their views of the obligations and responsibilities of modern American Jews diverge. Marx does not accept Grossbart's definition of the situation as "them against us." In an era in which the organized American Jewish community was emphasizing its ethnic solidarity, Nathan's exposure of Grossbart's pursuit of preferential treatment caused many readers to label the story anti-Semitic. For Marx, to shirk the fulfillment of one's duty as an American is to fail to fulfill a Jewish obligation as well. Thus, he repudiates Sheldon's charge that he is an anti-Semite because he does not help him escape assignment to combat in the Pacific.

The encounter between Grossbart and Marx is a struggle between two views of American Jewish life, realized as two different ways of seeing. In this story

about the demands American military training placed on Jews near the end of World War II, the soldier's life is presented visually: roll call, discipline, and medals take up much of the beginning of the story. What happens when a young Jewish soldier tries to avoid facing up to required basic military training appears as a sequence of brief encounters of small figures against a larger background. The European and Pacific theatres of combat bracket the theatrical space of Camp Crowder, in which these actors play out their roles. Grossbart's world is spatially limited; he is afraid of the open space of the military drill field. Marx's world encompasses the horizon as it takes into account the larger view of the conflict and the obligations of Jews and Americans.

"You Can't Tell a Man by the Song He Sings" and "Epstein"

Parallel visual contrasts also define the situation in the next two stories. The contrasting spaces in which events take place are carefully described. Setting and characterization are intertwined, as characters are placed in their social context by manners and dress. In **"You Can't Tell a Man by the Song He Sings"** classroom behavior becomes an index of social class; in **"Epstein"** a socialist button pinned to a teddy bear, baseball cards, a folk singer, a thin dress, stockings, and the absence of a coat on a chilly morning are details that mark the class positions and the historical commitments of different characters. In both stories such details define the historical moment in terms of the inflections of class, gender, and political allegiance of the fictional characters. These nuances of social position are encapsulated by the particular dialogue of each character, which locates him along the social spectrum. The plot generates encounters between characters from different groups, and the resulting confrontations bring these different linguistic habits and social manners, as they challenge the range of possibilities available, to a sharp focus.

In **"You Can't Tell a Man by the Song He Sings"** the friendship between Alberto Pelagutti, tough reform school kid, and the narrator cuts across class and ethnic lines. Despite their different attitudes to school and education they bond with the other boys to defeat Mr. Russo, the "occupations" teacher, by forcing him to let them sing "The Star Spangled Banner" in the middle of class. This episode serves as the context for the discovery that the system that has marked Albie as an ex-con has done the same for their teacher, Mr. Russo, blacklisting him as a communist. By the end of the story the narrator realizes that the telltale index cards which indelibly record past mistakes will catch up not only with Albie, the student, but even more shockingly with their teacher. The story ends by making the reader ask with the narrator whether "a man's history is his fate."

The same pattern of discovery informs the farcical **"Epstein."** Here the story turns on an irritation Epstein's wife discovers on his penis, the result of an illicit sexual encounter with a widow across the street. Encouraged by her daughter's sexual encounter with his nephew, which Epstein has accidentally seen, he seduces Ida Kaufman. When his wife, Goldie, discovers the irritation, she is convinced he has always been an unfaithful, philandering husband, and she demands a divorce—something unheard of in their Jewish neighborhood. As he tries to escape from her recriminations by seeking solace with Ida, Epstein collapses in her bedroom. His heart attack reconciles his wife to him. The young doctor in the ambulance assures Goldie it is not syphilis that Epstein has but "an irritation" that can be cured.

All of these stories begin with an encounter of people of unequal status. Then they progress to a possible friendship between them, and move to a tumultuous climax when their differing expectations clash head-on. In each case a secret is revealed that brings the original encounter full circle. Each story presents the conflict visually, so that "The Conversion of the Jews," for example, has Ozzie on top of a building demanding that his mother, friends, and rabbi kneel to keep him from jumping off. The vertical axis in this story, with Ozzie on top and Rabbi Binder kneeling below, reverses the expected social hierarchy.

"Eli, the Fanatic"

The structural principle of reversal is also at work in **"Eli, the Fanatic,"** the first major story about the Holocaust written by an American writer after the first wave of reporting that succeeded the end of World War II had come to a close. Roth observed that most American Jews in the decade and a half following the end of the war embraced the process of suburbanization and assimilation. In 1959 he probed the repressed shame and guilt Western Jews felt about the Holocaust, while other distinguished American Jewish writers did not deal with it as a major subject for almost another decade.

As a satirist Roth understands the importance of community life and communal norms: they are the necessary conditions for satire. In the era of the disintegration of urban neighborhoods and communities Roth knows that these norms exist for the most part as past events that have been repressed. In **"Eli, the Fanatic"** the arrival of the group of Holocaust survivors who organize a Yeshivah (a traditional school of advanced Jewish learning) in one of the large old houses in the peaceful suburb of Woodenton disturbs its placid surface. The traditional long black cloak of the Hasidic Jew which one of the survivors wears provokes the assimilating Jews of the town, as if it were a lure to bring them out of their hiding places. The satire of the story, like its comedy, derives from the excessive feelings this innocent figure stirs up. He arouses little comment among the other townspeople; to the Jews he is a red flag.

In the course of the story this survivor becomes the fictional double of Eli Peck, a young lawyer with a history of mental illness, who has been asked by his fellow Jews in Woodenton to force the survivors to close the Yeshivah and leave. The Jews have discovered that it is against the zoning laws to run a school in that area of town. After a long day of work in the city Eli confronts the head of the Yeshivah, Leo Tzuref, with that fact, only to be told that the nineteen people who are involved are all family members and live there. Leo's expressive body language forces Eli into unexpected negotiations. Eli finds himself trying to justify the concerns of his Jewish neighbors to Tzuref—whose name echoes both the Yiddish word for trouble, *tsuris,* and the Hebrew word for participation, joining, *(le)tsaref*—and the Yeshivah's needs to the Jews of Woodenton.

Eli's buddies are dismayed. Though they have left the city where such things happen for the quiet suburb, the disturbing city experiences that throw all kinds of people together every day have now followed them to Woodenton. Eli's effort to persuade them that the disturbances that have provoked them, especially the wandering figure in the long black cloak and hat from the Yeshivah, will shortly cease does not convince them. Pursuing his effort at mediation, Eli sends the survivor two of his suits, discovering in the process that his wife, Miriam, who is in her ninth month of pregnancy with their first child, sides fully with the other Jews of Woodenton. However, Eli's strategy seems to work: now the survivor wears Eli's green suit as he strolls about town and is no longer recognizable as different from all the other people of Woodenton. Eli begins to think of him as "greenie"; the nickname is not only descriptive of his suit, but as well evokes "greenhorn," the traditional word for the American Jewish immigrant compounded out of Yiddish and late-nineteenth-century American English usage. When Miriam goes into labor, Eli takes her to the hospital. Returning home, he finds that the survivor has sent him the black suit of clothes, including the ritual fringed undergarment of *tzitzit* in exchange.

Eli is irresistibly drawn to these clothes, finally putting them on and going to meet the "greenie" to show him what he looks like in the long black cloak, suit, hat, and fringed undergarment. Their meeting echoes a climactic moment in Sholem Aleichem's classic story "On Account of a Hat," in which the main character cannot recognize himself in a mirror because he has put on an officer's cap by mistake: "And then Eli had the strange notion that he was two people. Or that he was one person wearing two suits" (289). The encounter leads Eli to an understanding of some of the experiences of the Holocaust survivor, of which Tzuref has spoken earlier. Identifying with him, Eli has a revelation. Now he becomes the committed Jew—the "fanatic" of the title of the story, living up to "Eli," which means "my God" in classical Hebrew and was the name of the high priest of the Temple in 1 Samuel. In his black Hasidic traditional clothing Eli strolls deliberately through the town, making visible to his Jewish friends and neighbors the experiences they want to banish and have repressed in their hearts. As the cars screech to a stop and people call his name, Eli discovers his identity: "he knew who he was down to his marrow—they were telling him. Eli Peck. He wanted to say it a thousand times, a million times, he would walk forever in that black suit, as adults whispered of his strangeness and children made 'Shame . . . shame' with their fingers" (293). Then Eli walks to the hospital to see his newborn son. Looking at him through the glass wall that separates them, he imagines himself cutting down the suit for his son to wear, "whether the kid liked it or not!" (297), thereby defining Jewish tradition through this image of clothing.

The black suit accumulates additional meanings in the course of the story. His wife as well as his friends become convinced that Eli has had another attack of mental illness and call for Dr. Eckman, the psychiatrist, who has been a threatening presence in his life. Eli feels very clear about who he is for the first time in his life; his friends, however, cannot acknowledge his discovery. His sense of having come home at last makes no sense to them, for unlike Eli they do not pursue issues to their conclusions, preferring instead to keep things stable and "normal" by banishing unwanted cultural and personal memories. As the story concludes, Eli is grabbed by two interns, who call him rabbi at the same time that they administer a sedative: "The drug calmed his soul, but did not touch it down where the blackness had reached" (298).[4] The blackness with which the story ends becomes a complex image: it is both the traditional suit of clothes as an emblem of tradition which clothes the human being, and the horror of the Holocaust. It also brings into bold relief the shabbiness of the response of the other Jews of Woodenton, eliciting their self-hatred and fear. Thus, **"Eli, the Fanatic"** focuses on the self-imposed censorship of American suburban Jewish life, which depends upon the refusal to acknowledge the links between individual American Jews and the larger community of Jews, the *klal yisroel*—that is, the entire people of Israel. The recurring image of blackness builds in this story into a judgment of what the Jews of Woodenton want to repress.

"Eli, the Fanatic" is a cautionary fable about what happened in the 1950s to Jews as they tried to disappear into the suburbs and abandon their communal life. When the young Holocaust survivor moves through Woodenton in his long Hasidic black coat, the response of the Jewish suburb to the appearance of someone in the traditional clothing of religious Jews reveals that the effort to forget extends to the visible marks of their historic meaning. The name of their town—Woodenton—precisely expresses what they have done in anesthetizing themselves against the shocks of modern Jewish history.

Notes

1. Roth, *Goodbye, Columbus* (Boston: Houghton Mifflin, 1959) 3. Further references will be noted parenthetically.

2. The title of this chapter echoes that of an important essay by our late colleague, Professor Joseph H. Silverman.

3. For further discussion of the differences between Rabbi Binder and Ozzie, see Will Herberg, *Protestant, Catholic, Jew: An Essay in American Religious Sociology* (Garden City, NY: Doubleday, 1956), and J. M. Cuddihy, *The Ordeal of Civility: Freud, Marx, Levi-Strauss, and the Jewish Struggle with Modernity* (New York: Basic Books, 1974).

4. Roth made significant revisions to the ending of this story in the second edition, which is quoted here.

Jay Halio (essay date 1992)

SOURCE: Halio, Jay. "Nice Jewish Boys: The Comedy of *Goodbye, Columbus* and the Early Stories." *Philip Roth Revisited*, pp. 13-36. Boston: Twayne Publishers, 1992.

[*In the following excerpt, Halio discusses what he considers to be surprisingly mature comedy and social commentary in Roth's early stories in* Goodbye, Columbus.]

THE COMEDY OF "GOODBYE, COLUMBUS" AND THE EARLY STORIES

Roth's most famous protagonist, Alexander Portnoy, complains that he is living inside a Jewish joke and pleads with his psychiatrist, Dr. Spielvogel, to help get him out of it. Though at first he seems oblivious of it, Neil Klugman in **"Goodbye, Columbus"** lives inside a burlesque-show joke—a sexual tease that from the opening paragraph sets his hormones pumping wildly. He describes his first sight of Brenda Patimkin at the country club swimming pool, when she asks him to hold her glasses. After her dive, as Neil returns her glasses he gazes after her: "I watched her move off. Her hands suddenly appeared behind her. She caught the bottom of her suit between her thumb and index finger and flicked what flesh had been showing back where it belonged. My blood jumped."[1] Without any kind of formal introduction, Neil calls her that very evening for a date. Thus their affair begins.

That Neil is a "nice Jewish boy" who quickly captures the reader's sympathy is manifest from his background, his education, his current job, and his warm family relationships. Educated at the Newark Colleges of Rutgers University with a degree in philosophy, he makes no apologies for not having gone to an Ivy League school or anything so prestigious (Brenda is a Radcliffe undergraduate). An only child, he lives with his aunt and uncle and their daughter in a Jewish neighborhood of Newark, because his mother and father, afflicted with asthma, have immigrated to the aridity of Arizona. Neil is devoted to his surrogate family, especially his Aunt Gladys who, like any Jewish mama, worries about his food, his social behavior, and anything else that affects her loved ones. Like many nice Jewish boys, Neil is often impatient of her concern and desperately, sometimes bluntly, tries to reassure her so that she will leave him alone. He works at the Newark Public Library in a respectable position that promises early promotion to the kind of industrious, conscientious young man Neil appears to his immediate superiors to be.

But nice Jewish boys also have strong masculine glands, and Neil is no exception. When he first sees Brenda, no wonder his heart jumps. Although this is not an attraction Roth often deals with later (Neil is not enticed by the forbidden fruit a shiksa, or gentile woman, represents to an older generation of Jews), in its way the situation is still typical. Brenda is Jewish; it is at a Jewish country club that Neil meets her. But Jewish American Princess that she is (Neil, as narrator, never uses the phrase himself), Brenda is rich, spoiled, and smart, if somewhat shortsighted (literally and perhaps figuratively). She knows her attractions, and she knows how to use them.

And so when Neil calls her, Brenda does not put him off. Evidently without a current boyfriend (though she has had her share in the past), she allows Neil to meet her at tennis with her girlfriend, Laura Simpson ("Simp") Stolowitch. The game Brenda plays is an-

other good initial indication of her character. Cocky, confident, she wins the set from Simp, but not in the "one more game" she tells Neil it will take when he arrives. Though dusk is falling, and falls, the two battle on into the dark, giving Neil a further chance to size Brenda up. He is struck by her ferocious play, her unwillingness to let the set end in a tie, and her reluctance to rush the net and put herself in physical jeopardy: "Her passion for winning a point seemed outmatched by an even stronger passion for maintaining her beauty as it was" (**"Goodbye, Columbus"** [**"GC"**], 20). After the game is over, as they walk off the court together Neil falls a step behind Brenda, giving him another opportunity to "appreciate" her: "Her hands did not twitch at her bottom, but the form revealed itself, covered or not, under the closeness of her khaki Bermudas. There were two wet triangles on the back of her tiny-collared white polo shirt, right where her wings would have been if she'd had a pair. She wore, to complete the picture, a tartan belt, white socks, and white tennis sneakers" (**"GC,"** 21).

The suggestion of wings may be deliberately misleading, for Brenda is no angel, no more than Neil is, though to all outward appearances they are a nice Jewish couple.[2] Moreover, in Neil's romantic/erotic gaze the wings image may be justified. Falling under a spell, he ignores warnings against the temptation Brenda represents. Although he registers her eagerness to win, which later will have important consequences for them—or him—and is irritated by her flip reply to where she goes to school, he perseveres in his pursuit of her. Further warnings, such as Brenda's comments on living in Newark or on the nose job she has had ("I was pretty. Now I'm prettier"; **"GC,"** 23), are also registered—and ignored.

Neil counters her responses with sarcastic wit, which Brenda either doesn't get or criticizes as being "nasty." Intent on the relationship, which he finds challenging, he tries to recover "civility," more or less successfully. When he asks for a closer look at her nose, Brenda takes the gambit, on which she too seems intent, and says, as he peers at her, "If I let you kiss me would you stop being nasty?" (**"GC,"** 24). Whether or not this is another tease, or something more, Neil thinks he feels "a faint fluttering, as though something stirred so deep in her breasts, so far back it could make itself felt through her shirt. It was like the fluttering of wings." That the wings were so small, smaller than her breasts, does not bother him: "it would not take an eagle to carry me up those lousy hundred and eighty feet that make summer nights so much cooler in Short Hills [where Brenda lives] than they are in Newark" (**"GC,"** 24).

That is how it all starts; the few pages that constitute the first chapter of the novella present the basic contours of the story and its theme. About halfway through the book, however, the story takes a different twist, as the burlesque-show joke deepens into something else. As often happens to nice Jewish boys, what starts out as an affair turns into love—with all its attendant complications. As this aspect of the story unfolds, Neil's true character reveals itself, also involving complications, for the writer as well as the narrator. From this earliest stage in his career, Roth shows that he cannot resist the urge to develop the character of a *schlemiel*. That is what Neil Klugman, despite his surname (which means "clever fellow"), turns out to be, though about this aspect of his protagonist's character Roth seems to be somewhat ambivalent or uncertain.[3] On the one hand, he has developed and seems reluctant to surrender the sympathy Neil has earned; on the other hand, he finds all but irresistible the comedy latent in the predicament Neil gets himself into by falling in love with a girl like Brenda. But we are getting ahead of the story. Neil has still to meet Brenda's family, the Patimkins.

Mr. and Mrs. Patimkin are among the nouveau riche Jewish families that years earlier moved out of the city and into the suburbs. The fortune Mr. Patimkin made in the war by supplying sinks to army barracks is partly responsible for that; the rest is the result of his continuing hard work and shrewdness as a businessman who knows how to make a buck—lots of them. The Patimkin household thus comes in for the kind of satire that has since become a rich source for Roth's wit and humor—and his trademark, as viewed by many critics. When Brenda invites Neil to dinner for the first time, we see what lies ahead for him—and the Patimkins. The invitation comes after another day at the country club pool, where Brenda and Neil have disported themselves in the water and engaged in further erotic play. The invitation is spontaneous and, for Neil, unexpected, as he tries to explain to his naturally worried Aunt Gladys why he will not be home for dinner that night.

Neil has already met Brenda's older brother, Ron, at the pool. He is built on the lines of a Greek god, as Neil describes him: "suddenly, like a crew-cut Proteus rising from the sea, Ron Patimkin emerged from the lower depths we'd just inhabited and his immensity was before us" (**"GC,"** 29). Ron is a playful, harmless Proteus, not very bright, but amiable and, like all the Patimkins, athletic. The comic juxtapositions Roth uses to describe Ron he also uses to describe Mr. Patimkin at the dinner table: "He was tall, strong, ungrammatical, and a ferocious eater" (**"GC,"** 31). Brenda's kid sister is rather less amiable, not yet a princess but certainly a princess-in-training. Julie is "ten, round-faced, bright, who before dinner, while the other little girls on the street had been playing with jacks and

boys and each other, had been on the back lawn putting golf balls with her father." Though she is the handsomest of them all, Mrs. Patimkin appears ominous and arouses an immediate dislike, or fear, in Neil: "She was disastrously polite to me, and with her purple eyes, her dark hair, and large, persuasive frame, she gave me the feeling of some captive beauty, some wild princess, who has been tamed and made the servant of the king's daughter—who was Brenda" (**"GC,"** 31).

The comic potential of such a cast is great, and Roth exploits it fully and economically. Instead of transcribing the fragmented or garbled talk interrupting the Patimkins' energetic eating, he consolidates dialogue and description and presents them both in "one fell swoop." The result is just as funny as—perhaps funnier than—the actual talk, which the reader can easily imagine. Eating among these Brobdingnagians seems to reduce their guest, even to diminish him physically (or so he thinks), and gives early indications of the schlemiel that will emerge. The conflict between Mrs. Patimkin and Brenda also emerges, ever so subtly. In the midst of everything the erotic play continues, as Neil feels Brenda's fingers fondling his calf under the table.

After dinner the comedy continues, with somewhat darker overtones. Brenda describes her feelings about her mother and the jealousy between the two women, mother and daughter, which she calls "practically a case study" (**"GC,"** 35). An excellent tennis player in her youth, Mrs. Patimkin arouses Brenda's admiration for what she was—then. Now the two constantly battle about money, about clothes, about everything. Brenda's snobbery again shows itself, but Neil chooses to ignore it, afraid to "lift the cover and reveal that hideous emotion I always felt for her, and is the underside of love" (**"GC,"** 37). If Neil is falling in love with Brenda, he is nevertheless aware of the lust that has drawn him to her and keeps him by her side.

At this moment Julie interrupts, and another indication of Neil the schlemiel emerges, as he lets a basketball thrown at him bounce off his chest. Like Mr. Patimkin, Neil allows the child to win a game of "five and two," though a part of him desperately wants "to run little Julie into the ground" (**"GC,"** 38). Extremely self-conscious, he feels the gaze of the Patimkins and even Carlota, the black maid who served dinner. Feeling humiliated, Neil is reassured when Brenda says that even Ron, a star basketball player, lets Julie win.

The next morning Neil, at work in the library, has an experience that seems to comment on his involvement with Brenda and her family. As he goes to work he sees a little black boy in front of the library growling and snarling at the cement lions that guard the building. "Man, you's a coward," the boy says to one of them, and then growls again (**"GC,"** 42). Shortly afterward the boy enters the library and asks Neil where the "heart" section is. He means the *art* section, and Neil later finds him absorbed in a folio of Gauguin reproductions. The boy is struck by the serenity and beauty of the Tahitian women in the paintings: "These people, man, they sure does look cool," he says. "They ain't no yelling or shouting here, you could just see it." Turning the pages, he shows Neil another picture and says, "Man, that's the fuckin life" (**"GC,"** 47).

The boy's rapture is not quite what Neil feels about Brenda and Short Hills, but it's close. In fact, Neil makes an explicit comparison, as he daydreams about meeting Brenda that evening in Short Hills, "which I could see now, in my mind's eye, at dusk, rose-colored, like a Gauguin stream" (**"GC,"** 48). His rose-colored expectations are disappointed, however, for when he arrives Brenda and her family drive Ron to the airport, leaving Neil at home to baby-sit Julie. Angered by the imposition, he sends Julie off to watch television alone. His impulse is to leave quietly and return to Newark, where he feels he belongs, among his own humble people. But he doesn't leave. Instead, he explores the house, or rather the basement, where among other things he finds an unused bar with two dozen unopened bottles of Jack Daniels—"the bar of a wealthy man who never entertains drinking people, who himself does not drink, who, in fact, gets a fishy look from his wife when every several months he takes a shot of schnapps before dinner" (**"GC,"** 52)—further comic commentary on the middle-class Jewish household the Patimkins' represents. Wanting a drink now himself, Neil is afraid to break the seal of one of the unopened bottles. He muses that the bar had not seen a dirty glass since Ron's bar mitzvah and probably wouldn't see another until one of the children was married or engaged. He then finds an old refrigerator full of fruit, to which he helps himself until discovered by Julie, who surprises him in the act of eating a nectarine. The handful of cherries he has also taken he drops into his pocket, afraid of further discovery.

Neil gets his revenge against Julie for the interruption and the game of five and two when he unmercifully beats her at Ping-Pong in the basement recreation room. Actually, Julie quits in hysterics before he is able to score the final point. She is outraged that Neil, no longer under the gaze of the family, will not make concessions and let her win, as he and the others had always done before. He completes his revenge after the family has gone to bed that night, when he makes love to Brenda for the first time: "How can I describe loving Brenda?" he muses. "It was so sweet, as though

I'd finally scored that twenty-first point" (**"GC,"** 56). The juxtaposition of events is deliberate and reveals what the love affair is truly about: winning. The question is, Who is winning what?

In the episodes that follow Roth reemphasizes that the affair is a game—another aspect of the burlesque-show joke, or tease—and not truly love, despite Neil's longings and self-deceptions. First Neil plays games with an elderly, jowly gentleman who tries to check out the Gauguin book the little boy has been looking at during his daily trips to the library. Neil explains that the book has a "hold" on it and cannot be taken out. Later Neil and Brenda are at the country club; it is late evening, and they are alone. As the lights go out around the pool, Neil thinks they should be going home, but reassuring him it's all right to stay, Brenda starts asking him questions about himself—for the first time since they met. Although initially these are questions her mother wants answered, soon Brenda admits to her own curiosity, and then asks Neil if he loves her. He hesitates, and she says she will sleep with him anyway, whether he loves her or not. When he says he does not, she answers, "I want you to." He refers to his library job, but she seems untroubled by his humble occupation, and continues: "When you love me, there'll be nothing to worry about" (**"GC,"** 62). Then they begin playing pool games, hiding from each other for longer and longer intervals, until Neil, anxious, confesses, "I love you . . . I do" (**"GC,"** 64).

Gamesome, manipulative Brenda wins that one as she wins others. By now fully aware of what is happening, Neil seems not to care. They see each other every evening, make love whenever possible, and finally Brenda invites Neil to spend a week of his vacation at her house. Then they make love every night in her room. The day Neil arrives is the day Ron announces his engagement to Harriet, his girlfriend in Milwaukee, and the house plunges into turmoil preparing for a Labor Day wedding. Why the wedding is so rushed is not clear, though there are hints that Harriet may be pregnant. Neither is an explanation offered as to why the wedding is arranged by the groom's parents and not the bride's, following tradition. Perhaps no explanation is needed. Mr. Patimkin, the equivalent of a *nogid* (rich Jew of the shtetl; Gittleman, 168) enjoys showing off what his money can buy, and in any event Roth wants Neil to be a wedding guest.

Roth's introduction of these events, however, is not simply to find yet another opportunity for satiric comedy, which first Harriet's arrival and then the wedding celebration afford. He means to juxtapose Neil's affair with Brenda against Ron's wedding to Harriet so that the issue of marriage between Neil and Brenda can come to the fore, as it does. Rather than proposing marriage to Brenda, which is the way their relationship seems to be heading, Neil instead proposes that she get a diaphragm, thereby forcing quite a different kind of issue.

Brenda rejects Neil's proposal, claiming that they are OK as they are, but Neil presses her. Although the best argument he can offer is that a diaphragm will make sex more pleasurable for him as well as safer for her, he ultimately admits that he wants her to get one simply to please him, to yield to his desire. It is another contest of wills between them, another attempt by Neil to assert his manhood against Brenda's domineering spirit. In many other respects she has successfully led him around by the nose, so that by the time he is living in her house he has actually begun to look like her, not only in dress—sneakers, sweat socks, khaki Bermudas, and all—but in manner and deportment; he has begun to look the way she wants him to (**"GC,"** 81). He has started to fit into the Patimkin family, much to his Aunt Gladys's disgust but precisely as Brenda wants. It is time for Neil either to assert himself or to lose his manhood altogether.

Why, then, doesn't Neil ask Brenda to marry him? He is sure he loves her, and she him, but somehow things don't seem quite right, as she promised him they would be the night at the pool. Fearing that anything other than a resounding "Hallelujah!" to a marriage proposal would utterly daunt him, he proposes the diaphragm instead, hardly realizing how much more daring the latter would actually be. More evidence of the kind of schlemiel Neil is occurs in a scene at Patimkin Kitchen and Bathroom Sinks. There Neil watches in amazement as men load sinks onto a truck, tossing them to one another, oblivious of the danger of dropping them. Suddenly Neil imagines himself directing them and hears himself screaming warnings. His reverie continues: "Suppose Mr. Patimkin should come up to me and say, 'Okay, boy, you want to marry my daughter, let's see what you can do.' Well, he would see: in a moment that floor would be a shattered mosaic, a crunchy path of enamel. 'Klugman, what kind of worker are you? You work like you eat!' 'That's right, that's right, I'm a sparrow, let me go.' 'Don't you even know how to load and unload?' 'Mr. Patimkin, even breathing gives me trouble, sleep tires me out, let me go, let me go'" (**"GC,"** 103). Is this the real Neil Klugman? Where is the sensitive, clever young fellow Roth has been presenting to us? Where is the assertive, masculine chap who orders his lover to get fitted with a diaphragm? Is he capable only of stealing fruit and beating little Julie at Ping-Pong so long as no one is looking? or of telling transparent lies so that the black boy can enjoy his book in the library a little longer?

Obviously Neil is both men, and therein lies Roth's ambivalence toward his character[4] and the source—conscious or otherwise—of both subterranean and surface comedy. While Neil's wit can puncture the pretentiousness of the Patimkins and other social-climbing middle-class Jews, he is also vulnerable within himself. He lacks the *cojones* of a real man. Arguing vehemently with Brenda about the diaphragm, he eventually agrees not to force her to get one. Whereupon she does.

The victory that should have been Neil's therefore becomes Brenda's. She even makes him accompany her to New York to the doctor's office, though she does not force him to go in with her. And when she comes out and Neil does not see her carrying a package, he thinks she may have changed her mind. Actually, he is relieved, but then his emotion turns completely around when Brenda tells him she's wearing the device. "He said shall I wrap it up," she explains, "or will you take it with you?" Whereupon Neil cries, "Oh Brenda, I love you" (**"GC,"** 112).

Roth's ambivalence toward Neil is matched by Neil's toward Brenda and leads to further indications of his schlemielhood. Even as Brenda apparently yields to Neil's wishes and is fitted with the diaphragm, Neil wanders away to St. Patrick's Cathedral and indulges in a kind of prayer: "God, I said, I am twenty-three years old. I want to make the best of things. Now the doctor is about to wed Brenda to me, and I am not entirely certain this is all for the best. What is it I love, Lord? Why have I chosen? Who is Brenda? The race is to the swift. Should I have stopped to think?" Getting no answers, he perseveres, confessing his carnal and acquisitive nature and identifying it with God: "I am carnal, and I know You approve, I just know it. But how carnal can I get? I am acquisitive. Where do I turn now in my acquisitiveness? Where do we meet? Which prize is You?" Suddenly he feels ashamed and, still without an answer, walks out into the hubbub of Fifth Avenue, and hears, "Which prize do you think, *schmuck*? Gold dinnerware, sporting-goods trees, nectarines, garbage disposals, bumpless noses, Patimkin Sink, Bonwit Teller—" (**"GC,"** 111-12). The answer, which in his imagination Neil again insistently identifies with God, gets only a celestial belly laugh.

In later novels, preeminently in *Portnoy's Complaint* but also in *My Life as a Man* and in others, Roth develops ambivalence toward his protagonists for comic effect. His attitude can be related to the typical kind of Jewish humor in which Jews make fun of their own inconsistencies and contradictions, while frowning on anyone else's doing so. But Roth has other sources of humor. His excellent eye and ear capture, and his typewriter accurately transcribes, observations that not only are funny in themselves but serve as social commentary and as commentary too on the observer, in this instance Neil Klugman. Aunt Gladys is an excellent case in point, and though a minor character, she is surely a contender for the real heroine of the novella.

As against Neil's false sense of superiority and the Patimkin women's wealth and pretentiousness, Aunt Gladys stands as a model of common sense, hard work, wry humor, and shrewd perception. An early version of the typical Jewish mother in Roth's fiction, she partly eludes the stereotype by knowing how and when to stop nagging Neil, by her reduced role in the fiction (compare Sophie Portnoy later on), and by her innate stature as above all a decent, caring woman. Forever complaining about the work she has to do—for example, the four different meals she has to prepare at four different times for the members of her household, including herself—she simply gives vent to her feelings in a harmless, usually humorous way. Neil does not try to explain her odd dinnertime routine except to say that his aunt is "crazy" ("GC," 14). From his rationalist viewpoint it certainly seems that way, but underlying the "craziness" is a firm resolve to serve the needs of her loved ones. Neil's flip comment thus boomerangs. Witty as he is, her wit matches his but, more important, Aunt Gladys differs from Neil in the depths and strengths of her commitments. Funny in her remarks and her fractured syntax—"I'll see it I'll believe it" ("GC," 68)—she is not merely a figure of fun but a standard of humanity against which others in the novella, including Neil, pale.

Roth wisely does not sentimentalize Aunt Gladys; in fact, he strongly opposes sentimentality, as he shows in his satiric portrait of Ron Patimkin. Large and amiable, Ron is devoted to the "light classics" of André Kostelanetz and Mantovani but above all to the album that gives this story its title and theme. Lying on his bed after a basketball game in the evening, Ron enjoys listening to the graduation record narrated by "a Voice, bowel-deep and historic, the kind one associates with documentaries about the rise of Fascism" ("GC," 114). Nostalgia for the Class of '57 lulls Ron to sleep as he hums along with the band and the Voice intones "goodbye, Ohio State, goodbye, red and white, goodbye, Columbus . . . goodbye, Columbus . . . goodbye" ("GC," 116). The perfect ending to a perfect day.

At Ron and Harriet's wedding the family portraits Roth draws are not only funny in themselves; like that of Aunt Gladys, they say something about Neil and his priggishness and about the world he lives in. After describing Mrs. Patimkin's side of the family, Neil turns to Mr. Patimkin's half-brother, Leo, a traveling salesman who tells Neil the story of his life. The hu-

mor darkens here as, embittered by his lot in life (only two good things ever happened to him, and one he can hardly remember), Leo advises Neil that he has a good thing going with Brenda and should not "louse things up" ("GC," 129). The good thing Leo remembers is that his mother-in-law found a rent-controlled apartment in Queens for him and his wife. (Later he recalls the other good thing—Hannah Schreiber, whom he met in the army and who believed in "oral love"; "GC," 127.) The other guests, mostly Ron's friends and Harriet's, come in for their share of caricature—for example, Gloria Feldman, "a nervous, undernourished girl who continually looked down the front of her gown as though there was some sort of construction project going on under her clothes" ("GC," 121). But for most of the evening Neil dances with Brenda until, having drunk too much champagne, she gets sick in the ladies' room and falls asleep on a sofa in the lobby, while Neil listens to the rest of Leo's tale of woes.

Despite Uncle Leo's advice, Neil does louse things up. He does soon after the wedding, when Brenda leaves to go back to college. The Jewish New Year approaches, and unable to come home for the holidays, Brenda persuades Neil to take off from work and come to Boston, where she has reserved a hotel room for them. Obedient as ever, Neil wangles the days off and travels to Boston. Expecting a joyous reunion, he even contemplates matrimony ("GC," 137). But he is in for a shock. Confessing only to an "oversight," Brenda tells Neil that she has left her diaphragm at home, where her mother has found it.

The letters Brenda receives from her parents force her into a choice she apparently never thought she'd have to make. Her parents are bitterly disappointed in her and obviously have no use for Neil, but now Brenda must choose where her loyalties lie. It is hardly a difficult choice, given her love of luxury and ease—none of which Neil, as a librarian, could ever afford. The issue turns ludicrous as, prompted by a remark in her father's letter, the discussion focuses on whom Brenda will bring home for Thanksgiving: her roommate Linda from last year or Neil.

For his part Neil tries to make Brenda see that, consciously or not, she left the diaphragm at home because she *wanted* her mother to find it and so end the relationship. Although Brenda rejects this argument as so much "psychoanalytic crap" ("GC," 144), Neil has a point. But it no longer really matters. Things are over between them. Whether Brenda *can* see or not is irrelevant; myopic as ever, she here *refuses* to see.

Why Brenda acts as she does remains unexplained and is a little curious, since she seemed genuinely to want to be with Neil during the Jewish holidays and urged him to come to Boston. In Bernard Rodgers's analysis Brenda resembles Daisy in *The Great Gatsby:* like Jordan Baker, Daisy, and Tom Buchanan, she is one of those careless people who "smashed up things and creatures and then retreated back into their money or their vast carelessness . . . and let other people clean up the mess they made" (quoted in Rodgers, 44). Not that Neil has a big mess to clean up; Brenda will be welcomed back on more or less the same terms as before by her doting father and jealous mother.

All of this forces Neil—unable once again to "win" with Brenda—to see himself as he is. This he does literally by looking at his reflection in the front window of the Lamont Library. He does not especially like what he sees there any more than he liked the insight his meditation in St. Patrick's Cathedral had given him. Moreover, he seems puzzled by his motives and impulses:

> What was it inside me that had turned pursuit and clutching into love, and then turned it inside out again? What was it that had turned winning into losing, and losing—who knows?—into winning? I was sure I had loved Brenda, though standing there, I knew I couldn't any longer. And I knew it would be a long while before I made love to anyone the way I had made love to her. With anyone else, could I summon up such a passion? Whatever spawned my love for her, had that spawned such lust too? If she had only been slightly *not* Brenda . . . but then would I have loved her?
>
> ("GC," 147)

Like many of Roth's later protagonists, Neil is unable to resolve these questions. He ends by simply taking the train back to Newark in plenty of time to get to work on the morning of Rosh Hashanah, the start of the Ten Days of Penitence and one of the holiest days in the Jewish calendar.

None of the five short stories collected along with "**Goodbye, Columbus**" in Roth's first published volume has quite the same range of wit and humor as the novella. But if "**The Conversion of the Jews**" is in part a ludicrous melodrama and "**Epstein**" borders on the tragic, they also reveal not only Roth's own moral earnestness but his witty perception into the contradictions and inconsistencies of human lives—elements that can make men and women simultaneously comic and pathetic, funny and sad. In "**The Defender of the Faith**" Roth opened himself to accusations of anti-Semitism, or Jewish self-hate, accusations he has rejected, arguing vigorously in defense of the artist's freedom to pursue and present truth as he sees it and of the universal, not peculiarly Jewish, nature of his theme.[5] Yet the story is essentially comic, its humor underlying and occasionally covering over the darker elements of its characters and situations. "**You Can't**

Tell a Man by the Songs He Sings" has nothing particularly Jewish in it, but "**Eli, the Fanatic**" contains much of the dark humor found in "**The Defender of the Faith**."

"THE CONVERSION OF THE JEWS"

Little Ozzie Freedman is the kind of boy who, because of his independent spirit and relentlessly inquiring intellect, is constantly getting into trouble with his elders. The framework for "**The Conversion of the Jews**" is the *heder,* or Hebrew school, Ozzie attends and where he comes into conflict with his teacher, Rabbi Binder. What gets Ozzie into trouble is his insistence on following the logic of scripture even to the point of recognizing the possibility of a Virgin Birth. For a Jewish rabbi teaching a class of would-be bar mitzvah boys, this is surely asking too much. That Jesus was "historical . . . a person that lived like you and me" is as far as Rabbi Binder is willing to go. He insists that Jesus's birth, like anyone else's, had to come through human intercourse, not divine intervention. But Ozzie cannot resist the force of logic: if God could "create heaven and earth in six days, and make all the animals and the fish and the light in six days— the light especially," then he asks Rabbi Binder "why couldn't He let a woman have a baby without intercourse" (*GC* ["*Goodbye, Columbus*" *and Five Short Stories*], 152-53). For a third time Ozzie's mother is summoned to school to see the rabbi.

Roth plays Ozzie's stubborn inquisitiveness off against his friend Itzie's more practical, wise-guy attitudes and coarser diction: "Itzie preferred to keep *his* mother in the kitchen"; "'Sure it's impossible. That stuff's all bull. To have a baby you gotta get laid,' Itzie theologized" (*GC,* 151-52). The contrast is comic, underscored by Itzie's amazement, which he expresses in humorous gestures and exclamations of disbelief at his friend's temerity. But worse—or better—is yet to come.

That Friday night Ozzie resolves to tell his widowed mother about the summons to see Rabbi Binder, but not before she lights the Sabbath candles. A "round, tired, gray-haired penguin of a woman," in the act of lighting the candles she is transformed for Ozzie into a radiant being "who knew momentarily that God could do anything" (*GC,* 155). He is therefore all the more astonished when, after he tells her about what has happened at heder, for the first time in their life together she hits him across the face with her hand.

The comic contrast of earlier episodes between Ozzie and Itzie now turns somber. Tension mounts on the following Wednesday at heder when, during "free-discussion" time, Rabbi Binder calls on Ozzie to give the class "the advantage of his thought." Ozzie at first resists but, on repeated provocation from the rabbi, demands, "Why can't He make anything He wants to make!" (*GC,* 158). The question causes a commotion in the class, and Ozzie cries out repeatedly, "You don't know, you don't know," until, probably by accident, Rabbi Binder's hand catches Ozzie squarely on the nose, making it bleed.

In the ensuing uproar Ozzie runs onto the roof and locks the door behind him. He has no thoughts of suicide, but the image of him several stories up on top of the building strikes fear in the hearts of all who behold him. Arriving for her appointment, Ozzie's mother is instead greeted by her son on the roof, a crowd gathered below, fire trucks clanging, and a net spread out to catch the boy if he jumps. What a surprise! All pleas for Ozzie to come down fail, and Rabbi Binder's threats—"I'll give you three to come down"—are ludicrous. Mrs. Freedman's cry that her boy not be a martyr is taken over by Ozzie's classmates, who, led by Itzie and not understanding the term, egg him on with "Be a Martin, be a Martin" (*GC,* 167).

The farcical situation evokes increasing humor but seriousness too, as in the growing darkness of the autumn evening Ozzie makes first Rabbi Binder and then everyone else, including his mother, get on their knees. In this posture of gentile prayer Ozzie makes the rabbi, his mother, and even the poor old sexton, Yakov Blotnik, confess that "God can do Anything"—even make a child without intercourse. By now everyone is kneeling, and Ozzie finally extracts their promise never to "hit anybody about God" (*GC,* 169-70). Only then does he jump "right into the center of the yellow net that glowed in the evening's edge like an overgrown halo" (*GC,* 171).

Some critics, while generally admiring Roth's stories, find them a little too neat, too pat. Alfred Kazin, for example, believes that in **"The Conversion of the Jews"** Roth is too anxious not only to dramatize the conflict but to make the issue "absolutely clear"; he needs to find the creative writer's delight in "life for its own sake" and become less concerned with the design of his fable.[6] But Kazin seems to miss the point here: in the world of the child, simplicity rules, as it does for Ozzie Freedman. Therein also lies the humor of the story and its import: adult sophistications and their consequences are finally no match for the single-mindedness and courage of a little boy, for whom the logic of God's omnipotence and mercy overwhelms all other considerations. That recognition, literally and figuratively, brings the others to their knees.

"THE DEFENDER OF THE FAITH"

"The Conversion of the Jews," with its beatific ending, brought ample criticism to Roth from many in the Jewish community, who overlooked its comedy[7] and concentrated instead on what they regarded as anti-Semitism in the story. **"The Defender of the Faith"** contains fewer funny moments but, if anything, a sharper wit and a tough-mindedness that insist, both in the story and its telling, that Jews are in most respects like other human beings. If Malamud's recurrent theme is that "All men are Jews," then Roth's is that "All Jews are men,"[8] as illustrated in the fictional portrayal of Sergeant Nathan Marx and the three Jewish recruits whose basic training he supervises.

Rotated back to the United States shortly after the fighting ends in Europe in 1945, Sergeant Marx is a veteran and a war hero, with ribbons to prove it. He wins the admiration and respect of his commanding officer and others he associates with at Camp Crowder, Missouri, but Sheldon Grossbart is something else. Swiftly ascertaining that Marx, like himself, is Jewish, Grossbart begins requesting special treatment, at first in relatively minor matters but eventually in some of much greater importance. Playing on Marx's sense of guilt more than on any sense of solidarity he might have with his landsmen (that is, fellow Jews), Grossbart finagles special passes and exemptions from onerous duty for himself and two of his friends. When nothing else works, he writes letters—signing his father's name—to his parents' congressman. These prompt the commanding officer and higher authorities to inquire into such matters as the food that men brought up in kosher homes must eat.

Grossbart's cleverness—for example, his wishing Marx a "Good *shabbus,* sir!" as, exempted from a "G.I. party" (Friday-night barracks cleaning), he runs off to "Jewish Mass"—eventually backfires. Too smart by half, he manipulates not only Marx but others to the point of getting his orders changed from being shipped out to the Pacific (where the war is still raging) to being sent to Fort Monmouth, New Jersey, closer to his parents' home and certainly much safer. But this time Grossbart goes too far. Marx, furious, arranges to have someone else sent to New Jersey and Grossbart to the Pacific with the rest of the company.

The comedy in this story derives partly from the competition that develops between Grossbart and Marx, their contest of wit, a game that finally becomes deadly earnest. In this respect it resembles the games Neil and Brenda play in **"Goodbye, Columbus."** Grossbart is usually smart enough to know when to attack and when to retreat, when to show guts and when to act meekly, as in the Passover seder incident. But Marx is no dummy. Even his sense of guilt (at not being much of a Jew) has its limits. He realizes full well who and what Grossbart is and finally confronts him in a towering rage: "Grossbart, you're a liar! . . . You're a schemer and a crook. You've got no respect for anything. Nothing at all. Not for me, for the truth—not even for poor Halpern! You use us all—" (*GC,* 210). Discovering and then shifting Grossbart's orders are the final victory, however vindictive, that Roth awards Marx, who has certainly earned it.

If **The Conversion of the Jews"** appeared too simple or too clear to Alfred Kazin, the "moral complexity" of this story exhilarated him, for in it Roth shows "the Jew as individual, not the individual as Jew." Moreover, Roth "caught perfectly the drama of personal integrity in the face of group pressures that is so typical of American literature" (Kazin, 259). He does indeed. But the issue of Jewish identity, which Grossbart forces Sergeant Marx to face, and the conflicts that develop from it are Roth's own. Though they resemble situations in stories like Malamud's "Last of the Mohicans" and "The Lady of the Lake,"⁹ the humor is more sharply satiric and less fanciful. Furthermore, the ending puts the entire story in an utterly different perspective, when Marx hears Grossbart weeping behind him after their confrontation. As the private swallows hard, accepting his fate, Marx resists with all his will the impulse to turn and ask Grossbart's pardon. Struggling, Marx accepts his fate too. Thus, Roth deftly mingles comedy, satire, and pathos in an amalgam fully justified by the "moral complexity" of his tale.

"EPSTEIN"

Mixed comedy and pathos, melodrama and farce characterize **"Epstein"** also, though in different doses and for different purposes. So do moral earnestness and what appears to be, on the surface anyway, a kind of poetic justice not unlike that meted out at the end to Private Grossbart. Old, hardworking Lou Epstein's life is suddenly transformed after his nephew Michael comes to spend a weekend at his home. Epstein is at an extremely vulnerable point in a middle-aged man's life. His wife of many years, Goldie, is no longer as attractive as she once was. His son, Herbie, dead of polio early in life, is kept alive only in memory, and in the bedroom where his baseball pictures still hang on the wall. His daughter, Sheila, once a pretty child, at 23 is coarse and unlovely. Engaged to a folksinger, she is active politically and socially, her leftist values hardly reflecting those of her middle-class family.

Into this milieu Epstein's nephew enters, slipping inside the house at night with his date from across the street. At first Epstein thinks it is Sheila and her boyfriend, Marvin, and braces himself for the inevitable zippings and unzippings of their lovemaking in the living room. An unhandsome couple, they fill him with disgust, not lust. Usually he ignores their vigorous pantings and carryings on, but this night he goes downstairs to give them a piece of his mind. He is astonished to find not Sheila and Marvin but Michael and Linda, the girl from across the street, who make quite a different sight from the one he expected, one far more erotic and exciting.

Watching unseen and tingling all the while, Epstein at last tiptoes back upstairs. Until the couple leaves, however, he is unable to sleep, and no sooner have they gone than Sheila and her boyfriend arrive and the zippings begin all over again. Epstein ponders to himself: "The whole world . . . the whole young world, the ugly ones and the pretty ones, the fat and the skinny ones, zipping and unzipping!" He grabs his great shock of gray hair and yanks it until his scalp hurts, while beside him Goldie shuffles, mumbles, and pulls the blankets over her. "Butter! She's dreaming about butter," Epstein muses. "Recipes she dreams while the world zips." He finally closes his eyes and pounds himself "down down into an old man's sleep" (*GC,* 222).

Later Epstein wonders whether that evening or some other event was the beginning of his "big trouble." But he decides that it all began when it appeared to begin, when he saw Linda's mother, Ida Kaufman, waiting for a bus and offered her a lift. Only recently a neighbor, Ida was unlikely to remain in her house long, now that her husband had died and she had the house in Barnegat to go to. Epstein drives her there, attracted by her voluptuousness, and they carry on an affair for several weeks—until one night Epstein discovers a rash near his genitals.

The rash precipitates a crisis that nearly wrecks Epstein's family and his life. Trying to pass off the affliction as prickly heat, a sand rash, or something he picked up from a toilet seat in his paper bag factory, Epstein fails to convince Goldie, who is sure he has venereal disease. Turmoil ensues; Epstein is ordered out of the conjugal bedroom and into the spare bed in Herbie's room where, unable to sleep, he talks to Michael, reminiscing about the past. It is all both funny and sad: Epstein's arrival with his parents at Ellis Island; the early years with Goldie; Herbie; his estrangement from his brother, Michael's father, years ago. When the young man becomes judgmental, Epstein makes this apologia: "You're a boy, you don't understand. When they start taking things away from you, you reach out, you *grab*—maybe like a pig even, but you grab. And right, wrong, who knows! With tears in your eyes, who can even see the difference!" (*GC,* 235).

The next morning, Sunday, the family has quieted down, but the weekend routine has changed. Instead of Epstein, Marvin the folksinger goes out for lox and a newspaper. As coffee percolates and family members sit around the table, Lou enters and the turmoil resumes. So Epstein has his breakfast at the corner luncheonette. Afterward, wondering where he should go, he sees Ida in her backyard in shorts and a halter, hanging underwear on a clothesline. She smiles at him, and that determines his decision.

Catastrophe follows. At noon a siren goes off. When Goldie, Sheila, and the others see an ambulance across the street, they suddenly realize its import but do not fully grasp it until a stretcher emerges from Ida Kaufman's house with Epstein on it. Sex and stress have taken their toll: he has had a heart attack.

However melodramatic and contrived, the ending of the story is, again, not without its humor. At the sight of her stricken husband Goldie explodes into grief and concern characteristic of a matronly Jewish house wife. In the ambulance on the way to the hospital, the doctor tries to reassure her. When he comments, "A grown man can't act like a boy," Goldie puts her hands over her eyes and Lou opens his. Everything will be all right, the doctor says. "All he's got to do is live a normal life, normal for sixty" (*GC,* 243). Now Goldie reassures Lou, who cannot or will not talk; though he opens his mouth, his tongue—an image of enforced impotence—"hung over his teeth like a dead snake." He'll live, but it is the end. As for the rash—not a symptom of venereal disease after all—the doctor reassures Goldie that he can fix that up, too, "So it'll never come back."

Epstein's world, like Mr. Patimkin's in **"Goodbye, Columbus,"** is "one taken up entirely by the economics of *making it* in America, and of demonstrating that you have achieved something to those around you," as Sol Gittleman says (Gittleman, 170). Therein lies the tragedy. The pathetic part is how little Epstein has achieved, really, and the comedy derives from what he tries to grab for himself once he realizes how little the little that he has is. Ironically, even the little that he reaches for turns out to be too much. What happens to Epstein is partly the result of the disintegration of "kinship values," which have been the essence of Jewish survival through the centuries (Gittleman, 171), and Roth knows it. Far from attacking Jewish values, then, Roth through his satire is crying out for their realization and, presumably, their restoration in contemporary American life.

Roth's instrument of attack, here as in **"Goodbye, Columbus"** and in much of his later fiction, is satire, which after we stop laughing helps us better understand the incongruities that have set us laughing in the first place. On the one hand, it is incongruous that a 60-year-old man, Lou Epstein, should try to behave like his young nephew, for Lou is well past the age of "zippings." On the other hand, he has enough life left in him both to envy the young and to think he can emulate them. But the world knows better, he discovers, not so much to his chagrin as to his sorrow. Being carried out of his paramour's home across the street on a stretcher on a Sunday morning is comical, as Roth presents it. What is not so funny (though it has its humorous side) is the image of the future that Goldie holds out for Lou in the ambulance. Marvin and Sheila will marry and run the business, and he can retire. She'll take care of him and they can go someplace together. "Don't try to talk," she says. "I'll take care. You'll be better soon and we can go someplace. We can go to Saratoga, to the mineral baths, if you want. We'll just go, you and me—" (*GC,* 244). No wonder that, as she talks, Lou's eyes roll in his head.

"You Can't Tell a Man by the Songs He Sings"

According to critical consensus, the penultimate story in *Goodbye, Columbus* is the weakest. It is also the earliest of Roth's stories in the collection. Nevertheless, it has its humor too and its moral irony, though here the two are not as tightly interwoven as in the other stories. Jokes abound, as when the ex-con Albie Pelagutti, recently returned to high school, asks the boy sitting next to him for "the answer" while they are filling out an occupations questionnaire. Or when Albie turns up for a baseball game in an outlandish costume. Though he has bragged about his skill as a ballplayer, when a fly ball comes his way he lets it land on his chest instead of in his glove and he doesn't know the first thing about holding a bat at the plate.

The unnamed narrator (the boy who gives Albie "the answer" and the one who is duped into picking him for his ball team) learns a lot from Albie and from another ex-con, "Duke" Scarpa. Streetwise, they know when to assert themselves and when to run—for instance, when the cafeteria window accidentally gets broken while the three are horsing around. The ex-cons never make it through high school, but years later, when the Kefauver Committee investigates crime in the area, neither Pelagutti's nor Scarpa's name turns up in the papers. Instead, the well-meaning, decent occupations teacher, Mr. Russo, is victimized when another Senate committee swoops through the state. Refusing to answer some of the committee's questions, he is fired by the board of education for having been a Marxist during his college years. The point of the story becomes clear at the end, as the narrator contrasts Russo's fate with his own experience in the high school principal's office, where he was sent for breaking the cafeteria window. The principal had warned that the file card on which the disciplinary breach was recorded would follow the boy all through his life. Albie and Duke knew that; that is why they ran when the window was broken. The narrator had not run and was punished. Ironically, poor Russo was just discovering a fact of life that his pupils had learned much earlier, while still boys.

"ELI, THE FANATIC"

Like **"The Defender of the Faith," "Eli, the Fanatic"** is suffused with dark humor. The comedy derives from the contrasts and juxtapositions of an assimilated Jewish community in predominantly WASPish Woodenton suddenly confronted by an Orthodox Jewish yeshiva in its midst. The yeshiva consists of some 18 refugee children presided over by Leo Tzuref[10] and cared for by a nameless survivor of concentration camps. The affluent Jews who have moved to Woodenton in suburban New York—merchants as well as professionals and their families—are disturbed by the presence of this outlandish settlement and want it removed. Not only does the yeshiva violate the town's zoning ordinances, but, more significantly, it is acutely embarrassing for the town's assimilated Jewish residents. The harmony established between themselves and their Protestant neighbors is, they feel, endangered by the yeshiva and particularly by the strange greenhorn, a Hasid who marches around the town in his fantastic black garb shopping for the children. They therefore call on one of their own, Eli Peck, an attorney, to get the yeshiva to move.

Eli does his best under the most trying circumstances. Tzuref is stubborn and refuses to budge, making Eli feel as though he were persecuting the already-too-much-persecuted refugees from Hitler's Europe. Eli's sense of this oppression is repeatedly exacerbated by knowing that these are mainly children he is trying to remove, children who flee from the very sight of him as he walks over the grounds to negotiate with Tzuref. Nor does Eli's home life provide more than scant consolation for him (though it provides much humor for the reader), as the efforts of his very pregnant wife to "understand" Eli invariably have the opposite effect. Having suffered two nervous breakdowns earlier, Eli is by no means heartless or insensitive. He feels for Tzuref and the children, and he feels for his community, whose members increasingly pressure him to resolve the predicament they see themselves in.

Eli tries to compromise by offering Tzuref conditions: first, that the religious, educational, and social activities of the yeshiva of Woodenton be confined to the yeshiva grounds and, second, that yeshiva personnel who appear in public be attired in clothing usually associated with American life in the twentieth century (**GC,** 276). The reply Eli gets from Tzuref is typically succinct:

> Mr. Peck:
>
> The suit the gentleman wears is all he's got.
>
> Sincerely,
>
> Leo Tzuref, Headmaster

Eli therefore once more visits Tzuref at the yeshiva, again frightening the children, to discuss the situation. As usual, the room is dim, unlit by electricity (Tzuref eventually lights a candle). They argue at cross-purposes. Eli, rational, insists that the greenhorn could get another suit; they—he and his clients—will even pay for it, he suggests, smacking his hand to his billfold. Tzuref, otherwise motivated, also smacks his hand to his breast, at "not what lay under his coat, but deeper, under the ribs" (**GC,** 279). Eli's appeal is to the laws of the community; Tzuref's is to the heart, to God's law, not mortals'. He insists that since everything but the man's black suit has been taken away from him, the least the Woodenton Jews can do is suffer a little too.

At an impasse, the two end their discussion, and Eli, guilt-ridden, sneaks off into the night trying not to frighten the little children once more. He finally breaks the impasse in an unusual manner as his wife gives birth to their son in the hospital. He takes one of his best suits, wraps it up, and delivers it to the yeshiva. But the issue is not yet entirely resolved. Although the "greenie" wears Eli's clothes—good suit, hat, shoes, everything—and parades around the streets of Woodenton in them, to the astonished satisfaction of Eli's friends, that is not the end of the affair. Soon afterward, while Miriam is still in the hospital with the baby, Eli hears a noise outside his back door. There he finds the Bonwit Teller box he had used to pack his things deposited on his doorstep. In the box are the black clothes of the "greenie," complete with broken shoes, black hat, and *tsitsit,* the fringed garment worn by Orthodox Jewish men.

Slowly, as he dons the strange clothing, Eli begins to realize why it has been left there. This time when he leaves his house to go to the yeshiva, he scares not the children, who scarcely notice him, but his next-door neighbor, Harriet Knudson, who is busy painting the stones on her lawn pink. At the yeshiva he confronts the greenie, busy painting the porch columns white. Until Eli says "Shalom" he does not turn around, and when he does, recognition takes some time. As they gaze at each other, Eli has "the strange notion that he

[Eli] was two people. Or that he was one person wearing two suits. The greenie looked to be suffering from a similar confusion" (***GC***, 304)."[11]

In his "mixed-up condition" Eli reaches out to the greenie to fasten the button-down collar of his shirt, but the gesture frightens the poor man, who backs away in terror. Chasing after him, Eli finally corners him and yanks the man's hands away from his face, pleading with him to tell him what else it is he must do. The greenie, raising one hand to his chest and jamming it there, then points off to the horizon, toward the center of Woodenton. Not until the greenie repeats the gesture does Eli understand its significance, and he heads toward the town.

What happens then is both funny and poignant. Roth adeptly portrays the town in its everyday activity and dress, into which the figure of Eli Peck, now dressed as a Hasid, strides. The impact is stunning: "Horns blew, traffic jerked, as Eli made his way up Coach House Road" (***GC***, 307). But Eli perseveres, knowing that everyone thinks he is having another nervous breakdown. He knows he is not insane. If you *chose* to act crazy, he thinks, then you weren't crazy. "It's when you didn't choose. No, he wasn't flipping" (***GC***, 309). Soon afterward he remembers his wife in the hospital and, rejecting the idea of changing back into his own clothes, makes his way to her bedside.

Seeing him, Miriam is nearly beside herself:

> "Eli, why are you doing this to me! . . . *He's* not your fault," she explained. "Oh, Eli, sweetheart, why do you feel guilty about everything. Eli, change your clothes. I forgive you."
>
> "Stop forgiving me. Stop understanding me."
>
> "But I love you."
>
> "That's something else."
>
>   (***GC***, 310)

Love *is* something else, Eli has learned, and it passes understanding. He insists on seeing his newborn son, and as he contemplates the "reddened ball—*his* reddened ball" the interns come and tear off his coat, injecting him with a sedative. "The drug calmed his soul," the story ends, "but did not touch it down where the blackness had reached" (***GC***, 313).

"Eli, the Fanatic," the most powerful story in the collection, brings the volume full circle. Whereas **"Goodbye, Columbus"** ended with Neil Klugman rejecting love, rejecting religion, ready to start work on Rosh Hashanah, Eli Peck ends with a resolve not to let his wife, his neighbors, or his psychiatrist persuade him to renounce his actions. Through Tzuref and the greenie

and the children at the yeshiva, he has learned what none of the others appreciate: the meaning of sacrifice, sacrifice through love, which for Philip Roth appears to be the essence of Judaism. It has cost the greenie everything to end up in Woodenton dressed in a nice tweed suit and decent hat. It has cost Eli just as much to recognize the sacrifice, reciprocate it, and allow comedy to triumph.

Some commentators have criticized Roth for this story as they have done for the others, claiming his ignorance of Jewish tradition or, worse, his innate anti-Semitism and self-hatred. Sol Liptzin, for example, argues that no Hasid would surrender his traditional garb to appease the residents of a New York suburb: Rather, he would devoutly pray for them. This aspect, Liptzin maintains, shows Roth's "ignorance of the inner motivation and behavior of Jews."[12] Although perhaps technically correct, Liptzin's argument may be beside the point, which is partly to show the chasm between traditional and assimilationist Jews and the difficulty of any rapprochement. Whereas Liptzin claims that Roth is being "theatrical and not genuine," "genuine" seems to signify merely the literal, and, of course, Roth in writing imaginative literature is not being literal-minded. If he is "theatrical," then that is partly what makes the story succeed. It *is* good theater, make-believe, although make-believe dressed up in the trappings of reality.

The Jews of Woodenton, for example, are real enough. Though they speak English, they talk like Jews; Saul Bellow, for one, picked up the Yiddish rhythms that characterize their speech (Bellow, 79).[13] The streets of Woodenton look like real streets too; as Gittleman remarks, Coach House Road is "the ultimate suburban street, with a Colonial-styled supermarket" where the president of the Lions Club, "the epitome of proper, Gentile Woodenton," encounters Eli in his Hasidic dress (Gittleman, 155). The theatrics undoubtedly constitute much of the comedy; in fact, the story opens like the first scene of a play or film, as Eli approaches the yeshiva for his first meeting with Tzuref. Much of the story is in dialogue too, emphasizing the theatrics but also dramatizing the issues. In addition, it lets Roth display the kinds of wit that characterize both Tzuref and Eli, as they talk at cross-purposes during their initial conference and thereafter:

> "The law is the law," Tzuref said.
>
> "Exactly!" Eli had the urge to rise and walk about the room.
>
> "And then of course"—Tzuref made a pair of scales in the air with his hands—"The law is not the law. When is the law that is the law not the law?" He jiggled the scales. "And vice versa."
>
>   (***GC***, 265)

Roth's resolution of the conflict in "Eli, the Fanatic" may be factually or theologically inauthentic, but Eli's insight as well as his courage cannot be dismissed on those grounds. However unlikely, if not impossible, it might be for a Hasid to exchange clothes with a modern Jew in suburban New York, the exchange does provoke comedy on all sides. And underlying the comedy is the essential truth concerning the loss of values, of tradition and identity, that Eli Peck finally comes to recognize and, in his bizarre but necessary way, tries to restore.

Eli is without question a modern assimilationist Jew. But he is also a sensitive, caring person who knows only too well that an argument has two sides, that while defending one side you often wish you were on the other (*GC*, 268). In this story Roth shows both sides vividly and powerfully. If Eli changes sides at the end, he does so in full knowledge of what he is doing and why. If he is carried off finally with a hypodermic needle in his arm, Roth shows that changing sides may not be so easy after all; that the mores of a community cannot be violated with impunity; that society will have its revenges. "Okay, rabbi," one of the men in white coats calls out to Eli in the hospital. "Okay okay okay okay okay okay. . . . Okay okay everything's going to be okay" (*GC*, 313). But everything is not "okay"; the drug soothes Eli's soul, but insofar as it does not touch it "down where the blackness had reached," nothing is ultimately resolved. In this way Roth's comedy reveals both its depths and its complexity and shows him at the very beginning of his career, despite his years, to be a surprisingly mature writer.

Notes

1. *Goodbye, Columbus and Five Stories* (Boston: Houghton Mifflin, 1959), 13; hereafter cited in text as *GC*.

2. They seem the prototypes for young Nathan Zuckerman and Sharon Shatzky in "Salad Days," one of Peter Tarnopol's "Useful Fictions" in *My Life as a Man*.

3. In his review of the book ("The Swamp of Prosperity," *Commentary*, July 1959, 77; hereafter cited in text) Saul Bellow says that Neil descends from the *schlemazel*, or unlucky fellow, in Jewish literary tradition, as well as from the poor clerk in Gogol's story "The Overcoat" and the (relatively) "pure youth" of Sherwood Anderson's "I'm a Fool." But to me Neil seems closer to the Jewish *schlemiel*, the archetypal fool, a loser and a victim. In any case the two types are closely related.

4. In his analysis of "Goodbye, Columbus" in *Philip Roth* ([Boston: Twayne Publishers, 1978]; hereafter cited in text), 34-46, Bernard F. Rodgers, Jr.

sees Neil as both "a disapproving moralist" and "a libidinous slob." This dualism is at the heart of Neil's character, but Rodgers does not fully explore its comic implications.

5. See the discussion in chapter 6 and "Writing about Jews" in *Reading Myself and Others*, 157-67. Roth immediately earned the support of others, such as Saul Bellow, who urged him "to ignore all objections and to continue on his present course" (Bellow, "The Swamp of Prosperity," 79). He did.

6. Alfred Kazin, "Tough Minded Mr. Roth," in *Contemporaries* (Boston: Atlantic/Little, Brown, 1962), 262; hereafter cited in text. For some reason Kazin omitted this essay from the later edition of his book.

7. But see Guttmann, "Jewish Humor," in *The Comic Imagination*, ed. Rubin, 337-38, who says Roth rivals Saul Bellow "as a master of subtle irony" and uses this story as an example of his humor.

8. Sanford Pinsker, *The Comedy That "Hoits": An Essay on the Fiction of Philip Roth* (Columbia: University of Missouri Press, 1975), 4.

9. In *From Shtetl to Suburbia*, 156-61, Gittleman relates these stories to Roth's "Eli the Fanatic," which also treats the theme of Jewish identity.

10. Names here are significant. *Tsuref* sounds much like the Yiddish *tsurres* (sorrows, troubles); *Woodenton* suggests a stiff, "wooden" town; *Eli* recalls the priest in Israel who witnessed Hannah's distress (see 1 Samuel 1.1-28); and *Miriam* is the name of Aaron's sister, who led the women of Israel in rejoicing at the miracle of the Red Sea (Exodus 15.20-21).

11. In *Philip Roth* (London and New York: Methuen, 1982), 31, Hermione Lee compares Eli's "double" with Susskind, the character who makes Fidelman responsible for him in Malamud's story "Last Mohican."

12. Sol Liptzin, *The Jew in American Literature* (New York: Bloch, 1966), 228. Compare Pinsker, *The Comedy That "Hoits"*, 23, who cites Liptzin, and Rodgers, *Philip Roth*, 27-31, who analyzes the differences between Roth's Eli and the biblical Elijah he represents in the story.

13. Although Bellow quotes some of the dialogue between Eli and his friend Ted Heller to demonstrate the point, the speech of Artie Berg and Harry Shaw also demonstrates it; see *Goodbye, Columbus*, 270-73.

Selected Bibliography

Primary Sources

The Anatomy Lesson. New York: Farrar, Straus & Giroux, 1981.

The Breast. New York: Holt, Rinehart & Winston, 1972. Rev. Ed., New York: Farrar, Straus & Giroux, 1980.

The Counterlife. New York: Farrar, Straus & Giroux, 1987.

Deception. New York: Simon & Schuster, 1990.

The Facts: A Novelist's Autobiography. New York: Farrar, Straus & Giroux, 1988.

The Ghost Writer. New York: Farrar, Straus & Giroux, 1979.

Goodbye, Columbus and Five Stories. Boston: Houghton Mifflin, 1959.

The Great American Novel. New York: Holt, Rinehart & Winston, 1973.

Letting Go. New York: Random House, 1962.

My Life as a Man. New York: Farrar, Straus & Giroux, 1974.

Our Gang. New York: Random House, 1971.

Patrimony: A True Story. New York: Simon & Schuster, 1991.

Portnoy's Complaint. New York: Random House, 1969.

The Professor of Desire. New York: Farrar, Straus & Giroux, 1977.

Reading Myself and Others. New York: Farrar, Straus & Giroux, 1975.

When She Was Good. New York: Random House, 1967.

Zuckerman Bound. New York: Farrar, Straus & Giroux, 1985. Containing *The Ghost Writer, Zuckerman Unbound, The Anatomy Lesson,* and *Epilogue: The Prague Orgy.*

Zuckerman Unbound. New York: Farrar, Straus & Giroux, 1981.

SECONDARY SOURCES

Gittleman, Sol. *From Shtetl to Suburbia: The Family in Jewish Literary Imagination.* Boston: Beacon Press, 1978.

Guttman, Allen. "Jewish Humor." In *The Comic Imagination in American Literature,* edited by Louis D. Rubin, 329-38. New Brunswick, N.J.: Rutgers University Press, 1973.

Emily Miller Budick (essay date autumn 1996)

SOURCE: Miller Budick, Emily. "Philip Roth's Jewish Family Marx and the Defense of Faith." *Arizona Quarterly* 52, no. 3 (autumn 1996): 55-70.

[*In the following essay, Budick asserts that despite its reputation as a biting critique of American Jewry, "Defender of the Faith" is primarily a philosophical story that probes the meaning of faith and its defenses.*]

Hegel remarks somewhere that all facts and personages of great importance in world history occur, as it were, twice. He forgot to add: the first time as tragedy, the second as farce.

Karl Marx

Like Karl and Harpo, I was one of them.

Nathan Marx

Despite its notoriety, Philip Roth's **"Defender of the Faith"** has received very little sustained scholarly attention—perhaps because the story is so early and so apparently slight and obvious: seemingly nothing more than a story about loyalties divided across the hyphenation of American-Jewish identity. In fact, **"Defender of the Faith"** has become less important as a work of art, exactly anticipating the issues that swirled in the wake of its publication, than as a document in the history of Jewish American literary criticism. It was this text that produced within the Jewish community the charges of Jewish self-hatred that Roth has spent much of his career refuting.[1]

And yet **"Defender of the Faith"** is an exquisitely crafted, complexly philosophical story. It is not primarily, as most of its readers have assumed, a critique of American Jewry, although the story includes ample criticism of American Jews. Rather, it is a philosophical inquiry into the meaning of faith and its defenses, especially as such large philosophical issues evolve out of specific historical circumstances. **"Defender of the Faith"** is a model of the inseparability of text and context. It unravels its philosophical investigation under the precise pressures of one of the most painful historical events in either Jewish or world history: the Nazi extermination of almost the whole of European Jewry during World War II.

By explicitly invoking the events of the Holocaust, Roth's story constructs the stakes in its investigation into faith in such a way as to require the reader to decide exactly those issues that it makes seem undecidable. There is here a superfluity, almost an overdetermination, of political-literary relation. No reading of this story can be less than a defense of one faith or another. So proceeding, **"Defender of the Faith"** does nothing less than examine the conditions that set the stage for holocaustal events. At the same time, however, the story produces a philosophy of faith (and a comic faith, at that) that has everything to do with how human beings mediate against the fate that has just befallen the Jews. As we shall see, this story turns on the two terms *faith* and *fate* as governing human moral choice.

Roth's **"Defender"** [**"Defender of the Faith"**] centers on Nathan Marx, a Jewish sergeant in the U.S. army at the end of World War II (the fighting in Europe is already over), who is called upon to "defend" his (Jewish) "faith" by one of the Jewish soldiers under his command, one Sheldon Grossbart. Grossbart is the story's self-appointed "defender of the faith." What he does, he tells Marx, he does in the name of *religion*."[2] Accordingly, he makes several neither unreasonable nor unusual demands of the sergeant. By implication, he makes these demands as well of the nation that Sergeant Marx officially, institutionally, represents. In insisting on his right to attend Friday-night worship and to obtain leave to celebrate the Passover holiday, Grossbart is asking for nothing more, though nothing less, than the freedom of religious expression guaranteed him by the United States Constitution: "to be allowed to live as a Jew"—or, given the context in which the story occurs, to die as one (135).

The problem, of course, is that Grossbart is not an observant Jew, and is barely interested in Jewish community or identity, let alone in religion: he is merely trading on a shared ethnicity made more fraught by recent Jewish history. Grossbart wishes to achieve not parity with his fellow soldiers, but privilege and, ultimately (in the extremity of the military moment in which this story takes place), exemption. By placing his story in the context of the American army, Roth brings into view the intrinsic coerciveness of all social institutions (even in as pluralistic and free a society as the United States). He also, however, evokes the threats, internal and external, under which society itself exists, which (as much as any private or local faith) require our defending it. There is, at the moment of the story's action, a very real danger to the nation itself, which may well necessitate the individual's surrendering the right to defend his or her more private beliefs or interests.

As someone interested in the national good, and by extension, the universal values that the national good seems to represent, Nathan Marx would seem to emerge as the unchallenged defender of the faith in Roth's story. But the situation is not so simple. Set as they are against the recent devastation to European Jewry, Grossbart's demands, including his special claims on Marx's Jewish loyalties, are not easily set aside. And, as if bringing even closer to home the truth of Jewish endangerment, the captain of Marx's and Grossbart's unit (the supreme representative of America in this story) is indeed an anti-Semite and a racist (126, 133). America, the story suggests, may well constitute a threat to Jews, a threat not so very different from the threat recently posed and exacted in Germany. To complicate matters more, the rather sleazy Grossbart represents not only his own false interests, but also the legitimate concerns of one of his coreligionists, who is genuinely pious.

The story proceeds, from beginning to end, through such pairings of mutually exclusive alternatives, which make it almost impossible to answer the text's central challenge: how one defends a faith. That it is the anti-Semitic, racist Captain Barrett who reminds us that the participation of the American army on the European front helped save a Jewish remnant does not make this fact less true (136). The source does, however, render this statement in need of some complex double-thinking, especially in light of Grossbart's equally correct observation (also no less true for being articulated by Grossbart) that had German Jewry chosen to "stick together" the Holocaust might never have occurred (132). (Of course, for some interpreters of the Holocaust, Hannah Arendt and Bruno Bettelheim among them, it was precisely the Jews' sticking together that enabled Hitler to dispose of them so efficiently.) Jews are "pushy," Captain Barrett tells us only a few sentences after Grossbart has reminded us that German Jews may have fatally erred in allowing themselves to be "pushed around" (133, 132). Don't make "trouble," Captain Barrett cautions Grossbart (136), and Grossbart for the moment withdraws, not wanting to start any such "trouble": "that's the first thing they toss up to us" (136). (Grossbart says this earlier as well, in advance of Barrett's statement on page 126; "don't make trouble" is one of those coda of Jewish behavior in the diaspora, and the punch line of a good number of Jewish jokes.) Barrett levels his caution against Grossbart just at a moment in history when—in some views at least—had the Jews made more trouble, more of them might have survived.

In unrelenting repetition of irresolvable conflicts such as these, Roth's story lays bare the Solomonic possibility that we will decide issues of loyalty and faith only at the expense of cutting the living child in two. "Blood is blood," Grossbart says to Marx (137), trying to lay claim to particular ties of kinship. But, in the context of the very bloody world war still raging outside the United States, Grossbart's phrase exposes as well both the larger truth of universal human brotherhood and the human cost, in blood, when larger definitions of filiation are denied. When Marx actively intervenes—whether out of duty or revenge, it is perilously difficult but necessary to decide—to send Grossbart off to the Pacific, possibly to perish in the still-ferocious fighting there, it remains a real possibility that, in defending one faith—his faith in America, in freedom, in justice, and in fair play—he has sacrificed another equally vital, perhaps even more quintessential faith, the destruction of which he has witnessed, personally, during his tour of duty in Europe.

Thus, when Grossbart counters Marx with one more expression of his self-concern—"You call this watching out for *me*—what you did?"—and we, naturally enough, experience as much disgust as does Marx, we may still feel slightly uneasy, in light of the specifically Jewish catastrophe that has just occurred in Europe, about sacrificing, in the name of some abstract, universalist, even American idea of justice or law or ethics (watching out for all of us, as Marx claims to be doing), even one more Jewish life (149; emphasis added). Roth pushes an ethically difficult story almost to the point of moral torture when he works the plot so that Marx does not simply stand by and let Grossbart's "fate" happen to him, which in the context of the Holocaust would be problematical enough (150). Rather, Roth has Marx actively intervene to send Grossbart, if not to his death, then at least into danger on the Pacific front.

On some level, Roth seems to be constructing one of those familiar heart versus head problematics reminiscent of the fiction of Nathaniel Hawthorne. Thus, when Captain Barrett tells Sergeant Marx that he "judge[s] a man by what he shows me on the field of battle. . . . It's what he's got *here*" and "jerk[s] a thumb toward the buttons straining to hold his blouse across his belly," Marx thinks he is going to "point to his heart" (126). Instead Barrett announces "guts," which, placed as it is against Barrett's having just said that "I'd fight side by side with a nigger if the fella proved to me he was a man," doesn't quite seem like the right source for our moral wisdom. The story makes us ask once again, what prompts our loyalty and defines our faith? A display of guts, which not only proves men equal but proves them to be men, as if they must demonstrate to each other that they are men in the first place and therefore worthy of our loyalty and defense? (I choose my gender inflection purposely: this is a story about the American army and men.) Grossbart has no guts; are we meant to understand by that that it is okay for Marx to send him to his death, or for us to sympathize with this move? (German Jews seemed gutless to the Nazis, and also to many who have blamed the Jews since for what happened to them.) Or does faith imply something more subjective and irrational, something of the "heart," which binds us together, blood to blood, even against some sort of moral logic? Grossbart may be as heartless as he is gutless, but Marx is not, and it is very much to the point of this story whether he will decide to show moral guts or follow the less rational dictates of his heart.

Of course, we err on the side of sentimentality when we imagine that the heart doesn't exert its own compromising coercion. Like most of Roth's fiction, "Defender of the Faith" is trenchantly antisentimental, and we know Marx is in dire moral danger when he starts to wax "exceedingly tender about [him]self" (129), as when Grossbart's calling Mickey Halpern "my *leben*" reminds Marx of his grandmother: "'*Leben!*' My

grandmother's word for me!" he exclaims (132). Marx might, in this moment of nostalgia, stop to inquire what it means to call one's descendent one's life (*leben*). In his later fiction, Roth focuses on the ferocity of the Jewish parent's claim on the child, which calling him or her "my *leben*" implies. But even setting Roth's later investigations of this aside, Marx's sentimentalization of the Jewish parent is highly problematic. "Jewish parents worry," Marx explains to Barrett, carrying forward some of the sentimental mood evoked by overhearing the pet name. Again, Captain Barrett gets to voice the story's wisdom: "*All parents worry, for Christ's sake*," making us see the degree to which Marx's appeal, like Grossbart's, is racist (133). Of course, that "for Christ's sake," added so inevitably and unselfconsciously, reminds us that even our acknowledgments of brotherhood and universality represent their own investment in local, and exclusionary, truths.

Deciding matters of loyalty and faith on the basis of the heart alone just won't do. Nonetheless, to swing back once again on the story's incessant pendulum, what could it possibly mean to construct a human society on the basis of "guts," of proving oneself on the military battlefield? Or, for that matter, on the social or economic or cultural or moral battlefield? The question of defending faith seems to have everything, and finally nothing, to do with the difference between throwing in one's lot, unquestioningly, with one's people. Or, oppositionally, with making judgments that seem the very opposite of such a defense, discriminations, indeed, that seem a (gutsy) indictment and maybe even a betrayal of that faith. I did this for all of us, Marx explains to Grossbart, in direct rebuttal of Grossbart's claim to have done what he has done in the name of the Jews. And we are tempted, for the moment, to applaud Marx's bravery, his guts.

But who, exactly, is Marx's "all of us"? And does this "all of us" differ, in any substantive or structural way, from Grossbart's? Does it imply a different order or register of moral identification, transcending the narrow, special pleading of group loyalties? Or is Marx's "all of us" only a different (if larger) set of individuals, expressing merely a different faith that needs defending? In the final analysis, Marx's position may be no more oppositional, no less unquestioning, than Grossbart's. By this token, Marx, no less than Grossbart, is a self-appointed and rather grandiose defender of the faith, albeit not the faith called Judaism.

The historical joke that the title of Roth's story invokes directly exposes the dishonesty and self-concern of both Grossbart's and Marx's positions. The original "defender of the faith" was King Henry VIII, who was granted the title by the Pope not long before he broke with Rome and created a church of his own, an event that had direct implications for the Puritan Revolution in England and the subsequent settling of the American colonies. Given Roth's subversion of America's founding myths in **Goodbye, Columbus,** it seems likely that, in this story about American patriotism and war, Roth is thinking of that other defender of the faith. To defend a faith may well imply, Roth suggests, breaking (quite faithlessly) with another faith. It may involve inventing a new faith, which, in a process of infinite regress, will also need to be defended. Hence, the story's placement in that bastion of national defense, the American army. Are we doomed always to do the bidding of one "us" or another, to invent the requirements of a new faith even as we abandon the dictates of an old one?

In this context the extra reverberations provided by the name of Roth's major protagonist cannot be ignored. "Marx, you know, like Karl Marx," Grossbart says to Nathan, in his bid to force Marx to identify himself as a Jew: "The Marx Brothers. Those guys are all—M-a-r-x. Isn't that how *you* spell it, Sergeant?" And Nathan identifies fully, letter by letter: "M-a-r-x," he answers (125). Who, we are forced to ask, are these several, identically transcribed yet utterly different Marxes, appearing, in repeating performances, comically and tragically, on the stage of international politics and culture? "Karl and Harpo," Nathan says later; "I was one of them" (126). Which one, we might ask? And what is his familial connection to the Jewish family Marx? Philosopher, clown, or simple ordinary citizen?

Unlike most of Roth's fiction, **"Defender of the Faith"** is not especially comic and it is certainly not the broad slapstick conjured up by the reference to the Marx Brothers. Nonetheless, in its distance from the fighting in Europe, in its belatedness (Hitler is dead, the Nazis conquered), and in the smallness of its melodrama, it can easily be read as a parody of the large issues its title announces—which is itself part of the comedy. And one long, crucial segment of the story is in fact riotously funny, in the wildly insane manner of a Marx Brothers film. I refer to the sequence when Grossbart prevails upon Marx to give him a pass to celebrate the Passover seder with his aunt, one month after Passover is over (squeezing out of the word passover a neat new pun), a week before she's actually invited him to come to her home, and then ups the ante to include his two Jewish comrades in arms, Halpern and Fishbein, and then upon his return, brings Sergeant Marx, not a piece of gefilte fish as requested, but a (quite unkosher) Chinese egg roll. The sequence's crowding of errors and people, its substitutions of things and events (egg rolls for gefilte fish, Chinese restaurants for seders) recalls nothing so much

as classic Marx Brothers' mayhem—say, the cabin scene from *Night at the Opera.*

Why these allusions (implicit and explicit) to the Marx Brothers in what is otherwise not a comic tale? Why the mixture of the comic and the tragic in this story, the reunion (as it were) of the missing Marx (Karl) with the other three? (There was, of course, originally a fourth Marx brother, who subsequently fell out of their movies; whether or not this was in Roth's mind is, of course, impossible to say). In a recent essay about the Marx Brothers in the *London Review of Books,* Stanley Cavell has defined the comedy of their films in terms that help us locate the dimensions of Roth's own undertaking in **"Defender of the Faith."** The fantastic energy of the Marx Brothers, argues Cavell, derives from the fierce disequilibrium of the "pleasure" and "pain" effected by the movies' "puns." The "pain" of puns, Cavell goes on, is to "stop the forward motion of assertion, peel back the protective self-ignorance of words." It is the pain of "incessant thinking—thinking among the endless things there are to say, which of them we shall have for ever said, and not said, now. Their pleasure is the illusion that nothing is going unsaid. . . . An array of implication," Cavell continues,

> like the disarray of puns, will threaten anarchy, against a demand for autarchy; but both work to make what sense is to be made of a world whose sense is stolen, in which it is to be stolen back. Both show aspects of our victimisation by words, fools of them, but thereby show that there are, still, ordinary words, beyond and between us, whose lives we might imagine, which might share lives we can imagine—not simply signs and signals hovering over a destroyed landscape.

For Cavell the Marx Brothers, to invoke the Wittgensteinian text informing his language here, lead language back home again, and, in the process, they make of a "destroyed landscape" a home, a place of shared meanings, of shared living. Their movies are thus filled not only with humor but with hope, we might even say with faith, that human beings can thus steal back their birthright and begin the story anew. As Cavell also suggests in his essay, there is something specifically Jewish about the Marx Brothers' comedies, something having to do with the immigrant and the chaotic, but also liberating, place he or she occupies between worlds.[3]

In **"Defender of the Faith,"** as in the greater range of his writings, Roth makes his move toward Marx-like comedy, unsettling meanings, introducing arrays of implication, and leading language back home by breaking it open and ridding it of its pretenses and disguises. "You're a regular Messiah, aren't you?" Nathan quips sarcastically to Grossbart, who replies,

"That's a good one, Sergeant. . . . But who knows? Who can tell? Maybe you're the Messiah—a little bit" (138). And, at the penultimate moment of the story, when it is still in its comic upswing, Nathan entertains this possibility, in appropriately sacrilegious but compassionate terms: "Who was Nathan Marx to be such a penny pincher with kindness? Surely, I thought, the Messiah himself—if He should ever come—won't niggle over nickels and dimes. God willing, he'll hug and kiss" (145).

But Roth suggests that the destroyed, Holocaust-razed landscape of the world, after the extermination of six million Jews, cannot, especially in a work of Jewish fiction, so easily be reclaimed. More to the point, Nathan Marx, who can almost join in the punning, anarchy-producing, raucous comedy of recovery and redefinition, simply cannot keep the faith. Nathan makes the subtle but decisive turn from comedy to tragedy when, furious and enraged, he exits the sprawling scene of outlandish comedy ("Egg roll . . . Holy Christ, Chinese goddam egg roll" [147]) and enters into the final act of what he declares to be grim "fate": "With a kind of quiet nervousness, they polished shoes, shined belt buckles, squared away underwear, trying as best they could to accept their fate. Behind me, Grossbart swallowed hard, accepting his. And then, resisting with all my will an impulse to turn and seek pardon for my vindictiveness I accepted my own" (149-50).

"Closing [his] heart"—alternately referred to as "tight" and "hard" (142, 144)—Nathan, in this Passover drama, plays no role so much as that of pharaoh, that perverse agent of the divine, whose heart, we are told in the Bible, God repeatedly hardens. And this makes of Grossbart in this mini-scenario of exodus no less than the embodiment of the Jewish people. And its Christ: for, even though Roth keeps his story fundamentally Jewish, nonetheless, insofar as the issue given Marx to decide is whether to save Grossbart, or to damn him, the story has a Christian implication as well.

Readers, especially Jewish readers, who are disinclined toward a poetics of salvation, are likely to applaud Marx in his desire not to play the messiah. But like another fatherly military officer in American literary history with an erring "son," in another story about types and antitypes of salvation and about the necessity for maintaining military discipline at all costs, Nathan Marx declines becoming the messiah only to discover himself playing the even more exalted role of God the Father (**"Defender of the Faith"** explicitly places Marx and Grossbart in a father-son relationship). Refusing to become Grossbart's messiah, Nathan Marx becomes the messiah of "all of us." And when, like

Melville's Captain Vere, he refuses finally to "seek pardon" of the son, choosing instead to hide behind the protective self-ignorance of words like "accepting one's fate" ("Fated boy," Captain Vere says to Billy; "an angel of God. Yet the angel must hang"),[4] we may well feel that Nathan has exactly misunderstood what Melville's Captain Vere could also not quite fathom: that we are not actors in a cosmic drama, speaking our given lines, defending the faith, accepting our fate (and that of others), but rather, merely human beings of failed and flawed judgment, who simultaneously act out of "vindictiveness" and honor, and who might do well at least to seek the pardon of those whose lives we inevitably, irreparably, injure.[5]

If "defender of the faith" is one paradoxical, unexamined phrase on which the narrative turns, "accepting fate" is the other. What is "fate" that it should be or even can be accepted? And what does it mean to "accept" it? To surrender to it? Or to embrace it? Although accepting fate seems to be the heroic wisdom of this story, it is exactly the position that Roth's story (like his corpus as a whole) resists. It is what blocks and banishes in this story the comedic impulse that characterizes his other writings. It is what makes **"Defender,"** like "Billy Budd," tragedy. For in declaring his action inevitable, fated, Nathan Marx, like Captain Vere before him, and like that other defender of faith, Sheldon Grossbart, evades acknowledging his responsibility for what he has done. Having made a choice, he denies his having made it, denies that he has a choice in the matter at all.

In a discussion of one of the most central of America's philosophical texts, Thoreau's *Walden,* Cavell calls this condition of denying choice *fate.* Such fate, he suggests, is precisely the opposite of faith:

> The world is what meets the conditions of what we call our necessities—whether we have really found them to be ours or not. "The universe constantly and obediently answers to our conceptions." . . . In particular, we have determined that we shall be governed by fate—by something that denies for us the incessant exercise of our control. . . . What we have constructed is fate itself. That it never turns aside is merely what the word fate, or rather Atropos, means. And we are not fated to it; *we* can turn. We can learn a lesson . . . from . . . what happens, if we can for once learn something that does not merely confirm our worst fears instead of our confidence. . . . Your own is the path he [Thoreau] calls wisdom, confidence, faith. . . . One must advance "confidently in the direction of [one's] dreams." . . . Everybody more or less sees the sense of this. The question is how we are to find this path, have the trust to accept it, since everyone also more or less knows that it is an offer, a promise. We live by fate because we are "determined not to live by faith."[6]

Fate, Roth's story demonstrates, is only religion in a different guise, its god an impersonalization of deity just as coercive, just as demanding, just as angry, as the God it replaces. Fate, in other words, is that we construct for ourselves and for each other and oblige each other, with sacred oaths, to defend. Indeed, it is what faith becomes under the pressure of its having to be defended as opposed to its being declared or accepted, as faith. In view of the catastrophe that has just transpired in Europe, the protective self-ignorance of Marx's words is excruciating. And they recall all too powerfully the brother Marx who is neither straight man nor mute, neither clown nor victim, for whom there are no puns and no comedy to offset the grim determinism and fateful fatality of his words.

It is the presence of this other Marx on the scene of Roth's drama that compromises the comedy of Roth's story, as faith transforms itself into fate, and the story ends, not in Roth's typical—if dark—laughter, but in a silence far more harrowing, far less eloquent than Harpo's. That Karl Marx should haunt Roth's story is not difficult to understand. If fascism represented one grave threat to Jewish existence, Marxism represented another. Not only was Marx himself personally anti-Semitic and therefore a prototype of the self-hating Jew (exactly what Nathan Marx and his author are accused of), but Marxist ideology produced its own virulent anti-Semitism in the Russian Communist party, giving way not only to Communism's complicity with fascism in the Hitler-Stalin pact but to the infamous Show Trials of the Stalin Regime. Marxism, which embraced large, universal, moral truths addressed, like Nathan's, to *all* of us, provides the counterplot in Jewish history to Jewish assimilation (the German phenomenon American Jewry imitate, of which the story's protagonist is already a representative). If the Holocaust was one major event in the backdrop of Roth's youth, to which he continues throughout his career to respond, American Jewish socialism/Communism/Stalinism was the other. Indeed, it may be possible to trace some of the differences between Roth and his critics—like Irving Howe—and some of the affinities between Roth and other American Jewish intellectuals (like Lionel Trilling and Stanley Cavell) to the different political positions these figures take vis-à-vis American (Jewish) socialism. In **"Defender of the Faith,"** Nathan Marx does not represent, simply, the assimilated American Jew. He embodies one particular form that that assimilationism took, a form that was initially so promising that its later tragic implications, in particular for Jews, could hardly be taken lightly.

Is it part of the tragedy of the Jewish people, the story asks, their fate, perhaps, for Jews always to align themselves with the ideological systems that, in an effort to save the world, will seek to destroy the Jews, if not as individuals, then as a group? Charlie Chaplin's *The*

Great Dictator examines the highly comic, deeply tragic, internal relation between the Jew as clown/victim and as tyrant/dictator: the Jews, it would seem, are their own worst enemies, hopelessly committed to the defense of one faith or another, to their own destruction. In his own view of things, Nathan Marx can be either Jew or American. He cannot be both at once. He cannot explore and mobilize the comic potential of his multiple personae, the nesting egg of Marxes cracked open to reveal the many facets, not only of Jewish history but of the individual Jew within that history. In this singleness of his self-conception and purpose, Nathan Marx is a lot more like Sheldon Grossbart than he, or we, would like to think. Whichever Marx he is, Nathan, like Grossbart, follows, to its fateful conclusion, a script from which he will not turn aside.

Marx's error, it must be emphasized, is not in the choice he makes, even though we are made to see that his choice is problematic. Rather, it lies in his going behind "fate" to deny he has made a choice. On first glance, the final paragraph of the story seems an airtight defense of Marx's position, as Grossbart, Halpern, Fishbein are presented (at least by Marx) as accepting their fate. But, while it may well be the case that these soldiers, at this moment in the story, have no choice in what is about to happen to them, any more than they had any choice in their being drafted into the American army, nonetheless their defense of their country has, from the beginning, been a part of a social contract which itself acknowledges their participation in a made, prior choice. Certainly their parents, for the most part immigrant Jews who chose to come to America, made a choice, which as much obliges them to defend America as their Jewish origins oblige them to defend their other faith. It is significant, in this context, that Grossbart has his father sign a letter of protest that he himself writes: father and son are implicated in exactly the same choices in nearly the same ways. And so, too, is Nathan, whose being Jewish and American are choices in exactly the same way. Nathan may be born Jewish and American, and therefore seem to have no choice in the matter, but no one compels him to remain either one; no one decides for him now how he will act or speak in relation to Barrett or Grossbart, America or Judaism. To speak, then, with conviction, as a Jew or an American or an American Jew, Nathan Marx has to do more than act in accordance with what he understands to be American or Jewish or Jewish American values. He must admit his choice in the matter and speak through an identity that he consciously, deliberately embraces.

Even though Nathan Marx is the narrator of **"Defender of the Faith,"** too much is left unsaid by him for him to emerge the hero of the story. It is one of the text's more painful moments, for example, when Nathan, playing Groucho-like "straight man" to Captain Barrett, fails to respond to the captain's anti-Semitic and racist utterances (136). Nathan's voicelessness offers grim warning of what his silence at the end of the story may portend, when he expressly refuses to provide Grossbart with an explanation of his actions or to seek his pardon. But Philip Roth is not Nathan Marx, and it is important for this story that the issue for Roth is not merely Marx's behavior (which may, in fact, be correct), but his unwillingness to speak.

In **"Defender of the Faith"** Roth does more than dramatize the sufficiently complex dilemma of American Jewish loyalties, which could be taken as nothing more than one particular case of the general phenomenon of American hyphenation, relevant to any number of American ethnic and racial groups. Rather, Roth takes it upon himself to speak, unmistakably and unequivocally, *as a Jew*. And he says, as Jew, to other Jews, and to non-Jews as well, something about Jewish suffering and persecution, and, within that self-acknowledged context, something even more powerful and painful about Jewish choices and responsibilities, Jewish faith and fate. Roth, we might say, given the Marx-ist context of the story, produces (as Nathan Marx does not) a specifically Jewish asking of the question that Karl Marx himself had asked (and answered), long before Hitler asked (and answered) the same question. This is what Karl Marx himself called the "Jewish Question," the question of how and whether Jews will continue to exist upon the stage of world history, and what role they will play, and for whom, and whether they or someone else will direct them in their acting.

To adapt Captain Barrett's thinking on this matter, who or what are these Jews (of whom Grossbart is certainly one representative) to be making so much trouble, trouble that might well be thought to have led as directly to the Cold War (aren't all Jews, Communists? all Communists, Jews?) as it had to World War II. Indeed, for many individuals, at the end of the twentieth century, the Jews are still playing out this Question, largely (in the Western world) as someone else's question, and they are enacting it center stage (in the Middle East), as if somehow Western culture has still not reached its Final Solution vis-à-vis the Jews. In **"Defender of the Faith,"** Roth defends his faith as much by rendering the Jewish Question a *Jewish* question as by any insights he offers into faith itself. He retrieves the question, of faith and fate, not as something asked by someone else about the Jews, which is susceptible of one answer or another, but as one Jew painfully and passionately asking himself a question about himself, his people, and the world.

Roth owns up to Grossbart in a way that Nathan Marx will not, and he owns up to both of them as equally representative of Jewish claims and lapses. For Roth, the danger of defending faith and accepting fate is the same: both silence the individual voice. They surrender the telling and the doing of our lives to someone or something else, as if our lives were nothing more than answers to someone else's questions.

Still, Roth's gag of playing out Karl Marx's Jewish Question as a Marx Brothers comedy produces dangers of its own. The story may well spin out of control. It may gag on its own words, and leave us (like Grossbart and Marx, in the final scene) speechless. Roth does not wholly evade this danger. Nonetheless, by playing out his comedy of American Jewish identity under the shadow of the Holocaust, Roth, even as he evidences some of the profits of laughter, acknowledges its real costs as well. The definition of Roth's comedy, we might say, is "accepting fate" under protest, where such acceptance represents the very opposite of submission. His fiction "defends faith" exactly by refusing to defend it.

"Defender of the Faith" is not simply a story by a Jewish American writer about Jews and Jewish history. Rather, it is a fundamentally Jewish work of art and philosophy. Like the tradition of rabbinic midrash it recalls, it reads texts, including itself, through a ceaseless play of interpretive possibilities.[7] And without surrendering its commitment to the shared texts of our mutual lives and destinies, it defies determinism (fate) in order to lead language back home again to faith. In so proceeding, Roth's story takes back the fate of the Jews from those (including other Jews) who would determine that fate for them. He affirms a faith, the defense of which can only be in its perpetual reaffirmation.

Notes

1. As Alfred Kazin put it, the story is a "drama of personal integrity in the face of group pressures" (27)—quoted by Jay L. Halio in *Philip Roth Revisited* (New York: Twayne, 1992) 26-28, who is of the same opinion. Among those who agree are Sanford Pinsker, *The Comedy that "Hoits": An Essay on the Fiction of Philip Roth* (Columbia, Mo.: University of Missouri Press, 1975) 15-19; Hana Wirth-Nesher, "From Newark to Prague: Roth's Place in the American-Jewish Literary Tradition," in *Reading Philip Roth,* ed. Asher Z. Milbauer and Donald G. Watson (New York: Macmillan Press, 1988) 17-31 (reading of "Defender" 21-22); and Murray Baumgarten and Barbara Gottfried, *Understanding Philip Roth* (Columbia, S.C.: University of South Carolina Press, 1990) 48-51. Though Irving Howe was no advocate of Roth, he

considered "Defender of the Faith" the best of Roth's writings and provided a sensitive reading of it in "Philip Roth Reconsidered," *Commentary* December 1972: 66-77 (reading of "Defender" 72).

In "Writing About Jews," Roth discusses the sharp attack on his work, in particular concerning "Defender," which was mounted by the Jewish community—*Commentary* (December 1963): 446-52; reprinted in Roth, *Reading Myself and Others* (New York: Farrar, Straus, Giroux, 1975) 149-69. In the essay Roth reprints portions of the letters and articles written against him and his fiction; the April 1963 issue of *Commentary* contains responses to Roth's self-defense (7-18).

2. Philip Roth, *Goodbye, Columbus and Five Short Stories* (London: Penguin, 1964) 125; subsequent citations in text.

3. Stanley Cavell, "Nothing goes without saying: Stanley Cavell reads the Marx Brothers," *London Review of Books* 16 (6 January 1994): 3-5. By invoking the Yiddish theater and the experiences of his own (Jewish) immigrant father, Cavell also implies the specifically Jewish contexts of these movies.

4. Herman Melville, *Billy Budd, Sailor and Other Stories,* ed. Harold Beaver (London: Penguin, 1970) 377-78.

5. I read Melville's *Billy Budd* along these lines in *Fiction and Historical Consciousness: The American Romance Tradition* (New Haven: Yale University Press, 1989) 58-62.

6. Stanley Cavell, *The Senses of Walden* (San Francisco: North Point Press, 1981) 97-98.

7. For basic definitions of rabbinic midrash, especially in relation to contemporary literature and literary theory, see Geoffrey H. Hartman and Sanford Budick, *Midrash and Literature* (New Haven: Yale University Press, 1986).

Stephen Wade (essay date 1996)

SOURCE: Wade, Stephen. "From Klugman to Portnoy." *The Imagination in Transit,* pp. 26-34. Sheffield, England: Sheffield Academic Press, 1996.

[*In the following essay, Wade discusses Roth's use of social realism in his early works and examines the satirical depiction of postwar Jews in* Goodbye, Columbus *as well as Roth's broadening of his themes in subsequent novels.*]

A relevant starting point in an analysis of Roth's first four works involves some reference to social history. The keyword here is suburbia. The unifying context in all four books is that of the American suburbs, with the accretions of working class and 'respectable' middle class, cultural bohemians, graduates, secularized immigrants, all subject to the extensions of capitalism, social uniformity and religious doubt. The books contain portraits of family power-structures under stress; they deal with generational confrontation; they depict pathetic vignettes of various versions of human failure, yet they also carry wry humour, farcical entertainment, surreal dimensions and social realism.

It is helpful to consider the nature of the geographical and demographic changes inherent in suburban growth. The general trend in the 1950s, exhibited by the career of the builder William Levitt, was the acceleration of suburban building and a population shift from city to suburb of the mostly white middle classes, with a corresponding move of black Americans from the south to the north into the vacated cities. The historian, Richard Polenberg explains thus:

> The general contours of suburban development were shaped by the expansion of the automobile industry, the creation of a national highway system, the federal approach to insuring home mortgages, the application of mass-production techniques to the housing industry, and the decision of businessmen to decentralize their operations.[1]

The outstanding result of this population shift, as it impressed itself onto the writers of that period, was uniformity. Sociologists such as David Riesman talked of 'the lonely crowd' and 'the suburban sadness' and noted the consequences of suburbanization on the human, relational level in terms of deprivation in perception, stimulation and desire for betterment. Riesman commented: 'The suburb is like a fraternity house at a small college in which like-mindedness reverberates upon itself.'[2] With Roth and Jewish American writing in mind, the important aspect of these changes was how the Jewish sense of identity fared in the midst of this. There was a definite decline in ethnic self-concept and integration. Historians have pointed out that 'religion was replacing nationality' and that there was a fragmentation even within different Jewish communities. The scene where Mrs Patimkin questions Neil about his religious attitudes must be typical of this increasing feeling of difference within the Jewish American community:

> 'Are you interested in B'nai Brith?' she asked me. 'Ron is joining you know, as soon as he gets married.'
>
> 'I think I'll wait till then,' I said.
>
> . . . 'What temple do you belong to?' She asked in a moment.
>
> 'We used to belong to Hudson Street synagogue. Since my parents left, I haven't had much contact.'[3]

The trend was for ethnic groups in this new suburbia either to retain their ethnicity simply through religious practice, or to keep a distance and thus develop a sense of their superiority. The increasing presence of black Americans in the cities meant that other versions of difference and contradistinction would inevitably arrive. Neil's visit to the 'Patimkin Kitchen and Bathroom Sinks' factory gives us a glimpse of these social trends woven into the novella's themes. Neil describes the shouts of negro children playing in the streets which used to form a Jewish area with kosher delicatessens and so on. 'Now, in fact, the negroes were making the same migration,' he comments. The negro boy in the story who searches out the art books in the library where Neil works is used in the narrative to set up a textual opposition, and this is the first hint that Roth is developing from this background a profound social commentary, linked with an examination of himself and his first fictional persona.

Goodbye, Columbus (1959), a collection including the novella of that name and another five short stories, brought a varied range of responses in the reviews of the time. They mostly agreed on the social commentary, and on the sources of the style in Salinger and others, but few critics saw what Leslie Fiedler pointed out: that Roth received the young Jewish writer's accolade, the accusation of anti-semitism.[4]

Saul Bellow and others saw literary sources for Neil Klugman, but the real controversy came from two of the short stories, not the main novella. There is a great deal to say about this first extended work of fiction. First, it uses the device of the narrator observing a family who have attractiveness, vitality, energy as well as status and wealth. Neil reminds the reader of Nick in *The Great Gatsby* in this sense, or of Herr Issyvoo watching Mr Norris in Isherwood's *Mr Norris Changes Trains*. The device sets up various textual dialogic discourses which enable Roth to contrast action with passivity, rich with respectably poor, 'new' American mores against traditional Jewish family values. Most prominent of all, Roth interweaves a love story which lets him explore the sexual liberation inherent in the Patimkin's lifestyle. One reviewer considered that the issue of Brenda's diaphragm and the centrality of sex in the novella was all that Roth was interested in. Such are the blinkers worn by critics who only extract one thing—what they want to see. This latter response led to Roth eventually having to write a long apologia for something that he had never intended in the first place, so it would be useful here to insist on what the first book is really addressing.

The basis of the story concerns the narrator's place in a negative, life-denying milieu as he describes and annotates the allure of the Patimkins' world. It is the story of a seduction, but also, more broadly, an account of the acculturation of a new ego-identity for Roth's generation. In contrast to the aggressive, pushy, self-concerned atmosphere of the Patimkins' home. Aunt Gladys and Uncle Max, with whom Neil lives, represent values which suggest anachronism, passivity and anti-selfhood attributes. Aunt Gladys is depicted in a comic, satirical way; a mode of narration is employed that hints at self-parody and pastiche, almost at times an intonation of the comic monologue routine with which Portnoy delivers his story:

> Life was a throwing off for poor Aunt Gladys, her greatest joys were taking out the garbage, emptying her pantry, and making threadbare bundles for what she still referred to as the Poor Jews in Palestine. I only hope she dies with an empty refrigerator, otherwise she'll ruin eternity for everyone else.[5]

This is very much the narrative voice of Woody Allen's *Radio Days:* a device of distancing an oppositional voice in a text in order to place a privileged reading of the Other—in this case the Patimkins. What do they offer?

This forms the second element in the story: Neil sees Brenda as amazingly open, frank and receptive. Her direct, untroubled ability with words and her uncomplicated showing of affection wins him from the negating world of the past, of denial, and of communication through sub-texts. 'She was smiling there, at ME, down at the bottom of the swimming pool . . .'[6] and later in the same episode, she asks him,

> 'Where, do you get those fine shoulders? Do you play something?'
>
> 'No,' I said, 'I just grew up and they came with me.'
>
> 'I like your body. It's fine.'[7]

The Patimkin family are easy to see as satirical targets, but in the noisy dinner scene something else is clarified: they are what might be called Philistines from the cultured, restrained world of good manners represented by home. The meal is convivial and entirely without niceties or refinement. Apologies are not necessary. Eating in their family is part of another, alien concept of the family for Neil. It embraces tolerance even of rule-breaking. Of course, the test comes when their morality is stretched, and old attitudes emerge, but open sensuality and the free and unburdened relations in leisure and sport are what win him over. The reader is bound to include censure with the seemingly innocent laughter urged on him or her by the images of Aunt Gladys and her little domestic rituals.

The other element in the novella's narrative scheme is the Newark library. This, it can be argued, is the wide perspective opening the narrow, circumscribed world of the Jewish community and their concerns into middle ground America. The negro boy arrives in the tranquillity and repression of the library like a nervous tic on a comatose body. That 'body' has been established as a limbo, a lifeless purgatory in which youth will atrophy; the familiar Bellovian world of purgatorial chasms within the self emerges:

> The day began the same as any other. From behind the desk on the main floor, I watched the hot high-breasted teenage girls . . . The stairs were an imitation of a staircase somewhere in Versailles . . .[8]

His colleague John McKee is described as a brain-dead functionary, a bureaucrat who has no self beyond the walls of this artificial and inhuman place. It takes only a few pages of the novella to establish that the plot takes in a series of images like the above, hinting at the dying limbs of the body of Newark—and all references to urban, Europe-related culture show it as dead, or at least moribund. The Patimkins have stepped into another new America and Neil is taken in.

The strongest social comment, one could suggest, is the negro boy's significance. The initial conversation of Neil and the boy, fuddled by the 'heart/art' confusion, indicates that the McKee element wants to protect the shrine of art and culture from the newest Americans in the dream city. But Neil is redeemed as the new man with integrity:

> 'Those are VERY expensive books.'
>
> 'Don't be nervous, John. People are supposed to touch them.'
>
> 'There is touching,' said John sententiously, 'And there is touching . . .'[9]

In the end, however, the narrative's devices assert the familiar ambiguity of Jamesian mistrust. Neil's sad verdict on the disappearance of the negro boy might, ironically, be made about him too:

> But no, they were not his kind of artists. What had probably happened was that he had given up on the library and gone back to playing Willie Mays in the streets. He was better off, I thought. No sense carrying dreams of Tahiti in your head, if you can't afford the fare.[10]

This could equally be a reference to what Neil loses; how something in him leads inevitably to failure; in fact, the relentless sub-text of rebellion and satirical ridicule, lapsing at times into absurdity, leads to a conclusion in which Neil himself sees the failure as one of the ego-identity, not of any wider social forces. He asks himself how to look behind the image he sees, and 'catch whatever it was that looked through those eyes.'[11]

Goodbye, Columbus, then, is largely ironical, setting up oppositional contexts to counteract the narrator's desire to escape a perceived failure, a sense of the inevitable, created by his roots, his familial malaises and limitations of vision. The comment Neil makes about the group of young fresh-faced wives at the South Mountain reservation prompts a reading which seeks to broaden the imaginative locus of the novella's subject: 'These were the goddesses, and if I were Paris, I could not have been able to choose among them.' But the charm, he sees, is false. 'Their hair would always stay the colour they desired.'[12] The young man's fiction mixing self-identity and gentle satire finds a more complex conclusion. That was certainly something that fifties fiction was learning from the existential forays of the new Jewish American writers since Bellow.

Of course, there is also a lyrical, poetic quality to the prose; and the introspection of Neil's self-searchings finds powerful contrasts with the hard surface talk of business and money in the Patimkin world. It could be as much a disquisition on American capitalism and materialism as *The Great Gatsby,* with a twist of contemporaneity added. Irving Howe in a review of the time saw much of this, but said 'there is not enough imaginative transformation.'[13] However, the basis of the story pre-empts this: the lack of this is the point.

This is the ideal point to mention the beginnings of the furore against Roth's writing on Jewish themes: the two stories from the *Goodbye, Columbus* volume that attracted antagonism and misreadings are **'Defender of the Faith,'** and **'Epstein,'** and it should be pointed out here that the two stories make an interesting opening to the question of Roth's two polarities, the 'ethical Jew' and the 'good Jewish boy.' The necessary overview of Roth's writing up to *Portnoy's Complaint* in 1969 must begin with the meanings of the 'ethical Jew' term. It carries with it all the cultural and historical reference to the Jewish people as 'people of the book.' The intensely literate and literary habits of thought in the annotation and evaluation of the Hebrew Torah and associated scholarship, so minutely described in Potok's *The Chosen,* forms a part of this. From the socio-comic element in Roth's fiction we find the Jew as a version of Everyman in an allegory (Epstein is this), but from the fictions of the accretion of liberal American middle-class culture and the university art and writing circles, the playgoers and music-lovers, comes the issue of the place in the modern American novel of the established moralistic and intellectual values of the Jewish inheritance. Roth deals with this in some depth in *Letting Go,* but before Gabe Wallach and a more approachable, mainline existential storyline, Roth had to deal with the question of individuality within the Jewish structures of social allegiance, bonds and habits of character. This is why

'Defender of the Faith,' although only a social comedy with an underlying point about the identity of a minority, attracted such vilification and such extreme readings.

Many contemporary reviews mentioned anti-semitism, vulgarity and bad taste. Some damned by faint praise and sheer blandness. But Roth's essay *Writing about Jews* (from a lecture delivered originally in 1963) addresses the question of authorial intention: labyrinthine, virtually impossible to navigate so as to emerge into daylight. His basic defence was that a particular critic, Rabbi Seligson, wanted Jewish writing to be of only one type. The only acceptable writing was that which gave Judaism and Jewish culture and manners a 'good press.' Roth insists on the universal and his argument is admirably successful.

In the story, what is so contentious is, one could argue, a purely literary point. Fishbein and Grossbart are depicted as totally two-sided, ambiguous characters. The reader is asked to judge whether their demands on Nathan Marx are exploitative or humanly supportable. However one decides, the theme of the brotherhood of individuals in a setting of minority identity against a militaristic machine is unavoidably compelling. It is all the more so because that machine is so efficient and so non-human. We are asked to feel the family appeal of the slightest presence of Grossbart:

> 'The others went to sleep.' He took a deep, paternal breath. We sat silent for a while, and a homey feeling invaded my ugly little cubicle; the door was locked, the cat was out, the children were safely in bed.[14]

At several stages in the story, the interplay of stylistic and verbal registers force an effect of moving what is Jewish into the privileged textual placing of what is human. When Marx countermands Grossbart's reversal of the orders to send him into the combat-centred Pacific, and the plot leads to the final tragi-comic conclusion from this, the ambiguous dialogic functioning of the representation of Jewishness begs for judgment.

Roth even forces the debate into the open when Marx is losing patience with the scheming, recalcitrant but somehow likeable Grossbart.

> 'Come back here!' I called. He stopped and looked at me. 'Grossbart, why can't you be like the rest? Why do you have to stick out like a sore thumb?'
>
> 'Because I'm a Jew, Sergeant. I AM different. Better, maybe not. But different.'[15]

When Grossbart insists that it is a hard thing to be a Jew, the reader is forced to consider why it is that Marx is so opposite—and the conclusion is that Grossbart is a representative of the element of ethical Jew-

hood that Marx has cancelled out in himself in order to be a Sergeant in the US Army. In other words, Roth is entering the fictional areas where residual Jewishness persists: the aspects of identity that will always feel the presence and influence of that quality that Grossbart feels so keenly. One has to conclude, then, that Grossbart's final tears, the defeat of his strategies of survival and comfort as a Jew before his American nature, are somewhere near tragedy. The relationship is akin to that of Iago and Othello. In Shakespeare's play, both the emptiness inside Othello the racial outsider with power in the state, and the hatred within Iago the alienated insider have to be punished. Othello's, like Marx's, is that much worse because of the disintegration of a formerly ordered self. The cajolings and pleadings of those subject to power have brought changes in those with power but only because of what is already there. The residual Jewishness has been denied in Sergeant Nathan Marx. Marx's final comment, after all, is 'And then, resisting with all my will an impulse to seek pardon for my vindictiveness, I accepted my own.'[16]

In this same collection, **'The Conversion of the Jews'** is more openly about related themes. Young Ozzie in schul disobeys the rather poorly equipped Rabbi Binder, and a serious question from the boy on a serious point leads to a reversal of power. Ozzie forces a comic show-down and Rabbi Binder, in some ways like Marx, has to undergo a purifying embarrassment to attain forgiveness. It all came from the intransigent insistence on the pride of office and the vanity of status.

This may be seen in several stories: human frailties against dogma. It is there in the innocent story, **'Epstein,'** a simple comic tale of lust in an old man; of fornication in the neighbourhood. Chaucerian in its tone at times, the story is yet another example of how Roth simply writes of the way universal human traits are intensified in specific ethnic, racial or religious sub-groups, independent of any moral structures that might be applied. The lesson is given to us directly in the lecture/essay quoted earlier:

> Jews are people who are not what anti-Semites say they are. That was once a statement out of which a man might begin to construct an identity for himself; now it does not work so well, for it is difficult to act counter to the ways people expect you to act when fewer and fewer people define you by such expectations.[17]

It is useful to remind ourselves that Roth has commented on the fact that you can be charged with pleading your own life and calling it fiction; that is to say, inside Philip Roth's self, mixed inextricably in the writer and the man, are metaphorical means of conveying that 'world of forgetting' that has the potential to put versions of the 'ethical Jew' before us, just as Kafka's hero can become a huge insect when he wakes up in the morning and still be a version of Franz Kafka. Such a fundamental *donné* of artistic creation was overlooked by Roth's detractors at the time.

In a contemporary reading of this first book, a collection of stories and an impressive novella of social-realism mixed with comic modes, Roth began the long process of placing provocative and inventive personae within fictional discourse. The next three novels broaden this considerably, *Letting Go* and *When She Was Good* attempting more ambitious and centrally, archetypally American themes, while *Portnoy's Complaint* returns to the more microcosmic milieu of home and family.

In moving on to *Letting Go,* the critic faces multi-layered themes held together by the autobiographical imperative which urges a young writer to move into more ambitious areas. *When She Was Good* is eclectic in language and style, on the surface amorphous and with a naturalistic mood at times, but is not so intractable as has been suggested. This is a constructive point at which to review some of the overall qualities of the two novels. They have been judged as belonging to some vague interim period between the 'main' subject matter of Jewish American identity. They have also been assessed in terms of literary sources. Sol Gittelman, for instance, rightly pinpoints the quality of 'distance and detachment' in both novels, and goes on to say,

> *When She Was Good,* of course, is an act of imitation—imitation, as Roth admits, of James and Flaubert. However, an element of ventriloquism also enters here as Roth speaks through foreign faces in an alien voice, a psychic division . . .[18]

As Zuckerman says when addressing Roth in the last section of *The Facts*:

> It's as if you had worked it out in your mind, the formula for who you are, and this is it. Very neat—but where's the struggle, the STRUGGLING you? Maybe it was easy to get from Leslie Street to Newark Rutgers to Bucknell to Chicago . . . to be drawn to the possibilities of goy America and feel that you have all the freedom that anyone else has.[19]

It is helpful to consider this last comment with these two novels in mind. There may be imitation in both, but what is undeniably strong and interesting with the perspective of the mainstream direction of Roth's work in mind is that both novels concern entrapments in a failing American Dream. The almost intolerable inner failures and emotional walking wounded of *Letting Go* and the ubiquitous aroma of bland, aching loneliness

in *When She Was Good* belong firmly in their intellectual milieu. The studies therein may reflect Roth's own curiosity about goyim, but he achieved outstanding effects of hard realism; it could also be argued that the naturalism of Dreiser is not far away. Certainly, there is a sense of inevitability, of circumscribed lives in a frame of complex, relentlessly reductive forces emanating from an ideological process based in an acquisitive society. But one feels that the most productive critical approaches are in terms of seeing various patterns, examining the decline of familial cohesion and the traumas of living in a mechanistic age.

Letting Go operates on many levels: it is ambitiously comprehensive and Roth allows leisurely accounts of minutiae to extend into a series of emotional dead-ends for most central characters. However, three themes are particularly prominent. One over-riding interest is in the intellectual, academy-centred relationships: a version of the campus novel, but with a cold, objective view. The engagement of the intellectual with the occupational roles and status, as satirized in the figure of Spigliano, is used in the novel as a metaphor for a version of alienation within a postmodern condition. The first section introduces the other main theme—the vestiges of outmoded bonds of affection. Gabe's father and his circle are distanced as if from some other, distant world of dying values, similar to Neil's aunt's part in an eccentric human comedy that allows Roth an oppositional force of deep irony. In *Letting Go* the attachments to the old world are ritualistic, hollow motions, shadowing the reality like an absurd game. The third theme involves the emergence of the argument

Notes

1. R. Polenberg, *One Nation Divisible: Class, Race and Ethnicity in the United States since 1938* (London: Penguin, 1980), p. 129.

2. Quoted in Polenberg, *One Nation*, p. 135.

3. *Goodbye, Columbus*, p. 7.

4. L. A. Fiedler, 'The Image of Newark and the Indignities of Love: Notes on Philip Roth', *Midstream 5* (Summer 1959), pp. 96-99.

5. *Goodbye, Columbus*, p. 13.

6. *Goodbye, Columbus*, p. 20.

7. *Goodbye, Columbus*, p. 21.

8. *Goodbye, Columbus*, p. 31.

9. *Goodbye, Columbus*, p. 33.

10. *Goodbye, Columbus*, p. 93.

11. *Goodbye, Columbus*, p. 104.

12. *Goodbye, Columbus,* p. 76.

13. I. Howe, 'The Suburbs of Babylon', *New Republic* 140 (15 June, 1959), p. 17.

14. Roth, 'Defender of the Faith' in *Goodbye, Columbus,* p. 145.

15. *Goodbye, Columbus,* p. 141.

16. *Goodbye, Columbus,* p. 150.

17. Roth, 'Writing about Jews', in *Reading Myself and Others,* p. 165.

18. S. Gittelman, 'The Pecks of Woodenton, Long Island, Thirty Years Later: Another look at "Eli, the Fanatic"', *Studies in American Jewish Literature* 8.2 (Fall 1989), pp. 138-42.

19. *The Facts,* p. 165.

Theoharis C. Theoharis (essay date spring 1999)

SOURCE: Theoharis, Theoharis C. "'For with God All Things Are Possible': Philip Roth's 'The Conversion of the Jews.'" *Journal of the Short Story in English,* no. 32 (spring 1999): 69-75.

[*In the following essay, Theoharis discusses what he regards as Roth's elegant and comic portrayal of assimilation and identity in "The Conversion of the Jews."*]

The term "other" can express a relation of simple opposition—the reverse, "the other side of the coin," or a relation of simple identity—the additional, "the other penny." Very often, though, the relation presented by the "other" involves a complex and dynamic fusion of opposition and identity. Literature and philosophy and religion may reasonably be thought of as attempts to disclose the laws by which that fusion works, to make its energy our own. The natural sciences and the humanistic disciplines have long given the name "conversion" to the process by which opposition yields up identity. For centuries the phrase "conversion of the Jews" has been a trope for the pragmatically unlikely, the tragically impossible, the heroically resisted, the idealistically sought for event. Andrew Marvell plays wittily on all these meanings in his carpe diem love lyric "To his Coy Mistress." If the two had "World enough, and Time," the speaker promises gallantly, he would woo her indefinitely while she could, if she "please, refuse/Till the Conversion of the *Jews.*" The complex reversal invoked and forestalled by axiomatic reference to the "conversion of the Jews," is, of course, the acceptance by the Jews of Christ's, and Christianity's claim that Jesus is the fusion raising all oppositions into redemptive identity, that he is God for us and with us, our life, whether we are for him or not,

our joy if we are. Two faiths separated by a common dogma, monotheism, Christianity and Judaism are locked in a simple credal opposition—God is One, that One is Three. God is not only the unmultiplied other, but most crucially the unassimilable and unassimilating other for Jews; from Jesus forward, he is another one of us, any one of us, all of us, for Christians. The history of the Jews in Christian times has been a struggle with assimilation. They are the paradigmatic "other," always struggling with the simple and complex meaning of being different, and always bringing Christians to struggle with the same problem. Christians have carried out the struggle violently, almost entirely antagonistically, and mostly unsuccessfully; Jews have prevailed by suffering stubbornly and righteously past the Christian campaign of assimilation through annihilation. Wittily, elegantly, and with elemental humanistic dignity, Philip Roth takes all these matters up in the story of obdurate Ozzie Freedman's unconventionally righteous preparation for his Bar Mitzvah.

Ozzie, like Socrates, confronts the false necessities of his world by persistently exceeding them. As Roth puts it, "What Ozzie wanted to know was always different."[1] During afternoon Hebrew school, which Roth depicts with genially burlesque comedy, Ozzie has wanted to know something different three times. Each desire has ended in the dreaded summons of his mother to the Rabbi's office. The first time he required Rabbi Binder to resolve the contradiction between his instruction that the Jews are God's chosen people and the Declaration of Independence's claim that all men are created equal. When Binder offered a distinction between political and spiritual identities, Ozzie discounted it, insisting that what he wanted to know was something different. The implication Roth makes here is that Ozzie wanted to know why the Rabbi made the incoherent statement to begin with, not how he can get himself out of it, why, in other words, being Jewish can never mean being created equal. The second question is similar: why did his mother single out the eight Jewish deaths in a plane crash as tragic, ignoring the rest. To Binder's inadequate citation of cultural unity, Ozzie responds not only that he wanted to know something different, but when pressed to accept it, blurts out that he wishes all fifty-eight victims had been Jews. Mrs. Freedman is summoned again. The exasperated response again annuls the privilege of Jewish "difference," substituting a comically punitive, absurd compassion, a Marx brother's quip, along with the anger—if they all had been Jews, his cracked logic runs, there would be less of what Ozzie cannot understand and more compassion.

The third connundrum is the worst, and centers on the dividing line of Christianity and Judaism: the human and divine status of Jesus. If God is omnipotent, Ozzie asks, how can Binder claim that he could not father Jesus on Mary without intercourse? Roth makes much of the snickering comedy attending thirteen year-old male inquiry into this subject, as in this exchange: "'Sure its impossible. That stuff's all bull. To have a baby you gotta get laid,' Itzie theologized. 'Mary hadda get laid'" (Roth, *Goodbye, Columbus* [*Goodbye, Columbus and Five Short Stories*] [*R*], p. 140). As the story begins, Ozzie has not yet responded to Binder's evasive restatement that the historicity of Jesus excludes his divine status, except to say again that he wants to know something different. The implied object of inquiry here is how can being Jewish, an identity established in righteous worship of an omnipotent God, require a stiffnecked limitation of that omnipotence. The bulk of the action takes place on Wednesday afternoon, the day his mother has to come and account a third time to Binder for her son's insubordinate recalcitrance. Ozzie has told her why she's been summoned again, and her response, over Sabbath supper, has been to slap his face.

Before she arrives Ozzie and Binder have a blowout, in which Ozzie challenges the Rabbi with the question, "Why can't He make anything He wants to make?," and then assaults him with the rebellious insult "You don't know! You don't know anything about God!" (*R*, p. 146). Binder responds with an accidental blow to Ozzie's nose; a nosebleed, and a chase ensue, and the scene ends with Ozzie on the roof of the synagogue, and the other boys, with Binder, on the sidewalk staring up at him. Binder commands Ozzie to descend, unavailingly, at which point the dotty caretaker of the synagogue calls the fire department to get Ozzie off the roof, because he once got a cat off his roof that way. Going to the roof to flee repudiated and discredited religious instruction, Ozzie starts his real initiation into manhood. Accordingly, he's confused about what he's done, initially. The first question, Is it me up here?, yields quickly to a subtler pair—is the question Is it me on the roof, or Is it me who called Binder a bastard? The split inquiry presents the split status of the boy straining to become the man in Ozzie, and the division is quickly dispelled once his identity as defier is established by Binder's command that he descend immediately. Establishing him as Ozzie, the command ironically fills him with a feeling of peace and power. The first strain toward adulthood is finished, and the irenic potency it bestows will swell soon into comic resolution of Christian and Jewish theological and cultural difference as Ozzie compels, in his peculiar way, childrens' and adults' submission to his righteousness, his difference.

Enter the firemen. Roth turns the escalating circumstances deftly thematic by having Binder opportunistically respond to the fireman's appropriate but mistaken questions Is the kid nuts, Is he going to jump? with the terrified lie "Yes, Yes, I think so . . . He's been threatening to . . ." (*R*, p. 151). Ozzie registers Binder's cowardly fraud, and responds to the matter of fact fireman's challenge . . . jump or don't jump. "But don't waste our time, willya?" by playing with the power incompetent and indifferent adults have just accidentally and formally bestowed on him (*R*, p. 152). The moment is a comic masterpiece, and teasingly ethnic, sounding what Joyce in *Ulysses* calls the Jewish "accent of the ecstasy of catastrophe" in a sequence of events that fractures and preserves the formal logic of cause and effect.[2] To torment the Rabbi, impress his friends, lord it over the firemen, and match the new man he's becoming to the boy he still is, Ozzie calls back, "I'm going to jump" (*R*, p. 152). He runs back and forth on the roof, feigning to jump from one side and the other, pulling the crowd with him like a puppet-master. A competition then ensues, as Itzie, who's caught on to the anarchic power Ozzie wields, counters Binder's "Please don't jump," with his call for Ozzie to do so, a call taken up by all the other boys (*R*, p. 153). Eventually they reduce Binder to tears, in a triumph of the adolescent will.

Enter, at precisely that moment, the mother. When she asks Binder what Ozzie's doing on the roof, the Rabbi stays mute with humiliated fear and anguish. To her plea that Binder get Ozzie down from the roof and prevent him from accidentally killing himself, the Rabbi pleads impotence, explaining to Mrs. Freedman that Ozzie wants to kill himself to please the boys urging him to do so. The mother finishes the cleric's logic by calling her son down: "Don't be a martyr, my baby" (*R*, p. 155). Binder repeats this last plea to Ozzie, and the boys immediately turn the infantilizing parental counsel to their advantage. Following Itzie's lead they all shout out in chorus to their heroic rebel leader to gawhead and "Be a Martin, be a Martin . . ." (*R*, p. 155). Their ignorance of what they're asking, comically indicated by their changing of the sacred role into a common name, signals that Ozzie's championing of Jesus has reached a new ironic level in the story.

The scene Roth evokes here is from the three temptations Jesus undergoes in the wilderness before he starts his ministry.

Matthew 4, 5-7:

> Then the devil taketh him up into the holy city, and setteth him on a pinnacle of the temple, And saith unto him, If thou be the Son of God, cast thyself down: for it is written, He shall give his angels charge concerning thee: and in *their* hands they shall bear thee up, lest at

any time thou dash thy foot against a stone. Jesus said unto him, It is written again, Thou shalt not tempt the Lord thy God.

The logic of the story casts Binder as the original tempter here. He put Ozzie onto the pinnacle of the synagogue, and first put the idea of jumping into Ozzie's head. The boys have usurped and transformed that unintended seduction. The Rabbi doesn't want the martyrdom at all, unlike Satan; the boys do, but not exactly for Satan's reason. Unlike the Biblical seducer, they have the angels immediately at hand, those put upon firemen, and they are boys, and therefore can't belief in death and so don't envision or require any self-destruction in Ozzie's self-aggrandizing leap. The parental figures do, of course, see that death is really possible now, despite the firemen. Here Roth makes his criticism of Christian culture: its worship of martyrdom may too much resemble an incoherent adolescent frenzy delusionally aspiring to utopian and vain rebellion.

And where is Ozzie in all this? He's finally realized how strange the boys' request for him to jump is. The question he now poses to himself is no longer Is it me that counts up here on the roof, but "Is it us? . . . Is it us?" (*R*, p. 156). The issue, in other words, is cultural. Ozzie wonders if he can create an order of values for his fellows if he jumps. He asks himself if the singing would turn to dancing at his leap, if the jumping would stop anything in the culture of the parents or the boys. He has a fantasy of plucking a coin from the sun with an inscription do or don't written on it, and then hallucinates that each part of his body is taking a vote, independently of his will, on what he should do. The sun makes the decision for him, but not as he expected. The late afternoon gets suddenly darker, and the voices are subdued by the oncoming night. Ozzie makes his mother, the Rabbi, the boys, the caretaker and the firemen with their net all kneel. In this omnipotent posture he forces Binder to go through a catechism that ends with the Rabbi saying "God . . . can make a child without intercourse" (*R*, p. 157). The mother the caretaker and the boys and the firemen are then all forced to make the same confession to Ozzie, who then requires the multitude to confess singly and then in chorus that they believe in Jesus Christ. There is yet a triumph to compel. Ozzie turns an exhausted, weepy voice, his boy's voice which Roth says has the sound of an exhausted bellwringer's, to his mother, tells her she shouldn't hit him, or anybody ever about God, and when she asks him to come down, makes her promise first that she'll "never hit anybody about God" (*R*, p. 158). Although he's only asked the grey-haired madonna (Ozzie's earthly father is teasingly symbolically absent from the story through death) everyone kneeling in the street

makes the promise. Roth ends Ozzie's impossible performance this way.

> Once again there was silence.
>
> "I can come down now, Mamma," the boy on the roof finally said. He turned his head both ways as though checking the traffic lights. "Now I can come down . . ."
>
> And he did, right into the center of the yellow net that glowed in the evening's edge like an overgrown halo.
>
> (*R*, p. 158)

Both senses of "other"—the reverse and the additional—which were invoked at the beginning of this essay play through Ozzie's conversion of the Jews. He has compelled Binder to tell him the different thing he wanted to know, to reverse himself and admit that Jewish exclusiveness cannot bind God. This much is righteousness and converts Jews not to Christianity, but back to the ethos of loving and exemplary obedience to God which their status as "chosen" was meant to secure when it was first announced to Abraham. Ozzie's prophetic compelling of the crowd to confess belief in Jesus Christ is pure bravado, the exuberance of an Alexander in short pants, and certainly not an acceptance on their part or on his of Christian dogma or worship. Indeed the whole scene is a burlesque of both. Roth's comic reduction of salvation through martyrdom makes that much perfectly clear. But something Christian is required by the boy of his people, something Christians have consistently proved to be exemplary failures in, something Christians were told by Jesus himself was the basis of the law and the prophets. In his commandment that no one violate their neighbor for God's sake, Ozzie condenses what Jesus in Mark 12, 29-31 cites to demonstrate his authority as a religious teacher against the scribes, the Binders of his day, who view him as a subversive interloper.

> And Jesus answered him, The first of all the commandments is, Hear, O Israel; The Lord our God in one Lord: And thou shalt love the Lord thy God with all thy heart, and with all thy soul, and with all thy mind, and with all thy strength: this is the first commandment. And the second is like, namely this, Thou shalt love thy neighbour as thyself.

Jesus claims, and Christians believe, that he not only obeys and preaches these commandments, but exemplifies them uniquely by instantiating, in his living presence, the God who set them forth to establish the proper relation of human life to him. God is now no longer the reverse of you, but another one of you, and loving him should be all that more compelling, immediate, and pure. This fusion of otherness as difference and as similarity in the logic of the Incarnation is the conversion Jesus urged on his contemporary Jews.

Ozzie also feels himself to be an exemplary instantiation of God's power and peace, and the mixture of delusion and insight on his part may very well be Roth's final word in the story on Christ's mentality. But the ethos of the Incarnation is certainly included in the broken-hearted injunction Ozzie closes the story with. Thou shalt love thy neighbor as thyself Jesus says is like the first commandment, thou shalt love thy God exclusively and exhaustively. The identification here of exclusive and exhaustive love is the theological basis for the humanism, Christian in one aspect, Jewish in another, of Ozzie's belief, to which he converts the Jews, that "You should never hit anybody about God" (*R,* p. 158) Exclusive love of God means exhaustive love of humankind. Exclusive and exhaustive love are two sides of the one Jewish coin, and of the additional Christian coin, and of the coin that is Judeao-Christian. In Ozzie Freedman's glorious tantrum on the pinnacle of a synagogue, Philip Roth comically condenses a strife over Jewish "otherness" that has in many ways defined the Christian world as much as it has the Jewish one. Ozzie is able to turn martyrdom as a resolution of that strife into a boy-man's righteous game. Whoever has meditated on the cross might profit much from imagining the look on Ozzie's face as he leaps into the firemen's net that Roth has made this new man's halo.

Notes

1. Philip Roth, "The Conversion of the Jews" in *Goodbye, Columbus,* (New York: Vintage International, 1993), p. 141. The story originally appeared in *The New Yorker* in 1959.

2. James Joyce, *Ulysses,* (New York, Random House, 1961), p. 689.

Victoria Aarons (essay date fall 2000)

SOURCE: Aarons, Victoria. "Is It 'Good-for-the-Jews or No-Good-for-the-Jews'?: Philip Roth's Registry of Jewish Consciousness." *Shofar* 19, no. 1 (fall 2000): 7-18.

[*In the following essay, Aarons discusses "Eli, the Fanatic," focusing on the protagonist's ambivalence about his history and identity and arguing that Eli's doubleness reminds readers of the failure of reinvention.*]

When Eli Peck, Philip Roth's recalcitrant Jew in the short story **"Eli, the Fanatic,"** emerges from behind the supporting pillar of Woodenton's yeshiva, it is not his antagonist Leo Tzuref whom he encounters, but rather Eli himself, a far more ominous adversary. And it's a contest that Eli will ultimately lose, for Eli has

both mistaken and underestimated the relentless tenacity of his opponent. In a fictive conceit characteristic of Roth, we find in Eli a divided self, a protagonist whose attempts to reconstruct himself result in uneasy and often fantastic stratagems of self-deceiving disguise. Most notably since *Portnoy's Complaint*, Roth's protagonists have enacted a conscious dialectic, often intertextually, of reconstructing themselves as Jews or not as Jews. For Roth, a deeply suspicious and evasive assessment of Jewish identity is what it means to be a Jew in the latter half of the twentieth-century. This obsession with matters Jewish is shared equally by Roth's narrative voice and his characters. And, ironically, this compulsive preoccupation locates itself very simply, or not so simply, in the preposterous imposition of an untenable duality, by which, as Yakov Blotnik, the old janitor in Roth's **"The Conversion of the Jews,"** with unconditional conviction puts it, "things were either good-for-the-Jews or no-good-for-the-Jews."[1]

Roth's protagonists' comically neurotic attempts to transform themselves in and out of their Jewishness are both provoked and undermined by Roth's ironic and self-reflexive narrative intrusions. That is, narrative voice, typically in Roth, both speaks with exemplary neurotic self-consumption and, through parody, shows the ironic limitations of its own perspective. And surely, Roth's protagonists, too, are often themselves aware of their own faltering and suspicious attempts at self-fashioning. But when their conscious self-mocking and self-parodic assessment turns on itself, the exaggerated self-analysis becomes the unconscious wish fulfillment of desires long expunged and barely recognized. The performance on the stage of the self, where, in fact, the protagonist is often both actor and audience, is eclipsed, the performed self no longer an act, but a farcical self-impersonation, a kind of burlesque of contentious doubles in which fictive character becomes the symptomatic marker of near-hysterical fixation. Moreover, as *Portnoy*'s master narrative trope so cleverly revealed, narrative self-reflexivity and the Freudian master narrative of neurotic displacement have been prominent in Roth's fiction from the beginning. In **"Eli, the Fanatic,"** Roth makes Freudian tropes of neurotic displacement part of an allegory of post-war Jewish identity, much as his later fiction does. Such a refashioning of identity, for Roth, involves in part the fiction of the autonomous self, a postmodern amnesia, and in part the recurrent Jewish self-loathing that has long been the source of contention directed toward Roth's work.[2]

Roth's characters, thus, tend to be their own worst enemies. They find themselves in someone else, in doubles, making the threat two-fold, increasing the peril, the self imperiled by yet another self, its phobias redoubled. This complicated redoubling of unconscious motives in Roth is paradigmatically represented by the figure of Eli Peck, Eli, "the fanatic," who willfully becomes his double, inflicts himself on himself, makes of himself an imposing caricature of his own fears and conflicts.[3] So, characteristic of Roth's reluctant Jews, when their defenses no longer protect them from themselves, their response is to retreat, as does Eli Peck, into historical conditions of anxiety: they become Jews.

In this negotiation of the anxieties of the centuries and the attendant guilt that arises from "the return of the repressed"[4] and its super-egoistic call to collectivity, there are, as Nathan Marx, in **"Defender of the Faith,"** so wearily acknowledges, "strategies of aggression, but there are strategies of retreat as well."[5] When appointed by the Jews in suburban Woodenton, New York to disband the offending presence of the yeshiva—"what a nerve . . . this is the twentieth century"[6]—Eli Peck, attorney, pillar of the community, and spokesperson for the Woodenton Jews, reluctantly complies. He does so because Eli for so long has repressed his feelings for and consanguinity with a Jewish past from which he has falsely believed himself to be liberated. Eli, along with his wife and the suburban Jews of Woodenton, have remade themselves as middle-class Jews, so much so that they exchange their Judaism, their connection to a war-torn and shattered past, for a wished-for Gentile (and genteel) respectability. If repression involves the deflection of instinctual drives and impulses from their original aims to more socially valuable ones, then Eli gets it wrong: he confuses what is valuable with what is socially acceptable, acceptable, that is, to the "new" Woodenton, "long . . . the home of well-to-do Protestants," where now, since the war, "'there's a good healthy relationship in this town because it's modern Jews and Protestants . . . just people who respect each other, and leave each other be" (277-8). But the presence of the yeshiva, its eighteen children and two men, threatens this precarious coalescence, maintained only by benign neglect on the one hand and cautious acquiescence on the other.

Roth stages this conflict of past and present by making Leo Tzuref, headmaster of the yeshiva and visibly old-world protector of his vulnerable group of displaced persons, the main obstacle standing in the way of such a measured peace: "Have children ever been so safe in their beds? Parents—Eli wondered—so full in their stomachs?" (279). And Eli's desire to maintain the carefully-honed "peace and safety" of falsely pastoral Woodenton produces in him rationalizations that border on the pathological: "It was what his parents had asked for in the Bronx, and his grandparents in Poland, and theirs in Russia or Austria, or wherever else

they'd fled to or from. . . . And now they had it—the world was at last a place for families, even Jewish families. After all these centuries, maybe there just had to be this communal toughness—or numbness—to protect such a blessing. Maybe that was the trouble with the Jews all along—too soft . . . to live takes guts" (279-280). But "guts," courage, is something that Eli lacks, and his nagging suspicion that he can't quite be the "new" professional suburban Jew and his attendant self-loathing are directed, initially, at the mystifying Tzuref, slinking behind pillars, whispering in riddles, seemingly decapitated, threatening Eli with the return of his own decapitated conscience. What weighs on Eli so heavily is not only the weight of the present, but also the pull of the past, and so he defends himself, however ineffectually, against both.

So, when the well-defended Eli, armed with briefcase and sanctioned by zoning ordinances, invades the precarious sanctuary of the yeshiva's grounds, he mistakenly believes that it is Leo Tzuref with whom he must contend. The law that Eli encounters in the yeshiva is not the law of the "new" Woodenton, but rather the old law enshrouded in mysterious and troubling allegorical disguise in the figure of Leo Tzuref, a refugee from the past, who speaks in Talmudic riddles— "When is the law that is the law not the law?"—and who "cloud[s] the issue with issues" (251). Tzuref is here for Roth the embodiment of the old law, in Freud's terms, the religion of Moses, a guilt-laden reminder of a collective past and of the desire for a defining authority in the form of an idealizing of a past, of the idea of a past:

> The religion of Moses . . . had not disappeared without leaving a trace. A kind of memory of it had survived, obscured and distorted, perhaps. . . . And it was this tradition of a great past which continued to work in the background, as it were, which gradually gained more and more power over men's minds, and which finally succeeded . . . in calling back to life the religion of Moses which had been established and then abandoned long centuries earlier.
>
> ("Moses and Monotheism," p. 124)

This simultaneous disavowal of and yearning for a repressed Jewish past that Freud attributes to the Jewish psyche in Eli manifests itself in a tension between his inability to extricate himself from Leo Tzuref and the summons of the yeshiva and his defensive resistance in the name of progress to a law that would so uncomfortably take him back. Tzuref thus becomes the authorizing father, in Freud's terms, from whose will Eli retreats, and in this retreat his rejection of Judaism and the attendant self-punishment that accompanies this rejection are the poles of his undoing as a suburban Jewish success story. Thus Eli is plagued from the very start by his ambivalence, his desire constituted by Roth as fear.

And so it is Tzuref, the "father," the embodiment of the law, whom Eli clumsily fears. If Tzuref is the "father," then Eli is his only slightly distorted mirror image. In a singularly representative scene, each man, sitting across from the other, mimics each other's actions in a parody of self-assertion. With exaggerated deliberation, Eli

> removed Tzuref's letter from a manila folder. Tzuref removed Eli's letter from his pants pocket. Eli removed the carbon of his own letter from another manila folder. Tzuref removed Eli's first letter from his back pocket. Eli removed the carbon from his briefcase. Tzuref raised his palms.
>
> (264)

As if engaged in a game of poker, each man attempts to one-up the other. And despite Tzuref's willingness to engage Eli in contest, the conditions are preset for Tzuref's victory, or in any event, Eli's loss. For Tzuref is always in control, in large part because of Eli's necessary and unconscious projection of authority onto him, and from the very beginning the stage is set for Eli's repudiation of the "father," which at the end of the story "rectifies" itself in Eli's fanatical return to Judaism. Eli from the start senses his impotence and thus fears Tzuref for it. He feels persecuted by the figure of Tzuref, slightly sinister, an apparition appearing from behind the columns of the yeshiva, "halfway hidden" (250), accusatory, lying in wait for the unsuspecting Eli. But it is Eli himself who has all along been hiding in the shadows, lurking behind the columns and pillars of his conflicts of identity as an assimilated, "cultured" Jew. Eli's suppressed hostility toward the threatening Tzuref and his unexpressed desire to "slay" him, to overcome him, will become the catalyst for Eli's eventual failed attempts at exculpation by yielding to the higher demands placed upon him by his reactive desire to embrace a mythic Judaism.

So, when Eli climbs the mount from the safety of Woodenton's "progressive suburban community," where "Jews and Gentiles . . . live beside each other in amity" (261-2), to the menacing darkness of the yeshiva's grounds, where children "in their mysterious babble . . . run at the sight of him" (250, 253), he finds there not the source of the legal dispute, "a boarding school in a residential area" (251), but rather that from which he, himself, has been running. Tzuref's response to Eli's legal mandate to disband the yeshiva is as cryptic as the language of the children who play on the grounds and whose "babble— not mysterious to Tzuref, who smiled—entered the room like a third person," making Eli "shudder" and triangulating his wish for a simply oppositional encounter (250). The children's unintelligible language, foreign, that is, to Eli, takes human form, is anthropo-

morphized into the outsider, a symbol of difference, a secret unbreakable code by which Eli feels himself threatened, persecuted, ironically, by a group of vulnerable children.

This is an uneasy position in which Eli finds himself, but not without its unconscious gratification. Eli, legal spokesperson for the Jews of Woodenton, finds himself aligned, not against the Protestants, whose longstanding place in the community is never forgotten and with whom the Jews have "a good healthy relationship . . . no progroms," but instead against the yeshiva Jews, "religious fanatics . . . talking a dead language . . . making a big thing out of suffering," who threaten the middle-class social values and comfort of the Jews who guardedly live there (277-278). In a parody of identity politics, the Jews of Woodenton are to the yeshiva Jews what the Gentiles are to the Jews of Woodenton. The Woodenton yeshiva, ironically, is, indeed, "no-good-for-the-Jews," since it calls to attention that there are Jews, calls attention *to* the Jews as a flagrant symbol of difference. But it's Eli's own passive acquiescence to the will of the local assimilated community that brings him, donned in the accouterments of his professional disguise, the suit and the briefcase, to the yeshiva. Once there, however, Eli, the laws of the community buffeting his trespass upon the grounds of the yeshiva, encounters, much to his dismay, a far more imperious authority than the law with which he believes himself to be empowered. Once on the grounds of the yeshiva, the very foundation of Eli's world shifts. And as it does so, Roth stages a return to a distant mythic Jewish past, the ground itself for the moral authority Eli must so uncomfortably confront and the text upon which the "causal story" of repression coming undone will begin to unfold.[7]

The physical setting in which Roth places Eli is a measure of his psychic landscape. In approaching the yeshiva, Eli is taken back, against his will, to a kind of eerie, pre-lapsarian landscape, where the "jungle of hedges . . . the dark, untrampled horse path" both obscure his course and lure him there (249). From the beginning, Eli is anxious, burdened, fearful in advance of what he will find. And he is right to be so apprehensive, for once there he is unconsoled, clearly imperiled. For Roth, Eli is the perfect candidate to come apart on the grounds of the yeshiva, an agitated, immoderate man, who, previously in the midst of a nervous breakdown "sat in the bottom of the closet and chewed on [his] bedroom slippers" (271). Once at the yeshiva, disoriented, defensive, transgressive, Eli is pulled under by the tyrannous demands of the past and the present. And the ground he loses, the loose bearings that so tenuously tethered him to himself, cause him to take flight.

When it becomes clear to Eli that his aggressive litigious posture, precariously bolstered by city ordinances against "mountain goats, say, in [the] backyard" (276) and by the confident insistence of the community he represents, will not work on the immovable Tzuref, Eli retreats; he literally runs from the grounds of the yeshiva. But the "trope of flight," as Harold Bloom puts it, "is hardly literal language."⁸ Eli runs from himself, far less frightened by the figure of Tzuref than he is of his own repressed relations to his Jewish identity, despite the fact that he locates that fear in Tzuref.

Roth thus makes Tzuref the embodiment of both fear and conscience, an angry, vindictive god, who will not be fooled by Eli's protestations and rationalizations. Tzuref's responses, his gesticulations even, no matter how insignificant, are viewed by the obsessively guilt-ridden Eli as accusations. He anticipates, desires even, Tzuref's wrath and exoneration in the form of punishment. It is Tzuref who threatens Eli's professional demeanor, who strips him of his guise and who demands in no uncertain terms that Eli recognize himself in Tzuref and the other Jewish refugees: "Aach! You are us, we are you!" (265). Tzuref, however, leaves the punishment to Eli himself, a worse scenario than any Eli could have predicted, since then there is no idealized Jewish "father" to exonerate him.

Tzuref's mandate that Eli not only admit to the historical, contemporary, and habitual suffering of the Jews, but "try it. It's a little thing" (265), unnerves Eli. It does so because Tzuref's nagging reminder of Eli's connections and obligations prevent the safety of his repression and denial. It sets the stage for Eli's "conversion." The yeshiva is, for Eli, a dangerous place, exactly because being Eli, that is, being in an antagonistic relation to one's past, is, indeed, perilous. But Eli can't quite face his own fear; his defenses fail in the face of the imperious Tzuref. His "flight," as Herman Nunberg has explained it, is "a reaction to a danger," or to a perceived danger: "The displacement of the inner danger into the outer world makes possible an attempt at flight."⁹ Hence Eli displaces, transfers his sense of danger onto Tzuref, a likely candidate since he here represents the old law so palpably. But such an attempt to escape, as Nunberg warns, "is successful for a short period, but by no means permanently, since one cannot flee from oneself. . . . As the danger is fundamentally an inner one, he cannot bring about changes of reality in order to meet it; he has to change himself" (189). And so he does. When Eli stops resisting that which he fears and himself moves "in the shadows" of the yeshiva, rather than running from its occupants and their past, it is not to the "lights" of Woodenton that he is drawn, but rather back, back to his own deeply defended sense of a mythic Jewish

self. For Eli, the apostate, will become the "fanatic," like Nathan Marx, the "defender" of a faith from which he has turned.

It is typical of Roth's fiction that Eli's own dissembling, the sublimation of his own desires, ironically, brings about their expression, forces Eli to come into the open, to "realize," to fix upon his identity as a Jew, as "the fanatic." Eli, an all too willing disinheritor of that which will ultimately claim him, finds himself ambushed, both to his surprise and to his relief, by no less than his own feared denial of his belief in his Jewishness. He comes to feel, to borrow a phrase that Alan Berger uses in a related context, "the presence of an absence,"¹⁰ the very real presence of the missing because repressed part of himself, a Jewish past, which, for Eli, as for so many of Roth's characters—Henry Zuckerman remade as Hanoch in *The Counterlife,* or Roth, his own protagonist in Israel, whose double usurps his identity in *Operation Shylock,* for example—is enshrouded in mysterious and foreboding configurations, as flatly illusory as it is compelling.

But the shape of repression and the effort to maintain the deflection of the instinctual drives and impulses that the sublimated self hopes to control is even more arduous and preposterous than is giving in to them.¹¹ And so in order to recreate the presence of the absent or obliterated self, Eli must reinvent himself in the object, paradoxically, of that which he believes himself to fear most. This is what Sergeant Nathan Marx, in **"Defender of the Faith,"** finds in the duplicitous Sheldon Grossbart, who represents the worst in Jewish stereotypes, and what perhaps Roth himself discovers in embracing his father's decline and death in *Patrimony:* that only through stepping into the frame of one's fears can one hope to engage them and thus, ironically, reshape them, accepting, as Nathan Marx at the close of **"Defender of the Faith,"** so generously does, "my own" (200). Eli, too, face-to-face with his own partially eclipsed character, "the shock of having daylight turned off all at once . . . the color of blackness: a little stale, a little sour, a little old," accepts his own, "nothing that could overwhelm you" (285), looks to complete himself in that which he has phobically avoided. Eli, thus, finds himself, not surprisingly, in this radically depicted other, in the Hasidic Jew, whose clothes Eli literally will wear.

It is not surprising that it is the Hasidic Jew, dressed in the black garb of his European ancestors, who is the source of the town's fixation and the focus of Eli's fear. The man in "the black coat . . . the round-topped, wide-brimmed Talmudic hat . . . the beard . . . side-locks" (253) is viewed by the suburban Jews of Woodenton as the epitome of their seized-upon difference and consequent exclusion. His very presence in the town is a measure and felt reminder of what the suburban Jews have feared all along: that they will never be accepted, never made members of the club, so to speak. His "presence" in the town is a warning, a transgression, an uninvited and unwelcome phantom from the past, "a regular greenhorn . . . like in the Bronx the old guys who used to come around selling Hebrew trinkets" (255). But for Eli, the man in the Talmudic hat becomes the locus of his thwarted desires and repressed impulses, which, once recognized, cannot be eradicated.

Eli's initial response to the DP, who has lost everything in the war and who resides at the yeshiva, is to flee at the sight of him. In Eli's apprehensive and agitated state, the yeshiva Jew seems disembodied, "only a deep hollow of blackness." As he begins to take shape, however, his appearance is even more frightening for Eli, because in him, Eli sees the possibilities for his own long-hidden countenance, "his face . . . no older than Eli's" (253). When Eli, characteristically, misunderstands the Jew's gesture of lamentation, throwing open his arms in despair and supplication, for an embrace, an invitation to join him, to be him, Eli runs. Running from the sight of him, scurrying "toward the lights of Woodenton," false beacons of safety and providence, Eli attempts to run from himself, from an "absence," which becomes increasingly and unbearably palpable. The symptomatic retreat and avoidance, inevitably, predictably, become unfeasible, impossible to maintain. And so, ultimately, to combat his fear Eli faces it, becomes it, gives into it completely by "becoming" the Jew, "wearing" it, impersonating it until it becomes him, until, in fact, he mimics the man's cry of mourning, whose moan "stung and stung inside him . . . became a scream, louder, a song, a crazy song" (281).

While Leo Tzuref may be Eli's conscience, it is, rather, the man in the hat, "that hat which was the very cause of Eli's mission, the source of Woodenton's upset" (253), who comes to be Eli's alter ego, his unwitting double. And the hat, the very clothes worn by the Jew from the yeshiva, whose cry evokes in Eli "a feeling . . . for whose deepness he could find no word" (281), become the symbol of his repression, a tangible covering of Eli's identity. What Eli hears in the man's cry, "some feeling [that] crept into him" (280), is not unlike the call of "good shabbus" made to Nathan Marx in "Defender of the Faith." So well defended for so long, so inured against all emotion, "fortunate enough to develop an infantryman's heart, which, like his feet, at first aches and swells but finally grows horny enough for him to travel the weirdest paths without feeling a thing" (161), it only takes, for Nathan Marx, one seemingly insignificant word to evoke in him "a

deep memory . . . plunged down through all I had anesthetized . . . to what I suddenly remembered was myself" (170). It is only through recreating the Jew as "other," envisioned first as some inanimate "other," felt sound, disembodied "clothes," something outside of the self, that Roth's characters can step into their identity, can find themselves, again, as Jews. Eli dons the garb of the Hasidic Jew and so, in becoming him, becomes himself.[12] It is only through his identification with and replacement of the other, that Eli, the "fanatic," the Jew, becomes "the Jew," becomes that which he has repressed for so long. But one's repressed impulses are "more likely to emerge into consciousness when repression is weakened or when the content of the fantasy finds a close match in conscious thoughts, relationships, or situations . . . aggressive in nature."[13] So when Eli feels himself aggressively pursued, he can no longer resist; he is able, finally, to play out his fantasies in equally aggressive and exhibitionistic form.

Eli, pushed to the limits by his guilt, in the form of Leo Tzuref on the one side and his wife and the Woodenton Jews on the other, finds himself eclipsed by the Jew whom Roth intentionally refuses to name, his anonymity subsumed in his replacement of Eli. When Eli packs his best green suit and delivers the box of clothes to the orthodox Jew in the yeshiva, defining events are set in motion that cannot be arrested, and the one man will become the other. Not only does the Hasidic Jew attire himself in Eli's clothes, but he is mistaken for Eli: "Eli, it's Ted. . . . I turned around and I swear I thought it was you. But it was him. He still walks like he did, but the clothes, Eli, the clothes" (281). The clothes, indeed. The suit of clothes for both men becomes the symbol of loss and the misguided replacement for that loss.

For the gift of clothes is reciprocated, Eli's actions mirrored by the man who now looks like him, the Jew's actions mirrored by Eli. Eli's exchange of attire with the yeshiva Jew gives new and ironic meaning to the tired adage "the clothes make the man," since for both men this is both literally and metaphorically true. Each man sees a partially eclipsed version of himself in the other:

> The recognition took some time. He looked at what Eli wore. Up close, Eli looked at what he wore. And then Eli had the strange notion that he was two people. Or that he was one person wearing two suits.
>
> (289)

Eli's confusion of identities disturbingly augurs the question later posed to him: "you know you're still Eli, don't you" (297). But what it means to be Eli, for Eli himself, is not so easily answered nor circumnavigated. For one brief but cataclysmic moment, when Eli suits himself in the clothes of the orthodox Jew and parades through the town, the townspeople, Eli, and even the yeshiva Jew himself believe Eli to be other than what he is, believe him to be the man whom Eli took upon himself further to displace. Eli, dressed as the Jew, of course, displaces no one but himself: "'Sholom,' Eli whispered and zoomed off towards the hill" (288).

Eli, in defiant and thus regressive reaction against the noxious, self-serving attitude of his friends and neighbors, not only accepts the box of clothes left on his doorstep by the yeshiva Jew, but wears them throughout the town in a performative replay of his double's objectionable behavior. As Adam Phillips suggests, "as most of [Roth's] fictional heroes . . . know, there's no good performance—no performance, indeed—without indiscretion, or its possibility."[14] So Eli's performance is exhibitionistic; he "exposes" himself as the Jew, as he really is, the orthodox garb far less a disguise than was Eli's professional demeanor, but, at the same time, the orthodox garb a manic assumption of self-authenticating difference, itself a disguise, a covering up of the failed attempt at autonomy.

Exhibitionism, the act of attracting attention to oneself, is here, ironically, and in the circuitous fashion so typical to Roth, a matter of calling attention to oneself as other, which, paradoxically turns on itself, since by calling attention to the Jew, the very thing that Eli wanted to prevent, he calls attention to himself not only as Jew but as *the* Jew, a caricature of the Jew he might have been.[15] But this narrative that Eli has been composing for so long and which has taken an enormous toll on the erosion of his identity, falls apart in its development not so much of plot but rather of character, the making of character. Eli, all along, has attempted to construct his own character in the guise of what is expected of him, a consistent character whose composition bears out the reflection that others want to have of themselves. And, as Adam Phillips reminds us, "one lets people down—or 'deceives' them—when one refuses to be only one version of oneself." Since "consistency is compliance," and since Eli's fictional version of himself is always undermined by his punitive superego, he ultimately, vindictively even, alters the narrative dramatically, better to betray others than himself.[16]

Therefore, Eli must perform this exchange of identities in public, must expose himself to public scrutiny, because in doing so he both makes claims to an historical identity and exhibitionistically performs its exaggerated impossibility. Eli is finally able to locate himself within an authorized history of persecution, persecuted now less by his own fantasies and the inad-

equacies of his friends and of his wife, whose self-absorbed narcissism has throughout the story served as a foil to Eli's self-loathing. His identity is forever linked to the identity of another, the "other," the Jew, who, ironically, indelibly, is, indeed, none other than Eli himself. Eli's telling linguistic slip in defense of the proposed timetable for legal action taken against the yeshiva—"Just give me the day—them the day" (279)—suggests just how much he has come to identify with the yeshiva Jews, with, in fact, his own deeply embedded desire to transform himself into them, a "conversion" not outward, but inward, back into himself. The clothes he wears and accepts are a replacement for his own "as if they were the skin of his skin" (293), a language of kinship. Thus the clothes name him, redefine him if only to expose an impossible demand on his own historical conditions. If, as Jonathan Lear suggests, "unconscious motivation can be thought of as striving to be understood," and I think that it can, then Eli's appropriation of the Jew's clothes and identity is his unconscious self-subverting wish to change his own.[17]

But the replacement of identities is, of course, here far more complicated than is the replacement of clothes. While the "greenie" can, obligingly, attire himself in Eli's suit, the replacement can never make up for the loss of his own clothes, the suit that, after everything else has been taken away, "is all he's got":

> "A mother and a father?" Tzuref said. "No. A wife? No. A baby? A little ten-month-old baby? No! A village full of friends? A synagogue where you knew the feel of every seat under your paints? Where with your eyes closed you could smell the cloth of the Torah? . . . That leaves nothing, Mr. Peck. Absolutely nothing!"
>
> (264)

Eli's faltering acknowledgment, "I misunderstood," his belated recognition of the Jew's history, a set of circumstances that only willful evasion could ignore—"No news reached Woodenton" (264)—underscores the extent to which Eli has denied his Judaism, his connection and obligation to those whose identity he belatedly shares. But it also underscores the falseness, the self-deception of Tzuref, whose accession to the authority to the law here represents the punitive superego that Eli thinks he escapes in his belated and elated embracing of a Jewish history.

As he begins to dress himself in the Jew's clothes, his hoped-for exhilaration soon dissipates in the face of a reality Eli can hardly deny, a self-exposure which leaves Eli depleted: "What a silly disappointment to see yourself naked in a hat. Especially in that hat. He sighed, but could not rid himself of the great weakness that suddenly set on his muscles and joints, beneath the terrible weight of the stranger's strange hat" (285). Donning the clothes becomes an allegory for the impossibility of embracing the past in any simple or single way. Eli's attempts to step into a "new" identity are not as easily made as his stepping into the clothes left on his doorstep. Just as Eli's clothes cannot replace the losses suffered by the man who resides at the yeshiva, the Jew's suit of clothes cannot finally be a replacement for Eli's loss of identity, absence of history. And the shame that Eli experiences comes in large part from the recognition that, while the "greenie's" history was purloined, Eli has given up his willingly; he has no one to blame but himself, and he can't see clearly through the convolutions of history and repression.

And so Eli punishes himself. His masquerade throughout the town in the guise of the Hasidic Jew is, for Eli, self-inflicted punishment. For there is a point where Eli realizes that his actions are not irrevocable, that, in fact, he can "go inside and put on his clothes" and return to himself. And it is at this juncture that he makes a choice, perhaps for the first time, a defining, deafening moment in which he makes claims to himself. But Roth doesn't let us off so easily. Although Eli comforts himself by thinking that "if you chose to be crazy, then you weren't crazy" (295), it is wishful thinking, indeed. When, at the story's close, in full orthodox dress, Eli arrives at the hospital where his wife has just given birth to his first child, a son, he is carted off by the doctors, whose "white suits smelled, but not like Eli's." As with every fulfillment of the wish, including the wish to "be a Jew," the release of the repressed impulses is met with external opposition. But the drug given to him by the doctors, the drug intended to calm his nervous state, cannot quite "touch . . . down where the blackness had reached" (298). That untouchable place in Eli is here a metaphor for the unconscious, whose protective armor insulates it from the tranquilizing effects of the drug. It cannot, however, protect it from its own internal split, the fragmentation of self that Eli can't arrest.

In **"Eli, the Fanatic,"** Roth presents us with what can only be regarded as the American-Jewish dilemma for the "assimilated" Jew in the second half of the twentieth-century, a self-inflicted dilemma, which has gained continued momentum if not through the close of the century then certainly through Roth's maturing fiction. This dilemma that rests on identity, on a developing Jewish identity, is born from a deeply rooted ambivalence about the possibilities and consequences of refashioning the self in Jewish terms. Such latent anxieties, however, are but a deflection of what is perhaps the more insidious consequence of this ironic self-absorption, which can be seen in what Adam Phillips so insightfully identifies in his discussion of

Roth's protagonists, as the "catastrophe of the Second World War . . . the disowning of history, or the appropriation of other traditions."[18] Much of Roth's later fiction, for example, takes this catastrophic disavowal of history as a portent, perhaps, of the regressive and reactionary self-conceits and convoluted self-transformations for American Jews at the onset of the new century. Roth seizes upon the abandonment of a Jewish past as a metaphor for the disowning of Jewish identity, the source of much of his characters' angst. One can neither take the Jew out of history nor history—mythic, impending, or mundane—out of the individual Jew. But whether Eli's "conversion" is "good-for-the-Jews or no-good-for-the-Jews" is not so easily estimated or negotiated in the serpentine contortions of Philip Roth's contentious fictions.

Notes

1. Philip Roth, "The Conversion of the Jews," in *Goodbye, Columbus and Five Short Stories* (1959; Rpt., New York: Modern Library, 1966), p. 150.

2. See, most notably perhaps, Irving Howe's essay, "Philip Roth Reconsidered," in *Commentary* (December 1972): 69-77.

3. I would argue, in fact, that Roth's protagonist in "Eli, the Fanatic" might well be viewed as a precursor to later "doubles" that inhabit Roth's fiction, not in the least the recurring figure of Nathan Zuckerman.

4. In "Moses and Monotheism," Freud explains the "return of the repressed" as "something in a people's life which is past, lost to view, superseded, and which we venture to compare with what is repressed in the mental life of an individual" ("Moses and Monotheism," in *The Standard Edition of the Complete Psychological Works of Sigmund Freud,* trans. James Strachey [London: The Hogarth Press and The Institute of Psycho-Analysis, 1964], p. 132).

5. Philip Roth, "Defender of the Faith," in *Goodbye, Columbus and Five Short Stories,* p. 194. Subsequent references are noted in the text.

6. Philip Roth, "Eli, the Fanatic," in *Goodbye, Columbus and Five Short Stories,* pp. 253, 276. Subsequent references are noted in the text.

7. The philosopher and analyst Jonathan Lear, in his discussion of repression in *Love and Its Place in Nature: A Philosophical Interpretation of Freudian Psychoanalysis* (New York: Farrar, Straus & Giroux, 1990), suggests that an idea "even though repressed" may produce feelings and emotions that are brought into effect and that "[t]he point of repression, for Freud, is to prevent this causal story from unfolding" (87-8).

8. Harold Bloom, "Freud's Concepts of Defense and the Poetic Will," in *The Literary Freud: Mechanisms of Defense and the Poetic Will, Psychiatry and the Humanities,* vol. 4, Joseph H. Smith, M.D., editor (New Haven: Yale University Press, 1980), p. 5.

9. Herman Nunberg, M.D., *Principles of Psychoanalysis: Their Application to the Neuroses,* trans. Madlyn Kahr and Sidney Kahr, M.D. (New York: International Universities Press, Inc. 1955), p. 189.

10. Alan L. Berger, *Children of Job: American Second-Generation Witnesses to the Holocaust* (Albany: State University of New York Press, 1997), p. 2.

11. For summarily concise discussions of the functions of repression and sublimation, especially in terms of the directed deflection of drives to socially acceptable conduct, see *Psychoanalytic Terms and Concepts,* edited by Burness E. Moore, M.D., and Bernard D. Fine, M.D. (New Haven: The American Psychoanalytic Assoc. and Yale University Press, 1990), pp. 166-168 and 187-188.

12. This logic of becoming the "other" is expressed by Roth in the unusual essay "Juice or Gravy?: How I Met My Fate in a Cafeteria," in *New York Times Book Review* (September 18, 1994).

13. Moore and Fine, eds., *Psychoanalytic Terms and Concepts,* p. 94.

14. Adam Phillips, "Philip Roth's Patrimony," in *On Flirtation: Psychoanalytic Essays on the Uncommitted Life* (Cambridge: Harvard University Press, 1994), p. 168.

15. In the ironic fulfillment of Eli's wish, the playing-out of his desire, we are reminded of the protagonist Roth in *The Facts* (New York: Farrar, Straus & Giroux, 1988), whose wish is granted, in the form of his first wife's death by automobile accident; what he wanted to happen happened, but not because he wanted it.

16. Adam Phillips, "Philip Roth's Patrimony," in *On Flirtation,* pp. 168-9.

17. Lear, *Love and Its Place in Nature,* p. 215.

18. Adam Phillips, "Philip Roth's Patrimony," in *On Flirtation,* p. 172.

Thomas Fahy (essay date fall 2000)

SOURCE: Fahy, Thomas. "Filling the Love Vessel: Women and Religion in Philip Roth's Uncollected Short Fiction." *Shofar* 19, no. 1 (fall 2000): 117-26.

[*In the following essay, Fahy examines the portrayal of mother figures and heterosexual relationships in Roth's uncollected short fiction, which the critic says Roth used as a testing ground for his longer works.*]

"'Mamma, don't you see—you shouldn't hit me. [Rabbi Binder] shouldn't hit me. You shouldn't hit me about God, Mamma. You should never hit anybody about God—'"

—"The Conversion of the Jews"

Many of the boys and men in Philip Roth's stories feel pummeled by the expectations of strong maternal figures. These conflicted relationships between men and women (sons/mothers and husbands/wife-mothers) leave men feeling enervated sexually and spiritually, and foster a debilitating anger for women. This struggle, which appears throughout Roth's *œuvre,* is explored powerfully in his uncollected short fiction;[1] and these neglected pieces can offer readers insight into his exploration of heterosexual relationships and religion. With the publication of **"The Day It Snowed"** in the Fall 1954 issue of the *Chicago Review,* his short stories began appearing in journals, collections, and magazines for the next twenty years. Outside of five short stories included in his first book **Goodbye, Columbus** (1959), most of this work has remained uncollected and received little, if any, critical attention.[2]

Roth's male characters are often emasculated by mother-figures who make them feel inadequate as men (physically and sexually) and as Jews because they are not living up to certain expectations—expectations which include marrying within the Jewish community, upholding the faith, and being devoted to one's mother. Since many of these men perceive women as embodying a devout Judaism that excludes them, their inability to achieve some level of heterosexual romantic fulfillment raises questions about religious identity. As they become increasingly resentful of the cultural and religious pressures women police, they fetishize women's bodies, transforming them into grotesque, asexual beings. At the end of *Portnoy's Complaint,* for example, Alex explains: "My final downfall and humiliation—Naomi, The Jewish Pumpkin, The Heroine, that hardy, red-headed, freckled, ideological hunk of a girl! . . . I associate her instantly with my lost Pumpkin, when in physical type she is, of course, my mother. Coloring, size, even temperament, it turned out—a real fault-finder, a professional critic of me. . . . Why don't I marry her."[3] For Alex, Naomi embodies his mother's neverending criticism, a failed connection to Judaism, and sexual inadequacy. (When he tries to rape her, he gives up because he "can't get a hard-on in this place."[4]) Once he associates her sexual identity with his mother, his resentment is manifested, in part, through demeaning descriptions of her body. Throughout Roth's fiction, the conflation of lover and mother, both of whom uphold and represent Judaism, suggests that men have feminized their faith, and, in doing so, they often transfer their anger from one to the other.

The othering of women in Roth's fiction clearly reflects male anxieties about female power and control. Typically, as Simone de Beavoir explains in *The Second Sex*, women are seen as "others" in a patriarchal society. ". . . [S]he is the incidental, the inessential as opposed to the essential. He is the Subject, he is the Absolute—She is the Other."[5] Roth's short stories intensify this type of marginalization by transforming women's bodies into something grotesque or "freakish." More specifically, his narratives relegate women to the realm of the physically deformed in order to focus on the concerns of male characters. This physical othering suggests male resentment about the cultural and religious ostracism and disempowerment they feel from women and Judaism. Because men link their animosity for powerfully controlling women with the constraints of cultural and religious Judaism, a widening lacuna between them and their faith occurs. Subsequently, they often respond to this alienating and frustrating gulf by interpreting women's bodies as repulsive.

This section of *Portnoy's Complaint*, "In Exile," was anticipated in **"The Love Vessel,"** published in *The Dial* (Fall 1959). In this story, Sam Shachat's failed marriage, in which he felt controlled and emasculated by his wife, is the impetus for his journey to Israel. Like Alex Portnoy and Mickey Sabbath, Sam feels disconnected from his religious identity as a Jew and often looks to women (unsuccessfully) to fill voids in his emotional, cultural, and religious identity. His ineffectual search for some spiritual connection with Judaism, however, mirrors and intensifies the painful losses of his unsuccessful romantic relationships. He then projects his own self-loathing and anger at women, particularly through his descriptions of their bodies. Stories such as **"The Love Vessel"** can be seen as a testing ground for some of Roth's longer fiction, and in this way they offer an invaluable comparison with some of his novels by enhancing our understanding of maternal and heterosexual relationships in his fiction. This essay will examine the portrait of mother-figures and present Roth's short fiction as a valuable way to explore the intersection of heterosexual relationships and religion in his writing. I also hope that a discussion of some of these short pieces and their thematic connections with his novels will serve as a way to revivify some of this "lost" and neglected work.

MOTHERS AND SONS

For many of Roth's male protagonists, their troubles with women are defined by power struggles. In his short fiction about young boys, he often presents mother-figures as exerting intellectual and physical control similar to a type of religious coercion—one that demands unquestioned faith and obedience. His

first publications, **"The Day It Snowed"** and **"The Contest for Aaron Gold,"** were short fables about a mother and a maternal figure, respectively, who inadvertently hurt "their" boys by attempting to protect them from suffering. Like **"The Conversion of the Jews,"** published two years later, these stories depict the dangers of trying to force certain ideologies and behaviors onto children, and present a struggle for intellectual (and often physical) control divided along gender lines. Sydney's mother in **"The Day It Snowed"** has lied to her son about death in order to "spare" him, using the term "disappear" as a euphemism for death. As Alan Cooper explains in *Philip Roth and the Jews*, "[Sydney] is ignorant of any ritual or family custom into which to place [death] and of the questions that a real child would ask. He has no referents and no particular background. His childish speculations on the mystery of death convey no culture's memory or teachings."[6] Furthermore, his innocence has left him more open to pain because he doesn't have the knowledge to protect himself, and this vulnerability is maintained by his mother's intellectual and physical control. Sydney, more specifically, has not been allowed to leave his neighborhood and realizes that by looking for his stepfather "his mother would beat him because he should never have left the house in the first place."[7] Here, her intellectual control is enforced by the threat of physical punishment. When Sydney later learns from an old man that "to disappear is to die," he is ecstatic; though he has risked being punished, he believes he can now comfort his mother with the knowledge that his stepfather has not abandoned them: "'He hasn't disappeared—he died. He's dead, so it's O.K." (**"The Day It Snowed"** ["DS"], 43).

The story's melodramatic conclusion leaves both parties defeated and suggests a troubling connection between maternal and spiritual control. Immediately before Sydney's death, his mother was horrified by her son's new-found awareness, falling back into the car and "waving her arms in the air like some giant snake or octopus was squeezing the life out of her" (**"DS,"** 44). This odd and somewhat grotesque image can also be applied to Sydney's relationship with his mother, who has squeezed him like an octopus. His act of defiance has ruptured her physical and intellectual control over him—a break which leads both to his death ("the big black hearse . . . crushed the boy to the ground" ["DS," 44]) and her metaphoric one. Arguably, the fact that she has prevented Sydney from having any religious framework with which to understand death is in itself an act of religious control. The story makes no reference to any particular religion, implying that she is Sydney's primary source for moral and spiritual guidance. Also, the implication that she has hit Sydney to enforce her beliefs parallels events in **"The Conversion of the Jews."** In this work, Roth takes the embattled relationship between mother and son much further. Ozzie Freedman's mother and Rabbi Binder become one and the same—both hit Ozzie because he questions some of the tenets of Judaism. His "conversion," so to speak, is a rejection of Judaism as his mother and the Rabbi understand it. "'Mamma, don't you see—you shouldn't hit me. [Rabbi Binder] shouldn't hit me. You shouldn't hit me about God, Mamma. You should never hit anybody about God—.'"[8] Here there is an inextricable link between mother and Judaism, particularly the ways in which they enforce ideologies and religious beliefs. In both stories, mothers are a physically domineering, feminine force, who impose a belief-system on their children that must be accepted without question.

"The Contest for Aaron Gold," which does not explicitly address religious Judaism, also revolves around "maternal" control, but this time its control over sexual identity and artistic expression. (Unlike **"The Day It Snowed,"** it deals with Jewish characters.) The story begins when Werner Samuelson takes a summer job as a ceramics teacher in a camp for Jewish children. Roth juxtaposes Werner's sensitive, maternal concern for Aaron with Lefty Shulberg's masculinity and his role as swim teacher: "Lefty . . . bareheaded, his trousers tucked neatly into brown combat boots, marched at the front. . . . 'Suck that gut in Gold!'"[9] Lefty and the camp coordinator Mr. Steinberg also speculate about Aaron's and Werner's relationship in terms that feminize the narrator: "'Lefty tells me he sees how you hold the kid back. . . . I'd hate like hell to tell you what he said about you and that kid'" (**"The Contest for Aaron Gold"** [**"CAG"**], 557). And later in the story when Steinberg learns that Aaron is the only boy who has not finished a sculpture before parents' weekend, he more explicitly implies a quasi-sexual relationship: "'What kind of game are you and that little queer trying to play anyhow!'" (**"CAG,"** 559). Though these men most likely don't believe anything illicit is going on, their homophobic concern for Aaron's identity reflects anxieties about the potential harm art and maternal influence (Werner) pose to masculinity. Early in the story, for example, Steinberg tells Werner that "'Lefty tells me that the kid is kind of peculiar. Having a helluva time teaching him to swim.'" For Lefty and Steinberg, they fear that Aaron's interest in art, as nurtured by Werner, will make him "queer"; but they believe this can be overcome by controlling Aaron's outward behavior.[10] As Aaron innocently explains to Werner: "'The head counselor . . . says we gotta not play alone. Uncle Lefty says so too. It's no good for you'" (**"CAG,"** 554). For Lefty and Steinberg, the

success of the camp depends on Aaron's ability to appear "normal," which in this case means heterosexual and athletic, like all the other kids.

Even though the camp establishes a dichotomy between heterosexual masculinity and athleticism as good and the feminine and artistic as bad, Werner's artistic control and misunderstanding of Aaron's needs posit maternal control as a destructive force. Werner's gender inversion, which puts him in a type of maternal relationship with Aaron, is linked to his unwitting ability to stifle and control Aaron's artistic vision: "[Aaron] puttered with several knights for a while, then embarked upon a large one, a warrior knight standing and aiming his sword at something. For a while he couldn't decide what that something was. Werner said that since the something wasn't to be shown it didn't matter, but Aaron insisted that it did" (**"CAG,"** 555). Pressured by Steinberg and afraid that "Lefty would make Aaron Gold the most miserable kid in the world," Werner finishes Aaron's knight the evening before parents' day to prevent him from getting in trouble. Even though he recognizes Aaron's talent and dedication, he intellectualizes the boy's knight, ultimately misunderstanding his artistic vision. When he first sees the knight, for example, he feels its "spindly legs wouldn't have done him much service against a good, fast dragon," and, at the end of the story, he has put arms on it: "'you didn't expect him to fight without arms, did you?'" (**"CAG,"** 553, 561). This act of appropriating Aaron's art and reshaping it suggests that Werner, like Lefty and Steinberg, cannot get beyond his own expectations of what Aaron should do and be: masculine, heterosexual, and conventional. Ironically, as Aaron runs out the door of the ceramic's shop yelling "'You ruined him'" (**"CAG,"** 561), his only recourse for resisting Werner's artistic control is to join Lefty's anti-artistic, masculinist world. Like Sydney's mother, Werner's attempts to protect Aaron take the form of intellectual control and manipulation. Ultimately, Aaron is pushed away because his form of expression and sense of identity are not acceptable.

FILLING THE LOVE VESSEL

"The Love Vessel," written in 1959, explicitly reveals Roth's interest in the intersection of religion and women. At the outset of the story, Sam Shachat's attempt to find himself on a kibbutz has failed, adding to his growing list of disappointments: physical ugliness, rectal itching, dropping out of dental school and law school, and getting divorced. He begins by moving from West to East—a literal and symbolic attempt to move away from a Christian-centered culture to embrace Judaism. Though he left behind his ex-wife, America, and a primarily Christian culture, he ultimately returns to New York, feeling even more isolated from his cultural and spiritual identity. Before returning to America, a beekeeper, the only person he has gotten to know on the kibbutz, asks him to take a small container filled with dirt back to his mother: "'it would give her a kick to have some earth, she could have it thrown on her grave.'"[11] This earth-filled vessel offers Sam a chance to do something selfless, something for someone else. It also offers him a way to bridge the gap between himself and women/Judaism. The story's circular motion (West-East-West) reinforces Sam's inability to make progress in his relationships with Judaism and women. Unable to escape a pattern that has only caused self-abasement and pain, he resents the type of power that women and religion have over him—the power to make him feel like a failure.

Sam makes such a strong connection between women and religion that both Judaism and his wife-mother have the power to emasculate him. On one hand, his alienation from Judaism reinforces his sense of loss and impotence after the divorce. His failure to live on a kibbutz, for example, makes him feel disconnected from the powerful legacy of (male) Jewish history:

> In any other time would his own role have been any different? Would Noah have allowed him on board? And Solomon—while he threw big catered affairs, Sam would have been on some street corner, listening to the hot stories about the Queen. Far back in David's legions, with the supply corps probably, you would have found Sam Shachat.
>
> **("The Love Vessel" ["LV"], 432)**

Excluded from this catalogue of powerful men, he feels enervated, measuring himself against great men who have led others—while he has always been led. He also compares himself with the beekeeper, and the beekeeper's sexuality: "[His chest] was constructed like a ship's hull, great ribbing swelling it out. In his T-shirt, ragged khaki shorts, and Army boots, he was a sore sight for Sam's eyes. He looked so thriving" (**"LV,"** 425). For Sam and presumably other men, thriving sexuality can come from a strong connection to Judaism. And he lacks both. When the beekeeper tells him "'we're somewhat alike in what we think life is all about,'" Sam sadly responds: "'We're somewhat alike . . . except for one thing. We're different'" (**"LV,"** 431).

On the other hand, Sam's relationship with women also makes him feel like less of a man and less of a Jew. Specifically, Roth links Sam's marital problems with his conflicted cultural and religious identity. While in a French cathedral, Sam associates a type of apostasy with his failed marriage: "'I'm a weakling! An ingrate! . . . I told her—I don't! Oh her, her, her.

Feed me wheat germ all my life—I'm only flesh and bones!' The cross gleamed so, it seemed to leap another hundred feet. 'Oh, Lord, how could I screw up in such a short time!' Calling Christ Lord, he almost dropped the parcel" (**"LV,"** 438). At this moment, while thinking about his broken marriage, he temporarily abandons his faith. Without a sexual and spiritual/cultural identity, Sam is nothing but "flesh and bones," and the rest of his journey marks his gradual physical deterioration: "He took poor care of himself. His hair grew. His knuckles got dirty. He didn't eat right. He stopped using underarm deodorant" (**"LV,"** 440). Not surprisingly, as he feels more defeated physically, he begins attacking women on a physical level. By focusing on their physical deterioration, which Sam sees as comparable and often worse than his own, he tries to mitigate his own losses and pain.

Like Roth's short fiction about young boys and their mothers (**"The Day It Snowed," "Conversion of the Jews,"** and in some ways **"The Contest for Aaron Gold"**), this story creates a similar type of power dynamic in the way Sam perceives his wife-mother and women in general:

> Romance and hygiene! That was the first Mrs. Shachat all over. [Pauline] would batter him to bits at tennis, at home, in bed, and then try to build him up again with wheat germ, brewer's yeast, yogurt, viosterol capsules, and broiled liver for breakfast. *She so much wanted him to be the man.* Yet, there was something about him that encouraged her to be always talking his low blood-sugar level in public. (my emphasis)
>
> (**"LV,"** 436)

Sexually and physically, Pauline "batter[s] him to bits," tearing down his masculinity and leaving him resentful and angry. This type of emasculating relationship between husband and wife is also responsible for the beekeeper's violent contempt for his mother. He, who is the most positive Jewish man in the story, refers to her as "'a colossal hag, a selfish old son of a bitch if you ever saw one . . . The old bitch, she pushed my old man through six businesses till she murdered him with number seven. Diabetes and asthma have been killing her for years, she says' . . ." (**"LV,"** 427). The beekeeper is angry about his mother's manipulative and destructive power over his father. Their relationship, like Sam's physical submission to Pauline, suggests that marriage can have an enervating impact on men, fostering a great animosity for women. (Not surprisingly, the beekeeper, a model of masculinity for Sam, is virile, brave, and unmarried.) Sam and the beekeeper see heterosexual relationships and mother-figures as dangerous, and these feed an animosity that objectifies and desexualizes them (**"Epstein,"** another story from *Goodbye, Columbus,* also offers a prime example of this).

The beekeeper's antagonistic relationship with his mother has developed far beyond Ozzie's and Sydney's youthful rebelliousness. Yet both characters express their anger, in part, through physical descriptions of these women. Ozzie describes his mother as "a round, tired, gray-haired penguin of a woman whose gray skin had begun to feel the tug of gravity and the weight of her own history. . . . But when she lit candles she looked like something better; like a woman who knew momentarily that God could do anything" (**"Conversion of the Jews"** [**"CJ"**], 143). Similarly, the beekeeper refers to his mother as "a colossal hag. . . . She considers herself a very religious person—she shaved her head when she married my father, she's so Orthodox" (**"LV,"** 427). Ozzie's and the beekeeper's representations of their mothers are intimately connected with Judaism, showing the ways these women possess (or believe they possess) an unquestioning and unfailing commitment to their faith—the type of relationship Sam envies. At the same time, both of these characters disagree with the way their mothers understand, display, and/or enforce it; and their criticism, conscious or subconscious, appears in the narrative through demeaning physical descriptions.

Similarly, during Sam's travels back to New York, his perceptions of women become increasingly grotesque as his sense of failure increases. When looking at the chambermaid in Florence, for example, he notices that "[a]bove the battered shoes, her tubular calves took each five-inch rise with a tremor. Her breathing sounded like interference on a short-wave broadcast" (**"LV,"** 430). Sam clearly uses his portrayals of her to exert some degree of power and to feel better about himself. Later, when she is blamed for stealing the can of dirt and is fired, he notices that "[s]he looked up at him with one good eye and another that was filmy with a cataract. . . . *She was lower yet than him.* . . . Her lips and gums made eating noises when she spoke" (my emphasis) (**"LV,"** 433). For Sam, it is her physical appearance—her infirm, disfigured body—that makes her "lower" than he. Sam, who has wanted to measure everything by externals—muscles mean masculinity, living on a kibbutz demonstrates religious devotion, and physical beauty makes one important—creates a way of seeing the world that reinforces his own sense of failure. Women can't live up to his physical standards, and neither can he. After arriving in Paris, for example, he describes the wife of the American hotel owner as having "a scornful set of features" (**"LV,"** 435). Yet this woman chastises him for washing his socks in his room, which makes him recall the words of his step-father: "If you were half a man, you'd tell *Pauline* what to do" (**"LV,"** 437). Sam's masculinity, as measured by his inability to stand up to women, is even threatened by a brash, ugly woman.

His last measure of superiority has been taken away, offering him no solace from his feelings of cultural and religious marginality and sexual inferiority.

Much of Roth's fiction is driven by an impending confrontation between a male character and his wife/lover/mother. In one of the culminating scenes in *Sabbath's Theater*, Sabbath watches his wife Rosie having lesbian intercourse with Christa: "He had arrived at the loneliest moment of his life."[12] The defeated and broken Sabbath lets out a primal roar and pounds his fists like a gorilla against the house. This type of frustration and rage appears in varying levels for many of Roth's male characters—the beekeeper, Epstein, Alex Portnoy, Eli, and Sam. Unlike Sabbath, some characters seem to have the possibility for redemption. Ozzie jumps off the roof, returning to the world of his mother and Rabbi Binder, and Sam delivers the vessel to the beekeeper's mother. Ironically, in these cases, a renewed connection between a man and mother is essential "to save" these men. When Sam first describes the beekeeper's mother, he sees her as a repulsive physical object, and, throughout the story, he and the beekeeper have othered her on three levels: enervating wife, domineering mother, and physical beast. For example, he is suffocated by her strong medicated odor and describes her "hulking" body as draped across the bed in her dark apartment. Then "she came towering, toppling toward him. Sam stood and felt the weight press in. It came crushing down" (**"LV,"** 442). In the final scene, however, Roth uses the embrace and kiss between Sam and the beekeeper's mother to suggest that physical and emotional connections between men and women may offer some salve for male estrangement from their Jewish cultural and religious identity. By bringing the can of dirt from her son, Sam inadvertently repairs this broken relationship and "[carries] *some* task to a conclusion" (**"LV,"** 442). His perception of her changes at this moment. She moves from being this beastly creature to a "sobbing, only weeping . . . old lady" (**"LV,"** 442). Sam begins breaking down the self/other categories he has created to view the world, and, in doing so, he has the opportunity to feel and express emotional and physical tenderness: "Then his head moved up, his lids slowly closed over his throbbing eyes, and on his toes, he planted his lips to another's" (**"LV,"** 443).

Throughout Roth's fiction, the problems men have with their mothers and wives foster such a deep-seated animosity that the link between women and Judaism makes it impossible for these men to establish a meaningful connection with their religious and cultural identity. For these men, Judaism's association with mother-figures alienates them from their sense of cultural as well as sexual identity. So where do Roth's stories leave these men? They may be lost and alone, but perhaps Sam's embrace at the end of **"The Love Vessel"** offers an image of hope—suggesting the possibility for reconciliation between men and women, men and Judaism, and men and themselves . . . even if it does not occur within Roth's fiction.

Notes

1. See Appendix.

2. In the second chapter of *Philip Roth Revisited* (New York: Twayne Publishers, 1992), Jay Halio discusses the stories in *Goodbye, Columbus.* Bernard Rodgers, Jr., in *Philip Roth* (Boston: Twayne Publishers, 1978), mentions Roth's pieces from *Et Cetera,* Bucknell University's literary magazine, and Alan Cooper refers to "The Day It Snowed" in *Philip Roth and The Jews* (Albany State University of New York Press, 1996). See also Pierre Michel's "Philip Roth's Reductive Lens: From 'On the Air' to *My Life as a Man,"* *Revue des Langues Vivantes,* Vol. 42 (1976): 509-519.

3. Roth, *Portnoy's Complaint* (1969; rpt. New York: Touchstone, 1991), p. 271, 272.

4. Roth, *Portnoy,* 281.

5. Simone de Beauvoir, *The Second Sex,* trans. and ed. H. M. Parshley (1953; New York: Knopf, 1993), p. xi.

6. Cooper, *Philip Roth and the Jews,* p. 28.

7. Philip Roth, "The Day It Snowed," *Chicago Review,* Vol. 8, No. 4 (Fall 1954): 38. Hereafter cited as *DS.*

8. Philip Roth, "The Conversion of the Jews," *Goodbye, Columbus and Five Short Stories,* (New York: Vintage International, 1993), p. 158. Hereafter cited as *CJ.*

9. Philip Roth, "The Contest for Aaron Gold," rpt. in *Fifty Best American Short Stories* (Boston: Houghton Mifflin, 1965), p. 557. Hereafter cited as *CAG.*

10. The attitude that one "chooses" a sexual identity still underlies much homophobia today. In Roth's story, this fear is evident in the camp's desperate attempts to enforce heterosexual desire and "masculine" behaviors. As Eve Kosofsky Sedgwick explains in *Epistemology of the Closet* (Berkeley: University of California Press, 1990), "the scope of institutions whose programmatic undertaking is to prevent the development of gay people is unimaginably large. No major institutionalized discourse offers a firm resistance to that undertaking; in the United States, at any rate, most sites of the state, the military, education, law, penal institutions, the church, medicine, mass culture, and the mental health industries enforce it all but unquestioningly, and with little hesitation even at recourse to invasive violence" (p. 42).

11. Philip Roth, "The Love Vessel," *Dial 1* (Fall 1959), rpt. in *My Name Aloud: Jewish Stories by Jewish Writers,* ed. Harold U. Ribalow (South Brunswick: T. Yoseloff, 1969), p. 427. Hereafter cited as *LV.*

12. Philip Roth, *Sabbath's Theater* (New York: Houghton Mifflin, 1995), p. 438.

APPENDIX

UNCOLLECTED SHORT FICTION AND VIGNETTES

1) "The Day It Snowed." *Chicago Review,* Vol. 8 (1954): 34-45.

2) "The Contest for Aaron Gold." *Epoch,* Vol. 5-6 (1955): 37-50.

3) "Heard Melodies Are Sweeter." *Esquire* (August 1958): 58.

4) "Expect the Vandals." *Esquire* (December 1958): 208-228.

5) "The Love Vessel." *Dial 1* (1959): 41-68.

6) "The Mistaken." *American Judaism,* Vol. 10 (1960): 10.

7) "Novotny's Pain." *New Yorker* (October 27, 1962): 46-56.*

8) "Psychoanalytic Special." *Esquire* (November 1963): 106.

9) "On the Air." *New American Review,* Vol. 10 (1970): 7-49.

Collected Short Fiction

1) "The Conversion of the Jews." *Goodbye, Columbus* (1959).

2) "Defender of the Faith." *Goodbye, Columbus* (1959).

3) "Epstein." *Goodbye, Columbus* (1959).

4) "You Can't Tell a Man by the Song He Sings." *Goodbye, Columbus* (1959).

5) "Eli, the Fanatic." *Goodbye, Columbus* (1959).

6) "'I Always Wanted You to Admire My Fasting'; or Looking at Kafka." *Reading Myself and Others* (New York: Farrar, Straus and Giroux, 1975).

7) "The President Addresses the Nation." *Reading Myself and Others* (1975).

* "Novotny's Pain" was later revised and collected in *A Philip Roth Reader.*

Steven Milowitz (essay date 2000)

SOURCE: Milowitz, Steven. "Now Vee May Perhaps to Begin. Yes?" In *Philip Roth Considered,* pp. 1-21. New York: Garland Publishing, Inc., 2000.

[*In the following excerpt, Milowitz examines Roth's treatment of memory and the Holocaust in his short fiction and in selected novels.*]

When you admire a writer you become curious. You look for his secret. The clues to his puzzle.

—Philip Roth—*The Ghost Writer*

Powerlessness haunts post-Holocaust man. The knowledge that, ultimately, one has no power over one's life, that one can, in a moment, be labeled, numbered, and shipped off towards death creates a startling ever-present vulnerability. To know, intuitively, that all that one has and all that one is is contingent upon an undeclared power not intervening, not changing the rules of life—rules that were once assumed to be incontestable and unchallengeable—keeps one forever suspicious, forever unsure, embattled, entrapped. The truth of Joyce's declaration, "You could die just the same on a sunny day," becomes only one truth that inhabits and inhibits man. Precariousness is now not only a component of bodily well-being but of freedom, of the self's ability to create its own destiny. For those ever-aware of the nightmare of the Holocaust nothing can be assumed stable or sure. The freedom one feels today is only a reminder of that freedom's possible revocation.

The testimonies and poems of survivors and victims, the histories written and recorded, and the essays fashioned from those works, remark time and time again on the helplessness of man when he is deemed the inhuman enemy of a state's ideology. How to continue in light of that knowledge, how to find meaning, how to reinvigorate will, and how to reestablish choice, become essential questions. Fear replaces hope in the concentrationary universe, the universe not only of the Holocaust-proper but of the new world created from its ashes.

David Rousset was the first to use the phrase, "l'Univers concentrationaire," as Sidra Ezrahi reports (10). For him, as for Ezrahi, the phrase describes the "self-contained world" of the concentration camp and "all aspects of the Nazi operation which were part of the master plan of annihilation and therefore common to most of the ghettos and camps" (Ezrahi 10). I have expanded the phrase to represent not only the place and period of the incarceration and extermination but the altered universe that is born as a result of unprecedented evil. It is as though, after the camps, the universe itself is impaired: hopes die, beliefs are more difficult to hold fast to, a pale hangs over the world.

In *The Professor of Desire,* Philip Roth's ninth novel, David Kepesh, a man whose tumult has reached a point of diminution, a man whose life has suddenly been brightened by new hope, expresses a profound, nagging fear of an unknown and unknowable oppressor. Having spent the evening listening to a Holocaust survivor tell his tragic tale Kepesh sits with his

"innocent-beloved" girlfriend, Claire, and tells her the outline of "a simple Chekhov story" which describes his life: (261).

> Two old men come to the country to visit a healthy, handsome, young couple, brimming over with contentment. The young man is in his middle thirties, having recovered finally from the mistakes of his twenties. The young woman is in her twenties, the survivor of a painful youth and adolescence. They have every reason to believe they have come through. It looks and feels to both of them as though they have been saved, and inlarge part by one another. They are in love. But after dinner by candlelight, one of the old men tells of his life, about the utter ruination of a world, and about the blows that keep on coming. And that's it. The story ends just like this: her pretty head on his shoulder; his hand stroking her hair; their owlhooting; their constellations all in order—their medallions all in order; their guests in their freshly made beds; and their summer cottage, so cozy and inviting, just down the hill from where they sit together wondering about what they have to fear. Music is playing in the house. The most lovely music there is. 'And both of them knew that the most complicated and difficult part was only beginning'
>
> (259-260)

An ominous force, awakened by the survivor's oration, surrounds them. "Are you really frightened of something?" Claire asks Kepesh, after listening to his brooding summary (260). "I seem to be saying I am, don't I," he responds (260). As to what he's afraid of he tells her, "I don't know, really" (260). It is an unintelligible and uninterpretable fear rooted in history, ambiguous and menacing. It is the fear that Sydney, one of Roth's earliest protagonists, speaks of in Roth's first published story, **"The Day it Snowed,"** the fear excited by the naive observation which begins the tale: "Suddenly people began to disappear" (34). Roth's first published sentence resonates backward in time, resurrecting images still so vivid in 1959, images still undigested, still impossible to acclimate. Sydney's world is the world of the unexperienced and innocent child baffled by death's power. His vision articulates that of a young America shocked into awareness of systematic murder and dehumanization. Just as Sydney's first world is forever altered, turned "inside out," so too any post-Holocaust man's view of life is altered irretrievably (35).

"The Day it Snowed" is a story of the birth of the knowledge which presages death, as Sydney is, in a heavy-handed conclusion, "crushed" by a "big black hearse," a reminder not only of death's whale-like strength but of its allegiance with mechanization (44). The hearse announces the death of childhood and of the pastoral. Roth's first fictional landscape is a post-Holocaust, post-lapsarian, post-pastoral landscape, a landscape at once terrifying and empty. The world in Roth's work is one of surprises, one in which people disappear inexplicably, as simply as snow can fall, seemingly out of nowhere.

The world is, in Roth's words, "crooked and unreal;" it is a place wherein "one feels less and less power" over one's life (*Reading Myself and Others* [*RMAO*] 187). It is a place for which "the inevitable end is destruction, if not of all life, then of much that is valuable and civilized in life" (*RMAO* 187). This is the world that Roth thrusts his young protagonist into, only to have him quickly devoured by it.

In **"Goodbye, Columbus"** Neil Klugman recounts a dream about himself and a little black boy he has met at the library. The two outsiders are placed onto a boat that, under its own power, takes them off shore: "And though we did not want to go, the little boy and I," Neil explains, "the boat was moving and there was nothing we could do about it" (74). Like unwilling passengers on a destinationless boat, Roth's characters search for a way to regain control of their lives. But each character is struck with the "terrifying inkling," which Willard Carroll describes early in *When She Was Good,*" "that there were in the universe forces . . . immune to his charm . . . remote from his desires . . . estranged from human need and feeling" (5).

One feels oneself a potential victim of a numinous extrinsic power, a Kafkaesque fiend which threatens at every turn. Like Kafka, the young Peter Tarnopol, in *My Life as a Man,* wonders if his life will be one of "Eviction? Confusion? Disorder?" (244). For Peter, as Kafka expresses in his *Diary,* misery "happens whether you like or no," and whether you expect it or no (268). Returning to the home he had a day earlier moved away from, having momentarily forgotten that he now lives somewhere else, he is impaled with terror "to find the door . . . wide open and to hear men talking loudly inside" (244). His world, he feels, has suddenly been taken from him. This terror comes not simply because of a childish error of memory but more importantly it is born from a world view that recognizes the barbarity of life, the tenuousness of safety. "One minute it's sunlight and the next dark," explains Leo Patimkin (**"Goodbye, Columbus"** [**"GC"**] 113). "All of a sudden, pfft!' exclaims Epstein, "and things are changed" (218). The momentary nature of one's happiness and of one's comfort is a constant source of anxiety for the characters inhabiting Roth's texts.

Some give into dismay, becoming misanthropic shells, appearing "round-shouldered, burdened," as though in flight from "a captured city" (**GC** 118), and some "reach out" and "grab" whatever they can get their hands on, whatever momentarily salves their pain

("**Epstein**" [**"E"**] 221). Some latch onto an ideology and some embrace nihilism. Some mortify their flesh and some become all-consuming carnivores. And then some few manage to neither fall into despond nor to become salacious sybarites. Some manage to negotiate a tense balance between their opposing desires and drives, finding a way to live in the unsure and devalued universe.

In that universe not only are things changed in an instant but they are changed, ostensibly, without reason or meaning. "The power to alter the course of the age, of my life and your life, is actually vested nowhere," Roth quotes Benjamin Demott approvingly (*RMAO* 177). There seems, in many cases, no one to assign blame to for one's personal pain. The confusion Sydney feels in **"The Day It Snowed"** is exemplary of the confusion of many of Roth's subsequent protagonists. Sydney asks, "What did I do? Why does everybody have to disappear on me?" (42). The question foreshadows to Novotny's query, in "Novotny's Pain," Roth's 1962 story of a soldier with a recurring backache, as to why, "Good as he had been—industrious, devoted, resolute, self-sacrificing—he would never have the pleasure of being a husband . . . or a comfort to his mother in her old age?" (266). He wonders, "What had he done in his life to deserve this?" (270).

And Kepesh—the same Kepesh whose fears rest not even on the quietest, most peaceful, evening of the year—must ask himself, when miraculously, horribly, he is turned into a breast, "What does it mean? How could it have happened? In the entire history of the human race, why Professor Kepesh?" (27). Characters are thrown into situations that defy understanding, that defy logic, that defy words, that defy explanation. It is as if Hardy's malevolent 'immanant-will' rules the lives of these twentieth-century men. Though the doctors tell Kepesh he has experienced "a massive hormonal influx or an endocrinopathic catastrophe, and/or a hermaphroditic explosion of chromosomes," no one knows with any degree of certainty what has caused his disfigurement (13). "Evidently," Kepesh realizes," nothing that has happened can be blamed on anyone, not even on me" (53). As Roth states, "Not all the ingenuity of all the English teachers in all the English departments in America can put David Kepesh together again" (*RMAO* 69). Nathan Zuckerman's back pain, in *The Anatomy Lesson* is, like Novotny's pain and like Kepesh's transformation, unclassifiable and incurable, its source impossible to uncover. In 'Courting Disaster' Zuckerman admits, "I tended, like a student of high literature or a savage who paints his body blue, to see the migraines as standing for something, a disclosure or 'epiphany'" (*My Life as a Man* [*MLAM*]

55). But, as Zuckerman learns, quite often pain stands for nothing, has no retrievable cause, no substantive meaning. Things, simply, fall apart.

Epstein's rash is thought to be "prickly heat," a "sand rash" (212), or even "The syph" (216). Like the others before him Epstein insists "He was innocent," as if this declared innocence would cause the rash to disappear (217). 'Philip Roth,' in *Operation Shylock*, borrows the Jungian formulation, "the uncontrollability of real things," to express this unexplainable uninterpretability of life (237). Smilesburger calls it "Pipikism," "the antitragic force that inconsequentializes everything" (289). Giving it a name, though, does not contain or control it; nor does it soothe the fearful heart of those for whom it is a potential victimizer.

Connected to and working in tandem with all that oppresses invisibly and for no ostensible purpose are those discernible and recognizable powers that consciously and knowingly constrict man. They are what Roth refers to as "The Powers that Be," and range from the restrictive state to the restrictive religion, from the restrictive parent to the restrictive self (*RMAO* 3). When Epstein cries out in desperation, "When they start taking things away from you, you reach out, you grab," the "they" he attaches blame to are all those powers which conspire against the individual (221). "You Must Change Your Life," Rilke writes, and in Roth it is interpreted as a command. You, the powerless, the small, must change, a decree, not a suggestion.

In *Letting Go* Gabe Wallach comes in contact with Harry Bigoness, a representative figure for all the forces that stand above the individual, unswayed. Bigoness, Roth points out, "can't be moved by [Gabe's] intelligence, by his money, by his persuasiveness, by his moral code" (*Conversation with Philip Roth* [*CWPR*] 9). The Big Ones—the ones who are in control, whose strength appears limitless, whose impersonal authority and dispassion resonate in all lives, whose decrees are meted out, whose words are acted upon, whose language is corrupt and corrupting—are ubiquitous. Of Gabe's encounter with Bigoness, Roth states, "I wanted him to come up against, at the end of the book, something that was indeed larger than him, but something that had nothing to do with being more intelligent or even more charitable than he was" (*CWPR* 9).

Bigoness is a concrete illustration of that force that Willard comments upon, and that Sydney, Novotny, Kepesh, and Epstein feel haunting them in every shadow. Incarnations of Bigoness are revealed in the McCarthyite actions of Mr. Wendell, in "You Can't Tell a Man by the Song he Sings," who documents both teachers' and students' behaviors and opinions on "a big card" which, he assures everyone, "would follow [them] through life," and which portends disaster for the left-leaning Russo (246), in the residents of Woodenton, who force the quiescent Holocaust-survivor, "the greenie" (281), to give up his clothes, to whom he appears to ask, "The face is all right, I can keep it? (283), in what Alexander Portnoy refers to as "this Holy Protestant Empire" (43), in the officials and agents in Prague who follow both Kepesh and Zuckerman throughout their short visits, in the equally intrusive Israeli agents who tail 'Philip Roth' in Israel, in the Major League Baseball Association, the "Holy Baseball Empire," in *The Great American Novel*, which denies Smitty's entreaties, denies even Smitty's memories, and most hilariously in the figure of Tricky Dixon, in *Our Gang*, the personification of the tyrannical and the false, a parody of all political potentates, all dictators (16).

Dixon is the embodiment of what Norman Manea, in *On Clowns: The Dictator and the Artist*, calls "the white clown," the stark, cold, autocrat, exemplified for Manea in the figure of Nicolae Ceausescu (41). Manea contrasts the White Clown with Auguste the Fool, the subdued artist who "simply refuses" to let the White Clown dictate his life (49). But, Auguste is no dissident leading the charge against tyranny; he is, instead, the fearful, schlemiel-like man who, when forced into submission, must resist, who admits proudly, "I couldn't restrain myself" (8). It is this aspect of Manea's study that Roth finds most fascinating: "The battle not of the heroic but of the vulnerable, the weak and the unheroic to hang on and, stubbornly, against all odds, to resist their degradation" (*I Couldn't Restrain Myself* [*CRM*] 3). For Roth, "no moral endeavor is more astonishing" (3).

This same fascination with the weak, the ordinary, the decidedly human, coming in contact and doing battle with various forms of coercion informs Roth's own fiction. It is not so much the Dixons and the Bigoness that intrigue Roth as much as those who manage to see through their hypocrisy and their lies, who manage to live in truth, in Vaclav Havel's phrase.[1] To give in to the powers that be, to submit one's self to the preset patterns of society is no remarkable feat; It is, in fact, the norm. Roth's prose focuses on how and why certain individuals, however unexceptional, are able to, to some degree or other, retain individuality in the midst of what Manea calls "the derailment of humanity itself;" how they do battle with the lie and with those who present the lie as truth (*CRM* 3).

This essential concern of Roth's explains his interest in oppressed European writers from Kafka to Klima, writers who investigate the individual in extreme situations, in conflict with powerful dehumanizing and corrupt political systems. His own works bridge the gap between Europe and America, focusing on the less overt ways in which man is stripped of individuality.[2] In contrast to the obvious manipulation of an authoritarian state the American reality is more obtuse and complex. There is no clear White Clown, no single Dixon to place blame upon. Roth's work speaks of the more subtle ways in which man loses his self: conformity, banality, blind patriotism, cliche, stereotype, trivialization, mechanization, a laundry list of methods and enactors of, what Noam Chomsky calls "manufactured consent," the unquestioning and obedient trust in one's world (Said 302). What Chomsky sees as "the effects of a generation of indoctrination" Roth writes in response to, pitting his frightened, groping, protagonists against various automatizing agents (Said 302). From Sydney's mother, whose attempt to stifle his growth through euphemism and lie, to the Mossad, which asks 'Philip Roth' to censor himself, these agents act, often effectively, to keep the individual in line, under control, essentially imprisoned.

Again and again characters attempt to "cut loose from what binds and inhibits" them, most often doing battle with the twin imposing threats of "the oppressiveness of family feeling" and the "binding ideas" of religion, threats which stretch across the spectrum of body and mind, the heart and the head, and which are employed synecdochically for all that represses man (*RMAO* 9).

Both forms of pressure are present in Roth's early, celebrated story, "The Conversion of the Jews," a story used often to explain Roth's initial impetus to create, a story usually viewed as a "moral-fantasy" (Jones & Nance 28), or, as Roth puts it, a "day dream," wherein oppressors are "magically" (*CWPR* 85) humbled by the young Ozzie Freedman, the personification of "the urge for individualistic freedom" (Jones & Nance 29).

Ozzie rebels against the obfuscations of his mother and of Rabbi Marvin Binder, dissenting from the illogical dogma that the students who surround him accept without disquiet. Ozzie, unlike his fearful peers, is disinclined towards "closed-mouthedness," questioning Binder on Binder's easeful rejection of the Immaculate Conception: "Jesus is historical" (139). Ozzie, refusing to digest, unconsidered, the words of authority, asks Binder, "If [God] could create the heaven and earth in six days, and make all the animals and the fish and the light in six days . . . and He could pick the six days right out of nowhere, why couldn't He let a woman have a baby without having intercourse?" (140-141). Ozzie is a literalist, confused when lessons learned do not correspond with new lessons or with behavior. He has wondered "how Rabbi Binder could call the Jews 'The Chosen People' if the Declaration of Independence claimed all men to be created equal" (141), and why during "free-discussion time" he feels so unfree to express what is on his mind (144).

The suggestion, most critics make, is that Binder, Mrs. Freedman, and Yakov Blotnik—"the seventy-one-year old custodian" who mumbles incoherent prayers to himself and whose thought are "fractionated . . . simply: things were either good- for- the-Jews or no-good-for-the-Jews" (150)—"come to represent the narrow and sterile religiosity from which Ozzie wishes to escape" (McDaniel 85), and that Ozzie is a "spiritual activist" (McDaniel 82) who moves from a constricting spiritless world to "one of spiritual freedom" (Meeter 20). Bernard Rodgers is the primary proponent of the Ozzie/Roth parallel. He calls Ozzie's action a "revolt against . . . xenophobia and closed-mindedness" and likens it emphatically with "Roth's own artistic revolt" (22).

These readings, defensible though they are, miss the substance of both Ozzie's 'revolt' and Roth's artistic program. For these readers the story lacks any irony: Ozzie is heroic individualism and the three elders repressive society and religion. There is no doubt that Roth uses this story, on one level, to exact criticism on those platitudinous and doctrinaire religious and secular authorities who refuse to answer or consider questions, who expect acquiescence, and who mouth the words of God without understanding what they are saying. And yet these villains are less villainous than at first imagined.

"Rabbi Binder," we are reminded, "only looked dictatorial" (149). In fact he is an unimposing and easily humbled figure, who, against the group chant of "Jump," maintains his plea, "Don't Jump! Please, Don't Jump" (153). Mrs. Freedman, a widow, is presented as a gentle and sad figure who "didn't look like a chosen person," and who, though she strikes Ozzie does so "for the first time," and without vigor (143). And Yakov Blotnik is clearly no danger to anyone, saddled with an "old mind" which "hobbled slowly, as if on crutches" (150). Though they are, indeed, single-minded and cliche-ridden they are not formidable threats; rather, they are combatants easily vanquished.

Ozzie, in many ways, is the aggressor, not merely questioning his teacher's words but insisting that the answers he receives are not sufficient, constantly claiming, "What I wanted to know was different" (141). Their conflict is essentially generational, the elder secure and dogmatic, the youth quizzical and unsatisfied with anything but faultless logic. But, where Binder attempts to answer Ozzie again and again, albeit with banalities, Ozzie rejects his answers outright, firing the accusation, "You don't know! You don't know anything about God!" (146).

It is Ozzie, not Binder, who is described as feeling both "Peace" and "Power" (149). It is Ozzie who becomes a Christ figure dancing on the rooftop to the chant of his earnest disciples, "Be a Martin. Be a Martin" (155). It is Ozzie who forces all into the "Gentile posture of prayer" (157), and compels them to "say they all believed in Jesus Christ" (158). Ozzie renounces Binder's binding dogma in favor of Christianity's, replacing Binder's cliches with his own: "You should never hit anyone about God" (158) He becomes so sure, so finally certain, that he leaps from the rooftop without fear, a believer. Ozzie, who only wanted definitive answers finds his answers in the "catechizing" of the Jews, in the language of another religion (158). His rebellion is less than "a fragile one," as Sanford Pinsker asserts; it is a fundamentally empty rebellion, a rebellion not towards freedom but towards more restrictiveness (*The Comedy That Hoits* [*TCTH*] 14). Ozzie, who initially seems to be "protesting his individuality," loses his individuality not to Binder, Blotnik, or to his mother, but to his reliance on the language of established Christianity, the language of dogma, to his assertion of power and surety (Deer 357). The story turns in upon itself, ironizing the simplicity with which Ozzie seems to find freedom.

To claim Ozzie Freedman as the personification of the activist's revolt against constrictions is to apply a facile and superficial reading to a story that demands a more complex explication. The outward simplicity of the language that Roth employs seems to invite uncomplicated interpretations. Saul Bellow chastises **"The Conversion of the Jews"** for being "absolutely clear" (42), and Joseph Landis states, "The point is . . . altogether too clear (166). And Roth, in a 1966 interview, suggests that his reading of the story is no more sophisticated than many readers when he asserts that he is no longer "at one with the ideas and feelings that had caused it to be written" (*CWPR* 8). Roth's statement applies to a story that is only about the absolute rejection of authority, a story which enacts a revolt. If the more complex reading is applied the story is seen as questioning both authority and the individual, both the rebel as well as the object of the rebellion.

In any reading, though, Ozzie's revolt is not commensurate with Roth's artistic program, as Rodgers claims it to be. To argue that Binder, Blotnik, and Mrs. Freedman "personify all that Roth was determined to reject in the attitudes of the Jewish environment which had surrounded him for the first eighteen years of his life"

Rodgers paints a picture of Roth's work as overtly polemical, as didactic, as the work of a rebel rather than of an aesthete (22). Rodgers's claim is based on Roth's own argument that "an author's work can and should have a social impact" (61). He adds: "To Roth that impact would appear to be a subversive one" (61). Such a view of Roth places him side by side with Ozzie, a child attempting to overturn his world with an act of conversion. Roth is not such a simple subject. Rather than encouraging rebellion he investigates it in all its forms. Rather than derogating authority he questions and scrutinizes it. "I wouldn't write a book to win a fight," Roth contends, making clear his refusal to see art as a vehicle of rebellion (*CWPR* 193). "If you ask if I want my fiction to change anything in culture," Roth states, "the answer is still no," further subverting Rodgers's argument (*CWPR* 186). Roth, unlike Ozzie, embraces no position to overturn another. His fiction resonates with his "distrust of positions" of all kinds (*RMAO* 71). To see Roth's burgeoning writing as equivalent to Ozzie Freedman's escapade on the temple roof is to begin to study Roth from a mistaken angle.

Roth's first critics, those rabbis and readers who vehemently decried **"The Conversion of the Jews,"** **"Epstein,"** and **"Defender of the Faith,"** offered Roth a much more virulent disapprobation than Binder's for Ozzie, and Roth's response has been more considered and sophisticated, more tinged with irony and doubt, than Ozzie's intuitive response. Roth's early stories were called "dangerous, dishonest, and irresponsible" (*RMAO* 205). He was called an "anti-Semite" and "self-hating" (*RMAO* 25), and was accused of "informing" on Jews by representing the lecherous Grossbart, the lusting Epstein (**RMAO** 217). "You have earned the gratitude," wrote a rabbi, "of all who sustain their anti-Semitism on such conceptions of Jews as ultimately lead to the murder of six million in our time" (*RMAO* 218). "I hated you personally every sentence of your story," another reader wrote (*The Philip Roth Collection* [*PRC*]).[3] "Medieval Jews would have known what to do with him," a "rabbi and educator in New York City" voiced (*RMAO* 216). A literary discussion group wrote to *The New Yorker,* after studying **"Defender of the Faith,"** "We have discussed this story from every possible angle and we cannot escape the conclusion that it will do irreparable damage to the Jewish people" (*RMAO* 216). Requesting an answer to their complaints the group concluded, "Cliches like 'this being art' will not be acceptable" (*RMAO* 216).

Roth responded not with cliches but with unremitting earnestness, writing not only his 1963 essay, **"Writing about Jews,"** (which summarizes and addresses those complaints) but with detailed individual letters written to rabbis and other readers. He decried their narrowness of vision, their inability to see his stories as investigations of various types of Jewish men and woman, both righteous and limited, both driven and conscience-laden, both deceitful and forthright. His book was not simply a categorizing of the evils and weaknesses of Jews, not "rassenschande," but an attempt to "redeem the stereotype," to understand and uncover both the truths and falsities embedded in the stereotype, to explore Jews as human beings, fallible and real (*Second Dialogue in Israel* [*SDI*] 75). "The hope of the fiction writer is to tell the truth about experience and phenomena," Roth argues, in a draft to **"Writing about Jews,"** not hiding ugly truth and celebrating laudatory truth (11). To adhere to his critic's suggestions, to succumb to their fear of fomenting "fuel" for anti-Semite's fire (*RMAO* 206), to create art while constantly asking, "What will the goyim think?" is to allow one's freedom to be taken away, to allow a restriction to be placed upon the imagination, to turn one's work into agitprop (*RMAO* 212).

Likening his critics to McCarthyites and to the Russian government in its persecution of Boris Pasternak, he views their exercise as an attempt at "denying me my freedom and making me obedient to their will" (*WAJ-D* 11), arguing that "the only response there is to any restriction of liberties is 'No, I refuse'" (*RMAO* 221). Roth places the responsibility on the I, the individual, to hold fast to his sense of self by not adhering to the censoring powers, by 'writing in truth,' as Havel might term it.

Ozzie does not retain his self-hood in **"The Conversion of the Jews."** His recurring question, "Is it me? is it me?" reveals his loss of self (148). The language describing his actions on the roof indicate a boy out of control: "The question came to him," "he discovered himself no longer kneeling," "his arms flying every which way as though not his own," "he hadn't really headed for the roof as much as he'd been chased there" (151). He is a boy without volition, jumping because the crowd calls for it, using a language not his own. The individuality he asserts at the start of the story has disappeared. His revolt has failed. Roth's revolt is, by contrast, not only against the narrowness of his Jewish detractors but against narrowness in general. Roth resists all "untenable notions of right and wrong" (*RMAO* 206), using his fiction to locate "all that is beyond moral categorizing" (*RMAO* 207).

At the center of that resistance is an exploration of the self, the way in which a man holds back and falls victim to entrapment, the way in which a man entraps and liberates himself. **"You Must Change Your Life"** is not only a potential threat but, as Martin Green points out, a reminder of "the process of self-indictment" (*Philip Roth Reconsidered* [*PRR*] XXII).

The struggle inside is as perilous as the struggle outside, the powers that inhabit a man more trying than the powers that be.

For the writer the "imaginations' systems of constraints and habits of expression," and not the critics' disdain, offer the most profound problems (*RMAO* 13). It is the self's limits that need to be traversed if writing is to succeed. The writing self is stymied by guilt, by fear, by history, by experience, and by indissoluble literary paradigms. Roth claims that he writes and reads fiction "to be freed from my own suffocatingly narrow perspective on life" (*RMAO* 120). Elsewhere he states that successful literature "allows us for awhile to be free" (*WAJ-D* 6). Roth's work springs from this conception of literature as potentially liberating and transforming. Like his characters the urge, the necessity, to maintain individuality, whether in style or content, is Roth's most difficult and imperative task. "What is it to be what I am?" his characters ask themselves again and again, determined to discover themselves without recourse to a preconstructed formula (Introduction to **Goodbye, Columbus,** German Edition [*I-GC*] 1). The discovery of the self and the retention of individuality and freedom amidst a debasing and deindividualizing world and a tortured and confused body and mind are concerns central to Roth's artistic drive, concerns which spring forth from Roth's overriding interest in the Holocaust and its lingering effects on twentieth-century man.

In an interview about the Zuckerman trilogy with *The London Sunday Times,* in 1973, Roth says of the Holocaust, "If you take away that word—and with it the fact—none of these Zuckerman books would exist" (*RMAO* 136). In fact to take away that word would be to erase Roth's canon. For Roth the Holocaust is the contemporary equivalent of what Harold Bloom terms Kafka's "Judaism of the Negative" (12). What in Kafka is the understood as the darkness "of the future," becomes in Roth the darkness of the past (Bloom 12). What Kafka feared and imagined became real for Philip Roth's generation; the penal colony became the death camps.

Instead of recognizing Roth's essential concern with the Holocaust and with its power to hold sway over the next generation, critics tended to use the Holocaust as a linchpin for their criticisms of his work, insisting that Roth degraded the memory of the victims by his critical and all too human portrait of Jews. In those early expressions of outrage the Holocaust is consistently invoked. Marie Syrkin's words are representative of the barbs lodged at Roth. She calls *Portnoy's Complaint* a work "straight out of the Goebbels-Streicher script" (*RMAO* 300). As Roth sardonically points out, "Had she not been constrained by limits of space Syrkin might eventually have had me in the dock with the entire roster of Nuremberg defendants" (*RMAO* 300).

Critics like Syrkin contended that not enough time had passed to write so openly about Jews. Jews, they asserted, should be exempt from criticism, their recent history made them unique, separate from other men, needing to be insulated, written and spoken about referentially, only as passive victims and heroic sufferers. For Roth the fact of the Holocaust makes it essential not to stoop to propagandizing for the Jews, not to cower in fear of the repetition of history; to present Jews as men and women, not categories, as individuals, not indistinguishable members of a group. After all, what is the fundamental difference between the Nazi picture of Jews as "wicked," and wicked only, and the fearful Jewish claim that Jews are "perfect," and perfect only? (*Draft of Writing about Jews* [*WAJ-D*] 14).

Roth recognizes the validity of the fears expressed, just as he recognizes the anti-Semitic threat as real. "The difference between us," Roth writes of his critics, "is in how we choose to respond to the threat" (*WAJ-D* 13). While his critics espouse silence, prettified pictures, and timidity, Roth suggests vociferousness, honest, if sometimes ugly, pictures, and boldness as ways of exploring Jewish and American life after the Holocaust. It would be "an insult to the dead" six million to use their memory to stifle the artist's spirit (*RMAO* 221). For Roth, "The suggestion that we act willingly now the way certain Jews, in horror, grief, and shock, were forced to act then, provokes in me an outrage equaled only by my disbelief" (*WAJ-D* 15). To act as a victim when the victimization has ended is to hand the enemy a final victory. Roth's work is so centrally concerned with the I because it is the I that the Holocaust-architects tried to strip away. "Hitler killed nerve" (*WAJ-D* 18), argues Roth, and to allow nerve's death to infect the survivors is to "continue to be Hitler's victims" (*WAJ-D* 15). Roth's first responsibility, then, is to resist the impulse to censor himself in deference to the memory of the camps. The first I to liberate is the I of the writer.

As Sanford Pinsker points out, "If an older generation of American-Jewish writers had insisted, in Bernard Malamud's phrase, that 'All men are Jews!' Roth's vision was the converse-All Jews were also men" (*TCTH* 4). Roth individualizes men rather than grouping and universalizing them. Each Jew, in Roth, is differentiated from previous or future protagonists, each faces his own barriers, his own hurdles, and each responds according to his own strengths and limitations.

Many critics, including Irving Howe, find Roth's individualizing of Jews unconvincing, suggesting that Roth's Jews are de-judaized, their ties to Jewish tradition and history non-existent. Howe sees Roth as a writer submerging Jewish identity into assimilationist America, flaying the Jew from his roots, making him disappear into the mass, like Ellison's black paint disappears into a great American whiteness. Dorothy Seidman Bilik points to Roth's comments in a 1961 *Commentary* Symposium, to prove her point. In that debate Roth asked of Jews, "How are you connected to me as another man is not?" (351). However, rather than deciphered as a statement of disconnection from the Jews it is more accurately read as a declaration of connection to all men, not limited to Jews only. Jews are men, each attractive or repulsive on his own. This manner of viewing one's connection to Jews allows one a vaster perspective, allows one to deny that Jews are all one thing, all the same. "And that is a good thing," Roth states in the same symposium, "for it enables a man to choose to be a Jew," to embrace his Judaism and his history by choice rather than by being "turned into one, without his free accession" (351).

His embrace of Judaism is a complex embrace, not simply the throwing of arms blindly around all Jews and all the patriarchal Jewish beliefs and codes but a more considered embrace, an embrace tinged with questions and with thought. Roth does not renounce his Judaism, nor does he turn away from its discomforting realities. On the contrary, Roth's emphasis on the Jew as man, on the Jew as willful and complex, springs forth from a painful need to remember and delve into the Jewish past.

What the Nazis attempted to take from Jews, and indeed from everyone, Roth attempts to reinsert in his fiction, using the Holocaust as a lodestar to point to the hurdles man must overcome. The most seductive hurdle the Holocaust exposes is the hurdle of ideology, the belief in a fundamental, absolute, indubious truth, a truth one must ascribe to unquestionably. In its denial of self and in its elimination of choice the enactors of the Holocaust relied on a strict ideology to enforce their will. Ideology presents itself as the most malevolent force behind all that worked to devastate and dehumanize man in Nazi Germany. The Nazi ideology insisted that the Jews were less than human, that they were cancers that needed to be excised.

In Roth's work, characters move across the spectrum of ideology and nihilism. No single stance is satisfactory because each embodies an aspect of the Nazi philosophy. The Nazi doctrine was not only a call to ideology but, as David Hirsch points out, "a call for a return to a primordial past . . . a regression to chthonic Dionysian drunkenness" (265-6). It relied not only on the "systematic" and the "ordered" (Ezrahi 255) in man but on the "unshackled" in him as well

(Hirsch 265). The Nazis tried to harness neither side of man, allowing uncapped Dionysus to alternate with automatized and programed Apollo. No balance, no interplay, was reached between these contradictory sides of man. The Nazi, in this illustration, is half a man (though he feels himself to be whole, complete) turning one side of his self off while the other performs its horrendous duties. Roth's successful men and women find fullness in the tension between the two diverse sides of self, a tension lessened and engorged minute by minute but never subdued, never fully quieted. Unlike the Nazi, Roth's protagonist maintains a balance, unable and unwilling to allow either Dionysus or Apollo full control over him. He feels "painful points of friction," as Roth writes of the quintessential Rothian man, his father, a friction, he continues, "which yield[s], at its best, vitality, a dense and lively matrix of feeling and response" (*The Man in the Middle*, [*MIM*] A-32). The maintenance of this friction, this balance, creates countless dilemmas, neuroses, terrors, hurts, and fears, but its maintenance is the only way to exist in a concentrationary universe.

The balance extends to Roth's style as well as to his content. Roth rejects the temptation "to imitate" narrative techniques "verified by authority" (*RMAO* 8). He rejects "literary dogma" in favor of a more individual style, one which mixes genres, which mixes the past and the present, which mixes the vernacular and the literary, which uses models and breaks free from models, which forms new paradigms only to undermine and reconsider them. Speaking of *The Counterlife,* but useful for all his works, Roth notes, "The narratives are all awry but they have a unity" (*CWPR* 253). In that remark he locates the pull between form and formlessness, the need for both if a work is to have validity in the changed world. His works take literary techniques and genres—naturalism, realism, anti-realism, parody, satire, thriller, confession, love-story, biography, autobiography—and turn them in upon themselves, altering the reader's perspective by diverging from the established form, by undermining expectations. Roth's style, a cacophony, a hybrid, a bringing together and a stripping apart, can best be defined as impressionism, a style inextricably bound up with the individual, the I groping for vision, a style which both is aware of the ambiguity and unsurety of the world at the same time as it retains some solidity, some structure which holds back the urge for a deconstructionist denial of all form, all truth, all meaning.

The battle is between, what will be termed, Lonoffism and Pipikism, the ordered, ideological, strict, impotent, lifeless automaton and the "protean" (*Operation Shylock* [*OS*] 185), the nihilistic, "the senseless," the driven, the lustful, the uncontrolled, the unbound animal (*OS* 389). To keep the tension between the two

and to be aware of the split is to remain viable and vibrant, functioning and potent. To shut down one side and to give the other sovereignty is to fall into the cauldron of the concentrationary universe.

"The novelist," Roth says in an interview with Asher Z Milbauer and Donald G. Watson, "suffers from serious ignorance of his obsessional theme" (10). Whether Roth suffers from that ignorance is difficult to deduce, but it is clear that when a comprehensive survey of Roth's work is undertaken the Holocaust in all its manifestations, as history, as lesson, as harbinger, as memory, as coercer, as warning, is Roth's obsessional theme.

Unlike other American writers Roth was not hesitant to investigate imaginatively the stark facts of the Holocaust period. Sidra Ezrahi describes the "slow process by which the remote event eventually entered [American] literature (179). She notes that in America "few . . . writers possessed the resources from which an immediate response could be shaped" (176-177). The war literature of the forties, Ezrahi argues, "established the camps somewhere on the outer boundaries of human geography" (179). American literature of the late forties and fifties investigated "the fascist threat . . . but not the historical events of the Holocaust" (179). The fifties, she states, were taken up with "growing documentation by survivors and historians," but little substantive fiction was created (179). Ezrahi points to the trial of Adolph Eichmann in 1961 as "a watershed in the American perception of the Holocaust," the bell that awoke the slumbering or weary writers (180). And yet between 1958 and 1959 Philip Roth was already writing and re-writing a play, titled "A Coffin in Egypt," which confronts the Holocaust directly, exploring boldly the experience of a Jewish ghetto between 1941 and 1943.[4]

The play tells its story in three relatively short acts. Act One sets the scene in Vilna, Lithuania, October 1941. Solomon Kessler, a former clerk, a simple man, "a man who has been deprived all his life" (26), a "mediocre failure," has just been made Mayor of the Jews of Vilna, by the Nazi Colonel Holtz (60). He meets with the Jewish council to explain that he is now "in charge of the Jews" (6) Rabbi David Meyer, the Chancellor of the Yesivah, refuses to acknowledge Kessler, refuses to compromise, as he will throughout the play. Rabbi Joachim Smolenskin, a wise elderly man, recognizes the need for compromise, the need to retain some Jewish authority in the midst of what he admits is an incomprehensible situation. Leo Rosenfeld, a communist, refuses, like Meyer, to respect Kessler's rule, promising him a revolution of workers. Kessler is told by Holtz that he will be able to make Vilna a prospering, culturally alive village again as long as each month he sends a thousand Jews to the extermination camps. Holtz explains that in sending a sacrifice each month Kessler will save countless Jewish lives. Kessler resigns himself to Holtz's terms believing that "Fighting them is impossible" (17). The first act ends with the first "Action" (10). An old man, the last of the thousand, asks, "What did I do? Why?" as he stops midway to the train (20). He asks Smolenskin, "Rabbi, who can be buried in a strange place?" and the rabbi tells him of Joseph's burial in Egypt, far away from the promised homeland (21). The man is taken away and hit by a Nazi guard. Kessler smacks the guard, telling him, "Never lay one finger" (23). The train pulls away and the citizens of Vilna begin the mourner's prayer as Kessler screams, "Stop it! Stop mourning! I forbid mourning!" (23).

Act Two takes place in December 1942, in an ostensibly revitalized Vilna. The coffee shop is filled with Jews; music is playing. The theater, the schools, the restaurants, have been reopened, and, as Smolenskin says, It is all "Kessler's doing" (26). The two rabbis and Rosenfeld argue their various positions, Meyer and Rosenfeld secure in their rightness, Smolenskin consumed by doubt. Kessler enters the shop like a monarch, an air of confidence about him, magisterial, in control. He tells those assembled of his plan to save ten thousand Jewish lives. Five thousand workers are to be shipped to Kovno, which will become a "Jewish worker's city," and five thousand of Vilna's vagrants will then take their places at work (28). Kessler appoints Rosenfeld the leader of the workers in Kovno. Rosenfeld, accusing Kessler and the Nazis of "breaking the back of the resistance" by sending "the young" and "the strong" away from Vilna, declines the appointment (38). For his non-acquiescence Rosenfeld is arrested. The train for Kovno is loaded with healthy, optimistic men and women. Kessler and Meyer watch the train begin its trip, Kessler fiercely proud of his accomplishment, Meyer bitter, enraged at the decimation of his beloved Vilna. The train, suddenly, comes to a halt and the young Jews are led from the train and are massacred in a maze of machine-gun fire. Kessler, horrified, despondent, screams, "I didn't do it! I didn't do it!" (42). The act ends, once again, with the mourner's kaddish, chanted this time by Kessler himself.

Act Three takes place in August 1943. The Nazis are concerned about the approaching Russian army. Vilna, it seems, will soon be overrun. Holtz presents Kessler with a scheme whereby Kessler will assume guilt for all the evils perpetrated upon Vilna's Jews in return for an assisted escape to Sweden. Kessler, while thinking over Holtz's proposal, visits the ailing Smolenskin, who despairing, wants only to die. Kessler defends his actions, claiming that everything he did he did only to save Jews. He tells Smolenskin, "Every-

thing was black and some of us stood in front of the blackness, and we made some gestures" (58). Kessler leaves the dying rabbi to supervise what might be the last Action. He is told that they are one Jew short of their quota. Kessler moves to a microphone and addresses the crowd. "The Russians are coming," he tells them. "Go home. All of you, go home" (59). Powerless to have his words acted upon he joins the doomed Jews. The crowd begins to chant the mourner's prayer as Kessler disappears into the train.

"A Coffin in Egypt," written virtually simultaneously with the stories of *Goodbye, Columbus,* recreates the Holocaust universe while pointing towards the post-Holocaust universe that Roth's next works will take as their setting. The play begins with an overwhelming assertion of power: the imposition of a puppet government to both subjugate and palliate the frightened Jews of Vilna. Kessler's appointment is not put to a democratic vote; the Jewish council is dissolved in a moment. The power thrusts itself upon Kessler and the villagers, taking control of their lives. But that power is invisible, always at a distance, always removed. Kessler answers to Holtz, Holtz to an unseen Berlin. "I resent," Holtz tells Kessler, "that you are making this seem my idea" (13). "Kovno," he says later, "was Berlin" (48). But Berlin remains in the shadows. The power seems to emanate from nowhere.

It is not only invisible but uninterpretable. It seems to act counter-intuitively. "I don't even begin to understand," Smolenskin says. "Cossacks I've seen, pogroms I've seen. But this, giving people yellow cards, counting them off, putting them on trains, some still carrying their fiddles, their china" (17). There is no model, no precedent, to compare to the Nazi assault. All designations, all forms of knowledge and of language are undone. "What did I do?" cries the old man (20) In this new world innocence is no defense against punishment It is a world, as Primo Levi reports, in *Survival in Auschwitz,* without "Why" (7).[5]

It is a world where the strong are murdered and the mediocre are rewarded. It is a world where the definitions of good and evil are overturned. Are Kessler's actions good because they save lives or are they evil because they advance the Nazi campaign? Are Meyer and Rosenfeld good because they admonish Kessler or are they evil because they would rather submit everyone to a collective death. rather than compromise with an outside power and give up their own authority? The attack upon Vilna's citizens is more than an attack upon their bodies; it is an attack upon all that they have believed in, all that they have spoken, all that they know. It is an attack upon their sense of themselves, on their humanity. A mammoth power has arrived not only to conquer but to control, to strip its victims of their very status as human beings.

Each character reacts to this assault in a different manner, depending on his/her former life, preconceptions, and ardent beliefs. Rosenfeld uses communism as the redemptive ideology to challenge the Nazi ideology. To him Kessler is a "Fascist" (56). A true believer in the workers, in the coming of a world revolution, in Stalin as god-head, Rosenfeld promises Kessler, "There will be a new era" (56). Rosenfeld derives his strength from this belief, a belief which gives him the will to refuse Kessler at every turn, to mock and threaten him. But Rosenfeld's ideology is as limited as the Nazi ideology that he rebels against. He mimics Stalin and Lenin as Hitlerites mimic Hitler. He considers nothing, doubts nothing, sees the world in black and white. His revolt, then, is an empty one. Like Ozzie, he merely substitutes one ideology for another. He never aspires to individuality; his ideology keeps him strong but costs him his identity.

David Meyer's refusal is, like Rosenfeld's, initiated from ideological ground, his ideology being that of Orthodox Judaism. Meyer is forever quoting the bible, suggesting that martyrdom is the only solution for Vilna's Jews. For Meyer compromise is out of the question, those who do, whether they save lives or not, are collaborators, traitors to their religion. Smolenskin responds to Meyer's simplistic assertion of superiority, asking him, "How can you be so holy? How can the rest of us be so wicked?" (27). Meyer, like the Nazis, attempts to brand each man holy or unholy, hero or murderer, human or beast, "messiah" or "butcher" (36). There are no gradations. Ideology provides him with a sense of rightness, but it takes away his ability to consider, to think and rethink, making him robotized, inhuman, making him the epitome of the undone, victimized Jew.

Smolenskin resists the urge to condemn or criticize too quickly in favor of a more balanced and thoughtful approach to the unendurable situation. He is an appeaser, a realist, offering sympathy for the victims while maintaining his connection to those in charge. He tells Meyer, "A dead Jew helps nobody. We take from the Germans what life we can" (27). Smolenskin is a man of decency and of wisdom, his philosophy antagonistic to ideology.

But with his faith pulled out from under him, his town denuded, his fellow Jews at war with one another, he gives in to despair, banishing himself to his bedroom, hoping for death. When Kessler encourages him to recover the rabbi responds, "I don't have the ambition" (53). He has given up, surrendered himself to the degradation that has been foisted upon him. He appropriates the posture of a dying man though his health is fine. Nihilistically, he lies down and closes his eyes, becoming a martyr to hopelessness. Meyer and Rosen-

feld find sanctuary in ideology while Smolenskin finds his sanctuary in emptiness. All eviscerate their selves.

Solomon Kessler moves within both frames, only to escape from the binds of each to unfettered self-hood. Initially he is an empty vessel, a man whose heart is "a plug of iron," a man cut in half (15). "For thirty-seven years I went through life I didn't feel a thing," he remarks (39). He is an automaton, moving through each day by rote. Thrust into a position of power Kessler finds his missing half, he finds purpose. "I . . . believe in what I'm doing," he says with passion (39). He finds an alternative lifestyle to his previous structureless life. He develops faith in his power, believing it to be legitimate. When he announces his plan for Kovno he says triumphantly, "They have made a concession to me. To me!" (34). He tells the Nazi guards, "I'm in charge here" (23).

But Kessler's language betrays him. He tells a crowd, "The basis for existence in the ghetto is work," echoing the Nazi cliche, "Work makes man free," exposing the extent of his indoctrination into the Nazi lexicon and dogma. In the throes of power he displays his inherent impotence. He is a puppet, mouthing the oppressor's words, no more human than he was when a nonfeeling clerk. Kessler tells Smolenskin, "I suddenly was given a life, not of a bug" (55). He believes he has experienced a reverse metamorphosis, that he has finally become a man. But even in his expression of this found freedom he displays his debt to a controlling power. He is 'given' a life; he does not create or choose a life. As long as he acts as the Nazi representative he is never free.

It is when doubt enters his consciousness that he begins to extricate his self from its confinement. When Holtz asks him, towards the end of the play, "What have you been in this for in the first place?" he responds, "I don't know" (51). His belief in his role has evaporated and he is liberated. When he disobeys Holtz and tells the Jews to detrain he knows his life is in jeopardy, he knows his action will be ineffective, he knows that he has given up all roads to escape. His act of refusal is a potent act, an act born not from ideology nor from despair but from will. In the midst of the dehumanization of all that surrounds him he exercises choice thereby denying Holtz and Berlin their victory. Kessler finds, in the convergence of the twin sides of self, a freedom that no other character is able to uncover.

The battle Kessler undergoes augurs the battle Rothian man suffers time and time again, attempting to keep each side vibrant without relying on ideology or grabbing hold of nihilism. Ambiguity is the stance Rothian man finds most satisfactory, a questioning back not a rejection, a searching but not a discovery, a way of living with the "blackness" without allowing it to devour. The play itself ends ambiguously, a mourner's prayer spoken but for whom it is unclear. For Kessler? For the thousand on the train? For the mourners themselves? Or, perhaps, for the changed world, for the future, for the next generation whose duty it will be to recover meaning, to recover hope, to recover language, to recover faith, to recover the covenant, all without forgetting and without demeaning the memory.

In the end, the play asserts, it is the individual who is responsible for his own redemption. Roth's characters must risk appearing as fanatics to the world if they are to maintain their individual integrity. Two types of fanatics are illustrated and explored throughout Roth's work: The fanatic who follows blindly an ideology and the fanatic who rebels against conformity. To resist fanaticism of the first order Roth's characters must often embrace fanaticism of the second order, appearing insane to those indoctrinated many. Kessler's final action may appear as the gesture of a fanatic, the futile gesture of a man outside society, but it his his one authentic gesture, his one true assertion of self.

"A Coffin in Egypt" introduces the historical period that shapes the attitudes and visions of the characters and that shapes the very language of the texts themselves, the world that informs, impels, encourages, and entraps the next world. The situation in Vilna is not only the epitome of the situation of twentieth century man but is also the base memory that intrudes upon the more staid post-1945 world. When not involved in their own battles against disintegration Roth's characters are reflecting upon their separation from the world Vilna represents, and their connection to that world.

Never again will Roth make the Holocaust world his setting, never again will he so nakedly immerse himself in its horrors, but never will it cease to be the central subject of his work. It remains on the periphery, awakening, enervating, and informing. Its relative silence makes its force altogether more powerful.

The mix of silence and of speech is essential to Roth. His work is structured on dichotomy, on tension and balance. To write only and always about the Holocaust in its stark reality would serve to trivialize its weight, but to leave it out is impossible. Roth's work is assimilationist; it relies on a "two-way engagement," as Roth says of true assimilation: Silence and verbosity, head and heart, past and present, desire and conscience, ideology and nihilism, literature and life, all interact creating an explosion of lively tension, a burst of energy (*MIM* A-32). It is the energy of conversa-

tion, of commingling. The conversation reinvestigates history, reimagines time, reinterprets literature, spurns cliche and stereotype, dehumanization and vulnerability, to salvage a taste of truth.

The concentrationary universe removes certainty. It creates an abyss and warns against a descent into that abyss. It demands memory and demands that memory not inhibit truth. It makes authority suspect and the invisibility of authority portentous. The man in the concentrationary universe is anxious and uneasy, fundamentally powerless. How to overcome that powerlessness and write is Roth's first concern. With language so debased how is a writer to explore the multi-faceted altered world? It is this question which Sydney asks throughout **"The Day it Snowed"**: How to find words to comprehend what is incomprehensible. Language resists the attempt but the attempt must be made.

"Suddenly people began to disappear." We begin with that fact, stark and plain, and from that our investigation is set afloat. How? Why? History demands investigation, demands memory. The mourner's kaddish which ends Roth's early Holocaust play is a psalm of memory and it acts as an impetus for Roth's efforts. "You must not forget anything," Roth quotes his father, echoing Elie Wiesel's plaintive cry for remembrance (p. 238). To remember means not merely to record the facts but to retain the lessons.

This complex call for memory infects the whole of Roth's canon, from the young boy longing for truth to the writer questioning his motives and his debts. The Holocaust moves across Roth's work like an anomorphic design in a painting, hidden at first, but with the turn of the head and the focusing of the eyes it is readily apparent, huge, overwhelming.

Notes

1. Vaclav Havel, in his essay, "The power of the powerless," posits, "Living within the truth, as humanity's revolt against an enforced position, is . . . an attempt to regain control over one's own sense of responsibility" (62). Havel uses the dichotomy of "living within the truth" (55) and living "within the lie," the lie being the oppressive system which demands conformity (50). To live within the lie is not only to join willingly in the repressive government but to live obediently, anonymously, cowardly, unquestioningly, under that government. Havel recognizes the desire to "merge with the anonymous crowd and flow comfortably along with it down the river of psuedo-life" (55), the desire to turn one's head away from the truth of one's own enslavement, one's col-

laboration, but implores man to resist in any small way he can, to break "the rules of the game" and to therefore disrupt "the game as such" (56).

2. Since 1974 Roth has been General Editor of "Writer's from the Other Europe," a series of books written by Eastern European writers whose voices were, in many cases, virtually unheard in America. The series includes: Jerzy Andrezejewski's *Ashes and Diamonds,* Tadeusz Borowski's *This Way for the Gas, Ladies and Gentlemen,* Geza Csath's *Opium and Other Stories,* Bohumil Hrabal's *Closely Watched TTrains,* Danilo Kis's *A Tomb for Boris Davidovich,* Tadeusz Koniwicki's *A Dreambook for Our Time,* Milan Kundera's *The Book of Laughter and Forgetting, The Farewell Party,* and *Laughable Loves,* Bruno Schulz's *Sanatorium Under the Sign of the Hourglass,* and *The Street of Crocodiles,* and Ludvick Vaculik's *The Guinea Pigs.*

3. The Philip Roth Collection, in the Manuscript Division of the Library of Congress includes many unpublished letters to and from Roth, from which this has been extracted. It also includes unpublished manuscripts and drafts of stories and novels.

4. "A Coffin in Egypt" is included in The Philip Roth Collection. I have quoted from the third draft, written October 1959. Roth describes it as a "play" but its parenthetical directions suggest that he was also considering it as a film.

5. Levi attributes that comment to a Nazi guard, and so for many writers on the Holocaust the expression loses its validity; they do not want the terror defined by the persecutors but by the victims. Levi is a writer Roth has expressed great affection for. His poem 'Shema,' a stern call for memory, can be read as an epigraph to Roth's fiction. In *Patrimony* Roth writes of a 1986 interview with Levi: "Over the course of the four days together we had become mysteriously close friends—so close that when my time came to leave, Primo said, "'I don't know which of us is the younger brother and which is the older brother,' and we embraced emotionally as though we might never meet again. It turned out that we never did" (211).

Works Cited

Primary Sources

Books

American Pastoral. New York: Houghton Mifflin, 1997.

A Philip Roth Reader. Ed. Martin Green. New York: Farrar, Straus and Giroux, 1980.

Conversations with Philip Roth. Ed. George J. Searles. Jackson and London: University Press of Mississippi, 1992.

Deception. New York: Simon and Schuster, 1990.

Goodbye, Columbus. Boston: Houghton Mifflin Company, 1959.

Letting Go. New York: Random House, 1962.

My Life as a Man. New York: Penguin Books, 1985.

Operation Shylock. New York: Simon and Schuster, 1993.

Our Gang. New York: Random House, 1971.

Patrimony. New York: Simon and Schuster, 1991.

Portnoy's Complaint. New York: Random House, 1969.

Reading Myself and Others. New York: Penguin Books, 1985.

Sabbath's Theater. New York: Houghton Mifflin, 1995

The Anatomy Lesson. New York: Farrar, Straus and Giroux, 1981.

The Breast. New York: Penguin Books, 1985.

The Facts: A Novelist's Autobiography. New York: Farrar, Straus and Giroux, 1988.

The Ghost Writer. New York: Penguin Books, 1985.

When She Was Good. New York: Random House, 1967.

Zuckerman Bound. New York: Fawcett Crest, 1985.

Zuckerman Unbound. New York: Farrar, Staus and Giroux, 1981.

Essays, Interviews, Short-Stories, and Unpublished Manuscripts

"A Coffin in Egypt." Third draft ms. *The Philip Roth Collection* 28 Oct. 1959.

"A Conversation in Prague." *New York Review of Books* 12 April 1990: 14-22.

"Armando and the Fraud." *Et Cetera* Oct. 1953: 21-28.

"Author Meets the Critics." *Newsday* 28 March 1993: Fan Fare 40.

"Commentary Symposium." *Commentary* April 1961: 11-12.

"Defender of the Faith." *Goodbye, Columbus* 159-200.

"Eli, the Fanatic." *Goodbye, Columbus* 247-298.

"Epstein." *Goodbye, Columbus* 201-230.

"Goodbye, Columbus." *Goodbye, Columbus* 1-136.

"His Mistress's Voice." *Partisan Review* 53.2 (1986): 155-176.

"'I Always Wanted You to Admire My Fasting'; or, Looking at Kafka." *Reading Myself and Others* 303-326.

"I Couldn't Restrain Myself." *New York Times Book Review* 21 June 1992: 3.

"Imagining Jews." *Reading Myself and Others* 271-302.

"Introduction: Goodbye, Columbus, German Edition." *The Philip Roth Collection.*

"Juice or Gravy? How I Met My Fate in a Cafeteria." *New York Times Book Review* 18 Sept. 1994: 3.

"Novotny's Pain." *A Philip Roth Reader* 261-280.

"Oh, Ma, Let Me Join the National Guard." *New York Times* 24 Aug. 1988: A25.

"On the Air." *New American Review* 10 (1970): 7-49.

"Philip Roth Sees Double. And Maybe Triple, Too." *New York Times* 9 March 1993: C13.

"Positive Thinking on Pennsylvania Avenue." New Republic 3 June 1957: 10-11.

"Pro-Life Pro." *New York Review of Books* 17 Aug. 1989: 5.

"Second Dialogue in Israel." *Congress Bi-Weekly* 16 Sept. 1963: 4-85.

"Some New Jewish Stereotypes." *Reading Myself and Others* 193-203.

"The Box of Truths." *Et Cetera* Oct. 1952: 10-11.

"The Contest for Aaron Gold." *The Best American Short Stories: 1956.* Boston: Houghton Mifflin Company, 1956. 285-299.

"The Conversion of the Jews." *Goodbye, Columbus* 137-158.

"The Day it Snowed." *Chicago Review* 8 (1954): 34-45.

"The Fence." *Et Cetera* June 1953: 18.

"The Final Delivery of Mr. Thorn." *Et Cetera* Spring 1954: 20-28.

"The Last Jew." Draft ms. *The Philip Roth Collection.*

"The Mistaken." Ms. *The Philip Roth Collection.*

The Philip Roth Collection. The Manuscript Division of the Library of Congress, Washington D.C.

"The Prague Orgy." *Zuckerman Bound* 423-472.

"The Sex Fiend." Ms. *The Philip Roth Collection.*

"Writing About Jews." *Reading Myself and Others* 205-225.

"Writing About Jews—Draft." *The Philip Roth Collection.*

"Writing American Fiction." *Reading Myself and Others* 173-191.

"You Can't Tell a Man by the Songs He Sings." *Goodbye, Columbus* 231-246.

Secondary Sources

Appelfeld, Aharon. *Beyond Despair: Three Lectures and a Conversation with Philip Roth.* Trans. Jeffrey M. Green. New York: Fromm International Publishing Corporation, 1994.

Arendt, Hannah. *Eichmann in Jerusalem: A Report on the Banality of Evil.* New York: Penguin Books, 1964.

Babel, Isaac. *The Collected Stories.* Ed. and Trans. Walter Morison. New York: Penguin Books USA, 1955.

Barthes, Roland. *The Pleasure of the Text.* Trans. Richard Miller. New York: Hill and Wang, 1975.

Baumgarten, Murray, and Barbara Gottfried. *Understanding Philip Roth.* Columbia: University of South Carolina Press, 1990.

Beatty, Jack. "The Ghost Writer." *New Republic* 6 Oct. 1979: 36-40.

Bell. Pearl K. "Roth and Baldwin: Coming Home." *Commentary* Dec. 1979: 72-74.

Bellow, Saul. "The Swamp of Prosperity." *Commentary* July 1959: 77-79.

Berger, Alan L. *Crisis and Covenant: The Holocaust in American Jewish Fiction.* Albany: State University of New York Press, 1985.

Bettelheim, Bruno. *Surviving and Other Essays.* New York: Vintage Books, 1980.

Bilik, Dorothy Seidman. *Immigrant-Survivors.* Middletown, Connecticut: Wesleyan University Press, 1981.

Bloom, Harold. "Introduction." Modern Critical Interpretations: Franz Kafka's The Metamorphosis. Ed. Bloom. New York: Chelsea House Publishers, 1988. 1-19.

Brent, Jonathan. "The Unspeakable Self: Philip Roth and the Imagination." Milbauer and Watson 180-200.

Chekhov, Anton. *Plays.* Trans. Elisaveta Fen. New York: Penguin Books, 1959.

———.*The Darling and Other Stories.* Trans. Constance Garnett. London: Chatto and Windus, 1925.

Crane, Stephen. *Great Short Works of Stephen Crane.* New York: Harper and Row, 1968.

Deer, Irving, and Harriet Deer. "Philip Roth and the Crisis in American Fiction." *Minnesota Review* 6 (1966): 353-360.

Descartes, René. _The Cambridge Companion to Descartes._ ed. John Cottingham. Cambridge: Cambridge University Press, 1992.

Des Pres, Terrence. The Survivor: An Anatomy of Life in the Death Camps. New York: Pocket Books, 1976.

Edwards, Beverly. _Zuckerman Bound: The Artist in the Labyrinth._ Diss. Lehigh University, 1987. Ann Arbor, 1987. 8714665.

Ehre, Milton. _Isaac Babel._ Boston: G.K. Hall and Company, 1986.

Epstein, Joseph. "Too Much Even of Kreplach." _Hudson Review_ 33 (1980): 97-110.

Ezrahi, Sidra Dekoven. _By Words Alone: The Holocaust in Literature._ Chicago and London: The University of Chicago Press, 1980.

———. "Philip Roth's Diasporism: A Symposium." _Tikkun_ 8.3 (1993): 41-42.

Fowler, Marilyn Stachenfe. _The Prism of Self: The Fiction of Philip Roth._ Diss. University of California, San Diego, 1984. Ann Arbor: UMI, 1984. 8428917.

Fiedler, Leslie. _Fiedler on the Roof: Essays on Literature and Jewish Identity._ Boston: David R. godine, 1991.

Fitzgerald, F. Scott. _The Great Gatsby._ New York: Charles Scribner's Sons, 1925.

Foucalt, Michel. The Order of Things: An Archaeology of the Human Sciences. New York: Vintage Books, 1970.

Freud, Sigmund. "Contributions to the Psychology of Love." Sexuality and the Psychology of Love." Ed. Philip Rieff. New York: Collier Books, 1963. 39-76.

———. "The Infantile Genital Organization of the Libido." _Sexuality and the Psychology of Love_ 161-165.

Girgus, Sam R. "Portnoy's Prayer: Philip Roth and the American Unconscious." Milbauer and Watson 126-143.

Ginsburg, Allen. _Kaddish and Other Poems_ 1958-1960. San Francisco: City Lights Books, 1961.

Green, Martin. "Half a Lemon, Half an Egg." Milbauer and Watson 82-104.

———. "Introduction." _A Philip Roth Reader_ ix-xxiii.

Havel, Vaclav. _Living in Truth._ Ed. Jan Vladislav. London: Faber and faber, 1986.

Hirsch, David H. _The Deconstruction of Literature. Criticism after Auschwitz._ London: University Press of New England, 1991.

Howe, Irving. _A Critic's Notebook._ Ed. Nicholas Howe. New York San Diego London: Harcourt Brace and Company, 1994.

———. "Philip Roth Reconsidered." _Critical Essays on Philip Roth_ 229-244.

———. _Selected Writings_ 1950-1990. San Diego New York London: Harcourt Brace Jovanovich, Publishers, 1990.

———. "The Lost Young Intellectual." _Commentary_ Oct. 1946: 361-367.

———. "The Suburbs of Babylon." _New Republic_ 15 June 1958: 17-18.

———. _World of Our Fathers._ New York: Simon and Schuster, 1976.

Isaac, Dan. "Philip Roth: His Art and Its Origins." _Midstream_ March 1981: 47-48.

James, Henry. "The Author of Beltraffio." _The Figure in the Carpet and Other Stories_ 57-112.

———. "The Death of the Lion." _The Figure in the Carpet and Other Stories_ 259-304.

———. _The Figure in the Carpet and Other Stories._ Ed. Frank Kermode. New York: Penguin Books, 1986.

———. "The Figure in the Carpet." _The Figure in the Carpet and Other Stories_ 355-400.

———. "The Lesson of the Master." _The Figure in the Carpet and Other Stories_ 113-188.

———. "The Middle Years." _The Figure in the Carpet and Other Stories_ 233-258.

———. "The Private Life." _The Figure in the Carpet and Other Stories_ 189-232.

Joyce, James. _A Portrait of the Artist as a Young Man._ New York: Penguin Books, 1944.

Kafka, Franz. "A Little Fable." _The Basic Kafka._ New York: Pocket Books, 1979. 157.

———. "Selections from Diaries, 1911-1923." _The Basic Kafka_ 255-268.

———. "The Judgment." _Selected Stories of Franz Kafka._ Trans. Willa and Edwin Muir. New York: The Modern Library, 1952. 3-18.

Kakutani, Michiko. "With Reality Reeling, Pity the Poor Realist." _New York Times_ 22 June 1994: C13.

Karl, Frederick R. _American Fictions_ 1940-1980. New York: Harper and Row, 1983.

———. _Franz Kafka: Representative Man._ New York: Ticknor and Fields, 1991.

Kazin, Alfred. "Introduction." _By Words Alone_ ix-xiii.

Kundera, Milan. "Some Notes on Roth's My Life as a Man and The Professor of Desire." Milbauer and Watson 160-167.

———. The Art of the Novel. Trans. Linda Asher. New York: Grove Press, 1986.

Langer, Lawrence L. *Holocaust Testimonies: the ruins of memory*. New Haven: Yale University Press, 1991.

———. *The Holocaust and the Literary Imagination*. New Haven: Yale University Press, 1975.

———. *Versions of Survival: The Holocaust and the Human Spirit*. Albany: State University of New York Press, 1982.

Landis, Joseph L. "The Sadness of Philip Roth: An Interim Report." *Critical Essays on Philip Roth* 164-171.

Lee, Hermione. "Kiss and Tell." *New Republic* 30 April 1990: 39-42.

———. *Philip Roth*. London: Methuen, 1982.

Leonard, John. "Fathers and Ghosts." *Critical Essays on Philip Roth* 89-94.

Manea, Norman. *On Clowns: The Dictator and the Artist*. New York: Grove Weidenfeld, 1992.

Maloff, Saul. "Philip Roth and the Master's Voice: The Uses of Adversity." *Commonweal* 9 Nov. 1979: 628-631.

Marx, Leo. *The Machine in the Garden: Technology and the Pastoral Ideal in America*. London: Oxford University Press, 1964.

McDaniel, John Nobel. *Heroes in the Fiction of Philip Roth*. Diss. The Florida State University, 1972. Ann Arbor: UMI, 1972. 72-31,410.

Meeter, Glenn. *Philip Roth and Bernard Malamud: A Critical Essay*. Columbia: University of Missouri, 1973.

Milbauer, Asher Z., and Donald G. Watson, eds. *Reading Philip Roth*. New York: St. Martin's Press, 1988.

Nagel, James. *Stephen Crane and Literary Impressionism*. University Park and London: The Pennsylvania State University Press, 1980.

Nance, Guinevera A., and Judith Paterson Jones. *Philip Roth*. New York: Frederick Ungar Publishing Company, 1981.

Neel, Jasper. *Plato, Derrida, and Writing*. Carbondale and Edwardsville: Southern Illinois University Press, 1988.

O'Donnell, Patrick. "The Disappearing Text: Philip Roth's The Ghost Writer." *Contemporary Literature* xxiv. 3 (1983): 365-378.

Pinsker, Sanford, ed. *Critical Essays on Philip Roth*. Boston: G.K. Hall, 1982.

———. *The Comedy that Hoits: An Essay on the Fiction of Philip Roth*. Columbia: University of Missouri, 1975.

Plath, Sylvia. *Ariel*. New York: Harper and Row, 1965.

Quart, Barbara. "The Treatment of Women in the Work of Three Contemporary Jewish-American Writers: Mailer, Bellow, and Roth." Diss. New York University, 1979. *Dissertation Abstracts International* 40 (1979): 1472A.

Quart, Barbara Koenig. "The Rapacity of One Nearly Buried Alive." *Massachusetts Review* 24 (Autum 1984): 590-608.

Rodgers, Bernard F. *Philip Roth*. Boston: Twayne Publishers, 1978.

Rubin-Dorsky, Jeffrey. "Philip Roth's The Ghost Writer: Literary Heritage and Jewish Irreverence." *Studies in American Jewish Literature* 8.2 (Fall 1989): 168-185.

Said, Edward W. *Culture and Imperialism*. New York: Alfred A. Knopf, 1993.

Segev, Tom. *The Seventh Million: The Israelis and the Holocaust*. Trans. Haim Watzman. New York: Hill and Wang, 1993.

Schechner, Mark. "Philip Roth." *Critical Essays on Philip Roth* 117-132.

Steiner, George. *Language and Silence*. New York: Atheneum, 1966.

Tintner, Adeline. "Henry James as Roth's Ghost Writer." *Midstream* March 1981: 48-51.

———. "Hiding Behind James." *Midstream* April 1982: 49-53.

Tolstoy, Leo. "Tolstoy's Criticism on The Darling." *The Darling and Other Stories* 23-31.

Towers, Robert. "The Lesson of the Master." *New York Times Book Review* 2 Sept. 1979: 1.

Troyat, Henri. *Chekhov*. Trans. Michael Henry Heim. New York: Fawcett Columbine, 1986.

Tucker, Martin. "The Shape of Exile in Philip Roth, pr The Part is Always Apart." Milbauer and Watson 33-49.

Updike, John. "Recruiting Raw Nerves." *New Yorker* 15 March 1993: 109-112.

———. *Odd Jobs*. New York: Alfred A. Knopf, 1991.

Voelker, Joseph C. "Dedalian Sahdes: Philip Roth's The Ghost Writer." *Critical Essays on Philip Roth* 89-94.

Young, James. *Writing and Rewriting the Holocaust: Narrative and the Consequences of Interpretation*. Bloomington: Indiana University Press, 1988.

Hana Wirth-Nesher (essay date winter 2001)

SOURCE: Wirth-Nesher, Hana. "Resisting Allegory, or Reading "Eli, the Fanatic' in Tel Aviv." *Prooftexts: A*

Journal of Jewish Literary History 21, no. 1 (winter 2001): 103-12.

[*In the following essay, Wirth-Nesher discusses reactions by her Israeli students to reading "Eli, the Fanatic," noting the differences between their views regarding Roth's portrayal of Jewishness and those of American undergraduates.*]

If reading a work of fiction is like waking up in a foreign universe whose rules have to be deduced, whose logic has to be decoded, then the challenge of this estrangement is compounded when that universe looks like home. It is one thing to inform students that Isabel Archer's world collapses because James exposes her to a breach of etiquette that could only mean betrayal in a now defunct code of manners (her husband is seated while her best friend is standing); it is another to expose the unquestioned premises of the students' own world. Reader identification with a character or a situation may often block critical reading more than facilitate it. If it is the teacher's or the critic's work to minimize the gap created by temporal and spatial distance, by history and geography, what happens when the teacher travels in time and in space? How does this affect the reading? My immigration to Israel in the mid-1980s had just this unsettling effect on my reading and teaching of works that had become all too familiar. Israeli students often had a refreshingly new approach to American literature. Whereas American students, for example, were incredulous that Jefferson or Emerson could have had doubts about the viability of a fledgling nation and culture only two or three generations removed from its founding, Israeli students found that anxiety to be comprehensible in light of their own place in history. Among the many examples of such cross-cultural interpretation that I have encountered in the classroom over the years, the one that has both intrigued and disturbed me the most is Philip Roth's **"Eli, the Fanatic."**

The story was first published in *Commentary* in the late 1950s and later appeared in Roth's collection *Goodbye, Columbus.* Alarmed at the arrival of a group of religious Holocaust survivors who have moved into the pastoral suburb of Woodenton, the resident Jewish community designates Eli Peck to be their representative in conveying their concerns to the refugees—namely, that zoning regulations do not permit a yeshiva on the premises. To be more specific, Peck has been asked to negotiate with Leo Tzuref, the ultra-orthodox head of what he terms an "orphanage"—eighteen war orphans and another adult refugee who calls attention to himself by walking through the modern American suburb in his black caftan, *shtrayml,* and sidelocks, mutely submitting shopping lists on his errands for the "home." As Woodenton has only recently admitted Jews to its manicured lawns and split-level homes, the American-born Jews fear that the presence of caftaned refugees will jeopardize their hard-won affluence and grudging acceptance by their Protestant neighbors. As Artie Berg tells Eli, "If I want to live in Brownsville, Eli, I'll live in Brownsville." Others in the community are more graphic—they fear that the neighborhood will be overrun: "It's going to be a hundred little kids with little *yarmulkahs* chanting their Hebrew lessons on Coach House Road, and then it's not going to strike you as funny." For them, the Orthodox Jews ironically pose a threat of intermarriage: "Next thing they'll be after our daughters." So intent on demonizing this threat to their assimilation into the American dream, they insinuate that the yeshiva may be indulging in more than merely "hocus-pocus abracadabra stuff"—"I'd really like to find out what is going on up there."

In the wake of the Holocaust, this American Jewish community has no compunctions about putting the blame for antisemitism on the victims themselves: "There's going to be no pogroms in Woodenton, 'cause there's no fanatics, no crazy people." This accusation makes its way into the formal letter of complaint that Eli delivers to Tzuref:

> It is only since the war that Jews have been able to buy property here, and for Jews and Gentiles to live beside each other in amity. For this adjustment to be made, both Jews and Gentiles alike have had to give up some of their more extreme practices in order not to threaten or offend one another. . . . Perhaps if such conditions had existed in pre-war Europe, the persecution of the Jewish people, of which you and those 18 children have been victims, could not have been carried out with such success—in fact, might not have been carried out at all.

In the course of Eli's negotiations with Tzuref, he is convinced not only of the refugees' right to remain in Woodenton, but also of his own moral obligation to empathize with the survivors' sufferings and to perpetuate the civilization that has nearly been extinguished. This comes about mainly in his interactions with a third character, the mute "greenie," as he is called by the suburbanites, whose obtrusive traditional garb has become the trigger of the community's distress and insecurity, resulting in their demand that he adopt an "American" dress code. Only after Eli contributes his own impeccable designer clothing as a remedy does he realize that what the survivor had in mind was an *exchange,* not a gift that requires renunciation of a way of life. When Eli dons the black clothing of his double, including the hat, "for the first time in his life he *smelled* the color of blackness." And when he decides to pass this blackness on to his newborn son, entering the maternity ward in his full religious garb, his community brands him a fanatic, and the medical staff treats him as insane. Although he asserts his right to greet his newborn as he sees fit— "*I'm the father!*"—the doctor administers a tranquilizer that "calmed his soul, but did not touch down where the blackness had reached."

Any reading of this story will have to offer an interpretation of this "blackness" that is located so deeply within Eli that it is immune to the "treatment" that his American society administers. If we borrow from the discourse of identity politics, it appears to be an essential identity that he has recovered, one that has been there all along. It merely required a serious engagement with the greenie to reinstate it as a core identity for Eli. How is this achieved? And of what is this blackness constituted?

When I first taught this story more than twenty years ago in an American college, it seemed to me to be a fairly straightforward theme. Roth was satirizing post-World War II suburban Jewish America, with its reverence for mental health and therapy, upper-middle-class assimilation measured by designer labels and color-schemed landscaping, and well-heeled, well-bred Protestant America. Designated to represent his community in a legal struggle to remove Holocaust survivors on the pretext of zoning laws, Eli undergoes a transformation, a conversion of sorts, when he is faced with the vapid and callous attitudes of his neighbors. His exchange of clothing with his double is the sign of this crossing over to the side of collective memory and responsibility, an act that is diagnosed as a nervous breakdown. Surely this was an allegory about the perils of assimilation, about the moral price paid for turning one's back on one's heritage.

The evidence for this was ample. Wasn't Harriet Knudsen giving the stones on her lawn another coat of pink paint? Wasn't Eli's pregnant wife, Miriam, leaving him notes about her oedipal experiences with the baby? Didn't Ted Heller reveal a moronic literalness of the imagination by feeling superior to the biblical Abraham because he used an X-ray machine to measure his customers' feet?

> Look, I don't even know about this Sunday School business. Sundays I drive my oldest kid all the way to Scarsdale to learn Bible stories . . . and you know what she comes up with? This Abraham in the Bible was going to kill his own *kid* for a sacrifice. You call that religion? Today a guy like that, they'd lock him up.

Didn't Tzuref, the headmaster of the yeshiva with its eighteen orphans, represent morality over legality when he exposed the smokescreen of the zoning laws for further displacing his charges, this time by their

fellow Jews? "What you call the law, I call shame. The heart, Mr. Peck, the heart is the law!" Roth had written a fable for his time, and it was my duty as a teacher in a suburban American college to explicate the parable, to turn Roth's searchlight on the communities that my students complacently called home.

Furthermore, the story lent itself to neat structural and thematic explications, particularly in its self-evident binaries. On one side, the Jews of Woodenton—American, English-speaking, rational, affluent, comfortable, and inclined to base their judgments on the law and psychology; on the other side, the Holocaust survivors and displaced persons—European, Yiddish-speaking, emotional, poor, suffering, and inclined to base their judgments on morality and mercy. What did each of these communities want? The former, to keep a low profile so as not to jeopardize their standing in the American professional and upper middle class; the latter, to practice their religion and way of life in a safe haven after all their losses. For whom was Roth enlisting our sympathies? How could it be otherwise?

As long as I taught this story to readers who were the target of Roth's satire, it posed no particular difficulties for me. As the child of Holocaust survivors who never felt entirely at home on those manicured suburban lawns, I identified with Roth's exposé of postwar Jewish America, with his contempt for its smug materialism and its therapy-driven lifestyle. I could also identify with his character's need to be recognized by the mute Holocaust survivor, the man who moans and sheds tears but cannot speak to him. In a world that offered either pink rocks in the driveway or two tears on a silent face, the only humane option was to defer to the reality of the latter, to its call for moral action. In the ability to empathize with the victims of the Holocaust and to identify with the collective trauma of the Jewish people lay the only hope for a meaningful existence in 1950s America. The right kind of Jew, Roth's fable illustrated, turned his back on consumerism and donned the rags of a persecuted people in order to preserve its integrity. My students, fed on *Fiddler on the Roof* sentimentality for the lost world of the shtetl, were ripe for this reading.

But the plot thickened as I began to teach the same story at Tel Aviv University years later, after I had made Israel my home. As I was no longer teaching students who were familiar with Roth's milieu, what had previously seemed self-evident now seemed perplexing and even disturbing. It began with responses to Eli's double, the "Ḥaredi" who refuses to speak, whose inarticulate groan, which Eli tries to simulate, signifies Jewish suffering through the ages, culminating in the Holocaust survivor as quintessential Jew. With regard to this character, "Eli, the Fanatic" is a story that invites allegorization. Nameless and speech-less, the Haredi survivor has no personal features. He remains entirely a stick figure symbolizing loss: the sole survivor of a family that consisted of his parents, his wife, and his infant, poor and unprepared for life in America, and the subject of Nazi medical experiments that have left him incapable of fathering a family in the New World. A cipher for the unspeakable. American students did not hesitate to read him allegorically, to grant this mute dark figure surrounded by babbling social climbers the symbolic status of quintessential victim, so accustomed to violence that when Eli reaches out to button down the collar of his shirt, he flings his arms in front of his face expecting a blow. It is his darkness, his blackness, that Eli takes upon himself as a mission, to perpetuate in every generation, to pass on to his son. Flailing his own arms about in a rehearsal of the greenie's movements, Eli vows to be loyal to his legacy: "He felt those black clothes as if they were the skin of his skin." And when the doctors, dressed in white, yank off the jacket and slip the needle under his skin, the drug cannot reach that "blackness" that has come to signify his authentic Jewish self.

And this blackness, this being true to himself, is the crux of the matter. Secular Israeli students have simply not been willing to concede what had seemed commonplace to Americans—namely, the conflation of the two identities: the representative Jew as Holocaust survivor and as Haredi. Even if the two metonyms had appeared separately, they would have troubled Israeli readers who resist allegorizing these two identities.

Roth's perceptive observation in the 1950s that American Jewish identity would be derived from identification with and empathy for Europe's exterminated Jewish community has been realized on a scale hardly imagined at the time of writing. The last two decades have seen a proliferation of Holocaust memorials and museums in the United States to the extent that Jewish identity in America has been largely constituted by collective memory of trauma. History has caught up with Eli's fierce commitment to pass on a legacy in which Jewishness is synonymous with victimization. But the attitude toward Holocaust survivors in Israel in the 1950s contrasted sharply with attitudes in America. During the first few decades of Statehood, the Holocaust survivor was perceived to be the very antithesis of the desirable new Jew returned to his ancient homeland, because he was associated with passivity, effeminacy, and victimization. This attitude has changed dramatically in Israel. Since the Six-Day War, and more intensely since the Yom Kippur War, Israeli culture has come to see continuities where it had previously seen only ruptures, and has come to understand where it formerly was quick to judge. The writ-

ings of Aharon Appelfeld, David Grossman, Joshua Sobol, among many other authors, have contributed to this shift in awareness, so that it has become easier for Israeli readers to identify with the survivor character, a change in communal memory that brings them closer to American Jewish culture. But conflating the Holocaust survivor with the Haredi invests the latter with an allegorical dimension that meets with resistance. For the change in attitude toward the Haredi has been in the opposite direction. No longer a tiny minority perceived to be a saving remnant of a quaint way of life, a remnant for whom Ben-Gurion made special concessions during the early years of the State, the ultra-Orthodox community in Israel has become a significant and assertive presence, perceived to be a threat to Israel as a democratic modern state.

This resistance to allegory on the part of the Tel Aviv student results from his or her inability to identify with the Haredi character, given the tensions between these two communities in contemporary Israel. The question of who represents Jewishness in Israel today is ideological, political, and deeply emotional. The reader in Tel Aviv questions Roth's strategy of representing authentic Jewish identity as a convergence of ultra-Orthodox religious observance and a history of being persecuted. Whereas my American students, including those whom I continue to teach in the overseas program at Tel Aviv University, are not particularly troubled by Roth's metaphor of Jewishness and, in fact, continue to regard the Haredi nostalgically as an integral part of a folkloric Eastern European landscape populated by their recent ancestors, liberal Israeli students refuse to sign over their Jewishness to a sector of their society that they regard as a daily threat to their secular Jewish culture. From the Israeli perspective, there is an incongruity in the merging of the helpless Holocaust survivor with the politically powerful Haredi.

To read Roth in an American context is perhaps to recognize him as a Jewish writer who unhesitatingly uses the trope of the Haredi as a signifier of Jewishness. To read Roth in Israel is to recognize him as an American writer who locates Jewishness in Judaism. When viewed from Tel Aviv, Eli is less sympathetic, his born-again Judaism unsettling, even alarming. When viewed from Tel Aviv, Miriam Peck's desire for domestic fulfillment and psychological well-being seems almost attractive by comparison to her husband's, well, fanaticism: "Please, can't you learn to leave well enough alone? Can't we just have a family?" In Israel, where Jewish history is inescapable, where it permeates every aspect of life including the family, regulates the calendar, fuels political debate, and forges communal experience day in and day out, Miriam's desire to carve out a family space that eschews history and validates the inner life of the individual seems like a blessed interlude, too much to ask for. In America, on the other hand, where individual fulfillment and individual destiny are prized, Miriam's pleas must be measured against her responsibility—or, in her case, irresponsibility—to community, in this case to the Jewish people. "*He's* not your fault," she assures Eli, referring to the Holocaust survivor. "Why do you feel guilty about everything?"

Reading **"Eli, the Fanatic"** now, in this time and in this place, compels me to take a more historical approach to Roth's work than I had previously done, to see that it is of another time and another place. It is a tale of America in the 1950s, a brilliant satire about a community torn between the promise held out by America for individual self-fulfillment at the price of communal attenuation and its *own* pledge, in the shadow of the Holocaust, for collective responsibility and continuity. Roth presents the latter as an atavistic return to some primal darkness. Maybe reading Roth's story in an American community haunted by the specter of assimilation grants Eli a certain integrity, even courage. Maybe reading the story in an Israeli community haunted by the specter of fundamentalism and theocracy limits the reader's ability to empathize with the choice that he eventually makes.

And yet the Israeli reader is not immune to the story's claim on his empathy and would like to comply. This can be accomplished by another sort of allegory altogether: by playing down the survivor's historical and referential identity and transforming him, and the story, into a modernist, universalist, and existential text. Israeli students have pointed out that in the climactic scene between Eli and the greenie, white paint is splashed on them both, and that the latter conveys his message to Eli in pantomime. Moreover, "all [Eli] saw of the greenie's face were two white droplets stuck to each cheek." Pained by his double's visage of pain, distraught and helpless, Eli cries out, "Tell me, what can I do for you, I'll do it." The mute responds with hand gestures and with the same "two white tears." This moment triggers intertextual associations for Israeli students of literature who identify the mute as a Pierrot figure and the two mimes as Beckett's clowns or tramps, gesturing in a world devoid of meaning. The mute figure, in short, has been to the "heart of darkness"; unable to articulate the horrors that he has seen, he communicates solely by sighs, moans, flailing of arms, and tears. It is the modernist failure of language, the dark vision of the twentieth century, cast in a Jewish American landscape. The Haredi survivor can be read allegorically only if he is universalized out of the sphere of Israeli politics, and out of Jewishness altogether.

The universalist reading is simply further evidence that in "Eli, the Fanatic," Roth exposes and then unleashes in his readers the forces of demonization within the Jewish community. The refugees in Woodenton have been victims of the European demonization of the Jew. The American Jewish community has internalized this perspective and, in a classic illustration of self-hatred, has projected its own low self-esteem onto that segment of their group that represents aspects of their own identity that they would prefer to hide. Tzuref and his crew are simply too Jewish when viewed through the eyes of the Gentiles whom they are fanatic about pleasing, and appeasing. For them, religiously observant Jews are the "other." At first, Eli identifies exclusively with his Woodenton peers, so that when Tzuref tries to get him to take a personal stand, "But you, Mr. Peck, how about you?" he replies, "I am them, they are me, Mr. Tzuref." But Tzuref will have none of this equivocation: "Aach! You are us, we are you!" From Tzuref's point of view, the boundary that divides Jews from the non-Jewish world supersedes the boundaries within the Jewish world, and he expects to be treated compassionately by those he defines as part of his own group. Although they regard him as "other," he acts on the premise that they are all part of the same remnant of the Jewish people. Whereas there is a seemingly unbridgeable gap between the greenie and Eli, best expressed in Eli's desperate plea to "just *look* at me . . . please, say something, speak *English*," Eli adopts Tzuref's view when he dons the greenie's clothes and vows to pass on some mysterious Jewish identity associated with the capacity to suffer. ("You have the word 'suffer' in English?" Tzuref once asked him.) Roth's literary strategy for representing an inclusive Jewishness that resists the demonizing practiced by Eli's assimilationist peers is through the allegory of the Haredi survivor. This is a literary strategy that makes a great deal of sense in suburban New York in the 1950s, but it is highly charged when it is read in Israel at the beginning of the millennium.

I came to Israel in the 1980s reading Roth's story with the empathy and maybe even sentimentality that the Jewish American experience had made possible. The Haredi figure could be allegorized as authentic Jew with no misgivings, particularly in relation to the radical assimilation and self-denigration of Woodenton's vapid Jews. During the past twenty years, the Haredi has become a menacing and powerful presence in my life and in the lives of my students. For many secular Israelis, Tzuref and the greenie are as emphatically "other" as they are for Ted Heller in Woodenton. But times have changed in America as well, exemplified by the recent Beachwood, Ohio, zoning controversy that pitted Orthodox and non-Orthdox Jews against each other over the construction of "religious build-ings" by observant newcomers to the community. One of the greatest challenges for a Conservative or a Re-form Jew like myself living in Israel is not to suc-cumb to the demonizing of the Jewish "other," despite the knowledge that I am the demon for ultra-Orthodox Jewry. I have come to revise my reading of Roth's story in seemingly contradictory ways. On the one hand, it is necessary to historicize, to read it as a bril-liant document of 1950s Jewish America. On the other hand, I have also come to appreciate its double-edged qualities, its insistence on exposing not only the shal-lowness of a society that would dub Eli a fanatic for choosing a visible Jewish identity and a commitment to collective memory, but also its exposure of Eli him-self *as a fanatic.* Whereas the demonization of ultra-orthodox Jews by secular Israelis today has brought Roth's Woodenton closer to Tel Aviv, the demoniza-tion of non-Orthodox Jews by the Orthodox religious establishment makes any allegory of the Haredi as ge-neric Jew almost unimaginable and exerts extreme so-cial pressure on the dynamic of entering Roth's fic-tional world. Maybe **"Eli, the Fanatic"** is a far more wrenching story to teach in Tel Aviv today than in Pennsylvania twenty years ago because it forces Jew-ish Israeli students to regard *two* distant "others": Jew-ish Americans and ultra-Orthodox Jews. Sadly, it be-comes increasingly difficult to affirm Tzuref's words to Eli: "Aach! You are us, we are you!"

Peter L. Rudhytsky (essay date spring 2005)

SOURCE: Rudhytsky, Peter L. "'Goodbye, Columbus': Roth's Portrait of the Narcissist as a Young Man." *Twentieth-Century Literature* 51, no. 1 (spring 2005): 25-42.

[*In the following essay, Rudhytsky uses psychoanalytic techniques to examine the theme of the waning of mas-culine desire in "Goodbye, Columbus."*]

For all the undoubted virtuosity of the other five sto-ries in the collection, it is of course *Goodbye, Colum-bus* that is the pièce de résistance and the reason Philip Roth won the National Book Award for his first book. The novella certainly has a realistic dimension and shows Roth's equally keen ear and eye. Neil Klug-man, a recent graduate of Newark Colleges of Rutgers University, an Army veteran, and working at a dead-end job at the Newark public library, has a summer romance with Brenda Patimkin, a Radcliffe student and the daughter of wealthy parents living in the New Jersey suburb of Short Hills. It would be fatuous to deny that at least some of Neil's insecurity can be as-cribed to issues of class, or at least expresses itself in

his sensitivity to social slights. On their first date, Brenda's innocent remark, "We lived in Newark when I was a baby," makes Neil "suddenly angry" (12), pre-sumably because it reminds him how far the Patimkins have moved up the social ladder. Not for nothing does Brenda's nose job become a target of Neil's incessant razzing. But as the first fully developed exploration of Roth's quintessential theme of the waning of mascu-line desire, **"Goodbye, Columbus"** sounds depths that cannot be plumbed critically without the aid of psy-choanalysis.

In their first telephone conversation, after Neil has held Brenda's glasses at the swimming pool of the Green Lane Country Club but when she still does not know who he is, his description of his swarthy appear-ance leads her to ask him, "Are you a Negro?" (7). This equation of the middle-class Jew with the black reinforces Neil's sense of social inferiority, as when he later feels even more out of place amid the opu-lence of the Patimkins' home (40) than does their "Navaho-faced Negro" (21) maid, Carlota. Like the protagonists of Roth's other early stories, Neil is a "man in the middle," estranged both from his family of origin and from the Jewish establishment, just as Brenda experiences her own more privileged life as a "Hundred Years' War" (26) with *her* family, especially her mother. But, as I said, I think it would be a mis-take to reduce Neil's insecurity to factors of religion and class when it is ultimately ontological in nature and manifests itself most acutely in the sphere of love.

Roth develops the motif of Neil's "blackness" above all through his identification with the "small colored boy" (31) who comes to the library one day to look at the art books. The boy is drawn to an edition of Gauguin reproductions, with its enchanting images of Tahiti. Even on his first drive out of Newark to visit Brenda in Short Hills, Neil had felt that the slight el-evation in altitude "brought one closer to heaven" (8); and on the very day that he encounters the Negro boy at the library, Neil begins to see Short Hills "in my mind's eye, at dusk, rose-colored, like a Gauguin stream" (38). The equation of the Patimkins' opu-lence, despite its meretriciousness to which Neil is no less keenly responsive, with the lushness of Tahiti is evident in Neil's Marvellian apostrophe: "Oh Pa-timkin! Fruit grew in their refrigerator and sporting goods dropped from their trees!" (43).

The parallel established by Roth between the colored boy's fantasy of Tahiti and Neil's equally fantasy-drenched experience of Short Hills finds a more spe-cific counterpart in the parallel between Neil's am-bivalent desire for Brenda and the boy's insecure attachment to the actual book containing the Gauguin reproductions. For obscure reasons, Neil becomes alarmed when one day the boy does not show up at the library, and "as though in his place, a very old man appeared, white, smelling of Life Savers" (48), and tries to check out the same Gauguin volume. Stepping into action, Neil falsely tells the patron that someone has placed a hold on the book, and thus he cannot borrow it for the time being. "And so I was able," Neil reports, "not without flushing once or twice, to get the book back in the stacks."

Neil's behavior becomes comprehensible when he is seen to be trying to replace a lost object—or, in Lacanian terms, to fill a lack in his being—that he experiences in his relationship with Brenda. From the beginning, Neil is plagued by his fears of losing Brenda, which are the obverse of his extreme dependence on her. On their second meeting at the swimming pool, after she had allowed him to kiss her the previous evening, Neil avers while they are underwater together, "I didn't care for anything but Brenda" (16-17). He describes how "her breasts swam towards me like two pink-nosed fish and she let me hold them" (17). The prominence given to the breasts in Neil's attraction is a trademark of Roth's; and their aquatic communion leads Neil to imagine that the relationship might be permanent: "I felt she had made a promise to me about the summer, and, I hoped, beyond."

But no sooner do they get out of the water than Neil starts in with a reprise of the aggressiveness that he had shown the night before on the subject of nose jobs, when he asked whether Brenda's father was planning to get one too. (Brenda had told him that her brother Ron would be having his nose fixed in the fall.) Just as Brenda had responded then, "Why are you so nasty?" (13), and followed her query with the alluring offer, "If I let you kiss me would you stop being nasty?" (14), so again Brenda is driven to ask him, "Why do you always sound a little nasty to me?" (17). When she correctly calls his apology insincere, Neil shoots back, "Now you're being nasty to me," to which Brenda once more rejoins both accurately and magnanimously, "No. Just stating the facts. Let's not argue. I like you" (18).

The pattern established in these early interactions persists throughout their entire relationship. In their first major quarrel, precipitated when Neil asks Brenda to buy a diaphragm and she initially demurs, he demands: "Why are you being selfish?" (80). She responds: "Selfish? You're the one who's being selfish. It's your pleasure." The relationship weathers this storm, but the diaphragm proves to be its undoing in the end. Neil pays a visit to Brenda at Radcliffe over the Jewish holidays, and they sign into a hotel room as "Mr. and Mrs. Neil Klugman," with Brenda wearing a "thin gold band shining on her left hand" (125). Everything

seems fine until Brenda informs Neil that her mother has found the diaphragm, and Neil accuses Brenda of deliberately having left it behind where it would be found instead of bringing it with her to Boston. (The original plan had been for Brenda to come home over the holidays and see Neil in New Jersey. It apparently does not occur to him that if she had brought the diaphragm with her to college she might have put it to use with somebody else.) The exchange follows a by-now familiar script. Neil says, "Don't get angry," and Brenda answers: "You're the one who's angry" (130). As she reminds him,

> You're the one who from the very beginning was accusing me of things? Remember? . . . You kept acting as if I was going to run away from you every minute. And now you're doing it again, telling me I planted that thing on purpose.
>
> (134)

This cycle of tit-for-tat aggression is one of which Neil, like his creator, is intellectually aware, though he is unable to do anything to alter its seemingly ineluctable course. Disturbed by Brenda's casual remark that her mother "still thinks we live in Newark" (26), Neil succeeds for once in remaining silent: "I did not want to voice a word that would lift the cover and reveal that hideous emotion I always felt for her, and is the underside of love" (27). Since the narrative is written retrospectively, and Neil knows that he and Brenda are destined to break up, he drops a hint to the reader of what is to come: "It will not always *stay* the underside—but I am skipping ahead." Again, later, as Labor Day approaches and Neil has to face the prospect of Brenda's return to Radcliffe and the threat this poses to their relationship, he cannot suppress his foreboding that her departure "would be the end for me," even though he tells himself that "there'd been no hints of ending our affair from Brenda, and any suspicions I had, any uneasiness, was spawned in my own uneasy heart" (75-76).

The vicious cycle from which Neil cannot escape is that his extreme feelings of dependency on Brenda—his sense that she is his entire world—are exacerbated rather than assuaged by his hopes of permanence. This causes him to fear that she will disappear, leaving him with nothing, which in turn instigates him to provoke their break-up so that he can walk out on her before he is abandoned. The irony, of course, is that he thereby brings about the very thing he fears—the (repetition of the) loss of the love object, an exposure of the sense of lack in his being—but with the fig leaf to his pride that he is the master of his fate and not its victim.

Implicit in this interpretation of Neil's relationship with Brenda is that he casts her in a maternal role, symbolized concretely by her breasts but reflected more generally in his emotional dependence and insecurity. It is striking that Roth in his first major work simplifies the family background of his protagonist. Neil's parents are out of the picture, having moved to Tucson because of their asthma, and the 23-year-old is living with his aunt and uncle. There is no mention of any siblings. Uncle Max is a shadowy figure, but Aunt Gladys sees to it that Neil—as Roth reports his own childhood to have been in *The Facts*—is "the gorged beneficiary of overdevotion, overprotection, and oversurveillance" (*Facts* 93). The opening pages of **"Goodbye, Columbus"** show Aunt Gladys harping on food, pressuring Neil to eat more than he wants, accusing him of not liking what she has prepared.

Aunt Gladys, then, is only an attenuated version of the orally intrusive mother, but it is clear that Neil has stored up a sufficient supply of resentments, whether against her or against the absent mother for whom she is a surrogate. When he visits the Patimkins for the first time, Neil feels comfortable with Brenda's father, who reminds him of his own father without asthma, but he "did not like Mrs. Patimkin, though she was certainly the handsomest of all of us at the table" (21). At dinner, Mrs. Patimkin calls him Bill instead of Neil, while Mr. Patimkin was "not wholly successful in stifling a belch" (24), a breach of decorum that Neil finds ingratiating. Observing the owner of Patimkin Kitchen and Bathroom Sinks later in his undershirt, Neil reflects that "Brenda's old nose fitted him well" (28). Despite the gulf in social status between the two families, the Patimkins resemble the Klugmans in being under the thumb of a dominant mother-figure, while the father-figure is peripheral and weak. After giving himself a tour of the premises, Neil is struck that "in the entire house I hadn't seen one picture of Mr. Patimkin" (42).

Both Neil and Brenda, then, are in conflict with their mothers, and Neil seems to speak for both of them when he says, after Brenda proposes one morning that they go running together, "I think the bigger your lungs get the more you're supposed to hate your mother" (70). There is no reason to disbelieve Brenda when she says that her mother "hates" and is "jealous" (25) of her—neither Mrs. Patimkin's backhand nor her beauty are what they used to be—and their quarrels drive Brenda to tears: "'Oh, Mother!' and Brenda was crying. 'Why the hell are you like this!'" (65). When Neil lashes out at Brenda over her reluctance to get a diaphragm, calling her "a selfish egotistical bitch," he becomes identified in her mind with the image of the bad mother: "Why don't you and my mother take turns—one day she can plague me, the next you—" (82).

Despite the severity of Brenda's conflicts with her mother, she possesses a basic security and trust that

Neil sorely lacks. It is impossible to try to explain how this might have come about, though some people have an innate capacity to survive even quite severe traumas with remarkably little damage, while others are badly scarred by what might to an outside observer seem to be experiences within a normal range. The speculation does appear plausible that Brenda's attraction to Neil has something to do with the way he reminds her of her father, though there is no direct evidence for this in the text, which rather simply takes for granted the mystery of Brenda's acceptance of a most unlikely and difficult suitor.

Because only Neil's subjectivity is laid bare by the first-person narrative, the psychological origins of his susceptibility to the "hideous emotion" that starts as the "underside" of love before finally overmastering it are, as we have seen, much more thoroughly delineated. He can never rid himself of the fear that Brenda will, in her words, "run away . . . every minute." Swimming late at night in the country club pool, while Brenda waits alongside, Neil reveals that "I was sure when I left the water that Brenda would be gone. . . . I wanted to get back to Brenda, for I worried again— and there was no evidence, was there?—that if I stayed away too long she would not be there when I returned" (52-53). Finally, when Brenda herself climbs out after what seems to Neil an interminable swim in the cold pool, "I held her so tightly I almost dug my body into hers, 'I love you,' I said, 'I do'" (54).

Later on, when Brenda leaves briefly to accompany her family in picking up her brother's fiancée, Harriet, at the airport, Neil, tormented by the "suspicions" of his "uneasy heart," broods upon her imminent return to Radcliffe: "I felt open-stomached, as though I hadn't eaten for months" (77). He knows the feeling has nothing to do with his "caloric intake," but is rather "only a rumor of the hollowness that would come when Brenda was away." The sensation of emptiness caused by her absence is the "underside" of the fullness Neil feels when he sees her "two pink-nosed fish" swimming toward him at the bottom of the pool. Roth's use of oral imagery allows the reader to link this back to Aunt Gladys's badgering Neil about food, and thereby suggests that his emotional instability is an effect of his relationship to his mother-figure. And when Brenda does indeed return to college in the fall, although she has given him no reason to doubt that she remains deeply in love with him, Neil on a solitary drive into the country can experience the beauty that surrounds him only as the site of loss: "after a while everything, even the objects of nature, the trees, the clouds, the grass, the weeds, reminded me of Brenda" (119).

The downfall of Neil's relationship with Brenda, therefore, is caused not by his sexual jealousy of a rival but by the destructiveness that leads him, in Oscar Wilde's line from *The Ballad of Reading Gaol,* to "kill the thing he loves." To be sure, there is one hint of an outside threat in the person of Luther Ferrari, whom "Brenda had dated for a whole year in high school" (55), and Neil even confesses when he sees her greet her brother for the first time that "it ached me some when she kissed him on the face" (20). But these reactions are simply more manifestations of his insecurity. It would be quite another matter if Brenda were torn between Neil and a boyfriend at Harvard. Roth conspicuously omits any reference to the 23-year-old Neil's prior girlfriends, just as Neil does not fantasize about anyone else when he feels abandoned by Brenda. The conflict over the diaphragm, as I have noted, does not concern the possibility that Brenda might be sleeping with someone else, but arises solely from Neil's absurd suspicion that she deliberately left it at home where her mother would find it as a way of sabotaging *their* relationship. The text is not explicit on this point, but the clear impression is given that when Neil and Brenda sing "hesitant, clever, nervous, gentle dithyrambs about how we were beginning to feel towards one another" (19), this is a first love for both of them. For all practical purposes, the two of them are virgins.

In short, to put the matter in psychoanalytic terms, the issue that Roth is exploring in his first masterpiece is not the triangular constellation of the Oedipus complex, in which the father (or his surrogate) looms large as the son's rival, but the more primitive battle over survival that has only two participants and is thrashed out originally in the child's earliest experiences with the mother. That Neil's aunt calls him "Casanova" (4) when he places his first telephone call to Brenda is not inaccurate as a diagnosis and is certainly a harbinger of things to come in Roth, but even the compulsive promiscuity of a Tarnopol, Kepesh, Portnoy, or Zuckerman has its roots in the mother complex.

Having indicated how the fault lines in Neil's relationship with Brenda go back to disturbances in the preoedipal realm, I return now to what Melanie Klein would call his projective identification with the colored boy who comes to the library.[1] As I have suggested, not only does Neil incorporate the boy's fascination with Tahiti into his own fantasies about the Patimkins, but his anxiety lest the boy not find the Gauguin volume on the shelf can be understood as a displaced expression of the fear of loss that is the "underside" of his love for Brenda. It is as though, prompted by Brenda's question about whether he is a "Negro," Neil tries desperately to forestall the catastrophe he senses is inevitable in his own future by making sure that it does not happen to the boy.

Neil does succeed in keeping the Gauguin book out of the elderly white man's clutches not once but twice—

telling him when he comes back for it a second time that "it should be back any day" (59)—but the colored boy is no less obdurate than Neil in staging unhappy endings. When he shows up at the library later on the same day as the white man and asks to see "That Mr. Go-again's book"—that is, Mr. Repetition's—Neil pleads with him to check the book out himself and asks whether he has a library card. The boy refuses to cooperate with Neil's efforts to intervene on his behalf: "What you keep telling me take that book home for? At home somebody *dee-stroy* it" (60). When Neil warns him that "someday somebody's going to take that book out," the boy is unperturbed; and Neil leaves for his Labor Day vacation full of foreboding that the "jowly bastard would return to the library, and the colored kid's book would disappear" (60-61).

Once one recognizes that the colored boy is Neil's double and, as it were, an externalized representation of his unconscious, then his explanation for not checking out the book becomes charged with significance. His statement that the book would be destroyed at home—in addition to its literal meaning—is a metaphor for the violence in Neil's inner world and what he fears would happen to Brenda were he to marry her instead of leaving her "on the shelf." The tragedy, of course, for both the boy and Neil, is that by refusing to expose the beloved object to the full force of their destructive attacks, they are unable (as D. W. Winnicott explains in "The Use of an Object") to accept its independent existence in the realm of external reality, and they thereby guarantee that it will be permanently lost.[2]

Neil's second encounter with the colored boy and the "jowly" white man forms the backdrop to his "Goodbye, Columbus" dream, which is the psychological fulcrum of the novella. The dream takes place while he is on vacation visiting the Patimkins, a couple of days after he has heard the news that Ron and Harriet are getting married and, crucially, the night after Brenda has for the first time told him she loves him. Neil describes himself as "unsettled" by the dream, in which he was the captain and the colored boy his mate and only crew member on "an old sailing ship" (74). At first, they were "anchored in the harbor" of a Pacific island; it was "very sunny," and the dream was "pleasant." Suddenly, however, "the boat was moving and there was nothing we could do about it." The beautiful "Negresses" on the island came down to the shore and "began to throw leis at us and say 'Goodbye, Columbus . . . goodbye, Columbus . . . goodbye. . . .'" Distressed at the involuntary movement of the boat, Neil and the boy began to reproach one another: "he shouted at me that it was my fault and I shouted it was his for not having a library card." Soon, however, the island disappeared from view, and

Neil awakens with the feeling that "space was all out of proportion in the dream" (75).

It is only later, on the night before his wedding, that Ron plays for Neil in its entirety his "Columbus record" (102), which commemorates the athletic and other triumphs of the Class of 1957 at Ohio State University, including the thunderous ovation greeting Ron's own final appearance on the basketball court wearing a Buckeye uniform. At the time of his dream, Neil has caught only snatches of the record emanating from Ron's room, including "a deep kind of Edward R. Murrow gloomy voice" intoning the refrain *"goodbye, Columbus"* against a backdrop of "bells moaning evenly and soft patriotic music" (74); but what he has overheard has obviously left a memory trace on his unconscious mind.

The first, and most important, thing to say about Neil's dream is that it gives a double meaning to the title of Roth's novella, the ambiguity of which probably registers subliminally even on those who may never read the book. For whereas in Ron's recording the phrase "Goodbye, Columbus" is implicitly addressed by the graduating seniors to the city of their alma mater, in Neil's dream "Columbus" is no longer the city in Ohio but rather the explorer and discoverer of America after whom the city was named. Neil, that is, is himself Columbus in the dream, and the Negresses' goodbyes to him and the colored boy signify his imminent and involuntary departure from the "Tahiti" of the Patimkins' home in Short Hills and the loss of his paradisiacal love with Brenda.

That Neil should unconsciously identify himself with Columbus in his dream—and that Roth should consciously launch his career in the same fashion—becomes exceptionally poignant when viewed retrospectively in light of subsequent developments. When Roth seeks in *The Facts* to fathom the mystery of how he could have forsaken the eminently desirable "Gayle Milman"—his pseudonym for the Brenda Patimkin figure in his real life—for the disaster of his marriage to Margaret Martinson Williams, all he can say is that by September 1956 he had come to the conclusion that

> my voyage out—wherever it might be taking me—could no longer be impeded by this affair, which as I saw it, had inevitably to resolve itself into a marriage linking me with the safe enclosure of Jewish New Jersey.
>
> (89)

What Roth calls in *The Facts* his "voyage out" is concretely represented in his dream in **"Goodbye, Columbus"** by the departure of the ship from its Pacific

island harbor. The immense sadness and mutual recriminations between Neil and his double over who is at "fault" for the sudden movement of the boat make the dream the only place where Roth is unable to escape the guilt and depression for his abandonment of Brenda that he otherwise stoutly defends as having been necessary to his personal and artistic development. To leave Brenda, to renounce Tahiti, is to choose a life of sexual adventure—that is, "fucking"—over the "safe enclosure" of a marriage that might actually work.

It is, for better and worse, to become the author of *Portnoy's Complaint*. In one of the most frequently cited passages from that novel, Portnoy describes his relentless promiscuity to his analyst Spielvogel as a form of sociological research:

> What I'm saying, Doctor, is that I don't seem to stick my dick up these girls, as much as I stick it up their backgrounds—as though through fucking I will discover America. *Conquer* America—maybe that's more like it.
>
> (235)

Like Roth's reference to his "voyage out" in *The Facts,* this passage takes on its full meaning when it is read as a continuation of, and commentary on, Neil Klugman's dream in **"Goodbye, Columbus."** It is not surprising whom Portnoy should go on to name as the first of his forefathers to have stuck his dick up America's New-Found-Land: "Columbus, Captain Smith, Governor Winthrop, General Washington—now Portnoy."

If *The Facts* confirms that Neil's relationship with Brenda is grounded in Roth's personal experience, a biographical reading of Neil's dream in **"Goodbye, Columbus"** can be ventured with the aid of *Patrimony.* In this memoir of his father's life and death, Roth reveals that on the walls of the latter's apartment in Elizabeth were "two large reproductions (chosen for my parents nearly forty years back by my brother, who had been to art school) of Gauguin landscapes" (25). The mention of Gauguin is, of course, striking, and the parallel to **"Goodbye, Columbus"** is reinforced by the fact that the library book that captures the imagination of the colored boy is described as a *"large*-sized edition of Gauguin *reproductions"* (italics added). We enter here the realm of speculation, but surely images that had hung for 40 years in his parents' home must have affected Roth deeply. This in turn suggests that beneath the erotic component of Neil's Tahiti fantasy in **"Goodbye, Columbus"** is Roth's own longing for the lost paradise of his childhood, including the ambivalent wish for and fear of becoming fused once again with the body of his mother.

A second, even more far-reaching parallel is that between Neil's dream in **"Goodbye, Columbus"** and the dream of the "defunct warship drifting blindly into shore" (237) that Roth himself reports in *Patrimony* having had during the summer before his father's death. As in the case of the Gauguin allusions, where the words "large" and "reproduction" occur in both **"Goodbye, Columbus"** and *Patrimony,* there are specific verbal echoes between the two texts. In both the early novella (74-75) and the later memoir (235-36) the dream-narratives feature a "boat" that is "old," as well as a "harbor"; there is likewise emphasis on the "crew," though in *Patrimony* there was "no life on board," whereas in **"Goodbye, Columbus"** the only members are Neil and the colored boy. In both dreams, the ship moves involuntarily: in *Patrimony,* it "floated imperceptibly toward the shore," whereas in **"Goodbye, Columbus"** it was carried "further and further from the island." In both dreams, the mood, as Roth says in *Patrimony,* is "heartbreaking," and he wakes up "despondent and frightened and sad." In both cases, moreover, the ship is identified with the central figure: in *Patrimony,* he says, "my father *was* the ship," while in **"Goodbye, Columbus,"** Neil himself is symbolically equated with the ship that is being carried away from the "harbor" of Brenda. A final parallel, connected to the melancholy mood of both dreams, is that in *Patrimony* Roth describes the "ghostly hulk" of the ship as "the aftermath of a disaster," thereby projecting the dream forward into the period of his father's death, even though that event still lies some months in the future. In precisely similar fashion, Neil's dream in **"Goodbye, Columbus"** also takes place in the future perfect tense, after he will have broken up with Brenda.

Whether or not Roth actually dreamed the dream that he gives to Neil Klugman, as he dreamed the dream in *Patrimony,* is impossible to say. Clearly, he either dreamed Neil's dream or made it up, so either way it arose out of his unconscious, and thus its ontological status is of secondary importance. Still, the uncanny resemblances between the two dreams seem to me to weigh strongly in favor of the hypothesis that Roth did indeed have such a **"Goodbye, Columbus"** dream in real life, and that he can therefore in this respect be literally identified with his fictional protagonist. In any event, this juxtaposition of the two dreams separated by more than 30 years takes us into the heart of Roth's unconscious—into his imagination of disaster, his equation of separation with death, and the primordial screen memories of his childhood.

It remains for me now to trace out how the tragic ending of Neil's relationship to Brenda, foreshadowed by this anxiety-dream evoked by her declaration of love for him (as well as by the news of her brother's im-

pending marriage), plays itself out in the final sections of the novella. The next important episode is the quarrel arising from Neil's request that Brenda obtain a diaphragm. As I have noted, this leads to their first serious breach, though equilibrium is restored when Brenda later decides to give Neil what he wants. What is crucial to consider is how Neil's idea about the diaphragm occurs to him as a response to "the union of Harriet and Ron," which he says "reminded me that separation need not be a permanent state" (78). Indeed, Neil expressly affirms, "I wanted Brenda to marry me," though he immediately adds that marriage "was not what I proposed to her." Claiming to fear the possibility of rejection, or even being asked by Brenda to wait, Neil supposes that this is why he "proposed the surrogate, which turned out finally to be more daring than I knew at the time."

Neil's proposal concerning the diaphragm, then, is explicitly described as a "surrogate" for a marriage proposal, and the diaphragm itself is a substitute for the permanent commitment. In psychoanalytic terms, the diaphragm is a *symptom,* a classic example of a compromise formation that expresses at once his desire for and fear of marriage. The request reflects Neil's desire for marriage in that it is a bold step, a test of their relationship and of Brenda's feelings for him, and of course it has to do with sex. But it reflects his fear of marriage in that it is conspicuously not a marriage proposal, and indeed threatens to derail his and Brenda's progress toward this goal. Again, to borrow Freud's extremely helpful language, a process of *displacement* is at work, which shows by the similarity between the thing itself and the "surrogate" the force of Neil's desire, but also reveals by their difference the countervailing force of his fear. In another vicious circle, Neil's fear of separation, and the hope that it "need not be a permanent state," leads him to think of marriage; but his fear of commitment leads him to propose the diaphragm instead, which drives him back toward the isolation that initiated the merry-go-round with Brenda in the first place.

A further crucial feature of Neil's proposal about the diaphragm is that it is experienced by Brenda as degrading. "You think there would be something affairish about it," she says. "Last summer I went with this whore who I sent out to buy—" (82). It is this outburst that leads Neil to call her a "selfish egotistical bitch," and Brenda to respond by asking why he doesn't "take turns" with her mother in plaguing her. Given the hidden motives behind Neil's idea of this "surrogate" and the crude way he presents it to Brenda, there can be no doubt that she is right in her perceptions. Neil is indeed trying to turn her into a "whore," and their relationship into "something affairish."

If that is the case, the question then inevitably arises of why he would do this. The answer is that Neil desires to degrade Brenda precisely in order that she will be unfit to marry, and he will then be justified in rejecting her. In other words, he is creating the conditions that guarantee the relationship will fail, and he does so by imposing a humiliating test on the beloved. If she refuses to comply with his demand, she has shown (in his mind) that she does not love him; but if she passes the test, she has failed on a deeper level by her abjectness, which is bound over time to induce resentment in her and contempt in him. Either way, she remains for him an object of his fantasy rather than an independent person in her own right; and the relationship, instead of being based on mutual recognition, becomes a power struggle in which one party must win and the other lose. "I can't win, no matter what I say," Brenda exclaims in frustration; and the scene ends with Neil's reply: "'Yes you can,' I said. 'You have'" (85).

In Freud's classic psychoanalytic model based on the Oedipus complex, the son's desire for the mother is split into "sensual" and "affectionate" currents, and the interference of the incest taboo makes it difficult for a man to reunite these two currents of love in his feelings for the same woman in adult life.[3] From this standpoint, the problem Brenda poses for Neil is paradoxically that she is perfect: by affording him the possibility of integrating sex and love, passion and affection, she threatens to undo the split in the mother image that is his bulwark against the incest wish. As Neil ruminates on the final page of the narrative, "Whatever spawned my love for her, had that spawned such lust too? If she had only been slightly *not* Brenda . . ." (136). Here we see him celebrating Brenda as the one woman who can combine his "love" and "lust," but, by the twisted logic of the unconscious, must for that very reason be rejected. If only she had been different in some way, it might have lasted; but then she would had something wrong with her so it couldn't have lasted either.

After Neil and Brenda's initial quarrel over the diaphragm, the narrative moves inexorably to its denouement. Neil visits Brenda's father at his warehouse and later attends Ron's wedding to Harriet. On both occasions Mr. Patimkin sends clear signals that he would be glad to have Neil in the family, though a cynical note is struck at the wedding by Mr. Patimkin's half-brother Leo. Even while jocularly admonishing Neil "don't louse it up" (108) and assuring him that "next time we see you it'll be *your* wedding" (117), the intoxicated Leo complains both about his job as a traveling lightbulb salesman and the fact that his wife does not enjoy sex. He fondly recalls a time years ago in San Francisco when a woman with whom he took a

taxi ride told him in her room that "she believes in oral love" (116). Leo clearly expresses the negative pole of Neil's own ambivalence toward marriage and the lure of women who promise to satisfy him sexually in a way that his wife will not or cannot. Between Neil's visit to Patimkin Sinks and the wedding, Brenda changes her mind about the diaphragm, and Neil accompanies her to New York City where she has made a doctor's appointment. While Brenda is having her appointment, Neil wanders into St. Patrick's Cathedral and, in a continuation of his earlier allusion to the diaphragm as a "surrogate" for marriage, somewhat oddly prays to himself: "Now the doctor is about to wed Brenda and me, and I am not entirely certain this is all for the best. What is it I love, Lord?" (100).

The final section opens with Neil plunged into desolation after Brenda has returned to college. Back at his job at the Newark library, he notices that "Gauguin was gone, apparently charged out finally by the jowly man," and Neil wonders "what it had been like that day the colored kid had discovered the book was gone" (120). In the terms of my analysis, Neil's efforts to replace the lost object are doomed to fail, and he is confronted with the abiding sense of a lack in his being. Not having seen the boy again, he imagines that the boy blames the disappearance of the book on him, but then realizes that "I was confusing the dream I'd had with reality." In a summary judgment applicable to himself no less than the boy, Neil opines that the latter is "better off," and (with a probable reminiscence of Leo's comments at the wedding about not being able to enjoy cab rides because he is always watching the meter) there is "no sense carrying dreams of Tahiti in your head, if you can't afford the fare" (120).

In the concluding scene of the novella, Neil travels to Boston when Brenda is unable to come home for the Jewish holidays; and, as I have noted, they check into a hotel room as though they were man and wife, with Brenda wearing a "thin gold band" on her left hand. If Neil had a reason for fearing rejection earlier, he has not even a pretext now, and he realizes why he has come to Boston: "It was time to stop kidding about marriage" (126). But what starts out as their "wedding night" turns into disaster when Brenda shows him the letters she has received from both parents after her mother had found a certain unmentionable item while putting away Brenda's summer clothing. Her father's letter is kind and tells her to go out and buy a coat, while her mother's hysterically reproaches Brenda, "I don't know what we ever did that you should reward us this way" (129). Still, both parents seem to agree that Neil's having slept with Brenda while a guest in their home is unforgivable, and that their relationship must end.

Brenda is, of course, already upset and has been crying, but it is crucial to appreciate that her relationship with Neil is by no means necessarily over, despite her parents' misgivings. To speculate about what might have happened in a story that Roth did not write must remain hypothetical, but it is not far-fetched to imagine that if Neil had told Brenda he loved her and asked her to marry him, she would gladly have exchanged her pretend wedding band for the real thing. Then, when the officially engaged couple confronted her parents with a fait accompli, Brenda and her mother would have had a terrible fight, following which her father would have paid for a fabulous wedding. Neil would thereupon have taken his place beside Ron as a right-hand man in the family business and done his duty as the begetter of grandchildren to the great joy of all Klugmans and Patimkins.

This, however, is not what happens. On the contrary, as I have indicated, Neil blames Brenda for having left the diaphragm at home where her mother would find it. The conversation degenerates into mutual recriminations, in which Brenda is driven to exclaim, "Oh, Neil, don't start any of that psychoanalytic crap!" (134); and she reminds him that he has been attacking her since the beginning of their relationship. Soon they are both talking in the past tense about their love, and Neil picks up his bag and puts on his coat: "I think Brenda was crying too when I went out the door" (135).

Roth's realization of this scene is vividly realistic, but perhaps his greatest strength as a writer lies in the way he shows unconscious processes in action. What Neil is unable to see for himself Roth allows the reader to discern through his words and deeds. Neil relentlessly badgers Brenda with "psychoanalytic" interpretations of her allegedly unconsciously motivated behavior, but he does so as a way of not looking at his own unconscious agency in asking her to buy the diaphragm in the first place and in now attacking her when she is most vulnerable instead of embracing her and telling her he loves her. In succumbing to the "hideous emotion" that is no longer the "underside" of love but its conqueror, Neil becomes the consummate bad mother, or the desperate infant once again annihilating the mother who has been unable to survive his destructive attacks. The full "daring" of his proposal of the "surrogate" has been revealed, and the transformation of Brenda into a "selfish egotistical bitch" is complete. Only in his dream, where the phrase "goodbye, Columbus" falls into the unconscious and takes on a double meaning, can Neil accept responsibility for his fate. In waking life, it is always somebody else's fault.

After Neil walks out of Brenda's life, he heads with his suitcase for Harvard Yard, which he enters for the first time. It is night; he stops in front of Lamont Library, remembering that Brenda had told him its rest rooms had Patimkin sinks. Peering inside, Neil finds that the building is empty and sees his reflection in the glass. "Suddenly," he says, "I wanted to set down my suitcase and pick up a rock and heave it right through the glass," but instead "I simply looked at myself in the mirror the light made of the window" (135). Neil fantasizes being able to run around to the other side to "catch whatever it was that looked through those eyes," but he can see only his reflection, and "the outside of me gave up little information about the inside of me."

This disorienting experience leads Neil to ask some questions that will have a familiar ring to readers of Roth: "What was it inside me that had turned pursuit and clutching into love, and then turned it inside out again? What was it that had turned winning into losing, and losing—who knows—into winning?" Although Roth never manages to solve the central riddle of his life, there can be no denying the reality of Neil's loss—"I was sure I had loved Brenda, though standing there, I knew I couldn't any longer"—or the awareness that it will not be easy to find the complete package again: "And I knew it would be a long while before I made love to anyone the way I had made love to her" (136). Confounded by the impossibility of being satisfied either with Brenda or with any other woman who is in the least "*not* Brenda," Neil stares at his image in the darkening glass before his gaze pierces the library window to "a broken wall of books, imperfectly shelved."

What eludes Neil's power to put into words, Roth shows us through the rough magic of his art. The true tragedy, however, is that the insight Roth displays with supreme objectivity as a novelist into the psychic deformations of his protagonist—his insecurity, his anger, his incapacity for love—does not prevent him from sharing Neil's blindness to these same traits in his own character. Neil wants to fathom what is going on "inside" his head, but unless and until he confronts the guilt of his primitive battle for survival with the mother, he is condemned to behold only the "outside" and to try to blame his misfortunes on other people. His impulse to throw a rock through the mirror that should be a window is a manifestation of his predicament. Neil Klugman is not yet a writer, only someone who works in a library; but "the broken wall of books, imperfectly shelved," is an emblem of Roth's oeuvre to come. That it is a "wall" suggests its defensive function; that it is "broken" and "imperfectly shelved" captures the disorder of his life that even Roth's sublime achievement as an artist is unable to hold at bay. **"Goodbye, Columbus,"** the fully formed masterpiece with which Roth burst upon the world, is his portrait of the narcissist as a young man.

Notes

1. For a detailed overview of projective identification in the psychoanalytic literature, see Hinshel-

wood 179-208. The term was introduced by Klein in a 1952 addition to "Notes on Some Schizoid Mechanisms."

2. See Winnicott.

3. Freud 180. "On the Universal Tendency to Debasement in the Sphere of Love," as Strachey calls it in the *Standard Edition,* is the same essay, translated by Joan Riviere as "The Most Prevalent Form of Degradation in Erotic Life," read by Alexander Portnoy and that lends a title to a chapter of *Portnoy's Complaint.*

Works Cited

Freud, Sigmund. "On the Universal Tendency to Debasement in the Sphere of Love." 1912. *The Standard Edition of the Complete Psychological Works of Sigmund Freud.* Ed. and trans. James Strachey et al. Vol 11. London: Hogarth, 1957. 179-90.

Hinshelwood, R. D. *A Dictionary of Kleinian Thought.* 2nd ed. London: Free Association, 1991.

Klein, Melanie. "Notes on Some Schizoid Mechanisms." 1946. *The Writings of Melanie Klein.* Ed. Roger Money-Kyrle et al. Vol. 3. New York: Free Press, 1975. 1-24.

Roth, Philip. *The Facts: A Novelist's Autobiography.* 1988. New York: Vintage, 1997.

———. *Goodbye, Columbus and Five Short Stories.* 1959. New York: Vintage, 1987.

———. *Patrimony: A True Story.* 1991. New York: Vintage, 1996.

———. *Portnoy's Complaint.* 1969. New York: Vintage, 1994.

Winnicott, D. W. "The Use of an Object and Relating through Identifications." 1969. *Playing and Reality.* London: Tavistock, 1984. 86-94.

Jessica G. Rabin (essay date 2005)

SOURCE: Rabin, Jessica G. "Still (Resonant, Relevant, and) Crazy after All These Years: 'Goodbye, Columbus' and Five Short Stories." In *Philip Roth: New Perspectives on an American Author,* pp. 9-23. Westport, Conn.: Praeger, 2005.

[*In the following excerpt, Rabin claims that Roth's combination of ethnic particularity and American universality makes his early stories resonate forty-five years after their first publication.*]

What is it about the selections in Philip Roth's ***"Goodbye, Columbus" and Five Short Stories*** that has allowed them to transcend their original context and re-tain their relevance for future generations? These stories are not only still resonant, they are still fresh, lending themselves to new readings based on postmodern theories of identity, as well as evolving discussions of ethnicity, consumerism, and the American Dream. Although one strength of Roth's stories about Jewish Americans is that they engage both Jewish and non-Jewish (and, for that matter, both American and international) audiences, their ethnic grounding and rootedness in place contribute to their longevity. Indeed, in Roth's case it is arguably the combination of ethnic particularity and American universality that has lent Roth's first collection its staying power for nearly forty-five years.

The balance between the ethnic and the universal does not always come easy to Roth. In fact, he has never seemed to waver from the sentiments expressed early in his career when he announced: "I am not a Jewish writer; I am a writer who is a Jew" (qtd. in Ozick 158). Roth's concern is understandable. So-called ethnic novels have traditionally been considered less valuable as literature than works of mainstream American realism, causing aspiring minority-group novelists to feel pressure to move beyond group-specific experiences and pursue more universal themes (Ferraro 1, 3). Indeed, if Roth has persistently resisted classifying himself as a minority writer, he is in good company and has learned from the best. James Baldwin, whose texts Roth says he was reading during the 1950s (Preface xi), similarly disliked being pigeonholed as either a black writer or a gay writer (Leeming 45, 129). Instead, Baldwin believed that an American identity was the only salient one—for himself or any other American writer (Leeming 172). Here Baldwin's attitude provides an example of an ethnic writer's apparent wish to be valued solely as an artist, rather than being classified as an ethnic writer (Palumbo-Liu 194). And yet according to any number of theorists, ethnic identity is itself quintessentially American. Werner Sollors suggests that "in America, casting oneself as an outsider may in fact be considered a dominant cultural trait" (31), whereas Bruce Robbins points out that nearly all Americans can hyphenate (Asian American, Irish American, Italian American, etc.) (167). Thus as residents of a country of immigrants, all Americans have some connection to the experiences Roth portrays.

The eponymous novella **"Goodbye, Columbus"** relates a summer romance between Jewish young adults on opposite sides of the American Dream's proverbial tracks. Neil Klugman, a philosophy major and lower-middle-class librarian at the Newark Library, dates Brenda Patimkin, a Radcliffe student spending her summer vacation at home in the ritzy suburb of Short Hills. Although Neil stays for two weeks with Brenda's family, attends Brenda's brother's wedding, and even gets Brenda to agree to a diaphragm, the title's "goodbye" proves prophetic—the romance does not survive the summer.

Several important motifs in the novella tap into both ethnic and more universal western literary traditions. To begin with, Short Hills is represented as a Garden of Eden or as a Promised Land flowing with milk and honey (or in the vernacular, sporting goods and fresh fruit). The sporting goods trees frame the backyard of a magical paradise where "long lawns [. . .] seemed to be twirling water on themselves" (8). These trees don't seem to offer much in the way of knowledge, but Julie, Brenda's younger sister, has a temper tantrum in which she accuses Neil of "stealing fruit," an allegation that is immediately juxtaposed with Neil's report that "later that night, Brenda and I made love, our first time" (45). The next time Neil encounters the forbidden fruit, it is through his temptress: "Brenda led me to it herself," he reports (54). Their overindulgence in fruit produces gastrointestinal problems: "at last I cracked my frail bowel," Neil admits (54). Further, it deliberately taps into an American literary tradition, offering a twist on Hawthorne's scarlet letter: "at home, undressing for the second time that night, I would find red marks on the undersides of my feet" (56). A mark thus inscribed on the body apparently cannot be cleansed, despite repeated ritual immersions in the rarified water of the Short Hills Country Club's swimming pool. Such immersion, calling up the Jewish mikva or Christian baptism, suggests the possibility of sea change or being born again. But ultimately paradise is lost: Neil's eventual banishment from the Patimkin homestead constitutes expulsion from the Garden.

Roth also positions his characters within a particularly American literary and cultural tradition. Ron, an all-American jock, is a paragon of the boys of summer. He contemplates making a career of playing games by becoming a gym teacher, but ultimately decides to accept his "responsibilities" and live vicariously through his own children: "we're going to have a boy [. . .] and when he's about six months old I'm going to sit him down with a basketball in front of him, and a football, and a baseball, and then whichever one he reaches for, that's the one we're going to concentrate on" (61). In addition to the sports-as-life metaphor, Roth alludes to the American motifs of haunted houses and skeletons in the closet via the Patimkins' "not-to-be-buried past" (Peden BR4), embodied in the roomful of old furniture. You can take the Patimkins out of Newark, but you can't take Newark out of the Patimkins. Or as William Faulkner's Gavin Stevens so memorably says, "the past is never dead. It's not even past" (80).

Even the various family squabbles—relatively harmless in the case of Neil's family and potentially more volatile in Brenda's—relate to ethnic American iden-

tity. Becoming an American has been linked to other kinds of coming-of-age experiences, especially in the form of teenage rebellion against parents. Metaphorically, the would-be American rebels against his or her old-world parents in an attempt to assert individuality and independence.[1] Both Neil and Brenda try to distance themselves from old-world Newark, embodied for Neil in his aunt's speech and mannerisms and for Brenda in her mother's emphasis on participation in Jewish organizations and on thrift. The resultant disharmony between parents and children is itself a prominent feature of American culture—adolescent angst is not universal.[2] Hence both Neil's relatively gentle mocking of Gladys's worldview and Brenda's dramatic temper tantrums reinforce the themes of the struggle for American identity and the costs of the American Dream.

In questioning the attainment and desirability of the American Dream, Roth further suggests that the process of becoming American is ongoing for his characters. In important ways, Neil contains elements of both the individualist American hero and the prototypical ethnic American hero, a blending that might provide insight into Roth's own ambivalence about identification as well. Questions about what it means to be Jewish and American fall squarely in Neil's lap. As the ethnic American hero, Neil is saddled with what Betty Ann Burch calls "the burden of identity: What does it mean to be an American? Am I an American? Where do I fit in American society?" (56). Significantly, Neil is essentially an orphan, a typical experience in the ethnic American bildungsroman. In charting patterns for ethnic heroines, Mary Dearborn has argued that the heroine typically separates from her parents as a prerequisite for establishing an independent American identity (76). Furthermore, ethnic heroines often gain both American status and social mobility through "marrying up" in the form of a well-to-do American citizen. In an interesting twist on this stereotypical practice by women, Roth offers us a young man who is embarking on the path of Americanization and achievement of the American Dream through his association with a woman who has already made the journey, as Brenda reminds Neil more than once, "we lived in Newark when I was a baby" (12). Accordingly, Neil excises the influence of his parents and the lack of success they represent and similarly dismisses his caricatured aunt and uncle. When he meets Brenda, Neil casts off his family in one fell swoop: "my cousin Doris could peel away to nothing for all I cared, my Aunt Gladys have twenty feedings every night, my father and mother could roast away their asthma down in the furnace of Arizona, those penniless deserters—I didn't care for anything but Brenda" (16-17); anything, that is, except perhaps that which Brenda represents: success on American terms.

The prominence of the becoming American theme in Roth's novella additionally suggests Roth's awareness of and tacit agreement with the premise that American identity is not conferred simultaneously or automatically with citizenship. Rather it is ongoing and often incomplete. Writing in 1926, Henry Pratt Fairchild insists that "in fact, no immigrant immediately after arrival is ever a member of the new nationality"; rather, an immigrant "must devoutly wish to be Americanized" for the process to take place (141, 222). Thirty years later, Roth seems to offer a similar take on the topic. Even though he was born in America, Neil is still in some ways a person who is in the process of becoming American, and although they are further along in the process, the Patimkins are also still working on this goal: the Patimkin children will get nose jobs to remove the bodily inscription of their ethnicity, while Mr. Patimkin will retain his trademark bumpy nose and Mrs. Patimkin will fuss over meat and milk silverware. Although Europeans become Americans by crossing the Atlantic, and Jews become Americans by crossing from Newark shtetl to Short Hills mansion, Neil's aspirations towards American success and Patimkinization involve other types of crossings as well.

A major motif in American (and particularly ethnic American) literature, crossing recurs in several different forms throughout **"Goodbye, Columbus."** Although the characters are not of the immigrant generation that crossed from Europe to America, they make significant geographical and psychic crossings of their own. In a review contemporaneous with the novella's publication, William Peden observes that "Brenda's family has 'moved up' from Newark economically [. . .] and Neil has made the 'migration' intellectually" (BR4). Whereas Neil's parents have gone west, in a sort of horizontal move as opposed to Neil's vertical aspirations, his Aunt Gladys and Uncle Max remain in the old-world community, "sharing a Mounds bar in the cindery darkness of their alley" (9). If Newark is connected with the Jewish ghetto, suburban Short Hills clearly represents upward mobility: "Once I'd driven out of Newark, past Irvington and the packed-in tangle of railroad crossings, switchmen shacks, lumberyards, Dairy Queens, and used car lots, the night grew cooler. It was, in fact, as though the hundred and eighty feet that the suburbs rose in altitude above Newark brought one closer to heaven" (8). Neil's daily sojourns to Short Hills represent an important crossing for him; he is a migrant trying to decide if he will become an immigrant, a permanent resident. It is worth noting that Brenda never comes to visit Neil and his family; symbolically, this is a journey that is only supposed to occur in one direction—up, a "lousy hundred and eighty feet" up, to be specific (14).

The concept of migration, which the Patimkins embrace, Neil experiments with, and Gladys and Max resist, is itself fundamentally connected with American identity. Indeed the shared experience of journeying—physically or psychologically—forms a cornerstone of American cultural identity (Urgo 5, 55). Hence in moving from Newark to Short Hills, the Patimkins have essentially made the transition from foreigner to American. This conclusion is further supported by the finding that the twentieth-century America rise of "consumer culture" offered those who were not white Anglo-Saxon protestants an alternative means by which to "join the exclusive 'American race'" (Marren 18). Indeed, it is money that provides the Jewish Patimkins their portal to the American Dream, complete with country clubs, ostentatious weddings, and Ivy League schools.

Neil's journeys from Newark to Short Hills—culminating in his two weeks as full-time resident—constitute a literal and figurative climbing of the social scale and a manifestation of geographical crossing, but his sojourns take on other symbolic associations of crossing as well. Jonathan Dollimore points out that crossing suggests physical movement, hybridity, and disagreement, further noting that the expression "cross-dressing" disrupts simple either/or gender binaries (288). Although Neil does not cross-dress in the usual sense of the expression—he does not wear evening gowns or high-heeled shoes—he does adopt the dress of another culture, so to speak. Unpacking in the Patimkins' guest room, Neil strategically allows his single Brooks Brothers shirt to "linger on the bed a while" (63); shortly thereafter, he announces, "I sat down on my Brooks Brothers shirt and pronounced my own name out loud" (66). Similarly, when Brenda approvingly says to Neil, "you look like me. Except bigger" (70), we concur with Neil's hunch that this observation has ramifications for identity and integrity: "I had the feeling that Brenda was not talking about the accidents of our dress—if they were accidents. She meant, I was sure, that I was somehow beginning to look the way she wanted me to. Like herself" (70). Dress is an indicator both of social status and of group membership.[3] Hence Neil's uneasiness about Brenda's comment reflects his ambivalence about the potential costs of joining the Patimkin family; his dress is intimately bound up with his sense of personal identity.

When he begins to dress the part, Neil enters another realm that is closely associated with crossing, that of passing. Although the term *passing* is usually associated with race—generally the phenomenon of African Americans passing for white—Roth seems to borrow deliberately from the language of passing as he describes Neil's attempts to "become a Patimkin with ease" (120). (Passing will again become thematically significant in Roth's later fiction, particularly *The Human Stain* and *American Pastoral*.) By analogy, Neil's making the physical journey from Newark to Short

Hills and the psychological shift from Klugman to Patimkin jointly suggest the psychic journey from foreigner to American. By assimilating to American/Patimkin standards, Neil runs the very real risk of losing his own identity—in other words, his multiplying transformations destabilize any coherent or unitary sense of self, rendering him chameleon-like.[4]

Neil's attempt to pass for a Patimkin and his increasingly precarious sense of self call attention to identity politics in the novel. To begin with, it is worth noting that the Patimkin parents retain their Jewish identifiers, but they fail to pass their ethnic heritage to their assimilated children. While Mrs. Patimkin laments that Brenda has traded her status as "the best Hebrew student" (89) for American success at Radcliffe, Mr. Patimkin remarks "without anger," "they're *goyim*, my kids, that's how much they understand" (94). These tensions between ethnicity and assimilation form a point of connection between Roth's Jewish characters and the experiences of other ethnic groups, particularly African Americans, a relationship that James Baldwin also pondered at length. Driving to Patimkin Kitchen and Bathroom Sinks, Neil reflects that "the Negroes were making the same migration, following the steps of the Jews" (90). On an individual level, Neil's experiences are highlighted by the counterpoint of a foil character, the African American boy in the library.

Although Neil recognizes the boy is facing long odds in his desire to connect with European art and a middle-class lifestyle, Neil remains remarkably opaque to the parallels between the boy's situation and his own. In his first phone conversation with Brenda, Neil is quick to assure her that he is not "a Negro" (7), and yet in important ways Neil shares the experience of marginality. Although the boy is of significantly lower class than Neil and his status is further complicated by race, he calls attention to Neil's position in the Patimkin household. Just as Neil travels most evenings to Short Hills, the boy comes most days to the library; both are migrants, potential immigrants, and explorers reconnoitering a new world. The boy's attempts to make himself inconspicuous by tiptoeing have the opposite result, much as Neil's superhuman exertions to eat like a Patimkin never change Mr. Patimkin's initial conclusion that "he eats like a bird" (23). Furthermore, the little boy is out of his element in the library, linguistically and culturally. His heavy accent constitutes a language barrier, and communication difficulties are compounded by skepticism on the part of the other librarians, a distrust shared by the boy, who, not understanding how the system works, reacts with suspicion and hostility to Neil's well-meaning suggestion that he obtain a library card. Neil is similarly out of place in "fancy-shmancy" Short Hills (57). When Neil reflects, "I felt like Carlota; no, not even as comfortable as that" (40), he articulates a sense of being even lower on the social scale than the family's African American domestic. And yet while Neil's "sneaking-away time" dream subconsciously situates himself and the boy in the proverbial same boat (74), Neil does not seem to realize that Brenda can be taken from him just as easily as the boy's book can be checked out by another patron.

Indeed, Neil's ambiguous and liminal status as "Brenda's friend" (89) is further highlighted by the Gauguin motif introduced in the little boy's subplot. As an artist and a migrant who formed points of attachment to two different worlds but found complete acceptance in neither, Gauguin foregrounds the insider-outsider dilemma of being between worlds and the problems associated with the process of "self-nativising," or blurring the lines between subject and observer by participating in the activities of the group one is studying (Gambrell 22, 15). The two weeks Neil spends with the Patimkins comprise an insider-outsider experience, a sense Neil himself articulates when he describes himself as "the outsider who might one day be an insider" (94). And yet Mr. Patimkin's tolerance of Neil's idiosyncrasies reflects Mr. Patimkin's dismissal of Neil as essentially nonthreatening to the Patimkin worldview. Trying to be polite, Mr. Patimkin unwittingly shows that he does not consider Neil a potential insider: idealism, Mr. Patimkin explains, is "all right, you know, if you're a schoolteacher, or like you, you know, a student or something like that." In the Patimkin business world, however, "you need a little of the *gonif* in you" (94).

By the end of the novella, Neil will discover that the Patimkins thought of him as "a perfect stranger" to whom they were "nice enough" to offer their "hospitality" (129). Although Brenda shows herself unwilling to break with her family, and the African American boy presumably loses out on the American Dream because of his racial and socioeconomic marginality, Neil rejects the Patimkin compromises. Neil justifies the African American boy's apparent relinquishment of his aspirations by reflecting, "No sense carrying dreams of Tahiti in your head, if you can't afford the fare" (120). In his own case, Neil can conceivably afford the fare to Tahiti, but he chooses not to pay it. It is Neil who leaves Brenda alone in the hotel room.

Building on some of the same themes and concerns introduced in **"Goodbye, Columbus,"** the five short stories that follow additionally retain their freshness for contemporary readers through their focus on perception, performance, politics, and power. **"Conversion of the Jews," "Defender of the Faith," "Epstein," "You Can't Tell a Man by the Song He Sings,"** and **"Eli, the Fanatic"** present Jewish male protagonists of varying ages and acculturation: thirteen-year-old Hebrew School troublemaker, Ozzie Freedman; newly returned WWII veteran, Sergeant

Nathan Marx; sixty-year-old adulterer, Lou Epstein; a high school student (and unnamed narrator) who becomes friends with a trouble-making misfit; and suburban lawyer (and expectant father), Eli Peck. Furthermore, each protagonist is at a turning point or rite of passage, counterpointed by the experience of a foil or even a doppelganger, reiterating Neil's transitional summer and the projection of his "divided self" (Aarons 7) onto his foil. Ozzie is at the age of Bar Mitzvah and stands in opposition to Rabbi Binder; Marx is returning from war and plays against Grossbart; Epstein sees an earlier version of himself in his nephew Michael and has an affair with Michael's girlfriend's mother; the student embarking on his high school career scores similarly on a personality test to his ex-con classmate; and Eli Peck is on the verge of fatherhood when he meets and eventually becomes a "darker" version of himself, switching clothes with the Hasidic "greenie."

Neil majored in philosophy, and Ozzie Freedman of **"Conversion of the Jews"** seems to be heading in the same direction. His roof climbing notwithstanding, Ozzie's performance is basically semantic, and he has a history of getting himself into trouble with questions: "Mrs. Freedman had to see Rabbi Binder twice before about Ozzie's questions and this Wednesday at four-thirty would be the third time" (139). The story itself questions America's status as a land of possibility. Although his rigid and absolutist Hebrew school teacher, aptly named Rabbi Binder, is concerned with what actually happens, Ozzie always wants to know what is possible. This story further anticipates *The Counterlife* (1986) by focusing on perception, but here the perception is literal: fleeing imminent punishment from his instructor, Ozzie finds himself looking at his world from an unaccustomed perspective, the roof of his Hebrew School: "somehow when you're on a roof the darker it gets the less you can hear" (155).

In addition to focusing on perception, **"Conversion of the Jews"** is fundamentally about power: the omnipotence of God and the power of a little boy to manipulate his audience. To his friend Itzie's incredulous admiration, Ozzie says "intercourse" to Rabbi Binder (141); by the end of the story, Ozzie is eliciting equally scandalous verbal ejaculations from his audience: "he made them all say they believed in Jesus Christ—first one at a time, then all together" (158). Transgressing the American norm of keeping religion a private matter, Ozzie's performance also embodies the cliché of shouting it from the rooftops, or, in the Christian vernacular, "Go tell it on the mountain." And yet despite the apparent threat of a suicidal leap, Ozzie's stance is basically pacifist, as he makes a plea for the power of the word (with which God created the world) rather than the power of might: "Mamma, don't you see—

you shouldn't hit me. He shouldn't hit me. You shouldn't hit me about God, Mamma. You should never hit anybody about God—" (158).

At the same time that is promotes the power of language, the story suggests the ultimate absurdity of language. Although Mrs. Freedman beseeches her son, "Don't be a martyr, my baby," Ozzie's schoolmates encourage him to jump without even knowing what they are saying: "Be a Martin, be a Martin . . ." (155). This chant becomes a mantra without meaning, much like the prayers said by the janitor, old Yakov Blotnik, which, Ozzie hypothesizes, he "had been mumbling so steadily for so many years, [. . .] he had memorized the prayers and forgotten all about God" (144). The same could likely be said for the conversion Ozzie facilitates (or, given the logistics of the situation, coerces), as Naseeb Shaheen hypothesizes: "it is doubtful that Rabbi Binder or anyone else in the story underwent a lasting conversion experience" (378). Pacified by the words, however, Ozzie relents and comes down from the roof. Reflecting the basic satiric bent of the story, the would-be Christ figure ends a fallen angel—the "overgrown halo" of the firemen's net "glow[s]" beneath him instead of above (158).

At first glance, Sergeant Nathan Marx, in **"Defender of the Faith,"** has a dilemma that seems quite different from Ozzie's, and yet language, perception, and identity play an important role in his story as well. Joseph DaCrema reads language as foundational to the story, arguing that the story's "central conflict [. . .] is strongly figured in [Marx's] language patterns" (19) and noting that Marx's increased ethnic identification can be traced through his adoption of traditional Jewish words and linguistic mannerisms as the story progresses. Furthermore, Marx finds himself in the uncomfortable role of cultural translator or mediator: "the next morning, while chatting with Captain Barrett, I recounted the incident of the previous evening. Somehow, in the telling, it must have seemed to the Captain that I was not so much explaining Grossbart's position as defending it" (165-66). An officer, an American, and a Jew, Marx finds himself simultaneously belonging to several groups with mutually exclusive—or at least contradictory—goals and requirements.[5] Whereas Grossbart looks to Marx to privilege his Jewish identity in a show of ethnic/religious solidarity, abetted by post-Holocaust survivor's guilt, Marx's ultimate decision embodies the recognition that "identities are complex and multiple" (Appiah 110). In this context, Marx's betrayal of Grossbart, ostensibly calling in a "favor" to help out a "Jewish kid" (198) but actually undermining Grossbart's manipulations, seems to be an endorsement of personal integrity rather than of a single exclusionary category of identification. And hence Marx's final assertion, while referring to his fate, applies equally well to his evolving sense of identity: "I accepted my own" (200).

Marx reappears in new avatars in the next story as well, in Lou Epstein's soldier nephew Michael, on his way to the Monmouth base where Grossbart wanted to be sent, and in Epstein's daughter Sheila, whose "childhood teddy bear [. . . had] a VOTE SOCIAL-IST button pinned to its left ear" (203). Epstein himself, however, is a dirty old man who might well be, in fact, Leo Patimkin (Ben Patimkin's unsuccessful half-brother) grown older. Whereas Leo's crowning moment was "oral love" with Hannah Schreiber (116), Epstein initiates an adulterous affair in late middle age. And whereas Neil Klugman's scarlet letter appears on the cherry-stained soles of his feet, Epstein's inscription of sin materializes on the biblical site of the covenant, his syphilis-afflicted penis. Sexual ills in this story signify a crisis in continuity and therefore in the American Dream. Just as Ben Patimkin's ability to pass his legacy to his son is compromised by Ron's inability to unload a truck (93), Epstein loses his son Herbie to polio, quarrels with his brother, and is left with only a daughter ("a twenty-three-year-old woman with 'a social conscience'!" [205]) and her boyfriend ("the folk singer" [208]) to presumably carry on the family lineage and business; he finds himself "a year away from the retirement he had planned but with no heir to Epstein Paper Bag Company" (205). Epstein's attempts to rejuvenate himself by having an affair produce the opposite effect: he gets syphilis, which like Alzheimer's "softens the brain" (223), and he has a heart attack. But such rebellion actually reifies conventionality. His wife ceases her demands for a divorce and assures him that their daughter and the folk singer will institutionalize their relationship and live out the dream: "Sheila will marry Marvin and that'll be that. You won't have to sell, Lou, [the business will] be in the family. You can retire, rest, and Marvin can take over" (229). Perhaps. Or maybe Epstein's, like Ozzie's, is just another temporary conversion.

Whereas Epstein is at the end of his career (and, if his heart attack is any indication, perhaps near the end of his life), the nameless protagonist of **"You Can't Tell a Man by the Song He Sings"** is a high school freshman negotiating the American Dream by trying to find out what he is supposed to be when he grows up. This story parodies the Jewish faith in education as a means for social mobility, as the veneration for science implicit in the boast, "my son the doctor," is satirized in the high school "Occupations" class, which comprises a "mysterious but scientific" process of assessing "skills, deficiencies, tendencies, and psyches" (233) of nice Jewish boys and ex-cons alike. Furthermore, reformatory school alumnus Albie Pelagutti is a parody of the American Dream, predictably frustrating the speaker's expectations that "a bum like Pelagutti [could] be an all-American boy in the first place" (239).

Like **"Conversion of the Jews,"** which is also set in a school, this story suggests the absurdity of language, starting with the title itself, which sounds like it should be a famous saying but is not. (A Google search of "you can't tell a man . . ." retrieves everything from "by the color of his skin" to "by the cut of his clothes" to "is a candidate for kidney stones just by looking at him.") Similarly, the song the boys (not men) sing is playful and completely out of context in a school setting, popular but without any apparent purpose or underlying meaning. They sing it solely to irritate their teacher: *Don't sit under the apple treel With anyone else but me.* This rendition is immediately followed by the implicitly equally meaningless, *"Oh, say can you see, by the dawn's early light, what so proudly we hailed—"*(244). So much for John Dewey and the public schools system as a locus for Americanization. However, everyone gets an education in the limitations of the American way: Albie leaves school, the speaker gets a "criminal record" of his own, and the teacher loses his job after an encounter with the House Un-American Activities Committee.

Bringing the collection full circle, **"Eli, the Fanatic"** seems to encapsulate and further explore several of the issues raised in the other selections, including the tension between the public sphere and private life, the relationship between clothes and identity, the implications of survivor guilt, and the nature of postmodern identity. Unlike Ozzie, who doesn't mind shouting issues of personal belief and theology from the rooftops in a public display, the Jews of Woodenton consider religion a private matter. Therefore they are frustrated when their ability to pass is compromised by the reminder of unsuccessful passing, the assimilation to German life that nevertheless could not save the Jewish victims of the Holocaust. This reminder is embodied in the "greenie," a speechless refugee on whom the community projects its post-Holocaust guilt, fear, and anger (Aarons 14; Wirth-Nesher 110-111). Although the story pokes predictable fun at suburbanites trying to pass for WASPs (white Anglo-Saxon Protestants) and at the over-psychoanalyzed characters with their periodic nervous breakdowns, the most interesting episode occurs when Eli switches clothes with the greenie. As in "Goodbye, Columbus" when Neil recognizes his dressing like Brenda as an ominous sign, a potential sacrificing of his identity, Eli Peck embodies the truism of "clothes make the man." The changing of clothes suggests that Eli is trying on alternative identities, but it also prefigures current theories about the nature of postmodern identity. In particular, contemporary theories of gender identity can profitably be applied to ethnic/religious identity in the text. Judith Butler, for example, has asked, "To what extent is 'identity' a normative ideal rather than a descriptive feature of experience?" (16). She concludes that "gender proves to be performative. [. . .] There is no gender identity behind the expressions of gender" (25). In other words, gender is a behavior and has no essential existence when that behavior is not being performed. Arguably, the same could be said of Eli's apparent conversion to religious fanaticism; or rather, we might say, Eli's performance of religious fanaticism (in the form of Hasidic dress) confers upon him the identity of fanatic. Not recognizing the difference between essentialism and performativity, Eli's neighbors believe he *is* crazy and treat him accordingly: the men in white remove his dark jacket, inject him with a tranquilizer, and take him away.

Upon initial examination, the first and last texts in ***"Goodbye, Columbus" and Five Short Stories*** end in seemingly opposite places. Like so many American bildungsromans, from William Faulkner's "Barn Burning" to Richard Wright's "The Man Who Was Almost a Man," **"Goodbye, Columbus"** concludes with a young man's departure to an uncertain destination, whereas **"Eli, the Fanatic"** presents the opposite extreme: Eli is trapped, facing incarceration because of his unwillingness to conform. Indeed, Eli's commitment to his fanaticism suggests that he will live out the martyrdom that Ozzie Freedman (who is a freed man, the opposite of an imprisoned one) ultimately stops short of carrying out. And yet paradoxically Eli's rejection of social niceties is itself potentially liberating. In fact freedom—and not just money—is a crucial element of achieving the American Dream. As Lauren Berlant argues, "to be American [. . .] would be to inhabit a secure space liberated from identities and structures that seem to constrain what a person can do in history" (4). In this light, it is worth noting that all the protagonists in this collection chafe against authority and categorization in one way or another; furthermore, each makes his own proverbial separate peace.

Like protagonist, like author: on the thirtieth anniversary of the publication of his first collection, Philip Roth seems just as ambivalent about identification and categorization as he was in 1959. Looking back on his roots, his early works, and his general caginess, Roth says about himself, using the third person "unwittingly, he had activated the ambivalence that was to stimulate his imagination for years to come and establish the grounds for that necessary struggle from which his—no, my—fiction would spring" (Preface xiv). In shifting from third to first person, Roth makes a Nathan Marxist statement of owning himself, ambivalence and all. Perhaps it is the very ambivalence, uncertainty, and fluidity for protagonists and author alike (plus the timeless appeal of a good measure of general nuttiness) that has given ***"Goodbye, Columbus" and Five Short Stories*** and Roth himself their staying power: still resonant, relevant, and crazy after all these years.

Notes

1. Sollors points out that generational strife serves as a metaphor for Americanization: "many motifs of American culture stem from the stresses of adolescence and ethnogenesis (the individual and the collective 'coming of age' after separating from a parent/country), of urbanization, of immigration, and of social mobility" (211).

2. Mary Dearborn observes that "generational conflict is felt by many historians of ethnicity to be the most striking feature of ethnic American identity" (73).

3. Horace Kallen argues, "dress serves not only as a criterion of difference, but as a signal of identification [. . .] a ticket of admission and a sign of belonging" (13).

4. Sollors observes of these situations: "the writer, narrator, or character may begin to resemble a 'chameleon'" (251).

5. Alice Gambrell remarks on this phenomenon of "*multiple* affiliation: serial or simultaneous connections to more than one formation—and in many cases, to competing formations" (24).

Works Cited

Aarons, Victoria. "Is It 'Good-for-the-Jews or No-Good-for-the-Jews?': Philip Roth's Registry of Jewish Consciousness." *Shofar* 19 (2000): 7-18.

Appiah, Kwame Anthony. "African Identities." *Social Postmodernism: Beyond Identity Politics*. Ed. Linda Nicholson and Steven Seidman. Cambridge: Cambridge University Press, 1995. 103-115.

Berlant, Lauren. *The Queen of America Goes to Washington City*. Durham: Duke University Press, 1997.

Burch, Betty Ann. "Us and Them: Personal Reflections on Ethnic Literature." *Immigrant America: European Ethnicity in the United States*. Ed. Timothy Walch. New York: Garland, 1994. 55-62.

Butler, Judith. *Gender Trouble: Feminism and the Subversion of Identity*. New York: Routledge, 1990.

Dearborn, Mary V. *Pocahontas's Daughters: Gender and Ethnicity in American Culture*. New York: Oxford University Press, 1986.

DaCrema, Joseph. "Roth's 'Defender of the Faith.'" *Explicator* 39.1 (1980): 19-20.

Dollimore, Jonathan. *Sexual Dissidence*. New York: Clarendon, 1991.

Fairchild, Henry Pratt. *The Melting-Pot Mistake*. Boston: Little, Brown, and Company, 1926.

Faulkner, William. *Requiem for a Nun*. 1950. New York: Vintage, 1975.

Ferraro, Thomas J. *Ethnic Passages: Literary Immigrants in Twentieth-Century America*. Chicago: University of Chicago Press, 1993.

Gambrell, Alice. *Women Intellectuals, Modernism, and Difference.* Cambridge: Cambridge University Press, 1997.

Kallen, Horace M. *Cultural Pluralism and the American Idea: An Essay in Social Philosophy.* Philadelphia: University of Pennsylvania Press, 1956.

Leeming, David. *James Baldwin: A Biography.* New York: Knopf, 1994.

Marren, Susan Marie. "Passing for American: Establishing American Identity in the Work of James Weldon Johnson, F. Scott Fitzgerald, Nella Larsen and Gertrude Stein." Diss. University of Michigan, 1995.

Ozick, Cynthia. *Art and Ardor.* New York: Knopf, 1983.

Palumbo-Liu, David. "Universalisms and Minority Culture." *differences* 7.1 (1995): 188-208.

Peden, William. "In a Limbo Between Past and Present." *New York Times* 17 May 1959: BR4.

Robbins, Bruce. "The Weird Heights: On Cosmopolitanism, Feeling and Power." *differences* 7.1 (1995): 165-87.

Roth, Philip. *The Counterlife.* New York: Penguin, 1986.

———. *Goodbye, Columbus and Five Short Stories.* 1959. New York: Vintage, 1993.

———. "Preface to the Thirtieth Anniversary Edition." *Goodbye, Columbus and Five Short Stories.* 1959. Boston: Houghton Mifflin, 1989. xi-xiv.

Shaheen, Naseeb. "Binder Unbound, or, How Not to Convert the Jews." *Studies in Short Fiction* 13 (1976): 376-78.

Sollors, Werner. *Beyond Ethnicity: Consent and Descent in American Culture.* New York: Oxford University Press, 1986.

Urgo, Joseph R. *Willa Cather and the Myth of American Migration.* Urbana: University of Illinois Press, 1995.

Wirth-Nesher, Hana. "Resisting Allegory, or Reading 'Eli, the Fanatic' in Tel Aviv." *Prooftexts* 21 (2001): 103-112.

FURTHER READING

Criticism

Gilman, Sander L. "The Fanatic: Philip Roth and Hanif Kureishi Confront Success." *Comparative Literature* 58, no. 2 (spring 2006): 153-69.

> Compares the treatment of fanaticism and religious transformation in Roth's "Eli, the Fanatic" with that in "My Son the Fanatic," a short story by Anglo-Pakistani author Hanif Kureishi.

Milowitz, Steven. *Philip Roth Considered: The Concentrationary Universe of the American Universe.* New York: Garland Publishing, Inc., 2000, 229p.

> Overview of Roth's oeuvre, with interspersed discussions of his short stories.

How to Use This Index

The main references

```
Calvino, Italo
    1923-1985 ....... CLC 5, 8, 11, 22, 33, 39,
                              73; SSC 3, 48
```

list all author entries in the following Thomson Gale Literary Criticism series:

AAL = *Asian American Literature*
BG = *The Beat Generation: A Gale Critical Companion*
BLC = *Black Literature Criticism*
BLCS = *Black Literature Criticism Supplement*
CLC = *Contemporary Literary Criticism*
CLR = *Children's Literature Review*
CMLC = *Classical and Medieval Literature Criticism*
DC = *Drama Criticism*
FL = *Feminism in Literature: A Gale Critical Companion*
GL = *Gothic Literature: A Gale Critical Companion*
HLC = *Hispanic Literature Criticism*
HLCS = *Hispanic Literature Criticism Supplement*
HR = *Harlem Renaissance: A Gale Critical Companion*
LC = *Literature Criticism from 1400 to 1800*
NCLC = *Nineteenth-Century Literature Criticism*
NNAL = *Native North American Literature*
PC = *Poetry Criticism*
SSC = *Short Story Criticism*
TCLC = *Twentieth-Century Literary Criticism*
WLC = *World Literature Criticism, 1500 to the Present*
WLCS = *World Literature Criticism Supplement*

The cross-references

```
See also CA 85-88, 116; CANR 23, 61;
DAM NOV; DLB 196; EW 13; MTCW 1, 2;
RGSF 2; RGWL 2; SFW 4; SSFS 12
```

list all author entries in the following Thomson Gale biographical and literary sources:

AAYA = *Authors & Artists for Young Adults*
AFAW = *African American Writers*
AFW = *African Writers*
AITN = *Authors in the News*
AMW = *American Writers*
AMWR = *American Writers Retrospective Supplement*
AMWS = *American Writers Supplement*
ANW = *American Nature Writers*
AW = *Ancient Writers*
BEST = *Bestsellers*
BPFB = *Beacham's Encyclopedia of Popular Fiction: Biography and Resources*
BRW = *British Writers*
BRWS = *British Writers Supplement*
BW = *Black Writers*
BYA = *Beacham's Guide to Literature for Young Adults*
CA = *Contemporary Authors*
CAAS = *Contemporary Authors Autobiography Series*
CABS = *Contemporary Authors Bibliographical Series*
CAD = *Contemporary American Dramatists*
CANR = *Contemporary Authors New Revision Series*
CAP = *Contemporary Authors Permanent Series*
CBD = *Contemporary British Dramatists*
CCA = *Contemporary Canadian Authors*
CD = *Contemporary Dramatists*
CDALB = *Concise Dictionary of American Literary Biography*

CDALBS = *Concise Dictionary of American Literary Biography Supplement*
CDBLB = *Concise Dictionary of British Literary Biography*
CMW = *St. James Guide to Crime & Mystery Writers*
CN = *Contemporary Novelists*
CP = *Contemporary Poets*
CPW = *Contemporary Popular Writers*
CSW = *Contemporary Southern Writers*
CWD = *Contemporary Women Dramatists*
CWP = *Contemporary Women Poets*
CWRI = *St. James Guide to Children's Writers*
CWW = *Contemporary World Writers*
DA = *DISCovering Authors*
DA3 = *DISCovering Authors 3.0*
DAB = *DISCovering Authors: British Edition*
DAC = *DISCovering Authors: Canadian Edition*
DAM = *DISCovering Authors: Modules*
   DRAM: *Dramatists Module;* **MST:** *Most-studied Authors Module;*
   MULT: *Multicultural Authors Module;* **NOV:** *Novelists Module;*
   POET: *Poets Module;* **POP:** *Popular Fiction and Genre Authors Module*
DFS = *Drama for Students*
DLB = *Dictionary of Literary Biography*
DLBD = *Dictionary of Literary Biography Documentary Series*
DLBY = *Dictionary of Literary Biography Yearbook*
DNFS = *Literature of Developing Nations for Students*
EFS = *Epics for Students*
EXPN = *Exploring Novels*
EXPP = *Exploring Poetry*
EXPS = *Exploring Short Stories*
EW = *European Writers*
FANT = *St. James Guide to Fantasy Writers*
FW = *Feminist Writers*
GFL = *Guide to French Literature,* Beginnings to 1789, 1798 to the Present
GLL = *Gay and Lesbian Literature*
HGG = *St. James Guide to Horror, Ghost & Gothic Writers*
HW = *Hispanic Writers*
IDFW = *International Dictionary of Films and Filmmakers: Writers and Production Artists*
IDTP = *International Dictionary of Theatre: Playwrights*
LAIT = *Literature and Its Times*
LAW = *Latin American Writers*
JRDA = *Junior DISCovering Authors*
MAICYA = *Major Authors and Illustrators for Children and Young Adults*
MAICYAS = *Major Authors and Illustrators for Children and Young Adults Supplement*
MAWW = *Modern American Women Writers*
MJW = *Modern Japanese Writers*
MTCW = *Major 20th-Century Writers*
NCFS = *Nonfiction Classics for Students*
NFS = *Novels for Students*
PAB = *Poets: American and British*
PFS = *Poetry for Students*
RGAL = *Reference Guide to American Literature*
RGEL = *Reference Guide to English Literature*
RGSF = *Reference Guide to Short Fiction*
RGWL = *Reference Guide to World Literature*
RHW = *Twentieth-Century Romance and Historical Writers*
SAAS = *Something about the Author Autobiography Series*
SATA = *Something about the Author*
SFW = *St. James Guide to Science Fiction Writers*
SSFS = *Short Stories for Students*
TCWW = *Twentieth-Century Western Writers*
WLIT = *World Literature and Its Times*
WP = *World Poets*
YABC = *Yesterday's Authors of Books for Children*
YAW = *St. James Guide to Young Adult Writers*

Literary Criticism Series
Cumulative Author Index

20/1631
See Upward, Allen

A/C Cross
See Lawrence, T(homas) E(dward)

A. M.
See Megged, Aharon

Abasiyanik, Sait Faik 1906-1954
See Sait Faik
See also CA 231; CAAE 123

Abbey, Edward 1927-1989 .... **CLC 36, 59; TCLC 160**
See also AAYA 75; AMWS 13; ANW; CA 45-48; CAAS 128; CANR 2, 41, 131; DA3; DLB 256, 275; LATS 1:2; MTCW 2; MTFW 2005; TCWW 1, 2

Abbott, Edwin A. 1838-1926 .... **TCLC 139**
See also DLB 178

Abbott, Lee K(ittredge) 1947- .... **CLC 48**
See also CA 124; CANR 51, 101; DLB 130

Abe, Kobo 1924-1993 ...... **CLC 8, 22, 53, 81; SSC 61; TCLC 131**
See also CA 65-68; CAAS 140; CANR 24, 60; DAM NOV; DFS 14; DLB 182; EWL 3; MJW; MTCW 1, 2; MTFW 2005; NFS 22; RGWL 3; SFW 4

Abe Kobo
See Abe, Kobo

Abelard, Peter c. 1079-c. 1142 ..... **CMLC 11, 77**
See also DLB 115, 208

Abell, Kjeld 1901-1961 .... **CLC 15**
See also CA 191; CAAS 111; DLB 214; EWL 3

Abercrombie, Lascelles 1881-1938 .... **TCLC 141**
See also CAAE 112; DLB 19; RGEL 2

Abish, Walter 1931- .... **CLC 22; SSC 44**
See also CA 101; CANR 37, 114, 153; CN 3, 4, 5, 6; DLB 130, 227; MAL 5; RGHL

Abrahams, Peter (Henry) 1919- .... **CLC 4**
See also AFW; BW 1; CA 57-60; CANR 26, 125; CDWLB 3; CN 1, 2, 3, 4, 5, 6; DLB 117, 225; EWL 3; MTCW 1, 2; RGEL 2; WLIT 2

Abrams, M(eyer) H(oward) 1912- ... **CLC 24**
See also CA 57-60; CANR 13, 33; DLB 67

Abse, Dannie 1923- .... **CLC 7, 29; PC 41**
See also CA 53-56; 1; CANR 4, 46, 74, 124; CBD; CN 1, 2, 3; CP 1, 2, 3, 4, 5, 6, 7; DAB; DAM POET; DLB 27, 245; MTCW 2

Abutsu 1222(?)-1283 .... **CMLC 46**
See Abutsu-ni

Abutsu-ni
See Abutsu
See also DLB 203

Achebe, Albert Chinualumogu
See Achebe, Chinua

Achebe, Chinua 1930- .. **BLC 1; CLC 1, 3, 5, 7, 11, 26, 51, 75, 127, 152; WLC 1**
See also AAYA 15; AFW; BPFB 1; BRWC 2; BW 2, 3; CA 1-4R; CANR 6, 26, 47, 124; CDWLB 3; CLR 20; CN 1, 2, 3, 4, 5, 6, 7; CP 2, 3, 4, 5, 6, 7; CWRI 5; DA; DA3; DAB; DAC; DAM MST, MULT, NOV; DLB 117; DNFS 1; EWL 3; EXPN; EXPS; LAIT 2; LATS 1:2; MAICYA 1, 2; MTCW 1, 2; MTFW 2005; NFS 2; RGEL 2; RGSF 2; SATA 38, 40; SATA-Brief 38; SSFS 3, 13; TWA; WLIT 2; WWE 1

Acker, Kathy 1948-1997 .... **CLC 45, 111; TCLC 191**
See also AMWS 12; CA 122; CAAE 117; CAAS 162; CANR 55; CN 5, 6; MAL 5

Ackroyd, Peter 1949- .... **CLC 34, 52, 140**
See also BRWS 6; CA 127; CAAE 123; CANR 51, 74, 99, 132; CN 4, 5, 6, 7; DLB 155, 231; HGG; INT CA-127; MTCW 2; MTFW 2005; RHW; SATA 153; SUFW 2

Acorn, Milton 1923-1986 .... **CLC 15**
See also CA 103; CCA 1; CP 1, 2, 3, 4; DAC; DLB 53; INT CA-103

Adam de la Halle c. 1250-c. 1285 .... **CMLC 80**

Adamov, Arthur 1908-1970 .... **CLC 4, 25; TCLC 189**
See also CA 17-18; CAAS 25-28R; CAP 2; DAM DRAM; DLB 321; EWL 3; GFL 1789 to the Present; MTCW 1; RGWL 2, 3

Adams, Alice 1926-1999 .... **CLC 6, 13, 46; SSC 24**
See also CA 81-84; CAAS 179; CANR 26, 53, 75, 88, 136; CN 4, 5, 6; CSW; DLB 234; DLBY 1986; INT CANR-26; MTCW 1, 2; MTFW 2005; SSFS 14, 21

Adams, Andy 1859-1935 .... **TCLC 56**
See also TCWW 1, 2; YABC 1

Adams, (Henry) Brooks 1848-1927 .... **TCLC 80**
See also CA 193; CAAE 123

Adams, Douglas 1952-2001 .... **CLC 27, 60**
See also AAYA 4, 33; BEST 89:3; BYA 14; CA 106; CAAS 197; CANR 34, 64, 124; CPW; DA3; DAM POP; DLB 261; DLBY 1983; JRDA; MTCW 2; MTFW 2005; NFS 7; SATA 116; SATA-Obit 128; SFW 4

Adams, Francis 1862-1893 .... **NCLC 33**

Adams, Henry (Brooks) 1838-1918 .... **TCLC 4, 52**
See also AMW; CA 133; CAAE 104; CANR 77; DA; DAB; DAC; DAM MST; DLB 12, 47, 189, 284; EWL 3; MAL 5; MTCW 2; NCFS 1; RGAL 4; TUS

Adams, John 1735-1826 .... **NCLC 106**
See also DLB 31, 183

Adams, John Quincy 1767-1848 .. **NCLC 175**
See also DLB 37

Adams, Mary
See Phelps, Elizabeth Stuart

Adams, Richard (George) 1920- ... **CLC 4, 5, 18**
See also AAYA 16; AITN 1, 2; BPFB 1; BYA 5; CA 49-52; CANR 3, 35, 128; CLR 20, 121; CN 4, 5, 6, 7; DAM NOV; DLB 261; FANT; JRDA; LAIT 5; MAICYA 1, 2; MTCW 1, 2; NFS 11; SATA 7, 69; YAW

Adamson, Joy(-Friederike Victoria) 1910-1980 .... **CLC 17**
See also CA 69-72; CAAS 93-96; CANR 22; MTCW 1; SATA 11; SATA-Obit 22

Adcock, Fleur 1934- .... **CLC 41**
See also BRWS 12; CA 182; 25-28R, 182; 23; CANR 11, 34, 69, 101; CP 1, 2, 3, 4, 5, 6, 7; CWP; DLB 40; FW; WWE 1

Addams, Charles 1912-1988 .... **CLC 30**
See also CA 61-64; CAAS 126; CANR 12, 79

Addams, Charles Samuel
See Addams, Charles

Addams, (Laura) Jane 1860-1935 . **TCLC 76**
See also AMWS 1; CA 194; DLB 303; FW

Addison, Joseph 1672-1719 .... **LC 18**
See also BRW 3; CDBLB 1660-1789; DLB 101; RGEL 2; WLIT 3

Adler, Alfred (F.) 1870-1937 .... **TCLC 61**
See also CA 159; CAAE 119

Adler, C(arole) S(chwerdtfeger) 1932- .... **CLC 35**
See also AAYA 4, 41; CA 89-92; CANR 19, 40, 101; CLR 78; JRDA; MAICYA 1, 2; SAAS 15; SATA 26, 63, 102, 126; YAW

Adler, Renata 1938- .... **CLC 8, 31**
See also CA 49-52; CANR 95; CN 4, 5, 6; MTCW 1

Adorno, Theodor W(iesengrund) 1903-1969 .... **TCLC 111**
See also CA 89-92; CAAS 25-28R; CANR 89; DLB 242; EWL 3

Ady, Endre 1877-1919 .... **TCLC 11**
See also CAAE 107; CDWLB 4; DLB 215; EW 9; EWL 3

A.E. .... **TCLC 3, 10**
See Russell, George William
See also DLB 19

Aelfric c. 955-c. 1010 .... **CMLC 46**
See also DLB 146

Aeschines c. 390B.C.-c. 320B.C. .... **CMLC 47**
See also DLB 176

Aleshkovsky, Yuz .... **CLC 44**
  See Aleshkovsky, Joseph
  See also DLB 317

Alexander, Lloyd 1924-2007 .... **CLC 35**
  See also AAYA 1, 27; BPFB 1; BYA 5, 6,
  7, 9, 10, 11; CA 1-4R; CANR 1, 24, 38,
  55, 113; CLR 1, 5, 48; CWRI 5; DLB 52;
  FANT; JRDA; MAICYA 1, 2; MAICYAS
  1; MTCW 1; SAAS 19; SATA 3, 49, 81,
  129, 135; SUFW; TUS; WYA; YAW

Alexander, Lloyd Chudley
  See Alexander, Lloyd

Alexander, Meena 1951- .... **CLC 121**
  See also CA 115; CANR 38, 70, 146; CP 5,
  6, 7; CWP; DLB 323; FW

Alexander, Samuel 1859-1938 .... **TCLC 77**

Alexeiev, Konstantin
  See Stanislavsky, Constantin

Alexeyev, Constantin Sergeivich
  See Stanislavsky, Constantin

Alexeyev, Konstantin Sergeyevich
  See Stanislavsky, Constantin

Alexie, Sherman 1966- .... **CLC 96, 154;**
  NNAL; PC 53
    See also AAYA 28; BYA 15; CA 138;
    CANR 65, 95, 133; CN 7; DA3; DAM
    MULT; DLB 175, 206, 278; LATS 1:2;
    MTCW 2; MTFW 2005; NFS 17; SSFS
    18

al-Farabi 870(?)-950 .... **CMLC 58**
  See also DLB 115

Alfau, Felipe 1902-1999 .... **CLC 66**
  See also CA 137

Alfieri, Vittorio 1749-1803 .... **NCLC 101**
  See also EW 4; RGWL 2, 3; WLIT 7

Alfonso X 1221-1284 .... **CMLC 78**

Alfred, Jean Gaston
  See Ponge, Francis

Alger, Horatio, Jr. 1832-1899 .... **NCLC 8, 83**
  See also CLR 87; DLB 42; LAIT 2; RGAL
  4; SATA 16; TUS

Al-Ghazali, Muhammad ibn Muhammad
  1058-1111 .... **CMLC 50**
  See also DLB 115

Algren, Nelson 1909-1981 ..... **CLC 4, 10, 33;**
  SSC 33
    See also AMWS 9; BPFB 1; CA 13-16R;
    CAAS 103; CANR 20, 61; CDALB 1941-
    1968; CN 1, 2; DLB 9; DLBY 1981,
    1982, 2000; EWL 3; MAL 5; MTCW 1,
    2; MTFW 2005; RGAL 4; RGSF 2

al-Hariri, al-Qasim ibn 'Ali Abu
  Muhammad al-Basri
  1054-1122 .... **CMLC 63**
  See also RGWL 3

Ali, Ahmed 1908-1998 .... **CLC 69**
  See also CA 25-28R; CANR 15, 34; CN 1,
  2, 3, 4, 5; DLB 323; EWL 3

Ali, Tariq 1943- .... **CLC 173**
  See also CA 25-28R; CANR 10, 99, 161

Alighieri, Dante
  See Dante
  See also WLIT 7

al-Kindi, Abu Yusuf Ya'qub ibn Ishaq c.
  801-c. 873 .... **CMLC 80**

Allan, John B.
  See Westlake, Donald E.

Allan, Sidney
  See Hartmann, Sadakichi

Allan, Sydney
  See Hartmann, Sadakichi

Allard, Janet .... **CLC 59**

Allen, Edward 1948- .... **CLC 59**

Allen, Fred 1894-1956 .... **TCLC 87**

Allen, Paula Gunn 1939- .... **CLC 84, 202;**
  NNAL
    See also AMWS 4; CA 143; CAAE 112;
    CANR 63, 130; CWP; DA3; DAM
    MULT; DLB 175; FW; MTCW 2; MTFW
    2005; RGAL 4; TCWW 2

Allen, Roland
  See Ayckbourn, Alan

Allen, Sarah A.
  See Hopkins, Pauline Elizabeth

Allen, Sidney H.
  See Hartmann, Sadakichi

Allen, Woody 1935- .... **CLC 16, 52, 195**
  See also AAYA 10, 51; AMWS 15; CA 33-
  36R; CANR 27, 38, 63, 128; DAM POP;
  DLB 44; MTCW 1; SSFS 21

Allende, Isabel 1942- ... **CLC 39, 57, 97, 170;**
  HLC 1; SSC 65; WLCS
    See also AAYA 18, 70; CA 130; CAAE 125;
    CANR 51, 74, 129; CDWLB 3; CLR 99;
    CWW 2; DA3; DAM MULT, NOV; DLB
    145; DNFS 1; EWL 3; FL 1:5; FW; HW
    1, 2; INT CA-130; LAIT 5; LAWS 1;
    LMFS 2; MTCW 1, 2; MTFW 2005;
    NCFS 1; NFS 6, 18; RGSF 2; RGWL 3;
    SATA 163; SSFS 11, 16; WLIT 1

Alleyn, Ellen
  See Rossetti, Christina

Alleyne, Carla D. .... **CLC 65**

Allingham, Margery (Louise)
  1904-1966 .... **CLC 19**
  See also CA 5-8R; CAAS 25-28R; CANR
  4, 58; CMW 4; DLB 77; MSW; MTCW
  1, 2

Allingham, William 1824-1889 ...... **NCLC 25**
  See also DLB 35; RGEL 2

Allison, Dorothy E. 1949- .... **CLC 78, 153**
  See also AAYA 53; CA 140; CANR 66, 107;
  CN 7; CSW; DA3; FW; MTCW 2; MTFW
  2005; NFS 11; RGAL 4

Alloula, Malek .... **CLC 65**

Allston, Washington 1779-1843 .... **NCLC 2**
  See also DLB 1, 235

Almedingen, E. M. .... **CLC 12**
  See Almedingen, Martha Edith von
  See also SATA 3

Almedingen, Martha Edith von 1898-1971
  See Almedingen, E. M.
  See also CA 1-4R; CANR 1

Almodovar, Pedro 1949(?)- .... **CLC 114, 229;**
  HLCS 1
    See also CA 133; CANR 72, 151; HW 2

Almqvist, Carl Jonas Love
  1793-1866 .... **NCLC 42**

al-Mutanabbi, Ahmad ibn al-Husayn Abu
  al-Tayyib al-Jufi al-Kindi
  915-965 .... **CMLC 66**
  See Mutanabbi, Al-
  See also RGWL 3

Alonso, Damaso 1898-1990 .... **CLC 14**
  See also CA 131; CAAE 110; CAAS 130;
  CANR 72; DLB 108; EWL 3; HW 1, 2

Alov
  See Gogol, Nikolai (Vasilyevich)

al'Sadaawi, Nawal
  See El Saadawi, Nawal
  See also FW

al-Shaykh, Hanan 1945- .... **CLC 218**
  See Shaykh, al- Hanan
  See also CA 135; CANR 111; WLIT 6

Al Siddik
  See Rolfe, Frederick (William Serafino Aus-
  tin Lewis Mary)
  See also GLL 1; RGEL 2

Alta 1942- .... **CLC 19**
  See also CA 57-60

Alter, Robert B. 1935- .... **CLC 34**
  See also CA 49-52; CANR 1, 47, 100, 160

Alter, Robert Bernard
  See Alter, Robert B.

Alther, Lisa 1944- .... **CLC 7, 41**
  See also BPFB 1; CA 65-68; 30; CANR 12,
  30, 51; CN 4, 5, 6, 7; CSW; GLL 2;
  MTCW 1

Althusser, L.
  See Althusser, Louis

Althusser, Louis 1918-1990 .... **CLC 106**
  See also CA 131; CAAS 132; CANR 102;
  DLB 242

Altman, Robert 1925-2006 .... **CLC 16, 116**
  See also CA 73-76; CAAS 254; CANR 43

Alurista .... **HLCS 1; PC 34**
  See Urista (Heredia), Alberto (Baltazar)
  See also CA 45-48R; DLB 82; LLW

Alvarez, A. 1929- .... **CLC 5, 13**
  See also CA 1-4R; CANR 3, 33, 63, 101,
  134; CN 3, 4, 5, 6; CP 1, 2, 3, 4, 5, 6, 7;
  DLB 14, 40; MTFW 2005

Alvarez, Alejandro Rodriguez 1903-1965
  See Casona, Alejandro
  See also CA 131; CAAS 93-96; HW 1

Alvarez, Julia 1950- .... **CLC 93; HLCS 1**
  See also AAYA 25; AMWS 7; CA 147;
  CANR 69, 101, 133; DA3; DLB 282;
  LATS 1:2; LLW; MTCW 2; MTFW 2005;
  NFS 5, 9; SATA 129; WLIT 1

Alvaro, Corrado 1896-1956 .... **TCLC 60**
  See also CA 163; DLB 264; EWL 3

Amado, Jorge 1912-2001 ... **CLC 13, 40, 106,**
  232; HLC 1
    See also CA 77-80; CAAS 201; CANR 35,
    74, 135; CWW 2; DAM MULT, NOV;
    DLB 113, 307; EWL 3; HW 2; LAW;
    LAWS 1; MTCW 1, 2; MTFW 2005;
    RGWL 2, 3; TWA; WLIT 1

Ambler, Eric 1909-1998 .... **CLC 4, 6, 9**
  See also BRWS 4; CA 9-12R; CAAS 171;
  CANR 7, 38, 74; CMW 4; CN 1, 2, 3, 4,
  5, 6; DLB 77; MSW; MTCW 1, 2; TEA

Ambrose, Stephen E. 1936-2002 ... **CLC 145**
  See also AAYA 44; CA 1-4R; CAAS 209;
  CANR 3, 43, 57, 83, 105; MTFW 2005;
  NCFS 2; SATA 40, 138

Amichai, Yehuda 1924-2000 .. **CLC 9, 22, 57,**
  116; PC 38
    See also CA 85-88; CAAS 189; CANR 46,
    60, 99, 132; CWW 2; EWL 3; MTCW 1,
    2; MTFW 2005; PFS 24; RGHL; WLIT 6

Amichai, Yehudah
  See Amichai, Yehuda

Amiel, Henri Frederic 1821-1881 .... **NCLC 4**
  See also DLB 217

Amis, Kingsley 1922-1995 . **CLC 1, 2, 3, 5, 8,**
  13, 40, 44, 129
    See also AITN 2; BPFB 1; BRWS 2; CA
    9-12R; CAAS 150; CANR 8, 28, 54; CD-
    BLB 1945-1960; CN 1, 2, 3, 4, 5, 6; CP
    1, 2, 3, 4; DA; DA3; DAB; DAC; DAM
    MST, NOV; DLB 15, 27, 100, 139, 326;
    DLBY 1996; EWL 3; HGG; INT
    CANR-8; MTCW 1, 2; MTFW 2005;
    RGEL 2; RGSF 2; SFW 4

Amis, Martin 1949- ... **CLC 4, 9, 38, 62, 101,**
  213
    See also BEST 90:3; BRWS 4; CA 65-68;
    CANR 8, 27, 54, 73, 95, 132; CN 5, 6, 7;
    DA3; DLB 14, 194; EWL 3; INT CANR-
    27; MTCW 2; MTFW 2005

Ammianus Marcellinus c. 330-c.
  395 .... **CMLC 60**
  See also AW 2; DLB 211

Ammons, A.R. 1926-2001 .. **CLC 2, 3, 5, 8, 9,**
  25, 57, 108; PC 16
    See also AITN 1; AMWS 7; CA 9-12R;
    CAAS 193; CANR 6, 36, 51, 73, 107,
    156; CP 1, 2, 3, 4, 5, 6, 7; CSW; DAM
    POET; DLB 5, 165; EWL 3; MAL 5;
    MTCW 1, 2; PFS 19; RGAL 4; TCLE 1:1

Ammons, Archie Randolph
  See Ammons, A.R.

Amo, Tauraatua i
  See Adams, Henry (Brooks)

Amory, Thomas 1691(?)-1788 .... **LC 48**
  See also DLB 39

Aragon, Louis 1897-1982 .... **CLC 3, 22; TCLC 123**
See also CA 69-72; CAAS 108; CANR 28, 71; DAM NOV, POET; DLB 72, 258; EW 11; EWL 3; GFL 1789 to the Present; GLL 2; LMFS 2; MTCW 1, 2; RGWL 2, 3

Arany, Janos 1817-1882 .... **NCLC 34**

Aranyos, Kakay 1847-1910
See Mikszath, Kalman

Aratus of Soli c. 315B.C.-c. 240B.C. .... **CMLC 64**
See also DLB 176

Arbuthnot, John 1667-1735 .... **LC 1**
See also DLB 101

Archer, Herbert Winslow
See Mencken, H(enry) L(ouis)

Archer, Jeffrey 1940- .... **CLC 28**
See also AAYA 16; BEST 89:3; BPFB 1; CA 77-80; CANR 22, 52, 95, 136; CPW; DA3; DAM POP; INT CANR-22; MTFW 2005

Archer, Jeffrey Howard
See Archer, Jeffrey

Archer, Jules 1915- .... **CLC 12**
See also CA 9-12R; CANR 6, 69; SAAS 5; SATA 4, 85

Archer, Lee
See Ellison, Harlan

Archilochus c. 7th cent. B.C.- .... **CMLC 44**
See also DLB 176

Arden, John 1930- .... **CLC 6, 13, 15**
See also BRWS 2; CA 13-16R; 4; CANR 31, 65, 67, 124; CBD; CD 5, 6; DAM DRAM; DFS 9; DLB 13, 245; EWL 3; MTCW 1

Arenas, Reinaldo 1943-1990 .. **CLC 41; HLC 1; TCLC 191**
See also CA 128; CAAE 124; CAAS 133; CANR 73, 106; DAM MULT; DLB 145; EWL 3; GLL 2; HW 1; LAW; LAWS 1; MTCW 2; MTFW 2005; RGSF 2; RGWL 3; WLIT 1

Arendt, Hannah 1906-1975 .... **CLC 66, 98**
See also CA 17-20R; CAAS 61-64; CANR 26, 60; DLB 242; MTCW 1, 2

Aretino, Pietro 1492-1556 .... **LC 12**
See also RGWL 2, 3

Arghezi, Tudor .... **CLC 80**
See Theodorescu, Ion N.
See also CA 167; CDWLB 4; DLB 220; EWL 3

Arguedas, Jose Maria 1911-1969 .... **CLC 10, 18; HLCS 1; TCLC 147**
See also CA 89-92; CANR 73; DLB 113; EWL 3; HW 1; LAW; RGWL 2, 3; WLIT 1

Argueta, Manlio 1936- .... **CLC 31**
See also CA 131; CANR 73; CWW 2; DLB 145; EWL 3; HW 1; RGWL 3

Arias, Ron 1941- .... **HLC 1**
See also CA 131; CANR 81, 136; DAM MULT; DLB 82; HW 1, 2; MTCW 2; MTFW 2005

Ariosto, Lodovico
See Ariosto, Ludovico
See also WLIT 7

Ariosto, Ludovico 1474-1533 ... **LC 6, 87; PC 42**
See Ariosto, Lodovico
See also EW 2; RGWL 2, 3

Aristides
See Epstein, Joseph

Aristophanes 450B.C.-385B.C. .... **CMLC 4, 51; DC 2; WLCS**
See also AW 1; CDWLB 1; DA; DA3; DAB; DAC; DAM DRAM, MST; DFS 10; DLB 176; LMFS 1; RGWL 2, 3; TWA; WLIT 8

Aristotle 384B.C.-322B.C. .... **CMLC 31; WLCS**
See also AW 1; CDWLB 1; DA; DA3; DAB; DAC; DAM MST; DLB 176; RGWL 2, 3; TWA; WLIT 8

Arlt, Roberto (Godofredo Christophersen) 1900-1942 .... **HLC 1; TCLC 29**
See also CA 131; CAAE 123; CANR 67; DAM MULT; DLB 305; EWL 3; HW 1, 2; IDTP; LAW

Armah, Ayi Kwei 1939- . **BLC 1; CLC 5, 33, 136**
See also AFW; BRWS 10; BW 1; CA 61-64; CANR 21, 64; CDWLB 3; CN 1, 2, 3, 4, 5, 6, 7; DAM MULT, POET; DLB 117; EWL 3; MTCW 1; WLIT 2

Armatrading, Joan 1950- .... **CLC 17**
See also CA 186; CAAE 114

Armin, Robert 1568(?)-1615(?) .... **LC 120**

Armitage, Frank
See Carpenter, John (Howard)

Armstrong, Jeannette (C.) 1948- .... **NNAL**
See also CA 149; CCA 1; CN 6, 7; DAC; DLB 334; SATA 102

Arnette, Robert
See Silverberg, Robert

Arnim, Achim von (Ludwig Joachim von Arnim) 1781-1831 .. **NCLC 5, 159; SSC 29**
See also DLB 90

Arnim, Bettina von 1785-1859 ...... **NCLC 38, 123**
See also DLB 90; RGWL 2, 3

Arnold, Matthew 1822-1888 ..... **NCLC 6, 29, 89, 126; PC 5; WLC 1**
See also BRW 5; CDBLB 1832-1890; DA; DAB; DAC; DAM MST, POET; DLB 32, 57; EXPP; PAB; PFS 2; TEA; WP

Arnold, Thomas 1795-1842 .... **NCLC 18**
See also DLB 55

Arnow, Harriette (Louisa) Simpson 1908-1986 .... **CLC 2, 7, 18**
See also BPFB 1; CA 9-12R; CAAS 118; CANR 14; CN 2, 3, 4; DLB 6; FW; MTCW 1, 2; RHW; SATA 42; SATA-Obit 47

Arouet, Francois-Marie
See Voltaire

Arp, Hans
See Arp, Jean

Arp, Jean 1887-1966 .... **CLC 5; TCLC 115**
See also CA 81-84; CAAS 25-28R; CANR 42, 77; EW 10

Arrabal
See Arrabal, Fernando

Arrabal (Teran), Fernando
See Arrabal, Fernando
See also CWW 2

Arrabal, Fernando 1932- ... **CLC 2, 9, 18, 58**
See Arrabal (Teran), Fernando
See also CA 9-12R; CANR 15; DLB 321; EWL 3; LMFS 2

Arreola, Juan Jose 1918-2001 .... **CLC 147; HLC 1; SSC 38**
See also CA 131; CAAE 113; CAAS 200; CANR 81; CWW 2; DAM MULT; DLB 113; DNFS 2; EWL 3; HW 1, 2; LAW; RGSF 2

Arrian c. 89(?)-c. 155(?) .... **CMLC 43**
See also DLB 176

Arrick, Fran .... **CLC 30**
See Gaberman, Judie Angell
See also BYA 6

Arrley, Richmond
See Delany, Samuel R., Jr.

Artaud, Antonin (Marie Joseph) 1896-1948 .... **DC 14; TCLC 3, 36**
See also CA 149; CAAE 104; DA3; DAM DRAM; DFS 22; DLB 258, 321; EW 11; EWL 3; GFL 1789 to the Present; MTCW 2; MTFW 2005; RGWL 2, 3

Arthur, Ruth M(abel) 1905-1979 ..... **CLC 12**
See also CA 9-12R; CAAS 85-88; CANR 4; CWRI 5; SATA 7, 26

Artsybashev, Mikhail (Petrovich) 1878-1927 .... **TCLC 31**
See also CA 170; DLB 295

Arundel, Honor (Morfydd) 1919-1973 .... **CLC 17**
See also CA 21-22; CAAS 41-44R; CAP 2; CLR 35; CWRI 5; SATA 4; SATA-Obit 24

Arzner, Dorothy 1900-1979 .... **CLC 98**

Asch, Sholem 1880-1957 .... **TCLC 3**
See also CAAE 105; DLB 333; EWL 3; GLL 2; RGHL

Ascham, Roger 1516(?)-1568 .... **LC 101**
See also DLB 236

Ash, Shalom
See Asch, Sholem

Ashbery, John 1927- ... **CLC 2, 3, 4, 6, 9, 13, 15, 25, 41, 77, 125, 221; PC 26**
See Berry, Jonas
See also AMWS 3; CA 5-8R; CANR 9, 37, 66, 102, 132; CP 1, 2, 3, 4, 5, 6, 7; DA3; DAM POET; DLB 5, 165; DLBY 1981; EWL 3; INT CANR-9; MAL 5; MTCW 1, 2; MTFW 2005; PAB; PFS 11; RGAL 4; TCLE 1:1; WP

Ashdown, Clifford
See Freeman, R(ichard) Austin

Ashe, Gordon
See Creasey, John

Ashton-Warner, Sylvia (Constance) 1908-1984 .... **CLC 19**
See also CA 69-72; CAAS 112; CANR 29; CN 1, 2, 3; MTCW 1, 2

Asimov, Isaac 1920-1992 ..... **CLC 1, 3, 9, 19, 26, 76, 92**
See also AAYA 13; BEST 90:2; BPFB 1; BYA 4, 6, 7, 9; CA 1-4R; CAAS 137; CANR 2, 19, 36, 60, 125; CLR 12, 79; CMW 4; CN 1, 2, 3, 4, 5; CPW; DA3; DAM POP; DLB 8; DLBY 1992; INT CANR-19; JRDA; LAIT 5; LMFS 2; MAICYA 1, 2; MAL 5; MTCW 1, 2; MTFW 2005; RGAL 4; SATA 1, 26, 74; SCFW 1, 2; SFW 4; SSFS 17; TUS; YAW

Askew, Anne 1521(?)-1546 .... **LC 81**
See also DLB 136

Assis, Joaquim Maria Machado de
See Machado de Assis, Joaquim Maria

Astell, Mary 1666-1731 .... **LC 68**
See also DLB 252, 336; FW

Astley, Thea (Beatrice May) 1925-2004 .... **CLC 41**
See also CA 65-68; CAAS 229; CANR 11, 43, 78; CN 1, 2, 3, 4, 5, 6, 7; DLB 289; EWL 3

Astley, William 1855-1911
See Warung, Price

Aston, James
See White, T(erence) H(anbury)

Asturias, Miguel Angel 1899-1974 .... **CLC 3, 8, 13; HLC 1; TCLC 184**
See also CA 25-28; CAAS 49-52; CANR 32; CAP 2; CDWLB 3; DA3; DAM MULT, NOV; DLB 113, 290, 329; EWL 3; HW 1; LAW; LMFS 2; MTCW 1, 2; RGWL 2, 3; WLIT 1

Atares, Carlos Saura
See Saura (Atares), Carlos

Bagryana, Elisaveta .... **CLC 10**
See Belcheva, Elisaveta Lyubomirova
See also CA 178; CDWLB 4; DLB 147;
EWL 3

Bailey, Paul 1937- .... **CLC 45**
See also CA 21-24R; CANR 16, 62, 124;
CN 1, 2, 3, 4, 5, 6, 7; DLB 14, 271; GLL
2

Baillie, Joanna 1762-1851 ...... **NCLC 71, 151**
See also DLB 93; GL 2; RGEL 2

Bainbridge, Beryl 1934- ...... **CLC 4, 5, 8, 10,
14, 18, 22, 62, 130**
See also BRWS 6; CA 21-24R; CANR 24,
55, 75, 88, 128; CN 2, 3, 4, 5, 6, 7; DAM
NOV; DLB 14, 231; EWL 3; MTCW 1,
2; MTFW 2005

Baker, Carlos (Heard)
1909-1987 .... **TCLC 119**
See also CA 5-8R; CAAS 122; CANR 3,
63; DLB 103

Baker, Elliott 1922-2007 .... **CLC 8**
See also CA 45-48; CAAS 257; CANR 2,
63; CN 1, 2, 3, 4, 5, 6, 7

Baker, Elliott Joseph
See Baker, Elliott

Baker, Jean H. .... **TCLC 3, 10**
See Russell, George William

Baker, Nicholson 1957- .... **CLC 61, 165**
See also AMWS 13; CA 135; CANR 63,
120, 138; CN 6; CPW; DA3; DAM POP;
DLB 227; MTFW 2005

Baker, Ray Stannard 1870-1946 .... **TCLC 47**
See also CAAE 118

Baker, Russell 1925- .... **CLC 31**
See also BEST 89:4; CA 57-60; CANR 11,
41, 59, 137; MTCW 1, 2; MTFW 2005

Bakhtin, M.
See Bakhtin, Mikhail Mikhailovich

Bakhtin, M. M.
See Bakhtin, Mikhail Mikhailovich

Bakhtin, Mikhail
See Bakhtin, Mikhail Mikhailovich

Bakhtin, Mikhail Mikhailovich
1895-1975 .... **CLC 83; TCLC 160**
See also CA 128; CAAS 113; DLB 242;
EWL 3

Bakshi, Ralph 1938(?)- .... **CLC 26**
See also CA 138; CAAE 112; IDFW 3

Bakunin, Mikhail (Alexandrovich)
1814-1876 .... **NCLC 25, 58**
See also DLB 277

Baldwin, James 1924-1987 ... **BLC 1; CLC 1,
2, 3, 4, 5, 8, 13, 15, 17, 42, 50, 67, 90,
127; DC 1; SSC 10, 33, 98; WLC 1**
See also AAYA 4, 34; AFAW 1, 2; AMWR
2; AMWS 1; BPFB 1; BW 1; CA 1-4R;
CAAS 124; CABS 1; CAD; CANR 3, 24;
CDALB 1941-1968; CN 1, 2, 3, 4; CPW;
DA; DA3; DAB; DAC; DAM MST,
MULT, NOV, POP; DFS 11, 15; DLB 2,
7, 33, 249, 278; DLBY 1987; EWL 3;
EXPS; LAIT 5; MAL 5; MTCW 1, 2;
MTFW 2005; NCFS 4; NFS 4; RGAL 4;
RGSF 2; SATA 9; SATA-Obit 54; SSFS
2, 18; TUS

Baldwin, William c. 1515-1563 .... **LC 113**
See also DLB 132

Bale, John 1495-1563 .... **LC 62**
See also DLB 132; RGEL 2; TEA

Ball, Hugo 1886-1927 .... **TCLC 104**

Ballard, J.G. 1930- .... **CLC 3, 6, 14, 36, 137;
SSC 1, 53**
See also AAYA 3, 52; BRWS 5; CA 5-8R;
CANR 15, 39, 65, 107, 133; CN 1, 2, 3,
4, 5, 6, 7; DA3; DAM NOV, POP; DLB
14, 207, 261, 319; EWL 3; HGG; MTCW
1, 2; MTFW 2005; NFS 8; RGEL 2;
RGSF 2; SATA 93; SCFW 1, 2; SFW 4

Balmont, Konstantin (Dmitriyevich)
1867-1943 .... **TCLC 11**
See also CA 155; CAAE 109; DLB 295;
EWL 3

Baltausis, Vincas 1847-1910
See Mikszath, Kalman

Balzac, Honore de 1799-1850 ... **NCLC 5, 35,
53, 153; SSC 5, 59, 102; WLC 1**
See also DA; DA3; DAB; DAC; DAM
MST, NOV; DLB 119; EW 5; GFL 1789
to the Present; LMFS 1; RGSF 2; RGWL
2, 3; SSFS 10; SUFW; TWA

Bambara, Toni Cade 1939-1995 .... **BLC 1;
CLC 19, 88; SSC 35; TCLC 116;
WLCS**
See also AAYA 5, 49; AFAW 2; AMWS 11;
BW 2, 3; BYA 12, 14; CA 29-32R; CAAS
150; CANR 24, 49, 81; CDALBS; DA;
DA3; DAC; DAM MST, MULT; DLB 38,
218; EXPS; MAL 5; MTCW 1, 2; MTFW
2005; RGAL 4; RGSF 2; SATA 112; SSFS
4, 7, 12, 21

Bamdad, A.
See Shamlu, Ahmad

Bamdad, Alef
See Shamlu, Ahmad

Banat, D. R.
See Bradbury, Ray

Bancroft, Laura
See Baum, L(yman) Frank

Banim, John 1798-1842 .... **NCLC 13**
See also DLB 116, 158, 159; RGEL 2

Banim, Michael 1796-1874 .... **NCLC 13**
See also DLB 158, 159

Banjo, The
See Paterson, A(ndrew) B(arton)

Banks, Iain
See Banks, Iain M.
See also BRWS 11

Banks, Iain M. 1954- .... **CLC 34**
See Banks, Iain
See also CA 128; CAAE 123; CANR 61,
106; DLB 194, 261; EWL 3; HGG; INT
CA-128; MTFW 2005; SFW 4

Banks, Iain Menzies
See Banks, Iain M.

Banks, Lynne Reid .... **CLC 23**
See Reid Banks, Lynne
See also AAYA 6; BYA 7; CLR 86; CN 4,
5, 6

Banks, Russell 1940- . **CLC 37, 72, 187; SSC
42**
See also AAYA 45; AMWS 5; CA 65-68;
15; CANR 19, 52, 73, 118; CN 4, 5, 6, 7;
DLB 130, 278; EWL 3; MAL 5; MTCW
2; MTFW 2005; NFS 13

Banville, John 1945- .... **CLC 46, 118, 224**
See also CA 128; CAAE 117; CANR 104,
150; CN 4, 5, 6, 7; DLB 14, 271, 326;
INT CA-128

Banville, Theodore (Faullain) de
1832-1891 .... **NCLC 9**
See also DLB 217; GFL 1789 to the Present

Baraka, Amiri 1934- .... **BLC 1; CLC 1, 2, 3,
5, 10, 14, 33, 115, 213; DC 6; PC 4;
WLCS**
See Jones, LeRoi
See also AAYA 63; AFAW 1, 2; AMWS 2;
BW 2, 3; CA 21-24R; CABS 3; CAD;
CANR 27, 38, 61, 133; CD 3, 5, 6;
CDALB 1941-1968; CP 4, 5, 6, 7; CPW;
DA; DA3; DAC; DAM MST, MULT,
POET, POP; DFS 3, 11, 16; DLB 5, 7,
16, 38; DLBD 8; EWL 3; MAL 5; MTCW
1, 2; MTFW 2005; PFS 9; RGAL 4;
TCLE 1:1; TUS; WP

Baratynsky, Evgenii Abramovich
1800-1844 .... **NCLC 103**
See also DLB 205

Barbauld, Anna Laetitia
1743-1825 .... **NCLC 50, 185**
See also DLB 107, 109, 142, 158, 336;
RGEL 2

Barbellion, W. N. P. .... **TCLC 24**
See Cummings, Bruce F(rederick)

Barber, Benjamin R. 1939- .... **CLC 141**
See also CA 29-32R; CANR 12, 32, 64, 119

Barbera, Jack (Vincent) 1945- .... **CLC 44**
See also CA 110; CANR 45

Barbey d'Aurevilly, Jules-Amedee
1808-1889 .... **NCLC 1; SSC 17**
See also DLB 119; GFL 1789 to the Present

Barbour, John c. 1316-1395 .... **CMLC 33**
See also DLB 146

Barbusse, Henri 1873-1935 .... **TCLC 5**
See also CA 154; CAAE 105; DLB 65;
EWL 3; RGWL 2, 3

Barclay, Alexander c. 1475-1552 .... **LC 109**
See also DLB 132

Barclay, Bill
See Moorcock, Michael

Barclay, William Ewert
See Moorcock, Michael

Barea, Arturo 1897-1957 .... **TCLC 14**
See also CA 201; CAAE 111

Barfoot, Joan 1946- .... **CLC 18**
See also CA 105; CANR 141

Barham, Richard Harris
1788-1845 .... **NCLC 77**
See also DLB 159

Baring, Maurice 1874-1945 .... **TCLC 8**
See also CA 168; CAAE 105; DLB 34;
HGG

Baring-Gould, Sabine 1834-1924 ... **TCLC 88**
See also DLB 156, 190

Barker, Clive 1952- .... **CLC 52, 205; SSC 53**
See also AAYA 10, 54; BEST 90:3; BPFB
1; CA 129; CAAE 121; CANR 71, 111,
133; CPW; DA3; DAM POP; DLB 261;
HGG; INT CA-129; MTCW 1, 2; MTFW
2005; SUFW 2

Barker, George Granville
1913-1991 .... **CLC 8, 48; PC 77**
See also CA 9-12R; CAAS 135; CANR 7,
38; CP 1, 2, 3, 4, 5; DAM POET; DLB
20; EWL 3; MTCW 1

Barker, Harley Granville
See Granville-Barker, Harley
See also DLB 10

Barker, Howard 1946- .... **CLC 37**
See also CA 102; CBD; CD 5, 6; DLB 13,
233

Barker, Jane 1652-1732 .... **LC 42, 82**
See also DLB 39, 131

Barker, Pat 1943- .... **CLC 32, 94, 146**
See also BRWS 4; CA 122; CAAE 117;
CANR 50, 101, 148; CN 6, 7; DLB 271,
326; INT CA-122

Barker, Patricia
See Barker, Pat

Barlach, Ernst (Heinrich)
1870-1938 .... **TCLC 84**
See also CA 178; DLB 56, 118; EWL 3

Barlow, Joel 1754-1812 .... **NCLC 23**
See also AMWS 2; DLB 37; RGAL 4

Barnard, Mary (Ethel) 1909- .... **CLC 48**
See also CA 21-22; CAP 2; CP 1

Barnes, Djuna 1892-1982 .... **CLC 3, 4, 8, 11,
29, 127; SSC 3**
See Steptoe, Lydia
See also AMWS 3; CA 9-12R; CAAS 107;
CAD; CANR 16, 55; CN 1, 2; DLB 4, 9, 45; EWL 3; GLL 1; MAL 5;
MTCW 1, 2; MTFW 2005; RGAL 4;
TCLE 1:1; TUS

Barnes, Jim 1933- .... **NNAL**
See also CA 175; 108, 175; 28; DLB 175

Becker, Jurek 1937-1997 .... **CLC 7, 19**
See also CA 85-88; CAAS 157; CANR 60, 117; CWW 2; DLB 75, 299; EWL 3; RGHL

Becker, Walter 1950- .... **CLC 26**

Becket, Thomas a 1118(?)-1170 .... **CMLC 83**

Beckett, Samuel 1906-1989 ... **CLC 1, 2, 3, 4, 6, 9, 10, 11, 14, 18, 29, 57, 59, 83; DC 22; SSC 16, 74; TCLC 145; WLC 1**
See also BRWC 2; BRWR 1; BRWS 1; CA 5-8R; CAAS 130; CANR 33, 61; CBD; CDBLB 1945-1960; CN 1, 2, 3, 4; CP 1, 2, 3, 4; DA; DA3; DAB; DAC; DAM DRAM, MST, NOV; DFS 2, 7, 18; DLB 13, 15, 233, 319, 321, 329; DLBY 1990; EWL 3; GFL 1789 to the Present; LATS 1:2; LMFS 2; MTCW 1, 2; MTFW 2005; RGSF 2; RGWL 2, 3; SSFS 15; TEA; WLIT 4

Beckford, William 1760-1844 .... **NCLC 16**
See also BRW 3; DLB 39, 213; GL 2; HGG; LMFS 1; SUFW

Beckham, Barry (Earl) 1944- .... **BLC 1**
See also BW 1; CA 29-32R; CANR 26, 62; CN 1, 2, 3, 4, 5, 6; DAM MULT; DLB 33

Beckman, Gunnel 1910- .... **CLC 26**
See also CA 33-36R; CANR 15, 114; CLR 25; MAICYA 1, 2; SAAS 9; SATA 6

Becque, Henri 1837-1899 .... **DC 21; NCLC 3**
See also DLB 192; GFL 1789 to the Present

Becquer, Gustavo Adolfo
1836-1870 .... **HLCS 1; NCLC 106**
See also DAM MULT

Beddoes, Thomas Lovell 1803-1849 .. **DC 15; NCLC 3, 154**
See also BRWS 11; DLB 96

Bede c. 673-735 .... **CMLC 20**
See also DLB 146; TEA

Bedford, Denton R. 1907-(?) .... **NNAL**

Bedford, Donald F.
See Fearing, Kenneth (Flexner)

Beecher, Catharine Esther
1800-1878 .... **NCLC 30**
See also DLB 1, 243

Beecher, John 1904-1980 .... **CLC 6**
See also AITN 1; CA 5-8R; CAAS 105; CANR 8; CP 1, 2, 3

Beer, Johann 1655-1700 .... **LC 5**
See also DLB 168

Beer, Patricia 1924- .... **CLC 58**
See also CA 61-64; CAAS 183; CANR 13, 46; CP 1, 2, 3, 4, 5, 6; CWP; DLB 40; FW

Beerbohm, Max
See Beerbohm, (Henry) Max(imilian)

Beerbohm, (Henry) Max(imilian)
1872-1956 .... **TCLC 1, 24**
See also BRWS 2; CA 154; CAAE 104; CANR 79; DLB 34, 100; FANT; MTCW 2

Beer-Hofmann, Richard
1866-1945 .... **TCLC 60**
See also CA 160; DLB 81

Beg, Shemus
See Stephens, James

Begiebing, Robert J(ohn) 1946- .... **CLC 70**
See also CA 122; CANR 40, 88

Begley, Louis 1933- .... **CLC 197**
See also CA 140; CANR 98; DLB 299; RGHL; TCLE 1:1

Behan, Brendan (Francis)
1923-1964 .... **CLC 1, 8, 11, 15, 79**
See also BRWS 2; CA 73-76; CANR 33, 121; CBD; CDBLB 1945-1960; DAM DRAM; DFS 7; DLB 13, 233; EWL 3; MTCW 1, 2

Behn, Aphra 1640(?)-1689 .. **DC 4; LC 1, 30, 42, 135; PC 13; WLC 1**
See also BRWS 3; DA; DA3; DAB; DAC; DAM DRAM, MST, NOV, POET; DFS 16, 24; DLB 39, 80, 131; FW; TEA; WLIT 3

Behrman, S(amuel) N(athaniel)
1893-1973 .... **CLC 40**
See also CA 13-16; CAAS 45-48; CAD; CAP 1; DLB 7, 44; IDFW 3; MAL 5; RGAL 4

Bekederemo, J. P. Clark
See Clark Bekederemo, J.P.
See also CD 6

Belasco, David 1853-1931 .... **TCLC 3**
See also CA 168; CAAE 104; DLB 7; MAL 5; RGAL 4

Belcheva, Elisaveta Lyubomirova
1893-1991 .... **CLC 10**
See Bagryana, Elisaveta

Beldone, Phil "Cheech"
See Ellison, Harlan

Beleno
See Azuela, Mariano

Belinski, Vissarion Grigoryevich
1811-1848 .... **NCLC 5**
See also DLB 198

Belitt, Ben 1911- .... **CLC 22**
See also CA 13-16R; 4; CANR 7, 77; CP 1, 2, 3, 4, 5, 6; DLB 5

Belknap, Jeremy 1744-1798 .... **LC 115**
See also DLB 30, 37

Bell, Gertrude (Margaret Lowthian)
1868-1926 .... **TCLC 67**
See also CA 167; CANR 110; DLB 174

Bell, J. Freeman
See Zangwill, Israel

Bell, James Madison 1826-1902 .... **BLC 1; TCLC 43**
See also BW 1; CA 124; CAAE 122; DAM MULT; DLB 50

Bell, Madison Smartt 1957- ..... **CLC 41, 102, 223**
See also AMWS 10; BPFB 1; CA 183; 111, 183; CANR 28, 54, 73, 134; CN 5, 6, 7; CSW; DLB 218, 278; MTCW 2; MTFW 2005

Bell, Marvin (Hartley) 1937- .... **CLC 8, 31**
See also CA 21-24R; 14; CANR 59, 102; CP 1, 2, 3, 4, 5, 6, 7; DAM POET; DLB 5; MAL 5; MTCW 1; PFS 25

Bell, W. L. D.
See Mencken, H(enry) L(ouis)

Bellamy, Atwood C.
See Mencken, H(enry) L(ouis)

Bellamy, Edward 1850-1898 ..... **NCLC 4, 86, 147**
See also DLB 12; NFS 15; RGAL 4; SFW 4

Belli, Gioconda 1948- .... **HLCS 1**
See also CA 152; CANR 143; CWW 2; DLB 290; EWL 3; RGWL 3

Bellin, Edward J.
See Kuttner, Henry

Bello, Andres 1781-1865 .... **NCLC 131**
See also LAW

Belloc, (Joseph) Hilaire (Pierre Sebastien Rene Swanton) 1870-1953 .... **PC 24; TCLC 7, 18**
See also CA 152; CAAE 106; CLR 102; CWRI 5; DAM POET; DLB 19, 100, 141, 174; EWL 3; MTCW 2; MTFW 2005; SATA 112; WCH; YABC 1

Belloc, Joseph Peter Rene Hilaire
See Belloc, (Joseph) Hilaire (Pierre Sebastien Rene Swanton)

Belloc, Joseph Pierre Hilaire
See Belloc, (Joseph) Hilaire (Pierre Sebastien Rene Swanton)

Belloc, M. A.
See Lowndes, Marie Adelaide (Belloc)

Belloc-Lowndes, Mrs.
See Lowndes, Marie Adelaide (Belloc)

Bellow, Saul 1915-2005 ...... **CLC 1, 2, 3, 6, 8, 10, 13, 15, 25, 33, 34, 63, 79, 190, 200; SSC 14, 101; WLC 1**
See also AITN 2; AMW; AMWC 2; AMWR 2; BEST 89:3; BPFB 1; CA 5-8R; CAAS 238; CANR 29, 53, 95, 132; CDALB 1941-1968; CN 1, 2, 3, 4, 5, 6, 7; DA; DA3; DAB; DAC; DAM MST, NOV, POP; DLB 2, 28, 299, 329; DLBD 3; DLBY 1982; EWL 3; MAL 5; MTCW 1, 2; MTFW 2005; NFS 4, 14; RGAL 4; RGHL; RGSF 2; SSFS 12, 22; TUS

Belser, Reimond Karel Maria de 1929-
See Ruyslinck, Ward
See also CA 152

Bely, Andrey .... **PC 11; TCLC 7**
See Bugayev, Boris Nikolayevich
See also DLB 295; EW 9; EWL 3

Belyi, Andrei
See Bugayev, Boris Nikolayevich
See also RGWL 2, 3

Bembo, Pietro 1470-1547 .... **LC 79**
See also RGWL 2, 3

Benary, Margot
See Benary-Isbert, Margot

Benary-Isbert, Margot 1889-1979 .... **CLC 12**
See also CA 5-8R; CAAS 89-92; CANR 4, 72; CLR 12; MAICYA 1, 2; SATA 2; SATA-Obit 21

Benavente (y Martinez), Jacinto
1866-1954 .... **DC 26; HLCS 1; TCLC 3**
See also CA 131; CAAE 106; CANR 81; DAM DRAM, MULT; DLB 329; EWL 3; GLL 2; HW 1, 2; MTCW 1, 2

Benchley, Peter 1940-2006 .... **CLC 4, 8**
See also AAYA 14; AITN 2; BPFB 1; CA 17-20R; CAAS 248; CANR 12, 35, 66, 115; CPW; DAM NOV, POP; HGG; MTCW 1, 2; MTFW 2005; SATA 3, 89, 164

Benchley, Peter Bradford
See Benchley, Peter

Benchley, Robert (Charles)
1889-1945 .... **TCLC 1, 55**
See also CA 153; CAAE 105; DLB 11; MAL 5; RGAL 4

Benda, Julien 1867-1956 .... **TCLC 60**
See also CA 154; CAAE 120; GFL 1789 to the Present

Benedict, Ruth 1887-1948 .... **TCLC 60**
See also CA 158; CANR 146; DLB 246

Benedict, Ruth Fulton
See Benedict, Ruth

Benedikt, Michael 1935- .... **CLC 4, 14**
See also CA 13-16R; CANR 7; CP 1, 2, 3, 4, 5, 6, 7; DLB 5

Benet, Juan 1927-1993 .... **CLC 28**
See also CA 143; EWL 3

Benet, Stephen Vincent 1898-1943 ..... **PC 64; SSC 10, 86; TCLC 7**
See also AMWS 11; CA 152; CAAE 104; DA3; DAM POET; DLB 4, 48, 102, 249, 284; DLBY 1997; EWL 3; HGG; MAL 5; MTCW 2; MTFW 2005; RGAL 4; RGSF 2; SSFS 22; SUFW; WP; YABC 1

Benet, William Rose 1886-1950 ..... **TCLC 28**
See also CA 152; CAAE 118; DAM POET; DLB 45; RGAL 4

Benford, Gregory 1941- .... **CLC 52**
See also BPFB 1; CA 175; 69-72, 175; 27; CANR 12, 24, 49, 95, 134; CN 7; CSW; DLBY 1982; MTFW 2005; SCFW 2; SFW 4

Benford, Gregory Albert
See Benford, Gregory

Beti, Mongo .... **BLC 1; CLC 27**
See Biyidi, Alexandre
See also AFW; CANR 79; DAM MULT;
EWL 3; WLIT 2

Betjeman, John 1906-1984 ...... **CLC 2, 6, 10, 34, 43; PC 75**
See also BRW 7; CA 9-12R; CAAS 112;
CANR 33, 56; CDBLB 1945-1960; CP 1,
2, 3; DA3; DAB; DAM MST, POET;
DLB 20; DLBY 1984; EWL 3; MTCW 1,
2

Bettelheim, Bruno 1903-1990 .... **CLC 79; TCLC 143**
See also CA 81-84; CAAS 131; CANR 23,
61; DA3; MTCW 1, 2; RGHL

Betti, Ugo 1892-1953 .... **TCLC 5**
See also CA 155; CAAE 104; EWL 3;
RGWL 2, 3

Betts, Doris (Waugh) 1932- ..... **CLC 3, 6, 28; SSC 45**
See also CA 13-16R; CANR 9, 66, 77; CN
6, 7; CSW; DLB 218; DLBY 1982; INT
CANR-9; RGAL 4

Bevan, Alistair
See Roberts, Keith (John Kingston)

Bey, Pilaff
See Douglas, (George) Norman

Bialik, Chaim Nachman
1873-1934 .... **TCLC 25**
See Bialik, Hayyim Nahman
See also CA 170; EWL 3

Bialik, Hayyim Nahman
See Bialik, Chaim Nachman
See also WLIT 6

Bickerstaff, Isaac
See Swift, Jonathan

Bidart, Frank 1939- .... **CLC 33**
See also AMWS 15; CA 140; CANR 106;
CP 5, 6, 7

Bienek, Horst 1930- .... **CLC 7, 11**
See also CA 73-76; DLB 75

Bierce, Ambrose (Gwinett)
1842-1914(?) ..... **SSC 9, 72; TCLC 1, 7, 44; WLC 1**
See also AAYA 55; AMW; BYA 11; CA
139; CAAE 104; CANR 78; CDALB
1865-1917; DA; DA3; DAC; DAM MST;
DLB 11, 12, 23, 71, 74, 186; EWL 3;
EXPS; HGG; LAIT 2; MAL 5; RGAL 4;
RGSF 2; SSFS 9; SUFW 1

Biggers, Earl Derr 1884-1933 .... **TCLC 65**
See also CA 153; CAAE 108; DLB 306

Billiken, Bud
See Motley, Willard (Francis)

Billings, Josh
See Shaw, Henry Wheeler

Billington, (Lady) Rachel (Mary)
1942- .... **CLC 43**
See also AITN 2; CA 33-36R; CANR 44;
CN 4, 5, 6, 7

Binchy, Maeve 1940- .... **CLC 153**
See also BEST 90:1; BPFB 1; CA 134;
CAAE 127; CANR 50, 96, 134; CN 5, 6,
7; CPW; DA3; DAM POP; DLB 319; INT
CA-134; MTCW 2; MTFW 2005; RHW

Binyon, T(imothy) J(ohn)
1936-2004 .... **CLC 34**
See also CA 111; CAAS 232; CANR 28,
140

Bion 335B.C.-245B.C. .... **CMLC 39**

Bioy Casares, Adolfo 1914-1999 ... **CLC 4, 8, 13, 88; HLC 1; SSC 17, 102**
See Casares, Adolfo Bioy; Miranda, Javier;
Sacastru, Martin
See also CA 29-32R; CAAS 177; CANR
19, 43, 66; CWW 2; DAM MULT; DLB
113; EWL 3; HW 1, 2; LAW; MTCW 1,
2; MTFW 2005

Birch, Allison .... **CLC 65**

Bird, Cordwainer
See Ellison, Harlan

Bird, Robert Montgomery
1806-1854 .... **NCLC 1**
See also DLB 202; RGAL 4

Birkerts, Sven 1951- .... **CLC 116**
See also CA 176; 133, 176; 29; CAAE 128;
CANR 151; INT CA-133

Birney, (Alfred) Earle 1904-1995 .. **CLC 1, 4, 6, 11; PC 52**
See also CA 1-4R; CANR 5, 20; CN 1, 2,
3, 4; CP 1, 2, 3, 4, 5, 6; DAC; DAM MST,
POET; DLB 88; MTCW 1; PFS 8; RGEL
2

Biruni, al 973-1048(?) .... **CMLC 28**

Bishop, Elizabeth 1911-1979 ..... **CLC 1, 4, 9, 13, 15, 32; PC 3, 34; TCLC 121**
See also AMWR 2; AMWS 1; CA 5-8R;
CAAS 89-92; CABS 2; CANR 26, 61,
108; CDALB 1968-1988; CP 1, 2, 3; DA;
DA3; DAC; DAM MST, POET; DLB 5,
169; EWL 3; GLL 2; MAL 5; MBL;
MTCW 1, 2; PAB; PFS 6, 12; RGAL 4;
SATA-Obit 24; TUS; WP

Bishop, John 1935- .... **CLC 10**
See also CA 105

Bishop, John Peale 1892-1944 ..... **TCLC 103**
See also CA 155; CAAE 107; DLB 4, 9,
45; MAL 5; RGAL 4

Bissett, Bill 1939- .... **CLC 18; PC 14**
See also CA 69-72; 19; CANR 15; CCA 1;
CP 1, 2, 3, 4, 5, 6, 7; DLB 53; MTCW 1

Bissoondath, Neil (Devindra)
1955- .... **CLC 120**
See also CA 136; CANR 123; CN 6, 7;
DAC

Bitov, Andrei (Georgievich) 1937- ... **CLC 57**
See also CA 142; DLB 302

Biyidi, Alexandre 1932-
See Beti, Mongo
See also BW 1, 3; CA 124; CAAE 114;
CANR 81; DA3; MTCW 1, 2

Bjarme, Brynjolf
See Ibsen, Henrik (Johan)

Bjoernson, Bjoernstjerne (Martinius)
1832-1910 .... **TCLC 7, 37**
See also CAAE 104

Black, Benjamin
See Banville, John

Black, Robert
See Holdstock, Robert

Blackburn, Paul 1926-1971 .... **CLC 9, 43**
See also BG 1:2; CA 81-84; CAAS 33-36R;
CANR 34; CP 1; DLB 16; DLBY 1981

Black Elk 1863-1950 .... **NNAL; TCLC 33**
See also CA 144; DAM MULT; MTCW 2;
MTFW 2005; WP

Black Hawk 1767-1838 .... **NNAL**

Black Hobart
See Sanders, (James) Ed(ward)

Blacklin, Malcolm
See Chambers, Aidan

Blackmore, R(ichard) D(oddridge)
1825-1900 .... **TCLC 27**
See also CAAE 120; DLB 18; RGEL 2

Blackmur, R(ichard) P(almer)
1904-1965 .... **CLC 2, 24**
See also AMWS 2; CA 11-12; CAAS 25-
28R; CANR 71; CAP 1; DLB 63; EWL
3; MAL 5

Black Tarantula
See Acker, Kathy

Blackwood, Algernon (Henry)
1869-1951 .... **TCLC 5**
See also CA 150; CAAE 105; DLB 153,
156, 178; HGG; SUFW 1

Blackwood, Caroline (Maureen)
1931-1996 .... **CLC 6, 9, 100**
See also BRWS 9; CA 85-88; CAAS 151;
CANR 32, 61, 65; CN 3, 4, 5, 6; DLB 14,
207; HGG; MTCW 1

Blade, Alexander
See Hamilton, Edmond; Silverberg, Robert

Blaga, Lucian 1895-1961 .... **CLC 75**
See also CA 157; DLB 220; EWL 3

Blair, Eric (Arthur) 1903-1950 .... **TCLC 123**
See Orwell, George
See also CA 132; CAAE 104; DA; DA3;
DAB; DAC; DAM MST, NOV; MTCW
1, 2; MTFW 2005; SATA 29

Blair, Hugh 1718-1800 .... **NCLC 75**

Blais, Marie-Claire 1939- .... **CLC 2, 4, 6, 13, 22**
See also CA 21-24R; 4; CANR 38, 75, 93;
CWW 2; DAC; DAM MST; DLB 53;
EWL 3; FW; MTCW 1, 2; MTFW 2005;
TWA

Blaise, Clark 1940- .... **CLC 29**
See also AITN 2; CA 231; 53-56, 231; 3;
CANR 5, 66, 106; CN 4, 5, 6, 7; DLB 53;
RGSF 2

Blake, Fairley
See De Voto, Bernard (Augustine)

Blake, Nicholas
See Day Lewis, C(ecil)
See also DLB 77; MSW

Blake, Sterling
See Benford, Gregory

Blake, William 1757-1827 . **NCLC 13, 37, 57, 127, 173; PC 12, 63; WLC 1**
See also AAYA 47; BRW 3; BRWR 1; CD-
BLB 1789-1832; CLR 52; DA; DA3;
DAB; DAC; DAM MST, POET; DLB 93,
163; EXPP; LATS 1:1; LMFS 1; MAI-
CYA 1, 2; PAB; PFS 2, 12, 24; SATA 30;
TEA; WCH; WLIT 3; WP

Blanchot, Maurice 1907-2003 .... **CLC 135**
See also CA 144; CAAE 117; CAAS 213;
CANR 138; DLB 72, 296; EWL 3

Blasco Ibanez, Vicente 1867-1928 . **TCLC 12**
See Ibanez, Vicente Blasco
See also BPFB 1; CA 131; CAAE 110;
CANR 81; DA3; DAM NOV; EW 8;
EWL 3; HW 1, 2; MTCW 1

Blatty, William Peter 1928- .... **CLC 2**
See also CA 5-8R; CANR 9, 124; DAM
POP; HGG

Bleeck, Oliver
See Thomas, Ross (Elmore)

Blessing, Lee (Knowlton) 1949- .... **CLC 54**
See also CA 236; CAD; CD 5, 6; DFS 23

Blight, Rose
See Greer, Germaine

Blish, James (Benjamin) 1921-1975 . **CLC 14**
See also BPFB 1; CA 1-4R; CAAS 57-60;
CANR 3; CN 2; DLB 8; MTCW 1; SATA
66; SCFW 1, 2; SFW 4

Bliss, Frederick
See Card, Orson Scott

Bliss, Gillian
See Paton Walsh, Jill

Bliss, Reginald
See Wells, H(erbert) G(eorge)

Blixen, Karen (Christentze Dinesen)
1885-1962
See Dinesen, Isak
See also CA 25-28; CANR 22, 50; CAP 2;
DA3; DLB 214; LMFS 1; MTCW 1, 2;
SATA 44; SSFS 20

Bloch, Robert (Albert) 1917-1994 .... **CLC 33**
See also AAYA 29; CA 179; 5-8R, 179; 20;
CAAS 146; CANR 5, 78; DA3; DLB 44;
HGG; INT CANR-5; MTCW 2; SATA 12;
SATA-Obit 82; SFW 4; SUFW 1, 2

Bourjaily, Vance (Nye) 1922- .... **CLC 8, 62**
See also CA 1-4R; 1; CANR 2, 72; CN 1, 2, 3, 4, 5, 6, 7; DLB 2, 143; MAL 5

Bourne, Randolph S(illiman)
1886-1918 .... **TCLC 16**
See also AMW; CA 155; CAAE 117; DLB 63; MAL 5

Bova, Ben 1932- .... **CLC 45**
See also AAYA 16; CA 5-8R; 18; CANR 11, 56, 94, 111, 157; CLR 3, 96; DLBY 1981; INT CANR-11; MAICYA 1, 2; MTCW 1; SATA 6, 68, 133; SFW 4

Bova, Benjamin William
See Bova, Ben

Bowen, Elizabeth (Dorothea Cole)
1899-1973 . **CLC 1, 3, 6, 11, 15, 22, 118; SSC 3, 28, 66; TCLC 148**
See also BRWS 2; CA 17-18; CAAS 41-44R; CANR 35, 105; CAP 2; CDBLB 1945-1960; CN 1; DA3; DAM NOV; DLB 15, 162; EWL 3; EXPS; FW; HGG; MTCW 1, 2; MTFW 2005; NFS 13; RGSF 2; SSFS 5, 22; SUFW 1; TEA; WLIT 4

Bowering, George 1935- .... **CLC 15, 47**
See also CA 21-24R; 16; CANR 10; CN 7; CP 1, 2, 3, 4, 5, 6, 7; DLB 53

Bowering, Marilyn R(uthe) 1949- .... **CLC 32**
See also CA 101; CANR 49; CP 4, 5, 6, 7; CWP; DLB 334

Bowers, Edgar 1924-2000 .... **CLC 9**
See also CA 5-8R; CAAS 188; CANR 24; CP 1, 2, 3, 4, 5, 6, 7; CSW; DLB 5

Bowers, Mrs. J. Milton 1842-1914
See Bierce, Ambrose (Gwinett)

Bowie, David .... **CLC 17**
See Jones, David Robert

Bowles, Jane (Sydney) 1917-1973 ..... **CLC 3, 68**
See Bowles, Jane Auer
See also CA 19-20; CAAS 41-44R; CAP 2; CN 1; MAL 5

Bowles, Jane Auer
See Bowles, Jane (Sydney)
See also EWL 3

Bowles, Paul 1910-1999 ..... **CLC 1, 2, 19, 53; SSC 3, 98**
See also AMWS 4; CA 1-4R; 1; CAAS 186; CANR 1, 19, 50, 75; CN 1, 2, 3, 4, 5, 6; DA3; DLB 5, 6, 218; EWL 3; MAL 5; MTCW 1, 2; MTFW 2005; RGAL 4; SSFS 17

Bowles, William Lisle 1762-1850 . **NCLC 103**
See also DLB 93

Box, Edgar
See Vidal, Gore
See also GLL 1

Boyd, James 1888-1944 .... **TCLC 115**
See also CA 186; DLB 9; DLBD 16; RGAL 4; RHW

Boyd, Nancy
See Millay, Edna St. Vincent
See also GLL 1

Boyd, Thomas (Alexander)
1898-1935 .... **TCLC 111**
See also CA 183; CAAE 111; DLB 9; DLBD 16, 316

Boyd, William (Andrew Murray)
1952- .... **CLC 28, 53, 70**
See also CA 120; CAAE 114; CANR 51, 71, 131; CN 4, 5, 6, 7; DLB 231

Boyesen, Hjalmar Hjorth
1848-1895 .... **NCLC 135**
See also DLB 12, 71; DLBD 13; RGAL 4

Boyle, Kay 1902-1992 .... **CLC 1, 5, 19, 58, 121; SSC 5, 102**
See also CA 13-16R; 1; CAAS 140; CANR 29, 61, 110; CN 1, 2, 3, 4, 5; CP 1, 2, 3, 4, 5; DLB 4, 9, 48, 86; DLBY 1993; EWL 3; MAL 5; MTCW 1, 2; MTFW 2005; RGAL 4; RGSF 2; SSFS 10, 13, 14

Boyle, Mark
See Kienzle, William X.

Boyle, Patrick 1905-1982 .... **CLC 19**
See also CA 127

Boyle, T. C.
See Boyle, T. Coraghessan
See also AMWS 8

Boyle, T. Coraghessan 1948- ..... **CLC 36, 55, 90; SSC 16**
See Boyle, T. C.
See also AAYA 47; BEST 90:4; BPFB 1; CA 120; CANR 44, 76, 89, 132; CN 6, 7; CPW; DA3; DAM POP; DLB 218, 278; DLBY 1986; EWL 3; MAL 5; MTCW 2; MTFW 2005; SSFS 13, 19

Boz
See Dickens, Charles (John Huffam)

Brackenridge, Hugh Henry
1748-1816 .... **NCLC 7**
See also DLB 11, 37; RGAL 4

Bradbury, Edward P.
See Moorcock, Michael
See also MTCW 2

Bradbury, Malcolm (Stanley)
1932-2000 .... **CLC 32, 61**
See also CA 1-4R; CANR 1, 33, 91, 98, 137; CN 1, 2, 3, 4, 5, 6, 7; CP 1; DA3; DAM NOV; DLB 14, 207; EWL 3; MTCW 1, 2; MTFW 2005

Bradbury, Ray 1920- ... **CLC 1, 3, 10, 15, 42, 98, 235; SSC 29, 53; WLC 1**
See also AAYA 15; AITN 1, 2; AMWS 4; BPFB 1; BYA 4, 5, 11; CA 1-4R; CANR 2, 30, 75, 125; CDALB 1968-1988; CN 1, 2, 3, 4, 5, 6, 7; CPW; DA; DA3; DAB; DAC; DAM MST, NOV, POP; DLB 2, 8; EXPN; EXPS; HGG; LAIT 3, 5; LATS 1:2; LMFS 2; MAL 5; MTCW 1, 2; MTFW 2005; NFS 1, 22; RGAL 4; RGSF 2; SATA 11, 64, 123; SCFW 1, 2; SFW 4; SSFS 1, 20; SUFW 1, 2; TUS; YAW

Braddon, Mary Elizabeth
1837-1915 .... **TCLC 111**
See also BRWS 8; CA 179; CAAE 108; CMW 4; DLB 18, 70, 156; HGG

Bradfield, Scott 1955- .... **SSC 65**
See also CA 147; CANR 90; HGG; SUFW 2

Bradfield, Scott Michael
See Bradfield, Scott

Bradford, Gamaliel 1863-1932 .... **TCLC 36**
See also CA 160; DLB 17

Bradford, William 1590-1657 .... **LC 64**
See also DLB 24, 30; RGAL 4

Bradley, David (Henry), Jr. 1950- .... **BLC 1; CLC 23, 118**
See also BW 1, 3; CA 104; CANR 26, 81; CN 4, 5, 6, 7; DAM MULT; DLB 33

Bradley, John Ed 1958- .... **CLC 55**
See also CA 139; CANR 99; CN 6, 7; CSW

Bradley, John Edmund, Jr.
See Bradley, John Ed

Bradley, Marion Zimmer
1930-1999 .... **CLC 30**
See Chapman, Lee; Dexter, John; Gardner, Miriam; Ives, Morgan; Rivers, Elfrida
See also AAYA 40; BPFB 1; CA 57-60; 10; CAAS 185; CANR 7, 31, 51, 75, 107; CPW; DA3; DAM POP; DLB 8; FANT; FW; MTCW 1, 2; MTFW 2005; SATA 90, 139; SATA-Obit 116; SFW 4; SUFW 2; YAW

Bradshaw, John 1933- .... **CLC 70**
See also CA 138; CANR 61

Bradstreet, Anne 1612(?)-1672 .... **LC 4, 30, 130; PC 10**
See also AMWS 1; CDALB 1640-1865; DA; DA3; DAC; DAM MST, POET; DLB 24; EXPP; FW; PFS 6; RGAL 4; TUS; WP

Brady, Joan 1939- .... **CLC 86**
See also CA 141

Bragg, Melvyn 1939- .... **CLC 10**
See also BEST 89:3; CA 57-60; CANR 10, 48, 89, 158; CN 1, 2, 3, 4, 5, 6, 7; DLB 14, 271; RHW

Brahe, Tycho 1546-1601 .... **LC 45**
See also DLB 300

Braine, John (Gerard) 1922-1986 . **CLC 1, 3, 41**
See also CA 1-4R; CAAS 120; CANR 1, 33; CDBLB 1945-1960; CN 1, 2, 3, 4; DLB 15; DLBY 1986; EWL 3; MTCW 1

Braithwaite, William Stanley (Beaumont)
1878-1962 .... **BLC 1; HR 1:2; PC 52**
See also BW 1; CA 125; DAM MULT; DLB 50, 54; MAL 5

Bramah, Ernest 1868-1942 .... **TCLC 72**
See also CA 156; CMW 4; DLB 70; FANT

Brammer, Billy Lee
See Brammer, William

Brammer, William 1929-1978 .... **CLC 31**
See also CA 235; CAAS 77-80

Brancati, Vitaliano 1907-1954 .... **TCLC 12**
See also CAAE 109; DLB 264; EWL 3

Brancato, Robin F(idler) 1936- .... **CLC 35**
See also AAYA 9, 68; BYA 6; CA 69-72; CANR 11, 45; CLR 32; JRDA; MAICYA 2; MAICYAS 1; SAAS 9; SATA 97; WYA; YAW

Brand, Dionne 1953- .... **CLC 192**
See also BW 2; CA 143; CANR 143; CWP; DLB 334

Brand, Max
See Faust, Frederick (Schiller)
See also BPFB 1; TCWW 1, 2

Brand, Millen 1906-1980 .... **CLC 7**
See also CA 21-24R; CAAS 97-100; CANR 72

Branden, Barbara .... **CLC 44**
See also CA 148

Brandes, Georg (Morris Cohen)
1842-1927 .... **TCLC 10**
See also CA 189; CAAE 105; DLB 300

Brandys, Kazimierz 1916-2000 .... **CLC 62**
See also CA 239; EWL 3

Branley, Franklyn M(ansfield)
1915-2002 .... **CLC 21**
See also CA 33-36R; CAAS 207; CANR 14, 39; CLR 13; MAICYA 1, 2; SAAS 16; SATA 4, 68, 136

Brant, Beth (E.) 1941- .... **NNAL**
See also CA 144; FW

Brant, Sebastian 1457-1521 .... **LC 112**
See also DLB 179; RGWL 2, 3

Brathwaite, Edward Kamau
1930- .... **BLCS; CLC 11; PC 56**
See also BRWS 12; BW 2, 3; CA 25-28R; CANR 11, 26, 47, 107; CDWLB 3; CP 1, 2, 3, 4, 5, 6, 7; DAM POET; DLB 125; EWL 3

Brathwaite, Kamau
See Brathwaite, Edward Kamau

Brautigan, Richard (Gary)
1935-1984 .... **CLC 1, 3, 5, 9, 12, 34, 42; TCLC 133**
See also BPFB 1; CA 53-56; CAAS 113; CANR 34; CN 1, 2, 3; CP 1, 2, 3, 4; DA3; DAM NOV; DLB 2, 5, 206; DLBY 1980, 1984; FANT; MAL 5; MTCW 1; RGAL 4; SATA 56

Brave Bird, Mary .... **NNAL**
See Crow Dog, Mary

Braverman, Kate 1950- .... **CLC 67**
See also CA 89-92; CANR 141; DLB 335

Cabral de Melo Neto, Joao
1920-1999 .... **CLC 76**
See Melo Neto, Joao Cabral de
See also CA 151; DAM MULT; DLB 307;
LAW; LAWS 1

Cabrera Infante, G. 1929-2005 ... **CLC 5, 25,
45, 120; HLC 1; SSC 39**
See also CA 85-88; CAAS 236; CANR 29,
65, 110; CDWLB 3; CWW 2; DA3; DAM
MULT; DLB 113; EWL 3; HW 1, 2;
LAW; LAWS 1; MTCW 1, 2; MTFW
2005; RGSF 2; WLIT 1

Cabrera Infante, Guillermo
See Cabrera Infante, G.

Cade, Toni
See Bambara, Toni Cade

Cadmus and Harmonia
See Buchan, John

Caedmon fl. 658-680 .... **CMLC 7**
See also DLB 146

Caeiro, Alberto
See Pessoa, Fernando (Antonio Nogueira)

Caesar, Julius .... **CMLC 47**
See Julius Caesar
See also AW 1; RGWL 2, 3; WLIT 8

Cage, John (Milton), (Jr.)
1912-1992 .... **CLC 41; PC 58**
See also CA 13-16R; CAAS 169; CANR 9,
78; DLB 193; INT CANR-9; TCLE 1:1

Cahan, Abraham 1860-1951 .... **TCLC 71**
See also CA 154; CAAE 108; DLB 9, 25,
28; MAL 5; RGAL 4

Cain, G.
See Cabrera Infante, G.

Cain, Guillermo
See Cabrera Infante, G.

Cain, James M(allahan) 1892-1977 .. **CLC 3,
11, 28**
See also AITN 1; BPFB 1; CA 17-20R;
CAAS 73-76; CANR 8, 34, 61; CMW 4;
CN 1, 2; DLB 226; MAL 5; MSW;
MSW; MTCW 1; RGAL 4

Caine, Hall 1853-1931 .... **TCLC 97**
See also RHW

Caine, Mark
See Raphael, Frederic (Michael)

Calasso, Roberto 1941- .... **CLC 81**
See also CA 143; CANR 89

Calderon de la Barca, Pedro
1600-1681 . **DC 3; HLCS 1; LC 23, 136**
See also DFS 23; EW 2; RGWL 2, 3; TWA

Caldwell, Erskine 1903-1987 ... **CLC 1, 8, 14,
50, 60; SSC 19; TCLC 117**
See also AITN 1; AMW; BPFB 1; CA 1-4R;
1; CAAS 121; CANR 2, 33; CN 1, 2, 3,
4; DA3; DAM NOV; DLB 9, 86; EWL 3;
MAL 5; MTCW 1, 2; MTFW 2005;
RGAL 4; RGSF 2; TUS

Caldwell, (Janet Miriam) Taylor (Holland)
1900-1985 .... **CLC 2, 28, 39**
See also BPFB 1; CA 5-8R; CAAS 116;
CANR 5; DA3; DAM NOV, POP; DLBD
17; MTCW 2; RHW

Calhoun, John Caldwell
1782-1850 .... **NCLC 15**
See also DLB 3, 248

Calisher, Hortense 1911- ..... **CLC 2, 4, 8, 38,
134; SSC 15**
See also CA 1-4R; CANR 1, 22, 117; CN
1, 2, 3, 4, 5, 6, 7; DA3; DAM NOV; DLB
2, 218; INT CANR-22; MAL 5; MTCW
1, 2; MTFW 2005; RGAL 4; RGSF 2

Callaghan, Morley Edward
1903-1990 ..... **CLC 3, 14, 41, 65; TCLC
145**
See also CA 9-12R; CAAS 132; CANR 33,
73; CN 1, 2, 3, 4; DAC; DAM MST; DLB
68; EWL 3; MTCW 1, 2; MTFW 2005;
RGEL 2; RGSF 2; SSFS 19

Callimachus c. 305B.C.-c.
240B.C. .... **CMLC 18**
See also AW 1; DLB 176; RGWL 2, 3

Calvin, Jean
See Calvin, John
See also DLB 327; GFL Beginnings to 1789

Calvin, John 1509-1564 .... **LC 37**
See Calvin, Jean

Calvino, Italo 1923-1985 .... **CLC 5, 8, 11, 22,
33, 39, 73; SSC 3, 48; TCLC 183**
See also AAYA 58; CA 85-88; CAAS 116;
CANR 23, 61, 132; DAM NOV; DLB
196; EW 13; EWL 3; MTCW 1, 2; MTFW
2005; RGHL; RGSF 2; RGWL 2, 3; SFW
4; SSFS 12; WLIT 7

Camara Laye
See Laye, Camara
See also EWL 3

Camden, William 1551-1623 .... **LC 77**
See also DLB 172

Cameron, Carey 1952- .... **CLC 59**
See also CA 135

Cameron, Peter 1959- .... **CLC 44**
See also AMWS 12; CA 125; CANR 50,
117; DLB 234; GLL 2

Camoens, Luis Vaz de 1524(?)-1580
See Camoes, Luis de
See also EW 2

Camoes, Luis de 1524(?)-1580 . **HLCS 1; LC
62; PC 31**
See Camoens, Luis Vaz de
See also DLB 287; RGWL 2, 3

Campana, Dino 1885-1932 .... **TCLC 20**
See also CA 246; CAAE 117; DLB 114;
EWL 3

Campanella, Tommaso 1568-1639 .... **LC 32**
See also RGWL 2, 3

Campbell, John W(ood, Jr.)
1910-1971 .... **CLC 32**
See also CA 21-22; CAAS 29-32R; CANR
34; CAP 2; DLB 8; MTCW 1; SCFW 1,
2; SFW 4

Campbell, Joseph 1904-1987 .... **CLC 69;
TCLC 140**
See also AAYA 3, 66; BEST 89:2; CA 1-4R;
CAAS 124; CANR 3, 28, 61, 107; DA3;
MTCW 1, 2

Campbell, Maria 1940- .... **CLC 85; NNAL**
See also CA 102; CANR 54; CCA 1; DAC

Campbell, (John) Ramsey 1946- ..... **CLC 42;
SSC 19**
See also AAYA 51; CA 228; 57-60, 228;
CANR 7, 102; DLB 261; HGG; INT
CANR-7; SUFW 1, 2

Campbell, (Ignatius) Roy (Dunnachie)
1901-1957 .... **TCLC 5**
See also AFW; CA 155; CAAE 104; DLB
20, 225; EWL 3; MTCW 2; RGEL 2

Campbell, Thomas 1777-1844 .... **NCLC 19**
See also DLB 93, 144; RGEL 2

Campbell, Wilfred .... **TCLC 9**
See Campbell, William

Campbell, William 1858(?)-1918
See Campbell, Wilfred
See also CAAE 106; DLB 92

Campbell, William Edward March
1893-1954
See March, William
See also CAAE 108

Campion, Jane 1954- .... **CLC 95, 229**
See also AAYA 33; CA 138; CANR 87

Campion, Thomas 1567-1620 .... **LC 78**
See also CDBLB Before 1660; DAM POET;
DLB 58, 172; RGEL 2

Camus, Albert 1913-1960 ...... **CLC 1, 2, 4, 9,
11, 14, 32, 63, 69, 124; DC 2; SSC 9,
76; WLC 1**
See also AAYA 36; AFW; BPFB 1; CA 89-
92; CANR 131; DA; DA3; DAB; DAC;
DAM DRAM, MST, NOV; DLB 72, 321,
329; EW 13; EWL 3; EXPN; EXPS; GFL
1789 to the Present; LATS 1:2; LMFS 2;
MTCW 1, 2; MTFW 2005; NFS 6, 16;
RGHL; RGSF 2; RGWL 2, 3; SSFS 4;
TWA

Canby, Vincent 1924-2000 .... **CLC 13**
See also CA 81-84; CAAS 191

Cancale
See Desnos, Robert

Canetti, Elias 1905-1994 .. **CLC 3, 14, 25, 75,
86; TCLC 157**
See also CA 21-24R; CAAS 146; CANR
23, 61, 79; CDWLB 2; CWW 2; DA3;
DLB 85, 124, 329; EW 12; EWL 3;
MTCW 1, 2; MTFW 2005; RGWL 2, 3;
TWA

Canfield, Dorothea F.
See Fisher, Dorothy (Frances) Canfield

Canfield, Dorothea Frances
See Fisher, Dorothy (Frances) Canfield

Canfield, Dorothy
See Fisher, Dorothy (Frances) Canfield

Canin, Ethan 1960- .... **CLC 55; SSC 70**
See also CA 135; CAAE 131; DLB 335;
MAL 5

Cankar, Ivan 1876-1918 .... **TCLC 105**
See also CDWLB 4; DLB 147; EWL 3

Cannon, Curt
See Hunter, Evan

Cao, Lan 1961- .... **CLC 109**
See also CA 165

Cape, Judith
See Page, P(atricia) K(athleen)
See also CCA 1

Capek, Karel 1890-1938 .... **DC 1; SSC 36;
TCLC 6, 37; WLC 1**
See also CA 140; CAAE 104; CDWLB 4;
DA; DA3; DAB; DAC; DAM DRAM,
MST, NOV; DFS 7, 11; DLB 215; EW
10; EWL 3; MTCW 2; MTFW 2005;
RGSF 2; RGWL 2, 3; SCFW 1, 2; SFW 4

Capella, Martianus fl. 4th cent. - .. **CMLC 84**

Capote, Truman 1924-1984 . **CLC 1, 3, 8, 13,
19, 34, 38, 58; SSC 2, 47, 93; TCLC
164; WLC 1**
See also AAYA 61; AMWS 3; BPFB 1; CA
5-8R; CAAS 113; CANR 18, 62; CDALB
1941-1968; CN 1, 2, 3; CPW; DA; DA3;
DAB; DAC; DAM MST, NOV, POP;
DLB 2, 185, 227; DLBY 1980, 1984;
EWL 3; EXPS; GLL 1; LAIT 3; MAL 5;
MTCW 1, 2; MTFW 2005; NCFS 2;
RGAL 4; RGSF 2; SATA 91; SSFS 2;
TUS

Capra, Frank 1897-1991 .... **CLC 16**
See also AAYA 52; CA 61-64; CAAS 135

Caputo, Philip 1941- .... **CLC 32**
See also AAYA 60; CA 73-76; CANR 40,
135; YAW

Caragiale, Ion Luca 1852-1912 ...... **TCLC 76**
See also CA 157

Card, Orson Scott 1951- .... **CLC 44, 47, 50**
See also AAYA 11, 42; BPFB 1; BYA 5, 8;
CA 102; CANR 27, 47, 73, 102, 106, 133;
CLR 116; CPW; DA3; DAM POP; FANT;
INT CANR-27; MTCW 1, 2; MTFW
2005; NFS 5; SATA 83, 127; SCFW 2;
SFW 4; SUFW 2; YAW

Cardenal, Ernesto 1925- .... **CLC 31, 161;
HLC 1; PC 22**
See also CA 49-52; CANR 2, 32, 66, 138;
CWW 2; DAM MULT, POET; DLB 290;
EWL 3; HW 1, 2; LAWS 1; MTCW 1, 2;
MTFW 2005; RGWL 2, 3

Cather, Willa (Sibert) 1873-1947 . **SSC 2, 50; TCLC 1, 11, 31, 99, 132, 152; WLC 1**
See also AAYA 24; AMW; AMWC 1; AMWR 1; BPFB 1; CA 128; CAAE 104; CDALB 1865-1917; CLR 98; DA; DA3; DAB; DAC; DAM MST, NOV; DLB 9, 54, 78, 256; DLBD 1; EWL 3; EXPN; EXPS; FL 1:5; LAIT 3; LATS 1:1; MAL 5; MBL; MTCW 1, 2; MTFW 2005; NFS 2, 19; RGAL 4; RGSF 2; RHW; SATA 30; SSFS 2, 7, 16; TCWW 1, 2; TUS

Catherine II
See Catherine the Great
See also DLB 150

Catherine the Great 1729-1796 .... **LC 69**
See Catherine II

Cato, Marcus Porcius
234B.C.-149B.C. .... **CMLC 21**
See Cato the Elder

Cato, Marcus Porcius, the Elder
See Cato, Marcus Porcius

Cato the Elder
See Cato, Marcus Porcius
See also DLB 211

Catton, (Charles) Bruce 1899-1978 . **CLC 35**
See also AITN 1; CA 5-8R; CAAS 81-84; CANR 7, 74; DLB 17; MTCW 2; MTFW 2005; SATA 2; SATA-Obit 24

Catullus c. 84B.C.-54B.C. .... **CMLC 18**
See also AW 2; CDWLB 1; DLB 211; RGWL 2, 3; WLIT 8

Cauldwell, Frank
See King, Francis (Henry)

Caunitz, William J. 1933-1996 .... **CLC 34**
See also BEST 89:3; CA 130; CAAE 125; CAAS 152; CANR 73; INT CA-130

Causley, Charles (Stanley)
1917-2003 .... **CLC 7**
See also CA 9-12R; CAAS 223; CANR 5, 35, 94; CLR 30; CP 1, 2, 3, 4, 5; CWRI 5; DLB 27; MTCW 1; SATA 3, 66; SATA-Obit 149

Caute, (John) David 1936- .... **CLC 29**
See also CA 1-4R; 4; CANR 1, 33, 64, 120; CBD; CD 5, 6; CN 1, 2, 3, 4, 5, 6, 7; DAM NOV; DLB 14, 231

Cavafy, C(onstantine) P(eter) .... **PC 36; TCLC 2, 7**
See Kavafis, Konstantinos Petrou
See also CA 148; DA3; DAM POET; EW 8; EWL 3; MTCW 2; PFS 19; RGWL 2, 3; WP

Cavalcanti, Guido c. 1250-c.
1300 .... **CMLC 54**
See also RGWL 2, 3; WLIT 7

Cavallo, Evelyn
See Spark, Muriel

Cavanna, Betty .... **CLC 12**
See Harrison, Elizabeth (Allen) Cavanna
See also JRDA; MAICYA 1; SAAS 4; SATA 1, 30

Cavendish, Margaret Lucas
1623-1673 .... **LC 30, 132**
See also DLB 131, 252, 281; RGEL 2

Caxton, William 1421(?)-1491(?) .... **LC 17**
See also DLB 170

Cayer, D. M.
See Duffy, Maureen (Patricia)

Cayrol, Jean 1911-2005 .... **CLC 11**
See also CA 89-92; CAAS 236; DLB 83; EWL 3

Cela (y Trulock), Camilo Jose
See Cela, Camilo Jose
See also CWW 2

Cela, Camilo Jose 1916-2002 .... **CLC 4, 13, 59, 122; HLC 1; SSC 71**
See Cela (y Trulock), Camilo Jose
See also BEST 90:2; CA 21-24R; 10; CAAS 206; CANR 21, 32, 76, 139; DAM MULT;

DLB 322; DLBY 1989; EW 13; EWL 3; HW 1; MTCW 1, 2; MTFW 2005; RGSF 2; RGWL 2, 3

Celan, Paul .... **CLC 10, 19, 53, 82; PC 10**
See Antschel, Paul
See also CDWLB 2; DLB 69; EWL 3; RGHL; RGWL 2, 3

Celine, Louis-Ferdinand .. **CLC 1, 3, 4, 7, 9, 15, 47, 124**
See Destouches, Louis-Ferdinand
See also DLB 72; EW 11; EWL 3; GFL 1789 to the Present; RGWL 2, 3

Cellini, Benvenuto 1500-1571 .... **LC 7**
See also WLIT 7

Cendrars, Blaise .... **CLC 18, 106**
See Sauser-Hall, Frederic
See also DLB 258; EWL 3; GFL 1789 to the Present; RGWL 2, 3; WP

Centlivre, Susanna 1669(?)-1723 .... **DC 25; LC 65**
See also DLB 84; RGEL 2

Cernuda (y Bidon), Luis
1902-1963 .... **CLC 54; PC 62**
See also CA 131; CAAS 89-92; DAM POET; DLB 134; EWL 3; GLL 1; HW 1; RGWL 2, 3

Cervantes, Lorna Dee 1954- ..... **HLCS 1; PC 35**
See also CA 131; CANR 80; CP 7; CWP; DLB 82; EXPP; HW 1; LLW

Cervantes (Saavedra), Miguel de
1547-1616 .... **HLCS; LC 6, 23, 93; SSC 12; WLC 1**
See also AAYA 56; BYA 1, 14; DA; DAB; DAC; DAM MST, NOV; EW 2; LAIT 1; LATS 1:1; LMFS 1; NFS 8; RGSF 2; RGWL 2, 3; TWA

Cesaire, Aime 1913- ..... **BLC 1; CLC 19, 32, 112; DC 22; PC 25**
See also BW 2, 3; CA 65-68; CANR 24, 43, 81; CWW 2; DA3; DAM MULT, POET; DLB 321; EWL 3; GFL 1789 to the Present; MTCW 1, 2; MTFW 2005; WP

Chabon, Michael 1963- ... **CLC 55, 149; SSC 59**
See also AAYA 45; AMWS 11; CA 139; CANR 57, 96, 127, 138; DLB 278; MAL 5; MTFW 2005; NFS 25; SATA 145

Chabrol, Claude 1930- .... **CLC 16**
See also CA 110

Chairil Anwar
See Anwar, Chairil
See also EWL 3

Challans, Mary 1905-1983
See Renault, Mary
See also CA 81-84; CAAS 111; CANR 74; DA3; MTCW 2; MTFW 2005; SATA 23; SATA-Obit 36; TEA

Challis, George
See Faust, Frederick (Schiller)

Chambers, Aidan 1934- .... **CLC 35**
See also AAYA 27; CA 25-28R; CANR 12, 31, 58, 116; JRDA; MAICYA 1, 2; SAAS 12; SATA 1, 69, 108, 171; WYA; YAW

Chambers, James 1948-
See Cliff, Jimmy
See also CAAE 124

Chambers, Jessie
See Lawrence, D(avid) H(erbert Richards)
See also GLL 1

Chambers, Robert W(illiam)
1865-1933 .... **SSC 92; TCLC 41**
See also CA 165; DLB 202; HGG; SATA 107; SUFW 1

Chambers, (David) Whittaker
1901-1961 .... **TCLC 129**
See also CAAS 89-92; DLB 303

Chamisso, Adelbert von
1781-1838 .... **NCLC 82**
See also DLB 90; RGWL 2, 3; SUFW 1

Chance, James T.
See Carpenter, John (Howard)

Chance, John T.
See Carpenter, John (Howard)

Chandler, Raymond (Thornton)
1888-1959 .... **SSC 23; TCLC 1, 7, 179**
See also AAYA 25; AMWC 2; AMWS 4; BPFB 1; CA 129; CAAE 104; CANR 60, 107; CDALB 1929-1941; CMW 4; DA3; DLB 226, 253; DLBD 6; EWL 3; MAL 5; MSW; MTCW 1, 2; MTFW 2005; NFS 17; RGAL 4; TUS

Chang, Diana 1934- .... **AAL**
See also CA 228; CWP; DLB 312; EXPP

Chang, Eileen 1921-1995 .... **AAL; SSC 28; TCLC 184**
See Chang Ai-Ling; Zhang Ailing
See also CA 166

Chang, Jung 1952- .... **CLC 71**
See also CA 142

Chang Ai-Ling
See Chang, Eileen
See also EWL 3

Channing, William Ellery
1780-1842 .... **NCLC 17**
See also DLB 1, 59, 235; RGAL 4

Chao, Patricia 1955- .... **CLC 119**
See also CA 163; CANR 155

Chaplin, Charles Spencer
1889-1977 .... **CLC 16**
See Chaplin, Charlie
See also CA 81-84; CAAS 73-76

Chaplin, Charlie
See Chaplin, Charles Spencer
See also AAYA 61; DLB 44

Chapman, George 1559(?)-1634 . **DC 19; LC 22, 116**
See also BRW 1; DAM DRAM; DLB 62, 121; LMFS 1; RGEL 2

Chapman, Graham 1941-1989 .... **CLC 21**
See Monty Python
See also CA 116; CAAS 129; CANR 35, 95

Chapman, John Jay 1862-1933 .... **TCLC 7**
See also AMWS 14; CA 191; CAAE 104

Chapman, Lee
See Bradley, Marion Zimmer
See also GLL 1

Chapman, Walker
See Silverberg, Robert

Chappell, Fred (Davis) 1936- .... **CLC 40, 78, 162**
See also CA 198; 5-8R, 198; 4; CANR 8, 33, 67, 110; CN 6; CP 6, 7; CSW; DLB 6, 105; HGG

Char, Rene(-Emile) 1907-1988 .... **CLC 9, 11, 14, 55; PC 56**
See also CA 13-16R; CAAS 124; CANR 32; DAM POET; DLB 258; EWL 3; GFL 1789 to the Present; MTCW 1, 2; RGWL 2, 3

Charby, Jay
See Ellison, Harlan

Chardin, Pierre Teilhard de
See Teilhard de Chardin, (Marie Joseph) Pierre

Chariton fl. 1st cent. (?)- .... **CMLC 49**

Charlemagne 742-814 .... **CMLC 37**

Charles I 1600-1649 .... **LC 13**

Charriere, Isabelle de 1740-1805 .. **NCLC 66**
See also DLB 313

Chartier, Alain c. 1392-1430 .... **LC 94**
See also DLB 208

Chartier, Emile-Auguste
See Alain

NOV; DLB 10, 34, 98, 156; EWL 3; EXPN; EXPS; LAIT 2; LATS 1:1; LMFS 1; MTCW 1, 2; MTFW 2005; NFS 2, 16; RGEL 2; RGSF 2; SATA 27; SSFS 1, 12; TEA; WLIT 4

Conrad, Robert Arnold
See Hart, Moss

Conroy, Pat 1945- .... **CLC 30, 74**
See also AAYA 8, 52; AITN 1; BPFB 1; CA 85-88; CANR 24, 53, 129; CN 7; CPW; CSW; DA3; DAM NOV, POP; DLB 6; LAIT 5; MAL 5; MTCW 1, 2; MTFW 2005

Constant (de Rebecque), (Henri) Benjamin
1767-1830 .... **NCLC 6, 182**
See also DLB 119; EW 4; GFL 1789 to the Present

Conway, Jill K(er) 1934- .... **CLC 152**
See also CA 130; CANR 94

Conybeare, Charles Augustus
See Eliot, T(homas) S(tearns)

Cook, Michael 1933-1994 .... **CLC 58**
See also CA 93-96; CANR 68; DLB 53

Cook, Robin 1940- .... **CLC 14**
See also AAYA 32; BEST 90:2; BPFB 1; CA 111; CAAE 108; CANR 41, 90, 109; CPW; DA3; DAM POP; HGG; INT CA-111

Cook, Roy
See Silverberg, Robert

Cooke, Elizabeth 1948- .... **CLC 55**
See also CA 129

Cooke, John Esten 1830-1886 .... **NCLC 5**
See also DLB 3, 248; RGAL 4

Cooke, John Estes
See Baum, L(yman) Frank

Cooke, M. E.
See Creasey, John

Cooke, Margaret
See Creasey, John

Cooke, Rose Terry 1827-1892 ...... **NCLC 110**
See also DLB 12, 74

Cook-Lynn, Elizabeth 1930- .... **CLC 93; NNAL**
See also CA 133; DAM MULT; DLB 175

Cooney, Ray .... **CLC 62**
See also CBD

Cooper, Anthony Ashley 1671-1713 .. **LC 107**
See also DLB 101, 336

Cooper, Dennis 1953- .... **CLC 203**
See also CA 133; CANR 72, 86; GLL 1; HGG

Cooper, Douglas 1960- .... **CLC 86**

Cooper, Henry St. John
See Creasey, John

Cooper, J. California (?)- .... **CLC 56**
See also AAYA 12; BW 1; CA 125; CANR 55; DAM MULT; DLB 212

Cooper, James Fenimore
1789-1851 .... **NCLC 1, 27, 54**
See also AAYA 22; AMW; BPFB 1; CDALB 1640-1865; CLR 105; DA3; DLB 3, 183, 250, 254; LAIT 1; NFS 25; RGAL 4; SATA 19; TUS; WCH

Cooper, Susan Fenimore
1813-1894 .... **NCLC 129**
See also ANW; DLB 239, 254

Coover, Robert 1932- .. **CLC 3, 7, 15, 32, 46, 87, 161; SSC 15, 101**
See also AMWS 5; BPFB 1; CA 45-48; CANR 3, 37, 58, 115; CN 1, 2, 3, 4, 5, 6, 7; DAM NOV; DLB 2, 227; DLBY 1981; EWL 3; MAL 5; MTCW 1, 2; MTFW 2005; RGAL 4; RGSF 2

Copeland, Stewart (Armstrong)
1952- .... **CLC 26**

Copernicus, Nicolaus 1473-1543 .... **LC 45**

Coppard, A(lfred) E(dgar)
1878-1957 .... **SSC 21; TCLC 5**
See also BRWS 8; CA 167; CAAE 114; DLB 162; EWL 3; HGG; RGEL 2; RGSF 2; SUFW 1; YABC 1

Coppee, Francois 1842-1908 .... **TCLC 25**
See also CA 170; DLB 217

Coppola, Francis Ford 1939- ... **CLC 16, 126**
See also AAYA 39; CA 77-80; CANR 40, 78; DLB 44

Copway, George 1818-1869 .... **NNAL**
See also DAM MULT; DLB 175, 183

Corbiere, Tristan 1845-1875 .... **NCLC 43**
See also DLB 217; GFL 1789 to the Present

Corcoran, Barbara (Asenath)
1911- .... **CLC 17**
See also AAYA 14; CA 191; 21-24R, 191; 2; CANR 11, 28, 48; CLR 50; DLB 52; JRDA; MAICYA 2; MAICYAS 1; RHW; SAAS 20; SATA 3, 77; SATA-Essay 125

Cordelier, Maurice
See Giraudoux, Jean(-Hippolyte)

Corelli, Marie .... **TCLC 51**
See Mackay, Mary
See also DLB 34, 156; RGEL 2; SUFW 1

Corinna c. 225B.C.-c. 305B.C. ...... **CMLC 72**

Corman, Cid .... **CLC 9**
See Corman, Sidney
See also CA 2; CP 1, 2, 3, 4, 5, 6, 7; DLB 5, 193

Corman, Sidney 1924-2004
See Corman, Cid
See also CA 85-88; CAAS 225; CANR 44; DAM POET

Cormier, Robert 1925-2000 .... **CLC 12, 30**
See also AAYA 3, 19; BYA 1, 2, 6, 8, 9; CA 1-4R; CANR 5, 23, 76, 93; CDALB 1968-1988; CLR 12, 55; DA; DAB; DAC; DAM MST, NOV; DLB 52; EXPN; INT CANR-23; JRDA; LAIT 5; MAICYA 1, 2; MTCW 1, 2; MTFW 2005; NFS 2, 18; SATA 10, 45, 83; SATA-Obit 122; WYA; YAW

Corn, Alfred (DeWitt III) 1943- .... **CLC 33**
See also CA 179; 179; 25; CANR 44; CP 3, 4, 5, 6, 7; CSW; DLB 120, 282; DLBY 1980

Corneille, Pierre 1606-1684 .. **DC 21; LC 28, 135**
See also DAB; DAM MST; DFS 21; DLB 268; EW 3; GFL Beginnings to 1789; RGWL 2, 3; TWA

Cornwell, David
See le Carre, John

Cornwell, Patricia 1956- .... **CLC 155**
See also AAYA 16, 56; BPFB 1; CA 134; CANR 53, 131; CMW 4; CPW; CSW; DAM POP; DLB 306; MSW; MTCW 2; MTFW 2005

Cornwell, Patricia Daniels
See Cornwell, Patricia

Corso, Gregory 1930-2001 .... **CLC 1, 11; PC 33**
See also AMWS 12; BG 1:2; CA 5-8R; CAAS 193; CANR 41, 76, 132; CP 1, 2, 3, 4, 5, 6, 7; DA3; DLB 5, 16, 237; LMFS 2; MAL 5; MTCW 1, 2; MTFW 2005; WP

Cortazar, Julio 1914-1984 ... **CLC 2, 3, 5, 10, 13, 15, 33, 34, 92; HLC 1; SSC 7, 76**
See also BPFB 1; CA 21-24R; CANR 12, 32, 81; CDWLB 3; DA3; DAM MULT, NOV; DLB 113; EWL 3; EXPS; HW 1, 2; LAW; MTCW 1, 2; MTFW 2005; RGSF 2; RGWL 2, 3; SSFS 3, 20; TWA; WLIT 1

Cortes, Hernan 1485-1547 .... **LC 31**

Corvinus, Jakob
See Raabe, Wilhelm (Karl)

Corwin, Cecil
See Kornbluth, C(yril) M.

Cosic, Dobrica 1921- .... **CLC 14**
See also CA 138; CAAE 122; CDWLB 4; CWW 2; DLB 181; EWL 3

Costain, Thomas B(ertram)
1885-1965 .... **CLC 30**
See also BYA 3; CA 5-8R; CAAS 25-28R; DLB 9; RHW

Costantini, Humberto 1924(?)-1987 . **CLC 49**
See also CA 131; CAAS 122; EWL 3; HW 1

Costello, Elvis 1954- .... **CLC 21**
See also CA 204

Costenoble, Philostene
See Ghelderode, Michel de

Cotes, Cecil V.
See Duncan, Sara Jeannette

Cotter, Joseph Seamon Sr.
1861-1949 .... **BLC 1; TCLC 28**
See also BW 1; CA 124; DAM MULT; DLB 50

Couch, Arthur Thomas Quiller
See Quiller-Couch, Sir Arthur (Thomas)

Coulton, James
See Hansen, Joseph

Couperus, Louis (Marie Anne)
1863-1923 .... **TCLC 15**
See also CAAE 115; EWL 3; RGWL 2, 3

Coupland, Douglas 1961- .... **CLC 85, 133**
See also AAYA 34; CA 142; CANR 57, 90, 130; CCA 1; CN 7; CPW; DAC; DAM POP; DLB 334

Court, Wesli
See Turco, Lewis (Putnam)

Courtenay, Bryce 1933- .... **CLC 59**
See also CA 138; CPW

Courtney, Robert
See Ellison, Harlan

Cousteau, Jacques-Yves 1910-1997 .. **CLC 30**
See also CA 65-68; CAAS 159; CANR 15, 67; MTCW 1; SATA 38, 98

Coventry, Francis 1725-1754 .... **LC 46**

Coverdale, Miles c. 1487-1569 .... **LC 77**
See also DLB 167

Cowan, Peter (Walkinshaw)
1914-2002 .... **SSC 28**
See also CA 21-24R; CANR 9, 25, 50, 83; CN 1, 2, 3, 4, 5, 6, 7; DLB 260; RGSF 2

Coward, Noel (Peirce) 1899-1973 . **CLC 1, 9, 29, 51**
See also AITN 1; BRWS 2; CA 17-18; CAAS 41-44R; CANR 35, 132; CAP 2; CBD; CDBLB 1914-1945; DA3; DAM DRAM; DFS 3, 6; DLB 10, 245; EWL 3; IDFW 3, 4; MTCW 1, 2; MTFW 2005; RGEL 2; TEA

Cowley, Abraham 1618-1667 .... **LC 43**
See also BRW 2; DLB 131, 151; PAB; RGEL 2

Cowley, Malcolm 1898-1989 .... **CLC 39**
See also AMWS 2; CA 5-8R; CAAS 128; CANR 3, 55; CP 1, 2, 3, 4; DLB 4, 48; DLBY 1981, 1989; EWL 3; MAL 5; MTCW 1, 2; MTFW 2005

Cowper, William 1731-1800 ..... **NCLC 8, 94; PC 40**
See also BRW 3; DA3; DAM POET; DLB 104, 109; RGEL 2

Cox, William Trevor 1928-
See Trevor, William
See also CA 9-12R; CANR 4, 37, 55, 76, 102, 139; DAM NOV; INT CANR-37; MTCW 1, 2; MTFW 2005; TEA

Coyne, P. J.
See Masters, Hilary

Dorset
See Sackville, Thomas
Dos Passos, John (Roderigo)
1896-1970 ... **CLC 1, 4, 8, 11, 15, 25, 34, 82; WLC 2**
See also AMW; BPFB 1; CA 1-4R; CAAS 29-32R; CANR 3; CDALB 1929-1941; DA; DA3; DAB; DAC; DAM MST, NOV; DLB 4, 9, 274, 316; DLBD 1, 15; DLBY 1996; EWL 3; MAL 5; MTCW 1, 2; MTFW 2005; NFS 14; RGAL 4; TUS
Dossage, Jean
See Simenon, Georges (Jacques Christian)
Dostoevsky, Fedor Mikhailovich
1821-1881 .. **NCLC 2, 7, 21, 33, 43, 119, 167; SSC 2, 33, 44; WLC 2**
See Dostoevsky, Fyodor
See also AAYA 40; DA; DA3; DAB; DAC; DAM MST, NOV; EW 7; EXPN; NFS 3, 8; RGSF 2; RGWL 2, 3; SSFS 8; TWA
Dostoevsky, Fyodor
See Dostoevsky, Fedor Mikhailovich
See also DLB 238; LATS 1:1; LMFS 1, 2
Doty, M. R.
See Doty, Mark
Doty, Mark 1953(?)- .... **CLC 176; PC 53**
See also AMWS 11; CA 183; 161, 183; CANR 110; CP 7
Doty, Mark A.
See Doty, Mark
Doty, Mark Alan
See Doty, Mark
Doughty, Charles M(ontagu)
1843-1926 .... **TCLC 27**
See also CA 178; CAAE 115; DLB 19, 57, 174
Douglas, Ellen .... **CLC 73**
See Haxton, Josephine Ayres; Williamson, Ellen Douglas
See also CN 5, 6, 7; CSW; DLB 292
Douglas, Gavin 1475(?)-1522 .... **LC 20**
See also DLB 132; RGEL 2
Douglas, George
See Brown, George Douglas
See also RGEL 2
Douglas, Keith (Castellain)
1920-1944 .... **TCLC 40**
See also BRW 7; CA 160; DLB 27; EWL 3; PAB; RGEL 2
Douglas, Leonard
See Bradbury, Ray
Douglas, Michael
See Crichton, Michael
Douglas, (George) Norman
1868-1952 .... **TCLC 68**
See also BRW 6; CA 157; CAAE 119; DLB 34, 195; RGEL 2
Douglas, William
See Brown, George Douglas
Douglass, Frederick 1817(?)-1895 ..... **BLC 1; NCLC 7, 55, 141; WLC 2**
See also AAYA 48; AFAW 1, 2; AMWC 1; AMWS 3; CDALB 1640-1865; DA; DA3; DAC; DAM MST, MULT; DLB 1, 43, 50, 79, 243; FW; LAIT 2; NCFS 2; RGAL 4; SATA 29
Dourado, (Waldomiro Freitas) Autran
1926- .... **CLC 23, 60**
See also CA 25-28R, 179; CANR 34, 81; DLB 145, 307; HW 2
Dourado, Waldomiro Freitas Autran
See Dourado, (Waldomiro Freitas) Autran
Dove, Rita 1952- .. **BLCS; CLC 50, 81; PC 6**
See also AAYA 46; AMWS 4; BW 2; CA 109; 19; CANR 27, 42, 68, 76, 97, 132; CDALBS; CP 5, 6, 7; CSW; CWP; DA3; DAM MULT, POET; DLB 120; EWL 3; EXPP; MAL 5; MTCW 2; MTFW 2005; PFS 1, 15; RGAL 4

Dove, Rita Frances
See Dove, Rita
Doveglion
See Villa, Jose Garcia
Dowell, Coleman 1925-1985 .... **CLC 60**
See also CA 25-28R; CAAS 117; CANR 10; DLB 130; GLL 2
Dowson, Ernest (Christopher)
1867-1900 .... **TCLC 4**
See also CA 150; CAAE 105; DLB 19, 135; RGEL 2
Doyle, A. Conan
See Doyle, Sir Arthur Conan
Doyle, Sir Arthur Conan
1859-1930 ..... **SSC 12, 83, 95; TCLC 7; WLC 2**
See Conan Doyle, Arthur
See also AAYA 14; BRWS 2; CA 122; CAAE 104; CANR 131; CDBLB 1890-1914; CLR 106; CMW 4; DA; DA3; DAB; DAC; DAM MST, NOV; DLB 18, 70, 156, 178; EXPS; HGG; LAIT 2; MSW; MTCW 1, 2; MTFW 2005; RGEL 2; RGSF 2; RHW; SATA 24; SCFW 1, 2; SFW 4; SSFS 2; TEA; WCH; WLIT 4; WYA; YAW
Doyle, Conan
See Doyle, Sir Arthur Conan
Doyle, John
See Graves, Robert
Doyle, Roddy 1958- .... **CLC 81, 178**
See also AAYA 14; BRWS 5; CA 143; CANR 73, 128; CN 6, 7; DA3; DLB 194, 326; MTCW 2; MTFW 2005
Doyle, Sir A. Conan
See Doyle, Sir Arthur Conan
Dr. A
See Asimov, Isaac; Silverstein, Alvin; Silverstein, Virginia B(arbara Opshelor)
Drabble, Margaret 1939- ...... **CLC 2, 3, 5, 8, 10, 22, 53, 129**
See also BRWS 4; CA 13-16R; CANR 18, 35, 63, 112, 131; CDBLB 1960 to Present; CN 1, 2, 3, 4, 5, 6, 7; CPW; DA3; DAB; DAC; DAM MST, NOV, POP; DLB 14, 155, 231; EWL 3; FW; MTCW 1, 2; MTFW 2005; RGEL 2; SATA 48; TEA
Drakulic, Slavenka 1949- .... **CLC 173**
See also CA 144; CANR 92
Drakulic-Ilic, Slavenka
See Drakulic, Slavenka
Drapier, M. B.
See Swift, Jonathan
Drayham, James
See Mencken, H(enry) L(ouis)
Drayton, Michael 1563-1631 .... **LC 8**
See also DAM POET; DLB 121; RGEL 2
Dreadstone, Carl
See Campbell, (John) Ramsey
Dreiser, Theodore 1871-1945 .... **SSC 30; TCLC 10, 18, 35, 83; WLC 2**
See also AMW; AMWC 2; AMWR 2; BYA 15, 16; CA 132; CAAE 106; CDALB 1865-1917; DA; DA3; DAC; DAM MST, NOV; DLB 9, 12, 102, 137; DLBD 1; EWL 3; LAIT 2; LMFS 2; MAL 5; MTCW 1, 2; MTFW 2005; NFS 8, 17; RGAL 4; TUS
Dreiser, Theodore Herman Albert
See Dreiser, Theodore
Drexler, Rosalyn 1926- .... **CLC 2, 6**
See also CA 81-84; CAD; CANR 68, 124; CD 5, 6; CWD; MAL 5
Dreyer, Carl Theodor 1889-1968 ...... **CLC 16**
See also CAAS 116
Drieu la Rochelle, Pierre
1893-1945 .... **TCLC 21**
See also CA 250; CAAE 117; DLB 72; EWL 3; GFL 1789 to the Present

Drieu la Rochelle, Pierre-Eugene 1893-1945
See Drieu la Rochelle, Pierre
Drinkwater, John 1882-1937 .... **TCLC 57**
See also CA 149; CAAE 109; DLB 10, 19, 149; RGEL 2
Drop Shot
See Cable, George Washington
Droste-Hulshoff, Annette Freiin von
1797-1848 .... **NCLC 3, 133**
See also CDWLB 2; DLB 133; RGSF 2; RGWL 2, 3
Drummond, Walter
See Silverberg, Robert
Drummond, William Henry
1854-1907 .... **TCLC 25**
See also CA 160; DLB 92
Drummond de Andrade, Carlos
1902-1987 .... **CLC 18; TCLC 139**
See Andrade, Carlos Drummond de
See also CA 132; CAAS 123; DLB 307; LAW
Drummond of Hawthornden, William
1585-1649 .... **LC 83**
See also DLB 121, 213; RGEL 2
Drury, Allen (Stuart) 1918-1998 .... **CLC 37**
See also CA 57-60; CAAS 170; CANR 18, 52; CN 1, 2, 3, 4, 5, 6; INT CANR-18
Druse, Eleanor
See King, Stephen
Dryden, John 1631-1700 ..... **DC 3; LC 3, 21, 115; PC 25; WLC 2**
See also BRW 2; CDBLB 1660-1789; DA; DAB; DAC; DAM DRAM, MST, POET; DLB 80, 101, 131; EXPP; IDTP; LMFS 1; RGEL 2; TEA; WLIT 3
du Bellay, Joachim 1524-1560 .... **LC 92**
See also DLB 327; GFL Beginnings to 1789; RGWL 2, 3
Duberman, Martin 1930- .... **CLC 8**
See also CA 1-4R; CAD; CANR 2, 63, 137; CD 5, 6
Dubie, Norman (Evans) 1945- .... **CLC 36**
See also CA 69-72; CANR 12, 115; CP 3, 4, 5, 6, 7; DLB 120; PFS 12
Du Bois, W(illiam) E(dward) B(urghardt)
1868-1963 ..... **BLC 1; CLC 1, 2, 13, 64, 96; HR 1:2; TCLC 169; WLC 2**
See also AAYA 40; AFAW 1, 2; AMWC 1; AMWS 2; BW 1, 3; CA 85-88; CANR 34, 82, 132; CDALB 1865-1917; DA; DA3; DAC; DAM MST, MULT, NOV; DLB 47, 50, 91, 246, 284; EWL 3; EXPP; LAIT 2; LMFS 2; MAL 5; MTCW 1, 2; MTFW 2005; NCFS 1; PFS 13; RGAL 4; SATA 42
Dubus, Andre 1936-1999 ..... **CLC 13, 36, 97; SSC 15**
See also AMWS 7; CA 21-24R; CAAS 177; CANR 17; CN 5, 6; CSW; DLB 130; INT CANR-17; RGAL 4; SSFS 10; TCLE 1:1
Duca Minimo
See D'Annunzio, Gabriele
Ducharme, Rejean 1941- .... **CLC 74**
See also CAAS 165; DLB 60
du Chatelet, Emilie 1706-1749 .... **LC 96**
See Chatelet, Gabrielle-Emilie Du
Duchen, Claire .... **CLC 65**
Duclos, Charles Pinot- 1704-1772 .... **LC 1**
See also GFL Beginnings to 1789
Ducornet, Erica 1943-
See Ducornet, Rikki
See also CA 37-40R; CANR 14, 34, 54, 82; SATA 7
Ducornet, Rikki .... **CLC 232**
See Ducornet, Erica
Dudek, Louis 1918-2001 .... **CLC 11, 19**
See also CA 45-48; 14; CAAS 215; CANR 1; CP 1, 2, 3, 4, 5, 6, 7; DLB 88

Eberhart, Richard 1904-2005 ...... **CLC 3, 11, 19, 56; PC 76**
   See also AMW; CA 1-4R; CAAS 240; CANR 2, 125; CDALB 1941-1968; CP 1, 2, 3, 4, 5, 6, 7; DAM POET; DLB 48; MAL 5; MTCW 1; RGAL 4

Eberhart, Richard Ghormley
   See Eberhart, Richard

Eberstadt, Fernanda 1960- .... **CLC 39**
   See also CA 136; CANR 69, 128

Echegaray (y Eizaguirre), Jose (Maria Waldo) 1832-1916 .... **HLCS 1; TCLC 4**
   See also CAAE 104; CANR 32; DLB 329; EWL 3; HW 1; MTCW 1

Echeverria, (Jose) Esteban (Antonino)
   1805-1851 .... **NCLC 18**
   See also LAW

Echo
   See Proust, (Valentin-Louis-George-Eugene) Marcel

Eckert, Allan W. 1931- .... **CLC 17**
   See also AAYA 18; BYA 2; CA 13-16R; CANR 14, 45; INT CANR-14; MAICYA 2; MAICYAS 1; SAAS 21; SATA 29, 91; SATA-Brief 27

Eckhart, Meister 1260(?)-1327(?) .. **CMLC 9, 80**
   See also DLB 115; LMFS 1

Eckmar, F. R.
   See de Hartog, Jan

Eco, Umberto 1932- .... **CLC 28, 60, 142**
   See also BEST 90:1; BPFB 1; CA 77-80; CANR 12, 33, 55, 110, 131; CPW; CWW 2; DA3; DAM NOV, POP; DLB 196, 242; EWL 3; MSW; MTCW 1, 2; MTFW 2005; NFS 22; RGWL 3; WLIT 7

Eddison, E(ric) R(ucker)
   1882-1945 .... **TCLC 15**
   See also CA 156; CAAE 109; DLB 255; FANT; SFW 4; SUFW 1

Eddy, Mary (Ann Morse) Baker
   1821-1910 .... **TCLC 71**
   See also CA 174; CAAE 113

Edel, (Joseph) Leon 1907-1997 .. **CLC 29, 34**
   See also CA 1-4R; CAAS 161; CANR 1, 22, 112; DLB 103; INT CANR-22

Eden, Emily 1797-1869 .... **NCLC 10**

Edgar, David 1948- .... **CLC 42**
   See also CA 57-60; CANR 12, 61, 112; CBD; CD 5, 6; DAM DRAM; DFS 15; DLB 13, 233; MTCW 1

Edgerton, Clyde (Carlyle) 1944- ...... **CLC 39**
   See also AAYA 17; CA 134; CAAE 118; CANR 64, 125; CN 7; CSW; DLB 278; INT CA-134; TCLE 1:1; YAW

Edgeworth, Maria 1768-1849 ... **NCLC 1, 51, 158; SSC 86**
   See also BRWS 3; DLB 116, 159, 163; FL 1:3; FW; RGEL 2; SATA 21; TEA; WLIT 3

Edmonds, Paul
   See Kuttner, Henry

Edmonds, Walter D(umaux)
   1903-1998 .... **CLC 35**
   See also BYA 2; CA 5-8R; CANR 2; CWRI 5; DLB 9; LAIT 1; MAICYA 1, 2; MAL 5; RHW; SAAS 4; SATA 1, 27; SATA-Obit 99

Edmondson, Wallace
   See Ellison, Harlan

Edson, Margaret 1961- ...... **CLC 199; DC 24**
   See also CA 190; DFS 13; DLB 266

Edson, Russell 1935- .... **CLC 13**
   See also CA 33-36R; CANR 115; CP 2, 3, 4, 5, 6, 7; DLB 244; WP

Edwards, Bronwen Elizabeth
   See Rose, Wendy

Edwards, G(erald) B(asil)
   1899-1976 .... **CLC 25**
   See also CA 201; CAAS 110

Edwards, Gus 1939- .... **CLC 43**
   See also CA 108; INT CA-108

Edwards, Jonathan 1703-1758 ...... **LC 7, 54**
   See also AMW; DA; DAC; DAM MST; DLB 24, 270; RGAL 4; TUS

Edwards, Sarah Pierpont 1710-1758 .. **LC 87**
   See also DLB 200

Efron, Marina Ivanovna Tsvetaeva
   See Tsvetaeva (Efron), Marina (Ivanovna)

Egeria fl. 4th cent. - .... **CMLC 70**

Egoyan, Atom 1960- .... **CLC 151**
   See also AAYA 63; CA 157; CANR 151

Ehle, John (Marsden, Jr.) 1925- ...... **CLC 27**
   See also CA 9-12R; CSW

Ehrenbourg, Ilya (Grigoryevich)
   See Ehrenburg, Ilya (Grigoryevich)

Ehrenburg, Ilya (Grigoryevich)
   1891-1967 .... **CLC 18, 34, 62**
   See Erenburg, Il'ia Grigor'evich
   See also CA 102; CAAS 25-28R; EWL 3

Ehrenburg, Ilyo (Grigoryevich)
   See Ehrenburg, Ilya (Grigoryevich)

Ehrenreich, Barbara 1941- .... **CLC 110**
   See also BEST 90:4; CA 73-76; CANR 16, 37, 62, 117; DLB 246; FW; MTCW 1, 2; MTFW 2005

Eich, Gunter
   See Eich, Gunter
   See also RGWL 2, 3

Eich, Gunter 1907-1972 .... **CLC 15**
   See Eich, Gunter
   See also CA 111; CAAS 93-96; DLB 69, 124; EWL 3

Eichendorff, Joseph 1788-1857 .... **NCLC 8**
   See also DLB 90; RGWL 2, 3

Eigner, Larry .... **CLC 9**
   See Eigner, Laurence (Joel)
   See also CA 23; CP 1, 2, 3, 4, 5, 6; DLB 5; WP

Eigner, Laurence (Joel) 1927-1996
   See Eigner, Larry
   See also CA 9-12R; CAAS 151; CANR 6, 84; CP 7; DLB 193

Eilhart von Oberge c. 1140-c.
   1195 .... **CMLC 67**
   See also DLB 148

Einhard c. 770-840 .... **CMLC 50**
   See also DLB 148

Einstein, Albert 1879-1955 .... **TCLC 65**
   See also CA 133; CAAE 121; MTCW 1, 2

Eiseley, Loren
   See Eiseley, Loren Corey
   See also DLB 275

Eiseley, Loren Corey 1907-1977 .... **CLC 7**
   See Eiseley, Loren
   See also AAYA 5; ANW; CA 1-4R; CAAS 73-76; CANR 6; DLBD 17

Eisenstadt, Jill 1963- .... **CLC 50**
   See also CA 140

Eisenstein, Sergei (Mikhailovich)
   1898-1948 .... **TCLC 57**
   See also CA 149; CAAE 114

Eisner, Simon
   See Kornbluth, C(yril) M.

Eisner, Will 1917-2005 .... **CLC 237**
   See also AAYA 52; CA 108; CAAS 235; CANR 114, 140; MTFW 2005; SATA 31, 165

Eisner, William Erwin
   See Eisner, Will

Ekeloef, (Bengt) Gunnar
   1907-1968 .... **CLC 27; PC 23**
   See Ekelof, (Bengt) Gunnar
   See also CA 123; CAAS 25-28R; DAM POET

Ekelof, (Bengt) Gunnar 1907-1968
   See Ekeloef, (Bengt) Gunnar
   See also DLB 259; EW 12; EWL 3

Ekelund, Vilhelm 1880-1949 .... **TCLC 75**
   See also CA 189; EWL 3

Ekwensi, C. O. D.
   See Ekwensi, Cyprian (Odiatu Duaka)

Ekwensi, Cyprian (Odiatu Duaka)
   1921- .... **BLC 1; CLC 4**
   See also AFW; BW 2, 3; CA 29-32R; CANR 18, 42, 74, 125; CDWLB 3; CN 1, 2, 3, 4, 5, 6; CWRI 5; DAM MULT; DLB 117; EWL 3; MTCW 1, 2; RGEL 2; SATA 66; WLIT 2

Elaine .... **TCLC 18**
   See Leverson, Ada Esther

El Crummo
   See Crumb, R.

Elder, Lonne III 1931-1996 ..... **BLC 1; DC 8**
   See also BW 1, 3; CA 81-84; CAAS 152; CAD; CANR 25; DAM MULT; DLB 7, 38, 44; MAL 5

Eleanor of Aquitaine 1122-1204 ... **CMLC 39**

Elia
   See Lamb, Charles

Eliade, Mircea 1907-1986 .... **CLC 19**
   See also CA 65-68; CAAS 119; CANR 30, 62; CDWLB 4; DLB 220; EWL 3; MTCW 1; RGWL 3; SFW 4

Eliot, A. D.
   See Jewett, (Theodora) Sarah Orne

Eliot, Alice
   See Jewett, (Theodora) Sarah Orne

Eliot, Dan
   See Silverberg, Robert

Eliot, George 1819-1880 ...... **NCLC 4, 13, 23, 41, 49, 89, 118, 183; PC 20; SSC 72; WLC 2**
   See Evans, Mary Ann
   See also BRW 5; BRWC 1, 2; BRWR 2; CDBLB 1832-1890; CN 7; CPW; DA; DA3; DAB; DAC; DAM MST, NOV; DLB 21, 35, 55; FL 1:3; LATS 1:1; LMFS 1; NFS 17, 20; RGEL 2; RGSF 2; SSFS 8; TEA; WLIT 3

Eliot, John 1604-1690 .... **LC 5**
   See also DLB 24

Eliot, T(homas) S(tearns)
   1888-1965 ...... **CLC 1, 2, 3, 6, 9, 10, 13, 15, 24, 34, 41, 55, 57, 113; PC 5, 31; WLC 2**
   See also AAYA 28; AMW; AMWC 1; AMWR 1; BRW 7; BRWR 2; CA 5-8R; CAAS 25-28R; CANR 41; CBD; CDALB 1929-1941; DA; DA3; DAB; DAC; DAM DRAM, MST, POET; DFS 4, 13; DLB 7, 10, 45, 63, 245, 329; DLBY 1988; EWL 3; EXPP; LAIT 3; LATS 1:1; LMFS 1, 2; MAL 5; MTCW 1, 2; MTFW 2005; NCFS 5; PAB; PFS 1, 7, 20; RGAL 4; RGEL 2; TUS; WLIT 4; WP

Elisabeth of Schonau c.
   1129-1165 .... **CMLC 82**

Elizabeth 1866-1941 .... **TCLC 41**

Elizabeth I 1533-1603 .... **LC 118**
   See also DLB 136

Elkin, Stanley L. 1930-1995 ...... **CLC 4, 6, 9, 14, 27, 51, 91; SSC 12**
   See also AMWS 6; BPFB 1; CA 9-12R; CAAS 148; CANR 8, 46; CN 1, 2, 3, 4, 5, 6; CPW; DAM NOV, POP; DLB 2, 28, 218, 278; DLBY 1980; EWL 3; INT CANR-8; MAL 5; MTCW 1, 2; MTFW 2005; RGAL 4; TCLE 1:1

Elledge, Scott .... **CLC 34**

Eller, Scott
   See Shepard, Jim

Elliott, Don
   See Silverberg, Robert

Espada, Martin 1957- .... **PC 74**
See also CA 159; CANR 80; CP 7; EXPP;
LLW; MAL 5; PFS 13, 16

Espriella, Don Manuel Alvarez
See Southey, Robert

Espriu, Salvador 1913-1985 .... **CLC 9**
See also CA 154; CAAS 115; DLB 134;
EWL 3

Espronceda, Jose de 1808-1842 ..... **NCLC 39**

Esquivel, Laura 1950(?)- ... **CLC 141; HLCS 1**
See also AAYA 29; CA 143; CANR 68, 113,
161; DA3; DNFS 2; LAIT 3; LMFS 2;
MTCW 2; MTFW 2005; NFS 5; WLIT 1

Esse, James
See Stephens, James

Esterbrook, Tom
See Hubbard, L. Ron

Estleman, Loren D. 1952- .... **CLC 48**
See also AAYA 27; CA 85-88; CANR 27,
74, 139; CMW 4; CPW; DA3; DAM
NOV, POP; DLB 226; INT CANR-27;
MTCW 1, 2; MTFW 2005; TCWW 1, 2

Etherege, Sir George 1636-1692 . **DC 23; LC 78**
See also BRW 2; DAM DRAM; DLB 80;
PAB; RGEL 2

Euclid 306B.C.-283B.C. .... **CMLC 25**

Eugenides, Jeffrey 1960(?)- .... **CLC 81, 212**
See also AAYA 51; CA 144; CANR 120;
MTFW 2005; NFS 24

Euripides c. 484B.C.-406B.C. .... **CMLC 23, 51; DC 4; WLCS**
See also AW 1; CDWLB 1; DA; DA3;
DAB; DAC; DAM DRAM, MST; DFS 1,
4, 6; DLB 176; LAIT 1; LMFS 1; RGWL
2, 3; WLIT 8

Evan, Evin
See Faust, Frederick (Schiller)

Evans, Caradoc 1878-1945 ... **SSC 43; TCLC 85**
See also DLB 162

Evans, Evan
See Faust, Frederick (Schiller)

Evans, Marian
See Eliot, George

Evans, Mary Ann
See Eliot, George
See also NFS 20

Evarts, Esther
See Benson, Sally

Everett, Percival
See Everett, Percival L.
See also CSW

Everett, Percival L. 1956- .... **CLC 57**
See Everett, Percival
See also BW 2; CA 129; CANR 94, 134;
CN 7; MTFW 2005

Everson, R(onald) G(ilmour)
1903-1992 .... **CLC 27**
See also CA 17-20R; CP 1, 2, 3, 4; DLB 88

Everson, William (Oliver)
1912-1994 .... **CLC 1, 5, 14**
See Antoninus, Brother
See also BG 1:2; CA 9-12R; CAAS 145;
CANR 20; CP 2, 3, 4, 5; DLB 5, 16, 212;
MTCW 1

Evtushenko, Evgenii Aleksandrovich
See Yevtushenko, Yevgeny (Alexandrovich)
See also CWW 2; RGWL 2, 3

Ewart, Gavin (Buchanan)
1916-1995 .... **CLC 13, 46**
See also BRWS 7; CA 89-92; CAAS 150;
CANR 17, 46; CP 1, 2, 3, 4, 5, 6; DLB
40; MTCW 1

Ewers, Hanns Heinz 1871-1943 ..... **TCLC 12**
See also CA 149; CAAE 109

Ewing, Frederick R.
See Sturgeon, Theodore (Hamilton)

Exley, Frederick (Earl) 1929-1992 .... **CLC 6, 11**
See also AITN 2; BPFB 1; CA 81-84;
CAAS 138; CANR 117; DLB 143; DLBY
1981

Eynhardt, Guillermo
See Quiroga, Horacio (Sylvestre)

Ezekiel, Nissim (Moses) 1924-2004 .. **CLC 61**
See also CA 61-64; CAAS 223; CP 1, 2, 3,
4, 5, 6, 7; DLB 323; EWL 3

Ezekiel, Tish O'Dowd 1943- .... **CLC 34**
See also CA 129

Fadeev, Aleksandr Aleksandrovich
See Bulgya, Alexander Alexandrovich
See also DLB 272

Fadeev, Alexandr Alexandrovich
See Bulgya, Alexander Alexandrovich
See also EWL 3

Fadeyev, A.
See Bulgya, Alexander Alexandrovich

Fadeyev, Alexander .... **TCLC 53**
See Bulgya, Alexander Alexandrovich

Fagen, Donald 1948- .... **CLC 26**

Fainzil'berg, Il'ia Arnol'dovich
See Fainzilberg, Ilya Arnoldovich

Fainzilberg, Ilya Arnoldovich
1897-1937 .... **TCLC 21**
See Il'f, Il'ia
See also CA 165; CAAE 120; EWL 3

Fair, Ronald L. 1932- .... **CLC 18**
See also BW 1; CA 69-72; CANR 25; DLB
33

Fairbairn, Roger
See Carr, John Dickson

Fairbairns, Zoe (Ann) 1948- .... **CLC 32**
See also CA 103; CANR 21, 85; CN 4, 5,
6, 7

Fairfield, Flora
See Alcott, Louisa May

Fairman, Paul W. 1916-1977
See Queen, Ellery
See also CAAS 114; SFW 4

Falco, Gian
See Papini, Giovanni

Falconer, James
See Kirkup, James

Falconer, Kenneth
See Kornbluth, C(yril) M.

Falkland, Samuel
See Heijermans, Herman

Fallaci, Oriana 1930-2006 .... **CLC 11, 110**
See also CA 77-80; CAAS 253; CANR 15,
58, 134; FW; MTCW 1

Faludi, Susan 1959- .... **CLC 140**
See also CA 138; CANR 126; FW; MTCW
2; MTFW 2005; NCFS 3

Faludy, George 1913- .... **CLC 42**
See also CA 21-24R

Faludy, Gyoergy
See Faludy, George

Fanon, Frantz 1925-1961 ... **BLC 2; CLC 74; TCLC 188**
See also BW 1; CA 116; CAAS 89-92;
DAM MULT; DLB 296; LMFS 2; WLIT
2

Fanshawe, Ann 1625-1680 .... **LC 11**

Fante, John (Thomas) 1911-1983 .... **CLC 60; SSC 65**
See also AMWS 11; CA 69-72; CAAS 109;
CANR 23, 104; DLB 130; DLBY 1983

Far, Sui Sin .... **SSC 62**
See Eaton, Edith Maude
See also SSFS 4

Farah, Nuruddin 1945- ...... **BLC 2; CLC 53, 137**
See also AFW; BW 2, 3; CA 106; CANR
81, 148; CDWLB 3; CN 4, 5, 6, 7; DAM
MULT; DLB 125; EWL 3; WLIT 2

Fargue, Leon-Paul 1876(?)-1947 .... **TCLC 11**
See also CAAE 109; CANR 107; DLB 258;
EWL 3

Farigoule, Louis
See Romains, Jules

Farina, Richard 1936(?)-1966 .... **CLC 9**
See also CA 81-84; CAAS 25-28R

Farley, Walter (Lorimer)
1915-1989 .... **CLC 17**
See also AAYA 58; BYA 14; CA 17-20R;
CANR 8, 29, 84; DLB 22; JRDA; MAI-
CYA 1, 2; SATA 2, 43, 132; YAW

Farmer, Philip Jose 1918- .... **CLC 1, 19**
See also AAYA 28; BPFB 1; CA 1-4R;
CANR 4, 35, 111; DLB 8; MTCW 1;
SATA 93; SCFW 1, 2; SFW 4

Farquhar, George 1677-1707 .... **LC 21**
See also BRW 2; DAM DRAM; DLB 84;
RGEL 2

Farrell, J(ames) G(ordon)
1935-1979 .... **CLC 6**
See also CA 73-76; CAAS 89-92; CANR
36; CN 1, 2; DLB 14, 271, 326; MTCW
1; RGEL 2; RHW; WLIT 4

Farrell, James T(homas) 1904-1979 . **CLC 1, 4, 8, 11, 66; SSC 28**
See also AMW; BPFB 1; CA 5-8R; CAAS
89-92; CANR 9, 61; CN 1, 2; DLB 4, 9,
86; DLBD 2; EWL 3; MAL 5; MTCW 1,
2; MTFW 2005; RGAL 4

Farrell, Warren (Thomas) 1943- ...... **CLC 70**
See also CA 146; CANR 120

Farren, Richard J.
See Betjeman, John

Farren, Richard M.
See Betjeman, John

Fassbinder, Rainer Werner
1946-1982 .... **CLC 20**
See also CA 93-96; CAAS 106; CANR 31

Fast, Howard 1914-2003 .... **CLC 23, 131**
See also AAYA 16; BPFB 1; CA 181; 1-4R,
181; 18; CAAS 214; CANR 1, 33, 54, 75,
98, 140; CMW 4; CN 1, 2, 3, 4, 5, 6, 7;
CPW; DAM NOV; DLB 9; INT CANR-
33; LATS 1:1; MAL 5; MTCW 2; MTFW
2005; RHW; SATA 7; SATA-Essay 107;
TCWW 1, 2; YAW

Faulcon, Robert
See Holdstock, Robert

Faulkner, William (Cuthbert)
1897-1962 .... **CLC 1, 3, 6, 8, 9, 11, 14, 18, 28, 52, 68; SSC 1, 35, 42, 92, 97; TCLC 141; WLC 2**
See also AAYA 7; AMW; AMWR 1; BPFB
1; BYA 5, 15; CA 81-84; CANR 33;
CDALB 1929-1941; DA; DA3; DAB;
DAC; DAM MST, NOV; DLB 9, 11, 44,
102, 316, 330; DLBD 2; DLBY 1986,
1997; EWL 3; EXPN; EXPS; GL 2; LAIT
2; LATS 1:1; LMFS 2; MAL 5; MTCW
1, 2; MTFW 2005; NFS 4, 8, 13, 24;
RGAL 4; RGSF 2; SSFS 2, 5, 6, 12; TUS

Fauset, Jessie Redmon
1882(?)-1961 .. **BLC 2; CLC 19, 54; HR 1:2**
See also AFAW 2; BW 1; CA 109; CANR
83; DAM MULT; DLB 51; FW; LMFS 2;
MAL 5; MBL

Faust, Frederick (Schiller)
1892-1944 .... **TCLC 49**
See Brand, Max; Dawson, Peter; Frederick,
John
See also CA 152; CAAE 108; CANR 143;
DAM POP; DLB 256; TUS

Faust, Irvin 1924- .... **CLC 8**
See also CA 33-36R; CANR 28, 67; CN 1,
2, 3, 4, 5, 6, 7; DLB 2, 28, 218, 278;
DLBY 1980

Fawkes, Guy
See Benchley, Robert (Charles)

FitzGerald, Edward 1809-1883 ...... **NCLC 9, 153**
See also BRW 4; DLB 32; RGEL 2

Fitzgerald, F(rancis) Scott (Key)
1896-1940 ... **SSC 6, 31, 75; TCLC 1, 6, 14, 28, 55, 157; WLC 2**
See also AAYA 24; AITN 1; AMW; AMWC 2; AMWR 1; BPFB 1; CA 123; CAAE 110; CDALB 1917-1929; DA; DA3; DAB; DAC; DAM MST, NOV; DLB 4, 9, 86, 219, 273; DLBD 1, 15, 16; DLBY 1981, 1996; EWL 3; EXPN; EXPS; LAIT 3; MAL 5; MTCW 1, 2; MTFW 2005; NFS 2, 19, 20; RGAL 4; RGSF 2; SSFS 4, 15, 21; TUS

Fitzgerald, Penelope 1916-2000 . **CLC 19, 51, 61, 143**
See also BRWS 5; CA 85-88; 10; CAAS 190; CANR 56, 86, 131; CN 3, 4, 5, 6, 7; DLB 14, 194, 326; EWL 3; MTCW 2; MTFW 2005

Fitzgerald, Robert (Stuart)
1910-1985 .... **CLC 39**
See also CA 1-4R; CAAS 114; CANR 1; CP 1, 2, 3, 4; DLBY 1980; MAL 5

FitzGerald, Robert D(avid)
1902-1987 .... **CLC 19**
See also CA 17-20R; CP 1, 2, 3, 4; DLB 260; RGEL 2

Fitzgerald, Zelda (Sayre)
1900-1948 .... **TCLC 52**
See also AMWS 9; CA 126; CAAE 117; DLBY 1984

Flanagan, Thomas (James Bonner)
1923-2002 .... **CLC 25, 52**
See also CA 108; CAAS 206; CANR 55; CN 3, 4, 5, 6, 7; DLBY 1980; INT CA-108; MTCW 1; RHW; TCLE 1:1

Flaubert, Gustave 1821-1880 .... **NCLC 2, 10, 19, 62, 66, 135, 179, 185; SSC 11, 60; WLC 2**
See also DA; DA3; DAB; DAC; DAM MST, NOV; DLB 119, 301; EW 7; EXPS; GFL 1789 to the Present; LAIT 2; LMFS 1; NFS 14; RGSF 2; RGWL 2, 3; SSFS 6; TWA

Flavius Josephus
See Josephus, Flavius

Flecker, Herman Elroy
See Flecker, (Herman) James Elroy

Flecker, (Herman) James Elroy
1884-1915 .... **TCLC 43**
See also CA 150; CAAE 109; DLB 10, 19; RGEL 2

Fleming, Ian 1908-1964 .... **CLC 3, 30**
See also AAYA 26; BPFB 1; CA 5-8R; CANR 59; CDBLB 1945-1960; CMW 4; CPW; DA3; DAM POP; DLB 87, 201; MSW; MTCW 1, 2; MTFW 2005; RGEL 2; SATA 9; TEA; YAW

Fleming, Ian Lancaster
See Fleming, Ian

Fleming, Thomas 1927- .... **CLC 37**
See also CA 5-8R; CANR 10, 102, 155; INT CANR-10; SATA 8

Fleming, Thomas James
See Fleming, Thomas

Fletcher, John 1579-1625 .... **DC 6; LC 33**
See also BRW 2; CDBLB Before 1660; DLB 58; RGEL 2; TEA

Fletcher, John Gould 1886-1950 .... **TCLC 35**
See also CA 167; CAAE 107; DLB 4, 45; LMFS 2; MAL 5; RGAL 4

Fleur, Paul
See Pohl, Frederik

Flieg, Helmut
See Heym, Stefan

Flooglebuckle, Al
See Spiegelman, Art

Flora, Fletcher 1914-1969
See Queen, Ellery
See also CA 1-4R; CANR 3, 85

Flying Officer X
See Bates, H(erbert) E(rnest)

Fo, Dario 1926- .... **CLC 32, 109, 227; DC 10**
See also CA 116; CANR 68, 114, 134; CWW 2; DA3; DAM DRAM; DFS 23; DLB 330; DLBY 1997; EWL 3; MTCW 1, 2; MTFW 2005; WLIT 7

Foden, Giles 1967- .... **CLC 231**
See also CA 240; DLB 267; NFS 15

Fogarty, Jonathan Titulescu Esq.
See Farrell, James T(homas)

Follett, Ken 1949- .... **CLC 18**
See also AAYA 6, 50; BEST 89:4; BPFB 1; CA 81-84; CANR 13, 33, 54, 102, 156; CMW 4; CPW; DA3; DAM NOV, POP; DLB 87; DLBY 1981; INT CANR-33; MTCW 1

Follett, Kenneth Martin
See Follett, Ken

Fondane, Benjamin 1898-1944 ..... **TCLC 159**

Fontane, Theodor 1819-1898 . **NCLC 26, 163**
See also CDWLB 2; DLB 129; EW 6; RGWL 2, 3; TWA

Fonte, Moderata 1555-1592 .... **LC 118**

Fontenelle, Bernard Le Bovier de
1657-1757 .... **LC 140**
See also DLB 268, 313; GFL Beginnings to 1789

Fontenot, Chester .... **CLC 65**

Fonvizin, Denis Ivanovich
1744(?)-1792 .... **LC 81**
See also DLB 150; RGWL 2, 3

Foote, Horton 1916- .... **CLC 51, 91**
See also CA 73-76; CAD; CANR 34, 51, 110; CD 5, 6; CSW; DA3; DAM DRAM; DFS 20; DLB 26, 266; EWL 3; INT CANR-34; MTFW 2005

Foote, Mary Hallock 1847-1938 .. **TCLC 108**
See also DLB 186, 188, 202, 221; TCWW 2

Foote, Samuel 1721-1777 .... **LC 106**
See also DLB 89; RGEL 2

Foote, Shelby 1916-2005 .... **CLC 75, 224**
See also AAYA 40; CA 5-8R; CAAS 240; CANR 3, 45, 74, 131; CN 1, 2, 3, 4, 5, 6, 7; CPW; CSW; DA3; DAM NOV, POP; DLB 2, 17; MAL 5; MTCW 2; MTFW 2005; RHW

Forbes, Cosmo
See Lewton, Val

Forbes, Esther 1891-1967 .... **CLC 12**
See also AAYA 17; BYA 2; CA 13-14; CAAS 25-28R; CAP 1; CLR 27; DLB 22; JRDA; MAICYA 1, 2; RHW; SATA 2, 100; YAW

Forche, Carolyn 1950- .. **CLC 25, 83, 86; PC 10**
See also CA 117; CAAE 109; CANR 50, 74, 138; CP 4, 5, 6, 7; CWP; DA3; DAM POET; DLB 5, 193; INT CA-117; MAL 5; MTCW 2; MTFW 2005; PFS 18; RGAL 4

Forche, Carolyn Louise
See Forche, Carolyn

Ford, Elbur
See Hibbert, Eleanor Alice Burford

Ford, Ford Madox 1873-1939 ... **TCLC 1, 15, 39, 57, 172**
See Chaucer, Daniel
See also BRW 6; CA 132; CAAE 104; CANR 74; CDBLB 1914-1945; DA3; DAM NOV; DLB 34, 98, 162; EWL 3; MTCW 1, 2; RGEL 2; TEA

Ford, Henry 1863-1947 .... **TCLC 73**
See also CA 148; CAAE 115

Ford, Jack
See Ford, John

Ford, John 1586-1639 .... **DC 8; LC 68**
See also BRW 2; CDBLB Before 1660; DA3; DAM DRAM; DFS 7; DLB 58; IDTP; RGEL 2

Ford, John 1895-1973 .... **CLC 16**
See also AAYA 75; CA 187; CAAS 45-48

Ford, Richard 1944- .... **CLC 46, 99, 205**
See also AMWS 5; CA 69-72; CANR 11, 47, 86, 128; CN 5, 6, 7; CSW; DLB 227; EWL 3; MAL 5; MTCW 2; MTFW 2005; NFS 25; RGAL 4; RGSF 2

Ford, Webster
See Masters, Edgar Lee

Foreman, Richard 1937- .... **CLC 50**
See also CA 65-68; CAD; CANR 32, 63, 143; CD 5, 6

Forester, C(ecil) S(cott) 1899-1966 . **CLC 35; TCLC 152**
See also CA 73-76; CAAS 25-28R; CANR 83; DLB 191; RGEL 2; RHW; SATA 13

Forez
See Mauriac, Francois (Charles)

Forman, James
See Forman, James D(ouglas)

Forman, James D(ouglas) 1932- .... **CLC 21**
See also AAYA 17; CA 9-12R; CANR 4, 19, 42; JRDA; MAICYA 1, 2; SATA 8, 70; YAW

Forman, Milos 1932- .... **CLC 164**
See also AAYA 63; CA 109

Fornes, Maria Irene 1930- .... **CLC 39, 61, 187; DC 10; HLCS 1**
See also CA 25-28R; CAD; CANR 28, 81; CD 5, 6; CWD; DLB 7; HW 1, 2; INT CANR-28; LLW; MAL 5; MTCW 1; RGAL 4

Forrest, Leon (Richard)
1937-1997 .... **BLCS; CLC 4**
See also AFAW 2; BW 2; CA 89-92; 7; CAAS 162; CANR 25, 52, 87; CN 4, 5, 6; DLB 33

Forster, E(dward) M(organ)
1879-1970 ...... **CLC 1, 2, 3, 4, 9, 10, 13, 15, 22, 45, 77; SSC 27, 96; TCLC 125; WLC 2**
See also AAYA 2, 37; BRW 6; BRWR 2; BYA 12; CA 13-14; CAAS 25-28R; CANR 45; CAP 1; CDBLB 1914-1945; DA; DA3; DAB; DAC; DAM MST, NOV; DLB 34, 98, 162, 178, 195; DLBD 10; EWL 3; EXPN; LAIT 3; LMFS 1; MTCW 1, 2; MTFW 2005; NCFS 1; NFS 3, 10, 11; RGEL 2; RGSF 2; SATA 57; SUFW 1; TEA; WLIT 4

Forster, John 1812-1876 .... **NCLC 11**
See also DLB 144, 184

Forster, Margaret 1938- .... **CLC 149**
See also CA 133; CANR 62, 115; CN 4, 5, 6, 7; DLB 155, 271

Forsyth, Frederick 1938- .... **CLC 2, 5, 36**
See also BEST 89:4; CA 85-88; CANR 38, 62, 115, 137; CMW 4; CN 3, 4, 5, 6, 7; CPW; DAM NOV, POP; DLB 87; MTCW 1, 2; MTFW 2005

Forten, Charlotte L. 1837-1914 .... **BLC 2; TCLC 16**
See Grimke, Charlotte L(ottie) Forten
See also DLB 50, 239

Fortinbras
See Grieg, (Johan) Nordahl (Brun)

Foscolo, Ugo 1778-1827 .... **NCLC 8, 97**
See also EW 5; WLIT 7

Fosse, Bob 1927-1987
See Fosse, Robert L.
See also CAAE 110; CAAS 123

Fosse, Robert L. .... **CLC 20**
See Fosse, Bob

Froude, James Anthony
1818-1894 .... **NCLC 43**
See also DLB 18, 57, 144

Froy, Herald
See Waterhouse, Keith (Spencer)

Fry, Christopher 1907-2005 ... **CLC 2, 10, 14**
See also BRWS 3; CA 17-20R; 23; CAAS
240; CANR 9, 30, 74, 132; CBD; CD 5,
6; CP 1, 2, 3, 4, 5, 6, 7; DAM DRAM;
DLB 13; EWL 3; MTCW 1, 2; MTFW
2005; RGEL 2; SATA 66; TEA

Frye, (Herman) Northrop
1912-1991 .... **CLC 24, 70; TCLC 165**
See also CA 5-8R; CAAS 133; CANR 8,
37; DLB 67, 68, 246; EWL 3; MTCW 1,
2; MTFW 2005; RGAL 4; TWA

Fuchs, Daniel 1909-1993 .... **CLC 8, 22**
See also CA 81-84; 5; CAAS 142; CANR
40; CN 1, 2, 3, 4, 5; DLB 9, 26, 28;
DLBY 1993; MAL 5

Fuchs, Daniel 1934- .... **CLC 34**
See also CA 37-40R; CANR 14, 48

Fuentes, Carlos 1928- .. **CLC 3, 8, 10, 13, 22,**
41, 60, 113; HLC 1; SSC 24; WLC 2
See also AAYA 4, 45; AITN 2; BPFB 1;
CA 69-72; CANR 10, 32, 68, 104, 138;
CDWLB 3; CWW 2; DA; DA3; DAB;
DAC; DAM MST, MULT, NOV; DLB
113; DNFS 2; EWL 3; HW 1, 2; LAIT 3;
LATS 1:2; LAW; LAWS 1; LMFS 2;
MTCW 1, 2; MTFW 2005; NFS 8; RGSF
2; RGWL 2, 3; TWA; WLIT 1

Fuentes, Gregorio Lopez y
See Lopez y Fuentes, Gregorio

Fuertes, Gloria 1918-1998 .... **PC 27**
See also CA 178, 180; DLB 108; HW 2;
SATA 115

Fugard, (Harold) Athol 1932- . **CLC 5, 9, 14,**
25, 40, 80, 211; DC 3
See also AAYA 17; AFW; CA 85-88; CANR
32, 54, 118; CD 5, 6; DAM DRAM; DFS
3, 6, 10, 24; DLB 225; DNFS 1, 2; EWL
3; LATS 1:2; MTCW 1; MTFW 2005;
RGEL 2; WLIT 2

Fugard, Sheila 1932- .... **CLC 48**
See also CA 125

Fujiwara no Teika 1162-1241 .... **CMLC 73**
See also DLB 203

Fukuyama, Francis 1952- .... **CLC 131**
See also CA 140; CANR 72, 125

Fuller, Charles (H.), (Jr.) 1939- .... **BLC 2;**
CLC 25; DC 1
See also BW 2; CA 112; CAAE 108; CAD;
CANR 87; CD 5, 6; DAM DRAM,
MULT; DFS 8; DLB 38, 266; EWL 3;
INT CA-112; MAL 5; MTCW 1

Fuller, Henry Blake 1857-1929 .... **TCLC 103**
See also CA 177; CAAE 108; DLB 12;
RGAL 4

Fuller, John (Leopold) 1937- .... **CLC 62**
See also CA 21-24R; CANR 9, 44; CP 1, 2,
3, 4, 5, 6, 7; DLB 40

Fuller, Margaret
See Ossoli, Sarah Margaret (Fuller)
See also AMWS 2; DLB 183, 223, 239; FL
1:3

Fuller, Roy (Broadbent) 1912-1991 ... **CLC 4,**
28
See also BRWS 7; CA 5-8R; 10; CAAS
135; CANR 53, 83; CN 1, 2, 3, 4, 5; CP
1, 2, 3, 4, 5; CWRI 5; DLB 15, 20; EWL
3; RGEL 2; SATA 87

Fuller, Sarah Margaret
See Ossoli, Sarah Margaret (Fuller)

Fuller, Sarah Margaret
See Ossoli, Sarah Margaret (Fuller)
See also DLB 1, 59, 73

Fuller, Thomas 1608-1661 .... **LC 111**
See also DLB 151

Fulton, Alice 1952- .... **CLC 52**
See also CA 116; CANR 57, 88; CP 5, 6, 7;
CWP; DLB 193; PFS 25

Furphy, Joseph 1843-1912 .... **TCLC 25**
See Collins, Tom
See also CA 163; DLB 230; EWL 3; RGEL
2

Fuson, Robert H(enderson) 1927- .... **CLC 70**
See also CA 89-92; CANR 103

Fussell, Paul 1924- .... **CLC 74**
See also BEST 90:1; CA 17-20R; CANR 8,
21, 35, 69, 135; INT CANR-21; MTCW
1, 2; MTFW 2005

Futabatei, Shimei 1864-1909 .... **TCLC 44**
See Futabatei Shimei
See also CA 162; MJW

Futabatei Shimei
See Futabatei, Shimei
See also DLB 180; EWL 3

Futrelle, Jacques 1875-1912 .... **TCLC 19**
See also CA 155; CAAE 113; CMW 4

Gaboriau, Emile 1835-1873 .... **NCLC 14**
See also CMW 4; MSW

Gadda, Carlo Emilio 1893-1973 ...... **CLC 11;**
TCLC 144
See also CA 89-92; DLB 177; EWL 3;
WLIT 7

Gaddis, William 1922-1998 ... **CLC 1, 3, 6, 8,**
10, 19, 43, 86
See also AMWS 4; BPFB 1; CA 17-20R;
CAAS 172; CANR 21, 48, 148; CN 1, 2,
3, 4, 5, 6; DLB 2, 278; EWL 3; MAL 5;
MTCW 1, 2; MTFW 2005; RGAL 4

Gage, Walter
See Inge, William (Motter)

Gaiman, Neil 1960- .... **CLC 195**
See also AAYA 19, 42; CA 133; CANR 81,
129; CLR 109; DLB 261; HGG; MTFW
2005; SATA 85, 146; SFW 4; SUFW 2

Gaiman, Neil Richard
See Gaiman, Neil

Gaines, Ernest J. 1933- .. **BLC 2; CLC 3, 11,**
18, 86, 181; SSC 68
See also AAYA 18; AFAW 1, 2; AITN 1;
BPFB 2; BW 2, 3; BYA 6; CA 9-12R;
CANR 6, 24, 42, 75, 126; CDALB 1968-
1988; CLR 62; CN 1, 2, 3, 4, 5, 6, 7;
CSW; DA3; DAM MULT; DLB 2, 33,
152; DLBY 1980; EWL 3; EXPN; LAIT
5; LATS 1:2; MAL 5; MTCW 1, 2;
MTFW 2005; NFS 5, 7, 16; RGAL 4;
RGSF 2; RHW; SATA 86; SSFS 5; YAW

Gaitskill, Mary 1954- .... **CLC 69**
See also CA 128; CANR 61, 152; DLB 244;
TCLE 1:1

Gaitskill, Mary Lawrence
See Gaitskill, Mary

Gaius Suetonius Tranquillus
See Suetonius

Galdos, Benito Perez
See Perez Galdos, Benito
See also EW 7

Gale, Zona 1874-1938 .... **TCLC 7**
See also CA 153; CAAE 105; CANR 84;
DAM DRAM; DFS 17; DLB 9, 78, 228;
RGAL 4

Galeano, Eduardo 1940- ... **CLC 72; HLCS 1**
See also CA 29-32R; CANR 13, 32, 100,
163; HW 1

Galeano, Eduardo Hughes
See Galeano, Eduardo

Galiano, Juan Valera y Alcala
See Valera y Alcala-Galiano, Juan

Galilei, Galileo 1564-1642 .... **LC 45**

Gallagher, Tess 1943- .... **CLC 18, 63; PC 9**
See also CA 106; CP 3, 4, 5, 6, 7; CWP;
DAM POET; DLB 120, 212, 244; PFS 16

Gallant, Mavis 1922- ..... **CLC 7, 18, 38, 172;**
SSC 5, 78
See also CA 69-72; CANR 29, 69, 117;
CCA 1; CN 1, 2, 3, 4, 5, 6, 7; DAC; DAM
MST; DLB 53; EWL 3; MTCW 1, 2;
MTFW 2005; RGEL 2; RGSF 2

Gallant, Roy A(rthur) 1924- .... **CLC 17**
See also CA 5-8R; CANR 4, 29, 54, 117;
CLR 30; MAICYA 1, 2; SATA 4, 68, 110

Gallico, Paul (William) 1897-1976 ..... **CLC 2**
See also AITN 1; CA 5-8R; CAAS 69-72;
CANR 23; CN 1, 2; DLB 9, 171; FANT;
MAICYA 1, 2; SATA 13

Gallo, Max Louis 1932- .... **CLC 95**
See also CA 85-88

Gallois, Lucien
See Desnos, Robert

Gallup, Ralph
See Whitemore, Hugh (John)

Galsworthy, John 1867-1933 .... **SSC 22;**
TCLC 1, 45; WLC 2
See also BRW 6; CA 141; CAAE 104;
CANR 75; CDBLB 1890-1914; DA; DA3;
DAB; DAC; DAM DRAM, MST, NOV;
DLB 10, 34, 98, 162, 330; DLBD 16;
EWL 3; MTCW 2; RGEL 2; SSFS 3; TEA

Galt, John 1779-1839 .... **NCLC 1, 110**
See also DLB 99, 116, 159; RGEL 2; RGSF
2

Galvin, James 1951- .... **CLC 38**
See also CA 108; CANR 26

Gamboa, Federico 1864-1939 .... **TCLC 36**
See also CA 167; HW 2; LAW

Gandhi, M. K.
See Gandhi, Mohandas Karamchand

Gandhi, Mahatma
See Gandhi, Mohandas Karamchand

Gandhi, Mohandas Karamchand
1869-1948 .... **TCLC 59**
See also CA 132; CAAE 121; DA3; DAM
MULT; DLB 323; MTCW 1, 2

Gann, Ernest Kellogg 1910-1991 ..... **CLC 23**
See also AITN 1; BPFB 2; CA 1-4R; CAAS
136; CANR 1, 83; RHW

Gao Xingjian 1940- .... **CLC 167**
See Xingjian, Gao
See also MTFW 2005

Garber, Eric 1943(?)-
See Holleran, Andrew
See also CANR 89, 162

Garcia, Cristina 1958- .... **CLC 76**
See also AMWS 11; CA 141; CANR 73,
130; CN 7; DLB 292; DNFS 1; EWL 3;
HW 2; LLW; MTFW 2005

Garcia Lorca, Federico 1898-1936 ...... **DC 2;**
HLC 1; PC 3; TCLC 1, 7, 49, 181;
WLC 2
See Lorca, Federico Garcia
See also AAYA 46; CA 131; CAAE 104;
CANR 81; DA; DA3; DAB; DAC; DAM
DRAM, MST, MULT, POET; DFS 4, 10;
DLB 108; EWL 3; HW 1, 2; LATS 1:2;
MTCW 1, 2; MTFW 2005; TWA

Garcia Marquez, Gabriel 1928- .... **CLC 2, 3,**
8, 10, 15, 27, 47, 55, 68, 170; HLC 1;
SSC 8, 83; WLC 3
See also AAYA 3, 33; BEST 89:1, 90:4;
BPFB 2; BYA 12, 16; CA 33-36R; CANR
10, 28, 50, 75, 82, 128; CDWLB 3; CPW;
CWW 2; DA; DA3; DAB; DAC; DAM
MST, MULT, NOV, POP; DLB 113, 330;
DNFS 1, 2; EWL 3; EXPN; EXPS; HW
1, 2; LAIT 2; LATS 1:2; LAW; LAWS 1;
LMFS 2; MTCW 1, 2; MTFW 2005;
NCFS 3; NFS 1, 5, 10; RGSF 2; RGWL
2, 3; SSFS 1, 6, 16, 21; TWA; WLIT 1

Garcia Marquez, Gabriel Jose
See Garcia Marquez, Gabriel

Ghiselin, Brewster 1903-2001 .... **CLC 23**
See also CA 13-16R; 10; CANR 13; CP 1, 2, 3, 4, 5, 6, 7

Ghose, Aurabinda 1872-1950 .... **TCLC 63**
See Ghose, Aurobindo
See also CA 163

Ghose, Aurobindo
See Ghose, Aurabinda
See also EWL 3

Ghose, Zulfikar 1935- .... **CLC 42, 200**
See also CA 65-68; CANR 67; CN 1, 2, 3, 4, 5, 6, 7; CP 1, 2, 3, 4, 5, 6, 7; DLB 323; EWL 3

Ghosh, Amitav 1956- .... **CLC 44, 153**
See also CA 147; CANR 80, 158; CN 6, 7; DLB 323; WWE 1

Giacosa, Giuseppe 1847-1906 .... **TCLC 7**
See also CAAE 104

Gibb, Lee
See Waterhouse, Keith (Spencer)

Gibbon, Edward 1737-1794 .... **LC 97**
See also BRW 3; DLB 104, 336; RGEL 2

Gibbon, Lewis Grassic .... **TCLC 4**
See Mitchell, James Leslie
See also RGEL 2

Gibbons, Kaye 1960- .... **CLC 50, 88, 145**
See also AAYA 34; AMWS 10; CA 151; CANR 75, 127; CN 7; CSW; DA3; DAM POP; DLB 292; MTCW 2; MTFW 2005; NFS 3; RGAL 4; SATA 117

Gibran, Kahlil 1883-1931 . **PC 9; TCLC 1, 9**
See also CA 150; CAAE 104; DA3; DAM POET, POP; EWL 3; MTCW 2; WLIT 6

Gibran, Khalil
See Gibran, Kahlil

Gibson, Mel 1956- .... **CLC 215**

Gibson, William 1914- .... **CLC 23**
See also CA 9-12R; CAD; CANR 9, 42, 75, 125; CD 5, 6; DA; DAB; DAC; DAM DRAM, MST; DFS 2; DLB 7; LAIT 2; MAL 5; MTCW 2; MTFW 2005; SATA 66; YAW

Gibson, William 1948- .... **CLC 39, 63, 186, 192; SSC 52**
See also AAYA 12, 59; AMWS 16; BPFB 2; CA 133; CAAE 126; CANR 52, 90, 106; CN 6, 7; CPW; DA3; DAM POP; DLB 251; MTCW 2; MTFW 2005; SCFW 2; SFW 4

Gibson, William Ford
See Gibson, William

Gide, Andre (Paul Guillaume)
1869-1951 ...... **SSC 13; TCLC 5, 12, 36, 177; WLC 3**
See also CA 124; CAAE 104; DA; DA3; DAB; DAC; DAM MST, NOV; DLB 65, 321, 330; EW 8; EWL 3; GFL 1789 to the Present; MTCW 1, 2; MTFW 2005; NFS 21; RGSF 2; RGWL 2, 3; TWA

Gifford, Barry (Colby) 1946- .... **CLC 34**
See also CA 65-68; CANR 9, 30, 40, 90

Gilbert, Frank
See De Voto, Bernard (Augustine)

Gilbert, W(illiam) S(chwenck)
1836-1911 .... **TCLC 3**
See also CA 173; CAAE 104; DAM DRAM, POET; RGEL 2; SATA 36

Gilbert of Poitiers c. 1085-1154 .... **CMLC 85**

Gilbreth, Frank B(unker), Jr.
1911-2001 .... **CLC 17**
See also CA 9-12R; SATA 2

Gilchrist, Ellen (Louise) 1935- .. **CLC 34, 48, 143; SSC 14, 63**
See also BPFB 2; CA 116; CAAE 113; CANR 41, 61, 104; CN 4, 5, 6, 7; CPW; CSW; DAM POP; DLB 130; EWL 3; EXPS; MTCW 1, 2; MTFW 2005; RGAL 4; RGSF 2; SSFS 9

Giles, Molly 1942- .... **CLC 39**
See also CA 126; CANR 98

Gill, Eric .... **TCLC 85**
See Gill, (Arthur) Eric (Rowton Peter Joseph)

Gill, (Arthur) Eric (Rowton Peter Joseph)
1882-1940
See Gill, Eric
See also CAAE 120; DLB 98

Gill, Patrick
See Creasey, John

Gillette, Douglas .... **CLC 70**

Gilliam, Terry 1940- .... **CLC 21, 141**
See Monty Python
See also AAYA 19, 59; CA 113; CAAE 108; CANR 35; INT CA-113

Gilliam, Terry Vance
See Gilliam, Terry

Gillian, Jerry
See Gilliam, Terry

Gilliatt, Penelope (Ann Douglass)
1932-1993 .... **CLC 2, 10, 13, 53**
See also AITN 2; CA 13-16R; CAAS 141; CANR 49; CN 1, 2, 3, 4, 5; DLB 14

Gilligan, Carol 1936- .... **CLC 208**
See also CA 142; CANR 121; FW

Gilman, Charlotte (Anna) Perkins (Stetson)
1860-1935 ...... **SSC 13, 62; TCLC 9, 37, 117**
See also AAYA 75; AMWS 11; BYA 11; CA 150; CAAE 106; DLB 221; EXPS; FL 1:5; FW; HGG; LAIT 2; MBL; MTCW 2; MTFW 2005; RGAL 4; RGSF 2; SFW 4; SSFS 1, 18

Gilmour, David 1946- .... **CLC 35**

Gilpin, William 1724-1804 .... **NCLC 30**

Gilray, J. D.
See Mencken, H(enry) L(ouis)

Gilroy, Frank D(aniel) 1925- .... **CLC 2**
See also CA 81-84; CAD; CANR 32, 64, 86; CD 5, 6; DFS 17; DLB 7

Gilstrap, John 1957(?)- .... **CLC 99**
See also AAYA 67; CA 160; CANR 101

Ginsberg, Allen 1926-1997 .... **CLC 1, 2, 3, 4, 6, 13, 36, 69, 109; PC 4, 47; TCLC 120; WLC 3**
See also AAYA 33; AITN 1; AMWC 1; AMWS 2; BG 1:2; CA 1-4R; CAAS 157; CANR 2, 41, 63, 95; CDALB 1941-1968; CP 1, 2, 3, 4, 5, 6; DA; DA3; DAB; DAC; DAM MST, POET; DLB 5, 16, 169, 237; EWL 3; GLL 1; LMFS 2; MAL 5; MTCW 1, 2; MTFW 2005; PAB; PFS 5; RGAL 4; TUS; WP

Ginzburg, Eugenia .... **CLC 59**
See Ginzburg, Evgeniia

Ginzburg, Evgeniia 1904-1977
See Ginzburg, Eugenia
See also DLB 302

Ginzburg, Natalia 1916-1991 .... **CLC 5, 11, 54, 70; SSC 65; TCLC 156**
See also CA 85-88; CAAS 135; CANR 33; DFS 14; DLB 177; EW 13; EWL 3; MTCW 1, 2; MTFW 2005; RGHL; RGWL 2, 3

Giono, Jean 1895-1970 .... **CLC 4, 11; TCLC 124**
See also CA 45-48; CAAS 29-32R; CANR 2, 35; DLB 72, 321; EWL 3; GFL 1789 to the Present; MTCW 1; RGWL 2, 3

Giovanni, Nikki 1943- ...... **BLC 2; CLC 2, 4, 19, 64, 117; PC 19; WLCS**
See also AAYA 22; AITN 1; BW 2, 3; CA 29-32R; 6; CANR 18, 41, 60, 91, 130; CDALBS; CLR 6, 73; CP 2, 3, 4, 5, 6, 7; CSW; CWP; CWRI 5; DA; DA3; DAB; DAC; DAM MST, MULT, POET; DLB 5,

41; EWL 3; EXPP; INT CANR-18; MAICYA 1, 2; MAL 5; MTCW 1, 2; MTFW 2005; PFS 17; RGAL 4; SATA 24, 107; TUS; YAW

Giovene, Andrea 1904-1998 .... **CLC 7**
See also CA 85-88

Gippius, Zinaida (Nikolaevna) 1869-1945
See Hippius, Zinaida (Nikolaevna)
See also CA 212; CAAE 106

Giraudoux, Jean(-Hippolyte)
1882-1944 .... **TCLC 2, 7**
See also CA 196; CAAE 104; DAM DRAM; DLB 65, 321; EW 9; EWL 3; GFL 1789 to the Present; RGWL 2, 3; TWA

Gironella, Jose Maria (Pous)
1917-2003 .... **CLC 11**
See also CA 101; CAAS 212; EWL 3; RGWL 2, 3

Gissing, George (Robert)
1857-1903 .... **SSC 37; TCLC 3, 24, 47**
See also BRW 5; CA 167; CAAE 105; DLB 18, 135, 184; RGEL 2; TEA

Gitlin, Todd 1943- .... **CLC 201**
See also CA 29-32R; CANR 25, 50, 88

Giurlani, Aldo
See Palazzeschi, Aldo

Gladkov, Fedor Vasil'evich
See Gladkov, Fyodor (Vasilyevich)
See also DLB 272

Gladkov, Fyodor (Vasilyevich)
1883-1958 .... **TCLC 27**
See Gladkov, Fedor Vasil'evich
See also CA 170; EWL 3

Glancy, Diane 1941- .... **CLC 210; NNAL**
See also CA 225; 136, 225; 24; CANR 87, 162; DLB 175

Glanville, Brian (Lester) 1931- .... **CLC 6**
See also CA 5-8R; 9; CANR 3, 70; CN 1, 2, 3, 4, 5, 6, 7; DLB 15, 139; SATA 42

Glasgow, Ellen (Anderson Gholson)
1873-1945 .... **SSC 34; TCLC 2, 7**
See also AMW; CA 164; CAAE 104; DLB 9, 12; MAL 5; MBL; MTCW 2; MTFW 2005; RGAL 4; RHW; SSFS 9; TUS

Glaspell, Susan 1882(?)-1948 ..... **DC 10; SSC 41; TCLC 55, 175**
See also AMWS 3; CA 154; CAAE 110; DFS 8, 18, 24; DLB 7, 9, 78, 228; MBL; RGAL 4; SSFS 3; TCWW 2; TUS; YABC 2

Glassco, John 1909-1981 .... **CLC 9**
See also CA 13-16R; CAAS 102; CANR 15; CN 1, 2; CP 1, 2, 3; DLB 68

Glasscock, Amnesia
See Steinbeck, John (Ernst)

Glasser, Ronald J. 1940(?)- .... **CLC 37**
See also CA 209

Glassman, Joyce
See Johnson, Joyce

Gleick, James (W.) 1954- .... **CLC 147**
See also CA 137; CAAE 131; CANR 97; INT CA-137

Glendinning, Victoria 1937- .... **CLC 50**
See also CA 127; CAAE 120; CANR 59, 89; DLB 155

Glissant, Edouard (Mathieu)
1928- .... **CLC 10, 68**
See also CA 153; CANR 111; CWW 2; DAM MULT; EWL 3; RGWL 3

Gloag, Julian 1930- .... **CLC 40**
See also AITN 1; CA 65-68; CANR 10, 70; CN 1, 2, 3, 4, 5, 6

Glowacki, Aleksander
See Prus, Boleslaw

Guillen, Nicolas (Cristobal)
1902-1989 .... **BLC 2; CLC 48, 79; HLC 1; PC 23**
See also BW 2; CA 125; CAAE 116; CAAS 129; CANR 84; DAM MST, MULT, POET; DLB 283; EWL 3; HW 1; LAW; RGWL 2, 3; WP

Guillen y Alvarez, Jorge
See Guillen, Jorge

Guillevic, (Eugene) 1907-1997 .... CLC 33
See also CA 93-96; CWW 2

Guillois
See Desnos, Robert

Guillois, Valentin
See Desnos, Robert

Guimaraes Rosa, Joao 1908-1967 .... HLCS 2
See Rosa, Joao Guimaraes
See also CA 175; LAW; RGSF 2; RGWL 2, 3

Guiney, Louise Imogen
1861-1920 .... **TCLC 41**
See also CA 160; DLB 54; RGAL 4

Guinizelli, Guido c. 1230-1276 ...... CMLC 49
See Guinizzelli, Guido

Guinizzelli, Guido
See Guinizelli, Guido
See also WLIT 7

Guiraldes, Ricardo (Guillermo)
1886-1927 .... **TCLC 39**
See also CA 131; EWL 3; HW 1; LAW; MTCW 1

Gumilev, Nikolai (Stepanovich)
1886-1921 .... **TCLC 60**
See Gumilyov, Nikolay Stepanovich
See also CA 165; DLB 295

Gumilyov, Nikolay Stepanovich
See Gumilev, Nikolai (Stepanovich)
See also EWL 3

Gump, P. Q.
See Card, Orson Scott

Gunesekera, Romesh 1954- .... CLC 91
See also BRWS 10; CA 159; CANR 140; CN 6, 7; DLB 267, 323

Gunn, Bill .... **CLC 5**
See Gunn, William Harrison
See also DLB 38

Gunn, Thom(son William)
1929-2004 . **CLC 3, 6, 18, 32, 81; PC 26**
See also BRWS 4; CA 17-20R; CAAS 227; CANR 9, 33, 116; CDBLB 1960 to Present; CP 1, 2, 3, 4, 5, 6, 7; DAM POET; DLB 27; INT CANR-33; MTCW 1; PFS 9; RGEL 2

Gunn, William Harrison 1934(?)-1989
See Gunn, Bill
See also AITN 1; BW 1, 3; CA 13-16R; CAAS 128; CANR 12, 25, 76

Gunn Allen, Paula
See Allen, Paula Gunn

Gunnars, Kristjana 1948- .... CLC 69
See also CA 113; CCA 1; CP 6, 7; CWP; DLB 60

Gunter, Erich
See Eich, Gunter

Gurdjieff, G(eorgei) I(vanovich)
1877(?)-1949 .... **TCLC 71**
See also CA 157

Gurganus, Allan 1947- .... CLC 70
See also BEST 90:1; CA 135; CANR 114; CN 6, 7; CPW; CSW; DAM POP; GLL 1

Gurney, A. R.
See Gurney, A(lbert) R(amsdell), Jr.
See also DLB 266

Gurney, A(lbert) R(amsdell), Jr.
1930- .... **CLC 32, 50, 54**
See Gurney, A. R.
See also AMWS 5; CA 77-80; CAD; CANR 32, 64, 121; CD 5, 6; DAM DRAM; EWL 3

Gurney, Ivor (Bertie) 1890-1937 ... TCLC 33
See also BRW 6; CA 167; DLBY 2002; PAB; RGEL 2

Gurney, Peter
See Gurney, A(lbert) R(amsdell), Jr.

Guro, Elena (Genrikhovna)
1877-1913 .... **TCLC 56**
See also DLB 295

Gustafson, James M(oody) 1925- ... CLC 100
See also CA 25-28R; CANR 37

Gustafson, Ralph (Barker)
1909-1995 .... **CLC 36**
See also CA 21-24R; CANR 8, 45, 84; CP 1, 2, 3, 4, 5, 6; DLB 88; RGEL 2

Gut, Gom
See Simenon, Georges (Jacques Christian)

Guterson, David 1956- .... CLC 91
See also CA 132; CANR 73, 126; CN 7; DLB 292; MTCW 2; MTFW 2005; NFS 13

Guthrie, A(lfred) B(ertram), Jr.
1901-1991 .... **CLC 23**
See also CA 57-60; CAAS 134; CANR 24; CN 1, 2, 3; DLB 6, 212; MAL 5; SATA 62; SATA-Obit 67; TCWW 1, 2

Guthrie, Isobel
See Grieve, C(hristopher) M(urray)

Guthrie, Woodrow Wilson 1912-1967
See Guthrie, Woody
See also CA 113; CAAS 93-96

Guthrie, Woody .... **CLC 35**
See Guthrie, Woodrow Wilson
See also DLB 303; LAIT 3

Gutierrez Najera, Manuel
1859-1895 .... **HLCS 2; NCLC 133**
See also DLB 290; LAW

Guy, Rosa (Cuthbert) 1925- .... CLC 26
See also AAYA 4, 37; BW 2; CA 17-20R; CANR 14, 34, 83; CLR 13; DLB 33; DNFS 1; JRDA; MAICYA 1, 2; SATA 14, 62, 122; YAW

Gwendolyn
See Bennett, (Enoch) Arnold

H. D. .... **CLC 3, 8, 14, 31, 34, 73; PC 5**
See Doolittle, Hilda
See also FL 1:5

H. de V.
See Buchan, John

Haavikko, Paavo Juhani 1931- .. CLC 18, 34
See also CA 106; CWW 2; EWL 3

Habbema, Koos
See Heijermans, Herman

Habermas, Juergen 1929- .... CLC 104
See also CA 109; CANR 85, 162; DLB 242

Habermas, Jurgen
See Habermas, Juergen

Hacker, Marilyn 1942- ...... CLC 5, 9, 23, 72, 91; PC 47
See also CA 77-80; CANR 68, 129; CP 3, 4, 5, 6, 7; CWP; DAM POET; DLB 120, 282; FW; GLL 2; MAL 5; PFS 19

Hadewijch of Antwerp fl. 1250- ... CMLC 61
See also RGWL 3

Hadrian 76-138 .... CMLC 52

Haeckel, Ernst Heinrich (Philipp August)
1834-1919 .... **TCLC 83**
See also CA 157

Hafiz c. 1326-1389(?) .... CMLC 34
See also RGWL 2, 3; WLIT 6

Hagedorn, Jessica T(arahata)
1949- .... **CLC 185**
See also CA 139; CANR 69; CWP; DLB 312; RGAL 4

Haggard, H(enry) Rider
1856-1925 .... **TCLC 11**
See also BRWS 3; BYA 4, 5; CA 148; CAAE 108; CANR 112; DLB 70, 156, 174, 178; FANT; LMFS 1; MTCW 2; RGEL 2; RHW; SATA 16; SCFW 1, 2; SFW 4; SUFW 1; WLIT 4

Hagiosy, L.
See Larbaud, Valery (Nicolas)

Hagiwara, Sakutaro 1886-1942 .... PC 18; TCLC 60
See Hagiwara Sakutaro
See also CA 154; RGWL 3

Hagiwara Sakutaro
See Hagiwara, Sakutaro
See also EWL 3

Haig, Fenil
See Ford, Ford Madox

Haig-Brown, Roderick (Langmere)
1908-1976 .... **CLC 21**
See also CA 5-8R; CAAS 69-72; CANR 4, 38, 83; CLR 31; CWRI 5; DLB 88; MAICYA 1, 2; SATA 12; TCWW 2

Haight, Rip
See Carpenter, John (Howard)

Haij, Vera
See Jansson, Tove (Marika)

Hailey, Arthur 1920-2004 .... CLC 5
See also AITN 2; BEST 90:3; BPFB 2; CA 1-4R; CAAS 233; CANR 2, 36, 75; CCA 1; CN 1, 2, 3, 4, 5, 6, 7; CPW; DAM NOV, POP; DLB 88; DLBY 1982; MTCW 1, 2; MTFW 2005

Hailey, Elizabeth Forsythe 1938- ..... CLC 40
See also CA 188; 93-96, 188; 1; CANR 15, 48; INT CANR-15

Haines, John (Meade) 1924- .... CLC 58
See also AMWS 12; CA 17-20R; CANR 13, 34; CP 1, 2, 3, 4, 5; CSW; DLB 5, 212; TCLE 1:1

Ha Jin 1956- .... CLC 109
See Jin, Xuefei
See also CA 152; CANR 91, 130; DLB 244, 292; MTFW 2005; NFS 25; SSFS 17

Hakluyt, Richard 1552-1616 .... LC 31
See also DLB 136; RGEL 2

Haldeman, Joe 1943- .... CLC 61
See Graham, Robert
See also AAYA 38; CA 179; 53-56, 179; 25; CANR 6, 70, 72, 130; DLB 8; INT CANR-6; SCFW 2; SFW 4

Haldeman, Joe William
See Haldeman, Joe

Hale, Janet Campbell 1947- .... NNAL
See also CA 49-52; CANR 45, 75; DAM MULT; DLB 175; MTCW 2; MTFW 2005

Hale, Sarah Josepha (Buell)
1788-1879 .... **NCLC 75**
See also DLB 1, 42, 73, 243

Halevy, Elie 1870-1937 .... TCLC 104

Haley, Alex(ander Murray Palmer)
1921-1992 .... **BLC 2; CLC 8, 12, 76; TCLC 147**
See also AAYA 26; BPFB 2; BW 2, 3; CA 77-80; CAAS 136; CANR 61; CDALBS; CPW; CSW; DA; DA3; DAB; DAC; DAM MST, MULT, POP; DLB 38; LAIT 5; MTCW 1, 2; NFS 9

Haliburton, Thomas Chandler
1796-1865 .... **NCLC 15, 149**
See also DLB 11, 99; RGEL 2; RGSF 2

Hall, Donald 1928- ... CLC 1, 13, 37, 59, 151, 240; PC 70
See also AAYA 63; CA 5-8R; 7; CANR 2, 44, 64, 106, 133; CP 1, 2, 3, 4, 5, 6, 7; DAM POET; DLB 5; MAL 5; MTCW 2; MTFW 2005; RGAL 4; SATA 23, 97

Hall, Donald Andrew, Jr.
See Hall, Donald

Hall, Frederic Sauser
See Sauser-Hall, Frederic
Hall, James
See Kuttner, Henry
Hall, James Norman 1887-1951 ..... **TCLC 23**
See also CA 173; CAAE 123; LAIT 1;
RHW 1; SATA 21
Hall, Joseph 1574-1656 .... **LC 91**
See also DLB 121, 151; RGEL 2
Hall, Marguerite Radclyffe
See Hall, Radclyffe
Hall, Radclyffe 1880-1943 .... **TCLC 12**
See also BRWS 6; CA 150; CAAE 110;
CANR 83; DLB 191; MTCW 2; MTFW
2005; RGEL 2; RHW
Hall, Rodney 1935- .... **CLC 51**
See also CA 109; CANR 69; CN 6, 7; CP
1, 2, 3, 4, 5, 6, 7; DLB 289
Hallam, Arthur Henry
1811-1833 .... **NCLC 110**
See also DLB 32
Halldor Laxness .... **CLC 25**
See Gudjonsson, Halldor Kiljan
See also DLB 293; EW 12; EWL 3; RGWL
2, 3
Halleck, Fitz-Greene 1790-1867 .... **NCLC 47**
See also DLB 3, 250; RGAL 4
Halliday, Michael
See Creasey, John
Halpern, Daniel 1945- .... **CLC 14**
See also CA 33-36R; CANR 93; CP 3, 4, 5,
6, 7
Hamburger, Michael 1924-2007 ... **CLC 5, 14**
See also CA 196; 5-8R, 196; 4; CANR 2,
47; CP 1, 2, 3, 4, 5, 6, 7; DLB 27
Hamburger, Michael Peter Leopold
See Hamburger, Michael
Hamill, Pete 1935- .... **CLC 10**
See also CA 25-28R; CANR 18, 71, 127
Hamilton, Alexander
1755(?)-1804 .... **NCLC 49**
See also DLB 37
Hamilton, Clive
See Lewis, C.S.
Hamilton, Edmond 1904-1977 .... **CLC 1**
See also CA 1-4R; CANR 3, 84; DLB 8;
SATA 118; SFW 4
Hamilton, Elizabeth 1758-1816 ... **NCLC 153**
See also DLB 116, 158
Hamilton, Eugene (Jacob) Lee
See Lee-Hamilton, Eugene (Jacob)
Hamilton, Franklin
See Silverberg, Robert
Hamilton, Gail
See Corcoran, Barbara (Asenath)
Hamilton, (Robert) Ian 1938-2001 . **CLC 191**
See also CA 106; CAAS 203; CANR 41,
67; CP 1, 2, 3, 4, 5, 6, 7; DLB 40, 155
Hamilton, Jane 1957- .... **CLC 179**
See also CA 147; CANR 85, 128; CN 7;
MTFW 2005
Hamilton, Mollie
See Kaye, M.M.
Hamilton, (Anthony Walter) Patrick
1904-1962 .... **CLC 51**
See also CA 176; CAAS 113; DLB 10, 191
Hamilton, Virginia 1936-2002 .... **CLC 26**
See also AAYA 2, 21; BW 2, 3; BYA 1, 2,
8; CA 25-28R; CAAS 206; CANR 20, 37,
73, 126; CLR 1, 11, 40; DAM MULT;
DLB 33, 52; DLBY 2001; INT CANR-
20; JRDA; LAIT 5; MAICYA 1, 2; MAI-
CYAS 1; MTCW 1, 2; MTFW 2005;
SATA 4, 56, 79, 123; SATA-Obit 132;
WYA; YAW

Hammett, (Samuel) Dashiell
1894-1961 .... **CLC 3, 5, 10, 19, 47; SSC
17; TCLC 187**
See also AAYA 59; AITN 1; AMWS 4;
BPFB 2; CA 81-84; CANR 42; CDALB
1929-1941; CMW 4; DA3; DLB 226, 280;
DLBD 6; DLBY 1996; EWL 3; LAIT 3;
MAL 5; MSW; MTCW 1, 2; MTFW
2005; NFS 21; RGAL 4; RGSF 2; TUS
Hammon, Jupiter 1720(?)-1800(?) .... **BLC 2;
NCLC 5; PC 16**
See also DAM MULT, POET; DLB 31, 50
Hammond, Keith
See Kuttner, Henry
Hamner, Earl (Henry), Jr. 1923- ...... **CLC 12**
See also AITN 2; CA 73-76; DLB 6
Hampton, Christopher 1946- .... **CLC 4**
See also CA 25-28R; CD 5, 6; DLB 13;
MTCW 1
Hampton, Christopher James
See Hampton, Christopher
Hamsun, Knut .... **TCLC 2, 14, 49, 151**
See Pedersen, Knut
See also DLB 297, 330; EW 8; EWL 3;
RGWL 2, 3
Handke, Peter 1942- .... **CLC 5, 8, 10, 15, 38,
134; DC 17**
See also CA 77-80; CANR 33, 75, 104, 133;
CWW 2; DAM DRAM, NOV; DLB 85,
124; EWL 3; MTCW 1, 2; MTFW 2005;
TWA
Handy, W(illiam) C(hristopher)
1873-1958 .... **TCLC 97**
See also BW 3; CA 167; CAAE 121
Hanley, James 1901-1985 ..... **CLC 3, 5, 8, 13**
See also CA 73-76; CAAS 117; CANR 36;
CBD; CN 1, 2, 3; DLB 191; EWL 3;
MTCW 1; RGEL 2
Hannah, Barry 1942- .. **CLC 23, 38, 90; SSC
94**
See also BPFB 2; CA 110; CAAE 108;
CANR 43, 68, 113; CN 4, 5, 6, 7; CSW;
DLB 6, 234; INT CA-110; MTCW 1;
RGSF 2
Hannon, Ezra
See Hunter, Evan
Hansberry, Lorraine (Vivian)
1930-1965 ... **BLC 2; CLC 17, 62; DC 2**
See also AAYA 25; AFAW 1, 2; AMWS 4;
BW 1, 3; CA 109; CAAS 25-28R; CABS
3; CAD; CANR 58; CDALB 1941-1968;
CWD; DA; DA3; DAB; DAC; DAM
DRAM, MST, MULT; DFS 2; DLB 7, 38;
EWL 3; FL 1:6; FW; LAIT 4; MAL 5;
MTCW 1, 2; MTFW 2005; RGAL 4; TUS
Hansen, Joseph 1923-2004 .... **CLC 38**
See Brock, Rose; Colton, James
See also BPFB 2; CA 29-32R; 17; CAAS
233; CANR 16, 44, 66, 125; CMW 4;
DLB 226; GLL 1; INT CANR-16
Hansen, Karen V. 1955- .... **CLC 65**
See also CA 149; CANR 102
Hansen, Martin A(lfred)
1909-1955 .... **TCLC 32**
See also CA 167; DLB 214; EWL 3
Hanson, Kenneth O(stlin) 1922- .... **CLC 13**
See also CA 53-56; CANR 7; CP 1, 2, 3, 4,
5
Hardwick, Elizabeth 1916- .... **CLC 13**
See also AMWS 3; CA 5-8R; CANR 3, 32,
70, 100, 139; CN 4, 5, 6; CSW; DA3;
DAM NOV; DLB 6; MBL; MTCW 1, 2;
MTFW 2005; TCLE 1:1
Hardy, Thomas 1840-1928 .... **PC 8; SSC 2,
60; TCLC 4, 10, 18, 32, 48, 53, 72, 143,
153; WLC 3**
See also AAYA 69; BRW 6; BRWC 1, 2;
BRWR 1; CA 123; CAAE 104; CDBLB
1890-1914; DA; DA3; DAB; DAC; DAM
MST, NOV, POET; DLB 18, 19, 135, 284;

EWL 3; EXPN; EXPP; LAIT 2; MTCW
1, 2; MTFW 2005; NFS 3, 11, 15, 19; PFS
3, 4, 18; RGEL 2; RGSF 2; TEA; WLIT
4
Hare, David 1947- . **CLC 29, 58, 136; DC 26**
See also BRWS 4; CA 97-100; CANR 39,
91; CBD; CD 5, 6; DFS 4, 7, 16; DLB
13, 310; MTCW 1; TEA
Harewood, John
See Van Druten, John (William)
Harford, Henry
See Hudson, W(illiam) H(enry)
Hargrave, Leonie
See Disch, Thomas M.
**Hariri, Al- al-Qasim ibn 'Ali Abu
Muhammad al-Basri**
See al-Hariri, al-Qasim ibn 'Ali Abu Mu-
hammad al-Basri
Harjo, Joy 1951- ..... **CLC 83; NNAL; PC 27**
See also AMWS 12; CA 114; CANR 35,
67, 91, 129; CP 6, 7; CWP; DAM MULT;
DLB 120, 175; EWL 3; MTCW 2; MTFW
2005; PFS 15; RGAL 4
Harlan, Louis R(udolph) 1922- .... **CLC 34**
See also CA 21-24R; CANR 25, 55, 80
Harling, Robert 1951(?)- .... **CLC 53**
See also CA 147
Harmon, William (Ruth) 1938- .... **CLC 38**
See also CA 33-36R; CANR 14, 32, 35;
SATA 65
Harper, F. E. W.
See Harper, Frances Ellen Watkins
Harper, Frances E. W.
See Harper, Frances Ellen Watkins
Harper, Frances E. Watkins
See Harper, Frances Ellen Watkins
Harper, Frances Ellen
See Harper, Frances Ellen Watkins
Harper, Frances Ellen Watkins
1825-1911 ..... **BLC 2; PC 21; TCLC 14**
See also AFAW 1, 2; BW 1, 3; CA 125;
CAAE 111; CANR 79; DAM MULT,
POET; DLB 50, 221; MBL; RGAL 4
Harper, Michael S(teven) 1938- ... **CLC 7, 22**
See also AFAW 2; BW 1; CA 224; 33-36R,
224; CANR 24, 108; CP 2, 3, 4, 5, 6, 7;
DLB 41; RGAL 4; TCLE 1:1
Harper, Mrs. F. E. W.
See Harper, Frances Ellen Watkins
Harpur, Charles 1813-1868 .... **NCLC 114**
See also DLB 230; RGEL 2
Harris, Christie
See Harris, Christie (Lucy) Irwin
Harris, Christie (Lucy) Irwin
1907-2002 .... **CLC 12**
See also CA 5-8R; CANR 6, 83; CLR 47;
DLB 88; JRDA; MAICYA 1, 2; SAAS 10;
SATA 6, 74; SATA-Essay 116
Harris, Frank 1856-1931 .... **TCLC 24**
See also CA 150; CAAE 109; CANR 80;
DLB 156, 197; RGEL 2
Harris, George Washington
1814-1869 .... **NCLC 23, 165**
See also DLB 3, 11, 248; RGAL 4
Harris, Joel Chandler 1848-1908 ..... **SSC 19;
TCLC 2**
See also CA 137; CAAE 104; CANR 80;
CLR 49; DLB 11, 23, 42, 78, 91; LAIT 2;
MAICYA 1, 2; RGSF 2; SATA 100; WCH;
YABC 1
**Harris, John (Wyndham Parkes Lucas)
Beynon** 1903-1969
See Wyndham, John
See also CA 102; CAAS 89-92; CANR 84;
SATA 118; SFW 4
Harris, MacDonald .... **CLC 9**
See Heiney, Donald (William)

Harris, Mark 1922-2007 .... **CLC 19**
See also CA 5-8R; 3; CANR 2, 55, 83; CN 1, 2, 3, 4, 5, 6, 7; DLB 2; DLBY 1980

Harris, Norman .... **CLC 65**

Harris, (Theodore) Wilson 1921- .... **CLC 25, 159**
See also BRWS 5; BW 2, 3; CA 65-68; 16; CANR 11, 27, 69, 114; CDWLB 3; CN 1, 2, 3, 4, 5, 6, 7; CP 1, 2, 3, 4, 5, 6, 7; DLB 117; EWL 3; MTCW 1; RGEL 2

Harrison, Barbara Grizzuti
1934-2002 .... **CLC 144**
See also CA 77-80; CAAS 205; CANR 15, 48; INT CANR-15

Harrison, Elizabeth (Allen) Cavanna
1909-2001
See Cavanna, Betty
See also CA 9-12R; CAAS 200; CANR 6, 27, 85, 104, 121; MAICYA 2; SATA 142; YAW

Harrison, Harry (Max) 1925- .... **CLC 42**
See also CA 1-4R; CANR 5, 21, 84; DLB 8; SATA 4; SCFW 2; SFW 4

Harrison, James
See Harrison, Jim

Harrison, James Thomas
See Harrison, Jim

Harrison, Jim 1937- .... **CLC 6, 14, 33, 66, 143; SSC 19**
See also AMWS 8; CA 13-16R; CANR 8, 51, 79, 142; CN 5, 6; CP 1, 2, 3, 4, 5, 6; DLBY 1982; INT CANR-8; RGAL 4; TCWW 2; TUS

Harrison, Kathryn 1961- .... **CLC 70, 151**
See also CA 144; CANR 68, 122

Harrison, Tony 1937- .... **CLC 43, 129**
See also BRWS 5; CA 65-68; CANR 44, 98; CBD; CD 5, 6; CP 2, 3, 4, 5, 6, 7; DLB 40, 245; MTCW 1; RGEL 2

Harriss, Will(ard Irvin) 1922- .... **CLC 34**
See also CA 111

Hart, Ellis
See Ellison, Harlan

Hart, Josephine 1942(?)- .... **CLC 70**
See also CA 138; CANR 70, 149; CPW; DAM POP

Hart, Moss 1904-1961 .... **CLC 66**
See also CA 109; CAAS 89-92; CANR 84; DAM DRAM; DFS 1; DLB 7, 266; RGAL 4

Harte, (Francis) Bret(t)
1836(?)-1902 ... **SSC 8, 59; TCLC 1, 25; WLC 3**
See also AMWS 2; CA 140; CAAE 104; CANR 80; CDALB 1865-1917; DA; DA3; DAC; DAM MST; DLB 12, 64, 74, 79, 186; EXPS; LAIT 2; RGAL 4; RGSF 2; SATA 26; SSFS 3; TUS

Hartley, L(eslie) P(oles) 1895-1972 ... **CLC 2, 22**
See also BRWS 7; CA 45-48; CAAS 37-40R; CANR 33; CN 1; DLB 15, 139; EWL 3; HGG; MTCW 1, 2; MTFW 2005; RGEL 2; RGSF 2; SUFW 1

Hartman, Geoffrey H. 1929- .... **CLC 27**
See also CA 125; CAAE 117; CANR 79; DLB 67

Hartmann, Sadakichi 1869-1944 ... **TCLC 73**
See also CA 157; DLB 54

Hartmann von Aue c. 1170-c.
1210 .... **CMLC 15**
See also CDWLB 2; DLB 138; RGWL 2, 3

Hartog, Jan de
See de Hartog, Jan

Haruf, Kent 1943- .... **CLC 34**
See also AAYA 44; CA 149; CANR 91, 131

Harvey, Caroline
See Trollope, Joanna

Harvey, Gabriel 1550(?)-1631 .... **LC 88**
See also DLB 167, 213, 281

Harwood, Ronald 1934- .... **CLC 32**
See also CA 1-4R; CANR 4, 55, 150; CBD; CD 5, 6; DAM DRAM, MST; DLB 13

Hasegawa Tatsunosuke
See Futabatei, Shimei

Hasek, Jaroslav (Matej Frantisek)
1883-1923 .... **SSC 69; TCLC 4**
See also CA 129; CAAE 104; CDWLB 4; DLB 215; EW 9; EWL 3; MTCW 1, 2; RGSF 2; RGWL 2, 3

Hass, Robert 1941- ... **CLC 18, 39, 99; PC 16**
See also AMWS 6; CA 111; CANR 30, 50, 71; CP 3, 4, 5, 6, 7; DLB 105, 206; EWL 3; MAL 5; MTCW 2; RGAL 4; SATA 94; TCLE 1:1

Hastings, Hudson
See Kuttner, Henry

Hastings, Selina .... **CLC 44**
See also CA 257

Hastings, Selina Shirley
See Hastings, Selina

Hathorne, John 1641-1717 .... **LC 38**

Hatteras, Amelia
See Mencken, H(enry) L(ouis)

Hatteras, Owen .... **TCLC 18**
See Mencken, H(enry) L(ouis); Nathan, George Jean

Hauff, Wilhelm 1802-1827 .... **NCLC 185**
See also DLB 90; SUFW 1

Hauptmann, Gerhart (Johann Robert)
1862-1946 .... **SSC 37; TCLC 4**
See also CA 153; CAAE 104; CDWLB 2; DAM DRAM; DLB 66, 118, 330; EW 8; EWL 3; RGSF 2; RGWL 2, 3; TWA

Havel, Vaclav 1936- ..... **CLC 25, 58, 65, 123; DC 6**
See also CA 104; CANR 36, 63, 124; CD-WLB 4; CWW 2; DA3; DAM DRAM; DFS 10; DLB 232; EWL 3; LMFS 2; MTCW 1, 2; MTFW 2005; RGWL 3

Haviaras, Stratis .... **CLC 33**
See Chaviaras, Strates

Hawes, Stephen 1475(?)-1529(?) .... **LC 17**
See also DLB 132; RGEL 2

Hawkes, John 1925-1998 .. **CLC 1, 2, 3, 4, 7, 9, 14, 15, 27, 49**
See also BPFB 2; CA 1-4R; CAAS 167; CANR 2, 47, 64; CN 1, 2, 3, 4, 5, 6; DLB 2, 7, 227; DLBY 1980, 1998; EWL 3; MAL 5; MTCW 1, 2; MTFW 2005; RGAL 4

Hawking, S. W.
See Hawking, Stephen W.

Hawking, Stephen W. 1942- ..... **CLC 63, 105**
See also AAYA 13; BEST 89:1; CA 129; CAAE 126; CANR 48, 115; CPW; DA3; MTCW 2; MTFW 2005

Hawkins, Anthony Hope
See Hope, Anthony

Hawthorne, Julian 1846-1934 .... **TCLC 25**
See also CA 165; HGG

Hawthorne, Nathaniel 1804-1864 ... **NCLC 2, 10, 17, 23, 39, 79, 95, 158, 171; SSC 3, 29, 39, 89; WLC 3**
See also AAYA 18; AMW; AMWC 1; AMWR 1; BPFB 2; BYA 3; CDALB 1640-1865; CLR 103; DA; DA3; DAB; DAC; DAM MST, NOV; DLB 1, 74, 183, 223, 269; EXPN; EXPS; GL 2; HGG; LAIT 1, 20; NFS 1; RGAL 4; RGSF 2; SSFS 1, 7, 11, 15; SUFW 1; TUS; WCH; YABC 2

Hawthorne, Sophia Peabody
1809-1871 .... **NCLC 150**
See also DLB 183, 239

Haxton, Josephine Ayres 1921-
See Douglas, Ellen
See also CA 115; CANR 41, 83

Hayaseca y Eizaguirre, Jorge
See Echegaray (y Eizaguirre), Jose (Maria Waldo)

Hayashi, Fumiko 1904-1951 .... **TCLC 27**
See Hayashi Fumiko
See also CA 161

Hayashi Fumiko
See Hayashi, Fumiko
See also DLB 180; EWL 3

Haycraft, Anna 1932-2005
See Ellis, Alice Thomas
See also CA 122; CAAS 237; CANR 90, 141; MTCW 2; MTFW 2005

Hayden, Robert E(arl) 1913-1980 ..... **BLC 2; CLC 5, 9, 14, 37; PC 6**
See also AFAW 1, 2; AMWS 2; BW 1, 3; CA 69-72; CAAS 97-100; CABS 2; CANR 24, 75, 82; CDALB 1941-1968; CP 1, 2, 3; DA; DAC; DAM MST, MULT, POET; DLB 5, 76; EWL 3; EXPP; MAL 5; MTCW 1, 2; PFS 1; RGAL 4; SATA 19; SATA-Obit 26; WP

Haydon, Benjamin Robert
1786-1846 .... **NCLC 146**
See also DLB 110

Hayek, F(riedrich) A(ugust von)
1899-1992 .... **TCLC 109**
See also CA 93-96; CAAS 137; CANR 20; MTCW 1, 2

Hayford, J(oseph) E(phraim) Casely
See Casely-Hayford, J(oseph) E(phraim)

Hayman, Ronald 1932- .... **CLC 44**
See also CA 25-28R; CANR 18, 50, 88; CD 5, 6; DLB 155

Hayne, Paul Hamilton 1830-1886 . **NCLC 94**
See also DLB 3, 64, 79, 248; RGAL 4

Hays, Mary 1760-1843 .... **NCLC 114**
See also DLB 142, 158; RGEL 2

Haywood, Eliza (Fowler)
1693(?)-1756 .... **LC 1, 44**
See also BRWS 12; DLB 39; RGEL 2

Hazlitt, William 1778-1830 ...... **NCLC 29, 82**
See also BRW 4; DLB 110, 158; RGEL 2; TEA

Hazzard, Shirley 1931- .... **CLC 18, 218**
See also CA 9-12R; CANR 4, 70, 127; CN 1, 2, 3, 4, 5, 6, 7; DLB 289; DLBY 1982; MTCW 1

Head, Bessie 1937-1986 ...... **BLC 2; CLC 25, 67; SSC 52**
See also AFW; BW 2, 3; CA 29-32R; CAAS 119; CANR 25, 82; CDWLB 3; CN 1, 2, 3, 4; DA3; DAM MULT; DLB 117, 225; EWL 3; EXPS; FL 1:6; FW; MTCW 1, 2; MTFW 2005; RGSF 2; SSFS 5, 13; WLIT 2; WWE 1

Headon, (Nicky) Topper 1956(?)- ..... **CLC 30**

Heaney, Seamus 1939- . **CLC 5, 7, 14, 25, 37, 74, 91, 171, 225; PC 18; WLCS**
See also AAYA 61; BRWR 1; BRWS 2; CA 85-88; CANR 25, 48, 75, 91, 128; CD-BLB 1960 to Present; CP 1, 2, 3, 4, 5, 6, 7; DA3; DAB; DAM POET; DLB 40, 330; DLBY 1995; EWL 3; EXPP; MTCW 1, 2; MTFW 2005; PAB; PFS 2, 5, 8, 17; RGEL 2; TEA; WLIT 4

Hearn, (Patricio) Lafcadio (Tessima Carlos)
1850-1904 .... **TCLC 9**
See also CA 166; CAAE 105; DLB 12, 78, 189; HGG; MAL 5; RGAL 4

Hearne, Samuel 1745-1792 .... **LC 95**
See also DLB 99

Hearne, Vicki 1946-2001 .... **CLC 56**
See also CA 139; CAAS 201

Herris, Violet
See Hunt, Violet

Herrmann, Dorothy 1941- .... **CLC 44**
See also CA 107

Herrmann, Taffy
See Herrmann, Dorothy

Hersey, John 1914-1993 .. **CLC 1, 2, 7, 9, 40, 81, 97**
See also AAYA 29; BPFB 2; CA 17-20R;
CAAS 140; CANR 33; CDALBS; CN 1,
2, 3, 4, 5; CPW; DAM POP; DLB 6, 185,
278, 299; MAL 5; MTCW 1, 2; MTFW
2005; RGHL; SATA 25; SATA-Obit 76;
TUS

Herzen, Aleksandr Ivanovich
1812-1870 .... **NCLC 10, 61**
See also Herzen, Alexander

Herzen, Alexander
See Herzen, Aleksandr Ivanovich
See also DLB 277

Herzl, Theodor 1860-1904 .... **TCLC 36**
See also CA 168

Herzog, Werner 1942- .... **CLC 16, 236**
See also CA 89-92

Hesiod c. 8th cent. B.C.- .... **CMLC 5**
See also AW 1; DLB 176; RGWL 2, 3;
WLIT 8

Hesse, Hermann 1877-1962 ... **CLC 1, 2, 3, 6,
11, 17, 25, 69; SSC 9, 49; TCLC 148;
WLC 3**
See also AAYA 43; BPFB 2; CA 17-18;
CAP 2; CDWLB 2; DA; DA3; DAB;
DAC; DAM MST, NOV; DLB 66, 330;
EW 9; EWL 3; EXPN; LAIT 1; MTCW
1, 2; MTFW 2005; NFS 6, 15, 24; RGWL
2, 3; SATA 50; TWA

Hewes, Cady
See De Voto, Bernard (Augustine)

Heyen, William 1940- .... **CLC 13, 18**
See also CA 220; 33-36R, 220; 9; CANR
98; CP 3, 4, 5, 6, 7; DLB 5; RGHL

Heyerdahl, Thor 1914-2002 .... **CLC 26**
See also CA 5-8R; CAAS 207; CANR 5,
22, 66, 73; LAIT 4; MTCW 1, 2; MTFW
2005; SATA 2, 52

Heym, Georg (Theodor Franz Arthur)
1887-1912 .... **TCLC 9**
See also CA 181; CAAE 106

Heym, Stefan 1913-2001 .... **CLC 41**
See also CA 9-12R; CAAS 203; CANR 4;
CWW 2; DLB 69; EWL 3

Heyse, Paul (Johann Ludwig von)
1830-1914 .... **TCLC 8**
See also CA 209; CAAE 104; DLB 129,
330

Heyward, (Edwin) DuBose
1885-1940 .... **HR 1:2; TCLC 59**
See also CA 157; CAAE 108; DLB 7, 9,
45, 249; MAL 5; SATA 21

Heywood, John 1497(?)-1580(?) .... **LC 65**
See also DLB 136; RGEL 2

Heywood, Thomas 1573(?)-1641 .... **LC 111**
See also DAM DRAM; DLB 62; LMFS 1;
RGEL 2; TEA

Hiaasen, Carl 1953- .... **CLC 238**
See also CA 105; CANR 22, 45, 65, 113,
133; CMW 4; CPW; CSW; DA3; DLB
292; MTCW 2; MTFW 2005

Hibbert, Eleanor Alice Burford
1906-1993 .... **CLC 7**
See Holt, Victoria
See also BEST 90:4; CA 17-20R; CAAS
140; CANR 9, 28, 59; CMW 4; CPW;
DAM POP; MTCW 2; MTFW 2005;
RHW; SATA 2; SATA-Obit 74

Hichens, Robert (Smythe)
1864-1950 .... **TCLC 64**
See also CA 162; DLB 153; HGG; RHW;
SUFW

Higgins, Aidan 1927- .... **SSC 68**
See also CA 9-12R; CANR 70, 115, 148;
CN 1, 2, 3, 4, 5; DLB 14

Higgins, George V(incent)
1939-1999 .... **CLC 4, 7, 10, 18**
See also BPFB 2; CA 77-80; 5; CAAS 186;
CANR 17, 51, 89, 96; CMW 4; CN 2, 3,
4, 5, 6; DLB 2; DLBY 1981, 1998; INT
CANR-17; MSW; MTCW 1

Higginson, Thomas Wentworth
1823-1911 .... **TCLC 36**
See also CA 162; DLB 1, 64, 243

Higgonet, Margaret .... **CLC 65**

Highet, Helen
See MacInnes, Helen (Clark)

Highsmith, Patricia 1921-1995 ...... **CLC 2, 4,
14, 42, 102**
See Morgan, Claire
See also AAYA 48; BRWS 5; CA 1-4R;
CAAS 147; CANR 1, 20, 48, 62, 108;
CMW 4; CN 1, 2, 3, 4, 5; CPW; DA3;
DAM NOV, POP; DLB 306; MSW;
MTCW 1, 2; MTFW 2005

Highwater, Jamake (Mamake)
1942(?)-2001 .... **CLC 12**
See also AAYA 7, 69; BPFB 2; BYA 4; CA
65-68; 7; CAAS 199; CANR 10, 34, 84;
CLR 17; CWRI 5; DLB 52; DLBY 1985;
JRDA; MAICYA 1, 2; SATA 32, 69;
SATA-Brief 30

Highway, Tomson 1951- ...... **CLC 92; NNAL**
See also CA 151; CANR 75; CCA 1; CD 5,
6; CN 7; DAC; DAM MULT; DFS 2;
DLB 334; MTCW 2

Hijuelos, Oscar 1951- .... **CLC 65; HLC 1**
See also AAYA 25; AMWS 8; BEST 90:1;
CA 123; CANR 50, 75, 125; CPW; DA3;
DAM MULT, POP; DLB 145; HW 1, 2;
LLW; MAL 5; MTCW 2; MTFW 2005;
NFS 17; RGAL 4; WLIT 1

Hikmet, Nazim 1902-1963 .... **CLC 40**
See Nizami of Ganja
See also CA 141; CAAS 93-96; EWL 3;
WLIT 6

Hildegard von Bingen 1098-1179 . **CMLC 20**
See also DLB 148

Hildesheimer, Wolfgang 1916-1991 .. **CLC 49**
See also CA 101; CAAS 135; DLB 69, 124;
EWL 3; RGHL

Hill, Geoffrey (William) 1932- ...... **CLC 5, 8,
18, 45**
See also BRWS 5; CA 81-84; CANR 21,
89; CDBLB 1960 to Present; CP 1, 2, 3,
4, 5, 6, 7; DAM POET; DLB 40; EWL 3;
MTCW 1; RGEL 2; RGHL

Hill, George Roy 1921-2002 .... **CLC 26**
See also CA 122; CAAE 110; CAAS 213

Hill, John
See Koontz, Dean R.

Hill, Susan 1942- .... **CLC 4, 113**
See also CA 33-36R; CANR 29, 69, 129;
CN 2, 3, 4, 5, 6, 7; DAB; DAM MST,
NOV; DLB 14, 139; HGG; MTCW 1;
RHW

Hill, Susan Elizabeth
See Hill, Susan

Hillard, Asa G. III .... **CLC 70**

Hillerman, Tony 1925- .... **CLC 62, 170**
See also AAYA 40; BEST 89:1; BPFB 2;
CA 29-32R; CANR 21, 42, 65, 97, 134;
CMW 4; CPW; DA3; DAM POP; DLB
206, 306; MAL 5; MSW; MTCW 2;
MTFW 2005; RGAL 4; SATA 6; TCWW
2; YAW

Hillesum, Etty 1914-1943 .... **TCLC 49**
See also CA 137; RGHL

Hilliard, Noel (Harvey) 1929-1996 ... **CLC 15**
See also CA 9-12R; CANR 7, 69; CN 1, 2,
3, 4, 5, 6

Hillis, Rick 1956- .... **CLC 66**
See also CA 134

Hilton, James 1900-1954 .... **TCLC 21**
See also CA 169; CAAE 108; DLB 34, 77;
FANT; SATA 34

Hilton, Walter (?)-1396 .... **CMLC 58**
See also DLB 146; RGEL 2

Himes, Chester (Bomar) 1909-1984 .. **BLC 2;
CLC 2, 4, 7, 18, 58, 108; TCLC 139**
See also AFAW 2; AMWS 16; BPFB 2; BW
2; CA 25-28R; CAAS 114; CANR 22, 89;
CMW 4; CN 1, 2, 3; DAM MULT; DLB
2, 76, 143, 226; EWL 3; MAL 5; MSW;
MTCW 1, 2; MTFW 2005; RGAL 4

Himmelfarb, Gertrude 1922- .... **CLC 202**
See also CA 49-52; CANR 28, 66, 102

Hinde, Thomas .... **CLC 6, 11**
See Chitty, Thomas Willes
See also CN 1, 2, 3, 4, 5, 6; EWL 3

Hine, (William) Daryl 1936- .... **CLC 15**
See also CA 1-4R; 15; CANR 1, 20; CP 1,
2, 3, 4, 5, 6, 7; DLB 60

Hinkson, Katharine Tynan
See Tynan, Katharine

Hinojosa, Rolando 1929- .... **HLC 1**
See Hinojosa-Smith, Rolando
See also CA 131; 16; CANR 62; DAM
MULT; DLB 82; HW 1, 2; LLW; MTCW
2; MTFW 2005; RGAL 4

Hinton, S.E. 1950- .... **CLC 30, 111**
See also AAYA 2, 33; BPFB 2; BYA 2, 3;
CA 81-84; CANR 32, 62, 92, 133;
CDALBS; CLR 3, 23; CPW; DA; DA3;
DAB; DAC; DAM MST, NOV; JRDA;
LAIT 5; MAICYA 1, 2; MTCW 1, 2;
MTFW 2005; NFS 5, 9, 15, 16; SATA 19,
58, 115, 160; WYA; YAW

Hippius, Zinaida (Nikolaevna) .... **TCLC 9**
See Gippius, Zinaida (Nikolaevna)
See also DLB 295; EWL 3

Hiraoka, Kimitake 1925-1970
See Mishima, Yukio
See also CA 97-100; CAAS 29-32R; DA3;
DAM DRAM; GLL 1; MTCW 1, 2

Hirsch, E.D., Jr. 1928- .... **CLC 79**
See also CA 25-28R; CANR 27, 51, 146;
DLB 67; INT CANR-27; MTCW 1

Hirsch, Edward 1950- .... **CLC 31, 50**
See also CA 104; CANR 20, 42, 102; CP 6,
7; DLB 120; PFS 22

Hirsch, Eric Donald, Jr.
See Hirsch, E.D., Jr.

Hitchcock, Alfred (Joseph)
1899-1980 .... **CLC 16**
See also AAYA 22; CA 159; CAAS 97-100;
SATA 27; SATA-Obit 24

Hitchens, Christopher 1949- .... **CLC 157**
See also CA 152; CANR 89, 155

Hitchens, Christopher Eric
See Hitchens, Christopher

Hitler, Adolf 1889-1945 .... **TCLC 53**
See also CA 147; CAAE 117

Hoagland, Edward (Morley) 1932- .. **CLC 28**
See also ANW; CA 1-4R; CANR 2, 31, 57,
107; CN 1, 2, 3, 4, 5, 6, 7; DLB 6; SATA
51; TCWW 2

Hoban, Russell 1925- .... **CLC 7, 25**
See also BPFB 2; CA 5-8R; CANR 23, 37,
66, 114, 138; CLR 3, 69; CN 4, 5, 6, 7;
CWRI 5; DAM NOV; DLB 52; FANT;
MAICYA 1, 2; MTCW 1, 2; MTFW 2005;
SATA 1, 40, 78, 136; SFW 4; SUFW 2;
TCLE 1:1

Hobbes, Thomas 1588-1679 .... **LC 36**
See also DLB 151, 252, 281; RGEL 2

Hobbs, Perry
See Blackmur, R(ichard) P(almer)

Hobson, Laura Z(ametkin)
1900-1986 .... **CLC 7, 25**
See also BPFB 2; CA 17-20R; CAAS 118;
CANR 55; CN 1, 2, 3, 4; DLB 28; SATA
52

Hoccleve, Thomas c. 1368-c. 1437 ...... **LC 75**
See also DLB 146; RGEL 2

Hoch, Edward D(entinger) 1930-
See Queen, Ellery
See also CA 29-32R; CANR 11, 27, 51, 97;
CMW 4; DLB 306; SFW 4

Hochhuth, Rolf 1931- .... **CLC 4, 11, 18**
See also CA 5-8R; CANR 33, 75, 136;
CWW 2; DAM DRAM; DLB 124; EWL
3; MTCW 1, 2; MTFW 2005; RGHL

Hochman, Sandra 1936- .... **CLC 3, 8**
See also CA 5-8R; CP 1, 2, 3, 4, 5; DLB 5

Hochwaelder, Fritz 1911-1986 .... **CLC 36**
See Hochwalder, Fritz
See also CA 29-32R; CAAS 120; CANR
42; DAM DRAM; MTCW 1; RGWL 3

Hochwalder, Fritz
See Hochwaelder, Fritz
See also EWL 3; RGWL 2

Hocking, Mary (Eunice) 1921- .... **CLC 13**
See also CA 101; CANR 18, 40

Hodgins, Jack 1938- .... **CLC 23**
See also CA 93-96; CN 4, 5, 6, 7; DLB 60

Hodgson, William Hope
1877(?)-1918 .... **TCLC 13**
See also CA 164; CAAE 111; CMW 4; DLB
70, 153, 156, 178; HGG; MTCW 2; SFW
4; SUFW 1

Hoeg, Peter 1957- .... **CLC 95, 156**
See also CA 151; CANR 75; CMW 4; DA3;
DLB 214; EWL 3; MTCW 2; MTFW
2005; NFS 17; RGWL 3; SSFS 18

Hoffman, Alice 1952- .... **CLC 51**
See also AAYA 37; AMWS 10; CA 77-80;
CANR 34, 66, 100, 138; CN 4, 5, 6, 7;
CPW; DAM NOV; DLB 292; MAL 5;
MTCW 1, 2; MTFW 2005; TCLE 1:1

Hoffman, Daniel (Gerard) 1923- . **CLC 6, 13,
23**
See also CA 1-4R; CANR 4, 142; CP 1, 2,
3, 4, 5, 6, 7; DLB 5; TCLE 1:1

Hoffman, Eva 1945- .... **CLC 182**
See also AMWS 16; CA 132; CANR 146

Hoffman, Stanley 1944- .... **CLC 5**
See also CA 77-80

Hoffman, William 1925- .... **CLC 141**
See also CA 21-24R; CANR 9, 103; CSW;
DLB 234; TCLE 1:1

Hoffman, William M.
See Hoffman, William M(oses)
See also CAD; CD 5, 6

Hoffman, William M(oses) 1939- ..... **CLC 40**
See Hoffman, William M.
See also CA 57-60; CANR 11, 71

Hoffmann, E(rnst) T(heodor) A(madeus)
1776-1822 ..... **NCLC 2, 183; SSC 13, 92**
See also CDWLB 2; DLB 90; EW 5; GL 2;
RGSF 2; RGWL 2, 3; SATA 27; SUFW
1; WCH

Hofmann, Gert 1931-1993 .... **CLC 54**
See also CA 128; CANR 145; EWL 3;
RGHL

Hofmannsthal, Hugo von 1874-1929 ... **DC 4;
TCLC 11**
See also CA 153; CAAE 106; CDWLB 2;
DAM DRAM; DFS 17; DLB 81, 118; EW
9; EWL 3; RGWL 2, 3

Hogan, Linda 1947- ..... **CLC 73; NNAL; PC
35**
See also AMWS 4; ANW; BYA 12; CA 226;
120, 226; CANR 45, 73, 129; CWP; DAM
MULT; DLB 175; SATA 132; TCWW 2

Hogarth, Charles
See Creasey, John

Hogarth, Emmett
See Polonsky, Abraham (Lincoln)

Hogarth, William 1697-1764 .... **LC 112**
See also AAYA 56

Hogg, James 1770-1835 .... **NCLC 4, 109**
See also BRWS 10; DLB 93, 116, 159; GL
2; HGG; RGEL 2; SUFW 1

Holbach, Paul-Henri Thiry
1723-1789 .... **LC 14**
See also DLB 313

Holberg, Ludvig 1684-1754 .... **LC 6**
See also DLB 300; RGWL 2, 3

Holcroft, Thomas 1745-1809 .... **NCLC 85**
See also DLB 39, 89, 158; RGEL 2

Holden, Ursula 1921- .... **CLC 18**
See also CA 101; 8; CANR 22

Holderlin, (Johann Christian) Friedrich
1770-1843 .... **NCLC 16; PC 4**
See also CDWLB 2; DLB 90; EW 5; RGWL
2, 3

Holdstock, Robert 1948- .... **CLC 39**
See also CA 131; CANR 81; DLB 261;
FANT; HGG; SFW 4; SUFW 2

Holdstock, Robert P.
See Holdstock, Robert

Holinshed, Raphael fl. 1580- .... **LC 69**
See also DLB 167; RGEL 2

Holland, Isabelle (Christian)
1920-2002 .... **CLC 21**
See also AAYA 11, 64; CA 181; 21-24R;
CAAS 205; CANR 10, 25, 47; CLR 57;
CWRI 5; JRDA; LAIT 4; MAICYA 1, 2;
SATA 8, 70; SATA-Essay 103; SATA-Obit
132; WYA

Holland, Marcus
See Caldwell, (Janet Miriam) Taylor
(Holland)

Hollander, John 1929- .... **CLC 2, 5, 8, 14**
See also CA 1-4R; CANR 1, 52, 136; CP 1,
2, 3, 4, 5, 6, 7; DLB 5; MAL 5; SATA 13

Hollander, Paul
See Silverberg, Robert

Holleran, Andrew .... **CLC 38**
See Garber, Eric
See also CA 144; GLL 1

Holley, Marietta 1836(?)-1926 .... **TCLC 99**
See also CAAE 118; DLB 11; FL 1:3

Hollinghurst, Alan 1954- .... **CLC 55, 91**
See also BRWS 10; CA 114; CN 5, 6, 7;
DLB 207, 326; GLL 1

Hollis, Jim
See Summers, Hollis (Spurgeon, Jr.)

Holly, Buddy 1936-1959 .... **TCLC 65**
See also CA 213

Holmes, Gordon
See Shiel, M(atthew) P(hipps)

Holmes, John
See Souster, (Holmes) Raymond

Holmes, John Clellon 1926-1988 ...... **CLC 56**
See also BG 1:2; CA 9-12R; CAAS 125;
CANR 4; CN 1, 2, 3, 4; DLB 16, 237

Holmes, Oliver Wendell, Jr.
1841-1935 .... **TCLC 77**
See also CA 186; CAAE 114

Holmes, Oliver Wendell
1809-1894 .... **NCLC 14, 81; PC 71**
See also AMWS 1; CDALB 1640-1865;
DLB 1, 189, 235; EXPP; PFS 24; RGAL
4; SATA 34

Holmes, Raymond
See Souster, (Holmes) Raymond

Holt, Victoria
See Hibbert, Eleanor Alice Burford
See also BPFB 2

Holub, Miroslav 1923-1998 .... **CLC 4**
See also CA 21-24R; CAAS 169; CANR
10; CDWLB 4; CWW 2; DLB 232; EWL
3; RGWL 3

Holz, Detlev
See Benjamin, Walter

Homer c. 8th cent. B.C.- .... **CMLC 1, 16, 61;
PC 23; WLCS**
See also AW 1; CDWLB 1; DA; DA3;
DAB; DAC; DAM MST, POET; DLB
176; EFS 1; LAIT 1; LMFS 1; RGWL 2,
3; TWA; WLIT 8; WP

Hongo, Garrett Kaoru 1951- .... **PC 23**
See also CA 133; 22; CP 5, 6, 7; DLB 120,
312; EWL 3; EXPP; PFS 25; RGAL 4

Honig, Edwin 1919- .... **CLC 33**
See also CA 5-8R; 8; CANR 4, 45, 144; CP
1, 2, 3, 4, 5, 6, 7; DLB 5

Hood, Hugh (John Blagdon) 1928- . **CLC 15,
28; SSC 42**
See also CA 49-52; 17; CANR 1, 33, 87;
CN 1, 2, 3, 4, 5, 6, 7; DLB 53; RGSF 2

Hood, Thomas 1799-1845 .... **NCLC 16**
See also BRW 4; DLB 96; RGEL 2

Hooker, (Peter) Jeremy 1941- .... **CLC 43**
See also CA 77-80; CANR 22; CP 2, 3, 4,
5, 6, 7; DLB 40

Hooker, Richard 1554-1600 .... **LC 95**
See also BRW 1; DLB 132; RGEL 2

Hooker, Thomas 1586-1647 .... **LC 137**
See also DLB 24

hooks, bell 1952(?)- .... **CLC 94**
See also BW 2; CA 143; CANR 87, 126;
DLB 246; MTCW 2; MTFW 2005; SATA
115, 170

Hooper, Johnson Jones
1815-1862 .... **NCLC 177**
See also DLB 3, 11, 248; RGAL 4

Hope, A(lec) D(erwent) 1907-2000 .... **CLC 3,
51; PC 56**
See also BRWS 7; CA 21-24R; CAAS 188;
CANR 33, 74; CP 1, 2, 3, 4, 5; DLB 289;
EWL 3; MTCW 1, 2; MTFW 2005; PFS
8; RGEL 2

Hope, Anthony 1863-1933 .... **TCLC 83**
See also CA 157; DLB 153, 156; RGEL 2;
RHW

Hope, Brian
See Creasey, John

Hope, Christopher (David Tully)
1944- .... **CLC 52**
See also AFW; CA 106; CANR 47, 101;
CN 4, 5, 6, 7; DLB 225; SATA 62

Hopkins, Gerard Manley
1844-1889 .... **NCLC 17; PC 15; WLC 3**
See also BRW 5; BRWR 2; CDBLB 1890-
1914; DA; DA3; DAB; DAC; DAM MST,
POET; DLB 35, 57; EXPP; PAB; RGEL
2; TEA; WP

Hopkins, John (Richard) 1931-1998 .. **CLC 4**
See also CA 85-88; CAAS 169; CBD; CD
5, 6

Hopkins, Pauline Elizabeth
1859-1930 .... **BLC 2; TCLC 28**
See also AFAW 2; BW 2, 3; CA 141; CANR
82; DAM MULT; DLB 50

Hopkinson, Francis 1737-1791 .... **LC 25**
See also DLB 31; RGAL 4

Hopley-Woolrich, Cornell George 1903-1968
See Woolrich, Cornell
See also CA 13-14; CANR 58, 156; CAP 1;
CMW 4; DLB 226; MTCW 2

Horace 65B.C.-8B.C. .... **CMLC 39; PC 46**
See also AW 2; CDWLB 1; DLB 211;
RGWL 2, 3; WLIT 8

Horatio
See Proust, (Valentin-Louis-George-Eugene)
Marcel

**Horgan, Paul (George Vincent
O'Shaughnessy)** 1903-1995 .. **CLC 9, 53**
See also BPFB 2; CA 13-16R; CAAS 147;
CANR 9, 35; CN 1, 2, 3, 4, 5; DAM
NOV; DLB 102, 212; DLBY 1985; INT
CANR-9; MTCW 1, 2; MTFW 2005;
SATA 13; SATA-Obit 84; TCWW 1, 2

Horkheimer, Max 1895-1973 .... **TCLC 132**
　　See also CA 216; CAAS 41-44R; DLB 296
Horn, Peter
　　See Kuttner, Henry
Horne, Frank (Smith) 1899-1974 ...... **HR 1:2**
　　See also BW 1; CA 125; CAAS 53-56; DLB
　　51; WP
Horne, Richard Henry Hengist
　　1802(?)-1884 .... **NCLC 127**
　　See also DLB 32; SATA 29
Hornem, Horace Esq.
　　See Byron, George Gordon (Noel)
Horney, Karen (Clementine Theodore
　　Danielsen) 1885-1952 .... **TCLC 71**
　　See also CA 165; CAAE 114; DLB 246;
　　FW
Hornung, E(rnest) W(illiam)
　　1866-1921 .... **TCLC 59**
　　See also CA 160; CAAE 108; CMW 4;
　　DLB 70
Horovitz, Israel (Arthur) 1939- .... **CLC 56**
　　See also CA 33-36R; CAD; CANR 46, 59;
　　CD 5, 6; DAM DRAM; DLB 7; MAL 5
Horton, George Moses
　　1797(?)-1883(?) .... **NCLC 87**
　　See also DLB 50
Horvath, odon von 1901-1938
　　See von Horvath, Odon
　　See also EWL 3
Horvath, Oedoen von -1938
　　See von Horvath, Odon
Horwitz, Julius 1920-1986 .... **CLC 14**
　　See also CA 9-12R; CAAS 119; CANR 12
Horwitz, Ronald
　　See Harwood, Ronald
Hospital, Janette Turner 1942- .... **CLC 42,
　　145**
　　See also CA 108; CANR 48; CN 5, 6, 7;
　　DLB 325; DLBY 2002; RGSF 2
Hostos, E. M. de
　　See Hostos (y Bonilla), Eugenio Maria de
Hostos, Eugenio M. de
　　See Hostos (y Bonilla), Eugenio Maria de
Hostos, Eugenio Maria
　　See Hostos (y Bonilla), Eugenio Maria de
Hostos (y Bonilla), Eugenio Maria de
　　1839-1903 .... **TCLC 24**
　　See also CA 131; CAAE 123; HW 1
Houdini
　　See Lovecraft, H. P.
Houellebecq, Michel 1958- .... **CLC 179**
　　See also CA 185; CANR 140; MTFW 2005
Hougan, Carolyn 1943-2007 .... **CLC 34**
　　See also CA 139; CAAS 257
Household, Geoffrey (Edward West)
　　1900-1988 .... **CLC 11**
　　See also CA 77-80; CAAS 126; CANR 58;
　　CMW 4; CN 1, 2, 3, 4; DLB 87; SATA
　　14; SATA-Obit 59
Housman, A(lfred) E(dward)
　　1859-1936 .... **PC 2, 43; TCLC 1, 10;
　　WLCS**
　　See also AAYA 66; BRW 6; CA 125; CAAE
　　104; DA; DA3; DAB; DAC; DAM MST,
　　POET; DLB 19, 284; EWL 3; EXPP;
　　MTCW 1, 2; MTFW 2005; PAB; PFS 4,
　　7; RGEL 2; TEA; WP
Housman, Laurence 1865-1959 .... **TCLC 7**
　　See also CA 155; CAAE 106; DLB 10;
　　FANT; RGEL 2; SATA 25
Houston, Jeanne Wakatsuki 1934- .... **AAL**
　　See also AAYA 49; CA 232; 103, 232; 16;
　　CANR 29, 123; LAIT 4; SATA 78, 168;
　　SATA-Essay 168
Howard, Elizabeth Jane 1923- ..... **CLC 7, 29**
　　See also BRWS 11; CA 5-8R; CANR 8, 62,
　　146; CN 1, 2, 3, 4, 5, 6, 7

Howard, Maureen 1930- .... **CLC 5, 14, 46,
　　151**
　　See also CA 53-56; CANR 31, 75, 140; CN
　　4, 5, 6, 7; DLBY 1983; INT CANR-31;
　　MTCW 1, 2; MTFW 2005
Howard, Richard 1929- .... **CLC 7, 10, 47**
　　See also AITN 1; CA 85-88; CANR 25, 80,
　　154; CP 1, 2, 3, 4, 5, 6, 7; DLB 5; INT
　　CANR-25; MAL 5
Howard, Robert E 1906-1936 .... **TCLC 8**
　　See also BPFB 2; BYA 5; CA 157; CAAE
　　105; CANR 155; FANT; SUFW 1;
　　TCWW 1, 2
Howard, Robert Ervin
　　See Howard, Robert E
Howard, Warren F.
　　See Pohl, Frederik
Howe, Fanny (Quincy) 1940- .... **CLC 47**
　　See also CA 187; 117, 187; 27; CANR 70,
　　116; CP 6, 7; CWP; SATA-Brief 52
Howe, Irving 1920-1993 .... **CLC 85**
　　See also AMWS 6; CA 9-12R; CAAS 141;
　　CANR 21, 50; DLB 67; EWL 3; MAL 5;
　　MTCW 1, 2; MTFW 2005
Howe, Julia Ward 1819-1910 .... **TCLC 21**
　　See also CA 191; CAAE 117; DLB 1, 189,
　　235; FW
Howe, Susan 1937- .... **CLC 72, 152; PC 54**
　　See also AMWS 4; CA 160; CP 5, 6, 7;
　　CWP; DLB 120; FW; RGAL 4
Howe, Tina 1937- .... **CLC 48**
　　See also CA 109; CAD; CANR 125; CD 5,
　　6; CWD
Howell, James 1594(?)-1666 .... **LC 13**
　　See also DLB 151
Howells, W. D.
　　See Howells, William Dean
Howells, William D.
　　See Howells, William Dean
Howells, William Dean 1837-1920 ... **SSC 36;
　　TCLC 7, 17, 41**
　　See also AMW; CA 134; CAAE 104;
　　CDALB 1865-1917; DLB 12, 64, 74, 79,
　　189; LMFS 1; MAL 5; MTCW 2; RGAL
　　4; TUS
Howes, Barbara 1914-1996 .... **CLC 15**
　　See also CA 9-12R; 3; CAAS 151; CANR
　　53; CP 1, 2, 3, 4, 5, 6; SATA 5; TCLE 1:1
Hrabal, Bohumil 1914-1997 ...... **CLC 13, 67;
　　TCLC 155**
　　See also CA 106; 12; CAAS 156; CANR
　　57; CWW 2; DLB 232; EWL 3; RGSF 2
Hrabanus Maurus 776(?)-856 .... **CMLC 78**
　　See also DLB 148
Hrotsvit of Gandersheim c. 935-c.
　　1000 .... **CMLC 29**
　　See also DLB 148
Hsi, Chu 1130-1200 .... **CMLC 42**
Hsun, Lu
　　See Lu Hsun
Hubbard, L. Ron 1911-1986 .... **CLC 43**
　　See also AAYA 64; CA 77-80; CAAS 118;
　　CANR 52; CPW; DA3; DAM POP;
　　FANT; MTCW 2; MTFW 2005; SFW 4
Hubbard, Lafayette Ronald
　　See Hubbard, L. Ron
Huch, Ricarda (Octavia)
　　1864-1947 .... **TCLC 13**
　　See also CA 189; CAAE 111; DLB 66;
　　EWL 3
Huddle, David 1942- .... **CLC 49**
　　See also CA 57-60; 20; CANR 89; DLB
　　130
Hudson, Jeffrey
　　See Crichton, Michael
Hudson, W(illiam) H(enry)
　　1841-1922 .... **TCLC 29**
　　See also CA 190; CAAE 115; DLB 98, 153,
　　174; RGEL 2; SATA 35

Hueffer, Ford Madox
　　See Ford, Ford Madox
Hughart, Barry 1934- .... **CLC 39**
　　See also CA 137; FANT; SFW 4; SUFW 2
Hughes, Colin
　　See Creasey, John
Hughes, David (John) 1930-2005 ..... **CLC 48**
　　See also CA 129; CAAE 116; CAAS 238;
　　CN 4, 5, 6, 7; DLB 14
Hughes, Edward James
　　See Hughes, Ted
　　See also DA3; DAM MST, POET
Hughes, (James Mercer) Langston
　　1902-1967 ..... **BLC 2; CLC 1, 5, 10, 15,
　　35, 44, 108; DC 3; HR 1:2; PC 1, 53;
　　SSC 6, 90; WLC 3**
　　See also AAYA 12; AFAW 1, 2; AMWR 1;
　　AMWS 1; BW 1, 3; CA 1-4R; CAAS 25-
　　28R; CANR 1, 34, 82; CDALB 1929-
　　1941; CLR 17; DA; DA3; DAB; DAC;
　　DAM DRAM, MST, MULT, POET; DFS
　　6, 18; DLB 4, 7, 48, 51, 86, 228, 315;
　　EWL 3; EXPP; EXPS; JRDA; LAIT 3;
　　LMFS 2; MAICYA 1, 2; MAL 5; MTCW
　　1, 2; MTFW 2005; NFS 21; PAB; PFS 1,
　　3, 6, 10, 15; RGAL 4; RGSF 2; SATA 4,
　　33; SSFS 4, 7; TUS; WCH; WP; YAW
Hughes, Richard (Arthur Warren)
　　1900-1976 .... **CLC 1, 11**
　　See also CA 5-8R; CAAS 65-68; CANR 4;
　　CN 1, 2; DAM NOV; DLB 15, 161; EWL
　　3; MTCW 1; RGEL 2; SATA 8; SATA-
　　Obit 25
Hughes, Ted 1930-1998 . **CLC 2, 4, 9, 14, 37,
　　119; PC 7**
　　See Hughes, Edward James
　　See also BRWC 2; BRWR 2; BRWS 1; CA
　　1-4R; CAAS 171; CANR 1, 33, 66, 108;
　　CLR 3; CP 1, 2, 3, 4, 5, 6; DAB; DAC;
　　DLB 40, 161; EWL 3; EXPP; MAICYA
　　1, 2; MTCW 1, 2; MTFW 2005; PAB;
　　PFS 4, 19; RGEL 2; SATA 49; SATA-
　　Brief 27; SATA-Obit 107; TEA; YAW
Hugo, Richard
　　See Huch, Ricarda (Octavia)
Hugo, Richard F(ranklin)
　　1923-1982 .... **CLC 6, 18, 32; PC 68**
　　See also AMWS 6; CA 49-52; CAAS 108;
　　CANR 3; CP 1, 2, 3; DAM POET; DLB
　　5, 206; EWL 3; MAL 5; PFS 17; RGAL 4
Hugo, Victor (Marie) 1802-1885 .... **NCLC 3,
　　10, 21, 161; PC 17; WLC 3**
　　See also AAYA 28; DA; DA3; DAB; DAC;
　　DAM DRAM, MST, NOV, POET; DLB
　　119, 192, 217; EFS 2; EW 6; EXPN; GFL
　　1789 to the Present; LAIT 1, 2; NFS 5,
　　20; RGWL 2, 3; SATA 47; TWA
Huidobro, Vicente
　　See Huidobro Fernandez, Vicente Garcia
　　See also DLB 283; EWL 3; LAW
Huidobro Fernandez, Vicente Garcia
　　1893-1948 .... **TCLC 31**
　　See Huidobro, Vicente
　　See also CA 131; HW 1
Hulme, Keri 1947- .... **CLC 39, 130**
　　See also CA 125; CANR 69; CN 4, 5, 6, 7;
　　CP 6, 7; CWP; DLB 326; EWL 3; FW;
　　INT CA-125; NFS 24
Hulme, T(homas) E(rnest)
　　1883-1917 .... **TCLC 21**
　　See also BRWS 6; CA 203; CAAE 117;
　　DLB 19
Humboldt, Alexander von
　　1769-1859 .... **NCLC 170**
　　See also DLB 90
Humboldt, Wilhelm von
　　1767-1835 .... **NCLC 134**
　　See also DLB 90

Johnston, Jennifer (Prudence)
1930- .... **CLC 7, 150, 228**
See also CA 85-88; CANR 92; CN 4, 5, 6, 7; DLB 14

Joinville, Jean de 1224(?)-1317 ..... **CMLC 38**

Jolley, Elizabeth 1923-2007 ..... **CLC 46; SSC 19**
See also CA 127; 13; CAAS 257; CANR 59; CN 4, 5, 6, 7; DLB 325; EWL 3; RGSF 2

Jolley, Monica Elizabeth
See Jolley, Elizabeth

Jones, Arthur Llewellyn 1863-1947
See Machen, Arthur
See also CA 179; CAAE 104; HGG

Jones, D(ouglas) G(ordon) 1929- ..... **CLC 10**
See also CA 29-32R; CANR 13, 90; CP 1, 2, 3, 4, 5, 6, 7; DLB 53

Jones, David (Michael) 1895-1974 .... **CLC 2, 4, 7, 13, 42**
See also BRW 6; BRWS 7; CA 9-12R; CAAS 53-56; CANR 28; CDBLB 1945-1960; CP 1, 2; DLB 20, 100; EWL 3; MTCW 1; PAB; RGEL 2

Jones, David Robert 1947-
See Bowie, David
See also CA 103; CANR 104

Jones, Diana Wynne 1934- .... **CLC 26**
See also AAYA 12; BYA 6, 7, 9, 11, 13, 16; CA 49-52; CANR 4, 26, 56, 120; CLR 23, 120; DLB 161; FANT; JRDA; MAI-CYA 1, 2; MTFW 2005; SAAS 7; SATA 9, 70, 108, 160; SFW 4; SUFW 2; YAW

Jones, Edward P. 1950- .... **CLC 76, 223**
See also AAYA 71; BW 2, 3; CA 142; CANR 79, 134; CSW; MTFW 2005

Jones, Gayl 1949- ...... **BLC 2; CLC 6, 9, 131**
See also AFAW 1, 2; BW 2, 3; CA 77-80; CANR 27, 66, 122; CN 4, 5, 6, 7; CSW; DA3; DAM MULT; DLB 33, 278; MAL 5; MTCW 1, 2; MTFW 2005; RGAL 4

Jones, James 1921-1977 ...... **CLC 1, 3, 10, 39**
See also AITN 1, 2; AMWS 11; BPFB 2; CA 1-4R; CAAS 69-72; CANR 6; CN 1, 2; DLB 2, 143; DLBD 17; DLBY 1998; EWL 3; MAL 5; MTCW 1; RGAL 4

Jones, John J.
See Lovecraft, H. P.

Jones, LeRoi .... **CLC 1, 2, 3, 5, 10, 14**
See Baraka, Amiri
See also CN 1, 2; CP 1, 2, 3; MTCW 2

Jones, Louis B. 1953- .... **CLC 65**
See also CA 141; CANR 73

Jones, Madison 1925- .... **CLC 4**
See also CA 13-16R; 11; CANR 7, 54, 83, 158; CN 1, 2, 3, 4, 5, 6, 7; CSW; DLB 152

Jones, Madison Percy, Jr.
See Jones, Madison

Jones, Mervyn 1922- .... **CLC 10, 52**
See also CA 45-48; 5; CANR 1, 91; CN 1, 2, 3, 4, 5, 6, 7; MTCW 1

Jones, Mick 1956(?)- .... **CLC 30**

Jones, Nettie (Pearl) 1941- .... **CLC 34**
See also BW 2; CA 137; 20; CANR 88

Jones, Peter 1802-1856 .... **NNAL**

Jones, Preston 1936-1979 .... **CLC 10**
See also CA 73-76; CAAS 89-92; DLB 7

Jones, Robert F(rancis) 1934-2003 .... **CLC 7**
See also CA 49-52; CANR 2, 61, 118

Jones, Rod 1953- .... **CLC 50**
See also CA 128

Jones, Terence Graham Parry
1942- .... **CLC 21**
See Jones, Terry; Monty Python
See also CA 116; CAAE 112; CANR 35, 93; INT CA-116; SATA 127

Jones, Terry
See Jones, Terence Graham Parry
See also SATA 67; SATA-Brief 51

Jones, Thom (Douglas) 1945(?)- ..... **CLC 81; SSC 56**
See also CA 157; CANR 88; DLB 244; SSFS 23

Jong, Erica 1942- .... **CLC 4, 6, 8, 18, 83**
See also AITN 1; AMWS 5; BEST 90:2; BPFB 2; CA 73-76; CANR 26, 52, 75, 132; CN 3, 4, 5, 6, 7; CP 2, 3, 4, 5, 6, 7; CPW; DA3; DAM NOV, POP; DLB 2, 5, 28, 152; FW; INT CANR-26; MAL 5; MTCW 1, 2; MTFW 2005

Jonson, Ben(jamin) 1572(?)-1637 . **DC 4; LC 6, 33, 110; PC 17; WLC 3**
See also BRW 1; BRWC 1; BRWR 1; CD-BLB Before 1660; DA; DAB; DAC; DAM DRAM, MST, POET; DFS 4, 10; DLB 62, 121; LMFS 1; PFS 23; RGEL 2; TEA; WLIT 3

Jordan, June 1936-2002 .. **BLCS; CLC 5, 11, 23, 114, 230; PC 38**
See also AAYA 2, 66; AFAW 1, 2; BW 2, 3; CA 33-36R; CAAS 206; CANR 25, 70, 114, 154; CLR 10; CP 3, 4, 5, 6, 7; CWP; DAM MULT, POET; DLB 38; GLL 2; LAIT 5; MAICYA 1, 2; MTCW 1; SATA 4, 136; YAW

Jordan, June Meyer
See Jordan, June

Jordan, Neil 1950- .... **CLC 110**
See also CA 130; CAAE 124; CANR 54, 154; CN 4, 5, 6, 7; GLL 2; INT CA-130

Jordan, Neil Patrick
See Jordan, Neil

Jordan, Pat(rick M.) 1941- .... **CLC 37**
See also CA 33-36R; CANR 121

Jorgensen, Ivar
See Ellison, Harlan

Jorgenson, Ivar
See Silverberg, Robert

Joseph, George Ghevarughese .... **CLC 70**

Josephson, Mary
See O'Doherty, Brian

Josephus, Flavius c. 37-100 .... **CMLC 13**
See also AW 2; DLB 176; WLIT 8

Josiah Allen's Wife
See Holley, Marietta

Josipovici, Gabriel (David) 1940- ...... **CLC 6, 43, 153**
See also CA 224; 37-40R, 224; 8; CANR 47, 84; CN 3, 4, 5, 6, 7; DLB 14, 319

Joubert, Joseph 1754-1824 .... **NCLC 9**

Jouve, Pierre Jean 1887-1976 .... **CLC 47**
See also CA 252; CAAS 65-68; DLB 258; EWL 3

Jovine, Francesco 1902-1950 .... **TCLC 79**
See also DLB 264; EWL 3

Joyce, James (Augustine Aloysius)
1882-1941 .... **DC 16; PC 22; SSC 3, 26, 44, 64; TCLC 3, 8, 16, 35, 52, 159; WLC 3**
See also AAYA 42; BRW 7; BRWC 1; BRWR 1; BYA 11, 13; CA 126; CAAE 104; CDBLB 1914-1945; DA; DA3; DAB; DAC; DAM MST, NOV, POET; DLB 10, 19, 36, 162, 247; EWL 3; EXPN; EXPS; LAIT 3; LMFS 1, 2; MTCW 1, 2; MTFW 2005; NFS 7; RGSF 2; SSFS 1, 19; TEA; WLIT 4

Jozsef, Attila 1905-1937 .... **TCLC 22**
See also CA 230; CAAE 116; CDWLB 4; DLB 215; EWL 3

Juana Ines de la Cruz, Sor
1651(?)-1695 ... **HLCS 1; LC 5, 136; PC 24**
See also DLB 305; FW; LAW; RGWL 2, 3; WLIT 1

Juana Inez de La Cruz, Sor
See Juana Ines de la Cruz, Sor

Juan Manuel, Don 1282-1348 .... **CMLC 88**

Judd, Cyril
See Kornbluth, C(yril) M.; Pohl, Frederik

Juenger, Ernst 1895-1998 .... **CLC 125**
See Junger, Ernst
See also CA 101; CAAS 167; CANR 21, 47, 106; DLB 56

Julian of Norwich 1342(?)-1416(?) . **LC 6, 52**
See also BRWS 12; DLB 146; LMFS 1

Julius Caesar 100B.C.-44B.C.
See Caesar, Julius
See also CDWLB 1; DLB 211

Junger, Ernst
See Juenger, Ernst
See also CDWLB 2; EWL 3; RGWL 2, 3

Junger, Sebastian 1962- .... **CLC 109**
See also AAYA 28; CA 165; CANR 130; MTFW 2005

Juniper, Alex
See Hospital, Janette Turner

Junius
See Luxemburg, Rosa

Junzaburo, Nishiwaki
See Nishiwaki, Junzaburo
See also EWL 3

Just, Ward 1935- .... **CLC 4, 27**
See also CA 25-28R; CANR 32, 87; CN 6, 7; DLB 335; INT CANR-32

Just, Ward Swift
See Just, Ward

Justice, Donald (Rodney)
1925-2004 .... **CLC 6, 19, 102; PC 64**
See also AMWS 7; CA 5-8R; CAAS 230; CANR 26, 54, 74, 121, 122; CP 1, 2, 3, 4, 5, 6, 7; CSW; DAM POET; DLBY 1983; EWL 3; INT CANR-26; MAL 5; MTCW 2; PFS 14; TCLE 1:1

Juvenal c. 60-c. 130 .... **CMLC 8**
See also AW 2; CDWLB 1; DLB 211; RGWL 2, 3; WLIT 8

Juvenis
See Bourne, Randolph S(illiman)

K., Alice
See Knapp, Caroline

Kabakov, Sasha .... **CLC 59**

Kabir 1398(?)-1448(?) .... **LC 109; PC 56**
See also RGWL 2, 3

Kacew, Romain 1914-1980
See Gary, Romain
See also CA 108; CAAS 102

Kadare, Ismail 1936- .... **CLC 52, 190**
See also CA 161; EWL 3; RGWL 3

Kadohata, Cynthia (Lynn)
1956(?)- .... **CLC 59, 122**
See also AAYA 71; CA 140; CANR 124; CLR 121; SATA 155

Kafka, Franz 1883-1924 ... **SSC 5, 29, 35, 60; TCLC 2, 6, 13, 29, 47, 53, 112, 179; WLC 3**
See also AAYA 31; BPFB 2; CA 126; CAAE 105; CDWLB 2; DA; DA3; DAB; DAC; DAM MST, NOV; DLB 81; EW 9; EWL 3; EXPS; LATS 1:1; LMFS 2; MTCW 1, 2; MTFW 2005; NFS 7; RGSF 2; RGWL 2, 3; SFW 4; SSFS 3, 7, 12; TWA

Kahanovitch, Pinchas
See Der Nister

Kahanovitsch, Pinkhes
See Der Nister

Kahanovitsh, Pinkhes
See Der Nister

Kahn, Roger 1927- .... **CLC 30**
See also CA 25-28R; CANR 44, 69, 152; DLB 171; SATA 37

Kain, Saul
See Sassoon, Siegfried (Lorraine)

Keneally, Thomas 1935- .... **CLC 5, 8, 10, 14, 19, 27, 43, 117**
See also BRWS 4; CA 85-88; CANR 10, 50, 74, 130; CN 1, 2, 3, 4, 5, 6, 7; CPW; DA3; DAM NOV; DLB 289, 299, 326; EWL 3; MTCW 1, 2; MTFW 2005; NFS 17; RGEL 2; RGHL; RHW

Kennedy, A(lison) L(ouise) 1965- ... **CLC 188**
See also CA 213; 168, 213; CANR 108; CD 5, 6; CN 6, 7; DLB 271; RGSF 2

Kennedy, Adrienne (Lita) 1931- .... **BLC 2; CLC 66; DC 5**
See also AFAW 2; BW 2, 3; CA 103; 20; CABS 3; CAD; CANR 26, 53, 82; CD 5, 6; DAM MULT; DFS 9; DLB 38; FW; MAL 5

Kennedy, John Pendleton
1795-1870 .... **NCLC 2**
See also DLB 3, 248, 254; RGAL 4

Kennedy, Joseph Charles 1929-
See Kennedy, X. J.
See also CA 201; 1-4R, 201; CANR 4, 30, 40; CWRI 5; MAICYA 2; MAICYAS 1; SATA 14, 86, 130; SATA-Essay 130

Kennedy, William 1928- .. **CLC 6, 28, 34, 53, 239**
See also AAYA 1, 73; AMWS 7; BPFB 2; CA 85-88; CANR 14, 31, 76, 134; CN 4, 5, 6, 7; DA3; DAM NOV; DLB 143; DLBY 1985; EWL 3; INT CANR-31; MAL 5; MTCW 1, 2; MTFW 2005; SATA 57

Kennedy, X. J. .... **CLC 8, 42**
See Kennedy, Joseph Charles
See also AMWS 15; CA 9; CLR 27; CP 1, 2, 3, 4, 5, 6, 7; DLB 5; SAAS 22

Kenny, Maurice (Francis) 1929- ..... **CLC 87; NNAL**
See also CA 144; 22; CANR 143; DAM MULT; DLB 175

Kent, Kelvin
See Kuttner, Henry

Kenton, Maxwell
See Southern, Terry

Kenyon, Jane 1947-1995 .... **PC 57**
See also AAYA 63; AMWS 7; CA 118; CAAS 148; CANR 44, 69; CP 6, 7; CWP; DLB 120; PFS 9, 17; RGAL 4

Kenyon, Robert O.
See Kuttner, Henry

Kepler, Johannes 1571-1630 .... **LC 45**

Ker, Jill
See Conway, Jill K(er)

Kerkow, H. C.
See Lewton, Val

Kerouac, Jack 1922-1969 ...... **CLC 1, 2, 3, 5, 14, 29, 61; TCLC 117; WLC**
See Kerouac, Jean-Louis Lebris de
See also AAYA 25; AMWC 1; AMWS 3; BG 3; BPFB 2; CDALB 1941-1968; CP 1; CPW; DLB 2, 16, 237; DLBD 3; DLBY 1995; EWL 3; GLL 1; LATS 1:2; LMFS 2; MAL 5; NFS 8; RGAL 4; TUS; WP

Kerouac, Jean-Louis Lebris de 1922-1969
See Kerouac, Jack
See also AITN 1; CA 5-8R; CAAS 25-28R; CANR 26, 54, 95; DA; DA3; DAB; DAC; DAM MST, NOV, POET, POP; MTCW 1, 2; MTFW 2005

Kerr, (Bridget) Jean (Collins)
1923(?)-2003 .... **CLC 22**
See also CA 5-8R; CAAS 212; CANR 7; INT CANR-7

Kerr, M. E. .... **CLC 12, 35**
See Meaker, Marijane
See also AAYA 2, 23; BYA 1, 7, 8; CLR 29; SAAS 1; WYA

Kerr, Robert .... **CLC 55**

Kerrigan, (Thomas) Anthony 1918- .. **CLC 4, 6**
See also CA 49-52; 11; CANR 4

Kerry, Lois
See Duncan, Lois

Kesey, Ken 1935-2001 .... **CLC 1, 3, 6, 11, 46, 64, 184; WLC 3**
See also AAYA 25; BG 1:3; BPFB 2; CA 1-4R; CAAS 204; CANR 22, 38, 66, 124; CDALB 1968-1988; CN 1, 2, 3, 4, 5, 6, 7; CPW; DA; DA3; DAB; DAC; DAM MST, NOV, POP; DLB 2, 16, 206; EWL 3; EXPN; LAIT 4; MAL 5; MTCW 1, 2; MTFW 2005; NFS 2; RGAL 4; SATA 66; SATA-Obit 131; TUS; YAW

Kesselring, Joseph (Otto)
1902-1967 .... **CLC 45**
See also CA 150; DAM DRAM, MST; DFS 20

Kessler, Jascha (Frederick) 1929- ...... **CLC 4**
See also CA 17-20R; CANR 8, 48, 111; CP 1

Kettelkamp, Larry (Dale) 1933- .... **CLC 12**
See also CA 29-32R; CANR 16; SAAS 3; SATA 2

Key, Ellen (Karolina Sofia)
1849-1926 .... **TCLC 65**
See also DLB 259

Keyber, Conny
See Fielding, Henry

Keyes, Daniel 1927- .... **CLC 80**
See also AAYA 23; BYA 11; CA 181; 17-20R, 181; CANR 10, 26, 54, 74; DA; DA3; DAC; DAM MST, NOV; EXPN; LAIT 4; MTCW 2; MTFW 2005; NFS 2; SATA 37; SFW 4

Keynes, John Maynard
1883-1946 .... **TCLC 64**
See also CA 162, 163; CAAE 114; DLBD 10; MTCW 2; MTFW 2005

Khanshendel, Chiron
See Rose, Wendy

Khayyam, Omar 1048-1131 ... **CMLC 11; PC 8**
See Omar Khayyam
See also DA3; DAM POET; WLIT 6

Kherdian, David 1931- .... **CLC 6, 9**
See also AAYA 42; CA 192; 21-24R, 192; 2; CANR 39, 78; CLR 24; JRDA; LAIT 3; MAICYA 1, 2; SATA 16, 74; SATA-Essay 125

Khlebnikov, Velimir .... **TCLC 20**
See Khlebnikov, Viktor Vladimirovich
See also DLB 295; EW 10; EWL 3; RGWL 2, 3

Khlebnikov, Viktor Vladimirovich 1885-1922
See Khlebnikov, Velimir
See also CA 217; CAAE 117

Khodasevich, V.F.
See Khodasevich, Vladislav

Khodasevich, Vladislav
1886-1939 .... **TCLC 15**
See also CAAE 115; DLB 317; EWL 3

Khodasevich, Vladislav Felitsianovich
See Khodasevich, Vladislav

Kielland, Alexander Lange
1849-1906 .... **TCLC 5**
See also CAAE 104

Kiely, Benedict 1919-2007 . **CLC 23, 43; SSC 58**
See also CA 1-4R; CAAS 257; CANR 2, 84; CN 1, 2, 3, 4, 5, 6, 7; DLB 15, 319; TCLE 1:1

Kienzle, William X. 1928-2001 .... **CLC 25**
See also CA 93-96; 1; CAAS 203; CANR 9, 31, 59, 111; CMW 4; DA3; DAM POP; INT CANR-31; MSW; MTCW 1, 2; MTFW 2005

Kierkegaard, Soren 1813-1855 ..... **NCLC 34, 78, 125**
See also DLB 300; EW 6; LMFS 2; RGWL 3; TWA

Kieslowski, Krzysztof 1941-1996 .... **CLC 120**
See also CA 147; CAAS 151

Killens, John Oliver 1916-1987 .... **CLC 10**
See also BW 2; CA 77-80; 2; CAAS 123; CANR 26; CN 1, 2, 3, 4; DLB 33; EWL 3

Killigrew, Anne 1660-1685 .... **LC 4, 73**
See also DLB 131

Killigrew, Thomas 1612-1683 .... **LC 57**
See also DLB 58; RGEL 2

Kim
See Simenon, Georges (Jacques Christian)

Kincaid, Jamaica 1949- ...... **BLC 2; CLC 43, 68, 137, 234; SSC 72**
See also AAYA 13, 56; AFAW 2; AMWS 7; BRWS 7; BW 2, 3; CA 125; CANR 47, 59, 95, 133; CDALBS; CDWLB 3; CLR 63; CN 4, 5, 6, 7; DA3; DAM MULT, NOV; DLB 157, 227; DNFS 1; EWL 3; EXPS; FW; LATS 1:2; LMFS 2; MAL 5; MTCW 2; MTFW 2005; NCFS 1; NFS 3; SSFS 5, 7; TUS; WWE 1; YAW

King, Francis (Henry) 1923- .... **CLC 8, 53, 145**
See also CA 1-4R; CANR 1, 33, 86; CN 1, 2, 3, 4, 5, 6, 7; DAM NOV; DLB 15, 139; MTCW 1

King, Kennedy
See Brown, George Douglas

King, Martin Luther, Jr. 1929-1968 . **BLC 2; CLC 83; WLCS**
See also BW 2, 3; CA 25-28; CANR 27, 44; CAP 2; DA; DA3; DAB; DAC; DAM MST, MULT; LAIT 5; LATS 1:2; MTCW 1, 2; MTFW 2005; SATA 14

King, Stephen 1947- .... **CLC 12, 26, 37, 61, 113, 228; SSC 17, 55**
See also AAYA 1, 17; AMWS 5; BEST 90:1; BPFB 2; CA 61-64; CANR 1, 30, 52, 76, 119, 134; CN 7; CPW; DA3; DAM NOV, POP; DLB 143; DLBY 1980; HGG; JRDA; LAIT 5; MTCW 1, 2; MTFW 2005; RGAL 4; SATA 9, 55, 161; SUFW 1, 2; WYAS 1; YAW

King, Stephen Edwin
See King, Stephen

King, Steve
See King, Stephen

King, Thomas 1943- .... **CLC 89, 171; NNAL**
See also CA 144; CANR 95; CCA 1; CN 6, 7; DAC; DAM MULT; DLB 175, 334; SATA 96

Kingman, Lee .... **CLC 17**
See Natti, (Mary) Lee
See also CWRI 5; SAAS 3; SATA 1, 67

Kingsley, Charles 1819-1875 .... **NCLC 35**
See also CLR 77; DLB 21, 32, 163, 178, 190; FANT; MAICYA 1; MAICYAS 1; RGEL 2; WCH; YABC 2

Kingsley, Henry 1830-1876 .... **NCLC 107**
See also DLB 21, 230; RGEL 2

Kingsley, Sidney 1906-1995 .... **CLC 44**
See also CA 85-88; CAAS 147; CAD; DFS 14, 19; DLB 7; MAL 5; RGAL 4

Kingsolver, Barbara 1955- .... **CLC 55, 81, 130, 216**
See also AAYA 15; AMWS 7; CA 134; CAAE 129; CANR 60, 96, 133; CDALBS; CN 7; CPW; CSW; DA3; DAM POP; DLB 206; INT CA-134; LAIT 5; MTCW 2; MTFW 2005; NFS 5, 10, 12, 24; RGAL 4; TCLE 1:1

Korolenko, V.G.
See Korolenko, Vladimir G.
Korolenko, Vladimir
See Korolenko, Vladimir G.
Korolenko, Vladimir G.
1853-1921 .... **TCLC 22**
See also CAAE 121; DLB 277
Korolenko, Vladimir Galaktionovich
See Korolenko, Vladimir G.
Korzybski, Alfred (Habdank Skarbek)
1879-1950 .... **TCLC 61**
See also CA 160; CAAE 123
Kosinski, Jerzy 1933-1991 ..... **CLC 1, 2, 3, 6,**
10, 15, 53, 70
See also AMWS 7; BPFB 2; CA 17-20R;
CAAS 134; CANR 9, 46; CN 1, 2, 3, 4;
DA3; DAM NOV; DLB 2, 299; DLBY
1982; EWL 3; HGG; MAL 5; MTCW 1,
2; MTFW 2005; NFS 12; RGAL 4;
RGHL; TUS
Kostelanetz, Richard (Cory) 1940- .. **CLC 28**
See also CA 13-16R; 8; CANR 38, 77; CN
4, 5, 6; CP 2, 3, 4, 5, 6, 7
Kostrowitzki, Wilhelm Apollinaris de
1880-1918
See Apollinaire, Guillaume
See also CAAE 104
Kotlowitz, Robert 1924- .... **CLC 4**
See also CA 33-36R; CANR 36
Kotzebue, August (Friedrich Ferdinand) von
1761-1819 .... **NCLC 25**
See also DLB 94
Kotzwinkle, William 1938- ..... **CLC 5, 14, 35**
See also BPFB 2; CA 45-48; CANR 3, 44,
84, 129; CLR 6; CN 7; DLB 173; FANT;
MAICYA 1, 2; SATA 24, 70, 146; SFW
4; SUFW 2; YAW
Kowna, Stancy
See Szymborska, Wislawa
Kozol, Jonathan 1936- .... **CLC 17**
See also AAYA 46; CA 61-64; CANR 16,
45, 96; MTFW 2005
Kozoll, Michael 1940(?)- .... **CLC 35**
Kramer, Kathryn 19(?)- .... **CLC 34**
Kramer, Larry 1935- .... **CLC 42; DC 8**
See also CA 124; CAAE 124; CANR 60,
132; DAM POP; DLB 249; GLL 1
Krasicki, Ignacy 1735-1801 .... **NCLC 8**
Krasinski, Zygmunt 1812-1859 .... **NCLC 4**
See also RGWL 2, 3
Kraus, Karl 1874-1936 .... **TCLC 5**
See also CA 216; CAAE 104; DLB 118;
EWL 3
Kreve (Mickevicius), Vincas
1882-1954 .... **TCLC 27**
See also CA 170; DLB 220; EWL 3
Kristeva, Julia 1941- .... **CLC 77, 140**
See also CA 154; CANR 99; DLB 242;
EWL 3; FW; LMFS 2
Kristofferson, Kris 1936- .... **CLC 26**
See also CA 104
Krizanc, John 1956- .... **CLC 57**
See also CA 187
Krleza, Miroslav 1893-1981 .... **CLC 8, 114**
See also CA 97-100; CAAS 105; CANR
50; CDWLB 4; DLB 147; EW 11; RGWL
2, 3
Kroetsch, Robert (Paul) 1927- .... **CLC 5, 23,**
57, 132
See also CA 17-20R; CANR 8, 38; CCA 1;
CN 2, 3, 4, 5, 6, 7; CP 6, 7; DAC; DAM
POET; DLB 53; MTCW 1
Kroetz, Franz
See Kroetz, Franz Xaver
Kroetz, Franz Xaver 1946- .... **CLC 41**
See also CA 130; CANR 142; CWW 2;
EWL 3
Kroker, Arthur (W.) 1945- .... **CLC 77**
See also CA 161

Kroniuk, Lisa
See Berton, Pierre (Francis de Marigny)
Kropotkin, Peter (Aleksieevich)
1842-1921 .... **TCLC 36**
See Kropotkin, Petr Alekseevich
See also CA 219; CAAE 119
Kropotkin, Petr Alekseevich
See Kropotkin, Peter (Aleksieevich)
See also DLB 277
Krotkov, Yuri 1917-1981 .... **CLC 19**
See also CA 102
Krumb
See Crumb, R.
Krumgold, Joseph (Quincy)
1908-1980 .... **CLC 12**
See also BYA 1, 2; CA 9-12R; CAAS 101;
CANR 7; MAICYA 1, 2; SATA 1, 48;
SATA-Obit 23; YAW
Krumwitz
See Crumb, R.
Krutch, Joseph Wood 1893-1970 ..... **CLC 24**
See also ANW; CA 1-4R; CAAS 25-28R;
CANR 4; DLB 63, 206, 275
Krutzch, Gus
See Eliot, T(homas) S(tearns)
Krylov, Ivan Andreevich
1768(?)-1844 .... **NCLC 1**
See also DLB 150
Kubin, Alfred (Leopold Isidor)
1877-1959 .... **TCLC 23**
See also CA 149; CAAE 112; CANR 104;
DLB 81
Kubrick, Stanley 1928-1999 .... **CLC 16;**
TCLC 112
See also AAYA 30; CA 81-84; CAAS 177;
CANR 33; DLB 26
Kumin, Maxine 1925- .... **CLC 5, 13, 28, 164;**
PC 15
See also AITN 2; AMWS 4; ANW; CA
1-4R; 8; CANR 1, 21, 69, 115, 140; CP 2,
3, 4, 5, 6, 7; CWP; DA3; DAM POET;
DLB 5; EWL 3; EXPP; MTCW 1, 2;
MTFW 2005; PAB; PFS 18; SATA 12
Kundera, Milan 1929- . **CLC 4, 9, 19, 32, 68,**
115, 135, 234; SSC 24
See also AAYA 2, 62; BPFB 2; CA 85-88;
CANR 19, 52, 74, 144; CDWLB 4; CWW
2; DA3; DAM NOV; DLB 232; EW 13;
EWL 3; MTCW 1, 2; MTFW 2005; NFS
18; RGSF 2; RGWL 3; SSFS 10
Kunene, Mazisi 1930-2006 .... **CLC 85**
See also BW 1, 3; CA 125; CAAS 252;
CANR 81; CP 1, 6, 7; DLB 117
Kunene, Mazisi Raymond
See Kunene, Mazisi
Kunene, Mazisi Raymond Fakazi Mngoni
See Kunene, Mazisi
Kung, Hans .... **CLC 130**
See Kung, Hans
Kung, Hans 1928-
See Kung, Hans
See also CA 53-56; CANR 66, 134; MTCW
1, 2; MTFW 2005
Kunikida Doppo 1869(?)-1908
See Doppo, Kunikida
See also DLB 180; EWL 3
Kunitz, Stanley 1905-2006 ..... **CLC 6, 11, 14,**
148; PC 19
See also AMWS 3; CA 41-44R; CAAS 250;
CANR 26, 57, 98; CP 1, 2, 3, 4, 5, 6, 7;
DA3; DLB 48; INT CANR-26; MAL 5;
MTCW 1, 2; MTFW 2005; PFS 11;
RGAL 4
Kunitz, Stanley Jasspon
See Kunitz, Stanley
Kunze, Reiner 1933- .... **CLC 10**
See also CA 93-96; CWW 2; DLB 75;
EWL 3

Kuprin, Aleksander Ivanovich
1870-1938 .... **TCLC 5**
See Kuprin, Aleksandr Ivanovich; Kuprin,
Alexandr Ivanovich
See also CA 182; CAAE 104
Kuprin, Aleksandr Ivanovich
See Kuprin, Aleksander Ivanovich
See also DLB 295
Kuprin, Alexandr Ivanovich
See Kuprin, Aleksander Ivanovich
See also EWL 3
Kureishi, Hanif 1954- .. **CLC 64, 135; DC 26**
See also BRWS 11; CA 139; CANR 113;
CBD; CD 5, 6; CN 6, 7; DLB 194, 245;
GLL 2; IDFW 4; WLIT 4; WWE 1
Kurosawa, Akira 1910-1998 ..... **CLC 16, 119**
See also AAYA 11, 64; CA 101; CAAS 170;
CANR 46; DAM MULT
Kushner, Tony 1956- .... **CLC 81, 203; DC 10**
See also AAYA 61; AMWS 9; CA 144;
CAD; CANR 74, 130; CD 5, 6; DA3;
DAM DRAM; DFS 5; DLB 228; EWL 3;
GLL 1; LAIT 5; MAL 5; MTCW 2;
MTFW 2005; RGAL 4; RGHL; SATA 160
Kuttner, Henry 1915-1958 .... **TCLC 10**
See also CA 157; CAAE 107; DLB 8;
FANT; SCFW 1, 2; SFW 4
Kutty, Madhavi
See Das, Kamala
Kuzma, Greg 1944- .... **CLC 7**
See also CA 33-36R; CANR 70
Kuzmin, Mikhail (Alekseevich)
1872(?)-1936 .... **TCLC 40**
See also CA 170; DLB 295; EWL 3
Kyd, Thomas 1558-1594 .. **DC 3; LC 22, 125**
See also BRW 1; DAM DRAM; DFS 21;
DLB 62; IDTP; LMFS 1; RGEL 2; TEA;
WLIT 3
Kyprianos, Iossif
See Samarakis, Antonis
L. S.
See Stephen, Sir Leslie
Labe, Louise 1521-1566 .... **LC 120**
See also DLB 327
Labrunie, Gerard
See Nerval, Gerard de
La Bruyere, Jean de 1645-1696 .... **LC 17**
See also DLB 268; EW 3; GFL Beginnings
to 1789
LaBute, Neil 1963- .... **CLC 225**
See also CA 240
Lacan, Jacques (Marie Emile)
1901-1981 .... **CLC 75**
See also CA 121; CAAS 104; DLB 296;
EWL 3; TWA
Laclos, Pierre-Ambroise Francois
1741-1803 .... **NCLC 4, 87**
See also DLB 313; EW 4; GFL Beginnings
to 1789; RGWL 2, 3
Lacolere, Francois
See Aragon, Louis
La Colere, Francois
See Aragon, Louis
La Deshabilleuse
See Simenon, Georges (Jacques Christian)
Lady Gregory
See Gregory, Lady Isabella Augusta (Persse)
Lady of Quality, A
See Bagnold, Enid
La Fayette, Marie-(Madelaine Pioche de la
Vergne) 1634-1693 .... **LC 2**
See Lafayette, Marie-Madeleine
See also GFL Beginnings to 1789; RGWL
2, 3
Lafayette, Marie-Madeleine
See La Fayette, Marie-(Madelaine Pioche
de la Vergne)
See also DLB 268

Levine, Albert Norman
See Levine, Norman
See also CN 7

Levine, Norman 1923-2005 .... **CLC 54**
See Levine, Albert Norman
See also CA 73-76; 23; CAAS 240; CANR 14, 70; CN 1, 2, 3, 4, 5, 6; CP 1; DLB 88

Levine, Norman Albert
See Levine, Norman

Levine, Philip 1928- .. **CLC 2, 4, 5, 9, 14, 33, 118; PC 22**
See also AMWS 5; CA 9-12R; CANR 9, 37, 52, 116, 156; CP 1, 2, 3, 4, 5, 6, 7; DAM POET; DLB 5; EWL 3; MAL 5; PFS 8

Levinson, Deirdre 1931- .... **CLC 49**
See also CA 73-76; CANR 70

Levi-Strauss, Claude 1908- .... **CLC 38**
See also CA 1-4R; CANR 6, 32, 57; DLB 242; EWL 3; GFL 1789 to the Present; MTCW 1, 2; TWA

Levitin, Sonia (Wolff) 1934- .... **CLC 17**
See also AAYA 13, 48; CA 29-32R; CANR 14, 32, 79; CLR 53; JRDA; MAICYA 1, 2; SAAS 2; SATA 4, 68, 119, 131; SATA-Essay 131; YAW

Levon, O. U.
See Kesey, Ken

Levy, Amy 1861-1889 .... **NCLC 59**
See also DLB 156, 240

Lewes, George Henry 1817-1878 ... **NCLC 25**
See also DLB 55, 144

Lewis, Alun 1915-1944 .... **SSC 40; TCLC 3**
See also BRW 7; CA 188; CAAE 104; DLB 20, 162; PAB; RGEL 2

Lewis, C. Day
See Day Lewis, C(ecil)
See also CN 1

Lewis, Cecil Day
See Day Lewis, C(ecil)

Lewis, Clive Staples
See Lewis, C.S.

Lewis, C.S. 1898-1963 ... **CLC 1, 3, 6, 14, 27, 124; WLC 4**
See also AAYA 3, 39; BPFB 2; BRWS 3; BYA 15, 16; CA 81-84; CANR 33, 71, 132; CDBLB 1945-1960; CLR 3, 27, 109; CWRI 5; DA; DA3; DAB; DAC; DAM MST, NOV, POP; DLB 15, 100, 160, 255; EWL 3; FANT; JRDA; LMFS 2; MAICYA 1, 2; MTCW 1, 2; MTFW 2005; NFS 24; RGEL 2; SATA 13, 100; SCFW 1, 2; SFW 4; SUFW 1; TEA; WCH; WYA; YAW

Lewis, Janet 1899-1998 .... **CLC 41**
See Winters, Janet Lewis
See also CA 9-12R; CAAS 172; CANR 29, 63; CAP 1; CN 1, 2, 3, 4, 5, 6; DLBY 1987; RHW; TCWW 2

Lewis, Matthew Gregory 1775-1818 .... **NCLC 11, 62**
See also DLB 39, 158, 178; GL 3; HGG; LMFS 1; RGEL 2; SUFW

Lewis, (Harry) Sinclair 1885-1951 . **TCLC 4, 13, 23, 39; WLC 4**
See also AMW; AMWC 1; BPFB 2; CA 133; CAAE 104; CANR 132; CDALB 1917-1929; DA; DA3; DAB; DAC; DAM MST, NOV; DLB 9, 102, 284, 331; DLBD 1; EWL 3; LAIT 3; MAL 5; MTCW 1, 2; MTFW 2005; NFS 15, 19, 22; RGAL 4; TUS

Lewis, (Percy) Wyndham 1884(?)-1957 .. **SSC 34; TCLC 2, 9, 104**
See also BRW 7; CA 157; CAAE 104; DLB 15; EWL 3; FANT; MTCW 2; MTFW 2005; RGEL 2

Lewisohn, Ludwig 1883-1955 .... **TCLC 19**
See also CA 203; CAAE 107; DLB 4, 9, 28, 102; MAL 5

Lewton, Val 1904-1951 .... **TCLC 76**
See also CA 199; IDFW 3, 4

Leyner, Mark 1956- .... **CLC 92**
See also CA 110; CANR 28, 53; DA3; DLB 292; MTCW 2; MTFW 2005

Lezama Lima, Jose 1910-1976 .... **CLC 4, 10, 101; HLCS 2**
See also CA 77-80; CANR 71; DAM MULT; DLB 113, 283; EWL 3; HW 1, 2; LAW; RGWL 2, 3

L'Heureux, John (Clarke) 1934- ...... **CLC 52**
See also CA 13-16R; CANR 23, 45, 88; CP 1, 2, 3, 4; DLB 244

Li Ch'ing-chao 1081(?)-1141(?) .... **CMLC 71**

Liddell, C. H.
See Kuttner, Henry

Lie, Jonas (Lauritz Idemil) 1833-1908(?) .... **TCLC 5**
See also CAAE 115

Lieber, Joel 1937-1971 .... **CLC 6**
See also CA 73-76; CAAS 29-32R

Lieber, Stanley Martin
See Lee, Stan

Lieberman, Laurence (James) 1935- .... **CLC 4, 36**
See also CA 17-20R; CANR 8, 36, 89; CP 1, 2, 3, 4, 5, 6, 7

Lieh Tzu fl. 7th cent. B.C.-5th cent. B.C. .... **CMLC 27**

Lieksman, Anders
See Haavikko, Paavo Juhani

Lifton, Robert Jay 1926- .... **CLC 67**
See also CA 17-20R; CANR 27, 78, 161; INT CANR-27; SATA 66

Lightfoot, Gordon 1938- .... **CLC 26**
See also CA 242; CAAE 109

Lightfoot, Gordon Meredith
See Lightfoot, Gordon

Lightman, Alan P(aige) 1948- .... **CLC 81**
See also CA 141; CANR 63, 105, 138; MTFW 2005

Ligotti, Thomas (Robert) 1953- ...... **CLC 44; SSC 16**
See also CA 123; CANR 49, 135; HGG; SUFW 2

Li Ho 791-817 .... **PC 13**

Li Ju-chen c. 1763-c. 1830 .... **NCLC 137**

Lilar, Francoise
See Mallet-Joris, Francoise

Liliencron, Detlev
See Liliencron, Detlev von

Liliencron, Detlev von 1844-1909 .. **TCLC 18**
See also CAAE 117

Liliencron, Friedrich Adolf Axel Detlev von
See Liliencron, Detlev von

Liliencron, Friedrich Detlev von
See Liliencron, Detlev von

Lille, Alain de
See Alain de Lille

Lillo, George 1691-1739 .... **LC 131**
See also DLB 84; RGEL 2

Lilly, William 1602-1681 .... **LC 27**

Lima, Jose Lezama
See Lezama Lima, Jose

Lima Barreto, Afonso Henrique de 1881-1922 .... **TCLC 23**
See Lima Barreto, Afonso Henriques de
See also CA 181; CAAE 117; LAW

Lima Barreto, Afonso Henriques de
See Lima Barreto, Afonso Henrique de
See also DLB 307

Limonov, Eduard
See Limonov, Edward
See also DLB 317

Limonov, Edward 1944- .... **CLC 67**
See Limonov, Eduard
See also CA 137

Lin, Frank
See Atherton, Gertrude (Franklin Horn)

Lin, Yutang 1895-1976 .... **TCLC 149**
See also CA 45-48; CAAS 65-68; CANR 2; RGAL 4

Lincoln, Abraham 1809-1865 .... **NCLC 18**
See also LAIT 2

Lind, Jakov 1927-2007 ... **CLC 1, 2, 4, 27, 82**
See Landwirth, Heinz
See also CA 4; CAAS 257; DLB 299; EWL 3; RGHL

Lindbergh, Anne Morrow 1906-2001 .... **CLC 82**
See also BPFB 2; CA 17-20R; CAAS 193; CANR 16, 73; DAM NOV; MTCW 1, 2; MTFW 2005; SATA 33; SATA-Obit 125; TUS

Lindsay, David 1878(?)-1945 .... **TCLC 15**
See also CA 187; CAAE 113; DLB 255; FANT; SFW 4; SUFW 1

Lindsay, (Nicholas) Vachel 1879-1931 .... **PC 23; TCLC 17; WLC 4**
See also AMWS 1; CA 135; CAAE 114; CANR 79; CDALB 1865-1917; DA; DA3; DAC; DAM MST, POET; DLB 54; EWL 3; EXPP; MAL 5; RGAL 4; SATA 40; WP

Linke-Poot
See Doeblin, Alfred

Linney, Romulus 1930- .... **CLC 51**
See also CA 1-4R; CAD; CANR 40, 44, 79; CD 5, 6; CSW; RGAL 4

Linton, Eliza Lynn 1822-1898 .... **NCLC 41**
See also DLB 18

Li Po 701-763 .... **CMLC 2, 86; PC 29**
See also PFS 20; WP

Lipsius, Justus 1547-1606 .... **LC 16**

Lipsyte, Robert 1938- .... **CLC 21**
See also AAYA 7, 45; CA 17-20R; CANR 8, 57, 146; CLR 23, 76; DA; DAC; DAM MST, NOV; JRDA; LAIT 5; MAICYA 1, 2; SATA 5, 68, 113, 161; WYA; YAW

Lipsyte, Robert Michael
See Lipsyte, Robert

Lish, Gordon 1934- .... **CLC 45; SSC 18**
See also CA 117; CAAE 113; CANR 79, 151; DLB 130; INT CA-117

Lish, Gordon Jay
See Lish, Gordon

Lispector, Clarice 1925(?)-1977 .... **CLC 43; HLCS 2; SSC 34, 96**
See also CA 139; CAAS 116; CANR 71; CDWLB 3; DLB 113, 307; DNFS 1; EWL 3; FW; HW 2; LAW; RGSF 2; RGWL 2, 3; WLIT 1

Littell, Robert 1935(?)- .... **CLC 42**
See also CA 112; CAAE 109; CANR 64, 115, 162; CMW 4

Little, Malcolm 1925-1965
See Malcolm X
See also BW 1, 3; CA 125; CAAS 111; CANR 82; DA; DA3; DAB; DAC; DAM MST, MULT; MTCW 1, 2; MTFW 2005

Littlewit, Humphrey Gent.
See Lovecraft, H. P.

Litwos
See Sienkiewicz, Henryk (Adam Alexander Pius)

Liu, E. 1857-1909 .... **TCLC 15**
See also CA 190; CAAE 115; DLB 328

Lively, Penelope 1933- .... **CLC 32, 50**
See also BPFB 2; CA 41-44R; CANR 29, 67, 79, 131; CLR 7; CN 5, 6, 7; CWRI 5; DAM NOV; DLB 14, 161, 207, 326; FANT; JRDA; MAICYA 1, 2; MTCW 1, 2; MTFW 2005; SATA 7, 60, 101, 164; TEA

Lively, Penelope Margaret
See Lively, Penelope

Lowry, (Clarence) Malcolm
1909-1957 .... **SSC 31; TCLC 6, 40**
See also BPFB 2; BRWS 3; CA 131; CAAE
105; CANR 62, 105; CDBLB 1945-1960;
DLB 15; EWL 3; MTCW 1, 2; MTFW
2005; RGEL 2

Lowry, Mina Gertrude 1882-1966
See Loy, Mina
See also CA 113

Lowry, Sam
See Soderbergh, Steven

Loxsmith, John
See Brunner, John (Kilian Houston)

Loy, Mina .... **CLC 28; PC 16**
See Lowry, Mina Gertrude
See also DAM POET; DLB 4, 54; PFS 20

Loyson-Bridet
See Schwob, Marcel (Mayer Andre)

Lucan 39-65 .... **CMLC 33**
See also AW 2; DLB 211; EFS 2; RGWL 2,
3

Lucas, Craig 1951- .... **CLC 64**
See also CA 137; CAD; CANR 71, 109,
142; CD 5, 6; GLL 2; MTFW 2005

Lucas, E(dward) V(errall)
1868-1938 .... **TCLC 73**
See also CA 176; DLB 98, 149, 153; SATA
20

Lucas, George 1944- .... **CLC 16**
See also AAYA 1, 23; CA 77-80; CANR
30; SATA 56

Lucas, Hans
See Godard, Jean-Luc

Lucas, Victoria
See Plath, Sylvia

Lucian c. 125-c. 180 .... **CMLC 32**
See also AW 2; DLB 176; RGWL 2, 3

Lucilius c. 180B.C.-102B.C. .... **CMLC 82**
See also DLB 211

Lucretius c. 94B.C.-c. 49B.C. .... **CMLC 48**
See also AW 2; CDWLB 1; DLB 211; EFS
2; RGWL 2, 3; WLIT 8

Ludlam, Charles 1943-1987 .... **CLC 46, 50**
See also CA 85-88; CAAS 122; CAD;
CANR 72, 86; DLB 266

Ludlum, Robert 1927-2001 .... **CLC 22, 43**
See also AAYA 10, 59; BEST 89:1, 90:3;
BPFB 2; CA 33-36R; CAAS 195; CANR
25, 41, 68, 105, 131; CMW 4; CPW;
DA3; DAM NOV, POP; DLBY 1982;
MSW; MTCW 1, 2; MTFW 2005

Ludwig, Ken 1950- .... **CLC 60**
See also CA 195; CAD; CD 6

Ludwig, Otto 1813-1865 .... **NCLC 4**
See also DLB 129

Lugones, Leopoldo 1874-1938 .... **HLCS 2;**
TCLC 15
See also CA 131; CAAE 116; CANR 104;
DLB 283; EWL 3; HW 1; LAW

Lu Hsun .... **SSC 20; TCLC 3**
See Shu-Jen, Chou
See also EWL 3

Lukacs, George .... **CLC 24**
See Lukacs, Gyorgy (Szegeny von)

Lukacs, Gyorgy (Szegeny von) 1885-1971
See Lukacs, George
See also CA 101; CAAS 29-32R; CANR
62; CDWLB 4; DLB 215, 242; EW 10;
EWL 3; MTCW 1, 2

Luke, Peter (Ambrose Cyprian)
1919-1995 .... **CLC 38**
See also CA 81-84; CAAS 147; CANR 72;
CBD; CD 5, 6; DLB 13

Lunar, Dennis
See Mungo, Raymond

Lurie, Alison 1926- ..... **CLC 4, 5, 18, 39, 175**
See also BPFB 2; CA 1-4R; CANR 2, 17,
50, 88; CN 1, 2, 3, 4, 5, 6, 7; DLB 2;
MAL 5; MTCW 1; NFS 24; SATA 46,
112; TCLE 1:1

Lustig, Arnost 1926- .... **CLC 56**
See also AAYA 3; CA 69-72; CANR 47,
102; CWW 2; DLB 232, 299; EWL 3;
RGHL; SATA 56

Luther, Martin 1483-1546 .... **LC 9, 37**
See also CDWLB 2; DLB 179; EW 2;
RGWL 2, 3

Luxemburg, Rosa 1870(?)-1919 ..... **TCLC 63**
See also CAAE 118

Luzi, Mario (Egidio Vincenzo)
1914-2005 .... **CLC 13**
See also CA 61-64; CAAS 236; CANR 9,
70; CWW 2; DLB 128; EWL 3

L'vov, Arkady .... **CLC 59**

Lydgate, John c. 1370-1450(?) .... **LC 81**
See also BRW 1; DLB 146; RGEL 2

Lyly, John 1554(?)-1606 .... **DC 7; LC 41**
See also BRW 1; DAM DRAM; DLB 62,
167; RGEL 2

L'Ymagier
See Gourmont, Remy(-Marie-Charles) de

Lynch, B. Suarez
See Borges, Jorge Luis

Lynch, David 1946- .... **CLC 66, 162**
See also AAYA 55; CA 129; CAAE 124;
CANR 111

Lynch, David Keith
See Lynch, David

Lynch, James
See Andreyev, Leonid (Nikolaevich)

Lyndsay, Sir David 1485-1555 .... **LC 20**
See also RGEL 2

Lynn, Kenneth S(chuyler)
1923-2001 .... **CLC 50**
See also CA 1-4R; CAAS 196; CANR 3,
27, 65

Lynx
See West, Rebecca

Lyons, Marcus
See Blish, James (Benjamin)

Lyotard, Jean-Francois
1924-1998 .... **TCLC 103**
See also DLB 242; EWL 3

Lyre, Pinchbeck
See Sassoon, Siegfried (Lorraine)

Lytle, Andrew (Nelson) 1902-1995 ... **CLC 22**
See also CA 9-12R; CAAS 150; CANR 70;
CN 1, 2, 3, 4, 5, 6; CSW; DLB 6; DLBY
1995; RGAL 4; RHW

Lyttelton, George 1709-1773 .... **LC 10**
See also RGEL 2

Lytton of Knebworth, Baron
See Bulwer-Lytton, Edward (George Earle
Lytton)

Maas, Peter 1929-2001 .... **CLC 29**
See also CA 93-96; CAAS 201; INT CA-
93-96; MTCW 2; MTFW 2005

Mac A'Ghobhainn, Iain
See Smith, Iain Crichton

Macaulay, Catherine 1731-1791 .... **LC 64**
See also DLB 104, 336

Macaulay, (Emilie) Rose
1881(?)-1958 .... **TCLC 7, 44**
See also CAAE 104; DLB 36; EWL 3;
RGEL 2; RHW

Macaulay, Thomas Babington
1800-1859 .... **NCLC 42**
See also BRW 4; CDBLB 1832-1890; DLB
32, 55; RGEL 2

MacBeth, George (Mann)
1932-1992 .... **CLC 2, 5, 9**
See also CA 25-28R; CAAS 136; CANR
61, 66; CP 1, 2, 3, 4, 5; DLB 40; MTCW
1; PFS 8; SATA 4; SATA-Obit 70

MacCaig, Norman (Alexander)
1910-1996 .... **CLC 36**
See also BRWS 6; CA 9-12R; CANR 3, 34;
CP 1, 2, 3, 4, 5, 6; DAB; DAM POET;
DLB 27; EWL 3; RGEL 2

MacCarthy, Sir (Charles Otto) Desmond
1877-1952 .... **TCLC 36**
See also CA 167

MacDiarmid, Hugh .... **CLC 2, 4, 11, 19, 63;**
PC 9
See Grieve, C(hristopher) M(urray)
See also BRWS 12; CDBLB 1945-1960;
CP 1, 2; DLB 20; EWL 3; RGEL 2

MacDonald, Anson
See Heinlein, Robert A.

Macdonald, Cynthia 1928- .... **CLC 13, 19**
See also CA 49-52; CANR 4, 44, 146; DLB
105

MacDonald, George 1824-1905 .... **TCLC 9,**
113
See also AAYA 57; BYA 5; CA 137; CAAE
106; CANR 80; CLR 67; DLB 18, 163,
178; FANT; MAICYA 1, 2; RGEL 2;
SATA 33, 100; SFW 4; SUFW; WCH

Macdonald, John
See Millar, Kenneth

MacDonald, John D. 1916-1986 .. **CLC 3, 27,**
44
See also BPFB 2; CA 1-4R; CAAS 121;
CANR 1, 19, 60; CMW 4; CPW; DAM
NOV, POP; DLB 8, 306; DLBY 1986;
MSW; MTCW 1, 2; MTFW 2005; SFW 4

Macdonald, John Ross
See Millar, Kenneth

Macdonald, Ross ..... **CLC 1, 2, 3, 14, 34, 41**
See Millar, Kenneth
See also AMWS 4; BPFB 2; CN 1, 2, 3;
DLBD 6; MAL 5; MSW; RGAL 4

MacDougal, John
See Blish, James (Benjamin)

MacDougal, John
See Blish, James (Benjamin)

MacDowell, John
See Parks, Tim(othy Harold)

MacEwen, Gwendolyn (Margaret)
1941-1987 .... **CLC 13, 55**
See also CA 9-12R; CAAS 124; CANR 7,
22; CP 1, 2, 3, 4; DLB 53, 251; SATA 50;
SATA-Obit 55

Macha, Karel Hynek 1810-1846 .... **NCLC 46**

Machado (y Ruiz), Antonio
1875-1939 .... **TCLC 3**
See also CA 174; CAAE 104; DLB 108;
EW 9; EWL 3; HW 2; PFS 23; RGWL 2,
3

Machado de Assis, Joaquim Maria
1839-1908 .... **BLC 2; HLCS 2; SSC 24;**
TCLC 10
See also CA 153; CAAE 107; CANR 91;
DLB 307; LAW; RGSF 2; RGWL 2, 3;
TWA; WLIT 1

Machaut, Guillaume de c.
1300-1377 .... **CMLC 64**
See also DLB 208

Machen, Arthur .... **SSC 20; TCLC 4**
See Jones, Arthur Llewellyn
See also CA 179; DLB 156, 178; RGEL 2;
SUFW 1

Machiavelli, Niccolo 1469-1527 ... **DC 16; LC**
8, 36, 140; WLCS
See also AAYA 58; DA; DAB; DAC; DAM
MST; EW 2; LAIT 1; LMFS 1; NFS 9;
RGWL 2, 3; TWA; WLIT 7

MacInnes, Colin 1914-1976 .... **CLC 4, 23**
See also CA 69-72; CAAS 65-68; CANR
21; CN 1, 2; DLB 14; MTCW 1, 2; RGEL
2; RHW

Mallowan, Agatha Christie
See Christie, Agatha (Mary Clarissa)

Maloff, Saul 1922- .... **CLC 5**
See also CA 33-36R

Malone, Louis
See MacNeice, (Frederick) Louis

Malone, Michael (Christopher)
1942- .... **CLC 43**
See also CA 77-80; CANR 14, 32, 57, 114

Malory, Sir Thomas 1410(?)-1471(?) . **LC 11, 88; WLCS**
See also BRW 1; BRWR 2; CDBLB Before 1660; DA; DAB; DAC; DAM MST; DLB 146; EFS 2; RGEL 2; SATA 59; SATA-Brief 33; TEA; WLIT 3

Malouf, David 1934- .... **CLC 28, 86**
See also BRWS 12; CA 124; CANR 50, 76; CN 3, 4, 5, 6, 7; CP 1, 3, 4, 5, 6, 7; DLB 289; EWL 3; MTCW 2; MTFW 2005; SSFS 24

Malouf, George Joseph David
See Malouf, David

Malraux, (Georges-)Andre
1901-1976 .... **CLC 1, 4, 9, 13, 15, 57**
See also BPFB 2; CA 21-22; CAAS 69-72; CANR 34, 58; CAP 2; DA3; DAM NOV; DLB 72; EW 12; EWL 3; GFL 1789 to the Present; MTCW 1, 2; MTFW 2005; RGWL 2, 3; TWA

Malthus, Thomas Robert
1766-1834 .... **NCLC 145**
See also DLB 107, 158; RGEL 2

Malzberg, Barry N(athaniel) 1939- ... **CLC 7**
See also CA 61-64; 4; CANR 16; CMW 4; DLB 8; SFW 4

Mamet, David 1947- .. **CLC 9, 15, 34, 46, 91, 166; DC 4, 24**
See also AAYA 3, 60; AMWS 14; CA 81-84; CABS 3; CAD; CANR 15, 41, 67, 72, 129; CD 5, 6; DA3; DAM DRAM; DFS 2, 3, 6, 12, 15; DLB 7; EWL 3; IDFW 4; MAL 5; MTCW 1, 2; MTFW 2005; RGAL 4

Mamet, David Alan
See Mamet, David

Mamoulian, Rouben (Zachary)
1897-1987 .... **CLC 16**
See also CA 25-28R; CAAS 124; CANR 85

Mandelshtam, Osip
See Mandelstam, Osip (Emilievich)
See also EW 10; EWL 3; RGWL 2, 3

Mandelstam, Osip (Emilievich)
1891(?)-1943(?) .... **PC 14; TCLC 2, 6**
See Mandelshtam, Osip
See also CA 150; CAAE 104; MTCW 2; TWA

Mander, (Mary) Jane 1877-1949 ... **TCLC 31**
See also CA 162; RGEL 2

Mandeville, Bernard 1670-1733 .... **LC 82**
See also DLB 101

Mandeville, Sir John fl. 1350- ...... **CMLC 19**
See also DLB 146

Mandiargues, Andre Pieyre de .... **CLC 41**
See Pieyre de Mandiargues, Andre
See also DLB 83

Mandrake, Ethel Belle
See Thurman, Wallace (Henry)

Mangan, James Clarence
1803-1849 .... **NCLC 27**
See also RGEL 2

Maniere, J.-E.
See Giraudoux, Jean(-Hippolyte)

Mankiewicz, Herman (Jacob)
1897-1953 .... **TCLC 85**
See also CA 169; CAAE 120; DLB 26; IDFW 3, 4

Manley, (Mary) Delariviere
1672(?)-1724 .... **LC 1, 42**
See also DLB 39, 80; RGEL 2

Mann, Abel
See Creasey, John

Mann, Emily 1952- .... **DC 7**
See also CA 130; CAD; CANR 55; CD 5, 6; CWD; DLB 266

Mann, (Luiz) Heinrich 1871-1950 ... **TCLC 9**
See also CA 164, 181; CAAE 106; DLB 66, 118; EW 8; EWL 3; RGWL 2, 3

Mann, (Paul) Thomas 1875-1955 . **SSC 5, 80, 82; TCLC 2, 8, 14, 21, 35, 44, 60, 168; WLC 4**
See also BPFB 2; CA 128; CAAE 104; CANR 133; CDWLB 2; DA; DA3; DAB; DAC; DAM MST, NOV; DLB 66, 331; EW 9; EWL 3; GLL 1; LATS 1:1; LMFS 1; MTCW 1, 2; MTFW 2005; NFS 17; RGSF 2; RGWL 2, 3; SSFS 4, 9; TWA

Mannheim, Karl 1893-1947 .... **TCLC 65**
See also CA 204

Manning, David
See Faust, Frederick (Schiller)

Manning, Frederic 1882-1935 .... **TCLC 25**
See also CA 216; CAAE 124; DLB 260

Manning, Olivia 1915-1980 .... **CLC 5, 19**
See also CA 5-8R; CAAS 101; CANR 29; CN 1, 2; EWL 3; FW; MTCW 1; RGEL 2

Mannyng, Robert c. 1264-c.
1340 .... **CMLC 83**
See also DLB 146

Mano, D. Keith 1942- .... **CLC 2, 10**
See also CA 25-28R; 6; CANR 26, 57; DLB 6

Mansfield, Katherine .... **SSC 9, 23, 38, 81; TCLC 2, 8, 39, 164; WLC 4**
See Beauchamp, Kathleen Mansfield
See also BPFB 2; BRW 7; DAB; DLB 162; EWL 3; EXPS; FW; GLL 1; RGEL 2; RGSF 2; SSFS 2, 8, 10, 11; WWE 1

Manso, Peter 1940- .... **CLC 39**
See also CA 29-32R; CANR 44, 156

Mantecon, Juan Jimenez
See Jimenez (Mantecon), Juan Ramon

Mantel, Hilary 1952- .... **CLC 144**
See also CA 125; CANR 54, 101, 161; CN 5, 6, 7; DLB 271; RHW

Mantel, Hilary Mary
See Mantel, Hilary

Manton, Peter
See Creasey, John

Man Without a Spleen, A
See Chekhov, Anton (Pavlovich)

Manzano, Juan Francisco
1797(?)-1854 .... **NCLC 155**

Manzoni, Alessandro 1785-1873 ... **NCLC 29, 98**
See also EW 5; RGWL 2, 3; TWA; WLIT 7

Map, Walter 1140-1209 .... **CMLC 32**

Mapu, Abraham (ben Jekutiel)
1808-1867 .... **NCLC 18**

Mara, Sally
See Queneau, Raymond

Maracle, Lee 1950- .... **NNAL**
See also CA 149

Marat, Jean Paul 1743-1793 .... **LC 10**

Marcel, Gabriel Honore 1889-1973 . **CLC 15**
See also CA 102; CAAS 45-48; EWL 3; MTCW 1, 2

March, William .... **TCLC 96**
See Campbell, William Edward March
See also CA 216; DLB 9, 86, 316; MAL 5

Marchbanks, Samuel
See Davies, Robertson
See also CCA 1

Marchi, Giacomo
See Bassani, Giorgio

Marcus Aurelius
See Aurelius, Marcus
See also AW 2

Marguerite
See de Navarre, Marguerite

Marguerite d'Angouleme
See de Navarre, Marguerite
See also GFL Beginnings to 1789

Marguerite de Navarre
See de Navarre, Marguerite
See also RGWL 2, 3

Margulies, Donald 1954- .... **CLC 76**
See also AAYA 57; CA 200; CD 6; DFS 13; DLB 228

Marias, Javier 1951- .... **CLC 239**
See also CA 167; CANR 109, 139; DLB 322; HW 2; MTFW 2005

Marie de France c. 12th cent. - ..... **CMLC 8; PC 22**
See also DLB 208; FW; RGWL 2, 3

Marie de l'Incarnation 1599-1672 ...... **LC 10**

Marier, Captain Victor
See Griffith, D(avid Lewelyn) W(ark)

Mariner, Scott
See Pohl, Frederik

Marinetti, Filippo Tommaso
1876-1944 .... **TCLC 10**
See also CAAE 107; DLB 114, 264; EW 9; EWL 3; WLIT 7

Marivaux, Pierre Carlet de Chamblain de
1688-1763 .... **DC 7; LC 4, 123**
See also DLB 314; GFL Beginnings to 1789; RGWL 2, 3; TWA

Markandaya, Kamala .... **CLC 8, 38**
See Taylor, Kamala
See also BYA 13; CN 1, 2, 3, 4, 5, 6, 7; DLB 323; EWL 3

Markfield, Wallace (Arthur)
1926-2002 .... **CLC 8**
See also CA 69-72; 3; CAAS 208; CN 1, 2, 3, 4, 5, 6, 7; DLB 2, 28; DLBY 2002

Markham, Edwin 1852-1940 .... **TCLC 47**
See also CA 160; DLB 54, 186; MAL 5; RGAL 4

Markham, Robert
See Amis, Kingsley

Marks, J.
See Highwater, Jamake (Mamake)

Marks-Highwater, J.
See Highwater, Jamake (Mamake)

Markson, David M. 1927- .... **CLC 67**
See also CA 49-52; CANR 1, 91, 158; CN 5, 6

Markson, David Merrill
See Markson, David M.

Marlatt, Daphne (Buckle) 1942- .... **CLC 168**
See also CA 25-28R; CANR 17, 39; CN 6, 7; CP 4, 5, 6, 7; CWP; DLB 60; FW

Marley, Bob .... **CLC 17**
See Marley, Robert Nesta

Marley, Robert Nesta 1945-1981
See Marley, Bob
See also CA 107; CAAS 103

Marlowe, Christopher 1564-1593 . **DC 1; LC 22, 47, 117; PC 57; WLC 4**
See also BRW 1; BRWR 1; CDBLB Before 1660; DA; DA3; DAB; DAC; DAM DRAM, MST; DFS 1, 5, 13, 21; DLB 62; EXPP; LMFS 1; PFS 22; RGEL 2; TEA; WLIT 3

Marlowe, Stephen 1928- .... **CLC 70**
See Queen, Ellery
See also CA 13-16R; CANR 6, 55; CMW 4; SFW 4

Marmion, Shakerley 1603-1639 .... **LC 89**
See also DLB 58; RGEL 2

Marmontel, Jean-Francois 1723-1799 .. **LC 2**
See also DLB 314

Maron, Monika 1941- .... **CLC 165**
See also CA 201

Marot, Clement c. 1496-1544 .... **LC 133**
See also DLB 327; GFL Beginnings to 1789

Matthiessen, Peter 1927- ... **CLC 5, 7, 11, 32, 64**
See also AAYA 6, 40; AMWS 5; ANW; BEST 90:4; BPFB 2; CA 9-12R; CANR 21, 50, 73, 100, 138; CN 1, 2, 3, 4, 5, 6, 7; DA3; DAM NOV; DLB 6, 173, 275; MAL 5; MTCW 1, 2; MTFW 2005; SATA 27

Maturin, Charles Robert
1780(?)-1824 .... **NCLC 6, 169**
See also BRWS 8; DLB 178; GL 3; HGG; LMFS 1; RGEL 2; SUFW

Matute (Ausejo), Ana Maria 1925- .. **CLC 11**
See also CA 89-92; CANR 129; CWW 2; DLB 322; EWL 3; MTCW 1; RGSF 2

Maugham, W. S.
See Maugham, W(illiam) Somerset

Maugham, W(illiam) Somerset
1874-1965 .. **CLC 1, 11, 15, 67, 93; SSC 8, 94; WLC 4**
See also AAYA 55; BPFB 2; BRW 6; CA 5-8R; CAAS 25-28R; CANR 40, 127; CDBLB 1914-1945; CMW 4; DA; DA3; DAB; DAC; DAM DRAM, MST, NOV; DFS 22; DLB 10, 36, 77, 100, 162, 195; EWL 3; LAIT 3; MTCW 1, 2; MTFW 2005; NFS 23; RGEL 2; RGSF 2; SATA 54; SSFS 17

Maugham, William Somerset
See Maugham, W(illiam) Somerset

Maupassant, (Henri Rene Albert) Guy de
1850-1893 . **NCLC 1, 42, 83; SSC 1, 64; WLC 4**
See also BYA 14; DA; DA3; DAB; DAC; DAM MST; DLB 123; EW 7; EXPS; GFL 1789 to the Present; LAIT 2; LMFS 1; RGSF 2; RGWL 2, 3; SSFS 4, 21; SUFW; TWA

Maupin, Armistead 1944- .... **CLC 95**
See also CA 130; CAAE 125; CANR 58, 101; CPW; DA3; DAM POP; DLB 278; GLL 1; INT CA-130; MTCW 2; MTFW 2005

Maupin, Armistead Jones, Jr.
See Maupin, Armistead

Maurhut, Richard
See Traven, B.

Mauriac, Claude 1914-1996 .... **CLC 9**
See also CA 89-92; CAAS 152; CWW 2; DLB 83; EWL 3; GFL 1789 to the Present

Mauriac, Francois (Charles)
1885-1970 .... **CLC 4, 9, 56; SSC 24**
See also CA 25-28; CAP 2; DLB 65, 331; EW 10; EWL 3; GFL 1789 to the Present; MTCW 1, 2; MTFW 2005; RGWL 2, 3; TWA

Mavor, Osborne Henry 1888-1951
See Bridie, James
See also CAAE 104

Maxwell, Glyn 1962- .... **CLC 238**
See also CA 154; CANR 88; CP 6, 7; PFS 23

Maxwell, William (Keepers, Jr.)
1908-2000 .... **CLC 19**
See also AMWS 8; CA 93-96; CAAS 189; CANR 54, 95; CN 1, 2, 3, 4, 5, 6, 7; DLB 218, 278; DLBY 1980; INT CA-93-96; MAL 5; SATA-Obit 128

May, Elaine 1932- .... **CLC 16**
See also CA 142; CAAE 124; CAD; CWD; DLB 44

Mayakovski, Vladimir (Vladimirovich)
1893-1930 .... **TCLC 4, 18**
See also Maiakovskii, Vladimir; Mayakovsky, Vladimir
See also CA 158; CAAE 104; EWL 3; MTCW 2; MTFW 2005; SFW 4; TWA

Mayakovsky, Vladimir
See Mayakovski, Vladimir (Vladimirovich)
See also EW 11; WP

Mayhew, Henry 1812-1887 .... **NCLC 31**
See also DLB 18, 55, 190

Mayle, Peter 1939(?)- .... **CLC 89**
See also CA 139; CANR 64, 109

Maynard, Joyce 1953- .... **CLC 23**
See also CA 129; CAAE 111; CANR 64

Mayne, William (James Carter)
1928- .... **CLC 12**
See also AAYA 20; CA 9-12R; CANR 37, 80, 100; CLR 25, 123; FANT; JRDA; MAICYA 1, 2; MAICYAS 1; SAAS 11; SATA 6, 68, 122; SUFW 2; YAW

Mayo, Jim
See L'Amour, Louis

Maysles, Albert 1926- .... **CLC 16**
See also CA 29-32R

Maysles, David 1932-1987 .... **CLC 16**
See also CA 191

Mazer, Norma Fox 1931- .... **CLC 26**
See also AAYA 5, 36; BYA 1, 8; CA 69-72; CANR 12, 32, 66, 129; CLR 23; JRDA; MAICYA 1, 2; SAAS 1; SATA 24, 67, 105, 168; WYA; YAW

Mazzini, Guiseppe 1805-1872 .... **NCLC 34**

McAlmon, Robert (Menzies)
1895-1956 .... **TCLC 97**
See also CA 168; CAAE 107; DLB 4, 45; DLBD 15; GLL 1

McAuley, James Phillip 1917-1976 .. **CLC 45**
See also CA 97-100; CP 1, 2; DLB 260; RGEL 2

McBain, Ed
See Hunter, Evan
See also MSW

McBrien, William (Augustine)
1930- .... **CLC 44**
See also CA 107; CANR 90

McCabe, Patrick 1955- .... **CLC 133**
See also BRWS 9; CA 130; CANR 50, 90; CN 6, 7; DLB 194

McCaffrey, Anne 1926- .... **CLC 17**
See also AAYA 6, 34; AITN 2; BEST 89:2; BPFB 2; BYA 5; CA 227; 25-28R, 227; CANR 15, 35, 55, 96; CLR 49; CPW; DA3; DAM NOV, POP; DLB 8; JRDA; MAICYA 1, 2; MTCW 1, 2; MTFW 2005; SAAS 11; SATA 8, 70, 116, 152; SATA-Essay 152; SFW 4; SUFW 2; WYA; YAW

McCaffrey, Anne Inez
See McCaffrey, Anne

McCall, Nathan 1955(?)- .... **CLC 86**
See also AAYA 59; BW 3; CA 146; CANR 88

McCann, Arthur
See Campbell, John W(ood, Jr.)

McCann, Edson
See Pohl, Frederik

McCarthy, Charles, Jr.
See McCarthy, Cormac

McCarthy, Cormac 1933- .... **CLC 4, 57, 101, 204**
See also AAYA 41; AMWS 8; BPFB 2; CA 13-16R; CANR 10, 42, 69, 101, 161; CN 6, 7; CPW; CSW; DA3; DAM POP; DLB 6, 143, 256; EWL 3; LATS 1:2; MAL 5; MTCW 2; MTFW 2005; TCLE 1:2; TCWW 2

McCarthy, Mary (Therese)
1912-1989 .. **CLC 1, 3, 5, 14, 24, 39, 59; SSC 24**
See also AMW; BPFB 2; CA 5-8R; CAAS 129; CANR 16, 50, 64; CN 1, 2, 3, 4; DA3; DLB 2; DLBY 1981; EWL 3; FW; INT CANR-16; MAL 5; MBL; MTCW 1, 2; MTFW 2005; RGAL 4; TUS

McCartney, James Paul
See McCartney, Paul

McCartney, Paul 1942- .... **CLC 12, 35**
See also CA 146; CANR 111

McCauley, Stephen (D.) 1955- .... **CLC 50**
See also CA 141

McClaren, Peter .... **CLC 70**

McClure, Michael (Thomas) 1932- ... **CLC 6, 10**
See also BG 1:3; CA 21-24R; CAD; CANR 17, 46, 77, 131; CD 5, 6; CP 1, 2, 3, 4, 5, 6, 7; DLB 16; WP

McCorkle, Jill (Collins) 1958- .... **CLC 51**
See also CA 121; CANR 113; CSW; DLB 234; DLBY 1987; SSFS 24

McCourt, Frank 1930- .... **CLC 109**
See also AAYA 61; AMWS 12; CA 157; CANR 97, 138; MTFW 2005; NCFS 1

McCourt, James 1941- .... **CLC 5**
See also CA 57-60; CANR 98, 152

McCourt, Malachy 1931- .... **CLC 119**
See also SATA 126

McCoy, Horace (Stanley)
1897-1955 .... **TCLC 28**
See also AMWS 13; CA 155; CAAE 108; CMW 4; DLB 9

McCrae, John 1872-1918 .... **TCLC 12**
See also CAAE 109; DLB 92; PFS 5

McCreigh, James
See Pohl, Frederik

McCullers, (Lula) Carson (Smith)
1917-1967 .... **CLC 1, 4, 10, 12, 48, 100; SSC 9, 24, 99; TCLC 155; WLC 4**
See also AAYA 21; AMW; AMWC 2; BPFB 2; CA 5-8R; CAAS 25-28R; CABS 1, 3; CANR 18, 132; CDALB 1941-1968; DA; DA3; DAB; DAC; DAM MST, NOV; DFS 5, 18; DLB 2, 7, 173, 228; EWL 3; EXPS; FW; GLL 1; LAIT 3, 4; MAL 5; MBL; MTCW 1, 2; MTFW 2005; NFS 6, 13; RGAL 4; RGSF 2; SATA 27; SSFS 5; TUS; YAW

McCulloch, John Tyler
See Burroughs, Edgar Rice

McCullough, Colleen 1937- ...... **CLC 27, 107**
See also AAYA 36; BPFB 2; CA 81-84; CANR 17, 46, 67, 98, 139; CPW; DA3; DAM NOV, POP; MTCW 1, 2; MTFW 2005; RHW

McCunn, Ruthanne Lum 1946- .... **AAL**
See also CA 119; CANR 43, 96; DLB 312; LAIT 2; SATA 63

McDermott, Alice 1953- .... **CLC 90**
See also CA 109; CANR 40, 90, 126; CN 7; DLB 292; MTFW 2005; NFS 23

McElroy, Joseph 1930- .... **CLC 5, 47**
See also CA 17-20R; CANR 149; CN 3, 4, 5, 6, 7

McElroy, Joseph Prince
See McElroy, Joseph

McEwan, Ian 1948- .... **CLC 13, 66, 169**
See also BEST 90:4; BRWS 4; CA 61-64; CANR 14, 41, 69, 87, 132; CN 3, 4, 5, 6, 7; DAM NOV; DLB 14, 194, 319, 326; HGG; MTCW 1, 2; MTFW 2005; RGSF 2; SUFW 2; TEA

McFadden, David 1940- .... **CLC 48**
See also CA 104; CP 1, 2, 3, 4, 5, 6, 7; DLB 60; INT CA-104

McFarland, Dennis 1950- .... **CLC 65**
See also CA 165; CANR 110

McGahern, John 1934-2006 .... **CLC 5, 9, 48, 156; SSC 17**
See also CA 17-20R; CAAS 249; CANR 29, 68, 113; CN 1, 2, 3, 4, 5, 6, 7; DLB 14, 231, 319; MTCW 1

McGinley, Patrick (Anthony) 1937- . **CLC 41**
See also CA 127; CAAE 120; CANR 56; INT CA-127

McGinley, Phyllis 1905-1978 .... **CLC 14**
See also CA 9-12R; CAAS 77-80; CANR 19; CP 1, 2; CWRI 5; DLB 11, 48; MAL 5; PFS 9, 13; SATA 2, 44; SATA-Obit 24

Meredith, George 1828-1909 .. **PC 60; TCLC 17, 43**
See also CA 153; CAAE 117; CANR 80; CDBLB 1832-1890; DAM POET; DLB 18, 35, 57, 159; RGEL 2; TEA

Meredith, William 1919-2007 ...... **CLC 4, 13, 22, 55; PC 28**
See also CA 9-12R; 14; CANR 6, 40, 129; CP 1, 2, 3, 4, 5, 6, 7; DAM POET; DLB 5; MAL 5

Meredith, William Morris
See Meredith, William

Merezhkovsky, Dmitrii Sergeevich
See Merezhkovsky, Dmitry Sergeyevich
See also DLB 295

Merezhkovsky, Dmitry Sergeevich
See Merezhkovsky, Dmitry Sergeyevich
See also EWL 3

Merezhkovsky, Dmitry Sergeyevich
1865-1941 .... **TCLC 29**
See Merezhkovsky, Dmitrii Sergeevich; Merezhkovsky, Dmitry Sergeevich
See also CA 169

Merimee, Prosper 1803-1870 ... **NCLC 6, 65; SSC 7, 77**
See also DLB 119, 192; EW 6; EXPS; GFL 1789 to the Present; RGSF 2; RGWL 2, 3; SSFS 8; SUFW

Merkin, Daphne 1954- .... **CLC 44**
See also CA 123

Merleau-Ponty, Maurice
1908-1961 .... **TCLC 156**
See also CA 114; CAAS 89-92; DLB 296; GFL 1789 to the Present

Merlin, Arthur
See Blish, James (Benjamin)

Mernissi, Fatima 1940- .... **CLC 171**
See also CA 152; FW

Merrill, James 1926-1995 ...... **CLC 2, 3, 6, 8, 13, 18, 34, 91; PC 28; TCLC 173**
See also AMWS 3; CA 13-16R; CAAS 147; CANR 10, 49, 63, 108; CP 1, 2, 3, 4; DA3; DAM POET; DLB 5, 165; DLBY 1985; EWL 3; INT CANR-10; MAL 5; MTCW 1, 2; MTFW 2005; PAB; PFS 23; RGAL 4

Merrill, James Ingram
See Merrill, James

Merriman, Alex
See Silverberg, Robert

Merriman, Brian 1747-1805 .... **NCLC 70**

Merritt, E. B.
See Waddington, Miriam

Merton, Thomas (James)
1915-1968 . **CLC 1, 3, 11, 34, 83; PC 10**
See also AAYA 61; AMWS 8; CA 5-8R; CAAS 25-28R; CANR 22, 53, 111, 131; DA3; DLB 48; DLBY 1981; MAL 5; MTCW 1, 2; MTFW 2005

Merwin, W.S. 1927- ..... **CLC 1, 2, 3, 5, 8, 13, 18, 45, 88; PC 45**
See also AMWS 3; CA 13-16R; CANR 15, 51, 112, 140; CP 1, 2, 3, 4, 5, 6, 7; DAM POET; DLB 5, 169; EWL 3; INT CANR-15; MAL 5; MTCW 1, 2; MTFW 2005; PAB; PFS 5, 15; RGAL 4

Metastasio, Pietro 1698-1782 .... **LC 115**
See also RGWL 2, 3

Metcalf, John 1938- .... **CLC 37; SSC 43**
See also CA 113; CN 4, 5, 6, 7; DLB 60; RGSF 2; TWA

Metcalf, Suzanne
See Baum, L(yman) Frank

Mew, Charlotte (Mary) 1870-1928 .. **TCLC 8**
See also CA 189; CAAE 105; DLB 19, 135; RGEL 2

Mewshaw, Michael 1943- .... **CLC 9**
See also CA 53-56; CANR 7, 47, 147; DLBY 1980

Meyer, Conrad Ferdinand
1825-1898 .... **NCLC 81; SSC 30**
See also DLB 129; EW; RGWL 2, 3

Meyer, Gustav 1868-1932
See Meyrink, Gustav
See also CA 190; CAAE 117

Meyer, June
See Jordan, June

Meyer, Lynn
See Slavitt, David R(ytman)

Meyers, Jeffrey 1939- .... **CLC 39**
See also CA 186; 73-76, 186; CANR 54, 102, 159; DLB 111

Meynell, Alice (Christina Gertrude Thompson) 1847-1922 .... **TCLC 6**
See also CA 177; CAAE 104; DLB 19, 98; RGEL 2

Meyrink, Gustav .... **TCLC 21**
See Meyer, Gustav
See also DLB 81; EWL 3

Michaels, Leonard 1933-2003 ..... **CLC 6, 25; SSC 16**
See also AMWS 16; CA 61-64; CAAS 216; CANR 21, 62, 119; CN 3, 45, 6, 7; DLB 130; MTCW 1; TCLE 1:2

Michaux, Henri 1899-1984 .... **CLC 8, 19**
See also CA 85-88; CAAS 114; DLB 258; EWL 3; GFL 1789 to the Present; RGWL 2, 3

Micheaux, Oscar (Devereaux)
1884-1951 .... **TCLC 76**
See also BW 3; CA 174; DLB 50; TCWW 2

Michelangelo 1475-1564 .... **LC 12**
See also AAYA 43

Michelet, Jules 1798-1874 .... **NCLC 31**
See also EW 5; GFL 1789 to the Present

Michels, Robert 1876-1936 .... **TCLC 88**
See also CA 212

Michener, James A. 1907(?)-1997 . **CLC 1, 5, 11, 29, 60, 109**
See also AAYA 27; AITN 1; BEST 90:1; BPFB 2; CA 5-8R; CAAS 161; CANR 21, 45, 68; CN 1, 2, 3, 4, 5, 6; CPW; DA3; DAM NOV, POP; DLB 6; MAL 5; MTCW 1, 2; MTFW 2005; RHW; TCWW 1, 2

Mickiewicz, Adam 1798-1855 . **NCLC 3, 101; PC 38**
See also EW 5; RGWL 2, 3

Middleton, (John) Christopher
1926- .... **CLC 13**
See also CA 13-16R; CANR 29, 54, 117; CP 1, 2, 3, 4, 5, 6, 7; DLB 40

Middleton, Richard (Barham)
1882-1911 .... **TCLC 56**
See also CA 187; DLB 156; HGG

Middleton, Stanley 1919- .... **CLC 7, 38**
See also CA 25-28R; 23; CANR 21, 46, 81, 157; CN 1, 2, 3, 4, 5, 6, 7; DLB 14, 326

Middleton, Thomas 1580-1627 ...... **DC 5; LC 33, 123**
See also BRW 2; DAM DRAM, MST; DFS 18, 22; DLB 58; RGEL 2

Mieville, China 1972(?)- .... **CLC 235**
See also AAYA 52; CA 196; CANR 138; MTFW 2005

Migueis, Jose Rodrigues 1901-1980 . **CLC 10**
See also DLB 287

Mikszath, Kalman 1847-1910 .... **TCLC 31**
See also CA 170

Miles, Jack .... **CLC 100**
See also CA 200

Miles, John Russiano
See Miles, Jack

Miles, Josephine (Louise)
1911-1985 .... **CLC 1, 2, 14, 34, 39**
See also CA 1-4R; CAAS 116; CANR 2, 55; CP 1, 2, 3, 4; DAM POET; DLB 48; MAL 5; TCLE 1:2

Militant
See Sandburg, Carl (August)

Mill, Harriet (Hardy) Taylor
1807-1858 .... **NCLC 102**
See also FW

Mill, John Stuart 1806-1873 ... **NCLC 11, 58, 179**
See also CDBLB 1832-1890; DLB 55, 190, 262; FW 1; RGEL 2; TEA

Millar, Kenneth 1915-1983 .... **CLC 14**
See Macdonald, Ross
See also CA 9-12R; CAAS 110; CANR 16, 63, 107; CMW 4; CPW; DA3; DAM POP; DLB 2, 226; DLBD 6; DLBY 1983; MTCW 1, 2; MTFW 2005

Millay, E. Vincent
See Millay, Edna St. Vincent

Millay, Edna St. Vincent 1892-1950 ..... **PC 6, 61; TCLC 4, 49, 169; WLCS**
See Boyd, Nancy
See also AMW; CA 130; CAAE 104; CDALB 1917-1929; DA; DA3; DAB; DAC; DAM MST, POET; DLB 45, 249; EWL 3; EXPP; FL 1:6; MAL 5; MBL; MTCW 1, 2; MTFW 2005; PAB; PFS 3, 17; RGAL 4; TUS; WP

Miller, Arthur 1915-2005 ..... **CLC 1, 2, 6, 10, 15, 26, 47, 78, 179; DC 1; WLC 4**
See also AAYA 15; AITN 1; AMW; AMWC 1; CA 1-4R; CAAS 236; CABS 3; CAD; CANR 2, 30, 54, 76, 132; CD 5, 6; CDALB 1941-1968; DA; DA3; DAB; DAC; DAM DRAM, MST; DFS 1, 3, 8; DLB 7, 266; EWL 3; LAIT 1, 4; LATS 1:2; MAL 5; MTCW 1, 2; MTFW 2005; RGAL 4; RGHL; TUS; WYAS 1

Miller, Henry (Valentine)
1891-1980 .... **CLC 1, 2, 4, 9, 14, 43, 84; WLC 4**
See also AMW; BPFB 2; CA 9-12R; CAAS 97-100; CANR 33, 64; CDALB 1929-1941; CN 1, 2; DA; DA3; DAB; DAC; DAM MST, NOV; DLB 4, 9; DLBY 1980; EWL 3; MAL 5; MTCW 1, 2; MTFW 2005; RGAL 4; TUS

Miller, Hugh 1802-1856 .... **NCLC 143**
See also DLB 190

Miller, Jason 1939(?)-2001 .... **CLC 2**
See also AITN 1; CA 73-76; CAAS 197; CAD; CANR 130; DFS 12; DLB 7

Miller, Sue 1943- .... **CLC 44**
See also AMWS 12; BEST 90:3; CA 139; CANR 59, 91, 128; DA3; DAM POP; DLB 143

Miller, Walter M(ichael, Jr.)
1923-1996 .... **CLC 4, 30**
See also BPFB 2; CA 85-88; CANR 108; DLB 8; SCFW 1, 2; SFW 4

Millett, Kate 1934- .... **CLC 67**
See also AITN 1; CA 73-76; CANR 32, 53, 76, 110; DA3; DLB 246; FW; GLL 1; MTCW 1, 2; MTFW 2005

Millhauser, Steven 1943- ... **CLC 21, 54, 109; SSC 57**
See also CA 111; CAAE 110; CANR 63, 114, 133; CN 6, 7; DA3; DLB 2; FANT; INT CA-111; MAL 5; MTCW 2; MTFW 2005

Millhauser, Steven Lewis
See Millhauser, Steven

Millin, Sarah Gertrude 1889-1968 ... **CLC 49**
See also CA 102; CAAS 93-96; DLB 225; EWL 3

Milne, A. A. 1882-1956 .... **TCLC 6, 88**
See also BRWS 5; CA 133; CAAE 104; CLR 1, 26, 108; CMW 4; CWRI 5; DA3; DAB; DAC; DAM MST; DLB 10, 77, 100, 160; FANT; MAICYA 1, 2; MTCW 1, 2; MTFW 2005; RGEL 2; SATA 100; WCH; YABC 1

Milne, Alan Alexander
See Milne, A. A.

Milner, Ron(ald) 1938-2004 ..... **BLC 3; CLC 56**
See also AITN 1; BW 1; CA 73-76; CAAS 230; CAD; CANR 24, 81; CD 5, 6; DAM MULT; DLB 38; MAL 5; MTCW 1

Milnes, Richard Monckton
1809-1885 .... **NCLC 61**
See also DLB 32, 184

Milosz, Czeslaw 1911-2004 .... **CLC 5, 11, 22, 31, 56, 82; PC 8; WLCS**
See also AAYA 62; CA 81-84; CAAS 230; CANR 23, 51, 91, 126; CDWLB 4; CWW 2; DA3; DAM MST, POET; DLB 215, 331; EW 13; EWL 3; MTCW 1, 2; MTFW 2005; PFS 16; RGHL; RGWL 2, 3

Milton, John 1608-1674 ..... **LC 9, 43, 92; PC 19, 29; WLC 4**
See also AAYA 65; BRW 2; BRWR 2; CD-BLB 1660-1789; DA; DA3; DAB; DAC; DAM MST, POET; DLB 131, 151, 281; EFS 1; EXPP; LAIT 1; PAB; PFS 3, 17; RGEL 2; TEA; WLIT 3; WP

Min, Anchee 1957- .... **CLC 86**
See also CA 146; CANR 94, 137; MTFW 2005

Minehaha, Cornelius
See Wedekind, Frank

Miner, Valerie 1947- .... **CLC 40**
See also CA 97-100; CANR 59; FW; GLL 2

Minimo, Duca
See D'Annunzio, Gabriele

Minot, Susan (Anderson) 1956- ...... **CLC 44, 159**
See also AMWS 6; CA 134; CANR 118; CN 6, 7

Minus, Ed 1938- .... **CLC 39**
See also CA 185

Mirabai 1498(?)-1550(?) .... **PC 48**
See also PFS 24

Miranda, Javier
See Bioy Casares, Adolfo
See also CWW 2

Mirbeau, Octave 1848-1917 .... **TCLC 55**
See also CA 216; DLB 123, 192; GFL 1789 to the Present

Mirikitani, Janice 1942- .... **AAL**
See also CA 211; DLB 312; RGAL 4

Mirk, John (?)-c. 1414 .... **LC 105**
See also DLB 146

Miro (Ferrer), Gabriel (Francisco Victor)
1879-1930 .... **TCLC 5**
See also CA 185; CAAE 104; DLB 322; EWL 3

Misharin, Alexandr .... **CLC 59**

Mishima, Yukio ... **CLC 2, 4, 6, 9, 27; DC 1; SSC 4; TCLC 161; WLC 4**
See Hiraoka, Kimitake
See also AAYA 50; BPFB 2; GLL 1; MJW; RGSF 2; RGWL 2, 3; SSFS 5, 12

Mistral, Frederic 1830-1914 .... **TCLC 51**
See also CA 213; CAAE 122; DLB 331; GFL 1789 to the Present

Mistral, Gabriela
See Godoy Alcayaga, Lucila
See also DLB 283, 331; DNFS 1; EWL 3; LAW; RGWL 2, 3; WP

Mistry, Rohinton 1952- ... **CLC 71, 196; SSC 73**
See also BRWS 10; CA 141; CANR 86, 114; CCA 1; CN 6, 7; DAC; DLB 334; SSFS 6

Mitchell, Clyde
See Ellison, Harlan

Mitchell, Emerson Blackhorse Barney
1945- .... **NNAL**
See also CA 45-48

Mitchell, James Leslie 1901-1935
See Gibbon, Lewis Grassic
See also CA 188; CAAE 104; DLB 15

Mitchell, Joni 1943- .... **CLC 12**
See also CA 112; CCA 1

Mitchell, Joseph (Quincy)
1908-1996 .... **CLC 98**
See also CA 77-80; CAAS 152; CANR 69; CN 1, 2, 3, 4, 5, 6; CSW; DLB 185; DLBY 1996

Mitchell, Margaret (Munnerlyn)
1900-1949 .... **TCLC 11, 170**
See also AAYA 23; BPFB 2; BYA 1; CA 125; CAAE 109; CANR 55, 94; CDALBS; DA3; DAM NOV, POP; DLB 9; LAIT 2; MAL 5; MTCW 1, 2; MTFW 2005; NFS 9; RGAL 4; RHW; TUS; WYAS 1; YAW

Mitchell, Peggy
See Mitchell, Margaret (Munnerlyn)

Mitchell, S(ilas) Weir 1829-1914 .... **TCLC 36**
See also CA 165; DLB 202; RGAL 4

Mitchell, W(illiam) O(rmond)
1914-1998 .... **CLC 25**
See also CA 77-80; CAAS 165; CANR 15, 43; CN 1, 2, 3, 4, 5, 6; DAC; DAM MST; DLB 88; TCLE 1:2

Mitchell, William (Lendrum)
1879-1936 .... **TCLC 81**
See also CA 213

Mitford, Mary Russell 1787-1855 ... **NCLC 4**
See also DLB 110, 116; RGEL 2

Mitford, Nancy 1904-1973 .... **CLC 44**
See also BRWS 10; CA 9-12R; CN 1; DLB 191; RGEL 2

Miyamoto, (Chujo) Yuriko
1899-1951 .... **TCLC 37**
See Miyamoto Yuriko
See also CA 170, 174

Miyamoto Yuriko
See Miyamoto, (Chujo) Yuriko
See also DLB 180

Miyazawa, Kenji 1896-1933 .... **TCLC 76**
See Miyazawa Kenji
See also CA 157; RGWL 3

Miyazawa Kenji
See Miyazawa, Kenji
See also EWL 3

Mizoguchi, Kenji 1898-1956 .... **TCLC 72**
See also CA 167

Mo, Timothy (Peter) 1950- .... **CLC 46, 134**
See also CA 117; CANR 128; CN 5, 6, 7; DLB 194; MTCW 1; WLIT 4; WWE 1

Modarressi, Taghi (M.) 1931-1997 ... **CLC 44**
See also CA 134; CAAE 121; INT CA-134

Modiano, Patrick (Jean) 1945- .... **CLC 18, 218**
See also CA 85-88; CANR 17, 40, 115; CWW 2; DLB 83, 299; EWL 3; RGHL

Mofolo, Thomas (Mokopu)
1875(?)-1948 .... **BLC 3; TCLC 22**
See also AFW; CA 153; CAAE 121; CANR 83; DAM MULT; DLB 225; EWL 3; MTCW 2; MTFW 2005; WLIT 2

Mohr, Nicholasa 1938- .... **CLC 12; HLC 2**
See also AAYA 8, 46; CA 49-52; CANR 1, 32, 64; CLR 22; DAM MULT; DLB 145; HW 1, 2; JRDA; LAIT 5; LLW; MAICYA 2; MAICYAS 1; RGAL 4; SAAS 8; SATA 8, 97; SATA-Essay 113; WYA; YAW

Moi, Toril 1953- .... **CLC 172**
See also CA 154; CANR 102; FW

Mojtabai, A(nn) G(race) 1938- ..... **CLC 5, 9, 15, 29**
See also CA 85-88; CANR 88

Moliere 1622-1673 ..... **DC 13; LC 10, 28, 64, 125, 127; WLC 4**
See also DA; DA3; DAB; DAC; DAM DRAM, MST; DFS 13, 18, 20; DLB 268; EW 3; GFL Beginnings to 1789; LATS 1:1; RGWL 2, 3; TWA

Molin, Charles
See Mayne, William (James Carter)

Molnar, Ferenc 1878-1952 .... **TCLC 20**
See also CA 153; CAAE 109; CANR 83; CDWLB 4; DAM DRAM; DLB 215; EWL 3; RGWL 2, 3

Momaday, N. Scott 1934- ...... **CLC 2, 19, 85, 95, 160; NNAL; PC 25; WLCS**
See also AAYA 11, 64; AMWS 4; ANW; BPFB 2; BYA 12; CA 25-28R; CANR 14, 34, 68, 134; CDALBS; CN 2, 3, 4, 5, 6, 7; CPW; DA; DA3; DAB; DAC; DAM MST, MULT, NOV, POP; DLB 143, 175, 256; EWL 3; EXPP; INT CANR-14; LAIT 4; LATS 1:2; MAL 5; MTCW 1, 2; MTFW 2005; NFS 10; PFS 2, 11; RGAL 4; SATA 48; SATA-Brief 30; TCWW 1, 2; WP; YAW

Monette, Paul 1945-1995 .... **CLC 82**
See also AMWS 10; CA 139; CAAS 147; CN 6; GLL 1

Monroe, Harriet 1860-1936 .... **TCLC 12**
See also CA 204; CAAE 109; DLB 54, 91

Monroe, Lyle
See Heinlein, Robert A.

Montagu, Elizabeth 1720-1800 .... **NCLC 7, 117**
See also FW

Montagu, Mary (Pierrepont) Wortley
1689-1762 .... **LC 9, 57; PC 16**
See also DLB 95, 101; FL 1:1; RGEL 2

Montagu, W. H.
See Coleridge, Samuel Taylor

Montague, John (Patrick) 1929- ..... **CLC 13, 46**
See also CA 9-12R; CANR 9, 69, 121; CP 1, 2, 3, 4, 5, 6, 7; DLB 40; EWL 3; MTCW 1; PFS 12; RGEL 2; TCLE 1:2

Montaigne, Michel (Eyquem) de
1533-1592 .... **LC 8, 105; WLC 4**
See also DA; DAB; DAC; DAM MST; DLB 327; EW 2; GFL Beginnings to 1789; LMFS 1; RGWL 2, 3; TWA

Montale, Eugenio 1896-1981 ... **CLC 7, 9, 18; PC 13**
See also CA 17-20R; CAAS 104; CANR 30; DLB 114, 331; EW 11; EWL 3; MTCW 1; PFS 22; RGWL 2, 3; TWA; WLIT 7

Montesquieu, Charles-Louis de Secondat
1689-1755 .... **LC 7, 69**
See also DLB 314; EW 3; GFL Beginnings to 1789; TWA

Montessori, Maria 1870-1952 .... **TCLC 103**
See also CA 147; CAAE 115

Montgomery, (Robert) Bruce 1921(?)-1978
See Crispin, Edmund
See also CA 179; CAAS 104; CMW 4

Montgomery, L(ucy) M(aud)
1874-1942 .... **TCLC 51, 140**
See also AAYA 12; BYA 1; CA 137; CAAE 108; CLR 8, 91; DA3; DAC; DAM MST; DLB 92; DLBD 14; JRDA; MAICYA 1,

2; MTCW 2; MTFW 2005; RGEL 2;
SATA 100; TWA; WCH; WYA; YABC 1

Montgomery, Marion, Jr. 1925- .... **CLC 7**
See also AITN 1; CA 1-4R; CANR 3, 48,
162; CSW; DLB 6

Montgomery, Marion H. 1925-
See Montgomery, Marion, Jr.

Montgomery, Max
See Davenport, Guy (Mattison, Jr.)

Montherlant, Henry (Milon) de
1896-1972 .... **CLC 8, 19**
See also CA 85-88; CAAS 37-40R; DAM
DRAM; DLB 72, 321; EW 11; EWL 3;
GFL 1789 to the Present; MTCW 1

Monty Python
See Chapman, Graham; Cleese, John
(Marwood); Gilliam, Terry; Idle, Eric;
Jones, Terence Graham Parry; Palin,
Michael (Edward)
See also AAYA 7

Moodie, Susanna (Strickland)
1803-1885 .... **NCLC 14, 113**
See also DLB 99

Moody, Hiram 1961-
See Moody, Rick
See also CA 138; CANR 64, 112; MTFW
2005

Moody, Minerva
See Alcott, Louisa May

Moody, Rick .... **CLC 147**
See Moody, Hiram

Moody, William Vaughan
1869-1910 .... **TCLC 105**
See also CA 178; CAAE 110; DLB 7, 54;
MAL 5; RGAL 4

Mooney, Edward 1951-
See Mooney, Ted
See also CA 130

Mooney, Ted .... **CLC 25**
See Mooney, Edward

Moorcock, Michael 1939- ...... **CLC 5, 27, 58,
236**
See Bradbury, Edward P.
See also AAYA 26; CA 45-48; 5; CANR 2,
17, 38, 64, 122; CN 5, 6, 7; DLB 14, 231,
261, 319; FANT; MTCW 1, 2; MTFW
2005; SATA 93, 166; SCFW 1, 2; SFW 4;
SUFW 1, 2

Moorcock, Michael John
See Moorcock, Michael

Moore, Alan 1953- .... **CLC 230**
See also AAYA 51; CA 204; CANR 138;
DLB 261; MTFW 2005; SFW 4

Moore, Brian 1921-1999 ... **CLC 1, 3, 5, 7, 8,
19, 32, 90**
See Bryan, Michael
See also BRWS 9; CA 1-4R; CAAS 174;
CANR 1, 25, 42, 63; CCA 1; CN 1, 2, 3,
4, 5, 6; DAB; DAC; DAM MST; DLB
251; EWL 3; FANT; MTCW 1, 2; MTFW
2005; RGEL 2

Moore, Edward
See Muir, Edwin
See also RGEL 2

Moore, G. E. 1873-1958 .... **TCLC 89**
See also DLB 262

Moore, George Augustus
1852-1933 .... **SSC 19; TCLC 7**
See also BRW 6; CA 177; CAAE 104; DLB
10, 18, 57, 135; EWL 3; RGEL 2; RGSF
2

Moore, Lorrie .... **CLC 39, 45, 68**
See Moore, Marie Lorena
See also AMWS 10; CN 5, 6, 7; DLB 234;
SSFS 19

Moore, Marianne (Craig)
1887-1972 .... **CLC 1, 2, 4, 8, 10, 13, 19,
47; PC 4, 49; WLCS**
See also AMW; CA 1-4R; CAAS 33-36R;
CANR 3, 61; CDALB 1929-1941; CP 1;
DA; DA3; DAB; DAC; DAM MST,
POET; DLB 45; DLBD 7; EWL 3; EXPP;
FL 1:6; MAL 5; MBL; MTCW 1, 2;
MTFW 2005; PAB; PFS 14, 17; RGAL 4;
SATA 20; TUS; WP

Moore, Marie Lorena 1957- .... **CLC 165**
See Moore, Lorrie
See also CA 116; CANR 39, 83, 139; DLB
234; MTFW 2005

Moore, Michael 1954- .... **CLC 218**
See also AAYA 53; CA 166; CANR 150

Moore, Thomas 1779-1852 .... **NCLC 6, 110**
See also DLB 96, 144; RGEL 2

Moorhouse, Frank 1938- .... **SSC 40**
See also CA 118; CANR 92; CN 3, 4, 5, 6,
7; DLB 289; RGSF 2

Mora, Pat 1942- .... **HLC 2**
See also AMWS 13; CA 129; CANR 57,
81, 131; CLR 58; DAM MULT; DLB 209;
HW 1, 2; LLW; MAICYA 2; MTFW
2005; SATA 92, 134

Moraga, Cherrie 1952- ...... **CLC 126; DC 22**
See also CA 131; CANR 66, 154; DAM
MULT; DLB 82, 249; FW; GLL 1; HW 1,
2; LLW

Morand, Paul 1888-1976 .... **CLC 41; SSC 22**
See also CA 184; CAAS 69-72; DLB 65;
EWL 3

Morante, Elsa 1918-1985 .... **CLC 8, 47**
See also CA 85-88; CAAS 117; CANR 35;
DLB 177; EWL 3; MTCW 1, 2; MTFW
2005; RGHL; RGWL 2, 3; WLIT 7

Moravia, Alberto .... **CLC 2, 7, 11, 27, 46;
SSC 26**
See Pincherle, Alberto
See also DLB 177; EW 12; EWL 3; MTCW
2; RGSF 2; RGWL 2, 3; WLIT 7

More, Hannah 1745-1833 ...... **NCLC 27, 141**
See also DLB 107, 109, 116, 158; RGEL 2

More, Henry 1614-1687 .... **LC 9**
See also DLB 126, 252

More, Sir Thomas 1478(?)-1535 ... **LC 10, 32,
140**
See also BRWC 1; BRWS 7; DLB 136, 281;
LMFS 1; RGEL 2; TEA

Moreas, Jean .... **TCLC 18**
See Papadiamantopoulos, Johannes
See also GFL 1789 to the Present

Moreton, Andrew Esq.
See Defoe, Daniel

Morgan, Berry 1919-2002 .... **CLC 6**
See also CA 49-52; CAAS 208; DLB 6

Morgan, Claire
See Highsmith, Patricia
See also GLL 1

Morgan, Edwin (George) 1920- .... **CLC 31**
See also BRWS 9; CA 5-8R; CANR 3, 43,
90; CP 1, 2, 3, 4, 5, 6, 7; DLB 27

Morgan, (George) Frederick
1922-2004 .... **CLC 23**
See also CA 17-20R; CAAS 224; CANR
21, 144; CP 2, 3, 4, 5, 6, 7

Morgan, Harriet
See Mencken, H(enry) L(ouis)

Morgan, Jane
See Cooper, James Fenimore

Morgan, Janet 1945- .... **CLC 39**
See also CA 65-68

Morgan, Lady 1776(?)-1859 .... **NCLC 29**
See also DLB 116, 158; RGEL 2

Morgan, Robin (Evonne) 1941- .... **CLC 2**
See also CA 69-72; CANR 29, 68; FW;
GLL 2; MTCW 1; SATA 80

Morgan, Scott
See Kuttner, Henry

Morgan, Seth 1949(?)-1990 .... **CLC 65**
See also CA 185; CAAS 132

**Morgenstern, Christian (Otto Josef
Wolfgang)** 1871-1914 .... **TCLC 8**
See also CA 191; CAAE 105; EWL 3

Morgenstern, S.
See Goldman, William

Mori, Rintaro
See Mori Ogai
See also CAAE 110

Mori, Toshio 1910-1980 .... **AAL; SSC 83**
See also CA 244; CAAE 116; DLB 312;
RGSF 2

Moricz, Zsigmond 1879-1942 .... **TCLC 33**
See also CA 165; DLB 215; EWL 3

Morike, Eduard (Friedrich)
1804-1875 .... **NCLC 10**
See also DLB 133; RGWL 2, 3

Mori Ogai 1862-1922 .... **TCLC 14**
See Ogai
See also CA 164; DLB 180; EWL 3; RGWL
3; TWA

Moritz, Karl Philipp 1756-1793 .... **LC 2**
See also DLB 94

Morland, Peter Henry
See Faust, Frederick (Schiller)

Morley, Christopher (Darlington)
1890-1957 .... **TCLC 87**
See also CA 213; CAAE 112; DLB 9; MAL
5; RGAL 4

Morren, Theophil
See Hofmannsthal, Hugo von

Morris, Bill 1952- .... **CLC 76**
See also CA 225

Morris, Julian
See West, Morris L(anglo)

Morris, Steveland Judkins (?)-
See Wonder, Stevie

Morris, William 1834-1896 . **NCLC 4; PC 55**
See also BRW 5; CDBLB 1832-1890; DLB
18, 35, 57, 156, 178, 184; FANT; RGEL
2; SFW 4; SUFW

Morris, Wright (Marion) 1910-1998 . **CLC 1,
3, 7, 18, 37; TCLC 107**
See also AMW; CA 9-12R; CAAS 167;
CANR 21, 81; CN 1, 2, 3, 4, 5, 6; DLB
2, 206, 218; DLBY 1981; EWL 3; MAL
5; MTCW 1, 2; MTFW 2005; RGAL 4;
TCWW 1, 2

Morrison, Arthur 1863-1945 .... **SSC 40;
TCLC 72**
See also CA 157; CAAE 120; CMW 4;
DLB 70, 135, 197; RGEL 2

Morrison, Chloe Anthony Wofford
See Morrison, Toni

Morrison, James Douglas 1943-1971
See Morrison, Jim
See also CA 73-76; CANR 40

Morrison, Jim .... **CLC 17**
See Morrison, James Douglas

Morrison, John Gordon 1904-1998 ... **SSC 93**
See also CA 103; CANR 92; DLB 260

Morrison, Toni 1931- ..... **BLC 3; CLC 4, 10,
22, 55, 81, 87, 173, 194; WLC 4**
See also AAYA 1, 22, 61; AFAW 1, 2;
AMWC 1; AMWS 3; BPFB 2; BW 2, 3;
CA 29-32R; CANR 27, 42, 67, 113, 124;
CDALB 1968-1988; CLR 99; CN 3, 4, 5,
6, 7; CPW; DA; DA3; DAB; DAC; DAM
MST, MULT, NOV, POP; DLB 6, 33, 143,
331; DLBY 1981; EWL 3; EXPN; FL 1:6;
FW; GL 3; LAIT 2, 4; LATS 1:2; LMFS
2; MAL 5; MBL; MTCW 1, 2; MTFW
2005; NFS 1, 6, 8, 14; RGAL 4; RHW;
SATA 57, 144; SSFS 5; TCLE 1:2; TUS;
YAW

Musil, Robert (Edler von)
1880-1942 .... **SSC 18; TCLC 12, 68**
See also CAAE 109; CANR 55, 84; CD-WLB 2; DLB 81, 124; EW 9; EWL 3; MTCW 2; RGSF 2; RGWL 2, 3

Muske, Carol .... **CLC 90**
See Muske-Dukes, Carol (Anne)

Muske-Dukes, Carol (Anne) 1945-
See Muske, Carol
See also CA 203; 65-68, 203; CANR 32, 70; CWP; PFS 24

Musset, Alfred de 1810-1857 . **DC 27; NCLC 7, 150**
See also DLB 192, 217; EW 6; GFL 1789 to the Present; RGWL 2, 3; TWA

Musset, Louis Charles Alfred de
See Musset, Alfred de

Mussolini, Benito (Amilcare Andrea)
1883-1945 .... **TCLC 96**
See also CAAE 116

Mutanabbi, Al-
See al-Mutanabbi, Ahmad ibn al-Husayn Abu al-Tayyib al-Jufi al-Kindi
See also WLIT 6

My Brother's Brother
See Chekhov, Anton (Pavlovich)

Myers, L(eopold) H(amilton)
1881-1944 .... **TCLC 59**
See also CA 157; DLB 15; EWL 3; RGEL 2

Myers, Walter Dean 1937- .. **BLC 3; CLC 35**
See Myers, Walter M.
See also AAYA 4, 23; BW 2; BYA 6, 8, 11; CA 33-36R; CANR 20, 42, 67, 108; CLR 4, 16, 35, 110; DAM MULT, NOV; DLB 33; INT CANR-20; JRDA; LAIT 5; MAICYA 1, 2; MAICYAS 1; MTCW 2; MTFW 2005; SAAS 2; SATA 41, 71, 109, 157; SATA-Brief 27; WYA; YAW

Myers, Walter M.
See Myers, Walter Dean

Myles, Symon
See Follett, Ken

Nabokov, Vladimir (Vladimirovich)
1899-1977 .... **CLC 1, 2, 3, 6, 8, 11, 15, 23, 44, 46, 64; SSC 11, 86; TCLC 108, 189; WLC 4**
See also AAYA 45; AMW; AMWC 1; AMWR 1; BPFB 2; CA 5-8R; CAAS 69-72; CANR 20, 102; CDALB 1941-1968; CN 1, 2; CP 2; DA; DA3; DAB; DAC; DAM MST, NOV; DLB 2, 244, 278, 317; DLBD 3; DLBY 1980, 1991; EWL 3; EXPS; LATS 1:2; MAL 5; MTCW 1, 2; MTFW 2005; NCFS 4; NFS 9; RGAL 4; RGSF 2; SSFS 6, 15; TUS

Naevius c. 265B.C.-201B.C. .... **CMLC 37**
See also DLB 211

Nagai, Kafu .... **TCLC 51**
See Nagai, Sokichi
See also DLB 180

Nagai, Sokichi 1879-1959
See Nagai, Kafu
See also CAAE 117

Nagy, Laszlo 1925-1978 .... **CLC 7**
See also CA 129; CAAS 112

Naidu, Sarojini 1879-1949 .... **TCLC 80**
See also EWL 3; RGEL 2

Naipaul, Shiva 1945-1985 .... **CLC 32, 39; TCLC 153**
See also CA 112; CAAE 110; CAAS 116; CANR 33; CN 2, 3; DA3; DAM NOV; DLB 157; DLBY 1985; EWL 3; MTCW 1, 2; MTFW 2005

Naipaul, V.S. 1932- .. **CLC 4, 7, 9, 13, 18, 37, 105, 199; SSC 38**
See also BPFB 2; BRWS 1; CA 1-4R; CANR 1, 33, 51, 91, 126; CDBLB 1960 to Present; CDWLB 3; CN 1, 2, 3, 4, 5, 6, 7; DA3; DAB; DAC; DAM MST,

NOV; DLB 125, 204, 207, 326, 331; DLBY 1985, 2001; EWL 3; LATS 1:2; MTCW 1, 2; MTFW 2005; RGEL 2; RGSF 2; TWA; WLIT 4; WWE 1

Nakos, Lilika 1903(?)-1989 .... **CLC 29**

Napoleon
See Yamamoto, Hisaye

Narayan, R.K. 1906-2001 ...... **CLC 7, 28, 47, 121, 211; SSC 25**
See also BPFB 2; CA 81-84; CAAS 196; CANR 33, 61, 112; CN 1, 2, 3, 4, 5, 6, 7; DA3; DAM NOV; DLB 323; DNFS 1; EWL 3; MTCW 1, 2; MTFW 2005; RGEL 2; RGSF 2; SATA 62; SSFS 5; WWE 1

Nash, (Frediric) Ogden 1902-1971 . **CLC 23; PC 21; TCLC 109**
See also CA 13-14; CAAS 29-32R; CANR 34, 61; CAP 1; CP 1; DAM POET; DLB 11; MAICYA 1, 2; MAL 5; MTCW 1, 2; RGAL 4; SATA 2, 46; WP

Nashe, Thomas 1567-1601(?) .... **LC 41, 89**
See also DLB 167; RGEL 2

Nathan, Daniel
See Dannay, Frederic

Nathan, George Jean 1882-1958 .... **TCLC 18**
See Hatteras, Owen
See also CA 169; CAAE 114; DLB 137; MAL 5

Natsume, Kinnosuke
See Natsume, Soseki

Natsume, Soseki 1867-1916 .... **TCLC 2, 10**
See Natsume Soseki; Soseki
See also CA 195; CAAE 104; RGWL 2, 3; TWA

Natsume Soseki
See Natsume, Soseki
See also DLB 180; EWL 3

Natti, (Mary) Lee 1919-
See Kingman, Lee
See also CA 5-8R; CANR 2

Navarre, Marguerite de
See de Navarre, Marguerite

Naylor, Gloria 1950- ..... **BLC 3; CLC 28, 52, 156; WLCS**
See also AAYA 6, 39; AFAW 1, 2; AMWS 8; BW 2, 3; CA 107; CANR 27, 51, 74, 130; CN 4, 5, 6, 7; CPW; DA; DA3; DAC; DAM MST, MULT, NOV, POP; DLB 173; EWL 3; FW; MAL 5; MTCW 1, 2; MTFW 2005; NFS 4, 7; RGAL 4; TCLE 1:2; TUS

Neal, John 1793-1876 .... **NCLC 161**
See also DLB 1, 59, 243; FW; RGAL 4

Neff, Debra .... **CLC 59**

Neihardt, John Gneisenau
1881-1973 .... **CLC 32**
See also CA 13-14; CANR 65; CAP 1; DLB 9, 54, 256; LAIT 2; TCWW 1, 2

Nekrasov, Nikolai Alekseevich
1821-1878 .... **NCLC 11**
See also DLB 277

Nelligan, Emile 1879-1941 .... **TCLC 14**
See also CA 204; CAAE 114; DLB 92; EWL 3

Nelson, Willie 1933- .... **CLC 17**
See also CA 107; CANR 114

Nemerov, Howard 1920-1991 .... **CLC 2, 6, 9, 36; PC 24; TCLC 124**
See also AMW; CA 1-4R; CAAS 134; CABS 2; CANR 1, 27, 53; CN 1, 2, 3; CP 1, 2, 3, 4, 5; DAM POET; DLB 5, 6; DLBY 1983; EWL 3; INT CANR-27; MAL 5; MTCW 1, 2; MTFW 2005; PFS 10, 14; RGAL 4

Nepos, Cornelius c. 99B.C.-c. 24B.C. .... **CMLC 89**
See also DLB 211

Neruda, Pablo 1904-1973 .. **CLC 1, 2, 5, 7, 9, 28, 62; HLC 2; PC 4, 64; WLC 4**
See also CA 19-20; CAAS 45-48; CANR 131; CAP 2; DA; DA3; DAB; DAC; DAM MST, MULT, POET; DLB 283, 331; DNFS 2; EWL 3; HW 1; LAW; MTCW 1, 2; MTFW 2005; PFS 11; RGWL 2, 3; TWA; WLIT 1; WP

Nerval, Gerard de 1808-1855 ... **NCLC 1, 67; PC 13; SSC 18**
See also DLB 217; EW 6; GFL 1789 to the Present; RGSF 2; RGWL 2, 3

Nervo, (Jose) Amado (Ruiz de)
1870-1919 .... **HLCS 2; TCLC 11**
See also CA 131; CAAE 109; DLB 290; EWL 3; HW 1; LAW

Nesbit, Malcolm
See Chester, Alfred

Nessi, Pio Baroja y
See Baroja, Pio

Nestroy, Johann 1801-1862 .... **NCLC 42**
See also DLB 133; RGWL 2, 3

Netterville, Luke
See O'Grady, Standish (James)

Neufeld, John (Arthur) 1938- .... **CLC 17**
See also AAYA 11; CA 25-28R; CANR 11, 37, 56; CLR 52; MAICYA 1, 2; SAAS 3; SATA 6, 81, 131; SATA-Essay 131; YAW

Neumann, Alfred 1895-1952 .... **TCLC 100**
See also CA 183; DLB 56

Neumann, Ferenc
See Molnar, Ferenc

Neville, Emily Cheney 1919- .... **CLC 12**
See also BYA 2; CA 5-8R; CANR 3, 37, 85; JRDA; MAICYA 1, 2; SAAS 2; SATA 1; YAW

Newbound, Bernard Slade 1930-
See Slade, Bernard
See also CA 81-84; CANR 49; CD 5; DAM DRAM

Newby, P(ercy) H(oward)
1918-1997 .... **CLC 2, 13**
See also CA 5-8R; CAAS 161; CANR 32, 67; CN 1, 2, 3, 4, 5, 6; DAM NOV; DLB 15, 326; MTCW 1; RGEL 2

Newcastle
See Cavendish, Margaret Lucas

Newlove, Donald 1928- .... **CLC 6**
See also CA 29-32R; CANR 25

Newlove, John (Herbert) 1938- .... **CLC 14**
See also CA 21-24R; CANR 9, 25; CP 1, 2, 3, 4, 5, 6, 7

Newman, Charles 1938-2006 .... **CLC 2, 8**
See also CA 21-24R; CAAS 249; CANR 84; CN 3, 4, 5, 6

Newman, Charles Hamilton
See Newman, Charles

Newman, Edwin (Harold) 1919- ...... **CLC 14**
See also AITN 1; CA 69-72; CANR 5

Newman, John Henry 1801-1890 . **NCLC 38, 99**
See also BRWS 7; DLB 18, 32, 55; RGEL 2

Newton, (Sir) Isaac 1642-1727 ...... **LC 35, 53**
See also DLB 252

Newton, Suzanne 1936- .... **CLC 35**
See also BYA 7; CA 41-44R; CANR 14; JRDA; SATA 5, 77

New York Dept. of Ed. .... **CLC 70**

Nexo, Martin Andersen
1869-1954 .... **TCLC 43**
See also CA 202; DLB 214; EWL 3

Nezval, Vitezslav 1900-1958 .... **TCLC 44**
See also CAAE 123; CDWLB 4; DLB 215; EWL 3

Ng, Fae Myenne 1957(?)- .... **CLC 81**
See also BYA 11; CA 146

O'Brian, Patrick 1914-2000 .... **CLC 152**
  See also AAYA 55; BRWS 12; CA 144;
  CAAS 187; CANR 74; CPW; MTCW 2;
  MTFW 2005; RHW
O'Brien, Darcy 1939-1998 .... **CLC 11**
  See also CA 21-24R; CAAS 167; CANR 8,
  59
O'Brien, Edna 1932- ..... **CLC 3, 5, 8, 13, 36,**
  65, 116, 237; SSC 10, 77
  See also BRWS 5; CA 1-4R; CANR 6, 41,
  65, 102; CDBLB 1960 to Present; CN 1,
  2, 3, 4, 5, 6, 7; DA3; DAM NOV; DLB
  14, 231, 319; EWL 3; FW; MTCW 1, 2;
  MTFW 2005; RGSF 2; WLIT 4
O'Brien, Fitz-James 1828-1862 ..... **NCLC 21**
  See also DLB 74; RGAL 4; SUFW
O'Brien, Flann .... **CLC 1, 4, 5, 7, 10, 47**
  See O Nuallain, Brian
  See also BRWS 2; DLB 231; EWL 3;
  RGEL 2
O'Brien, Richard 1942- .... **CLC 17**
  See also CA 124
O'Brien, Tim 1946- .... **CLC 7, 19, 40, 103,**
  211; SSC 74
  See also AAYA 16; AMWS 5; CA 85-88;
  CANR 40, 58, 133; CDALBS; CN 5, 6,
  7; CPW; DA3; DAM POP; DLB 152;
  DLBD 9; DLBY 1980; LATS 1:2; MAL
  5; MTCW 2; MTFW 2005; RGAL 4;
  SSFS 5, 15; TCLE 1:2
Obstfelder, Sigbjoern 1866-1900 .... **TCLC 23**
  See also CAAE 123
O'Casey, Sean 1880-1964 .... **CLC 1, 5, 9, 11,**
  15, 88; DC 12; WLCS
  See also BRW 7; CA 89-92; CANR 62;
  CBD; CDBLB 1914-1945; DA3; DAB;
  DAC; DAM DRAM, MST; DFS 19; DLB
  10; EWL 3; MTCW 1, 2; MTFW 2005;
  RGEL 2; TEA; WLIT 4
O'Cathasaigh, Sean
  See O'Casey, Sean
Occom, Samson 1723-1792 .... **LC 60; NNAL**
  See also DLB 175
Occomy, Marita (Odette) Bonner
  1899(?)-1971
  See Bonner, Marita
  See also BW 2; CA 142; DFS 13; DLB 51,
  228
Ochs, Phil(ip David) 1940-1976 .... **CLC 17**
  See also CA 185; CAAS 65-68
O'Connor, Edwin (Greene)
  1918-1968 .... **CLC 14**
  See also CA 93-96; CAAS 25-28R; MAL 5
O'Connor, (Mary) Flannery
  1925-1964 .... **CLC 1, 2, 3, 6, 10, 13, 15,**
  21, 66, 104; SSC 1, 23, 61, 82; TCLC
  132; WLC 4
  See also AAYA 7; AMW; AMWR 2; BPFB
  3; BYA 16; CA 1-4R; CANR 3, 41;
  CDALB 1941-1968; DA; DA3; DAB;
  DAC; DAM MST, NOV; DLB 2, 152;
  DLBD 12; DLBY 1980; EWL 3; EXPS;
  LAIT 5; MAL 5; MBL; MTCW 1, 2;
  MTFW 2005; NFS 3, 21; RGAL 4; RGSF
  2; SSFS 2, 7, 10, 19; TUS
O'Connor, Frank .... **CLC 23; SSC 5**
  See O'Donovan, Michael Francis
  See also DLB 162; EWL 3; RGSF 2; SSFS
  5
O'Dell, Scott 1898-1989 .... **CLC 30**
  See also AAYA 3, 44; BPFB 3; BYA 1, 2,
  3, 5; CA 61-64; CAAS 129; CANR 12,
  30, 112; CLR 1, 16; DLB 52; JRDA;
  MAICYA 1, 2; SATA 12, 60, 134; WYA;
  YAW
Odets, Clifford 1906-1963 ..... **CLC 2, 28, 98;**
  DC 6
  See also AMWS 2; CA 85-88; CAD; CANR
  62; DAM DRAM; DFS 3, 17, 20; DLB 7,
  26; EWL 3; MAL 5; MTCW 1, 2; MTFW
  2005; RGAL 4; TUS

O'Doherty, Brian 1928- .... **CLC 76**
  See also CA 105; CANR 108
O'Donnell, K. M.
  See Malzberg, Barry N(athaniel)
O'Donnell, Lawrence
  See Kuttner, Henry
O'Donovan, Michael Francis
  1903-1966 .... **CLC 14**
  See O'Connor, Frank
  See also CA 93-96; CANR 84
Oe, Kenzaburo 1935- .. **CLC 10, 36, 86, 187;**
  SSC 20
  See Oe Kenzaburo
  See also CA 97-100; CANR 36, 50, 74, 126;
  DA3; DAM NOV; DLB 182, 331; DLBY
  1994; LATS 1:2; MJW; MTCW 1, 2;
  MTFW 2005; RGSF 2; RGWL 2, 3
Oe Kenzaburo
  See Oe, Kenzaburo
  See also CWW 2; EWL 3
O'Faolain, Julia 1932- .... **CLC 6, 19, 47, 108**
  See also CA 81-84; 2; CANR 12, 61; CN 2,
  3, 4, 5, 6, 7; DLB 14, 231, 319; FW;
  MTCW 1; RHW
O'Faolain, Sean 1900-1991 ...... **CLC 1, 7, 14,**
  32, 70; SSC 13; TCLC 143
  See also CA 61-64; CAAS 134; CANR 12,
  66; CN 1, 2, 3, 4; DLB 15, 162; MTCW
  1, 2; MTFW 2005; RGEL 2; RGSF 2
O'Flaherty, Liam 1896-1984 .... **CLC 5, 34;**
  SSC 6
  See also CA 101; CAAS 113; CANR 35;
  CN 1, 2, 3; DLB 36, 162; DLBY 1984;
  MTCW 1, 2; MTFW 2005; RGEL 2;
  RGSF 2; SSFS 5, 20
Ogai
  See Mori Ogai
  See also MJW
Ogilvy, Gavin
  See Barrie, J(ames) M(atthew)
O'Grady, Standish (James)
  1846-1928 .... **TCLC 5**
  See also CA 157; CAAE 104
O'Grady, Timothy 1951- .... **CLC 59**
  See also CA 138
O'Hara, Frank 1926-1966 .... **CLC 2, 5, 13,**
  78; PC 45
  See also CA 9-12R; CAAS 25-28R; CANR
  33; DA3; DAM POET; DLB 5, 16, 193;
  EWL 3; MAL 5; MTCW 1, 2; MTFW
  2005; PFS 8, 12; RGAL 4; WP
O'Hara, John (Henry) 1905-1970 . **CLC 1, 2,**
  3, 6, 11, 42; SSC 15
  See also AMW; BPFB 3; CA 5-8R; CAAS
  25-28R; CANR 31, 60; CDALB 1929-
  1941; DAM NOV; DLB 9, 86, 324; DLBD
  2; EWL 3; MAL 5; MTCW 1, 2; MTFW
  2005; NFS 11; RGAL 4; RGSF 2
O'Hehir, Diana 1929- .... **CLC 41**
  See also CA 245
Ohiyesa
  See Eastman, Charles A(lexander)
Okada, John 1923-1971 .... **AAL**
  See also BYA 14; CA 212; DLB 312; NFS
  25
Okigbo, Christopher 1930-1967 .... **BLC 3;**
  CLC 25, 84; PC 7; TCLC 171
  See also AFW; BW 1, 3; CA 77-80; CANR
  74; CDWLB 3; DAM MULT, POET; DLB
  125; EWL 3; MTCW 1, 2; MTFW 2005;
  RGEL 2
Okigbo, Christopher Ifenayichukwu
  See Okigbo, Christopher
Okri, Ben 1959- .... **CLC 87, 223**
  See also AFW; BRWS 5; BW 2, 3; CA 138;
  CAAE 130; CANR 65, 128; CN 5, 6, 7;
  DLB 157, 231, 319, 326; EWL 3; INT
  CA-138; MTCW 2; MTFW 2005; RGSF
  2; SSFS 20; WLIT 2; WWE 1

Olds, Sharon 1942- .. **CLC 32, 39, 85; PC 22**
  See also AMWS 10; CA 101; CANR 18,
  41, 66, 98, 135; CP 5, 6, 7; CPW; CWP;
  DAM POET; DLB 120; MAL 5; MTCW
  2; MTFW 2005; PFS 17
Oldstyle, Jonathan
  See Irving, Washington
Olesha, Iurii
  See Olesha, Yuri (Karlovich)
  See also RGWL 2
Olesha, Iurii Karlovich
  See Olesha, Yuri (Karlovich)
  See also DLB 272
Olesha, Yuri (Karlovich) 1899-1960 . **CLC 8;**
  SSC 69; TCLC 136
  See Olesha, Iurii; Olesha, Iurii Karlovich;
  Olesha, Yury Karlovich
  See also CA 85-88; EW 11; RGWL 3
Olesha, Yury Karlovich
  See Olesha, Yuri (Karlovich)
  See also EWL 3
Oliphant, Mrs.
  See Oliphant, Margaret (Oliphant Wilson)
  See also SUFW
Oliphant, Laurence 1829(?)-1888 .. **NCLC 47**
  See also DLB 18, 166
Oliphant, Margaret (Oliphant Wilson)
  1828-1897 .... **NCLC 11, 61; SSC 25**
  See Oliphant, Mrs.
  See also BRWS 10; DLB 18, 159, 190;
  HGG; RGEL 2; RGSF 2
Oliver, Mary 1935- ... **CLC 19, 34, 98; PC 75**
  See also AMWS 7; CA 21-24R; CANR 9,
  43, 84, 92, 138; CP 4, 5, 6, 7; CWP; DLB
  5, 193; EWL 3; MTFW 2005; PFS 15
Olivier, Laurence (Kerr) 1907-1989 . **CLC 20**
  See also CA 150; CAAE 111; CAAS 129
Olsen, Tillie 1912-2007 .... **CLC 4, 13, 114;**
  SSC 11
  See also AAYA 51; AMWS 13; BYA 11;
  CA 1-4R; CAAS 256; CANR 1, 43, 74,
  132; CDALBS; CN 2, 3, 4, 5, 6, 7; DA;
  DA3; DAB; DAC; DAM MST; DLB 28,
  206; DLBY 1980; EWL 3; EXPS; FW;
  MAL 5; MTCW 1, 2; MTFW 2005;
  RGAL 4; RGSF 2; SSFS 1; TCLE 1:2;
  TCWW 2; TUS
Olson, Charles (John) 1910-1970 .. **CLC 1, 2,**
  5, 6, 9, 11, 29; PC 19
  See also AMWS 2; CA 13-16; CAAS 25-
  28R; CABS 2; CANR 35, 61; CAP 1; CP
  1; DAM POET; DLB 5, 16, 193; EWL 3;
  MAL 5; MTCW 1, 2; RGAL 4; WP
Olson, Toby 1937- .... **CLC 28**
  See also CA 65-68; 11; CANR 9, 31, 84;
  CP 3, 4, 5, 6, 7
Olyesha, Yuri
  See Olesha, Yuri (Karlovich)
Olympiodorus of Thebes c. 375-c.
  430 .... **CMLC 59**
Omar Khayyam
  See Khayyam, Omar
  See also RGWL 2, 3
Ondaatje, Michael 1943- ..... **CLC 14, 29, 51,**
  76, 180; PC 28
  See also AAYA 66; CA 77-80; CANR 42,
  74, 109, 133; CN 5, 6, 7; CP 1, 2, 3, 4, 5,
  6, 7; DA3; DAB; DAC; DAM MST; DLB
  60, 323, 326; EWL 3; LATS 1:2; LMFS
  2; MTCW 2; MTFW 2005; NFS 23; PFS
  8, 19; TCLE 1:2; TWA; WWE 1
Ondaatje, Philip Michael
  See Ondaatje, Michael
Oneal, Elizabeth 1934-
  See Oneal, Zibby
  See also CA 106; CANR 28, 84; MAICYA
  1, 2; SATA 30, 82; YAW

Petrakis, Harry Mark 1923- .... **CLC 3**
  See also CA 9-12R; CANR 4, 30, 85, 155;
  CN 1, 2, 3, 4, 5, 6, 7

Petrarch 1304-1374 .... **CMLC 20; PC 8**
  See also DA3; DAM POET; EW 2; LMFS
  1; RGWL 2, 3; WLIT 7

Petronius c. 20-66 .... **CMLC 34**
  See also AW 2; CDWLB 1; DLB 211;
  RGWL 2, 3; WLIT 8

Petrov, Evgeny .... **TCLC 21**
  See Kataev, Evgeny Petrovich

Petry, Ann (Lane) 1908-1997 .. **CLC 1, 7, 18;**
  TCLC 112
  See also AFAW 1, 2; BPFB 3; BW 1, 3;
  BYA 2; CA 5-8R; 6; CAAS 157; CANR
  4, 46; CLR 12; CN 1, 2, 3, 4, 5, 6; DLB
  76; EWL 3; JRDA; LAIT 1; MAICYA 1,
  2; MAICYAS 1; MTCW 1; RGAL 4;
  SATA 5; SATA-Obit 94; TUS

Petursson, Halligrimur 1614-1674 .... **LC 8**

Peychinovich
  See Vazov, Ivan (Minchov)

Phaedrus c. 15B.C.-c. 50 .... **CMLC 25**
  See also DLB 211

Phelps (Ward), Elizabeth Stuart
  See Phelps, Elizabeth Stuart
  See also FW

Phelps, Elizabeth Stuart
  1844-1911 .... **TCLC 113**
  See Phelps (Ward), Elizabeth Stuart
  See also CA 242; DLB 74

Philips, Katherine 1632-1664 . **LC 30; PC 40**
  See also DLB 131; RGEL 2

Philipson, Ilene J. 1950- .... **CLC 65**
  See also CA 219

Philipson, Morris H. 1926- .... **CLC 53**
  See also CA 1-4R; CANR 4

Phillips, Caryl 1958- ..... **BLCS; CLC 96, 224**
  See also BRWS 5; BW 2; CA 141; CANR
  63, 104, 140; CBD; CD 5, 6; CN 5, 6, 7;
  DA3; DAM MULT; DLB 157; EWL 3;
  MTCW 2; MTFW 2005; WLIT 4; WWE
  1

Phillips, David Graham
  1867-1911 .... **TCLC 44**
  See also CA 176; CAAE 108; DLB 9, 12,
  303; RGAL 4

Phillips, Jack
  See Sandburg, Carl (August)

Phillips, Jayne Anne 1952- .... **CLC 15, 33,**
  139; SSC 16
  See also AAYA 57; BPFB 3; CA 101;
  CANR 24, 50, 96; CN 4, 5, 6, 7; CSW;
  DLBY 1980; INT CANR-24; MTCW 1,
  2; MTFW 2005; RGAL 4; RGSF 2; SSFS
  4

Phillips, Richard
  See Dick, Philip K.

Phillips, Robert (Schaeffer) 1938- .... **CLC 28**
  See also CA 17-20R; 13; CANR 8; DLB
  105

Phillips, Ward
  See Lovecraft, H. P.

Philostratus, Flavius c. 179-c.
  244 .... **CMLC 62**

Piccolo, Lucio 1901-1969 .... **CLC 13**
  See also CA 97-100; DLB 114; EWL 3

Pickthall, Marjorie L(owry) C(hristie)
  1883-1922 .... **TCLC 21**
  See also CAAE 107; DLB 92

Pico della Mirandola, Giovanni
  1463-1494 .... **LC 15**
  See also LMFS 1

Piercy, Marge 1936- .... **CLC 3, 6, 14, 18, 27,**
  62, 128; PC 29
  See also BPFB 3; CA 187; 21-24R; 187; 1;
  CANR 13, 43, 66, 111; CN 3, 4, 5, 6, 7;
  CP 1, 2, 3, 4, 5, 6, 7; CWP; DLB 120,
  227; EXPP; FW; MAL 5; MTCW 1, 2;
  MTFW 2005; PFS 9, 22; SFW 4

Piers, Robert
  See Anthony, Piers

Pieyre de Mandiargues, Andre 1909-1991
  See Mandiargues, Andre Pieyre de
  See also CA 103; CAAS 136; CANR 22,
  82; EWL 3; GFL 1789 to the Present

Pilnyak, Boris 1894-1938 . **SSC 48; TCLC 23**
  See Vogau, Boris Andreyevich
  See also EWL 3

Pinchback, Eugene
  See Toomer, Jean

Pincherle, Alberto 1907-1990 ...... **CLC 11, 18**
  See Moravia, Alberto
  See also CA 25-28R; CAAS 132; CANR
  33, 63, 142; DAM NOV; MTCW 1;
  MTFW 2005

Pinckney, Darryl 1953- .... **CLC 76**
  See also BW 2, 3; CA 143; CANR 79

Pindar 518(?)B.C.-438(?)B.C. .... **CMLC 12;**
  PC 19
  See also AW 1; CDWLB 1; DLB 176;
  RGWL 2

Pineda, Cecile 1942- .... **CLC 39**
  See also CA 118; DLB 209

Pinero, Arthur Wing 1855-1934 .... **TCLC 32**
  See also CA 153; CAAE 110; DAM DRAM;
  DLB 10; RGEL 2

Pinero, Miguel (Antonio Gomez)
  1946-1988 .... **CLC 4, 55**
  See also CA 61-64; CAAS 125; CAD;
  CANR 29, 90; DLB 266; HW 1; LLW

Pinget, Robert 1919-1997 .... **CLC 7, 13, 37**
  See also CA 85-88; CAAS 160; CWW 2;
  DLB 83; EWL 3; GFL 1789 to the Present

Pink Floyd
  See Barrett, (Roger) Syd; Gilmour, David;
  Mason, Nick; Waters, Roger; Wright, Rick

Pinkney, Edward 1802-1828 .... **NCLC 31**
  See also DLB 248

Pinkwater, D. Manus
  See Pinkwater, Daniel Manus

Pinkwater, Daniel
  See Pinkwater, Daniel Manus

Pinkwater, Daniel M.
  See Pinkwater, Daniel Manus

Pinkwater, Daniel Manus 1941- .... **CLC 35**
  See also AAYA 1, 46; BYA 9; CA 29-32R;
  CANR 12, 38, 89, 143; CLR 4; CSW;
  FANT; JRDA; MAICYA 1, 2; SAAS 3;
  SATA 8, 46, 76, 114, 158; SFW 4; YAW

Pinkwater, Manus
  See Pinkwater, Daniel Manus

Pinsky, Robert 1940- .... **CLC 9, 19, 38, 94,**
  121, 216; PC 27
  See also AMWS 6; CA 29-32R; 4; CANR
  58, 97, 138; CP 3, 4, 5, 6, 7; DA3; DAM
  POET; DLBY 1982, 1998; MAL 5;
  MTCW 2; MTFW 2005; PFS 18; RGAL
  4; TCLE 1:2

Pinta, Harold
  See Pinter, Harold

Pinter, Harold 1930- .. **CLC 1, 3, 6, 9, 11, 15,**
  27, 58, 73, 199; DC 15; WLC 4
  See also BRWR 1; BRWS 1; CA 5-8R;
  CANR 33, 65, 112, 145; CBD; CD 5, 6;
  CDBLB 1960 to Present; CP 1; DA; DA3;
  DAB; DAC; DAM DRAM, MST; DFS 3,
  5, 7, 14; DLB 13, 310, 331; EWL 3;
  IDFW 3, 4; LMFS 2; MTCW 1, 2; MTFW
  2005; RGEL 2; RGHL; TEA

Piozzi, Hester Lynch (Thrale)
  1741-1821 .... **NCLC 57**
  See also DLB 104, 142

Pirandello, Luigi 1867-1936 .. **DC 5; SSC 22;**
  TCLC 4, 29, 172; WLC 4
  See also CA 153; CAAE 104; CANR 103;
  DA; DA3; DAB; DAC; DAM DRAM,
  MST; DFS 4, 9; DLB 264, 331; EW 8;
  EWL 3; MTCW 2; MTFW 2005; RGSF
  2; RGWL 2, 3; WLIT 7

Pirsig, Robert M(aynard) 1928- ... **CLC 4, 6,**
  73
  See also CA 53-56; CANR 42, 74; CPW 1;
  DA3; DAM POP; MTCW 1, 2; MTFW
  2005; SATA 39

Pisan, Christine de
  See Christine de Pizan

Pisarev, Dmitrii Ivanovich
  See Pisarev, Dmitry Ivanovich
  See also DLB 277

Pisarev, Dmitry Ivanovich
  1840-1868 .... **NCLC 25**
  See Pisarev, Dmitrii Ivanovich

Pix, Mary (Griffith) 1666-1709 .... **LC 8**
  See also DLB 80

Pixerecourt, (Rene Charles) Guilbert de
  1773-1844 .... **NCLC 39**
  See also DLB 192; GFL 1789 to the Present

Plaatje, Sol(omon) T(shekisho)
  1878-1932 .... **BLCS; TCLC 73**
  See also BW 2, 3; CA 141; CANR 79; DLB
  125, 225

Plaidy, Jean
  See Hibbert, Eleanor Alice Burford

Planche, James Robinson
  1796-1880 .... **NCLC 42**
  See also RGEL 2

Plant, Robert 1948- .... **CLC 12**

Plante, David 1940- .... **CLC 7, 23, 38**
  See also CA 37-40R; CANR 12, 36, 58, 82,
  152; CN 2, 3, 4, 5, 6, 7; DAM NOV;
  DLBY 1983; INT CANR-12; MTCW 1

Plante, David Robert
  See Plante, David

Plath, Sylvia 1932-1963 ..... **CLC 1, 2, 3, 5, 9,**
  11, 14, 17, 50, 51, 62, 111; PC 1, 37;
  WLC 4
  See also AAYA 13; AMWR 2; AMWS 1;
  BPFB 3; CA 19-20; CANR 34, 101; CAP
  2; CDALB 1941-1968; DA; DA3; DAB;
  DAC; DAM MST, POET; DLB 5, 6, 152;
  EWL 3; EXPN; EXPP; FL 1:6; FW; LAIT
  4; MAL 5; MBL; MTCW 1, 2; MTFW
  2005; NFS 1; PAB; PFS 1, 15; RGAL 4;
  SATA 96; TUS; WP; YAW

Plato c. 428B.C.-347B.C. .... **CMLC 8, 75;**
  WLCS
  See also AW 1; CDWLB 1; DA; DA3;
  DAB; DAC; DAM MST; DLB 176; LAIT
  1; LATS 1:1; RGWL 2, 3; WLIT 8

Platonov, Andrei
  See Klimentov, Andrei Platonovich

Platonov, Andrei Platonovich
  See Klimentov, Andrei Platonovich
  See also DLB 272

Platonov, Andrey Platonovich
  See Klimentov, Andrei Platonovich
  See also EWL 3

Platt, Kin 1911- .... **CLC 26**
  See also AAYA 11; CA 17-20R; CANR 11;
  JRDA; SAAS 17; SATA 21, 86; WYA

Plautus c. 254B.C.-c. 184B.C. .... **CMLC 24,**
  92; DC 6
  See also AW 1; CDWLB 1; DLB 211;
  RGWL 2, 3; WLIT 8

Plick et Plock
  See Simenon, Georges (Jacques Christian)

Plieksans, Janis
  See Rainis, Janis

Plimpton, George 1927-2003 .... **CLC 36**
  See also AITN 1; AMWS 16; CA 21-24R;
  CAAS 224; CANR 32, 70, 103, 133; DLB
  185, 241; MTCW 1, 2; MTFW 2005;
  SATA 10; SATA-Obit 150

Pliny the Elder c. 23-79 .... **CMLC 23**
  See also DLB 211

Pliny the Younger c. 61-c. 112 ...... **CMLC 62**
  See also AW 2; DLB 211

Plomer, William Charles Franklin
1903-1973 .... **CLC 4, 8**
See also AFW; BRWS 11; CA 21-22; CANR
34; CAP 2; CN 1; CP 1, 2; DLB 20, 162,
191, 225; EWL 3; MTCW 1; RGEL 2;
RGSF 2; SATA 24

Plotinus 204-270 .... **CMLC 46**
See also CDWLB 1; DLB 176

Plowman, Piers
See Kavanagh, Patrick (Joseph)

Plum, J.
See Wodehouse, P(elham) G(renville)

Plumly, Stanley (Ross) 1939- .... **CLC 33**
See also CA 110; CAAE 108; CANR 97;
CP 3, 4, 5, 6, 7; DLB 5, 193; INT CA-
110

Plumpe, Friedrich Wilhelm
See Murnau, F.W.

Plutarch c. 46-c. 120 .... **CMLC 60**
See also AW 2; CDWLB 1; DLB 176;
RGWL 2, 3; TWA; WLIT 8

Po Chu-i 772-846 .... **CMLC 24**

Podhoretz, Norman 1930- .... **CLC 189**
See also AMWS 8; CA 9-12R; CANR 7,
78, 135

Poe, Edgar Allan 1809-1849 ..... **NCLC 1, 16,
55, 78, 94, 97, 117; PC 1, 54; SSC 1,
22, 34, 35, 54, 88; WLC 4**
See also AAYA 14; AMW; AMWC 1;
AMWR 2; BPFB 3; BYA 5, 11; CDALB
1640-1865; CMW 4; DA; DA3; DAB;
DAC; DAM MST, POET; DLB 3, 59, 73,
74, 248, 254; EXPP; EXPS; GL 3; HGG;
LAIT 2; LATS 1:1; LMFS 1; MSW; PAB;
PFS 1, 3, 9; RGAL 4; RGSF 2; SATA 23;
SCFW 1, 2; SFW 4; SSFS 2, 4, 7, 8, 16;
SUFW; TUS; WP; WYA

Poet of Titchfield Street, The
See Pound, Ezra (Weston Loomis)

Poggio Bracciolini, Gian Francesco
1380-1459 .... **LC 125**

Pohl, Frederik 1919- .... **CLC 18; SSC 25**
See also AAYA 24; CA 188; 61-64, 188; 1;
CANR 11, 37, 81, 140; CN 1, 2, 3, 4, 5,
6; DLB 8; INT CANR-11; MTCW 1, 2;
MTFW 2005; SATA 24; SCFW 1, 2; SFW
4

Poirier, Louis 1910-
See Gracq, Julien
See also CA 126; CAAE 122; CANR 141

Poitier, Sidney 1927- .... **CLC 26**
See also AAYA 60; BW 1; CA 117; CANR
94

Pokagon, Simon 1830-1899 .... **NNAL**
See also DAM MULT

Polanski, Roman 1933- .... **CLC 16, 178**
See also CA 77-80

Poliakoff, Stephen 1952- .... **CLC 38**
See also CA 106; CANR 116; CBD; CD 5,
6; DLB 13

Police, The
See Copeland, Stewart (Armstrong); Summers, Andy

Polidori, John William
1795-1821 .... **NCLC 51; SSC 97**
See also DLB 116; HGG

Poliziano, Angelo 1454-1494 .... **LC 120**
See also WLIT 7

Pollitt, Katha 1949- .... **CLC 28, 122**
See also CA 122; CAAE 120; CANR 66,
108; MTCW 1, 2; MTFW 2005

Pollock, (Mary) Sharon 1936- .... **CLC 50**
See also CA 141; CANR 132; CD 5; CWD;
DAC; DAM DRAM, MST; DFS 3; DLB
60; FW

Pollock, Sharon 1936- .... **DC 20**
See also CD 6

Polo, Marco 1254-1324 .... **CMLC 15**
See also WLIT 7

Polonsky, Abraham (Lincoln)
1910-1999 .... **CLC 92**
See also CA 104; CAAS 187; DLB 26; INT
CA-104

Polybius c. 200B.C.-c. 118B.C. ...... **CMLC 17**
See also AW 1; DLB 176; RGWL 2, 3

Pomerance, Bernard 1940- .... **CLC 13**
See also CA 101; CAD; CANR 49, 134;
CD 5, 6; DAM DRAM; DFS 9; LAIT 2

Ponge, Francis 1899-1988 .... **CLC 6, 18**
See also CA 85-88; CAAS 126; CANR 40,
86; DAM POET; DLBY 2002; EWL 3;
GFL 1789 to the Present; RGWL 2, 3

Poniatowska, Elena 1932- . **CLC 140; HLC 2**
See also CA 101; CANR 32, 66, 107, 156;
CDWLB 3; CWW 2; DAM MULT; DLB
113; EWL 3; HW 1, 2; LAWS 1; WLIT 1

Pontoppidan, Henrik 1857-1943 .... **TCLC 29**
See also CA 170; DLB 300, 331

Ponty, Maurice Merleau
See Merleau-Ponty, Maurice

Poole, Josephine .... **CLC 17**
See Helyar, Jane Penelope Josephine
See also SAAS 2; SATA 5

Popa, Vasko 1922-1991 . **CLC 19; TCLC 167**
See also CA 148; CAAE 112; CDWLB 4;
DLB 181; EWL 3; RGWL 2, 3

Pope, Alexander 1688-1744 ...... **LC 3, 58, 60,
64; PC 26; WLC 5**
See also BRW 3; BRWC 1; BRWR 1; CD-
BLB 1660-1789; DA; DA3; DAB; DAC;
DAM MST, POET; DLB 95, 101, 213;
EXPP; PAB; PFS 12; RGEL 2; WLIT 3;
WP

Popov, Evgenii Anatol'evich
See Popov, Yevgeny
See also DLB 285

Popov, Yevgeny .... **CLC 59**
See Popov, Evgenii Anatol'evich

Poquelin, Jean-Baptiste
See Moliere

Porete, Marguerite (?)-1310 .... **CMLC 73**
See also DLB 208

Porphyry c. 233-c. 305 .... **CMLC 71**

Porter, Connie (Rose) 1959(?)- .... **CLC 70**
See also AAYA 65; BW 2, 3; CA 142;
CANR 90, 109; SATA 81, 129

Porter, Gene(va Grace) Stratton .. **TCLC 21**
See Stratton-Porter, Gene(va Grace)
See also BPFB 3; CAAE 112; CWRI 5;
RHW

Porter, Katherine Anne 1890-1980 ... **CLC 1,
3, 7, 10, 13, 15, 27, 101; SSC 4, 31, 43**
See also AAYA 42; AITN 2; AMW; BPFB
3; CA 1-4R; CAAS 101; CANR 1, 65;
CDALBS; CN 1, 2; DA; DA3; DAB;
DAC; DAM MST, NOV; DLB 4, 9, 102;
DLBD 12; DLBY 1980; EWL 3; EXPS;
LAIT 3; MAL 5; MBL; MTCW 1, 2;
MTFW 2005; NFS 14; RGAL 4; RGSF 2;
SATA 39; SATA-Obit 23; SSFS 1, 8, 11,
16, 23; TCWW 2; TUS

Porter, Peter (Neville Frederick)
1929- .... **CLC 5, 13, 33**
See also CA 85-88; CP 1, 2, 3, 4, 5, 6, 7;
DLB 40, 289; WWE 1

Porter, William Sydney 1862-1910
See Henry, O.
See also CA 131; CAAE 104; CDALB
1865-1917; DA; DA3; DAB; DAC; DAM
MST; DLB 12, 78, 79; MTCW 1, 2;
MTFW 2005; TUS; YABC 2

Portillo (y Pacheco), Jose Lopez
See Lopez Portillo (y Pacheco), Jose

Portillo Trambley, Estela 1927-1998 .. **HLC 2**
See Trambley, Estela Portillo
See also CANR 32; DAM MULT; DLB
209; HW 1

Posey, Alexander (Lawrence)
1873-1908 .... **NNAL**
See also CA 144; CANR 80; DAM MULT;
DLB 175

Posse, Abel .... **CLC 70**
See also CA 252

Post, Melville Davisson
1869-1930 .... **TCLC 39**
See also CA 202; CAAE 110; CMW 4

Potok, Chaim 1929-2002 ... **CLC 2, 7, 14, 26,
112**
See also AAYA 15, 50; AITN 1, 2; BPFB 3;
BYA 1; CA 17-20R; CAAS 208; CANR
19, 35, 64, 98; CLR 92; CN 4, 5, 6; DA3;
DAM NOV; DLB 28, 152; EXPN; INT
CANR-19; LAIT 4; MTCW 1, 2; MTFW
2005; NFS 4; RGHL; SATA 33, 106;
SATA-Obit 134; TUS; YAW

Potok, Herbert Harold -2002
See Potok, Chaim

Potok, Herman Harold
See Potok, Chaim

Potter, Dennis (Christopher George)
1935-1994 .... **CLC 58, 86, 123**
See also BRWS 10; CA 107; CAAS 145;
CANR 33, 61; CBD; DLB 233; MTCW 1

Pound, Ezra (Weston Loomis)
1885-1972 .. **CLC 1, 2, 3, 4, 5, 7, 10, 13,
18, 34, 48, 50, 112; PC 4; WLC 5**
See also AAYA 47; AMW; AMWR 1; CA
5-8R; CAAS 37-40R; CANR 40; CDALB
1917-1929; CP 1; DA; DA3; DAB; DAC;
DAM MST, POET; DLB 4, 45, 63; DLBD
15; EFS 2; EWL 3; EXPP; LMFS 2; MAL
5; MTCW 1, 2; MTFW 2005; PAB; PFS
2, 8, 16; RGAL 4; TUS; WP

Povod, Reinaldo 1959-1994 .... **CLC 44**
See also CA 136; CAAS 146; CANR 83

Powell, Adam Clayton, Jr.
1908-1972 .... **BLC 3; CLC 89**
See also BW 1, 3; CA 102; CAAS 33-36R;
CANR 86; DAM MULT

Powell, Anthony 1905-2000 ... **CLC 1, 3, 7, 9,
10, 31**
See also BRW 7; CA 1-4R; CAAS 189;
CANR 1, 32, 62, 107; CDBLB 1945-
1960; CN 1, 2, 3, 4, 5, 6; DLB 15; EWL
3; MTCW 1, 2; MTFW 2005; RGEL 2;
TEA

Powell, Dawn 1896(?)-1965 .... **CLC 66**
See also CA 5-8R; CANR 121; DLBY 1997

Powell, Padgett 1952- .... **CLC 34**
See also CA 126; CANR 63, 101; CSW;
DLB 234; DLBY 01

Powell, (Oval) Talmage 1920-2000
See Queen, Ellery
See also CA 5-8R; CANR 2, 80

Power, Susan 1961- .... **CLC 91**
See also BYA 14; CA 160; CANR 135; NFS
11

Powers, J(ames) F(arl) 1917-1999 ..... **CLC 1,
4, 8, 57; SSC 4**
See also CA 1-4R; CAAS 181; CANR 2,
61; CN 1, 2, 3, 4, 5, 6; DLB 130; MTCW
1; RGAL 4; RGSF 2

Powers, John J(ames) 1945-
See Powers, John R.
See also CA 69-72

Powers, John R. .... **CLC 66**
See Powers, John J(ames)

Powers, Richard 1957- .... **CLC 93**
See also AMWS 9; BPFB 3; CA 148;
CANR 80; CN 6, 7; MTFW 2005; TCLE
1:2

Powers, Richard S.
See Powers, Richard

Pownall, David 1938- .... **CLC 10**
See also CA 89-92, 180; 18; CANR 49, 101;
CBD; CD 5, 6; CN 4, 5, 6, 7; DLB 14

Powys, John Cowper 1872-1963 ... **CLC 7, 9, 15, 46, 125**
See also CA 85-88; CANR 106; DLB 15, 255; EWL 3; FANT; MTCW 1, 2; MTFW 2005; RGEL 2; SUFW

Powys, T(heodore) F(rancis)
1875-1953 .... **TCLC 9**
See also BRWS 8; CA 189; CAAE 106; DLB 36, 162; EWL 3; FANT; RGEL 2; SUFW

Pozzo, Modesta
See Fonte, Moderata

Prado (Calvo), Pedro 1886-1952 ... **TCLC 75**
See also CA 131; DLB 283; HW 1; LAW

Prager, Emily 1952- .... **CLC 56**
See also CA 204

Pratchett, Terry 1948- .... **CLC 197**
See also AAYA 19, 54; BPFB 3; CA 143; CANR 87, 126; CLR 64; CN 6, 7; CPW; CWRI 5; FANT; MTFW 2005; SATA 82, 139; SFW 4; SUFW 2

Pratolini, Vasco 1913-1991 .... **TCLC 124**
See also CA 211; DLB 177; EWL 3; RGWL 2, 3

Pratt, E(dwin) J(ohn) 1883(?)-1964 . **CLC 19**
See also CA 141; CAAS 93-96; CANR 77; DAC; DAM POET; DLB 92; EWL 3; RGEL 2; TWA

Premchand .... **TCLC 21**
See Srivastava, Dhanpat Rai
See also EWL 3

Prescott, William Hickling
1796-1859 .... **NCLC 163**
See also DLB 1, 30, 59, 235

Preseren, France 1800-1849 .... **NCLC 127**
See also CDWLB 4; DLB 147

Preussler, Otfried 1923- .... **CLC 17**
See also CA 77-80; SATA 24

Prevert, Jacques (Henri Marie)
1900-1977 .... **CLC 15**
See also CA 77-80; CAAS 69-72; CANR 29, 61; DLB 258; EWL 3; GFL 1789 to the Present; IDFW 3, 4; MTCW 1; RGWL 2, 3; SATA-Obit 30

Prevost, (Antoine Francois)
1697-1763 .... **LC 1**
See also DLB 314; EW 4; GFL Beginnings to 1789; RGWL 2, 3

Price, Reynolds 1933- .. **CLC 3, 6, 13, 43, 50, 63, 212; SSC 22**
See also AMWS 6; CA 1-4R; CANR 1, 37, 57, 87, 128; CN 1, 2, 3, 4, 5, 6, 7; CSW; DAM NOV; DLB 2, 218, 278; EWL 3; INT CANR-37; MAL 5; MTFW 2005; NFS 18

Price, Richard 1949- .... **CLC 6, 12**
See also CA 49-52; CANR 3, 147; CN 7; DLBY 1981

Prichard, Katharine Susannah
1883-1969 .... **CLC 46**
See also CA 11-12; CANR 33; CAP 1; DLB 260; MTCW 1; RGEL 2; RGSF 2; SATA 66

Priestley, J(ohn) B(oynton)
1894-1984 .... **CLC 2, 5, 9, 34**
See also BRW 7; CA 9-12R; CAAS 113; CANR 33; CDBLB 1914-1945; CN 1, 2, 3; DA3; DAM DRAM, NOV; DLB 10, 34, 77, 100, 139; DLBY 1984; EWL 3; MTCW 1, 2; MTFW 2005; RGEL 2; SFW 4

Prince 1958- .... **CLC 35**
See also CA 213

Prince, F(rank) T(empleton)
1912-2003 .... **CLC 22**
See also CA 101; CAAS 219; CANR 43, 79; CP 1, 2, 3, 4, 5, 6, 7; DLB 20

Prince Kropotkin
See Kropotkin, Peter (Aleksieevich)

Prior, Matthew 1664-1721 .... **LC 4**
See also DLB 95; RGEL 2

Prishvin, Mikhail 1873-1954 .... **TCLC 75**
See Prishvin, Mikhail Mikhailovich

Prishvin, Mikhail Mikhailovich
See Prishvin, Mikhail
See also DLB 272; EWL 3

Pritchard, William H(arrison)
1932- .... **CLC 34**
See also CA 65-68; CANR 23, 95; DLB 111

Pritchett, V(ictor) S(awdon)
1900-1997 ... **CLC 5, 13, 15, 41; SSC 14**
See also BPFB 3; BRWS 3; CA 61-64; CAAS 157; CANR 31, 63; CN 1, 2, 3, 4, 5, 6; DA3; DAM NOV; DLB 15, 139; EWL 3; MTCW 1, 2; MTFW 2005; RGEL 2; RGSF 2; TEA

Private 19022
See Manning, Frederic

Probst, Mark 1925- .... **CLC 59**
See also CA 130

Procaccino, Michael
See Cristofer, Michael

Proclus c. 412-c. 485 .... **CMLC 81**

Prokosch, Frederic 1908-1989 ...... **CLC 4, 48**
See also CA 73-76; CAAS 128; CANR 82; CN 1, 2, 3, 4; CP 1, 2, 3, 4; DLB 48; MTCW 2

Propertius, Sextus c. 50B.C.-c. 16B.C. .... **CMLC 32**
See also AW 2; CDWLB 1; DLB 211; RGWL 2, 3; WLIT 8

Prophet, The
See Dreiser, Theodore

Prose, Francine 1947- .... **CLC 45, 231**
See also AMWS 16; CA 112; CAAE 109; CANR 46, 95, 132; DLB 234; MTFW 2005; SATA 101, 149

Protagoras c. 490B.C.-420B.C. ...... **CMLC 85**
See also DLB 176

Proudhon
See Cunha, Euclides (Rodrigues Pimenta) da

Proulx, Annie
See Proulx, E. Annie

Proulx, E. Annie 1935- .... **CLC 81, 158**
See also AMWS 7; BPFB 3; CA 145; CANR 65, 110; CN 6, 7; CPW 1; DA3; DAM POP; DLB 335; MAL 5; MTCW 2; MTFW 2005; SSFS 18, 23

Proulx, Edna Annie
See Proulx, E. Annie

Proust, (Valentin-Louis-George-Eugene) Marcel 1871-1922 ..... **SSC 75; TCLC 7, 13, 33; WLC 5**
See also AAYA 58; BPFB 3; CA 120; CAAE 104; CANR 110; DA; DA3; DAB; DAC; DAM MST, NOV; DLB 65; EW 8; EWL 3; GFL 1789 to the Present; MTCW 1, 2; MTFW 2005; RGWL 2, 3; TWA

Prowler, Harley
See Masters, Edgar Lee

Prudentius, Aurelius Clemens 348-c. 405 .... **CMLC 78**
See also EW 1; RGWL 2, 3

Prudhomme, Rene Francois Armand
1839-1907
See Sully Prudhomme, Rene-Francois-Armand
See also CA 170

Prus, Boleslaw 1845-1912 .... **TCLC 48**
See also RGWL 2, 3

Pryor, Aaron Richard
See Pryor, Richard

Pryor, Richard 1940-2005 .... **CLC 26**
See also CA 152; CAAE 122; CAAS 246

Pryor, Richard Franklin Lenox Thomas
See Pryor, Richard

Przybyszewski, Stanislaw
1868-1927 .... **TCLC 36**

Pseudo-Dionysius the Areopagite fl. c. 5th cent. - .... **CMLC 89**
See also DLB 115

Pteleon
See Grieve, C(hristopher) M(urray)
See also DAM POET

Puckett, Lute
See Masters, Edgar Lee

Puig, Manuel 1932-1990 .... **CLC 3, 5, 10, 28, 65, 133; HLC 2**
See also BPFB 3; CA 45-48; CANR 2, 32, 63; CDWLB 3; DA3; DAM MULT; DLB 113; DNFS 1; EWL 3; GLL 1; HW 1, 2; LAW; MTCW 1, 2; MTFW 2005; RGWL 2, 3; TWA; WLIT 1

Pulitzer, Joseph 1847-1911 .... **TCLC 76**
See also CAAE 114; DLB 23

Purchas, Samuel 1577(?)-1626 .... **LC 70**
See also DLB 151

Purdy, A(lfred) W(ellington)
1918-2000 .... **CLC 3, 6, 14, 50**
See also CA 81-84; 17; CAAS 189; CANR 42, 66; CP 1, 2, 3, 4, 5, 6, 7; DAC; DAM MST, POET; DLB 88; PFS 5; RGEL 2

Purdy, James (Amos) 1923- .... **CLC 2, 4, 10, 28, 52**
See also AMWS 7; CA 33-36R; 1; CANR 19, 51, 132; CN 1, 2, 3, 4, 5, 6, 7; DLB 2, 218; EWL 3; INT CANR-19; MAL 5; MTCW 1; RGAL 4

Pure, Simon
See Swinnerton, Frank Arthur

Pushkin, Aleksandr Sergeevich
See Pushkin, Alexander (Sergeyevich)
See also DLB 205

Pushkin, Alexander (Sergeyevich)
1799-1837 .... **NCLC 3, 27, 83; PC 10; SSC 27, 55, 99; WLC 5**
See Pushkin, Aleksandr Sergeevich
See also DA; DA3; DAB; DAC; DAM DRAM, MST, POET; EW 5; EXPS; RGSF 2; RGWL 2, 3; SATA 61; SSFS 9; TWA

P'u Sung-ling 1640-1715 .... **LC 49; SSC 31**

Putnam, Arthur Lee
See Alger, Horatio, Jr.

Puttenham, George 1529(?)-1590 ...... **LC 116**
See also DLB 281

Puzo, Mario 1920-1999 .... **CLC 1, 2, 6, 36, 107**
See also BPFB 3; CA 65-68; CAAS 185; CANR 4, 42, 65, 99, 131; CN 1, 2, 3, 4, 5, 6; CPW; DA3; DAM NOV, POP; DLB 6; MTCW 1, 2; MTFW 2005; NFS 16; RGAL 4

Pygge, Edward
See Barnes, Julian

Pyle, Ernest Taylor 1900-1945
See Pyle, Ernie
See also CA 160; CAAE 115

Pyle, Ernie .... **TCLC 75**
See Pyle, Ernest Taylor
See also DLB 29; MTCW 2

Pyle, Howard 1853-1911 .... **TCLC 81**
See also AAYA 57; BYA 2, 4; CA 137; CAAE 109; CLR 22, 117; DLB 42, 188; DLBD 13; LAIT 1; MAICYA 1, 2; SATA 16, 100; WCH; YAW

Pym, Barbara (Mary Crampton)
1913-1980 .... **CLC 13, 19, 37, 111**
See also BPFB 3; BRWS 2; CA 13-14; CAAS 97-100; CANR 13, 34; CAP 1; DLB 14, 207; DLBY 1987; EWL 3; MTCW 1, 2; MTFW 2005; RGEL 2; TEA

Pynchon, Thomas 1937- .. CLC 2, 3, 6, 9, 11, 18, 33, 62, 72, 123, 192, 213; SSC 14, 84; WLC 5
See also AMWS 2; BEST 90:2; BPFB 3; CA 17-20R; CANR 22, 46, 73, 142; CN 1, 2, 3, 4, 5, 6, 7; CPW 1; DA; DA3; DAB; DAC; DAM MST, NOV, POP; DLB 2, 173; EWL 3; MAL 5; MTCW 1, 2; MTFW 2005; NFS 23; RGAL 4; SFW 4; TCLE 1:2; TUS

Pythagoras c. 582B.C.-c. 507B.C. . CMLC 22
See also DLB 176

Q
See Quiller-Couch, Sir Arthur (Thomas)

Qian, Chongzhu
See Ch'ien, Chung-shu

Qian, Sima 145B.C.-c. 89B.C. .... CMLC 72

Qian Zhongshu
See Ch'ien, Chung-shu
See also CWW 2; DLB 328

Qroll
See Dagerman, Stig (Halvard)

Quarles, Francis 1592-1644 .... LC 117
See also DLB 126; RGEL 2

Quarrington, Paul (Lewis) 1953- ..... CLC 65
See also CA 129; CANR 62, 95

Quasimodo, Salvatore 1901-1968 .... CLC 10; PC 47
See also CA 13-16; CAAS 25-28R; CAP 1; DLB 114, 332; EW 12; EWL 3; MTCW 1; RGWL 2, 3

Quatermass, Martin
See Carpenter, John (Howard)

Quay, Stephen 1947- .... CLC 95
See also CA 189

Quay, Timothy 1947- .... CLC 95
See also CA 189

Queen, Ellery .... CLC 3, 11
See Dannay, Frederic; Davidson, Avram (James); Deming, Richard; Fairman, Paul W.; Flora, Fletcher; Hoch, Edward D(entinger); Kane, Henry; Lee, Manfred B.; Marlowe, Stephen; Powell, (Oval) Talmage; Sheldon, Walter J(ames); Sturgeon, Theodore (Hamilton); Tracy, Don(ald Fiske); Vance, Jack
See also BPFB 3; CMW 4; MSW; RGAL 4

Queen, Ellery, Jr.
See Dannay, Frederic; Lee, Manfred B.

Queneau, Raymond 1903-1976 ..... CLC 2, 5, 10, 42
See also CA 77-80; CAAS 69-72; CANR 32; DLB 72, 258; EW 12; EWL 3; GFL 1789 to the Present; MTCW 1, 2; RGWL 2, 3

Quevedo, Francisco de 1580-1645 .... LC 23

Quiller-Couch, Sir Arthur (Thomas) 1863-1944 .... TCLC 53
See also CA 166; CAAE 118; DLB 135, 153, 190; HGG; RGEL 2; SUFW 1

Quin, Ann 1936-1973 .... CLC 6
See also CA 9-12R; CAAS 45-48; CANR 148; CN 1; DLB 14, 231

Quin, Ann Marie
See Quin, Ann

Quincey, Thomas de
See De Quincey, Thomas

Quindlen, Anna 1953- .... CLC 191
See also AAYA 35; CA 138; CANR 73, 126; DA3; DLB 292; MTCW 2; MTFW 2005

Quinn, Martin
See Smith, Martin Cruz

Quinn, Peter 1947- .... CLC 91
See also CA 197; CANR 147

Quinn, Peter A.
See Quinn, Peter

Quinn, Simon
See Smith, Martin Cruz

Quintana, Leroy V. 1944- ...... HLC 2; PC 36
See also CA 131; CANR 65, 139; DAM MULT; DLB 82; HW 1, 2

Quintilian c. 40-c. 100 .... CMLC 77
See also AW 2; DLB 211; RGWL 2, 3

Quintillian 0035-0100 .... CMLC 77

Quiroga, Horacio (Sylvestre) 1878-1937 ... HLC 2; SSC 89; TCLC 20
See also CA 131; CAAE 117; DAM MULT; EWL 3; HW 1; LAW; MTCW 1; RGSF 2; WLIT 1

Quoirez, Francoise 1935-2004 .... CLC 9
See Sagan, Francoise
See also CA 49-52; CAAS 231; CANR 6, 39, 73; MTCW 1, 2; MTFW 2005; TWA

Raabe, Wilhelm (Karl) 1831-1910 . TCLC 45
See also CA 167; DLB 129

Rabe, David (William) 1940- .. CLC 4, 8, 33, 200; DC 16
See also CA 85-88; CABS 3; CAD; CANR 59, 129; CD 5, 6; DAM DRAM; DFS 3, 8, 13; DLB 7, 228; EWL 3; MAL 5

Rabelais, Francois 1494-1553 .... LC 5, 60; WLC 5
See also DA; DAB; DAC; DAM MST; DLB 327; EW 2; GFL Beginnings to 1789; LMFS 1; RGWL 2, 3; TWA

Rabi'a al-'Adawiyya c. 717-c. 801 .... CMLC 83
See also DLB 311

Rabinovitch, Sholem 1859-1916
See Sholom Aleichem
See also CAAE 104

Rabinyan, Dorit 1972- .... CLC 119
See also CA 170; CANR 147

Rachilde
See Vallette, Marguerite Eymery; Vallette, Marguerite Eymery
See also EWL 3

Racine, Jean 1639-1699 .... LC 28, 113
See also DA3; DAB; DAM MST; DLB 268; EW 3; GFL Beginnings to 1789; LMFS 1; RGWL 2, 3; TWA

Radcliffe, Ann (Ward) 1764-1823 ... NCLC 6, 55, 106
See also DLB 39, 178; GL 3; HGG; LMFS 1; RGEL 2; SUFW 1; WLIT 3

Radclyffe-Hall, Marguerite
See Hall, Radclyffe

Radiguet, Raymond 1903-1923 ...... TCLC 29
See also CA 162; DLB 65; EWL 3; GFL 1789 to the Present; RGWL 2, 3

Radnoti, Miklos 1909-1944 .... TCLC 16
See also CA 212; CAAE 118; CDWLB 4; DLB 215; EWL 3; RGHL; RGWL 2, 3

Rado, James 1939- .... CLC 17
See also CA 105

Radvanyi, Netty 1900-1983
See Seghers, Anna
See also CA 85-88; CAAS 110; CANR 82

Rae, Ben
See Griffiths, Trevor

Raeburn, John (Hay) 1941- .... CLC 34
See also CA 57-60

Ragni, Gerome 1942-1991 .... CLC 17
See also CA 105; CAAS 134

Rahv, Philip .... CLC 24
See Greenberg, Ivan
See also DLB 137; MAL 5

Raimund, Ferdinand Jakob 1790-1836 .... NCLC 69
See also DLB 90

Raine, Craig (Anthony) 1944- .. CLC 32, 103
See also CA 108; CANR 29, 51, 103; CP 3, 4, 5, 6, 7; DLB 40; PFS 7

Raine, Kathleen (Jessie) 1908-2003 .. CLC 7, 45
See also CA 85-88; CAAS 218; CANR 46, 109; CP 1, 2, 3, 4, 5, 6, 7; DLB 20; EWL 3; MTCW 1; RGEL 2

Rainis, Janis 1865-1929 .... TCLC 29
See also CA 170; CDWLB 4; DLB 220; EWL 3

Rakosi, Carl .... CLC 47
See Rawley, Callman
See also CA 5; CAAS 228; CP 1, 2, 3, 4, 5, 6, 7; DLB 193

Ralegh, Sir Walter
See Raleigh, Sir Walter
See also BRW 1; RGEL 2; WP

Raleigh, Richard
See Lovecraft, H. P.

Raleigh, Sir Walter 1554(?)-1618 .... LC 31, 39; PC 31
See Ralegh, Sir Walter
See also CDBLB Before 1660; DLB 172; EXPP; PFS 14; TEA

Rallentando, H. P.
See Sayers, Dorothy L(eigh)

Ramal, Walter
See de la Mare, Walter (John)

Ramana Maharshi 1879-1950 .... TCLC 84

Ramoacn y Cajal, Santiago 1852-1934 .... TCLC 93

Ramon, Juan
See Jimenez (Mantecon), Juan Ramon

Ramos, Graciliano 1892-1953 .... TCLC 32
See also CA 167; DLB 307; EWL 3; HW 2; LAW; WLIT 1

Rampersad, Arnold 1941- .... CLC 44
See also BW 2, 3; CA 133; CAAE 127; CANR 81; DLB 111; INT CA-133

Rampling, Anne
See Rice, Anne
See also GLL 2

Ramsay, Allan 1686(?)-1758 .... LC 29
See also DLB 95; RGEL 2

Ramsay, Jay
See Campbell, (John) Ramsey

Ramuz, Charles-Ferdinand 1878-1947 .... TCLC 33
See also CA 165; EWL 3

Rand, Ayn 1905-1982 ...... CLC 3, 30, 44, 79; WLC 5
See also AAYA 10; AMWS 4; BPFB 3; BYA 12; CA 13-16R; CAAS 105; CANR 27, 73; CDALBS; CN 1, 2, 3; CPW; DA; DA3; DAC; DAM MST, NOV, POP; DLB 227, 279; MTCW 1, 2; MTFW 2005; NFS 10, 16; RGAL 4; SFW 4; TUS; YAW

Randall, Dudley (Felker) 1914-2000 . BLC 3; CLC 1, 135
See also BW 1, 3; CA 25-28R; CAAS 189; CANR 23, 82; CP 1, 2, 3, 4, 5; DAM MULT; DLB 41; PFS 5

Randall, Robert
See Silverberg, Robert

Ranger, Ken
See Creasey, John

Rank, Otto 1884-1939 .... TCLC 115

Ransom, John Crowe 1888-1974 .. CLC 2, 4, 5, 11, 24; PC 61
See also AMW; CA 5-8R; CAAS 49-52; CANR 6, 34; CDALBS; CP 1, 2; DA3; DAM POET; DLB 45, 63; EWL 3; EXPP; MAL 5; MTCW 1, 2; MTFW 2005; RGAL 4; TUS

Rao, Raja 1908-2006 .... CLC 25, 56; SSC 99
See also CA 73-76; CAAS 252; CANR 51; CN 1, 2, 3, 4, 5, 6; DAM NOV; DLB 323; EWL 3; MTCW 1, 2; MTFW 2005; RGEL 2; RGSF 2

Raphael, Frederic (Michael) 1931- ... **CLC 2, 14**
See also CA 1-4R; CANR 1, 86; CN 1, 2, 3, 4, 5, 6, 7; DLB 14, 319; TCLE 1:2
Raphael, Lev 1954- .... **CLC 232**
See also CA 134; CANR 72, 145; GLL 1
Ratcliffe, James P.
See Mencken, H(enry) L(ouis)
Rathbone, Julian 1935- .... **CLC 41**
See also CA 101; CANR 34, 73, 152
Rattigan, Terence (Mervyn)
1911-1977 .... **CLC 7; DC 18**
See also BRWS 7; CA 85-88; CAAS 73-76; CBD; CDBLB 1945-1960; DAM DRAM; DFS 8; DLB 13; IDFW 3, 4; MTCW 1, 2; RGEL 2
Ratushinskaya, Irina 1954- .... **CLC 54**
See also CA 129; CANR 68; CWW 2
Raven, Simon (Arthur Noel)
1927-2001 .... **CLC 14**
See also CA 81-84; CAAS 197; CANR 86; CN 1, 2, 3, 4, 5, 6; DLB 271
Ravenna, Michael
See Welty, Eudora
Rawley, Callman 1903-2004
See Rakosi, Carl
See also CA 21-24R; CAAS 228; CANR 12, 32, 91
Rawlings, Marjorie Kinnan
1896-1953 .... **TCLC 4**
See also AAYA 20; AMWS 10; ANW; BPFB 3; BYA 3; CA 137; CAAE 104; CANR 74; CLR 63; DLB 9, 22, 102; DLBD 17; JRDA; MAICYA 1, 2; MAL 5; MTCW 2; MTFW 2005; RGAL 4; SATA 100; WCH; YABC 1; YAW
Ray, Satyajit 1921-1992 .... **CLC 16, 76**
See also CA 114; CAAS 137; DAM MULT
Read, Herbert Edward 1893-1968 ..... **CLC 4**
See also BRW 6; CA 85-88; CANR 25-28R; DLB 20, 149; EWL 3; PAB; RGEL 2
Read, Piers Paul 1941- .... **CLC 4, 10, 25**
See also CA 21-24R; CANR 38, 86, 150; CN 2, 3, 4, 5, 6, 7; DLB 14; SATA 21
Reade, Charles 1814-1884 .... **NCLC 2, 74**
See also DLB 21; RGEL 2
Reade, Hamish
See Gray, Simon (James Holliday)
Reading, Peter 1946- .... **CLC 47**
See also BRWS 8; CA 103; CANR 46, 96; CP 5, 6, 7; DLB 40
Reaney, James 1926- .... **CLC 13**
See also CA 41-44R; 15; CANR 42; CD 5, 6; CP 1, 2, 3, 4, 5, 6, 7; DAC; DAM MST; DLB 68; RGEL 2; SATA 43
Rebreanu, Liviu 1885-1944 .... **TCLC 28**
See also CA 165; DLB 220; EWL 3
Rechy, John 1934- ..... **CLC 1, 7, 14, 18, 107; HLC 2**
See also CA 195; 5-8R, 195; 4; CANR 6, 32, 64, 152; CN 1, 2, 3, 4, 5, 6, 7; DAM MULT; DLB 122, 278; DLBY 1982; HW 1, 2; INT CANR-6; LLW; MAL 5; RGAL 4
Rechy, John Francisco
See Rechy, John
Redcam, Tom 1870-1933 .... **TCLC 25**
Reddin, Keith 1956- .... **CLC 67**
See also CAD; CD 6
Redgrove, Peter (William)
1932-2003 .... **CLC 6, 41**
See also BRWS 6; CA 1-4R; CAAS 217; CANR 3, 39, 77; CP 1, 2, 3, 4, 5, 6, 7; DLB 40; TCLE 1:2
Redmon, Anne .... **CLC 22**
See Nightingale, Anne Redmon
See also DLBY 1986
Reed, Eliot
See Ambler, Eric

Reed, Ishmael 1938- ..... **BLC 3; CLC 2, 3, 5, 6, 13, 32, 60, 174; PC 68**
See also AFAW 1, 2; AMWS 10; BPFB 3; BW 2, 3; CA 21-24R; CANR 25, 48, 74, 128; CN 1, 2, 3, 4, 5, 6, 7; CP 1, 2, 3, 4, 5, 6, 7; CSW; DA3; DAM MULT; DLB 2, 5, 33, 169, 227; DLBD 8; EWL 3; LMFS 2; MAL 5; MSW; MTCW 1, 2; MTFW 2005; PFS 6; RGAL 4; TCWW 2
Reed, John (Silas) 1887-1920 .... **TCLC 9**
See also CA 195; CAAE 106; MAL 5; TUS
Reed, Lou .... **CLC 21**
See Firbank, Louis
Reese, Lizette Woodworth
1856-1935 .... **PC 29; TCLC 181**
See also CA 180; DLB 54
Reeve, Clara 1729-1807 .... **NCLC 19**
See also DLB 39; RGEL 2
Reich, Wilhelm 1897-1957 .... **TCLC 57**
See also CA 199
Reid, Christopher (John) 1949- .... **CLC 33**
See also CA 140; CANR 89; CP 4, 5, 6, 7; DLB 40; EWL 3
Reid, Desmond
See Moorcock, Michael
Reid Banks, Lynne 1929-
See Banks, Lynne Reid
See also AAYA 49; CA 1-4R; CANR 6, 22, 38, 87; CLR 24; CN 1, 2, 3, 7; JRDA; MAICYA 1, 2; SATA 22, 75, 111, 165; YAW
Reilly, William K.
See Creasey, John
Reiner, Max
See Caldwell, (Janet Miriam) Taylor (Holland)
Reis, Ricardo
See Pessoa, Fernando (Antonio Nogueira)
Reizenstein, Elmer Leopold
See Rice, Elmer (Leopold)
See also EWL 3
Remarque, Erich Maria 1898-1970 . **CLC 21**
See also AAYA 27; BPFB 3; CA 77-80; CAAS 29-32R; CDWLB 2; DA; DA3; DAB; DAC; DAM MST, NOV; DLB 56; EWL 3; EXPN; LAIT 3; MTCW 1, 2; MTFW 2005; NFS 4; RGHL; RGWL 2, 3
Remington, Frederic S(ackrider)
1861-1909 .... **TCLC 89**
See also CA 169; CAAE 108; DLB 12, 186, 188; SATA 41; TCWW 2
Remizov, A.
See Remizov, Aleksei (Mikhailovich)
Remizov, A. M.
See Remizov, Aleksei (Mikhailovich)
Remizov, Aleksei (Mikhailovich)
1877-1957 .... **TCLC 27**
See Remizov, Alexey Mikhaylovich
See also CA 133; CAAE 125; DLB 295
Remizov, Alexey Mikhaylovich
See Remizov, Aleksei (Mikhailovich)
See also EWL 3
Renan, Joseph Ernest 1823-1892 . **NCLC 26, 145**
See also GFL 1789 to the Present
Renard, Jules(-Pierre) 1864-1910 .. **TCLC 17**
See also CA 202; CAAE 117; GFL 1789 to the Present
Renart, Jean fl. 13th cent. - .... **CMLC 83**
Renault, Mary .... **CLC 3, 11, 17**
See Challans, Mary
See also BPFB 3; BYA 2; CN 1, 2, 3; DLBY 1983; EWL 3; GLL 1; LAIT 1; RGEL 2; RHW

Rendell, Ruth 1930- .... **CLC 28, 48**
See Vine, Barbara
See also BPFB 3; BRWS 9; CA 109; CANR 32, 52, 74, 127, 162; CN 5, 6, 7; CPW; DAM POP; DLB 87, 276; INT CANR-32; MSW; MTCW 1, 2; MTFW 2005
Rendell, Ruth Barbara
See Rendell, Ruth
Renoir, Jean 1894-1979 .... **CLC 20**
See also CA 129; CAAS 85-88
Rensie, Willis
See Eisner, Will
Resnais, Alain 1922- .... **CLC 16**
Revard, Carter 1931- .... **NNAL**
See also CA 144; CANR 81, 153; PFS 5
Reverdy, Pierre 1889-1960 .... **CLC 53**
See also CA 97-100; CAAS 89-92; DLB 258; EWL 3; GFL 1789 to the Present
Rexroth, Kenneth 1905-1982 .... **CLC 1, 2, 6, 11, 22, 49, 112; PC 20**
See also BG 1:3; CA 5-8R; CAAS 107; CANR 14, 34, 63; CDALB 1941-1968; CP 1, 2, 3; DAM POET; DLB 16, 48, 165, 212; DLBY 1982; EWL 3; INT CANR-14; MAL 5; MTCW 1, 2; MTFW 2005; RGAL 4
Reyes, Alfonso 1889-1959 .... **HLCS 2; TCLC 33**
See also CA 131; EWL 3; HW 1; LAW
Reyes y Basoalto, Ricardo Eliecer Neftali
See Neruda, Pablo
Reymont, Wladyslaw (Stanislaw)
1868(?)-1925 .... **TCLC 5**
See also CAAE 104; DLB 332; EWL 3
Reynolds, John Hamilton
1794-1852 .... **NCLC 146**
See also DLB 96
Reynolds, Jonathan 1942- .... **CLC 6, 38**
See also CA 65-68; CANR 28
Reynolds, Joshua 1723-1792 .... **LC 15**
See also DLB 104
Reynolds, Michael S(hane)
1937-2000 .... **CLC 44**
See also CA 65-68; CAAS 189; CANR 9, 89, 97
Reznikoff, Charles 1894-1976 .... **CLC 9**
See also AMWS 14; CA 33-36; CAAS 61-64; CAP 2; CP 1, 2; DLB 28, 45; RGHL; WP
Rezzori, Gregor von
See Rezzori d'Arezzo, Gregor von
Rezzori d'Arezzo, Gregor von
1914-1998 .... **CLC 25**
See also CA 136; CAAE 122; CAAS 167
Rhine, Richard
See Silverstein, Alvin; Silverstein, Virginia B(arbara Opshelor)
Rhodes, Eugene Manlove
1869-1934 .... **TCLC 53**
See also CA 198; DLB 256; TCWW 1, 2
R'hoone, Lord
See Balzac, Honore de
Rhys, Jean 1890-1979 .... **CLC 2, 4, 6, 14, 19, 51, 124; SSC 21, 76**
See also BRWS 2; CA 25-28R; CAAS 85-88; CANR 35, 62; CDBLB 1945-1960; CDWLB 3; CN 1, 2; DA3; DAM NOV; DLB 36, 117, 162; DNFS 2; EWL 3; LATS 1:1; MTCW 1, 2; MTFW 2005; NFS 19; RGEL 2; RGSF 2; RHW; TEA; WWE 1
Ribeiro, Darcy 1922-1997 .... **CLC 34**
See also CA 33-36R; CAAS 156; EWL 3
Ribeiro, Joao Ubaldo (Osorio Pimentel)
1941- .... **CLC 10, 67**
See also CA 81-84; CWW 2; EWL 3
Ribman, Ronald (Burt) 1932- .... **CLC 7**
See also CA 21-24R; CAD; CANR 46, 80; CD 5, 6

Saba, Umberto 1883-1957 .... **TCLC 33**
  See also CA 144; CANR 79; DLB 114;
  EWL 3; RGWL 2, 3

Sabatini, Rafael 1875-1950 .... **TCLC 47**
  See also BPFB 3; CA 162; RHW

Sabato, Ernesto 1911- ... **CLC 10, 23; HLC 2**
  See also CA 97-100; CANR 32, 65; CD-
  WLB 2; CWW 2; DAM MULT; DLB 145;
  EWL 3; HW 1, 2; LAW; MTCW 1, 2;
  MTFW 2005

Sa-Carneiro, Mario de 1890-1916 . **TCLC 83**
  See also DLB 287; EWL 3

Sacastru, Martin
  See Bioy Casares, Adolfo
  See also CWW 2

Sacher-Masoch, Leopold von
  1836(?)-1895 .... **NCLC 31**

Sachs, Hans 1494-1576 .... **LC 95**
  See also CDWLB 2; DLB 179; RGWL 2, 3

Sachs, Marilyn 1927- .... **CLC 35**
  See also AAYA 2; BYA 6; CA 17-20R;
  CANR 13, 47, 150; CLR 2; JRDA; MAI-
  CYA 1, 2; SAAS 2; SATA 3, 68, 164;
  SATA-Essay 110; WYA; YAW

Sachs, Marilyn Stickle
  See Sachs, Marilyn

Sachs, Nelly 1891-1970 .. **CLC 14, 98; PC 78**
  See also CA 17-18; CAAS 25-28R; CANR
  87; CAP 2; DLB 332; EWL 3; MTCW 2;
  MTFW 2005; PFS 20; RGHL; RGWL 2,
  3

Sackler, Howard (Oliver)
  1929-1982 .... **CLC 14**
  See also CA 61-64; CAAS 108; CAD;
  CANR 30; DFS 15; DLB 7

Sacks, Oliver 1933- .... **CLC 67, 202**
  See also CA 53-56; CANR 28, 50, 76, 146;
  CPW; DA3; INT CANR-28; MTCW 1, 2;
  MTFW 2005

Sacks, Oliver Wolf
  See Sacks, Oliver

Sackville, Thomas 1536-1608 .... **LC 98**
  See also DAM DRAM; DLB 62, 132;
  RGEL 2

Sadakichi
  See Hartmann, Sadakichi

Sa'dawi, Nawal al-
  See El Saadawi, Nawal
  See also CWW 2

Sade, Donatien Alphonse Francois
  1740-1814 .... **NCLC 3, 47**
  See also DLB 314; EW 4; GFL Beginnings
  to 1789; RGWL 2, 3

Sade, Marquis de
  See Sade, Donatien Alphonse Francois

Sadoff, Ira 1945- .... **CLC 9**
  See also CA 53-56; CANR 5, 21, 109; DLB
  120

Saetone
  See Camus, Albert

Safire, William 1929- .... **CLC 10**
  See also CA 17-20R; CANR 31, 54, 91, 148

Sagan, Carl 1934-1996 .... **CLC 30, 112**
  See also AAYA 2, 62; CA 25-28R; CAAS
  155; CANR 11, 36, 74; CPW; DA3;
  MTCW 1, 2; MTFW 2005; SATA 58;
  SATA-Obit 94

Sagan, Francoise .... **CLC 3, 6, 9, 17, 36**
  See Quoirez, Francoise
  See also CWW 2; DLB 83; EWL 3; GFL
  1789 to the Present; MTCW 2

Sahgal, Nayantara (Pandit) 1927- .... **CLC 41**
  See also CA 9-12R; CANR 11, 88; CN 1,
  2, 3, 4, 5, 6, 7; DLB 323

Said, Edward W. 1935-2003 .... **CLC 123**
  See also CA 21-24R; CAAS 220; CANR
  45, 74, 107, 131; DLB 67; MTCW 2;
  MTFW 2005

Saint, H(arry) F. 1941- .... **CLC 50**
  See also CA 127

St. Aubin de Teran, Lisa 1953-
  See Teran, Lisa St. Aubin de
  See also CA 126; CAAE 118; CN 6, 7; INT
  CA-126

Saint Birgitta of Sweden c.
  1303-1373 .... **CMLC 24**

Sainte-Beuve, Charles Augustin
  1804-1869 .... **NCLC 5**
  See also DLB 217; EW 6; GFL 1789 to the
  Present

Saint-Exupery, Antoine de
  1900-1944 .... **TCLC 2, 56, 169; WLC**
  See also AAYA 63; BPFB 3; BYA 3; CA
  132; CAAE 108; CLR 10; DA3; DAM
  NOV; DLB 72; EW 12; EWL 3; GFL
  1789 to the Present; LAIT 3; MAICYA 1,
  2; MTCW 1, 2; MTFW 2005; RGWL 2,
  3; SATA 20; TWA

**Saint-Exupery, Antoine Jean Baptiste Marie
  Roger de**
  See Saint-Exupery, Antoine de

St. John, David
  See Hunt, E. Howard

St. John, J. Hector
  See Crevecoeur, Michel Guillaume Jean de

Saint-John Perse
  See Leger, (Marie-Rene Auguste) Alexis
  Saint-Leger
  See also EW 10; EWL 3; GFL 1789 to the
  Present; RGWL 2

Saintsbury, George (Edward Bateman)
  1845-1933 .... **TCLC 31**
  See also CA 160; DLB 57, 149

Sait Faik .... **TCLC 23**
  See Abasiyanik, Sait Faik

Saki .... **SSC 12; TCLC 3; WLC 5**
  See Munro, H(ector) H(ugh)
  See also BRWS 6; BYA 11; LAIT 2; RGEL
  2; SSFS 1; SUFW

Sala, George Augustus 1828-1895 . **NCLC 46**

Saladin 1138-1193 .... **CMLC 38**

Salama, Hannu 1936- .... **CLC 18**
  See also CA 244; EWL 3

Salamanca, J(ack) R(ichard) 1922- .. **CLC 4,
  15**
  See also CA 193; 25-28R, 193

Salas, Floyd Francis 1931- .... **HLC 2**
  See also CA 119; 27; CANR 44, 75, 93;
  DAM MULT; DLB 82; HW 1, 2; MTCW
  2; MTFW 2005

Sale, J. Kirkpatrick
  See Sale, Kirkpatrick

Sale, John Kirkpatrick
  See Sale, Kirkpatrick

Sale, Kirkpatrick 1937- .... **CLC 68**
  See also CA 13-16R; CANR 10, 147

Salinas, Luis Omar 1937- ... **CLC 90; HLC 2**
  See also AMWS 13; CA 131; CANR 81,
  153; DAM MULT; DLB 82; HW 1, 2

Salinas (y Serrano), Pedro
  1891(?)-1951 .... **TCLC 17**
  See also CAAE 117; DLB 134; EWL 3

Salinger, J.D. 1919- . **CLC 1, 3, 8, 12, 55, 56,
  138; SSC 2, 28, 65; WLC 5**
  See also AAYA 2, 36; AMW; AMWC 1;
  BPFB 3; CA 5-8R; CANR 39, 129;
  CDALB 1941-1968; CLR 18; CN 1, 2, 3,
  4, 5, 6, 7; CPW 1; DA; DA3; DAB; DAC;
  DAM MST, NOV, POP; DLB 2, 102, 173;
  EWL 3; EXPN; LAIT 4; MAICYA 1, 2;
  MAL 5; MTCW 1, 2; MTFW 2005; NFS
  1; RGAL 4; RGSF 2; SATA 67; SSFS 17;
  TUS; WYA; YAW

Salisbury, John
  See Caute, (John) David

Sallust c. 86B.C.-35B.C. .... **CMLC 68**
  See also AW 2; CDWLB 1; DLB 211;
  RGWL 2, 3

Salter, James 1925- .. **CLC 7, 52, 59; SSC 58**
  See also AMWS 9; CA 73-76; CANR 107,
  160; DLB 130

Saltus, Edgar (Everton) 1855-1921 . **TCLC 8**
  See also CAAE 105; DLB 202; RGAL 4

Saltykov, Mikhail Evgrafovich
  1826-1889 .... **NCLC 16**
  See also DLB 238:

Saltykov-Shchedrin, N.
  See Saltykov, Mikhail Evgrafovich

Samarakis, Andonis
  See Samarakis, Antonis
  See also EWL 3

Samarakis, Antonis 1919-2003 .... **CLC 5**
  See Samarakis, Andonis
  See also CA 25-28R; 16; CAAS 224; CANR
  36

Sanchez, Florencio 1875-1910 .... **TCLC 37**
  See also CA 153; DLB 305; EWL 3; HW 1;
  LAW

Sanchez, Luis Rafael 1936- .... **CLC 23**
  See also CA 128; DLB 305; EWL 3; HW 1;
  WLIT 1

Sanchez, Sonia 1934- .... **BLC 3; CLC 5, 116,
  215; PC 9**
  See also BW 2, 3; CA 33-36R; CANR 24,
  49, 74, 115; CLR 18; CP 2, 3, 4, 5, 6, 7;
  CSW; CWP; DA3; DAM MULT; DLB 41;
  DLBD 8; EWL 3; MAICYA 1, 2; MAL 5;
  MTCW 1, 2; MTFW 2005; SATA 22, 136;
  WP

Sancho, Ignatius 1729-1780 .... **LC 84**

Sand, George 1804-1876 ..... **NCLC 2, 42, 57,
  174; WLC 5**
  See also DA; DA3; DAB; DAC; DAM
  MST, NOV; DLB 119, 192; EW 6; FL 1:3;
  FW; GFL 1789 to the Present; RGWL 2,
  3; TWA

Sandburg, Carl (August) 1878-1967 . **CLC 1,
  4, 10, 15, 35; PC 2, 41; WLC 5**
  See also AAYA 24; AMW; BYA 1, 3; CA
  5-8R; CAAS 25-28R; CANR 35; CDALB
  1865-1917; CLR 67; DA; DA3; DAB;
  DAC; DAM MST, POET; DLB 17, 54,
  284; EWL 3; EXPP; LAIT 2; MAICYA 1,
  2; MAL 5; MTCW 1, 2; MTFW 2005;
  PAB; PFS 3, 6, 12; RGAL 4; SATA 8;
  TUS; WCH; WP; WYA

Sandburg, Charles
  See Sandburg, Carl (August)

Sandburg, Charles A.
  See Sandburg, Carl (August)

Sanders, (James) Ed(ward) 1939- .... **CLC 53**
  See Sanders, Edward
  See also BG 1:3; CA 13-16R; 21; CANR
  13, 44, 78; CP 1, 2, 3, 4, 5, 6, 7; DAM
  POET; DLB 16, 244

Sanders, Edward
  See Sanders, (James) Ed(ward)
  See also DLB 244

Sanders, Lawrence 1920-1998 .... **CLC 41**
  See also BEST 89:4; BPFB 3; CA 81-84;
  CAAS 165; CANR 33, 62; CMW 4;
  CPW; DA3; DAM POP; MTCW 1

Sanders, Noah
  See Blount, Roy (Alton), Jr.

Sanders, Winston P.
  See Anderson, Poul

Sandoz, Mari(e Susette) 1900-1966 .. **CLC 28**
  See also CA 1-4R; CAAS 25-28R; CANR
  17, 64; DLB 9, 212; LAIT 2; MTCW 1,
  2; SATA 5; TCWW 1, 2

Sandys, George 1578-1644 .... **LC 80**
  See also DLB 24, 121

Saner, Reg(inald Anthony) 1931- .... **CLC 9**
  See also CA 65-68; CP 3, 4, 5, 6, 7

Cumulative Author Index

Schnitzler, Arthur 1862-1931 ..... **DC 17; SSC 15, 61; TCLC 4**
See also CAAE 104; CDWLB 2; DLB 81, 118; EW 8; EWL 3; RGSF 2; RGWL 2, 3

Schoenberg, Arnold Franz Walter 1874-1951 .... **TCLC 75**
See also CA 188; CAAE 109

Schonberg, Arnold
See Schoenberg, Arnold Franz Walter

Schopenhauer, Arthur 1788-1860 . **NCLC 51, 157**
See also DLB 90; EW 5

Schor, Sandra (M.) 1932(?)-1990 ..... **CLC 65**
See also CAAS 132

Schorer, Mark 1908-1977 .... **CLC 9**
See also CA 5-8R; CAAS 73-76; CANR 7; CN 1, 2; DLB 103

Schrader, Paul (Joseph) 1946- . **CLC 26, 212**
See also CA 37-40R; CANR 41; DLB 44

Schreber, Daniel 1842-1911 .... **TCLC 123**

Schreiner, Olive (Emilie Albertina) 1855-1920 .... **TCLC 9**
See also AFW; BRWS 2; CA 154; CAAE 105; DLB 18, 156, 190, 225; EWL 3; FW; RGEL 2; TWA; WLIT 2; WWE 1

Schulberg, Budd (Wilson) 1914- .. **CLC 7, 48**
See also BPFB 3; CA 25-28R; CANR 19, 87; CN 1, 2, 3, 4, 5, 6, 7; DLB 6, 26, 28; DLBY 1981, 2001; MAL 5

Schulman, Arnold
See Trumbo, Dalton

Schulz, Bruno 1892-1942 .. **SSC 13; TCLC 5, 51**
See also CA 123; CAAE 115; CANR 86; CDWLB 4; DLB 215; EWL 3; MTCW 2; MTFW 2005; RGSF 2; RGWL 2, 3

Schulz, Charles M. 1922-2000 .... **CLC 12**
See also AAYA 39; CA 9-12R; CAAS 187; CANR 6, 132; INT CANR-6; MTFW 2005; SATA 10; SATA-Obit 118

Schulz, Charles Monroe
See Schulz, Charles M.

Schumacher, E(rnst) F(riedrich) 1911-1977 .... **CLC 80**
See also CA 81-84; CAAS 73-76; CANR 34, 85

Schumann, Robert 1810-1856 ...... **NCLC 143**

Schuyler, George Samuel 1895-1977 . **HR 1:3**
See also BW 2; CA 81-84; CAAS 73-76; CANR 42; DLB 29, 51

Schuyler, James Marcus 1923-1991 .. **CLC 5, 23**
See also CA 101; CAAS 134; CP 1, 2, 3, 4, 5; DAM POET; DLB 5, 169; EWL 3; INT CA-101; MAL 5; WP

Schwartz, Delmore (David) 1913-1966 ... **CLC 2, 4, 10, 45, 87; PC 8**
See also AMWS 2; CA 17-18; CAAS 25-28R; CANR 35; CAP 2; DLB 28, 48; EWL 3; MAL 5; MTCW 1, 2; MTFW 2005; PAB; RGAL 4; TUS

Schwartz, Ernst
See Ozu, Yasujiro

Schwartz, John Burnham 1965- .... **CLC 59**
See also CA 132; CANR 116

Schwartz, Lynne Sharon 1939- .... **CLC 31**
See also CA 103; CANR 44, 89, 160; DLB 218; MTCW 2; MTFW 2005

Schwartz, Muriel A.
See Eliot, T(homas) S(tearns)

Schwarz-Bart, Andre 1928-2006 .... **CLC 2, 4**
See also CA 89-92; CAAS 253; CANR 109; DLB 299; RGHL

Schwarz-Bart, Simone 1938- . **BLCS; CLC 7**
See also BW 2; CA 97-100; CANR 117; EWL 3

Schwerner, Armand 1927-1999 .... **PC 42**
See also CA 9-12R; CAAS 179; CANR 50, 85; CP 2, 3, 4, 5, 6; DLB 165

Schwitters, Kurt (Hermann Edward Karl Julius) 1887-1948 .... **TCLC 95**
See also CA 158

Schwob, Marcel (Mayer Andre) 1867-1905 .... **TCLC 20**
See also CA 168; CAAE 117; DLB 123; GFL 1789 to the Present

Sciascia, Leonardo 1921-1989 .. **CLC 8, 9, 41**
See also CA 85-88; CAAS 130; CANR 35; DLB 177; EWL 3; MTCW 1; RGWL 2, 3

Scoppettone, Sandra 1936- .... **CLC 26**
See Early, Jack
See also AAYA 11, 65; BYA 8; CA 5-8R; CANR 41, 73, 157; GLL 1; MAICYA 2; MAICYAS 1; SATA 9, 92; WYA; YAW

Scorsese, Martin 1942- .... **CLC 20, 89, 207**
See also AAYA 38; CA 114; CAAE 110; CANR 46, 85

Scotland, Jay
See Jakes, John

Scott, Duncan Campbell 1862-1947 .... **TCLC 6**
See also CA 153; CAAE 104; DAC; DLB 92; RGEL 2

Scott, Evelyn 1893-1963 .... **CLC 43**
See also CA 104; CAAS 112; CANR 64; DLB 9, 48; RHW

Scott, F(rancis) R(eginald) 1899-1985 .... **CLC 22**
See also CA 101; CAAS 114; CANR 87; CP 1, 2, 3, 4; DLB 88; INT CA-101; RGEL 2

Scott, Frank
See Scott, F(rancis) R(eginald)

Scott, Joan .... **CLC 65**

Scott, Joanna 1960- .... **CLC 50**
See also CA 126; CANR 53, 92

Scott, Paul (Mark) 1920-1978 ...... **CLC 9, 60**
See also BRWS 1; CA 81-84; CAAS 77-80; CANR 33; CN 1, 2; DLB 14, 207, 326; EWL 3; MTCW 1; RGEL 2; RHW; WWE 1

Scott, Ridley 1937- .... **CLC 183**
See also AAYA 13, 43

Scott, Sarah 1723-1795 .... **LC 44**
See also DLB 39

Scott, Sir Walter 1771-1832 .... **NCLC 15, 69, 110; PC 13; SSC 32; WLC 5**
See also AAYA 22; BRW 4; BYA 2; CD-BLB 1789-1832; DA; DAB; DAC; DAM MST, NOV, POET; DLB 93, 107, 116, 144, 159; GL 3; HGG; LAIT 1; RGEL 2; RGSF 2; SSFS 10; SUFW 1; TEA; WLIT 3; YABC 2

Scribe, (Augustin) Eugene 1791-1861 . **DC 5; NCLC 16**
See also DAM DRAM; DLB 192; GFL 1789 to the Present; RGWL 2, 3

Scrum, R.
See Crumb, R.

Scudery, Georges de 1601-1667 .... **LC 75**
See also GFL Beginnings to 1789

Scudery, Madeleine de 1607-1701 .. **LC 2, 58**
See also DLB 268; GFL Beginnings to 1789

Scum
See Crumb, R.

Scumbag, Little Bobby
See Crumb, R.

Seabrook, John
See Hubbard, L. Ron

Seacole, Mary Jane Grant 1805-1881 .... **NCLC 147**
See also DLB 166

Sealy, I(rwin) Allan 1951- .... **CLC 55**
See also CA 136; CN 6, 7

Search, Alexander
See Pessoa, Fernando (Antonio Nogueira)

Sebald, W(infried) G(eorg) 1944-2001 .... **CLC 194**
See also BRWS 8; CA 159; CAAS 202; CANR 98; MTFW 2005; RGHL

Sebastian, Lee
See Silverberg, Robert

Sebastian Owl
See Thompson, Hunter S.

Sebestyen, Igen
See Sebestyen, Ouida

Sebestyen, Ouida 1924- .... **CLC 30**
See also AAYA 8; BYA 7; CA 107; CANR 40, 114; CLR 17; JRDA; MAICYA 1, 2; SAAS 10; SATA 39, 140; WYA; YAW

Sebold, Alice 1963(?)- .... **CLC 193**
See also AAYA 56; CA 203; MTFW 2005

Second Duke of Buckingham
See Villiers, George

Secundus, H. Scriblerus
See Fielding, Henry

Sedges, John
See Buck, Pearl S(ydenstricker)

Sedgwick, Catharine Maria 1789-1867 .... **NCLC 19, 98**
See also DLB 1, 74, 183, 239, 243, 254; FL 1:3; RGAL 4

Sedulius Scottus 9th cent. -c. 874 .. **CMLC 86**

Seelye, John (Douglas) 1931- .... **CLC 7**
See also CA 97-100; CANR 70; INT CA-97-100; TCWW 1, 2

Seferiades, Giorgos Stylianou 1900-1971
See Seferis, George
See also CA 5-8R; CAAS 33-36R; CANR 5, 36; MTCW 1

Seferis, George .... **CLC 5, 11; PC 66**
See Seferiades, Giorgos Stylianou
See also DLB 332; EW 12; EWL 3; RGWL 2, 3

Segal, Erich (Wolf) 1937- .... **CLC 3, 10**
See also BEST 89:1; BPFB 3; CA 25-28R; CANR 20, 36, 65, 113; CPW; DAM POP; DLBY 1986; INT CANR-20; MTCW 1

Seger, Bob 1945- .... **CLC 35**

Seghers, Anna .... **CLC 7**
See Radvanyi, Netty
See also CDWLB 2; DLB 69; EWL 3

Seidel, Frederick (Lewis) 1936- .... **CLC 18**
See also CA 13-16R; CANR 8, 99; CP 1, 2, 3, 4, 5, 6, 7; DLBY 1984

Seifert, Jaroslav 1901-1986 . **CLC 34, 44, 93; PC 47**
See also CA 127; CDWLB 4; DLB 215, 332; EWL 3; MTCW 1, 2

Sei Shonagon c. 966-1017(?) ..... **CMLC 6, 89**

Sejour, Victor 1817-1874 .... **DC 10**
See also DLB 50

Sejour Marcou et Ferrand, Juan Victor
See Sejour, Victor

Selby, Hubert, Jr. 1928-2004 ..... **CLC 1, 2, 4, 8; SSC 20**
See also CA 13-16R; CAAS 226; CANR 33, 85; CN 1, 2, 3, 4, 5, 6, 7; DLB 2, 227; MAL 5

Selzer, Richard 1928- .... **CLC 74**
See also CA 65-68; CANR 14, 106

Sembene, Ousmane
See Ousmane, Sembene
See also AFW; EWL 3; WLIT 2

Senancour, Etienne Pivert de 1770-1846 .... **NCLC 16**
See also DLB 119; GFL 1789 to the Present

Sender, Ramon (Jose) 1902-1982 ...... **CLC 8; HLC 2; TCLC 136**
See also CA 5-8R; CAAS 105; CANR 8; DAM MULT; DLB 322; EWL 3; HW 1; MTCW 1; RGWL 2, 3

Shepard, James R.
See Shepard, Jim

Shepard, Jim 1956- .... **CLC 36**
See also AAYA 73; CA 137; CANR 59, 104, 160; SATA 90, 164

Shepard, Lucius 1947- .... **CLC 34**
See also CA 141; CAAE 128; CANR 81, 124; HGG; SCFW 2; SFW 4; SUFW 2

Shepard, Sam 1943- .... **CLC 4, 6, 17, 34, 41, 44, 169; DC 5**
See also AAYA 1, 58; AMWS 3; CA 69-72; CABS 3; CAD; CANR 22, 120, 140; CD 5, 6; DA3; DAM DRAM; DFS 3, 6, 7, 14; DLB 7, 212; EWL 3; IDFW 3, 4; MAL 5; MTCW 1, 2; MTFW 2005; RGAL 4

Shepherd, Jean (Parker)
1921-1999 .... **TCLC 177**
See also AAYA 69; AITN 2; CA 77-80; CAAS 187

Shepherd, Michael
See Ludlum, Robert

Sherburne, Zoa (Lillian Morin)
1912-1995 .... **CLC 30**
See also AAYA 13; CA 1-4R; CAAS 176; CANR 3, 37; MAICYA 1, 2; SAAS 18; SATA 3; YAW

Sheridan, Frances 1724-1766 .... **LC 7**
See also DLB 39, 84

Sheridan, Richard Brinsley
1751-1816 . **DC 1; NCLC 5, 91; WLC 5**
See also BRW 3; CDBLB 1660-1789; DA; DAB; DAC; DAM DRAM, MST; DFS 15; DLB 89; WLIT 3

Sherman, Jonathan Marc 1968- .... **CLC 55**
See also CA 230

Sherman, Martin 1941(?)- .... **CLC 19**
See also CA 123; CAAE 116; CAD; CANR 86; CD 5, 6; DFS 20; DLB 228; GLL 1; IDTP; RGHL

Sherwin, Judith Johnson
See Johnson, Judith (Emlyn)
See also CANR 85; CP 2, 3, 4, 5; CWP

Sherwood, Frances 1940- .... **CLC 81**
See also CA 220; 146, 220; CANR 158

Sherwood, Robert E(mmet)
1896-1955 .... **TCLC 3**
See also CA 153; CAAE 104; CANR 86; DAM DRAM; DFS 11, 15, 17; DLB 7, 26, 249; IDFW 3, 4; MAL 5; RGAL 4

Shestov, Lev 1866-1938 .... **TCLC 56**

Shevchenko, Taras 1814-1861 .... **NCLC 54**

Shiel, M(atthew) P(hipps)
1865-1947 .... **TCLC 8**
See Holmes, Gordon
See also CA 160; CAAE 106; DLB 153; HGG; MTCW 2; MTFW 2005; SCFW 1, 2; SFW 4; SUFW

Shields, Carol 1935-2003 .. **CLC 91, 113, 193**
See also AMWS 7; CA 81-84; CAAS 218; CANR 51, 74, 98, 133; CCA 1; CN 6, 7; CPW; DA3; DAC; DLB 334; MTCW 2; MTFW 2005; NFS 23

Shields, David 1956- .... **CLC 97**
See also CA 124; CANR 48, 99, 112, 157

Shields, David Jonathan
See Shields, David

Shiga, Naoya 1883-1971 .... **CLC 33; SSC 23; TCLC 172**
See Shiga Naoya
See also CA 101; CAAS 33-36R; MJW; RGWL 3

Shiga Naoya
See Shiga, Naoya
See also DLB 180; EWL 3; RGWL 3

Shilts, Randy 1951-1994 .... **CLC 85**
See also AAYA 19; CA 127; CAAE 115; CAAS 144; CANR 45; DA3; GLL 1; INT CA-127; MTCW 2; MTFW 2005

Shimazaki, Haruki 1872-1943
See Shimazaki Toson
See also CA 134; CAAE 105; CANR 84; RGWL 3

Shimazaki Toson .... **TCLC 5**
See Shimazaki, Haruki
See also DLB 180; EWL 3

Shirley, James 1596-1666 .... **DC 25; LC 96**
See also DLB 58; RGEL 2

Shirley Hastings, Selina
See Hastings, Selina

Sholokhov, Mikhail (Aleksandrovich)
1905-1984 .... **CLC 7, 15**
See also CA 101; CAAS 112; DLB 272, 332; EWL 3; MTCW 1, 2; MTFW 2005; RGWL 2, 3; SATA-Obit 36

Sholom Aleichem 1859-1916 .... **SSC 33; TCLC 1, 35**
See Rabinovitch, Sholem
See also DLB 333; TWA

Shone, Patric
See Hanley, James

Showalter, Elaine 1941- .... **CLC 169**
See also CA 57-60; CANR 58, 106; DLB 67; FW; GLL 2

Shreve, Susan
See Shreve, Susan Richards

Shreve, Susan Richards 1939- .... **CLC 23**
See also CA 49-52; 5; CANR 5, 38, 69, 100, 159; MAICYA 1, 2; SATA 46, 95, 152; SATA-Brief 41

Shue, Larry 1946-1985 .... **CLC 52**
See also CA 145; CAAS 117; DAM DRAM; DFS 7

Shu-Jen, Chou 1881-1936
See Lu Hsun
See also CAAE 104

Shulman, Alix Kates 1932- .... **CLC 2, 10**
See also CA 29-32R; CANR 43; FW; SATA 7

Shuster, Joe 1914-1992 .... **CLC 21**
See also AAYA 50

Shute, Nevil .... **CLC 30**
See Norway, Nevil Shute
See also BPFB 3; DLB 255; NFS 9; RHW; SFW 4

Shuttle, Penelope (Diane) 1947- .... **CLC 7**
See also CA 93-96; CANR 39, 84, 92, 108; CP 3, 4, 5, 6, 7; CWP; DLB 14, 40

Shvarts, Elena 1948- .... **PC 50**
See also CA 147

Sidhwa, Bapsi 1939-
See Sidhwa, Bapsy (N.)
See also CN 6, 7; DLB 323

Sidhwa, Bapsy (N.) 1938- .... **CLC 168**
See Sidhwa, Bapsi
See also CA 108; CANR 25, 57; FW

Sidney, Mary 1561-1621 .... **LC 19, 39**
See Sidney Herbert, Mary

Sidney, Sir Philip 1554-1586 .... **LC 19, 39, 131; PC 32**
See also BRW 1; BRWR 2; CDBLB Before 1660; DA; DA3; DAB; DAC; DAM MST, POET; DLB 167; EXPP; PAB; RGEL 2; TEA; WP

Sidney Herbert, Mary
See Sidney, Mary
See also DLB 167

Siegel, Jerome 1914-1996 .... **CLC 21**
See Siegel, Jerry
See also CA 169; CAAE 116; CAAS 151

Siegel, Jerry
See Siegel, Jerome
See also AAYA 50

Sienkiewicz, Henryk (Adam Alexander Pius)
1846-1916 .... **TCLC 3**
See also CA 134; CAAE 104; CANR 84; DLB 332; EWL 3; RGSF 2; RGWL 2, 3

Sierra, Gregorio Martinez
See Martinez Sierra, Gregorio

Sierra, Maria de la O'LeJarraga Martinez
See Martinez Sierra, Maria

Sigal, Clancy 1926- .... **CLC 7**
See also CA 1-4R; CANR 85; CN 1, 2, 3, 4, 5, 6, 7

Siger of Brabant 1240(?)-1284(?) . **CMLC 69**
See also DLB 115

Sigourney, Lydia H.
See Sigourney, Lydia Howard (Huntley)
See also DLB 73, 183

Sigourney, Lydia Howard (Huntley)
1791-1865 .... **NCLC 21, 87**
See Sigourney, Lydia H.; Sigourney, Lydia Huntley
See also DLB 1

Sigourney, Lydia Huntley
See Sigourney, Lydia Howard (Huntley)
See also DLB 42, 239, 243

Siguenza y Gongora, Carlos de
1645-1700 .... **HLCS 2; LC 8**
See also LAW

Sigurjonsson, Johann
See Sigurjonsson, Johann

Sigurjonsson, Johann 1880-1919 ... **TCLC 27**
See also CA 170; DLB 293; EWL 3

Sikelianos, Angelos 1884-1951 .... **PC 29; TCLC 39**
See also EWL 3; RGWL 2, 3

Silkin, Jon 1930-1997 .... **CLC 2, 6, 43**
See also CA 5-8R; 5; CANR 89; CP 1, 2, 3, 4, 5, 6; DLB 27

Silko, Leslie 1948- ...... **CLC 23, 74, 114, 211; NNAL; SSC 37, 66; WLCS**
See also AAYA 14; AMWS 4; ANW; BYA 12; CA 122; CAAE 115; CANR 45, 65, 118; CN 4, 5, 6, 7; CP 4, 5, 6, 7; CPW 1; CWP; DA; DA3; DAC; DAM MST, MULT, POP; DLB 143, 175, 256, 275; EWL 3; EXPP; EXPS; LAIT 4; MAL 5; MTCW 2; MTFW 2005; NFS 4; PFS 9, 16; RGAL 4; RGSF 2; SSFS 4, 8, 10, 11; TCWW 1, 2

Sillanpaa, Frans Eemil 1888-1964 ... **CLC 19**
See also CA 129; CAAS 93-96; DLB 332; EWL 3; MTCW 1

Sillitoe, Alan 1928- .. **CLC 1, 3, 6, 10, 19, 57, 148**
See also AITN 1; BRWS 5; CA 191; 9-12R, 191; 2; CANR 8, 26, 55, 139; CDBLB 1960 to Present; CN 1, 2, 3, 4, 5, 6; CP 1, 2, 3, 4, 5; DLB 14, 139; EWL 3; MTCW 1, 2; MTFW 2005; RGEL 2; RGSF 2; SATA 61

Silone, Ignazio 1900-1978 .... **CLC 4**
See also CA 25-28; CAAS 81-84; CANR 34; CAP 2; DLB 264; EW 12; EWL 3; MTCW 1; RGSF 2; RGWL 2, 3

Silone, Ignazione
See Silone, Ignazio

Silver, Joan Micklin 1935- .... **CLC 20**
See also CA 121; CAAE 114; INT CA-121

Silver, Nicholas
See Faust, Frederick (Schiller)

Silverberg, Robert 1935- .... **CLC 7, 140**
See also AAYA 24; BPFB 3; BYA 7, 9; CA 186; 1-4R, 186; 3; CANR 1, 20, 36, 85, 140; CLR 59; CN 6, 7; CPW; DAM POP; DLB 8; INT CANR-20; MAICYA 1, 2; MTCW 1, 2; MTFW 2005; SATA 13, 91; SATA-Essay 104; SCFW 1, 2; SFW 4; SUFW 2

Silverstein, Alvin 1933- .... **CLC 17**
See also CA 49-52; CANR 2; CLR 25; JRDA; MAICYA 1, 2; SATA 8, 69, 124

Smart, Elizabeth 1913-1986 .... **CLC 54**
    See also CA 81-84; CAAS 118; CN 4; DLB 88

Smiley, Jane 1949- ...... **CLC 53, 76, 144, 236**
    See also AAYA 66; AMWS 6; BPFB 3; CA 104; CANR 30, 50, 74, 96, 158; CN 6, 7; CPW 1; DA3; DAM POP; DLB 227, 234; EWL 3; INT CANR-30; MAL 5; MTFW 2005; SSFS 19

Smiley, Jane Graves
    See Smiley, Jane

Smith, A(rthur) J(ames) M(arshall)
    1902-1980 .... **CLC 15**
    See also CA 1-4R; CAAS 102; CANR 4; CP 1, 2, 3; DAC; DLB 88; RGEL 2

Smith, Adam 1723(?)-1790 .... **LC 36**
    See also DLB 104, 252, 336; RGEL 2

Smith, Alexander 1829-1867 .... **NCLC 59**
    See also DLB 32, 55

Smith, Anna Deavere 1950- .... **CLC 86**
    See also CA 133; CANR 103; CD 5, 6; DFS 2, 22

Smith, Betty (Wehner) 1904-1972 .... **CLC 19**
    See also AAYA 72; BPFB 3; BYA 3; CA 5-8R; CAAS 33-36R; DLBY 1982; LAIT 3; RGAL 4; SATA 6

Smith, Charlotte (Turner)
    1749-1806 .... **NCLC 23, 115**
    See also DLB 39, 109; RGEL 2; TEA

Smith, Clark Ashton 1893-1961 .... **CLC 43**
    See also CA 143; CANR 81; FANT; HGG; MTCW 2; SCFW 1, 2; SFW 4; SUFW

Smith, Dave .... **CLC 22, 42**
    See Smith, David (Jeddie)
    See also CA 7; CP 3, 4, 5, 6, 7; DLB 5

Smith, David (Jeddie) 1942-
    See Smith, Dave
    See also CA 49-52; CANR 1, 59, 120; CSW; DAM POET

Smith, Iain Crichton 1928-1998 .... **CLC 64**
    See also BRWS 9; CA 21-24R; CAAS 171; CN 1, 2, 3, 4, 5, 6; CP 1, 2, 3, 4, 5, 6; DLB 40, 139, 319; RGSF 2

Smith, John 1580(?)-1631 .... **LC 9**
    See also DLB 24, 30; TUS

Smith, Johnston
    See Crane, Stephen (Townley)

Smith, Joseph, Jr. 1805-1844 .... **NCLC 53**

Smith, Kevin 1970- .... **CLC 223**
    See also AAYA 37; CA 166; CANR 131

Smith, Lee 1944- .... **CLC 25, 73**
    See also CA 119; CAAE 114; CANR 46, 118; CN 7; CSW; DLB 143; DLBY 1983; EWL 3; INT CA-119; RGAL 4

Smith, Martin
    See Smith, Martin Cruz

Smith, Martin Cruz 1942- .. **CLC 25; NNAL**
    See also BEST 89:4; BPFB 3; CA 85-88; CANR 6, 23, 43, 65, 119; CMW 4; CPW; DAM MULT, POP; HGG; INT CANR-23; MTCW 2; MTFW 2005; RGAL 4

Smith, Patti 1946- .... **CLC 12**
    See also CA 93-96; CANR 63

Smith, Pauline (Urmson)
    1882-1959 .... **TCLC 25**
    See also DLB 225; EWL 3

Smith, Rosamond
    See Oates, Joyce Carol

Smith, Sheila Kaye
    See Kaye-Smith, Sheila

Smith, Stevie 1902-1971 .... **CLC 3, 8, 25, 44; PC 12**
    See also BRWS 2; CA 17-18; CAAS 29-32R; CANR 35; CAP 2; CP 1; DAM POET; DLB 20; EWL 3; MTCW 1, 2; PAB; PFS 3; RGEL 2; TEA

Smith, Wilbur 1933- .... **CLC 33**
    See also CA 13-16R; CANR 7, 46, 66, 134; CPW; MTCW 1, 2; MTFW 2005

Smith, William Jay 1918- .... **CLC 6**
    See also AMWS 13; CA 5-8R; CANR 44, 106; CP 1, 2, 3, 4, 5, 6, 7; CSW; CWRI 5; DLB 5; MAICYA 1, 2; SAAS 22; SATA 2, 68, 154; SATA-Essay 154; TCLE 1:2

Smith, Woodrow Wilson
    See Kuttner, Henry

Smith, Zadie 1975- .... **CLC 158**
    See also AAYA 50; CA 193; MTFW 2005

Smolenskin, Peretz 1842-1885 .... **NCLC 30**

Smollett, Tobias (George) 1721-1771 ... **LC 2, 46**
    See also BRW 3; CDBLB 1660-1789; DLB 39, 104; RGEL 2; TEA

Snodgrass, W.D. 1926- .... **CLC 2, 6, 10, 18, 68; PC 74**
    See also AMWS 6; CA 1-4R; CANR 6, 36, 65, 85; CP 1, 2, 3, 4, 5, 6; DAM POET; DLB 5; MAL 5; MTCW 1, 2; MTFW 2005; RGAL 4; TCLE 1:2

Snorri Sturluson 1179-1241 .... **CMLC 56**
    See also RGWL 2, 3

Snow, C(harles) P(ercy) 1905-1980 ... **CLC 1, 4, 6, 9, 13, 19**
    See also BRW 7; CA 5-8R; CAAS 101; CANR 28; CDBLB 1945-1960; CN 1, 2; DAM NOV; DLB 15, 77; DLBD 17; EWL 3; MTCW 1, 2; MTFW 2005; RGEL 2; TEA

Snow, Frances Compton
    See Adams, Henry (Brooks)

Snyder, Gary 1930- . **CLC 1, 2, 5, 9, 32, 120; PC 21**
    See also AAYA 72; AMWS 8; ANW; BG 1:3; CA 17-20R; CANR 30, 60, 125; CP 1, 2, 3, 4, 5, 6, 7; DA3; DAM POET; DLB 5, 16, 165, 212, 237, 275; EWL 3; MAL 5; MTCW 2; MTFW 2005; PFS 9, 19; RGAL 4; WP

Snyder, Zilpha Keatley 1927- .... **CLC 17**
    See also AAYA 15; BYA 1; CA 252; 9-12R, 252; CANR 38; CLR 31, 121; JRDA; MAICYA 1, 2; SAAS 2; SATA 1, 28, 75, 110, 163; SATA-Essay 112, 163; YAW

Soares, Bernardo
    See Pessoa, Fernando (Antonio Nogueira)

Sobh, A.
    See Shamlu, Ahmad

Sobh, Alef
    See Shamlu, Ahmad

Sobol, Joshua 1939- .... **CLC 60**
    See Sobol, Yehoshua
    See also CA 200; RGHL

Sobol, Yehoshua 1939-
    See Sobol, Joshua
    See also CWW 2

Socrates 470B.C.-399B.C. .... **CMLC 27**

Soderberg, Hjalmar 1869-1941 ...... **TCLC 39**
    See also DLB 259; EWL 3; RGSF 2

Soderbergh, Steven 1963- .... **CLC 154**
    See also AAYA 43; CA 243

Soderbergh, Steven Andrew
    See Soderbergh, Steven

Sodergran, Edith (Irene) 1892-1923
    See Soedergran, Edith (Irene)
    See also CA 202; DLB 259; EW 11; EWL 3; RGWL 2, 3

Soedergran, Edith (Irene)
    1892-1923 .... **TCLC 31**
    See Sodergran, Edith (Irene)

Softly, Edgar
    See Lovecraft, H. P.

Softly, Edward
    See Lovecraft, H. P.

Sokolov, Alexander V(sevolodovich) 1943-
    See Sokolov, Sasha
    See also CA 73-76

Sokolov, Raymond 1941- .... **CLC 7**
    See also CA 85-88

Sokolov, Sasha .... **CLC 59**
    See Sokolov, Alexander V(sevolodovich)
    See also CWW 2; DLB 285; EWL 3; RGWL 2, 3

Solo, Jay
    See Ellison, Harlan

Sologub, Fyodor .... **TCLC 9**
    See Teternikov, Fyodor Kuzmich
    See also EWL 3

Solomons, Ikey Esquir
    See Thackeray, William Makepeace

Solomos, Dionysios 1798-1857 .... **NCLC 15**

Solwoska, Mara
    See French, Marilyn

Solzhenitsyn, Aleksandr I. 1918- .. **CLC 1, 2, 4, 7, 9, 10, 18, 26, 34, 78, 134, 235; SSC 32; WLC 5**
    See Solzhenitsyn, Aleksandr Isayevich
    See also AAYA 49; AITN 1; BPFB 3; CA 69-72; CANR 40, 65, 116; DA; DA3; DAB; DAC; DAM MST, NOV; DLB 302, 332; EW 13; EXPS; LAIT 4; MTCW 1, 2; MTFW 2005; NFS 6; RGSF 2; RGWL 2, 3; SSFS 9; TWA

Solzhenitsyn, Aleksandr Isayevich
    See Solzhenitsyn, Aleksandr I.
    See also CWW 2; EWL 3

Somers, Jane
    See Lessing, Doris

Somerville, Edith Oenone
    1858-1949 .... **SSC 56; TCLC 51**
    See also CA 196; DLB 135; RGEL 2; RGSF 2

Somerville & Ross
    See Martin, Violet Florence; Somerville, Edith Oenone

Sommer, Scott 1951- .... **CLC 25**
    See also CA 106

Sommers, Christina Hoff 1950- ...... **CLC 197**
    See also CA 153; CANR 95

Sondheim, Stephen (Joshua) 1930- . **CLC 30, 39, 147; DC 22**
    See also AAYA 11, 66; CA 103; CANR 47, 67, 125; DAM DRAM; LAIT 4

Sone, Monica 1919- .... **AAL**
    See also DLB 312

Song, Cathy 1955- .... **AAL; PC 21**
    See also CA 154; CANR 118; CWP; DLB 169, 312; EXPP; FW; PFS 5

Sontag, Susan 1933-2004 ... **CLC 1, 2, 10, 13, 31, 105, 195**
    See also AMWS 3; CA 17-20R; CAAS 234; CANR 25, 51, 74, 97; CN 1, 2, 3, 4, 5, 6, 7; CPW; DA3; DAM POP; DLB 2, 67; EWL 3; MAL 5; MBL; MTCW 1, 2; MTFW 2005; RGAL 4; RHW; SSFS 10

Sophocles 496(?)B.C.-406(?)B.C. .... **CMLC 2, 47, 51, 86; DC 1; WLCS**
    See also AW 1; CDWLB 1; DA; DA3; DAB; DAC; DAM DRAM, MST; DFS 1, 4, 8, 24; DLB 176; LAIT 1; LATS 1:1; LMFS 1; RGWL 2, 3; TWA; WLIT 8

Sordello 1189-1269 .... **CMLC 15**

Sorel, Georges 1847-1922 .... **TCLC 91**
    See also CA 188; CAAE 118

Sorel, Julia
    See Drexler, Rosalyn

Sorokin, Vladimir .... **CLC 59**
    See Sorokin, Vladimir Georgievich
    See also CA 258

Sorokin, Vladimir Georgievich
    See Sorokin, Vladimir
    See also DLB 285

Starbuck, George (Edwin)
1931-1996 .... **CLC 53**
See also CA 21-24R; CAAS 153; CANR
23; CP 1, 2, 3, 4, 5, 6; DAM POET

Stark, Richard
See Westlake, Donald E.

Statius c. 45-c. 96 .... **CMLC 91**
See also AW 2; DLB 211

Staunton, Schuyler
See Baum, L(yman) Frank

Stead, Christina (Ellen) 1902-1983 ... **CLC 2, 5, 8, 32, 80**
See also BRWS 4; CA 13-16R; CAAS 109;
CANR 33, 40; CN 1, 2, 3; DLB 260;
EWL 3; FW; MTCW 1, 2; MTFW 2005;
RGEL 2; RGSF 2; WWE 1

Stead, William Thomas
1849-1912 .... **TCLC 48**
See also CA 167

Stebnitsky, M.
See Leskov, Nikolai (Semyonovich)

Steele, Richard 1672-1729 .... **LC 18**
See also BRW 3; CDBLB 1660-1789; DLB
84, 101; RGEL 2; WLIT 3

Steele, Timothy (Reid) 1948- .... **CLC 45**
See also CA 93-96; CANR 16, 50, 92; CP
5, 6, 7; DLB 120, 282

Steffens, (Joseph) Lincoln
1866-1936 .... **TCLC 20**
See also CA 198; CAAE 117; DLB 303;
MAL 5

Stegner, Wallace (Earle) 1909-1993 .. **CLC 9, 49, 81; SSC 27**
See also AITN 1; AMWS 4; ANW; BEST
90:3; BPFB 3; CA 1-4R; 9; CAAS 141;
CANR 1, 21, 46; CN 1, 2, 3, 4, 5; DAM
NOV; DLB 9, 206, 275; DLBY 1993;
EWL 3; MAL 5; MTCW 1, 2; MTFW
2005; RGAL 4; TCWW 1, 2; TUS

Stein, Gertrude 1874-1946 .... **DC 19; PC 18; SSC 42; TCLC 1, 6, 28, 48; WLC 5**
See also AAYA 64; AMW; AMWC 2; CA
132; CAAE 104; CANR 108; CDALB
1917-1929; DA; DA3; DAB; DAC; DAM
MST, NOV, POET; DLB 4, 54, 86, 228;
DLBD 15; EWL 3; EXPS; FL 1:6; GLL
1; MAL 5; MBL; MTCW 1, 2; MTFW
2005; NCFS 4; RGAL 4; RGSF 2; SSFS
5; TUS; WP

Steinbeck, John (Ernst) 1902-1968 ... **CLC 1, 5, 9, 13, 21, 34, 45, 75, 124; SSC 11, 37, 77; TCLC 135; WLC 5**
See also AAYA 12; AMW; BPFB 3; BYA 2,
3; CA 1-4R; CAAS 25-28R; CANR 1,
35; CDALB 1929-1941; DA; DA3; DAB;
DAC; DAM DRAM, MST, NOV; DLB 7,
9, 212, 275, 309, 332; DLBD 2; EWL 3;
EXPS; LAIT 3; MAL 5; MTCW 1, 2;
MTFW 2005; NFS 1, 5, 7, 17, 19; RGAL
4; RGSF 2; RHW; SATA 9; SSFS 3, 6,
22; TCWW 1, 2; TUS; WYA; YAW

Steinem, Gloria 1934- .... **CLC 63**
See also CA 53-56; CANR 28, 51, 139;
DLB 246; FL 1:1; FW; MTCW 1, 2;
MTFW 2005

Steiner, George 1929- .... **CLC 24, 221**
See also CA 73-76; CANR 31, 67, 108;
DAM NOV; DLB 67, 299; EWL 3;
MTCW 1, 2; MTFW 2005; RGHL; SATA
62

Steiner, K. Leslie
See Delany, Samuel R., Jr.

Steiner, Rudolf 1861-1925 .... **TCLC 13**
See also CAAE 107

Stendhal 1783-1842 .... **NCLC 23, 46, 178; SSC 27; WLC 5**
See also DA; DA3; DAB; DAC; DAM
MST, NOV; DLB 119; EW 5; GFL 1789
to the Present; RGWL 2, 3; TWA

Stephen, Adeline Virginia
See Woolf, (Adeline) Virginia

Stephen, Sir Leslie 1832-1904 .... **TCLC 23**
See also BRW 5; CAAE 123; DLB 57, 144,
190

Stephen, Sir Leslie
See Stephen, Sir Leslie

Stephen, Virginia
See Woolf, (Adeline) Virginia

Stephens, James 1882(?)-1950 .... **SSC 50; TCLC 4**
See also CA 192; CAAE 104; DLB 19, 153,
162; EWL 3; FANT; RGEL 2; SUFW

Stephens, Reed
See Donaldson, Stephen R(eeder)

Stephenson, Neal 1959- .... **CLC 220**
See also AAYA 38; CA 122; CANR 88, 138;
CN 7; MTFW 2005; SFW 4

Steptoe, Lydia
See Barnes, Djuna
See also GLL 1

Sterchi, Beat 1949- .... **CLC 65**
See also CA 203

Sterling, Brett
See Bradbury, Ray; Hamilton, Edmond

Sterling, Bruce 1954- .... **CLC 72**
See also CA 119; CANR 44, 135; CN 7;
MTFW 2005; SCFW 2; SFW 4

Sterling, George 1869-1926 .... **TCLC 20**
See also CA 165; CAAE 117; DLB 54

Stern, Gerald 1925- .... **CLC 40, 100**
See also AMWS 9; CA 81-84; CANR 28,
94; CP 3, 4, 5, 6, 7; DLB 105; RGAL 4

Stern, Richard (Gustave) 1928- ... **CLC 4, 39**
See also CA 1-4R; CANR 1, 25, 52, 120;
CN 1, 2, 3, 4, 5, 6, 7; DLB 218; DLBY
1987; INT CANR-25

Sternberg, Josef von 1894-1969 .... **CLC 20**
See also CA 81-84

Sterne, Laurence 1713-1768 .... **LC 2, 48; WLC 5**
See also BRW 3; BRWC 1; CDBLB 1660-
1789; DA; DAB; DAC; DAM MST, NOV;
DLB 39; RGEL 2; TEA

Sternheim, (William Adolf) Carl
1878-1942 .... **TCLC 8**
See also CA 193; CAAE 105; DLB 56, 118;
EWL 3; IDTP; RGWL 2, 3

Stevens, Margaret Dean
See Aldrich, Bess Streeter

Stevens, Mark 1951- .... **CLC 34**
See also CA 122

Stevens, Wallace 1879-1955 . **PC 6; TCLC 3, 12, 45; WLC 5**
See also AMW; AMWR 1; CA 124; CAAE
104; CDALB 1929-1941; DA; DA3;
DAB; DAC; DAM MST, POET; DLB 54;
EWL 3; EXPP; MAL 5; MTCW 1, 2;
PAB; PFS 13, 16; RGAL 4; TUS; WP

Stevenson, Anne (Katharine) 1933- .. **CLC 7, 33**
See also BRWS 6; CA 17-20R; 9; CANR 9,
33, 123; CP 3, 4, 5, 6, 7; CWP; DLB 40;
MTCW 1; RHW

Stevenson, Robert Louis (Balfour)
1850-1894 ...... **NCLC 5, 14, 63; SSC 11, 51; WLC 5**
See also AAYA 24; BPFB 3; BRW 5;
BRWC 1; BRWR 1; BYA 1, 2, 4, 13; CD-
BLB 1890-1914; CLR 10, 11, 107; DA;
DA3; DAB; DAC; DAM MST, NOV;
DLB 18, 57, 141, 156, 174; DLBD 13;
GL 3; HGG; JRDA; LAIT 1, 3; MAICYA
1, 2; NFS 11, 20; RGEL 2; RGSF 2;
SATA 100; SUFW; TEA; WCH; WLIT 4;
WYA; YABC 2; YAW

Stewart, J(ohn) I(nnes) M(ackintosh)
1906-1994 .... **CLC 7, 14, 32**
See Innes, Michael
See also CA 85-88; 3; CAAS 147; CANR
47; CMW 4; CN 1, 2, 3, 4, 5; MTCW 1,
2

Stewart, Mary (Florence Elinor)
1916- .... **CLC 7, 35, 117**
See also AAYA 29, 73; BPFB 3; CA 1-4R;
CANR 1, 59, 130; CMW 4; CPW; DAB;
FANT; RHW; SATA 12; YAW

Stewart, Mary Rainbow
See Stewart, Mary (Florence Elinor)

Stifle, June
See Campbell, Maria

Stifter, Adalbert 1805-1868 .. **NCLC 41; SSC 28**
See also CDWLB 2; DLB 133; RGSF 2;
RGWL 2, 3

Still, James 1906-2001 .... **CLC 49**
See also CA 65-68; 17; CAAS 195; CANR
10, 26; CSW; DLB 9; DLBY 01; SATA
29; SATA-Obit 127

Sting 1951-
See Sumner, Gordon Matthew
See also CA 167

Stirling, Arthur
See Sinclair, Upton

Stitt, Milan 1941- .... **CLC 29**
See also CA 69-72

Stockton, Francis Richard 1834-1902
See Stockton, Frank R.
See also AAYA 68; CA 137; CAAE 108;
MAICYA 1, 2; SATA 44; SFW 4

Stockton, Frank R. .... **TCLC 47**
See Stockton, Francis Richard
See also BYA 4, 13; DLB 42, 74; DLBD
13; EXPS; SATA-Brief 32; SSFS 3;
SUFW; WCH

Stoddard, Charles
See Kuttner, Henry

Stoker, Abraham 1847-1912
See Stoker, Bram
See also CA 150; CAAE 105; DA; DA3;
DAC; DAM MST, NOV; HGG; MTFW
2005; SATA 29

Stoker, Bram . **SSC 62; TCLC 8, 144; WLC 6**
See Stoker, Abraham
See also AAYA 23; BPFB 3; BRWS 3; BYA
5; CDBLB 1890-1914; DAB; DLB 304;
GL 3; LATS 1:1; NFS 18; RGEL 2;
SUFW; TEA; WLIT 4

Stolz, Mary 1920-2006 .... **CLC 12**
See also AAYA 8, 73; AITN 1; CA 5-8R;
CAAS 255; CANR 13, 41, 112; JRDA;
MAICYA 1, 2; SAAS 3; SATA 10, 71,
133; YAW

Stolz, Mary Slattery
See Stolz, Mary

Stone, Irving 1903-1989 .... **CLC 7**
See also AITN 1; BPFB 3; CA 1-4R; 3;
CAAS 129; CANR 1, 23; CN 1, 2, 3, 4;
CPW; DA3; DAM POP; INT CANR-23;
MTCW 1, 2; MTFW 2005; RHW; SATA
3; SATA-Obit 64

Stone, Oliver 1946- .... **CLC 73**
See also AAYA 15, 64; CA 110; CANR 55,
125

Stone, Oliver William
See Stone, Oliver

Stone, Robert 1937- .... **CLC 5, 23, 42, 175**
See also AMWS 5; BPFB 3; CA 85-88;
CANR 23, 66, 95; CN 4, 5, 6, 7; DLB
152; EWL 3; INT CANR-23; MAL 5;
MTCW 1; MTFW 2005

Stone, Ruth 1915- .... **PC 53**
See also CA 45-48; CANR 2, 91; CP 5, 6,
7; CSW; DLB 105; PFS 19

Suso, Heinrich c. 1295-1366 .... **CMLC 87**
Sutcliff, Rosemary 1920-1992 .... **CLC 26**
　See also AAYA 10; BYA 1, 4; CA 5-8R;
　CAAS 139; CANR 37; CLR 1, 37; CPW;
　DAB; DAC; DAM MST, POP; JRDA;
　LATS 1:1; MAICYA 1, 2; MAICYAS 1;
　RHW; SATA 6, 44, 78; SATA-Obit 73;
　WYA; YAW
Sutro, Alfred 1863-1933 .... **TCLC 6**
　See also CA 185; CAAE 105; DLB 10;
　RGEL 2
Sutton, Henry
　See Slavitt, David R(ytman)
Suzuki, D. T.
　See Suzuki, Daisetz Teitaro
Suzuki, Daisetz T.
　See Suzuki, Daisetz Teitaro
Suzuki, Daisetz Teitaro
　1870-1966 .... **TCLC 109**
　See also CA 121; CAAS 111; MTCW 1, 2;
　MTFW 2005
Suzuki, Teitaro
　See Suzuki, Daisetz Teitaro
Svevo, Italo .... **SSC 25; TCLC 2, 35**
　See Schmitz, Aron Hector
　See also DLB 264; EW 8; EWL 3; RGWL
　2, 3; WLIT 7
Swados, Elizabeth 1951- .... **CLC 12**
　See also CA 97-100; CANR 49, 163; INT
　CA-97-100
Swados, Elizabeth A.
　See Swados, Elizabeth
Swados, Harvey 1920-1972 .... **CLC 5**
　See also CA 5-8R; CAAS 37-40R; CANR
　6; CN 1; DLB 2, 335; MAL 5
Swados, Liz
　See Swados, Elizabeth
Swan, Gladys 1934- .... **CLC 69**
　See also CA 101; CANR 17, 39; TCLE 1:2
Swanson, Logan
　See Matheson, Richard (Burton)
Swarthout, Glendon (Fred)
　1918-1992 .... **CLC 35**
　See also AAYA 55; CA 1-4R; CAAS 139;
　CANR 1, 47; CN 1, 2, 3, 4, 5; LAIT 5;
　SATA 26; TCWW 1, 2; YAW
Swedenborg, Emanuel 1688-1772 ..... **LC 105**
Sweet, Sarah C.
　See Jewett, (Theodora) Sarah Orne
Swenson, May 1919-1989 ...... **CLC 4, 14, 61,**
　106; PC 14
　See also AMWS 4; CA 5-8R; CAAS 130;
　CANR 36, 61, 131; CP 1, 2, 3, 4; DA;
　DAB; DAC; DAM MST, POET; DLB 5;
　EXPP; GLL 2; MAL 5; MTCW 1, 2;
　MTFW 2005; PFS 16; SATA 15; WP
Swift, Augustus
　See Lovecraft, H. P.
Swift, Graham 1949- .... **CLC 41, 88, 233**
　See also BRWC 2; BRWS 5; CA 122;
　CAAE 117; CANR 46, 71, 128; CN 4, 5,
　6, 7; DLB 194, 326; MTCW 2; MTFW
　2005; NFS 18; RGSF 2
Swift, Jonathan 1667-1745 ..... **LC 1, 42, 101;**
　PC 9; WLC 6
　See also AAYA 41; BRW 3; BRWC 1;
　BRWR 1; BYA 5, 14; CDBLB 1660-1789;
　CLR 53; DA; DA3; DAB; DAC; DAM
　MST, NOV, POET; DLB 39, 95, 101;
　EXPN; LAIT 1; NFS 6; RGEL 2; SATA
　19; TEA; WCH; WLIT 3
Swinburne, Algernon Charles
　1837-1909 ... **PC 24; TCLC 8, 36; WLC**
　6
　See also BRW 5; CA 140; CAAE 105; CD-
　BLB 1832-1890; DA; DA3; DAB; DAC;
　DAM MST, POET; DLB 35, 57; PAB;
　RGEL 2; TEA

Swinfen, Ann .... **CLC 34**
　See also CA 202
Swinnerton, Frank (Arthur)
　1884-1982 .... **CLC 31**
　See also CA 202; CAAS 108; CN 1, 2, 3;
　DLB 34
Swinnerton, Frank Arthur
　1884-1982 .... **CLC 31**
　See also CAAS 108; DLB 34
Swithen, John
　See King, Stephen
Sylvia
　See Ashton-Warner, Sylvia (Constance)
Symmes, Robert Edward
　See Duncan, Robert
Symonds, John Addington
　1840-1893 .... **NCLC 34**
　See also DLB 57, 144
Symons, Arthur 1865-1945 .... **TCLC 11**
　See also CA 189; CAAE 107; DLB 19, 57,
　149; RGEL 2
Symons, Julian (Gustave)
　1912-1994 .... **CLC 2, 14, 32**
　See also CA 49-52; 3; CAAS 147; CANR
　3, 33, 59; CMW 4; CN 1, 2, 3, 4, 5; CP 1,
　3, 4; DLB 87, 155; DLBY 1992; MSW;
　MTCW 1
Synge, (Edmund) J(ohn) M(illington)
　1871-1909 .... **DC 2; TCLC 6, 37**
　See also BRW 6; BRWR 1; CA 141; CAAE
　104; CDBLB 1890-1914; DAM DRAM;
　DFS 18; DLB 10, 19; EWL 3; RGEL 2;
　TEA; WLIT 4
Syruc, J.
　See Milosz, Czeslaw
Szirtes, George 1948- .... **CLC 46; PC 51**
　See also CA 109; CANR 27, 61, 117; CP 4,
　5, 6, 7
Szymborska, Wislawa 1923- ... **CLC 99, 190;**
　PC 44
　See also CA 154; CANR 91, 133; CDWLB
　4; CWP; CWW 2; DA3; DLB 232, 332;
　DLBY 1996; EWL 3; MTCW 2; MTFW
　2005; PFS 15; RGHL; RGWL 3
T. O., Nik
　See Annensky, Innokenty (Fyodorovich)
Tabori, George 1914- .... **CLC 19**
　See also CA 49-52; CANR 4, 69; CBD; CD
　5, 6; DLB 245; RGHL
Tacitus c. 55-c. 117 .... **CMLC 56**
　See also AW 2; CDWLB 1; DLB 211;
　RGWL 2, 3; WLIT 8
Tagore, Rabindranath 1861-1941 .... **PC 8;**
　SSC 48; TCLC 3, 53
　See also CA 120; CAAE 104; DA3; DAM
　DRAM, POET; DLB 323, 332; EWL 3;
　MTCW 1, 2; MTFW 2005; PFS 18; RGEL
　2; RGSF 2; RGWL 2, 3; TWA
Taine, Hippolyte Adolphe
　1828-1893 .... **NCLC 15**
　See also EW 7; GFL 1789 to the Present
Talayesva, Don C. 1890-(?) .... **NNAL**
Talese, Gay 1932- .... **CLC 37, 232**
　See also AITN 1; CA 1-4R; CANR 9, 58,
　137; DLB 185; INT CANR-9; MTCW 1,
　2; MTFW 2005
Tallent, Elizabeth 1954- .... **CLC 45**
　See also CA 117; CANR 72; DLB 130
Tallmountain, Mary 1918-1997 .... **NNAL**
　See also CA 146; CAAS 161; DLB 193
Tally, Ted 1952- .... **CLC 42**
　See also CA 124; CAAE 120; CAD; CANR
　125; CD 5, 6; INT CA-124
Talvik, Heiti 1904-1947 .... **TCLC 87**
　See also EWL 3

Tamayo y Baus, Manuel
　1829-1898 .... **NCLC 1**
Tammsaare, A(nton) H(ansen)
　1878-1940 .... **TCLC 27**
　See also CA 164; CDWLB 4; DLB 220;
　EWL 3
Tam'si, Tchicaya U
　See Tchicaya, Gerald Felix
Tan, Amy 1952- ...... **AAL; CLC 59, 120, 151**
　See also AAYA 9, 48; AMWS 10; BEST
　89:3; BPFB 3; CA 136; CANR 54, 105,
　132; CDALBS; CN 6, 7; CPW 1; DA3;
　DAM MULT, NOV, POP; DLB 173, 312;
　EXPN; FL 1:6; FW; LAIT 3, 5; MAL 5;
　MTCW 2; MTFW 2005; NFS 1, 13, 16;
　RGAL 4; SATA 75; SSFS 9; YAW
Tandem, Carl Felix
　See Spitteler, Carl
Tandem, Felix
　See Spitteler, Carl
Tanizaki, Jun'ichiro 1886-1965 ... **CLC 8, 14,**
　28; SSC 21
　See Tanizaki Jun'ichiro
　See also CA 93-96; CAAS 25-28R; MJW;
　MTCW 2; MTFW 2005; RGSF 2; RGWL
　2
Tanizaki Jun'ichiro
　See Tanizaki, Jun'ichiro
　See also DLB 180; EWL 3
Tannen, Deborah 1945- .... **CLC 206**
　See also CA 118; CANR 95
Tannen, Deborah Frances
　See Tannen, Deborah
Tanner, William
　See Amis, Kingsley
Tante, Dilly
　See Kunitz, Stanley
Tao Lao
　See Storni, Alfonsina
Tapahonso, Luci 1953- .... **NNAL; PC 65**
　See also CA 145; CANR 72, 127; DLB 175
Tarantino, Quentin (Jerome)
　1963- .... **CLC 125, 230**
　See also AAYA 58; CA 171; CANR 125
Tarassoff, Lev
　See Troyat, Henri
Tarbell, Ida M(inerva) 1857-1944 . **TCLC 40**
　See also CA 181; CAAE 122; DLB 47
Tardieu d'Esclavelles,
　Louise-Florence-Petronille
　See Epinay, Louise d'
Tarkington, (Newton) Booth
　1869-1946 .... **TCLC 9**
　See also BPFB 3; BYA 3; CA 143; CAAE
　110; CWRI 5; DLB 9, 102; MAL 5;
　MTCW 2; RGAL 4; SATA 17
Tarkovskii, Andrei Arsen'evich
　See Tarkovsky, Andrei (Arsenyevich)
Tarkovsky, Andrei (Arsenyevich)
　1932-1986 .... **CLC 75**
　See also CA 127
Tartt, Donna 1964(?)- .... **CLC 76**
　See also AAYA 56; CA 142; CANR 135;
　MTFW 2005
Tasso, Torquato 1544-1595 .... **LC 5, 94**
　See also EFS 2; EW 2; RGWL 2, 3; WLIT
　7
Tate, (John Orley) Allen 1899-1979 .. **CLC 2,**
　4, 6, 9, 11, 14, 24; PC 50
　See also AMW; CA 5-8R; CAAS 85-88;
　CANR 32, 108; CN 1, 2; CP 1, 2; DLB 4,
　45, 63; DLBD 17; EWL 3; MAL 5;
　MTCW 1, 2; MTFW 2005; RGAL 4;
　RHW
Tate, Ellalice
　See Hibbert, Eleanor Alice Burford

Tate, James (Vincent) 1943- ..... **CLC 2, 6, 25**
See also CA 21-24R; CANR 29, 57, 114;
CP 1, 2, 3, 4, 5, 6, 7; DLB 5, 169; EWL
3; PFS 10, 15; RGAL 4; WP

Tate, Nahum 1652(?)-1715 .... **LC 109**
See also DLB 80; RGEL 2

Tauler, Johannes c. 1300-1361 ...... **CMLC 37**
See also DLB 179; LMFS 1

Tavel, Ronald 1940- .... **CLC 6**
See also CA 21-24R; CAD; CANR 33; CD
5, 6

Taviani, Paolo 1931- .... **CLC 70**
See also CA 153

Taylor, Bayard 1825-1878 .... **NCLC 89**
See also DLB 3, 189, 250, 254; RGAL 4

Taylor, C(ecil) P(hilip) 1929-1981 .... **CLC 27**
See also CA 25-28R; CAAS 105; CANR
47; CBD

Taylor, Edward 1642(?)-1729 . **LC 11; PC 63**
See also AMW; DA; DAB; DAC; DAM
MST, POET; DLB 24; EXPP; RGAL 4;
TUS

Taylor, Eleanor Ross 1920- .... **CLC 5**
See also CA 81-84; CANR 70

Taylor, Elizabeth 1912-1975 .... **CLC 2, 4, 29;
SSC 100**
See also CA 13-16R; CANR 9, 70; CN 1,
2; DLB 139; MTCW 1; RGEL 2; SATA
13

Taylor, Frederick Winslow
1856-1915 .... **TCLC 76**
See also CA 188

Taylor, Henry (Splawn) 1942- .... **CLC 44**
See also CA 33-36R; 7; CANR 31; CP 6, 7;
DLB 5; PFS 10

Taylor, Kamala 1924-2004
See Markandaya, Kamala
See also CA 77-80; CAAS 227; MTFW
2005; NFS 13

Taylor, Mildred D. 1943- .... **CLC 21**
See also AAYA 10, 47; BW 1; BYA 3, 8;
CA 85-88; CANR 25, 115, 136; CLR 9,
59, 90; CSW; DLB 52; JRDA; LAIT 3;
MAICYA 1, 2; MTFW 2005; SAAS 5;
SATA 135; WYA; YAW

Taylor, Peter (Hillsman) 1917-1994 .. **CLC 1,
4, 18, 37, 44, 50, 71; SSC 10, 84**
See also AMWS 5; BPFB 3; CA 13-16R;
CAAS 147; CANR 9, 50; CN 1, 2, 3, 4,
5; CSW; DLB 218, 278; DLBY 1981,
1994; EWL 3; EXPS; INT CANR-9;
MAL 5; MTCW 1, 2; MTFW 2005; RGSF
2; SSFS 9; TUS

Taylor, Robert Lewis 1912-1998 .... **CLC 14**
See also CA 1-4R; CAAS 170; CANR 3,
64; CN 1, 2; SATA 10; TCWW 1, 2

Tchekhov, Anton
See Chekhov, Anton (Pavlovich)

Tchicaya, Gerald Felix 1931-1988 .. **CLC 101**
See Tchicaya U Tam'si
See also CA 129; CAAS 125; CANR 81

Tchicaya U Tam'si
See Tchicaya, Gerald Felix
See also EWL 3

Teasdale, Sara 1884-1933 .... **PC 31; TCLC 4**
See also CA 163; CAAE 104; DLB 45;
GLL 1; PFS 14; RGAL 4; SATA 32; TUS

Tecumseh 1768-1813 .... **NNAL**
See also DAM MULT

Tegner, Esaias 1782-1846 .... **NCLC 2**

Teilhard de Chardin, (Marie Joseph) Pierre
1881-1955 .... **TCLC 9**
See also CA 210; CAAE 105; GFL 1789 to
the Present

Temple, Ann
See Mortimer, Penelope (Ruth)

Tennant, Emma (Christina) 1937- .. **CLC 13,
52**
See also BRWS 9; CA 65-68; 9; CANR 10,
38, 59, 88; CN 3, 4, 5, 6, 7; DLB 14;
EWL 3; SFW 4

Tenneshaw, S. M.
See Silverberg, Robert

Tenney, Tabitha Gilman
1762-1837 .... **NCLC 122**
See also DLB 37, 200

Tennyson, Alfred 1809-1892 ... **NCLC 30, 65,
115; PC 6; WLC 6**
See also AAYA 50; BRW 4; CDBLB 1832-
1890; DA; DA3; DAB; DAC; DAM MST,
POET; DLB 32; EXPP; PAB; PFS 1, 2, 4,
11, 15, 19; RGEL 2; TEA; WLIT 4; WP

Teran, Lisa St. Aubin de .... **CLC 36**
See St. Aubin de Teran, Lisa

Terence c. 184B.C.-c. 159B.C. ...... **CMLC 14;
DC 7**
See also AW 1; CDWLB 1; DLB 211;
RGWL 2, 3; TWA; WLIT 8

Teresa de Jesus, St. 1515-1582 .... **LC 18**

Teresa of Avila, St.
See Teresa de Jesus, St.

Terkel, Louis .... **CLC 38**
See Terkel, Studs
See also AAYA 32; AITN 1; MTCW 2; TUS

Terkel, Studs 1912-
See Terkel, Louis
See also CA 57-60; CANR 18, 45, 67, 132;
DA3; MTCW 1, 2; MTFW 2005

Terry, C. V.
See Slaughter, Frank G(ill)

Terry, Megan 1932- .... **CLC 19; DC 13**
See also CA 77-80; CABS 3; CAD; CANR
43; CD 5, 6; CWD; DFS 18; DLB 7, 249;
GLL 2

Tertullian c. 155-c. 245 .... **CMLC 29**

Tertz, Abram
See Sinyavsky, Andrei (Donatevich)
See also RGSF 2

Tesich, Steve 1943(?)-1996 .... **CLC 40, 69**
See also CA 105; CAAS 152; CAD; DLBY
1983

Tesla, Nikola 1856-1943 .... **TCLC 88**

Teternikov, Fyodor Kuzmich 1863-1927
See Sologub, Fyodor
See also CAAE 104

Tevis, Walter 1928-1984 .... **CLC 42**
See also CA 113; SFW 4

Tey, Josephine .... **TCLC 14**
See Mackintosh, Elizabeth
See also DLB 77; MSW

Thackeray, William Makepeace
1811-1863 ...... **NCLC 5, 14, 22, 43, 169;
WLC 6**
See also BRW 5; BRWC 2; CDBLB 1832-
1890; DA; DA3; DAB; DAC; DAM MST,
NOV; DLB 21, 55, 159, 163; NFS 13;
RGEL 2; SATA 23; TEA; WLIT 3

Thakura, Ravindranatha
See Tagore, Rabindranath

Thames, C. H.
See Marlowe, Stephen

Tharoor, Shashi 1956- .... **CLC 70**
See also CA 141; CANR 91; CN 6, 7

Thelwall, John 1764-1834 .... **NCLC 162**
See also DLB 93, 158

Thelwell, Michael Miles 1939- .... **CLC 22**
See also BW 2; CA 101

Theobald, Lewis, Jr.
See Lovecraft, H. P.

Theocritus c. 310B.C.- .... **CMLC 45**
See also AW 1; DLB 176; RGWL 2, 3

Theodorescu, Ion N. 1880-1967
See Arghezi, Tudor
See also CAAS 116

Theriault, Yves 1915-1983 .... **CLC 79**
See also CA 102; CANR 150; CCA 1;
DAC; DAM MST; DLB 88; EWL 3

Theroux, Alexander (Louis) 1939- .... **CLC 2,
25**
See also CA 85-88; CANR 20, 63; CN 4, 5,
6, 7

Theroux, Paul 1941- .... **CLC 5, 8, 11, 15, 28,
46, 159**
See also AAYA 28; AMWS 8; BEST 89:4;
BPFB 3; CA 33-36R; CANR 20, 45, 74,
133; CDALBS; CN 1, 2, 3, 4, 5, 6, 7; CP
1; CPW 1; DA3; DAM POP; DLB 2, 218;
EWL 3; HGG; MAL 5; MTCW 1, 2;
MTFW 2005; RGAL 4; SATA 44, 109;
TUS

Thesen, Sharon 1946- .... **CLC 56**
See also CA 163; CANR 125; CP 5, 6, 7;
CWP

Thespis fl. 6th cent. B.C.- .... **CMLC 51**
See also LMFS 1

Thevenin, Denis
See Duhamel, Georges

Thibault, Jacques Anatole Francois
1844-1924
See France, Anatole
See also CA 127; CAAE 106; DA3; DAM
NOV; MTCW 1, 2; TWA

Thiele, Colin 1920-2006 .... **CLC 17**
See also CA 29-32R; CANR 12, 28, 53,
105; CLR 27; CP 1, 2; DLB 289; MAI-
CYA 1, 2; SAAS 2; SATA 14, 72, 125;
YAW

Thistlethwaite, Bel
See Wetherald, Agnes Ethelwyn

Thomas, Audrey (Callahan) 1935- .... **CLC 7,
13, 37, 107; SSC 20**
See also AITN 2; CA 237; 21-24R, 237; 19;
CANR 36, 58; CN 2, 3, 4, 5, 6, 7; DLB
60; MTCW 1; RGSF 2

Thomas, Augustus 1857-1934 .... **TCLC 97**
See also MAL 5

Thomas, D.M. 1935- ..... **CLC 13, 22, 31, 132**
See also BPFB 3; BRWS 4; CA 61-64; 11;
CANR 17, 45, 75; CDBLB 1960 to
Present; CN 4, 5, 6, 7; CP 1, 2, 3, 4, 5, 6,
7; DA3; DLB 40, 207, 299; HGG; INT
CANR-17; MTCW 1, 2; MTFW 2005;
RGHL; SFW 4

Thomas, Dylan (Marlais) 1914-1953 .... **PC 2,
52; SSC 3, 44; TCLC 1, 8, 45, 105;
WLC 6**
See also AAYA 45; BRWS 1; CA 120;
CAAE 104; CANR 65; CDBLB 1945-
1960; DA; DA3; DAB; DAC; DAM
DRAM, MST, POET; DLB 13, 20, 139;
EWL 3; EXPP; LAIT 3; MTCW 1, 2;
MTFW 2005; PAB; PFS 1, 3, 8; RGEL 2;
RGSF 2; SATA 60; TEA; WLIT 4; WP

Thomas, (Philip) Edward 1878-1917 . **PC 53;
TCLC 10**
See also BRW 6; BRWS 3; CA 153; CAAE
106; DAM POET; DLB 19, 98, 156, 216;
EWL 3; PAB; RGEL 2

Thomas, Joyce Carol 1938- .... **CLC 35**
See also AAYA 12, 54; BW 2, 3; CA 116;
CAAE 113; CANR 48, 114, 135; CLR 19;
DLB 33; INT CA-116; JRDA; MAICYA
1, 2; MTCW 1, 2; MTFW 2005; SAAS 7;
SATA 40, 78, 123, 137; SATA-Essay 137;
WYA; YAW

Thomas, Lewis 1913-1993 .... **CLC 35**
See also ANW; CA 85-88; CAAS 143;
CANR 38, 60; DLB 275; MTCW 1, 2

Thomas, M. Carey 1857-1935 .... **TCLC 89**
See also FW

Thomas, Paul
See Mann, (Paul) Thomas

Thomas, Piri 1928- .... **CLC 17; HLCS 2**
See also CA 73-76; HW 1; LLW

Turgenev, Ivan (Sergeevich)
1818-1883 ..... **DC 7; NCLC 21, 37, 122; SSC 7, 57; WLC 6**
See also AAYA 58; DA; DAB; DAC; DAM MST, NOV; DFS 6; DLB 238, 284; EW 6; LATS 1:1; NFS 16; RGSF 2; RGWL 2, 3; TWA

Turgot, Anne-Robert-Jacques
1727-1781 .... **LC 26**
See also DLB 314

Turner, Frederick 1943- .... **CLC 48**
See also CA 227; 73-76, 227; 10; CANR 12, 30, 56; DLB 40, 282

Turton, James
See Crace, Jim

Tutu, Desmond M(pilo) 1931- .. **BLC 3; CLC 80**
See also BW 1, 3; CA 125; CANR 67, 81; DAM MULT

Tutuola, Amos 1920-1997 ..... **BLC 3; CLC 5, 14, 29; TCLC 188**
See also AFW; BW 2, 3; CA 9-12R; CAAS 159; CANR 27, 66; CDWLB 3; CN 1, 2, 3, 4, 5, 6; DA3; DAM MULT; DLB 125; DNFS 2; EWL 3; MTCW 1, 2; MTFW 2005; RGEL 2; WLIT 2

Twain, Mark .... **SSC 6, 26, 34, 87; TCLC 6, 12, 19, 36, 48, 59, 161, 185; WLC 6**
See Clemens, Samuel Langhorne
See also AAYA 20; AMW; AMWC 1; BPFB 3; BYA 2, 3, 11, 14; CLR 58, 60, 66; DLB 11; EXPN; EXPS; FANT; LAIT 2; MAL 5; NCFS 4; NFS 1, 6; RGAL 4; RGSF 2; SFW 4; SSFS 1, 7, 16, 21; SUFW; TUS; WCH; WYA; YAW

Tyler, Anne 1941- . **CLC 7, 11, 18, 28, 44, 59, 103, 205**
See also AAYA 18, 60; AMWS 4; BEST 89:1; BPFB 3; BYA 12; CA 9-12R; CANR 11, 33, 53, 109, 132; CDALBS; CN 1, 2, 3, 4, 5, 6, 7; CPW; CSW; DAM NOV; POP; DLB 6, 143; DLBY 1982; EWL 3; EXPN; LATS 1:2; MAL 5; MBL; MTCW 1, 2; MTFW 2005; NFS 2, 7, 10; RGAL 4; SATA 7, 90, 173; SSFS 17; TCLE 1:2; TUS; YAW

Tyler, Royall 1757-1826 .... **NCLC 3**
See also DLB 37; RGAL 4

Tynan, Katharine 1861-1931 .... **TCLC 3**
See also CA 167; CAAE 104; DLB 153, 240; FW

Tyndale, William c. 1484-1536 .... **LC 103**
See also DLB 132

Tyutchev, Fyodor 1803-1873 .... **NCLC 34**

Tzara, Tristan 1896-1963 .... **CLC 47; PC 27; TCLC 168**
See also CA 153; CAAS 89-92; DAM POET; EWL 3; MTCW 2

Uchida, Yoshiko 1921-1992 .... **AAL**
See also AAYA 16; BYA 2, 3; CA 13-16R; CAAS 139; CANR 6, 22, 47, 61; CDALBS; CLR 6, 56; CWRI 5; DLB 312; JRDA; MAICYA 1, 2; MTCW 1, 2; MTFW 2005; SAAS 1; SATA 1, 53; SATA-Obit 72

Udall, Nicholas 1504-1556 .... **LC 84**
See also DLB 62; RGEL 2

Ueda Akinari 1734-1809 .... **NCLC 131**

Uhry, Alfred 1936- .... **CLC 55**
See also CA 133; CAAE 127; CAD; CANR 112; CD 5, 6; CSW; DA3; DAM DRAM, POP; DFS 11, 15; INT CA-133; MTFW 2005

Ulf, Haerved
See Strindberg, (Johan) August

Ulf, Harved
See Strindberg, (Johan) August

Ulibarri, Sabine R(eyes)
1919-2003 .... **CLC 83; HLCS 2**
See also CA 131; CAAS 214; CANR 81; DAM MULT; DLB 82; HW 1, 2; RGSF 2

Unamuno (y Jugo), Miguel de
1864-1936 .. **HLC 2; SSC 11, 69; TCLC 2, 9, 148**
See also CA 131; CAAE 104; CANR 81; DAM MULT, NOV; DLB 108, 322; EW 8; EWL 3; HW 1, 2; MTCW 1, 2; MTFW 2005; RGSF 2; RGWL 2, 3; SSFS 20; TWA

Uncle Shelby
See Silverstein, Shel

Undercliffe, Errol
See Campbell, (John) Ramsey

Underwood, Miles
See Glassco, John

Undset, Sigrid 1882-1949 .. **TCLC 3; WLC 6**
See also CA 129; CAAE 104; DA; DA3; DAB; DAC; DAM MST, NOV; DLB 293, 332; EW 9; EWL 3; FW; MTCW 1, 2; MTFW 2005; RGWL 2, 3

Ungaretti, Giuseppe 1888-1970 ... **CLC 7, 11, 15; PC 57**
See also CA 19-20; CAAS 25-28R; CAP 2; DLB 114; EW 10; EWL 3; PFS 20; RGWL 2, 3; WLIT 7

Unger, Douglas 1952- .... **CLC 34**
See also CA 130; CANR 94, 155

Unsworth, Barry (Forster) 1930- .... **CLC 76, 127**
See also BRWS 7; CA 25-28R; CANR 30, 54, 125; CN 6, 7; DLB 194, 326

Updike, John 1932- . **CLC 1, 2, 3, 5, 7, 9, 13, 15, 23, 34, 43, 70, 139, 214; SSC 13, 27; WLC 6**
See also AAYA 36; AMW; AMWC 1; AMWR 1; BPFB 3; BYA 12; CA 1-4R; CABS 1; CANR 4, 33, 51, 94, 133; CDALB 1968-1988; CN 1, 2, 3, 4, 5, 6, 7; CP 1, 2, 3, 4, 5, 6, 7; CPW 1; DA; DA3; DAB; DAC; DAM MST, NOV, POET, POP; DLB 2, 5, 143, 218, 227; DLBD 3; DLBY 1980, 1982, 1997; EWL 3; EXPP; HGG; MAL 5; MTCW 1, 2; MTFW 2005; NFS 12, 24; RGAL 4; RGSF 2; SSFS 3, 19; TUS

Updike, John Hoyer
See Updike, John

Upshaw, Margaret Mitchell
See Mitchell, Margaret (Munnerlyn)

Upton, Mark
See Sanders, Lawrence

Upward, Allen 1863-1926 .... **TCLC 85**
See also CA 187; CAAE 117; DLB 36

Urdang, Constance (Henriette)
1922-1996 .... **CLC 47**
See also CA 21-24R; CANR 9, 24; CP 1, 2, 3, 4, 5, 6; CWP

Urfe, Honore d' 1567(?)-1625 .... **LC 132**
See also DLB 268; GFL Beginnings to 1789; RGWL 2, 3

Uriel, Henry
See Faust, Frederick (Schiller)

Uris, Leon 1924-2003 .... **CLC 7, 32**
See also AITN 1, 2; BEST 89:2; BPFB 3; CA 1-4R; CAAS 217; CANR 1, 40, 65, 123; CN 1, 2, 3, 4, 5, 6; CPW 1; DA3; DAM NOV, POP; MTCW 1, 2; MTFW 2005; RGHL; SATA 49; SATA-Obit 146

Urista (Heredia), Alberto (Baltazar)
1947- .... **HLCS 1**
See Alurista
See also CA 182; CANR 2, 32; HW 1

Urmuz
See Codrescu, Andrei

Urquhart, Guy
See McAlmon, Robert (Menzies)

Urquhart, Jane 1949- .... **CLC 90**
See also CA 113; CANR 32, 68, 116, 157; CCA 1; DAC; DLB 334

Usigli, Rodolfo 1905-1979 .... **HLCS 1**
See also CA 131; DLB 305; EWL 3; HW 1; LAW

Usk, Thomas (?)-1388 .... **CMLC 76**
See also DLB 146

Ustinov, Peter (Alexander)
1921-2004 .... **CLC 1**
See also AITN 1; CA 13-16R; CAAS 225; CANR 25, 51; CBD; CD 5, 6; DLB 13; MTCW 2

U Tam'si, Gerald Felix Tchicaya
See Tchicaya, Gerald Felix

U Tam'si, Tchicaya
See Tchicaya, Gerald Felix

Vachss, Andrew 1942- .... **CLC 106**
See also CA 214; 118, 214; CANR 44, 95, 153; CMW 4

Vachss, Andrew H.
See Vachss, Andrew

Vachss, Andrew Henry
See Vachss, Andrew

Vaculik, Ludvik 1926- .... **CLC 7**
See also CA 53-56; CANR 72; CWW 2; DLB 232; EWL 3

Vaihinger, Hans 1852-1933 .... **TCLC 71**
See also CA 166; CAAE 116

Valdez, Luis (Miguel) 1940- ..... **CLC 84; DC 10; HLC 2**
See also CA 101; CAD; CANR 32, 81; CD 5, 6; DAM MULT; DFS 5; DLB 122; EWL 3; HW 1; LAIT 4; LLW

Valenzuela, Luisa 1938- .... **CLC 31, 104; HLCS 2; SSC 14, 82**
See also CA 101; CANR 32, 65, 123; CDWLB 3; CWW 2; DAM MULT; DLB 113; EWL 3; FW; HW 1, 2; LAW; RGSF 2; RGWL 3

Valera y Alcala-Galiano, Juan
1824-1905 .... **TCLC 10**
See also CAAE 106

Valerius Maximus fl. 20- .... **CMLC 64**
See also DLB 211

Valery, (Ambroise) Paul (Toussaint Jules)
1871-1945 .... **PC 9; TCLC 4, 15**
See also CA 122; CAAE 104; DA3; DAM POET; DLB 258; EW 8; EWL 3; GFL 1789 to the Present; MTCW 1, 2; MTFW 2005; RGWL 2, 3; TWA

Valle-Inclan, Ramon (Maria) del
1866-1936 .... **HLC 2; TCLC 5**
See del Valle-Inclan, Ramon (Maria)
See also CA 153; CAAE 106; CANR 80; DAM MULT; DLB 134; EW 8; EWL 3; HW 2; RGSF 2; RGWL 2, 3

Vallejo, Antonio Buero
See Buero Vallejo, Antonio

Vallejo, Cesar (Abraham)
1892-1938 .... **HLC 2; TCLC 3, 56**
See also CA 153; CAAE 105; DAM MULT; DLB 290; EWL 3; HW 1; LAW; RGWL 2, 3

Valles, Jules 1832-1885 .... **NCLC 71**
See also DLB 123; GFL 1789 to the Present

Vallette, Marguerite Eymery
1860-1953 .... **TCLC 67**
See Rachilde
See also CA 182; DLB 123, 192

Valle Y Pena, Ramon del
See Valle-Inclan, Ramon (Maria) del

Van Ash, Cay 1918-1994 .... **CLC 34**
See also CA 220

Vanbrugh, Sir John 1664-1726 .... **LC 21**
See also BRW 2; DAM DRAM; DLB 80; IDTP; RGEL 2

Van Campen, Karl
See Campbell, John W(ood, Jr.)

Villehardouin, Geoffroi de
1150(?)-1218(?) .... **CMLC 38**
Villiers, George 1628-1687 .... **LC 107**
See also DLB 80; RGEL 2
Villiers de l'Isle Adam, Jean Marie Mathias Philippe Auguste 1838-1889 ... **NCLC 3; SSC 14**
See also DLB 123, 192; GFL 1789 to the Present; RGSF 2
Villon, Francois 1431-1463(?) . **LC 62; PC 13**
See also DLB 208; EW 2; RGWL 2, 3; TWA
Vine, Barbara .... **CLC 50**
See Rendell, Ruth
See also BEST 90:4
Vinge, Joan (Carol) D(ennison)
1948- .... **CLC 30; SSC 24**
See also AAYA 32; BPFB 3; CA 93-96; CANR 72; SATA 36, 113; SFW 4; YAW
Viola, Herman J(oseph) 1938- .... **CLC 70**
See also CA 61-64; CANR 8, 23, 48, 91; SATA 126
Violis, G.
See Simenon, Georges (Jacques Christian)
Viramontes, Helena Maria 1954- .... **HLCS 2**
See also CA 159; DLB 122; HW 2; LLW
Virgil
See Vergil
See also CDWLB 1; DLB 211; LAIT 1; RGWL 2, 3; WLIT 8; WP
Visconti, Luchino 1906-1976 .... **CLC 16**
See also CA 81-84; CAAS 65-68; CANR 39
Vitry, Jacques de
See Jacques de Vitry
Vittorini, Elio 1908-1966 .... **CLC 6, 9, 14**
See also CA 133; CAAS 25-28R; DLB 264; EW 12; EWL 3; RGWL 2, 3
Vivekananda, Swami 1863-1902 .... **TCLC 88**
Vizenor, Gerald Robert 1934- .... **CLC 103; NNAL**
See also CA 205; 13-16R, 205; 22; CANR 5, 21, 44, 67; DAM MULT; DLB 175, 227; MTCW 2; MTFW 2005; TCWW 2
Vizinczey, Stephen 1933- .... **CLC 40**
See also CA 128; CCA 1; INT CA-128
Vliet, R(ussell) G(ordon)
1929-1984 .... **CLC 22**
See also CA 37-40R; CAAS 112; CANR 18; CP 2, 3
Vogau, Boris Andreyevich 1894-1938
See Pilnyak, Boris
See also CA 218; CAAE 123
Vogel, Paula A. 1951- .... **CLC 76; DC 19**
See also CA 108; CAD; CANR 119, 140; CD 5, 6; CWD; DFS 14; MTFW 2005; RGAL 4
Voigt, Cynthia 1942- .... **CLC 30**
See also AAYA 3, 30; BYA 1, 3, 6, 7, 8; CA 106; CANR 18, 37, 40, 94, 145; CLR 13, 48; INT CANR-18; JRDA; LAIT 5; MAICYA 1, 2; MAICYAS 1; MTFW 2005; SATA 48, 79, 116, 160; SATA-Brief 33; WYA; YAW
Voigt, Ellen Bryant 1943- .... **CLC 54**
See also CA 69-72; CANR 11, 29, 55, 115; CP 5, 6, 7; CSW; CWP; DLB 120; PFS 23
Voinovich, Vladimir 1932- .. **CLC 10, 49, 147**
See also CA 81-84; 12; CANR 33, 67, 150; CWW 2; DLB 302; MTCW 1
Voinovich, Vladimir Nikolaevich
See Voinovich, Vladimir
Vollmann, William T. 1959- ...... **CLC 89, 227**
See also CA 134; CANR 67, 116; CN 7; CPW; DA3; DAM NOV, POP; MTCW 2; MTFW 2005
Voloshinov, V. N.
See Bakhtin, Mikhail Mikhailovich

Voltaire 1694-1778 . **LC 14, 79, 110; SSC 12; WLC 6**
See also BYA 13; DA; DA3; DAB; DAC; DAM DRAM, MST; DLB 314; EW 4; GFL Beginnings to 1789; LATS 1:1; LMFS 2; NFS 7; RGWL 2, 3; TWA
von Aschendrof, Baron Ignatz
See Ford, Ford Madox
von Chamisso, Adelbert
See Chamisso, Adelbert von
von Daeniken, Erich 1935- .... **CLC 30**
See also AITN 1; CA 37-40R; CANR 17, 44
von Daniken, Erich
See von Daeniken, Erich
von Eschenbach, Wolfram c. 1170-c.
1220 .... **CMLC 5**
See Eschenbach, Wolfram von
See also CDWLB 2; DLB 138; EW 1; RGWL 2
von Hartmann, Eduard
1842-1906 .... **TCLC 96**
von Hayek, Friedrich August
See Hayek, F(riedrich) A(ugust von)
von Heidenstam, (Carl Gustaf) Verner
See Heidenstam, (Carl Gustaf) Verner von
von Heyse, Paul (Johann Ludwig)
See Heyse, Paul (Johann Ludwig von)
von Hofmannsthal, Hugo
See Hofmannsthal, Hugo von
von Horvath, Odon
See von Horvath, Odon
von Horvath, Odon
See von Horvath, Odon
von Horvath, Odon 1901-1938 .... **TCLC 45**
See von Horvath, Oedoen
See also CA 194; CAAE 118; DLB 85, 124; RGWL 2, 3
von Horvath, Oedoen
See von Horvath, Odon
See also CA 184
von Kleist, Heinrich
See Kleist, Heinrich von
Vonnegut, Kurt, Jr.
See Vonnegut, Kurt
Vonnegut, Kurt 1922-2007 .... **CLC 1, 2, 3, 4, 5, 8, 12, 22, 40, 60, 111, 212; SSC 8; WLC 6**
See also AAYA 6, 44; AITN 1; AMWS 2; BEST 90:4; BPFB 3; BYA 3, 14; CA 1-4R; CANR 1, 25, 49, 75, 92; CDALB 1968-1988; CN 1, 2, 3, 4, 5, 6, 7; CPW 1; DA; DA3; DAB; DAC; DAM MST, NOV, POP; DLB 2, 8, 152; DLBD 3; DLBY 1980; EWL 3; EXPN; EXPS; LAIT 4; LMFS 2; MAL 5; MTCW 1, 2; MTFW 2005; NFS 3; RGAL 4; SCFW; SFW 4; SSFS 5; TUS; YAW
Von Rachen, Kurt
See Hubbard, L. Ron
von Sternberg, Josef
See Sternberg, Josef von
Vorster, Gordon 1924- .... **CLC 34**
See also CA 133
Vosce, Trudie
See Ozick, Cynthia
Voznesensky, Andrei (Andreievich)
1933- .... **CLC 1, 15, 57**
See Voznesensky, Andrey
See also CA 89-92; CANR 37; CWW 2; DAM POET; MTCW 1
Voznesensky, Andrey
See Voznesensky, Andrei (Andreievich)
See also EWL 3
Wace, Robert c. 1100-c. 1175 .... **CMLC 55**
See also DLB 146

Waddington, Miriam 1917-2004 .... **CLC 28**
See also CA 21-24R; CAAS 225; CANR 12, 30; CCA 1; CP 1, 2, 3, 4, 5, 6, 7; DLB 68
Wagman, Fredrica 1937- .... **CLC 7**
See also CA 97-100; INT CA-97-100
Wagner, Linda W.
See Wagner-Martin, Linda (C.)
Wagner, Linda Welshimer
See Wagner-Martin, Linda (C.)
Wagner, Richard 1813-1883 ..... **NCLC 9, 119**
See also DLB 129; EW 6
Wagner-Martin, Linda (C.) 1936- .... **CLC 50**
See also CA 159; CANR 135
Wagoner, David (Russell) 1926- .... **CLC 3, 5, 15; PC 33**
See also AMWS 9; CA 1-4R; 3; CANR 2, 71; CN 1, 2, 3, 4, 5, 6, 7; CP 1, 2, 3, 4, 5, 6, 7; DLB 5, 256; SATA 14; TCWW 1, 2
Wah, Fred(erick James) 1939- .... **CLC 44**
See also CA 141; CAAE 107; CP 1, 6, 7; DLB 60
Wahloo, Per 1926-1975 .... **CLC 7**
See also BPFB 3; CA 61-64; CANR 73; CMW; MSW
Wahloo, Peter
See Wahloo, Per
Wain, John (Barrington) 1925-1994 . **CLC 2, 11, 15, 46**
See also CA 5-8R; 4; CAAS 145; CANR 23, 54; CDBLB 1960 to Present; CN 1, 2, 3, 4, 5; CP 1, 2, 3, 4, 5; DLB 15, 27, 139, 155; EWL 3; MTCW 1, 2; MTFW 2005
Wajda, Andrzej 1926- .... **CLC 16, 219**
See also CA 102
Wakefield, Dan 1932- .... **CLC 7**
See also CA 211; 21-24R, 211; 7; CN 4, 5, 6, 7
Wakefield, Herbert Russell
1888-1965 .... **TCLC 120**
See also CA 5-8R; CANR 77; HGG; SUFW
Wakoski, Diane 1937- ...... **CLC 2, 4, 7, 9, 11, 40; PC 15**
See also CA 216; 13-16R, 216; 1; CANR 9, 60, 106; CP 1, 2, 3, 4, 5, 6, 7; CWP; DAM POET; DLB 5; INT CANR-9; MAL 5; MTCW 2; MTFW 2005
Wakoski-Sherbell, Diane
See Wakoski, Diane
Walcott, Derek 1930- ... **BLC 3; CLC 2, 4, 9, 14, 25, 42, 67, 76, 160; DC 7; PC 46**
See also BW 2; CA 89-92; CANR 26, 47, 75, 80, 130; CBD; CD 5, 6; CDWLB 3; CP 1, 2, 3, 4, 5, 6, 7; DA3; DAB; DAC; DAM MST, MULT, POET; DLB 117, 332; DLBY 1981; DNFS 1; EFS 1; EWL 3; LMFS 2; MTCW 1, 2; MTFW 2005; PFS 6; RGEL 2; TWA; WWE 1
Waldman, Anne (Lesley) 1945- .... **CLC 7**
See also BG 1:3; CA 37-40R; 17; CANR 34, 69, 116; CP 1, 2, 3, 4, 5, 6, 7; CWP; DLB 16
Waldo, E. Hunter
See Sturgeon, Theodore (Hamilton)
Waldo, Edward Hamilton
See Sturgeon, Theodore (Hamilton)
Walker, Alice 1944- ...... **BLC 3; CLC 5, 6, 9, 19, 27, 46, 58, 103, 167; PC 30; SSC 5; WLCS**
See also AAYA 3, 33; AFAW 1, 2; AMWS 3; BEST 89:4; BPFB 3; BW 2, 3; CA 37-40R; CANR 9, 27, 49, 66, 82, 131; CDALB 1968-1988; CN 4, 5, 6, 7; CPW; CSW; DA; DA3; DAB; DAC; DAM MST, MULT, NOV, POET, POP; DLB 6, 33, 143; EWL 3; EXPN; EXPS; FL 1:6; FW; INT CANR-27; LAIT 3; MAL 5; MBL; MTCW 1, 2; MTFW 2005; NFS 5; RGAL 4; RGSF 2; SATA 31; SSFS 2, 11; TUS; YAW

Waugh, Evelyn (Arthur St. John)
1903-1966 .. **CLC 1, 3, 8, 13, 19, 27, 44, 107; SSC 41; WLC 6**
See also BPFB 3; BRW 7; CA 85-88; CAAS 25-28R; CANR 22; CDBLB 1914-1945; DA; DA3; DAB; DAC; DAM MST, NOV, POP; DLB 15, 162, 195; EWL 3; MTCW 1, 2; MTFW 2005; NFS 13, 17; RGEL 2; RGSF 2; TEA; WLIT 4

Waugh, Harriet 1944- .... **CLC 6**
See also CA 85-88; CANR 22

Ways, C. R.
See Blount, Roy (Alton), Jr.

Waystaff, Simon
See Swift, Jonathan

Webb, Beatrice (Martha Potter)
1858-1943 .... **TCLC 22**
See also CA 162; CAAE 117; DLB 190; FW

Webb, Charles (Richard) 1939- .... **CLC 7**
See also CA 25-28R; CANR 114

Webb, Frank J. .... **NCLC 143**
See also DLB 50

Webb, James, Jr.
See Webb, James

Webb, James 1946- .... **CLC 22**
See also CA 81-84; CANR 156

Webb, James H.
See Webb, James

Webb, James Henry
See Webb, James

Webb, Mary Gladys (Meredith)
1881-1927 .... **TCLC 24**
See also CA 182; CAAS 123; DLB 34; FW; RGEL 2

Webb, Mrs. Sidney
See Webb, Beatrice (Martha Potter)

Webb, Phyllis 1927- .... **CLC 18**
See also CA 104; CANR 23; CCA 1; CP 1, 2, 3, 4, 5, 6, 7; CWP; DLB 53

Webb, Sidney (James) 1859-1947 .. **TCLC 22**
See also CA 163; CAAE 117; DLB 190

Webber, Andrew Lloyd .... **CLC 21**
See Lloyd Webber, Andrew
See also DFS 7

Weber, Lenora Mattingly
1895-1971 .... **CLC 12**
See also CA 19-20; CAAS 29-32R; CAP 1; SATA 2; SATA-Obit 26

Weber, Max 1864-1920 .... **TCLC 69**
See also CA 189; CAAE 109; DLB 296

Webster, John 1580(?)-1634(?) ...... **DC 2; LC 33, 84, 124; WLC 6**
See also BRW 2; CDBLB Before 1660; DA; DAB; DAC; DAM DRAM, MST; DFS 17, 19; DLB 58; IDTP; RGEL 2; WLIT 3

Webster, Noah 1758-1843 .... **NCLC 30**
See also DLB 1, 37, 42, 43, 73, 243

Wedekind, Benjamin Franklin
See Wedekind, Frank

Wedekind, Frank 1864-1918 .... **TCLC 7**
See also CA 153; CAAE 104; CANR 121, 122; CDWLB 2; DAM DRAM; DLB 118; EW 8; EWL 3; LMFS 2; RGWL 2, 3

Wehr, Demaris .... **CLC 65**

Weidman, Jerome 1913-1998 .... **CLC 7**
See also AITN 2; CA 1-4R; CAAS 171; CAD; CANR 1; CD 1, 2, 3, 4, 5; DLB 28

Weil, Simone (Adolphine)
1909-1943 .... **TCLC 23**
See also CA 159; CAAE 117; EW 12; EWL 3; FW; GFL 1789 to the Present; MTCW 2

Weininger, Otto 1880-1903 .... **TCLC 84**

Weinstein, Nathan
See West, Nathanael

Weinstein, Nathan von Wallenstein
See West, Nathanael

Weir, Peter (Lindsay) 1944- .... **CLC 20**
See also CA 123; CAAE 113

Weiss, Peter (Ulrich) 1916-1982 .. **CLC 3, 15, 51; TCLC 152**
See also CA 45-48; CAAS 106; CANR 3; DAM DRAM; DFS 3; DLB 69, 124; EWL 3; RGHL; RGWL 2, 3

Weiss, Theodore (Russell)
1916-2003 .... **CLC 3, 8, 14**
See also CA 189; 9-12R, 189; 2; CAAS 216; CANR 46, 94; CP 1, 2, 3, 4, 5, 6, 7; DLB 5; TCLE 1:2

Welch, (Maurice) Denton
1915-1948 .... **TCLC 22**
See also BRWS 8, 9; CA 148; CAAE 121; RGEL 2

Welch, James (Phillip) 1940-2003 ..... **CLC 6, 14, 52; NNAL; PC 62**
See also CA 85-88; CAAS 219; CANR 42, 66, 107; CN 5, 6, 7; CP 2, 3, 4, 5, 6, 7; CPW; DAM MULT, POP; DLB 175, 256; LATS 1:1; NFS 23; RGAL 4; TCWW 1, 2

Weldon, Fay 1931- . **CLC 6, 9, 11, 19, 36, 59, 122**
See also BRWS 4; CA 21-24R; CANR 16, 46, 63, 97, 137; CDBLB 1960 to Present; CN 3, 4, 5, 6, 7; CPW; DAM POP; DLB 14, 194, 319; EWL 3; FW; HGG; INT CANR-16; MTCW 1, 2; MTFW 2005; RGEL 2; RGSF 2

Wellek, Rene 1903-1995 .... **CLC 28**
See also CA 5-8R; 7; CAAS 150; CANR 8; DLB 63; EWL 3; INT CANR-8

Weller, Michael 1942- .... **CLC 10, 53**
See also CA 85-88; CAD; CD 5, 6

Weller, Paul 1958- .... **CLC 26**

Wellershoff, Dieter 1925- .... **CLC 46**
See also CA 89-92; CANR 16, 37

Welles, (George) Orson 1915-1985 .. **CLC 20, 80**
See also AAYA 40; CA 93-96; CAAS 117

Wellman, John McDowell 1945-
See Wellman, Mac
See also CA 166; CD 5

Wellman, Mac .... **CLC 65**
See Wellman, John McDowell; Wellman, John McDowell
See also CAD; CD 6; RGAL 4

Wellman, Manly Wade 1903-1986 ... **CLC 49**
See also CA 1-4R; CAAS 118; CANR 6, 16, 44; FANT; SATA 6; SATA-Obit 47; SFW 4; SUFW

Wells, Carolyn 1869(?)-1942 .... **TCLC 35**
See also CA 185; CAAE 113; CMW 4; DLB 11

Wells, H(erbert) G(eorge) 1866-1946 . **SSC 6, 70; TCLC 6, 12, 19, 133; WLC 6**
See also AAYA 18; BPFB 3; BRW 6; CA 121; CAAE 110; CDBLB 1914-1945; CLR 64; DA; DA3; DAB; DAC; DAM MST, NOV; DLB 34, 70, 156, 178; EWL 3; EXPS; HGG; LAIT 3; LMFS 2; MTCW 1, 2; MTFW 2005; NFS 17, 20; RGEL 2; RGSF 2; SATA 20; SCFW 1, 2; SFW 4; SSFS 3; SUFW; TEA; WCH; WLIT 4; YAW

Wells, Rosemary 1943- .... **CLC 12**
See also AAYA 13; BYA 7, 8; CA 85-88; CANR 48, 120; CLR 16, 69; CWRI 5; MAICYA 1, 2; SAAS 1; SATA 18, 69, 114, 156; YAW

Wells-Barnett, Ida B(ell)
1862-1931 .... **TCLC 125**
See also CA 182; DLB 23, 221

Welsh, Irvine 1958- .... **CLC 144**
See also CA 173; CANR 146; CN 7; DLB 271

Welty, Eudora 1909-2001 .... **CLC 1, 2, 5, 14, 22, 33, 105, 220; SSC 1, 27, 51; WLC 6**
See also AAYA 48; AMW; AMWR 1; BPFB 3; CA 9-12R; CAAS 199; CABS 1; CANR 32, 65, 128; CDALB 1941-1968; CN 1, 2, 3, 4, 5, 6, 7; CSW; DA; DA3; DAB; DAC; DAM MST, NOV; DLB 2, 102, 143; DLBD 12; DLBY 1987, 2001; EWL 3; EXPS; HGG; LAIT 3; MAL 5; MBL; MTCW 1, 2; MTFW 2005; NFS 13, 15; RGAL 4; RGSF 2; RHW; SSFS 2, 10; TUS

Welty, Eudora Alice
See Welty, Eudora

Wen I-to 1899-1946 .... **TCLC 28**
See also EWL 3

Wentworth, Robert
See Hamilton, Edmond

Werfel, Franz (Viktor) 1890-1945 ... **TCLC 8**
See also CA 161; CAAE 104; DLB 81, 124; EWL 3; RGWL 2, 3

Wergeland, Henrik Arnold
1808-1845 .... **NCLC 5**

Wersba, Barbara 1932- .... **CLC 30**
See also AAYA 2, 30; BYA 6, 12, 13; CA 182; 29-32R, 182; CANR 16, 38; CLR 3, 78; DLB 52; JRDA; MAICYA 1, 2; SAAS 2; SATA 1, 58; SATA-Essay 103; WYA; YAW

Wertmueller, Lina 1928- .... **CLC 16**
See also CA 97-100; CANR 39, 78

Wescott, Glenway 1901-1987 .. **CLC 13; SSC 35**
See also CA 13-16R; CAAS 121; CANR 23, 70; CN 1, 2, 3, 4; DLB 4, 9, 102; MAL 5; RGAL 4

Wesker, Arnold 1932- .... **CLC 3, 5, 42**
See also CA 1-4R; 7; CANR 1, 33; CBD; CD 5, 6; CDBLB 1960 to Present; DAB; DAM DRAM; DLB 13, 310, 319; EWL 3; MTCW 1; RGEL 2; TEA

Wesley, Charles 1707-1788 .... **LC 128**
See also DLB 95; RGEL 2

Wesley, John 1703-1791 .... **LC 88**
See also DLB 104

Wesley, Richard (Errol) 1945- .... **CLC 7**
See also BW 1; CA 57-60; CAD; CANR 27; CD 5, 6; DLB 38

Wessel, Johan Herman 1742-1785 .... **LC 7**
See also DLB 300

West, Anthony (Panther)
1914-1987 .... **CLC 50**
See also CA 45-48; CAAS 124; CANR 3, 19; CN 1, 2, 3, 4; DLB 15

West, C. P.
See Wodehouse, P(elham) G(renville)

West, Cornel 1953- .... **BLCS; CLC 134**
See also CA 144; CANR 91, 159; DLB 246

West, Cornel Ronald
See West, Cornel

West, Delno C(loyde), Jr. 1936- .... **CLC 70**
See also CA 57-60

West, Dorothy 1907-1998 ...... **HR 1:3; TCLC 108**
See also BW 2; CA 143; CAAS 169; DLB 76

West, (Mary) Jessamyn 1902-1984 ... **CLC 7, 17**
See also CA 9-12R; CAAS 112; CANR 27; CN 1, 2, 3; DLB 6; DLBY 1984; MTCW 1, 2; RGAL 4; RHW; SATA-Obit 37; TCWW 2; TUS; YAW

West, Morris L(anglo) 1916-1999 ..... **CLC 6, 33**
See also BPFB 3; CA 5-8R; CAAS 187; CANR 24, 49, 64; CN 1, 2, 3, 4, 5, 6; CPW; DLB 289; MTCW 1, 2; MTFW 2005

Cumulative Author Index

Wilbur, Richard 1921- .. **CLC 3, 6, 9, 14, 53, 110; PC 51**
See also AAYA 72; AMWS 3; CA 1-4R; CABS 2; CANR 2, 29, 76, 93, 139; CDALBS; CP 1, 2, 3, 4, 5, 6, 7; DA; DAB; DAC; DAM MST, POET; DLB 5, 169; EWL 3; EXPP; INT CANR-29; MAL 5; MTCW 1, 2; MTFW 2005; PAB; PFS 11, 12, 16; RGAL 4; SATA 9, 108; WP

Wilbur, Richard Purdy
See Wilbur, Richard

Wild, Peter 1940- .... **CLC 14**
See also CA 37-40R; CP 1, 2, 3, 4, 5, 6, 7; DLB 5

Wilde, Oscar (Fingal O'Flahertie Wills)
1854(?)-1900 .... **DC 17; SSC 11, 77; TCLC 1, 8, 23, 41, 175; WLC 6**
See also AAYA 49; BRW 5; BRWC 1, 2; BRWR 2; BYA 15; CA 119; CAAE 104; CANR 112; CDBLB 1890-1914; CLR 114; DA; DA3; DAB; DAC; DAM DRAM, MST, NOV; DFS 4, 8, 9, 21; DLB 10, 19, 34, 57, 141, 156, 190; EXPS; FANT; GL 3; LATS 1:1; NFS 20; RGEL 2; RGSF 2; SATA 24; SSFS 7; SUFW; TEA; WCH; WLIT 4

Wilder, Billy .... **CLC 20**
See Wilder, Samuel
See also AAYA 66; DLB 26

Wilder, Samuel 1906-2002
See Wilder, Billy
See also CA 89-92; CAAS 205

Wilder, Stephen
See Marlowe, Stephen

Wilder, Thornton (Niven)
1897-1975 .. **CLC 1, 5, 6, 10, 15, 35, 82; DC 1, 24; WLC 6**
See also AAYA 29; AITN 2; AMW; CA 13-16R; CAAS 61-64; CAD; CANR 40, 132; CDALBS; CN 1, 2; DA; DA3; DAB; DAC; DAM DRAM, MST, NOV; DFS 1, 4, 16; DLB 4, 7, 9, 228; DLBY 1997; EWL 3; LAIT 3; MAL 5; MTCW 1, 2; MTFW 2005; NFS 24; RGAL 4; RHW; WYAS 1

Wilding, Michael 1942- ...... **CLC 73; SSC 50**
See also CA 104; CANR 24, 49, 106; CN 4, 5, 6, 7; DLB 325; RGSF 2

Wiley, Richard 1944- .... **CLC 44**
See also CA 129; CAAE 121; CANR 71

Wilhelm, Kate .... **CLC 7**
See Wilhelm, Katie
See also AAYA 20; BYA 16; CA 5; DLB 8; INT CANR-17; SCFW 2

Wilhelm, Katie 1928-
See Wilhelm, Kate
See also CA 37-40R; CANR 17, 36, 60, 94; MTCW 1; SFW 4

Wilkins, Mary
See Freeman, Mary E(leanor) Wilkins

Willard, Nancy 1936- .... **CLC 7, 37**
See also BYA 5; CA 89-92; CANR 10, 39, 68, 107, 152; CLR 5; CP 2, 3, 4, 5; CWP; CWRI 5; DLB 5, 52; FANT; MAICYA 1, 2; MTCW 1; SATA 37, 71, 127; SATA-Brief 30; SUFW 2; TCLE 1:2

William of Malmesbury c. 1090B.C.-c.
1140B.C. .... **CMLC 57**

William of Moerbeke c. 1215-c.
1286 .... **CMLC 91**

William of Ockham 1290-1349 ..... **CMLC 32**

Williams, Ben Ames 1889-1953 ..... **TCLC 89**
See also CA 183; DLB 102

Williams, Charles
See Collier, James Lincoln

Williams, Charles (Walter Stansby)
1886-1945 .... **TCLC 1, 11**
See also BRWS 9; CA 163; CAAE 104; DLB 100, 153, 255; FANT; RGEL 2; SUFW 1

Williams, C.K. 1936- .... **CLC 33, 56, 148**
See also CA 37-40R; 26; CANR 57, 106; CP 1, 2, 3, 4, 5, 6, 7; DAM POET; DLB 5; MAL 5

Williams, Ella Gwendolen Rees
See Rhys, Jean

Williams, (George) Emlyn
1905-1987 .... **CLC 15**
See also CA 104; CAAS 123; CANR 36; DAM DRAM; DLB 10, 77; IDTP; MTCW 1

Williams, Hank 1923-1953 .... **TCLC 81**
See Williams, Hiram King

Williams, Helen Maria
1761-1827 .... **NCLC 135**
See also DLB 158

Williams, Hiram Hank
See Williams, Hank

Williams, Hiram King
See Williams, Hank
See also CA 188

Williams, Hugo (Mordaunt) 1942- ... **CLC 42**
See also CA 17-20R; CANR 45, 119; CP 1, 2, 3, 4, 5, 6, 7; DLB 40

Williams, J. Walker
See Wodehouse, P(elham) G(renville)

Williams, John A(lfred) 1925- . **BLC 3; CLC 5, 13**
See also AFAW 2; BW 2, 3; CA 195; 53-56, 195; 3; CANR 6, 26, 51, 118; CN 1, 2, 3, 4, 5, 6, 7; CSW; DAM MULT; DLB 2, 33; EWL 3; INT CANR-6; MAL 5; RGAL 4; SFW 4

Williams, Jonathan (Chamberlain)
1929- .... **CLC 13**
See also CA 9-12R; 12; CANR 8, 108; CP 1, 2, 3, 4, 5, 6, 7; DLB 5

Williams, Joy 1944- .... **CLC 31**
See also CA 41-44R; CANR 22, 48, 97; DLB 335

Williams, Norman 1952- .... **CLC 39**
See also CA 118

Williams, Roger 1603(?)-1683 .... **LC 129**
See also DLB 24

Williams, Sherley Anne 1944-1999 ... **BLC 3; CLC 89**
See also AFAW 2; BW 2, 3; CA 73-76; CAAS 185; CANR 25, 82; DAM MULT, POET; DLB 41; INT CANR-25; SATA 78; SATA-Obit 116

Williams, Shirley
See Williams, Sherley Anne

Williams, Tennessee 1911-1983 . **CLC 1, 2, 5, 7, 8, 11, 15, 19, 30, 39, 45, 71, 111; DC 4; SSC 81; WLC 6**
See also AAYA 31; AITN 1, 2; AMW; AMWC 1; CA 5-8R; CAAS 108; CABS 3; CAD; CANR 31, 132; CDALB 1941-1968; CN 1, 2, 3; DA; DA3; DAB; DAC; DAM DRAM, MST; DFS 17; DLB 7; DLBD 4; DLBY 1983; EWL 3; GLL 1; LAIT 4; LATS 1:2; MAL 5; MTCW 1, 2; MTFW 2005; RGAL 4; TUS

Williams, Thomas (Alonzo)
1926-1990 .... **CLC 14**
See also CA 1-4R; CAAS 132; CANR 2

Williams, William C.
See Williams, William Carlos

Williams, William Carlos
1883-1963 .... **CLC 1, 2, 5, 9, 13, 22, 42, 67; PC 7; SSC 31; WLC 6**
See also AAYA 46; AMW; AMWR 1; CA 89-92; CANR 34; CDALB 1917-1929; DA; DA3; DAB; DAC; DAM MST, POET; DLB 4, 16, 54, 86; EWL 3; EXPP; MAL 5; MTCW 1, 2; MTFW 2005; NCFS 4; PAB; PFS 1, 6, 11; RGAL 4; RGSF 2; TUS; WP

Williamson, David (Keith) 1942- ..... **CLC 56**
See also CA 103; CANR 41; CD 5, 6; DLB 289

Williamson, Ellen Douglas 1905-1984
See Douglas, Ellen
See also CA 17-20R; CAAS 114; CANR 39

Williamson, Jack .... **CLC 29**
See Williamson, John Stewart
See also CA 8; DLB 8; SCFW 1, 2

Williamson, John Stewart 1908-2006
See Williamson, Jack
See also CA 17-20R; CAAS 255; CANR 23, 70, 153; SFW 4

Willie, Frederick
See Lovecraft, H. P.

Willingham, Calder (Baynard, Jr.)
1922-1995 .... **CLC 5, 51**
See also CA 5-8R; CAAS 147; CANR 3; CN 1, 2, 3, 4, 5; CSW; DLB 2, 44; IDFW 3, 4; MTCW 1

Willis, Charles
See Clarke, Arthur C.

Willy
See Colette, (Sidonie-Gabrielle)

Willy, Colette
See Colette, (Sidonie-Gabrielle)
See also GLL 1

Wilmot, John 1647-1680 .... **LC 75; PC 66**
See Rochester
See also BRW 2; DLB 131; PAB

Wilson, A.N. 1950- .... **CLC 33**
See also BRWS 6; CA 122; CAAE 112; CANR 156; CN 4, 5, 6, 7; DLB 14, 155, 194; MTCW 2

Wilson, Andrew Norman
See Wilson, A.N.

Wilson, Angus (Frank Johnstone)
1913-1991 . **CLC 2, 3, 5, 25, 34; SSC 21**
See also BRWS 1; CA 5-8R; CAAS 134; CANR 21; CN 1, 2, 3, 4; DLB 15, 139, 155; EWL 3; MTCW 1, 2; MTFW 2005; RGEL 2; RGSF 2

Wilson, August 1945-2005 .. **BLC 3; CLC 39, 50, 63, 118, 222; DC 2; WLCS**
See also AAYA 16; AFAW 2; AMWS 8; BW 2, 3; CA 122; CAAE 115; CAAS 244; CAD; CANR 42, 54, 76, 128; CD 5, 6; DA; DA3; DAB; DAC; DAM DRAM, MST, MULT; DFS 3, 7, 15, 17, 24; DLB 228; EWL 3; LAIT 4; LATS 1:2; MAL 5; MTCW 1, 2; MTFW 2005; RGAL 4

Wilson, Brian 1942- .... **CLC 12**

Wilson, Colin (Henry) 1931- .... **CLC 3, 14**
See also CA 1-4R; 5; CANR 1, 22, 33, 77; CMW 4; CN 1, 2, 3, 4, 5, 6; DLB 14, 194; HGG; MTCW 1; SFW 4

Wilson, Dirk
See Pohl, Frederik

Wilson, Edmund 1895-1972 .. **CLC 1, 2, 3, 8, 24**
See also AMW; CA 1-4R; CAAS 37-40R; CANR 1, 46, 110; CN 1; DLB 63; EWL 3; MAL 5; MTCW 1, 2; MTFW 2005; RGAL 4; TUS

Wilson, Ethel Davis (Bryant)
1888(?)-1980 .... **CLC 13**
See also CA 102; CN 1, 2; DAC; DAM POET; DLB 68; MTCW 1; RGEL 2

Wilson, Harriet
See Wilson, Harriet E. Adams
See also DLB 239

Wilson, Harriet E.
See Wilson, Harriet E. Adams
See also DLB 243

Wouk, Herman 1915- .... **CLC 1, 9, 38**
    See also BPFB 2, 3; CA 5-8R; CANR 6,
    33, 67, 146; CDALBS; CN 1, 2, 3, 4, 5,
    6; CPW; DA3; DAM NOV, POP; DLBY
    1982; INT CANR-6; LAIT 4; MAL 5;
    MTCW 1, 2; MTFW 2005; NFS 7; TUS

Wright, Charles 1935- ... **CLC 6, 13, 28, 119,
    146**
    See also AMWS 5; CA 29-32R; 7; CANR
    23, 36, 62, 88, 135; CP 3, 4, 5, 6, 7; DLB
    165; DLBY 1982; EWL 3; MTCW 1, 2;
    MTFW 2005; PFS 10

Wright, Charles Stevenson 1932- ..... **BLC 3;
    CLC 49**
    See also BW 1; CA 9-12R; CANR 26; CN
    1, 2, 3, 4, 5, 6, 7; DAM MULT, POET;
    DLB 33

Wright, Frances 1795-1852 .... **NCLC 74**
    See also DLB 73

Wright, Frank Lloyd 1867-1959 .... **TCLC 95**
    See also AAYA 33; CA 174

Wright, Harold Bell 1872-1944 .... **TCLC 183**
    See also BPFB 3; CAAE 110; DLB 9;
    TCWW 2

Wright, Jack R.
    See Harris, Mark

Wright, James (Arlington)
    1927-1980 .... **CLC 3, 5, 10, 28; PC 36**
    See also AITN 2; AMWS 3; CA 49-52;
    CAAS 97-100; CANR 4, 34, 64;
    CDALBS; CP 1, 2; DAM POET; DLB 5,
    169; EWL 3; EXPP; MAL 5; MTCW 1,
    2; MTFW 2005; PFS 7, 8; RGAL 4; TUS;
    WP

Wright, Judith 1915-2000 ... **CLC 11, 53; PC
    14**
    See also CA 13-16R; CAAS 188; CANR
    31, 76, 93; CP 1, 2, 3, 4, 5, 6, 7; CWP;
    DLB 260; EWL 3; MTCW 1, 2; MTFW
    2005; PFS 8; RGEL 2; SATA 14; SATA-
    Obit 121

Wright, L(aurali) R. 1939- .... **CLC 44**
    See also CA 138; CMW 4

Wright, Richard (Nathaniel)
    1908-1960 ... **BLC 3; CLC 1, 3, 4, 9, 14,
    21, 48, 74; SSC 2; TCLC 136, 180;
    WLC 6**
    See also AAYA 5, 42; AFAW 1, 2; AMW;
    BPFB 3; BW 1; BYA 2; CA 108; CANR
    64; CDALB 1929-1941; DA; DA3; DAB;
    DAC; DAM MST, MULT, NOV; DLB 76,
    102; DLBD 2; EWL 3; EXPN; LAIT 3,
    4; MAL 5; MTCW 1, 2; MTFW 2005;
    NCFS 1; NFS 1, 7; RGAL 4; RGSF 2;
    SSFS 3, 9, 15, 20; TUS; YAW

Wright, Richard B(ruce) 1937- .... **CLC 6**
    See also CA 85-88; CANR 120; DLB 53

Wright, Rick 1945- .... **CLC 35**

Wright, Rowland
    See Wells, Carolyn

Wright, Stephen 1946- .... **CLC 33**
    See also CA 237

Wright, Willard Huntington 1888-1939
    See Van Dine, S. S.
    See also CA 189; CAAE 115; CMW 4;
    DLBD 16

Wright, William 1930- .... **CLC 44**
    See also CA 53-56; CANR 7, 23, 154

Wroth, Lady Mary 1587-1653(?) .... **LC 30,
    139; PC 38**
    See also DLB 121

Wu Ch'eng-en 1500(?)-1582(?) .... **LC 7**

Wu Ching-tzu 1701-1754 .... **LC 2**

Wulfstan c. 10th cent. -1023 .... **CMLC 59**

Wurlitzer, Rudolph 1938(?)- .... **CLC 2, 4, 15**
    See also CA 85-88; CN 4, 5, 6, 7; DLB 173

Wyatt, Sir Thomas c. 1503-1542 . **LC 70; PC
    27**
    See also BRW 1; DLB 132; EXPP; PFS 25;
    RGEL 2; TEA

Wycherley, William 1640-1716 .... **LC 8, 21,
    102, 136**
    See also BRW 2; CDBLB 1660-1789; DAM
    DRAM; DLB 80; RGEL 2

Wyclif, John c. 1330-1384 .... **CMLC 70**
    See also DLB 146

Wylie, Elinor (Morton Hoyt)
    1885-1928 .... **PC 23; TCLC 8**
    See also AMWS 1; CA 162; CAAE 105;
    DLB 9, 45; EXPP; MAL 5; RGAL 4

Wylie, Philip (Gordon) 1902-1971 ... **CLC 43**
    See also CA 21-22; CAAS 33-36R; CAP 2;
    CN 1; DLB 9; SFW 4

Wyndham, John .... **CLC 19**
    See Harris, John (Wyndham Parkes Lucas)
    Beynon
    See also DLB 255; SCFW 1, 2

Wyss, Johann David Von
    1743-1818 .... **NCLC 10**
    See also CLR 92; JRDA; MAICYA 1, 2;
    SATA 29; SATA-Brief 27

Xenophon c. 430B.C.-c. 354B.C. ... **CMLC 17**
    See also AW 1; DLB 176; RGWL 2, 3;
    WLIT 8

Xingjian, Gao 1940-
    See Gao Xingjian
    See also CA 193; DFS 21; DLB 330;
    RGWL 3

Yakamochi 718-785 .... **CMLC 45; PC 48**

Yakumo Koizumi
    See Hearn, (Patricio) Lafcadio (Tessima
    Carlos)

Yamada, Mitsuye (May) 1923- .... **PC 44**
    See also CA 77-80

Yamamoto, Hisaye 1921- .... **AAL; SSC 34**
    See also CA 214; DAM MULT; DLB 312;
    LAIT 4; SSFS 14

Yamauchi, Wakako 1924- .... **AAL**
    See also CA 214; DLB 312

Yanez, Jose Donoso
    See Donoso (Yanez), Jose

Yanovsky, Basile S.
    See Yanovsky, V(assily) S(emenovich)

Yanovsky, V(assily) S(emenovich)
    1906-1989 .... **CLC 2, 18**
    See also CA 97-100; CAAS 129

Yates, Richard 1926-1992 .... **CLC 7, 8, 23**
    See also AMWS 11; CA 5-8R; CAAS 139;
    CANR 10, 43; CN 1, 2, 3, 4, 5; DLB 2,
    234; DLBY 1981, 1992; INT CANR-10;
    SSFS 24

Yau, John 1950- .... **PC 61**
    See also CA 154; CANR 89; CP 4, 5, 6, 7;
    DLB 234, 312

Yearsley, Ann 1753-1806 .... **NCLC 174**
    See also DLB 109

Yeats, W. B.
    See Yeats, William Butler

Yeats, William Butler 1865-1939 . **PC 20, 51;
    TCLC 1, 11, 18, 31, 93, 116; WLC 6**
    See also AAYA 48; BRW 6; BRWR 1; CA
    127; CAAE 104; CANR 45; CDBLB
    1890-1914; DA; DA3; DAB; DAC; DAM
    DRAM, MST, POET; DLB 10, 19, 98,
    156, 332; EWL 3; EXPP; MTCW 1, 2;
    MTFW 2005; NCFS 3; PAB; PFS 1, 2, 5,
    7, 13, 15; RGEL 2; TEA; WLIT 4; WP

Yehoshua, A.B. 1936- .... **CLC 13, 31**
    See also CA 33-36R; CANR 43, 90, 145;
    CWW 2; EWL 3; RGHL; RGSF 2; RGWL
    3; WLIT 6

Yehoshua, Abraham B.
    See Yehoshua, A.B.

Yellow Bird
    See Ridge, John Rollin

Yep, Laurence 1948- .... **CLC 35**
    See also AAYA 5, 31; BYA 7; CA 49-52;
    CANR 1, 46, 92, 161; CLR 3, 17, 54;
    DLB 52, 312; FANT; JRDA; MAICYA 1,
    2; MAICYAS 1; SATA 7, 69, 123, 176;
    WYA; YAW

Yep, Laurence Michael
    See Yep, Laurence

Yerby, Frank G(arvin) 1916-1991 ..... **BLC 3;
    CLC 1, 7, 22**
    See also BPFB 3; BW 1, 3; CA 9-12R;
    CAAS 136; CANR 16, 52; CN 1, 2, 3, 4,
    5; DAM MULT; DLB 76; INT CANR-16;
    MTCW 1; RGAL 4; RHW

Yesenin, Sergei Aleksandrovich
    See Esenin, Sergei

Yevtushenko, Yevgeny (Alexandrovich)
    1933- ...... **CLC 1, 3, 13, 26, 51, 126; PC
    40**
    See Evtushenko, Evgenii Aleksandrovich
    See also CA 81-84; CANR 33, 54; DAM
    POET; EWL 3; MTCW 1; RGHL

Yezierska, Anzia 1885(?)-1970 .... **CLC 46**
    See also CA 126; CAAS 89-92; DLB 28,
    221; FW; MTCW 1; RGAL 4; SSFS 15

Yglesias, Helen 1915- .... **CLC 7, 22**
    See also CA 37-40R; 20; CANR 15, 65, 95;
    CN 4, 5, 6, 7; INT CANR-15; MTCW 1

Yokomitsu, Riichi 1898-1947 .... **TCLC 47**
    See also CA 170; EWL 3

Yonge, Charlotte (Mary)
    1823-1901 .... **TCLC 48**
    See also CA 163; CAAE 109; DLB 18, 163;
    RGEL 2; SATA 17; WCH

York, Jeremy
    See Creasey, John

York, Simon
    See Heinlein, Robert A.

Yorke, Henry Vincent 1905-1974 ..... **CLC 13**
    See Green, Henry
    See also CA 85-88; CAAS 49-52

Yosano, Akiko 1878-1942 ... **PC 11; TCLC 59**
    See also CA 161; EWL 3; RGWL 3

Yoshimoto, Banana .... **CLC 84**
    See Yoshimoto, Mahoko
    See also AAYA 50; NFS 7

Yoshimoto, Mahoko 1964-
    See Yoshimoto, Banana
    See also CA 144; CANR 98, 160; SSFS 16

Young, Al(bert James) 1939- ... **BLC 3; CLC
    19**
    See also BW 2, 3; CA 29-32R; CANR 26,
    65, 109; CN 2, 3, 4, 5, 6, 7; CP 1, 2, 3, 4,
    5, 6, 7; DAM MULT; DLB 33

Young, Andrew (John) 1885-1971 ...... **CLC 5**
    See also CA 5-8R; CANR 7, 29; CP 1;
    RGEL 2

Young, Collier
    See Bloch, Robert (Albert)

Young, Edward 1683-1765 .... **LC 3, 40**
    See also DLB 95; RGEL 2

Young, Marguerite (Vivian)
    1909-1995 .... **CLC 82**
    See also CA 13-16; CAAS 150; CAP 1; CN
    1, 2, 3, 4, 5, 6

Young, Neil 1945- .... **CLC 17**
    See also CA 110; CCA 1

Young Bear, Ray A. 1950- ... **CLC 94; NNAL**
    See also CA 146; DAM MULT; DLB 175;
    MAL 5

Yourcenar, Marguerite 1903-1987 ... **CLC 19,
    38, 50, 87**
    See also BPFB 3; CA 69-72; CANR 23, 60,
    93; DAM NOV; DLB 72; DLBY 1988;
    EW 12; EWL 3; GFL 1789 to the Present;
    GLL 1; MTCW 1, 2; MTFW 2005;
    RGWL 2, 3

Literary Criticism Series
Cumulative Topic Index

This index lists all topic entries in Thomson Gale's *Children's Literature Review* (CLR), *Classical and Medieval Literature Criticism* (CMLC), *Contemporary Literary Criticism* (CLC), *Drama Criticism* (DC), *Literature Criticism from 1400 to 1800* (LC), *Nineteenth-Century Literature Criticism* (NCLC), *Short Story Criticism* (SSC), and *Twentieth-Century Literary Criticism* (TCLC). The index also lists topic entries in the Gale Critical Companion Collection, which includes the following publications: *The Beat Generation* (BG), *Feminism in Literature* (FL), *Gothic Literature* (GL), and *Harlem Renaissance* (HR).

Topic Index

Topic Index

SSC Cumulative Nationality Index

ALGERIAN

Camus, Albert **9**

AMERICAN

Abish, Walter **44**
Adams, Alice (Boyd) **24**
Aiken, Conrad (Potter) **9**
Alcott, Louisa May **27, 98**
Algren, Nelson **33**
Anderson, Sherwood **1, 46, 91**
Apple, Max (Isaac) **50**
Auchincloss, Louis (Stanton) **22**
Baldwin, James (Arthur) **10, 33, 98**
Bambara, Toni Cade **35**
Banks, Russell **42**
Barnes, Djuna **3**
Barth, John (Simmons) **10, 89**
Barthelme, Donald **2, 55**
Bass, Rick **60**
Beattie, Ann **11**
Bellow, Saul **14, 101**
Benét, Stephen Vincent **10, 86**
Berriault, Gina **30**
Betts, Doris (Waugh) **45**
Bierce, Ambrose (Gwinett) **9, 72**
Bowles, Paul (Frederick) **3, 98**
Boyle, Kay **5, 102**
Boyle, T(homas) Coraghessan **16**
Bradbury, Ray (Douglas) **29, 53**
Bradfield, Scott **65**
Bukowski, Charles **45**
Cable, George Washington **4**
Caldwell, Erskine (Preston) **19**
Calisher, Hortense **15**
Canin, Ethan **70**
Capote, Truman **2, 47, 93**
Carver, Raymond **8, 51**
Cather, Willa (Sibert) **2, 50**
Chabon, Michael **59**
Chambers, Robert W. **92**
Chandler, Raymond (Thornton) **23**
Cheever, John **1, 38, 57**
Chesnutt, Charles W(addell) **7, 54**
Chopin, Kate **8, 68**
Cisneros, Sandra **32, 72**
Coover, Robert (Lowell) **15, 101**
Cowan, Peter (Walkinshaw) **28**
Crane, Stephen (Townley) **7, 56, 70**
Danticat, Edwige **100**
Davenport, Guy (Mattison Jr.) **16**
Davis, Rebecca (Blaine) Harding **38**
Dick, Philip K. **57**
Dixon, Stephen **16**
Dreiser, Theodore (Herman Albert) **30**
Dubus, André **15**
Dunbar, Paul Laurence **8**
Dybek, Stuart **55**
Elkin, Stanley L(awrence) **12**
Ellison, Harlan (Jay) **14**
Ellison, Ralph (Waldo) **26, 79**
Fante, John **65**
Farrell, James T(homas) **28**

Faulkner, William (Cuthbert) **1, 35, 42, 92, 97**
Fisher, Rudolph **25**
Fitzgerald, F(rancis) Scott (Key) **6, 31, 75**
Ford, Richard **56**
Freeman, Mary E(leanor) Wilkins **1, 47**
Gaines, Ernest J. **68**
Gardner, John (Champlin) Jr. **7**
Garland, (Hannibal) Hamlin **18**
Garrett, George (Palmer) **30**
Gass, William H(oward) **12**
Gibson, William (Ford) **52**
Gilchrist, Ellen (Louise) **14, 63**
Gilman, Charlotte (Anna) Perkins (Stetson) **13, 62**
Glasgow, Ellen (Anderson Gholson) **34**
Glaspell, Susan **41**
Gordon, Caroline **15**
Gordon, Mary **59**
Grau, Shirley Ann **15**
Hammett, (Samuel) Dashiell **17**
Hannah, Barry **94**
Harris, Joel Chandler **19**
Harrison, James (Thomas) **19**
Harte, (Francis) Bret(t) **8, 59**
Hawthorne, Nathaniel **3, 29, 39, 89**
Heinlein, Robert A(nson) **55**
Hemingway, Ernest (Miller) **1, 25, 36, 40, 63**
Henderson, Zenna (Chlarson) **29**
Henry, O. **5, 49**
Howells, William Dean **36**
Hughes, (James) Langston **6, 90**
Hurston, Zora Neale **4, 80**
Huxley, Aldous (Leonard) **39**
Irving, Washington **2, 37**
Jackson, Shirley **9, 39**
James, Henry **8, 32, 47**
Jewett, (Theodora) Sarah Orne **6, 44**
Johnson, Denis **56**
Jones, Thom (Douglas) **56**
Kelly, Robert **50**
Kincaid, Jamaica **72**
King, Stephen (Edwin) **17, 55**
Lahiri, Jhumpa **96**
Lardner, Ring(gold) W(ilmer) **32**
Le Guin, Ursula K(roeber) **12, 69**
Ligotti, Thomas (Robert) **16**
Lish, Gordon (Jay) **18**
London, Jack **4, 49**
Lovecraft, H(oward) P(hillips) **3, 52**
Maclean, Norman (Fitzroy) **13**
Malamud, Bernard **15**
Marshall, Paule **3**
Mason, Bobbie Ann **4, 101**
McCarthy, Mary (Therese) **24**
McCullers, (Lula) Carson (Smith) **9, 24, 99**
McPherson, James Alan **95**
Melville, Herman **1, 17, 46, 95**
Michaels, Leonard **16**
Millhauser, Steven **57**
Mori, Toshio **83**
Murfree, Mary Noailles **22**
Nabokov, Vladimir (Vladimirovich) **11, 86**

Nin, Anaïs **10**
Norris, (Benjamin) Frank(lin Jr.) **28**
Oates, Joyce Carol **6, 70**
O'Brien, Tim **74**
O'Connor, Frank **5**
O'Connor, (Mary) Flannery **1, 23, 61, 82**
O'Hara, John (Henry) **15**
Olsen, Tillie **11**
Ozick, Cynthia **15, 60**
Page, Thomas Nelson **23**
Paley, Grace **8**
Pancake, Breece D'J **61**
Parker, Dorothy (Rothschild) **2, 101**
Perelman, S(idney) J(oseph) **32**
Phillips, Jayne Anne **16**
Poe, Edgar Allan **1, 22, 34, 35, 54, 88**
Pohl, Frederik **25**
Porter, Katherine Anne **4, 31, 43**
Powers, J(ames) F(arl) **4**
Price, (Edward) Reynolds **22**
Pynchon, Thomas (Ruggles Jr.) **14, 84**
Roth, Philip (Milton) **26, 102**
Salinger, J(erome) D(avid) **2, 28, 65**
Salter, James **58**
Saroyan, William **21**
Selby, Hubert Jr. **20**
Silko, Leslie (Marmon) **37, 66**
Singer, Isaac Bashevis **3, 53**
Spencer, Elizabeth **57**
Spofford, Harriet Prescott **87**
Stafford, Jean **26, 86**
Stegner, Wallace (Earle) **27**
Stein, Gertrude **42**
Steinbeck, John (Ernst) **11, 37, 77**
Stuart, Jesse (Hilton) **31**
Styron, William **25**
Suckow, Ruth **18**
Taylor, Peter (Hillsman) **10, 84**
Thomas, Audrey (Callahan) **20**
Thurber, James (Grover) **1, 47**
Toomer, Jean **1, 45**
Trilling, Lionel **75**
Twain, Mark (Clemens, Samuel) **6, 26, 34, 87**
Updike, John (Hoyer) **13, 27**
Vinge, Joan (Carol) D(ennison) **24**
Vonnegut, Kurt Jr. **8**
Walker, Alice (Malsenior) **5, 97**
Wallace, David Foster **68**
Warren, Robert Penn **4, 58**
Welty, Eudora **1, 27, 51**
Wescott, Glenway **35**
West, Nathanael **16**
Wharton, Edith (Newbold Jones) **6, 84**
Wideman, John Edgar **62**
Williams, William Carlos **31**
Williams, Tennessee **81**
Wister, Owen **100**
Wodehouse, P(elham) G(renville) **2**
Wolfe, Thomas (Clayton) **33**
Wolff, Tobias **63**
Woolson, Constance Fenimore **90**

523

SSC-102 Title Index